World Political

Equatorial scale 1: 95 000 000 (main map)

— international boundary
• capital city

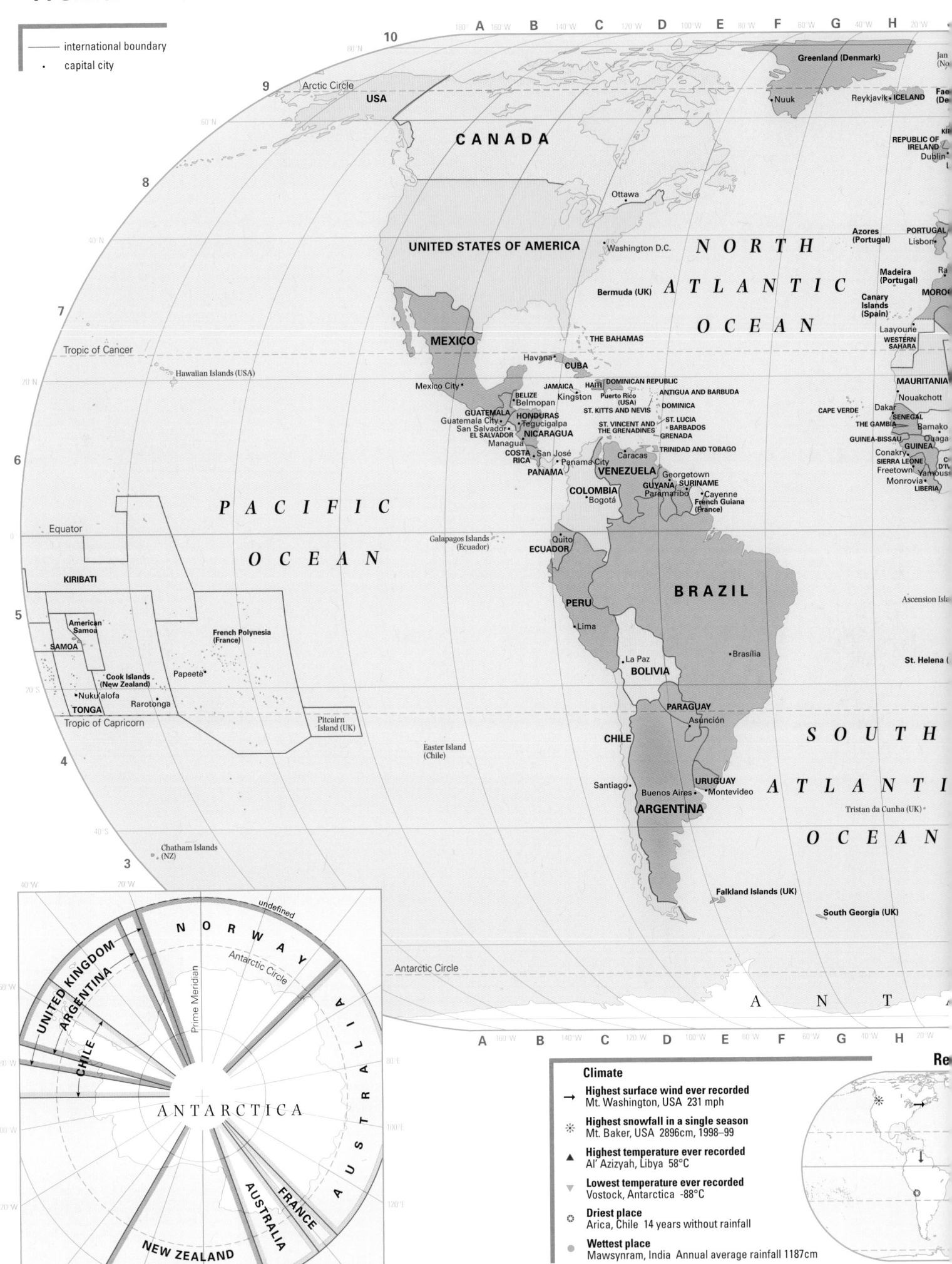

10 9 8 7 6 5 4 3

A B C D E F G H

Greenland (Denmark)
• Nuuk
Reykjavik • **ICELAND**
Jan (No...
Fae
(De...

USA

Arctic Circle

CANADA

REPUBLIC OF IRELAND
Dublin •

• Ottawa

UNITED STATES OF AMERICA
• Washington D.C.

N O R T H

A T L A N T I C

O C E A N

Azores (Portugal)
PORTUGAL
Lisbon •

Madeira (Portugal)
Ra

MORO

Bermuda (UK)

Tropic of Cancer

MEXICO

THE BAHAMAS

Havana •
CUBA

Hawaiian Islands (USA)

Laayoune
WESTERN SAHARA

MAURITANIA

Mexico City •
JAMAICA
HAITI
DOMINICAN REPUBLIC
BELIZE
Kingston
Puerto Rico (USA)
ANTIGUA AND BARBUDA
DOMINICA
• Nouakchott

GUATEMALA
Belmopan
ST. KITTS AND NEVIS
ST. LUCIA
BARBADOS
GRENADA
CAPE VERDE
Dakar
SENEGAL
THE GAMBIA
Bamako

Guatemala City •
HONDURAS
Tegucigalpa
ST. VINCENT AND THE GRENADINES
Ouaga
San Salvador • **NICARAGUA**
EL SALVADOR
Managua •
TRINIDAD AND TOBAGO
GUINEA-BISSAU
GUINEA
Conakry
SIERRA LEONE
CO
D'I

COSTA San José •
RICA
• Panama City
Caracas •
VENEZUELA
Georgetown
Freetown
Yamous
Monrovia
LIBERIA

PANAMA

COLOMBIA
• Bogotá
GUYANA SURINAME
Paramaribo •
• Cayenne
French Guiana (France)

Galapagos Islands (Ecuador)
Quito •
ECUADOR

Equator

PACIFIC

KIRIBATI

O C E A N

American Samoa

SAMOA

French Polynesia (France)

PERU
• Lima

B R A Z I L

Ascension Isla

Cook Islands (New Zealand)
Papeete •
• Brasília

Nuku'alofa
Rarotonga •
La Paz •
BOLIVIA

St. Helena

TONGA

Tropic of Capricorn

Pitcairn Island (UK)

PARAGUAY
Asunción •

Easter Island (Chile)

CHILE

S O U T H

A T L A N T I

Santiago •
URUGUAY
Buenos Aires • • Montevideo

Tristan da Cunha (UK) •

O C E A N

ARGENTINA

Chatham Islands (NZ)

Falkland Islands (UK)

South Georgia (UK)

Antarctic Circle

A N T

T

Inset map (Antarctica)

N O R W A Y
undefined
Antarctic Circle
UNITED KINGDOM
ARGENTINA
Prime Meridian
A U S T R A L I A
CHILE
A N T A R C T I C A
FRANCE
AUSTRALIA
NEW ZEALAND

Climate

→ **Highest surface wind ever recorded**
Mt. Washington, USA 231 mph

✳ **Highest snowfall in a single season**
Mt. Baker, USA 2896cm, 1998–99

▲ **Highest temperature ever recorded**
Al' Azizyah, Libya 58°C

▽ **Lowest temperature ever recorded**
Vostock, Antarctica -88°C

❂ **Driest place**
Arica, Chile 14 years without rainfall

● **Wettest place**
Mawsynram, India Annual average rainfall 1187cm

Re

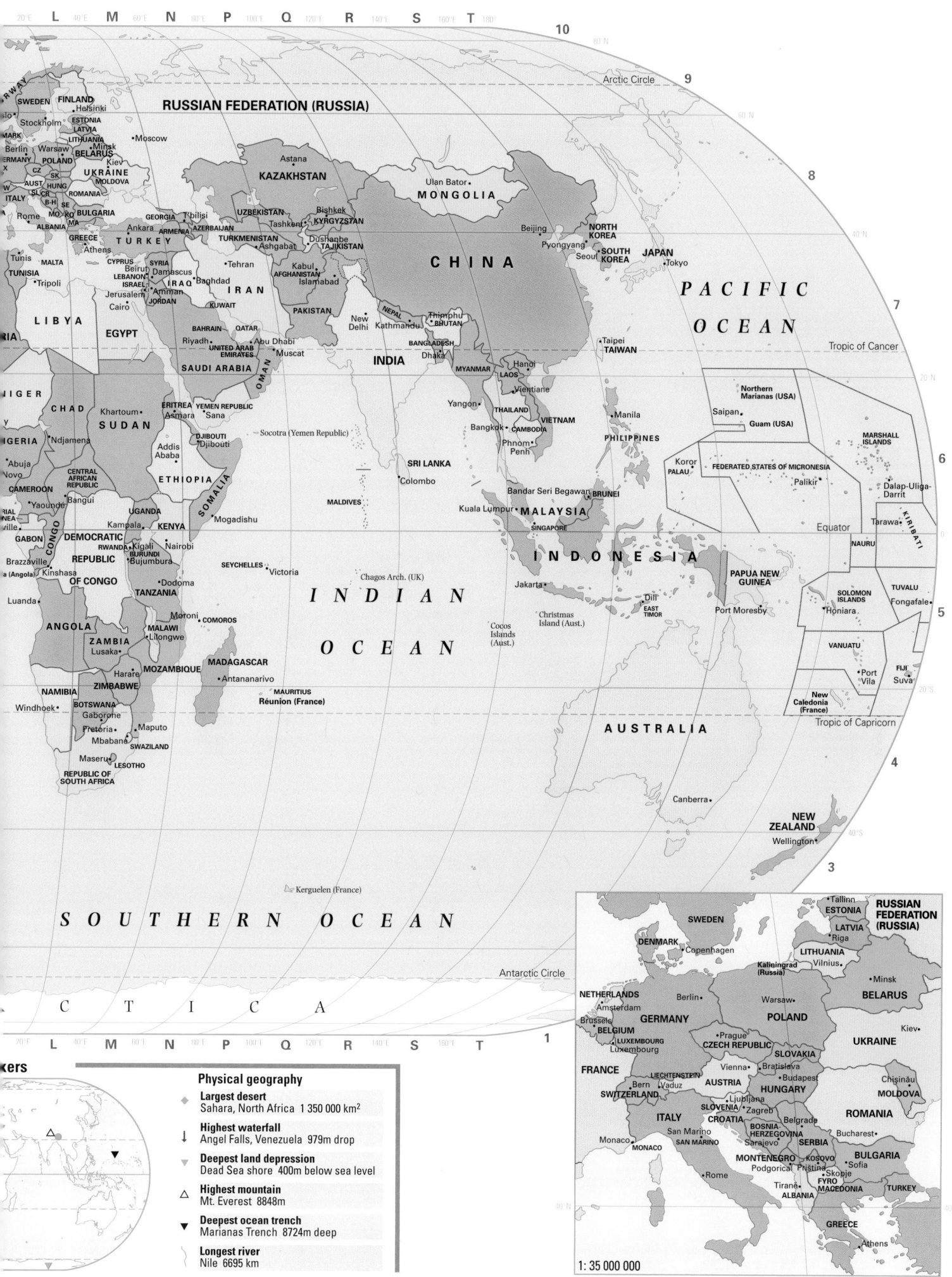

CANADIAN OXFORD
World
Atlas

— 6TH EDITION —

Quentin H. Stanford
GENERAL EDITOR

OXFORD
UNIVERSITY PRESS

2 Contents

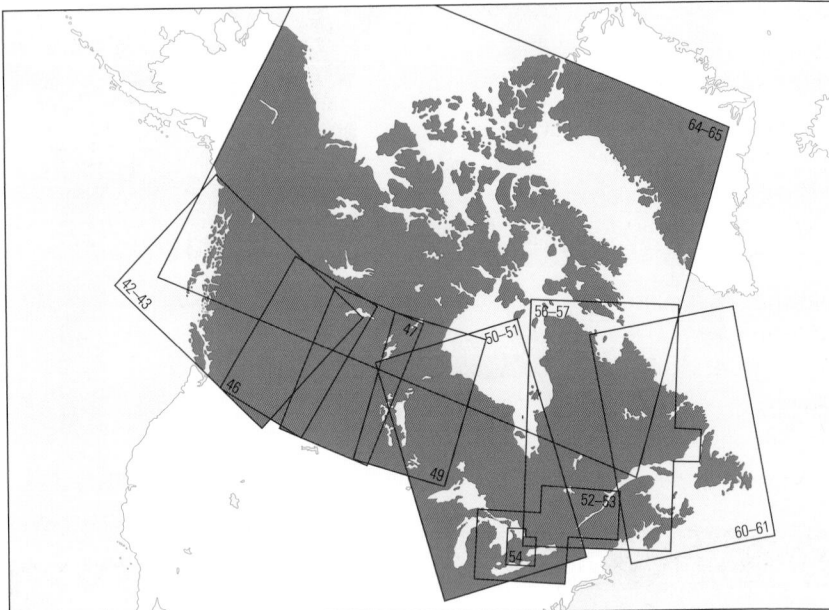

topographic maps of Canada

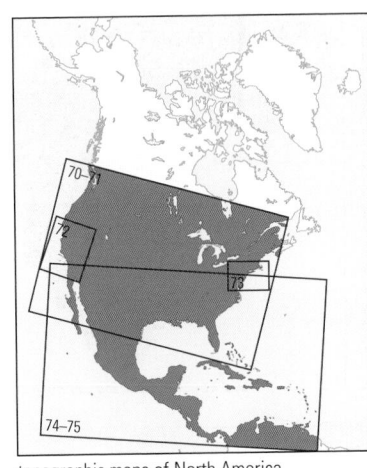

topographic maps of North America

topographic map of South America

Contents 3

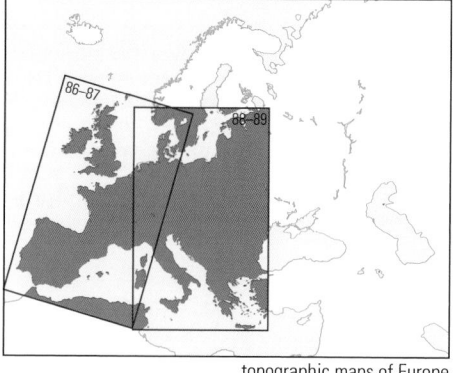
topographic maps of Europe

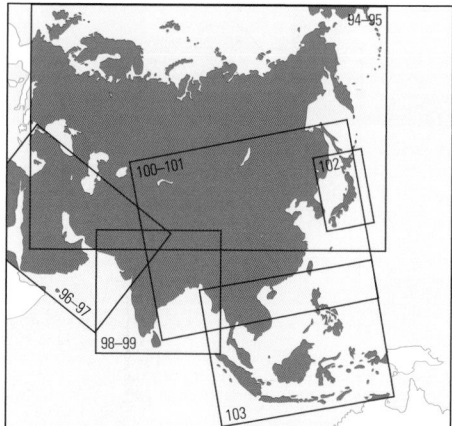
topographic maps of Asia

topographic map of Africa

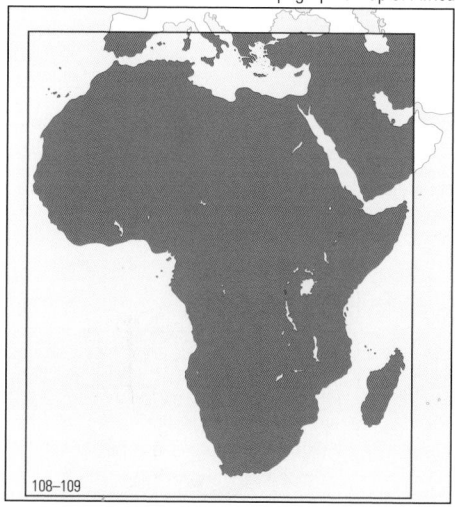

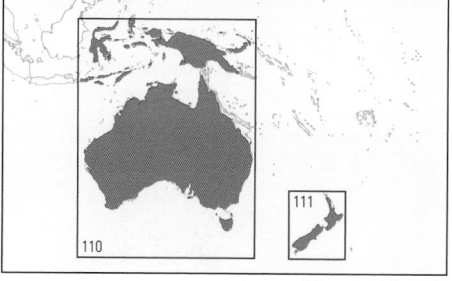
topographic map of Oceania

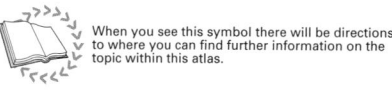
When you see this symbol there will be directions to where you can find further information on the topic within this atlas.

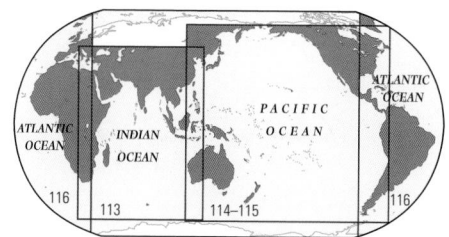
topographic maps of the Oceans

4 Types of maps

Maps are representations of the Earth's surface on a flat piece of paper. Maps can include such diverse information as the location of places, the depiction of economic and social data, the type and location of transportation routes, and the portrayal of change through time. Maps are everywhere; we come across them in everyday situations such as malls, schools, road atlases, and increasingly on the Internet. These pictures of the Earth's surface find many ways to attract our attention, orient our inquiries, and ultimately help direct our lives. An effective map is like a narrative — an open-ended and dynamic story that creates a dialogue between it and the user. It is not a straight forward text to be read; rather, it is a series of questions to be asked, ideas to be explored, and preconceptions to be challenged.

The two principal kinds of maps used in this atlas are topographic and thematic maps. Examples of these are shown below. In addition to these types of map, other devices can be used to show information about the Earth. These include globes (a spherical model of the Earth), plans (showing small areas), cross-sections (vertical views), and charts (navigational maps). Satellite imagery has also become an increasingly important means of understanding phenomena on the Earth's surface, and an introduction to the topic can be found on page 9.

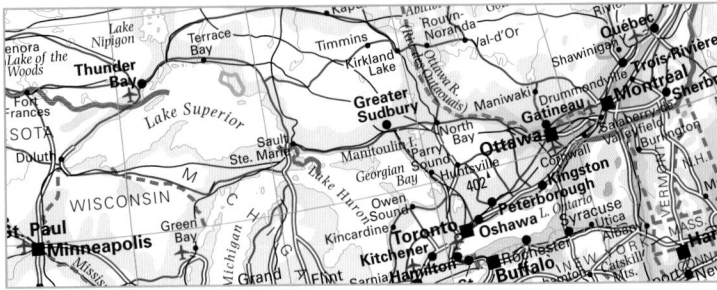

Topographic maps, also known as physical-political maps, are the general purpose maps in most atlases and provide a variety of information such as political boundaries, roads and railways, cities and towns, and the features of the physical landscape. Legends for the topographic maps in this atlas are expained on the opposite page.

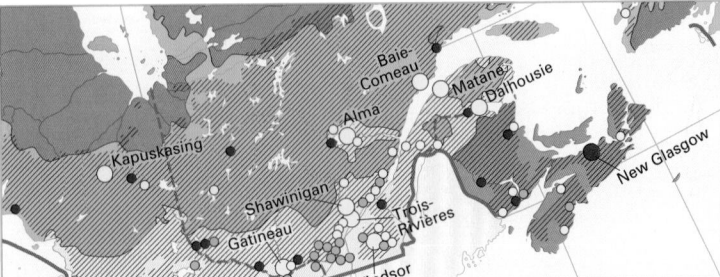

Thematic maps provide information about a variety of specific topics such as agriculture, climate, trade, and quality of life. Many different kinds of symbols are used for this purpose; the main ones are detailed in the section below.

Symbols on thematic maps

Point symbols

Distribution map
Each dot or circle represents a specific quantity.
From p36

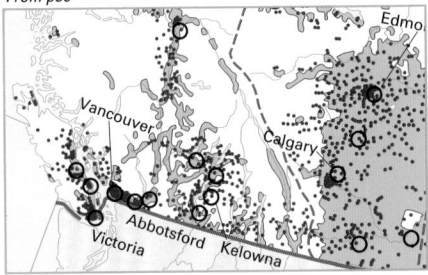

Symbol map
Different shapes, sizes, and colours are used to show, for example, economic or social data.
From p28

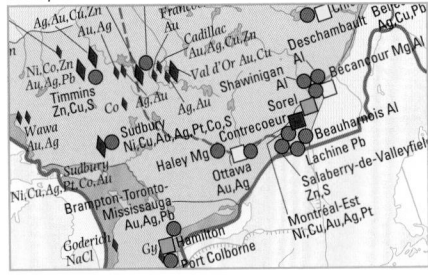

Proportional symbol map
The size or division of the symbol is used to represent quantities.
From p30

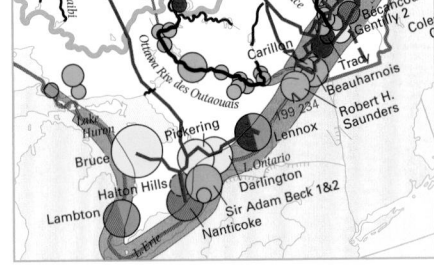

Line symbols

Transfer and transportation map
Lines represent routes or direction of movement.
From p29

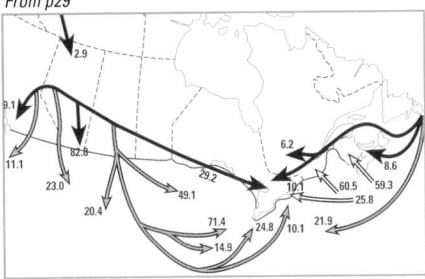

Isoline map
Lines connect places of equal value e.g. temperature (isotherms) or land height (contours).
From p17

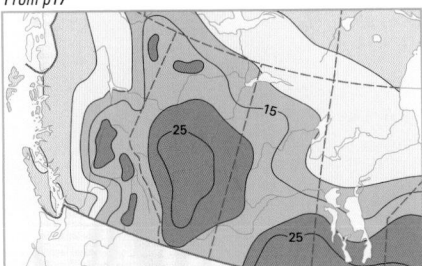

Flowline map
The thickness of the line is proportional to the quantity of what is being transferred.
From p144

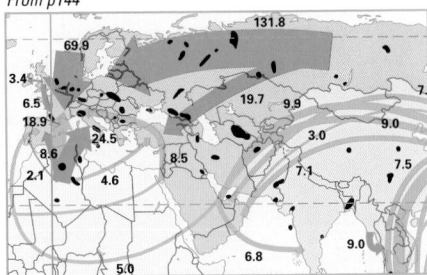

Area symbols

Choropleth map
Graduated colours or shades are used to represent variations in the information being presented.
From p32

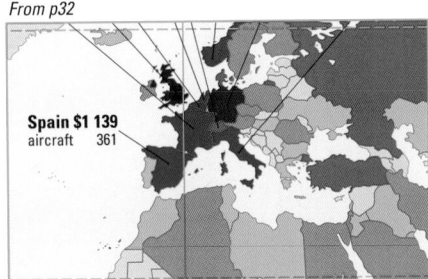

Special purpose map
Colours or shading are used to show different features such as soil types or geology.
From p14

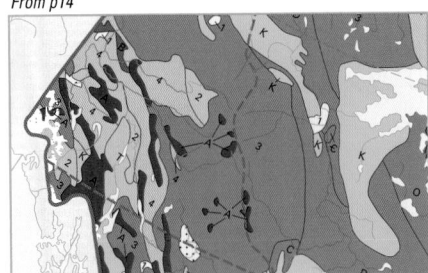

Political map
Colours have no meaning but are simply used to show where one country ends and another begins.
From p118

In the atlas, supplementary information complementing the topics illustrated by maps is provided in the form of tables, graphs, diagrams, satellite images, and text insets. Further information can be found in the two statistical appendixes of Canadian and World data, which begin on page 155.

opographic maps show the main features of the physical landscape
s well as settlements, communications, and boundaries. Background
olours show the height of the land.

here are small differences in the symbols and colours used for the
aps of Canada and those for the rest of the world.

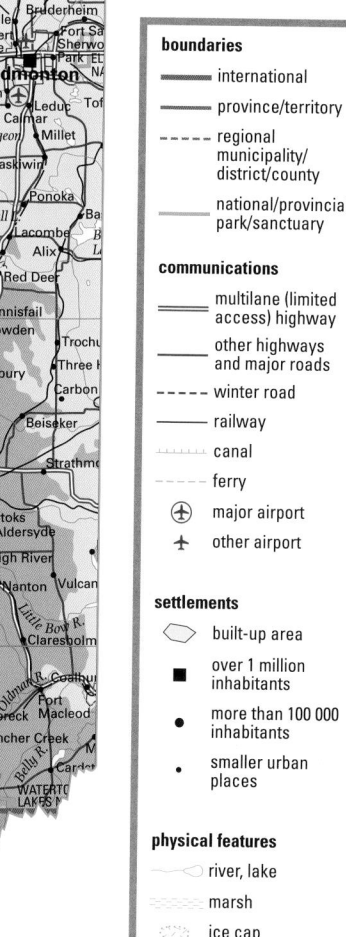

Canadian maps

boundaries

━━━ international

━━━ province/territory

- - - regional municipality/ district/county

━━━ national/provincial park/sanctuary

communications

═══ multilane (limited access) highway

━━━ other highways and major roads

- - - winter road

━━━ railway

┼┼┼┼ canal

- - - ferry

⊕ major airport

✈ other airport

settlements

⬡ built-up area

■ over 1 million inhabitants

● more than 100 000 inhabitants

• smaller urban places

physical features

~⟋ river, lake

marsh

ice cap

Non-Canadian maps

boundaries

━━━ international

- - - disputed

━━━ internal

communications

═══ expressway

━━━ major road

━━━ railway

┼┼┼┼ canal

✈ major airport

settlements

⬡ built-up area

■ over 1 million inhabitants

● more than 100 000 inhabitants

• smaller cities

physical features

⟋ river, lake

seasonal river

seasonal lake

marsh

salt lake

salt pan

ice cap

sand dunes

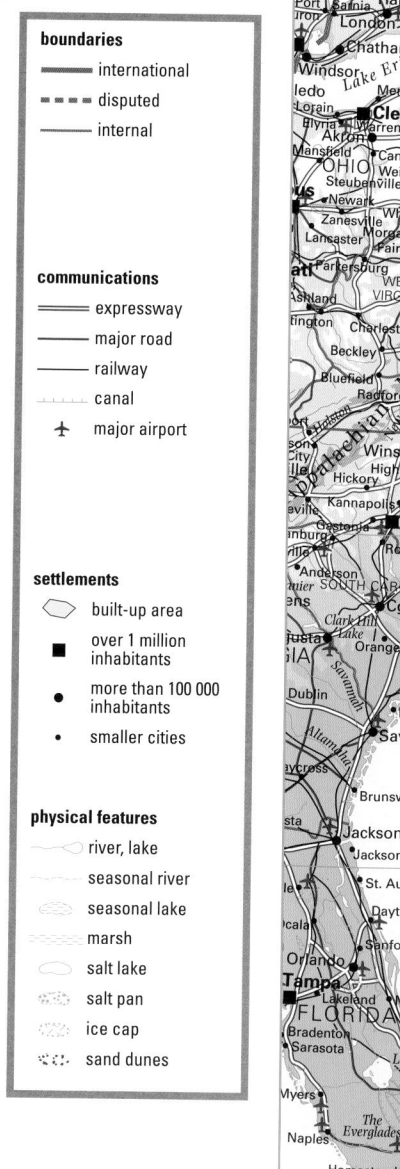

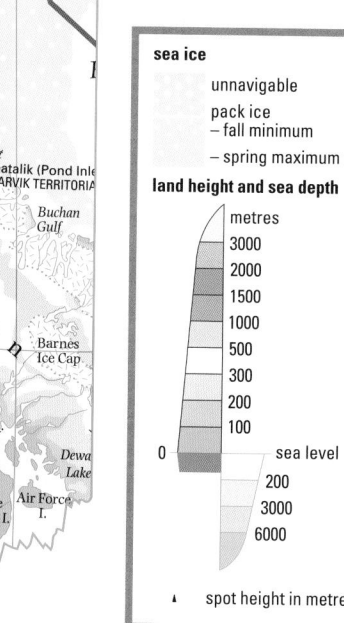

sea ice

unnavigable

pack ice
– fall minimum
– spring maximum

land height and sea depth

metres
3000
2000
1500
1000
500
300
200
100
0 sea level
200
3000
6000

▴ spot height in metres

Scale

Scale is shown by a representative fraction and a scale line.

Scale 1: 5 000 000

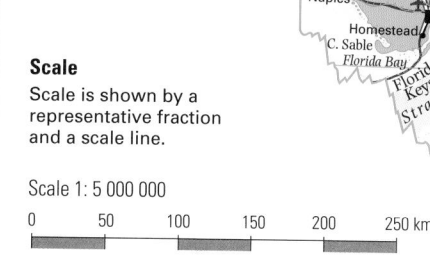

0   50   100   150   200   250 km

Sea ice

White stipple patterns over the sea colour show the seasonal extent of sea ice.

Land height and sea depth

Colours on topographic maps refer only to the height of the land or the depth of the sea. They do not give information about land use or other aspects of the environment.

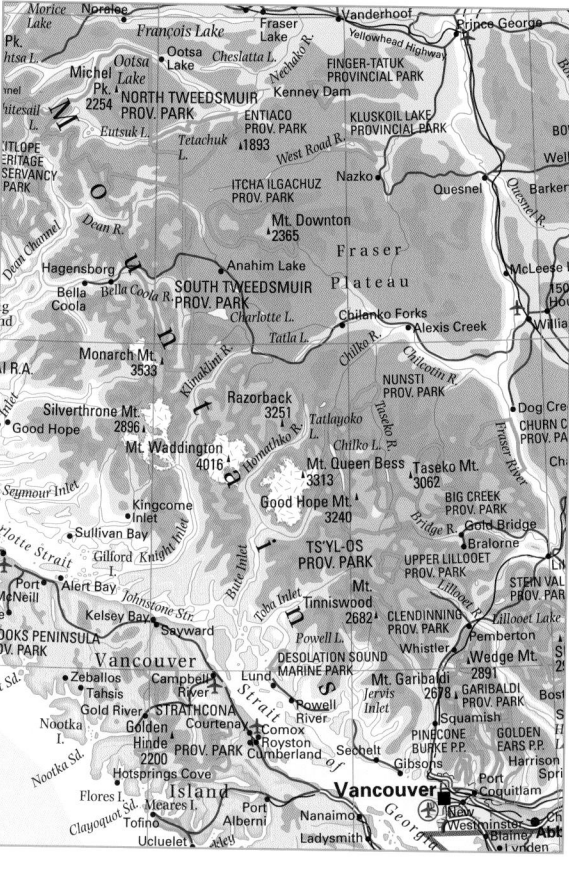

Place names

Anglicized spellings are used. Former names (where places have recently changed their names), and alternative spellings are shown in brackets.

This atlas has been designed for English speaking readers and so all places have been named using the Roman alphabet.

Type style

Contrasting type styles are used to show the difference between physical features, settlements, and administrative areas.

Physical features are separated into two categories, land and water. Land features are shown as roman type:

e.g.   Coast Mountains

Water features are shown in italics:

e.g.   *Hudson Bay (Baie d'Hudson)*

Peaks are shown in condensed type:

e.g.   Mt. Logan 5951

Settlement names are shown in upper and lower case:

e.g.   Hamilton

Administrative areas are shown in capital letters:

e.g.   ONTARIO

The importance of places is shown by the size of the type and whether the type face is bold or medium:

e.g.   **Ottawa**   Calgary   Louisbourg

On the Canadian maps all Census Metropolitan Areas (CMAs) are shown in bold.

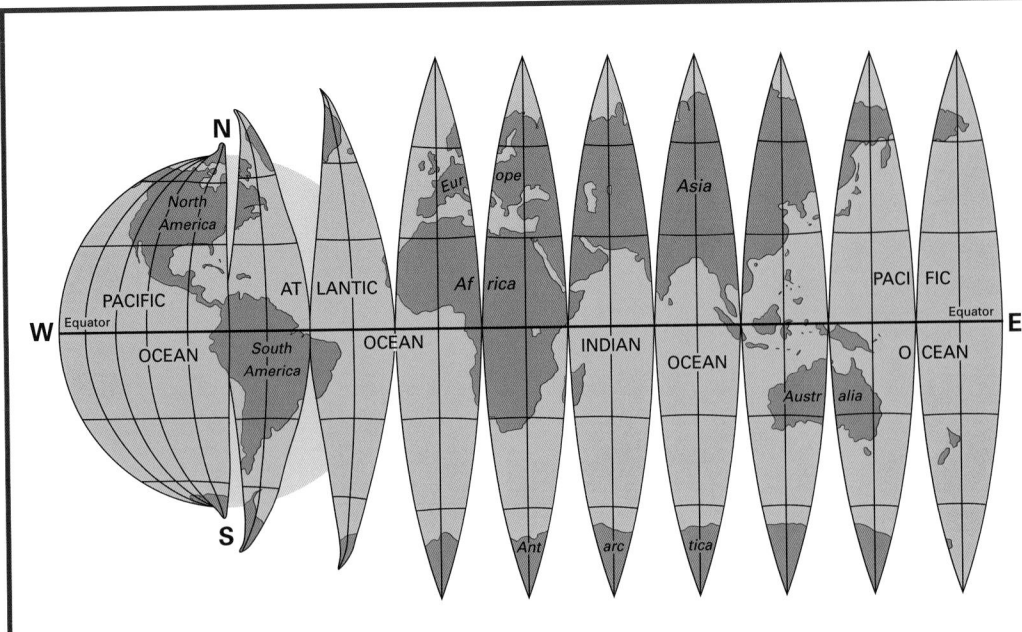

The most accurate way of looking at the Earth's land and sea areas is to use a globe. Globes, however, are not always available and are seldom large enough to show much detail. Thus, for most uses, maps are more convenient. To create a map it is necessary to transfer the surface of the globe on to a flat surface. In theory, as the diagram shows, it is necessary to unpeel strips (also known as gores) from the globe's surface, but such a method has obvious drawbacks. Since it is impossible to flatten the curved surface of the Earth without stretching or cutting part of it, it is necessary to employ other methods in order to produce an orderly system of parallels and meridians on which a map can be drawn. Such systems are referred to as **map projections**.

There are two main types of projections: **equal area projections**, where the area of any territory is shown in correct size proportion to other areas, and **conformal projections**, where the emphasis is on showing the shape correctly. No map can be both equal area and conformal, though some projections are designed to minimize distortions in both area and shape.

Polar projections give a good view of the poles. Most other projections do not show Antarctica or the Arctic Ocean accurately.

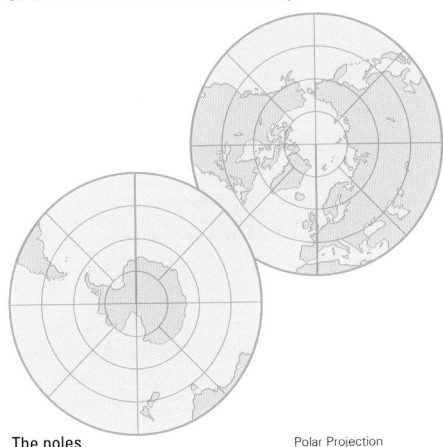

The poles   Polar Projection

The **Oblique Aitoff projection**, created by David Aitoff in 1889, is an equal area projection. The arrangement of the land masses allows a good view of routes in the northern hemisphere. The position of North America and Asia on either side of the Arctic is shown clearly.

—— major air routes

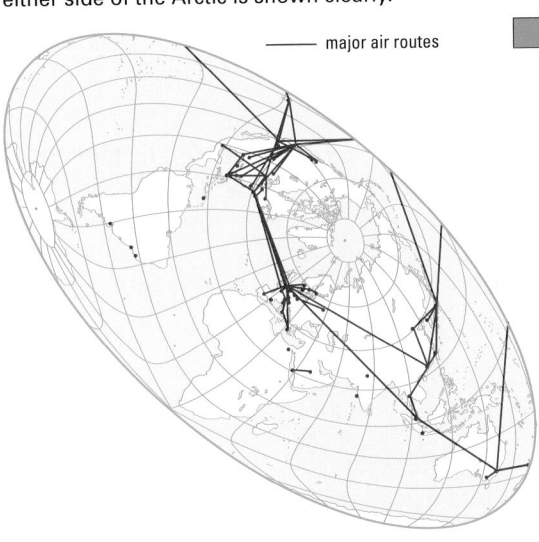

Major air routes   Oblique Aitoff Projection

Mercator's projection is a conformal projection and was initially designed by Gerhardus Mercator in 1569 to be used for navigation. Any straight line on the map is a line of constant compass bearing. Straight lines are not the shortest routes, however. Shape is accurate on a Mercator projection but the size of the land masses is distorted. Land is shown larger the further away it is from the equator. (For example, Alaska is shown four times larger than its actual size).

—— line of constant compass bearing

----- shortest route

Eckert IV projection was designed by the German cartographer Max Eckert (1868–1938). It is an equal area projection, showing the true area of places in relation to each other. This projection is often used in this atlas, the maps permitting fair comparisons to be made between areas of the world.

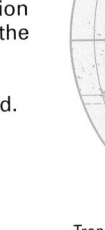 tropical forest

Gall's projection represents a compromise between equal area and conformal. A modified version is sometimes used in this atlas as a general world map. This map shows plate boundaries.

—— plate boundaries

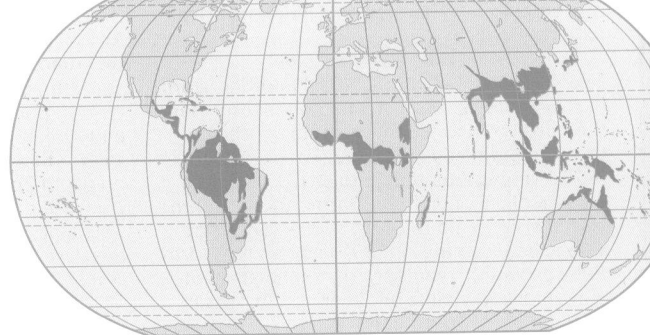

Navigation chart   Mercator's Proje

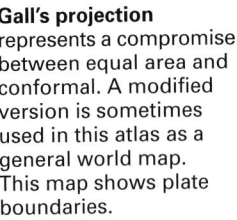

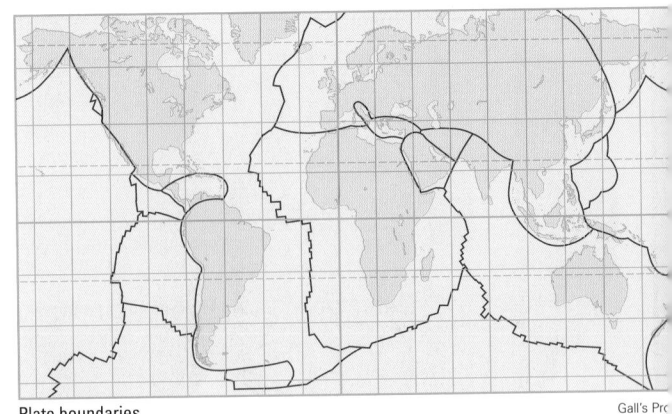

Tropical forest   Eckert IV Proj

Plate boundaries   Gall's Pro

There are two methods used in the atlas to locate places on maps. Both are shown in the gazetteer (geographical index) on pages 192–231 at the back of the atlas.

The first method is by grid code, where a blue grid (graticule) is superimposed on each topographic map. Each rectangle of the grid is identified vertically by a letter and horizontally by a number. Following each place name in the alphabetical gazetteer is a page number in bold and a letter and number combination (e.g., A2 or D5). This reference gives the page on which the place can be found and the specific rectangle on that page where the place is located. A single rectangle on a map may contain many place names, so it may take some diligence to find a specific place.

More instructions on using the gazetteer are on page 192 of this atlas.

The second method of determining location is by latitude and longitude. Since the Earth is a sphere, a locational grid requires fixed points of reference. The north and south poles, representing the axis of the Earth's rotation, act as these fixed points. A global grid based on these points allows us to pinpoint any place on Earth. The grid consists of two sets of lines. Those running east and west are called "parallels of latitude", and those extending north and south are called "meridians of longitude". Each line is given a value in angular measurement in degrees, minutes, and seconds (see diagram below). For more information on the global grid, see the box below.

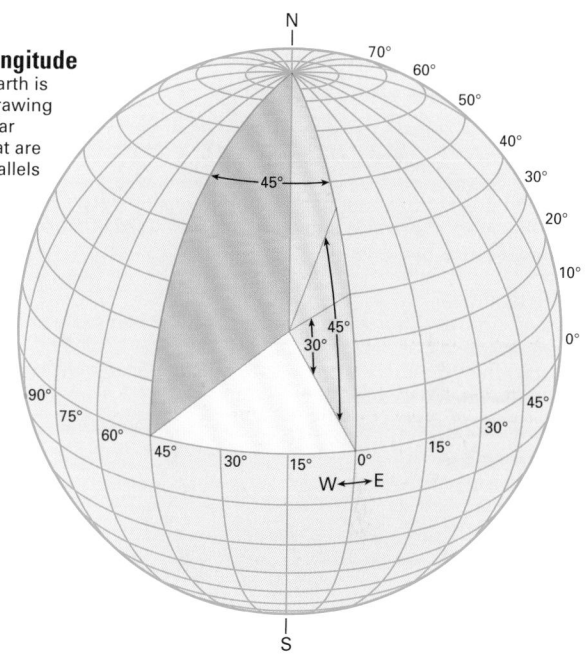

Latitude and longitude
A portion of the Earth is cut away in this drawing to show the angular measurements that are used to locate parallels and meridians.

This true-colour satellite image shows North and South America as they would appear from space 35 000 km (22 000 miles) above the Earth. The image is a combination of data from two satellites, so that it shows land surface data and a snapshot of the Earth's clouds.

Parallels of latitude are concentric circles that get smaller in diameter from the equator to the poles. The distance between the parallels remains constant; one degree equals 60 nautical miles (111 km). They are used to determine locations north (N) or south (S) of the equator. The equator is at latitude 0°. The poles are at latitudes 90°N and 90°S.

The Tropics of Cancer (23°26'N) and Capricorn (23°26'S) are parallels of latitude that represent the northern and southern limits of the sun appearing directly overhead. The Arctic (66°33'N) and Antarctic Circles (66°33'S) are also parallels of latitude. During the northern winter solstice (in December) the sun is not visible between the Arctic Circle and the North Pole; during the southern winter solstice (in June) it is not visible between the Antarctic Circle and the South Pole.

Meridians of longitude pass through both poles, intersecting all parallels of latitude at right angles. The distance between meridians gets smaller from a maximum distance at the equator to zero at the poles. Meridians are used to determine locations east (E) and west (W) of the prime meridian, and are numbered from 0° to 180° in both directions from the prime meridian. While the equator serves as a natural starting point for latitude, there is no such natural point for longitude; therefore in 1884, a meridian passing through Greenwich in the United Kingdom was chosen as the prime meridian (0°). On the opposite side of the globe from the prime meridian is the International Date Line, at 180° longitude. Travellers crossing the Date Line from east to west lose a day, while those crossing west to east repeat a day. The designations of 0° and 180° were made to implement the system of Standard Time.

The equator divides the Earth into halves: the northern hemisphere and the southern hemisphere. The prime meridian and the 180° meridian together also divide the Earth into halves: the western hemisphere and the eastern hemisphere.

Lines of latitude and longitude together form a grid. Any position on the surface of the Earth can be located accurately using this grid.

To locate places more precisely, each degree of latitude or longitude can be divided into 60 minutes, and each minute into 60 seconds. A location specified in degrees, minutes, and seconds (for example, 44°25'14"N, 80°45'36"W) describes a location to within a few metres.

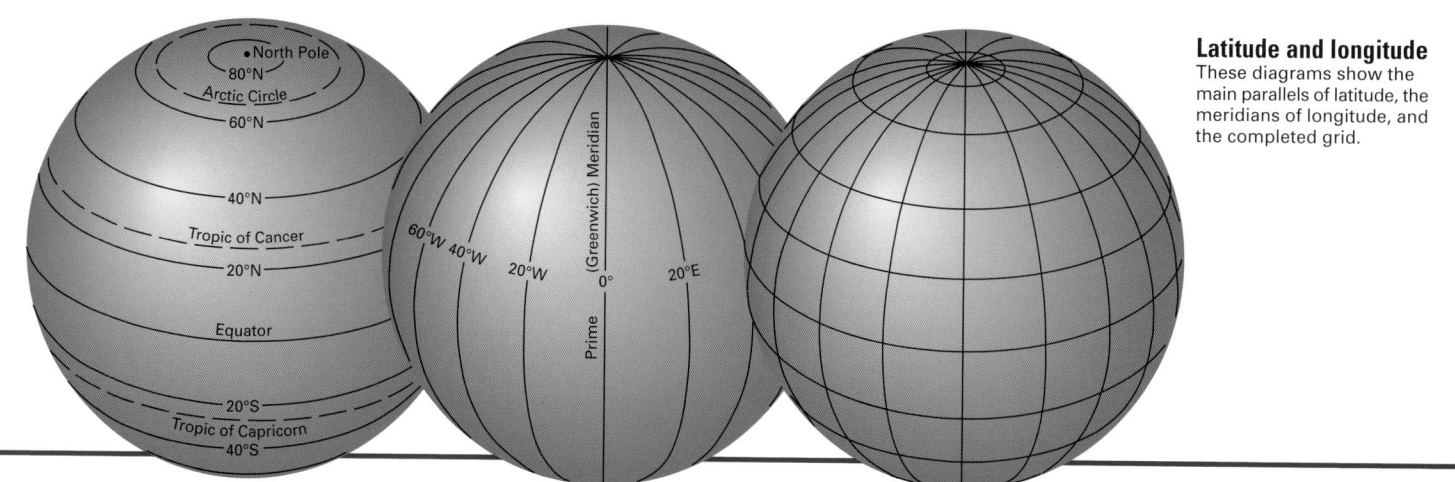

Latitude and longitude
These diagrams show the main parallels of latitude, the meridians of longitude, and the completed grid.

8 Scale and direction

Scale

Every map and globe has a scale to indicate how much the area on the map has been reduced from its actual size on the Earth's surface. Thus, the map scale indicates the proportion (or ratio) between a distance on a map and the corresponding distance on the Earth's surface.

Scale can be shown in three ways:

The scale statement

1 cm to 5 km   means 1 centimetre on the map represents five kilometres on the Earth's surface.

The representative fraction (RF)

1: 500 000   means 1 centimetre on the map represents 500 000 centimetres on the Earth's surface, or one of any unit of measurement represents 500 000 of the same units.

The linear scale

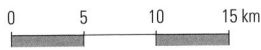

which is a measured line divided into units representing distances on the Earth.

It is important to understand the **relationship between scale and area**. In this atlas, Canada is shown mainly on maps that are at a larger scale than the rest of the world.

For example:
All of northern Africa appears on page 108 at a scale of 1: 26 000 000, while British Columbia, on pages 42–43, has a scale of 1: 5 000 000. We know from the scale that the African map shows a greater area, but how much greater?

The table shows that as the scale doubles, the area it represents increases four times. Thus a square centimetre on the Africa map represents an area more than twenty-seven times larger than a square centimetre on the British Columbia map.

Scale	Scale statement	Area of 1 cm²
1: 10 000	1 cm to 0.1 km	0.01 km²
1: 20 000	1 cm to 0.2 km	0.04 km²
1: 100 000	1 cm to 1 km	1 km²
1: 200 000	1 cm to 2 km	4 km²
1: 5 000 000	1 cm to 50 km	2500 km²
1: 10 000 000	1 cm to 100 km	10 000 km²
1: 20 000 000	1 cm to 200 km	40 000 km²

The scale of a map will determine the type and amount of information that can be shown. Larger scale maps (1: 1 000 000 or less) show a smaller area of the Earth than smaller scales (more than 1: 1 000 000). In this atlas, the Canadian urban plans covering the area of a single city have a scale of 1: 300 000, most of the regional Canadian maps covering an entire province have a scale of 1: 5 000 000, and some of those showing the entire Earth's surface have a scale of 1: 95 000 000 or greater. See below for examples of these maps in this atlas.

1: 300 000 scale
Suitable for urban plans.
From p55

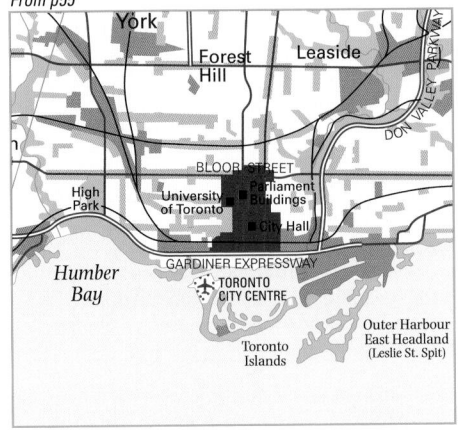

1: 5 000 000 scale
Suitable for maps of the Canadian provinces.
From p51

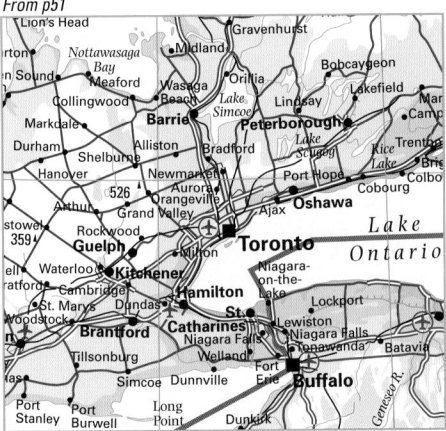

1: 95 000 000 scale
Suitable for maps of the world.
From p120

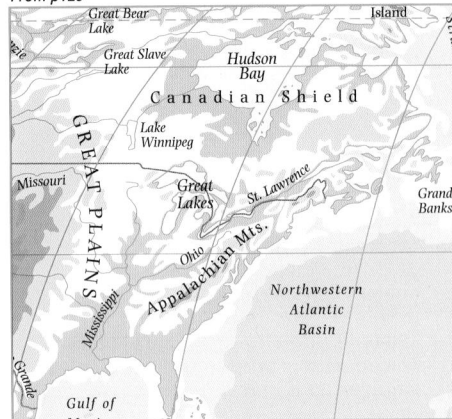

Direction

A direction can be expressed in two ways:

1. In terms of north, east, south, and west (the cardinal points of the compass) and various points between, such as east south east or north west (the intermediate points). These are shown on the diagram of the compass rose.

2. In terms of degrees (as a bearing), ranging through the values of the compass from 0° (north), 90° (east), 180° (south) to 359° (one degree west of north). These are also shown on the compass rose diagram.

The North Pole, where all meridians of longitude converge, is referred to as true or geographic north. Likewise, the South Pole is known as the true or geographic south. By convention, most maps are oriented so that true (geographic) north occurs toward the top of the map. Thus, when we refer to north and south on most maps, we are speaking of these poles.

There are also magnetic north and south poles. The magnetic north pole is presently located to the north of Ellesmere Island in the Canadian Arctic *(see pages 40–41)* and is moving about 24 km a year in a north-easterly direction. On a magnetic compass, the north arrow points to this pole.

Compass rose

In the atlas, the cardinal points (north, east, south, and west) can be determined from the parallels and meridians. Thus all parallels run north and south, and meridians east and west. Intermediate directions require the application of the compass rose or the use of bearings. Direction using bearings can be determined using a protractor.

Maps are devices created to capture phenomena on the Earth's surface in a simplified and accessible form. Depending on the size of the area being captured, the best position for starting to create a map is an elevated vantage point. In the past, views from hills and trees, drawn with paper and pencil, were used to create maps; more recently, photographs from cameras in hot-air balloons and airplanes were used. Today, using digital technology from satellites, we have a constant supply of images covering the entire globe. Technology has always been the close companion of the cartographer in the quest to accurately and effectively capture aspects of the environment.

Since the 1950s, artificial satellites have been in orbit around the Earth. These satellites are positioned at never-before-accessible vantage points high above the Earth. Soaring far above the reconnaissance airplanes used in the first half of the 20th century, the satellites quickly showed their capabilities. From hundreds of kilometres away, humans had their first look at the 'four corners' of the Earth.

As sophisticated as this technology might appear, at its core is one simple element: the camera. A satellite camera contains a series of sensors that are not unlike state-of-the-art digital cameras. These sensors can record information about the environment across a range of both the visible and non-visible parts of the electromagnetic spectrum (see diagram at the top right of this page). Like night-vision goggles, some cameras contain sensors that can detect heat energy (infrared); others contain sensors for energy within the radar portion of the electromagnetic spectrum. Theses sensors are "eyes in the sky", which capture a view of the Earth at a moment in time and allow the user the opportunity to interpret that landscape.

There are many satellites used for Earth observation. Some are privately funded, while others, such as military and environmental satellites, are funded by governments. Some of the satellite images in this atlas were taken by a satellite that orbits the Earth at an altitude of

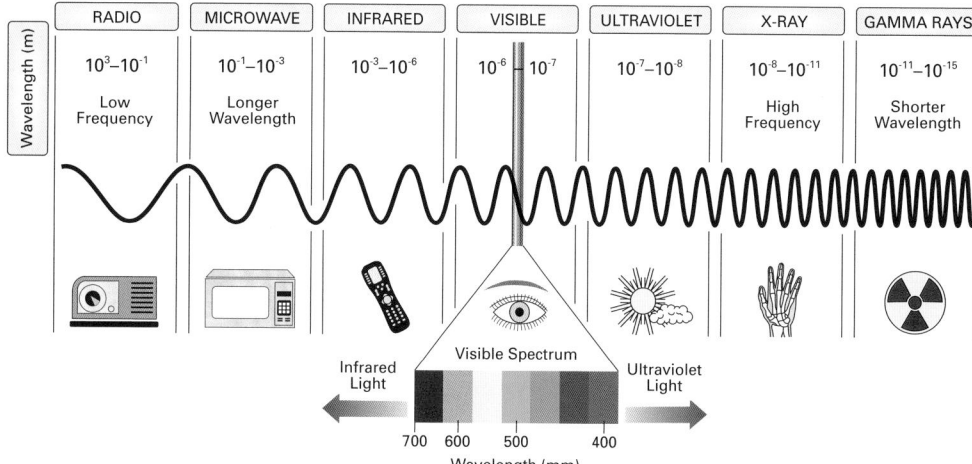

The electromagnetic spectrum
A simple diagram of the electromagnetic spectrum.

450 km and has a proven ground resolution of 60 cm, meaning that objects larger than 60 cm on the surface of the Earth can be seen in the images it produces. This orbit allows the satellite to revisit the same location each day. Much of this imagery is shown in natural colours to resemble a digital photograph of the Earth's surface.

To record a scene, the satellite must be positioned over the area of interest. Most satellites are in a sun-synchronous orbit, meaning they are over the same area of the Earth at roughly the same time each day, and always when that area is in daylight. As the sun's energy strikes the surface of the planet, the sensors on the satellite capture the reflected energy. Each sensor on the satellite is responsible for capturing specific wavelengths of energy. The sensors produce a matrix of numbers for each image. This raw data is sent back to ground stations, where it is processed to create usable images such as those in this atlas.

The various objects that make up the Earth's surface such as rocks, soil, vegetation, water, and

human artifacts (such as buildings), all absorb and reflect different wavelengths and amounts of energy. The differences in energy absorption and reflection — called a spectral signature — make it possible to distinguish one object from another in an image. For example, a forest may emit some energy at the visible green wavelength, but much more energy in the infrared range. On a satellite image, specific colours are chosen to display these different wavelengths of energy. The result is called a "false-colour composite", where the high levels of infrared energy from a forest could appear red, while urban areas appear blue-green. These images can also be shown in "true colour" to produce realistic landsurface colours. Nearly all of the images used in this atlas are true-colour images.

Satellite imagery has many applications, including environmental monitoring, resource management, disaster preparedness, land-use planning, forest inventories, energy exploration and monitoring, transportation, and security. Most important of all, satellite images are used in the creation of maps.

Vancouver
An oblique satellite view of much of the Lower Mainland of British Columbia from Howe Sound in the north to Point Roberts (part of the USA) in the south.

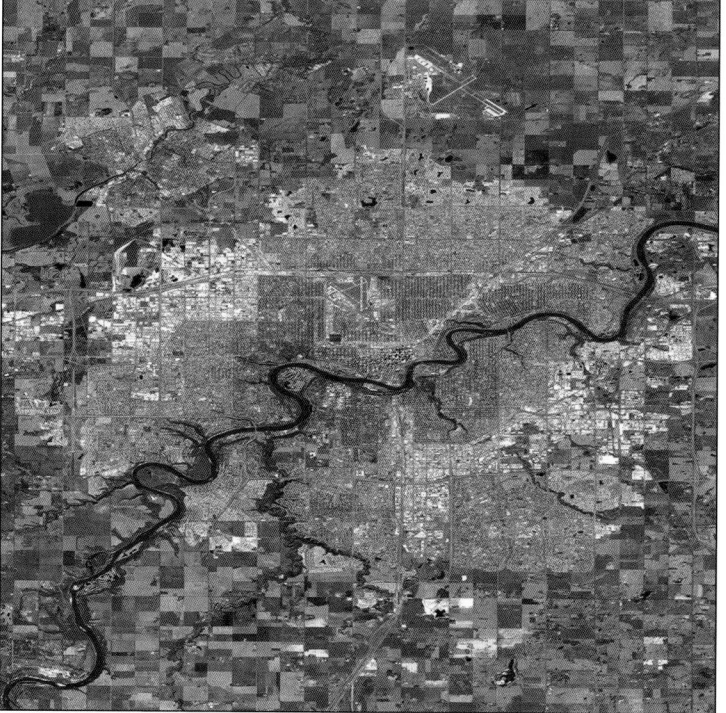

Edmonton
A vertical satellite view of Edmonton, Alberta bisected by the North Saskatchewan River.

Solar System

Our solar system comprises the sun and eight planets, their 162 moons, three dwarf planets (with four known moons), and thousands of small bodies including asteroids, meteoroids, comets, and interplanetary dust.

The main component of the solar system is the sun, which contains 99.86% of the system's known mass and dominates the system with its gravity. The sun's large mass makes it dense enough to sustain nuclear fusion, releasing enormous amounts of energy. Most of this energy is radiated into space as electromagnetic radiation, including visible light. Jupiter and Saturn together account for more than 90% of the solar system's remaining mass.

Light travels at 299 460 kilometres per second, or 10 trillion kilometres in one year. This distance is known as a light-year. It takes 8 minutes and 17 seconds for light to travel from the sun to the Earth, and about 5.5 hours for light to travel from the sun to the farthest extent of our solar system.

The Milky Way is a spiral galaxy containing at least 200 billion stars, and is approximately 100 000 light-years in diameter. Our sun is a medium-sized star in the Milky Way. Our solar system is located on one of the outer spirals of the galaxy, 28 000 light-years from the galactic centre. The closest star to the Earth outside our solar system, Proxima Centauri, is 4.22 light-years away. Of the known galaxies, one of the farthest from the Earth, called Quasar PKS 2000-330, is more than 13 billion light-years away; the light we see from it comes from a time close to when the universe was born.

All parts of the universe are in constant motion. The entire Milky Way rushes through space at 600 kilometres per second, or 2 160 000 kilometres per hour. It spins around its galactic centre at 800 000 kilometres per hour. The Earth revolves around the sun at 106 300 kilometres per hour, and completes one revolution every 365.26 days. The Earth rotates on its axis once every 23 hours and 56 minutes at 1 600 kilometres per hour at the equator; the rotational speed diminishes toward the poles.

Hubble/GALEX/Spitzer composite image of M81
This image combines data from the Hubble Space Telescope, the Spitzer Space Telescope, and the Galaxy Evolution Explorer (GALEX) missions.

	Neptune	Uranus	Saturn	Jupiter	Mars	Earth	Venus	Mercury
mean distance from the sun, in million km	4 497	2 870	1 427	778	228	150	108	58
time to orbit the sun, in days	60 275	30 660	10 767	4 343	687	365	225	88
diameter, in km	48 400	52 000	120 000	142 800	6 794	12 756	12 104	4 878
period of rotation, in days	0.67	0.45	0.42	0.41	1.02	0.99	243.0	58.67

Pluto (5.9 billion km from the sun) has been reclassified as a dwarf planet; Ceres (414 million km from the sun), and Eris (10.3 billion km from the sun) are also classified as dwarf planets.

Human use of Earth space

Satellites can be placed in different orbits around the Earth. For each satellite purpose there is a preferred orbit.

Low orbits

Satellites in low orbit (300–800 km) must travel rapidly (27 000 km/h) in order to overcome gravity. Satellites that observe the planet, such as those involved in remote sensing, weather, telephone, and data communication, use these orbits, as well as the International Space Station, which orbits the Earth at 354 km.

Polar orbits

These satellites, usually in a low orbit of 700 to 800 km, provide a more global view of the Earth, passing each latitude at approximately the same time through each season.

Elliptical or eccentric orbits

Often used for satellites designed to study particular areas of the Earth and needing to spend long periods over a chosen area.

Geostationary orbits

At 35 880 km above the equator, these are the highest orbits. They enable satellites to view a large area of the Earth. Each orbit takes 24 hours, the same time that it takes the Earth to rotate on its axis; they remain in the same position relative to the Earth. Communications and weather satellites use these orbits.

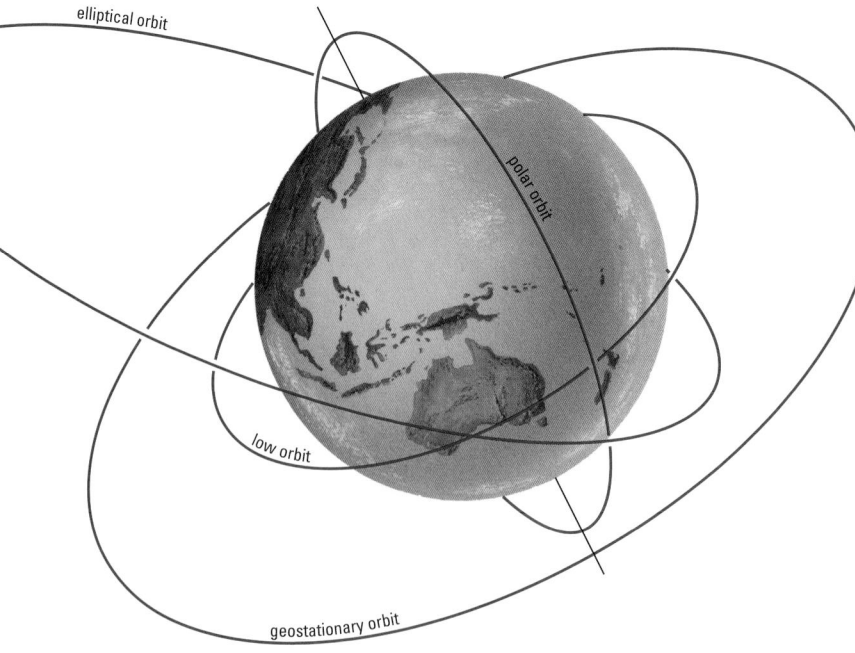

elliptical orbit

polar orbit

low orbit

geostationary orbit

The diagram shows how the Earth revolves around the sun every 365.25 days, while rotating on a tilted axis of 23.5° every 24 hours. The Earth's revolution on its tilted axis causes the four seasons, while its rotation causes day and night.

The Earth revolves around the sun following an elliptical, or slightly egg-shaped, orbit. Thus the distance between the Earth and the sun varies, from a maximum of 152 million kilometres on July 4 to a minimum of 147 million kilometres on January 3. However, this variation has little effect on temperatures on Earth.

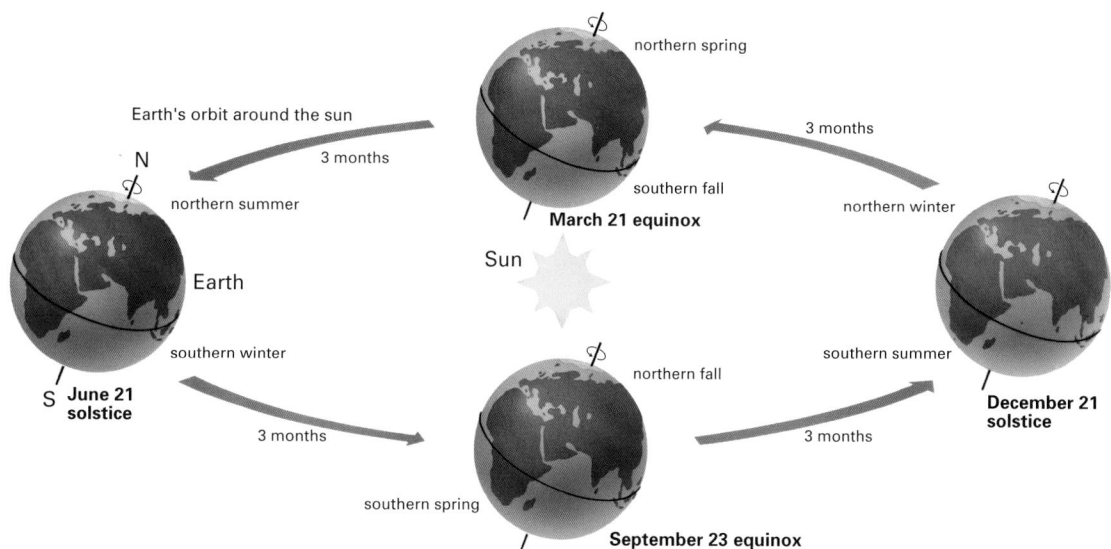

The diagram of the Earth in June and December shows the variations in the length of day and night. In June, the northern hemisphere is tilted at 23.5° towards the sun and as a result it receives more hours of sunshine. The sun's rays strike the Earth's atmosphere over the northern hemisphere more directly than at other times of the year, resulting in summer, with its warm temperatures.

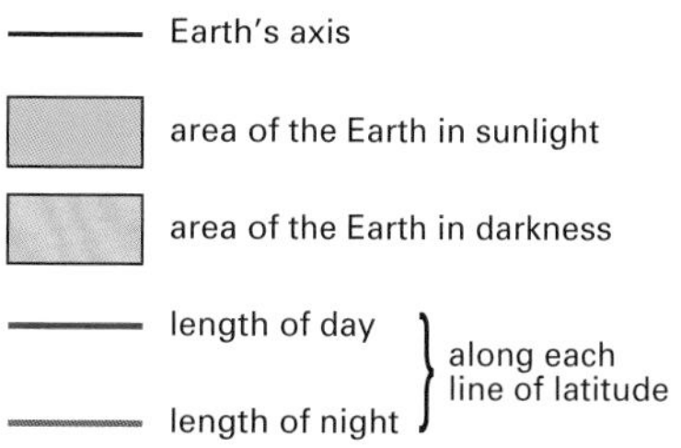

Earth's axis

area of the Earth in sunlight

area of the Earth in darkness

length of day } along each line of latitude
length of night }

Six months later, the Earth has revolved halfway around the sun. Now the southern hemisphere is tilted at 23.5° towards the sun. Thus in December it is summer in the southern hemisphere, while it is winter in the northern hemisphere.

June 21

23.5° tilt

North Pole
6 months daylight

short night/long day

Arctic Circle (66.5°N)
24 hours daylight

days and nights of equal length

Tropic of Cancer (23.5°N)
13.5 hours daylight

long night/short day

Equator (0°)
12 hours daylight

Tropic of Capricorn (23.5°S)
10.5 hours daylight

South Pole
6 months darkness

Antarctic Circle (66.5°S)
24 hours darkness

rays of the sun

December 21

23.5° tilt

Arctic Circle (66.5°N)
24 hours darkness

North Pole
6 months darkness

Tropic of Cancer (23.5°N)
10.5 hours daylight

short day/long night

Equator (0°)
12 hours daylight

days and nights of equal length

Tropic of Capricorn (23.5°S)
13.5 hours daylight

long day/short night

Antarctic Circle (66.5°S)
24 hours daylight

South Pole
6 months daylight

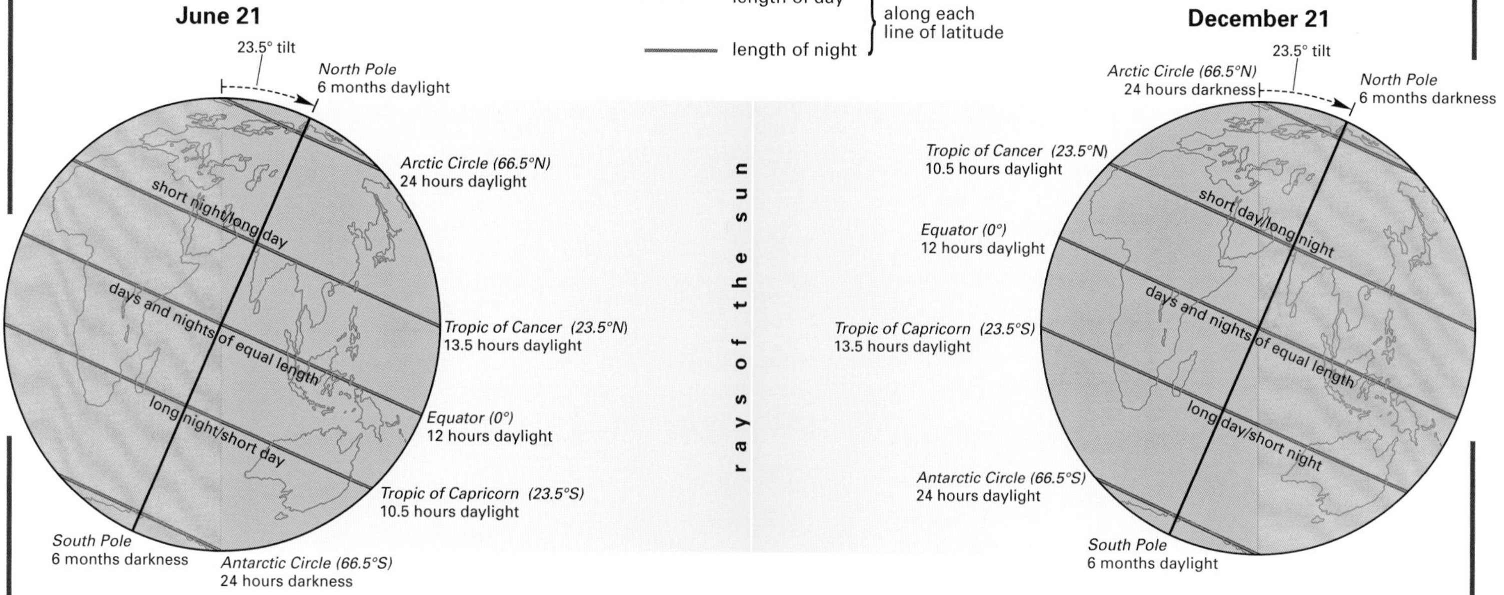

The graph shows the time of sunrise and sunset for selected latitudes in both hemispheres (red for south latitudes and blue for north) over the year. It illustrates that changes in the number of hours of daylight are greater with increased latitude.

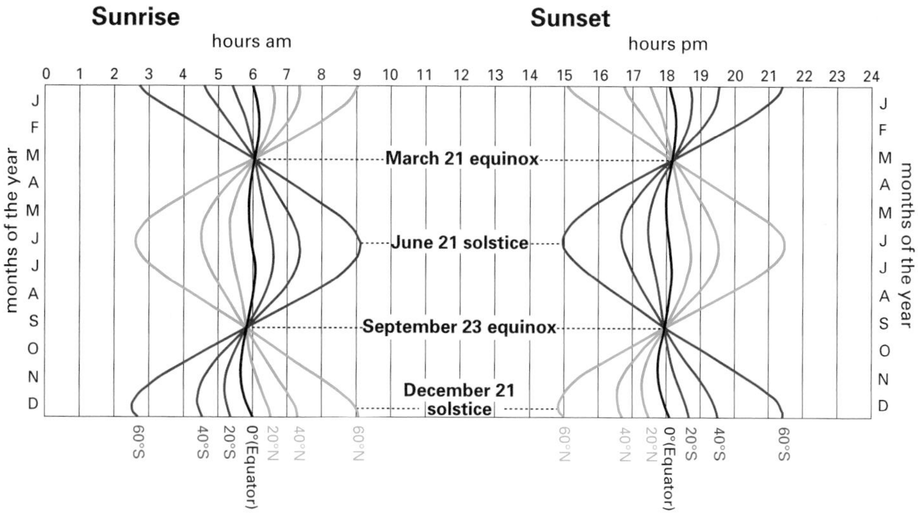

Sunrise

hours am

Sunset

hours pm

months of the year

J F M A M J J A S O N D

0 1 2 3 4 5 6 7 8 9 10 11 12 13 14 15 16 17 18 19 20 21 22 23 24

March 21 equinox

June 21 solstice

September 23 equinox

December 21 solstice

60°S 40°S 20°S 0°(Equator) 20°N 40°N 60°N

60°N 40°N 20°N 0°(Equator) 20°S 40°S 60°S

In the northern hemisphere at the summer solstice, the sun never sets north of the Arctic Circle. At the same time, the sun never rises south of the Antarctic Circle. The opposite occurs at the northern hemisphere's winter solstice. Places near the equator experience little variation in the length of day and night throughout the year.

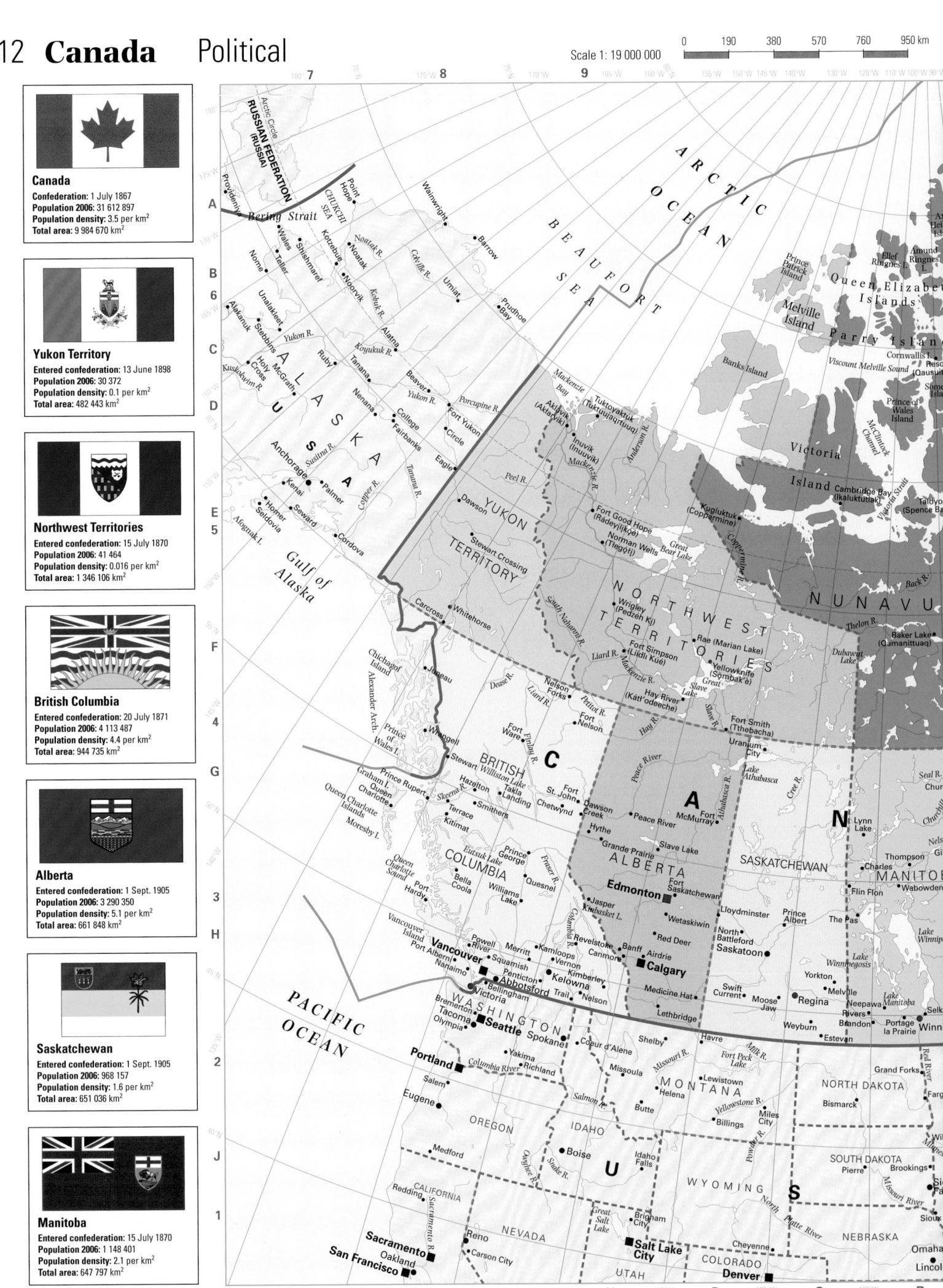

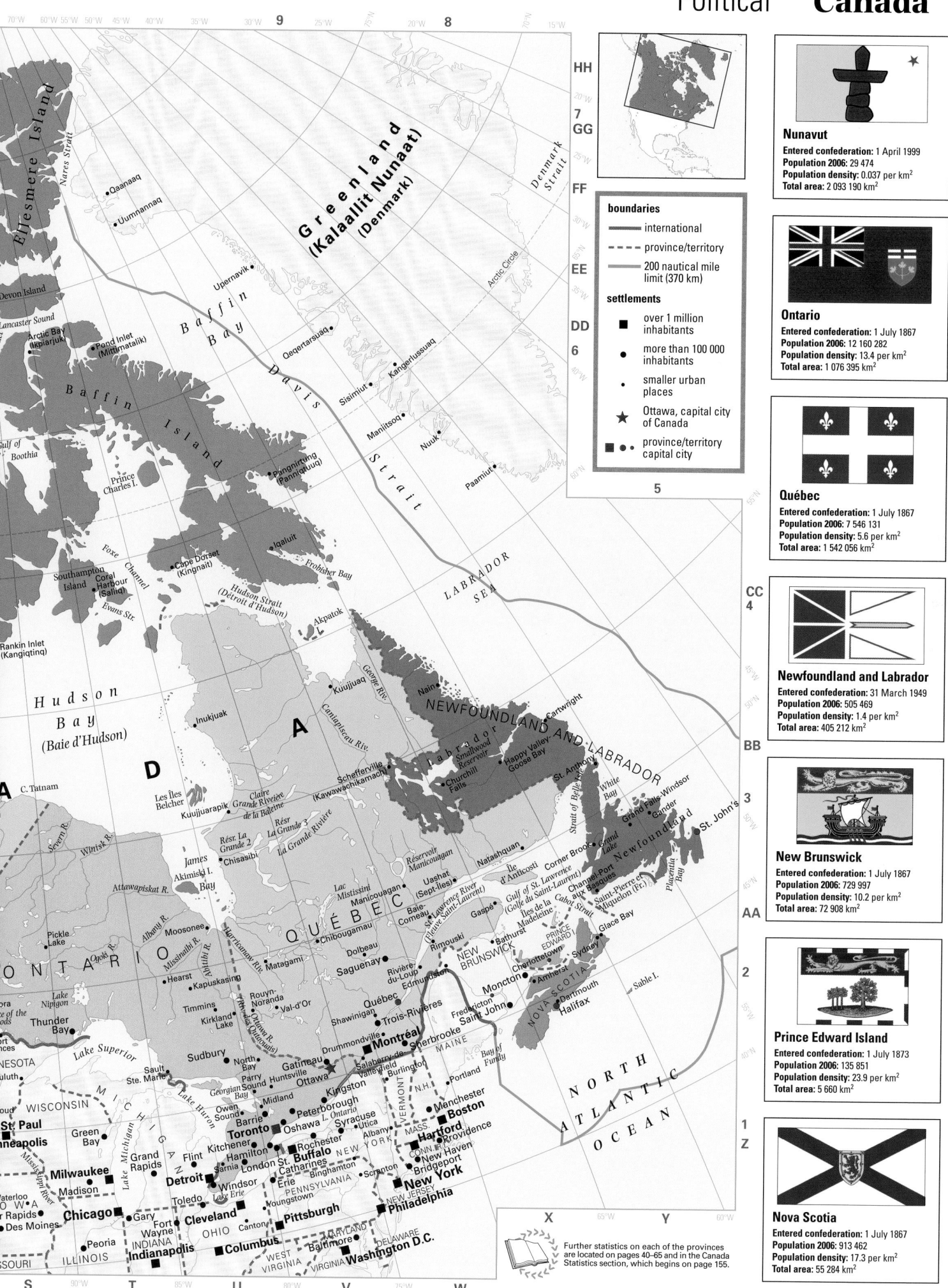

Further statistics on each of the provinces are located on pages 40–65 and in the Canada Statistics section, which begins on page 155.

boundaries

- international
- province/territory
- 200 nautical mile limit (370 km)

settlements

- ■ over 1 million inhabitants
- ● more than 100 000 inhabitants
- • smaller urban places
- ★ Ottawa, capital city of Canada
- ■•• province/territory capital city

Nunavut
Entered confederation: 1 April 1999
Population 2006: 29 474
Population density: 0.037 per km²
Total area: 2 093 190 km²

Ontario
Entered confederation: 1 July 1867
Population 2006: 12 160 282
Population density: 13.4 per km²
Total area: 1 076 395 km²

Québec
Entered confederation: 1 July 1867
Population 2006: 7 546 131
Population density: 5.6 per km²
Total area: 1 542 056 km²

Newfoundland and Labrador
Entered confederation: 31 March 1949
Population 2006: 505 469
Population density: 1.4 per km²
Total area: 405 212 km²

New Brunswick
Entered confederation: 1 July 1867
Population 2006: 729 997
Population density: 10.2 per km²
Total area: 72 908 km²

Prince Edward Island
Entered confederation: 1 July 1873
Population 2006: 135 851
Population density: 23.9 per km²
Total area: 5 660 km²

Nova Scotia
Entered confederation: 1 July 1867
Population 2006: 913 462
Population density: 17.3 per km²
Total area: 55 284 km²

© Oxford University Press

Scale 1: 24 000 000

0   240   480   720 km

Cenozoic

	Quaternary (Pleistocene and Recent)	Alluvium, glacial drift. (All Canada was affected by Pleistocene glaciation).
1	Tertiary	Sedimentary rocks (sandstone, shale, conglomerate, coal measures). Volcanic rocks (basalt, andesite) associated with sedimentary rocks.

Mesozoic

K	Cretaceous	Mainly sedimentary rocks (sandstone, shale, conglomerate), oil and natural gas, coal, tar sand, bentonite.
J	Jurassic	Sedimentary and volcanic rocks (argillite, greywacke, sandstone, andesite, volcanic breccia, tuff), oil.
T	Triassic	Sedimentary and volcanic rocks (argillite, quartzite, limestone, andesite, volcanic breccia, tuff), may include oil and natural gas.
2	undivided	

Paleozoic

C	Carboniferous and Permian	Mainly sedimentary rocks (sandstone, limestone, shale, conglomerate), some volcanic rocks; coal measures, oil and natural gas, gypsum.
D	Devonian	Sedimentary and volcanic rocks (shale, limestone, dolomite, conglomerate, sandstone, volcanic rocks), salt; oil and natural gas.
S	Silurian	Mainly sedimentary rocks (sandstone, shale, limestone, conglomerate, dolomite), some volcanic rocks; gypsum, salt; oil and natural gas.
O	Ordovician	Sedimentary rocks (limestone, dolomite, shale, argillite, sandstone, quartzite, grit); oil and natural gas.
Є	Cambrian	Sedimentary rocks (dolomite, limestone, shale, chert, quartzite, sandstone, conglomerate).
3	undivided	

Pre Cambrian

| 4 | Proterozoic | Mainly sedimentary and volcanic rocks and derived metamorphic rocks (shale, argillite, slate, chert, limestone, dolomite, sandstone, quartzite, arkose, greywacke, conglomerate; schists, gneiss, greenstone, andesite, basalt, trachyte; tuff, volcanic breccia; iron formation). |
| 5 | Archean | Mainly sedimentary and derived metamorphic rocks (argillite, slate, arkose, quartzite, greywacke, conglomerate, sedimentary gneiss and schist). Associated with areas of mainly volcanic and derived metamorphic rocks (andesite, dacite, basalt; rhyolite, trachyte, volcanic breccia and tuff; greenstone schist, hornblende gneiss; iron formation). |

Intrusive rocks

Paleozoic, Mesozoic, and Cenozoic

| A | Mainly acid rocks (granodiorite, quartz monzonite, quartz diorite; granite, syenite). Some areas of basic and ultrabasic rocks (gabbro, pyroxenite, serpentine). |

Pre Cambrian — Proterozoic and Archean

| B | Mainly acid rocks (granodiorite, granite, quartz diorite; granite gneiss), including some granitized sedimentary and volcanic rock. Some areas of basic and ultrabasic rocks (anorthosite, gabbro, diabase sills, and dykes). |

Glacial effect on landforms

existing glaciers
areas of glacial erosion and deposition
generally unglaciated areas
areas once covered by seas
areas once covered by lakes

ice cap

Scale 1 : 90 000 000

Geological time scale

(to nearest million years)

present	63	135	180	230	345	405	425	500	600	over 4.4 billion
Quaternary and Tertiary	Cretaceous	Jurassic	Triassic	Carboniferous and Permian	Devonian		Ordovician	Cambrian	Pre Cambrian	

Silurian

Arctic Circle

© Oxford University Press

Scale 1: 24 000 000

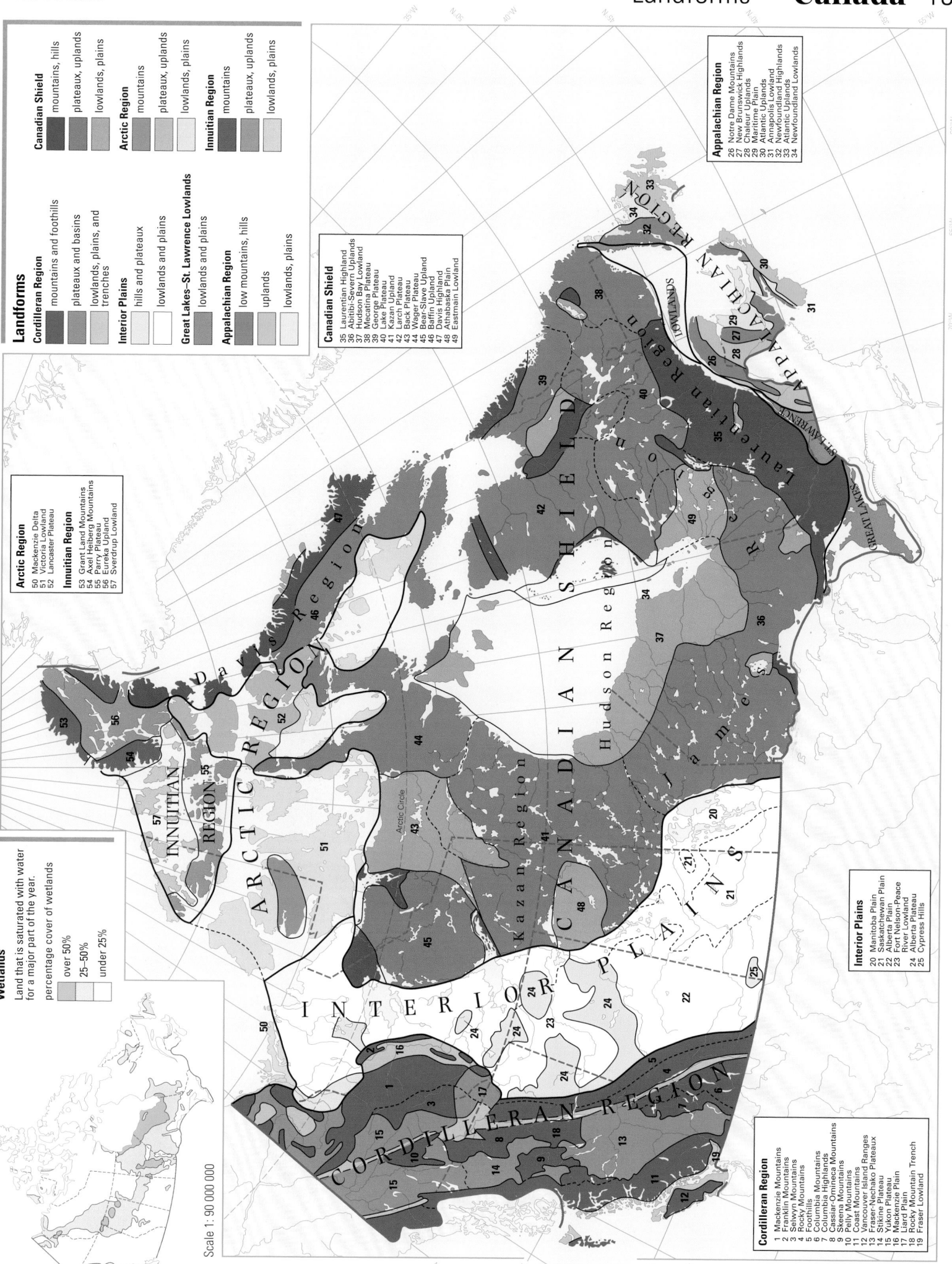

Landforms

Canadian Shield
- mountains, hills
- plateaux, uplands
- lowlands, plains

Arctic Region
- mountains
- plateaux, uplands
- lowlands, plains

Innuitian Region
- mountains
- plateaux, uplands
- lowlands, plains

Cordilleran Region
- mountains and foothills
- plateaux and basins
- lowlands, plains, and trenches

Interior Plains
- hills and plateaux
- lowlands and plains

Great Lakes–St. Lawrence Lowlands
- lowlands and plains

Appalachian Region
- low mountains, hills
- uplands
- lowlands, plains

Canadian Shield
35 Laurentian Highland
36 Abitibi-Severn Uplands
37 Hudson-Severn Uplands
38 Hudson Bay Lowland
39 Mecatina Plateau
39 George Plateau
40 Lake Plateau
41 Kazan Upland
42 Larch Plateau
43 Back Plateau
44 Wager Plateau
45 Bear-Slave Upland
46 Baffin Upland
47 Davis Highland
48 Athabaska Plain
49 Eastmain Lowland

Appalachian Region
26 Notre Dame Mountains
27 New Brunswick Highlands
28 Chaleur Uplands
29 Maritime Plain
30 Atlantic Uplands
31 Annapolis Lowland
32 Newfoundland Highlands
33 Atlantic Uplands
34 Newfoundland Lowlands

Arctic Region
50 Mackenzie Delta
51 Victoria Lowland
52 Lancaster Plateau

Innuitian Region
53 Grant Land Mountains
54 Axel Heiberg Mountains
55 Parry Plateau
56 Eureka Upland
57 Sverdrup Lowland

Interior Plains
20 Manitoba Plain
21 Saskatchewan Plain
22 Alberta Plain
23 Fort Nelson-Peace River Lowland
24 Alberta Plateau
25 Cypress Hills

Cordilleran Region
1 Mackenzie Mountains
2 Franklin Mountains
3 Selwyn Mountains
4 Rocky Mountains
5 Foothills
6 Columbia Mountains
7 Columbia Highlands
8 Cassiar-Omineca Mountains
9 Skeena Mountains
10 Pelly Mountains
11 Coast Mountains
12 Vancouver Island Ranges
13 Fraser-Nechako Plateaux
14 Stikine Plateau
15 Yukon Plateau
16 Mackenzie Plain
17 Liard Plain
18 Alberta Plateau
19 Fraser Lowland

Wetlands

Land that is saturated with water for a major part of the year.

percentage cover of wetlands
- over 50%
- 25–50%
- under 25%

Scale 1: 90 000 000

Zenithal Equidistant Projection © Oxford University Press

Heating the Earth

The Greenhouse Effect

The greenhouse effect is a naturally occurring process that enables the atmosphere to retain heat. Without it, the Earth's average temperature would be -18°C instead of the present +15°C. Climate change is attributed in large measure to increased levels of greenhouse gases largely due to human activity. Information on this subject for Canada occurs on page 25 and for the world on pages 124 and 128.

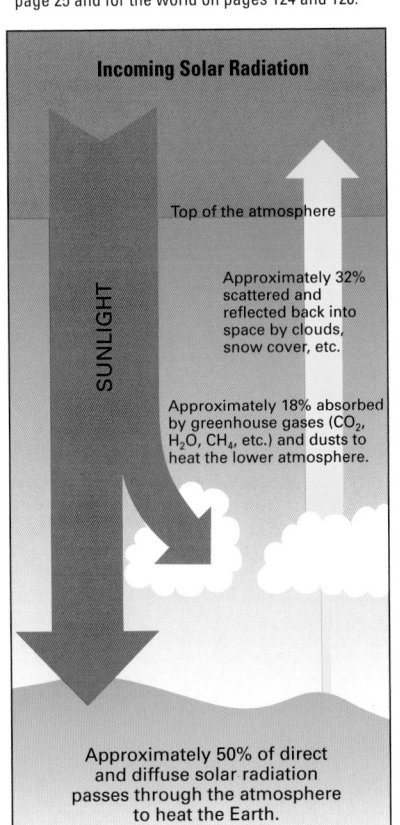

Incoming Solar Radiation

Top of the atmosphere

SUNLIGHT

Approximately 32% scattered and reflected back into space by clouds, snow cover, etc.

Approximately 18% absorbed by greenhouse gases (CO_2, H_2O, CH_4, etc.) and dusts to heat the lower atmosphere.

Approximately 50% of direct and diffuse solar radiation passes through the atmosphere to heat the Earth.

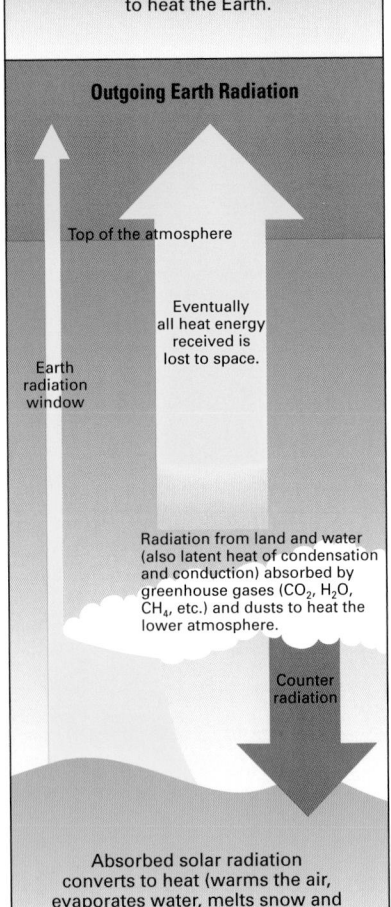

Outgoing Earth Radiation

Top of the atmosphere

Eventually all heat energy received is lost to space.

Earth radiation window

Radiation from land and water (also latent heat of condensation and conduction) absorbed by greenhouse gases (CO_2, H_2O, CH_4, etc.) and dusts to heat the lower atmosphere.

Counter radiation

Absorbed solar radiation converts to heat (warms the air, evaporates water, melts snow and ice), is used in photosynthesis, is released into the atmosphere, and ultimately is lost to space.

Temperature

Isotherms

°Celsius

- 20
- 15
- 10
- 5
- 0
- -10
- -20
- -30
- -35

Isotherms join places having the same average monthly temperature.

Isolines, as seen on the other maps on these pages, join places having the same average temperature range, precipitation, etc.

Permafrost

The state of the ground (soil or rock) that remains below 0°C for more than a year.

approximate southern limit of:

—— continuous permafrost (90–100% underlain by permafrost)

- - - discontinuous permafrost (10–90% underlain by permafrost)

Cross-section showing a typical permafrost distribution in Northern Canada

Limits of continuous and discontinuous permafrost are shown on the map above.

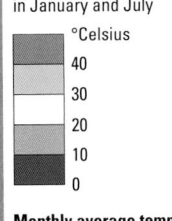

N ←

active layer   1-2m   2-3m

permafrost   45m   1-2m

400m   unfrozen ground

continuous permafrost   discontinuous permafrost

Temperature range

The difference between the average daily mean temperature in January and July

°Celsius

- 40
- 30
- 20
- 10
- 0

Monthly average temperatures for selected Canadian locations can be determined from the climate graphs on page 19 and the data in tables 84, 85 and 86 on pages 182–183.

Scale 1: 45 000 000

Zenithal Equidistant Projection
© Oxford University Press

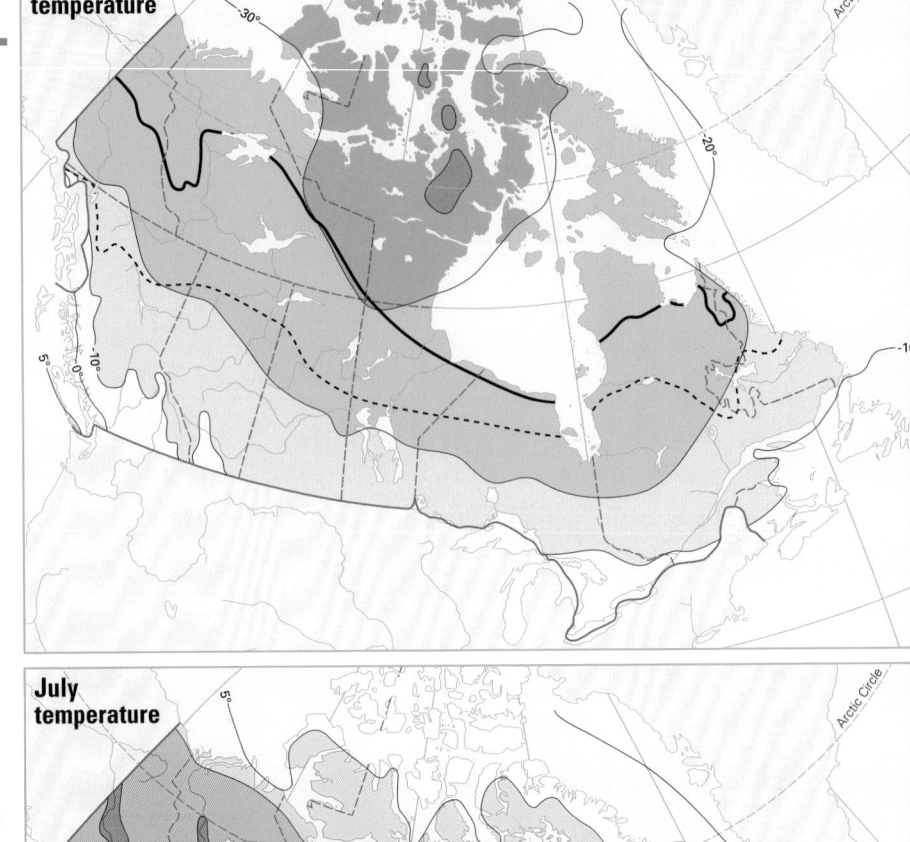

January temperature

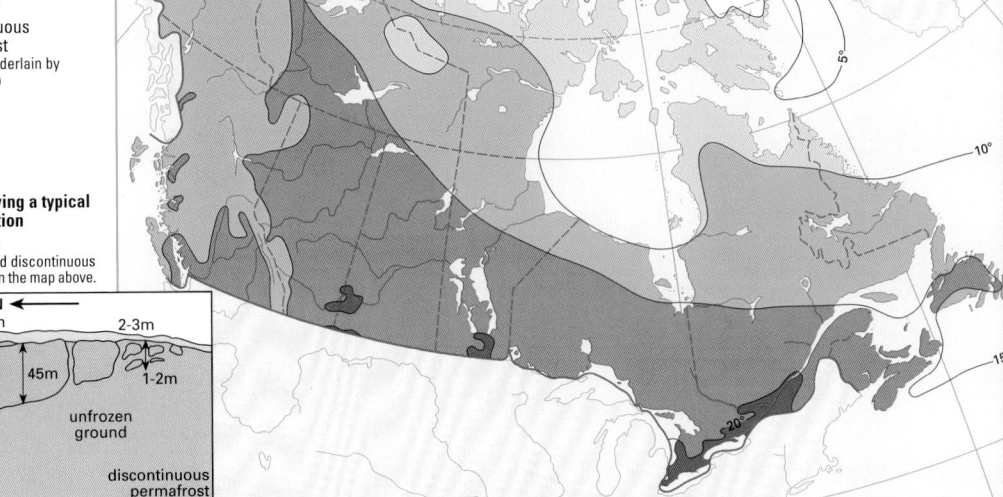

July temperature

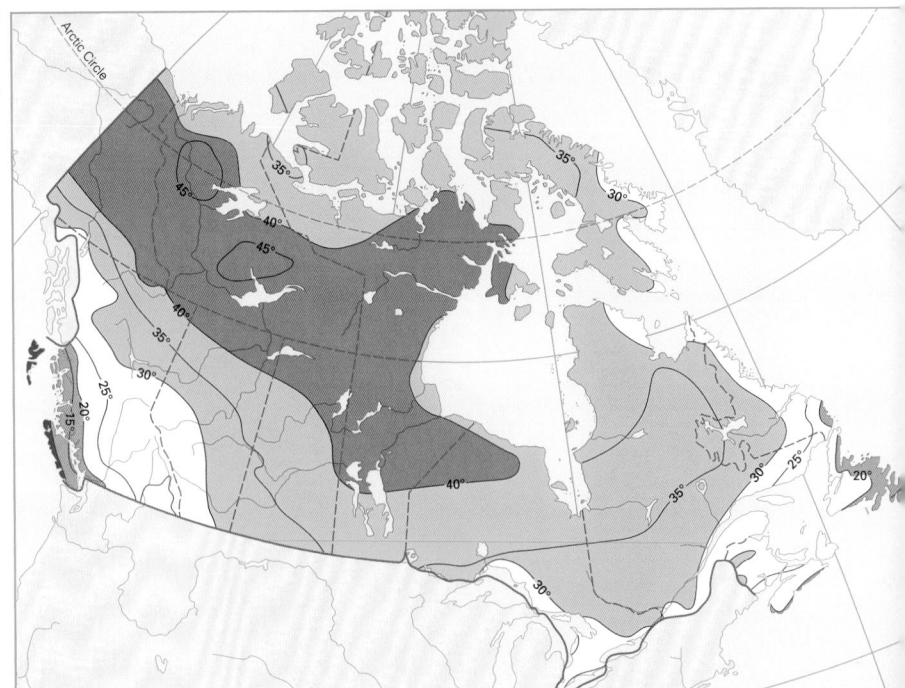

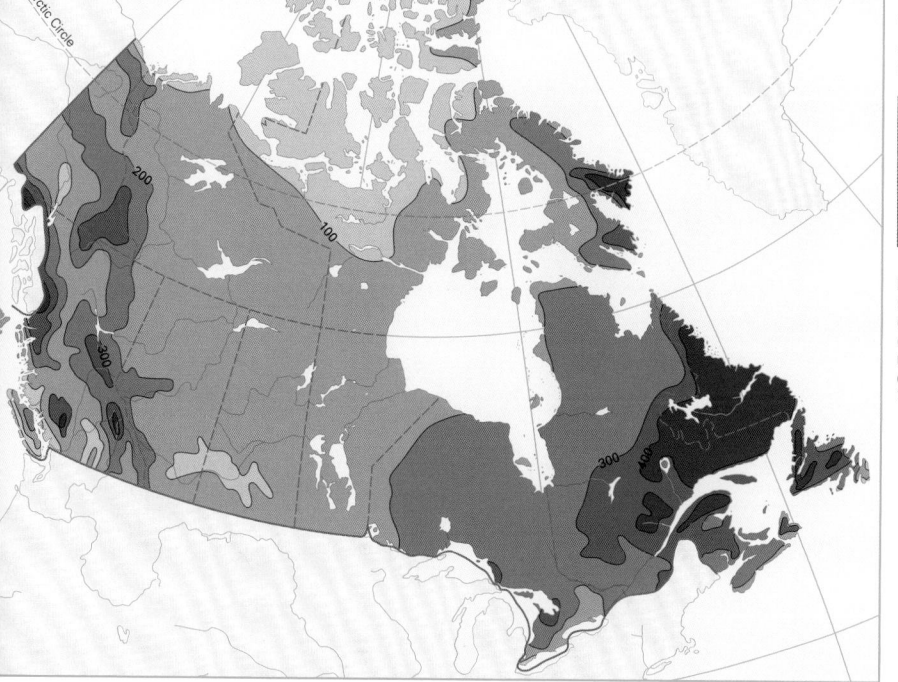

Precipitation

mean annual
precipitation

mm
2000
1000
750
500
250
0

**Monthly average
precipitation** for
selected Canadian
locations can be
determined from the
climate graphs on
page 19 and the data
in tables 84, 85 and 86
on pages 182–183.

Snow

mean annual
snowfall

cm	
	more than 400
	300–400
	200–300
	100–200
	less than 100

Precipitation includes
rain, snow, sleet, hail,
etc. Snowfall is
converted to water
using a 10 to 1 ratio
e.g., 10 cm of snow =
1 cm of rain.

Thunderstorms

average annual
number of days with
thunderstorms

days
20
10
5

Thunderstorms are
transient sometimes
violent storms caused
by strong rising air
currents resulting in
thunder, lightning,
heavy rain, and
sometimes hail and
high winds.

Scale 1: 45 000 000

Zenithal Equidistant Projection
© Oxford University Press

Air masses and winds

prevailing winds

- continental arctic
- maritime arctic
- maritime polar
- maritime tropical

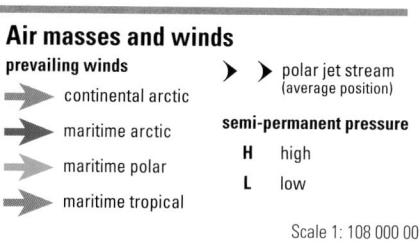

polar jet stream
(average position)

semi-permanent pressure

H high
L low

Scale 1: 108 000 000

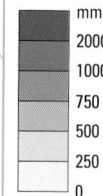

Winter

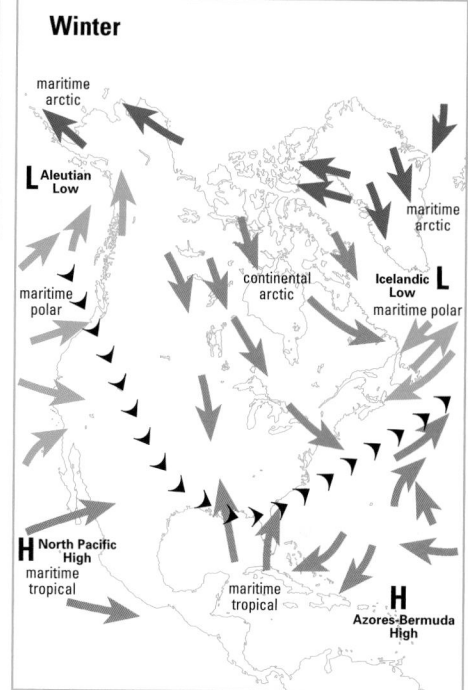

maritime arctic

L Aleutian Low

maritime polar

continental arctic

maritime arctic

Icelandic Low **L**

maritime polar

H North Pacific High
maritime tropical

maritime tropical

maritime tropical

H

H Azores-Bermuda High

Summer

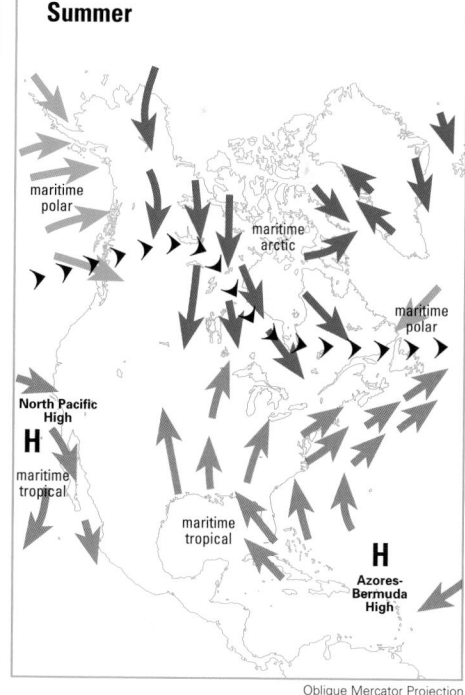

maritime polar

maritime arctic

maritime polar

North Pacific High

H

maritime tropical

maritime tropical

maritime tropical

H Azores-Bermuda High

Oblique Mercator Projection

The term **air mass** denotes a mass of air usually
several thousands of kilometres in extent, with
similar temperature characteristics. Their
boundaries are marked by frontal surfaces, along
which mid latitude cyclonic storms occur.

Jet streams are high altitude streams of rapidly
moving air, characterized by large stationary or
slow moving waves. They circle the Earth and
change locations with the seasons. They are
associated with the fronts between air masses,
and thus have a major influence on surface
weather.

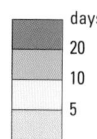

Humidex

The humidex was developed in Canada in 1965. Its purpose is to combine temperature and humidity into one number to reflect how hot humid weather is perceived by the average person.

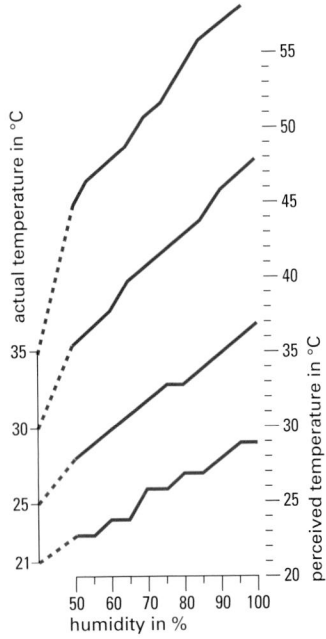

Humidex	Degree of discomfort
over 54	heat stroke imminent
45–54	dangerous
40–45	great discomfort
30–40	some discomfort
under 30	no discomfort

UV Index

The UV Index is a measure of the intensity of the sun's ultraviolet radiation in the sunburning spectrum. As the index increases, the sun's rays do more harm to skin, eyes, and the immune system, and it becomes necessary to take more precautions to protect exposed skin. In Canada, the UV forecast is issued twice daily for 47 locations. The risks from exposure to ultraviolet radiation have increased in recent years due to the thinning of the ozone layer.

UV Index	Description	Sun protection action
over 11	Extreme	take full precautions — unprotected skin will be damaged and can burn in minutes
8–10	Very high	extra precautions required — unprotected skin will be damaged and can burn quickly
6–7	High	protection required — UV damages the skin and can cause sunburn
3–5	Moderate	take precautions — hat, sunglasses and sunscreen
0–2	Low	minimal sun protection required for normal activity

Canadian weather records

highest air temperature	45°C Midale and Yellow Grass, Sask. *5 July 1937*
lowest air temperature	-63°C Snag, Y.T. *3 February 1947*
coldest month	-47.9°C Eureka, N.W.T. *February 1979*
highest sea-level pressure	107.96 kPa Dawson, Y.T. *2 February 1989*
lowest sea-level pressure	94.02 kPa St. Anthony, Nfld. *20 January 1977*
greatest precipitation in 24 hours	489.2 mm Ucluelet Brynnor Mines, B.C. *6 October 1967*
greatest precipitation in one month	2235.5 mm Swanson Bay, B.C. *November 1917*
greatest precipitation in one year	9479 mm Henderson Lake, B.C. *1977*
greatest average annual precipitation	6655 mm Henderson Lake, B.C.
least precipitation in one year	12.7 mm Arctic Bay, N.W.T. *1949*
greatest snowfall in one season	2446.5 cm Revelstoke, B.C. *1971–1972*
highest average annual number of thunderstorm days	34 days London, Ont.

Growing season

average annual length of the growing season in number of days, assuming the growing season is that part of the year when the mean daily temperature is greater than 5.6°C

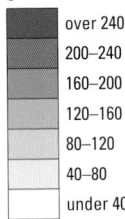

- over 240
- 200–240
- 160–200
- 120–160
- 80–120
- 40–80
- under 40

Scale 1: 45 000 000
Zenithal Equidistant Projection

Sunshine

average annual hours

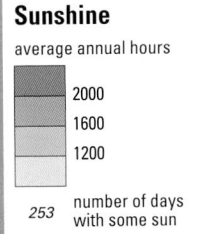

- 2000
- 1600
- 1200

253 number of days with some sun

The use of renewable sources such as solar, wind, geothermal, tide, and wave energy to produce electricity will continue to increase in importance to replace non-renewable sources and combat global warming.

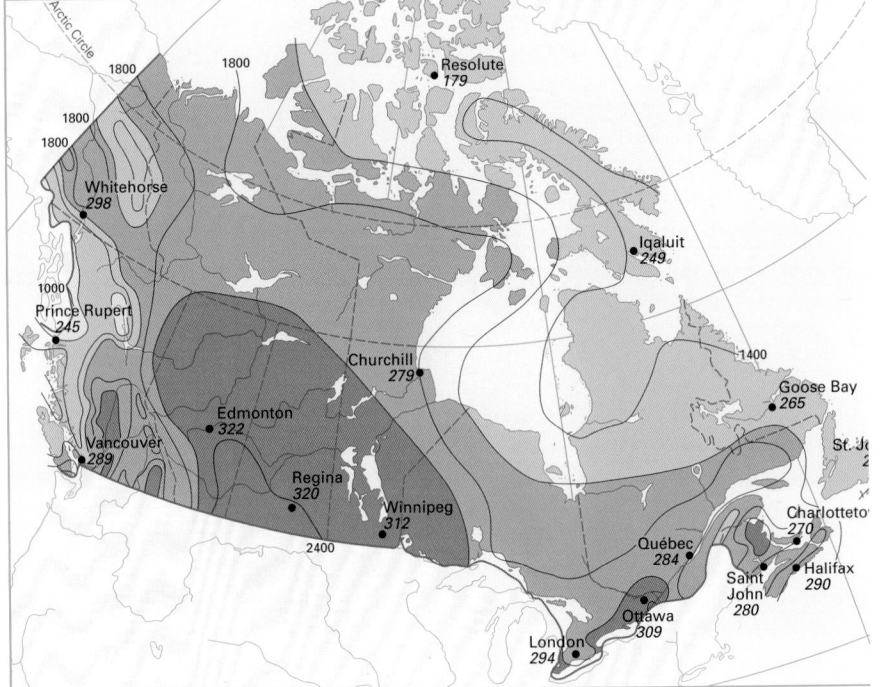

Resolute *179*
Whitehorse *298*
Iqaluit *249*
Prince Rupert *245*
Churchill *279*
Goose Bay *265*
St. J…
Edmonton *322*
Vancouver *289*
Regina *320*
Winnipeg *312*
Charlotteto… *270*
Québec *284*
Saint John *280*
Halifax *290*
Ottawa *309*
London *294*

January wind chill

5% chance of having a wind chill value worse than the value shown

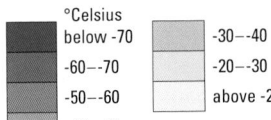

°Celsius
- below -70
- -60–-70
- -50–-60
- -40–-50
- -30–-40
- -20–-30
- above -20

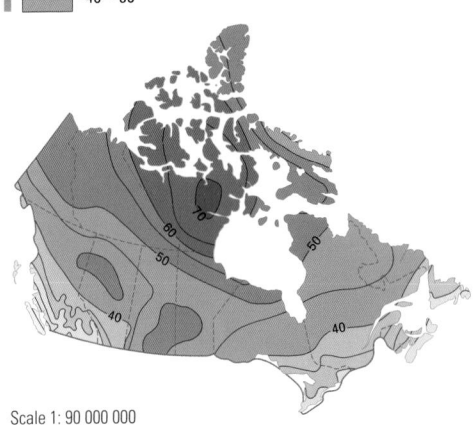

Scale 1: 90 000 000

Wind chill equivalent temperature

Wind chill is a measure of the wind's cooling effect, as on exposed flesh. So as not to confuse it with actual temperature, wind chill is expressed as a temperature index, without the degree symbol.

	actual air temperature in °C								
	5	0	-5	-10	-15	-20	-25	-30	-35
5	4	-2	-7	-13	-19	-24	-30	-36	-41
10	3	-3	-9	-15	-21	-27	-33	-39	-45
15	2	-4	-11	-17	-23	-29	-35	-41	-48
20	1	-5	-12	-18	-24	-31	-37	-43	-49
25	1	-6	-12	-19	-25	-32	-38	-45	-51
30	0	-7	-13	-20	-26	-33	-39	-46	-52
35	0	-7	-14	-20	-27	-33	-40	-47	-53
40	-1	-7	-14	-21	-27	-34	-41	-48	-54
45	-1	-8	-15	-21	-28	-35	-42	-48	-55
50	-1	-8	-15	-22	-29	-35	-42	-49	-56
55	-2	-9	-15	-22	-29	-36	-43	-50	-57
60	-2	-9	-16	-23	-30	-37	-43	-50	-57

wind speed at 10 metres in km/h

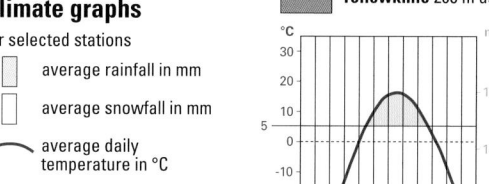

Climate graphs
for selected stations

- average rainfall in mm
- average snowfall in mm
- average daily temperature in °C
- growing season*
- asl above sea level

10 mm of snowfall is the water equivalent of 1 mm of rainfall

* that part of the year when average daily temperature remains above 5.6°C

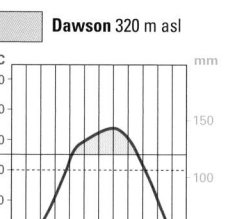
Dawson 320 m asl
Annual precipitation 306.0 mm

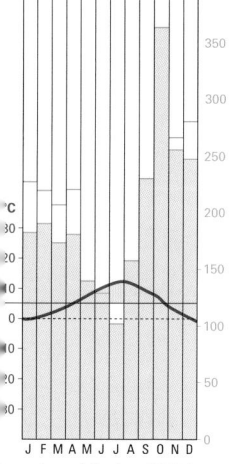
Prince Rupert 34 m asl
Annual precipitation 2 551.6 mm

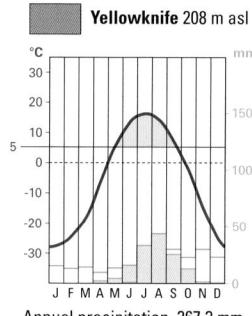
Yellowknife 208 m asl
Annual precipitation 267.3 mm

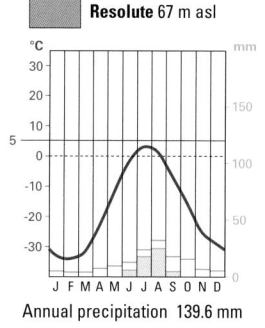
Resolute 67 m asl
Annual precipitation 139.6 mm

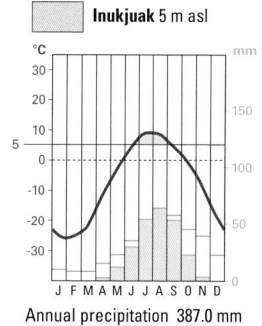
Inukjuak 5 m asl
Annual precipitation 387.0 mm

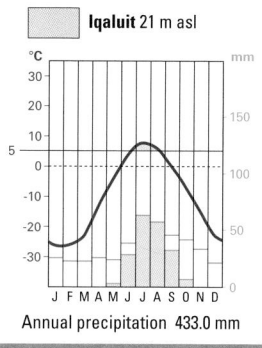
Iqaluit 21 m asl
Annual precipitation 433.0 mm

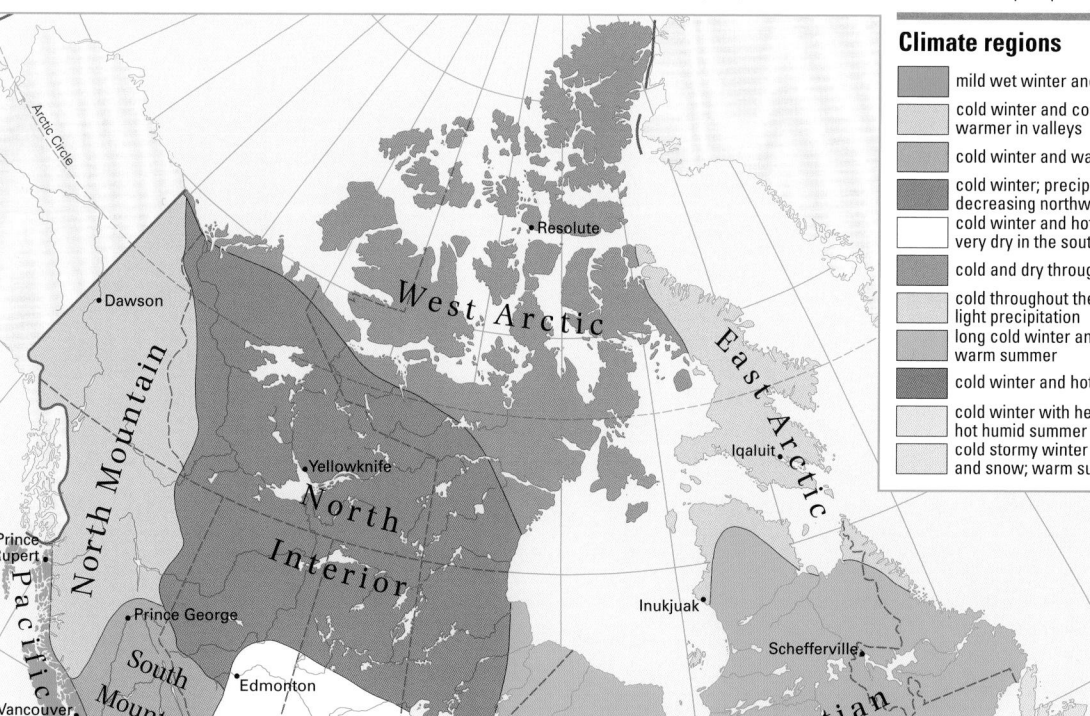

Climate regions
- mild wet winter and warm summer
- cold winter and cool summer; warmer in valleys
- cold winter and warm summer
- cold winter; precipitation decreasing northwards
- cold winter and hot summer; very dry in the south
- cold and dry throughout the year
- cold throughout the year; light precipitation
- long cold winter and short warm summer
- cold winter and hot summer
- cold winter with heavy snowfalls; hot humid summer
- cold stormy winter with heavy rain and snow; warm summer

Additional climate statistics for 28 Canadian locations can be found on pages 182 and 183, while similar data for 21 other global locations is on page 127.

© Oxford University Press

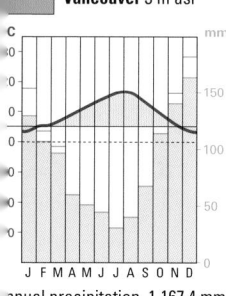
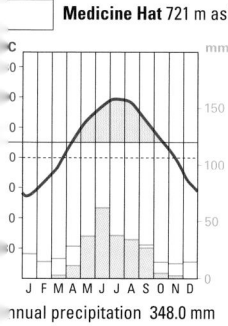

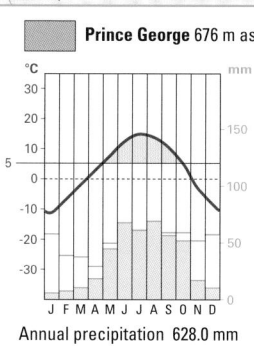
Vancouver 3 m asl
Annual precipitation 1 167.4 mm

Prince George 676 m asl
Annual precipitation 628.0 mm

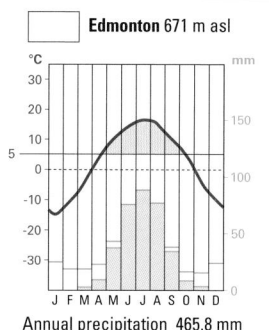
Edmonton 671 m asl
Annual precipitation 465.8 mm

Schefferville 522 m asl
Annual precipitation 769.0 mm

Halifax 32 m asl
Annual precipitation 1 473.5 mm

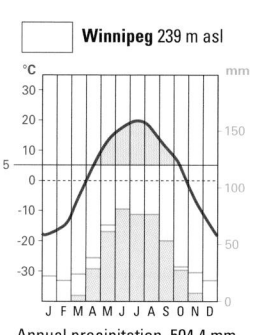
Medicine Hat 721 m asl
Annual precipitation 348.0 mm

Winnipeg 239 m asl
Annual precipitation 504.4 mm

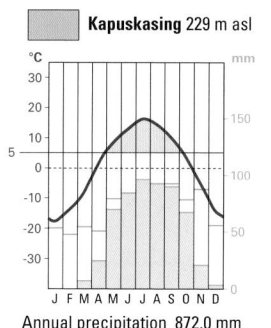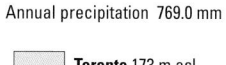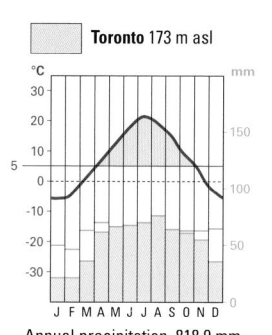
Kapuskasing 229 m asl
Annual precipitation 872.0 mm

Toronto 173 m asl
Annual precipitation 818.9 mm

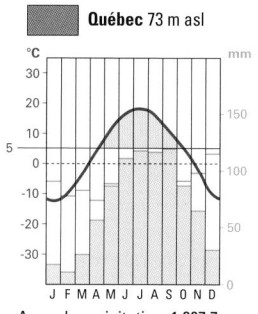
Québec 73 m asl
Annual precipitation 1 207.7 mm

Scale 1: 24 000 000

0 240 480 720 km

Main tree species

Black Spruce, White Spruce, Balsam Fir,
Jack Pine, White Birch, Trembling Aspen

Black Spruce, White Spruce, Tamarack

Trembling Aspen, Willow

Alpine Fir, Engelmann Spruce,
Lodgepole Pine

Douglas Fir, Lodgepole Pine,
Ponderosa Pine, Trembling Aspen

Western Red Cedar, Western Hemlock,
Douglas Fir, Sitka Spruce

Western Red Cedar, Western Hemlock,
Western Red Pine

Beech, Sugar Maple, Black Walnut,
Hickory, Red Oak, White Elm, Butternut

Eastern White Pine, Eastern Hemlock,
Red Pine, Yellow Birch, Sugar Maple, Oak

Red Spruce, Balsam Fir, Maple, Spruce
Yellow Birch, Red Pine, White Pine,

Trembling Aspen, Willow, Bur Oak

Vegetation regions

Boreal (mainly forest)

Boreal (forest and
barren ground)

Boreal (forest and
grassland)

Subalpine

Montane

Coast

Columbia

Deciduous

Great Lakes–
St. Lawrence

Acadian

Grassland

area of commercial forest (more than 50% of the total land area)

Tundra

Alpine sedges/grasses
and shrubs

Dwarf shrubs/sedges/
lichen/heath

Arctic stony lichen/heath

Rock desert

ice cap

Pulp, paper, and board mills

pulp only

pulp and paper or pulp and board

paper, board, or paper and board

over 500 000   under 500 000
tonnes/year   tonnes/year

93% of Canada's forests is publicly owned, 77% is under provincial or territorial
jurisdiction, and the rest is under federal control. About 80% of the harvesting
takes place on public lands following policies, legislation, and regulations set
down by the 10 provinces and three territories.

Further information on this topic
is located in the Canada Statistics
section, which begins on page 155.

Natural disturbances such as fire, wind, snow, insects, and fungi
are an important and necessary part of forest health. They remove
old or otherwise susceptible trees, recycle nutrients, and provide
habitat and food for wildlife. They can, however, have serious
economic repercussions if they become severe. For example, by
2005, the Mountain Pine Beetle infestation in British Columbia
had affected 8.7 million hectares. Beetle outbreaks are also
increasingly frequent in Alberta's pine forests. Altogether, on a
national scale, the forest area defoliated by insects and beetle-
killed trees totalled 13.1 million hectares in 2004. In 2005, some
7 438 fires burned 1.7 million hectares of forest, compared to
the 10-year average of 2.4 million hectares.

Western Hemlock

Red Oak

Sugar Maple

Trembling Aspen

White Birch

Western Red Cedar

Eastern White Pine

Douglas Fir

Black Spruce

Balsam Fir

Jack Pine

White Spruce

New Glasgow

Matane

Dalhousie

Baie-
Comeau

Alma

Trois-
Rivières

Windsor

Shawinigan

Gatineau

Thorold

Brampton

Kapuskasing

Dryden

Bovie

Peace River

Campbell
River

Crofton

© Oxford University Press

Scale 1: 35 000 000

| 0 | 350 | 700 | 1050 km |

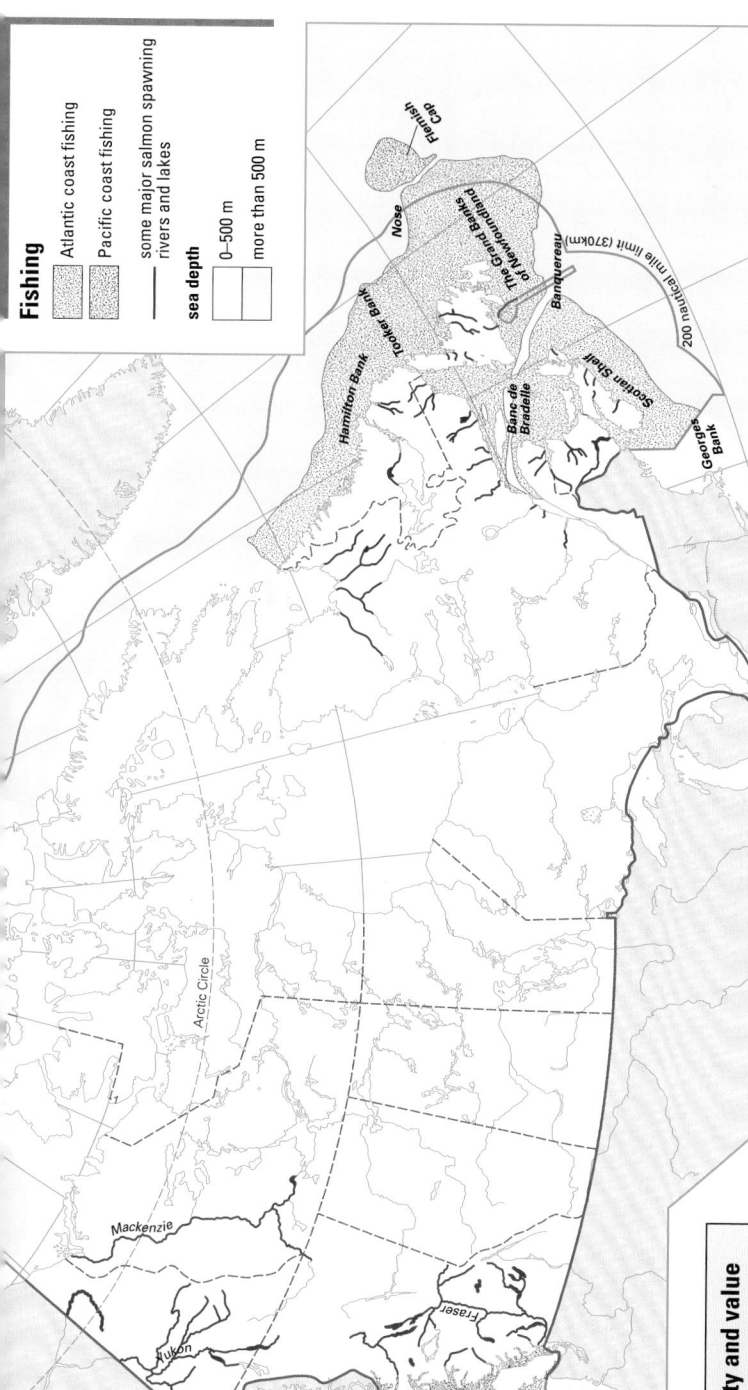

Fishing
- Atlantic coast fishing
- Pacific coast fishing
- some major salmon spawning rivers and lakes

sea depth
- 0–500 m
- more than 500 m

Flemish Cap
Nose
The Grand Banks of Newfoundland
Hamilton Bank
Hopedale Bank
Banquereau
Scotian Shelf
Banc de Bradelle
Georges Bank
200 nautical mile limit (370km)
Arctic Circle
Mackenzie
Fraser
Yukon
200 nautical mile limit (370km)

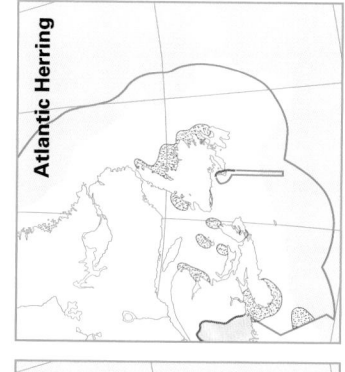

Atlantic Herring

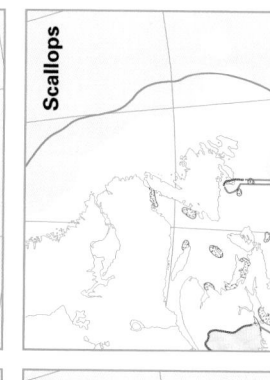

Scallops

Atlantic Cod

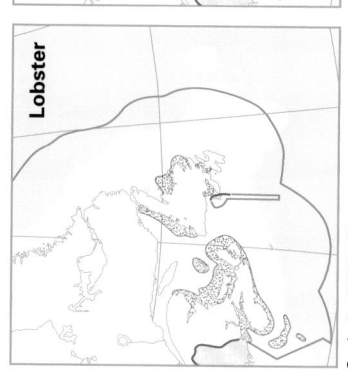

Lobster

Scale 1: 45 000 000

Aquaculture value by species, 2005
% of total value

salmon 76.0%
restocking 1.2%
other shellfish 1.3%
mussels 4.6%
oysters 2.3%
clams 1.2%
other finfish 10.5%
trout 2.9%

Total production 154 993 tonnes
Total value $715.1 million

In July 1992, the federal government announced a moratorium on the northern cod fishery to rebuild the stock of this species. Moratoria apply to other groundfish, such as haddock, redfish, and plaice, in certain areas, while the government sets out each year a Total Allowable Catch (TAC) for most other groundfish as well as other species.

According to the UN Food and Agriculture Organization, over 70% of the world's fish species are either fully exploited or being depleted. In the last decade in the North Atlantic region, commercial fish populations of cod, hake, haddock, and flounder have fallen by as much as 95%. Overfishing and destructive fishing techniques are the principal causes of the depletion of fish stocks, as well as the endangerment of marine mammals and entire aquatic ecosystems.

Fish catches by quantity and value

	quantity (000 tonnes)		value ($000 000)	
	1990	2006	1990	2006
Lobster	47.9	52.1	232.2	618.1
Crab	29.2	102.2	59.2	236.7
Shrimp	40.0	179.5	85.4	270.5
Scallop	83.4	63.1	87.4	85.9
Herring	301.3	182.1	110.8	55.6
Halibut	7.5	9.1	31.9	59.1
Hake	94.6	112.6	20.4	38.8
Cod	401.3	28.2	247.2	38.2
Salmon	97.1	23.5	266.6	58.2
All species	1 624.8	1 030.7	1 432.0	1 755.8

Major world fishing countries, 2004
(000 tonnes of catch in live weight)

China	17 271
Peru	9 621
Chile	5 326
USA	4 995
Indonesia	4 882
Japan	4 517
India	3 624
Russia	3 000
Thailand	2 845
Norway	2 671
Philippines	2 215
Vietnam	1 879
Iceland	1 750
Myanmar	1 587
South Korea	1 584
Mexico	1 478
Malaysia	1 340
Canada	1 191
Bangladesh	1 187
Denmark	1 090
Argentina	951
World total	96 462

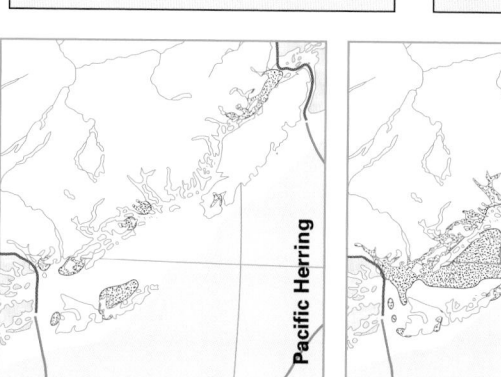

Pacific Cod

Pacific Halibut

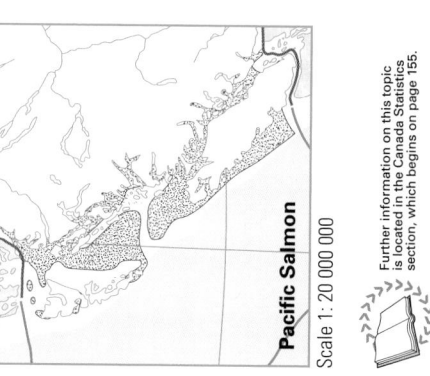

Pacific Herring

Pacific Salmon

Scale 1: 20 000 000

Further information on this topic is located in the Canada Statistics section, which begins on page 155.

Scale 1: 35 000 000

0   350   700   1050 km

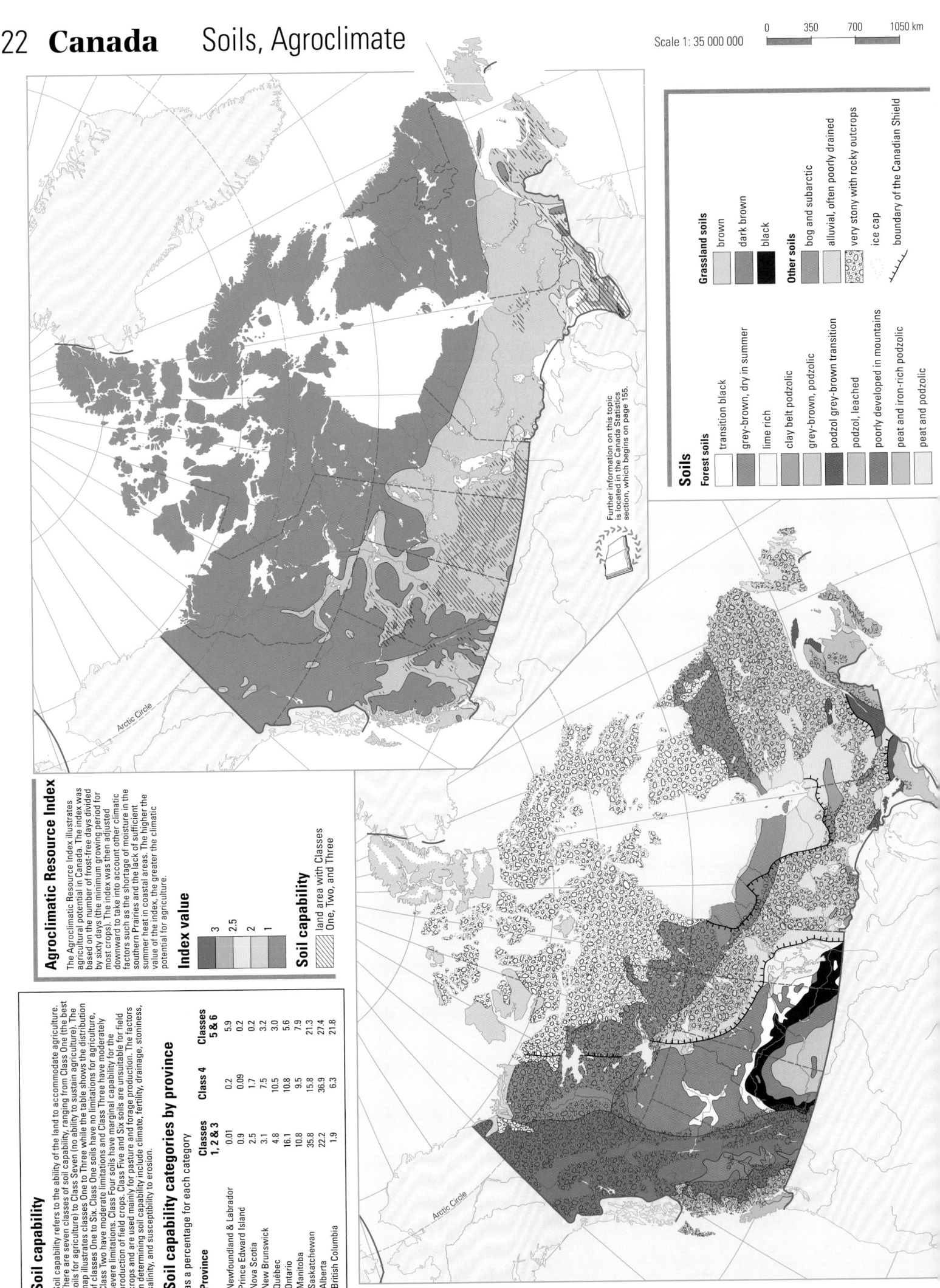

Further information on this topic is located in the Canada Statistics section, which begins on page 155.

Soils

Forest soils

- transition black
- grey-brown, dry in summer
- lime rich
- clay belt podzolic
- grey-brown, podzolic
- podzol grey-brown transition
- podzol, leached
- poorly developed in mountains
- peat and iron-rich podzolic
- peat and podzolic

Grassland soils

- brown
- dark brown
- black

Other soils

- bog and subarctic
- alluvial, often poorly drained
- very stony with rocky outcrops
- ice cap
- boundary of the Canadian Shield

Agroclimatic Resource Index

The Agroclimatic Resource Index illustrates agricultural potential in Canada. The index was based on the number of frost-free days divided by sixty days (the minimum growing period for most crops). The index was then adjusted downward to take into account other climatic factors such as the shortage of moisture in the southern Prairies and the lack of sufficient summer heat in coastal areas. The higher the value of the index, the greater the climatic potential for agriculture.

Index value

- 3
- 2.5
- 2
- 1

Soil capability

- land area with Classes One, Two, and Three

Soil capability

Soil capability refers to the ability of the land to accommodate agriculture. There are seven classes of soil capability, ranging from Class One (the best soils for agriculture) to Class Seven (no ability to sustain agriculture). The map illustrates classes One to Three while the table shows the distribution of classes One to Six. Class One soils have no limitations for agriculture, Class Two have moderate limitations and Class Three have moderately severe limitations. Class Four soils have marginal capability for the production of field crops. Class Five and Six soils are unsuitable for field crops and are used mainly for pasture and forage production. The factors in determining soil capability include climate, fertility, drainage, stoniness, salinity, and susceptibility to erosion.

Soil capability categories by province

as a percentage for each category

Province	Classes 1, 2 & 3	Class 4	Classes 5 & 6
Newfoundland & Labrador	0.01	0.2	5.9
Prince Edward Island	0.9	0.09	0.2
Nova Scotia	2.5	1.7	0.2
New Brunswick	3.1	7.5	3.2
Québec	4.8	10.5	3.0
Ontario	16.1	10.8	5.6
Manitoba	10.8	9.5	7.9
Saskatchewan	35.8	15.8	21.3
Alberta	22.2	36.9	27.4
British Columbia	1.9	6.3	21.8

Arctic Circle

Zenithal Equidistant Projection

© Oxford University Press

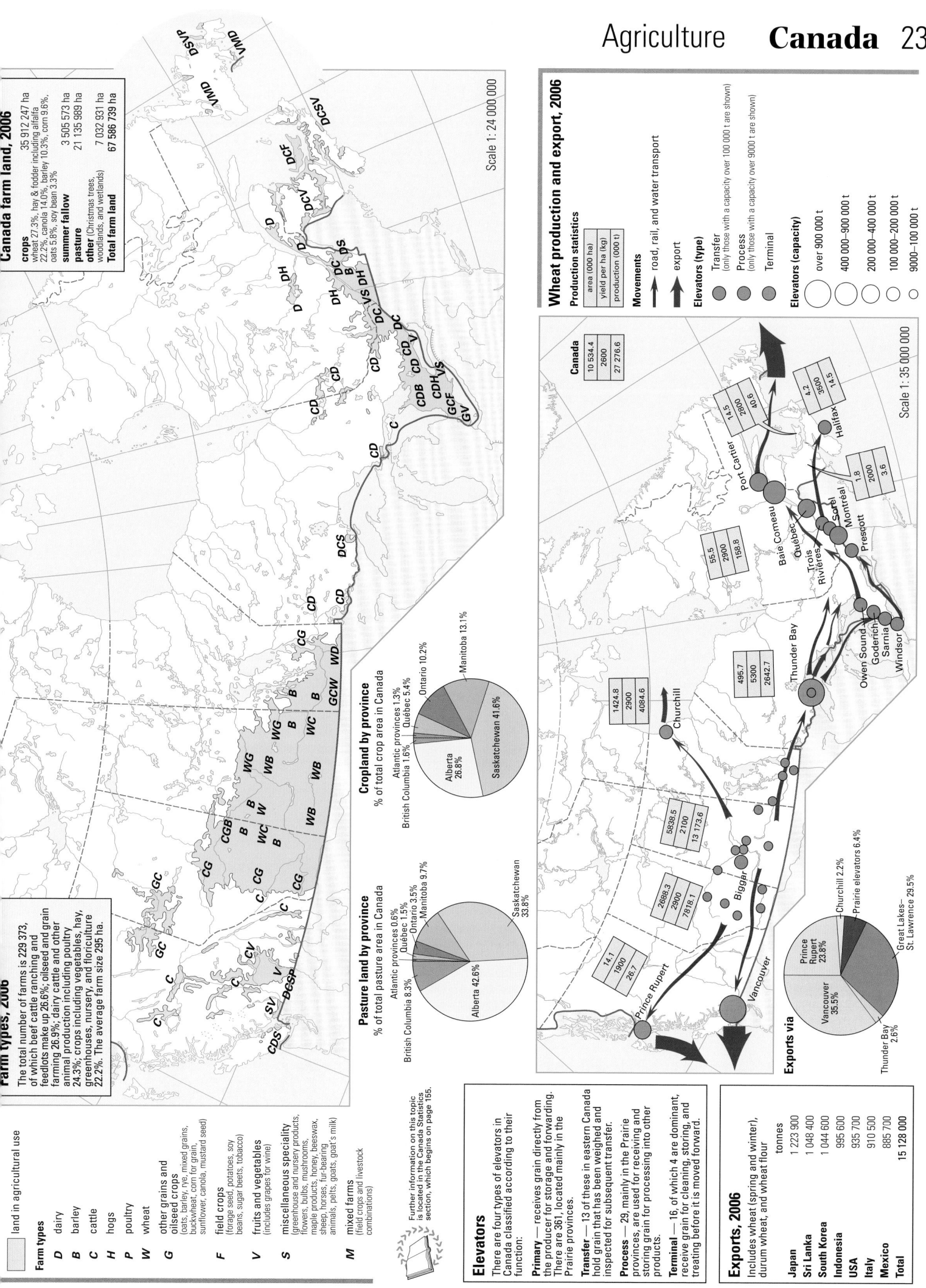

Canada farm land, 2006

crops — 35 912 247 ha
wheat 27.3%, hay & fodder including alfalfa 22.2%, canola 14.0%, barley 10.3%, corn 9.6%, oats 5.8%, soy bean 3.3%

summer fallow — 3 505 573 ha

pasture — 21 135 989 ha

other (Christmas trees, woodlands, and wetlands) — 7 032 931 ha

Total farm land — 67 586 739 ha

Farm types, 2006

The total number of farms is 229 373, of which beef cattle ranching and feedlots make up 26.6%; oilseed and grain farming 26.9%; dairy cattle and other animal production including poultry 24.3%; crops including vegetables, hay, greenhouses, nursery, and floriculture 22.2%. The average farm size 295 ha.

land in agricultural use

Farm types

- **D** dairy
- **B** barley
- **C** cattle
- **H** hogs
- **P** poultry
- **W** wheat
- **G** other grains and oilseed crops (oats, barley, rye, mixed grains, buckwheat, corn for grain, sunflower, canola, mustard seed)
- **F** field crops (forage seed, potatoes, soy beans, sugar beets, tobacco)
- **V** fruits and vegetables (includes grapes for wine)
- **S** miscellaneous speciality (greenhouse and nursery products, flowers, bulbs, mushrooms, maple products, honey, beeswax, sheep, horses, fur-bearing animals, pelts, goats, goat's milk)
- **M** mixed farms (field crops and livestock combinations)

Further information on this topic is located in the Canada Statistics section, which begins on page 155.

Scale 1 : 24 000 000

Pasture land by province
% of total pasture area in Canada

British Columbia 8.3%
Atlantic provinces 0.6%
Québec 1.5%
Ontario 3.5%
Manitoba 9.7%
Saskatchewan 33.8%
Alberta 42.6%

Cropland by province
% of total crop area in Canada

British Columbia 1.6%
Atlantic provinces 1.3%
Québec 5.4%
Ontario 10.2%
Manitoba 13.1%
Alberta 26.8%
Saskatchewan 41.6%

Elevators

There are four types of elevators in Canada classified according to their function:

Primary — receives grain directly from the producer for storage and forwarding. There are 361, located mainly in the Prairie provinces.

Transfer — 13 of these in eastern Canada hold grain that has been weighed and inspected for subsequent transfer.

Process — 29, mainly in the Prairie provinces, are used for receiving and storing grain for processing into other products.

Terminal — 16, of which 4 are dominant, receive grain for cleaning, storing, and treating before it is moved forward.

Wheat production and export, 2006

Production statistics

area (000 ha)	
yield per ha (kg)	
production (000 t)	

Canada

10 534.4
2600
27 276.6

Movements
road, rail, and water transport
▲ Transfer
▲ export

Elevators (type)
● Transfer (only those with a capacity over 100 000 t are shown)
● Process (only those with a capacity over 9000 t are shown)
● Terminal

Elevators (capacity)
○ over 900 000 t
○ 400 000–900 000 t
○ 200 000–400 000 t
○ 100 000–200 000 t
○ 9000–100 000 t

Scale 1 : 35 000 000

Exports, 2006

Includes wheat (spring and winter), durum wheat, and wheat flour

	tonnes
Japan	1 223 900
Sri Lanka	1 048 400
South Korea	1 044 600
Indonesia	995 600
USA	935 700
Italy	910 500
Mexico	885 700
Total	15 128 000

Exports via

Vancouver 35.5%
Prince Rupert 23.8%
Thunder Bay 2.6%
Churchill 2.2%
Prairie elevators 6.4%
Great Lakes–St. Lawrence 29.5%

Scale 1: 35 000 000

0   350   700   1050 km

Earthquakes

magnitudes greater than 5.5 on the Richter scale

● epicentre

Landslides and avalanches

in the 20th century involving loss of life

+ major landslides and avalanches

Tornadoes

average annual frequency of tornadoes per 10 000 km²

over 7.5
2.5–7.5
1.0–2.5

Earthquakes

Earthquakes are caused by the shifting of the Earth's plates (see page 123). Canada is one of the least affected countries in the world.

Other natural disasters

Tsunamis

Tsunamis are sea waves produced by earthquakes or volcanic eruptions. They can travel across the open oceans at speeds as high as 450 km/h and reach heights on the shore as great as 30 m. Damaging tsunamis are relatively rare along Canadian coastlines; the last serious one occurred in British Columbia in 1964, causing considerable damage with waves up to 6 m.

Volcanoes

While there has been only one documented volcanic eruption in Canada, there are many dormant volcanoes in western Canada, particularly northwestern British Columbia.

Drought

Drought is an extended period of below-average precipitation. It can result in huge losses of both crops and livestock and severely depleted water supplies. Generally, the lower an area's average annual precipitation, the more vulnerable it is to drought. Global warming is believed to be an important factor in the increased frequency and severity of droughts around the globe. One of the worst droughts in Canada occurred in 1988, when an estimated $1.8 billion in damage resulted in areas stretching from southern Alberta to southern Ontario.

Flooding

○ designated flood risk areas

Hail

average annual number of days with hail

over 3
1–3

Fog

visibility less than half a nautical mile in July, measured in percentage frequency

over 40
20–40
5–20

Landslides and avalanches

Landslides and avalanches involve mass movements of rock, soil, and snow and can take many different forms. While particularly common in mountainous regions, they can occur anywhere that the subsurface conditions on sloping lands are unstable.

Tornadoes

Tornadoes are rotating columns of high velocity winds (which can exceed 200 km/h) that reach the ground as funnel-shaped clouds. While their path on the ground is seldom very wide and usually completely unpredictable, almost everything in its path — trees, buildings, and other structures — may be destroyed.

Freezing rain

Freezing rain can cause serious damage. An ice storm in January 1998 moved across southern Ontario, southern Quebec, and parts of New Brunswick resulting in property damage, damage to forests, and loss of life. Ice storms of this severity are rare (see inset).

Freezing rain

freezing rain accumulations in mm between January 4–10 1998

mm
100
80
60
40

Scale 1: 19 000 000

Fog

Fog forms when warm humid air is cooled below its dew point. The waters off Canada's eastern coast are particularly vulnerable. Here the warm air associated with the Gulf Stream meets the colder air associated with the southward-moving Labrador Current.

Hail

Hail occurs in the warm updrafts of thunderstorms usually between May and October. Hail can strike the ground at 130 km/h and result in severe damage to crops, buildings, and vehicles. One of the costliest natural disasters in Canada was a hailstorm in the Calgary area in September 1991 in which insured damage was estimated at $400 million.

Almost all of Canada except the far north may experience hailstorms. Areas that have hail on average more than one day a year are shown on the map.

Flooding

Flooding is a natural phenomenon made worse by human changes to the natural environment, such as the destruction of vegetation cover. Floods most often occur during spring thaw or after heavy rains. Some notable floods: Red River in 1950 and 1997; the Saguenay region in July 1996.

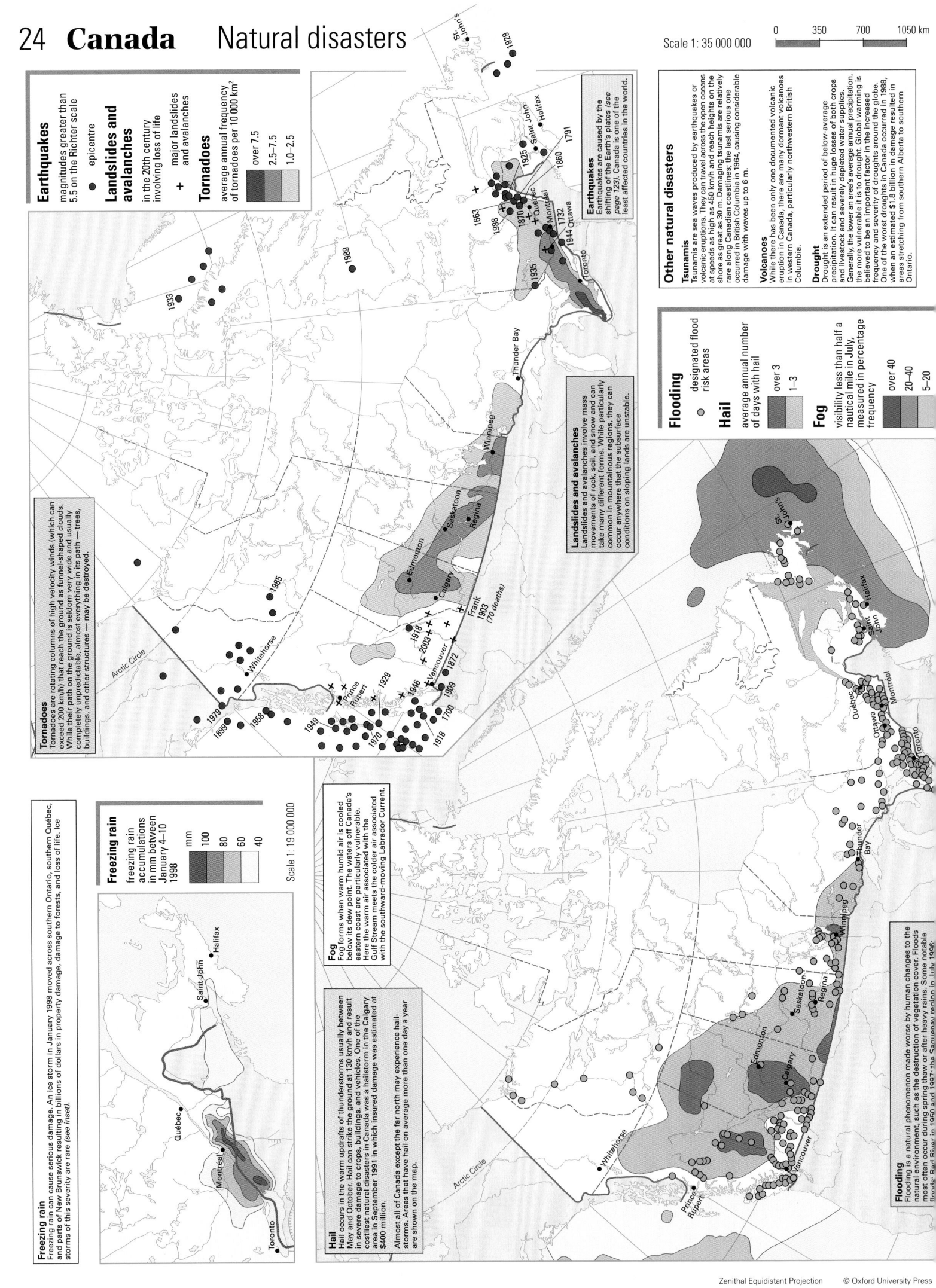

Zenithal Equidistant Projection

© Oxford University Press

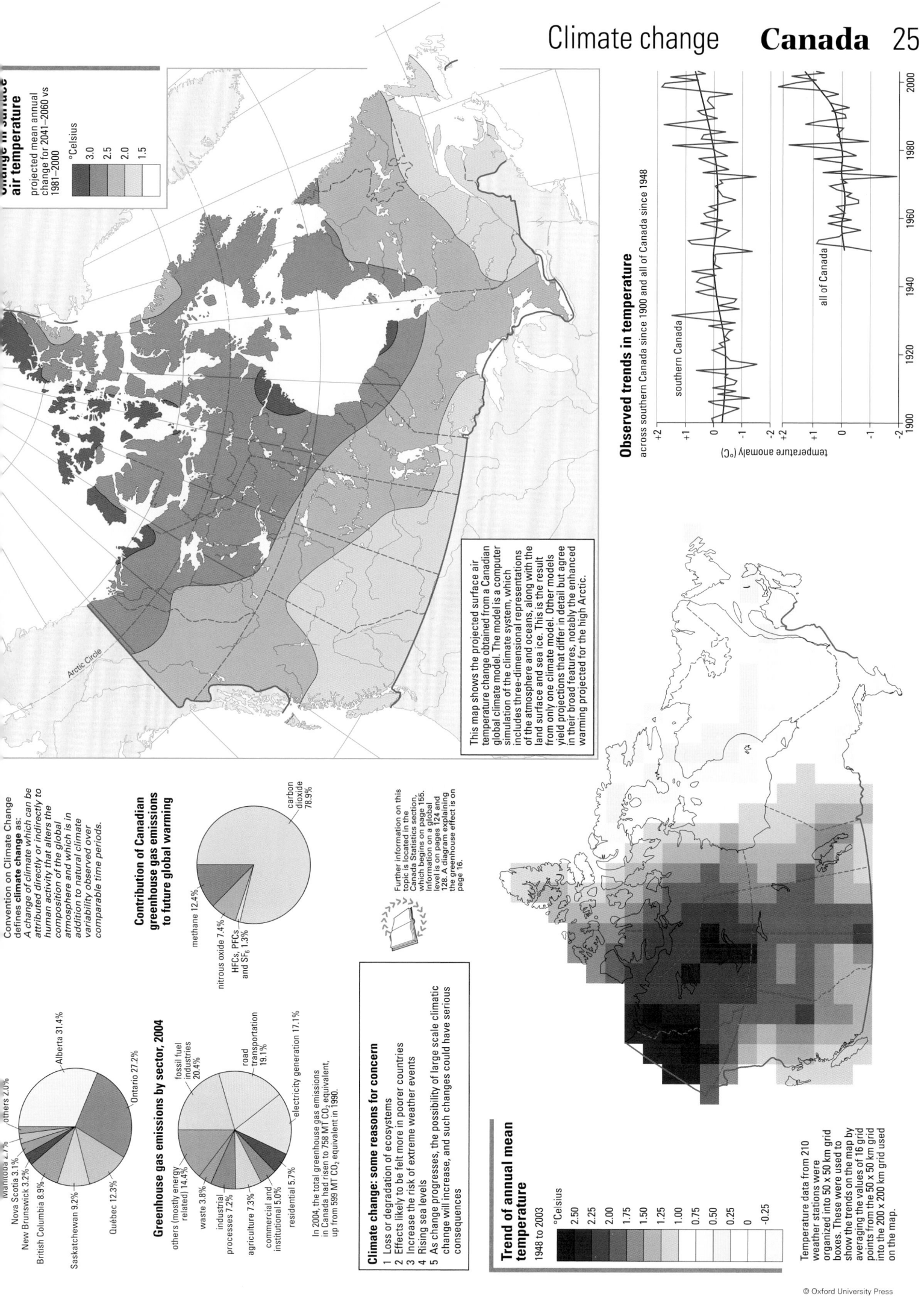

Observed trends in temperature
across southern Canada since 1900 and all of Canada since 1948

southern Canada

all of Canada

temperature anomaly (°C)

Change in surface air temperature
projected mean annual change for 2041–2060 vs 1981–2000

°Celsius
3.0
2.5
2.0
1.5

This map shows the projected surface air temperature change obtained from a Canadian global climate model. The model is a computer simulation of the climate system, which includes three-dimensional representations of the atmosphere and oceans, along with the land surface and sea ice. This is the result from only one climate model. Other models yield projections that differ in detail but agree in their broad features, notably the enhanced warming projected for the high Arctic.

Convention on Climate Change defines **climate change** as:
A change of climate which can be attributed directly or indirectly to human activity that alters the composition of the global atmosphere and which is in addition to natural climate variability observed over comparable time periods.

Contribution of Canadian greenhouse gas emissions to future global warming

carbon dioxide 78.9%
methane 12.4%
nitrous oxide 7.4%
HFCs, PFCs and SF$_6$ 1.3%

Further information on this topic is located in the Canada Statistics section, which begins on page 105. Information on a global level is on pages 124 and 128. A diagram explaining the greenhouse effect is on page 16.

others 2.7%
Alberta 31.4%
Manitoba 2.7%
Nova Scotia 3.1%
New Brunswick 3.2%
British Columbia 8.9%
Saskatchewan 9.2%
Québec 12.3%
Ontario 27.2%

Greenhouse gas emissions by sector, 2004

others (mostly energy related) 14.4%
fossil fuel industries 20.4%
waste 3.8%
industrial processes 7.2%
agriculture 7.3%
commercial and institutional 5.0%
residential 5.7%
road transportation 19.1%
electricity generation 17.1%

In 2004, the total greenhouse gas emissions in Canada had risen to 758 MT CO₂ equivalent, up from 599 MT CO₂ equivalent in 1990.

Climate change: some reasons for concern

1 Loss or degradation of ecosystems
2 Effects likely to be felt more in poorer countries
3 Increase the risk of extreme weather events
4 Rising sea levels
5 As change progresses, the possibility of large scale climatic change will increase, and such changes could have serious consequences

Trend of annual mean temperature
1948 to 2003

°Celsius
2.50
2.25
2.00
1.75
1.50
1.25
1.00
0.75
0.50
0.25
0
-0.25

Temperature data from 210 weather stations were organized into 50 x 50 km grid boxes. These were used to show the trends on the map by averaging the values of 16 grid points from the 50 x 50 km grid into the 200 x 200 km grid used on the map.

© Oxford University Press

Scale 1: 23 000 000

0   230   460   69

Terrestrial ecozones

A large or more or less environmentally homogeneous area in terms of landforms, water, soils, vegetation, climate, wildlife, and various human uses that are ecologically related. Considerable variation may occur within an ecozone and boundaries between them are seldom sharply defined.

- Taiga Shield
- Hudson Plain
- Southern Arctic
- Northern Arctic
- Arctic Cordillera
- Montane Cordillera
- Pacific Maritime
- Boreal Cordillera
- Taiga Cordillera
- Taiga Plain
- Atlantic Maritime
- Mixed-Wood Plain
- Boreal Shield
- Prairie
- Boreal Plain

Population by ecozone, 2001

Ecozone	Land area (km²)	Population	Density (person/km²)
Atlantic Maritime	192 017	2 557 685	13.216
Mixed-Wood Plain	107 017	15 631 830	146.068
Boreal Shield	1 640 949	2 821 808	1.033
Prairie	443 159	4 222 569	9.528
Boreal Plain	668 664	771 205	1.153
Montane Cordillera	474 753	859 134	1.810
Pacific Maritime	196 200	3 027 206	15.429
Boreal Cordillera	459 864	30 690	0.067
Taiga Cordillera	264 213	370	0.001
Taiga Plain	569 363	20 726	0.036
Taiga Shield	1 122 504	38 116	0.034
Hudson Plain	359 546	9 530	0.027
Southern Arctic	702 542	14 470	0.021
Northern Arctic	1 371 340	20 451	0.015
Arctic Cordillera	234 708	1 304	0.006

Further information on this topic is located in the Canada Statistics

Endangered species

There are five classifications of endangered species:

EX Extinct — species that no longer exist

EXT Extirpated — species that no longer exist in the wild in Canada, but live elsewhere

E Endangered — species facing imminent extinction or extirpation

T Threatened — species that are likely to become endangered in Canada if limiting factors are not reversed

S Special Concern — species with characteristics that make them particularly sensitive to human activities or natural events

In 2007 in Canada, there were more than 521 species of mammals, birds, reptiles, amphibians, fish, and plants listed in these five categories. Only selected species of birds, mammals, reptiles, and amphibians are shown here.

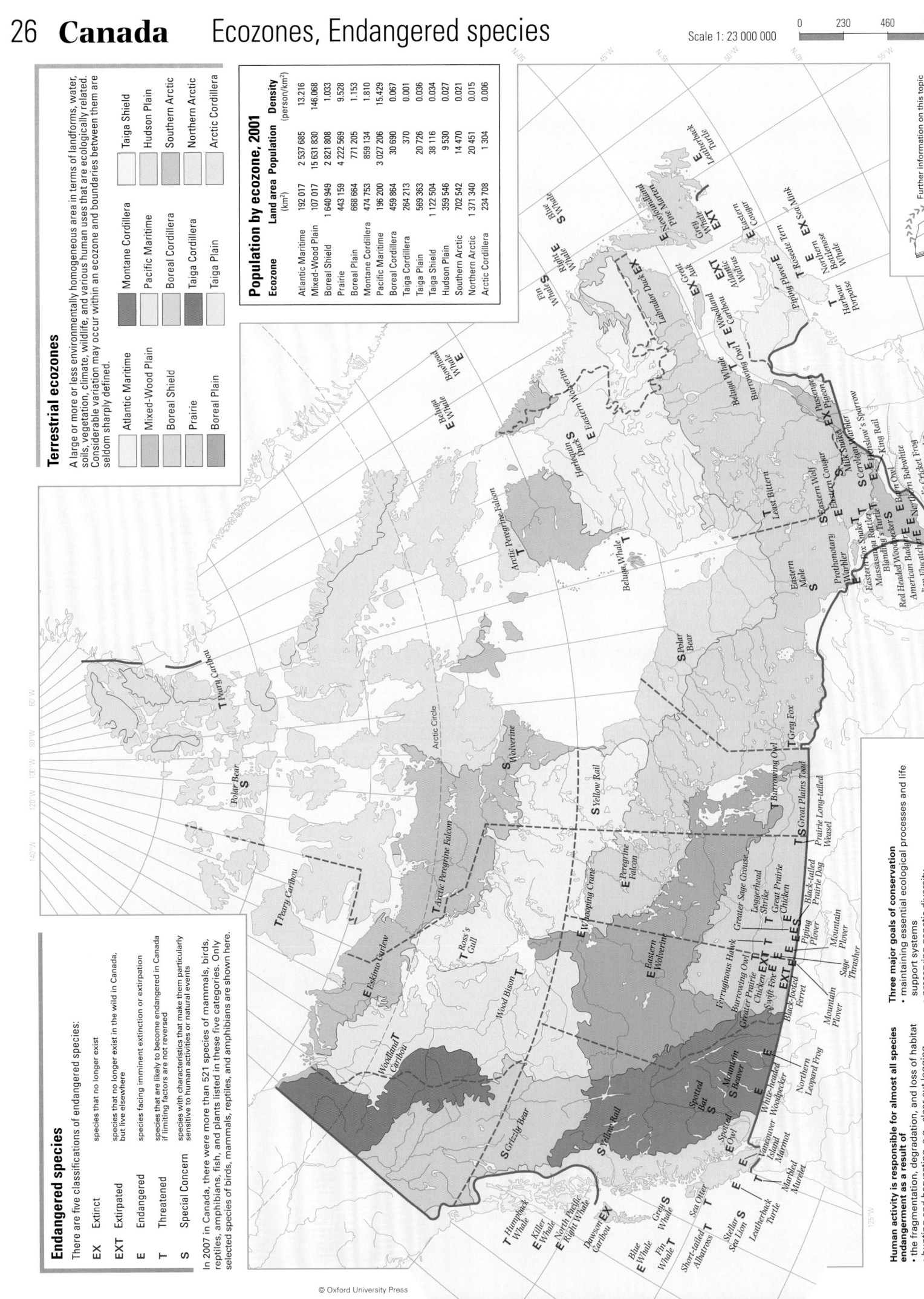

Human activity is responsible for almost all species endangerment as a result of
- the fragmentation, degradation, and loss of habitat
- hunting and harvesting, e.g., clear-cut logging

Three major goals of conservation
- maintaining essential ecological processes and life support systems
- preserving genetic diversity

© Oxford University Press

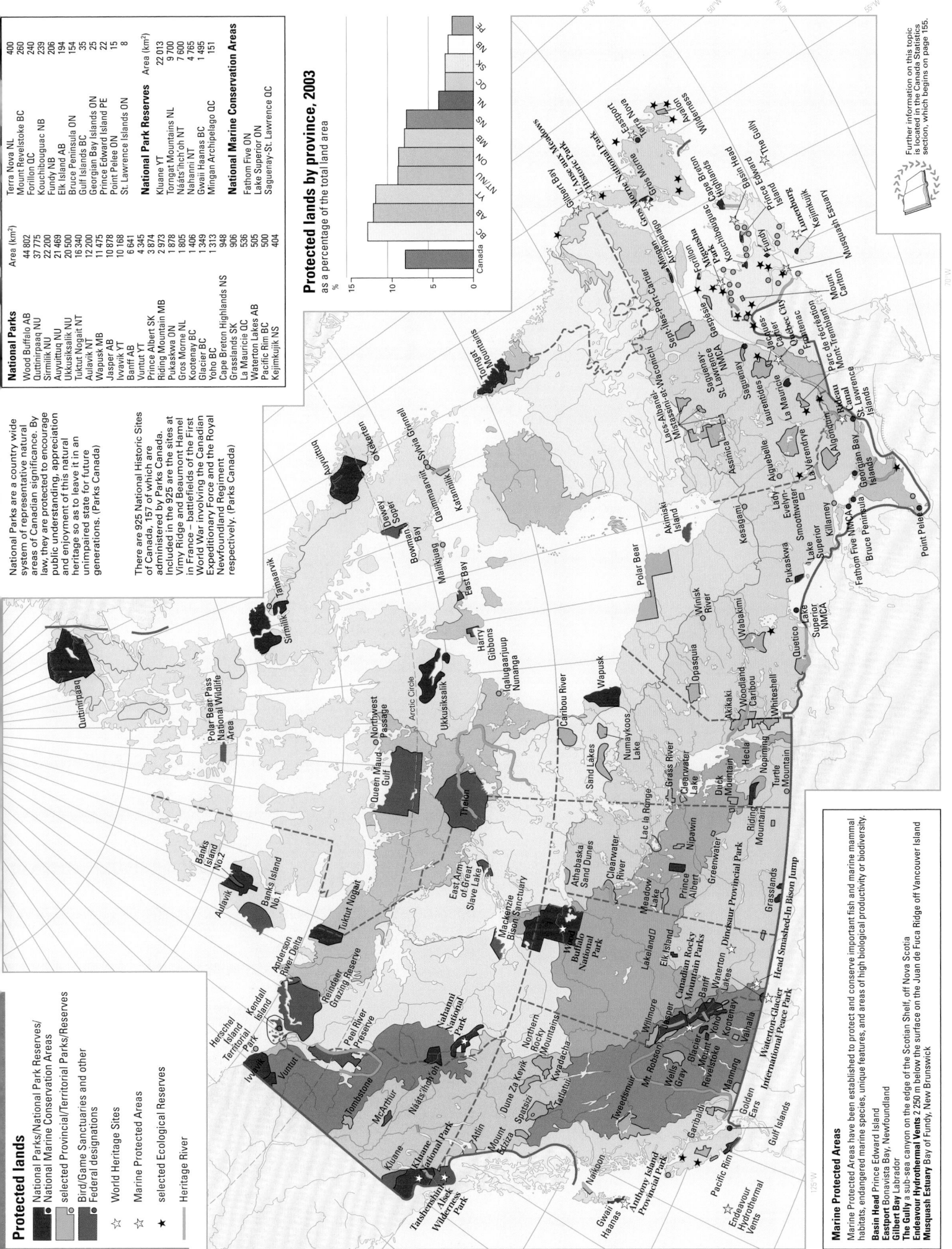

Protected lands

- National Parks/National Park Reserves/National Marine Conservation Areas
- selected Provincial/Territorial Parks/Reserves
- Bird/Game Sanctuaries and other
- Federal designations
- ☆ World Heritage Sites
- ★ Marine Protected Areas
- ● selected Ecological Reserves
- — Heritage River

National Parks are a country wide system of representative natural areas of Canadian significance. By law, they are protected to encourage public understanding, appreciation and enjoyment of this natural heritage so as to leave it in an unimpaired state for future generations. (Parks Canada)

There are 925 National Historic Sites of Canada, 157 of which are administered by Parks Canada. Included in the 925 are the sites at Vimy Ridge and Beaumont Hamel in France – battlefields of the First World War involving the Canadian Expeditionary Force and the Royal Newfoundland Regiment respectively. (Parks Canada)

National Parks

	Area (km²)
Wood Buffalo AB	44 802
Quttinirpaaq NU	37 775
Sirmilik NU	22 200
Auyuittuq NU	21 469
Ukkusiksalik NU	20 500
Tuktut Nogait NT	16 340
Aulavik NT	12 200
Wapusk MB	11 475
Jasper AB	10 878
Iwavik YT	10 168
Banff AB	6 641
Vuntut YT	4 345
Prince Albert SK	3 874
Riding Mountain MB	2 973
Pukaskwa ON	1 878
Gros Morne NL	1 805
Kootenay BC	1 406
Glacier BC	1 349
Yoho BC	1 313
Cape Breton Highlands NS	948
Grasslands SK	906
La Mauricie QC	536
Waterton Lakes AB	505
Pacific Rim BC	500
Kejimkujik NS	404
Terra Nova NL	400
Mount Revelstoke BC	260
Forillon QC	240
Kouchibouguac NB	239
Fundy NB	206
Elk Island AB	194
Bruce Peninsula ON	154
Gulf Islands BC	35
Georgian Bay Islands ON	25
Prince Edward Island PE	22
Point Pelee ON	15
St. Lawrence Islands ON	8

National Park Reserves

	Area (km²)
Kluane YT	22 013
Torngat Mountains NL	9 700
Nááts'ihch'oh NT	7 600
Nahanni NT	4 765
Gwaii Haanas BC	1 495
Mingan Archipelago QC	151

National Marine Conservation Areas

- Fathom Five ON
- Lake Superior ON
- Saguenay-St. Lawrence QC

Protected lands by province, 2003
as a percentage of the total land area

Marine Protected Areas

Marine Protected Areas have been established to protect and conserve important fish and marine mammal habitats, endangered marine species, unique features, and areas of high biological productivity or biodiversity.

Basin Head Prince Edward Island
Eastport Bonavista Bay, Newfoundland
Gilbert Bay Labrador
The Gully a sub-sea canyon on the edge of the Scotian Shelf, off Nova Scotia
Endeavour Hydrothermal Vents 2 250 m below the surface on the Juan de Fuca Ridge off Vancouver Island
Musquash Estuary Bay of Fundy, New Brunswick

Further information on this topic is located in the Canada Statistics section, which begins on page 155.

Zenithal Equidistant Projection   © Oxford University Press

Scale 1: 23 000 000

0 230 460 690 km

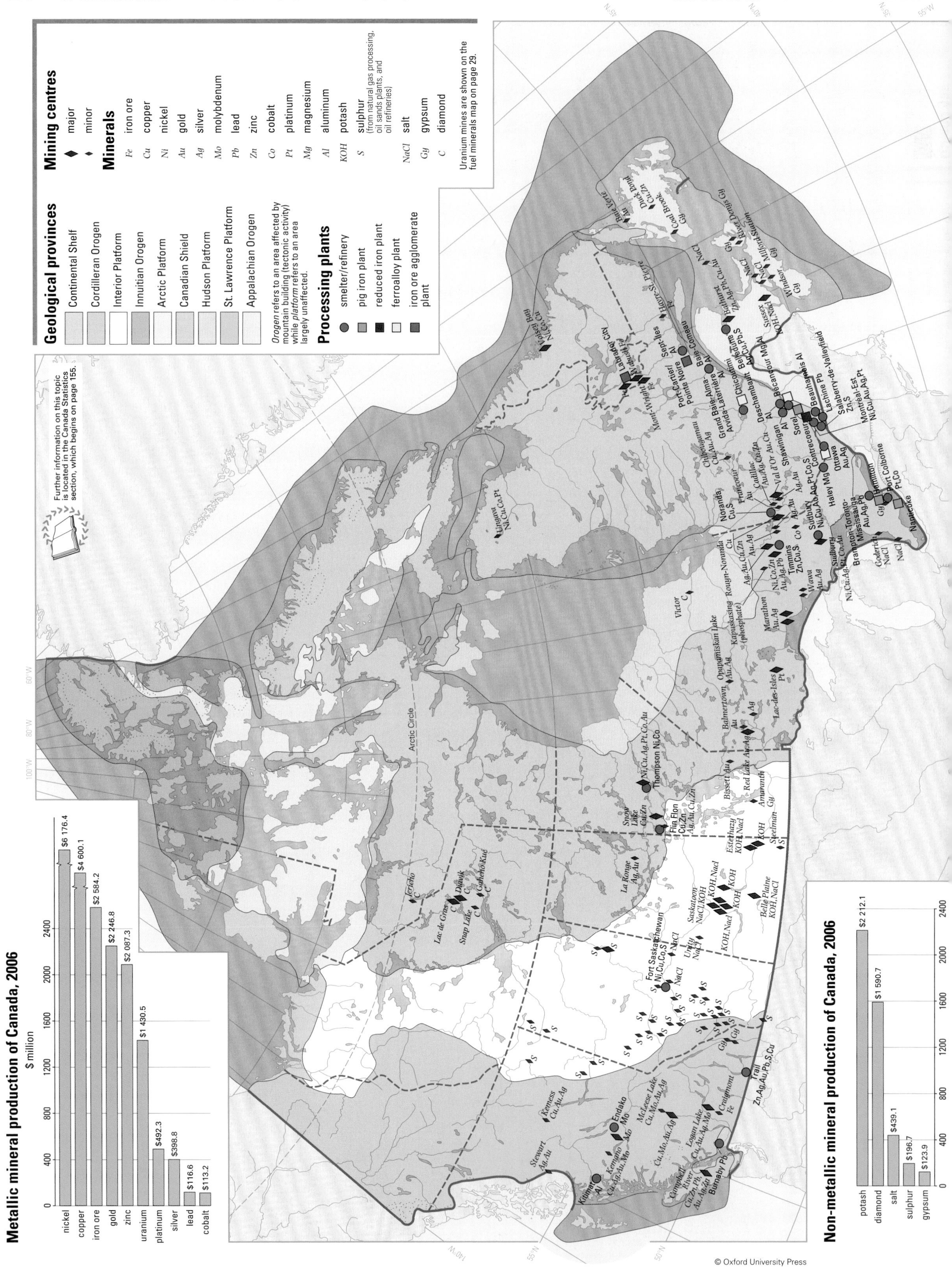

Mining centres
- ◆ major
- ◆ minor

Minerals
Fe	iron ore	
Cu	copper	
Ni	nickel	
Au	gold	
Ag	silver	
Mo	molybdenum	
Pb	lead	
Zn	zinc	
Co	cobalt	
Pt	platinum	
Mg	magnesium	
Al	aluminium	
KOH	potash	
S	sulphur (from natural gas processing, oil sands plants, and oil refineries)	
NaCl	salt	
Gy	gypsum	
C	diamond	

Uranium mines are shown on the fuel minerals map on page 29.

Geological provinces
- Continental Shelf
- Cordilleran Orogen
- Interior Platform
- Innuitian Orogen
- Arctic Platform
- Canadian Shield
- Hudson Platform
- St. Lawrence Platform
- Appalachian Orogen

Orogen refers to an area affected by mountain building (tectonic activity) while *platform* refers to an area largely unaffected.

Processing plants
- ● smelter/refinery
- ● pig iron plant
- ■ reduced iron plant
- □ ferroalloy plant
- ◼ iron ore agglomerate plant

Further information on this topic is located in the Canada Statistics section, which begins on page 155.

Metallic mineral production of Canada, 2006
$ million

nickel	$6 176.4
copper	$4 600.1
iron ore	$2 584.2
gold	$2 246.8
zinc	$2 087.3
uranium	$1 430.5
platinum	$492.3
silver	$398.8
lead	$116.6
cobalt	$113.2

Non-metallic mineral production of Canada, 2006

potash	$2 212.1
diamond	$1 590.7
salt	$439.1
sulphur	$196.7
gypsum	$123.9

© Oxford University Press

Oil and gas

- oil field
- oil sands deposits (surface and non-surface)
- oil pipeline
- gas field
- gas pipeline
- gas pipeline proposed

Oil refineries

capacity in barrels per day
- ◯ more than 100 000
- ◯ 25 000–100 000
- ○ 5000–25 000

Coal

producing mines of over 1 million tonnes per annum
- ▪ mine
- coal exports
- coal imports

Uranium mines

- ▲ mine
- ▴ mill
- △ processing plant

Orogen refers to an area affected by mountain building (tectonic activity) while *platform* refers to an area largely unaffected.

Further information on this topic is located in the Canada Statistics section, which begins on page 155.

Geological provinces

- Continental Shelf
- Cordilleran Orogen
- Interior Platform
- Innuitian Orogen
- Arctic Platform
- Canadian Shield
- Hudson Platform
- St. Lawrence Platform
- Appalachian Orogen

billion cubic metres per day
- interprovincial
- export

thousand cubic metres per day
- interprovincial
- export
- import

Coal consumption by province, 2005

- Alberta 44.7%
- Ontario 27.6%
- Saskatchewan 19.8%
- New Brunswick 4.3%
- Nova Scotia 2.2%
- Québec 1.4%

Total consumption was 58 million tonnes, of which 93% was used for electricity generation.

coal imports 21 million tonnes

Most of imported coal enters Canada via the USA ports of Toledo, Sandusky, Ashtabula, and Conneaut.

from (million tonnes)
USA 17.7
Colombia 2.6
Venezuela 0.7

coal exports 26.2 million tonnes

to (million tonnes)
Europe 7.8
Japan 7.5
South Korea 4.9
South America 2.3
also USA and Mexico

TRANSCANADA

INTERPROVINCIAL

TRANSMISSION

TRANSMOUNTAIN

WESTCOAST

Arctic fields are non-producing

Mackenzie Delta fields are non-producing

McClean Lake
Cigar Lake
Rabbit Lake
McArthur River
Key Lake

Skate
Cisco
Hecla
Drake
Ibbit

Norman Wells
Zama
Rainbow Lake
Keg River
Clarke Lake
Buick Creek
Boundary Lake
Peejay
Kaybob
South Edson
Strachan
Braeau
Pembina–Westpem
Swan Hills
Suffield
Hatton
Coleville
Smiley
Frobisher
Dollard
Coutadam
D'Orleille

Taylor
Montias
Prince George
Prince Rupert
Vancouver
North Burnaby
Burnaby

Lloydminster (refinery)
Lloydminster (oilfield)
Regina
Virden
Weyburn
Midale

Port Hope
Nanticoke
Sarnia (3)
Montréal (5)
Lévis
Saint John
Dartmouth
Come by Chance

Hibernia
White Rose
Terra Nova
Hebron
North Triumph
Venture

Arctic Circle

© Oxford University Press   Zenithal Equidistant Projection

Scale 1: 23 000 000

0 230 460 690 km

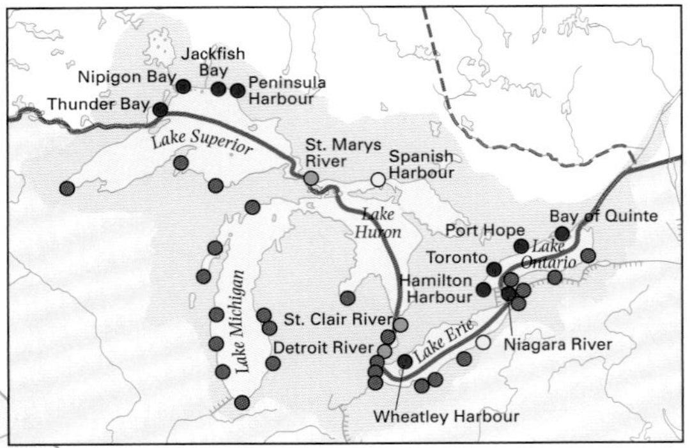

Areas of pollution concern in the Great Lakes

Great Lakes drainage basin

- binational
- Canada
- USA
- areas in recovery

The Great Lakes Basin is home to approximately 40 million people (30% of Canada's population and 50% of Canada's manufacturing output. The ecological health of the Great Lakes is critical to its long-term uses, including manufacturing, shipping, tourism, recreation, agriculture, water for domestic consumption, and energy production. These uses, as well as the related growth in population, have placed the basin under enormous stress, creating serious pollution problems. See the map for principal areas of concern.

(Great Lakes inset — labels)

Bay of Quinte, Lake Ontario, Niagara River, Port Hope, Toronto, Hamilton Harbour, Wheatley Harbour, Lake Erie, St. Clair River, Detroit River, Peninsula Harbour, St. Marys Spanish Harbour, Jackfish Bay, Nipigon Bay, Thunder Bay, Lake Superior, Lake Huron, Lake Michigan

Electricity generating stations

Installed capacity (MW)

- over 5000
- 2000–5000
- 1000–1999
- 500–999
- 100–499
- under construction
- * tidal power plant of capacity 20 MW

Fuel type

- hydro
- coal
- gas
- oil
- uranium (nuclear)
- cogeneration

Transmission line corridors

- over 400 kV
- over 400 kV proposed

There are hundreds of additional electricity generating stations, each of which has an installed capacity of less than 100 MW. An increasing number involve emerging technologies in energy production, which in 2006 made up 3% of all electricity production in Canada. Wind contributes the largest amount, with 149 MW installed and 2 780 MW under construction or proposed.

Further information on this topic is located in the Canada Statistics section, which begins on page 155.

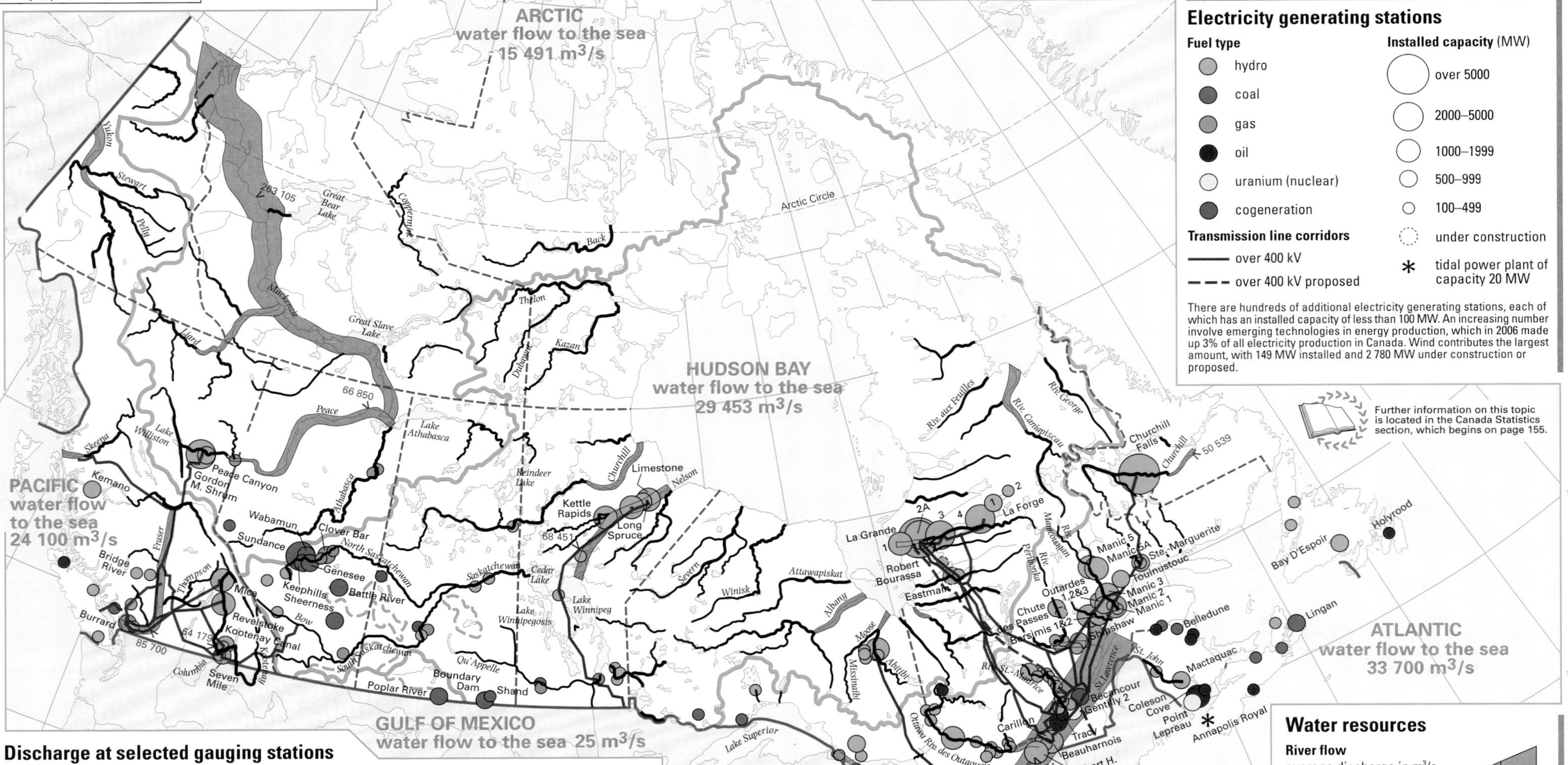

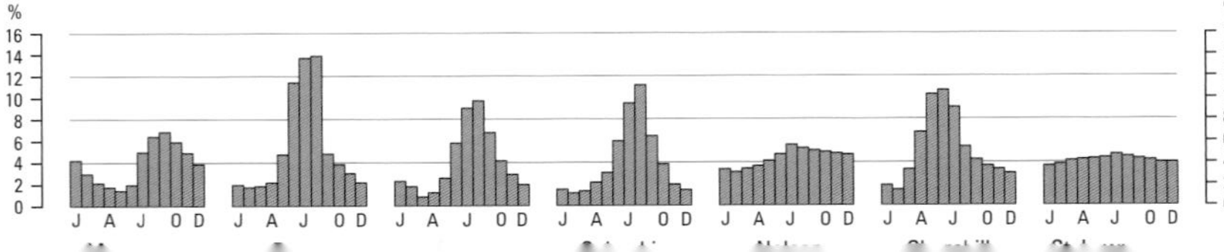

Water resources

River flow

average discharge in m³/s

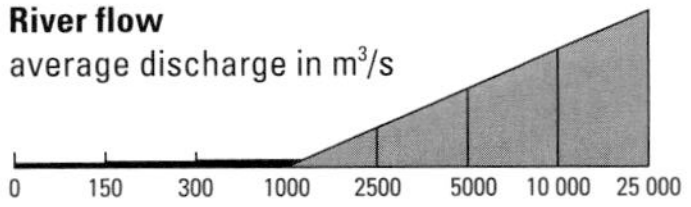

- gauging station average flow (10⁶ m³)
- ocean drainage area
- internal drainage area

Canada has 7% of the world's renewable water

0 150 300 1000 2500 5000 10 000 25 000

Electricity trade, 2005

gigawatt hours (GW.h)*

- interprovincial transfers
- exports to US
- imports from US

* one GW.h = one million KW.h

Scale 1: 90 000 000

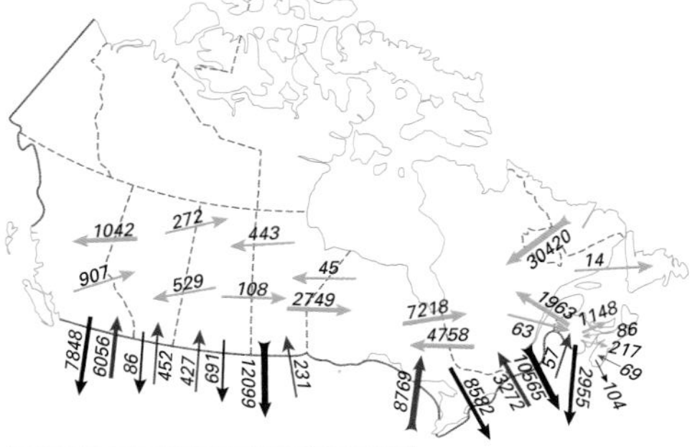

Total electricity production	568 900 GW.h
Electricity exports	42 900 GW.h
Electricity imports	19 300 GW.h

Discharge at selected gauging stations

average monthly runoff as a percentage of the total

(gauging stations are shown on the main map: >)

(Map region labels)

ARCTIC water flow to the sea 15 491 m³/s

HUDSON BAY water flow to the sea 29 453 m³/s

ATLANTIC water flow to the sea 33 700 m³/s

GULF OF MEXICO water flow to the sea 25 m³/s

PACIFIC water flow to the sea 24 100 m³/s

(Generating station / river labels)

Churchill Falls, Manic 5, Manic 3, Manic 2, Manic 1, La Forge, La Grande, Robert Bourassa, Eastmain, Outardes 2 & 3, Bersimis 1 & 2, Beaumont, Beauharnois, Carillon, Robert H. Saunders, Lennox, Pickering, Darlington, Sir Adam Beck 1 & 2, Nanticoke, Bruce, Lambton, Holyrood, Lingan, Belledune, Macagnac, St. John, Point Lepreau, Annapolis Royal, Bay D'Espoir

Limestone, Long Spruce, Kettle Rapids, Cedar Lake, Lake Winnipeg, Lake Winnipegosis, Grand Rapids, Shand, Boundary Dam, Poplar River

Kemano, Peace Canyon, Gordon M. Shrum, Mica, Revelstoke, Kootenay Canal, Seven Mile, Bridge River, Burrard, Clover Bar, Genesee, Keephills, Sundance, Sheerness, Wabamun, Battle River

Lake Athabasca, Great Slave Lake, Great Bear Lake, Mackenzie, Peace, Athabasca, North Saskatchewan, South Saskatchewan, Churchill, Nelson, Back, Thelon, Kazan, Dubawnt, Coppermine, Yukon, Pelly, Stewart, Liard, Fraser, Thompson, Lake Williston

Riv. George, Riv. Caniapiscau, Riv. Manicouagan, Riv. Péribonka, Riv. aux Feuilles, Riv. des Outaouais, Attawapiskat, Albany, Moose, Missinaibi, Abitibi, Winisk, Severn, Qu'Appelle, Bow

© Oxford University Press

Scale 1: 21 500 000

0   215   430   645 km

Manufacturing industries, 2006

The colour indicates the major industrial group and the numbers indicate important manufacturing subdivisions in some groups.

food, beverages, and tobacco
1 food
2 beverages and tobacco

textiles and clothing
3 textile mills
4 textile mill products
5 clothing

leather and allied products
6 leather and allied products

wood
7 wood products
8 furniture and related products

paper
9 paper
10 printing and related activities

chemicals
11 petroleum and coal products
12 chemicals

plastics and rubber

non-metallic minerals

metals
13 primary metals
14 fabricated metal products

machinery
15 machinery
16 computer and electronic products
17 electrical equipment, appliances, and components
18 transportation equipment

others
including the above industrial groups where the value added is less than 5% of the total or where the information is not available for reasons of confidentiality

\$217 279 million value added by manufacturing

The value of manufactured goods shipped, less the cost of materials and supplies used, including fuel and electricity.

Canada
\$217 279 million* value added by manufacturing

labels around pie chart: others, food, beverages, and tobacco, textiles and clothing, wood, paper, chemicals, plastics and rubber, non-metallic minerals, metals, machinery

Further information on this topic is located in the Canada Statistics section, which begins on page 155.

Newfoundland and Labrador
\$1 328 million

Prince Edward Island
\$471 million

Nova Scotia
\$3 774 million

New Brunswick
\$3 553 million

Québec
\$54 753 million

Ontario
\$105 508 million

Manitoba
\$6 452 million

Saskatchewan
\$3 153 million

Alberta
\$19 649 million

British Columbia
\$18 605 million

Nunavut
\$2.0 million

Northwest Territories
\$15.3 million

Yukon Territory
\$14.8 million

Arctic Circle

Selected CMAs, 2003
value added by manufacturing (\$000 000)

Toronto	46 153	Calgary	3 778
Montréal	24 151	Winnipeg	3 539
Vancouver	7 914	Ottawa–Gatineau	2 817
Edmonton	6 067	Regina	850
London	5 795	Halifax	752
Hamilton	5 361	St. John's	276

Manufacturing centres

These centres include Census Metropolitan Areas (CMAs), specified census agglomerations, and selected municipalities. Manufacturing outside CMAs, towns, and cities is not shown.

● dominant
● major
● secondary
• minor

© Oxford University Press   Zenithal Equidistant Projection

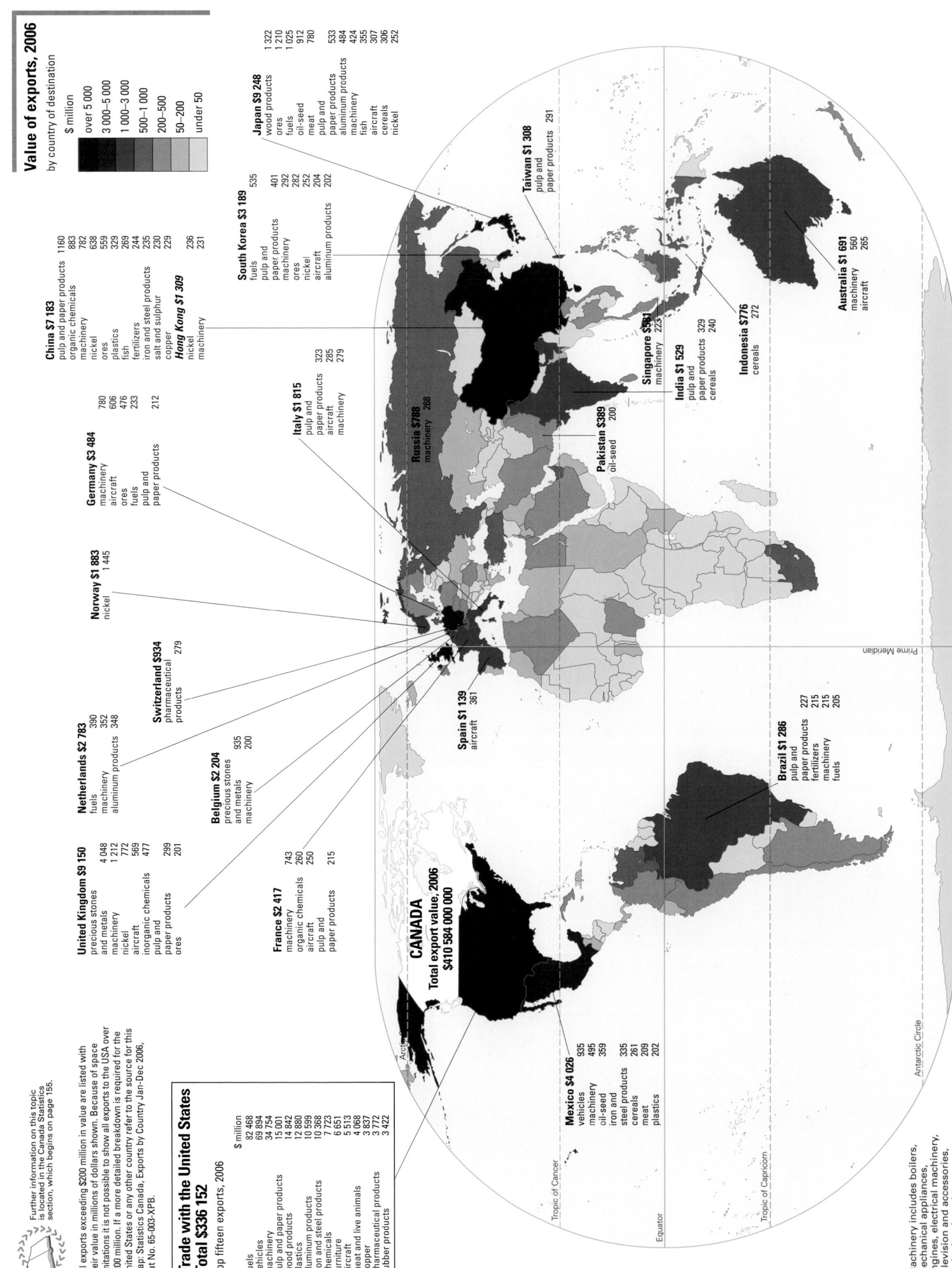

Value of exports, 2006
by country of destination

$ million

- over 5 000
- 3 000–5 000
- 1 000–3 000
- 500–1 000
- 200–500
- 50–200
- under 50

All exports exceeding $200 million in value are listed with their value in millions of dollars shown. Because of space limitations it is not possible to show all exports to the USA over $200 million. If a more detailed breakdown is required for the United States or any other country refer to the source for this map: Statistics Canada, Exports by Country Jan–Dec 2006, Cat No. 65-003-XPB.

Further information on this topic is located in the Canada Statistics section, which begins on page 155.

Trade with the United States
Total $336 152

top fifteen exports, 2006

	$ million
fuels	82 468
vehicles	69 894
machinery	34 754
pulp and paper products	15 001
wood products	14 842
plastics	12 880
aluminum products	10 599
iron and steel products	10 368
chemicals	7 723
furniture	6 651
aircraft	5 513
meat and live animals	4 068
copper	3 837
pharmaceutical products	3 772
rubber products	3 422

CANADA
Total export value, 2006
$410 584 000 000

Mexico $4 026
vehicles	935
machinery	495
oil-seed	359
iron and steel products	335
cereals	261
meat	209
plastics	202

Japan $9 248
wood products	1 322
ores	1 210
fuels	1 025
oil-seed	912
meat	780
pulp and paper products	533
aluminum products	484
machinery	424
fish	355
aircraft	307
cereals	306
nickel	252

China $7 183
pulp and paper products	1160
organic chemicals	883
machinery	638
nickel	559
ores	329
plastics	269
fish	244
fertilizers	235
iron and steel products	230
salt and sulphur	229
copper	

South Korea $3 189
fuels	535
pulp and paper products	401
machinery	292
ores	282
nickel	252
aircraft	204
aluminum products	202

Taiwan $1 308
pulp and paper products	291

Hong Kong $1 309
nickel	236
machinery	231

Germany $3 484
machinery	780
aircraft	606
ores	476
fuels	233
pulp and paper products	212

Italy $1 815
pulp and paper products	323
aircraft	285
machinery	279

Russia $788
machinery	268

Singapore $981
machinery	223

India $1 529
pulp and paper products	329
cereals	240

Indonesia $776
cereals	272

Australia $1 691
machinery	560
aircraft	265

Pakistan $389
oil-seed	200

Norway $1 883
nickel	1 445

Switzerland $934
pharmaceutical products	279

United Kingdom $9 150
precious stones and metals	4 048
machinery	1 212
nickel	772
aircraft	569
inorganic chemicals	477
pulp and paper products	299
ores	201

Netherlands $2 783
fuels	390
machinery	352
aluminum products	348

Belgium $2 204
precious stones and metals	935
machinery	200

France $2 417
machinery	743
organic chemicals	260
aircraft	250
pulp and paper products	215

Spain $1 139
aircraft	361

Brazil $1 286
pulp and paper products	227
fertilizers	215
machinery	215
fuels	205

Prime Meridian

Arctic Circle

Tropic of Cancer

Equator

Tropic of Capricorn

Antarctic Circle

Machinery includes boilers, mechanical appliances, engines, electrical machinery, television and accessories, and related products.

Scale 1: 160 000 000

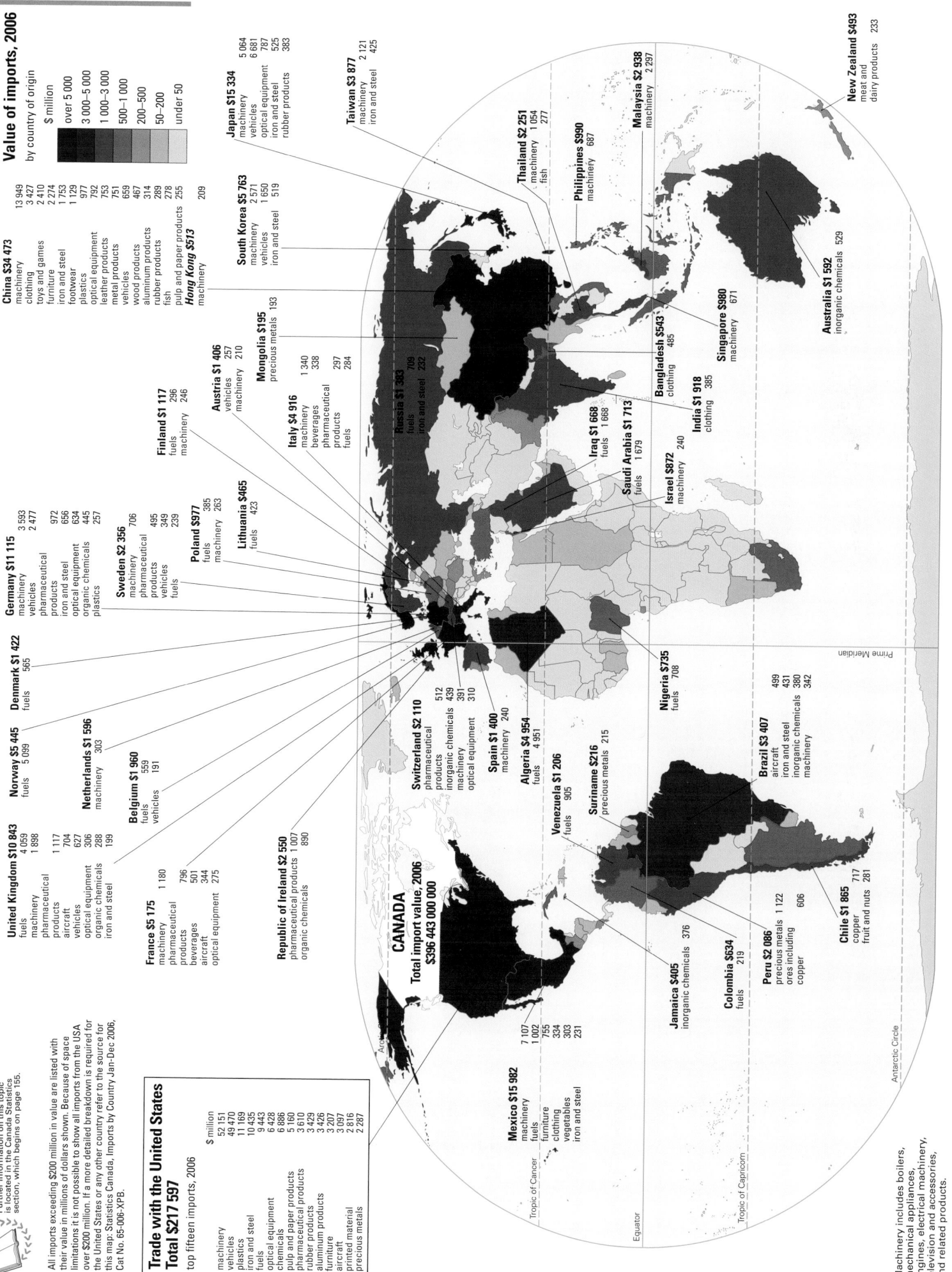

Value of imports, 2006
by country of origin

$ million

- over 5 000
- 3 000–5 000
- 1 000–3 000
- 500–1 000
- 200–500
- 50–200
- under 50

Further information on this topic is located in the Canada Statistics section, which begins on page 155.

All imports exceeding $200 million in value are listed with their value in millions of dollars shown. Because of space limitations it is not possible to show all imports from the USA over $200 million. If a more detailed breakdown is required for the United States or any other country refer to the source for this map: Statistics Canada, Imports by Country Jan–Dec 2006, Cat No. 65-006-XPB.

Trade with the United States
Total $217 597

top fifteen imports, 2006

	$ million
machinery	52 151
vehicles	49 470
plastics	11 169
iron and steel	10 435
fuels	9 443
optical equipment	6 428
chemicals	6 886
pulp and paper products	5 160
pharmaceutical products	3 610
rubber products	3 429
aluminum products	3 426
furniture	3 207
aircraft	3 097
printed material	2 816
precious metals	2 287

China $34 473

machinery	13 949
clothing	3 427
toys and games	2 410
furniture	2 274
iron and steel	1 753
footwear	1 129
plastics	977
optical equipment	792
leather products	753
metal products	751
vehicles	659
wood products	467
aluminum products	314
rubber products	289
fish	278
pulp and paper products	255

Hong Kong $513
machinery 209

Japan $15 334
machinery	5 064
vehicles	6 681
optical equipment	787
iron and steel	525
rubber products	383

Taiwan $3 877
| machinery | 2 121 |
| iron and steel | 425 |

South Korea $5 763
machinery	2 571
vehicles	1 650
iron and steel	519

Mongolia $195
precious metals 193

Thailand $2 251
| machinery | 1 054 |
| fish | 277 |

Philippines $990
machinery 687

Malaysia $2 938
machinery 2 297

New Zealand $493
meat and dairy products 233

Bangladesh $543
clothing 485

Singapore $980
machinery 671

India $1 918
clothing 385

Israel $872
machinery 240

Saudi Arabia $1 713
fuels 1 679

Iraq $1 668
fuels 1 668

Australia $1 592
inorganic chemicals 529

Italy $4 916
machinery	1 340
beverages	338
pharmaceutical products	297
fuels	284

Austria $1 406
| vehicles | 257 |
| machinery | 210 |

Russia $1 383
| fuels | 709 |
| iron and steel | 232 |

Finland $1 117
| fuels | 296 |
| machinery | 246 |

Poland $977
| fuels | 385 |
| machinery | 263 |

Lithuania $465
fuels 423

Sweden $2 356
machinery	706
pharmaceutical products	495
vehicles	349
fuels	239

Germany $11 115
machinery	3 593
vehicles	2 477
pharmaceutical products	972
iron and steel	656
optical equipment	634
organic chemicals	445
plastics	257

Denmark $1 422
fuels 565

Norway $5 445
fuels 5 099

Netherlands $1 596
machinery 303

Belgium $1 960
| fuels | 559 |
| vehicles | 191 |

United Kingdom $10 843
fuels	4 059
machinery	1 898
pharmaceutical products	1 117
aircraft	704
vehicles	627
optical equipment	306
organic chemicals	288
iron and steel	199

France $5 175
machinery	1 180
pharmaceutical products	796
beverages	501
aircraft	344
optical equipment	275

Republic of Ireland $2 550
| pharmaceutical products | 1 007 |
| organic chemicals | 890 |

Switzerland $2 110
pharmaceutical products	512
inorganic chemicals	439
machinery	391
optical equipment	310

Spain $1 400
machinery 240

Algeria $4 954
fuels 4 951

Nigeria $735
fuels 708

Venezuela $1 206
fuels 905

Suriname $216
precious metals 215

Brazil $3 407
aircraft	499
iron and steel	431
inorganic chemicals	380
machinery	342

Peru $2 086
| precious metals | 1 122 |
| ores including copper | 606 |

Chile $1 865
| copper | 717 |
| fruit and nuts | 281 |

Colombia $634
fuels 219

Jamaica $405
inorganic chemicals 376

Mexico $15 982
machinery	7 107
fuels	1 002
furniture	755
clothing	334
vegetables	303
iron and steel	231

CANADA
Total import value, 2006
$396 443 000 000

Tropic of Cancer

Equator

Tropic of Capricorn

Antarctic Circle

Arctic Circle

Prime Meridian

Machinery includes boilers, mechanical appliances, engines, electrical machinery, television and accessories, and related products.

© Oxford University Press   Eckert IV Projection

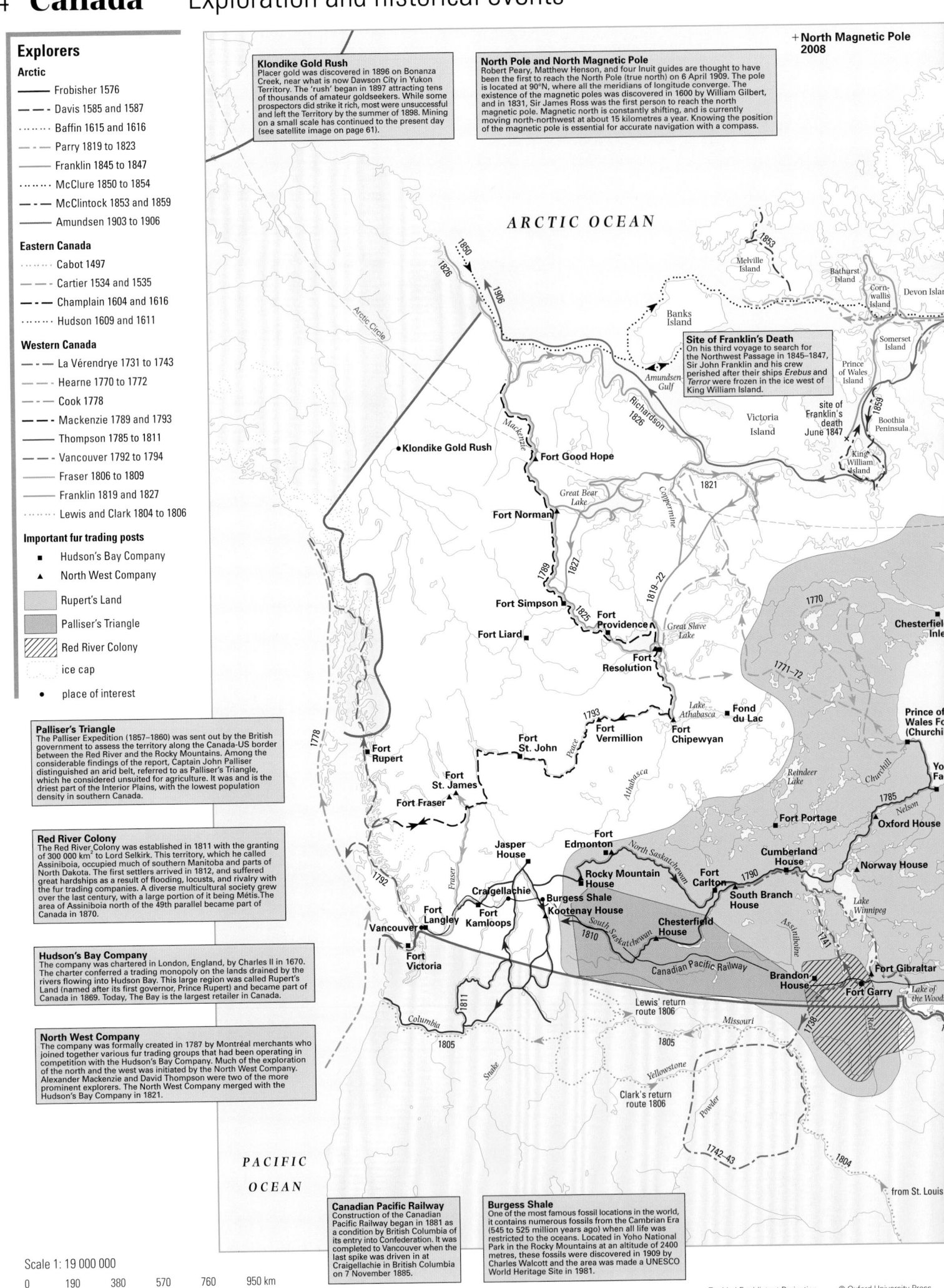

Explorers

Arctic
— Frobisher 1576
–·– Davis 1585 and 1587
······ Baffin 1615 and 1616
–·– Parry 1819 to 1823
— Franklin 1845 to 1847
····· McClure 1850 to 1854
– – – McClintock 1853 and 1859
—— Amundsen 1903 to 1906

Eastern Canada
······ Cabot 1497
–·– Cartier 1534 and 1535
–··– Champlain 1604 and 1616
······ Hudson 1609 and 1611

Western Canada
–·– La Vérendrye 1731 to 1743
–·– Hearne 1770 to 1772
–·– Cook 1778
– – Mackenzie 1789 and 1793
— Thompson 1785 to 1811
– – Vancouver 1792 to 1794
— Fraser 1806 to 1809
— Franklin 1819 and 1827
······ Lewis and Clark 1804 to 1806

Important fur trading posts
■ Hudson's Bay Company
▲ North West Company

▢ Rupert's Land
▢ Palliser's Triangle
▨ Red River Colony
⬚ ice cap

● place of interest

Palliser's Triangle
The Palliser Expedition (1857–1860) was sent out by the British government to assess the territory along the Canada-US border between the Red River and the Rocky Mountains. Among the considerable findings of the report, Captain John Palliser distinguished an arid belt, referred to as Palliser's Triangle, which he considered unsuited for agriculture. It was and is the driest part of the Interior Plains, with the lowest population density in southern Canada.

Red River Colony
The Red River Colony was established in 1811 with the granting of 300 000 km² of land to Lord Selkirk. This territory, which he called Assiniboia, occupied much of southern Manitoba and parts of North Dakota. The first settlers arrived in 1812, and suffered great hardships as a result of flooding, locusts, and rivalry with the fur trading companies. A diverse multicultural society grew over the last century, with a large portion of it being Métis. The area of Assiniboia north of the 49th parallel became part of Canada in 1870.

Hudson's Bay Company
The company was chartered in London, England, by Charles II in 1670. The charter conferred a trading monopoly on the lands drained by the rivers flowing into Hudson Bay. This large region was called Rupert's Land (named after its first governor, Prince Rupert) and became part of Canada in 1869. Today, The Bay is the largest retailer in Canada.

North West Company
The company was formally created in 1787 by Montréal merchants who joined together various fur trading groups that had been operating in competition with the Hudson's Bay Company. Much of the exploration of the north and the west was initiated by the North West Company. Alexander Mackenzie and David Thompson were two of the more prominent explorers. The North West Company merged with the Hudson's Bay Company in 1821.

Klondike Gold Rush
Placer gold was discovered in 1896 on Bonanza Creek, near what is now Dawson City in Yukon Territory. The 'rush' began in 1897 attracting tens of thousands of amateur goldseekers. While some prospectors did strike it rich, most were unsuccessful and left the Territory by the summer of 1898. Mining on a small scale has continued to the present day (see satellite image on page 61).

North Pole and North Magnetic Pole
Robert Peary, Matthew Henson, and four Inuit guides are thought to have been the first to reach the North Pole (true north) on 6 April 1909. The pole is located at 90°N, where all the meridians of longitude converge. The existence of the magnetic poles was discovered in 1600 by William Gilbert, and in 1831, Sir James Ross was the first person to reach the north magnetic pole. Magnetic north is constantly shifting, and is currently moving north-northwest at about 15 kilometres a year. Knowing the position of the magnetic pole is essential for accurate navigation with a compass.

+ North Magnetic Pole 2008

Site of Franklin's Death
On his third voyage to search for the Northwest Passage in 1845–1847, Sir John Franklin and his crew perished after their ships *Erebus* and *Terror* were frozen in the ice west of King William Island.

ARCTIC OCEAN

Melville Island
Bathurst Island
Cornwallis Island
Devon Island
Banks Island
Somerset Island
Prince of Wales Island
Boothia Peninsula
King William Island
Victoria Island
site of Franklin's death June 1847
Chesterfield Inlet

Arctic Circle
Klondike Gold Rush
Fort Good Hope
Fort Norman
Great Bear Lake
Fort Simpson
Fort Liard
Fort Providence
Fort Resolution
Great Slave Lake
Fort St. John
Fort Vermillion
Fort Chipewyan
Lake Athabasca
Fond du Lac
Reindeer Lake
Prince of Wales Fort (Churchill)
York Factory
Fort Portage
Oxford House
Cumberland House
Norway House
Fort Carlton
South Branch House
Rocky Mountain House
Fort Edmonton
Jasper House
Craigellachie
Burgess Shale
Kootenay House
Fort Kamloops
Fort Langley
Vancouver
Fort Victoria
Chesterfield House
Brandon House
Fort Garry
Fort Gibraltar
Lake of the Woods
Lake Winnipeg

Mackenzie
Richardson
Coppermine
Peace
Athabasca
Churchill
Nelson
North Saskatchewan
South Saskatchewan
Assiniboine
Red
Fraser
Columbia
Snake
Missouri
Yellowstone
Powder
Canadian Pacific Railway

Lewis' return route 1806
Clark's return route 1806
from St. Louis

PACIFIC OCEAN

Canadian Pacific Railway
Construction of the Canadian Pacific Railway began in 1881 as a condition by British Columbia of its entry into Confederation. It was completed to Vancouver when the last spike was driven in at Craigellachie in British Columbia on 7 November 1885.

Burgess Shale
One of the most famous fossil locations in the world, it contains numerous fossils from the Cambrian Era (545 to 525 million years ago) when all life was restricted to the oceans. Located in Yoho National Park in the Rocky Mountains at an altitude of 2400 metres, these fossils were discovered in 1909 by Charles Walcott and the area was made a UNESCO World Heritage Site in 1981.

Scale 1: 19 000 000
0   190   380   570   760   950 km

Zenithal Equidistant Projection   © Oxford University Press

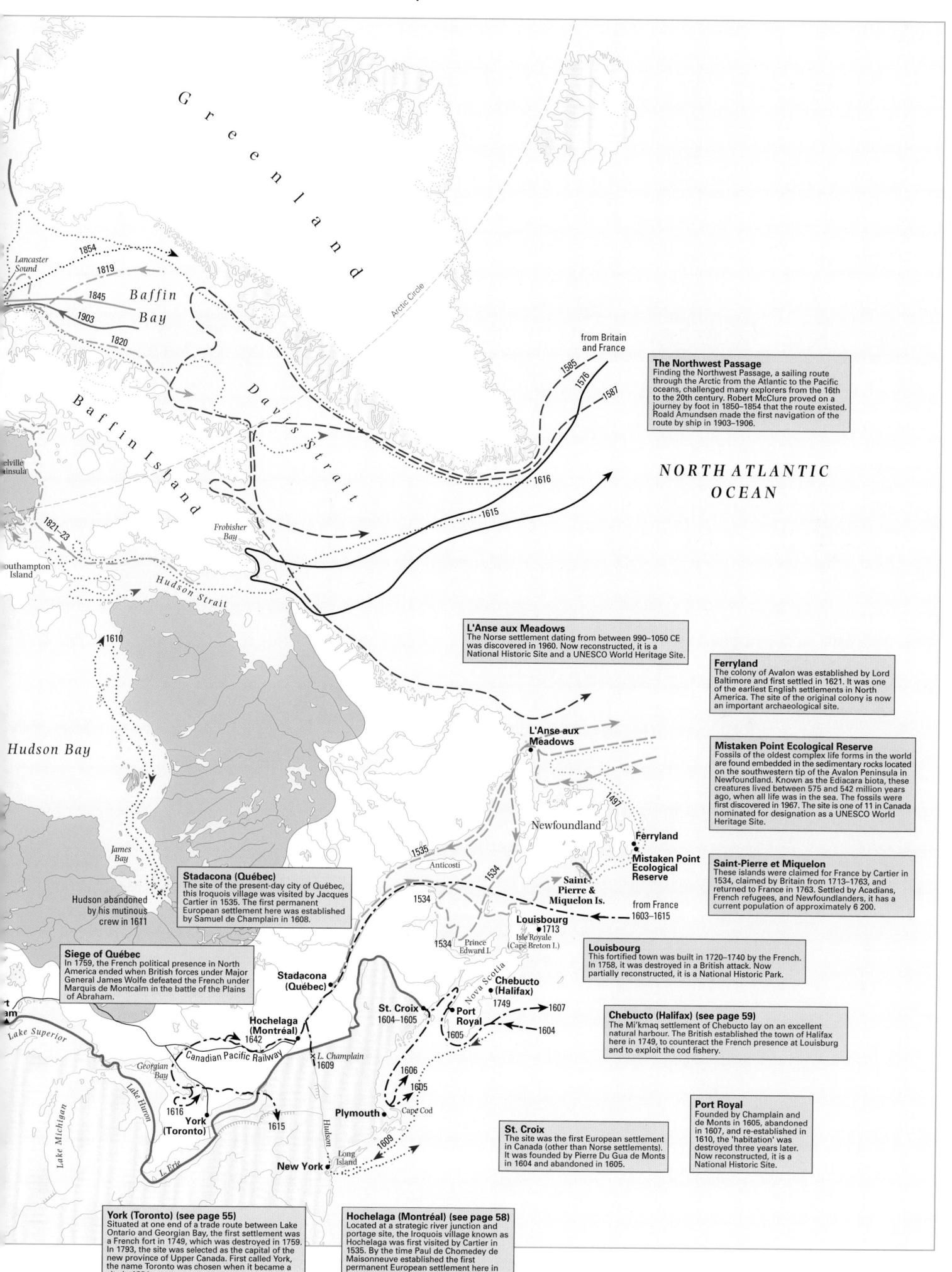

The Northwest Passage
Finding the Northwest Passage, a sailing route through the Arctic from the Atlantic to the Pacific oceans, challenged many explorers from the 16th to the 20th century. Robert McClure proved on a journey by foot in 1850–1854 that the route existed. Roald Amundsen made the first navigation of the route by ship in 1903–1906.

L'Anse aux Meadows
The Norse settlement dating from between 990–1050 CE was discovered in 1960. Now reconstructed, it is a National Historic Site and a UNESCO World Heritage Site.

Ferryland
The colony of Avalon was established by Lord Baltimore and first settled in 1621. It was one of the earliest English settlements in North America. The site of the original colony is now an important archaeological site.

Mistaken Point Ecological Reserve
Fossils of the oldest complex life forms in the world are found embedded in the sedimentary rocks located on the southwestern tip of the Avalon Peninsula in Newfoundland. Known as the Ediacara biota, these creatures lived between 575 and 542 million years ago, when all life was in the sea. The fossils were first discovered in 1967. The site is one of 11 in Canada nominated for designation as a UNESCO World Heritage Site.

Saint-Pierre et Miquelon
These islands were claimed for France by Cartier in 1534, claimed by Britain from 1713–1763, and returned to France in 1763. Settled by Acadians, French refugees, and Newfoundlanders, it has a current population of approximately 6 200.

Stadacona (Québec)
The site of the present-day city of Québec, this Iroquois village was visited by Jacques Cartier in 1535. The first permanent European settlement here was established by Samuel de Champlain in 1608.

Siege of Québec
In 1759, the French political presence in North America ended when British forces under Major General James Wolfe defeated the French under Marquis de Montcalm in the battle of the Plains of Abraham.

Louisbourg
This fortified town was built in 1720–1740 by the French. In 1758, it was destroyed in a British attack. Now partially reconstructed, it is a National Historic Park.

Chebucto (Halifax) (see page 59)
The Mi'kmaq settlement of Chebucto lay on an excellent natural harbour. The British established the town of Halifax here in 1749, to counteract the French presence at Louisbourg and to exploit the cod fishery.

Port Royal
Founded by Champlain and de Monts in 1605, abandoned in 1607, and re-established in 1610, the 'habitation' was destroyed three years later. Now reconstructed, it is a National Historic Site.

St. Croix
The site was the first European settlement in Canada (other than Norse settlements). It was founded by Pierre Du Gua de Monts in 1604 and abandoned in 1605.

York (Toronto) (see page 55)
Situated at one end of a trade route between Lake Ontario and Georgian Bay, the first settlement was a French fort in 1749, which was destroyed in 1759. In 1793, the site was selected as the capital of the new province of Upper Canada. First called York, the name Toronto was chosen when it became a city in 1834.

Hochelaga (Montréal) (see page 58)
Located at a strategic river junction and portage site, the Iroquois village known as Hochelaga was first visited by Cartier in 1535. By the time Paul de Chomedey de Maisonneuve established the first permanent European settlement here in 1642, Hochelaga had disappeared.

© Oxford University Press

Scale 1 : 45 000 000

Scale 1 : 22 500 000

0   225   450   675 km

Population distribution, 1901

one dot represents 1000 people

Boundaries, 1901

——— international

——— province/territory

The total population of Canada in 1901 was 5 371 300.

NEWFOUNDLAND

PRINCE EDWARD ISLAND

NOVA SCOTIA

NEW BRUNSWICK

QUÉBEC

ONTARIO

DISTRICT OF UNGAVA

DISTRICT OF KEEWATIN

DISTRICT OF MACKENZIE

DISTRICT OF ATHABASKA

DISTRICT OF SASKATCHEWAN

DISTRICT OF ALBERTA

DISTRICT OF ASSINIBOIA

MANITOBA

BRITISH COLUMBIA

YUKON

2006 Census

Total population of Canada was 31 612 897 of which 80% were classified as urban. Between 2001 and 2006 the population grew at the rate of 1.08% per year.

Further information on this topic is located in the Canada Statistics section which begins on page 155.

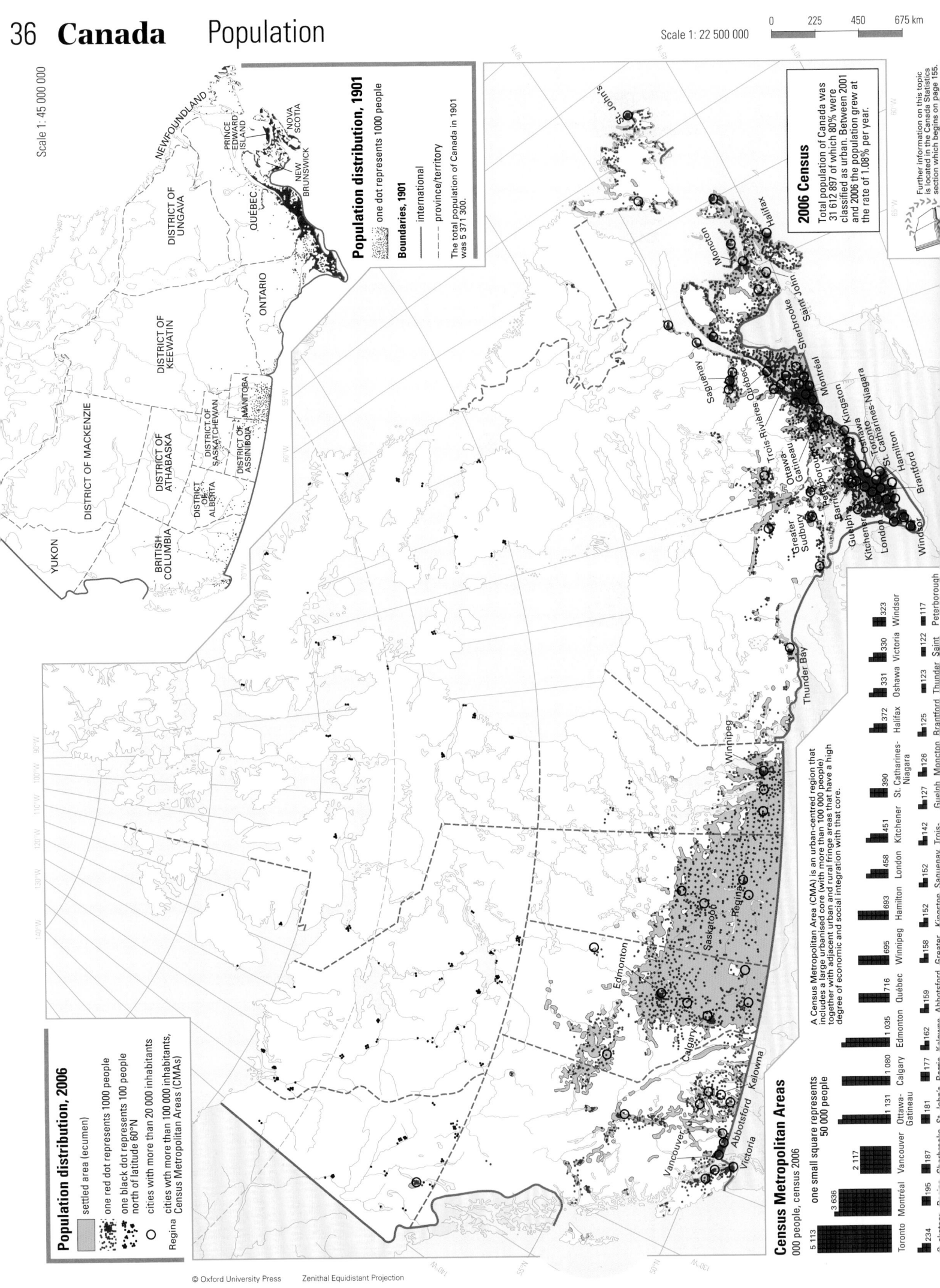

St. John's

Halifax

Moncton

Saint John

Sherbrooke

Saguenay

Québec

Trois-Rivières

Montréal

Gatineau

Ottawa

Kingston

Oshawa

Toronto

St. Catharines-Niagara

Hamilton

Peterborough

Barrie

Brantford

Guelph

Kitchener

London

Windsor

Greater Sudbury

Thunder Bay

Winnipeg

Regina

Saskatoon

Edmonton

Calgary

Kelowna

Abbotsford

Victoria

Vancouver

Population distribution, 2006

settled area (ecumen)

one red dot represents 1000 people

one black dot represents 100 people north of latitude 60°N

○ cities with more than 20 000 inhabitants

○ Regina cities with more than 100 000 inhabitants, Census Metropolitan Areas (CMAs)

Census Metropolitan Areas

000 people, census 2006

one small square represents 50 000 people

5 113	Toronto
3 636	Montréal
2 117	Vancouver
1 131	Ottawa-Gatineau
1 080	Calgary
1 035	Edmonton
716	Québec
695	Winnipeg
693	Hamilton
458	London
451	Kitchener
390	St. Catharines-Niagara
372	Halifax
331	Oshawa
330	Victoria
323	Windsor
234	
195	
187	
181	
177	
162	
159	
158	
152	
152	
142	
127	Guelph
126	Moncton
123	Brantford
122	Thunder Bay
117	Peterborough

Saint John

A Census Metropolitan Area (CMA) is an urban-centred region that includes a large urbanised core (with more than 100 000 people) together with adjacent urban and rural fringe areas that have a high degree of economic and social integration with that core.

© Oxford University Press   Zenithal Equidistant Projection

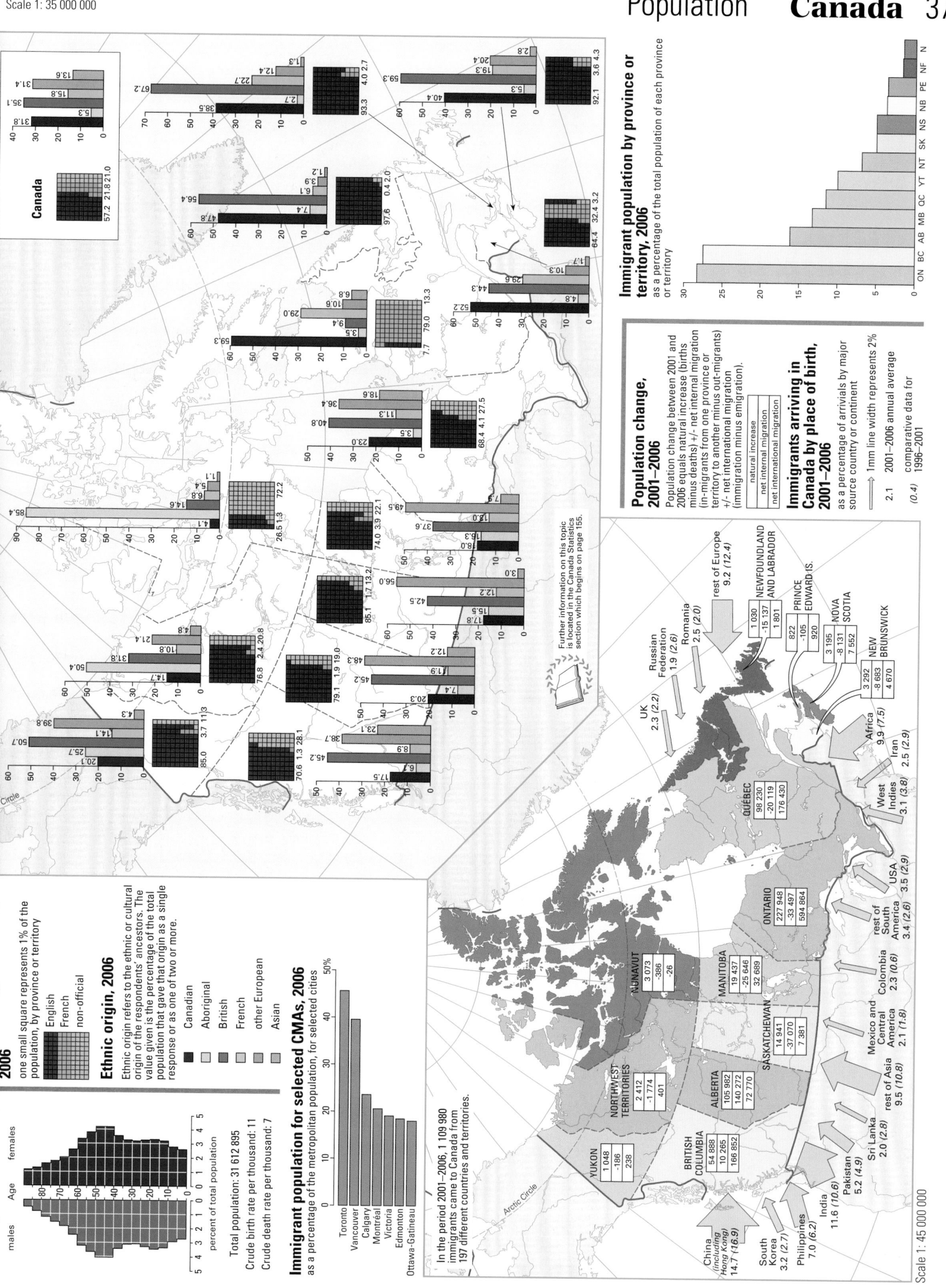

The 2006 Census recorded over 60 different languages spoken by Aboriginal peoples. Among Canada's First Nations, 29% could speak an Aboriginal language—51% of those living on reserves and 12% of those living off reserves. The languages with the largest number of speakers were Ojibwa (30 255), Oji-Cree (12 435), and Cree (87 285), (all members of the Algonquin family). Among the 50 485 Inuit, 34 345 were Inuktitut speakers.

Aboriginal languages by community

Distribution of Aboriginal communities categorized by the 11 major language families.

○ Algonquian	○ Kutenai
○ Athapaskan	○ Salish
○ Dakota (Siouan)	● Tlingit
○ Haida	○ Tsimshian
○ Inuktitut	● Wakashan
● Iroquoian	

Scale 1: 40 000 000

Aboriginal peoples, 2006
% of total Aboriginal population

First Nations 59.5%

more than one Aboriginal group or registered Indian without reporting an Aboriginal identity 2.9%

Inuit 4.3%

Métis 33.2%

Total population of Canada: 31 241 030
Total Aboriginal population: 1 172 790 (3.8%)

Where the Aboriginal population live, 2006

Inuit
urban 37.6%
reserve 0.9%
rural 61.5%

Métis
reserve 1.1%
rural 29.5%
urban 69.4%

First Nations
urban 44.7%
rural 12.2%
reserve 43.1%

Inuit population, 2006

Inuit regions (Inuit Nunaat)

	Inuvialuit
	Nunatsiavut
	Nunavik
	Nunavut

Census Subdivisions (CSDs) with a population of more than 250 Inuit identity people
● over 1000
· 250–1000

Scale 1: 78 000 000

Métis population, 2006

Census Subdivisions (CSDs) with a population of more than 250 Métis identity people
● over 1000
· 250–1000

First Nations population, 2006

Census Subdivisions (CSDs) with a population of more than 250 First Nations identity people
● over 1000
· 250–1000

Further information on this topic is located in the Canada Statistics section, which begins on page 155.

Zenithal Equidistant Projection

© Oxford University Press

Scale 1: 78 000 000

The Dominion of Canada was formed in 1867 and included the provinces of Nova Scotia, New Brunswick, Québec, and Ontario. The North-Western Territory, Rupert's Land, and Manitoba were added in 1870; British Columbia in 1871; Prince Edward Island in 1873; Saskatchewan and Alberta in 1905; and Newfoundland in 1949. The territory of Nunavut was created on 1 April 1999. On 6 December 2001, Newfoundland's name was officially changed to Newfoundland and Labrador.

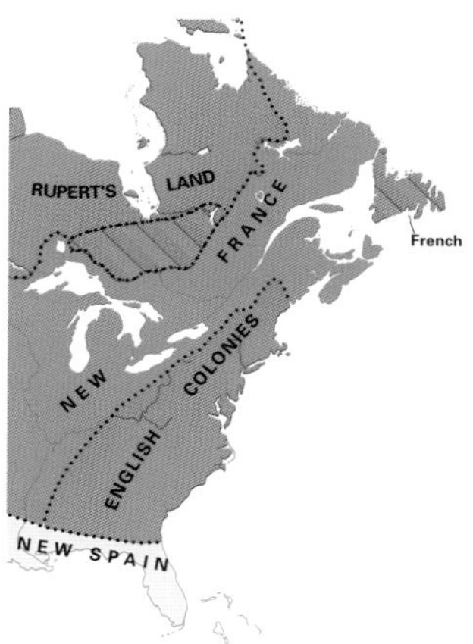

The small islands known formally as the Collectivité Territoriale de Saint-Pierre-et-Miquelon (population 6125 and area 215 km²), off the southern coast of Newfoundland, are a part of France and are all that remains of the former colonial territory of New France.

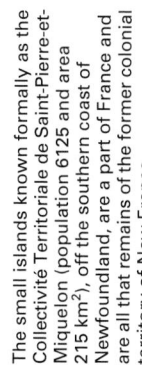

1791

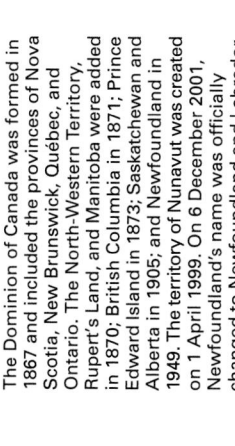

1763

1667

1667, 1763 and 1791

Boundaries

- English
- French
- disputed
- Spanish
- American
- unclaimed land

- ·········· colonial/territorial
- —— undefined
- —— district
- - - - province
- —— international

© Oxford University Press

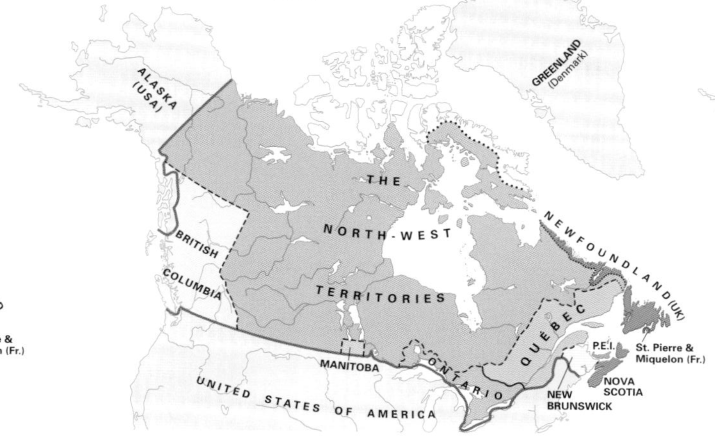

1889

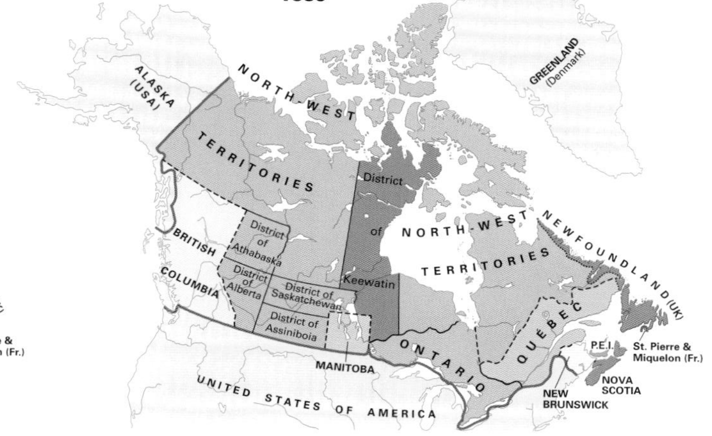

1873

1867

1949/2001

1912

1905

Scale 1: 19 000 000

| 0 | 190 | 380 | 570 | 760 | 950 km |

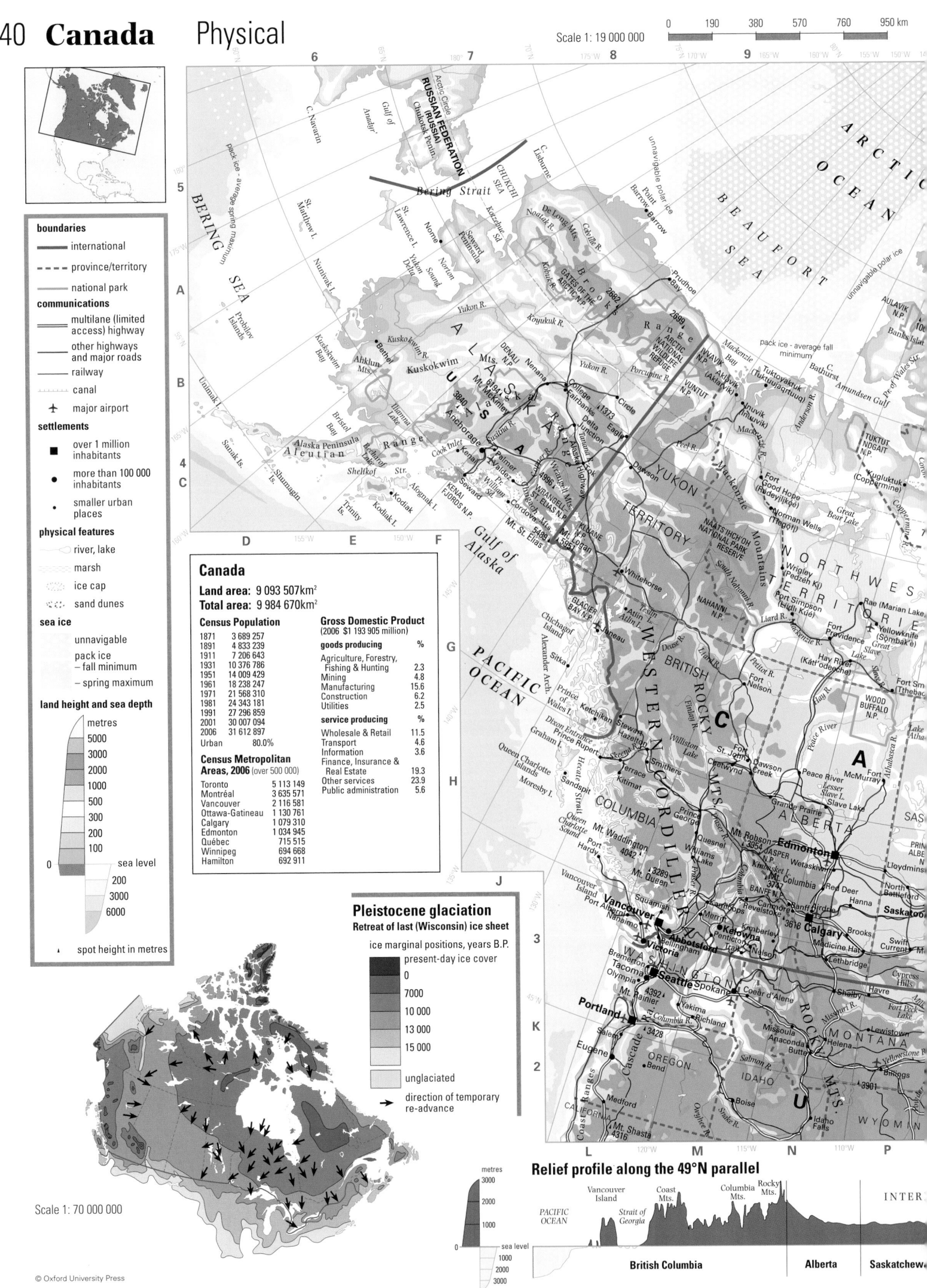

boundaries

— international
--- province/territory
— national park

communications

═══ multilane (limited access) highway
─── other highways and major roads
┈┈┈ railway
┈┼┈ canal
✈ major airport

settlements

■ over 1 million inhabitants
● more than 100 000 inhabitants
• smaller urban places

physical features

river, lake
marsh
ice cap
sand dunes

sea ice

unnavigable
pack ice
– fall minimum
– spring maximum

land height and sea depth

metres
5000
3000
2000
1000
500
300
200
100
sea level
200
3000
6000

▴ spot height in metres

Canada

Land area: 9 093 507km²
Total area: 9 984 670km²

Census Population

1871	3 689 257
1891	4 833 239
1911	7 206 643
1931	10 376 786
1951	14 009 429
1961	18 238 247
1971	21 568 310
1981	24 343 181
1991	27 296 859
2001	30 007 094
2006	31 612 897
Urban	80.0%

Census Metropolitan Areas, 2006 (over 500 000)

Toronto	5 113 149
Montréal	3 635 571
Vancouver	2 116 581
Ottawa-Gatineau	1 130 761
Calgary	1 079 310
Edmonton	1 034 945
Québec	715 515
Winnipeg	694 668
Hamilton	692 911

Gross Domestic Product
(2006 $1 193 905 million)

goods producing	%
Agriculture, Forestry, Fishing & Hunting	2.3
Mining	4.8
Manufacturing	15.6
Construction	6.2
Utilities	2.5

service producing	%
Wholesale & Retail	11.5
Transport	4.6
Information	3.6
Finance, Insurance & Real Estate	19.3
Other services	23.9
Public administration	5.6

Pleistocene glaciation
Retreat of last (Wisconsin) ice sheet

ice marginal positions, years B.P.

	present-day ice cover
	0
	7000
	10 000
	13 000
	15 000
	unglaciated

→ direction of temporary re-advance

Scale 1: 70 000 000

Relief profile along the 49°N parallel

metres	
3000	
2000	
1000	
sea level	
1000	
2000	
3000	

PACIFIC OCEAN — Vancouver Island — Strait of Georgia — Coast Mts. — Columbia Mts. — Rocky Mts. — INTER...

British Columbia — **Alberta** — **Saskatchew...**

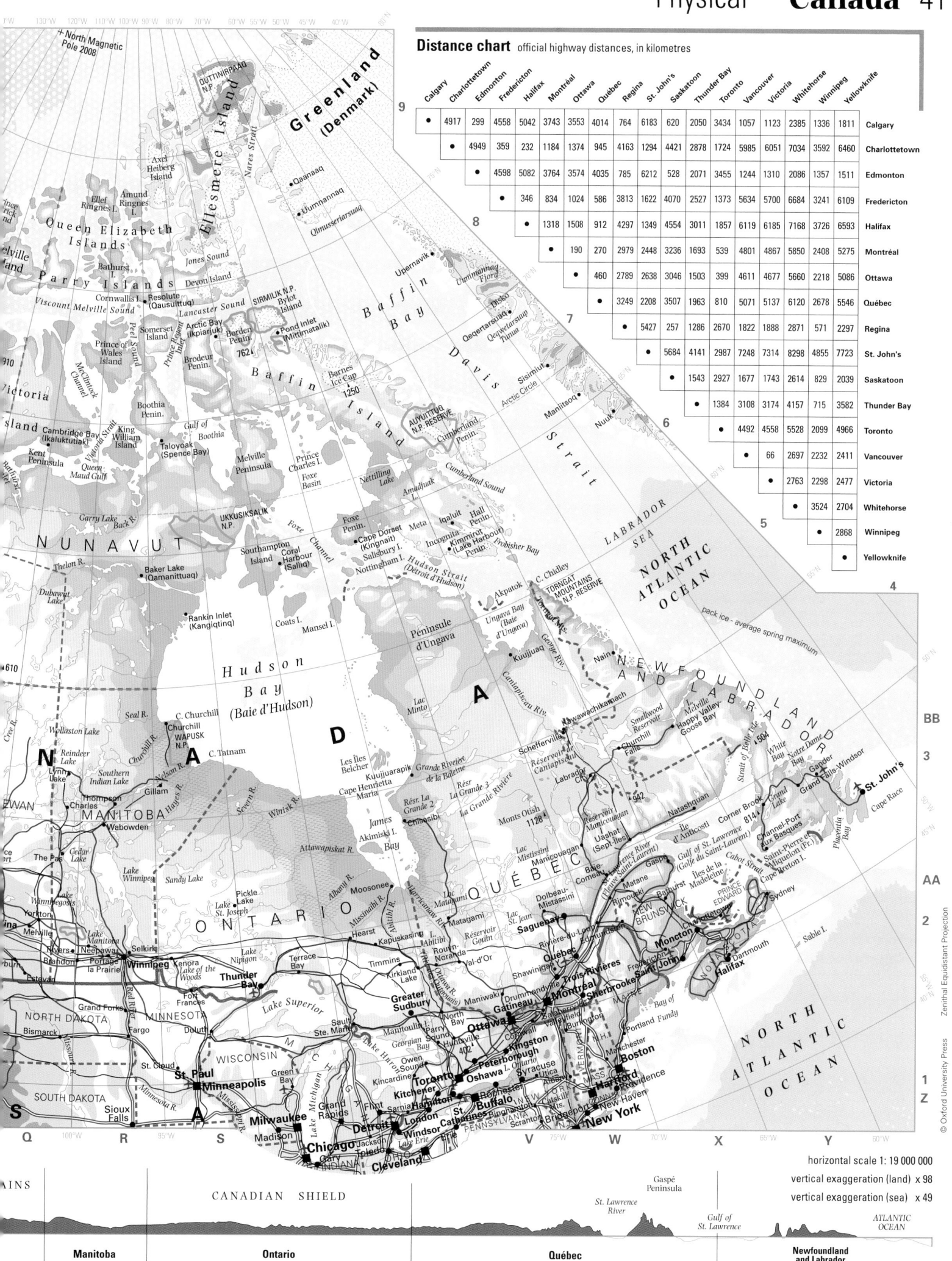

Distance chart official highway distances, in kilometres

	Calgary	Charlottetown	Edmonton	Fredericton	Halifax	Montréal	Ottawa	Québec	Regina	St. John's	Saskatoon	Thunder Bay	Toronto	Vancouver	Victoria	Whitehorse	Winnipeg	Yellowknife	
•	4917	299	4558	5042	3743	3553	4014	764	6183	620	2050	3434	1057	1123	2385	1336	1811	Calgary
	•	4949	359	232	1184	1374	945	4163	1294	4421	2878	1724	5985	6051	7034	3592	6460	Charlottetown
		•	4598	5082	3764	3574	4035	785	6212	528	2071	3455	1244	1310	2086	1357	1511	Edmonton
			•	346	834	1024	586	3813	1622	4070	2527	1373	5634	5700	6684	3241	6109	Fredericton
				•	1318	1508	912	4297	1349	4554	3011	1857	6119	6185	7168	3726	6593	Halifax
					•	190	270	2979	2448	3236	1693	539	4801	4867	5850	2408	5275	Montréal
						•	460	2789	2638	3046	1503	399	4611	4677	5660	2218	5086	Ottawa
							•	3249	2208	3507	1963	810	5071	5137	6120	2678	5546	Québec
								•	5427	257	1286	2670	1822	1888	2871	571	2297	Regina
									•	5684	4141	2987	7248	7314	8298	4855	7723	St. John's
										•	1543	2927	1677	1743	2614	829	2039	Saskatoon
											•	1384	3108	3174	4157	715	3582	Thunder Bay
												•	4492	4558	5528	2099	4966	Toronto
													•	66	2697	2232	2411	Vancouver
														•	2763	2298	2477	Victoria
															•	3524	2704	Whitehorse
																•	2868	Winnipeg
																	•	Yellowknife

horizontal scale 1: 19 000 000

vertical exaggeration (land) x 98

vertical exaggeration (sea) x 49

© Oxford University Press

Zenithal Equidistant Projection

CANADIAN SHIELD

Manitoba | Ontario | Québec | Newfoundland and Labrador

physical features

marsh
ice cap

sea ice

unnavigable
pack ice
–fall minimum
–spring maximum

land height and sea depth

metres
3000
2000
1500
1000
500
300
200
100
0 sea level
200
3000
6000

spot height
in metres

boundaries

international
province/territory
national park/
provincial park

communications

multilane (limited
access) highway
other highways
and major roads
railway
canal
ferry
major airport
other airport

settlements

built-up area
over 1 million
inhabitants
more than 100 000
inhabitants
smaller urban places

Scale 1: 2 000 000

0 20 40 60 80 100 km

Conical Orthomorphic Projection   © Oxford University Press

British Columbia

Land area: 925 186km²
Total area: 944 735km²
(9.5% of Canada)

Census Population

1871	36 247
1891	98 173
1911	392 480
1931	694 263
1951	1 165 210
1971	2 184 620
1991	3 282 061
2001	3 907 738
2006	4 113 487
Urban	85.4%

Census Metropolitan Areas, 2006

Abbotsford	159 020
Vancouver	2 116 581
Victoria (capital)	330 088

Other important urban centres, 2006

Chilliwack	80 892
Kamloops	92 882
Kelowna	162 276
Nanaimo	92 361
Prince George	83 225
Vernon	55 418

Gross Domestic Product
(2006 $136 050 million)

goods producing	%
Agriculture	0.8
Forestry	2.8
Fishing, Hunting, & Trapping	0.07
Mining incl. oil & gas	2.6
Utilities	1.9
Construction	6.4
Manufacturing	11.1

service producing	%
Wholesale & Retail trade	12.1
Transportation & Warehousing	6.6
Information & Cultural industries	4.4
Finance, Insurance & Real estate	22.8
Other services	23.5
Public administration	5.1

Scale 1: 5 000 000

0   50   100   150   200   250 km

© Oxford University Press

Scale 1 : 300 000

0   3   6   9   12   15 km

Vancouver map

boundaries
- – – – province
- ------ county/regional municipality/ district

communications
- multilane (limited access) highway
- other highways and major roads
- railway
- canal
- ✈ major airport
- ✈ other airport

physical features
- river, lake
- marsh
- —50— contours
- ▲ spot height in metres

land use
- central business district
- other major commercial areas
- industrial
- residential
- major parks and open spaces
- non-urban

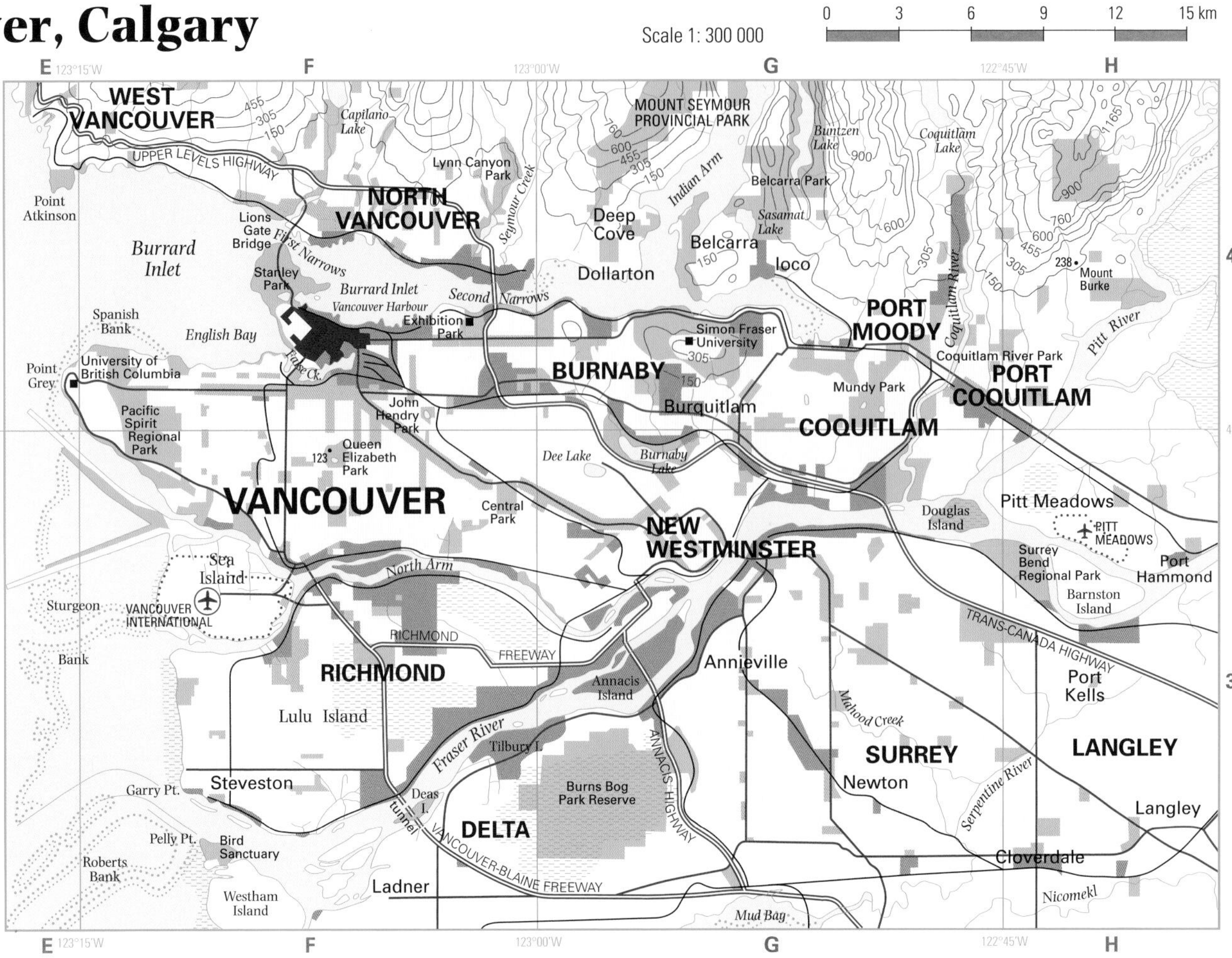

WEST VANCOUVER
NORTH VANCOUVER
MOUNT SEYMOUR PROVINCIAL PARK
Point Atkinson
Capilano Lake
Lynn Canyon Park
Buntzen Lake
Coquitlam Lake
Burrard Inlet
Lions Gate Bridge
Stanley Park
First Narrows
Seymour Creek
Deep Cove
Belcarra Park
Belcarra
Sasamat Lake
Ioco
Mount Burke
Spanish Bank
English Bay
Second Narrows
Burrard Inlet
Vancouver Harbour
Exhibition Park
Dollarton
Simon Fraser University
PORT MOODY
Coquitlam River Park
Coquitlam River
Point Grey
University of British Columbia
Trout Ck.
BURNABY
Burquitlam
Mundy Park
COQUITLAM
PORT COQUITLAM
Pacific Spirit Regional Park
John Hendry Park
Queen Elizabeth Park
123
Dee Lake
Burnaby Lake
VANCOUVER
Central Park
NEW WESTMINSTER
Douglas Island
Pitt Meadows
PITT MEADOWS
Pitt River
Sea Island
North Arm
RICHMOND FREEWAY
Annieville
Surrey Bend Regional Park
Port Hammond
Barnston Island
VANCOUVER INTERNATIONAL
Sturgeon Bank
RICHMOND
Lulu Island
Annacis Island
Methood Creek
TRANS-CANADA HIGHWAY
Port Kells
Garry Pt.
Fraser River
Tilbury I.
ANNACIS HIGHWAY
SURREY
Newton
LANGLEY
Steveston
Deas I.
Burns Bog Park Reserve
Serpentine River
Langley
Pelly Pt.
Bird Sanctuary
Tunnel
DELTA
VANCOUVER-BLAINE FREEWAY
Cloverdale
Roberts Bank
Westham Island
Ladner
Mud Bay
Nicomekl

Calgary

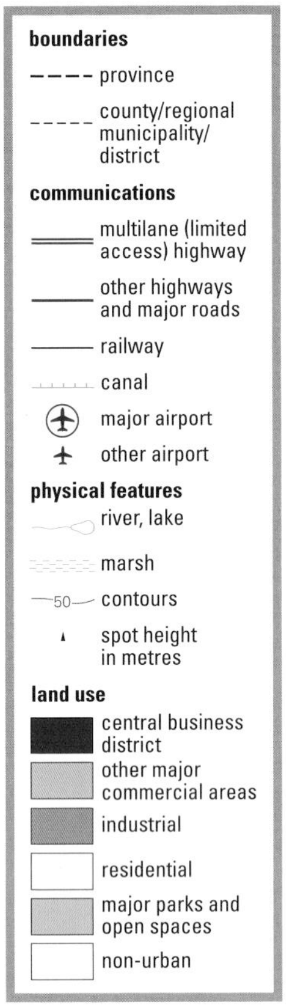

Calgary
In this image of the rapidly expanding city of Calgary, the Bow River (B) and Nose Hill (N) are prominent features.

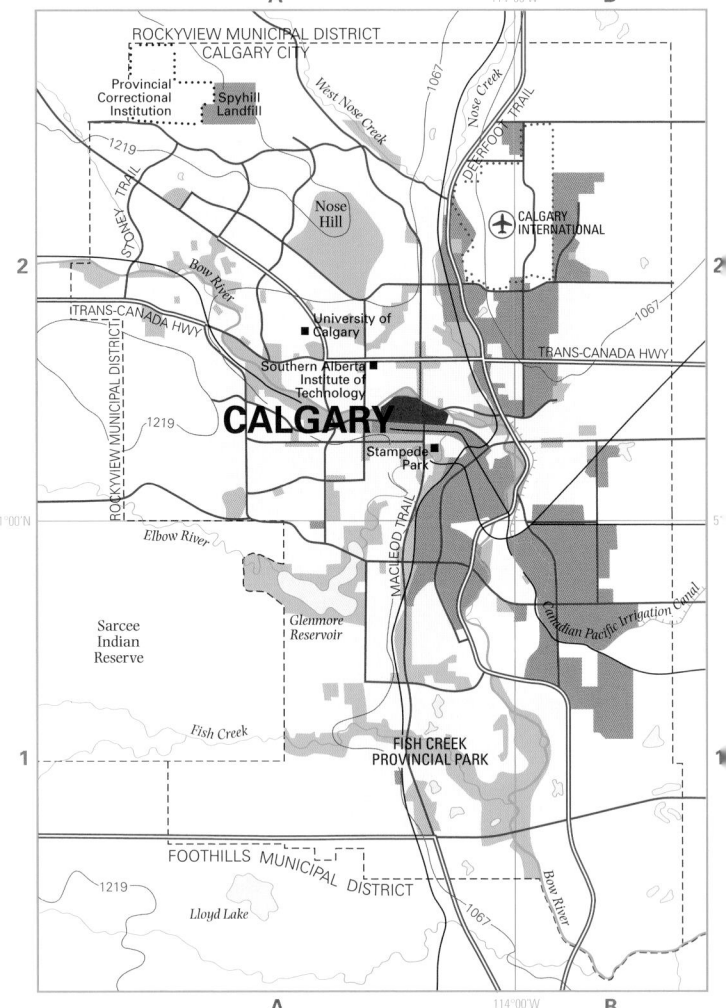

ROCKYVIEW MUNICIPAL DISTRICT
CALGARY CITY
Provincial Correctional Institution
Spyhill Landfill
West Nose Creek
Nose Creek
DEERFOOT TRAIL
STONEY TRAIL
Nose Hill
CALGARY INTERNATIONAL
Bow River
TRANS-CANADA HWY
University of Calgary
TRANS-CANADA HWY
Southern Alberta Institute of Technology
CALGARY
Stampede Park
ROCKYVIEW MUNICIPAL DISTRICT
MACLEOD TRAIL
Elbow River
Sarcee Indian Reserve
Glenmore Reservoir
Canadian Pacific Irrigation Canal
Fish Creek
FISH CREEK PROVINCIAL PARK
FOOTHILLS MUNICIPAL DISTRICT
Lloyd Lake
Bow River

Vancouver

Stanley Park, English Bay, Burrard Inlet, and False Creek (F) surround the central business district of Vancouver.

Victoria

In this image of central Victoria, the Parliament Buildings (P) are visible at the eastern end of Victoria Harbour.

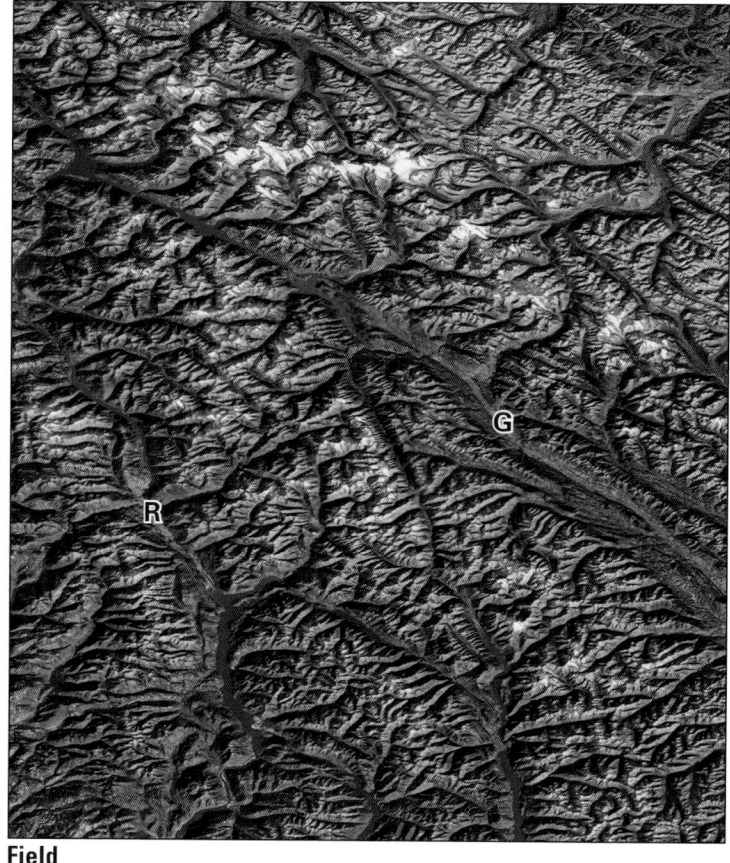

Field

This image shows (from east to west) the Rocky, Purcell, Selkirk, and Monashee Mountains. Golden (G) and Revelstoke (R) are located both on the Columbia River and on the route of the first transcontinental railway.

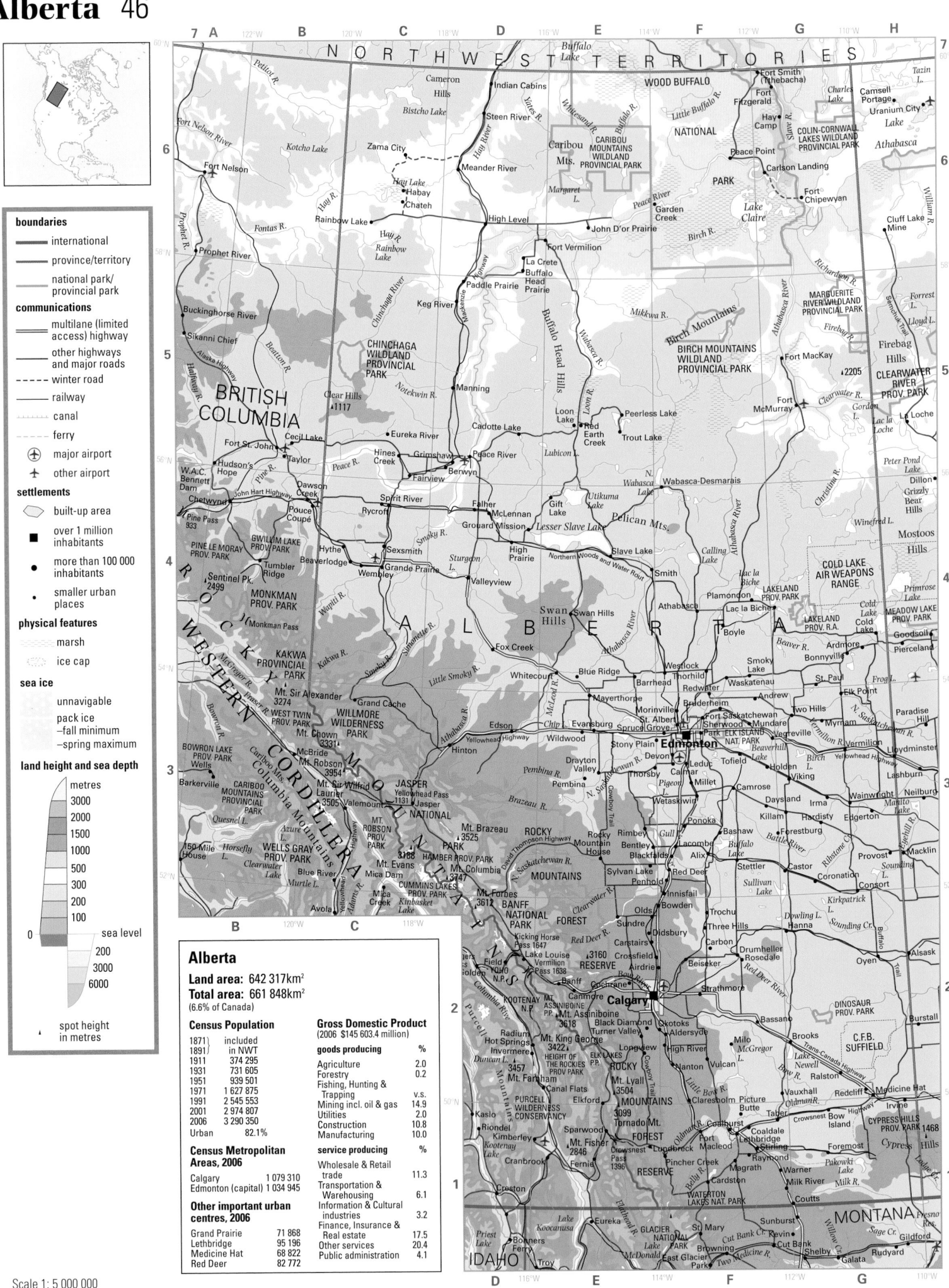

boundaries

	international
	province/territory
	national park/ provincial park

communications

	multilane (limited access) highway
	other highways and major roads
	winter road
	railway
	canal
	ferry
✈	major airport
✈	other airport

settlements

	built-up area
■	over 1 million inhabitants
●	more than 100 000 inhabitants
•	smaller urban places

physical features

| | marsh |
| | ice cap |

sea ice

| | unnavigable |
| | pack ice –fall minimum –spring maximum |

land height and sea depth

metres
3000
2000
1500
1000
500
300
200
100
0 — sea level
200
3000
6000

▲ spot height in metres

Alberta

Land area: 642 317km²
Total area: 661 848km²
(6.6% of Canada)

Census Population

1871	included
1891	in NWT
1911	374 295
1931	731 605
1951	939 501
1971	1 627 875
1991	2 545 553
2001	2 974 807
2006	3 290 350
Urban	82.1%

Census Metropolitan Areas, 2006

| Calgary | 1 079 310 |
| Edmonton (capital) | 1 034 945 |

Other important urban centres, 2006

Grand Prairie	71 868
Lethbridge	95 196
Medicine Hat	68 822
Red Deer	82 772

Gross Domestic Product
(2006 $145 603.4 million)

goods producing	%
Agriculture	2.0
Forestry	0.2
Fishing, Hunting & Trapping	v.s.
Mining incl. oil & gas	14.9
Utilities	2.0
Construction	10.8
Manufacturing	10.0
service producing	**%**
Wholesale & Retail trade	11.3
Transportation & Warehousing	6.1
Information & Cultural industries	3.2
Finance, Insurance & Real estate	17.5
Other services	20.4
Public administration	4.1

Scale 1: 5 000 000

0 50 100 150 200 250 km

Conical Orthomorphic Projection   © Oxford University Press

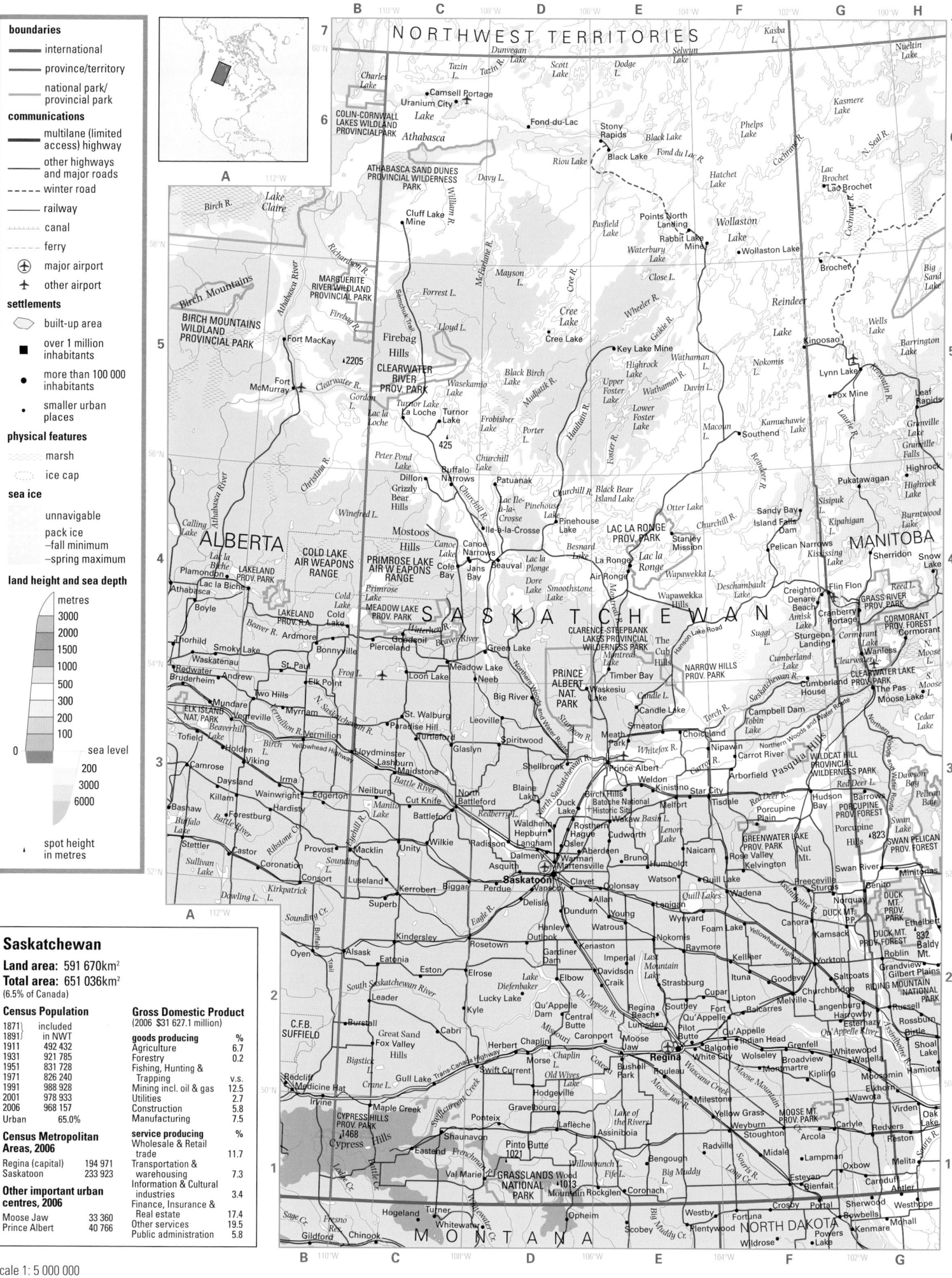

boundaries
— international
— province/territory
— national park/ provincial park

communications
— multilane (limited access) highway
— other highways and major roads
--- winter road
— railway
⊦⊦⊦ canal
--- ferry
✈ major airport
✈ other airport

settlements
⬡ built-up area
■ over 1 million inhabitants
● more than 100 000 inhabitants
• smaller urban places

physical features
marsh
ice cap

sea ice
unnavigable
pack ice
–fall minimum
–spring maximum

land height and sea depth

metres
3000
2000
1500
1000
500
300
200
100
0 sea level
200
3000
6000

▲ spot height in metres

Saskatchewan

Land area: 591 670km²
Total area: 651 036km²
(6.5% of Canada)

Census Population

1871	included
1891	in NWT
1911	492 432
1931	921 785
1951	831 728
1971	826 240
1991	988 928
2001	978 933
2006	968 157
Urban	65.0%

Census Metropolitan Areas, 2006

Regina (capital)	194 971
Saskatoon	233 923

Other important urban centres, 2006

Moose Jaw	33 360
Prince Albert	40 766

Gross Domestic Product
(2006 $31 627.1 million)

goods producing	%
Agriculture	6.7
Forestry	0.2
Fishing, Hunting & Trapping	v.s.
Mining incl. oil & gas	12.5
Utilities	2.7
Construction	5.8
Manufacturing	7.5

service producing	%
Wholesale & Retail trade	11.7
Transportation & warehousing	7.3
Information & Cultural industries	3.4
Finance, Insurance & Real estate	17.4
Other services	19.5
Public administration	5.8

Scale 1: 5 000 000

50 100 150 200 250 km

Conical Orthomorphic Projection
© Oxford University Press

Scale 1: 300 000

0   3   6   9   12   15 km

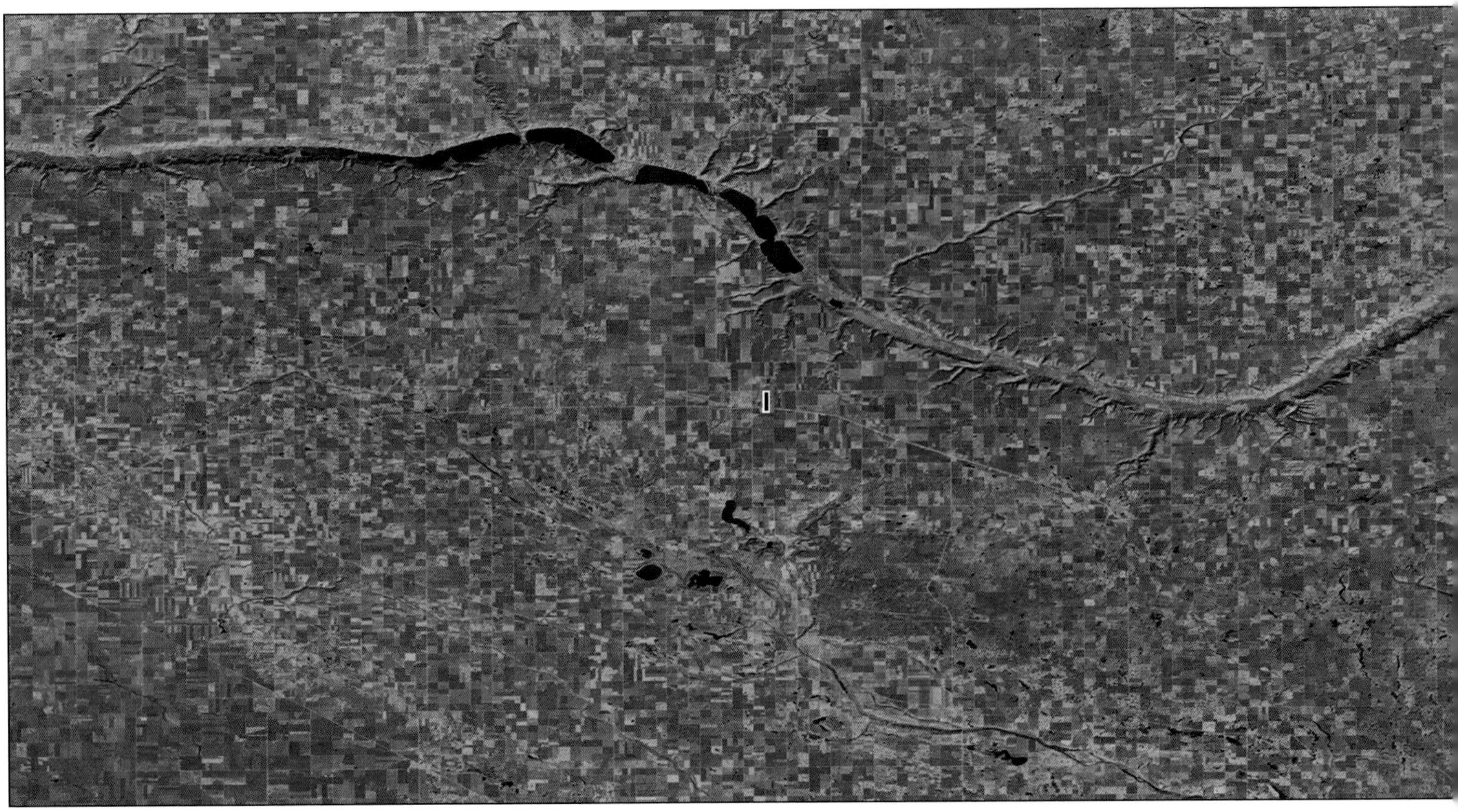

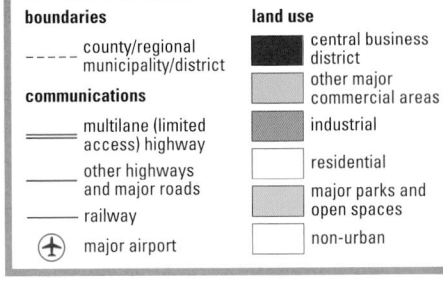

Central Saskatchewan

The image covers a large area of central Saskatchewan east of Regina, with the Qu'Appelle River in the north. The pattern of squares illustrates the division of these lands, beginning in 1872, into square townships of 36 square miles (93.2 km²) consisting of 36 sections of 640 acres each (259 ha), which were further subdivided into 160-acre lots (65 ha). The colour gradations indicate different crops and stages in their growth. The location of Indian Head (I), a small town with a population of 2000, 69 km east of Regina, is indicated.

boundaries	land use
- - - county/regional municipality/district	central business district
communications	other major commercial areas
═══ multilane (limited access) highway	industrial
─── other highways and major roads	residential
── railway	major parks and open spaces
✈ major airport	non-urban

Winnipeg

Winnipeg was first established near the junction of the Red and Assiniboine Rivers (A). This image includes almost the entire built-up area of the city. The airport is shown in the northwest and the Winnipeg Floodway (F) is apparent in the southeast.

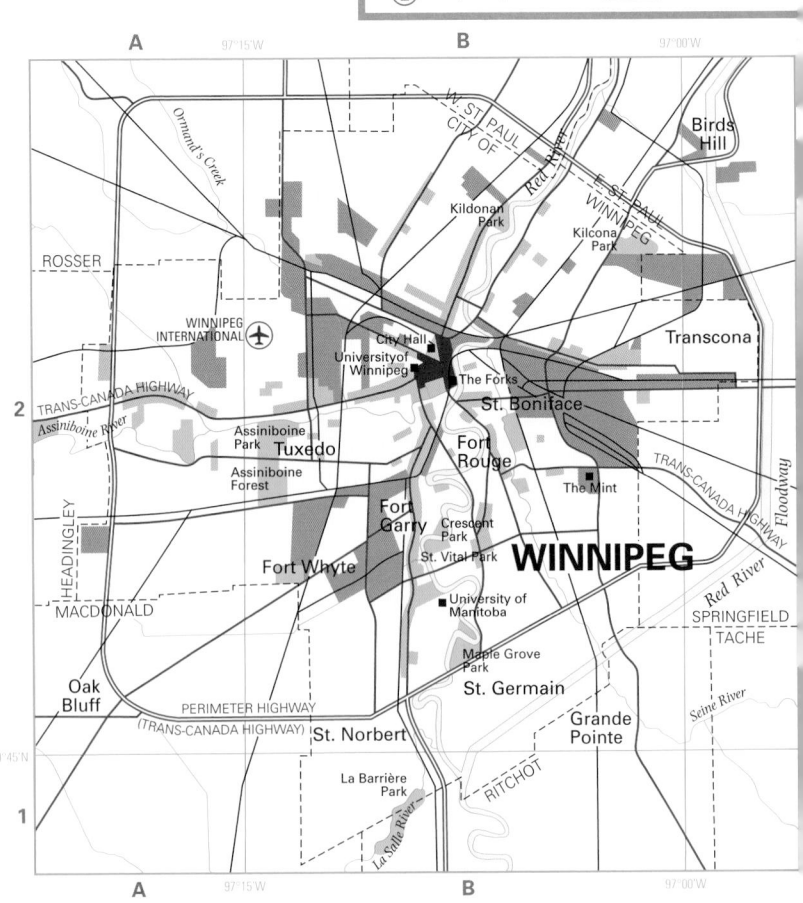

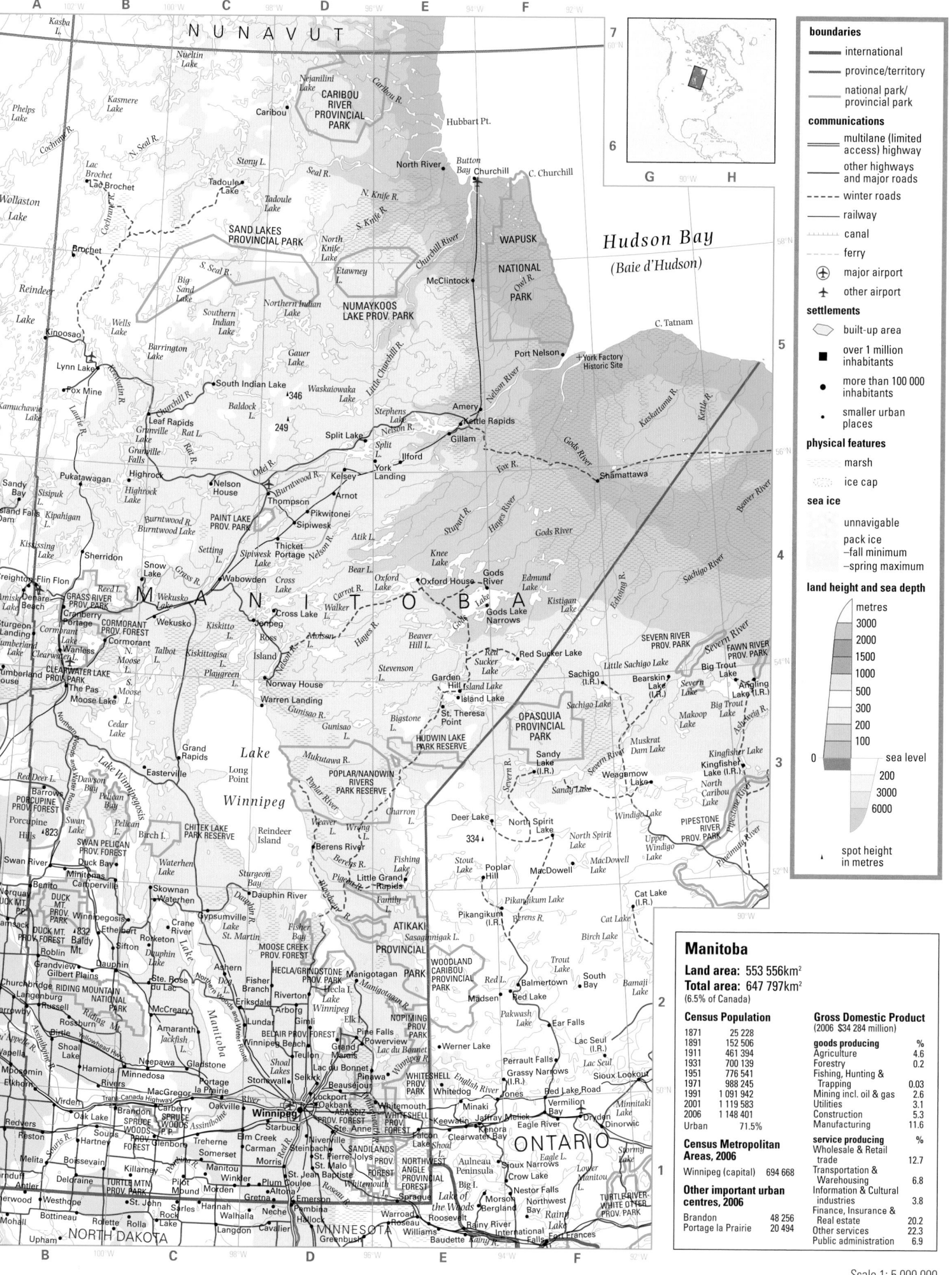

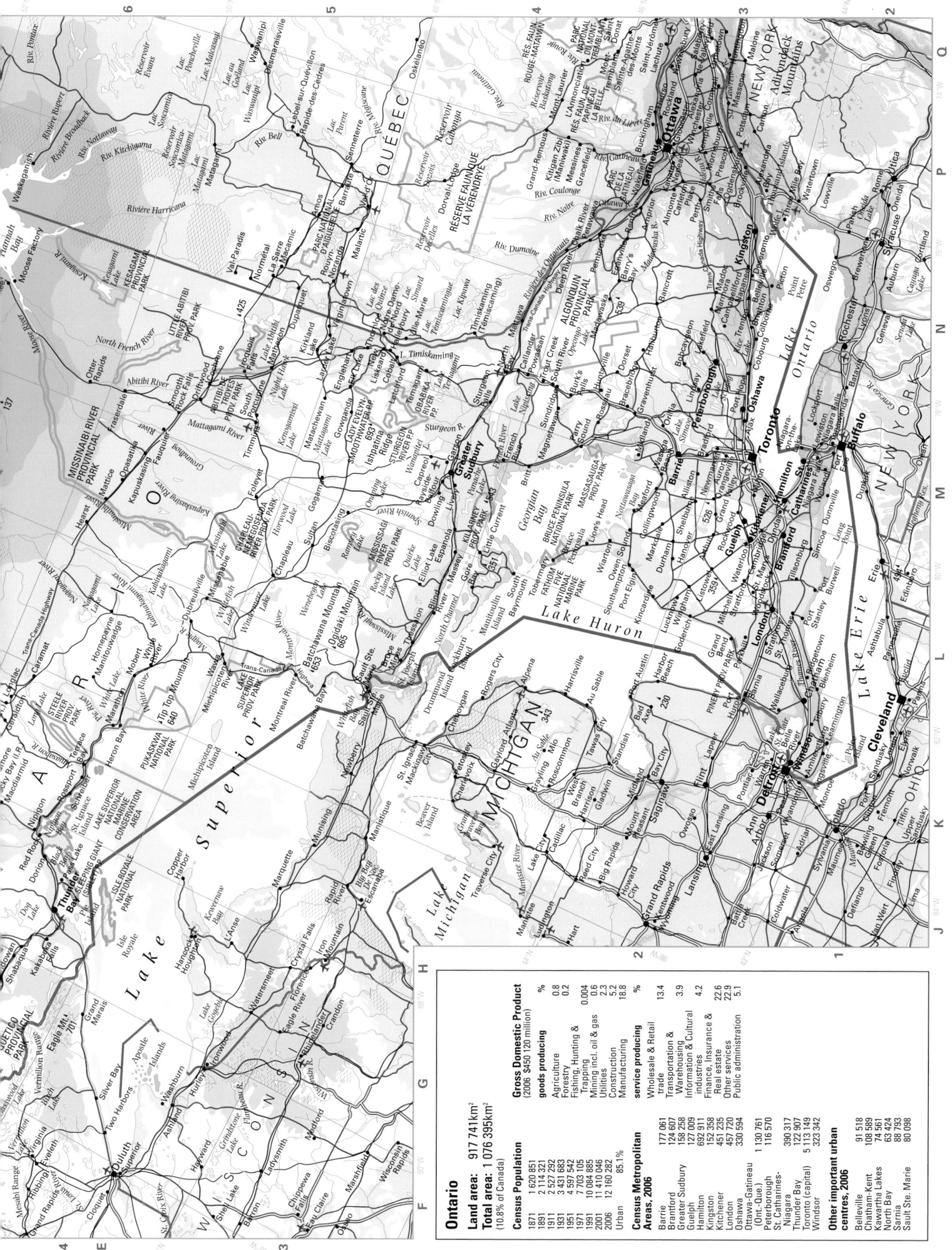

Ontario

Land area: 917 741 km²
Total area: 1 076 395 km²
(10.8% of Canada)

Census Population

Year	Population
1871	1 620 851
1891	2 114 321
1911	2 527 292
1931	3 431 683
1951	4 597 542
1971	7 703 105
1991	10 084 885
2001	11 410 046
2006	12 160 282
Urban	85.1%

Census Metropolitan Areas, 2006

Barrie	177 061
Brantford	124 607
Greater Sudbury	158 258
Guelph	127 009
Hamilton	692 911
Kingston	152 358
Kitchener	451 235
London	457 720
Oshawa	330 594
Ottawa-Gatineau (Ont.-Que.)	1 130 761
Peterborough	116 570
St. Catharines-Niagara	390 317
Thunder Bay	122 907
Toronto (capital)	5 113 149
Windsor	323 342

Other important urban centres, 2006

Belleville	91 518
Chatham-Kent	108 589
Kawartha Lakes	74 561
North Bay	63 424
Sarnia	88 793
Sault Ste. Marie	80 098

Gross Domestic Product
(2006 $450 120 million)

goods producing	%
Agriculture	0.8
Forestry	0.2
Fishing, Hunting & Trapping	0.004
Mining incl. oil & gas	0.6
Utilities	2.3
Construction	5.2
Manufacturing	18.8

service producing	%
Wholesale & Retail trade	13.4
Transportation & Warehousing	3.9
Information & Cultural industries	4.2
Finance, Insurance & Real estate	22.6
Other services	22.9
Public administration	5.1

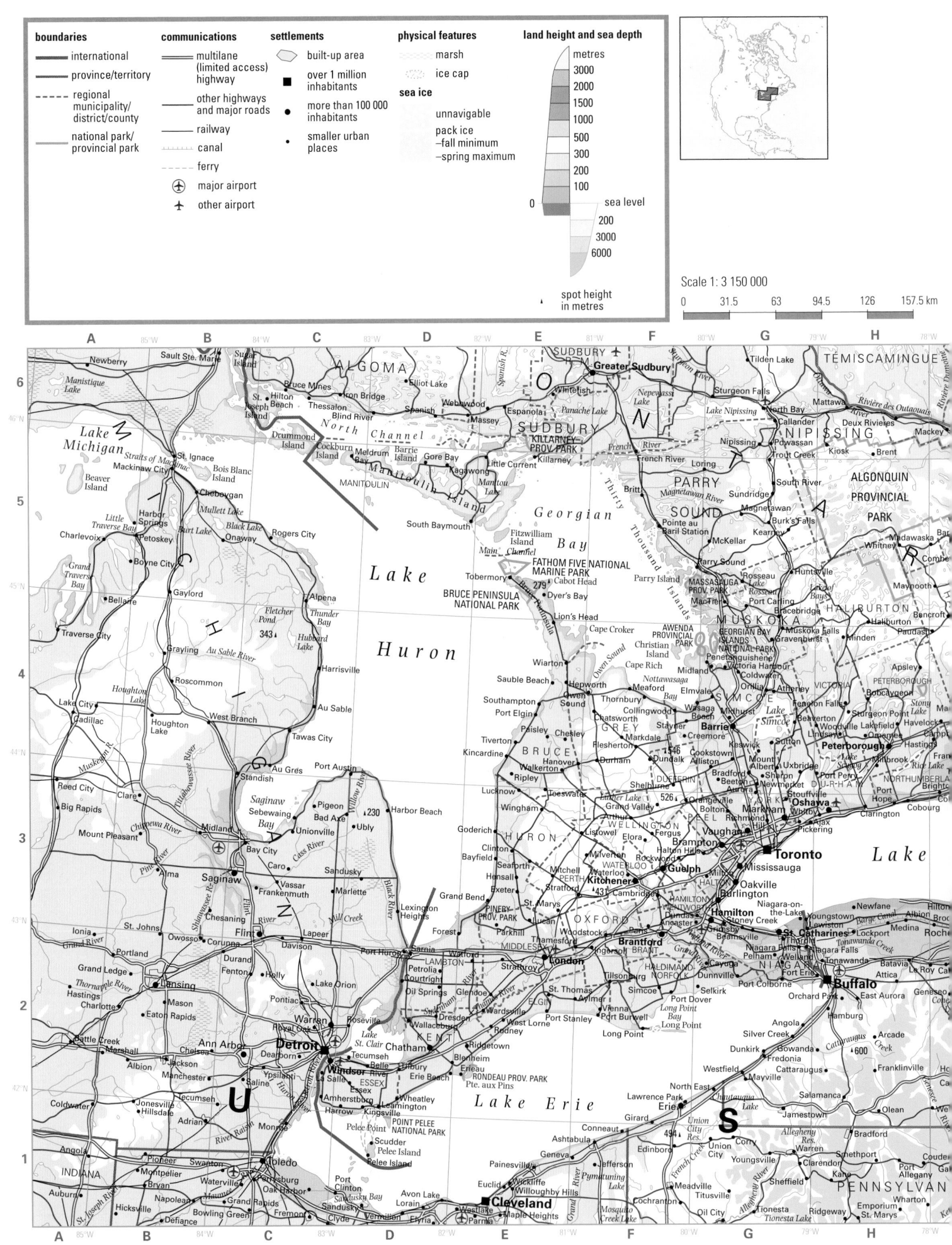

boundaries
- international
- province/territory
- regional municipality/ district/county
- national park/ provincial park

communications
- multilane (limited access) highway
- other highways and major roads
- railway
- canal
- ferry
- ✈ major airport
- ✈ other airport

settlements
- built-up area
- ■ over 1 million inhabitants
- ● more than 100 000 inhabitants
- • smaller urban places

physical features
- marsh
- ice cap

sea ice
- unnavigable
- pack ice –fall minimum –spring maximum

land height and sea depth

metres
3000
2000
1500
1000
500
300
200
100
sea level
200
3000
6000

spot height in metres

Scale 1: 3 150 000

0   31.5   63   94.5   126   157.5 km

Conical Orthomorphic Projection   © Oxford University Press

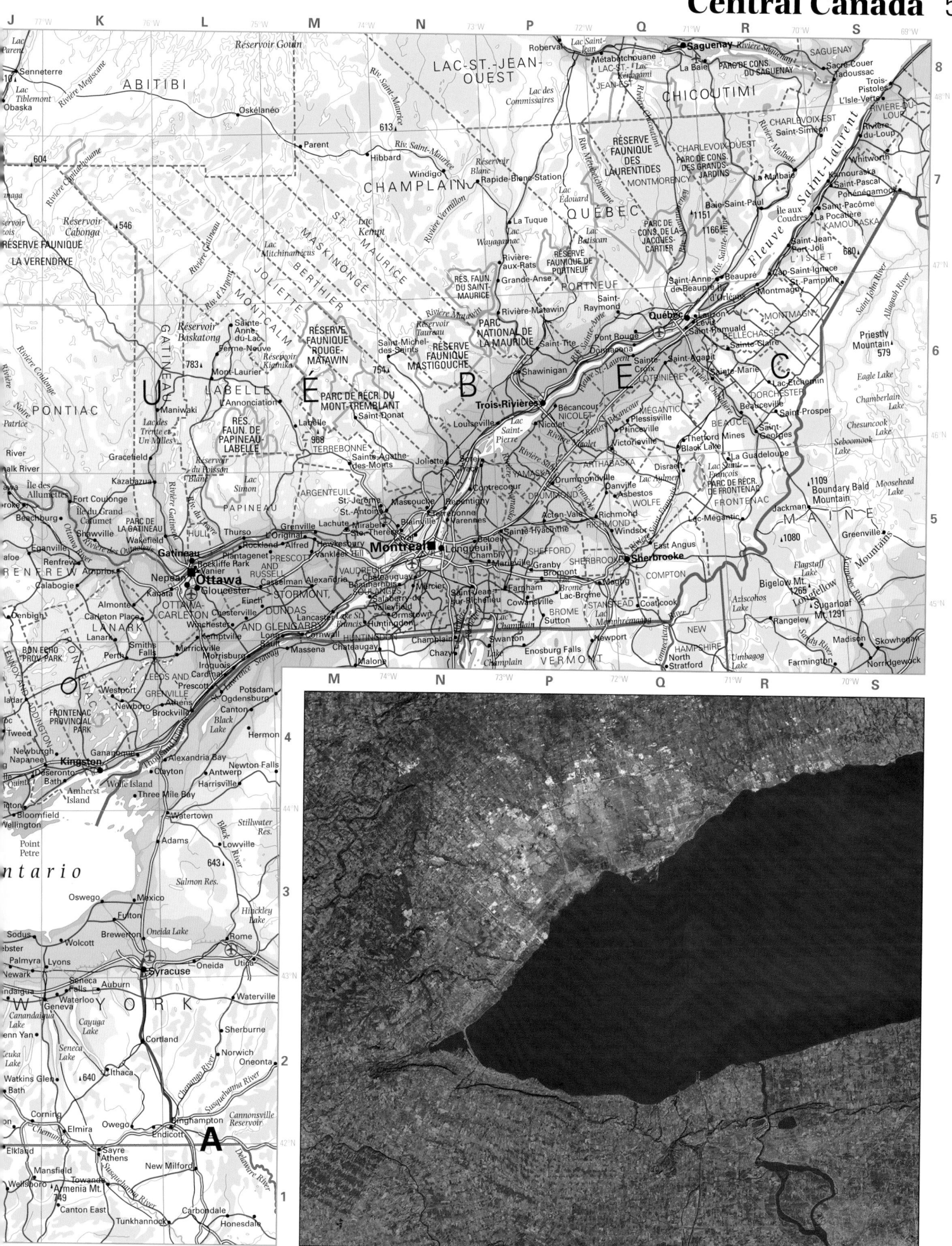

Golden Horseshoe

The Golden Horseshoe extends from Niagara Falls through Hamilton and Toronto, to Oshawa in the east. The Niagara River, separating Canada and the United States, and the Niagara Escarpment are clearly defined south of Lake Ontario.

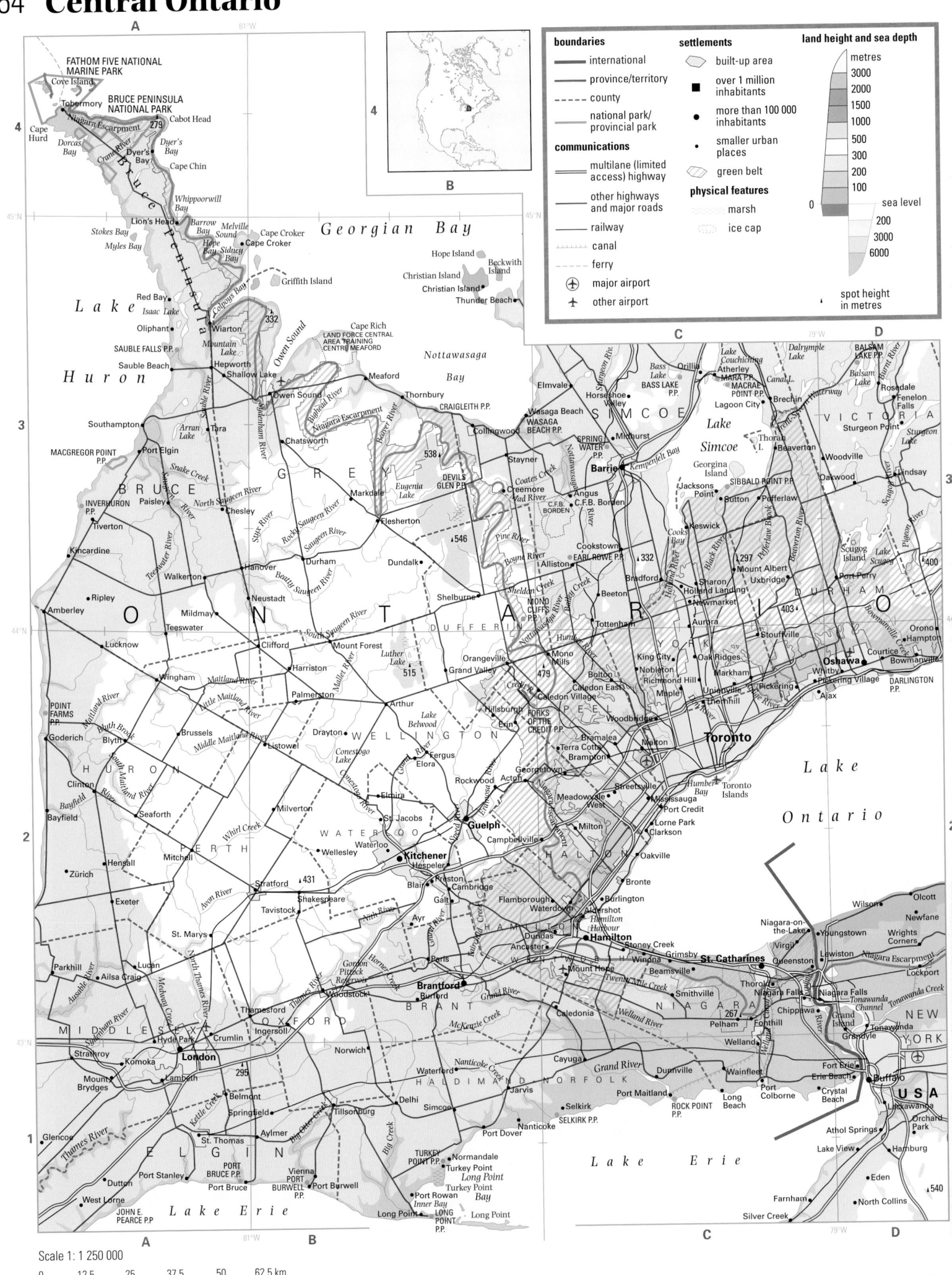

Scale 1: 1 250 000

0   12.5   25   37.5   50   62.5 km

Conical Orthomorphic Projection

© Oxford University Press

Scale 1 : 300 000

0   3   6   9   12   15 km

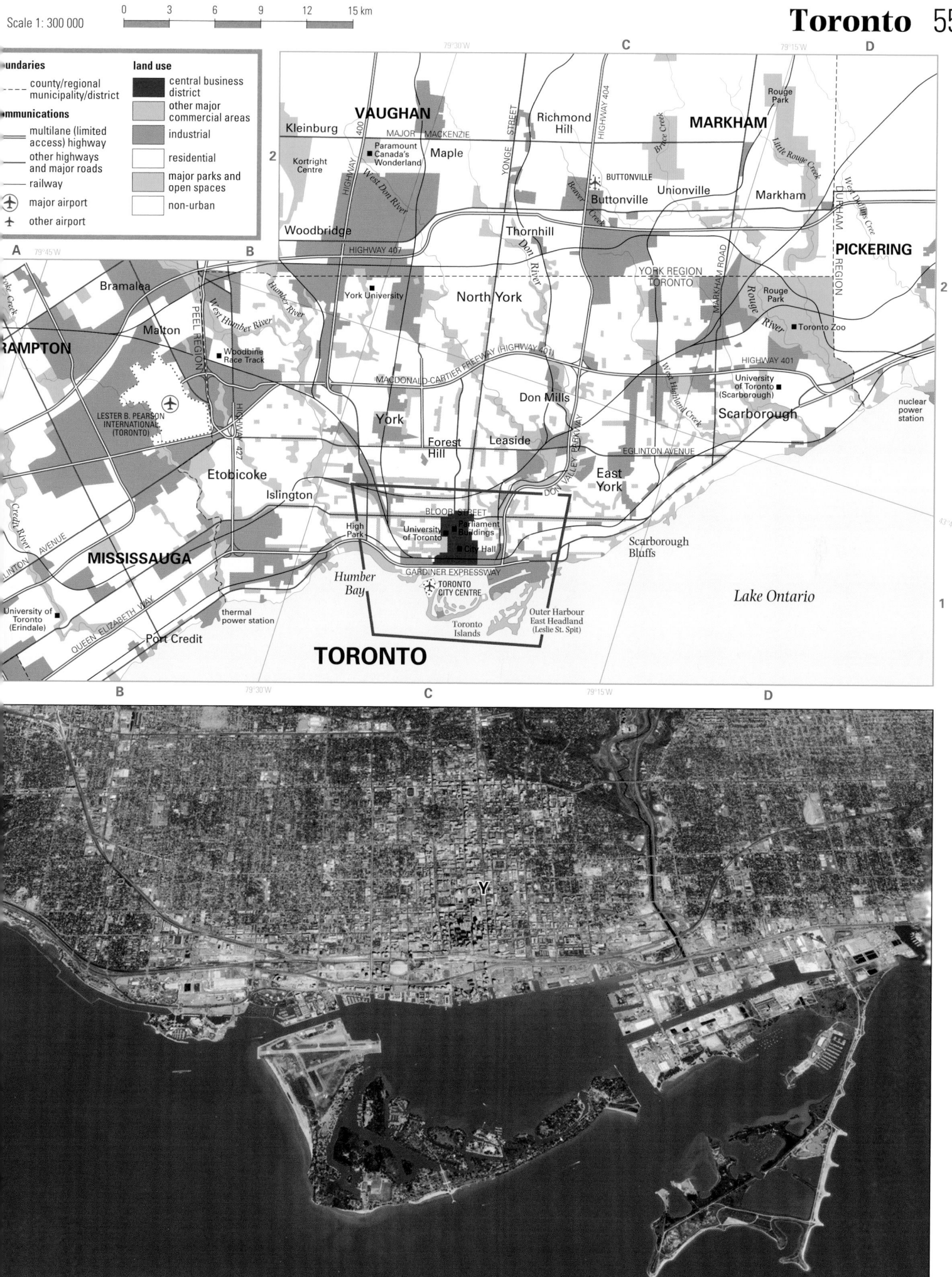

boundaries
- - - - county/regional
municipality/district

communications
══════ multilane (limited
access) highway
────── other highways
and major roads
──── railway
✈ major airport
✈ other airport

land use
- central business
district
- other major
commercial areas
- industrial
- residential
- major parks and
open spaces
- non-urban

VAUGHAN
Kleinburg
Kortright Centre
Paramount Canada's Wonderland
Maple
Woodbridge
HIGHWAY 400
West Don River
HIGHWAY 407

MAJOR MACKENZIE
YONGE STREET
Richmond Hill
HIGHWAY 404
BUTTONVILLE
Buttonville
Unionville
Thornhill
Don River
Beaver Creek

MARKHAM
Bruce Creek
Little Rouge Creek
Markham
Rouge Park
DURHAM REGION

York University
North York
YORK REGION
TORONTO
Rouge River
Rouge Park
Toronto Zoo

PICKERING
West Duffins Creek

BRAMPTON
Bramalea
Malton
Woodbine Race Track
West Humber River
Humber River
PEEL REGION

MACDONALD-CARTIER FREEWAY (HIGHWAY 401)
Don Mills
West Highland Creek
HIGHWAY 401
University of Toronto (Scarborough)
Scarborough
nuclear power station

Credit River
HIGHWAY 427
York
Forest Hill
Leaside
Don Valley Parkway
EGLINTON AVENUE
Etobicoke
Islington
East York
Scarborough Bluffs

MISSISSAUGA
QUEEN ELIZABETH WAY
DIXIE ROAD
University of Toronto (Erindale)
thermal power station
Port Credit

High Park
University of Toronto
BLOOR STREET
Parliament Buildings
City Hall
GARDINER EXPRESSWAY
TORONTO CITY CENTRE
Humber Bay
Toronto Islands

Outer Harbour East Headland (Leslie St. Spit)
Scarborough Bluffs

TORONTO
Lake Ontario

79°45'W · 79°30'W · 79°15'W
43°45'N

Toronto Central Toronto is divided by Yonge Street (Y), which was constructed shortly after the founding of York (Toronto) in 1793.

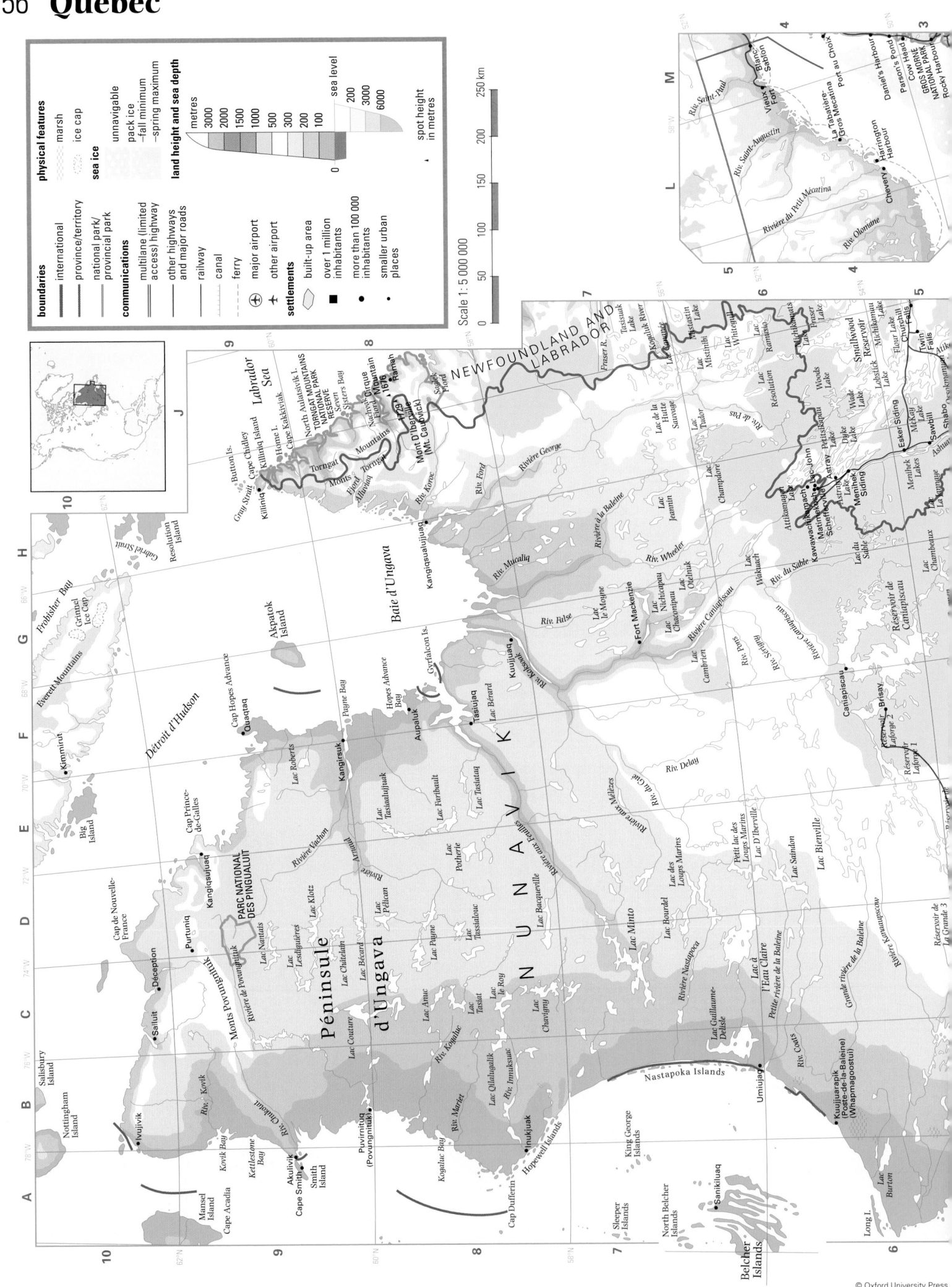

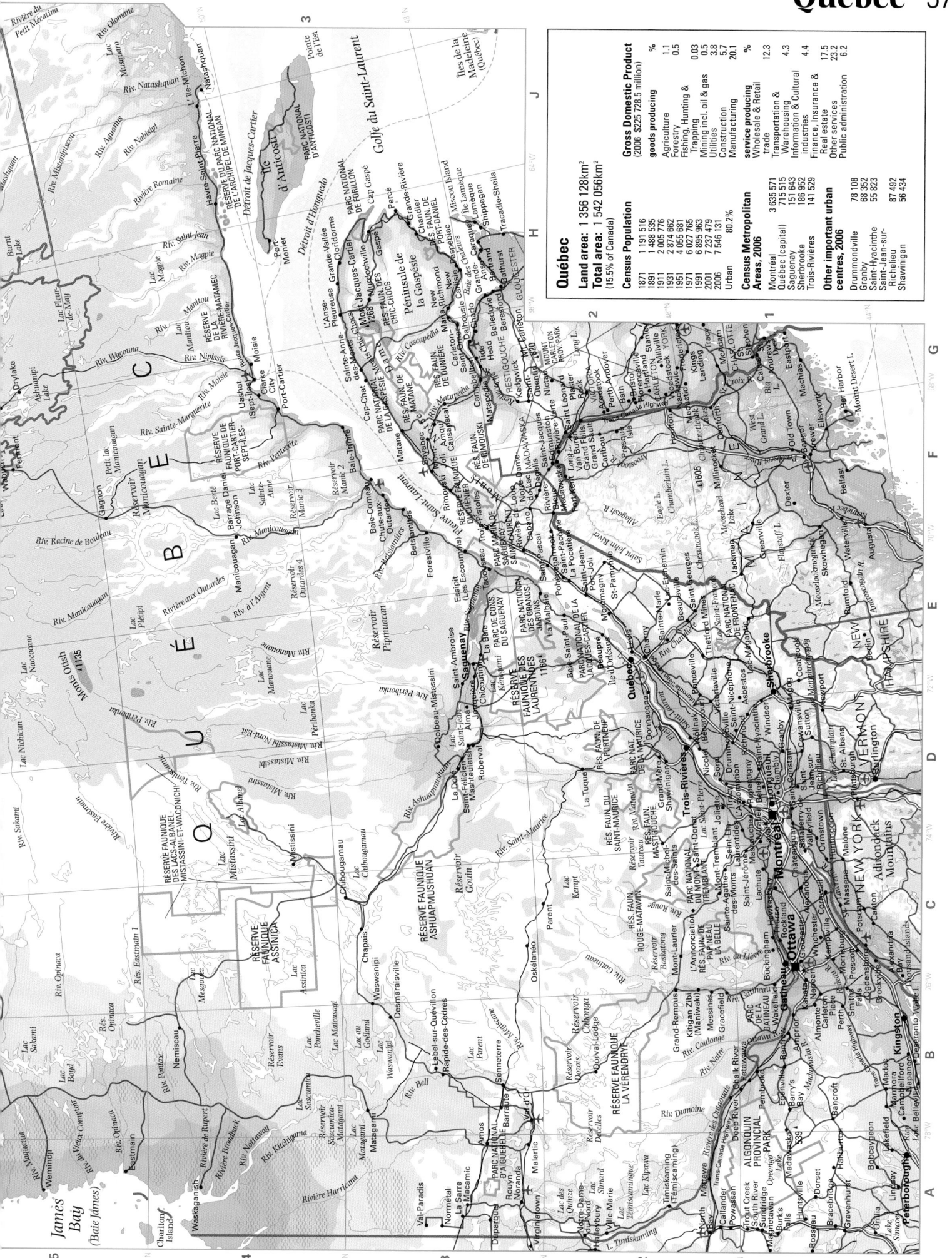

Québec

Land area: 1 356 128km²
Total area: 1 542 056km²
(15.5% of Canada)

Census Population

1871	1 191 516
1891	1 488 535
1911	2 005 776
1931	2 874 662
1951	4 055 681
1971	6 027 765
1991	6 895 963
2001	7 237 479
2006	7 546 131
Urban	80.2%

Census Metropolitan Areas, 2006

Montréal	3 635 571
Québec (capital)	715 515
Saguenay	151 643
Sherbrooke	186 952
Trois-Rivières	141 529

Other important urban centres, 2006

Drummondville	78 108
Granby	68 352
Saint-Hyacinthe	55 823
Saint-Jean-sur-Richelieu	87 492
Shawinigan	56 434

Gross Domestic Product
(2006 $225 728.5 million)

goods producing	%
Agriculture	1.1
Forestry	0.5
Fishing, Hunting & Trapping	0.03
Mining incl. oil & gas	0.5
Utilities	3.8
Construction	5.7
Manufacturing	20.1

service producing	%
Wholesale & Retail trade	12.3
Transportation & Warehousing	4.3
Information & Cultural industries	4.4
Finance, Insurance & Real estate	17.5
Other services	23.2
Public administration	6.2

Conical Orthomorphic Projection

Scale 1: 300 000

0   3   6   9   12   15 km

boundaries

--- – ---   province

- - - -   county/regional
municipality/
district

communications

══════   multilane (limited
access) highway

─────   other highways
and major roads

─────   railway

·······   canal

✈   major airport

✈   other airport

physical features

─────   river, lake

≈≈≈≈≈   marsh

—50—   contours

▲   spot height
in metres

land use

■   central business
district

▨   other major
commercial areas

▨   industrial

□   residential

▨   major parks and
open spaces

□   non-urban

Blainville
Lorraine
Sainte-Thérèse
AÉROPORT INT.
DE MONTRÉAL
(MIRABEL)
Rosemère
CO. TERREBONNE
CO. DEUX MONTAGNES
AUTOROUTE DES LAURENTIDES
Boisbriand
Sainte-Rose
VILLE DE LAVAL
Île Jésus
Rivière des Mille Îles
Saint-François
Saint-Vincent-de-Paul
Rivière des Prairies
Pointe-aux-Trembles
Anjou
AUTOROUTE FÉLIX-LECLERC
CO. CHAMBLY
Parc de récréation des Îles-de-Boucherville
Île Sainte-Thérèse
Varennes
Duvernay
Saint Leonard
AUTOROUTE LAVAL
AUTOROUTE CHOMEDEY
Pont-Viau
Laval-des-Rapides
Chomedey
Sainte-Dorothée
RUE SHERBROOKE
tunnel
AUTOROUTE JEAN-LESAGE
Stade Olympique
Montréal
MONTRÉAL
Île Ste Hélène
SAINT-HUBERT
LONGUEUIL
Laval-Ouest
Sainte-Eustache
Deux-Montagnes
Sainte-Marthe-sur-le-Lac
Rivière du Chêne
Saint-Laurent
Parc du Mont-Royal
Université de Montréal
Université McGill
Westmount
Île de
AUTOROUTE MÉTROPOLITAINE
Parc québecois d'Oka
Île Bizard
Lac des Deux Montagnes
Parc Cap-Saint-Jacques
AÉROPORT INT.
DE MONTRÉAL (DORVAL)
Verdun
Île des Soeurs
AUTOROUTE DES CANTONS DE L'EST
CO. LA PRAIRIE
Aboretum Morgan
Baie de Valois
Dorval
Île Dorval
Parc Angrignon
LaSalle
Île aux Hérons
Fleuve Saint-Laurent
TRANS-CANADA HIGHWAY
Beaconsfield
Lac Saint Louis
Kahnawake
Rapides de Lachine
Sainte-Catherine
St. Lawrence Seaway
La Prairie
Candiac
Île Lynch
L'Île-Perrot
RÉSERVE INDIENNE KAHNAWAKE

Montréal

The entire urban region of Montréal is visible in the image. Mont-Royal (M) is a prominent feature and the route of the St. Lawrence Seaway (S) can be seen along the south shore of the St. Lawrence.

M
S

© Oxford University Press

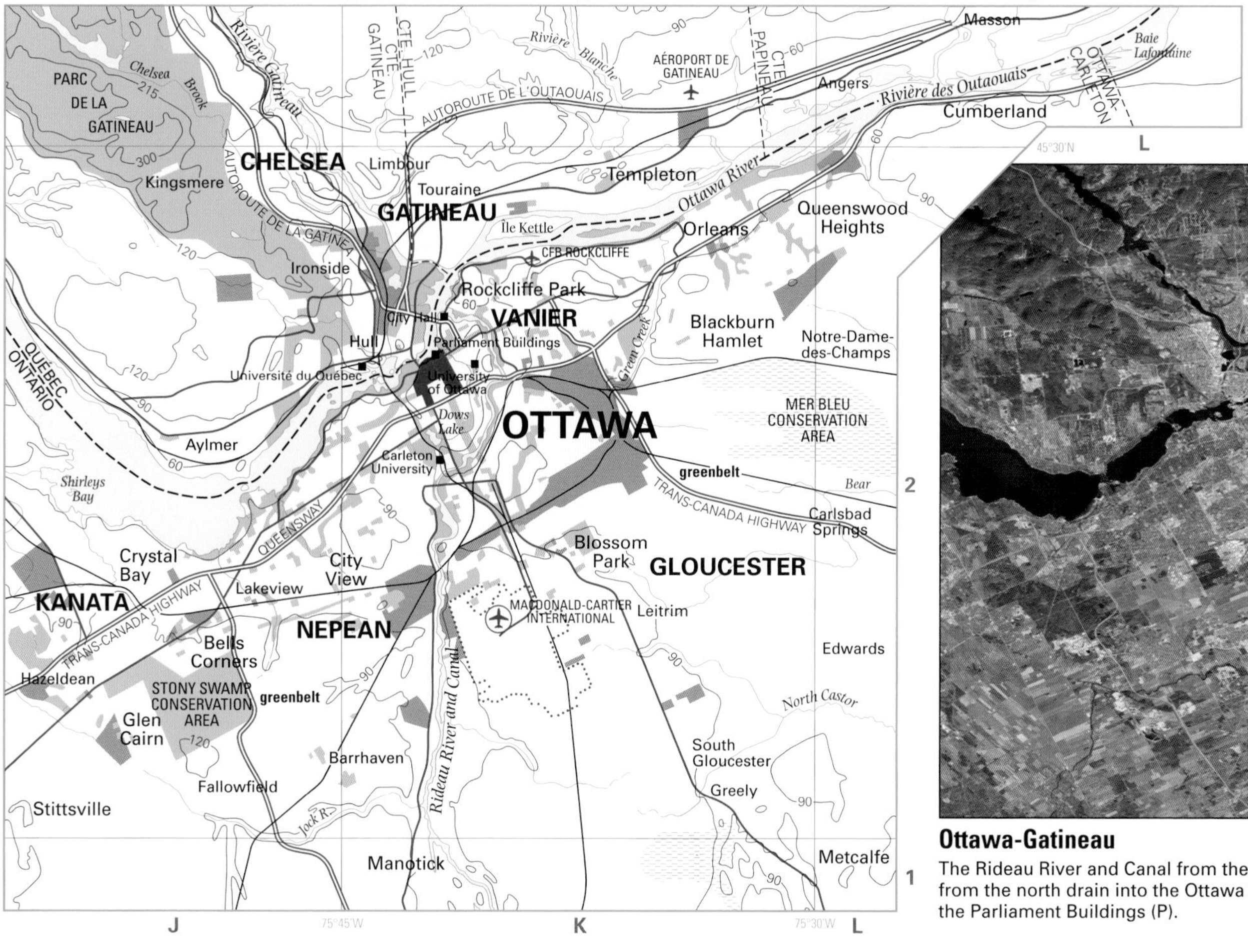

Ottawa

PARC DE LA GATINEAU
Chelsea 215
Kingsmere
CHELSEA
Limbour
Touraine
GATINEAU
Ironside
Île Kettle
CFB ROCKCLIFFE
Rockcliffe Park
City Hall
VANIER
Hull
Parliament Buildings
Université du Québec
University of Ottawa
Dows Lake
OTTAWA
Aylmer
Carleton University
Shirleys Bay
QUÉBEC ONTARIO
AUTOROUTE DE L'OUTAOUAIS
AUTOROUTE DE LA GATINEAU
Rivière Gatineau
Chelsea Brook
Rivière Blanche
AÉROPORT DE GATINEAU
Ottawa River
Templeton
Orleans
Queenswood Heights
Blackburn Hamlet
Notre-Dame-des-Champs
Masson
Baie Lafontaine
Angers
Rivière des Outaouais
Cumberland
Green Creek
MER BLEU CONSERVATION AREA
greenbelt
Bear
TRANS-CANADA HIGHWAY
Carlsbad Springs
Crystal Bay
Lakeview
City View
Blossom Park
GLOUCESTER
KANATA
Hazeldean
Bells Corners
NEPEAN
STONY SWAMP CONSERVATION AREA
greenbelt
Glen Cairn
Barrhaven
Fallowfield
Stittsville
Manotick
Jock R.
Rideau River and Canal
QUEENSWAY
MACDONALD-CARTIER INTERNATIONAL
Leitrim
Edwards
North Castor
South Gloucester
Greely
Metcalfe
CTÉ HULL CTÉ GATINEAU
CTÉ PAPINEAU
OTTAWA CARLETON

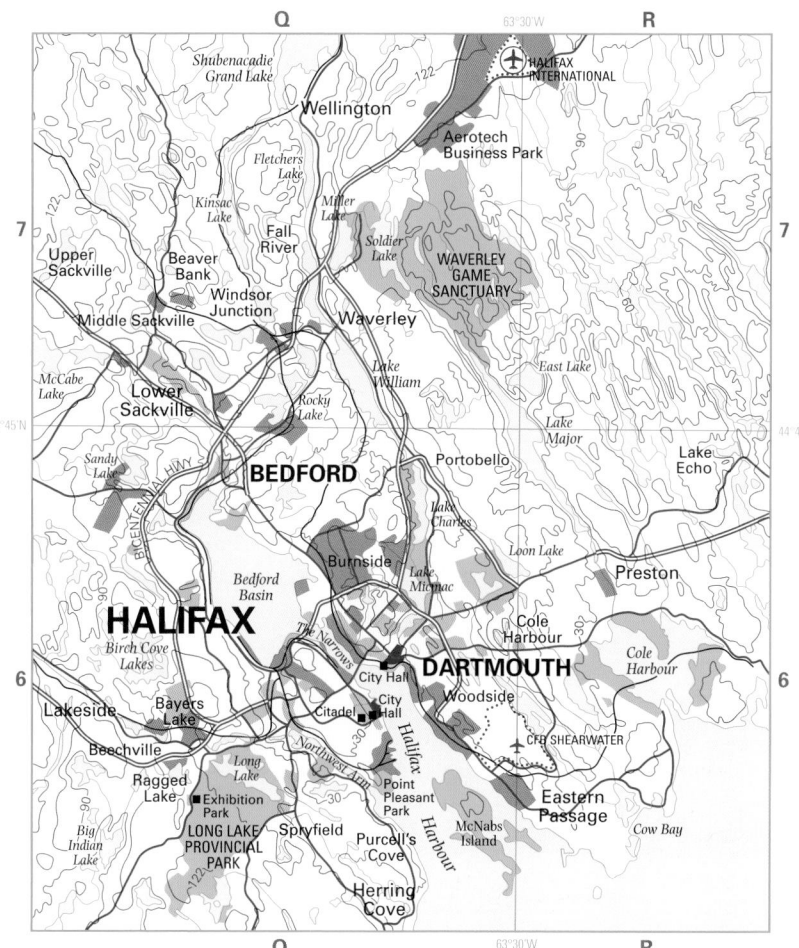

Ottawa-Gatineau

The Rideau River and Canal from the south and the Gatineau River from the north drain into the Ottawa River, just downstream from the Parliament Buildings (P).

Halifax

Halifax Harbour and Bedford Basin separate the cities of Halifax and Dartmouth.

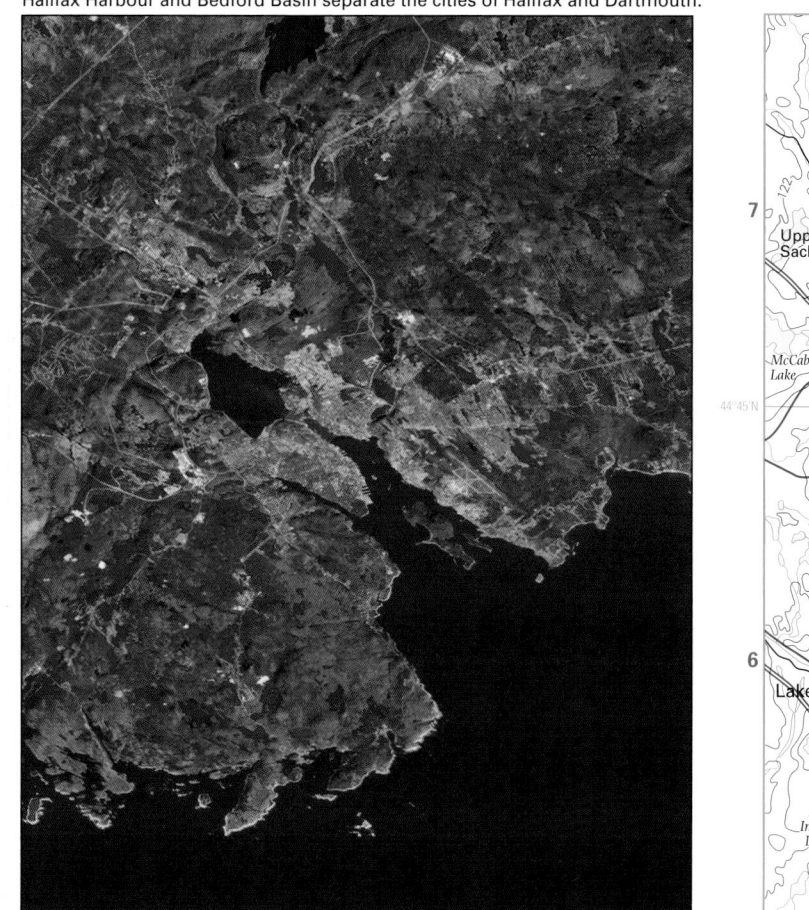

Shubenacadie Grand Lake
Wellington
HALIFAX INTERNATIONAL
Aerotech Business Park
Fletchers Lake
Kinsac Lake
Miller Lake
Upper Sackville
Beaver Bank
Fall River
Soldier Lake
WAVERLEY GAME SANCTUARY
Windsor Junction
Waverley
Middle Sackville
Lake William
McCabe Lake
Lower Sackville
Rocky Lake
East Lake
Sandy Lake
BEDFORD
Portobello
Lake Major
Lake Echo
Lake Charles
Lake Micmac
Burnside
Loon Lake
Preston
BICENTENNIAL HWY
Bedford Basin
HALIFAX
Birch Cove Lakes
The Narrows
DARTMOUTH
Cole Harbour
Lakeside
Bayers Lake
City Hall
City Hall
Citadel
Woodside
CFB SHEARWATER
Beechville
Northwest Arm
Halifax Harbour
Cole Harbour
Ragged Lake
Long Lake
Point Pleasant Park
McNabs Island
Eastern Passage
Big Indian Lake
Exhibition Park
Spryfield
Purcell's Cove
Cow Bay
LONG LAKE PROVINCIAL PARK
Herring Cove

Legend

boundaries
- international
- province/territory
- county
- national park/provincial park

communications
- multilane (limited access) highway
- other highways and major roads
- winter road
- railway
- canal
- ferry
- ✈ major airport
- ⊕ other airport

settlements
- built-up area
- ■ over 1 million inhabitants
- ● more than 100 000 inhabitants
- • smaller urban places

physical features
- marsh
- ice cap

sea ice
- unnavigable
- pack ice
- — fall minimum
- — spring maximum

land height and sea depth (metres)
3000, 2000, 1500, 1000, 500, 300, 200, 100, 0 sea level, 200, 3000, 6000

spot height in metres

Newfoundland and Labrador

Land area: 373 872km²
Total area: 405 212km²
(4.1% of Canada)

Census Population

Year	Population
1871	152 500
1891	202 040
1911	242 619
1931	281 500
1951	361 416
1971	522 105
1991	568 474
2001	512 930
2006	505 469
Urban	57.8%

Census Metropolitan Area, 2006
St. John's (capital) 181 113

Other important urban centre, 2006
Corner Brook 26 623

Gross Domestic Product (2006 $14 088.6 million)

goods producing	%
Agriculture	0.4
Forestry	0.5
Fishing, Hunting, & Trapping	1.7
Mining incl. oil & gas	18.7
Utilities	3.2
Construction	5.8
Manufacturing	6.5

service producing	%
Wholesale & Retail trade	9.1
Transportation & Warehousing	3.6
Information & Cultural industries	3.9
Finance, Insurance & Real estate	14.5
Other services	20.9
Public administration	8.3

Nova Scotia

Land area: 53 338km²
Total area: 55 284km²
(0.6% of Canada)

Census Population

Year	Population
1871	387 800
1891	450 396
1911	492 338
1931	512 846
1951	642 584
1971	788 960
1991	899 942
2001	908 007
2006	913 462
Urban	55.5%

Census Metropolitan Area, 2006
Halifax (capital) 372 858

Other important urban centres, 2006
Cape Breton 105 928
Truro 45 077

Gross Domestic Product (2006 $23 689 million)

goods producing	%
Agriculture	0.9
Forestry	0.5
Fishing, Hunting, & Trapping	1.4
Mining incl. oil & gas	2.4
Utilities	2.2
Construction	6.2
Manufacturing	8.9

service producing	%
Wholesale & Retail trade	11.8
Transportation & Warehousing	4.4
Information & Cultural industries	4.5
Finance, Insurance & Real estate	22.1
Other services	24.9
Public administration	10.2

Prince Edward Island

Land area: 5 660km²
Total area: 5 660km²
(0.1% of Canada)

Census Population

Year	Population
1871	94 021
1891	109 078
1911	93 728
1931	88 038
1951	98 429
1971	110 640
1991	129 765
2001	135 294
2006	135 851
Urban	45.0%

Important urban centres, 2006
Charlottetown (capital) 58 625
Summerside 16 153

Gross Domestic Product (2006 $3 205.5 million)

goods producing	%
Agriculture	3.8
Forestry	0.4
Fishing, Hunting, & Trapping	2.3
Mining incl. oil & gas	0.05
Utilities	0.8
Construction	5.9
Manufacturing	11.4

service producing	%
Wholesale & Retail trade	10.9
Transportation & Warehousing	2.8
Information & Cultural industries	4.1
Finance, Insurance & Real estate	19.9
Other services	25.4
Public administration	12.3

New Brunswick

Land area: 71 450km²
Total area: 72 908km²
(0.7% of Canada)

Census Population

Year	Population
1871	285 594
1891	321 236
1911	351 889
1931	408 219
1951	515 697
1971	634 556
1991	723 900
2001	729 498
2006	729 997
Urban	51.1%

Census Metropolitan Areas, 2006
Moncton 126 424
Saint John 122 389

Other important urban centre, 2006
Fredericton (capital) 85 688

Gross Domestic Product (2006 $19 749.1 million)

goods producing	%
Agriculture	1.9
Forestry	2.0
Fishing, Hunting, & Trapping	0.6
Mining incl. oil & gas	1.1
Utilities	2.9
Construction	6.5
Manufacturing	15.6

service producing	%
Wholesale & Retail trade	11.4
Transportation & Warehousing	5.4
Information & Cultural industries	4.1
Finance, Insurance & Real estate	17.7
Other services	21.5
Public administration	9.4

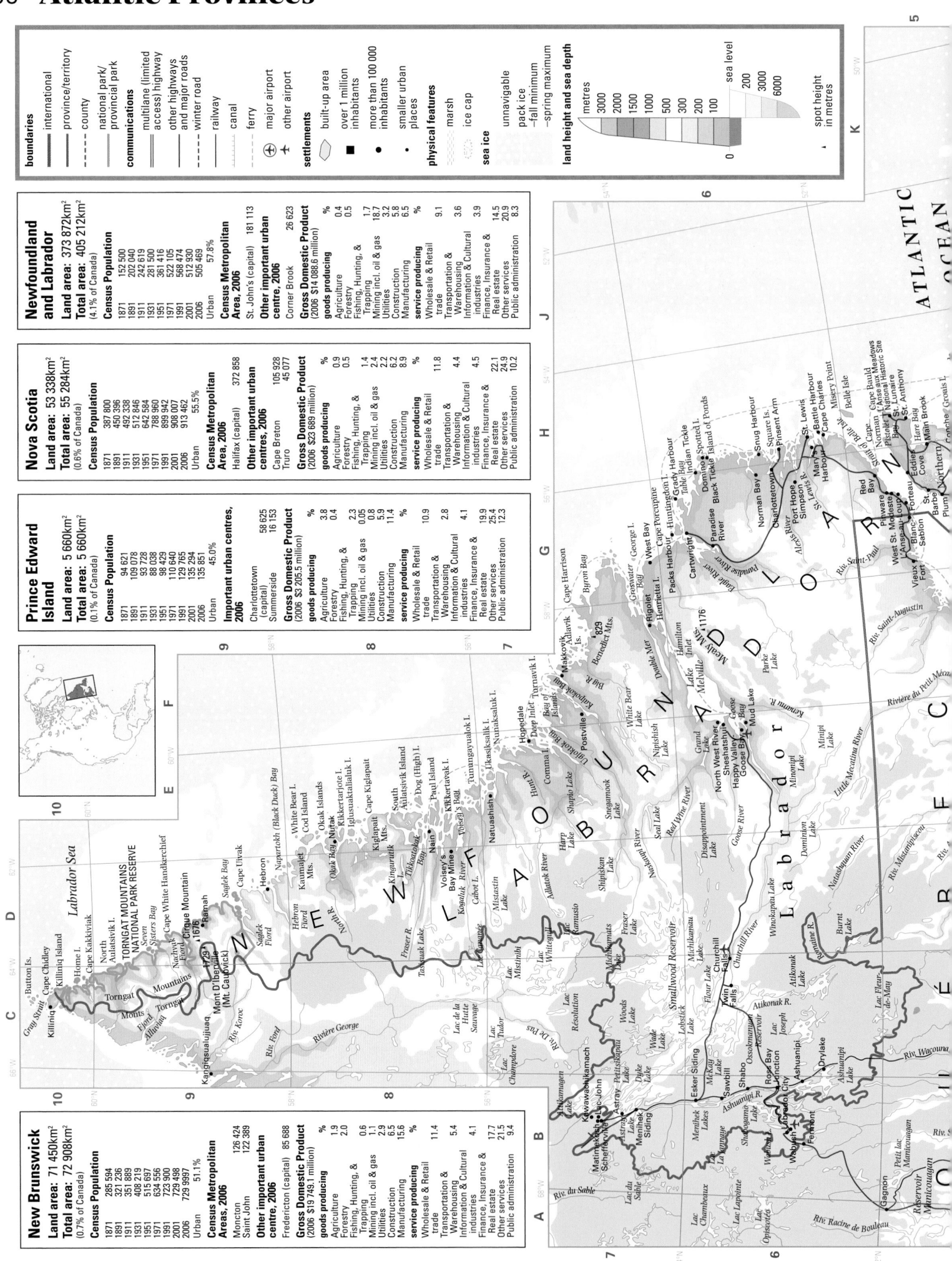

Conical Orthomorphic Projection   © Oxford University Press

Nova Scotia and Prince Edward Island

Scale 1 : 3 150 000

0   31.5   63   94.5   126   157.5 km

Scale 1 : 5 000 000

0   50   100   150   200   250 km

The boundary between the sedimentary plains and the Canadian Shield is evident on this image. The lakes, remnants of glaciation, formed along the border between these two geological provinces. Bobcaygeon (B) and Fenelon Falls (F) are identified at either end of Sturgeon Lake.

Beloeil (B) is located on the Richelieu River between Mont St-Bruno and Mont St-Hilaire, two of the eight Monteregian Hills, which rise 200 to 400 m above the surrounding lowland. The long lots associated with the seigneurial system are also evident.

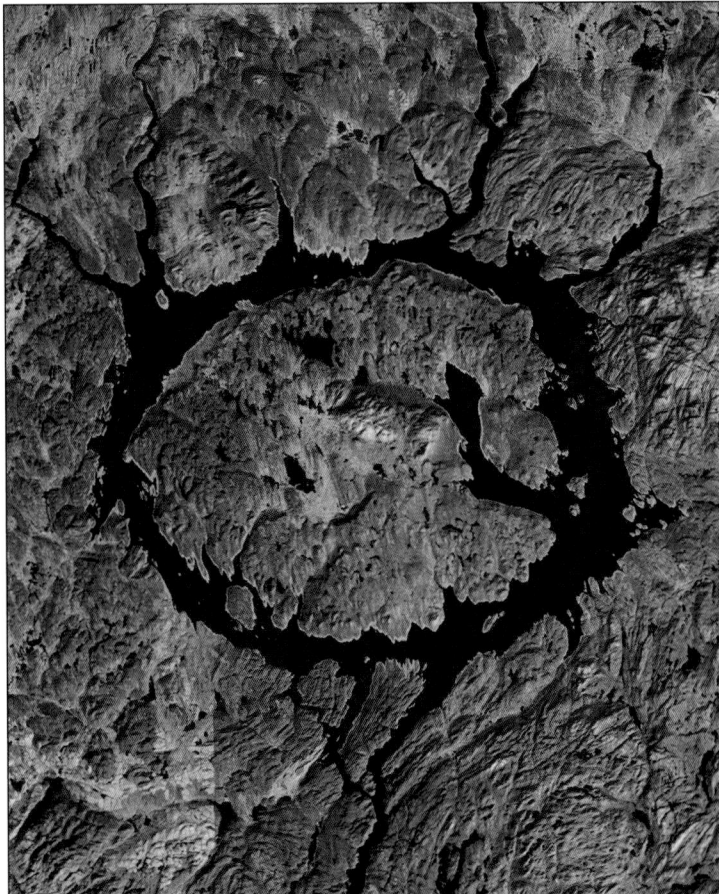

The Manicouagan Crater, one of the largest known impact craters, was created by an asteroid striking the Earth approximately 210 million years ago. Its crater, about 70 km wide, has been preserved in the hard rock of the Canadian Shield.

Québec City, founded in 1608, is the only walled city in North America, which led to its declaration as a UNESCO World Heritage Site. The Plains of Abraham are identified; the old city and its walls are just to the northeast.

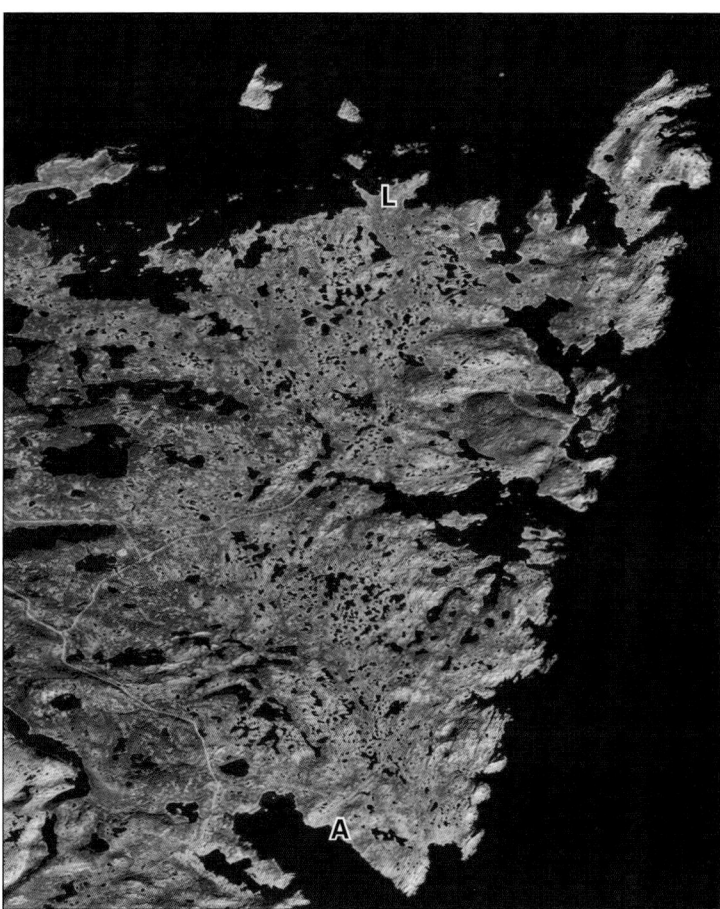

St. John's, Canada's oldest city (first permanent settlement 1605), is situated on the rugged coast of the Avalon Peninsula. Cape Spear, the most easterly point in North America, lies south and east of the city. Signal Hill (S) is a prominent St. John's landmark.

L'Anse aux Meadows (L) is famous as the site of the first European settlement in North America. It is believed that Vikings under Leif Ericsson settled here around 1000 CE. It is recognized as a UNESCO World Heritage Site. The town of St. Anthony (A) is marked for reference.

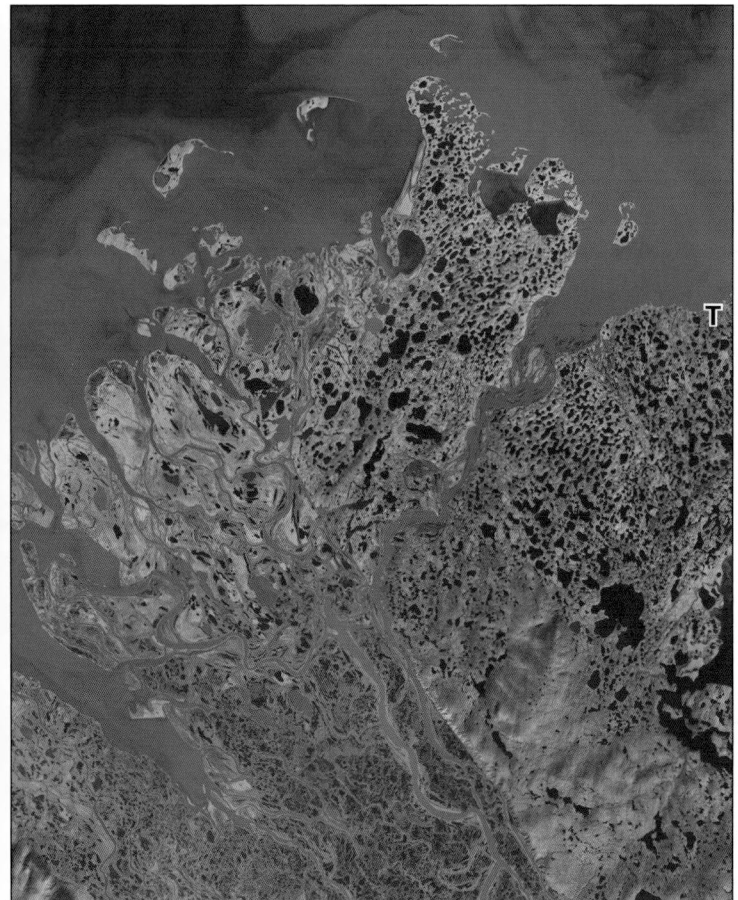

The Mackenzie Delta (13 500 km²) was formed by deposition from Canada's longest river. The rivers, lakes, and floodplains of the delta support diverse natural flora and fauna. Tuktoyaktuk (T), the largest settlement on the coast, is indicated.

Dawson City on the Yukon River came into existence during the Klondike gold rush in the late 1890s. While the early rush ended quickly, gold has been mined from placer deposits ever since, and the gravel ridges left by this process are evident in the valleys of the Klondike River (K) and Bonanza Creek (B).

Yukon Territory

Land area: 474 391km²
Total area: 482 443km²
(4.8% of Canada)

Census Population

1911	8 512
1931	4 230
1951	9 096
1971	18 390
1991	27 797
2001	28 674
2006	30 372
Urban	59.7%

Important urban centre, 2006

Whitehorse (capital) 22 898

Gross Domestic Product
(2006 $1 199.7 million)

goods producing	%
Agriculture	v.s.
Forestry	0.03
Fishing, Hunting, & Trapping	v.s.
Mining incl. oil & gas	6.3
Utilities	1.4
Construction	9.1
Manufacturing	0.3

service producing	%
Wholesale & Retail trade	9.9
Transportation & Warehousing	3.3
Information & Cultural industries	4.6
Finance, Insurance & Real estate	19.3
Other services	24.4
Public administration	23.7

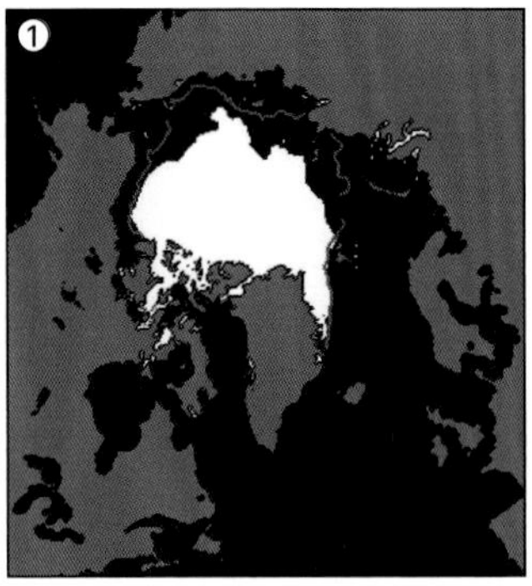

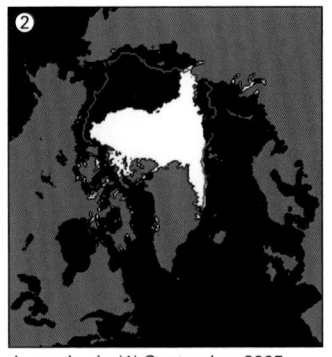

The two maps show the extent of the Arctic sea ice in (1) September 2005 (5.32 million km²) and (2) September 2007 (4.13 million km²). The pink line shows the median ice edge based on data from 1979 to 2000 (median coverage 6.74 million km²).

boundaries

— international
— province/territory
— national/provincial park/sanctuary

communications

═ multilane (limited access) highway
— other highways and major roads
---- winter road
— railway
✈ major airport
✈ other airport

settlements

● more than 1000 inhabitants
○ less than 1000 inhabitants

physical features

marsh
ice cap

sea ice

unnavigable
pack ice
–fall minimum
–spring maximum

land height and sea depth

metres
3000
2000
1000
500
300
200
100
0 — sea level
200
3000
6000

▲ spot height in metres

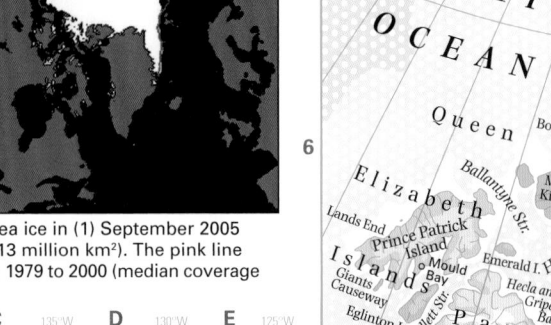

Scale 1: 12 000 000

0   120   240   360   480   600 km

Conical Orthomorphic Projection   © Oxford University Press

Nunavut

Land area: 1 936 113km²
Total area: 2 093 190km²
(21.0% of Canada)

Census Population

2001	26 745
2006	29 474
Urban	43.4%

Important urban centre, 2006

Iqaluit (capital)   6 184

Gross Domestic Product
(2006 $928.8 million)

goods producing	%
Agriculture	0.0
Forestry	0.0
Fishing, Hunting, & Trapping	0.1
Mining incl. oil & gas	4.2
Utilities	0.7
Construction	17.9
Manufacturing	0.2
service producing	**%**
Wholesale & Retail trade	4.2
Transportation & Warehousing	3.0
Information & Cultural industries	5.3
Finance, Insurance & Real estate	15.1
Other services	22.3
Public administration	25.7

Northwest Territories

Land area: 1 183 085km²
Total area: 1 346 106km²
(13.5% of Canada)

Census Population

1871	56 446*
1891	98 967*
1911	6 507
1931	9 316
1951	16 004
1971	34 805
1991	57 649
2001	37 360
2006	41 464
Urban	58.4%

*includes Saskatchewan and Alberta

Important urban centre, 2006

Yellowknife (capital)   18 700

Gross Domestic Product
(2006 $4 021.8 million)

goods producing	%
Agriculture	v.s.
Forestry	0.02
Fishing, Hunting, & Trapping	v.s.
Mining incl. oil & gas	49.7
Utilities	1.1
Construction	11.3
Manufacturing	0.1
service producing	**%**
Wholesale & Retail trade	3.3
Transportation & Warehousing	4.0
Information & Cultural industries	2.3
Finance, Insurance & Real estate	9.8
Other services	11.6
Public administration	9.1

60°N   80°N   80°N   0°

Arctic Circle

USA
ALASKA

GREENLAND
(Denmark)

YUKON
TERRITORY

NORTHWEST TERRITORIES

NUNAVUT

BRITISH
COLUMBIA

■ Nuuk

ALBERTA

SASKATCHEWAN

MANITOBA

C A N A D A

Vancouver

Seattle
WASHINGTON

OREGON

IDAHO

MONTANA

NORTH DAKOTA

ONTARIO

QUÉBEC

PRINCE
EDWARD
ISLAND

St. Pierre
& Miquelon
(France)

San
Francisco

NEVADA

WYOMING

SOUTH DAKOTA

MINNESOTA

WISCONSIN

NEW
BRUNSWICK

MAINE

NOVA SCOTIA

CALIFORNIA

UTAH

COLORADO

NEBRASKA

IOWA

MICHIGAN

●Ottawa ■ Montréal
Toronto
Detroit

VT/
N.H.
NEW YORK

Los Angeles

UNITED STATES OF AMERICA

KANSAS

MISSOURI

ILLINOIS INDIANA OHIO

PENNSYLVANIA

New York

MASS.
C. R.I.
N.J.

ARIZONA

NEW
MEXICO

OKLAHOMA

KENTUCKY

W.V.

Washington D.C.
MD. DEL.

Philadelphia

Tropic of Cancer

TEXAS

ARKANSAS

TENNESSEE

VIRGINIA

NORTH CAROLINA

●Dallas

MISS. ALABAMA GEORGIA

SOUTH
CAROLINA

Houston

LOUISIANA

Bermuda
(UK)

Monterray

New
Orleans

FLORIDA

THE BAHAMAS

MEXICO

Miami ●

■ Nassau

Guadalajara

Havana ■

C U B A

Turks &
Caicos Is.(UK)

Virgin Is. (USA)
Virgin Is. (UK)

■ México City

Cayman Is.
(UK)

Kingston ■

**DOMINICAN
REPUBLIC**

Puerto
Rico(USA)

Anguilla (UK)

ST. KITTS AND NEVIS
ANTIGUA &
BARBUDA

Belmopan

HAITI

Santo
Domingo

San
Juan

Guadeloupe (France)

GUATEMALA
BELIZE

JAMAICA

Port-au-
Prince

DOMINICA
Martinique (France)
ST. LUCIA

Guatemala ■

HONDURAS

Monserrat (UK)

San Salvador
EL SALVADOR

Tegucigalpa

ST. VINCENT &
THE GRENADINES

BARBADOS

NICARAGUA

Aruba
(Neth.)

GRENADA

Managua

Netherlands
Antilles
(Neth.)

Port of Spain

San José

■ Panamá

TRINIDAD &
TOBAGO

COSTA RICA

PANAMA

COLOMBIA

VENEZUELA

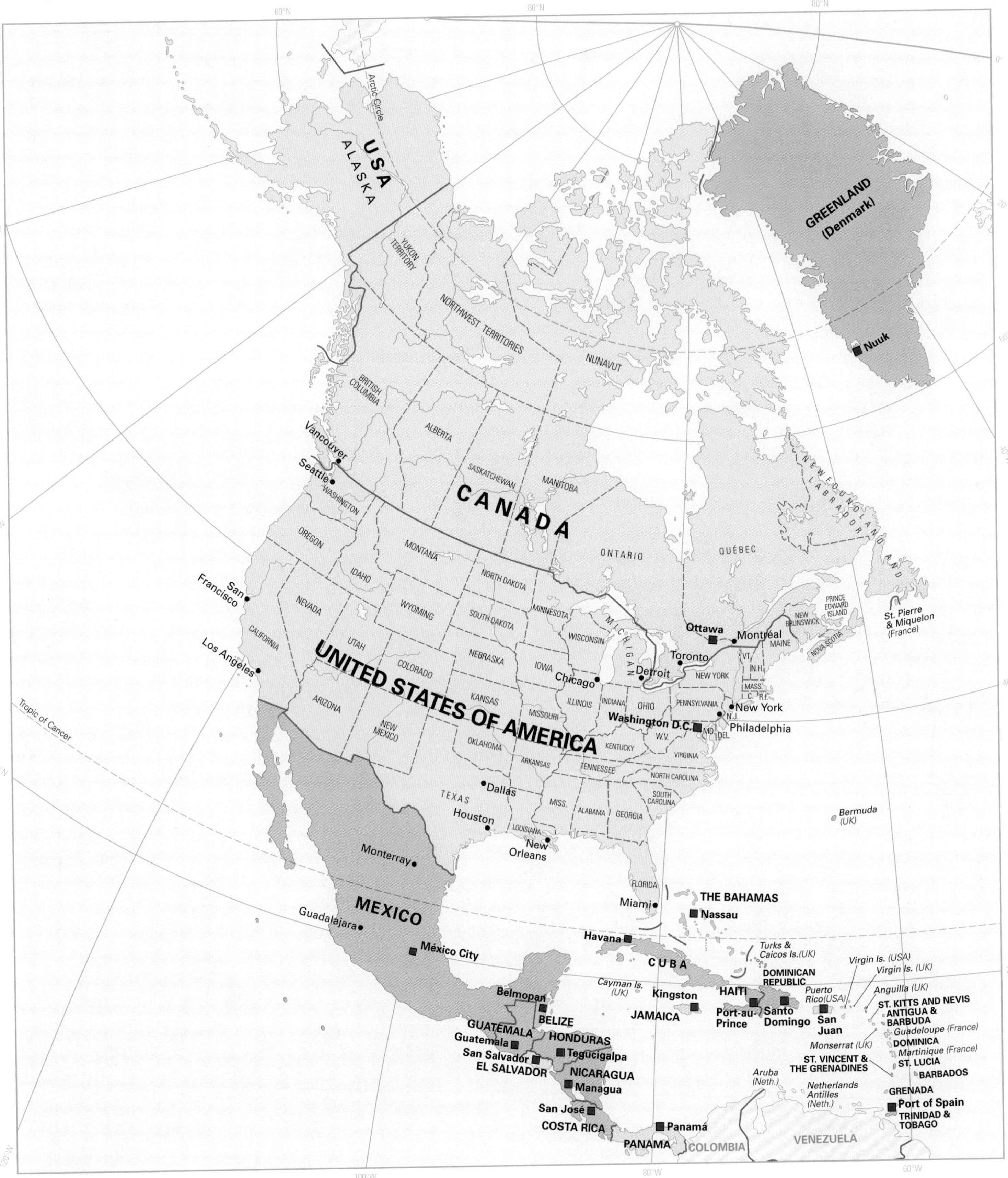

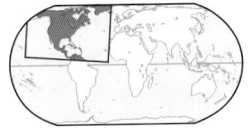

Scale 1: 40 000 000

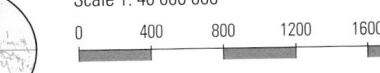

0   400   800   1200   1600   2000 km

C.	CONNECTICUT
DEL.	DELAWARE
MASS.	MASSACHUSETTS
MD.	MARYLAND
MISS.	MISSISSIPPI
N.H.	NEW HAMPSHIRE
N.J.	NEW JERSEY
R.I.	RHODE ISLAND
VT.	VERMONT
W.V.	WEST VIRGINIA

—— international boundary
---- internal boundary
■ capital city
● other important city

Oblique Mercator Projection   © Oxford University Press

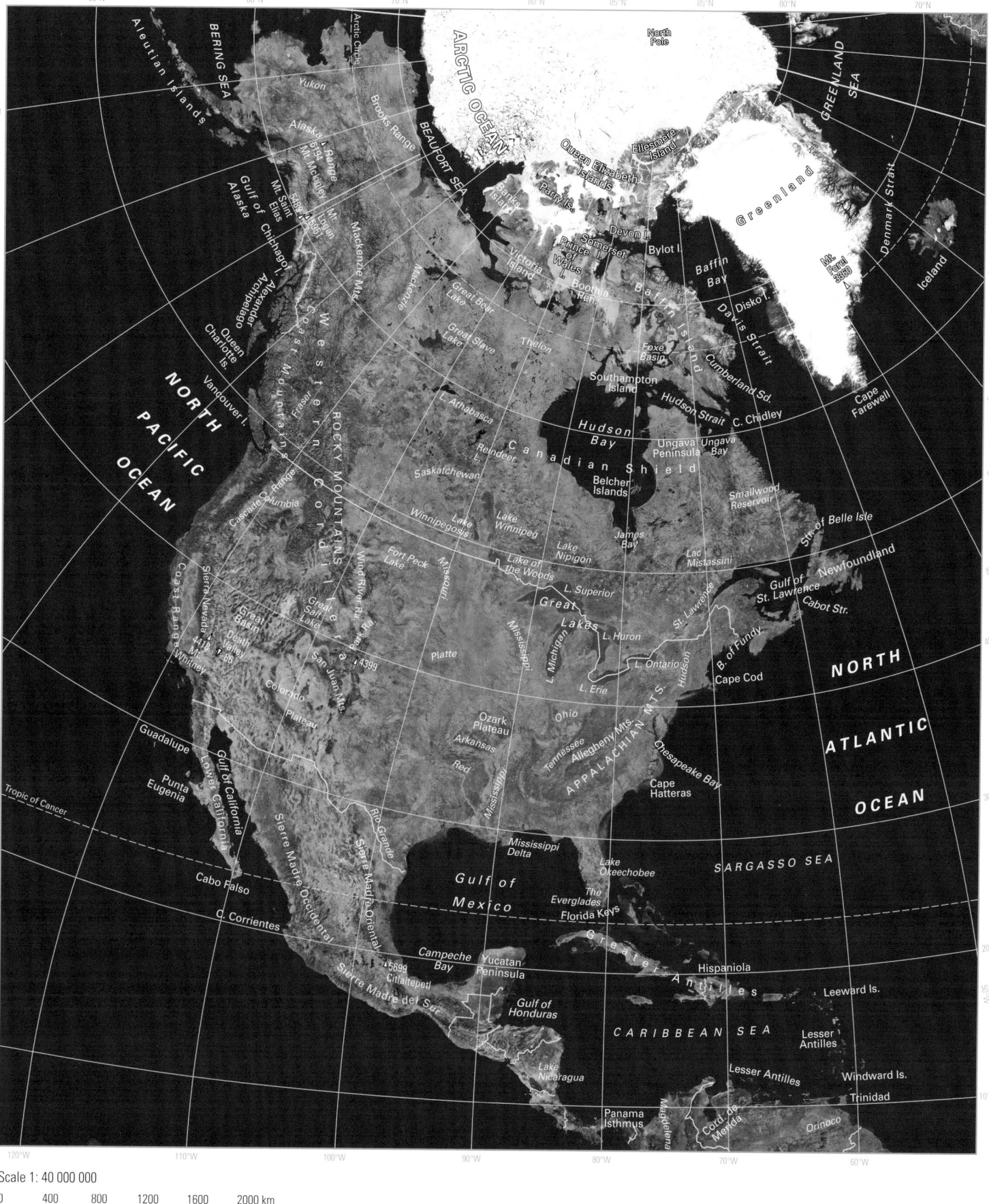

ARCTIC OCEAN

North Pole

BERING SEA

Aleutian Islands

Yukon

Brooks Range

Arctic Circle

BEAUFORT SEA

Banks Island

Queen Elizabeth Islands

Parry Is.

Ellesmere Island

GREENLAND SEA

Greenland

Denmark Strait

10°E

Iceland

10°W

Mt. Forel 3360

20°W

Alaska Range

Mt. McKinley 6194

Mt. Logan 5959

Mackenzie Mts.

Mt. Saint Elias 5489

Gulf of Alaska

Alexander Archipelago

Chichagof I.

Queen Charlotte Is.

Vancouver I.

Somerset I.

Prince of Wales I.

Victoria Island

Devon I.

Bylot I.

Baffin Bay

Disko I.

Davis Strait

Cape Farewell

Boothia Pen.

Baffin Island

Cumberland Sd.

C. Chidley

30°W

NORTH PACIFIC OCEAN

Coast Mountains

Fraser

Mackenzie

Great Bear Lake

Great Slave Lake

Thelon

Foxe Basin

Hudson Strait

Southampton Island

Ungava Peninsula

Ungava Bay

40°W

Western Cordillera

ROCKY MOUNTAINS

Reindeer L.

Saskatchewan

Canadian Shield

Hudson Bay

Belcher Islands

James Bay

Smallwood Reservoir

Str. of Belle Isle

50°W

Cascade

Columbia

Winnipegosis

Lake Winnipeg

Lake Nipigon

Lac Mistassini

Gulf of St. Lawrence

Newfoundland

Coast Range

Sierra Nevada

Great Basin

Great Salt Lake

Fort Peck Lake

Wind River Ra.

Lake of the Woods

L. Superior

Great Lakes

St. Lawrence

Cabot Str.

Death Valley -86

4418

Mt. Whitney

4399

San Juan Mts.

Missouri

Mississippi

Platte

L. Michigan

L. Huron

L. Erie

L. Ontario

Hudson

B. of Fundy

Cape Cod

NORTH ATLANTIC OCEAN

Colorado

Plateau

Ozark Plateau

Arkansas

Red

Ohio

Tennessee

Allegheny Mts.

APPALACHIAN MTS.

Chesapeake Bay

Cape Hatteras

Guadalupe

Punta Eugenia

Gulf of California

Lower California

Sierra Madre Occidental

Rio Grande

Mississippi Delta

Lake Okeechobee

SARGASSO SEA

Tropic of Cancer

20°N

Cabo Falso

C. Corrientes

Gulf of Mexico

The Everglades

Florida Keys

Sierra Madre Oriental

Campeche Bay

Yucatan Peninsula

Citlaltepetl 5699

Greater Antilles

Hispaniola

Leeward Is.

30°W

Sierra Madre del Sur

Gulf of Honduras

CARIBBEAN SEA

Lesser Antilles

Lesser Antilles

Windward Is.

Trinidad

Lake Nicaragua

Panama Isthmus

Cord. de Mérida

Magdalena

Orinoco

Scale 1: 40 000 000

0   400   800   1200   1600   2000 km

Oblique Mercator Projection   © Oxford University Press

January temperature

actual surface temperature

°Celsius
25
20
15
10
5
0
-10
-20
-30

• climate station
(average January temperature)

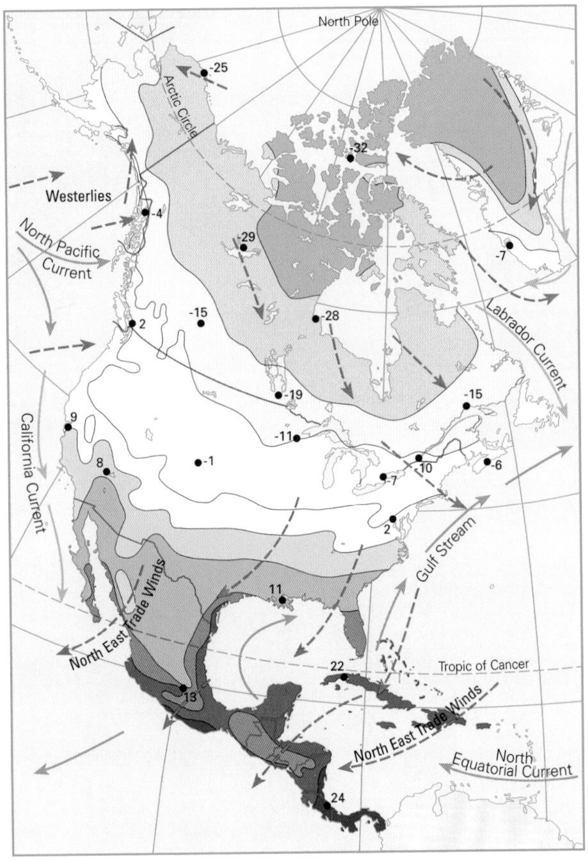

-25
-32
Westerlies
-4
North Pacific Current
-29
-15
-28
2
-19
-11
-7
-15
-10
-6
9
8
-1
2
California Current
North East Trade Winds
11
22
Tropic of Cancer
13
North East Trade Winds
24
North Equatorial Current
Gulf Stream
Labrador Current
Arctic Circle
North Pole

→ warm sea current   → cold sea current   --→ prevailing wind

July temperature

actual surface temperature

°Celsius
30
25
20
15
10
5
0
-10

• climate station
(average July temperature)

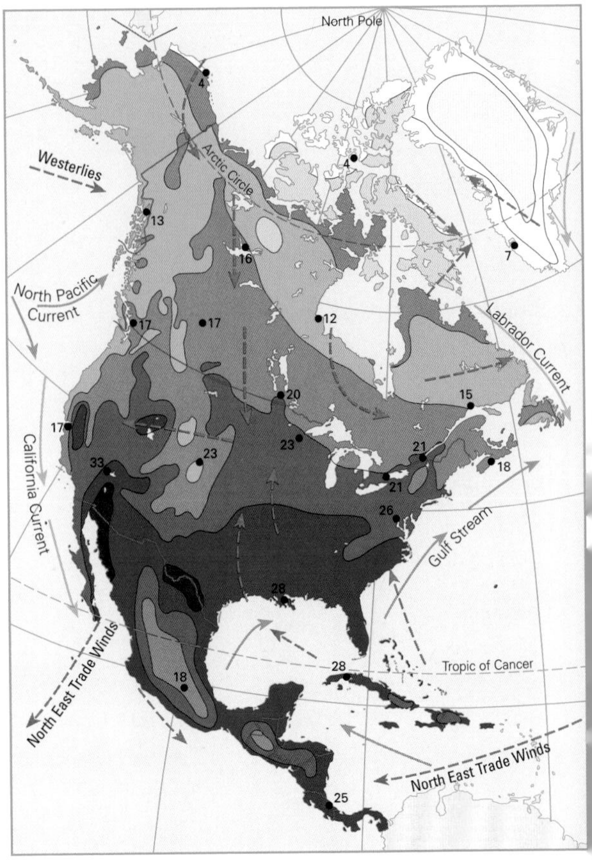

4
Westerlies
13
16
North Pacific Current
17
17
12
7
20
15
17
23
23
21
18
33
21
26
28
California Current
North East Trade Winds
18
28
Tropic of Cancer
28
25
North East Trade Winds
Gulf Stream
Labrador Current
Arctic Circle
North Pole

→ warm sea current   → cold sea current   --→ prevailing wind

Precipitation

average annual precipitation

mm
3000
2000
1000
500
250
0

• climate station
(average annual precipitation)

Barrow 112
Resolute 131
Juneau 1379
Yellowknife 267
Nuuk (Godthåb) 756
Arctic Circle
Vancouver 1113
Edmonton 466
Churchill 402
San Francisco 503
Winnipeg 526
Denver 393
Minneapolis St. Paul 719
Montréal 946
Sept-Îles 1125
Las Vegas 104
Toronto 762
Halifax 1491
Washington D.C. 1064
New Orleans 1572
Tropic of Cancer
Mexico City 749
Havana 1190
Limón 3384
North Pole

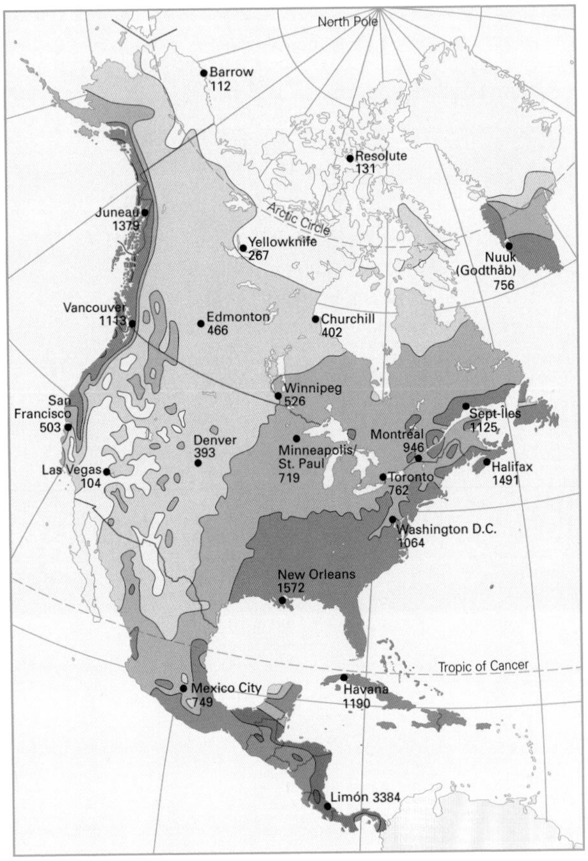

Natural vegetation

the type of vegetation that would occur naturally without interference by people

- coniferous forest
- mixed forest
- tropical rain forest
- tropical grasslands
- thorn forest
- temperate grasslands
- semi-desert
- tundra
- ice
- mountains

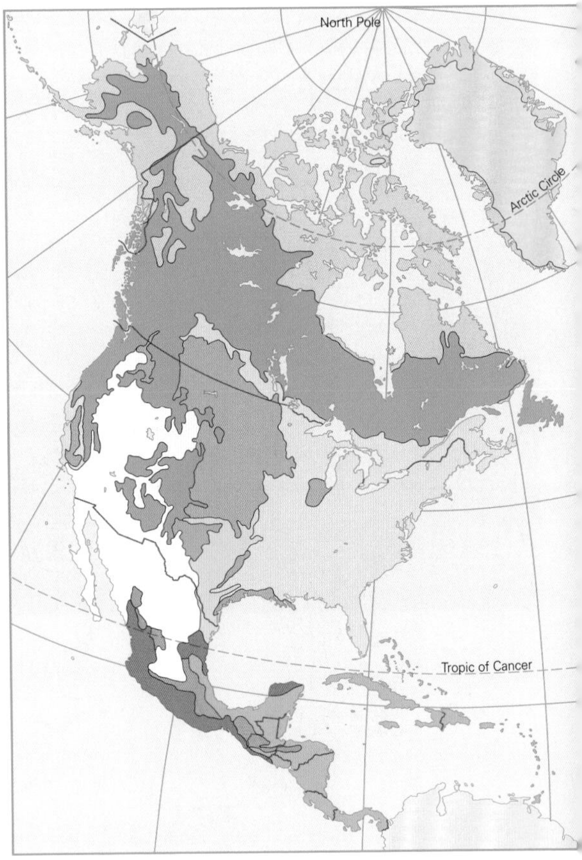

North Pole
Arctic Circle
Tropic of Cancer

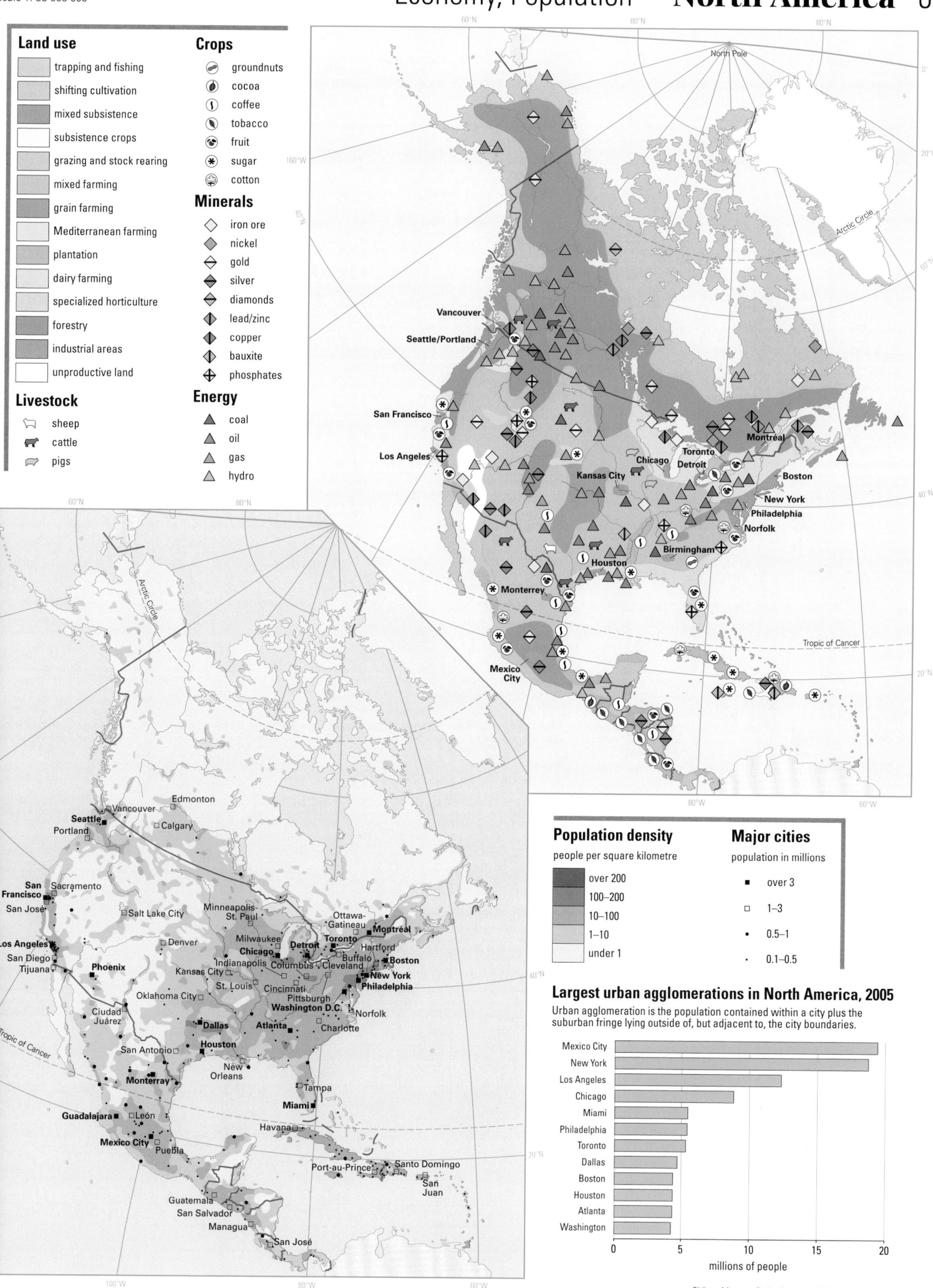

Land use

- trapping and fishing
- shifting cultivation
- mixed subsistence
- subsistence crops
- grazing and stock rearing
- mixed farming
- grain farming
- Mediterranean farming
- plantation
- dairy farming
- specialized horticulture
- forestry
- industrial areas
- unproductive land

Livestock

- sheep
- cattle
- pigs

Crops

- groundnuts
- cocoa
- coffee
- tobacco
- fruit
- sugar
- cotton

Minerals

- iron ore
- nickel
- gold
- silver
- diamonds
- lead/zinc
- copper
- bauxite
- phosphates

Energy

- coal
- oil
- gas
- hydro

Population density

people per square kilometre

- over 200
- 100–200
- 10–100
- 1–10
- under 1

Major cities

population in millions

- over 3
- 1–3
- 0.5–1
- 0.1–0.5

Largest urban agglomerations in North America, 2005

Urban agglomeration is the population contained within a city plus the suburban fringe lying outside of, but adjacent to, the city boundaries.

Mexico City
New York
Los Angeles
Chicago
Miami
Philadelphia
Toronto
Dallas
Boston
Houston
Atlanta
Washington

0   5   10   15   20

millions of people

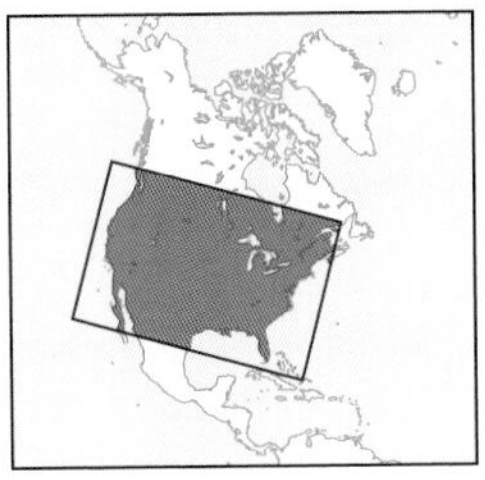

boundaries

	international
-----	disputed
	internal

communications

	expressway
	major road
	railway
	canal
✈	major airport

settlements

■	over 1 million inhabitants
●	more than 100 000 inhabitants
•	smaller towns

physical features

- river, lake
- seasonal river
- seasonal lake
- marsh
- salt lake
- salt pan
- ice cap
- sand dunes

sea ice

- unnavigable
- pack ice
  – fall minimum
  – spring maximum

land height and sea depth

metres
5000
3000
2000
1000
500
300
200
100
0 — sea level
200
3000
6000

▲ spot height in metres

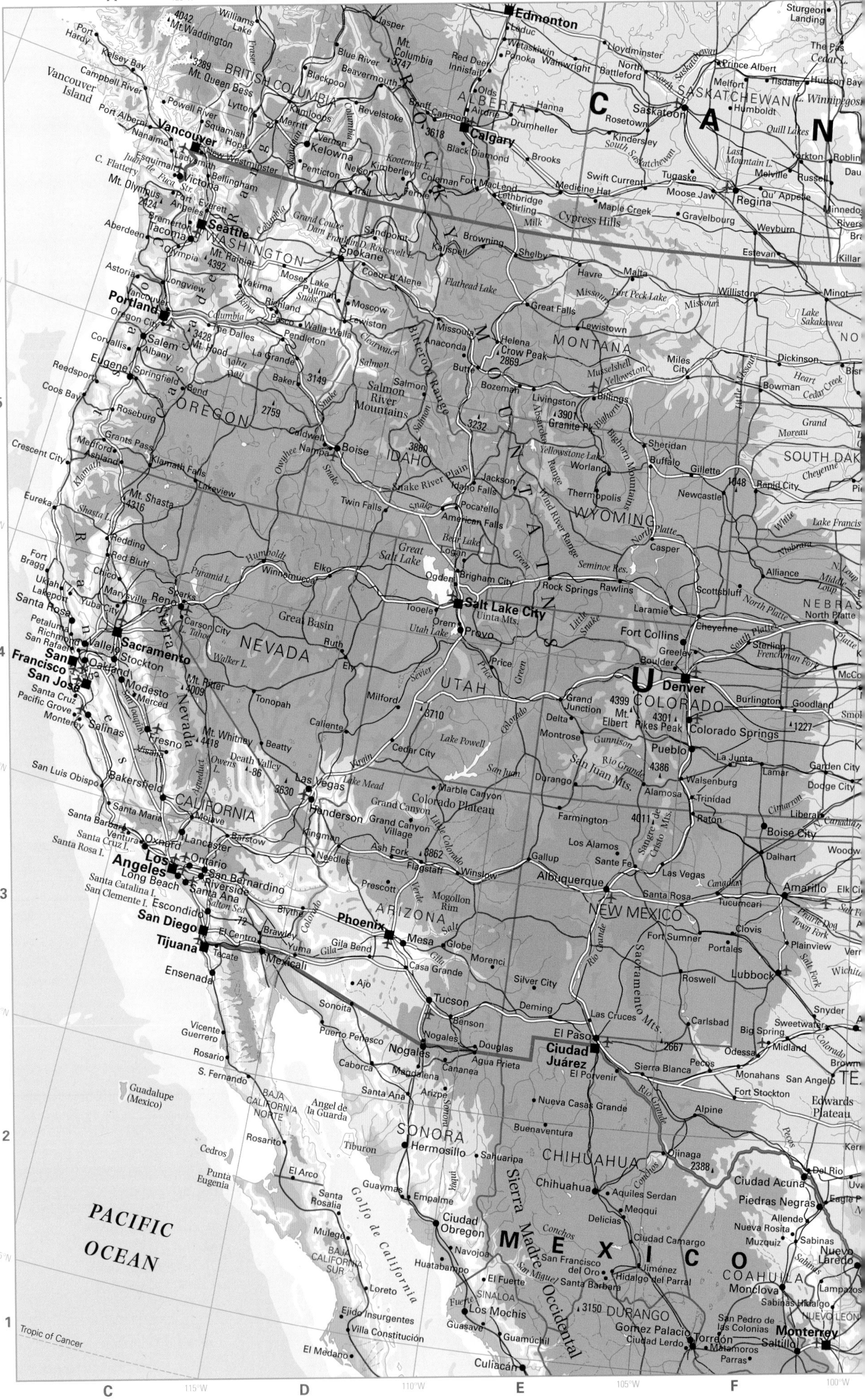

PACIFIC OCEAN

Scale 1: 12 500 000

0   125   250   375   500   625 km

Conical Orthomorphic Projection

© Oxford University Press

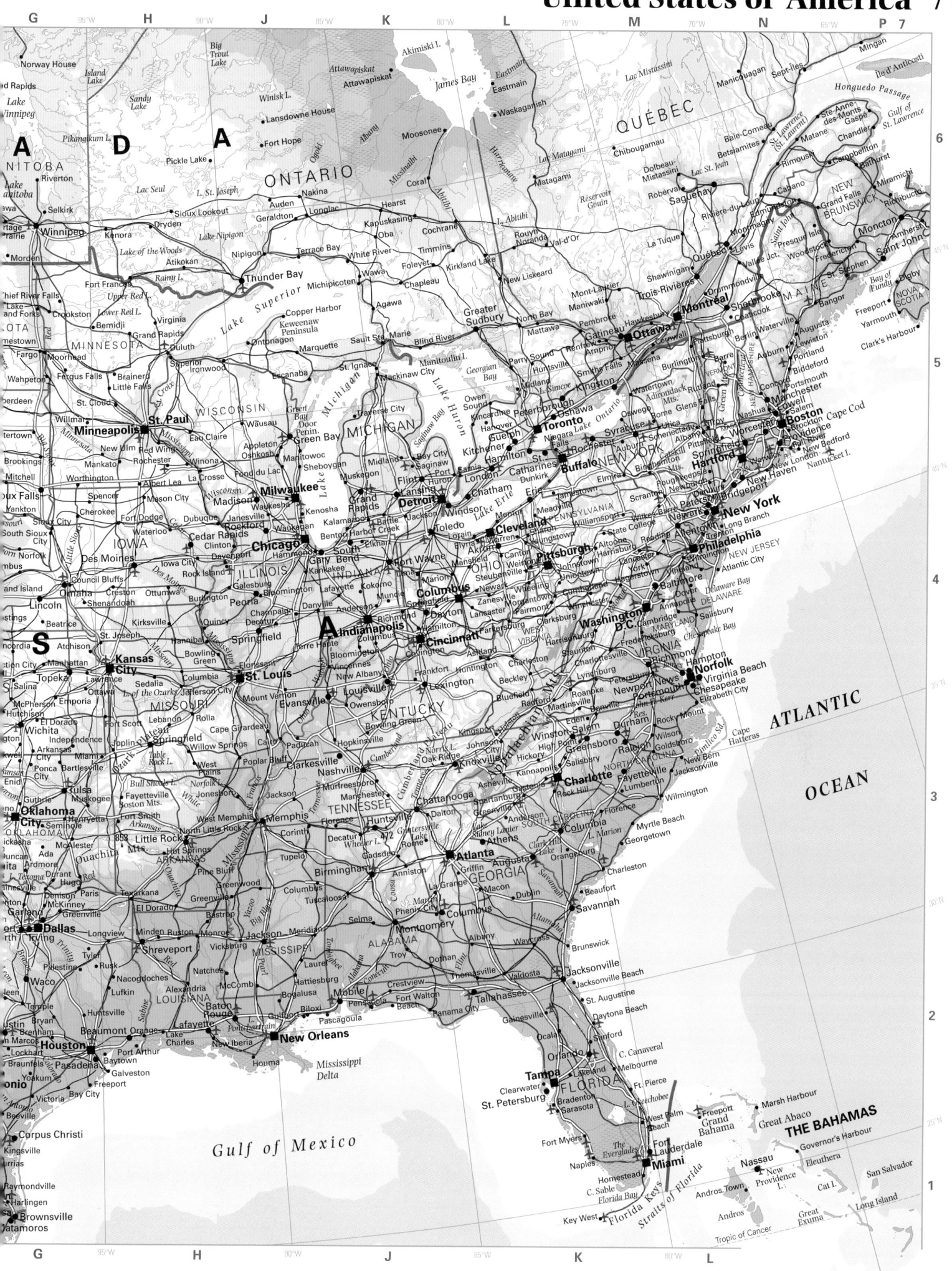

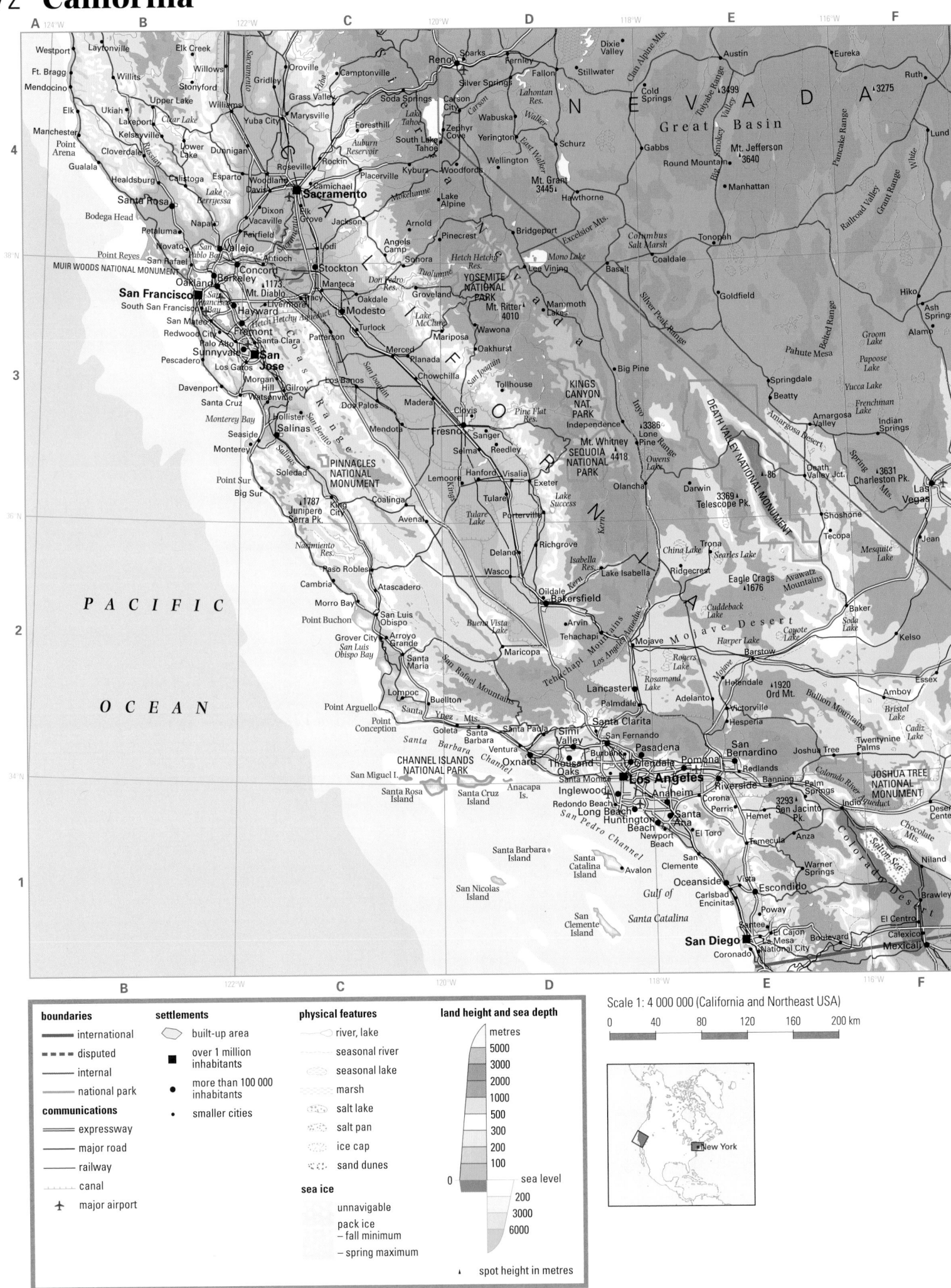

Scale 1: 4 000 000 (California and Northeast USA)

0   40   80   120   160   200 km

boundaries
—— international
- - - disputed
—— internal
—— national park

communications
══ expressway
—— major road
—— railway
╫ canal
✈ major airport

settlements
⬡ built-up area
◼ over 1 million inhabitants
● more than 100 000 inhabitants
• smaller cities

physical features
river, lake
seasonal river
seasonal lake
marsh
salt lake
salt pan
ice cap
sand dunes

sea ice
unnavigable
pack ice
– fall minimum
– spring maximum

land height and sea depth
metres
5000
3000
2000
1000
500
300
200
100
0 sea level
200
3000
6000

▲ spot height in metres

Conical Orthomorphic Projection   © Oxford University Press

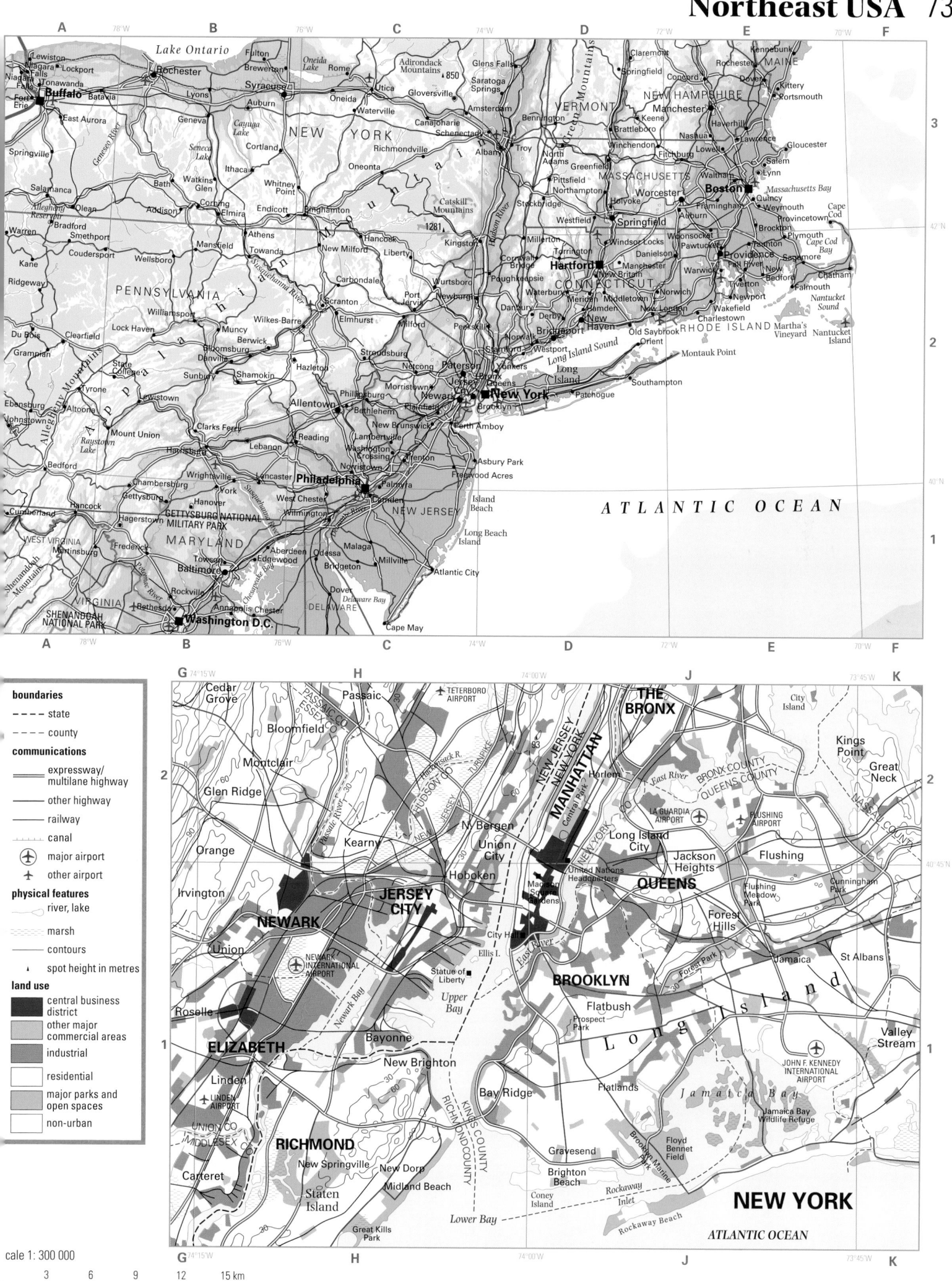

Main map (Northeast USA):

Lake Ontario

Lewiston, Niagara Falls, Lockport, Tonawanda, Buffalo, Fort Erie, East Aurora, Batavia, Rochester, Lyons, Geneva, Springville, Salamanca, Olean, Bradford, Smethport, Coudersport, Wellsboro, Warren, Kane, Ridgeway, Du Bois, Clearfield, Grampian, Ebensburg, Johnstown, Altoona, Tyrone, State College, Mount Union, Bedford, Cumberland, Hancock, Bethesda

Fulton, Brewerton, Oneida Lake, Rome, Syracuse, Oneida, Auburn, Cortland, Waterville, Canajoharie, Utica, Gloversville, Amsterdam, Schenectady, Albany, Troy

Adirondack Mountains 850, Glens Falls, Saratoga Springs

NEW YORK, PENNSYLVANIA, Cayuga Lake, Seneca Lake, Ithaca, Bath, Watkins Glen, Whitney Point, Corning, Elmira, Addison, Endicott, Binghamton, Mansfield, Towanda, Athens, Williamsport, Lock Haven, Muncy, Berwick, Bloomsburg, Danville, Sunbury, Shamokin, Lewistown, Harrisburg, Lebanon, Reading

Richmondville, Oneonta, New Milford, Hancock, Liberty, Carbondale, Scranton, Wilkes-Barre, Hazleton, Stroudsburg, Netcong, Phillipsburg, Allentown, Bethlehem, Easton

Catskill Mountains 1281, Kingston, Wurtsboro, Port Jervis, Milford, Newburgh, Poughkeepsie, Peekskill, Morristown

Hudson River, Stockbridge, Millerton, Torrington, Cornwall Bridge, Danbury, Waterbury, Derby, Bridgeport, Norwalk, Westport, Stamford, Yonkers, Paterson, Jersey City, Newark, New York, Brooklyn, Queens, Bronx

VERMONT, Bennington, North Adams, Greenfield, Pittsfield, Northampton, Westfield, Holyoke, Springfield, Hartford, New Britain, Meriden, Middletown, Hamden, New Haven, CONNECTICUT

Claremont, Springfield, Concord, Winchendon, Fitchburg, Worcester, Auburn, Framingham, NEW HAMPSHIRE, MASSACHUSETTS, Manchester, Nashua, Lowell, Lawrence, Haverhill, Waltham, Boston

Rochester, Dover, Kennebunk, MAINE, Kittery, Portsmouth, Gloucester, Salem, Lynn, Quincy, Weymouth, Brockton, Provincetown, Plymouth, Massachusetts Bay, Cape Cod, Cape Cod Bay, Sagamore

Windsor Locks, Manchester, Danielson, Norwich, New London, Old Saybrook, Orient, Pawtucket, Providence, Warwick, Woonsocket, Fall River, New Bedford, RHODE ISLAND, Newport, Tiverton, Wakefield, Charlestown, Chatham, Falmouth, Martha's Vineyard, Nantucket Sound, Nantucket Island

Long Island Sound, Long Island, Montauk Point, Southampton, Patchogue

Greene Mountains, Green Mountains

Susquehanna River, Genesee River, Allegheny River, Alleghany Reservoir, Raystown Lake

APPALACHIAN, Alleghany Mountains, Appalachian Mountains

WEST VIRGINIA, Martinsburg, Shenandoah Mountains, VIRGINIA, SHENANDOAH NATIONAL PARK, Frederick, Hagerstown, Chambersburg, Gettysburg, GETTYSBURG NATIONAL MILITARY PARK, Hanover, York, Wrightsville, Lancaster, West Chester, Wilmington, MARYLAND, Towson, Baltimore, Aberdeen, Edgewood, Rockville, Annapolis, Chester, Bethesda, Washington D.C., Dover, DELAWARE, Delaware Bay, Cape May

Morristown, New Brunswick, Perth Amboy, Asbury Park, Freewood Acres, NEW JERSEY, Washington Crossing, Lambertville, Trenton, Norristown, Philadelphia, Camden, Palmyra, Island Beach, Long Beach Island, Malaga, Bridgeton, Millville, Atlantic City, Odessa

ATLANTIC OCEAN

78°W, 76°W, 74°W, 72°W, 70°W, 47°N, 42°N, 40°N

A B C D E F, 3 2 1

Inset map (New York City):

Cedar Grove, Passaic, PASSAIC CO, ESSEX CO, Teterboro Airport, THE BRONX, City Island, Kings Point, Great Neck, Bloomfield, Montclair, Glen Ridge, Orange, Kearny, N Bergen, Union City, Hackensack R., HUDSON CO, MANHATTAN, NEW JERSEY, NEW YORK, Harlem, Central Park, BRONX COUNTY, QUEENS COUNTY, La Guardia Airport, Flushing Airport, Flushing, Irvington, Hoboken, Long Island City, Jackson Heights, Cunningham Park, NEWARK, JERSEY CITY, United Nations Headquarters, Madison Square Gardens, QUEENS, Forest Hills, Union, City Hall, Ellis I., Flushing Meadow Park, NEWARK INTERNATIONAL AIRPORT, Statue of Liberty, East River, Jamaica, St Albans, Roselle, Newark Bay, BROOKLYN, Forest Park, ELIZABETH, Upper Bay, Flatbush, Prospect Park, Long Island, Linden, LINDEN AIRPORT, Bayonne, New Brighton, Flatlands, Valley Stream, JOHN F. KENNEDY INTERNATIONAL AIRPORT, UNION CO, MIDDLESEX CO, RICHMOND, Bay Ridge, Jamaica Bay, Jamaica Bay Wildlife Refuge, New Springville, New Dorp, KINGS COUNTY, RICHMOND COUNTY, Gravesend, Floyd Bennett Field, Carteret, Midland Beach, Brighton Beach, Brooklyn Marine, Staten Island, Great Kills Park, Coney Island, Rockaway Inlet, Rockaway Beach, NEW YORK, Lower Bay, ATLANTIC OCEAN

74°15'W, 74°00'W, 73°45'W, 40°45'N

G H J K, 2 1

Legend

boundaries
— international
--- disputed
— internal

communications
═ expressway
— major road
— railway
⊦⊦⊦ canal
✈ major airport

settlements
■ over 1 million inhabitants
● more than 100 000 inhabitants
• smaller cities

physical features
~ river, lake
seasonal river
seasonal lake
marsh
salt lake
salt pan
ice cap
sand dunes

land height and sea depth

metres
5000
3000
2000
1000
500
300
200
100
sea level
0   200
3000
6000

▲ spot height in metres

Map labels

UNITED STATES / Mexico region:

Los Angeles, Long Beach, San Diego, Tijuana, Ensenada, Mexicali, Riverside, San Bernardino, Oxnard, San Clemente I., Vicente Guerrero, Rosario, S. Fernando, Guadalupe (Mexico), Cedros, Punta Eugenia, Santa Rosalía, Mulegé, Guaymas, Empalme, La Paz, Cabo San Lucas, San José del Cabo, El Médano, Villa Constitución, Tiburón, Ángel de la Guarda, El Arco, Rosarito

Phoenix, Mesa, Tucson, Casa Grande, Ajo, Nogales, El Centro, Gila, Yuma, S. Felipe, Puerto Peñasco, Caborca, Sonoita, Cananea, Agua Prieta, Magdalena, Arizpe, Hermosillo, Ciudad Obregón, Navojoa, Los Mochis, Guamúchil, Culiacán, Quilá, Mazatlán

COLORADO, Colorado Plateau, Grand Canyon, Kingman, Ash Fork, Prescott, Winslow, Gallup, Farmington, Durango, San Juan, Durango, NEW MEXICO, Albuquerque, Santa Fe, Las Vegas, Tucumcari, Clovis, Roswell, Carlsbad, El Paso, Ciudad Juárez, Las Cruces, Deming, Nueva Casas Grandes, Chihuahua, Aquiles Serdán, Hidalgo del Parral, San Francisco del Oro, Santa Bárbara

KANSAS, Great Bend, Garden City, Dodge City, Liberal, Wichita, Hutchinson, Arkansas City, Ponca City, Enid, OKLAHOMA City, Woodward, Altus, Lawton, Duncan, Ardmore, McAlester, Muskogee, Tulsa

MISSOURI, Topeka, Salina, Emporia, Jefferson City, Columbia, St. Louis, ILLINOIS, Evansville, Springfield, Cape Girardeau, Poplar Bluff, INDIANAPOLIS, Indiana

ARKANSAS, Fort Smith, Fayetteville, Little Rock, Pine Bluff, El Dorado, Texarkana, Monroe, Shreveport, Alexandria

TEXAS, Amarillo, Plainview, Lubbock, Snyder, Sweetwater, Abilene, Odessa, Pecos, Fort Stockton, Del Rio, San Angelo, Edwards Plateau, Killeen, Austin, Waco, Fort Worth, Dallas, Irving, Garland, Greenville, Paris, Longview, Tyler, Beaumont, Houston, Pasadena, Galveston, San Antonio, Corpus Christi, McAllen, Harlingen, Brownsville, Laredo

TENNESSEE, Nashville, Memphis, Florence, Tupelo, Columbus, Birmingham, Tuscaloosa, ALABAMA, Montgomery, MISSISSIPPI, Jackson, Vicksburg, Natchez, Meridian, Laurel, Hattiesburg, LOUISIANA, Baton Rouge, Lafayette, Lake Charles, Port Arthur, New Orleans, Biloxi, Mobile, Pascagoula

Piedras Negras, Nueva Rosita, Sabinas, Monclova, San Pedro de las Colonias, Gómez Palacio, Torreón, Ciudad Lerdo, Matamoros, Parras, Saltillo, Monterrey, Reynosa, Matamoros, Nuevo Laredo, Lampazos, Sabinas Hidalgo, Linares, Hidalgo, Ciudad Victoria, La Pesca, Laguna Madre

Durango, El Salto, Río Grande, Sombrerete, Fresnillo, Zacatecas, Villanueva, Matehuala, San Luis Potosí, Río Verde, Cárdenas, Ciudad Mante, Tamazunchale, Tula, Ciudad Madero, Tampico, Aldama

Tepic, Santiago Ixcuintla, Islas Marías, Pto. Vallarta, Cabo Corrientes, Ameca, Tepatitlán, Guadalajara, Lago de Chapala, Aguascalientes, León, Irapuato, Celaya, Querétaro, Salamanca, Acámbaro, Morelia, Toluca, Mexico City, Netzahualcóyotl, Ixtapaluca, Ixtaccíhuatl, Popocatépetl, Puebla, Cuernavaca, Cuautla, Xochimilco, Pachuca, Jalapa Enríquez, Veracruz, Córdoba, Orizaba, San Andrés Tuxtla

PACIFIC OCEAN

Colima, Manzanillo, Uruapan, Apatzingán, Playa Azul, Ixtapa-Zihuatanejo, Acapulco, Chilpancingo, Iguala, Tehuacán, Acatlán, Tierra Blanca, Oaxaca, Tuxtepec, Jamiltepec, Puerto Escondido, Pochutla, Tehuantepec, Ixtepec, Juchitán, Tonalá, Pijijiapan, Huixtla, Tapachula, Quezaltenango, Mazatenango, Ahuachapán, Sonsonate

Gulf of Mexico, Bahía de Campeche, Progreso, Mérida, Tizimín, Pisté, Valladolid, Cozumel, Isla Cozumel, Campeche, Champotón, Escárcega, Chetumal, Felipe Carrillo Puerto, Yucatan, BELIZE, Belize, Belmopan, Flores, Punta Gorda, Pto. Barrios, Puerto Cortés, GUATEMALA, Cobán, San Pedro Sula, Santa Rosa, Chiquimula, Zacapa, S. Cristóbal, Comitán, Tuxtla Gutiérrez, Villahermosa, Minatitlán, Coatzacoalcos, Frontera, Ciudad del Carmen, Istmo de Tehuantepec, Palomares, Acayucan

Guatemala City, Antigua, EL SALVADOR, San Salvador, Nueva San Salvador, Santa Ana, San Vicente, San Miguel, Usulután, Choluteca, HONDURAS, Tegucigalpa, Chinandega, León, Managua, Masaya, Granada, Golfo de Honduras

Leeward Islands Scale 1:5 000 000

Anguilla (UK), The Valley, St. Martin (Fr.), St. Maarten (Neths.), St. Barthélemy (Fr.), St. Eustatius (Neths.), St. Kitts, Nevis, Basseterre, ST. KITTS AND NEVIS, Plymouth, Montserrat (UK), Codrington, Barbuda, ANTIGUA AND BARBUDA, St. John's, Antigua, Falmouth, Grande Terre, Basse Terre, Guadeloupe Passage, Les Abymes, Pointe-à-Pitre, Soufrière, GUADELOUPE (Fr.), Basse-Terre, Marie Galente, Dominica Passage, Portsmouth, Marigot, DOMINICA, Roseau, Morne Diablotins

Windward Islands Scale 1:5 000 000

Mt. Pelée, Ste. Marie, Fort-de-France, Le François, MARTINIQUE (Fr.), Rivière-Pilote, St. Lucia Channel, Castries, ST. LUCIA, Vieux Fort, St. Vincent Passage, Chateaubelair, St. Vincent, Kingstown, Bequia, Mustique, Canouan, Union, ST. VINCENT AND THE GRENADINES, Carriacou, GRENADA, St. George's, Speightstown, Bridgetown, BARBADOS

© Oxford University Press

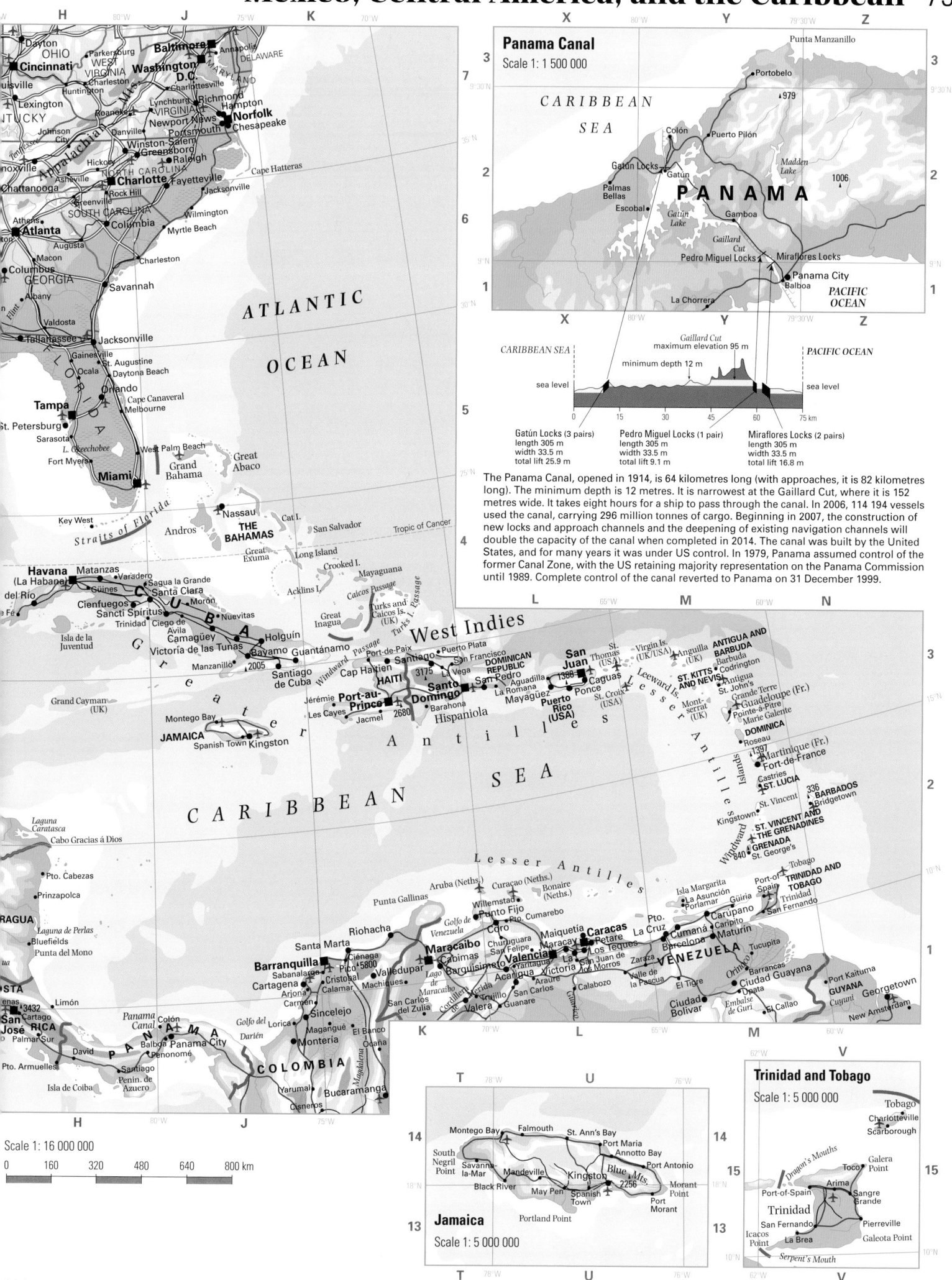

EL SALVADOR
NICARAGUA
COSTA RICA
PANAMA

Barranquilla
Maracaibo
Caracas
Valencia
VENEZUELA
Medellín
Georgetown
GUYANA
Paramaribo
SURINAME
Cayenne
Cali
Bogotá
French Guiana
(France)
COLOMBIA

Equator
0°

Galapagos Islands
(Ecuador)
Quito
ECUADOR
Guayaquil
Manaus
Belém
Rocas Island
(Brazil)
Fortaleza
Fernando de
Noronha
(Brazil)
Iquitos

PERU
B R A Z I L
Recife

Lima
Salvador

Arequipa
BOLIVIA
La Paz
Brasília
Santa
Cruz
Sucre

PARAGUAY
Rio de
Janeiro
20°S

Antofagasta
São Paulo
Tropic of Capricorn
Asunción

Porto Alegre

Córdoba
URUGUAY
Rosario
Juan Fernandez Is.
(Chile)
Santiago
Buenos Aires
Montevideo
ARGENTINA
Concepción
Mar del Plata

Stanley
Falkland Islands
(UK)
South Georgia
(UK)
Punta Arenas

Scale 1: 36 000 000

0   360   720   1080   1440   1800 km

| international boundary |
| internal boundary |
| ■ capital city |
| • other important city |

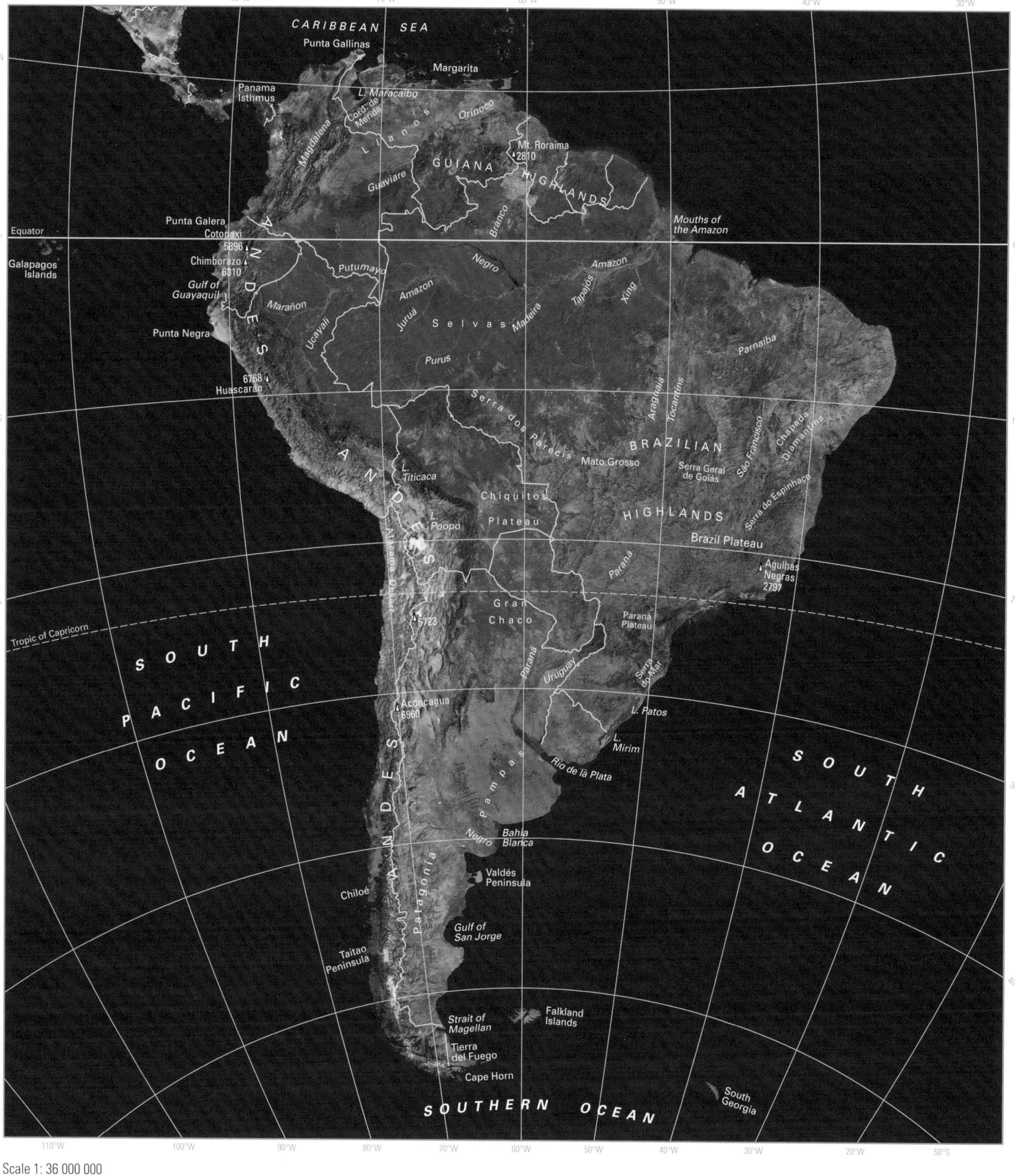

CARIBBEAN SEA
Punta Gallinas
Margarita
Panama Isthmus
L. Maracaibo
Cord. de Merida
Orinoco
Magdalena
Llanos
GUIANA HIGHLANDS
Mt. Roraima 2810
Guaviare
Branco
Mouths of the Amazon
Equator
Punta Galera
Cotopaxi 5896
Chimborazo 6310
Putumayo
Negro
Amazon
Galapagos Islands
Gulf of Guayaquil
Marañon
Amazon
Tapajós
Xing
ANDES
Ucayali
Juruá
Purus
Selvas
Madeira
Parnaiba
Punta Negra
6768 Huascaran
Serra dos Parecis
BRAZILIAN
L. Titicaca
Mato Grosso
Serra Geral de Goiás
São Francisco
Chapada Diamantina
ANDES
Chiquitos Plateau
L. Poopo
HIGHLANDS
Serra do Espinhaço
Atacama Desert
Brazil Plateau
Agulhas Negras 2797
6723
Gran Chaco
Paraná
Paraná Plateau
Tropic of Capricorn
SOUTH
Paraná
Uruguay
Serra do Mar
PACIFIC
Aconcagua 6960
L. Patos
SOUTH
OCEAN
ANDES
L. Mirim
ATLANTIC
Pampas
Rio de la Plata
OCEAN
Negro
Bahia Blanca
Chiloé
Valdés Peninsula
Patagonia
Gulf of San Jorge
Taitao Peninsula
Strait of Magellan
Falkland Islands
Tierra del Fuego
Cape Horn
South Georgia
SOUTHERN   OCEAN

Scale 1: 36 000 000

0   360   720   1080   1440   1800 km

Scale 1: 70 000 000

January temperature

actual surface temperature

°Celsius
- 25
- 20
- 15
- 10
- 5

• climate station (average January temperature)

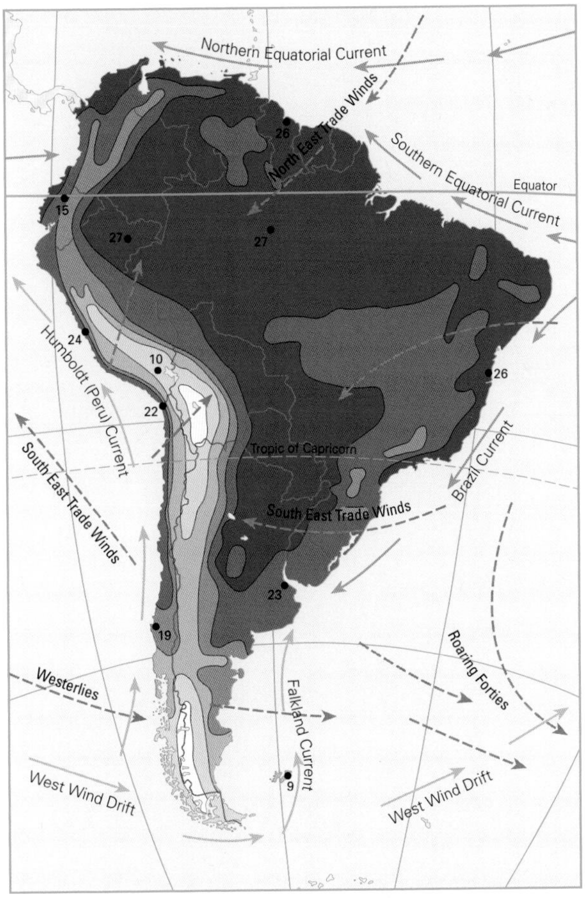

Northern Equatorial Current
North East Trade Winds
Southern Equatorial Current
Equator
15
27
27
26
Humboldt (Peru) Current
24
10
22
Tropic of Capricorn
South East Trade Winds
South East Trade Winds
Brazil Current
26
23
19
Westerlies
Falkland Current
Roaring Forties
9
West Wind Drift
West Wind Drift

→ warm sea current → cold sea current --→ prevailing wind

July temperature

actual surface temperature

°Celsius
- 25
- 20
- 15
- 10
- 5
- 0

• climate station (average July temperature)

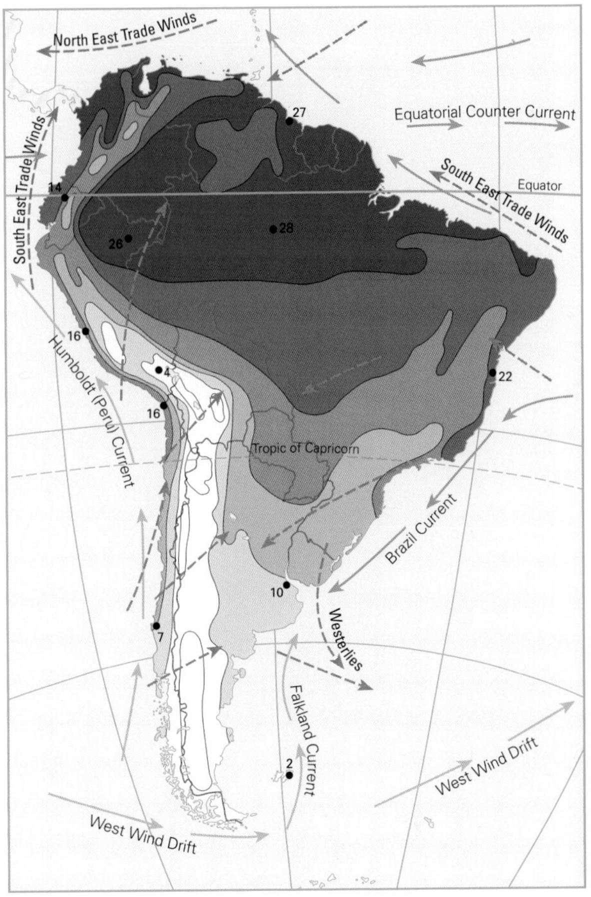

North East Trade Winds
South East Trade Winds
Equatorial Counter Current
South East Trade Winds
Equator
27
14
28
26
16
Humboldt (Peru) Current
4
16
22
Tropic of Capricorn
10
7
Brazil Current
Westerlies
Falkland Current
2
West Wind Drift
West Wind Drift

→ warm sea current → cold sea current --→ prevailing wind

Precipitation

average annual precipitation

mm
- 3000
- 2000
- 1000
- 500
- 250
- 0

• climate station (average annual precipitation)

Georgetown 2262
Equator
Quito 1086
Iquitos 2879
Manaus 1811
Lima 43
Juliaca 609
Arica 0
Ilhéus 2045
Tropic of Capricorn
Chillan 1107
Buenos Aires 950
Stanley 681

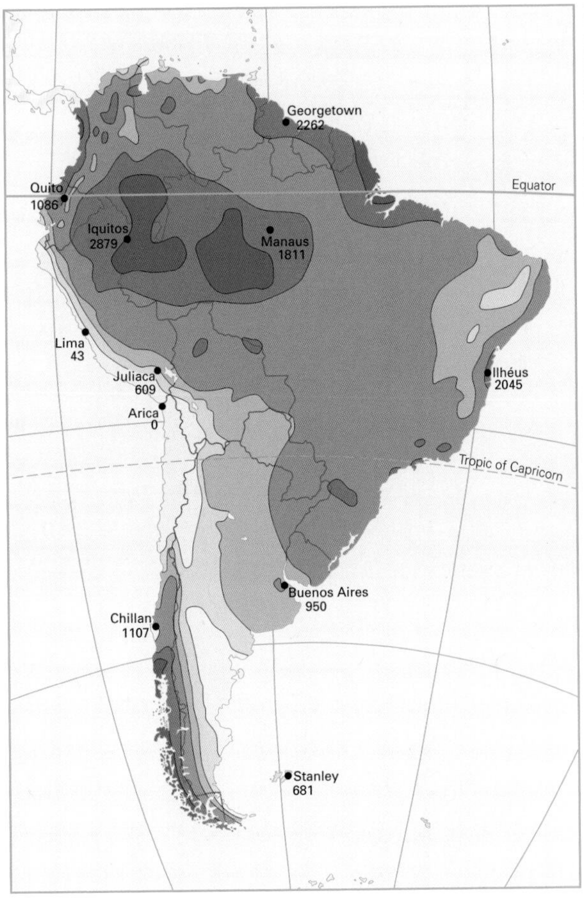

Natural vegetation

the type of vegetation that would occur naturally without interference by people

- mixed forest
- tropical rain forest
- tropical grasslands
- evergreens and shrubs
- thorn forest
- temperate grasslands
- semi-desert
- desert
- mountains

Equator

Tropic of Capricorn

Oblique Mercator Projection © Oxford University Pr

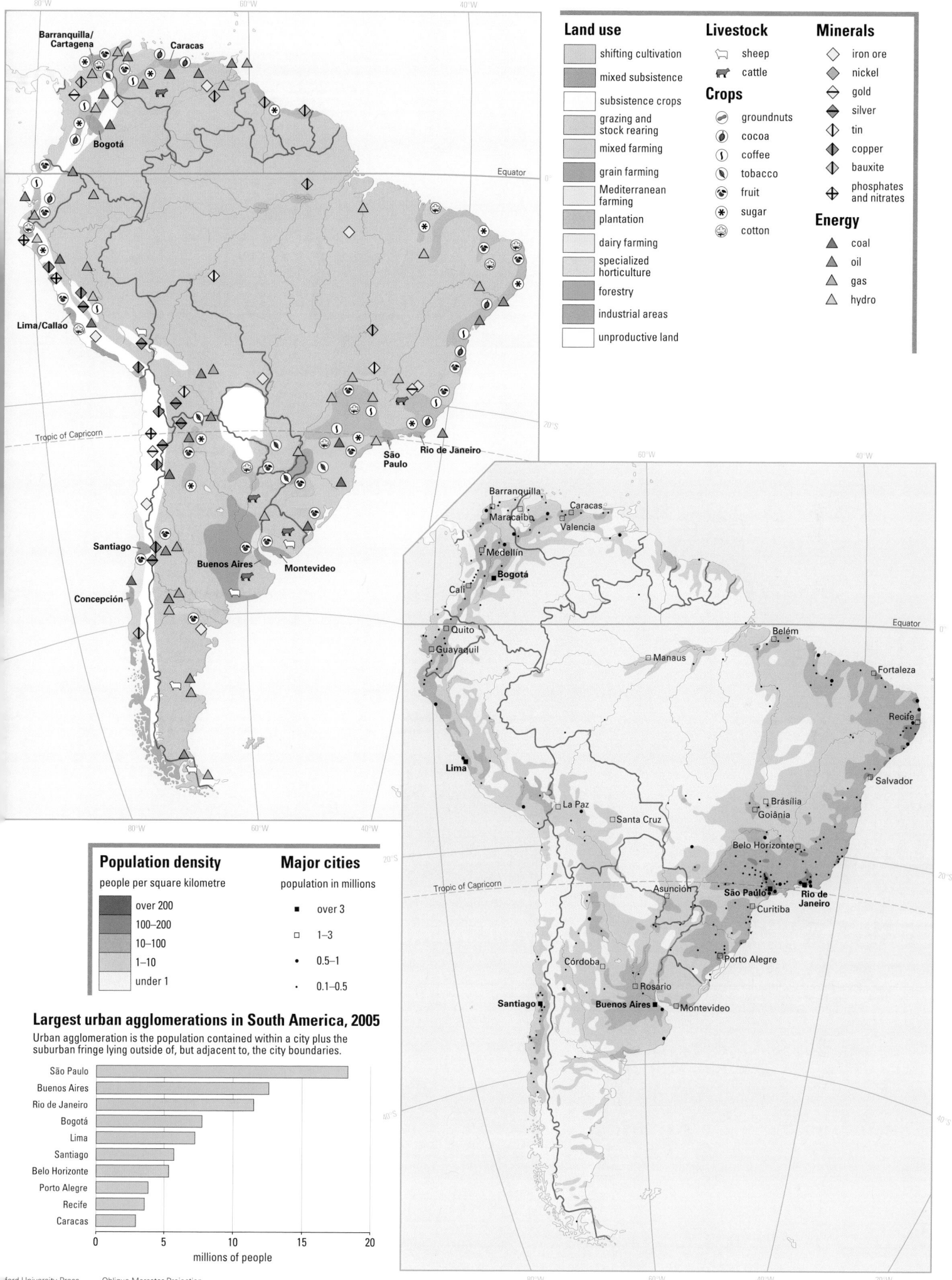

Land use
- shifting cultivation
- mixed subsistence
- subsistence crops
- grazing and stock rearing
- mixed farming
- grain farming
- Mediterranean farming
- plantation
- dairy farming
- specialized horticulture
- forestry
- industrial areas
- unproductive land

Livestock
- sheep
- cattle

Crops
- groundnuts
- cocoa
- coffee
- tobacco
- fruit
- sugar
- cotton

Minerals
- iron ore
- nickel
- gold
- silver
- tin
- copper
- bauxite
- phosphates and nitrates

Energy
- coal
- oil
- gas
- hydro

Population density
people per square kilometre
- over 200
- 100–200
- 10–100
- 1–10
- under 1

Major cities
population in millions
- over 3
- 1–3
- 0.5–1
- 0.1–0.5

Largest urban agglomerations in South America, 2005
Urban agglomeration is the population contained within a city plus the suburban fringe lying outside of, but adjacent to, the city boundaries.

São Paulo
Buenos Aires
Rio de Janeiro
Bogotá
Lima
Santiago
Belo Horizonte
Porto Alegre
Recife
Caracas

0   5   10   15   20
millions of people

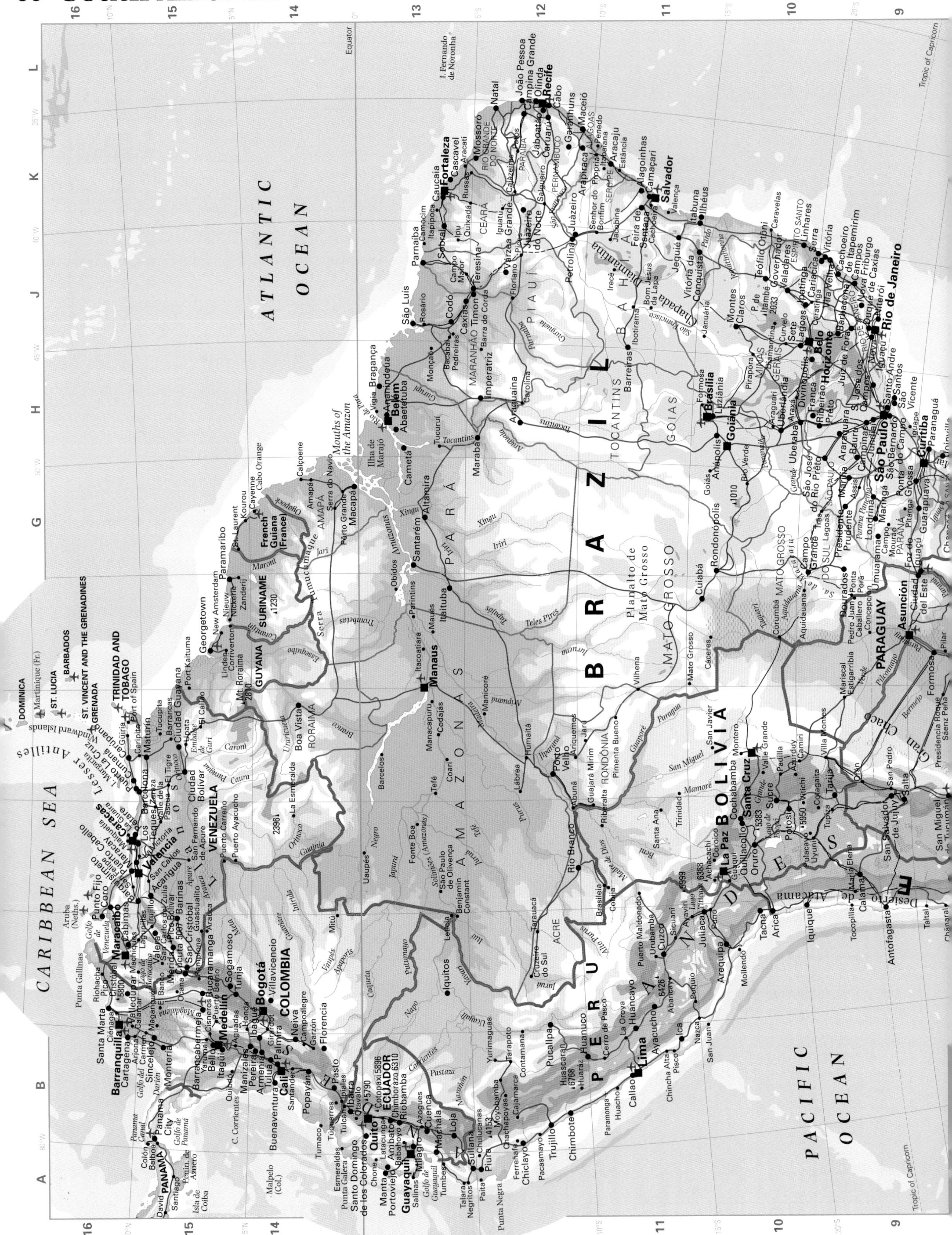

ATLANTIC OCEAN

PACIFIC OCEAN

CARIBBEAN SEA

B R A Z I L

COLOMBIA

VENEZUELA

GUYANA

SURINAME

French Guiana (France)

ECUADOR

PERU

BOLIVIA

PARAGUAY

CHILE

ARGENTINA

URUGUAY

PANAMA

DOMINICA
Martinique (Fr.)
ST. LUCIA
BARBADOS
ST. VINCENT AND THE GRENADINES
GRENADA
TRINIDAD AND TOBAGO

Lesser Antilles

Windward Islands

AMAZONAS

PARÁ

MATO GROSSO

MATO GROSSO DO SUL

GOIÁS

MINAS GERAIS

BAHIA

PIAUÍ

MARANHÃO

CEARÁ

RIO GRANDE DO NORTE

PARAÍBA

PERNAMBUCO

ALAGOAS

SERGIPE

TOCANTINS

RONDÔNIA

ACRE

RORAIMA

AMAPÁ

Mouths of the Amazon

Tropic of Capricorn

Equator

Bogotá · Medellín · Cali · Quito · Guayaquil · Lima · La Paz · Santa Cruz · Asunción · São Paulo · Rio de Janeiro · Belo Horizonte · Brasília · Goiânia · Salvador · Recife · Fortaleza · Belém · Manaus · Caracas · Maracaibo · Barranquilla · Cartagena

© Oxford University Press

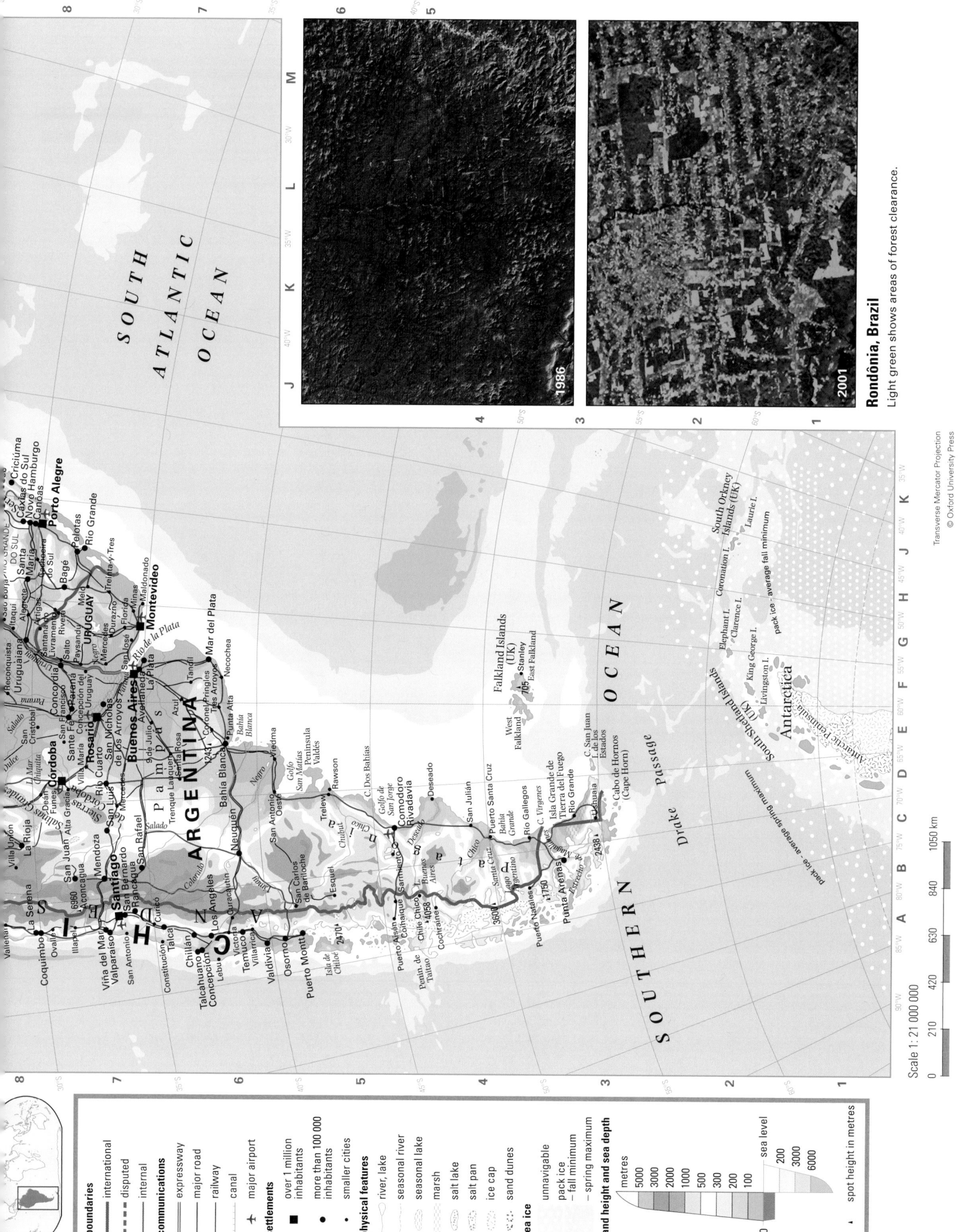

Rondônia, Brazil
Light green shows areas of forest clearance.

1986

2001

Scale 1 : 21 000 000

Transverse Mercator Projection

© Oxford University Press

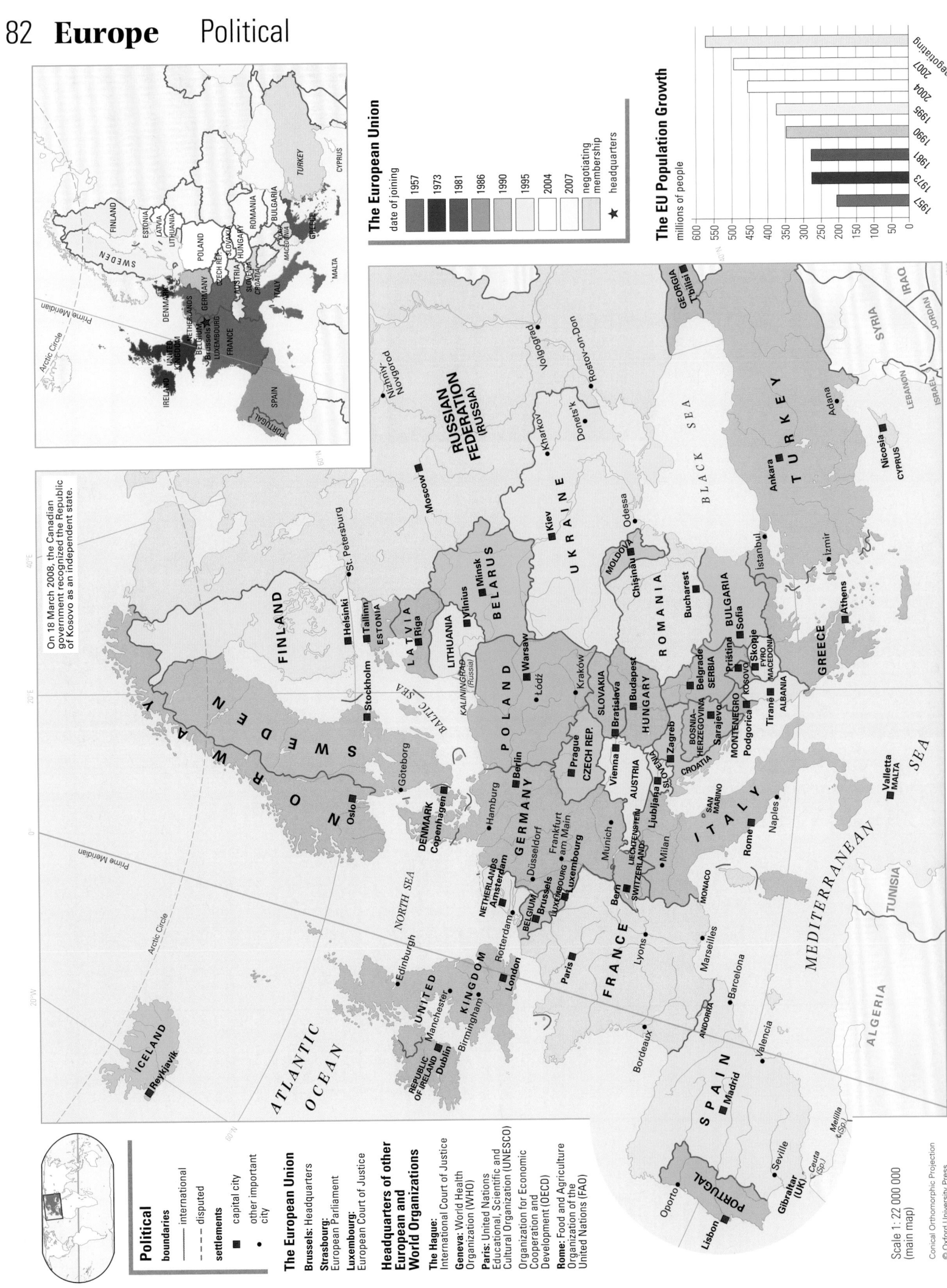

The European Union

date of joining

1957
1973
1981
1986
1990
1995
2004
2007
negotiating membership
★ headquarters

The EU Population Growth

millions of people

600 550 500 450 400 350 300 250 200 150 100 50 0

1957
1973
1981
1990
1995
2004
2007
negotiating

On 18 March 2008, the Canadian government recognized the Republic of Kosovo as an independent state.

Political

boundaries
— international
– – – disputed

settlements
■ capital city
● other important city

The European Union
Brussels: Headquarters
Strasbourg: European Parliament
Luxembourg: European Court of Justice

Headquarters of other European and World Organizations
The Hague: International Court of Justice
Geneva: World Health Organization (WHO)
Paris: United Nations Educational, Scientific and Cultural Organization (UNESCO) Organization for Economic Cooperation and Development (OECD)
Rome: Food and Agriculture Organization of the United Nations (FAO)

Scale 1: 22 000 000 (main map)

Conical Orthomorphic Projection

© Oxford University Press

Conical Orthomorphic Projection   © Oxford University Press

URAL MOUNTAINS

Pechora

Ural

Caspian Sea

Lake Urmia

Tigris

Euphrates

Mt Ararat 5123

Lake Van

Toros Dağları

Kola Peninsula

WHITE SEA

Lake Onega

Rybinsk Reservoir

Central Russian Uplands

Tsimlyansk Reservoir

Volga

Donets

Mt Elbrus 5642

Caucasus

SEA OF AZOV

Crimea

BLACK SEA

Bosporus

Anatolian Plateau

Lake Tuz

Cyprus

Rhodes

Lapland

Inarijärvi

Lake Ladoga

Lake Peipus

Gulf of Finland

Saimaassika

G. of Riga

Dnepr

Dnepr

Vistula

CARPATHIANS

Danube

Balkan Mts

Rodopi Planina

SEA OF MARMARA

Dardanelles

AEGEAN SEA

Crete

2917 Mt Olympus

Cyclades

Peloponnese

Pindhos Mountains

Corfu

Scandinavia

Lofoten Islands

Gulf of Bothnia

Åland

Gotland

Öland

BALTIC SEA

Lake Mälaren

Lake Vänern

Lake Vättern

Bornholm

Stora

North European Plain

Tatry Mts

Bohemian Massif

Danube

2548

Hungarian Basin

Dinaric Alps

ADRIATIC SEA

Gulf of Taranto

IONIAN SEA

Taranto

Jostedalsbreen

Porsgrunn

Hardanger Fjell

Skagerrak

Kattegat

Sjælland

Fyn

Jylland

Vyland

Frisian Islands

IJsselmeer

Rhine

Harz Mts

Erzgebirge

1603

Schwäbische Alb

Tauern

Alps

Bodensee

APENNINI

1277 Vesuvius

TYRRHENIAN SEA

Mt Etna 3323

Sicily

Malta

G. of Gabès

GREENLAND SEA

Arctic Circle

Faroe Islands

Shetland Islands

Orkney Islands

C. Wrath

Southern Uplands

NORTH SEA

British Isles

Great Britain

Pennines

The Wash

Frisian Islands

Strait of Dover

Ardennes

Vosges

Jura

Schwarzwald

Rhine

4807 Mont Blanc

L. Geneva

Alpes Maritimes

LIGURIAN SEA

Corsica

Sardinia

Gulf of Lyons

MEDITERRANEAN SEA

Prime Meridian

Iceland

Vatnajökull

2119 Hekla

ATLANTIC OCEAN

Outer Hebrides

Ben Nevis 1344

Grampians

Central Plain

Malin Head

Ireland

St. George's Channel

Cambrian Mts

Great Britain

English Channel

Channel Islands

Cotentin

Brittany Pen.

Seine

Paris Basin

Massif Central

Bay of Biscay

Pyrénées 3404

Ebro

Cantabrian Mts

Central Cordilleras

Central Cordillera

La Mancha

Balearic Islands

Menorca

Mallorca

Ibiza

Sierra Morena

Baetic Cordillera

Betica Cordillera

Str. of Gibraltar

Grand Erg Occidental

ATLAS MOUNTAINS

C. Finisterre

C. de São Vicente

T. C. Bon

Tunis

Scale 1:22 000 000

0   220   440   660   880   1100 km

Scale 1: 50 000 000

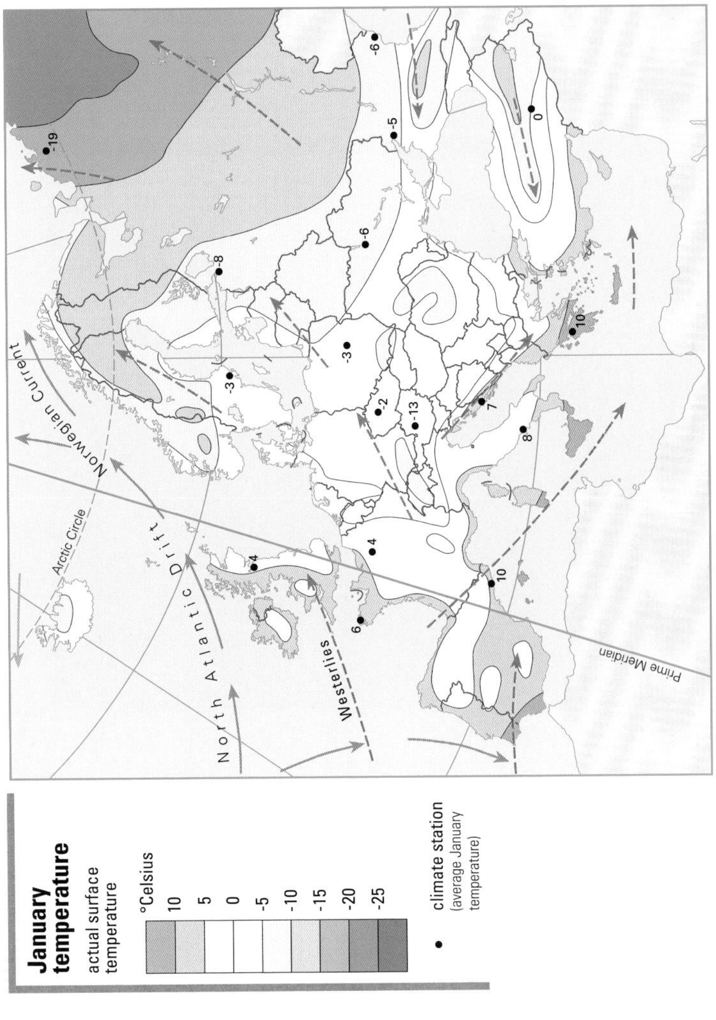

© Oxford University Press

Conical Orthomorphic Projection

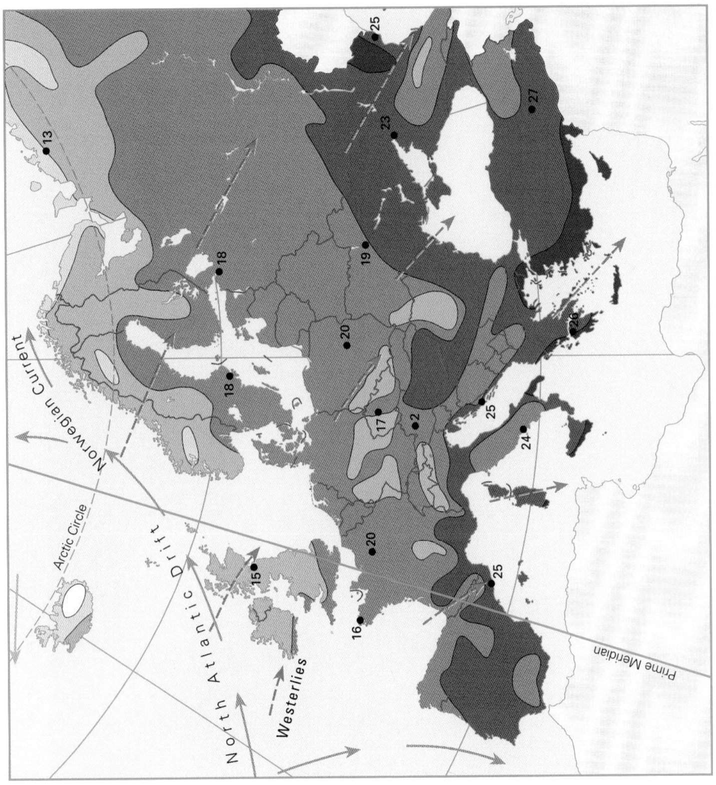

July temperature

actual surface temperature

°Celsius
25
20
15
10
5

● climate station (average July temperature)

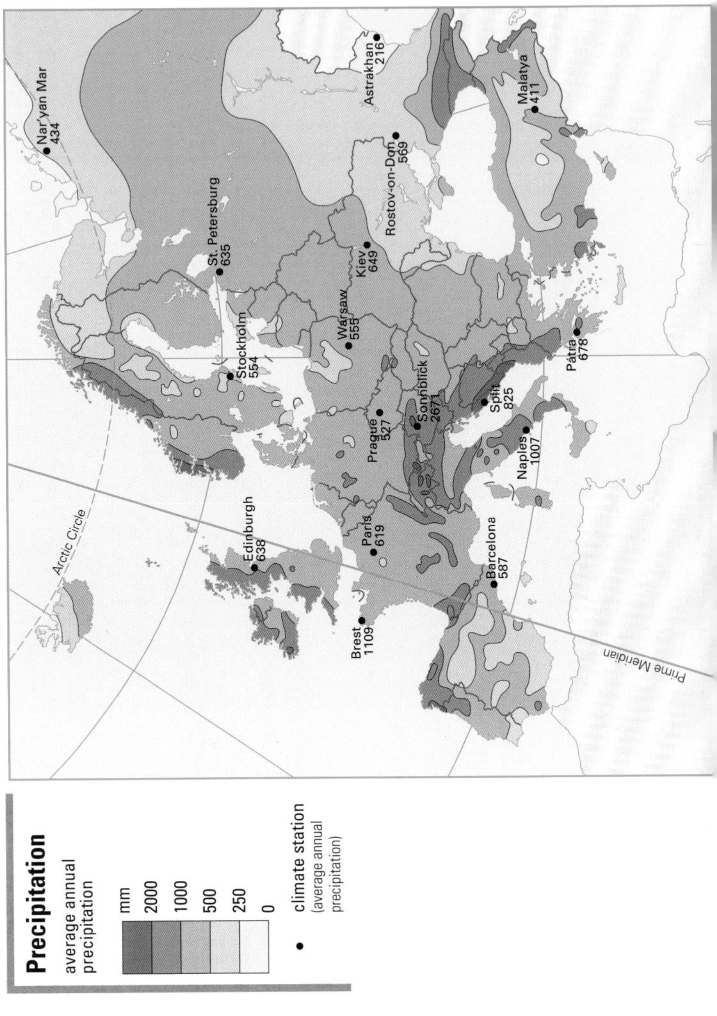

Station values (July temperature map):
13, 25, 27, 23, 18, 19, 20, 18, 25, 17, 2, 25, 24, 20, 15, 16, 25

January temperature

actual surface temperature

°Celsius
10
5
0
-5
-10
-15
-20
-25

● climate station (average January temperature)

Station values (January temperature map):
-19, -6, -5, 0, -8, -6, -8, -3, -10, -2, -13, -3, 7, 8, 4, 4, 10, 6

Norwegian Current
North Atlantic Drift
Westerlies
Arctic Circle
Prime Meridian

prevailing wind
cold sea current
warm sea current

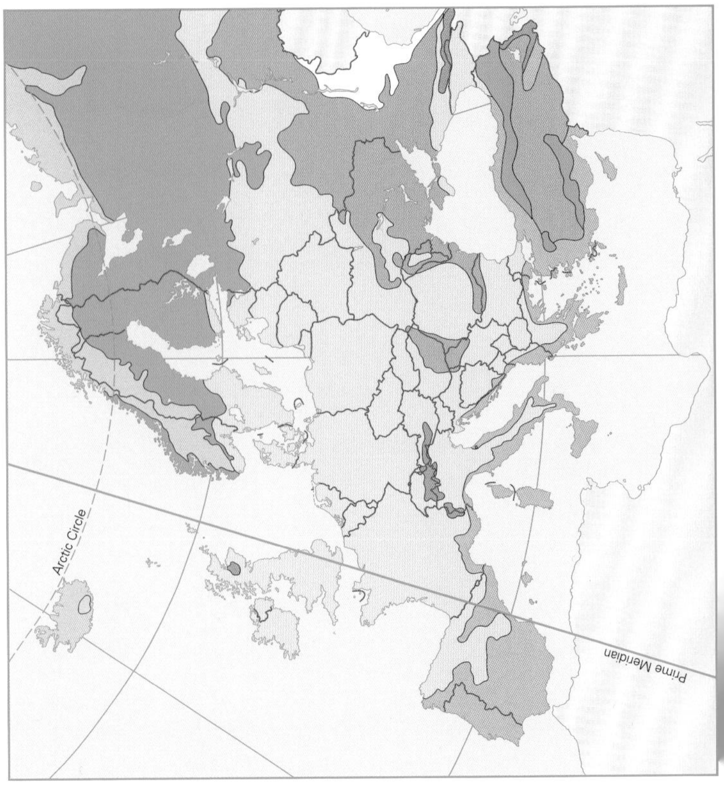

Natural vegetation

the type of vegetation that would occur naturally without interference by people

■ coniferous forest
□ mixed forest
■ evergreens and shrubs
■ temperate grasslands
□ semi-desert
□ tundra
□ ice
■ mountains

Precipitation

average annual precipitation

mm
2000
1000
500
250
0

● climate station (average annual precipitation)

Climate stations (Precipitation map):
Nar'yan Mar 434
Astrakhan 216
Malatya 411
St. Petersburg 635
Rostov-von-Don 569
Warsaw 555
Kiev 649
Stockholm 554
Sonnblick 2671
Patra 678
Prague 527
Split 825
Edinburgh 638
Paris 619
Naples 1007
Barcelona 587
Brest 1109

Scale 1: 35 000 000

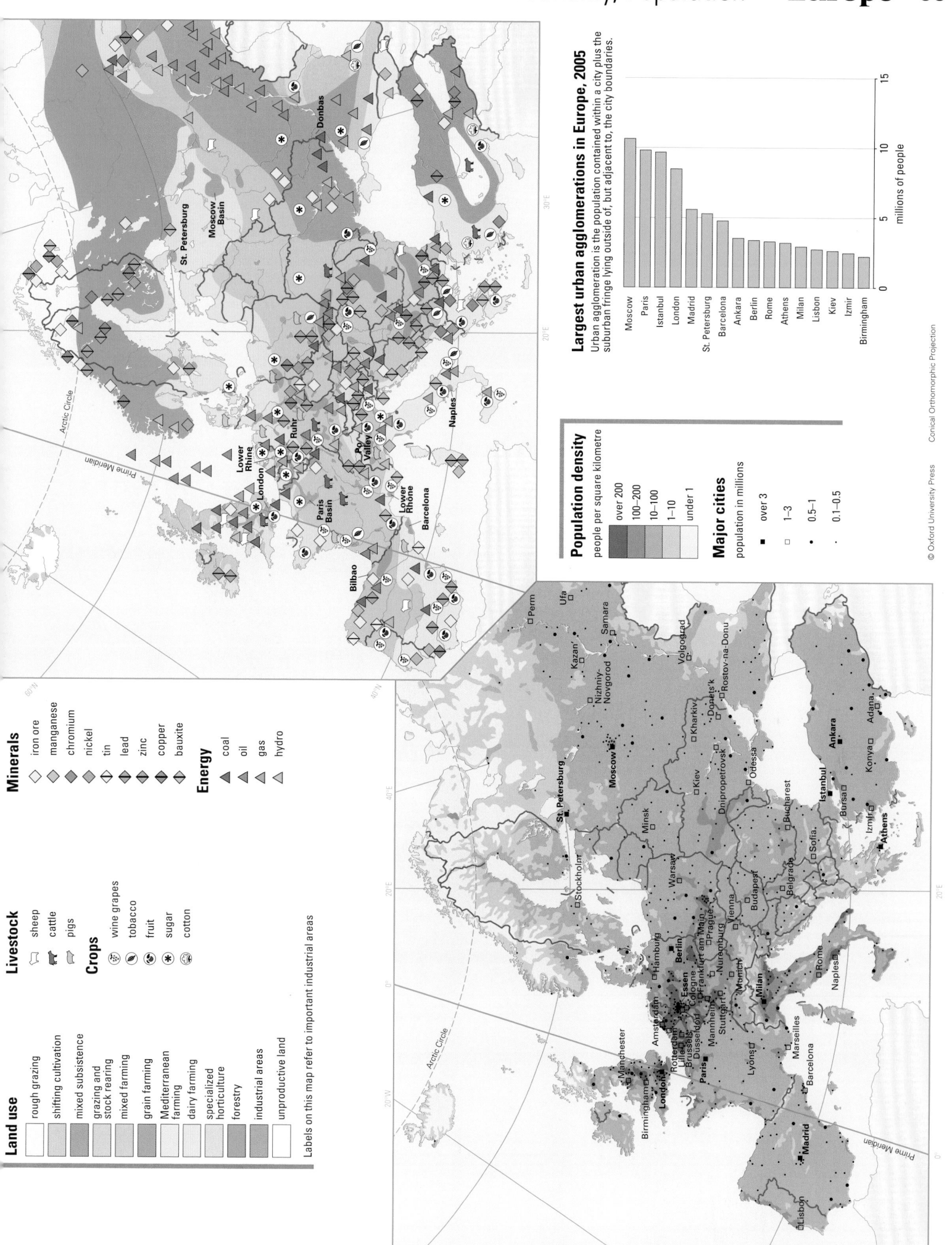

Largest urban agglomerations in Europe, 2005

An urban agglomeration is the population contained within a city plus the population lying outside of, but adjacent to, the city boundaries.

millions of people

Moscow
Paris
Istanbul
London
Madrid
St. Petersburg
Barcelona
Ankara
Berlin
Rome
Athens
Milan
Lisbon
Kiev
Izmir
Birmingham

Population density

people per square kilometre

| over 200 |
| 100–200 |
| 10–100 |
| 1–10 |
| under 1 |

Major cities

population in millions

■ over 3
□ 1–3
● 0.5–1
· 0.1–0.5

© Oxford University Press

Conical Orthomorphic Projection

Land use

| rough grazing |
| shifting cultivation |
| mixed subsistence |
| grazing and stock rearing |
| mixed farming |
| grain farming |
| Mediterranean farming |
| dairy farming |
| specialized horticulture |
| forestry |
| industrial areas |
| unproductive land |

Labels on this map refer to important industrial areas

Livestock

sheep
cattle
pigs

Crops

wine grapes
tobacco
fruit
sugar
cotton

Minerals

iron ore
manganese
chromium
nickel
tin
lead
zinc
copper
bauxite

Energy

coal
oil
gas
hydro

St. Petersburg

Moscow
Basin

Donbas

London
Lower
Rhine
Ruhr
Paris
Basin
Po
Valley
Lower
Rhône
Barcelona
Bilbao
Naples

Arctic Circle
Prime Meridian

Perm
Ufa
Samara
Kazan'
Nizhniy-
Novgorod
Volgograd
St Petersburg
Moscow
Kharkiv
Donets'k
Rostov-na-Donu
Kiev
Dnipropetrovsk
Odessa
Minsk
Bucharest
Warsaw
Stockholm
Sofia
Belgrade
Budapest
Vienna
Prague
Hamburg
Berlin
Frankfurt am Main
Nuremberg
Munich
Milan
Manchester
Amsterdam
Rotterdam
Brussels
Düsseldorf
Essen
Cologne
Mannheim
Stuttgart
Birmingham
London
Paris
Lyons
Marseilles
Barcelona
Rome
Naples
Madrid
Lisbon
Ankara
Adana
Konya
Istanbul
Bursa
Izmir
Athens

Arctic Circle
Prime Meridian

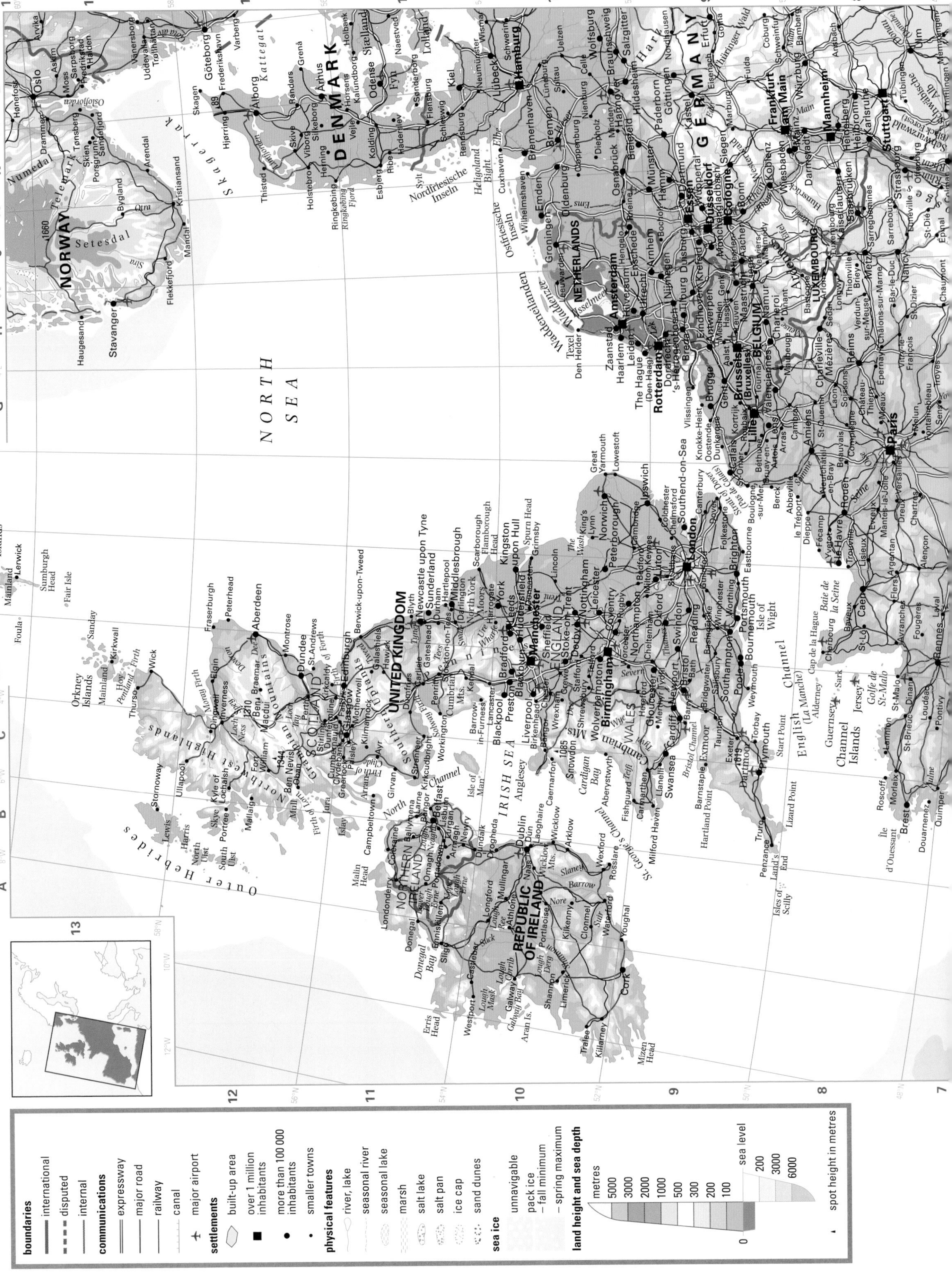

NORWAY

DENMARK

NORTH SEA

NETHERLANDS

GERMANY

BELGIUM

LUXEMBOURG

NORTHERN IRELAND

REPUBLIC OF IRELAND

UNITED KINGDOM

SCOTLAND

WALES

ENGLAND

IRISH SEA

English Channel

Channel Islands

Paris

London

boundaries
— international
— – – disputed
— internal

communications
— expressway
— major road
— railway
— canal
+ major airport

settlements
built-up area
■ over 1 million inhabitants
● more than 100 000 inhabitants
• smaller towns

physical features
river, lake
seasonal river
seasonal lake
marsh
salt lake
salt pan
ice cap
sand dunes

sea ice
unnavigable
pack ice
— fall minimum
— spring maximum

land height and sea depth

metres	
5000	3000
3000	2000
2000	1000
1000	500
500	300
300	200
200	100
sea level	0

sea level
200
3000
6000

▲ spot height in metres

Scale 1:6 750 000

0   67.5   135   202.5   270   337.5 km

Conical Orthomorphic Projection

© Oxford University Press

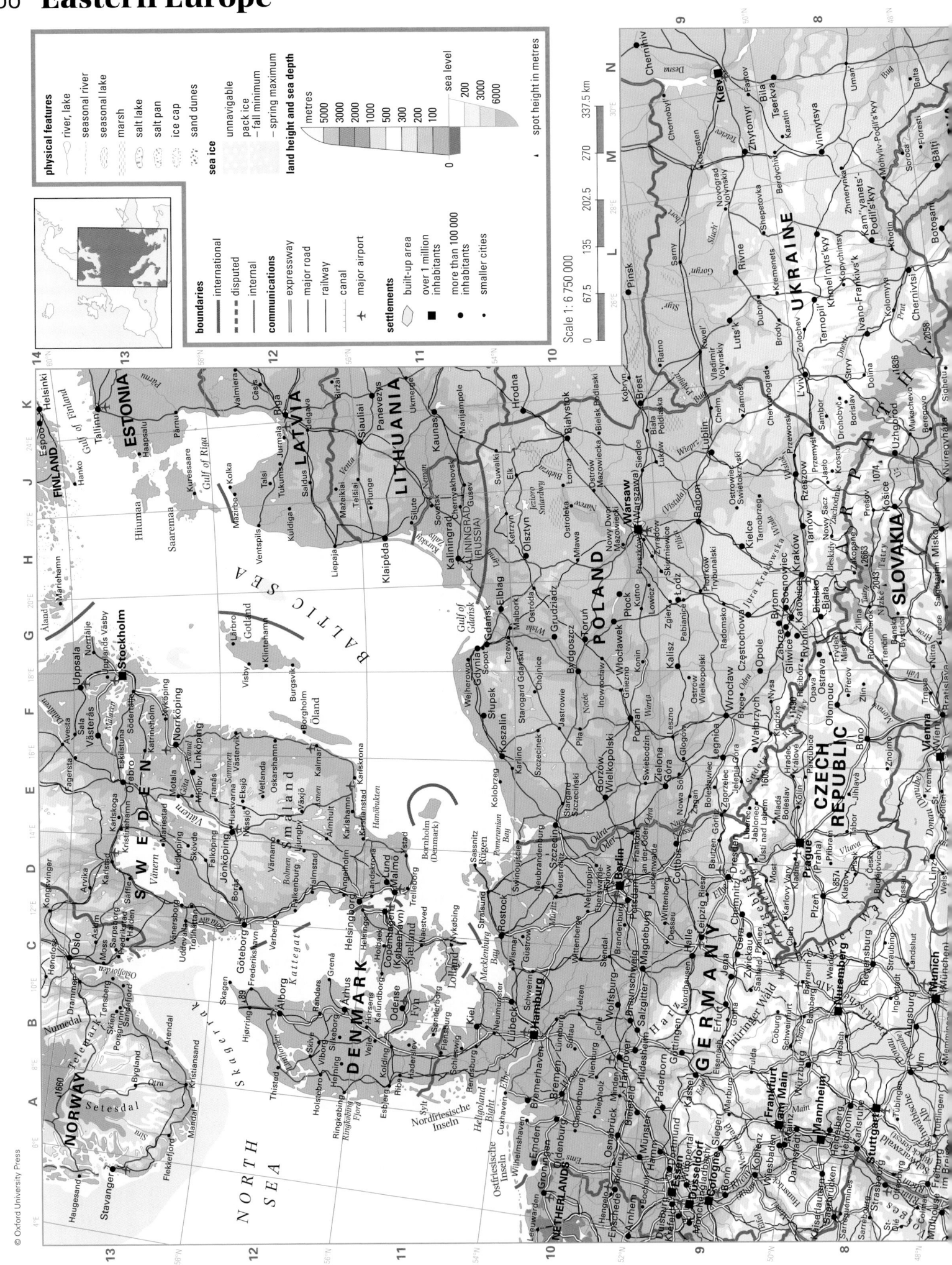

physical features
river, lake
seasonal river
seasonal lake
marsh
salt lake
salt pan
ice cap
sand dunes

sea ice
unnavigable
pack ice
– fall minimum
– spring maximum

land height and sea depth

metres
5000
3000
2000
1000
500
300
200
100
sea level

spot height in metres

metres
200
3000
6000
0

boundaries
international
disputed
internal

communications
expressway
major road
railway
canal
+ major airport

settlements
built-up area
over 1 million inhabitants
more than 100 000 inhabitants
smaller cities

Scale 1: 6 750 000

0   67.5   135   202.5   270   337.5 km

© Oxford University Press

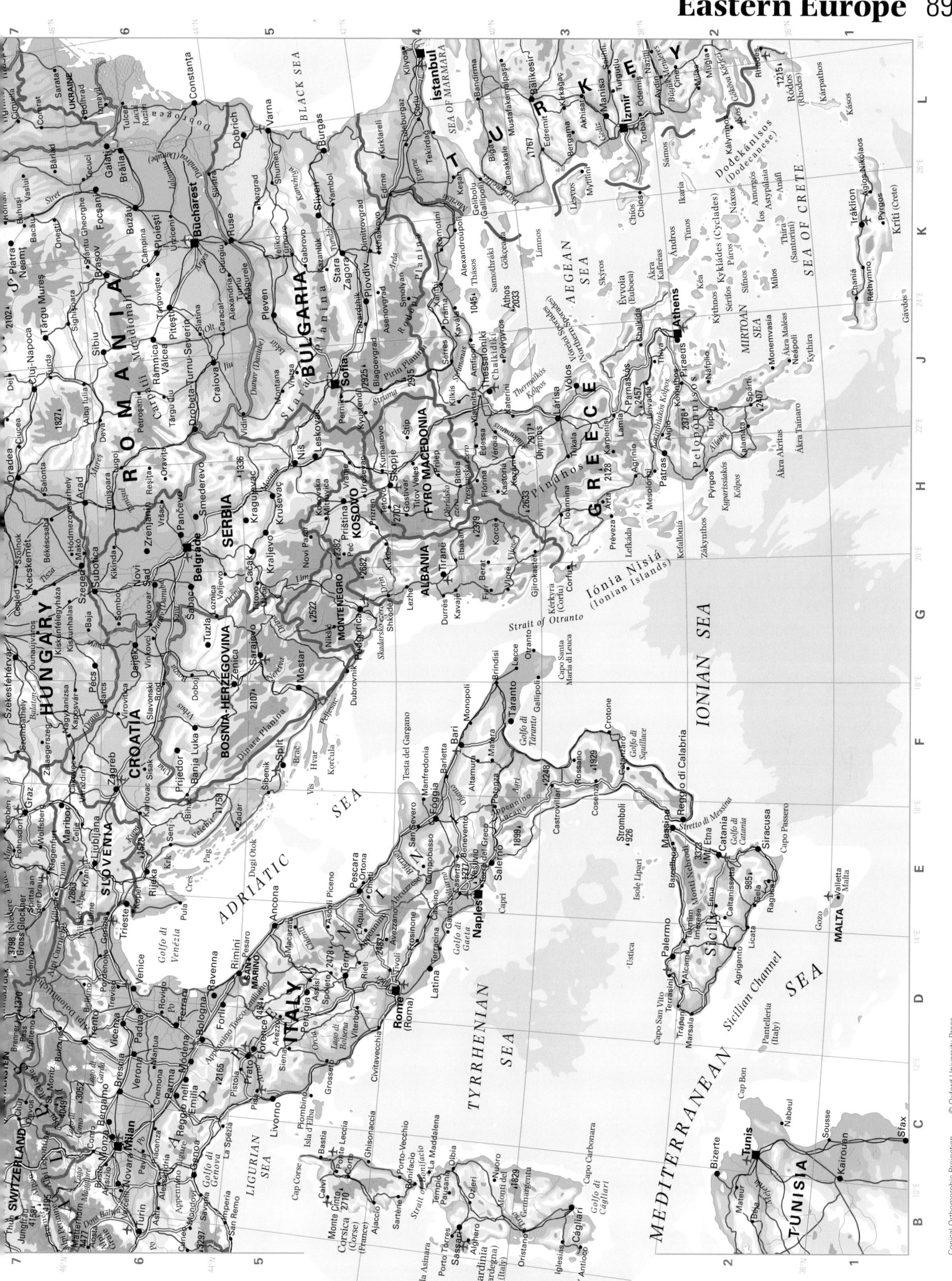

Scale 1 : 60 000 000

ARCTIC OCEAN

North Pole

RUSSIAN FEDERATION (RUSSIA)

Prime Meridian

NORWAY
SWEDEN
FINLAND

UNITED KINGDOM
FRANCE
GERMANY
POLAND
BELARUS
UKRAINE
ITALY
ROMANIA
E U R O P E
GREECE

St. Petersburg

Kaliningrad (part of Russian Federation)

● Nizhniy-Novgorod
■ Moscow
● Perm
● Chelyabinsk
● Omsk
● Novosibirsk

Istanbul
Ankara ■
Izmir
TURKEY
Adana
● Volgograd

GEORGIA
Tbilisi ■
ARMENIA
Yerevan ■
AZERBAIJAN
Baku ■
Tabriz

LEBANON
Aleppo
Beirut ●
SYRIA
Damascus ■
ISRAEL
Jerusalem ■
Amman ■
JORDAN
IRAQ
Baghdad ■

KAZAKHSTAN
■ Astana

UZBEKISTAN
TURKMENISTAN
Tashkent ■
● Almaty
Bishkek ■
KYRGYZSTAN
Ashgabat ■
Dushanbe ■
TAJIKISTAN

Ulan Bator ■
MONGOLIA

● Harbin
● Shenyang

NORTH KOREA
Pyongyang ■
Seoul ■
SOUTH KOREA
● Pusan

Kuril Islands (Russia)
Administered by Russia. Claimed by Japan

● Sapporo

■ Tokyo
Osaka ● JAPAN
Fukuoka

Mashhad ●
Tehran ■
Eşfahān ●
IRAN
Shīrāz ●

Kabul ■
AFGHANISTAN

● Ürümqi

Beijing ■
Tianjin ●

Lanzhou ●
C H I N A
Xi'an ●

● Shanghai
Wuhan ●
Chongqing ●

Tropic of Cancer

Ryukyu Islands (Japan)

KUWAIT
Kuwait ■
Manama ■
BAHRAIN
Riyadh ■
QATAR
Doha ■
SAUDI ARABIA
Abu Dhabi ■
UNITED ARAB EMIRATES
Muscat ■
Jedda ●

Islamabad ■
Jammu & Kashmir
Lahore ●
PAKISTAN
Karachi ●

New Delhi ■
NEPAL
Kathmandu ■
BHUTAN
Thimphu ■

Taibei ■
TAIWAN

Guangzhou ●
Hong Kong ●

PACIFIC OCEAN

EGYPT
Sana ■
YEMEN REPUBLIC
OMAN

Ahmadabad ●
Varanasi ●
Dhaka ■
BANGLADESH
Kolkata ●

SOMALIA
DJIBOUTI

Socotra (Yemen Rep.)

Mumbai ●
I N D I A
Hyderabad ●

MYANMAR
Yangon ■
Hanoi ■
LAOS
Vientiane ■

Manila ■ Quezon City ●
PHILIPPINES

Equator

Lakshadweep (India)

Bangalore ●
Chennai ●

Andaman Islands (India)

THAILAND
Bangkok ■
VIETNAM
CAMBODIA
Phnom Penh ■
Hô Chi Minh ●

MALDIVES
■ Colombo
SRI LANKA
Nicobar Islands (India)

■ Malé

BRUNEI
Bandar Seri Begawan ■

Kuala Lumpur ■
Medan ●
M A L A Y S I A
SINGAPORE ●

I N D O N E S I A

I N D I A N
O C E A N

● Palembang
Jakarta ■
Semarang ●
Surabaya ●
Bandung ●

Ujung Pandang ●
Dili ■
EAST TIMOR

AUSTRALIA
Tropic of Capricorn

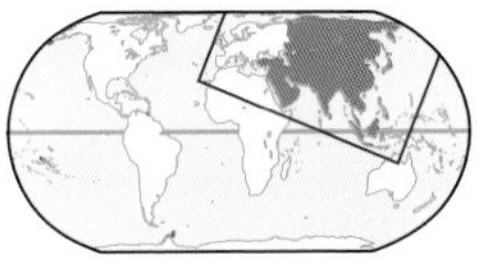

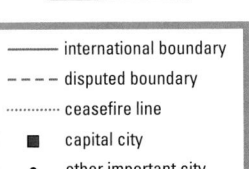

Scale 1 : 55 000 000

0   550   1100   1650   2200   2750 km

—— international boundary
- - - disputed boundary
········· ceasefire line
■ capital city
● other important city

Zenithal Equal Area Projection

© Oxford University Press

North Pole

ARCTIC OCEAN

Ireland

Prime Meridian

Lofoten Islands

Franz Josef Land

Svalbard

BARENTS SEA

Bering Strait

Wrangel

Chukotk Range

Arctic Circle

Koryak Range

BERING SEA

180°

Great Britain

NORTH

Scandinavia

G. of Bothnia

Kola Peninsula

WHITE SEA

Novaya Zemlya

KARA SEA

Severnaya Zemlya

LAPTEV SEA

New Siberian Islands

Kolyma Lowland

Vakhoyansk Range

Cherskiy Range

3147

Kolyma (Gydan) Range

Kamchatka

160°E

BALTIC SEA

North European Plain

Lake Peipus

Lake Ladoga

Lake Onega

Kanin Peninsula

G. of Ob

Taymyr Peninsula

Central Siberian

Lena

SEA OF OKHOSTK

Sakhalin

Kuril Islands

40°N

Hungarian Plain

CARPATHIANS

Central Russian Uplands

Dnepr

Ural Mountains

Ob'

Tobol

Yenisey

Siberian Lowland

Plateau

Stanovoy Range

Amur

Sikhote Alin

Hokkaido

Dniestr

Don

Volga

SEA OF AZOV

BLACK SEA

Caucasus

Mt. Elbrus 5642

Irtysh

Kazakh Upland

Lake Balkhash

Western Sayan

Tannu Ola

Eastern Sayan

Yablonovy Range

Greater Khingan Range

Lake Baykal

SEA OF JAPAN

Honshu

Mt. Fuji 3776

Anatolian Plateau

Toros Dağları

5123 Mt. Ararat

Lake Urmia

Caspian Sea

Aral Sea

Syr Darya

Kyzyl Kum

Altai Mountains

Gobi Desert

Bo Hai

Shandong Peninsula

YELLOW SEA

Shikoku

Kyushu

CYPRUS

Zagros Mts.

Mesopotamia

Elburz Mts.

Dasht-e Kavir

Kara Bogaz Gol

Karakum

Ust Urt Plateau

Amu Darya

Tian Shan

Dzungarian Basin

Turfan Depression 154

Ala Shan

Qilian Shan

Nan Shan

Ryukyu Islands

EAST CHINA SEA

Dead Sea

Syrian Desert

An Nafud

Dasht-e Lut

Qullai Ismoili Somoni

Pamirs

Tarim Basin

Altun Shan

Qaidam Basin

Amne Machin Shan

Bayan Har Shan

Xiqing Shan

Sichuan Basin

Chang Jiang (Yangtze)

Poyang Hu

Dongting Hu

Wuyi Shan

Taiwan Strait

Hindu Kush

6611

Karakoram

K2

Ladakh Ra.

Gandise Shan

Plateau of Tibet

Nyainqentanglha Shan

Mt. Everest 8848

Nan Ling

Taiwan

PACIFIC

Red Sea

Arabian Peninsula

Persian Gulf

Str. of Hormuz

Gulf of Oman

Indus

Thar Desert

Himalaya

Ganga

Brahmaputra

Irrawaddy

Gulf of Tongking

Leizhou Peninsula

OCEAN

140°E

20°N

Rub' al Khāli

Rann of Kachchh

Satpura Ra.

Mouths of the Ganga

Hainan

SOUTH CHINA SEA

Luzon

PHILIPPINE SEA

Tropic of Cancer

Asir Mountains

Hadhramaut

Gulf of Aden

Socotra

ARABIAN SEA

Western Ghats

Malabar

Deccan

Eastern Ghats

Coromandel Coast

Bay of Bengal

ANDAMAN SEA

Andaman Islands

Tonle Sap

Gulf of Thailand

Annam Range

Mekong

Mindoro

Panay

Negros

Palawan

SULU SEA

Mindanao

Samar

Equator

Cape Comorin

2518 Pidurutalagala

Nicobar Islands

Isthmus of Kra

Malay Peninsula

4094 Kinabalu

CELEBES SEA

Halmahera

INDIAN

Mentawai Islands

Strait of Malacca

Sumatra

3805

Borneo

Sulawesi

Seram

New Guinea

OCEAN

JAVA SEA

BANDA SEA

ARAFURA SEA

Java

Bali

Lesser Sunda Islands

Flores

Timor

TIMOR SEA

Arnhem Land

Scale 1: 55 000 000

0   550   1100   1650   2200   2750 km

January temperature

actual surface temperature

°Celsius
25
20
15
10
5
0
−10
−20
−30
−40
−50

● climate station (average January temperature)

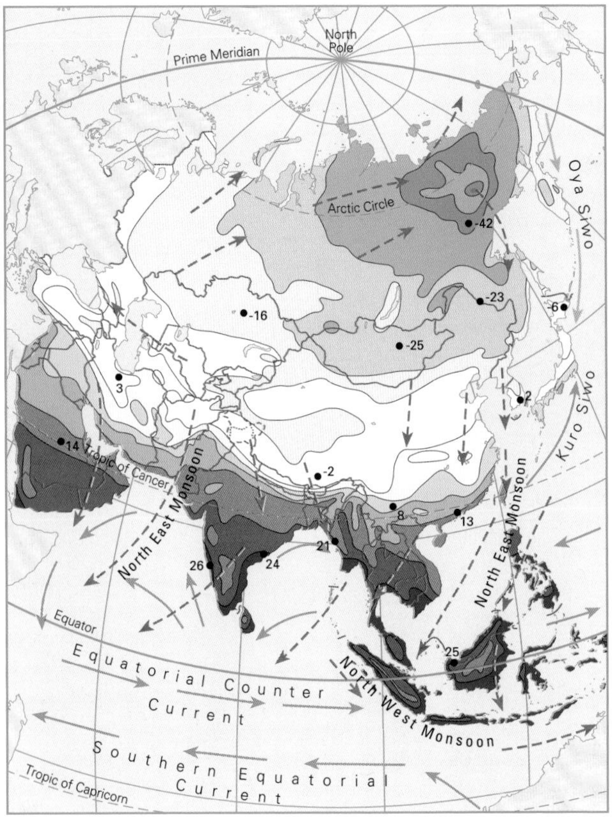

Prime Meridian
North Pole
Arctic Circle
Oya Siwo
Kuro Siwo
Tropic of Cancer
North East Monsoon
North West Monsoon
Equator
Equatorial Counter Current
Southern Equatorial Current
Tropic of Capricorn

−42
−23
−6
−16
−25
3
2
−2
−14
8
13
26
24
21
25

→ warm sea current → cold sea current - -→ prevailing wind

July temperature

actual surface temperature

°Celsius
35
30
25
20
15
10
5
0

● climate station (average July temperature)

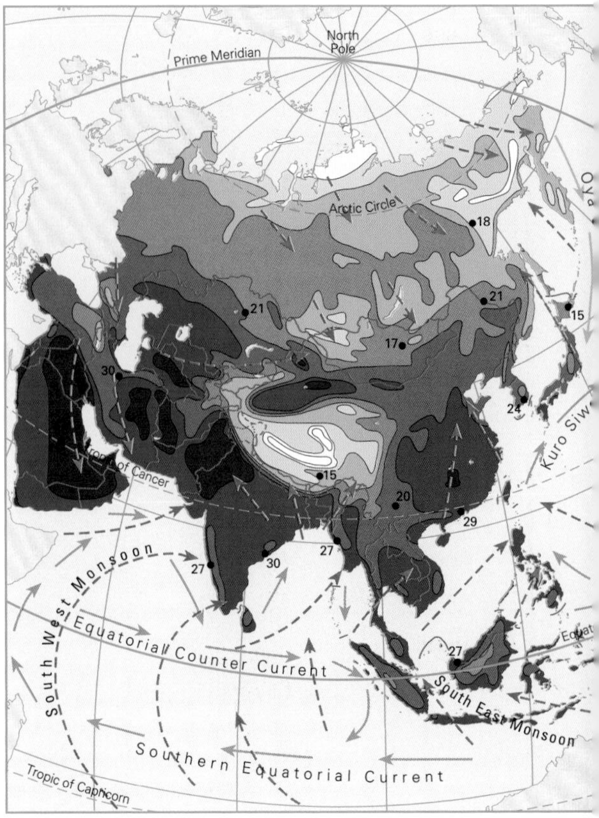

Prime Meridian
North Pole
Arctic Circle
Oya
Kuro Siwo
Tropic of Cancer
South West Monsoon
Equatorial Counter Current
South East Monsoon
Southern Equatorial Current
Tropic of Capricorn
Equator

18
21
21
15
17
30
15
20
27
29
27
30
27

→ warm sea current → cold sea current - -→ prevailing wind

Precipitation

average annual precipitation

mm
3000
2000
1000
500
250
0

● climate station (average annual precipitation)

Prime Meridian
North Pole
Arctic Circle
Tropic of Cancer
Equator
Tropic of Capricorn

Ust' Maya 313
Blagoveshchensk 575
Kushiro 1044
Astana 318
Ulan Bator 217
Pusan 1474
Tehran 230
Riyadh 101
Lhasa 421
Kunming 1008
Guangzhou 1683
Sittwe 4555
Goa 2813
Vishakhapatnam 955
Kuching 4155

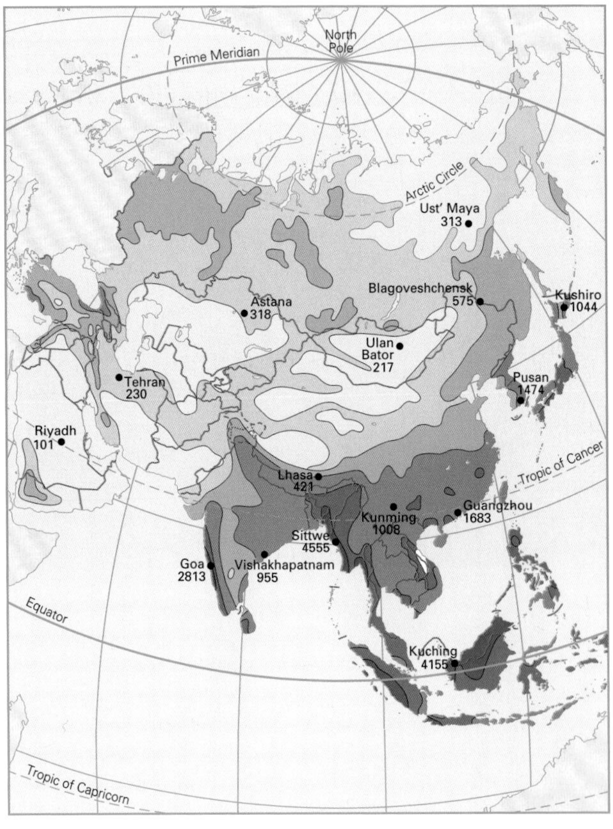

Natural vegetation

the type of vegetation that would occur naturally without interference by people

coniferous forest
mixed forest
tropical rain forest
evergreens and shrubs
thorn forest
temperate grasslands
semi-desert
desert
tundra
mountains

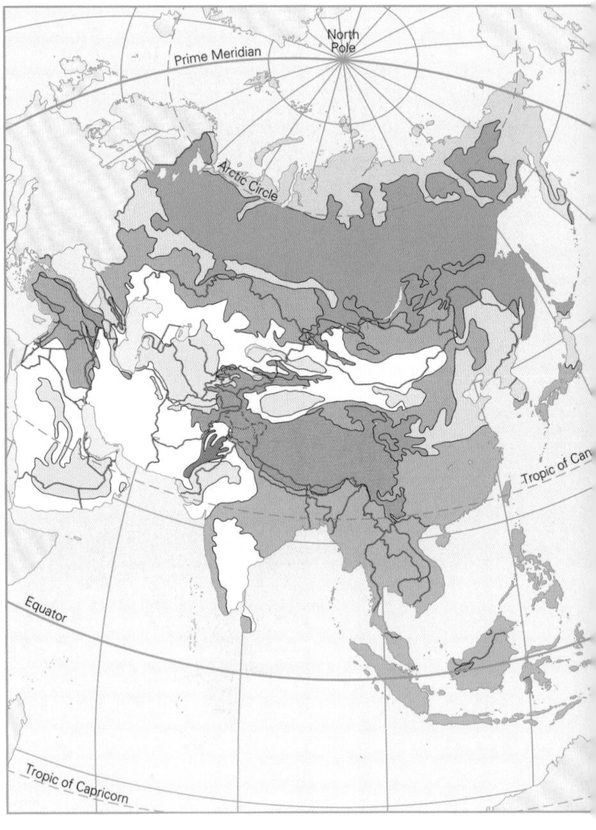

Prime Meridian
North Pole
Arctic Circle
Tropic of Cancer
Equator
Tropic of Capricorn

Scale 1: 75 000 000

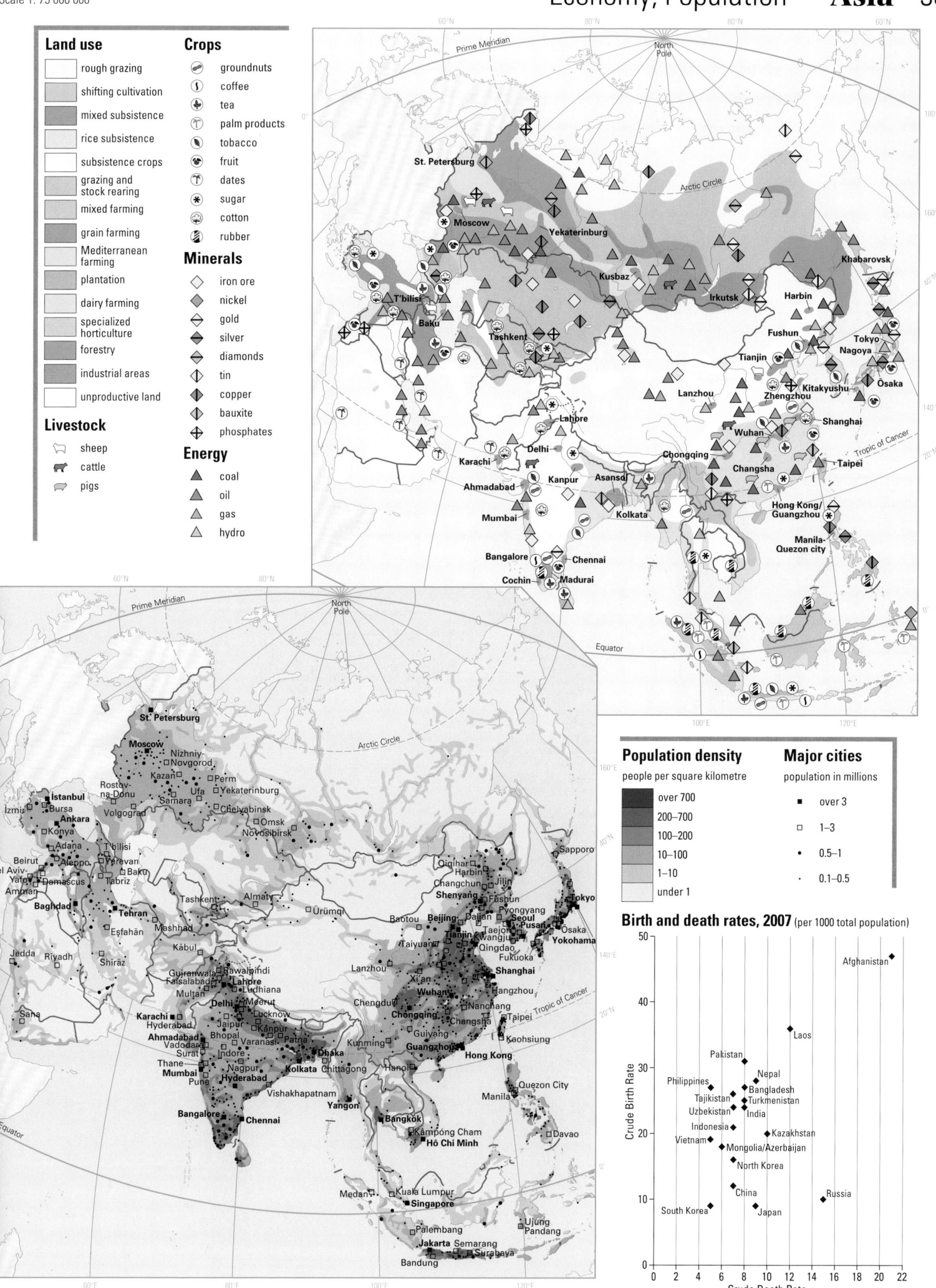

Land use

rough grazing
shifting cultivation
mixed subsistence
rice subsistence
subsistence crops
grazing and stock rearing
mixed farming
grain farming
Mediterranean farming
plantation
dairy farming
specialized horticulture
forestry
industrial areas
unproductive land

Livestock

sheep
cattle
pigs

Crops

groundnuts
coffee
tea
palm products
tobacco
fruit
dates
sugar
cotton
rubber

Minerals

iron ore
nickel
gold
silver
diamonds
tin
copper
bauxite
phosphates

Energy

coal
oil
gas
hydro

Population density

people per square kilometre

over 700
200–700
100–200
10–100
1–10
under 1

Major cities

population in millions

■ over 3
□ 1–3
• 0.5–1
· 0.1–0.5

Birth and death rates, 2007 (per 1000 total population)

Crude Birth Rate / Crude Death Rate

Afghanistan
Laos
Pakistan
Nepal
Philippines
Bangladesh
Tajikistan Turkmenistan
Uzbekistan India
Indonesia Kazakhstan
Vietnam Mongolia/Azerbaijan
North Korea
China Russia
South Korea Japan

Zenithal Equal Area Projection

© Oxford University Press

boundaries

- ═══ international
- ┅┅┅ disputed
- •••••• line of control
- ─── internal

communications

- ═══ expressway
- ─── major road
- ─── railway
- ┼┼┼┼ canal
- ✈ major airport

settlements

- ■ over 1 million inhabitants
- ● more than 100 000 inhabitants
- • smaller towns

physical features

- river, lake
- seasonal river
- seasonal lake
- marsh
- salt lake
- salt pan
- ice cap
- sand dunes

sea ice

- unnavigable
- pack ice
  – fall minimum
  – spring maximum

land height and sea depth

metres
5000
3000
2000
1000
500
300
200
100
0 sea level
200
3000
6000

▲ spot height in metres

Scale 1: 25 000 000

0 250 500 750 1000 1250 km

Conical Orthomorphic Projection

© Oxford University Press

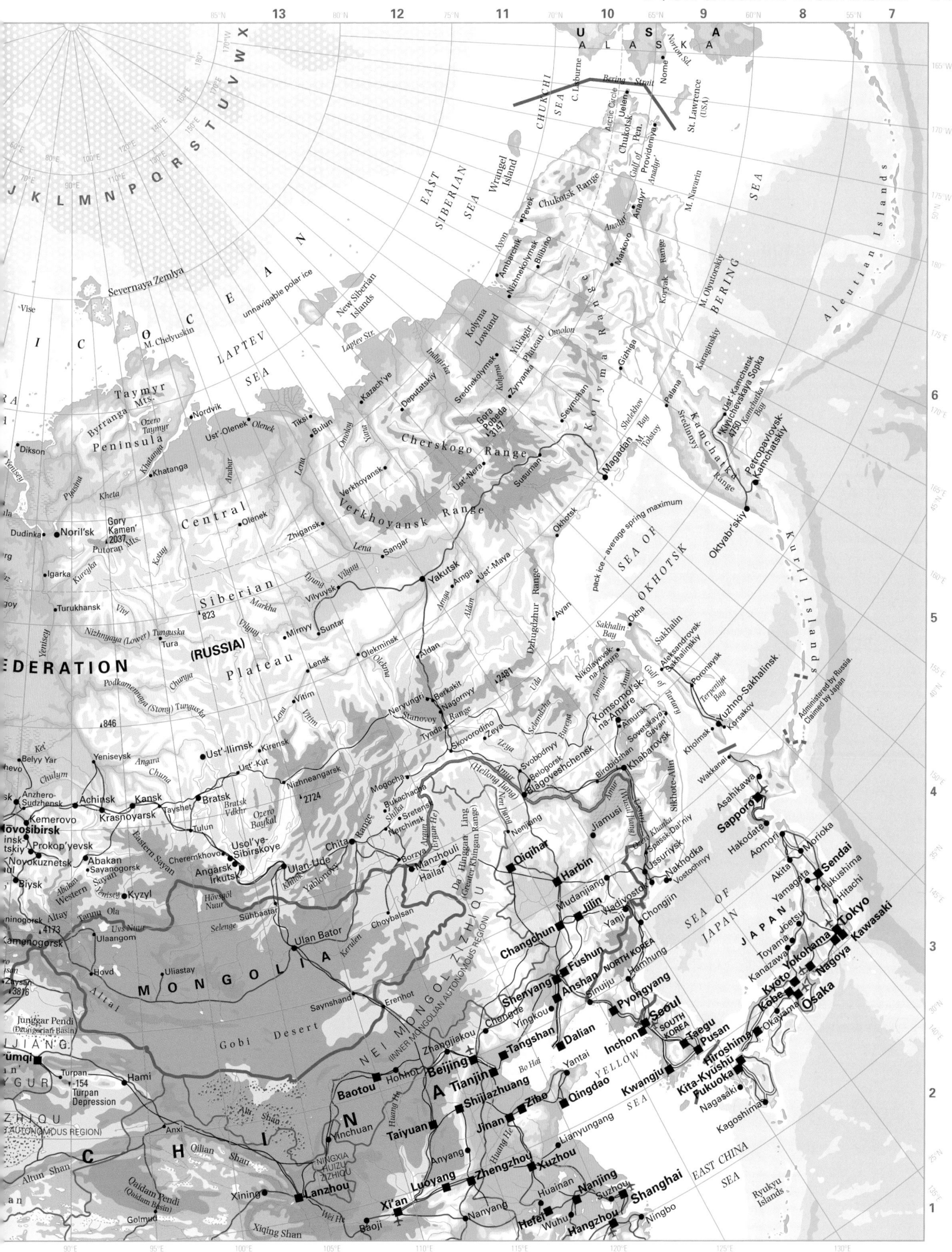

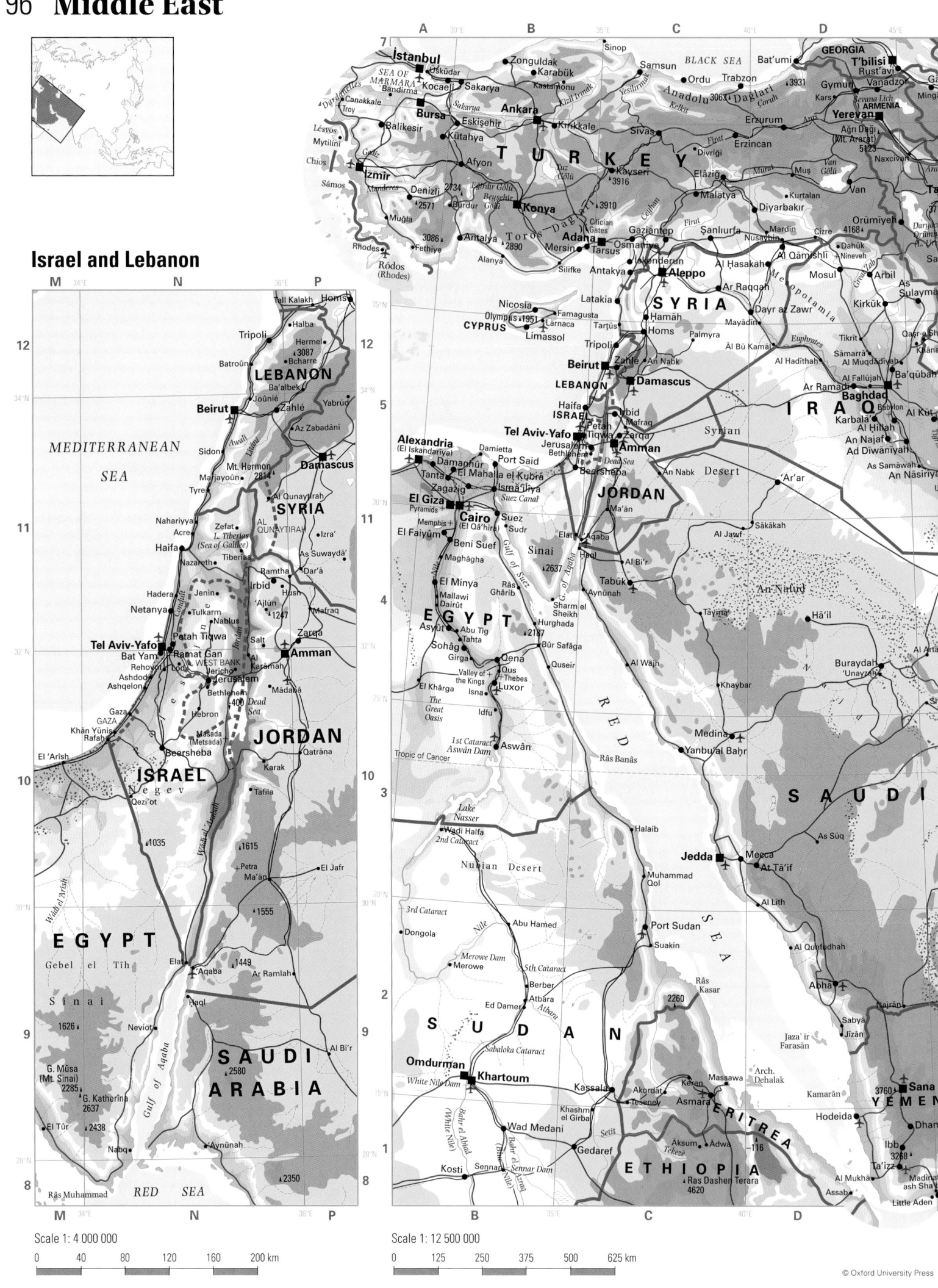

Israel and Lebanon

Scale 1 : 4 000 000

| 0 | 40 | 80 | 120 | 160 | 200 km |

Scale 1 : 12 500 000

| 0 | 125 | 250 | 375 | 500 | 625 km |

© Oxford University Press

Map labels

Caspian Sea
Zaliv Kara-Bogaz Gol
Sumqayıt
Baku
RBAIJAN
Länkäran
Astara
Ardabil
Rasht
Zanjan
Qazvin
Karaj
Tehran
Damavand
Damavand 5671
Elburz Mountains
Semnān
Qom
Hamadān
Arāk
Qom
Kāshān
Khorramābād
Esfahān
Qomisheh
Dezful 4548
Ahvāz
Yazd
Bāfq
Khorramshahr
Bandar Khomeyni
Shirāz
Kāzerūn
Zarand
Kermān
Rafsanjān
Neyriz
Kuwait
Al Fuhayhil
KUWAIT
Khārg
Būshehr
Jahrom
Lār
Kangan
Persian Gulf
Al Jubayl
Ad Dammam
Dhahran
BAHRAIN
Manama
QATAR
Al Mubarraz
Al Hufūf
Doha
RIYADH
Abu Dhabi
UNITED ARAB EMIRATES
Al Buraymi
Al Ayn
Sharjah
Ajman
Dubai
Ra's al Khaymah
Bandar-e Lengeh
Bandar-e 'Abbās
Str. of Hormuz
OMAN
Jāsk
Ibri
Nazwā
Jabal Akhdar 3018
Matrah
Muscat
Sūr
Ra's al Hadd
ARABIA
Rub' Al Khali
Umm as Samim
OMAN
Ra's Madrakah
Kuria Muria Is.
Salalah
Hadhramaut
Say'ūn
W. al Masilah
Ra's Fartak
EPUBLIC
2112
Habbān
Mukalla
Gulf of Aden
Hadiboh
Socotra (Yemen)
'Abd al Kūri
Gulf of Oman
ARABIAN SEA
Tropic of Cancer

TURKMENISTAN
Nebitdag
Krasnovodsk
Gyzylarbat
Ashgabat
Atrek
Bandar-e Torkeman
Gorgān
Sabzevār
Neyshābūr
Mashhad
3147
Sarakhs
Tedzhen
Mary
Kerki
Chärdzhev
UZBEKISTAN
Bukhara
Kattakurgan
Samarkand
Navoi
Kagan
Karshi
Termez
Amudar'ya (Oxus)
TAJIKISTAN
Dushanbe
Vakhsh
Khorog
Pamirs
CHINA
K2 8611
JAMMU AND KASHMIR
Gilgit
Indus
8126
Chitral
Dir
7690
Chaghcharān
Herāt
Hari Rud
Gushgy
Bālā Morghāb
Meymaneh
Sar-e Pol
Sheberghān
Andkhvoy
Mazār-e Sharīf
Khānābād
Kondūz
Baghlān
Feyzābād
AFGHANISTAN
5143
Kābul
Kabul
Charikar
Jalālabād
Khyber Pass
Peshawar
Mardan
Wah
Islamabad
Rawalpindi
Jhelum
Gujrat
Gujranwala
Sialkot
Jammu
Srinagar
Ghazni
Gardēz
Kohat
Bannu
Miram Shah
Dera Ismail Khan
Mianwali
Sargodha
Faisalabad
Lahore
Amritsar
Kasur
Okara
PUNJAB
Koh-i-Mazar 3788
Shindan
Farah Rud
Farāh
Khash
Dasht-i-Margo
Zābol
Helmand
Dōri
Kandahār
Qila Saifullah
Zargun 3578
Quetta 2641
Chaman
Zhob
Jhang Maghiana
Sahiwal
Multan
Bahawalpur
Gangānagar
Registan
Nushki
Sibi
Jacobabad
Shikarpur
Sukkur
Khairpur
Rahimyar Khan
Bikaner
Dasht-e Lut
Tabas
Birjand
Zāhedān
Bam
4420
Khāsh
Saravan
Irānshahr
Chāgai Hills
Dalbandin
Kharan
Kalat
Bela
Balūchistan
2293
Larkana
Sind
Jaisalmer
Jodhpur
RAJASTHAN
Thar Desert
Makrān
Kech
Chāh Bahār
Mouths of the Indus
Karachi
Hab
Kotri
Mirpur Khas
Hyderabad
Rann of Kachchh
GUJARAT
Bhuj
Kandla
Jamnagar
Morbi
Rajkot
Bhavnagar
Porbandar
Kathiawar
Veraval
Diu
G. of Kachchh
Patan

Legend

boundaries
— international
--- disputed
···· line of control
— internal

communications
expressway
major road
railway
canal
✈ major airport

settlements
built-up area
■ over 1 million inhabitants
● more than 100 000 inhabitants
• smaller towns

physical features
river, lake
seasonal river
seasonal lake
marsh
salt lake
salt pan
ice cap
sand dunes

sea ice
unnavigable
pack ice
 – fall minimum
 – spring maximum

land height and sea depth
metres
5000
3000
2000
1000
500
300
200
100
0 sea level
200
3000
6000
sea level
▴ spot height in metres

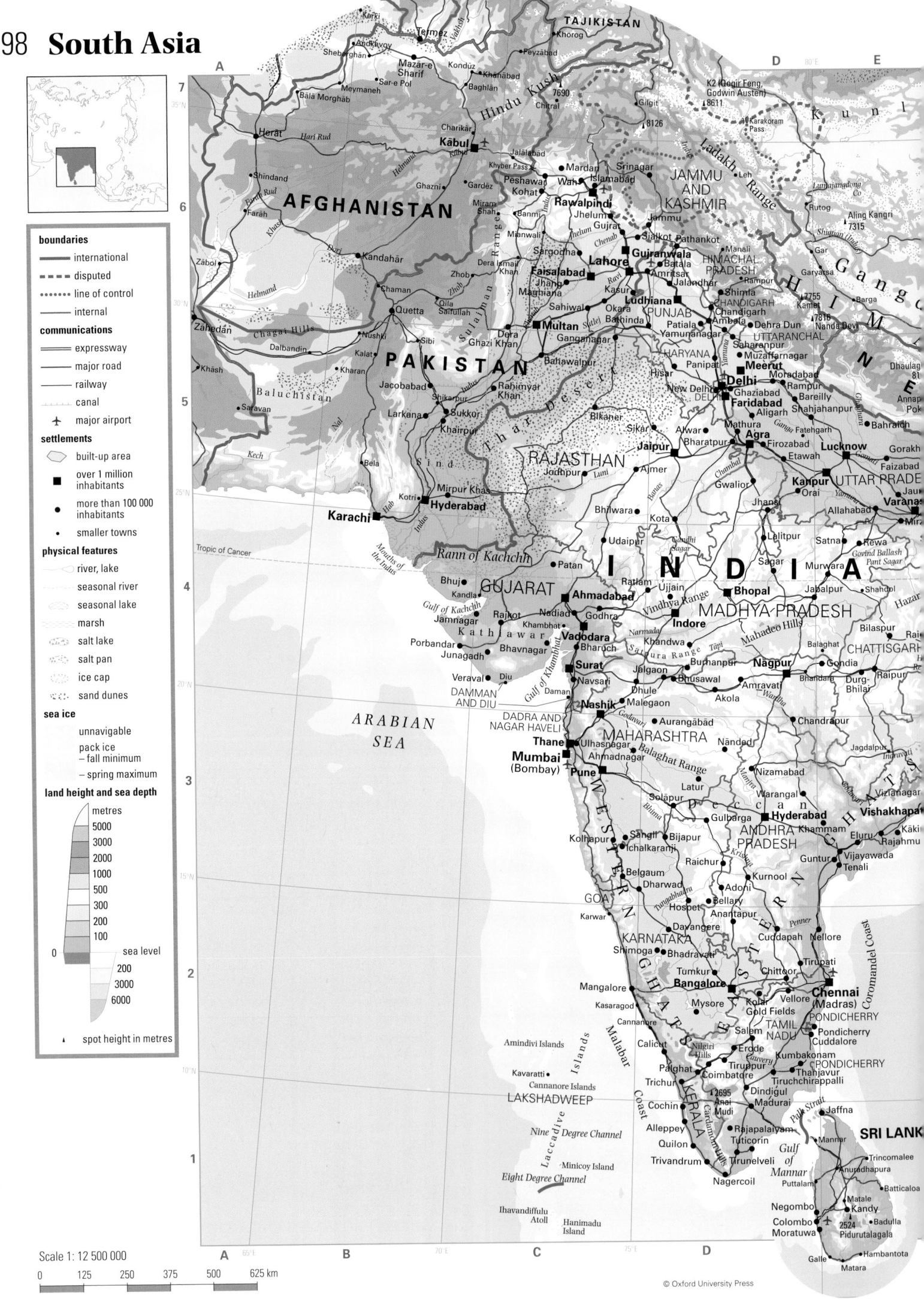

boundaries
———— international
------ disputed
·········· line of control
——— internal
communications
===== expressway
——— major road
——— railway
+++++ canal
✈ major airport
settlements
⬡ built-up area
■ over 1 million inhabitants
● more than 100 000 inhabitants
· smaller towns
physical features
river, lake
seasonal river
seasonal lake
marsh
salt lake
salt pan
ice cap
sand dunes
sea ice
unnavigable
pack ice
– fall minimum
– spring maximum
land height and sea depth
metres
5000
3000
2000
1000
500
300
200
100
0 sea level
200
3000
6000
▲ spot height in metres

Scale 1: 12 500 000

0   125   250   375   500   625 km

© Oxford University Press

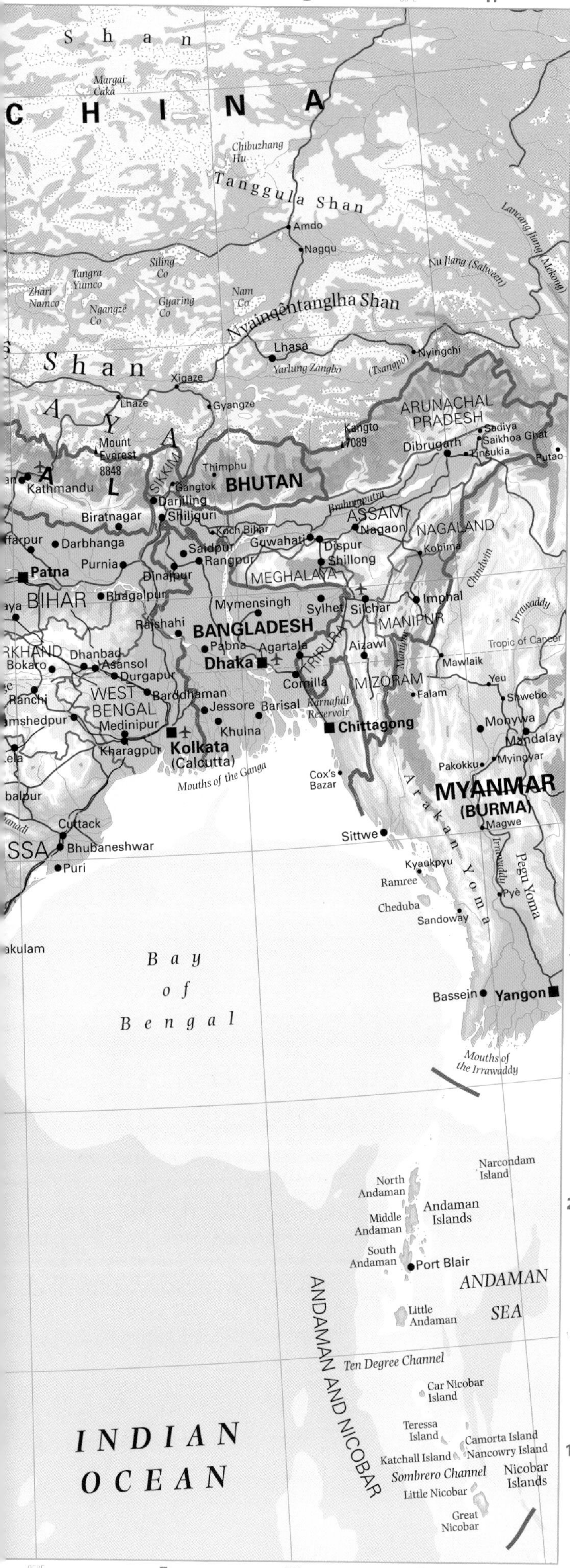

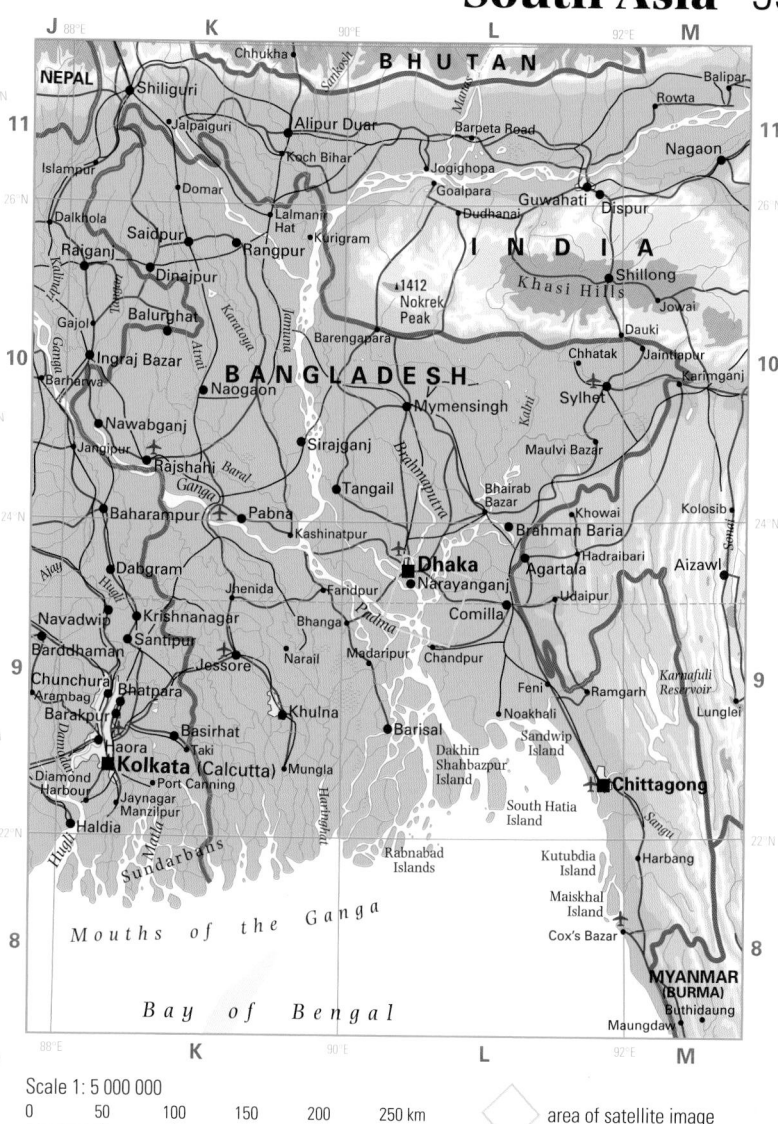

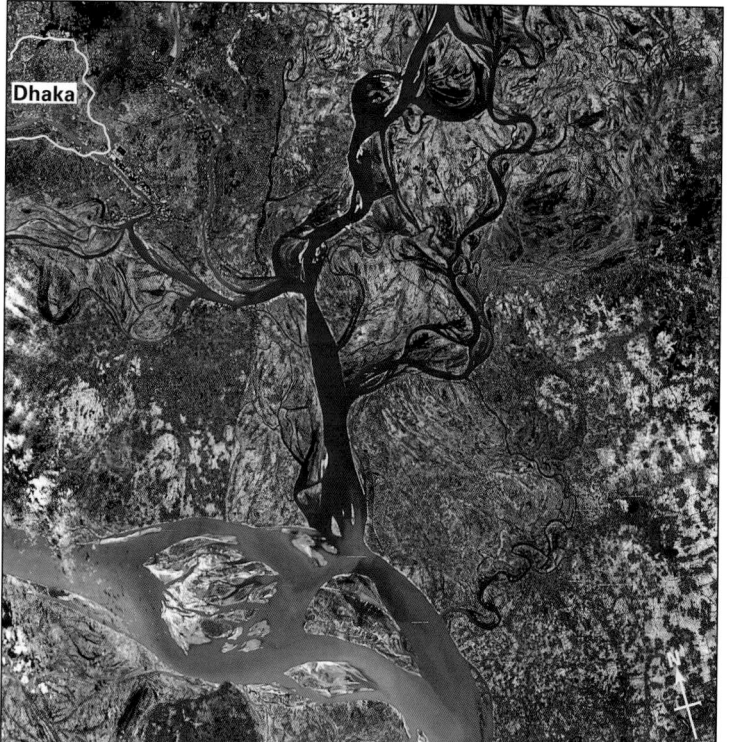

Ganges Delta, Bangladesh

In this false colour image, vegetation is red, and water is dark blue but paler where rich in silt.

Scale 1 : 5 000 000

0   50   100   150   200   250 km

◇ area of satellite image

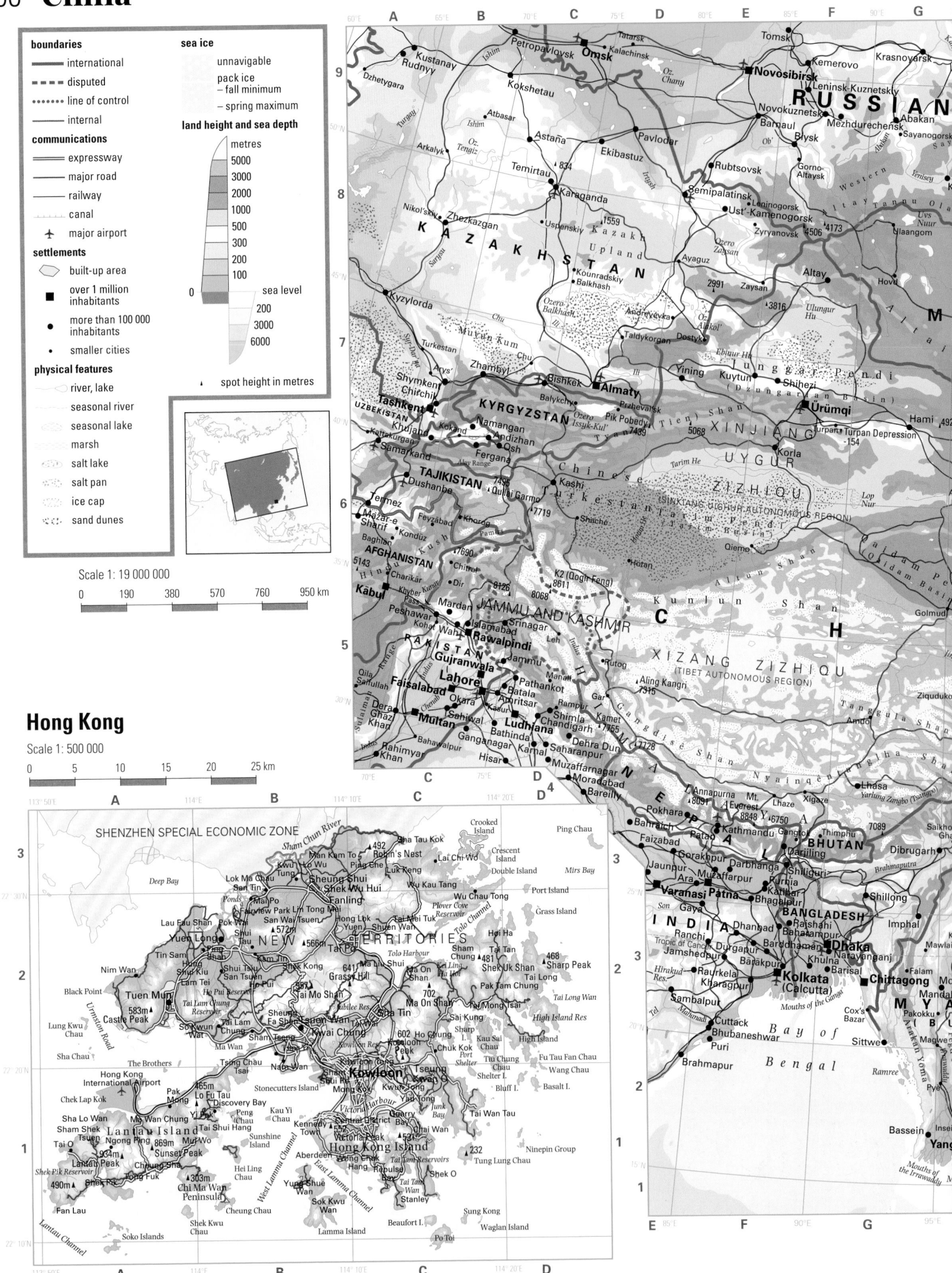

Hong Kong

Scale 1: 500 000

0 5 10 15 20 25 km

Gauss Conformal Projection

© Oxford University Press

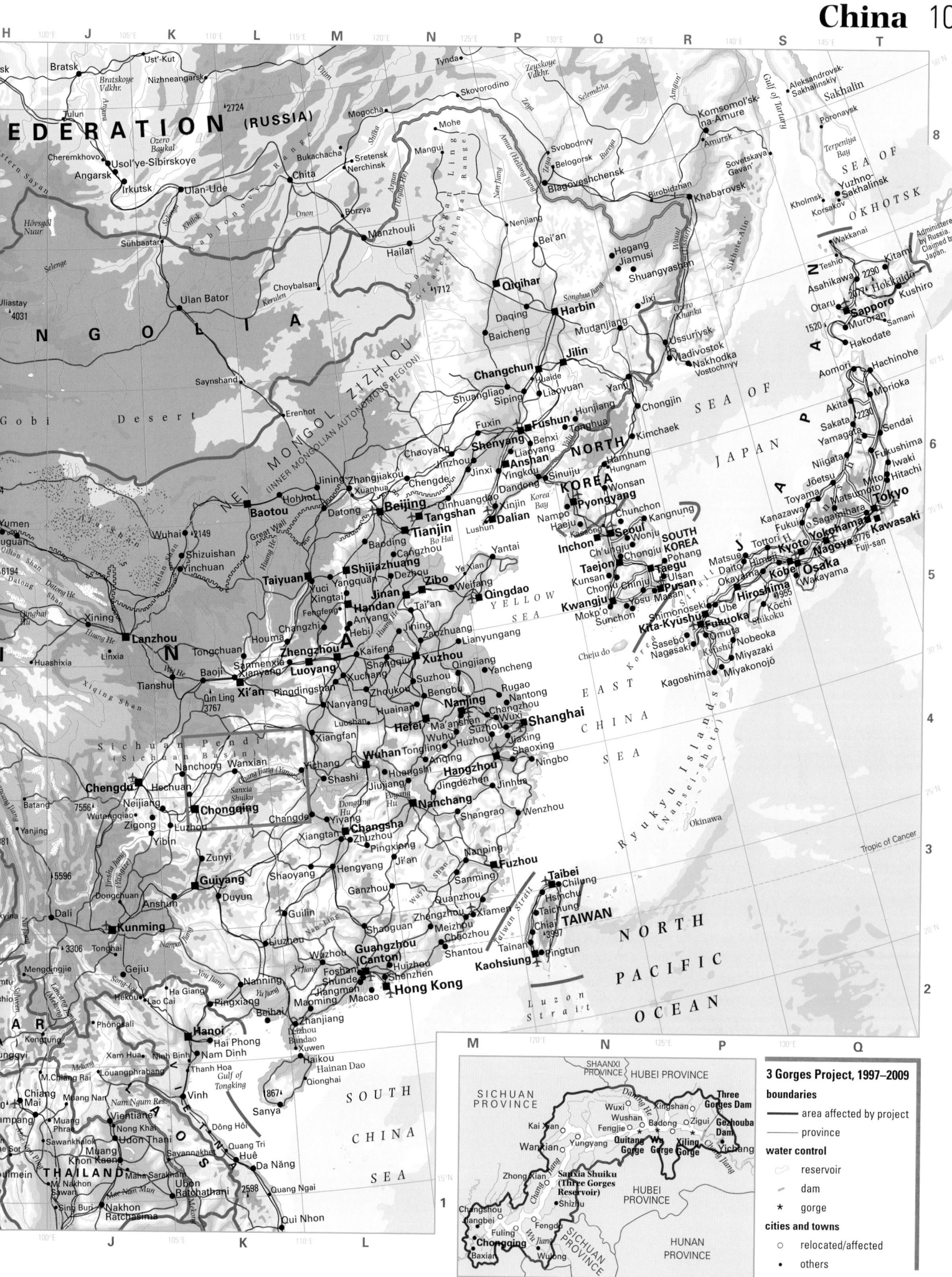

3 Gorges Project, 1997–2009

boundaries

━━━ area affected by project

─── province

water control

reservoir

dam

★ gorge

cities and towns

○ relocated/affected

• others

SHAANXI PROVINCE

HUBEI PROVINCE

SICHUAN PROVINCE

Wuxi

Xingshan

Three Gorges Dam

Kai Xian

Wushan

Badong

Zigui

Fengjie

Gezhouba Dam

Wanxian

Yungyang

Qutang Gorge · **Wu Gorge** · **Xiling Gorge**

Yichang

Zhong Xian

Sanxia Shuiku (Three Gorges Reservoir)

Shizhu

HUBEI PROVINCE

Changshou

Fengdu

Changbei

Chongqing

Fuling

Wu Jiang

HUNAN PROVINCE

Baxian

Wulong

SICHUAN PROVINCE

© Oxford University Press   Conical Orthomorphic Projection

Scale 1: 8 000 000   Conic Projection

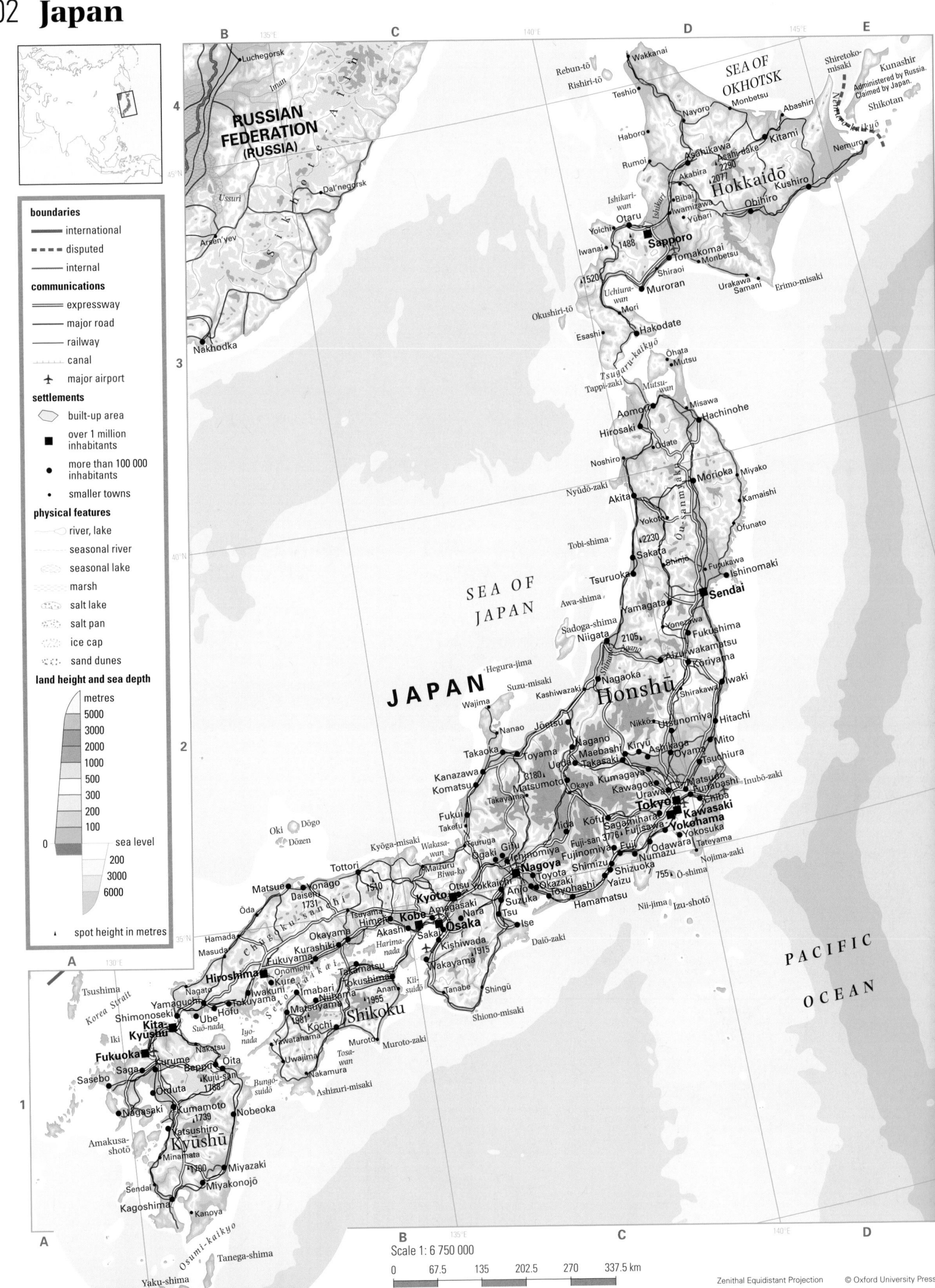

boundaries
━━━ international
╌╌╌ disputed
─── internal
communications
═══ expressway
─── major road
─── railway
┽┽┽ canal
✈ major airport
settlements
⬡ built-up area
■ over 1 million inhabitants
● more than 100 000 inhabitants
• smaller towns
physical features
river, lake
seasonal river
seasonal lake
marsh
salt lake
salt pan
ice cap
sand dunes
land height and sea depth

metres
5000
3000
2000
1000
500
300
200
100
sea level
200
3000
6000

▲ spot height in metres

RUSSIAN
FEDERATION
(RUSSIA)

Luchegorsk
Iman
Ussuri
Dal'negorsk
Arsen'yev
Nakhodka

SEA OF
OKHOTSK

Shiretoko-misaki
Kunashir
Administered by Russia.
Claimed by Japan.
Shikotan
Nemuro-kaikyō

Rebun-tō
Rishiri-tō
Wakkanai
Teshio
Nayoro
Monbetsu
Abashiri
Haboro
Asahikawa
Kitami
Rumoi
Akabira
Asahi-dake 2290
Hokkaidō
2077
Bibai
Iwamizawa
Kushiro
Ishikari-wan
Yūbari
Obihiro
Yoichi
Otaru
Sapporo
1488
Tomakomai
Iwanai
1520
Shiraoi
Monbetsu
Uchiura-wan
Muroran
Urakawa
Samani
Erimo-misaki
Okushiri-tō
Mori
Esashi
Hakodate
Tsugaru-kaikyō
Ōhata
Mutsu
Tappi-zaki
Mutsu-wan
Aomori
Misawa
Hachinohe
Hirosaki
Ōdate
Noshiro
Morioka
Miyako
Nyūdō-zaki
Ou-sanmyaku
Kamaishi
Akita
Yokote
2230
Ofunato
Tobi-shima
Sakata
Shinjō
Ishinomaki
Tsuruoka
Yamagata
Sendai
Awa-shima
Yonezawa
Fukushima
Sadoga-shima
2105
Aizu-wakamatsu
Kōriyama
Niigata
Agano
Nagaoka
Iwaki
Shirakawa
Honshū
Kashiwazaki
Nikkō
Utsunomiya
Hitachi
Jōetsu
Nagano
Maebashi
Kiryū
Ashikaga
Mito
Takaoka
Toyama
Takasaki
Oyama
Tsuchiura
Kanazawa
Ueda
Kumagaya
Matsudo
Komatsu
Matsumoto
Kawagoe
Funabashi
3180
Okaya
Urawa
Chiba
Fukui
Takayama
Iida
Tokyo
Takefu
Gifu
Kōfu
Kawasaki
Tsuruga
Ōgaki
Sagamihara
Yokohama
Ichinomiya
Fuji-san 3776
Fujinomiya
Yokosuka
Ichinomiya
Nagoya
Fuji
Odawara
Tateyama
Ōtsu
Yokkaichi
Shimizu
Numazu
Nojima-zaki
Kyoto
Toyota
Okazaki
Shizuoka
Kōbe
Amagasaki
Nara
Suzuka
Toyohashi
Yaizu
755
Ō-shima
Himeji
Akashi
Sakai
Osaka
Tsu
Hamamatsu
Nii-jima
Izu-shotō
Kishiwada
Ise
Daiō-zaki
Wakayama
1915

SEA OF
JAPAN

JAPAN

Heguri-jima
Suzu-misaki
Wajima
Nanao

Oki
Dōgo
Dōzen
Kyōga-misaki
Wakasa-wan
Maizuru
Biwa-ko

Matsue
Yonago
Daisen 1731
Tsuyama
Tottori
1510
Ōda
Chūgoku-sanchi
Hamada
Masuda

PACIFIC
OCEAN

Tsushima
Korea Strait
Iki

Yamaguchi
Shimonoseki
Kita-Kyūshū
Ube
Hōfu
Suō-nada
Fukuoka
Saga
Nagato
Tokuyama
Iwakuni
Kure
Onomichi
Hiroshima
Fukuyama
Kurashiki
Okayama
Seto-naikai
Takamatsu
Tokushima
Harima-nada
Anan
Kii-suidō
Imabari
Niihama
Matsuyama
1955
Iyo-nada
Kōchi
1981
Shikoku
Muroto
Tanabe
Shingū
Shiono-misaki
Yawatahama
Muroto-zaki
Nakatsu
Ōita
Uwajima
Tosa-wan
Beppu
Kuju-san 1788
Nobeoka
Bungo-suidō
Ashizuri-misaki
Nakamura
Sasebo
Kurume
Ōmuta
Kumamoto
1739
Amakusa-shotō
Yatsushiro
Minamata
1700
Miyazaki
Kyūshū
Miyakonojō
Sendai
Kanoya
Kagoshima
Osumi-kaikyō
Tanega-shima
Yaku-shima
Nagasaki
Oita
Kuju-san

Scale 1: 6 750 000
0 67.5 135 202.5 270 337.5 km

Zenithal Equidistant Projection
© Oxford University Press

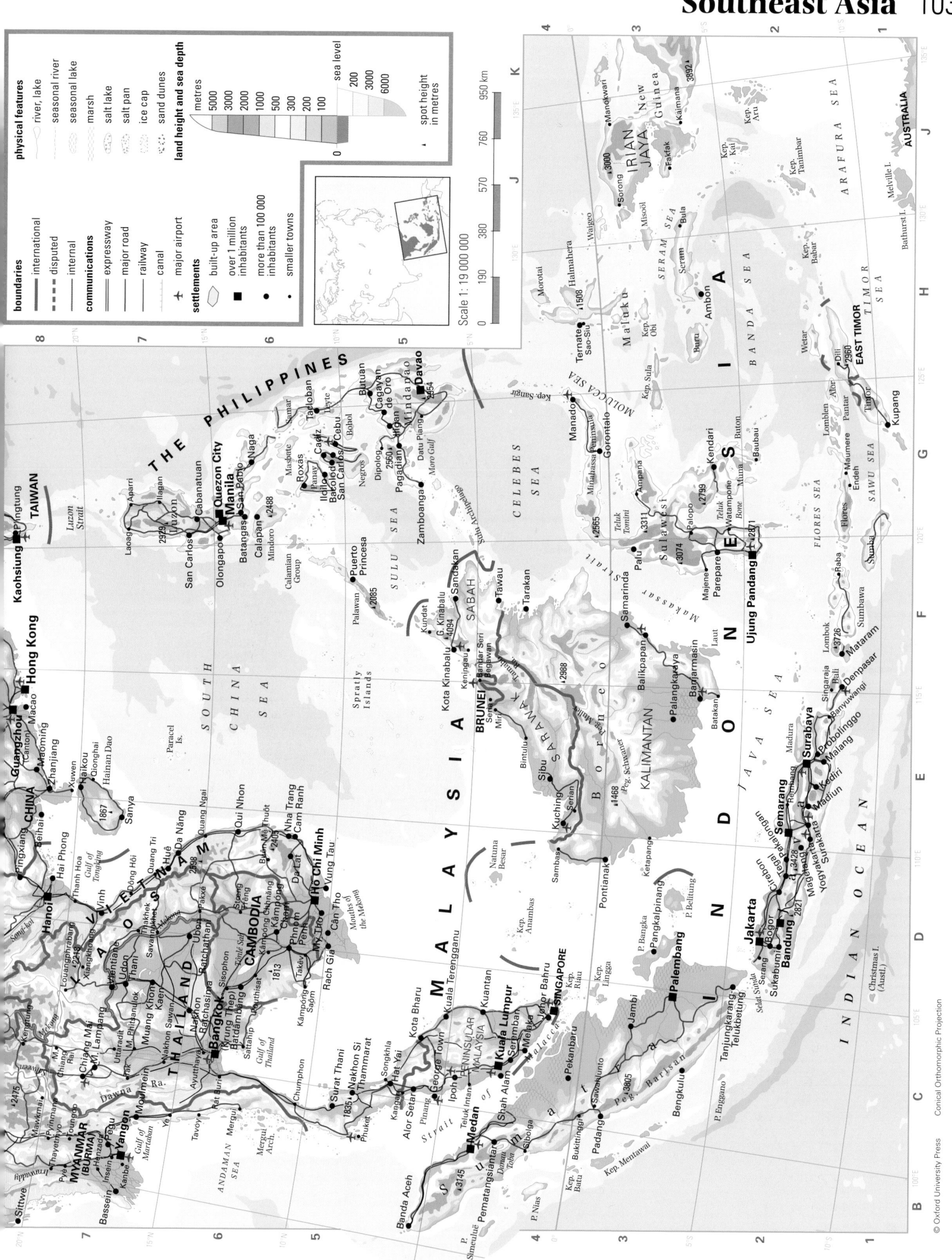

Conical Orthomorphic Projection

boundaries
international
disputed
internal
communications
expressway
major road
railway
canal
✈ major airport
settlements
built-up area
■ over 1 million inhabitants
■ more than 100 000 inhabitants
• smaller towns

physical features
river, lake
seasonal river
seasonal lake
marsh
salt lake
salt pan
ice cap
sand dunes

land height and sea depth
metres
5000
3000
2000
1000
500
300
200
100
sea level
200
3000
6000
▲ spot height in metres

Scale 1:19 000 000

0   190   380   570   760   950 km

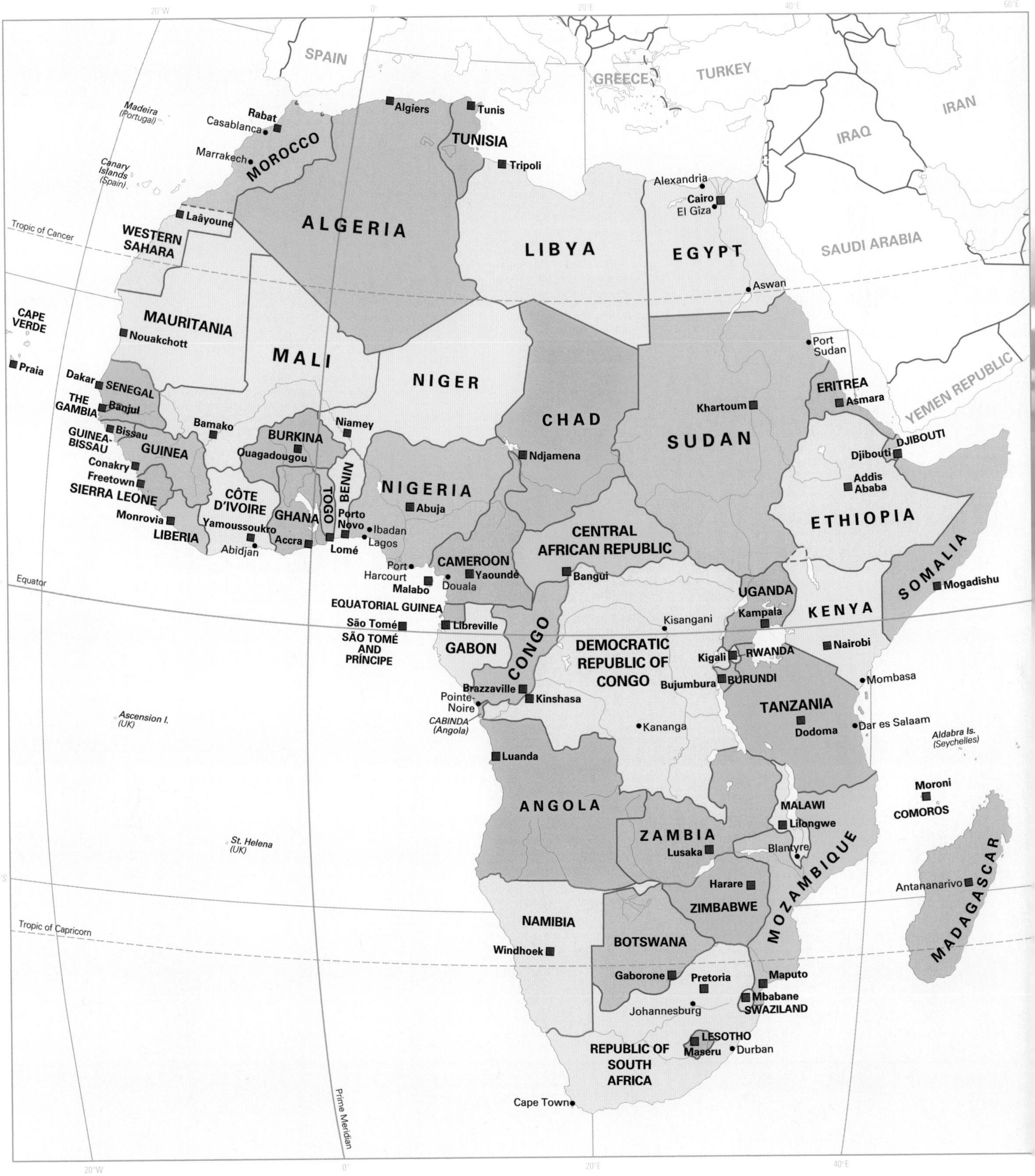

SPAIN

GREECE TURKEY

IRAN

IRAQ

Madeira
(Portugal)

■ Rabat
Casablanca
■ Algiers
■ Tunis
MOROCCO
TUNISIA
Marrakech
■ Tripoli

Alexandria
SAUDI ARABIA
■ Cairo
El Gîza
YEMEN REPUBLIC

Canary
Islands
(Spain)
Tropic of Cancer
■ Laâyoune
WESTERN
SAHARA

ALGERIA
LIBYA
EGYPT

20°N

CAPE
VERDE
MAURITANIA
■ Nouakchott
Aswan

Port
Sudan
ERITREA
■ Asmara

■ Praia
Dakar
SENEGAL
MALI
NIGER
Khartoum
DJIBOUTI
Djibouti ■

THE
GAMBIA
■ Banjul
Bamako
Niamey
CHAD
SUDAN
Addis
Ababa
Bissau
BURKINA
Ndjamena
GUINEA-
BISSAU
GUINEA
Ouagadougou
BENIN
Conakry
Freetown
NIGERIA
■ Abuja
ETHIOPIA
SIERRA LEONE
CÔTE
D'IVOIRE
TOGO
GHANA
Porto
Novo
Ibadan
SOMALIA
Monrovia
Yamoussoukro
Accra
Lagos
CENTRAL
AFRICAN REPUBLIC
■ Mogadishu
LIBERIA
Abidjan
Lomé
Port
Harcourt
CAMEROON
■ Bangui
UGANDA
Equator
Malabo
Yaoundé
Douala
Kisangani
Kampala
KENYA
EQUATORIAL GUINEA
■ Nairobi
São Tomé
■ Libreville
CONGO
Kigali
RWANDA
SÃO TOMÉ
AND
PRÍNCIPE
GABON
DEMOCRATIC
REPUBLIC OF
CONGO
Bujumbura
BURUNDI
Mombasa
Brazzaville
Pointe-
Noire
■ Kinshasa
TANZANIA
Aldabra Is.
(Seychelles)
Ascension I.
(UK)
CABINDA
(Angola)
Kananga
Dodoma
Dar es Salaam
■ Luanda
Moroni
St. Helena
(UK)
ANGOLA
MALAWI
COMOROS
■ Lilongwe
ZAMBIA
Blantyre
MADAGASCAR
20°S
Lusaka
MOZAMBIQUE
Harare
Antananarivo
Tropic of Capricorn
NAMIBIA
ZIMBABWE
Maputo
Windhoek
BOTSWANA
Gaborone
Pretoria
Mbabane
SWAZILAND
Johannesburg
LESOTHO
Maseru
Durban
REPUBLIC OF
SOUTH
AFRICA
Prime Meridian
Cape Town

20°W
0°
20°E
40°E

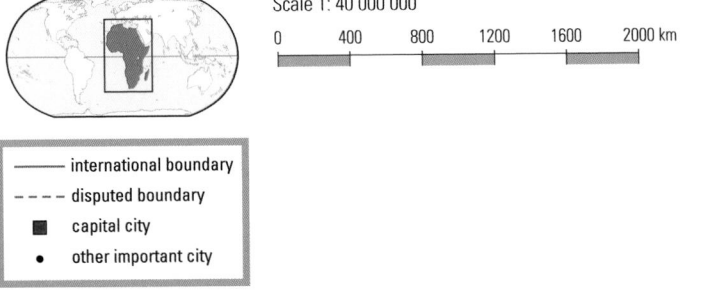

Scale 1: 40 000 000

0   400   800   1200   1600   2000 km

——— international boundary
----- disputed boundary
■ capital city
● other important city

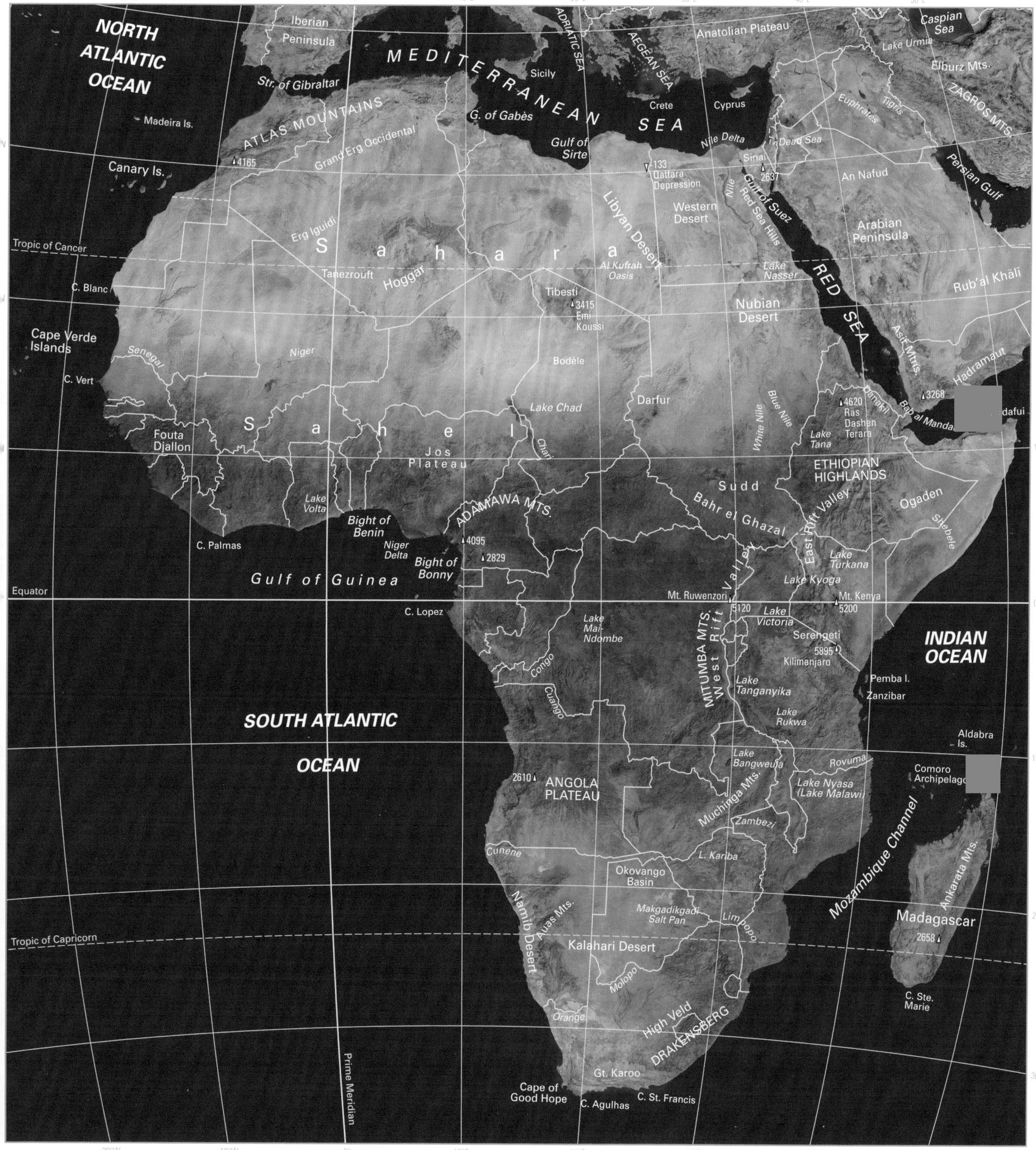

NORTH
ATLANTIC
OCEAN

Iberian
Peninsula

M E D I T E R R A N E A N   S E A

ADRIATIC SEA

AEGEAN SEA

Anatolian Plateau

Lake Urmia

Caspian
Sea

Elburz Mts.

ZAGROS MTS.

Str. of Gibraltar

ATLAS MOUNTAINS

Sicily

Crete

Cyprus

Madeira Is.

G. of Gabès

Gulf of
Sirte

Grand Erg Occidental

Nile Delta

Dead Sea

Euphrates

Tigris

Canary Is.

▲4165

Sinai

Gulf of Suez

An Nafud

Persian Gulf

Tropic of Cancer

Erg Iguidi

S   a   h   a   r   a

▽133
Qattara
Depression

Western
Desert

Libyan Desert

▲2637

Arabian
Peninsula

C. Blanc

Tanezrouft

Hoggar

Al Kufrah
Oasis

Nile

Red Sea Hills

Rub' al Khāli

Cape Verde
Islands

Niger

▲3415
Emi
Koussi

Tibesti

Lake Nasser

R E D   S E A

C. Vert

Senegal

Bodélé

Nubian
Desert

Asir Mts.

Hadramaut

▲3268

S   a   h   e   l

Lake Chad

Darfur

Blue Nile

White Nile

▲4620
Ras
Dashen
Terara

Danakil

Bab al Mandab

dafui

Fouta
Djallon

Chari

Jos
Plateau

Lake
Tana

ETHIOPIAN
HIGHLANDS

Lake
Volta

Sudd

Bahr el Ghazal

East Rift Valley

Ogaden

Shebele

Bight of
Benin

ADAMAWA MTS.

▲4095

Niger
Delta

C. Palmas

Bight of
Bonny

▲2829

Lake Turkana

Lake Kyoga

Equator

Gulf of Guinea

Mt. Ruwenzori
▲5120

Mt. Kenya
▲5200

INDIAN
OCEAN

C. Lopez

Lake
Mai-
Ndombe

Lake
Victoria

Serengeti

Congo

MITUMBA MTS.

West Rift Valley

Kilimanjaro
▲5895

Pemba I.

Zanzibar

SOUTH ATLANTIC

Cuango

Lake
Tanganyika

Aldabra
Is.

OCEAN

Lake
Rukwa

Lake
Bangweulu

Rovuma

Comoro
Archipelago

2610▲

ANGOLA
PLATEAU

Muchinga Mts.

Lake Nyasa
(Lake Malawi)

Zambezi

Mozambique Channel

Cunene

L. Kariba

Okovango
Basin

Namib Desert

Auas Mts.

Makgadikgadi
Salt Pan

Limpopo

Madagascar

▲2658

Tropic of Capricorn

Kalahari Desert

Molopo

Ankarata Mts.

Orange

High Veld

DRAKENSBERG

C. Ste.
Marie

Cape of
Good Hope

Gt. Karoo

C. Agulhas

C. St. Francis

Prime Meridian

Scale 1: 40 000 000

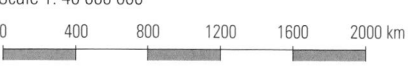

0   400   800   1200   1600   2000 km

The Sahel is a narrow band of semi-arid land south
of the Sahara that suffers from problems associated
with desertification. See page 130 for more
information about desertification.

© Oxford University Press   Zenithal Equal Area Projection

Rainfall variability in the Sahel, 1950–2004
0 equals the long term average. Variability is shown as standard deviations above and below this average.

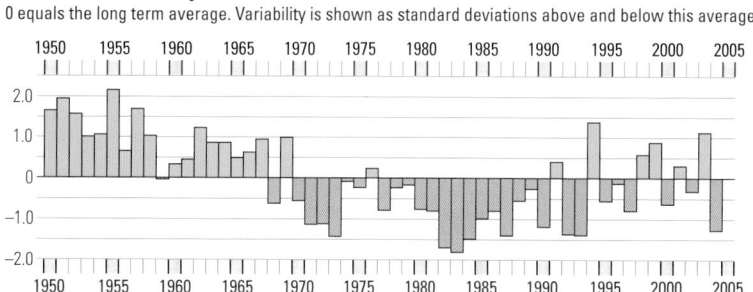

Scale 1: 90 000 000

January temperature

actual surface temperature

°Celsius

- 30
- 25
- 20
- 15
- 10
- 5

● climate station
(average January temperature)

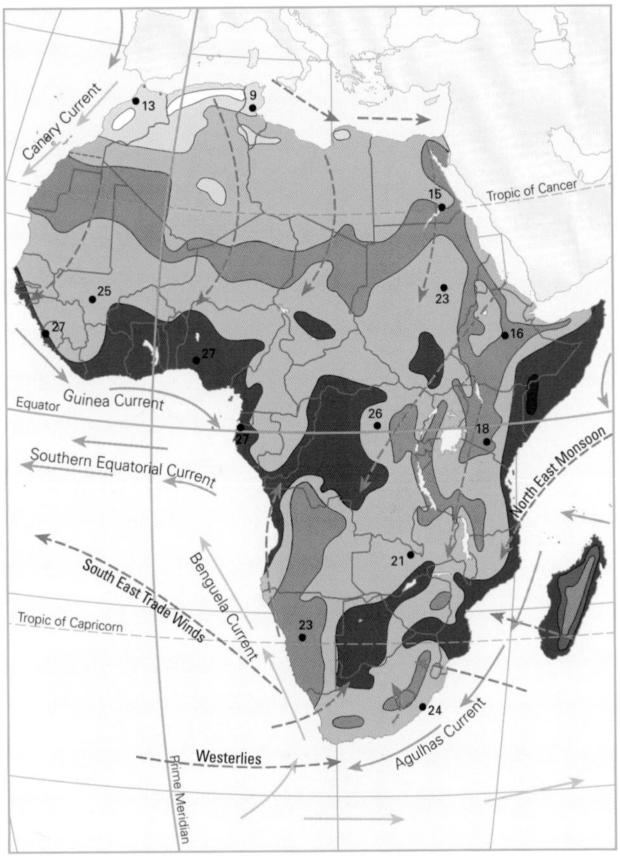

Canary Current
13
9
Tropic of Cancer
15
25
23
27
16
27
Equator Guinea Current
26
18
Southern Equatorial Current
North East Monsoon
South East Trade Winds
Benguela Current
21
Tropic of Capricorn
23
Westerlies
24
Aguilhas Current
Prime Meridian

→ warm sea current → cold sea current ---→ prevailing wind

July temperature

actual surface temperature

°Celsius

- 35
- 30
- 25
- 20
- 15
- 10
- 5

● climate station
(average July temperature)

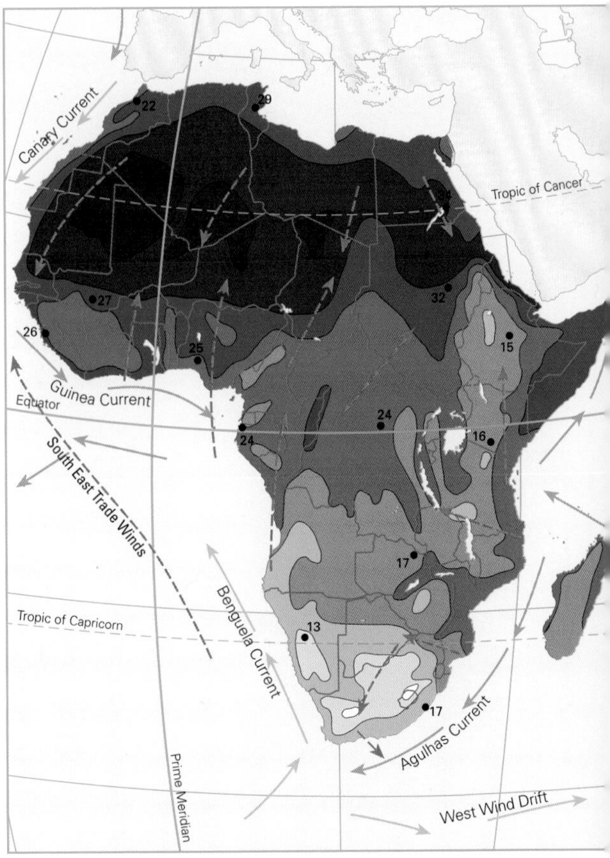

Canary Current
22
29
Tropic of Cancer
27
32
26
25
15
Equator Guinea Current
24
24
16
South East Trade Winds
17
Benguela Current
Tropic of Capricorn
13
17
Aguilhas Current
Prime Meridian
West Wind Drift

→ warm sea current → cold sea current ---→ prevailing wind

Precipitation

average annual precipitation

mm

- 3000
- 2000
- 1000
- 500
- 250
- 0

● climate station
(average annual precipitation)

Rabat 556
Gafsa 195
Aswan 0
Tropic of Cancer
Khartoum 161
Bamako 878
Freetown 2946
Ibadan 1121
Addis Ababa 1256
Equator
Libreville 2841
Kisangani 1704
Nairobi 1063
Ndola 1234
Tropic of Capricorn
Windhoek 362
Prime Meridian
Durban 1008

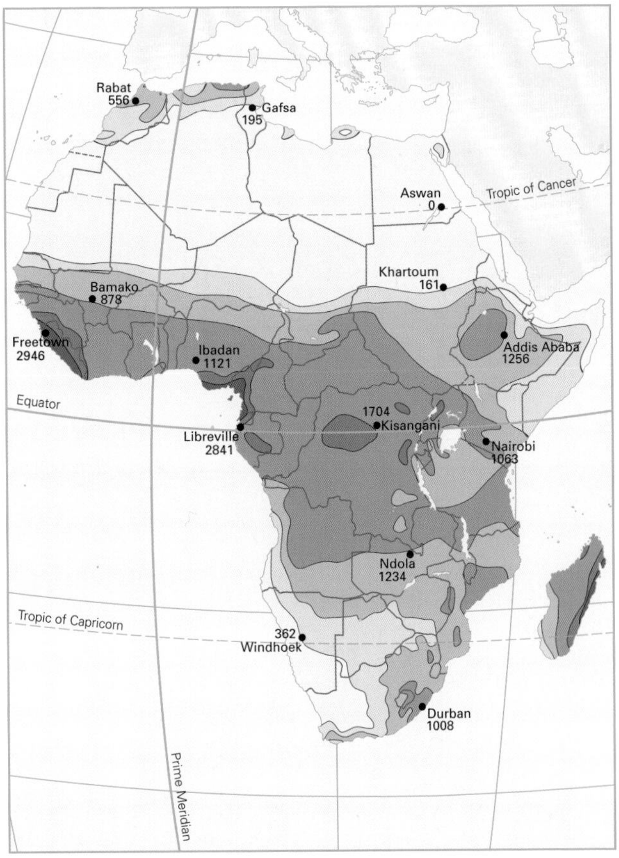

Natural vegetation

the type of vegetation that would occur naturally without interference by people

- tropical rain forest
- tropical grasslands
- evergreens and shrubs
- thorn forest
- temperate grasslands
- semi-desert
- desert
- mountains

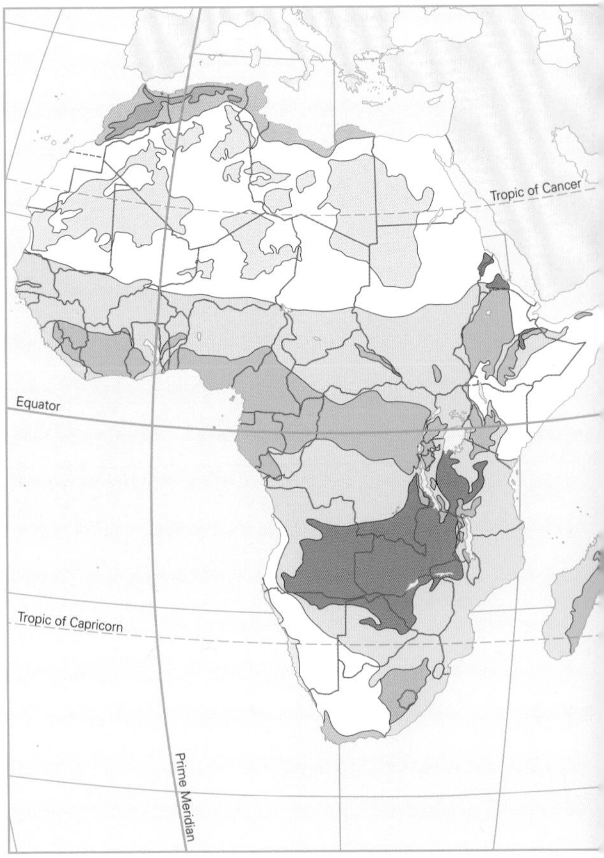

Tropic of Cancer
Equator
Tropic of Capricorn
Prime Meridian

Zenithal Equal Area Projection   © Oxford University Pr

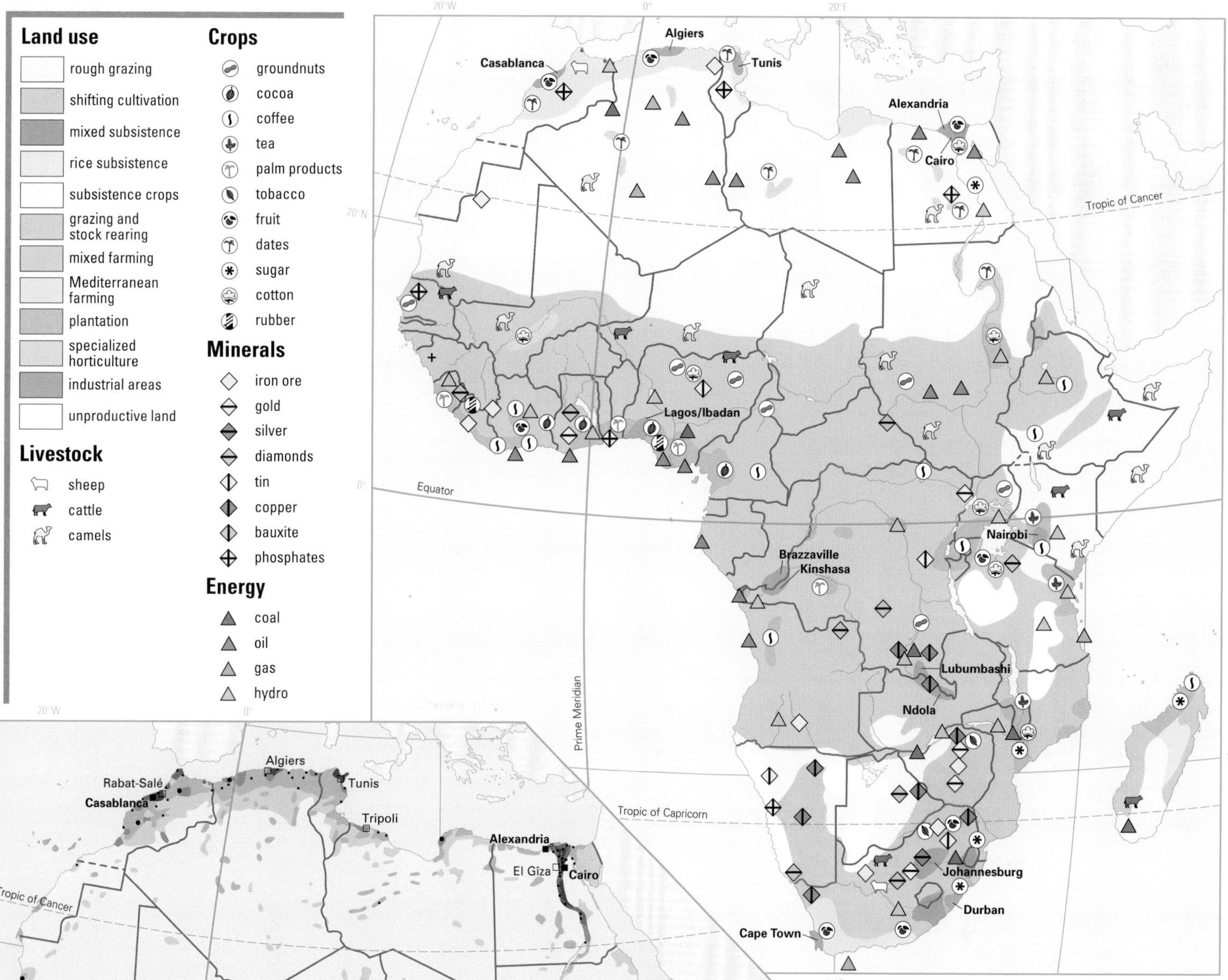

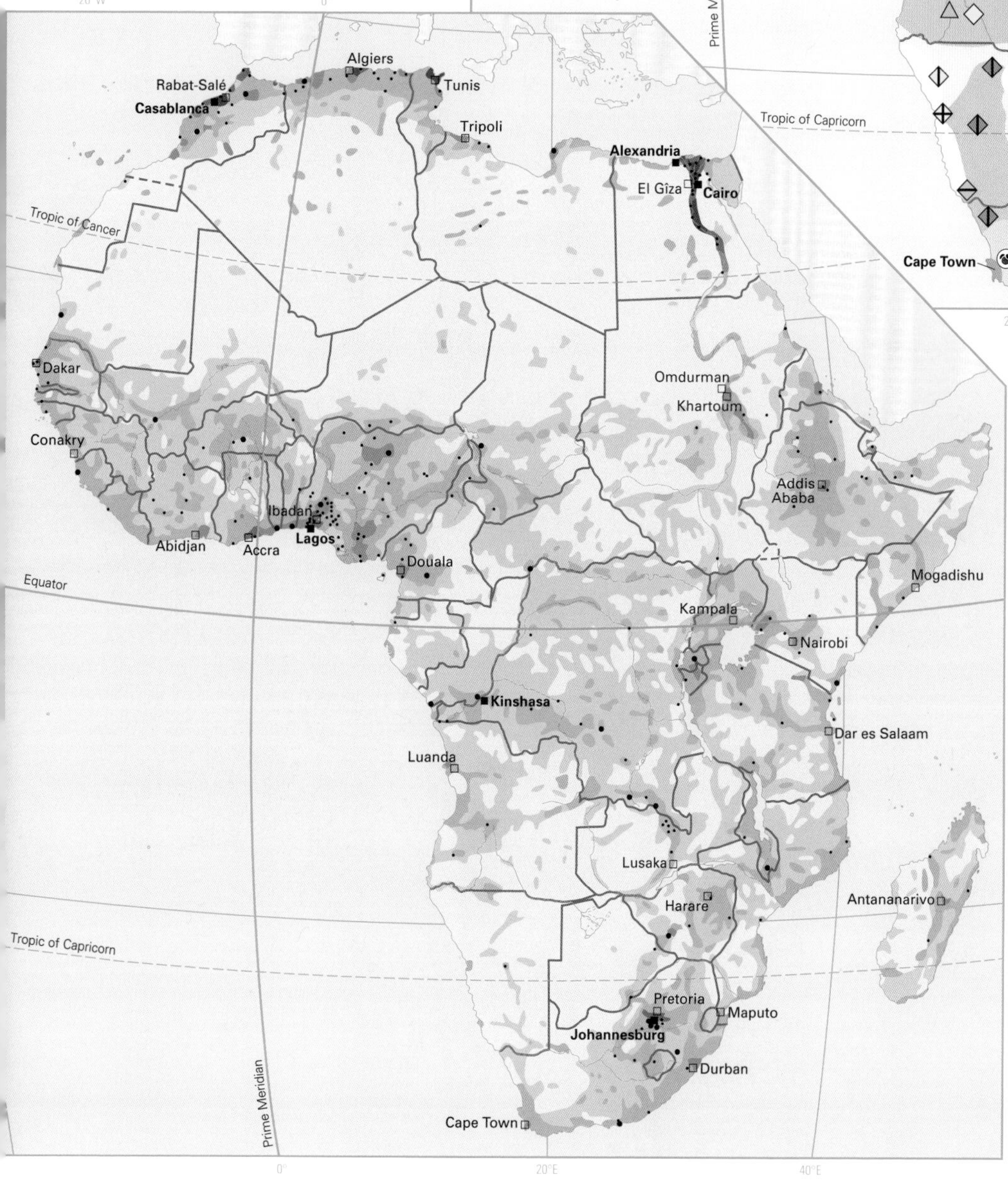

Land use

- rough grazing
- shifting cultivation
- mixed subsistence
- rice subsistence
- subsistence crops
- grazing and stock rearing
- mixed farming
- Mediterranean farming
- plantation
- specialized horticulture
- industrial areas
- unproductive land

Livestock

- sheep
- cattle
- camels

Crops

- groundnuts
- cocoa
- coffee
- tea
- palm products
- tobacco
- fruit
- dates
- sugar
- cotton
- rubber

Minerals

- iron ore
- gold
- silver
- diamonds
- tin
- copper
- bauxite
- phosphates

Energy

- coal
- oil
- gas
- hydro

Main map labels

Casablanca, Algiers, Tunis, Alexandria, Cairo, Lagos/Ibadan, Brazzaville, Kinshasa, Nairobi, Lubumbashi, Ndola, Johannesburg, Durban, Cape Town

Tropic of Cancer, Equator, Prime Meridian, Tropic of Capricorn

Population map labels

Rabat-Salé, Algiers, Tunis, Casablanca, Tripoli, Alexandria, El Gîza, Cairo, Dakar, Conakry, Omdurman, Khartoum, Addis Ababa, Ibadan, Lagos, Abidjan, Accra, Douala, Mogadishu, Kampala, Nairobi, Kinshasa, Dar es Salaam, Luanda, Lusaka, Harare, Antananarivo, Pretoria, Maputo, Johannesburg, Durban, Cape Town

Population density

people per square kilometre

- over 700
- 200–700
- 100–200
- 10–100
- 1–10
- under 1

Major cities

population in millions

- over 3
- 1–3
- 0.5–1
- 0.1–0.5

Projected population growth of selected African cities, 2005–2015

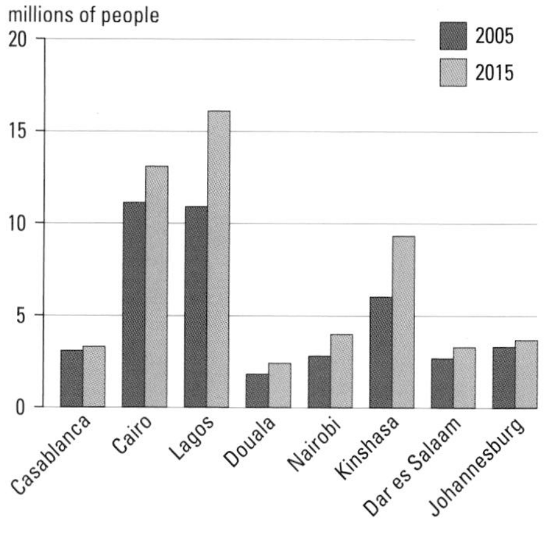

millions of people

- 2005
- 2015

Cities: Casablanca, Cairo, Lagos, Douala, Nairobi, Kinshasa, Dar es Salaam, Johannesburg

Zenithal Equal Area Projection

© Oxford University Press

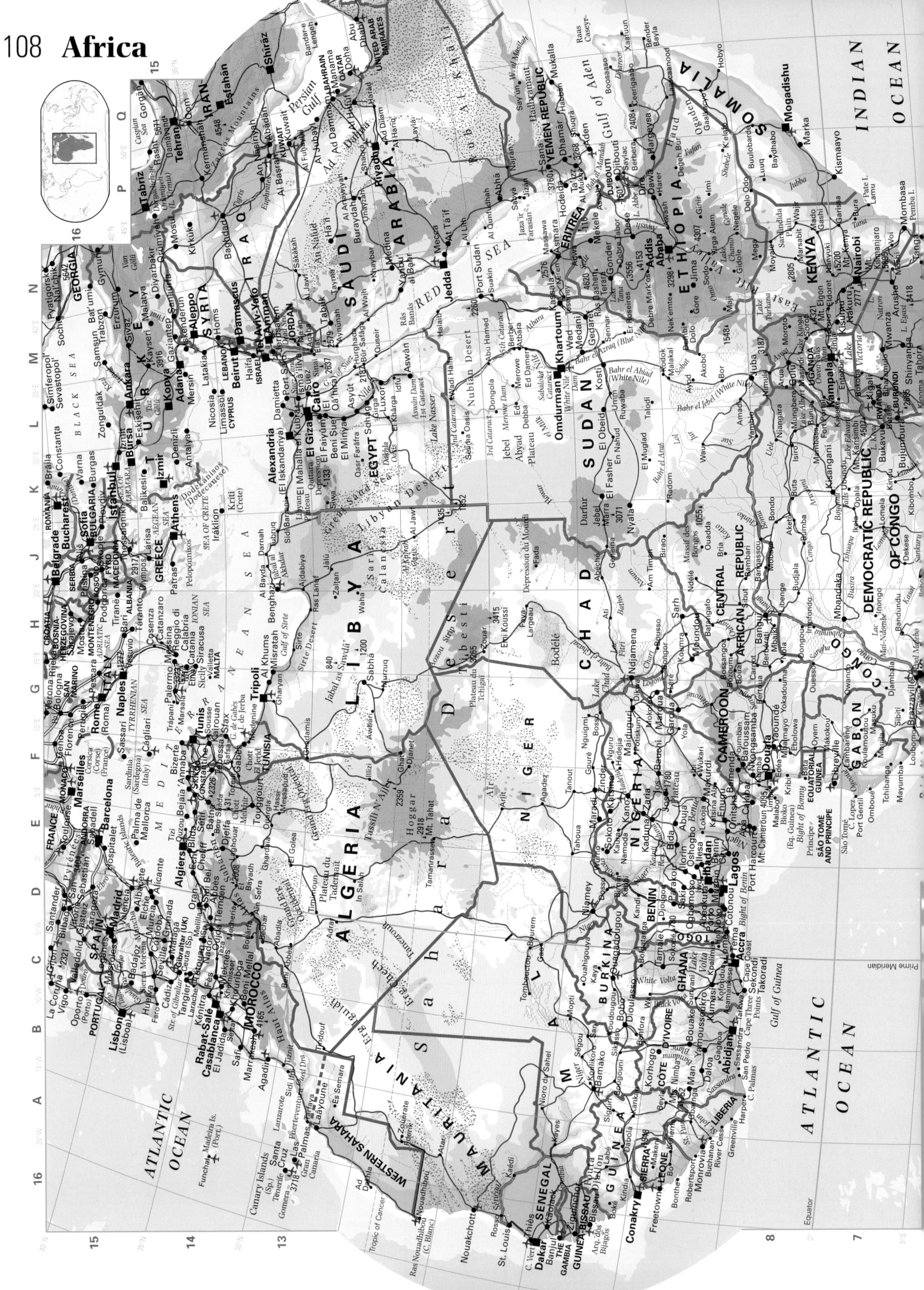

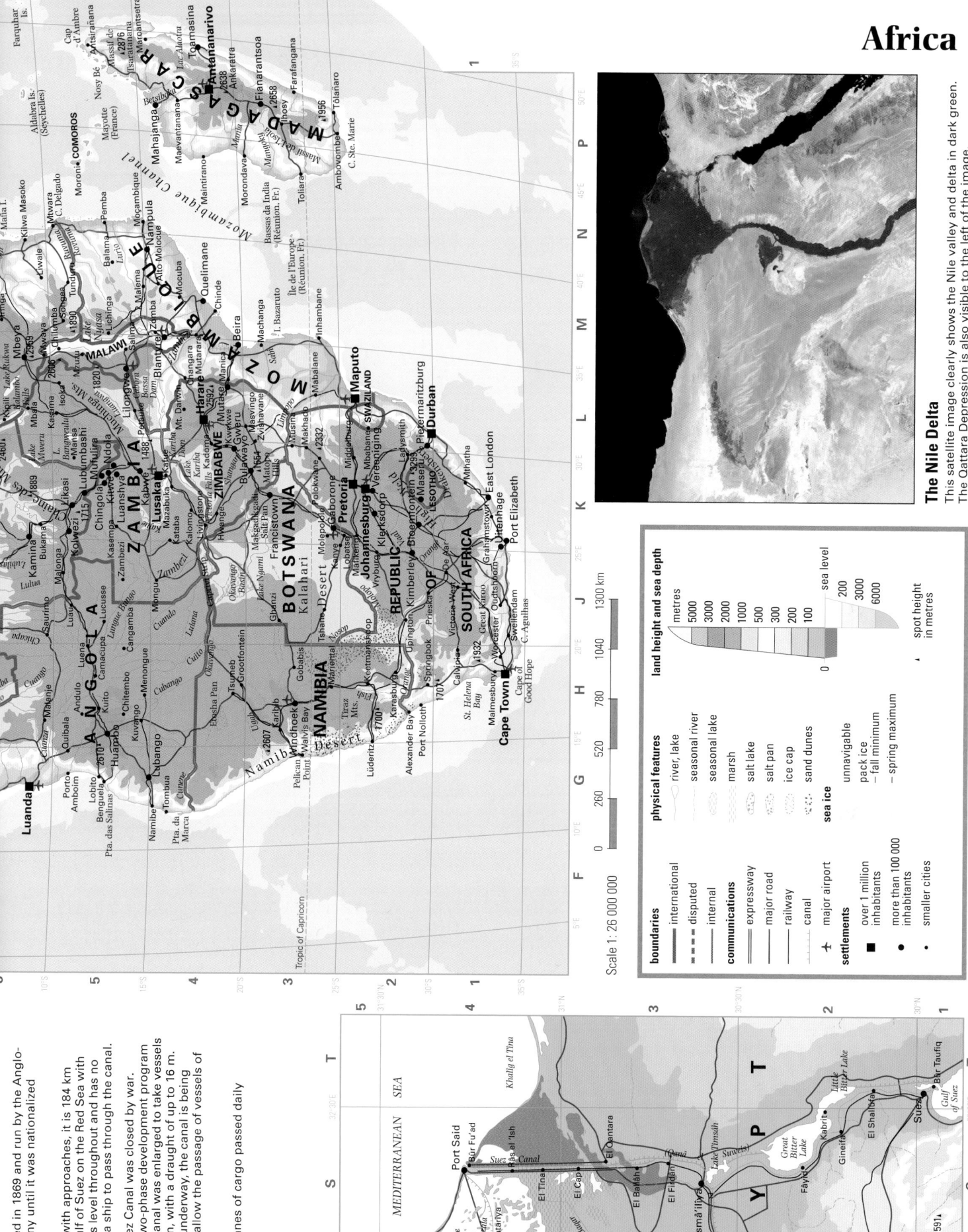

The Nile Delta

This satellite image clearly shows the Nile valley and delta in dark green. The Qattara Depression is also visible to the left of the image.

Scale 1 : 26 000 000

0   260   520   780   1040   1300 km

boundaries

— international
---- disputed
— internal

communications

expressway
major road
railway
canal
✈ major airport

settlements

■ over 1 million inhabitants
● more than 100 000 inhabitants
· smaller cities

physical features

river, lake
seasonal river
seasonal lake
marsh
salt lake
salt pan
ice cap
sand dunes

sea ice

unnavigable
pack ice
– fall minimum
– spring maximum

land height and sea depth

metres
5000
3000
2000
1000
500
300
200
100
0
sea level

200
3000
6000

▲ spot height in metres

Zenithal Equal Area Projection   © Oxford University Press

Suez Canal

The Suez Canal was opened in 1869 and run by the Anglo-French Suez Canal Company until it was nationalized by Egypt in 1956.

The canal is 173 km long (with approaches, it is 184 km long), and connects the Gulf of Suez on the Red Sea with the Mediterranean Sea. It is level throughout and has no locks. It takes 12 hours for a ship to pass through the canal.

From 1967 to 1975, the Suez Canal was closed by war. In 1980, the first part of a two-phase development program was completed when the canal was enlarged to take vessels of up to 150 000 DWT laden, with a draught of up to 16 m. In the second phase, now underway, the canal is being deepened and widened to allow the passage of vessels of up to 180 000 DWT.

On average, 1.7 million tonnes of cargo passed daily through the canal in 2006.

Scale 1 : 1 500 000

0   15   30   45 km

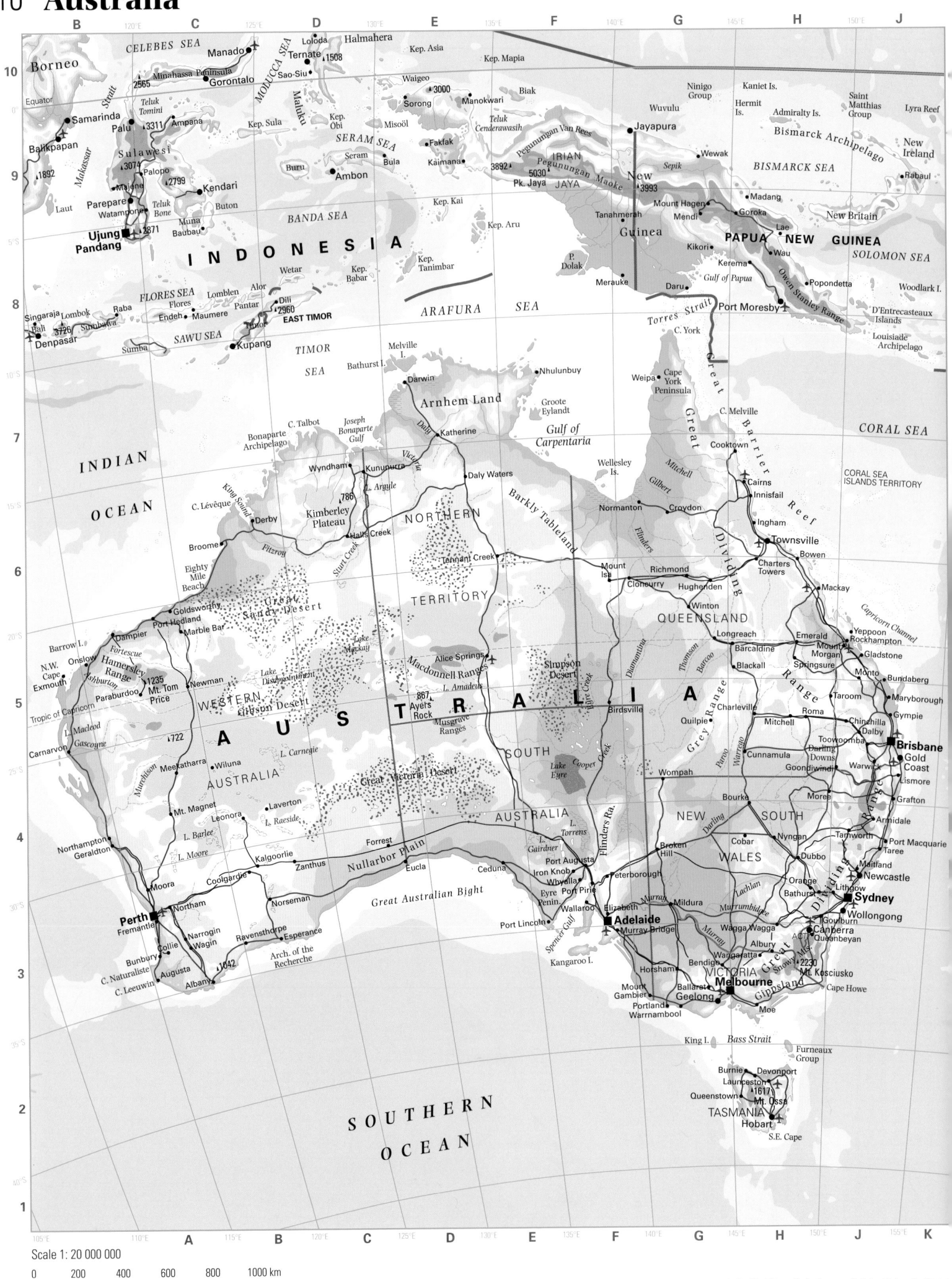

Scale 1: 20 000 000

0   200   400   600   800   1000 km

Zenithal Equidistant Projection

© Oxford University Press

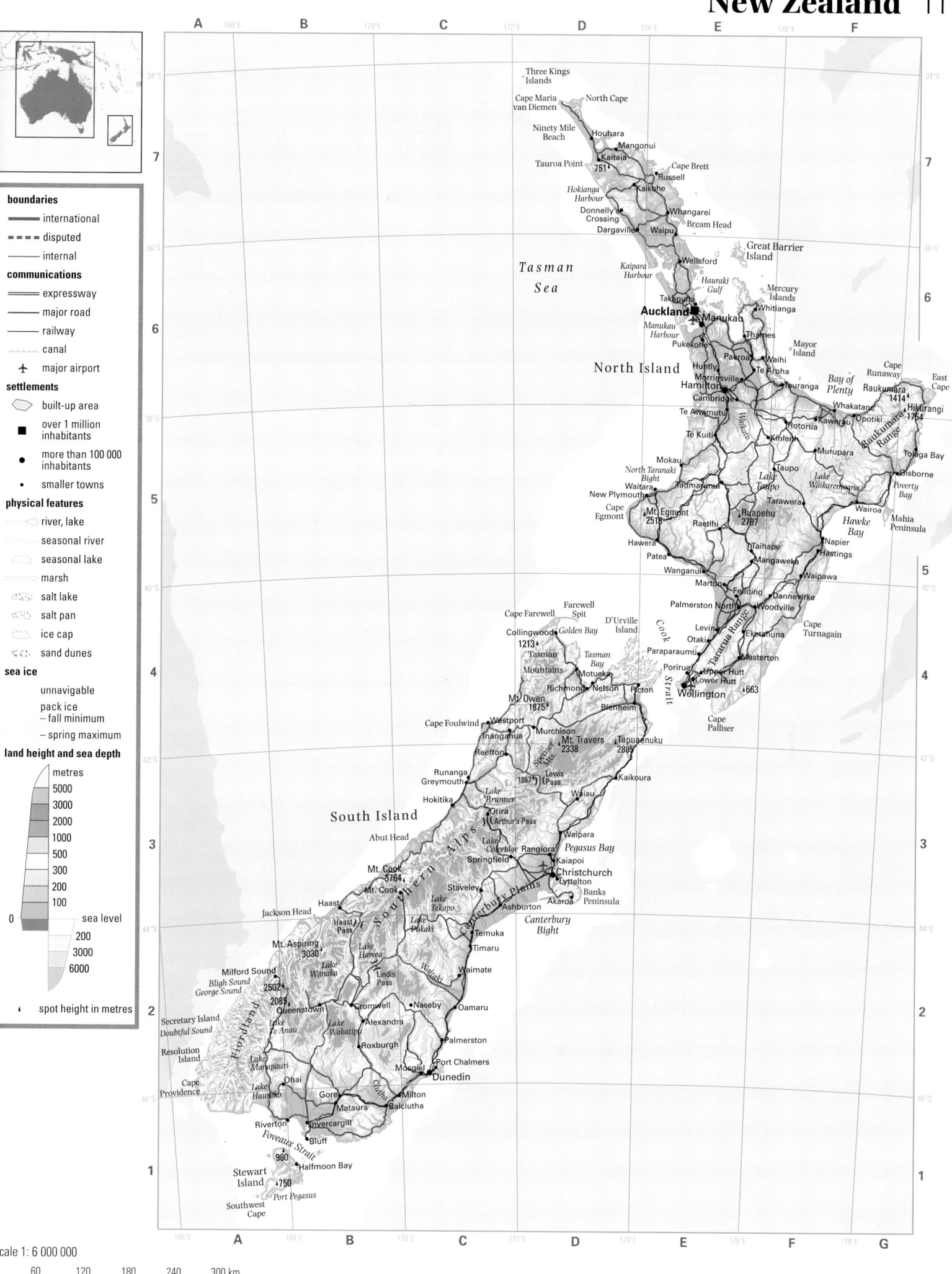

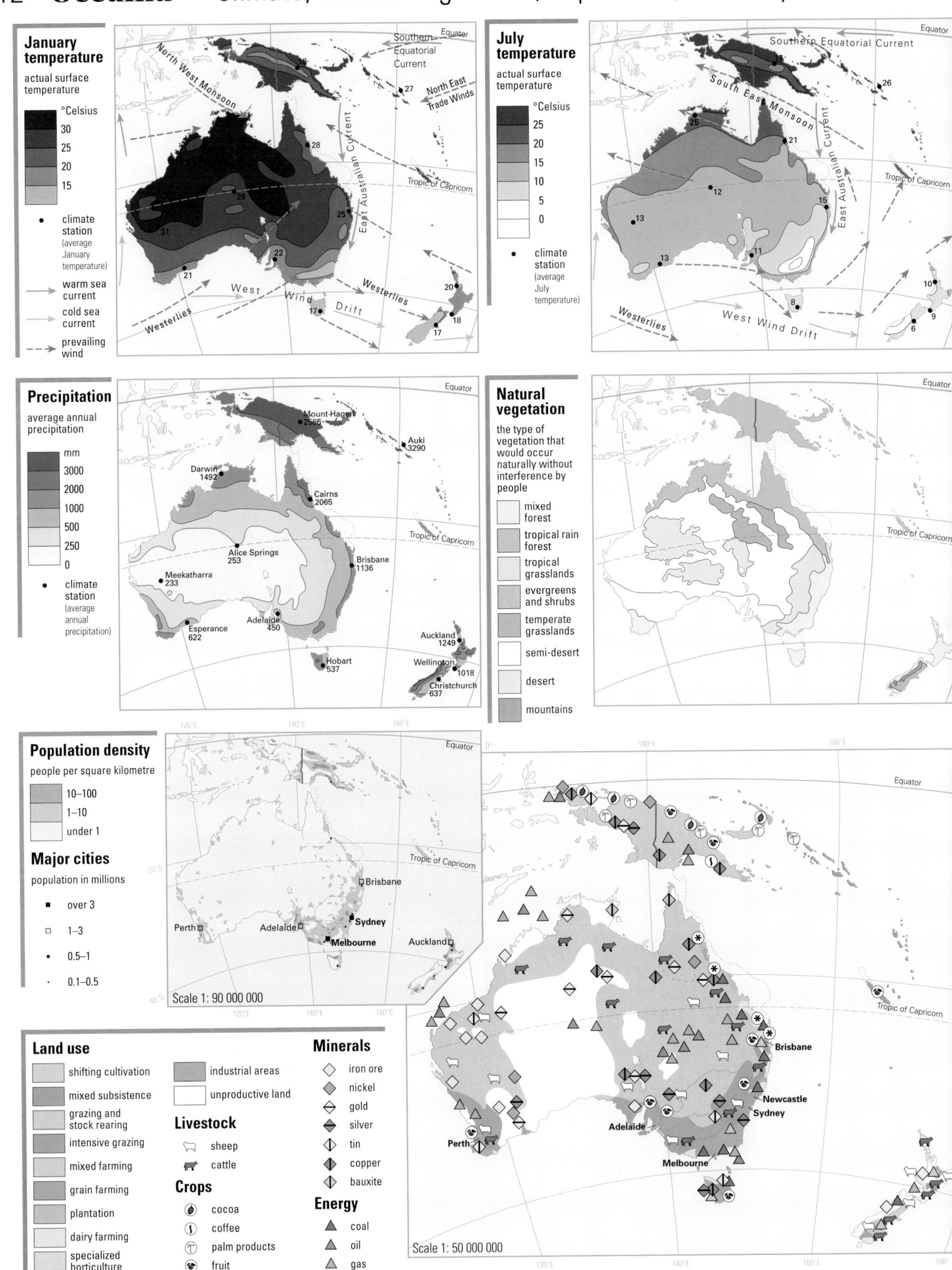

January temperature

actual surface temperature

°Celsius
30
25
20
15

● climate station (average January temperature)

→ warm sea current

→ cold sea current

--→ prevailing wind

North West Monsoon
Southern Equatorial Current
North East Trade Winds
Equator
East Australian Current
Tropic of Capricorn
West Wind Drift
Westerlies
Westerlies

July temperature

actual surface temperature

°Celsius
25
20
15
10
5
0

● climate station (average July temperature)

Southern Equatorial Current
South East Monsoon
Equator
East Australian Current
Tropic of Capricorn
Westerlies
West Wind Drift

Precipitation

average annual precipitation

mm
3000
2000
1000
500
250
0

● climate station (average annual precipitation)

Mount Hagen 2588
Auki 3290
Darwin 1492
Cairns 2065
Alice Springs 253
Brisbane 1136
Meekatharra 233
Esperance 622
Adelaide 450
Hobart 537
Auckland 1249
Wellington 1018
Christchurch 637
Equator
Tropic of Capricorn

Natural vegetation

the type of vegetation that would occur naturally without interference by people

mixed forest
tropical rain forest
tropical grasslands
evergreens and shrubs
temperate grasslands
semi-desert
desert
mountains

Equator
Tropic of Capricorn

Population density

people per square kilometre

10–100
1–10
under 1

Major cities

population in millions

■ over 3
□ 1–3
● 0.5–1
· 0.1–0.5

Brisbane
Perth
Adelaide
Sydney
Melbourne
Auckland

Equator
Tropic of Capricorn

Scale 1: 90 000 000

Land use

shifting cultivation
mixed subsistence
grazing and stock rearing
intensive grazing
mixed farming
grain farming
plantation
dairy farming
specialized horticulture
forestry
industrial areas
unproductive land

Livestock
🐑 sheep
🐄 cattle

Crops
⊚ cocoa
Ⓢ coffee
Ⓣ palm products
⊛ fruit
✳ sugar

Minerals
◇ iron ore
◇ nickel
◇ gold
◇ silver
◇ tin
◇ copper
◇ bauxite

Energy
▲ coal
▲ oil
▲ gas
▲ hydro

Perth
Adelaide
Melbourne
Newcastle
Sydney
Brisbane

Equator
Tropic of Capricorn

Scale 1: 50 000 000

Modified Zenithal Equidistant Projection   © Oxford University Press

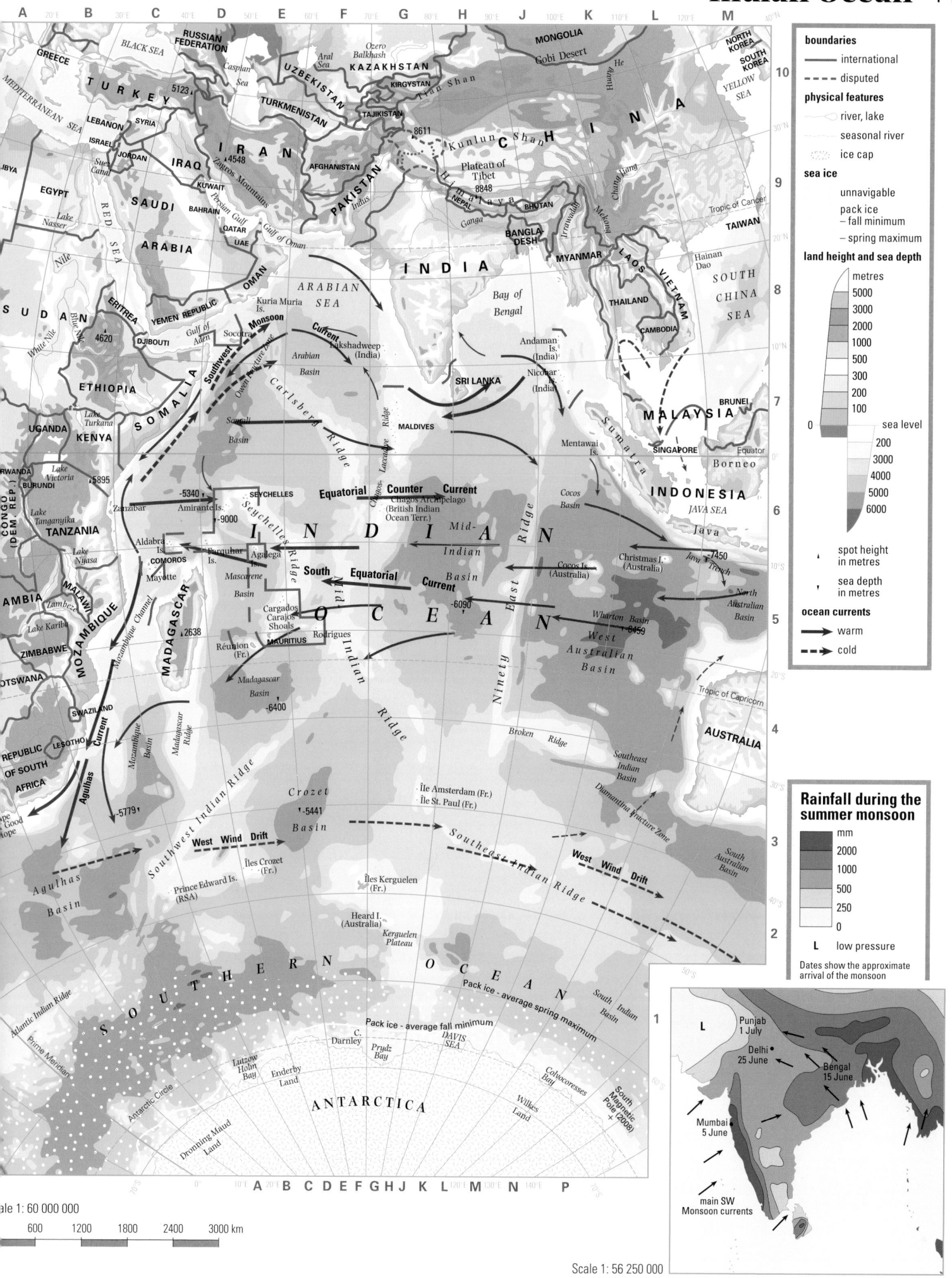

Oxford University Press   Modified Zenithal Equidistant Projection

boundaries
— international
- - - disputed

physical features
river, lake
seasonal river
ice cap

sea ice
unnavigable
pack ice
– fall minimum
– spring maximum

land height and sea depth
metres
5000
3000
2000
1000
500
300
200
100
0 — sea level
200
3000
4000
5000
6000

spot height in metres
sea depth in metres

ocean currents
→ warm
--→ cold

Rainfall during the summer monsoon
mm
2000
1000
500
250
0

L low pressure

Dates show the approximate arrival of the monsoon

Scale 1: 60 000 000

600 1200 1800 2400 3000 km

Scale 1: 56 250 000

Map labels

GREECE, TURKEY, MEDITERRANEAN SEA, BLACK SEA, RUSSIAN FEDERATION, LEBANON, SYRIA, ISRAEL, JORDAN, IRAQ, IRAN, KUWAIT, BAHRAIN, QATAR, UAE, SAUDI ARABIA, EGYPT, LIBYA, SUDAN, ERITREA, YEMEN REPUBLIC, DJIBOUTI, ETHIOPIA, SOMALIA, UGANDA, KENYA, TANZANIA, CONGO (DEM. REP.), RWANDA, BURUNDI, ZAMBIA, MALAWI, MOZAMBIQUE, ZIMBABWE, BOTSWANA, SWAZILAND, LESOTHO, REPUBLIC OF SOUTH AFRICA, MADAGASCAR, COMOROS

UZBEKISTAN, TURKMENISTAN, KAZAKHSTAN, KIRGYSTAN, TAJIKISTAN, AFGHANISTAN, PAKISTAN, NEPAL, BHUTAN, INDIA, BANGLADESH, MYANMAR, MONGOLIA, CHINA, LAOS, THAILAND, VIETNAM, CAMBODIA, TAIWAN, NORTH KOREA, SOUTH KOREA, MALAYSIA, BRUNEI, SINGAPORE, INDONESIA, SRI LANKA, AUSTRALIA

ARABIAN SEA, RED SEA, Gulf of Aden, Gulf of Oman, Persian Gulf, Bay of Bengal, SOUTH CHINA SEA, YELLOW SEA, JAVA SEA, SOUTHERN OCEAN, INDIAN OCEAN

Caspian Sea, Aral Sea, Ozero Balkhash, Lake Nasser, Lake Turkana, Lake Victoria, Lake Tanganyika, Lake Nyasa, Lake Kariba

Nile, White Nile, Blue Nile, Zambezi, Indus, Ganga, Tian Shan, Zagros Mountains, Plateau of Tibet, Gobi Desert, Kunlun Shan, Himalaya, Chang Jiang, Mekong, Irrawaddy, Huang He

Kuria Muria Is., Socotra, Lakshadweep (India), Maldives, Seychelles, Amirante Is., Aldabra Is., Farquhar Is., Agalega Is., Mascarene, Cargados Carajos Shoals, Mauritius, Rodrigues, Réunion (Fr.), Zanzibar, Mayotte, Andaman Is. (India), Nicobar Is. (India), Mentawai Is., Cocos Is. (Australia), Christmas I. (Australia), Sumatra, Borneo, Java, Hainan Dao, Chagos Archipelago (British Indian Ocean Terr.)

Carlsberg Ridge, Owen Fracture Zone, Chagos-Laccadive Ridge, Seychelles Ridge, Mid-Indian Ridge, East Ridge, Ninety East Ridge, Mid Indian Ridge, Madagascar Ridge, Southwest Indian Ridge, Southeast Indian Ridge, Broken Ridge, Kerguelen Plateau, Atlantic Indian Ridge, Diamantina Fracture Zone

Arabian Basin, Somali Basin, Mascarene Basin, Madagascar Basin, Agulhas Basin, Crozet Basin, Mozambique Basin, Cocos Basin, Wharton Basin, North Australian Basin, West Australian Basin, Southeast Indian Basin, South Australian Basin, South Indian Basin, Central Indian Basin

Southwest Monsoon Current, Equatorial Counter Current, South Equatorial Current, Agulhas Current, Mozambique Current, West Wind Drift, Madagascar Current

Île Amsterdam (Fr.), Île St. Paul (Fr.), Îles Crozet (Fr.), Prince Edward Is. (RSA), Îles Kerguelen (Fr.), Heard I. (Australia), ANTARCTICA, Dronning Maud Land, Enderby Land, Wilkes Land, Prydz Bay, DAVIS SEA, C. Darnley, Lutzow Holm Bay, Coats Land, South Magnetic Pole + (2008), Antarctic Circle, Prime Meridian

Tropic of Cancer, Equator, Tropic of Capricorn

5123, 4548, 8611, 8848, 4620, 5895, 4620, -5340, -9000, -5779, -2638, -6400, -5441, -6090, -6459, -7450, Pack ice – average spring maximum, Pack ice – average fall minimum

Rainfall inset (India)
L
Punjab 1 July
Delhi 25 June
Bengal 15 June
Mumbai 5 June
main SW Monsoon currents

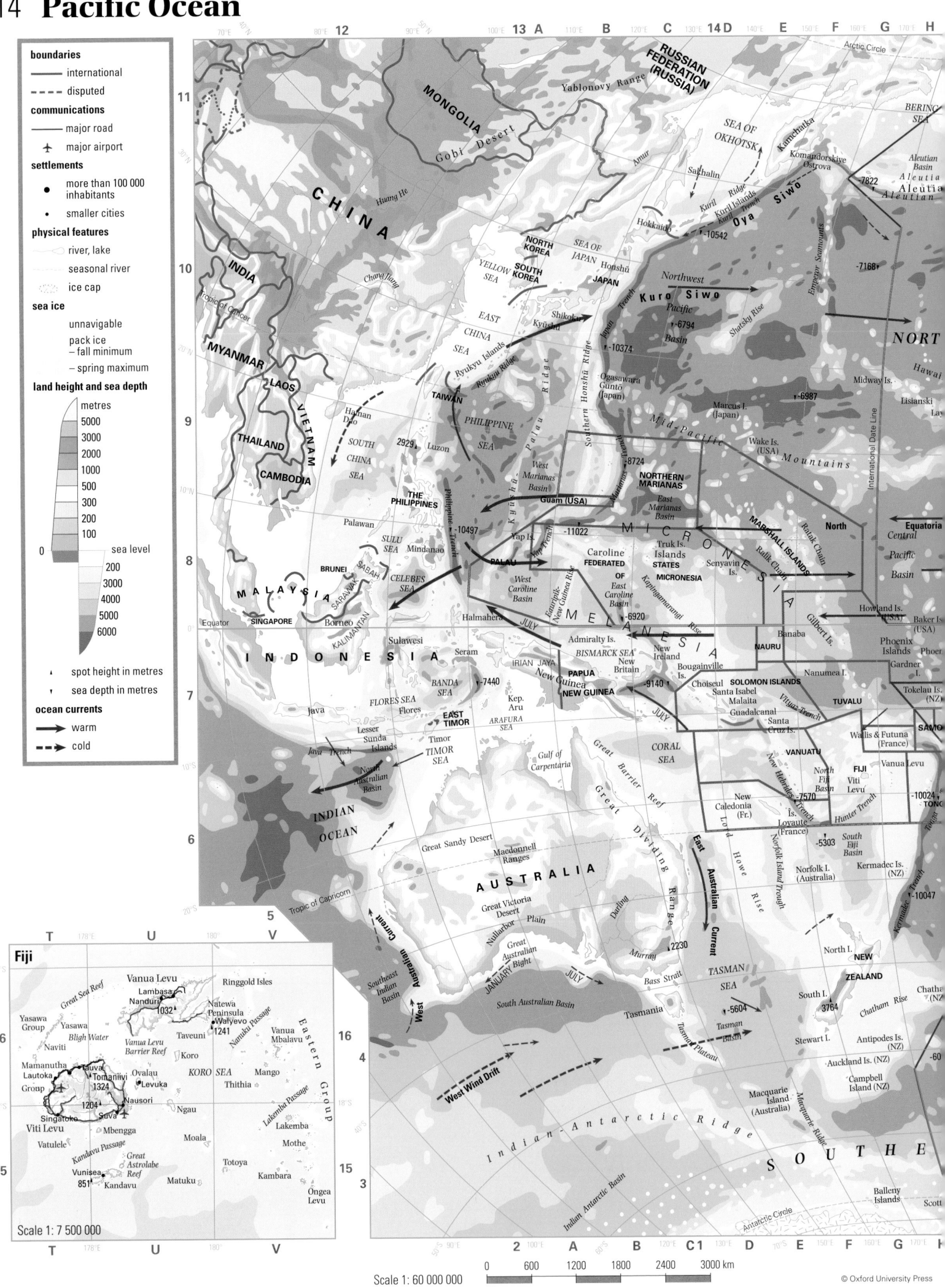

boundaries
— international
-- disputed

communications
— major road
✈ major airport

settlements
● more than 100 000 inhabitants
• smaller cities

physical features
~ river, lake
· · seasonal river
ice cap

sea ice
unnavigable
pack ice
– fall minimum
– spring maximum

land height and sea depth
metres
5000
3000
2000
1000
500
300
200
100
0 sea level
200
3000
4000
5000
6000

▲ spot height in metres
▼ sea depth in metres

ocean currents
→ warm
⇢ cold

Fiji

Scale 1: 7 500 000

Scale 1: 60 000 000

0 600 1200 1800 2400 3000 km

© Oxford University Press

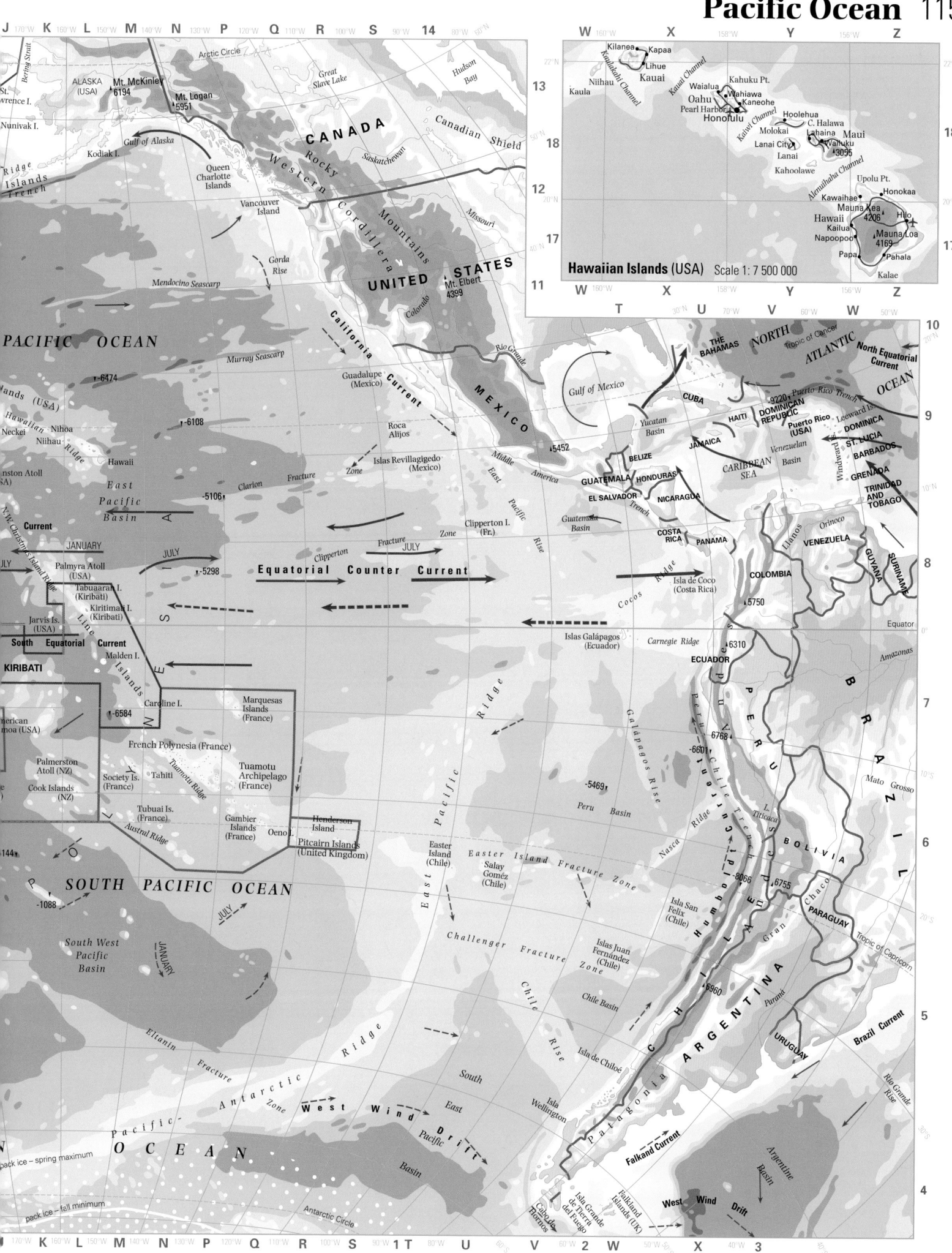

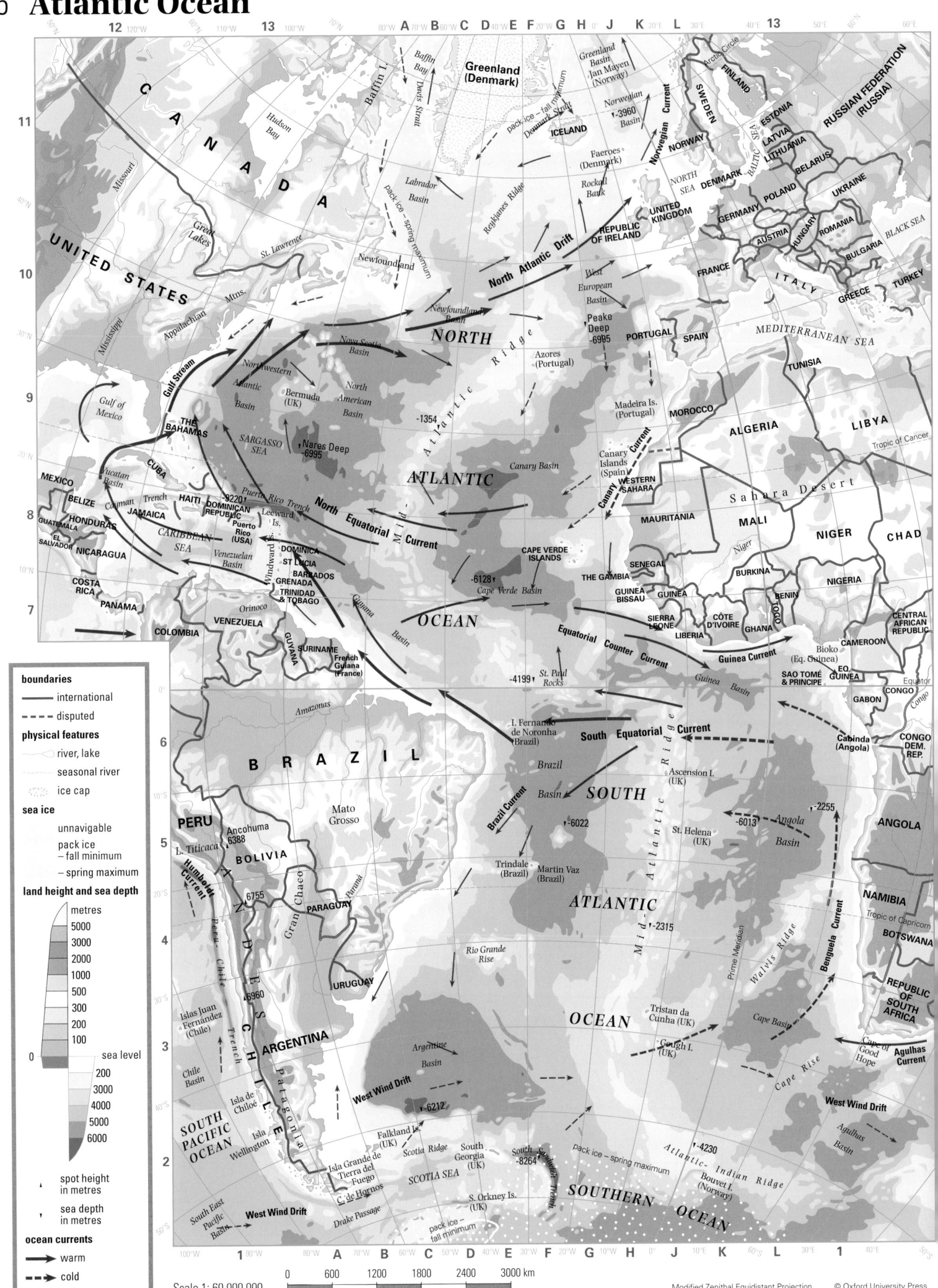

boundaries
— international
--- disputed

physical features
river, lake
seasonal river
ice cap

sea ice
unnavigable
pack ice
– fall minimum
– spring maximum

land height and sea depth
metres
5000
3000
2000
1000
500
300
200
100
0 — sea level
200
3000
4000
5000
6000

spot height in metres
sea depth in metres

ocean currents
→ warm
⇢ cold

Scale 1: 60 000 000

0 600 1200 1800 2400 3000 km

Modified Zenithal Equidistant Projection   © Oxford University Press

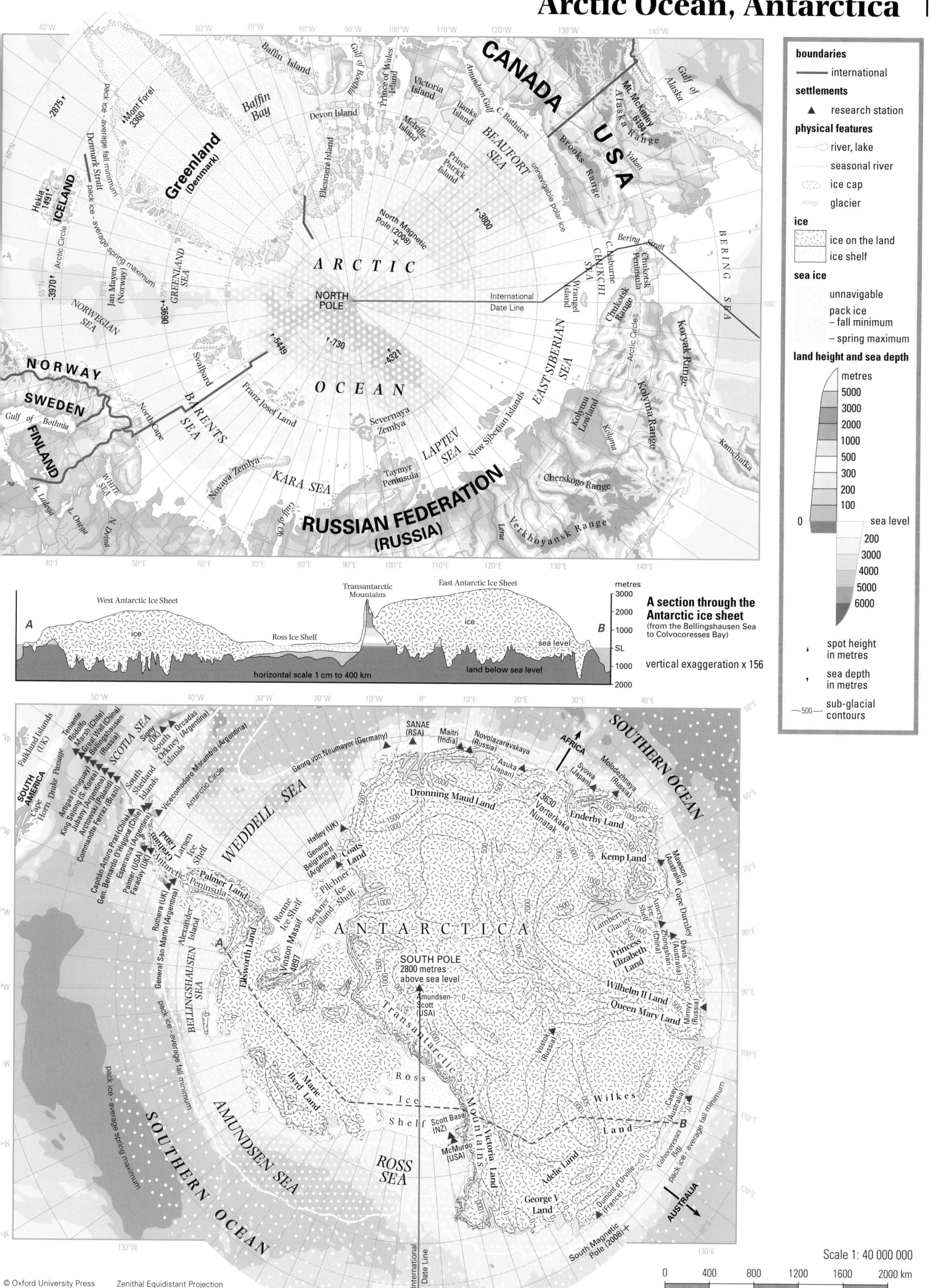

Equatorial scale 1: 95 000 000 (main map)

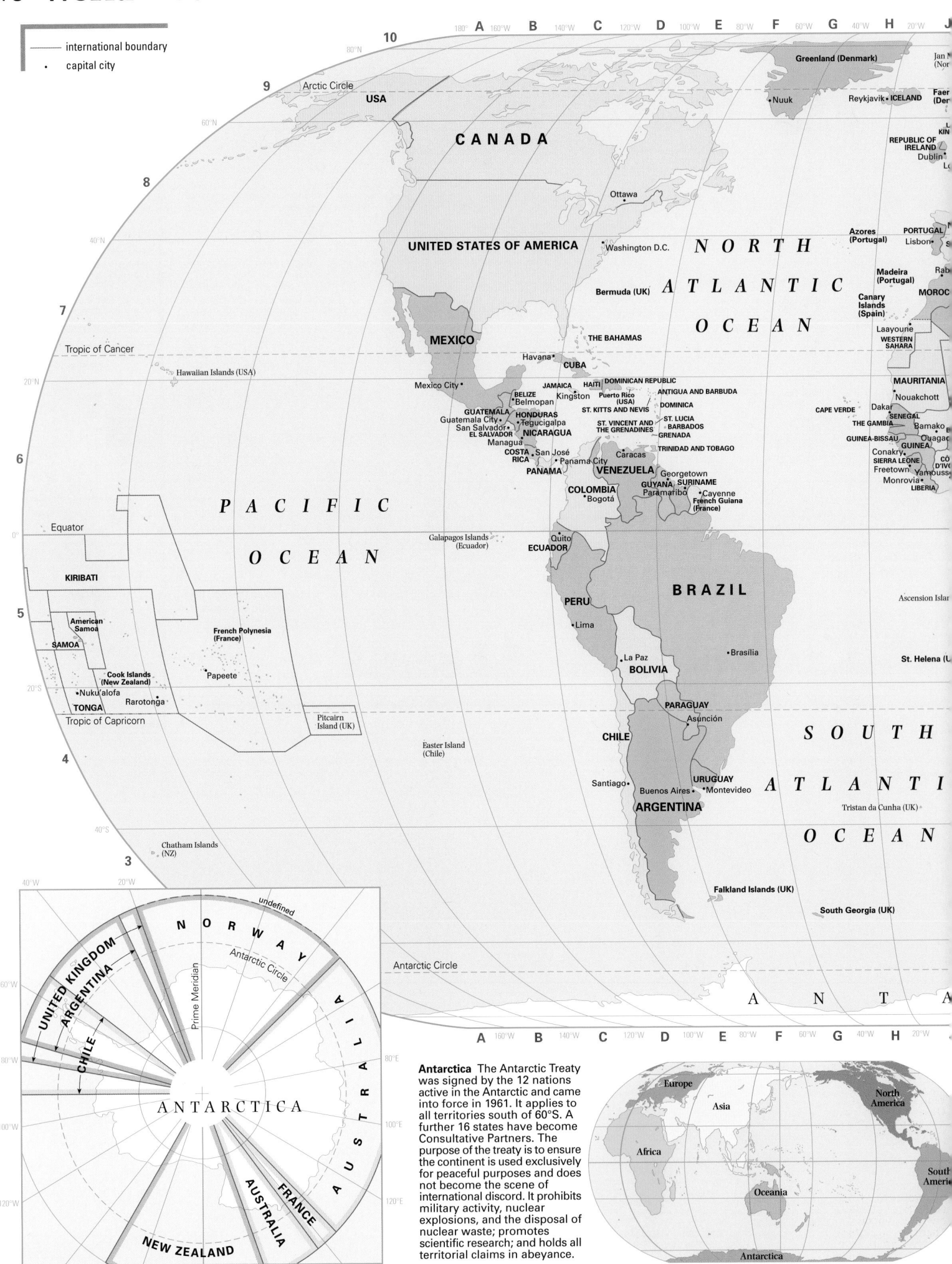

international boundary
capital city

Map labels (main map):

Greenland (Denmark)
Jan M. (Nor)
Nuuk
Reykjavik • ICELAND
Faer (Der)
Arctic Circle
USA
CANADA
REPUBLIC OF IRELAND
Dublin
Lo
Ottawa
UNITED STATES OF AMERICA
Washington D.C.
NORTH ATLANTIC OCEAN
Azores (Portugal)
PORTUGAL
Lisbon
Madeira (Portugal)
Bermuda (UK)
MOROC
Tropic of Cancer
Canary Islands (Spain)
Rab
MEXICO
THE BAHAMAS
Laayoune
WESTERN SAHARA
Hawaiian Islands (USA)
Havana
CUBA
MAURITANIA
Mexico City
DOMINICAN REPUBLIC
Nouakchott
JAMAICA
HAITI
BELIZE
Puerto Rico (USA)
ANTIGUA AND BARBUDA
CAPE VERDE
Dakar
SENEGAL
Belmopan
Kingston
DOMINICA
THE GAMBIA
Bamako
GUATEMALA
HONDURAS
ST. KITTS AND NEVIS
ST. LUCIA
GUINEA-BISSAU
GUINEA
Ouagad
Guatemala City
Tegucigalpa
ST. VINCENT AND
BARBADOS
Conakry
CÔ
San Salvador
THE GRENADINES
GRENADA
SIERRA LEONE
D'IVO
EL SALVADOR
NICARAGUA
Freetown
Yamouss
Managua
TRINIDAD AND TOBAGO
Monrovia
LIBERIA
COSTA RICA
San José
Cáracas
PANAMA
Panama City
VENEZUELA
Georgetown
COLOMBIA
GUYANA
SURINAME
Bogotá
Paramaribo
Cayenne
French Guiana (France)
PACIFIC OCEAN
Galapagos Islands (Ecuador)
Quito
ECUADOR
Ascension Islan
Equator
KIRIBATI
PERU
BRAZIL
American Samoa
Lima
SAMOA
La Paz
Brasília
St. Helena (U
Cook Islands (New Zealand)
Papeete
BOLIVIA
Nuku'alofa
TONGA
Rarotonga
PARAGUAY
Tropic of Capricorn
Pitcairn Island (UK)
Asunción
SOUTH
Easter Island (Chile)
CHILE
ATLANTI
Chatham Islands (NZ)
Santiago
URUGUAY
Buenos Aires
Montevideo
OCEAN
ARGENTINA
Tristan da Cunha (UK)
Falkland Islands (UK)
South Georgia (UK)
Antarctic Circle
A N T A

Antarctica inset:

NORWAY
undefined
UNITED KINGDOM
ARGENTINA
Antarctic Circle
CHILE
Prime Meridian
ANTARCTICA
AUSTRALIA
AUSTRALIA
FRANCE
NEW ZEALAND

Antarctica The Antarctic Treaty was signed by the 12 nations active in the Antarctic and came into force in 1961. It applies to all territories south of 60°S. A further 16 states have become Consultative Partners. The purpose of the treaty is to ensure the continent is used exclusively for peaceful purposes and does not become the scene of international discord. It prohibits military activity, nuclear explosions, and the disposal of nuclear waste; promotes scientific research; and holds all territorial claims in abeyance.

World inset:

Europe
Asia
North America
Africa
Oceania
South Americ
Antarctica

© Oxford University Press

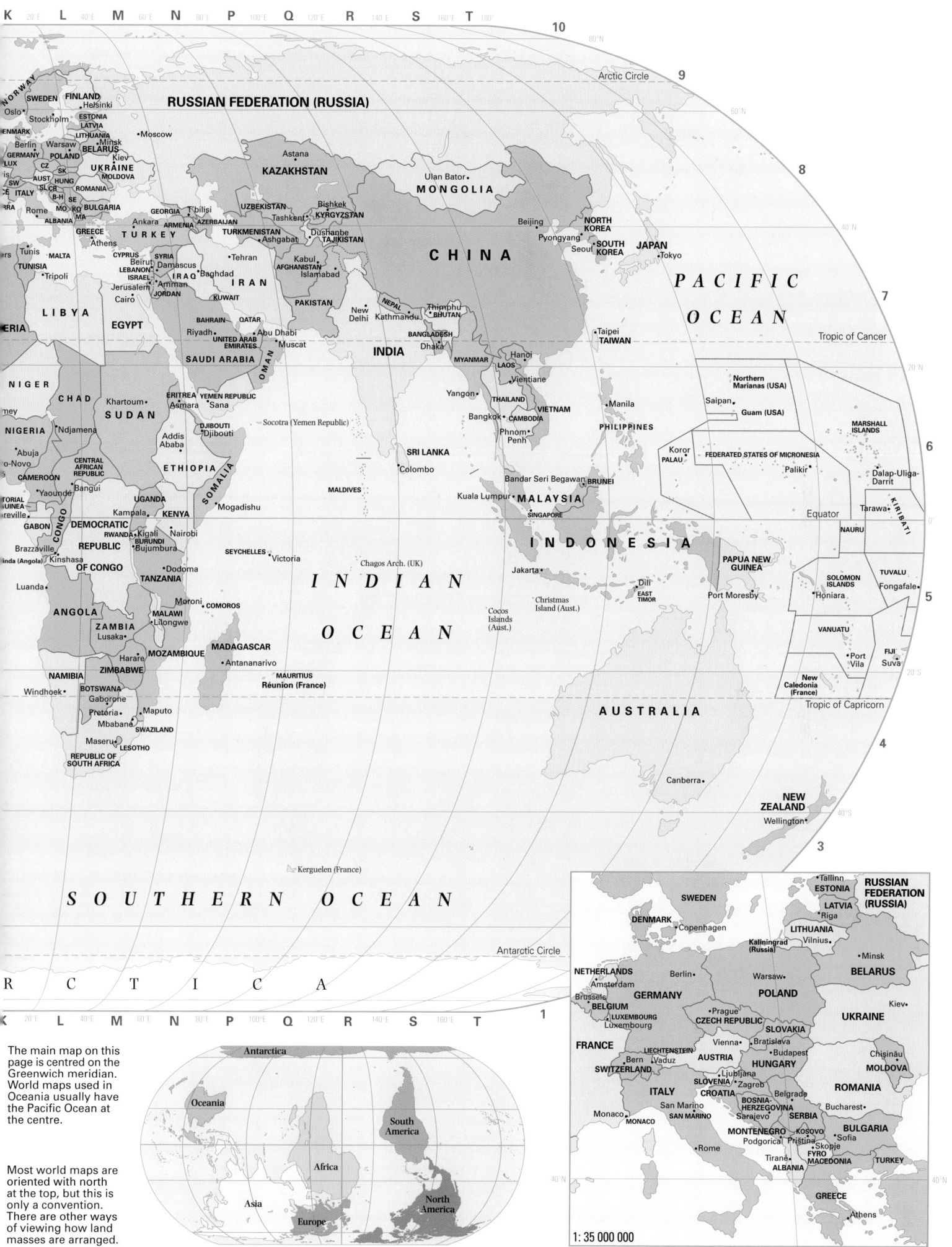

RUSSIAN FEDERATION (RUSSIA)

NORWAY
SWEDEN FINLAND
Oslo • Helsinki
Stockholm ESTONIA
DENMARK LATVIA
Berlin LITHUANIA • Moscow
GERMANY POLAND Minsk
LUX BELARUS
CZ Warsaw Kiev
SK UKRAINE
AUST HUNG MOLDOVA
ITALY B-H RO ROMANIA KAZAKHSTAN
Rome SE BULGARIA Astana
ALBANIA MA MO
GREECE GEORGIA UZBEKISTAN Bishkek
Athens Ankara ARMENIA T'bilisi KYRGYZSTAN MONGOLIA
TURKEY AZERBAIJAN Tashkent Ulan Bator
Tunis MALTA TURKMENISTAN Dushanbe
TUNISIA CYPRUS SYRIA Ashgabat TAJIKISTAN
LEBANON Beirut Damascus Tehran Kabul Islamabad Beijing NORTH
ISRAEL IRAQ Baghdad AFGHANISTAN KOREA JAPAN
Jerusalem Amman IRAN CHINA Pyongyang
Cairo JORDAN KUWAIT PAKISTAN SOUTH Seoul Tokyo
KOREA
LIBYA EGYPT BAHRAIN QATAR Riyadh New PACIFIC
ERIA Delhi NEPAL Thimphu
UNITED ARAB Abu Dhabi Kathmandu BHUTAN Taipei OCEAN
EMIRATES Muscat BANGLADESH TAIWAN
NIGER CHAD SUDAN Khartoum SAUDI ARABIA OMAN INDIA Dhaka
Asmara Sana MYANMAR Hanoi
mey ERITREA YEMEN REPUBLIC LAOS
NIGERIA Ndjamena Socotra (Yemen Republic) Vientiane
Abuja DJIBOUTI Addis THAILAND VIETNAM Manila
o-Novo CENTRAL Ababa Djibouti Yangon Bangkok CAMBODIA PHILIPPINES
CAMEROON AFRICAN ETHIOPIA SRI LANKA Phnom
Yaoundé REPUBLIC SOMALIA Colombo Penh Bandar Seri Begawan BRUNEI
TORIAL Bangui UGANDA MALDIVES Kuala Lumpur MALAYSIA
reville GABON KENYA SINGAPORE
CONGO DEMOCRATIC RWANDA Kigali Nairobi SEYCHELLES Victoria INDONESIA
nda (Angola) REPUBLIC BURUNDI Bujumbura Chagos Arch. (UK) Jakarta
Brazzaville OF CONGO Dodoma
Kinshasa TANZANIA INDIAN Christmas
Luanda Moroni COMOROS Island (Aust.) Dili
ANGOLA MALAWI Lilongwe OCEAN Cocos EAST
ZAMBIA Blantyre MADAGASCAR Islands TIMOR
Lusaka MOZAMBIQUE Antananarivo (Aust.)
NAMIBIA ZIMBABWE Harare MAURITIUS AUSTRALIA
Windhoek BOTSWANA Réunion (France)
Gaborone Maputo
Pretoria SWAZILAND
Mbabane
Maseru LESOTHO
REPUBLIC OF
SOUTH AFRICA

10
9
Arctic Circle
80°N
60°N
40°N
8
20°N
Tropic of Cancer
Equator
7
6
Northern
Marianas (USA)
Saipan
Guam (USA) MARSHALL
ISLANDS
FEDERATED STATES OF MICRONESIA
Koror Palikir Dalap-Uliga-
PALAU Darrit
KIRIBATI
Tarawa
NAURU
PAPUA NEW TUVALU
GUINEA Fongafale
SOLOMON
ISLANDS
Honiara
Port Moresby VANUATU FIJI
Port Suva
Vila
New
Caledonia
(France)
Tropic of Capricorn
Canberra
NEW
ZEALAND
Wellington
5
4
3

INDIAN
OCEAN

SOUTHERN OCEAN

Kerguelen (France)

Antarctic Circle

ARCTICA

The main map on this
page is centred on the
Greenwich meridian.
World maps used in
Oceania usually have
the Pacific Ocean at
the centre.

Most world maps are
oriented with north
at the top, but this is
only a convention.
There are other ways
of viewing how land
masses are arranged.

Antarctica
Oceania
South
America
Africa
Asia Europe
North
America

SWEDEN Tallinn RUSSIAN
ESTONIA FEDERATION
DENMARK Copenhagen LATVIA (RUSSIA)
Riga
LITHUANIA
Kaliningrad Vilnius
(Russia) Minsk
NETHERLANDS Berlin
Amsterdam Warsaw BELARUS
Brussels GERMANY POLAND
BELGIUM LUXEMBOURG Prague Kiev
Luxembourg CZECH REPUBLIC UKRAINE
SLOVAKIA
FRANCE LIECHTENSTEIN Vienna Bratislava
AUSTRIA Budapest Chişinău
SWITZERLAND Vaduz HUNGARY MOLDOVA
Bern Ljubljana
SLOVENIA Zagreb ROMANIA
ITALY CROATIA Belgrade
San Marino BOSNIA- Bucharest
HERZEGOVINA SERBIA
Monaco SAN MARINO Sarajevo BULGARIA
MONACO Kosovo Sofia
MONTENEGRO Skopje
Rome Podgorica Pristina
Tiranë FYRO TURKEY
ALBANIA MACEDONIA
GREECE
Athens

1 : 35 000 000

© Oxford University Press   Eckert IV Projection

Equatorial scale 1: 95 000 000

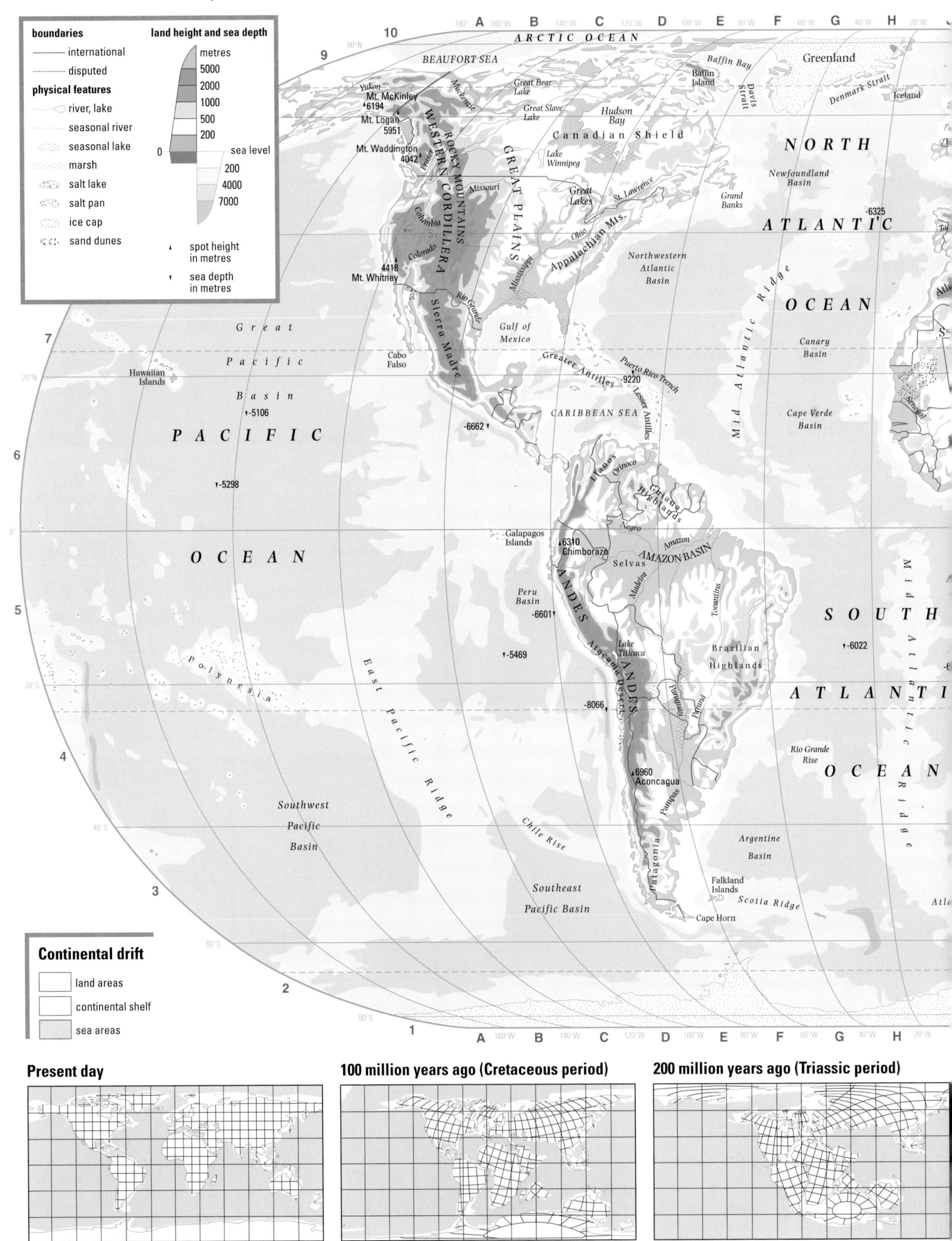

boundaries
— international
---- disputed

physical features
river, lake
seasonal river
seasonal lake
marsh
salt lake
salt pan
ice cap
sand dunes

land height and sea depth
metres
5000
2000
1000
500
200
0 sea level
200
4000
7000

spot height in metres
sea depth in metres

Continental drift
land areas
continental shelf
sea areas

Present day

100 million years ago (Cretaceous period)

200 million years ago (Triassic period)

© Oxford University Press

The equatorial circumference of the globe is 40 075 km

World's largest islands (km²)

Greenland (Denmark)	2 175 500
New Guinea (Indonesia/ Papua New Guinea)	792 500
Borneo (Brunei/Indonesia/ Malaysia)	725 500
Madagascar (Republic of Madagascar)	587 000
Baffin (Canada)	507 500
Sumatra (Indonesia)	470 000
Honshū (Japan)	227 400
Great Britain (UK)	218 100
Victoria (Canada)	217 300
Ellesmere (Canada)	196 200

World's longest rivers (km)

Nile (Africa)	6 690
Amazon (South America)	6 400
Chang Jiang (Yangtze) (Asia)	6 300
Mississippi-Missouri (North America)	5 970
Yenisey-Angara (Asia)	5 500
Huang He (Asia)	5 500
Ob' (Asia)	5 410
Congo-Chambeshi (Africa)	4 700
Amur (Asia)	4 480
Lena (Asia)	4 400
Mackenzie-Peace (Canada)	4 240

World's largest lakes (km²)

Caspian Sea (Asia)*	371 000
Lake Superior (Canada/USA)	82 100
Lake Victoria (Africa)	69 500
Lake Huron (Canada/USA)	59 600
Lake Michigan (USA)	57 800
Lake Tanganyika (Africa)	32 900
Great Bear Lake (Canada)	31 300
Ozero Baykal (Asia)	30 500
Lake Nyasa (Africa)	28 900
Great Slave Lake (Canada)	28 600
Lake Erie (Canada/USA)	25 700

*Despite being saline it is considered a lake by geographers as it is land-locked.

Highest mountain on each continent (m)

Asia	Mt Everest (China/Nepal)	8 848
Africa	Mt Kilimanjaro (Tanzania)	5 895
North America	Mt McKinley (USA)	6 194
South America	Aconcagua (Argentina)	6 960
Antarctica	Vinson Massif	4 897
Europe	Mt Elbrus (Georgia/Russia)	5 642
Australia	Mt Kosciusko (Australia)	2 230
Oceania	Pk Jaya (Papua New Guinea)	5 030
Canada	Mt Logan	5 951

Continents (km²)

Asia	43 998 000
Africa	29 800 000
North America	24 255 000
South America	17 663 000
Antarctica	13 209 000
Europe	9 699 000
Australia	7 687 000
World surface area (water 71%, land 29%)	510 072 000

Oceans (km²)

Pacific	155 557 000
Atlantic	76 762 000
Indian	68 556 000
Southern	20 327 000
Arctic	14 056 000

Equatorial scale 1: 130 000 000

Plate tectonics
plate boundaries
ridge zones (moving apart)
trench zones (colliding)
passive
transform faults
direction of plate movement
volcanoes active between 1900 and 2000
areas of deep focus earthquakes
EURASIAN PLATE
HELLENIC PLATE
IRANIAN PLATE
ARABIAN PLATE
AFRICAN PLATE
East African Rift System
CARIBBEAN PLATE
COCOS PLATE
NASCA PLATE
Peru-Chile Trench
SOUTH AMERICAN PLATE
Mid-Atlantic Ridge
INDIAN
Indian Ocean Ridge
Mid-Atlantic Ridge
ANTARCTIC PLATE
SCOTIA PLATE
ANTARCTIC PLATE

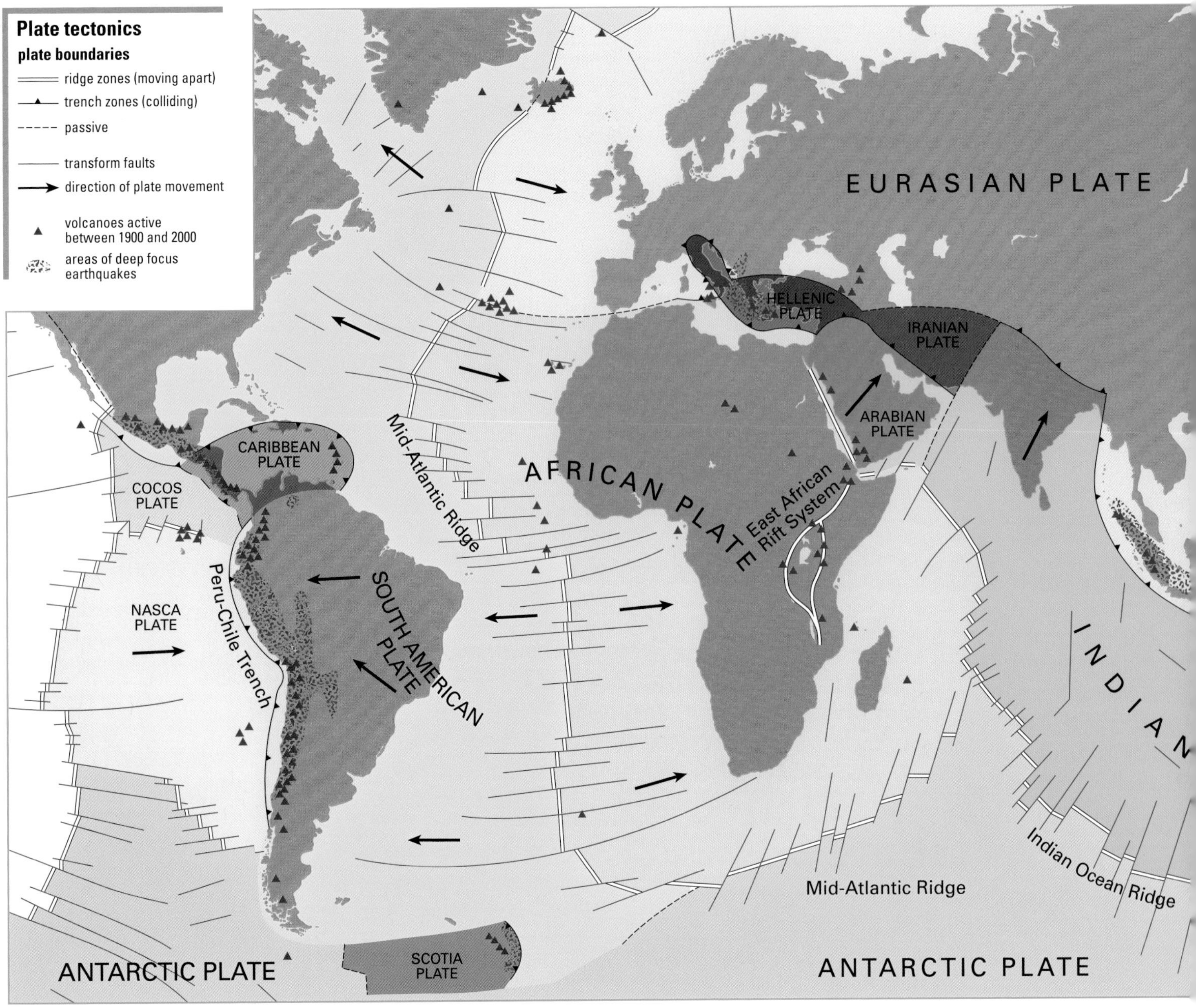

Structure of the Earth

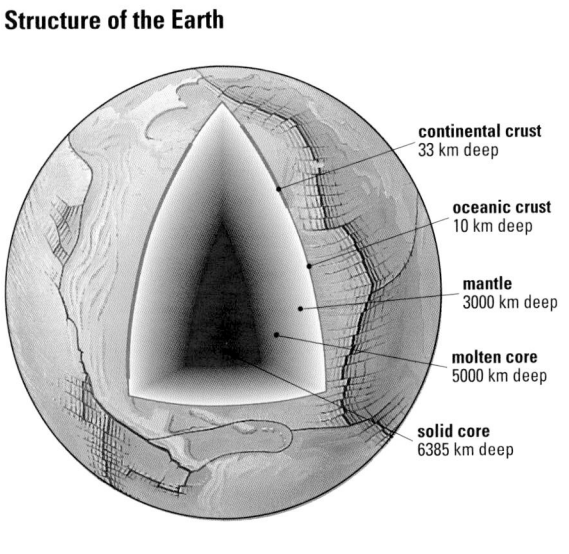

continental crust
33 km deep
oceanic crust
10 km deep
mantle
3000 km deep
molten core
5000 km deep
solid core
6385 km deep

Cross section of a strato volcano

(e.g. Mt. Vesuvius, Italy)

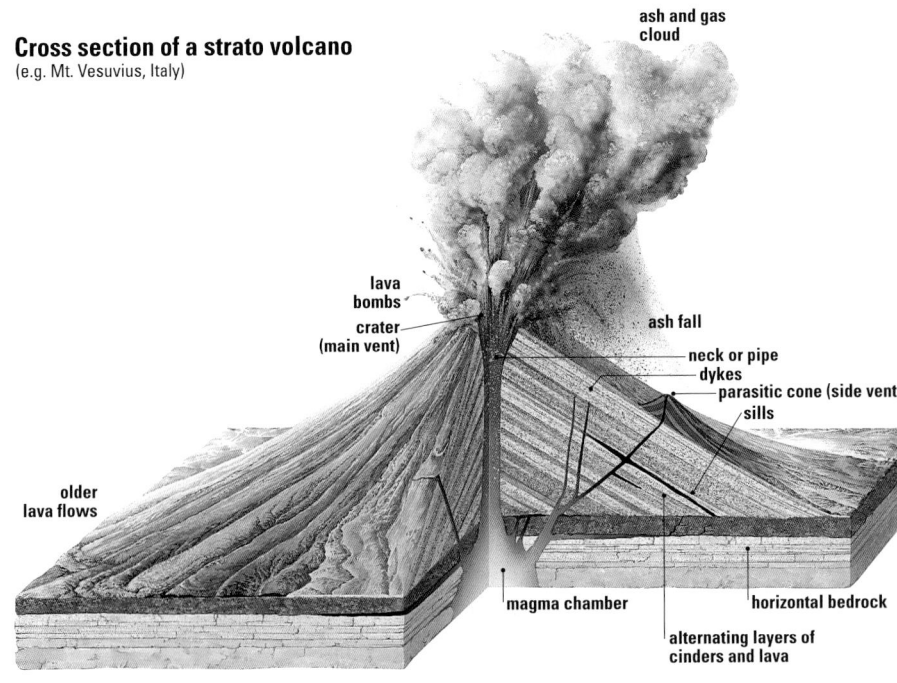

ash and gas cloud
lava bombs
crater (main vent)
ash fall
neck or pipe
dykes
parasitic cone (side vent
sills
older lava flows
magma chamber
horizontal bedrock
alternating layers of cinders and lava

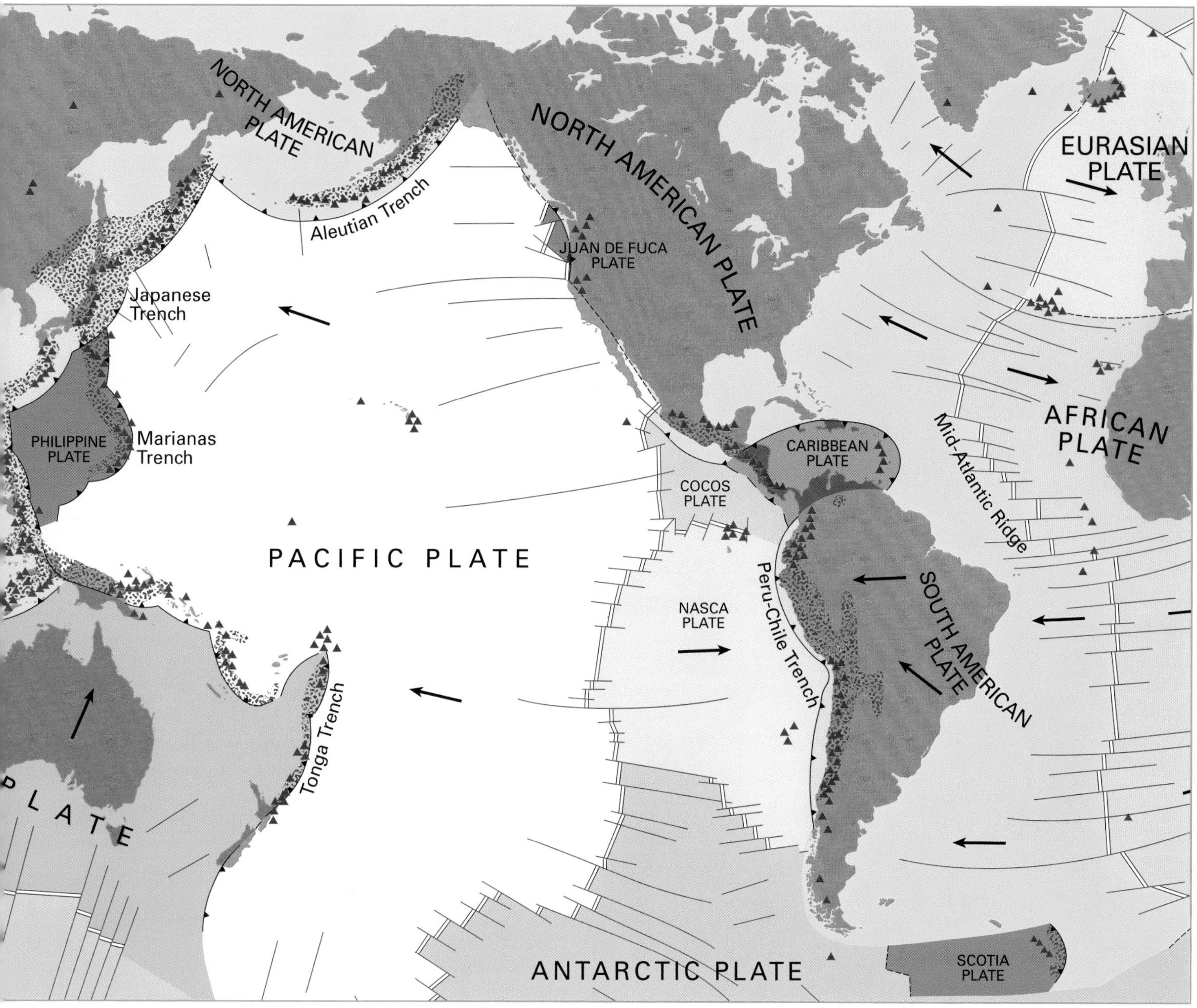

NORTH AMERICAN PLATE
Aleutian Trench
NORTH AMERICAN PLATE
JUAN DE FUCA PLATE
EURASIAN PLATE
Japanese Trench
PHILIPPINE PLATE
Marianas Trench
CARIBBEAN PLATE
COCOS PLATE
AFRICAN PLATE
Mid-Atlantic Ridge
PACIFIC PLATE
NASCA PLATE
Peru-Chile Trench
SOUTH AMERICAN PLATE
Tonga Trench
PLATE
ANTARCTIC PLATE
SCOTIA PLATE

ridge zone
transform fault
direction of plate movement
area of deep focus earthquakes
volcano
trench zone
COCOS PLATE
Galapagos Islands
Andes
Amazon
Atlantic Ocean
PACIFIC PLATE
NASCA PLATE
SOUTH AMERICAN PLATE
oceanic crust
upper part of mantle
continental crust

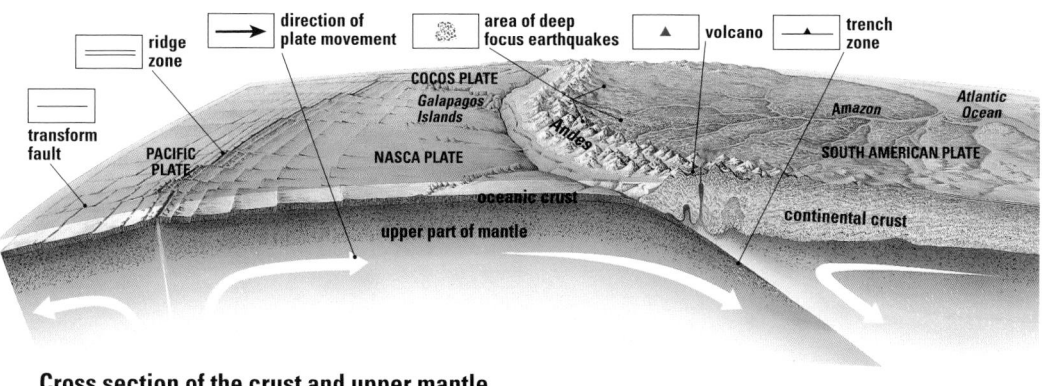

Cross section of the crust and upper mantle

100–150 km

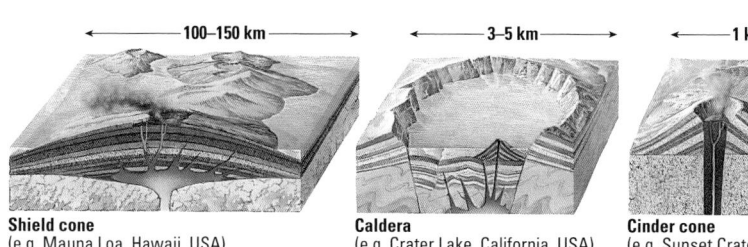

Shield cone
(e.g. Mauna Loa, Hawaii, USA)

3–5 km

Caldera
(e.g. Crater Lake, California, USA)

1 km

Cinder cone
(e.g. Sunset Crater, Arizona, USA)

Deadliest earthquakes, 1990–2006

force measured on the Richter scale

Year	Place	Force	Deaths
1990	Northwestern Iran	7.7	37 000
1990	Luzon, Philippines	7.7	1660
1991	Afghanistan/Pakistan	6.8	1000
1991	Uttar Pradesh, India	6.1	1500
1992	Erzincan, Turkey	6.7	2000
1992	Flores Island, Indonesia	7.5	2500
1993	Maharashtra, India	6.3	9800
1994	Cauca, Colombia	6.8	1000
1995	Kobe, Japan	7.2	5500
1995	Sakhalin Island, Russia	7.6	2000
1997	Ardabil, Iran	unknown	>1000
1997	Khorash, Iran	7.1	>1600
1998	Takhar, Afghanistan	6.1	>3800
1998	Northeastern Afghanistan	7.1	>3000
1999	Western Colombia	6.0	1124
1999	Izmit, Turkey	7.4	>17 000
1999	Central Taiwan	7.6	2295
2001	Gujarat, India	6.9	>20 000
2002	Baghlan, Afghanistan	6.0	>2000
2003	Northern Algeria	6.8	>2266
2003	Southeastern Iran	6.6	31 000
2004	Sumatra, Indonesia	9.1	>283 100
2005	Northern Pakistan	6.0	>86 000
2006	Java, Indonesia	6.3	>5 749

 Eckert IV Projection

January temperature

actual surface temperature

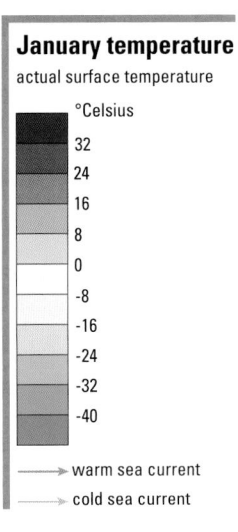

°Celsius

- 32
- 24
- 16
- 8
- 0
- -8
- -16
- -24
- -32
- -40

→ warm sea current
→ cold sea current

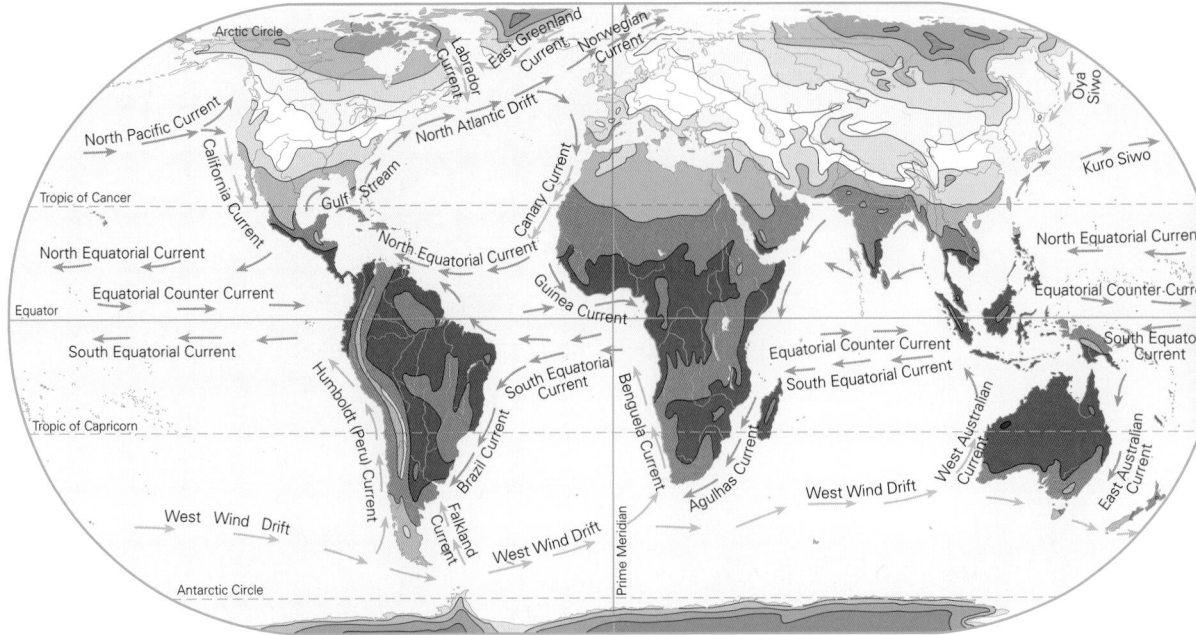

July temperature

actual surface temperature

°Celsius

- 32
- 24
- 16
- 8
- 0
- -8
- -16
- -24
- -32
- -40

→ warm sea current
→ cold sea current

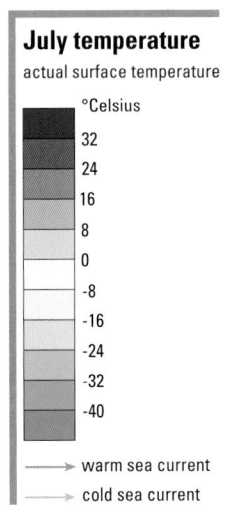

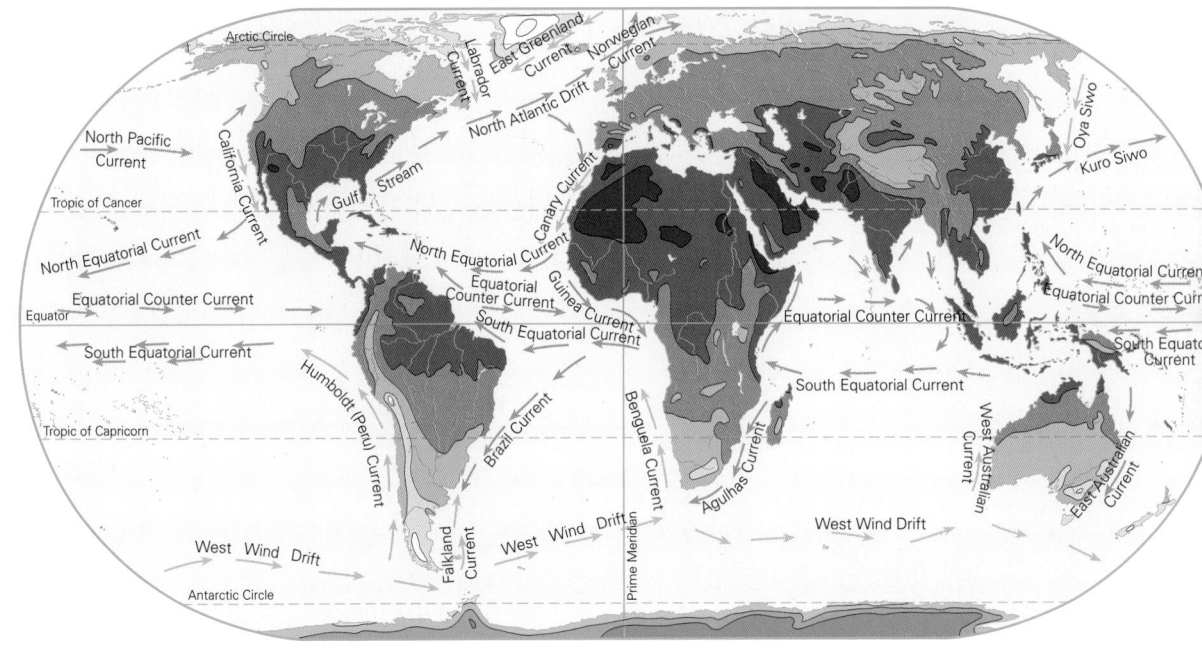

Global warming

predicted annual mean
temperature increase
by 2050

°Celsius

- 4.5
- 4.0
- 3.5
- 3.0
- 2.5
- 2.0
- 1.5
- 1.0

This map shows the projected
increase in temperature
obtained from a global climate
model. This is the result from
only one climate model. Other
models yield projections that
differ in detail but agree in their
broad features.

Further information on climate
change is located on page 128 and
for Canada on pages 16 and 25.

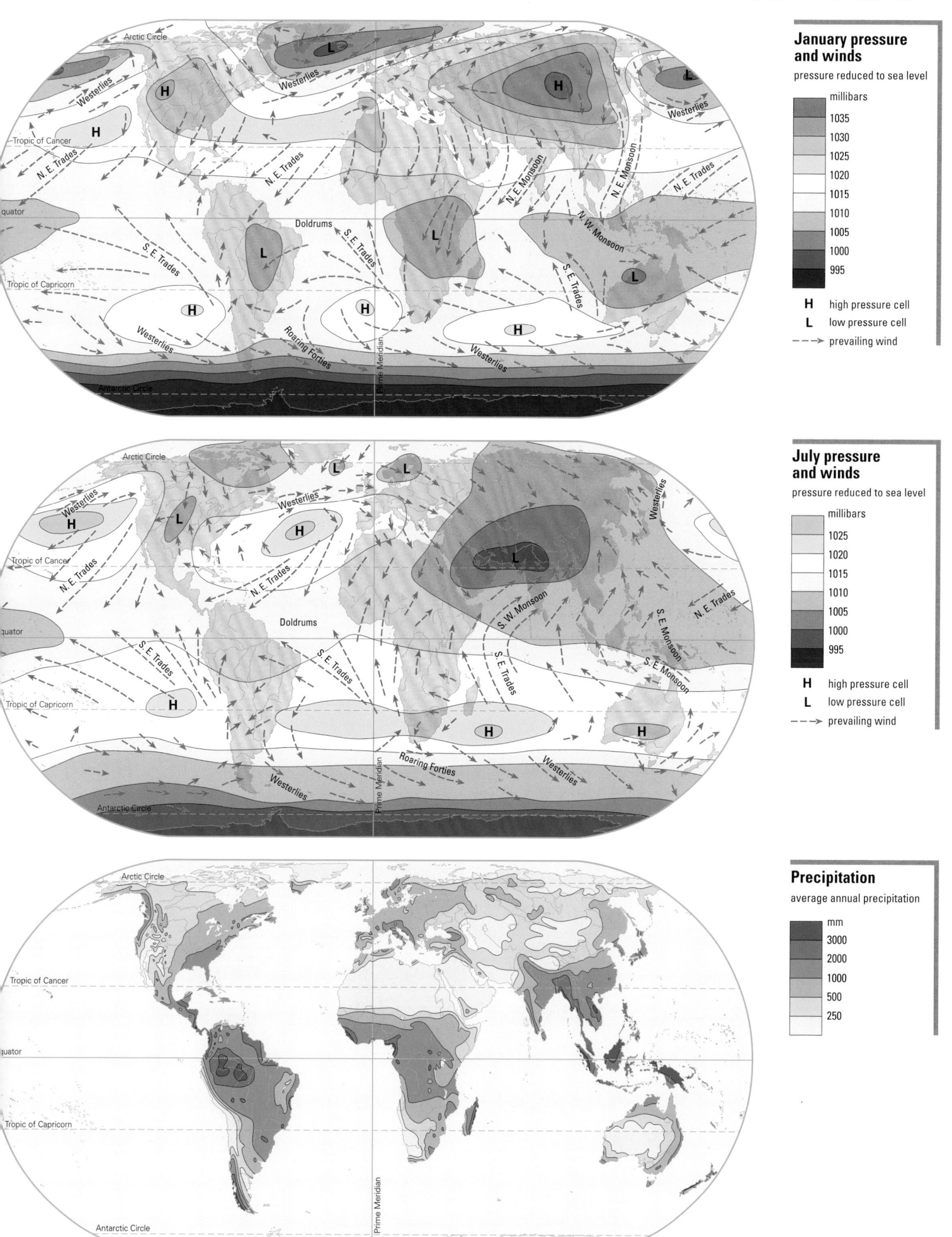

January pressure and winds

pressure reduced to sea level

millibars
1035
1030
1025
1020
1015
1010
1005
1000
995

H   high pressure cell
L   low pressure cell
--> prevailing wind

July pressure and winds

pressure reduced to sea level

millibars
1025
1020
1015
1010
1005
1000
995

H   high pressure cell
L   low pressure cell
--> prevailing wind

Precipitation

average annual precipitation

mm
3000
2000
1000
500
250

Equatorial scale 1: 190 000 000

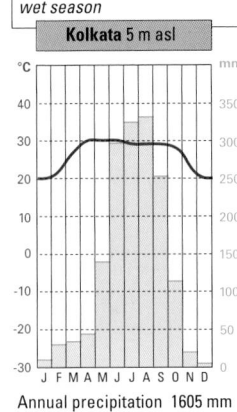

Tropical equatorial
hot and wet
rain all year

Singapore 10 m asl

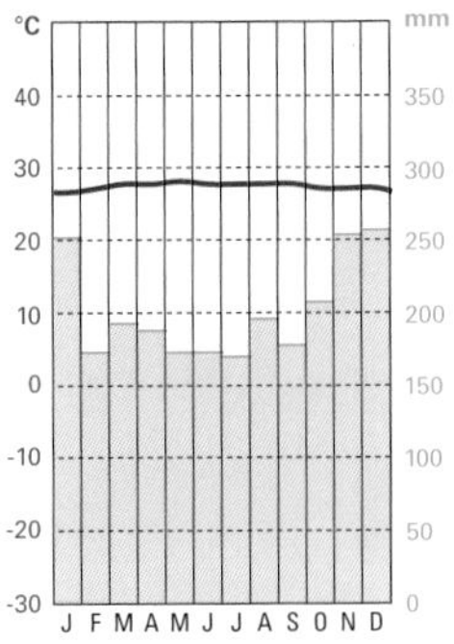

Annual precipitation 2415 mm

Tropical monsoon
hot and wet
pronounced summer wet season

Kolkata 5 m asl

Annual precipitation 1605 mm

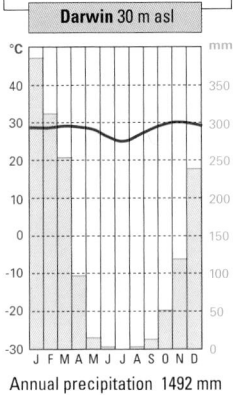

Tropical wet and dry
hot
winter dry season

Darwin 30 m asl

Annual precipitation 1492 mm

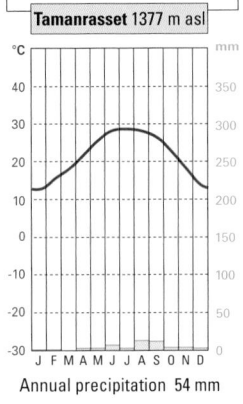

Arid desert
very dry
little reliable precipitation

Tamanrasset 1377 m asl

Annual precipitation 54 mm

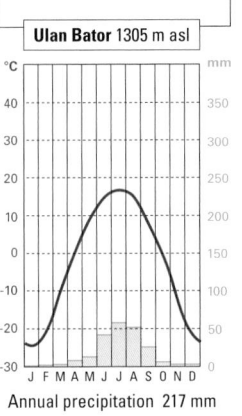

Semi-arid – steppe
very dry
low precipitation

Ulan Bator 1305 m asl

Annual precipitation 217 mm

Temperate mediterranea
mild winters
winter precipitation

Seville 8 m asl

Annual precipitation 534 mm

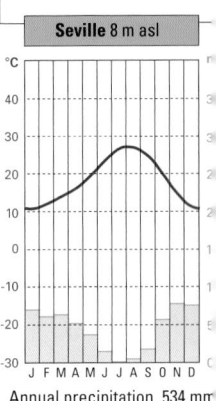

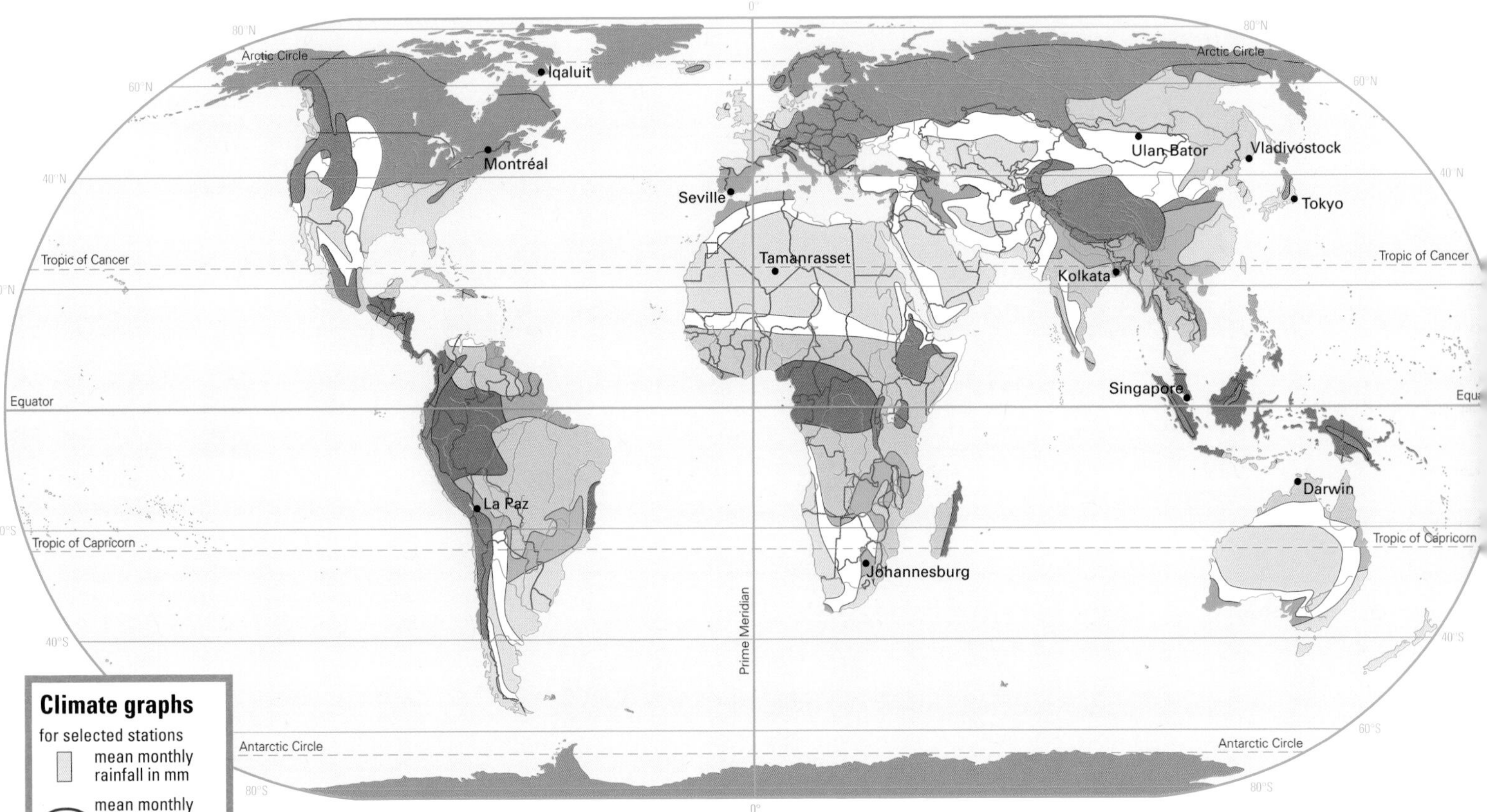

Climate graphs
for selected stations

mean monthly rainfall in mm

mean monthly temperature in °C

asl above sea level

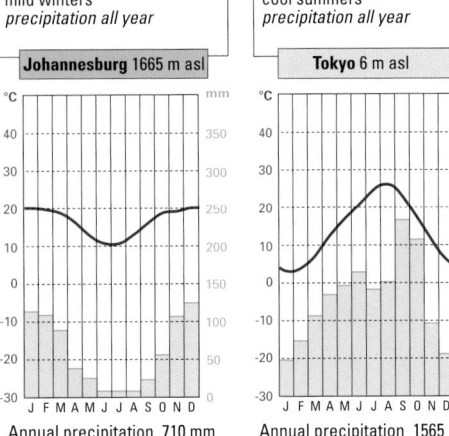

Temperate humid
mild winters
precipitation all year

Johannesburg 1665 m asl

Annual precipitation 710 mm

Temperate marine
cool summers
precipitation all year

Tokyo 6 m asl

Annual precipitation 1565 mm

Continental
large seasonal temperature range *precipitation decreases poleward*

Montréal 57 m asl

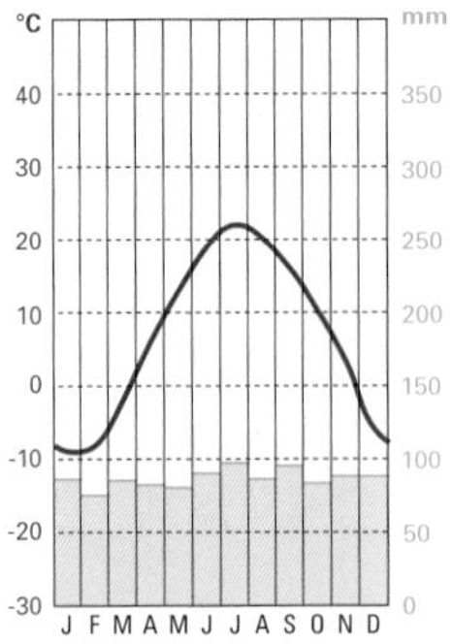

Annual precipitation 1047 mm

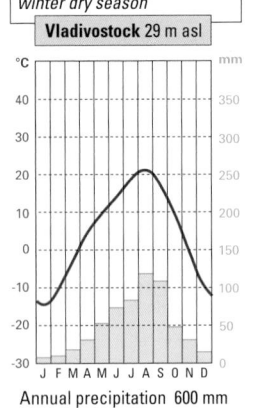

Continental
large seasonal temperature range *winter dry season*

Vladivostock 29 m asl

Annual precipitation 600 mm

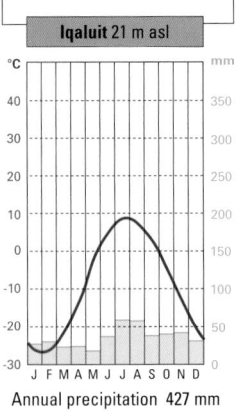

Polar
long cold winters
low precipitation

Iqaluit 21 m asl

Annual precipitation 427 mm

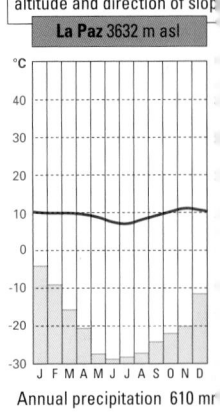

Mountain
variable temperatures and precipitation depending on altitude and direction of slop

La Paz 3632 m asl

Annual precipitation 610 mm

Eckert IV Projection   © Oxford University Press

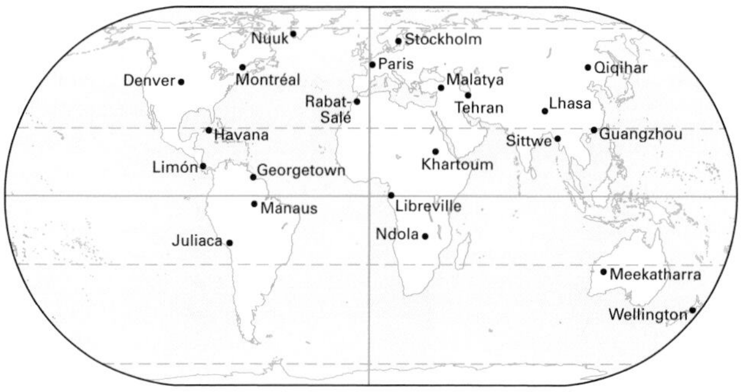

Climate data

Averages are for 1961–1990

Denver 1626 m		climate station and its height above sea level
Temperature (°C)	high	average daily maximum temperature
	mean	average monthly temperature
	low	average daily minimum temperature
Precipitation (mm)		average monthly precipitation

enver, USA 1626 m

		Jan	Feb	Mar	Apr	May	Jun	Jul	Aug	Sep	Oct	Nov	Dec	YEAR
emperature (°C)	high	6.2	8.1	11.2	16.6	21.6	27.4	31.2	29.9	24.9	19.1	11.4	6.9	17.9
	mean	-1.3	0.8	3.9	9.0	14.0	19.4	23.1	21.9	16.8	10.8	3.9	-0.6	10.1
	low	-8.8	-6.6	-3.4	1.4	6.4	11.3	14.8	13.8	8.7	2.4	-3.7	-8.1	2.4
recipitation (mm)		13	15	33	43	61	46	49	38	32	25	22	16	393

eorgetown, Guyana 2 m

		Jan	Feb	Mar	Apr	May	Jun	Jul	Aug	Sep	Oct	Nov	Dec	YEAR
emperature (°C)	high	28.6	28.9	29.2	29.5	29.4	29.2	29.6	30.2	30.8	30.8	30.2	29.1	29.6
	mean	26.1	26.4	26.7	27.0	26.8	26.5	26.6	27.0	27.5	27.6	27.2	26.4	26.8
	low	23.6	23.9	24.2	24.4	24.3	23.8	23.5	23.8	24.2	24.4	24.2	23.8	24.0
recipitation (mm)		185	89	111	141	286	328	268	201	98	107	186	262	2262

uangzhou, China 42 m

		Jan	Feb	Mar	Apr	May	Jun	Jul	Aug	Sep	Oct	Nov	Dec	YEAR
emperature (°C)	high	18.3	18.4	21.6	25.5	29.4	31.3	32.7	32.6	31.4	28.6	24.4	20.5	26.2
	mean	13.3	14.3	17.7	21.9	25.6	27.3	28.5	28.3	27.1	24.0	19.4	15.0	21.9
	low	5.0	6.6	10.7	16.1	20.7	23.5	25.7	25.2	22.6	17.6	11.9	6.5	16.0
recipitation (mm)		43	65	85	182	284	258	228	221	172	79	42	24	1683

avana, Cuba 50 m

		Jan	Feb	Mar	Apr	May	Jun	Jul	Aug	Sep	Oct	Nov	Dec	YEAR
emperature (°C)	high	25.8	26.1	27.6	28.6	29.8	30.5	31.3	31.6	31.0	29.2	27.7	26.5	28.8
	mean	22.2	22.4	23.7	24.8	26.1	26.9	27.6	27.8	27.4	26.2	24.5	23.0	25.2
	low	18.6	18.6	19.7	20.9	22.4	23.4	23.8	24.1	23.8	23.0	21.3	19.5	21.6
recipitation (mm)		64	69	46	54	98	182	106	100	144	181	88	58	1190

uliaca, Peru 3827 m

		Jan	Feb	Mar	Apr	May	Jun	Jul	Aug	Sep	Oct	Nov	Dec	YEAR
emperature (°C)	high	16.7	16.7	16.5	16.8	16.6	16.0	16.0	17.0	17.6	18.6	18.8	17.7	17.1
	mean	10.2	10.1	9.9	8.7	6.4	4.5	4.3	5.8	8.1	9.5	10.2	10.4	8.2
	low	3.6	3.5	3.2	0.6	-3.8	-7.0	-7.5	-5.4	-1.4	0.3	1.5	3.0	-0.8
recipitation (mm)		133	109	99	43	10	3	2	6	22	41	55	86	609

hartoum, Sudan 380 m

		Jan	Feb	Mar	Apr	May	Jun	Jul	Aug	Sep	Oct	Nov	Dec	YEAR
emperature (°C)	high	30.8	33.0	36.8	40.1	41.9	41.3	38.4	37.3	39.1	39.3	35.2	31.8	37.1
	mean	23.2	25.0	28.7	31.9	34.5	34.3	32.1	31.5	32.5	32.4	28.1	24.5	29.9
	low	15.6	17.0	20.5	23.6	27.1	27.3	25.9	25.3	26.0	25.5	21.0	17.1	22.7
recipitation (mm)		0	0	0	0.5	4	5	46	75	25	5	1	0	161

hasa, China 3650 m

		Jan	Feb	Mar	Apr	May	Jun	Jul	Aug	Sep	Oct	Nov	Dec	YEAR
emperature (°C)	high	6.9	9.0	12.1	15.6	19.3	22.7	22.1	21.1	19.7	16.3	11.2	7.7	15.3
	mean	-2.1	1.1	4.6	8.1	11.9	15.5	15.3	14.5	12.8	8.1	2.2	-1.7	7.5
	low	-10.1	-6.8	-3.0	0.9	5.0	9.3	10.1	9.4	7.5	1.3	-4.9	-9.0	0.8
recipitation (mm)		1	1	2	5	27	72	119	123	58	10	2	1	421

breville, Gabon 15 m

		Jan	Feb	Mar	Apr	May	Jun	Jul	Aug	Sep	Oct	Nov	Dec	YEAR
emperature (°C)	high	29.5	30.0	30.2	30.1	29.4	27.6	26.4	26.8	27.5	28.0	28.4	29.0	28.6
	mean	26.8	27.0	27.1	26.6	26.7	25.4	24.3	24.3	25.4	25.7	25.9	26.2	26.0
	low	24.1	24.0	23.9	23.1	24.0	23.2	22.1	21.8	23.4	23.4	23.4	23.4	23.3
recipitation (mm)		250	243	363	339	247	54	7	14	104	427	490	303	2841

món, Costa Rica 3 m

		Jan	Feb	Mar	Apr	May	Jun	Jul	Aug	Sep	Oct	Nov	Dec	YEAR
emperature (°C)	high	27.9	28.6	29.6	29.6	28.5	27.5	27.7	27.7	27.2	27.0	27.1	27.7	28.0
	mean	24.0	24.3	25.0	25.8	26.1	25.9	25.2	25.6	25.7	25.4	25.1	24.3	25.2
	low	20.3	20.3	20.9	21.6	22.2	22.3	22.1	22.1	22.2	21.9	21.6	20.9	21.5
ecipitation (mm)		319	201	193	287	281	276	408	289	163	198	367	402	3384

alatya, Turkey 849 m

		Jan	Feb	Mar	Apr	May	Jun	Jul	Aug	Sep	Oct	Nov	Dec	YEAR
emperature (°C)	high	2.9	5.3	11.1	18.2	23.5	29.2	33.8	33.4	28.9	20.9	11.8	5.7	18.7
	mean	-0.4	1.5	6.9	13.0	17.8	22.9	27.0	26.5	22.0	14.8	7.6	2.4	13.5
	low	-3.2	-1.7	2.4	7.7	11.8	16.1	19.8	19.4	15.2	9.5	3.7	-0.3	8.4
ecipitation (mm)		42	36	60	61	50	22	3	2	6	40	47	42	411

anaus, Brazil 84 m

		Jan	Feb	Mar	Apr	May	Jun	Jul	Aug	Sep	Oct	Nov	Dec	YEAR
emperature (°C)	high	30.5	30.4	30.6	30.7	30.8	31.0	31.3	32.6	32.9	32.8	32.1	31.3	31.4
	mean	26.1	26.0	26.1	26.3	26.3	26.4	26.5	27.0	27.5	27.6	27.3	26.7	26.7
	low	23.1	23.1	23.2	23.3	23.3	23.0	22.7	23.0	23.5	23.7	23.7	23.5	23.3
recipitation (mm)		260	288	314	300	256	114	88	58	83	126	183	217	2287

Meekatharra, Australia 518 m

		Jan	Feb	Mar	Apr	May	Jun	Jul	Aug	Sep	Oct	Nov	Dec	YEAR
Temperature (°C)	high	38.1	36.5	34.5	29.2	23.6	19.7	18.9	21.0	25.4	29.4	33.1	36.5	28.8
	mean	31.2	30.1	28.0	23.2	17.8	14.3	13.2	14.8	18.4	22.2	25.9	29.3	22.4
	low	24.3	23.7	21.5	17.1	11.9	8.9	7.5	8.5	11.4	15.0	18.6	22.1	15.9
Precipitation (mm)		26	30	22	17	27	36	25	12	6	7	14	11	233

Montréal, Canada 57 m

		Jan	Feb	Mar	Apr	May	Jun	Jul	Aug	Sep	Oct	Nov	Dec	YEAR
Temperature (°C)	high	-5.7	-4.4	1.6	10.6	18.5	23.6	26.1	24.8	19.9	13.3	5.4	-3.0	10.9
	mean	-10.3	-8.8	-2.4	5.7	12.9	18.0	20.8	19.4	14.5	8.3	1.6	-6.9	6.1
	low	-14.6	-13.5	-6.7	0.8	7.4	12.9	15.6	14.3	9.6	4.1	-1.5	-10.8	1.5
Precipitation (mm)		63.3	56.4	67.6	74.8	68.3	82.5	85.6	100.3	86.5	75.4	93.4	85.6	939.7

Ndola, Zambia 1270 m

		Jan	Feb	Mar	Apr	May	Jun	Jul	Aug	Sep	Oct	Nov	Dec	YEAR
Temperature (°C)	high	26.6	26.9	27.4	27.5	26.6	25.1	25.2	27.5	30.5	31.5	29.4	27.0	27.6
	mean	20.8	20.8	21.0	20.5	18.6	16.5	16.7	19.2	22.5	23.7	22.5	21.0	20.3
	low	17.1	17.1	16.5	14.4	10.8	7.9	7.8	10.2	13.6	16.2	17.1	17.2	13.8
Precipitation (mm)		29.3	249	170	46	4	1	0	0	3	32	130	306	1234

Nuukv, Greenland 70 m

		Jan	Feb	Mar	Apr	May	Jun	Jul	Aug	Sep	Oct	Nov	Dec	YEAR
Temperature (°C)	high	-4.4	-4.5	-4.8	-0.8	3.5	7.7	10.6	9.9	6.3	1.7	-1.0	-3.3	1.7
	mean	-7.4	-7.8	-8.0	-3.9	0.6	3.9	6.5	6.1	3.5	-0.6	-3.6	-6.2	-1.4
	low	-10.1	-10.6	-10.6	-6.1	-1.5	1.3	3.8	3.8	1.6	-2.5	-5.8	-8.7	-3.8
Precipitation (mm)		39	47	50	46	55	62	82	89	88	70	74	54	756

Paris, France 65 m

		Jan	Feb	Mar	Apr	May	Jun	Jul	Aug	Sep	Oct	Nov	Dec	YEAR
Temperature (°C)	high	6.0	7.6	10.8	14.4	18.2	21.5	24.0	23.8	20.8	16.0	10.1	6.8	15.0
	mean	3.4	4.2	6.6	9.5	13.2	16.4	18.4	18.0	15.3	11.4	6.7	4.2	10.6
	low	0.9	1.3	2.9	5.0	8.3	11.2	12.9	12.7	10.6	7.7	3.8	1.7	6.6
Precipitation (mm)		54	46	54	47	63	58	84	52	54	56	56	56	650

Qiqihar, China 148 m

		Jan	Feb	Mar	Apr	May	Jun	Jul	Aug	Sep	Oct	Nov	Dec	YEAR
Temperature (°C)	high	-12.7	-7.8	2.3	12.9	21.0	26.2	27.8	26.1	20.1	11.1	-1.3	-10.4	9.6
	mean	-19.2	-14.8	-4.5	6.1	14.4	20.3	22.8	20.9	14.0	4.8	-7.1	-16.2	3.5
	low	-24.5	-20.9	-11.0	-0.9	7.3	14.2	17.9	16.2	8.5	-0.7	-12.0	-21.2	-2.3
Precipitation (mm)		1	2	5	15	31	64	138	94	45	19	4	3	421

Rabat-Salé, Morocco 75 m

		Jan	Feb	Mar	Apr	May	Jun	Jul	Aug	Sep	Oct	Nov	Dec	YEAR
Temperature (°C)	high	17.2	17.7	19.2	20.0	22.1	24.1	26.8	27.1	26.4	24.0	20.6	17.7	21.9
	mean	12.6	13.1	14.2	15.2	17.4	19.8	22.2	22.4	21.5	19.0	15.9	13.2	17.2
	low	8.0	8.6	9.2	10.4	12.7	15.4	17.6	17.7	16.7	14.1	11.1	8.7	12.5
Precipitation (mm)		77	74	61	62	25	7	1	1	6	44	97	101	556

Sittwe, Myanmar 5 m

		Jan	Feb	Mar	Apr	May	Jun	Jul	Aug	Sep	Oct	Nov	Dec	YEAR
Temperature (°C)	high	28.0	29.4	31.4	34.1	31.5	29.5	28.9	28.9	30.1	31.1	30.3	28.5	30.1
	mean	21.4	22.7	24.8	28.9	28.3	27.1	26.8	26.7	27.4	27.6	25.7	22.6	25.8
	low	14.7	15.9	18.2	23.6	25.1	24.6	24.7	24.5	24.6	24.0	21.0	16.6	21.5
Precipitation (mm)		11	8	5	44	268	1091	1155	1025	537	289	105	17	4555

Stockholm, Sweden 52 m

		Jan	Feb	Mar	Apr	May	Jun	Jul	Aug	Sep	Oct	Nov	Dec	YEAR
Temperature (°C)	high	-0.7	-0.6	3.0	8.6	15.7	20.7	21.9	20.4	15.1	9.9	4.5	1.1	10.0
	mean	-2.8	-3.0	0.1	4.6	10.7	15.6	17.2	16.2	11.9	7.5	2.6	-1.0	6.6
	low	-5.0	-5.3	-2.7	1.1	6.3	11.3	13.4	12.7	9.0	5.3	0.7	-3.2	3.6
Precipitation (mm)		39	27	26	30	30	45	72	66	55	50	53	46	539

Tehran, Iran 1191 m

		Jan	Feb	Mar	Apr	May	Jun	Jul	Aug	Sep	Oct	Nov	Dec	YEAR
Temperature (°C)	high	7.2	9.9	15.4	21.9	28.0	34.1	36.8	35.4	31.5	24.0	16.5	9.8	22.5
	mean	3.0	5.3	10.3	16.4	22.1	27.5	30.4	29.2	25.3	18.5	11.6	5.6	17.1
	low	-1.1	0.7	5.2	10.9	16.1	20.9	24.0	23.0	19.2	12.9	6.7	1.3	11.7
Precipitation (mm)		37	34	37	28	15	3	3	1	1	14	21	36	230

Wellington, New Zealand 8 m

		Jan	Feb	Mar	Apr	May	Jun	Jul	Aug	Sep	Oct	Nov	Dec	YEAR
Temperature (°C)	high	21.3	21.1	19.8	17.3	14.8	12.8	12.0	12.7	14.2	15.9	17.8	19.6	16.6
	mean	17.8	17.7	16.6	14.3	11.9	10.1	9.2	9.8	11.2	12.8	14.5	16.4	13.5
	low	14.4	14.3	13.5	11.3	9.1	7.3	6.4	6.9	8.3	9.7	11.3	13.2	10.5
Precipitation (mm)		67	48	76	87	99	113	111	106	82	81	74	74	1018

Jan Feb Mar Apr May Jun Jul Aug Sep Oct Nov Dec YEAR

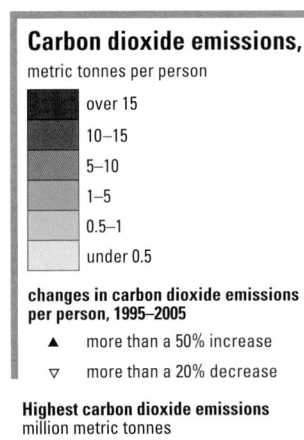

Carbon dioxide emissions, 2005
metric tonnes per person

- over 15
- 10–15
- 5–10
- 1–5
- 0.5–1
- under 0.5

changes in carbon dioxide emissions per person, 1995–2005

▲ more than a 50% increase

▽ more than a 20% decrease

Highest carbon dioxide emissions
million metric tonnes

USA	5 957.0
China	5 322.7
Russian Federation	1 696.0
Japan	1 230.4
India	1 165.7
Germany	844.2
Canada	631.3
United Kingdom	577.2
South Korea	499.6
Italy	466.6
World	28 192.7

Summary of atmospheric greenhouse gases

Gas	Anthropogenic sources	Concentrations preindustrial 1860	2004	Annual rate of increase 1994–2004	Lifetime in atmosphere	Contribution to global warming
carbon dioxide (CO_2)	fossil fuels, deforestation, soil destruction	286–288 ppm	377 ppm	1.9 ppm (0.5%)	50-200 years	54%
methane (CH_4)	domesticated livestock, biomass, rice cultivation, oil and gas production, mining	848 ppb	1784 ppb	3.7 ppb (0.2%)	12 +/–3 years	12%
halocarbons e.g., chlorofluorocarbons (CFC 11 & 12) and hydro-fluorocarbons (HFC)	refrigeration, air conditioning, solvents, aerosols	0 0	263 CFC 11 544 CFC 12 ppt	11 ppt (5.0%) CFC 11 19 ppt (5.0%) CFC 12	10s to 100s years	21%
nitrous oxide (N_2O)	fossil fuels, deforestation, fertilizer use	285 ppb	318 ppb	0.8 ppb (0.3%)	114 years	6%
ozone and other trace gases (O_3)	photochemicals, processes, cars, power plants, solvents	25 ppb	29 ppb	unknown	hours to days in upper troposphere	7%

ppm = parts per million; ppb = parts per billion; ppt = parts per trillion
Halocarbons are carbon compounds containing halogens such as chlorine, fluorine, and bromine. They are a product of human activities.
Each greenhouse gas differs in its ability to absorb heat in the atmosphere. CFCs and HFCs are the most heat absorbent. CH_4 traps 27 times and N_2O 270 times more heat than CO_2.

Climate change

The Earth's climate naturally changes over long periods of time. Many scientists now believe that these natural cycles have been interrupted by a rise in the temperature in the lower atmosphere as a consequence of human activity; predictions indicate this trend will continue and may accelerate. The primary cause of rising temperatures is related to the greenhouse effect (see page 16). Increasing amounts of carbon dioxide and other greenhouse gases are being added to the atmosphere as a result of burning fossil fuels, increased road and air transport, and the cutting down of forests makes the problem even worse.

Scientific models that attempt to understand future climate changes predict that rising temperatures will not occur uniformly, while precipitation will increase in some areas and decrease in others. Some of the reasons why we should be concerned about climate change are described on page 27. While it is practically impossible to know the specifics of the changes in climate that will occur in the future, the scientific principles are clear and our knowledge of more detailed implications is rapidly developing. However, uncertainties remain and the possibility of surprises cannot be ruled out.

World temperature forecast 2000–2100

Based on three scenarios from the Intergovernmental Panel on Climate Change which look at population and economic growth, technological change, and associated CO_2 emissions

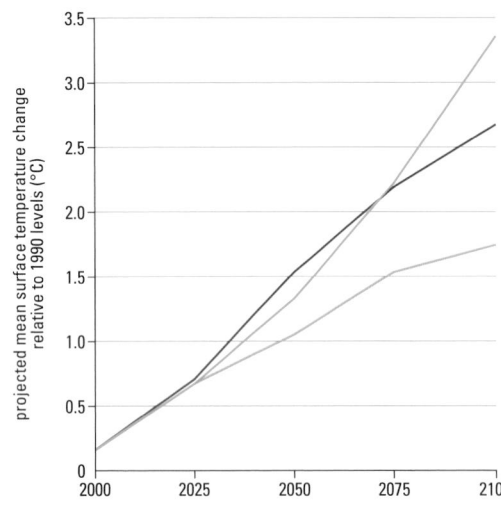

projected mean surface temperature change relative to 1990 levels (°C)

assumes rapid population and economic growth combined with a reliance on fossil and non-fossil energy

assumes high population growth but lower economic growth and less globalization

assumes some reduction in emissions through increased efficiency and improvement in technology

Global CO2 emissions by sector
% of world total

- other 4%
- other fuel consumption 10%
- electricity and heat 32%
- land use changes and forestry 24%
- manufacturing and construction 13%
- transportation 17%

Further information on climate change is located on page 124 and for Canada on pages 16 and 25.

© Oxford University Press

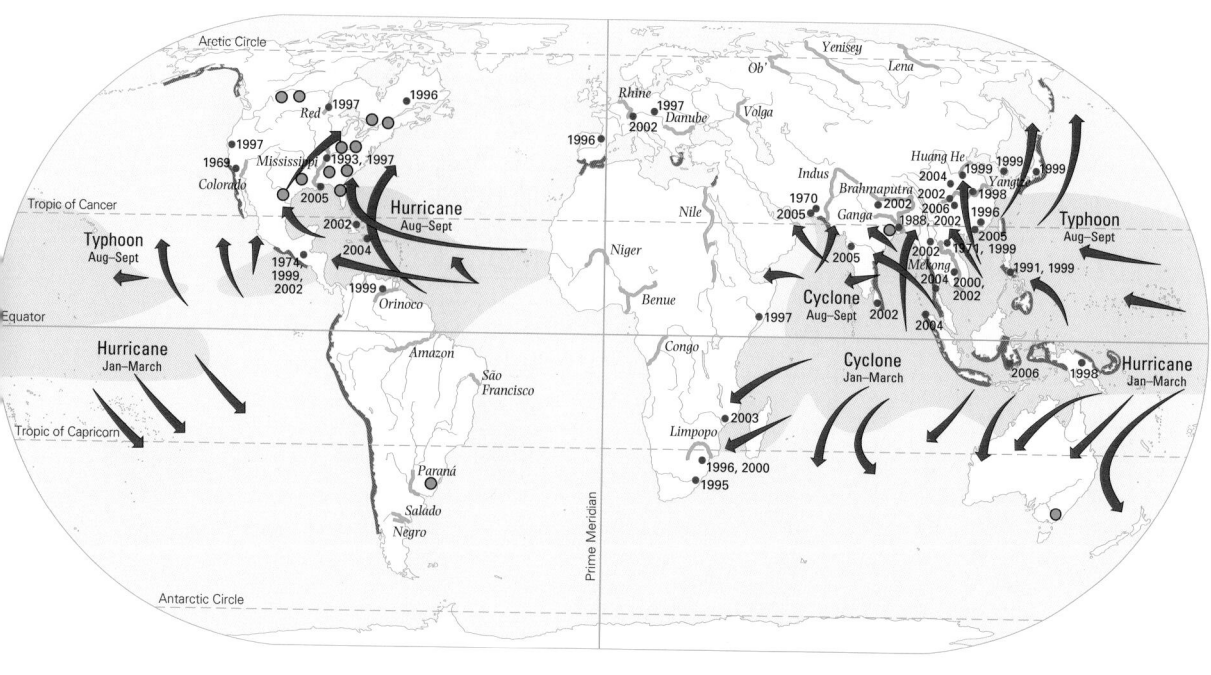

Storms and floods

→ paths of revolving tropical storms

areas affected by tropical storms

coasts vulnerable to tsunamis (seismic sea waves)

major river flood plains susceptible to flooding

• major floods

● areas affected by tornadoes

Distribution of the Earth's water

	Volume (km³)	Average residence time
Oceans and seas	1 370 000 000	4 000+ years
Glaciers and ice caps	30 000 000	1000s of years
Groundwater	4 000 000–60 000 000	from days to tens of thousands of years
Atmospheric water	113 000	8 to 10 days
Freshwater lakes	125 000	days to years
Saline lakes and inland seas	104 000	–
River channels	1 700	2 weeks
Swamps and marshes	3 600	years
Biological water (in plants and animals)	65 000	a few days
Moisture in soil	65 000	2 weeks to 1 year

Hurricane Katrina
Winds in this hurricane reached 280 km per hour and caused 1 836 deaths. 29 August 2005.

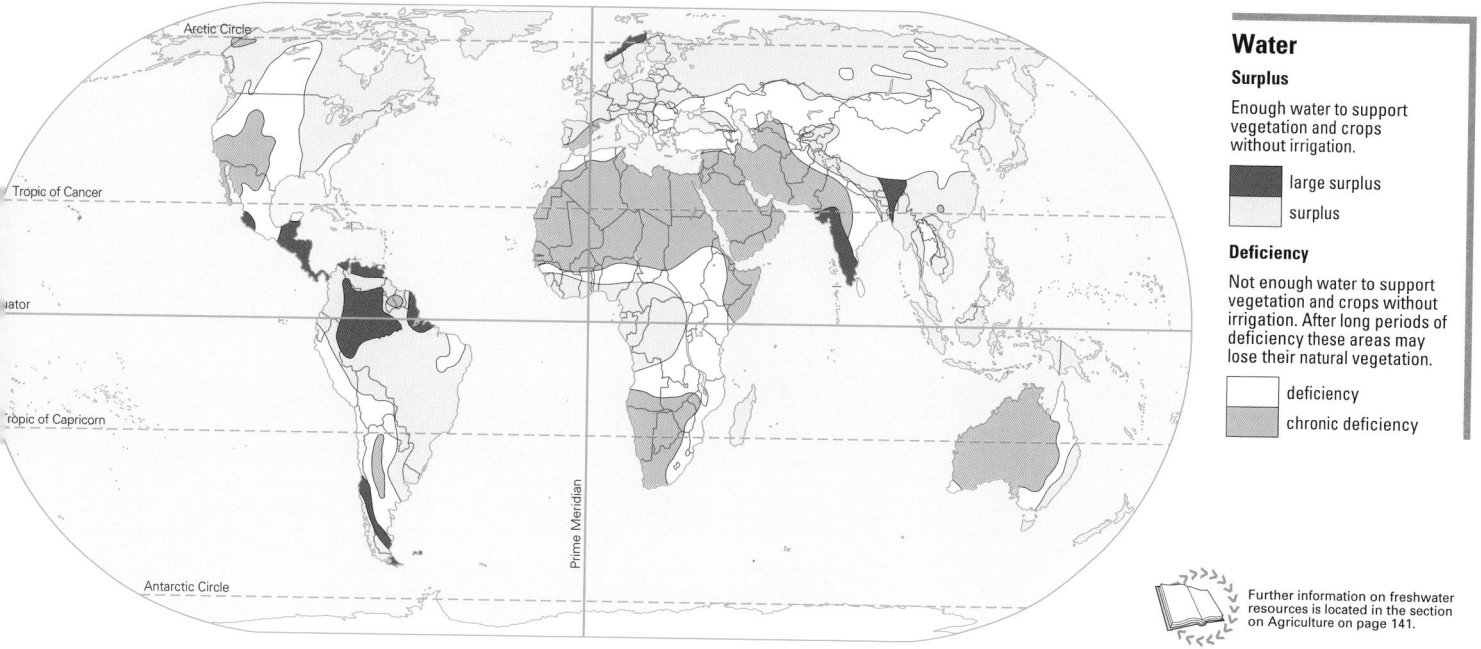

Water

Surplus

Enough water to support vegetation and crops without irrigation.

large surplus

surplus

Deficiency

Not enough water to support vegetation and crops without irrigation. After long periods of deficiency these areas may lose their natural vegetation.

deficiency

chronic deficiency

Further information on freshwater resources is located in the section on Agriculture on page 141.

Global aridity and drought probability

- **Extreme arid deserts**
  100% drought probability with exceptionally rare rainy spells

- **Arid deserts**
  shifting dunes and irregular moist years, drought dominating up to 90–95% of the time

- **Extremely arid areas**
  fine earth lowland areas with droughts dominating up to 60–70% of the time

- **Very frequent droughts**
  areas of semi-desert with the probability of droughts for 40–50% of the time

- **Frequent droughts**
  areas of dry steppe and savanna with the probability of droughts 20–25% of the time

- **Rare droughts**
  areas of steppe, prairie, and savanna with the probability of droughts 10–15% of the time

- **Sporadic very rare droughts**
  areas with the probability of droughts 3–5% of the time

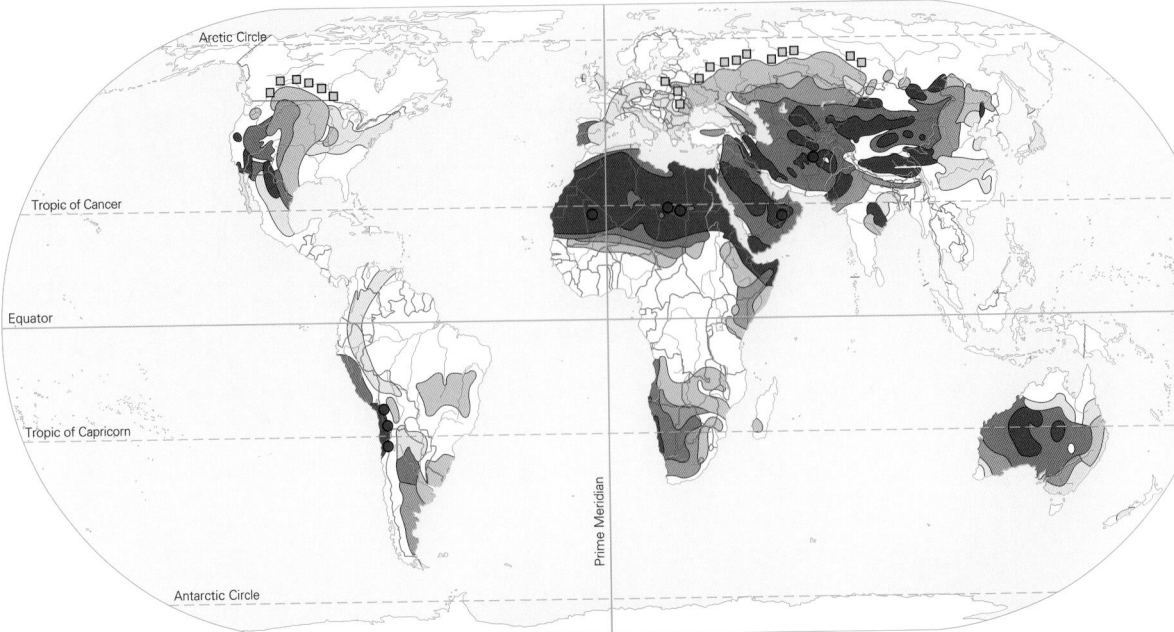

Drought and desertification

Drought begins with a deficiency of precipitation over an extended period, relative to a long-term average. It is naturally occurring phenomenon and may occur in any climatic region, though it is rare in the wet topics. Drought may also result from or be intensified by human activity, and is generally believed to be one consequence of global warming.

Desertification is caused by drought, together with human activity in arid, semi-arid, and sub-humid areas. Pressure from growing populations in these fragile ecosystems intensifies the impact of drought, resulting in permanent land degradation and widespread poverty. Though estimates vary, as much as 15% of the world's population and 25% of the world's land areas are affected by desertification.

Aral Sea, Central Asia, 1989–2003

The Aral Sea on the Kazakhstan-Uzbekistan border is a salt lake whose level is maintained by the Amudar'ya and Syrdar'ya rivers. Over the past several decades, the surface area has declined by more than 50 per cent, mainly because of the diversion of water from the two rivers for agricultural purposes. At the same time, its salt content has increased five times, and the lake is now severely polluted.

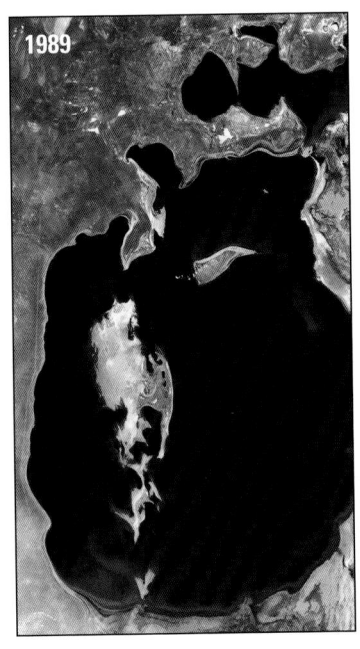

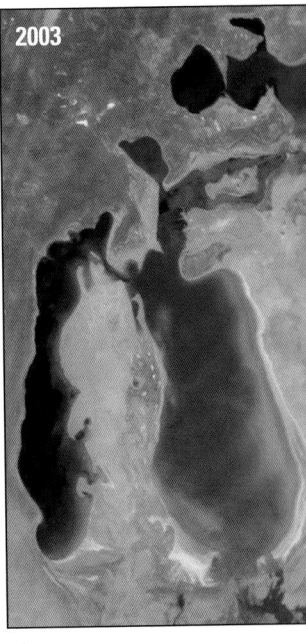

Desertification and tropical deforestation

- existing areas of desert
- areas with a high risk of becoming deserts
- areas with a moderate risk of becoming deserts
- existing areas of tropical rain forest
- former areas of tropical rain forest

Countries losing greatest areas of forest, average per year for 2000–2005 (000 hectares)

Brazil	3 103
Indonesia	1 871
Sudan	589
Myanmar	466
Zambia	445
Tanzania	412
Nigeria	410
Congo, Dem. Rep.	319
Zimbabwe	313
Venezuela	288

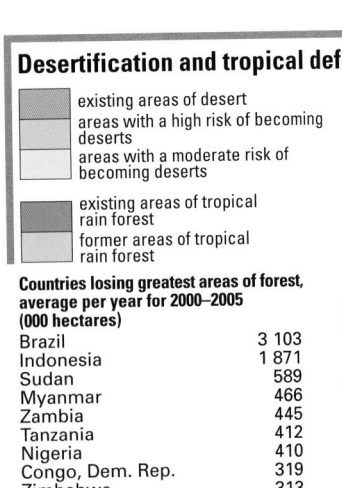

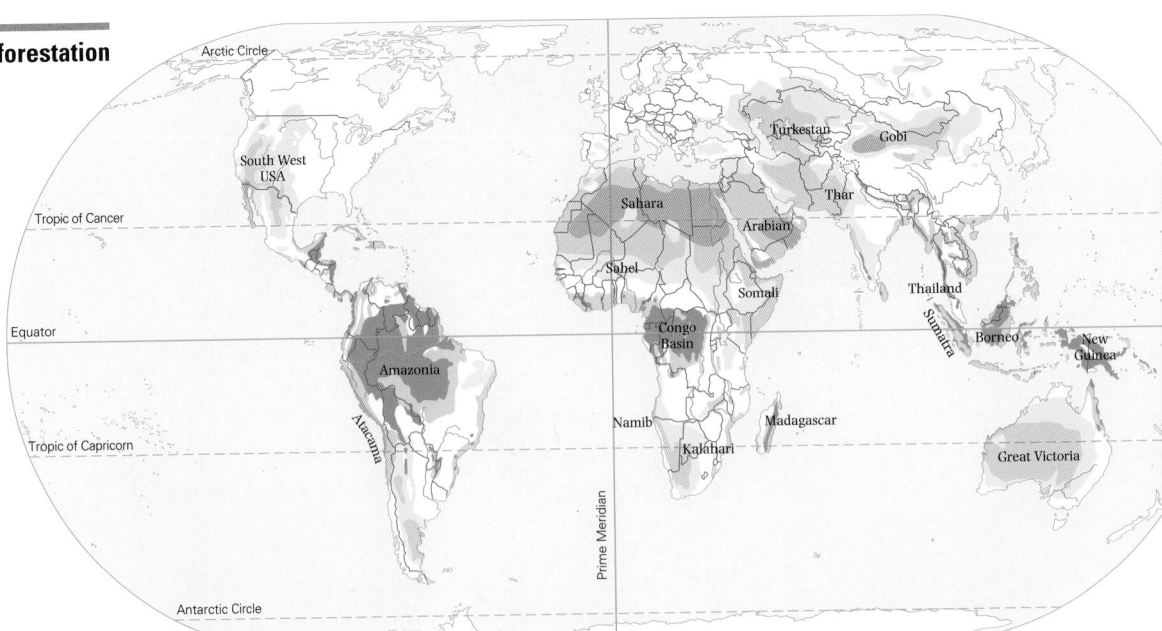

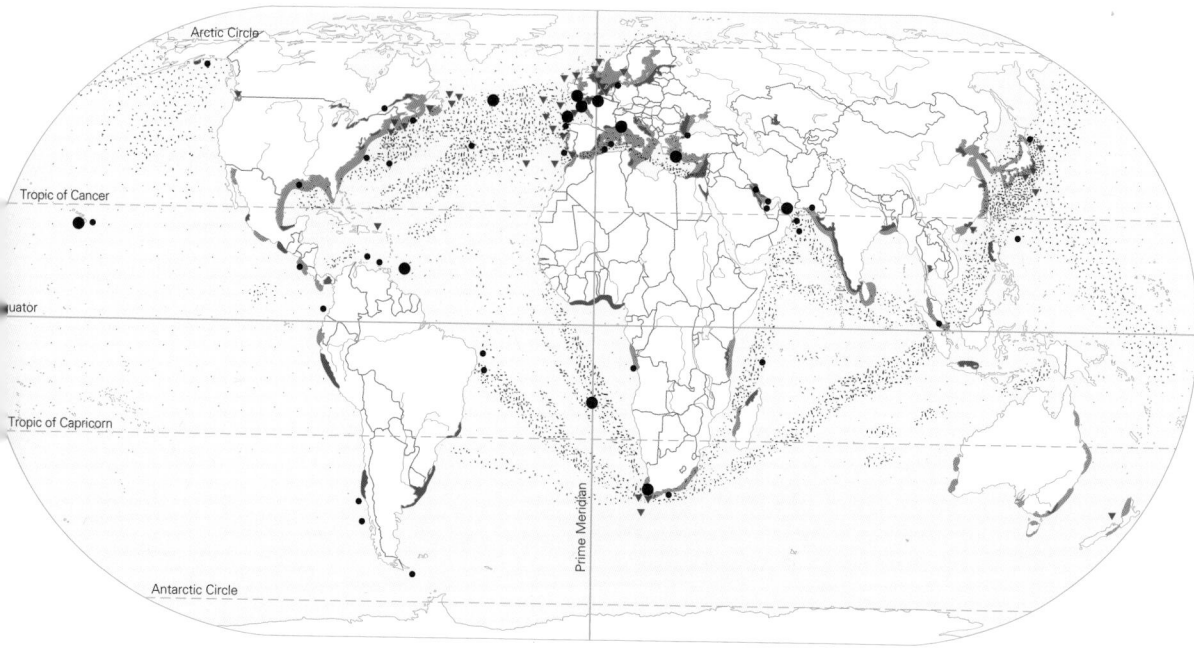

Sea pollution

Major oil spills

●   over 100 000 tonnes

•   under 100 000 tonnes

▨   frequent oil slicks from shipping

Other sea pollution

▰   severe pollution

▱   moderate pollution

▼   deep sea dump sites

Major oil spills (000 tonnes)

1979	*Ixtoc 1* well blowout, Gulf of Mexico	467
1979	Collision of *Atlantic Empress* and *Aegean Captain*, off Tobago, Caribbean	138
1983	*Nowruz* well blowout, Persian Gulf	267
1989	*Exxon Valdez* spills oil off the coast of Alaska	37
1991	Release of oil by Iraqi troops, *Sea Island* terminal, Persian Gulf	800
2002	*Prestige* oil tanker sinks off the coast of Spain	63
2003	*Tasman Spirit* tanker spills oil in Karachi Port, Pakistan	30

The world's top ten most endangered river basins

As identified by WWF with the primary threat facing each river basin

Over-extraction

Ganges, South Asia

Rio Grande/Rio Bravo del Norte, North America–Central America

Dams and infrastructure

Danube, Europe

Río de la Plata, South America

Salween, Southeast Asia

Invasive species

Murray–Darling, Australia

Climate change

Indus, South Asia

Nile–Lake Victoria, Africa

Over-fishing

Mekong (Lancang), Southeast Asia

Pollution

Yangtze, East Asia

The Antarctic ozone 'hole'

Three dimensional image of ozone depletion over Antarctica in September, 1998. The lowest ozone concentration is shown in blue.

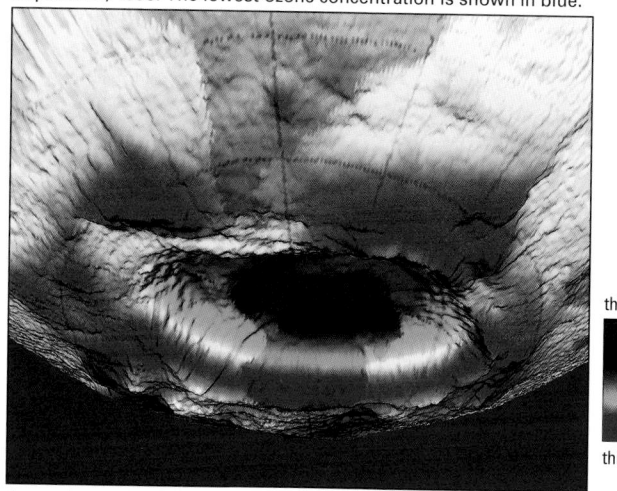

thinnest ozone

thickest ozone

Ozone in the stratosphere absorbs harmful ultraviolet rays. Pollutants in the air destroy ozone, making it thinner. Strong winds and intense cold concentrate the effects of pollutants, so that ozone is thinnest over Antarctica in spring.

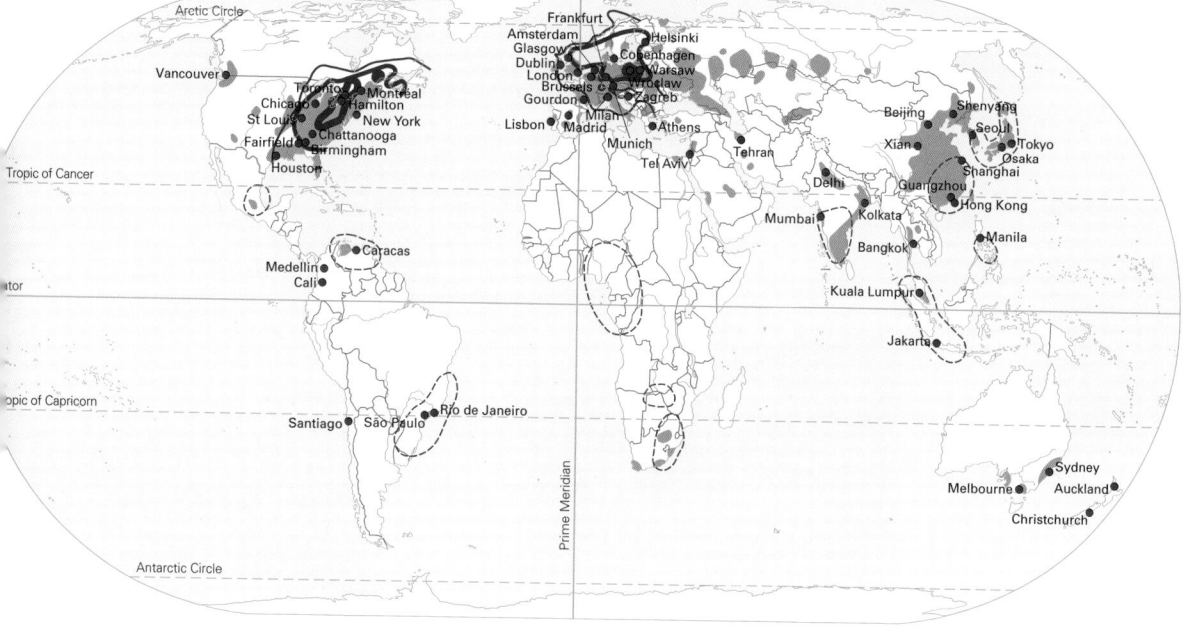

Acid rain

Sulphur and nitrogen emissions

Oxides of sulphur and nitrogen produced by burning fossil fuel react with rain to form dilute sulphuric and nitric acids

▨   areas with high levels of fossil fuel burning

•   cities where sulphur dioxide emissions are recorded and exceed World Health Organization recommended levels

Areas of acid rain deposition

Annual mean values of pH in precipitation

▬▬   pH less than 4.2 (most acidic)

——   pH 4.2–4.6

—   pH 4.6–5.0

⊂⊃   other areas where acid rain is becoming a problem

Lower pH values are more acidic. 'Clean' rain water is slightly acidic with a pH of 5.6. The pH scale is logarithmic, so that a value of 4.6 is ten times as acidic as normal rain.

Equatorial scale 1: 105 000 000

Ecosystems

vegetation types are those which would occur naturally without interference by people

coniferous forest
cone bearing trees

deciduous and mixed forest
leaf shedding and coniferous trees

tropical rain forest
many species of lush, tall trees

tropical grasslands (savannah)
tall grass parkland with scattered trees

evergreen trees and shrubs
plants and small trees with leathery leaves

thorn forest
low trees and shrubs with spines or thorns

temperate grasslands
prairies, steppes, pampas, and veld

semi-desert
short grasses and drought-resistant scrub

desert
sand and stones, very little vegetation

tundra
moss and lichen, with few trees

ice
no vegetation

mountains
thin soils, steep slopes, and high altitude affects type of vegetation

ice
Aerial view of Jameson Land, towards Liverpool Land, Greenland

deciduous and mixed forest
Mixed forest, Trois-Rivières, Québec, Canada

temperate grasslands
Prairie, South Dakota, USA

tropical rain forest
Monteverde Cloud Forest Reserve, Costa Rica

evergreen trees and shrubs
Coastal maquis vegetation, Albufeira, Algarve, Portugal

desert
Waved sand dunes, Sahara Desert, Algeria

Map labels:
Polar Bear
Jameson Land Greenland
Grey Wolf
Arctic Circle
Steller's Sea Lion
Grizzly Bear
Vancouver Island Marmot
Right Whale
Trois-Rivières Canada
South Dakota USA
Bison
Right Whale
Fin Whale
Algarve Portugal
Mexican Prairie Dog
Ocelot
Red Wolf
Florida Cougar
Manitee
Volcano Rabbit
Western Giant Eland
Monteverde Cloud Forest Reserve Costa Rica
Mountain Tapir
Jaguar
Hybrid Spider Monkey
Golden Headed Lion Tamarin
Vicuna
Maned Three-toed Sloth
Marine Otter
Blue Whale
Fin Whale

180° 160°W 140°W 120°W 100°W 80°W 60°W 40°W 20°W
80°N
60°N
40°N
Tropic of Cancer
Equator
Tropic of Capricorn
Antarctic Circle

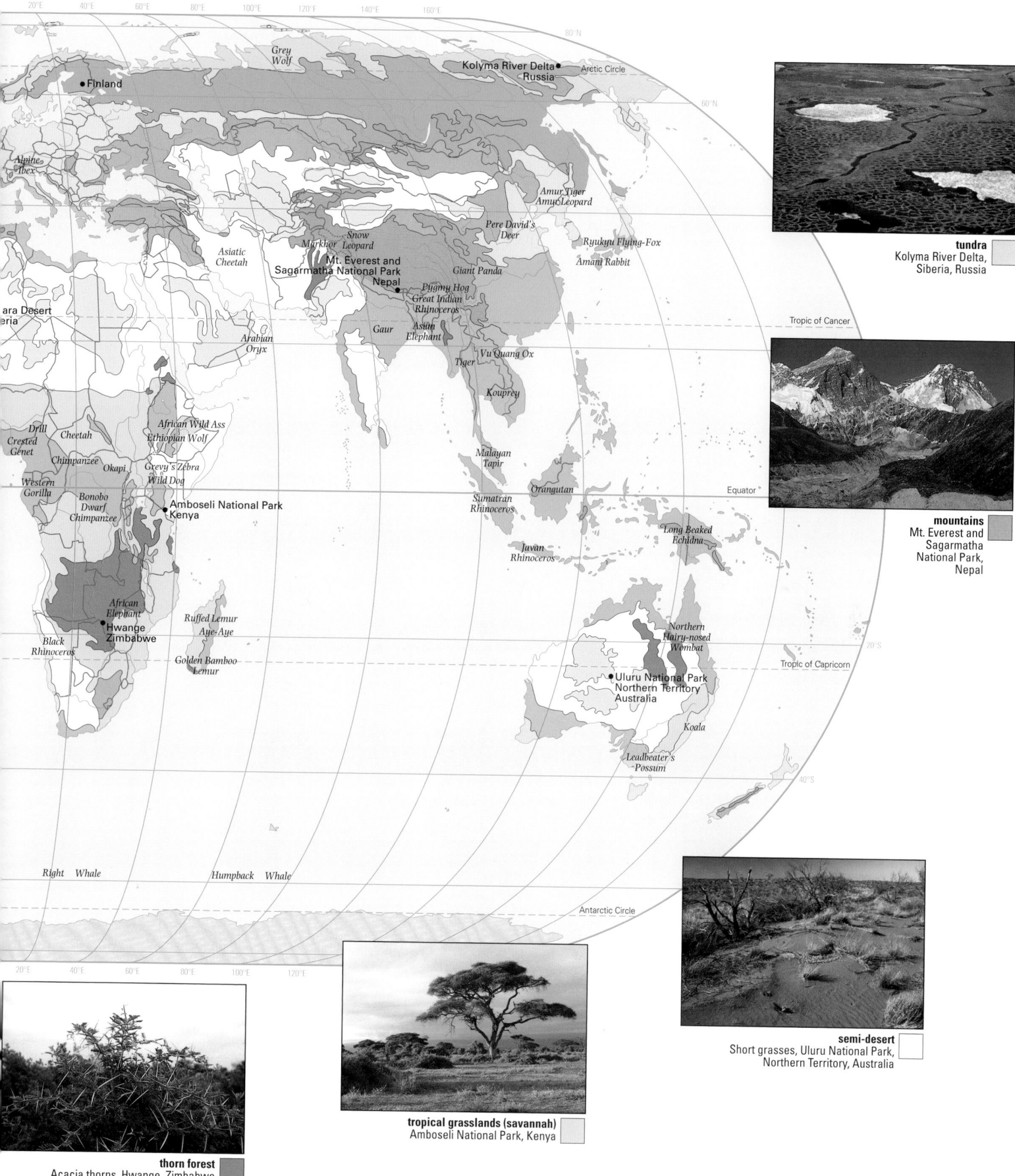

coniferous forest
Forest track, Finland

Endangered species

Human activity is primarily responsible for the loss of habitat resulting in the extinction, endangerment, and vulnerability of many species of animals, birds, fish, reptiles, and plants (definitions and Canadian examples are found on page 26). The names on the map represent only a small selection of animals that are classified as endangered.

tundra
Kolyma River Delta,
Siberia, Russia

mountains
Mt. Everest and
Sagarmatha
National Park,
Nepal

semi-desert
Short grasses, Uluru National Park,
Northern Territory, Australia

tropical grasslands (savannah)
Amboseli National Park, Kenya

thorn forest
Acacia thorns, Hwange, Zimbabwe

Map labels

Grey Wolf
Kolyma River Delta, Russia
Finland
Alpine Ibex
Asiatic Cheetah
Amur Tiger
Amur Leopard
Pere David's Deer
Ryukyu Flying-Fox
Markhor
Snow Leopard
Mt. Everest and Sagarmatha National Park, Nepal
Giant Panda
Amani Rabbit
..ara Desert ..eria
Arabian Oryx
Pygmy Hog
Great Indian Rhinoceros
Gaur
Asian Elephant
Vu Quang Ox
Tiger
Kouprey
Drill
Cheetah
African Wild Ass
Ethiopian Wolf
Crested Genet
Chimpanzee
Okapi
Grevy's Zebra
Wild Dog
Malayan Tapir
Western Gorilla
Bonobo Dwarf Chimpanzee
Amboseli National Park, Kenya
Orangutan
Equator
Sumatran Rhinoceros
Long Beaked Echidna
African Elephant
Ruffed Lemur
Aye-Aye
Javan Rhinoceros
Hwange Zimbabwe
Northern Hairy-nosed Wombat
Black Rhinoceros
Golden Bamboo Lemur
Uluru National Park Northern Territory Australia
Koala
Leadbeater's Possum
Right Whale
Humpback Whale

Eckert IV Projection   © Oxford University Press

Scale 1: 125 000 000

Population density

people per square kilometre

- over 200
- 100–200
- 50–100
- 5–50
- 1–5
- under 1

Major cities

population in millions

- ■ over 10
- ⊡ 5–10
- □ 1–5

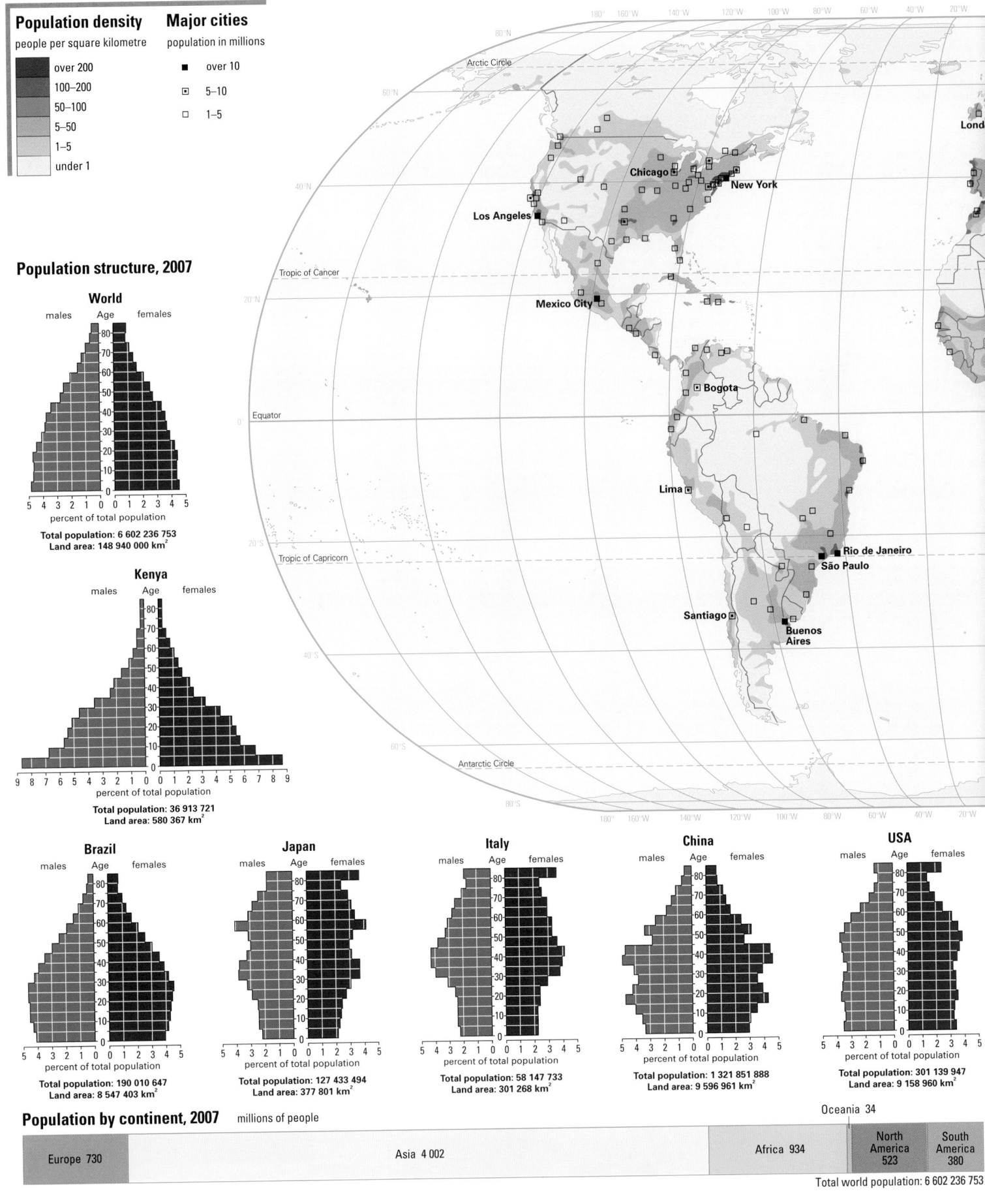

Population structure, 2007

World

males Age females

percent of total population

Total population: 6 602 236 753
Land area: 148 940 000 km²

Kenya

males Age females

percent of total population

Total population: 36 913 721
Land area: 580 367 km²

Brazil

males Age females

percent of total population

Total population: 190 010 647
Land area: 8 547 403 km²

Japan

males Age females

percent of total population

Total population: 127 433 494
Land area: 377 801 km²

Italy

males Age females

percent of total population

Total population: 58 147 733
Land area: 301 268 km²

China

males Age females

percent of total population

Total population: 1 321 851 888
Land area: 9 596 961 km²

USA

males Age females

percent of total population

Total population: 301 139 947
Land area: 9 158 960 km²

Population by continent, 2007   millions of people

Europe 730	Asia 4 002	Africa 934	North America 523	South America 380

Oceania 34

Total world population: 6 602 236 753

Land area by continent   thousands of square kilometres

Europe 10 498	Asia 44 387	Africa 30 335	Oceania 8 503	North America 24 241	South America 17 832	Antarctica 13 340

Total world land area: 148 940 000 km²

Eckert IV Projection   © Oxford University Press

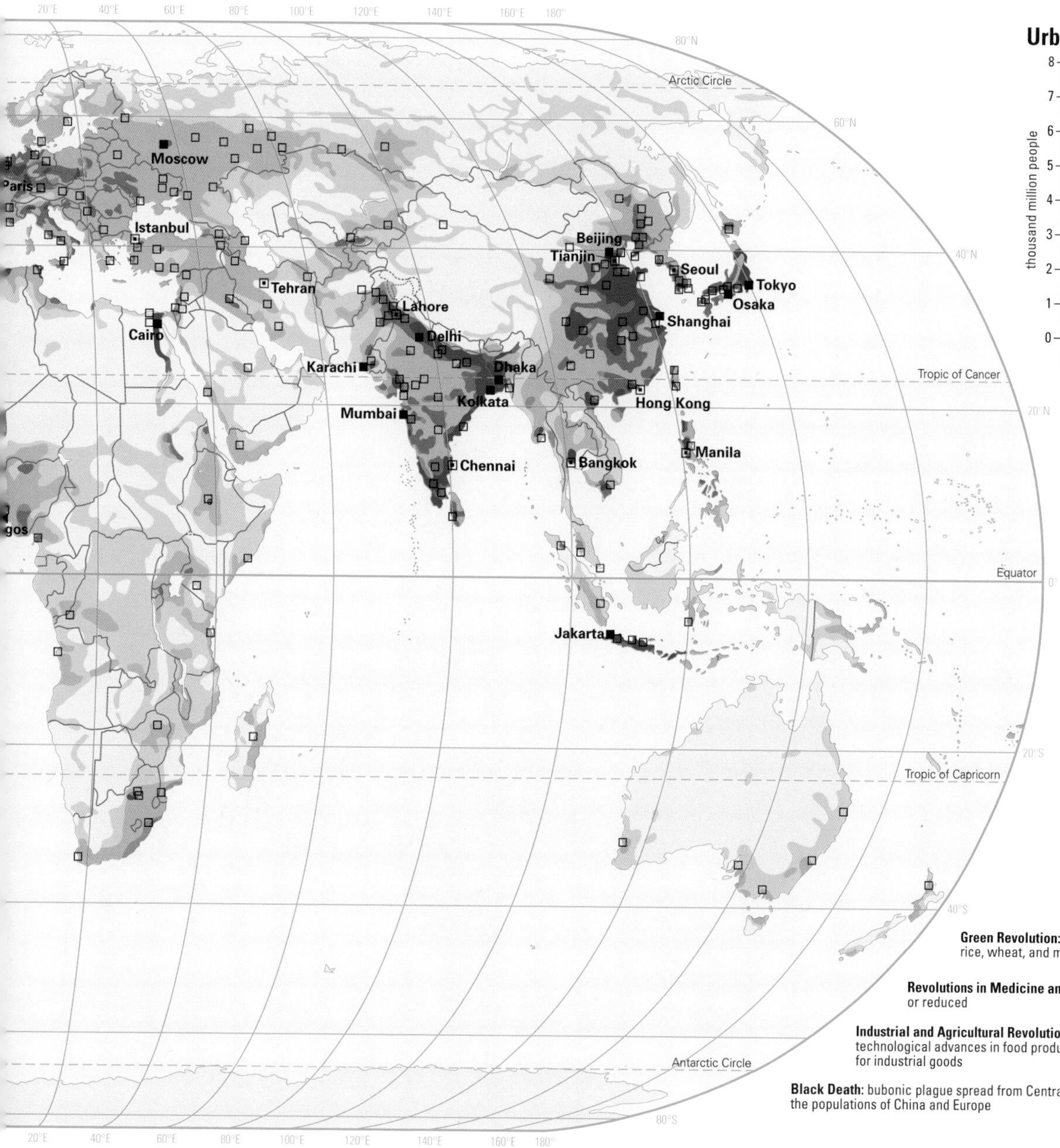

Moscow
Paris
Istanbul
Tehran
Cairo
Lahore
Delhi
Karachi
Dhaka
Kolkata
Mumbai
Chennai
Beijing
Tianjin
Seoul
Tokyo
Osaka
Shanghai
Hong Kong
Manila
Bangkok
Jakarta
gos
Arctic Circle
Tropic of Cancer
Equator
Tropic of Capricorn
Antarctic Circle
80°N
60°N
40°N
20°N
0°
20°S
40°S
80°S
20°E
40°E
60°E
80°E
100°E
120°E
140°E
160°E
180°

Urban and rural population, 1950–2030

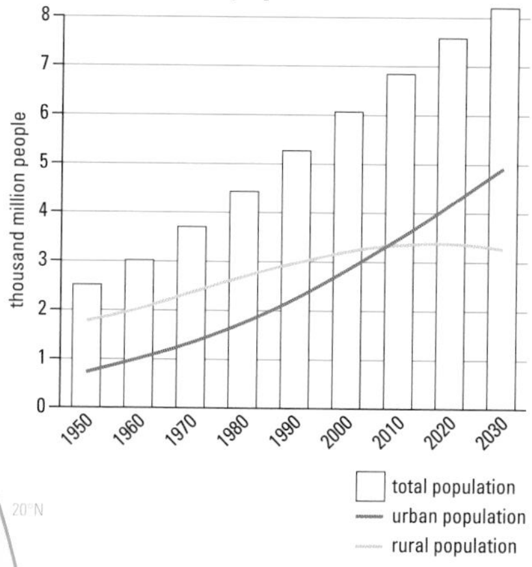

thousand million people
0
1
2
3
4
5
6
7
8
1950
1960
1970
1980
1990
2000
2010
2020
2030
total population
urban population
rural population

In 1950 there were two cities with more than 10 million inhabitants: New York and Tokyo. In 2007 there are 20 cities that have passed the 10 million mark, with Tokyo being the largest at over 35 million.

World population growth

Past growth (1 CE to 2007)

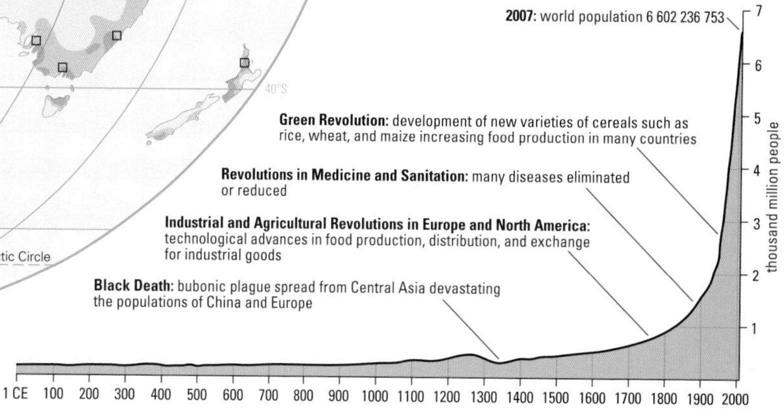

2007: world population 6 602 236 753
Green Revolution: development of new varieties of cereals such as rice, wheat, and maize increasing food production in many countries
Revolutions in Medicine and Sanitation: many diseases eliminated or reduced
Industrial and Agricultural Revolutions in Europe and North America: technological advances in food production, distribution, and exchange for industrial goods
Black Death: bubonic plague spread from Central Asia devastating the populations of China and Europe
thousand million people
1
2
3
4
5
6
7
1 CE
100
200
300
400
500
600
700
800
900
1000
1100
1200
1300
1400
1500
1600
1700
1800
1900
2000

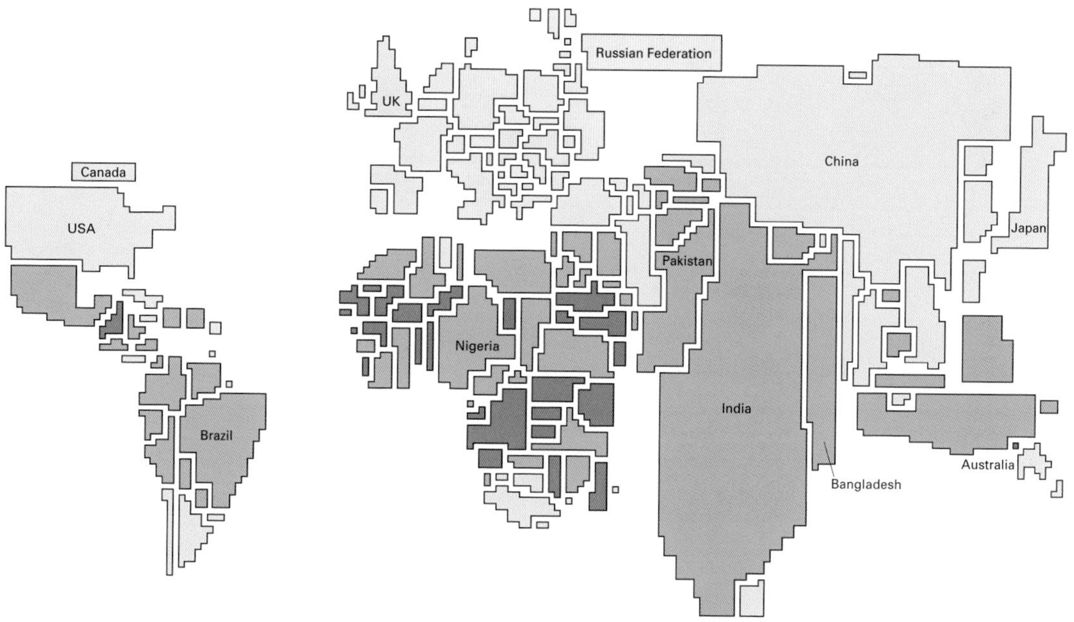

Russian Federation
UK
Canada
USA
China
Japan
Pakistan
Nigeria
India
Brazil
Bangladesh
Australia

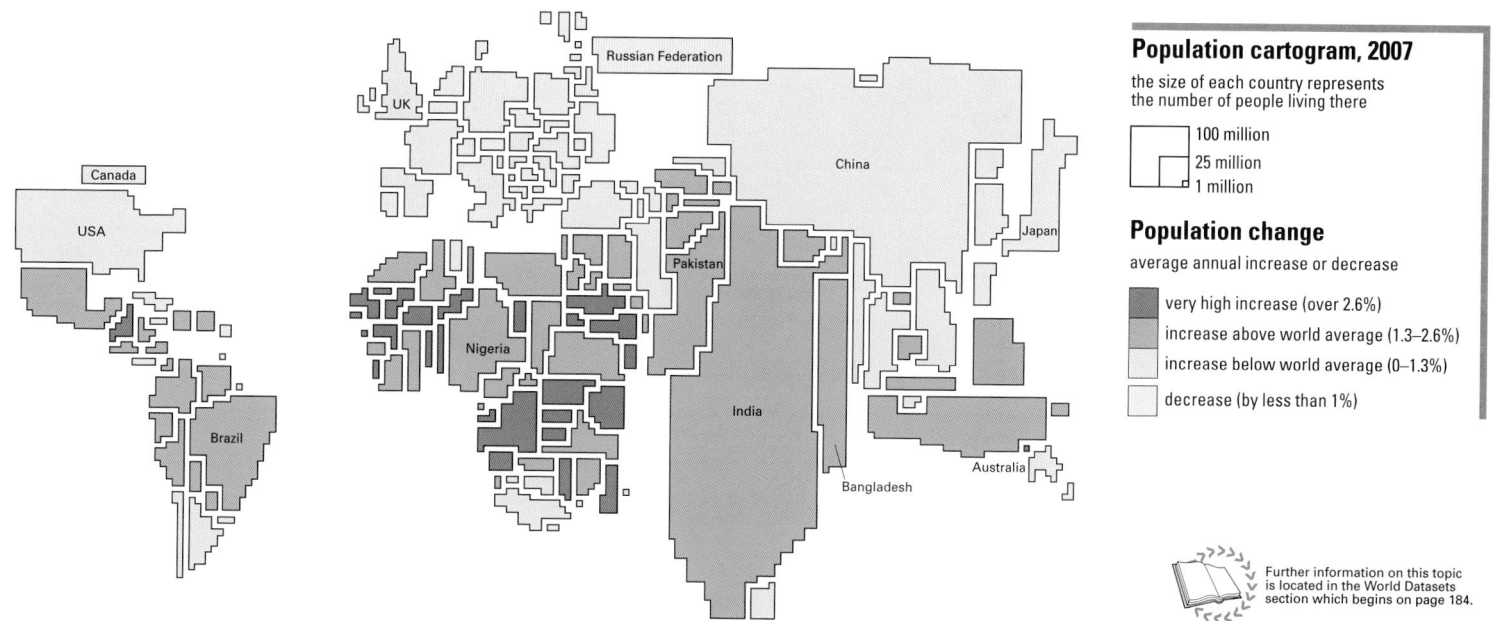

Population cartogram, 2007

the size of each country represents the number of people living there

100 million
25 million
1 million

Population change

average annual increase or decrease

- very high increase (over 2.6%)
- increase above world average (1.3–2.6%)
- increase below world average (0–1.3%)
- decrease (by less than 1%)

Further information on this topic is located in the World Datasets section which begins on page 184.

Scale 1: 240 000 000

Population change, 1997–2007

percentage population gain or loss

- over 40% gain
- 30–40% gain
- 20–30% gain
- 10–20% gain
- under 10% gain
- 0–20% loss

Highest population gain

United Arab Emirates	61.8%
Liberia	45.2%
Afghanistan	43.5%
Kuwait	41.9%
Yemen Republic	40.4%
Canada	**10.2%**

Highest population loss

Trinidad and Tobago	-7.2%
Latvia	-7.2%
Ukraine	-8.1%
Bulgaria	-9.2%
Montserrat	-14.1%

Population change refers to the growth or decline of a national population over the period 1997 to 2007 resulting from natural increase (births - deaths) and net migration (immigration - emigration).

Fertility rate, 2007

average number of children born to women of childbearing age

- over 6 children
- 5–5.9 children
- 4–4.9 children
- 3–3.9 children
- 2–2.9 children
- 1–1.9 children
- o countries with over 40% of the total population under the age of 15 in 2007

Largest families	**Number of children**
Niger	7.1
Afghanistan	6.8
Angola	6.8
Burundi	6.8
Somalia	6.8
Uganda	6.8
Canada	**1.5**

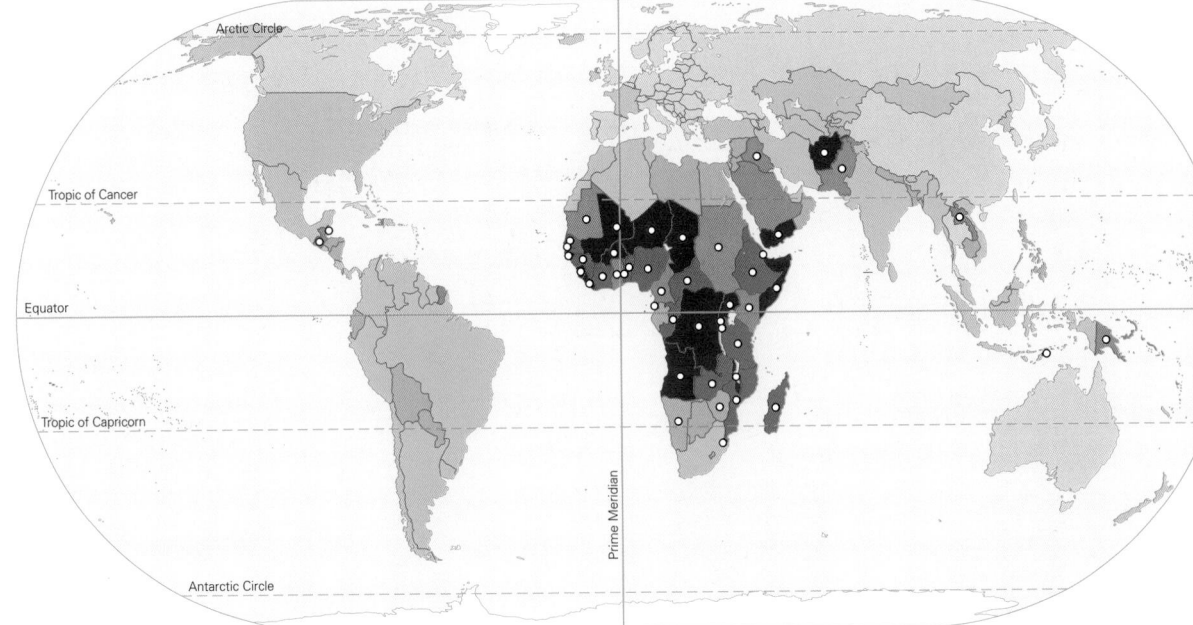

Urban population

percentage of the population living in urban areas

- over 80%
- 60–80%
- 40–60%
- 20–40%
- under 20%
- no data

Most urban in 2005	
Singapore	100.0%
Kuwait	98.3%
Belgium	97.2%
Bahrain	96.5%
Qatar	95.4%
Canada	**80.1%**

Least urban in 2005	
Sierra Leone	15.1%
Papua New Guinea	13.4%
Uganda	12.6%
Bhutan	11.1%
Burundi	10.0%

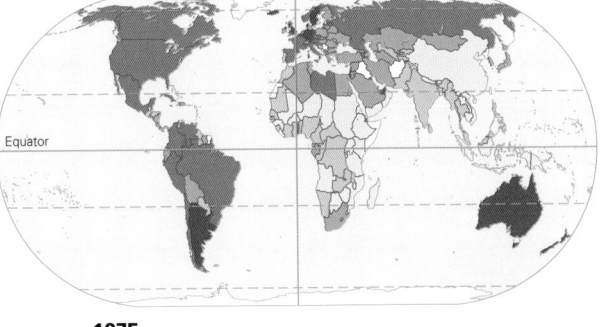

1975

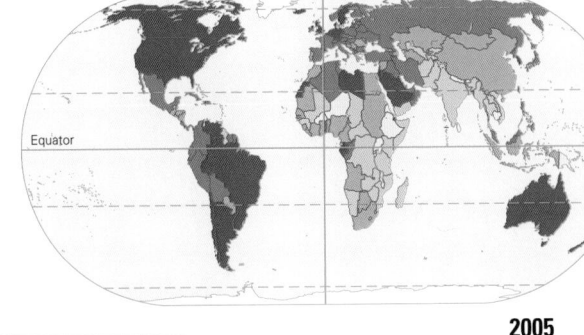

2005

projected **2015**

Further information on this topic is located in the World Datasets section, which begins on page 184.

Eckert IV Projection

© Oxford University Press

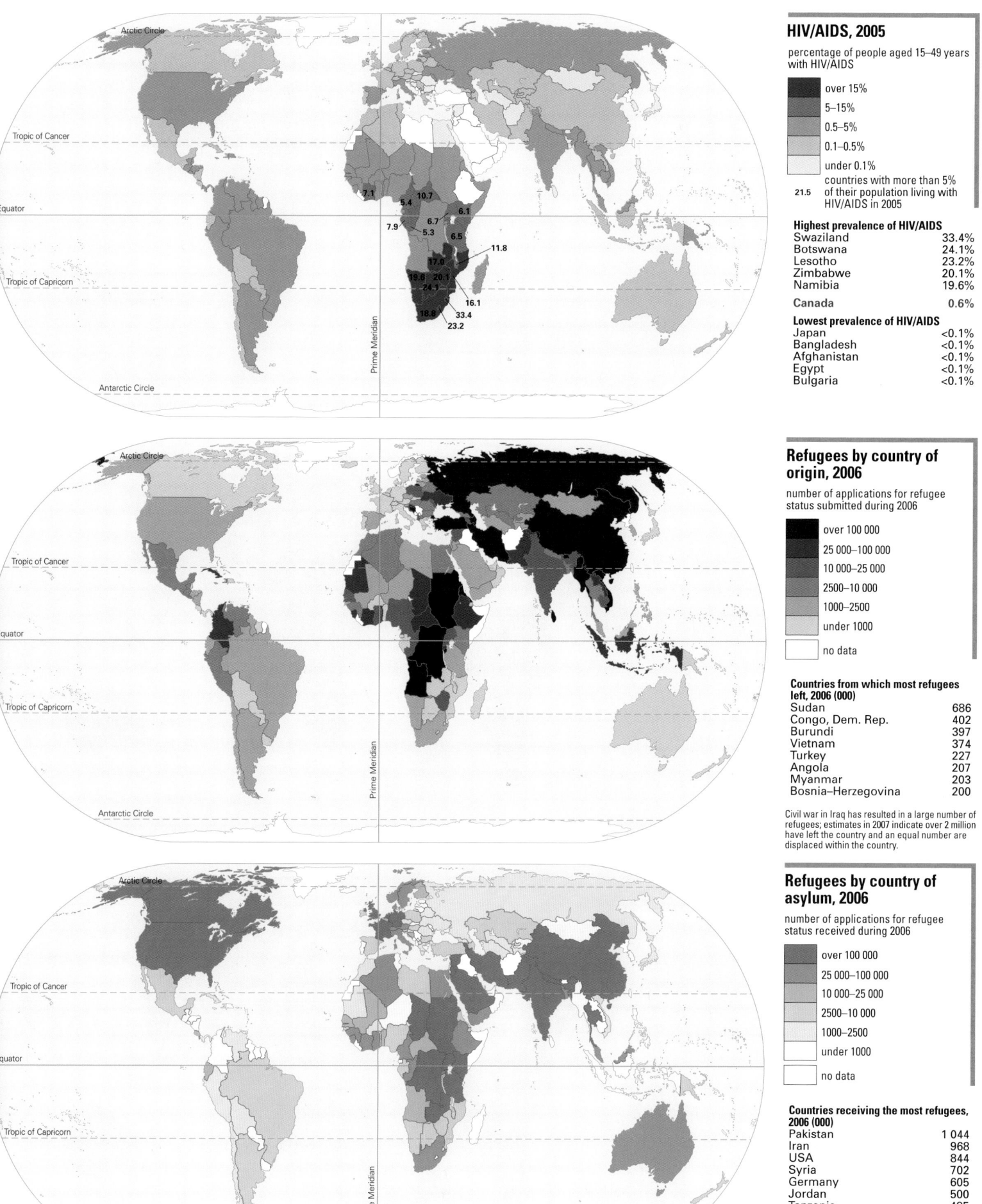

HIV/AIDS, 2005

percentage of people aged 15–49 years with HIV/AIDS

- over 15%
- 5–15%
- 0.5–5%
- 0.1–0.5%
- under 0.1%

21.5 countries with more than 5% of their population living with HIV/AIDS in 2005

Highest prevalence of HIV/AIDS

Swaziland	33.4%
Botswana	24.1%
Lesotho	23.2%
Zimbabwe	20.1%
Namibia	19.6%
Canada	0.6%

Lowest prevalence of HIV/AIDS

Japan	<0.1%
Bangladesh	<0.1%
Afghanistan	<0.1%
Egypt	<0.1%
Bulgaria	<0.1%

Refugees by country of origin, 2006

number of applications for refugee status submitted during 2006

- over 100 000
- 25 000–100 000
- 10 000–25 000
- 2500–10 000
- 1000–2500
- under 1000
- no data

Countries from which most refugees left, 2006 (000)

Sudan	686
Congo, Dem. Rep.	402
Burundi	397
Vietnam	374
Turkey	227
Angola	207
Myanmar	203
Bosnia–Herzegovina	200

Civil war in Iraq has resulted in a large number of refugees; estimates in 2007 indicate over 2 million have left the country and an equal number are displaced within the country.

Refugees by country of asylum, 2006

number of applications for refugee status received during 2006

- over 100 000
- 25 000–100 000
- 10 000–25 000
- 2500–10 000
- 1000–2500
- under 1000
- no data

Countries receiving the most refugees, 2006 (000)

Pakistan	1 044
Iran	968
USA	844
Syria	702
Germany	605
Jordan	500
Tanzania	485
United Kingdom	302
Canada	152

Purchasing power, 2005

Purchasing Power Parity (PPP) in $US based on Gross Domestic Product (GDP) per person, adjusted for the local cost of living

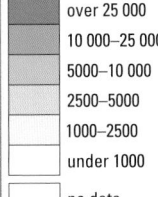

- over 25 000
- 10 000–25 000
- 5000–10 000
- 2500–5000
- 1000–2500
- under 1000
- no data

Highest purchasing power

Luxembourg	$60 228
United States	$41 890
Norway	$41 420
Ireland	$38 505
Iceland	$36 510
Canada	$33 375

Lowest purchasing power

Niger	$781
Tanzania	$744
Congo, Democratic Republic	$714
Burundi	$699
Malawi	$667

Literacy and schooling, 2005

percentage of people aged 15 and above who can, with understanding, both read and write a short, simple statement on their everyday life

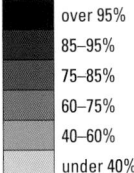

- over 95%
- 85–95%
- 75–85%
- 60–75%
- 40–60%
- under 40%
- ○ countries that spend a greater percentage of their GDP on the military than on education

Highest literacy levels

Georgia	100.0%
Cuba	99.8%
Estonia	99.8%
Latvia	99.7%
Slovenia	99.7%
Canada	99.0%

Lowest literacy levels

Niger	28.7%
Afghanistan	28.0%
Chad	25.7%
Mali	24.0%
Burkina	23.8%

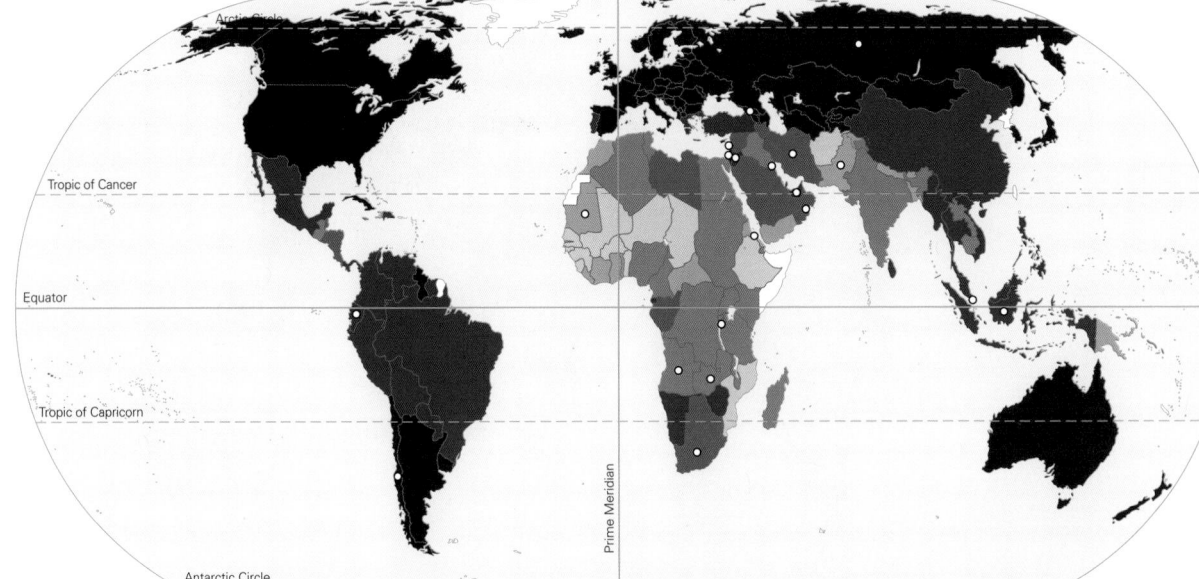

Life expectancy, 2005

average expected lifespan of babies born in 2005

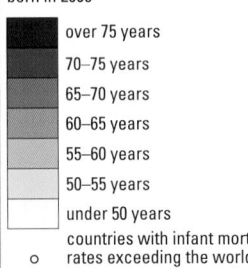

- over 75 years
- 70–75 years
- 65–70 years
- 60–65 years
- 55–60 years
- 50–55 years
- under 50 years
- ○ countries with infant mortality rates exceeding the world average of 52 per 1000 live births

Highest life expectancy

	Years
Japan	82
Iceland	81
Switzerland	81
Australia	80
Spain	80
Canada	80

Lowest life expectancy

Angola	41
Sierra Leone	41
Swaziland	40
Zambia	40
Zimbabwe	40

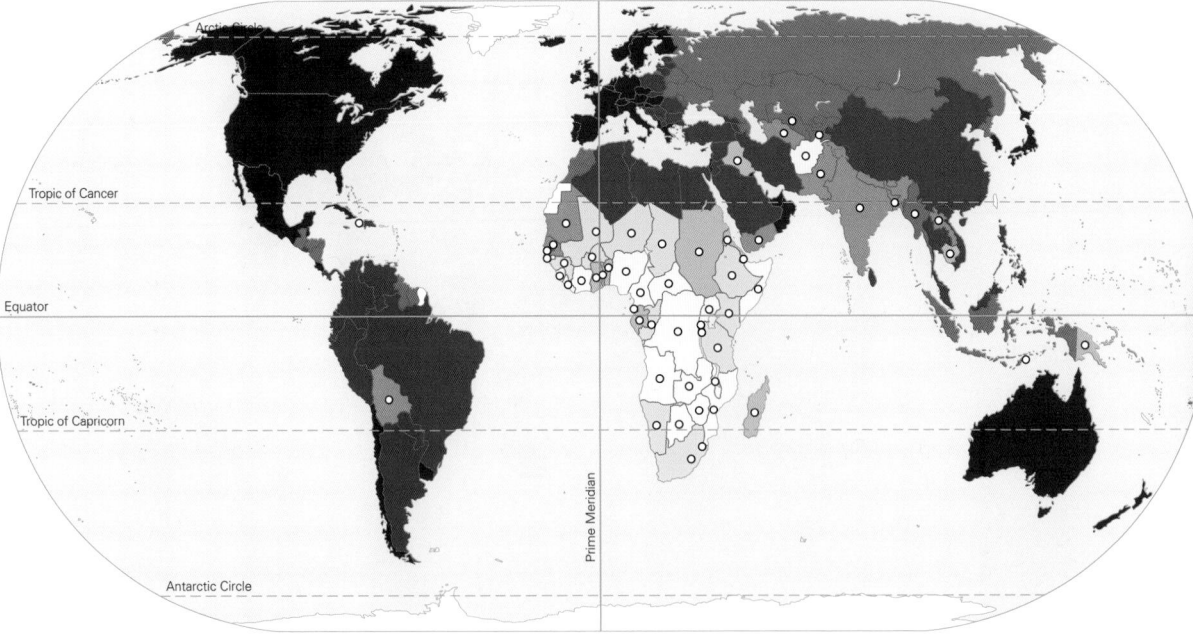

Further information on this topic is located in the World Datasets section which begins on page 184.

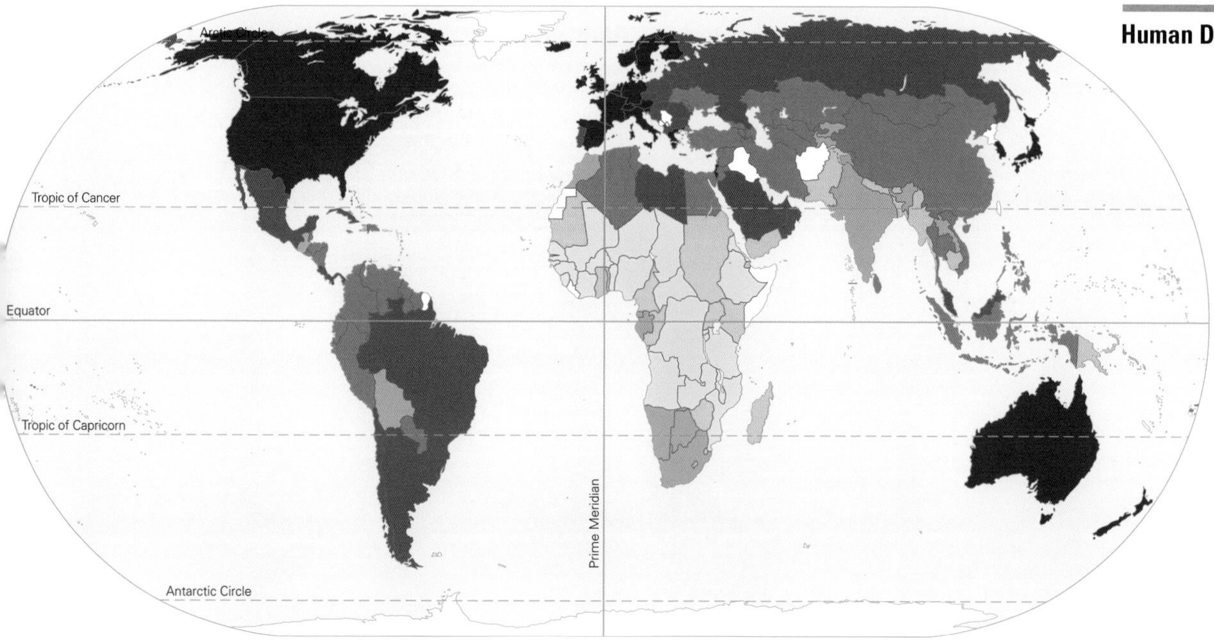

Human Development Index (HDI), 2005

HDI measures a country's relative social and economic progress. It combines life expectancy, adult literacy, average number of years of schooling, and purchasing power.

over 0.9	high HDI
0.8–0.9	
0.7–0.8	
0.6–0.7	medium HDI
0.5–0.6	
under 0.5	low HDI

Highest HDI
Iceland	0.968
Norway	0.968
Australia	0.962
Canada	0.961
Ireland	0.959

Lowest HDI
Mali	0.380
Niger	0.374
Guinea-Bissau	0.374
Burkina	0.370
Sierra Leone	0.336

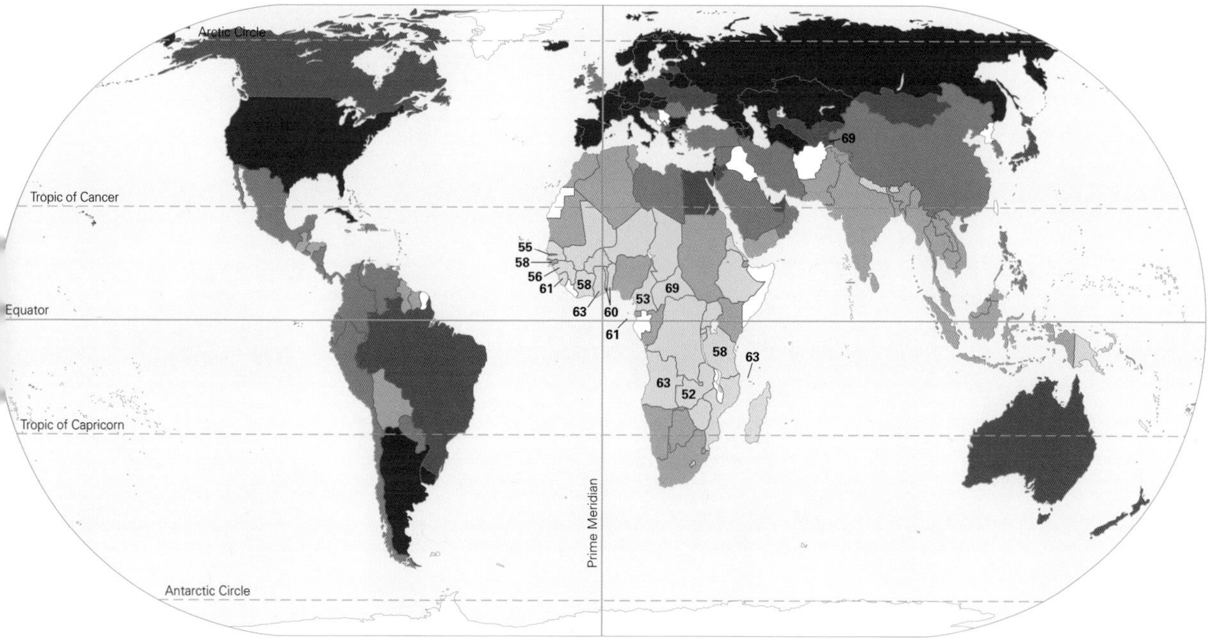

Medical care, 2004

number of doctors per 100 000 people

over 300
200–300
100–200
10–100
under 10

55   countries where more than 50% of children under five have been treated for Malaria in 2005

Most doctors per 100 000 people
Italy	606
Cuba	591
United States	549
St. Lucia	518
Belarus	450
Canada	214

Fewest doctors per 100 000 people
Chad	3
Niger	3
Rwanda	2
Tanzania	2
Mozambique	2
Malawi	1

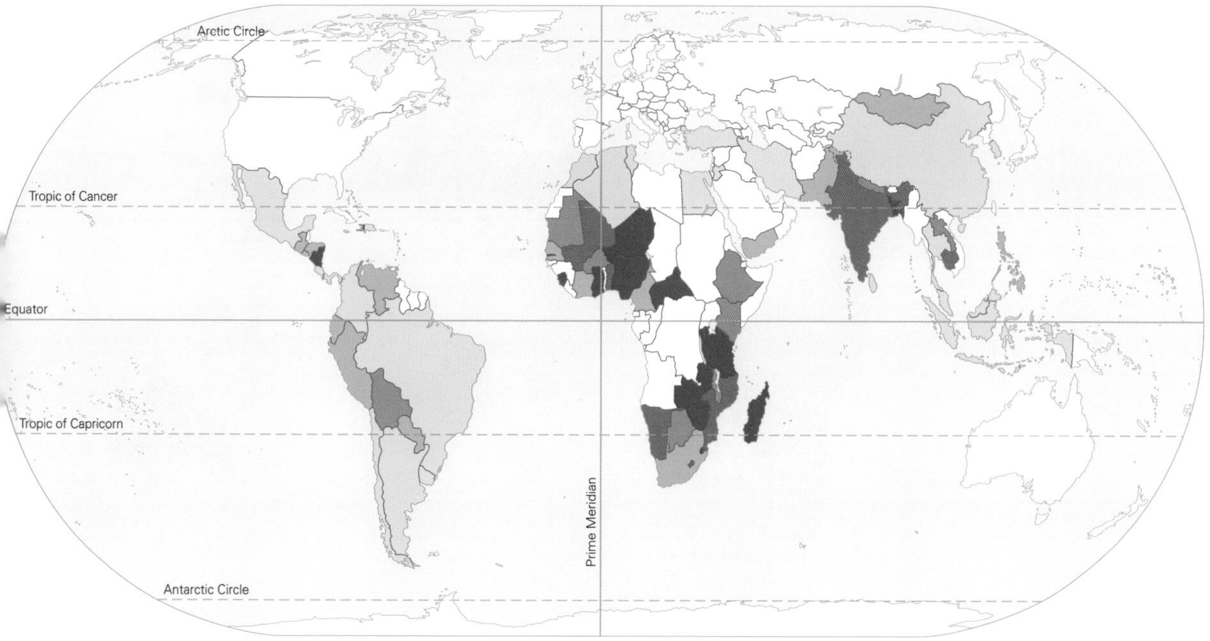

Poverty, 2005

percentage of population living on less than $1 per day

over 40%
30–40%
20–30
10–20%
under 10%

At the beginning of the 21st century, it is estimated that 1.1 billion people were living on less than $1 per day — the majority of them children.
In 2000 the member states of the UN adopted the Millennium Declaration that would provide targets and accountability mechanisms to enable poor people to improve their lives. The eight goals were: eradicate extreme poverty and hunger; achieve universal primary education; promote gender equality; reduce child mortality; improve maternal health; combat HIV/AIDS, malaria, and other diseases; ensure environmental sustainability; and develop a global partnership for development.

Agriculture

Commercial farming

- cereals dominant
- mixed farming and dairy
- mixed farming, fruit and vegetables
- mixed farming, cash crops
- ranching and stock raising

Mainly subsistence farming

- staples: cassava, yam, potatoes
- staples: millet, sorghum, barley, rye
- nomadic herding

Small holding

- rice dominant
- other cereals dominant
- mixed farming and livestock
- mixed farming, fruit and vegetables
- mixed farming, cash crops
- stock raising

Forests

- commercially exploited

Non-agricultural land

- ice, tundra, swamp, desert, montane, and coniferous forest

Scale 1: 190 000 000

Agriculture's contribution to Gross Domestic Product (GDP)

percentage of GDP, for selected countries, 2005 (GDP is the annual total value of all goods and services in a country, excluding transactions with other countries)

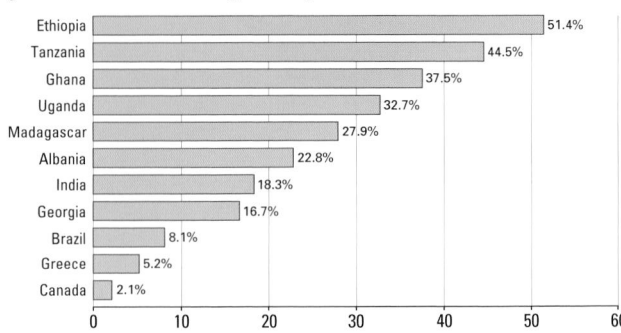

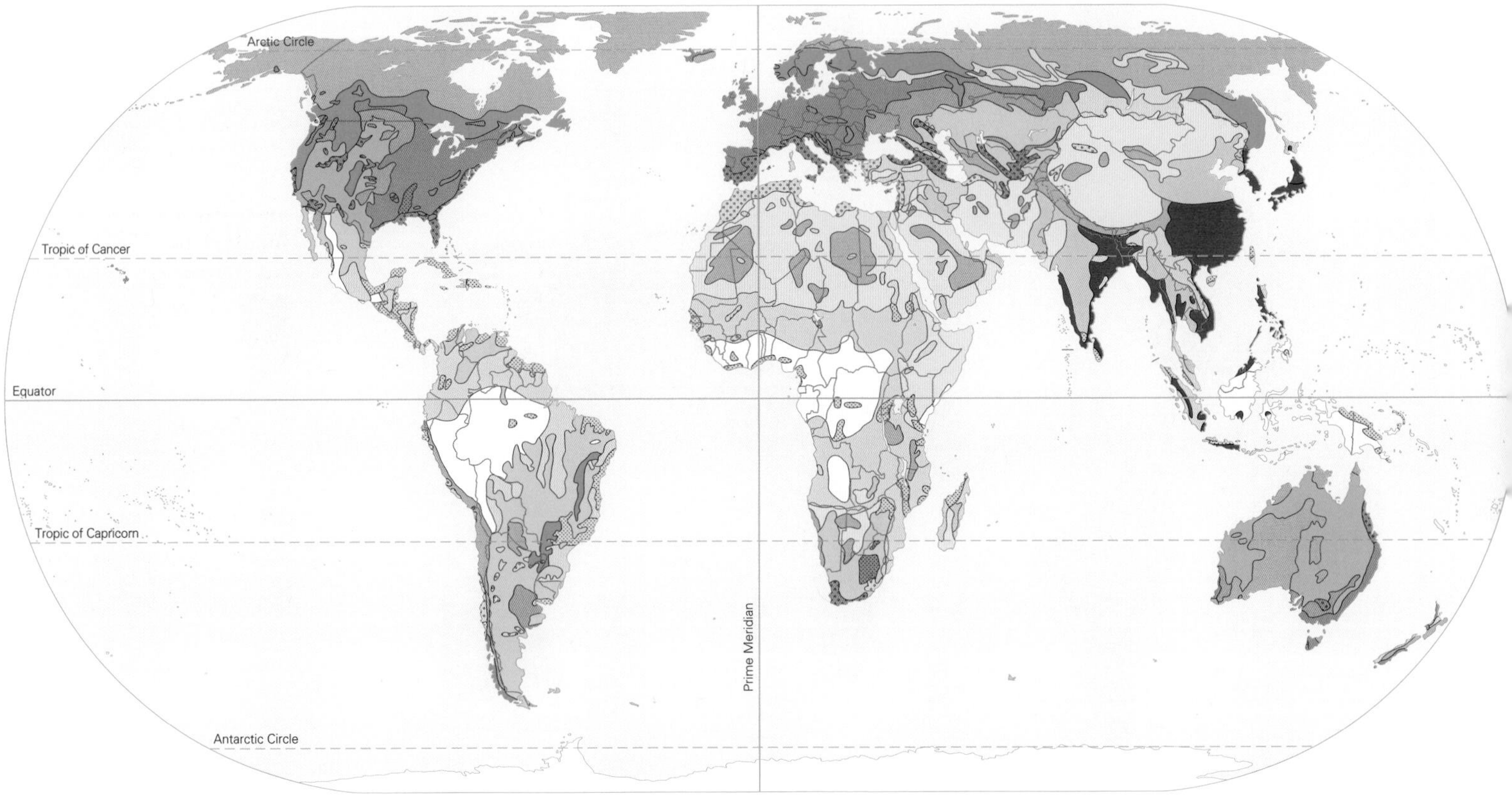

Country	Percentage
Ethiopia	51.4%
Tanzania	44.5%
Ghana	37.5%
Uganda	32.7%
Madagascar	27.9%
Albania	22.8%
India	18.3%
Georgia	16.7%
Brazil	8.1%
Greece	5.2%
Canada	2.1%

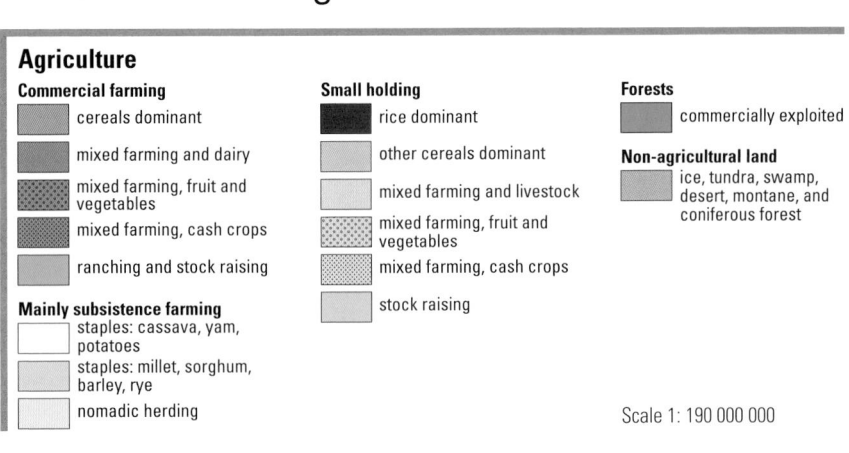

Food consumption, 2005

average daily food intake in calories per person

- more than 3500 calories
- 3000–3500 calories
- 2500–3000 calories
- 2000–2500 calories
- less than 2000 calories
- o countries with more than 25% of the total population classified by the UN as undernourished (2000–2003)

Highest food consumption

Romania	4 125
Austria	4 023
Italy	3 730
Israel	3 695
France	3 681
Canada	3 486

Lowest food consumption

Malawi	1 729
Burundi	1 693
Yemen	1 590
Ethiopia	1 582
Congo, Democratic Republic	1 398

Scale 1: 240 000 000

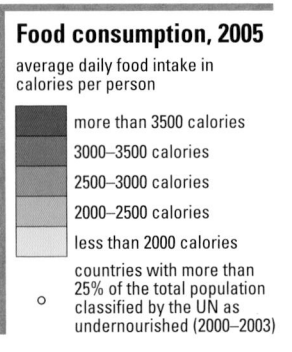

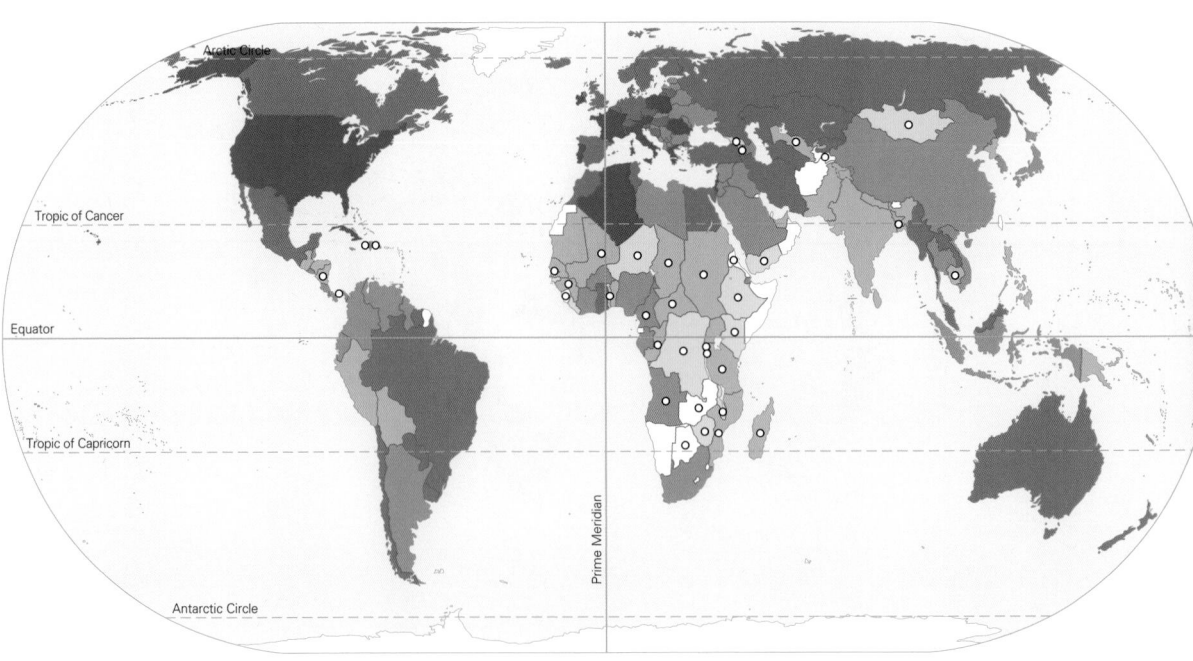

Eckert IV Projection   © Oxford University Press

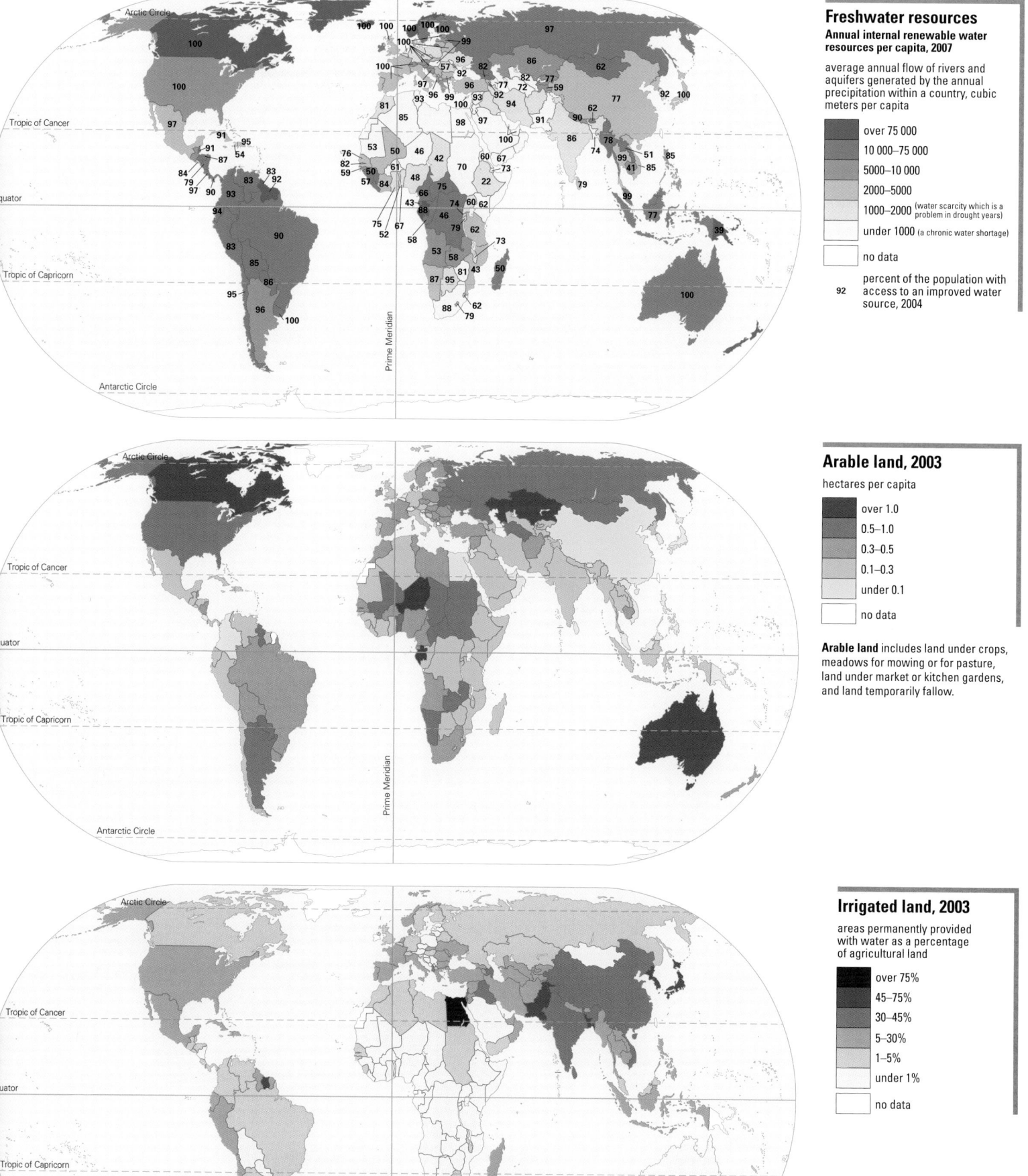

Freshwater resources

Annual internal renewable water resources per capita, 2007

average annual flow of rivers and aquifers generated by the annual precipitation within a country, cubic meters per capita

- over 75 000
- 10 000–75 000
- 5000–10 000
- 2000–5000
- 1000–2000 (water scarcity which is a problem in drought years)
- under 1000 (a chronic water shortage)
- no data

92 percent of the population with access to an improved water source, 2004

Arable land, 2003

hectares per capita

- over 1.0
- 0.5–1.0
- 0.3–0.5
- 0.1–0.3
- under 0.1
- no data

Arable land includes land under crops, meadows for mowing or for pasture, land under market or kitchen gardens, and land temporarily fallow.

Irrigated land, 2003

areas permanently provided with water as a percentage of agricultural land

- over 75%
- 45–75%
- 30–45%
- 5–30%
- 1–5%
- under 1%
- no data

Further information on this topic is located in the World Datasets section which begins on page 184.

Industrialization, 2006

Industrialized high income economies
Most people live in cities and have high standards of living based on manufacturing and services. High levels of energy consumption

Industrializing upper-middle income economies
Manufacturing and industrial development are growing alongside traditional economies. Most people have rising incomes.

Industrializing lower-middle income economies
Manufacturing and industrial development are growing alongside traditional economies. As a consequence, a middle-income class is emerging, though most people have relatively low incomes.

Agricultural low income economies
Most people live in rural areas and depend on agriculture. Little industrial development. Low incomes.

○ more than 40% of the population living below the national poverty line

International aid, 2005

Official development assistance (ODA) given or received per person in $US

Countries giving aid

over $100 per person

$50–$100 per person

under $50 per person

Countries receiving aid

under $10 per person

$10–$100 per person

over $100 per person

The economy becomes dependent on financial grants or loans from other, wealthier countries.

Countries giving most aid (total $US)
USA	$27 622 000 000
Japan	$13 147 000 000
United Kingdom	$10 767 000 000
Germany	$10 082 000 000
Canada	$3 756 000 000

Countries receiving most aid (total $US)
Nigeria	$6 437 300 000
Indonesia	$2 523 500 000
Ethiopia	$1 937 300 000
Vietnam	$1 904 900 000

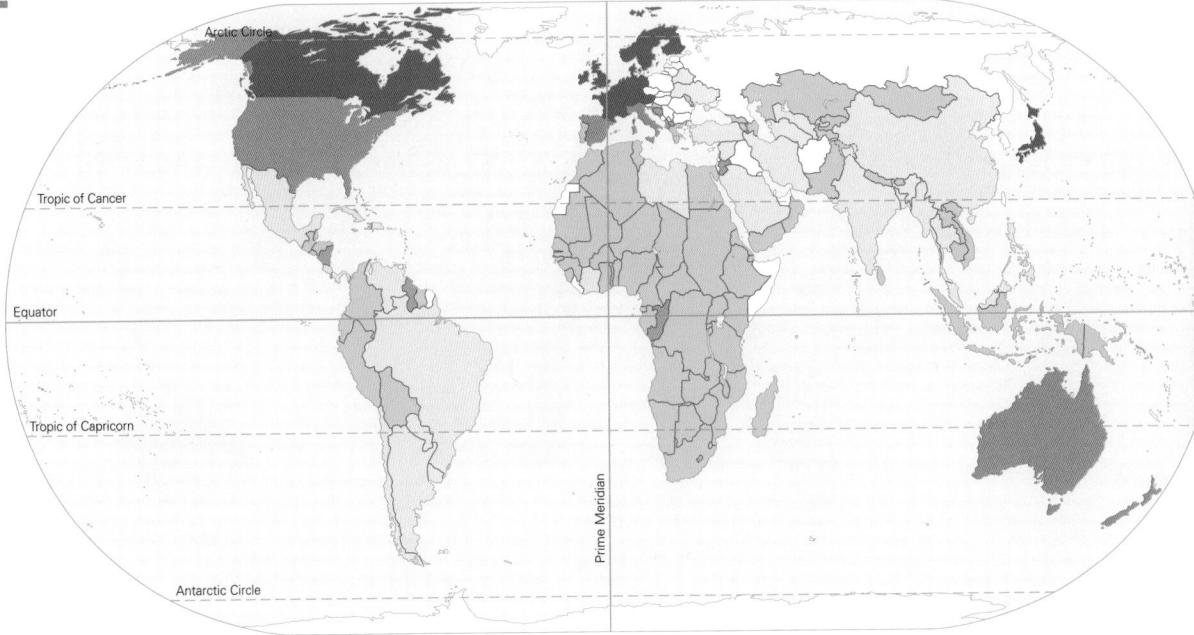

Employment

percentage of the labour force

over 80%

60–80%

30–60%

10–30%

under 10%

no data

Scale 1: 480 000 000

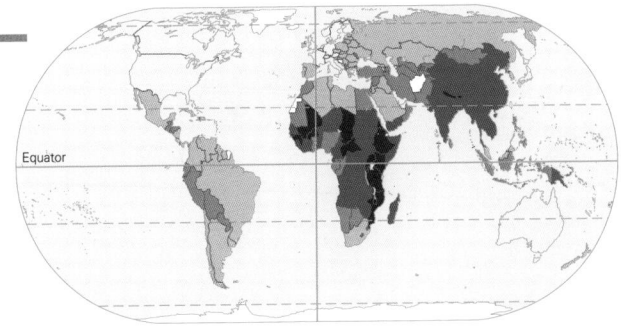

Agriculture

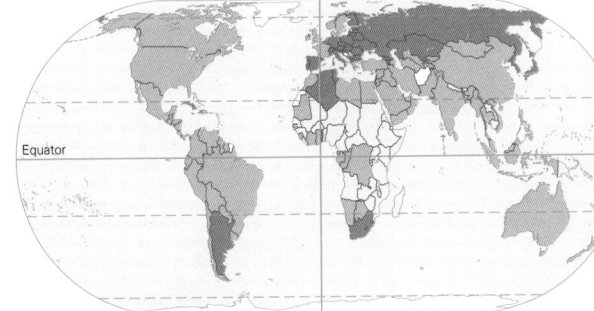

Industry

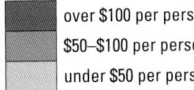
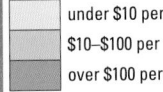
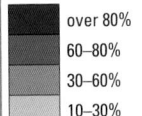

Services

Further information on this topic is located in the World Datasets section which begins on page 184.

Eckert IV Projection   © Oxford University Press

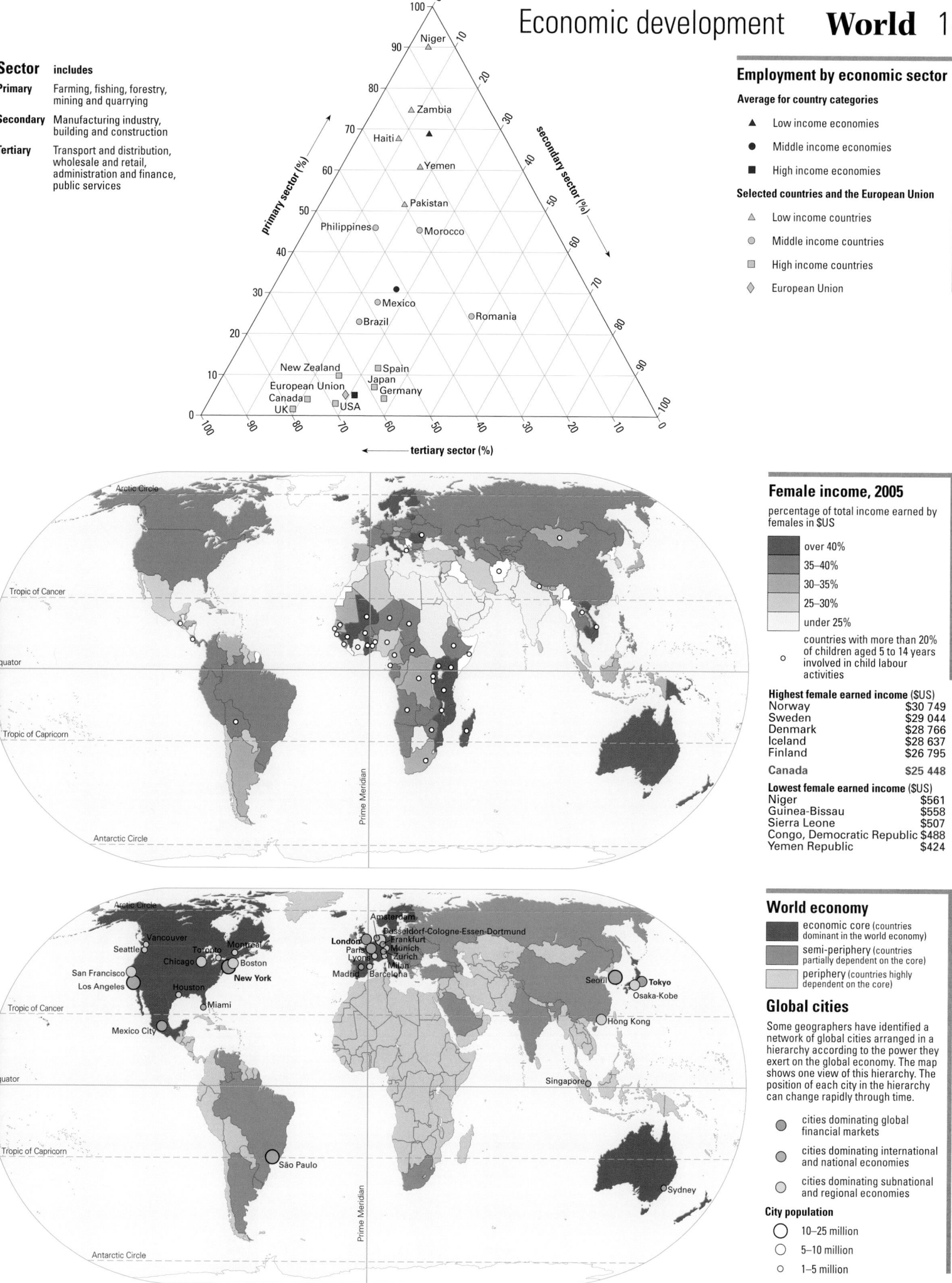

Sector | **includes**
Primary | Farming, fishing, forestry, mining and quarrying
Secondary | Manufacturing industry, building and construction
Tertiary | Transport and distribution, wholesale and retail, administration and finance, public services

Niger
Zambia
Haiti
Yemen
Pakistan
Philippines
Morocco
Mexico
Brazil
Romania
New Zealand
Spain
European Union
Japan
Canada
Germany
UK
USA

primary sector (%)
secondary sector (%)
tertiary sector (%)

Employment by economic sector

Average for country categories

▲ Low income economies
● Middle income economies
■ High income economies

Selected countries and the European Union

△ Low income countries
○ Middle income countries
□ High income countries
◇ European Union

Female income, 2005

percentage of total income earned by females in $US

over 40%
35–40%
30–35%
25–30%
under 25%

○ countries with more than 20% of children aged 5 to 14 years involved in child labour activities

Highest female earned income ($US)
Norway | $30 749
Sweden | $29 044
Denmark | $28 766
Iceland | $28 637
Finland | $26 795

Canada | $25 448

Lowest female earned income ($US)
Niger | $561
Guinea-Bissau | $558
Sierra Leone | $507
Congo, Democratic Republic | $488
Yemen Republic | $424

World economy

economic core (countries dominant in the world economy)
semi-periphery (countries partially dependent on the core)
periphery (countries highly dependent on the core)

Global cities

Some geographers have identified a network of global cities arranged in a hierarchy according to the power they exert on the global economy. The map shows one view of this hierarchy. The position of each city in the hierarchy can change rapidly through time.

○ cities dominating global financial markets
○ cities dominating international and national economies
○ cities dominating subnational and regional economies

City population

○ 10–25 million
○ 5–10 million
○ 1–5 million

Source: J. Friedmann, *World Cities in a World-System.* (Cambridge: Cambridge University Press, 1995), p.24.

Arctic Circle
Tropic of Cancer
Equator
Tropic of Capricorn
Antarctic Circle
Prime Meridian

Vancouver
Seattle
San Francisco
Los Angeles
Toronto
Montreal
Chicago
Boston
New York
Houston
Miami
Mexico City
São Paulo
Amsterdam
Düsseldorf-Cologne-Essen-Dortmund
London
Paris
Frankfurt
Munich
Lyons
Zürich
Milan
Madrid
Barcelona
Seoul
Tokyo
Osaka-Kobe
Hong Kong
Singapore
Sydney

© Oxford University Press

Scale 1: 240 000 000

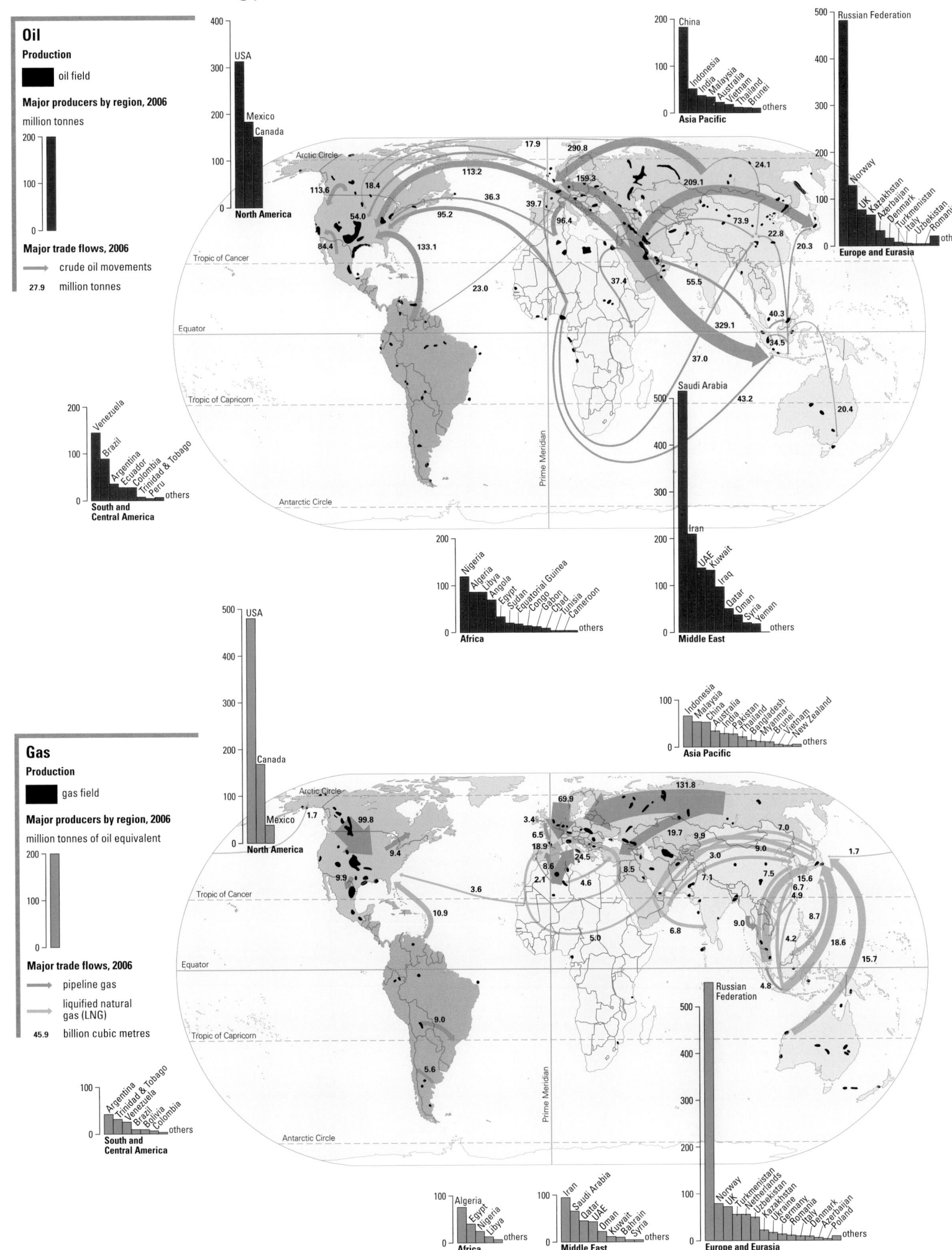

Eckert IV Projection   © Oxford University Press

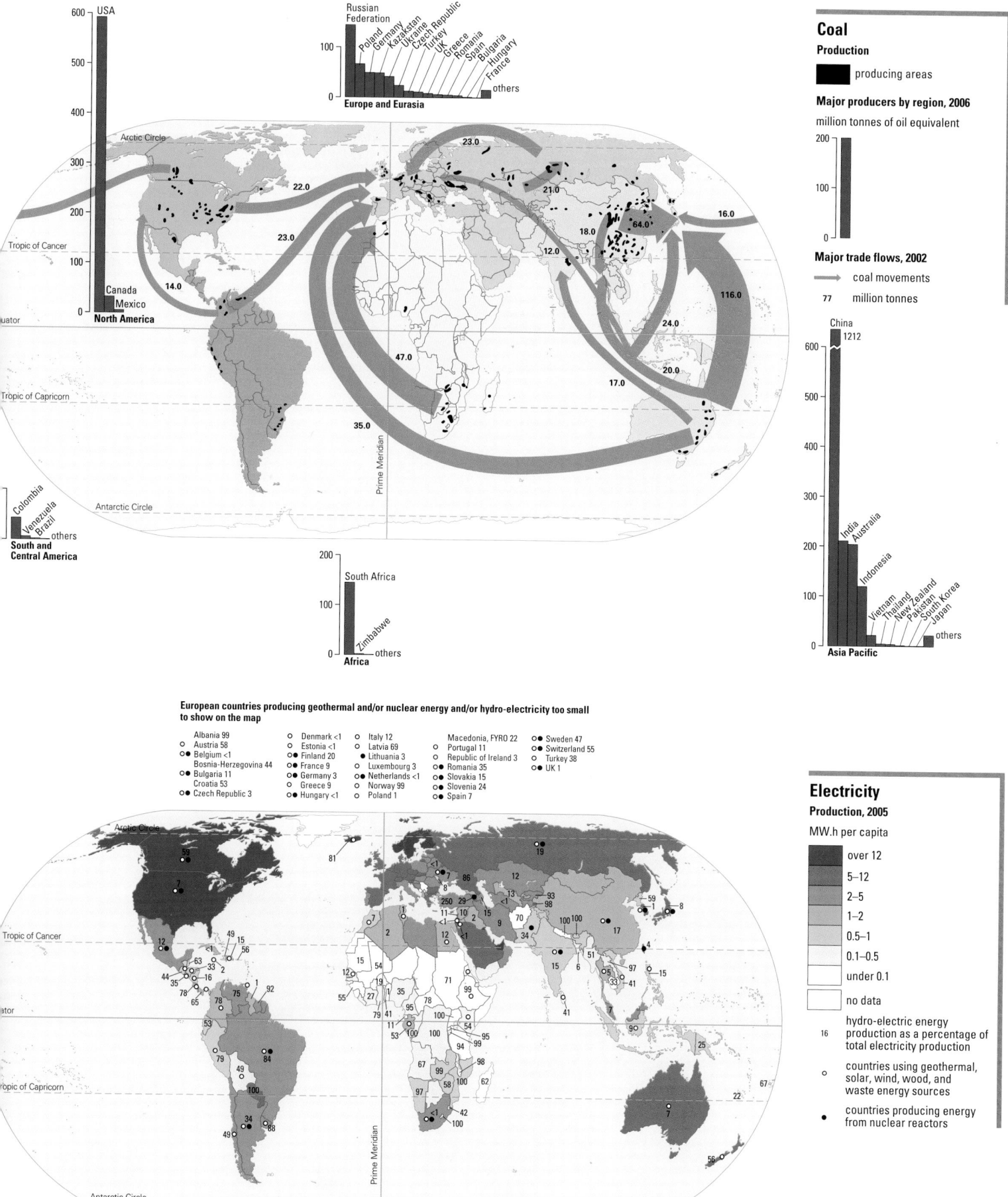

Coal

Production

■ producing areas

Major producers by region, 2006

million tonnes of oil equivalent

Major trade flows, 2002

→ coal movements

77 million tonnes

North America
USA
Canada
Mexico

Europe and Eurasia
Russian Federation
Poland
Germany
Kazakstan
Ukraine
Czech Republic
Turkey
UK
Greece
Romania
Spain
Bulgaria
Hungary
France
others

South and Central America
Colombia
Venezuela
Brazil
others

Africa
South Africa
Zimbabwe
others

Asia Pacific
China 1212
India
Australia
Indonesia
Vietnam
Thailand
New Zealand
Pakistan
South Korea
Japan
others

Coal trade flow values on map: 23.0, 22.0, 21.0, 18.0, 16.0, 14.0, 12.0, 64.0, 116.0, 24.0, 20.0, 47.0, 17.0, 35.0

European countries producing geothermal and/or nuclear energy and/or hydro-electricity too small to show on the map

○ Albania 99	○ Denmark <1	○ Italy 12	Macedonia, FYRO 22	○● Sweden 47
○ Austria 58	○ Estonia <1	○ Latvia 69	○ Portugal 11	○● Switzerland 55
○● Belgium <1	○● Finland 20	● Lithuania 3	○ Republic of Ireland 3	○ Turkey 38
Bosnia-Herzegovina 44	○● France 9	○ Luxembourg 3	○● Romania 35	○● UK 1
○● Bulgaria 11	○● Germany 3	○ Netherlands <1	○● Slovakia 15	
Croatia 53	○ Greece 9	● Norway 99	○● Slovenia 24	
○● Czech Republic 3	○● Hungary <1	○ Poland 1	○● Spain 7	

Electricity

Production, 2005

MW.h per capita

■	over 12
■	5–12
■	2–5
■	1–2
■	0.5–1
■	0.1–0.5
□	under 0.1
□	no data

16 hydro-electric energy production as a percentage of total electricity production

○ countries using geothermal, solar, wind, wood, and waste energy sources

● countries producing energy from nuclear reactors

Energy production, 2005

kg oil equivalent per person

- over 25 000
- 2500–25 000
- 1000–2500
- 100–1000
- under 100
- no data

Highest energy producers
kg oil equivalent per person

Qatar	117 511
Kuwait	60 340
Brunei	58 253
Norway	57 630
United Arab Emirates	41 859
Equatorial Guinea	41 283
Trinidad and Tobago	28 628
Saudi Arabia	27 583
Oman	23 411
Libya	17 089
Bahrain	16 747
Canada	14 774
Turkmenistan	14 182
Australia	13 806
Gabon	10 554

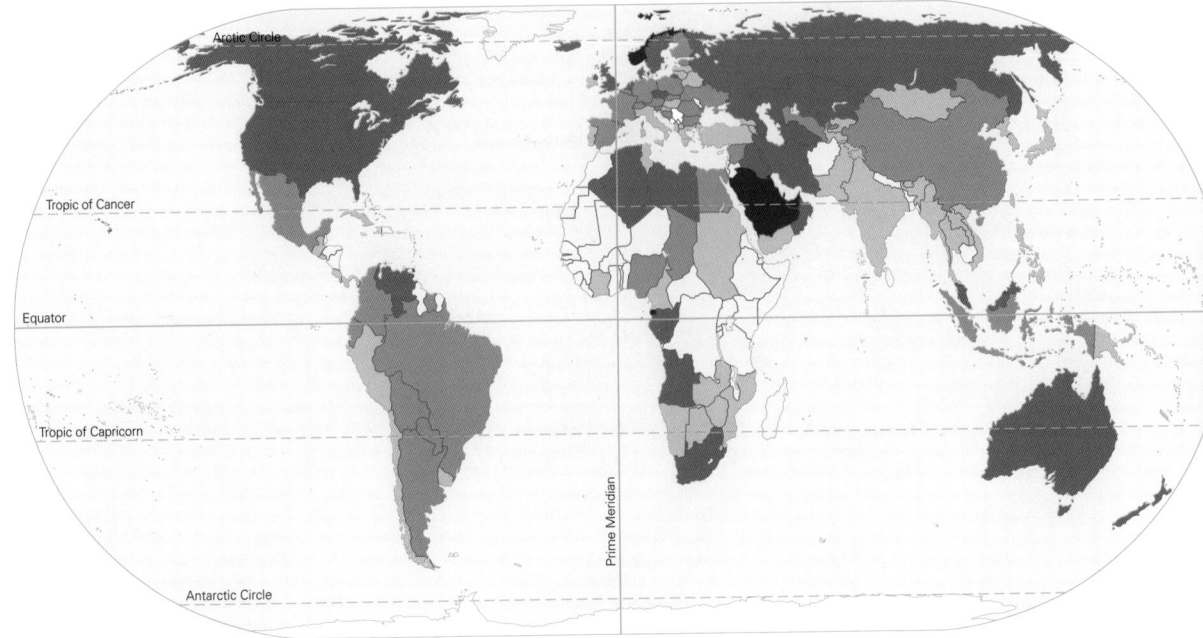

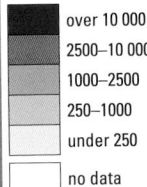

- North America
- Central and South America
- Europe and Eurasia
- Middle East
- Africa
- Asia Pacific

Oil reserves
Proven recoverable reserves
World total: 165 000 000 000 tonnes

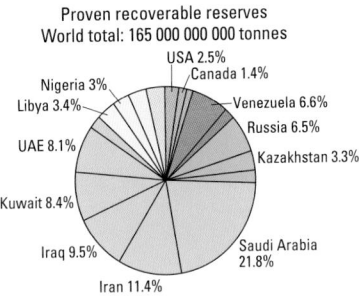

USA 2.5%
Canada 1.4%
Venezuela 6.6%
Nigeria 3%
Russia 6.5%
Libya 3.4%
Kazakhstan 3.3%
UAE 8.1%
Kuwait 8.4%
Iraq 9.5%
Saudi Arabia 21.8%
Iran 11.4%

Gas reserves
Proven recoverable reserves
World total: 180 200 000 000 000 m³

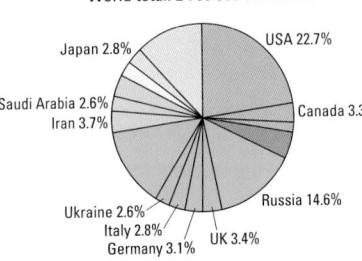

USA 3.2%
Canada 0.9%
Venezuela 2.4%
Algeria 2.5%
Nigeria 2.9%
Russia 26.4%
Qatar 14.1%
Iran 15.3%

Coal reserves
Proven recoverable reserves
World total: 909 064 000 000 tonnes

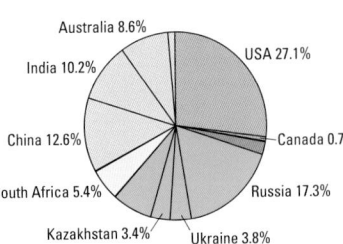

Australia 8.6%
USA 27.1%
India 10.2%
China 12.6%
Canada 0.7
South Africa 5.4%
Russia 17.3%
Kazakhstan 3.4%
Ukraine 3.8%

Oil consumption
World total: 3 861 300 000 tonnes

South Korea 2.7%
India 3.1%
USA 24.6%
Japan 6.3%
China 8.5%
Canada 2.6%
Mexico 2.3%
Brazil 2.3%
Iran 2.0%
Russia 3.2%
Saudi Arabia 2.3%
Germany 3.2%
Spain 2.0%
France 2.4%
UK 2.1%
Italy 2.2%

Gas consumption
World total: 2 780 300 000 000 m³

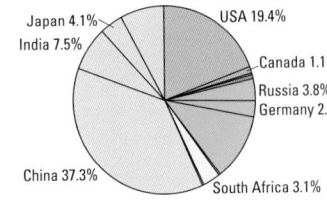

Japan 2.8%
USA 22.7%
Saudi Arabia 2.6%
Canada 3.3%
Iran 3.7%
Ukraine 2.6%
Russia 14.6%
Italy 2.8%
UK 3.4%
Germany 3.1%

Coal consumption
World total: 2 957 000 000 tonnes oil equivalent

Japan 4.1%
USA 19.4%
India 7.5%
Canada 1.1%
Russia 3.8%
Germany 2.8
China 37.3%
South Africa 3.1%

Energy consumption, 2005

kg oil equivalent per person

- over 10 000
- 2500–10 000
- 1000–2500
- 250–1000
- under 250
- no data

Highest energy consumers
kg oil equivalent per person

Qatar	26 555
Bahrain	15 769
United Arab Emirates	12 702
Trinidad and Tobago	12 624
Iceland	12 238
Canada	11 075

Lowest energy consumers
kg oil equivalent per person

Burundi	26
Mali	22
Afghanistan	16
Cambodia	15
Chad	7

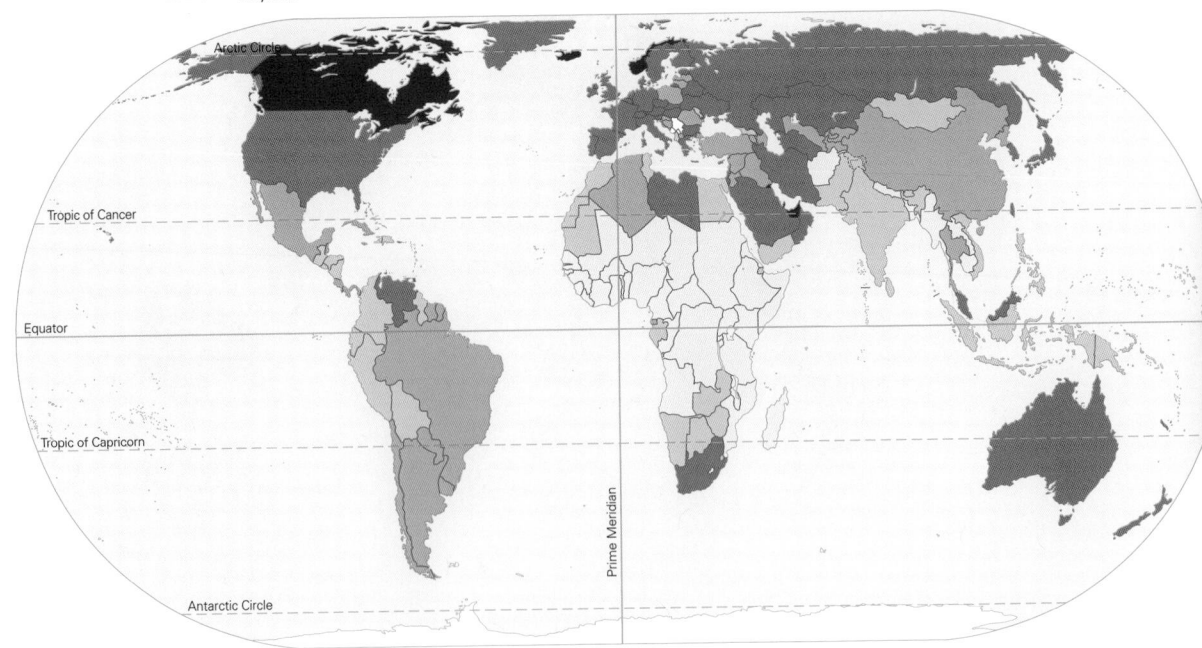

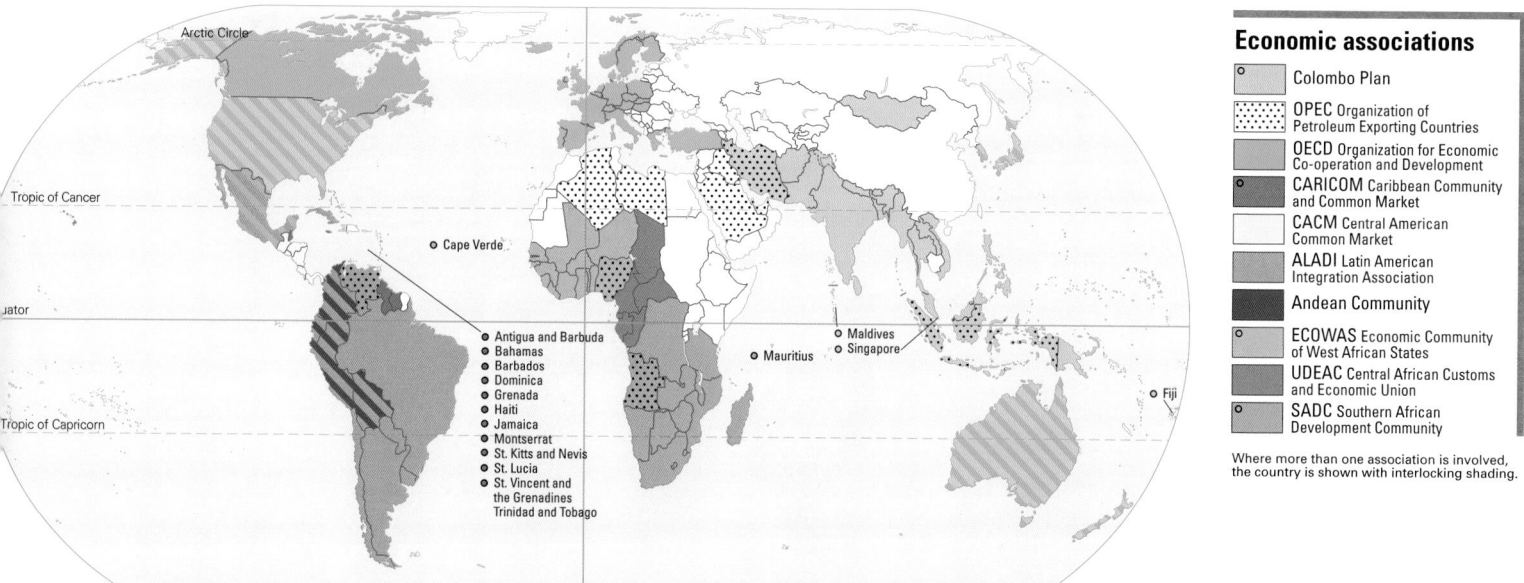

Economic associations

- Colombo Plan
- OPEC Organization of Petroleum Exporting Countries
- OECD Organization for Economic Co-operation and Development
- CARICOM Caribbean Community and Common Market
- CACM Central American Common Market
- ALADI Latin American Integration Association
- Andean Community
- ECOWAS Economic Community of West African States
- UDEAC Central African Customs and Economic Union
- SADC Southern African Development Community

Where more than one association is involved, the country is shown with interlocking shading.

Antigua and Barbuda
Bahamas
Barbados
Dominica
Grenada
Haiti
Jamaica
Montserrat
St. Kitts and Nevis
St. Lucia
St. Vincent and the Grenadines
Trinidad and Tobago

Cape Verde
Maldives
Singapore
Mauritius
Fiji

WTO World Trade Organization

- WTO World Trade Organization

Antigua and Barbuda	Maldives
Bahamas	Malta
Bahrain	Mauritius
Barbados	Nauru
Brunei	Qatar
Burundi	St. Kitts and Nevis
Cyprus	St. Lucia
Dominica	St. Vincent and
Fiji	the Grenadines
Grenada	Samoa
Haiti	Seychelles
Israel	Singapore
Jamaica	Solomon Islands
Kiribati	Tonga
Kuwait	Trinidad and Tobago
Liechtenstein	Tuvalu
Luxembourg	Vanuatu

- Commonwealth of Nations

Commonwealth of Nations

UNCTAD
United Nations Conference on Trade and Development

Almost all nations (193) are now members

EU
European Union

For members see page 82.

United Nations
The following countries are **non-members**

Northern Marianas
Taiwan
Vatican City†
Western Sahara

† observer status

Headquarters of selected world organizations

Brussels:
The European Union
North Atlantic Treaty Organization (NATO)

The Hague:
International Court of Justice

New York:
United Nations

Paris:
United Nations Educational, Scientific and Cultural Organization (UNESCO)
Organization for Economic Co-operation and Development (OECD)

Rome:
Food and Agriculture Organization of the United Nations (FAO)

Geneva:
World Health Organization (WHO)
World Trade Organization (WTO)

Washington:
Organization of American States (OAS)

Addis Ababa:
African Union (AU)

Cairo:
Arab League

Singapore:
Asia Pacific Economic Co-operation (APEC)

Strasbourg:
Council of Europe
European Parliament

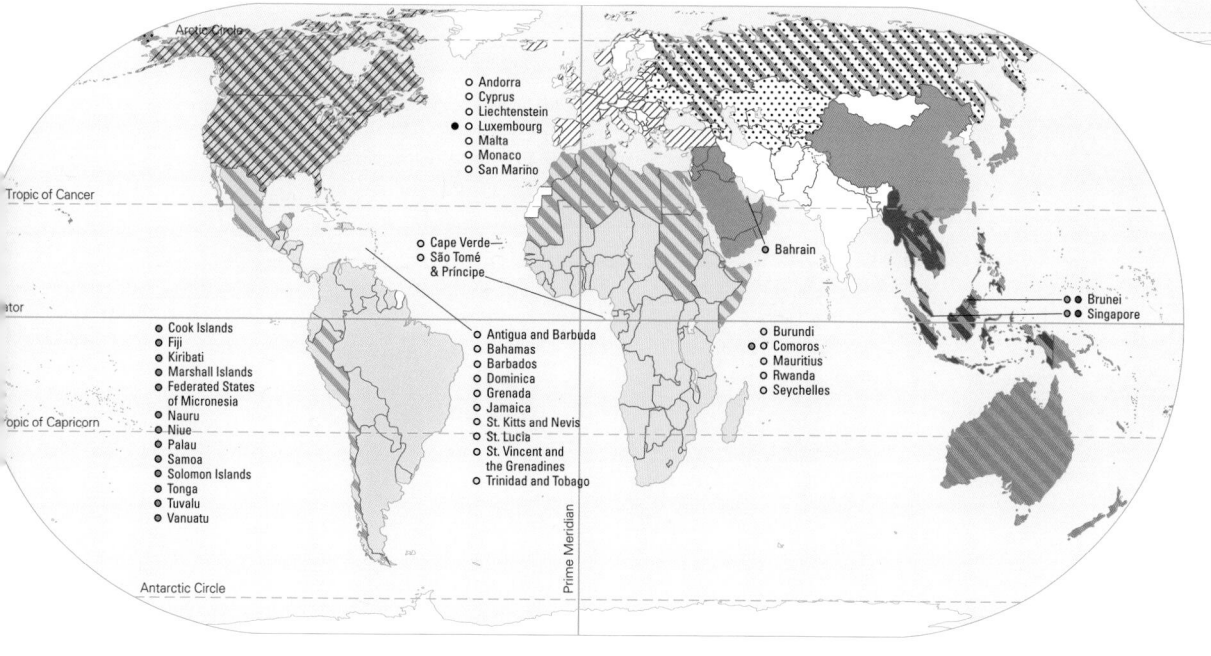

Andorra
Cyprus
Liechtenstein
Luxembourg
Malta
Monaco
San Marino

Cook Islands
Fiji
Kiribati
Marshall Islands
Federated States of Micronesia
Nauru
Niue
Palau
Samoa
Solomon Islands
Tonga
Tuvalu
Vanuatu

Cape Verde
São Tomé & Príncipe

Antigua and Barbuda
Bahamas
Barbados
Dominica
Grenada
Jamaica
St. Kitts and Nevis
St. Lucia
St. Vincent and the Grenadines
Trinidad and Tobago

Bahrain

Brunei
Singapore

Burundi
Comoros
Mauritius
Rwanda
Seychelles

International organizations

- South Pacific Forum
- ASEAN Association of South East Asian Nations
- OAS Organization of American States
- Arab League
- AU African Union
- NATO North Atlantic Treaty Organization
- Council of Europe
- APEC Asia Pacific Economic Co-operation
- CIS Commonwealth of Independent States

Where more than one organization is involved, the country is shown with interlocking shading.

Time zones

Minus numbers show hours behind Greenwich Mean Time (GMT). Plus numbers show hours ahead of GMT.

- even numbers of hours difference from GMT
- odd numbers of hours difference from GMT
- half an hour difference from adjacent zone
- less than half an hour difference from adjacent zone

Longitude is measured from the **prime meridian**, which passes through Greenwich. There are 24 standard time zones, each spanning 15° of longitude. Many of the boundaries of these time zones have been adjusted to follow political borders.

The **international date line** marks the point where one calendar day ends and another begins. A traveller crossing from east to west moves forward one day. Crossing from west to east, the calendar goes back one day.

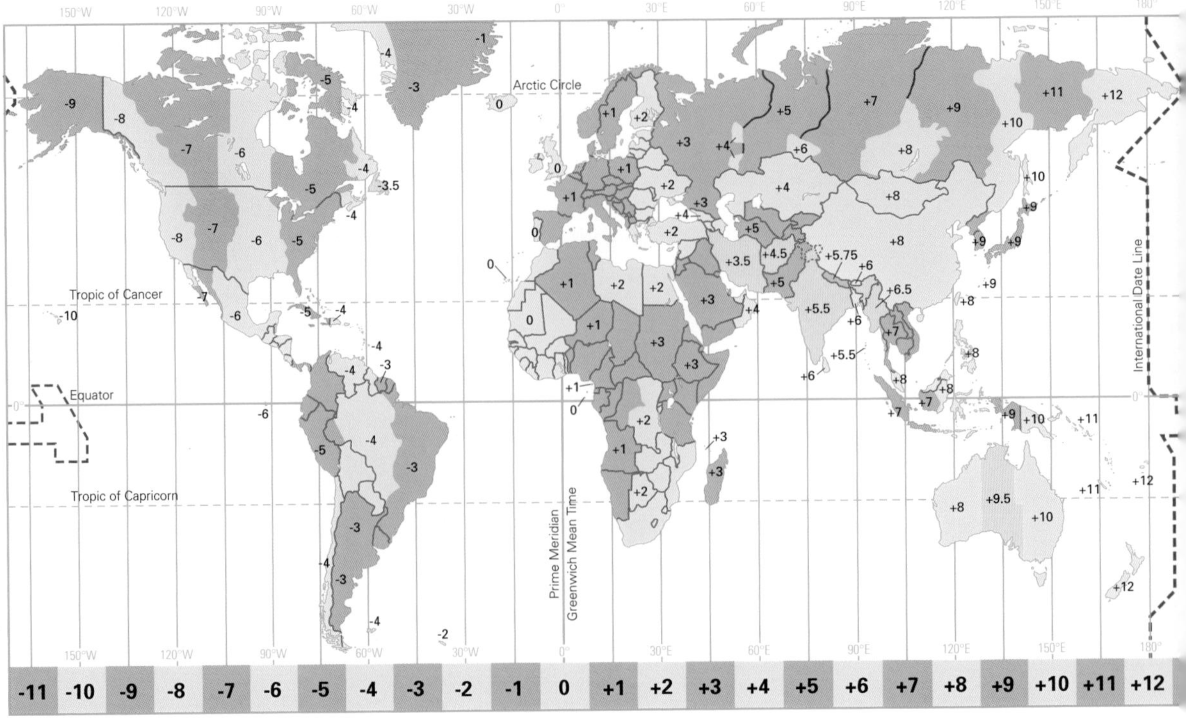

| -11 | -10 | -9 | -8 | -7 | -6 | -5 | -4 | -3 | -2 | -1 | 0 | +1 | +2 | +3 | +4 | +5 | +6 | +7 | +8 | +9 | +10 | +11 | +12 |

Online access, 2007

Percentage of population having Internet access

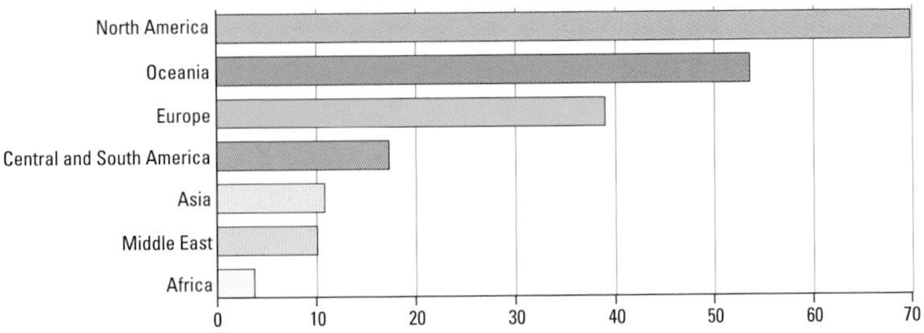

- North America
- Oceania
- Europe
- Central and South America
- Asia
- Middle East
- Africa

0 10 20 30 40 50 60 70

Internet users, 2007

There are 1114 million Internet users worldwide

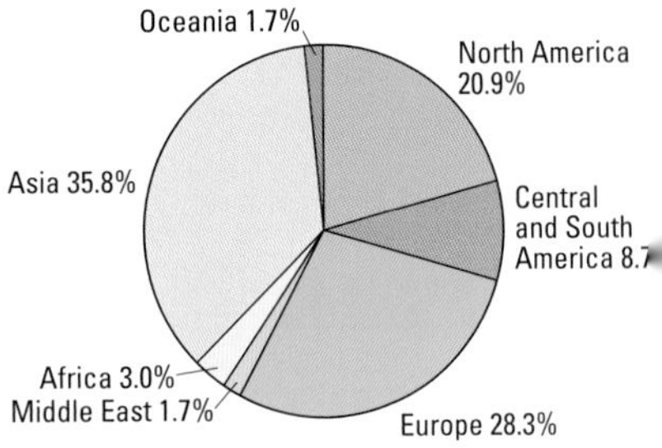

- Oceania 1.7%
- North America 20.9%
- Central and South America 8.7
- Europe 28.3%
- Middle East 1.7%
- Africa 3.0%
- Asia 35.8%

Internet users, 2007

per 10 000 people

- over 2500
- 1000–2500
- 250–1000
- 100–250
- 25–100
- under 25

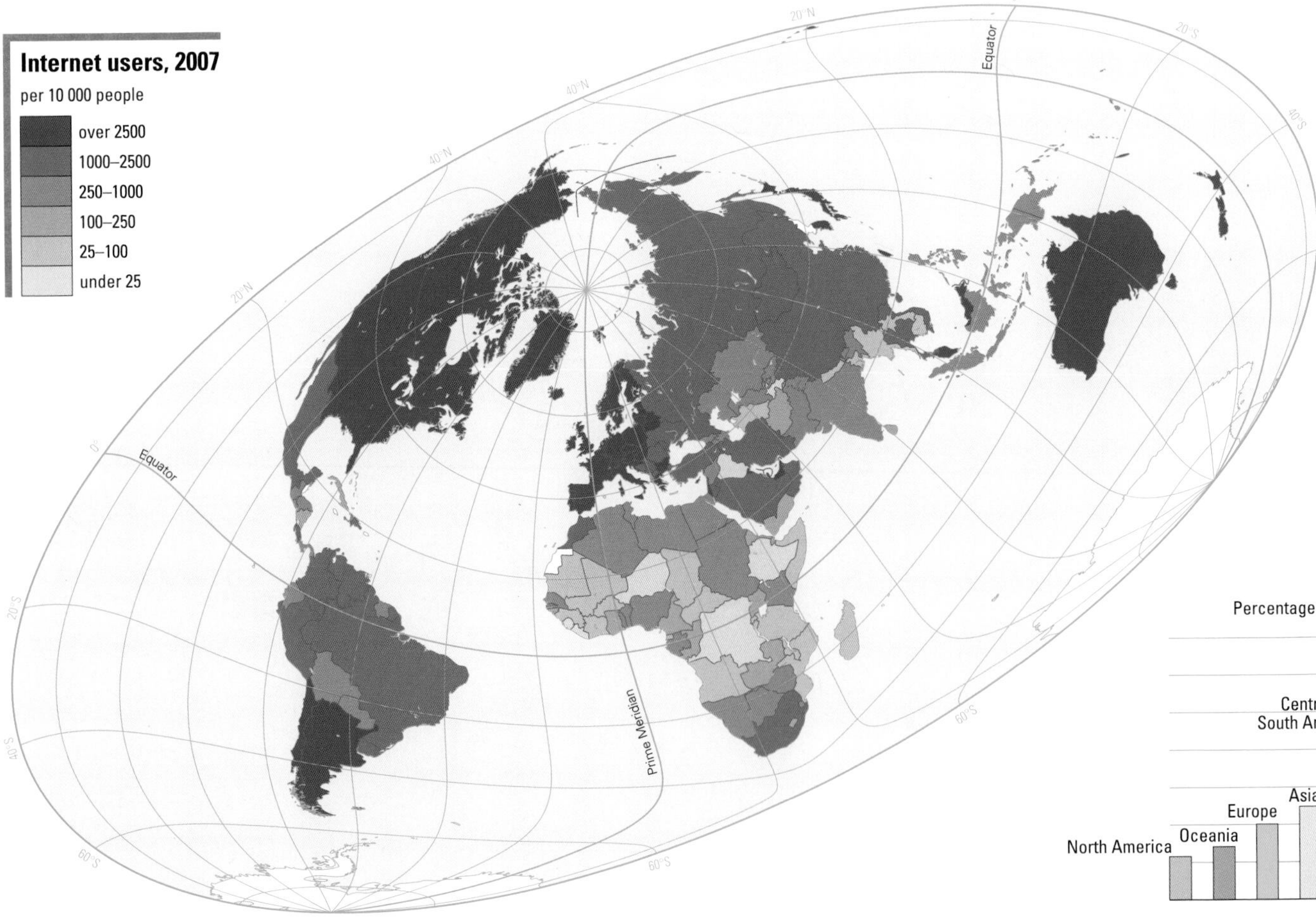

Internet growth 2000–200

Percentage increase in Internet use

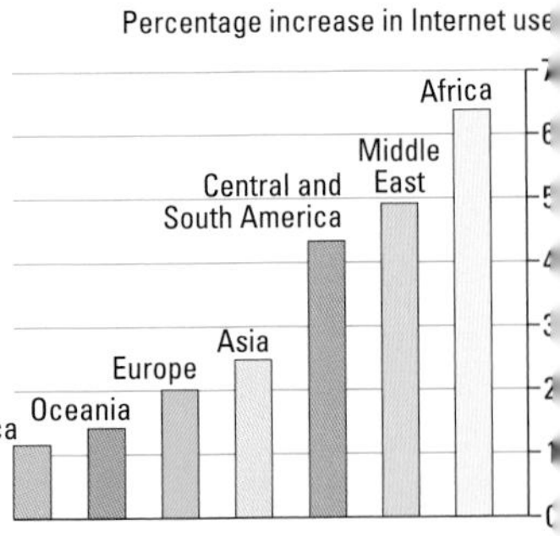

- North America
- Oceania
- Europe
- Asia
- Central and South America
- Middle East
- Africa

Gall Projection (Timezones)   Aitoff Projection   © Oxford University Press

World trade cartogram, 2006

the size of each country represents its share of total world trade

- 1% of world trade
- 0.01% of world trade

Change in share of world trade, 1996–2006

over 50%	
5–50%	growth
0–5% growth or decline	little or no change
5–50%	decline
over 50%	

Only those countries with more than 0.01% share in world trade are shown

Leading exporters
highest percentage share of world exports

China	10.7%
Germany	9.2%
United States	8.6%
Japan	5.4%
France	4.1%
Canada	3.2%

Highest importers
highest percentage share of world imports

United States	15.5%
China	9.1%
Germany	7.3%
United Kingdom	5.0%
Japan	4.7%
Canada	3.2%

Transport

Air transport

— major air route
• major airport

Sea transport

— major shipping lane
• major port

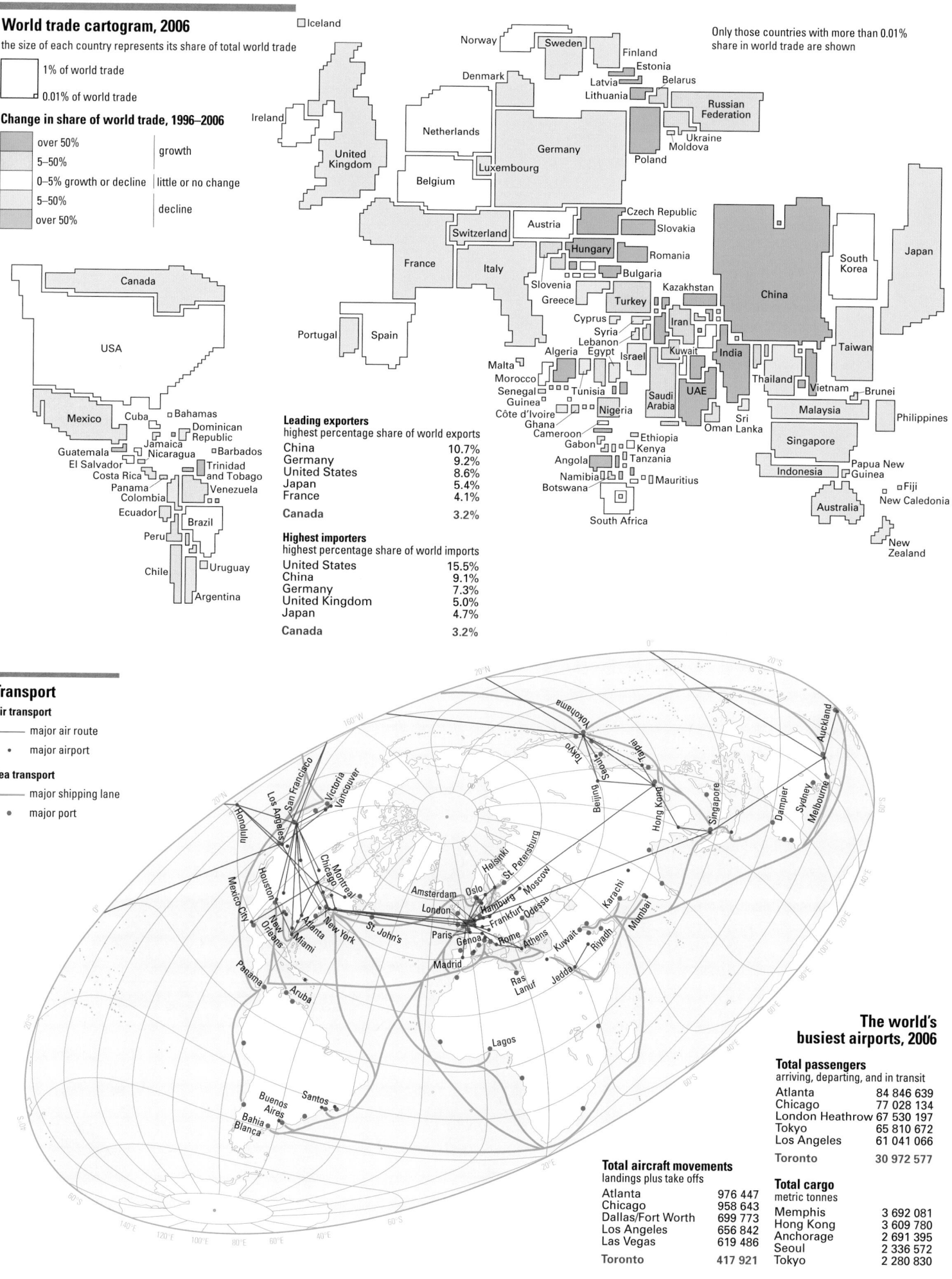

The world's busiest airports, 2006

Total passengers
arriving, departing, and in transit

Atlanta	84 846 639
Chicago	77 028 134
London Heathrow	67 530 197
Tokyo	65 810 672
Los Angeles	61 041 066
Toronto	30 972 577

Total aircraft movements
landings plus take offs

Atlanta	976 447
Chicago	958 643
Dallas/Fort Worth	699 773
Los Angeles	656 842
Las Vegas	619 486
Toronto	417 921

Total cargo
metric tonnes

Memphis	3 692 081
Hong Kong	3 609 780
Anchorage	2 691 395
Seoul	2 336 572
Tokyo	2 280 830

Scale 1: 125 000 000 (main map)

Selected tourist destinations

The locations shown represent a limited selection of important tourism sites.

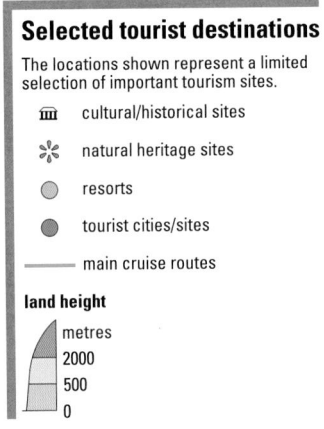

- 🏛 cultural/historical sites
- ❋ natural heritage sites
- ⊙ resorts
- ⬤ tourist cities/sites
- ── main cruise routes

land height

metres	
2000	
500	
0	

Top tourist destinations, 2006

	arrivals (000)	% change 2005–2006
France	79 100	4.2
Spain	58 500	4.5
USA	51 100	3.8
China	49 600	6.0
Italy	41 100	12.4
United Kingdom	30 700	9.3
Germany	23 600	9.6
Mexico	21 400	-2.6
Austria	20 300	1.5
Russia	20 200	1.3
Canada	**18 300**	**-2.7**

Market share, 2006

percentage of all international tourist arrivals

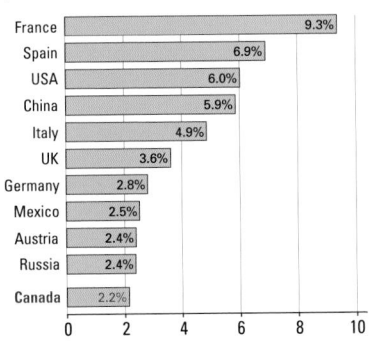

France	9.3%
Spain	6.9%
USA	6.0%
China	5.9%
Italy	4.9%
UK	3.6%
Germany	2.8%
Mexico	2.5%
Austria	2.4%
Russia	2.4%
Canada	2.2%

Earnings from tourism, 2005

tourist receipts in million $US

- over 5000
- 1000–5000
- 250–1000
- 100–250
- under 100
- no data

Highest tourist earnings (million)

USA	$122 944
China	$53 185
Spain	$52 960
France	$42 167
United Kingdom	$39 573
Canada	$15 830

The government of Canada maintains a regularly updated travel advisory for all countries of the world at www.voyage.gc.ca. In February 2008, warnings to avoid either non-essential or all travel were posted for 58 countries.

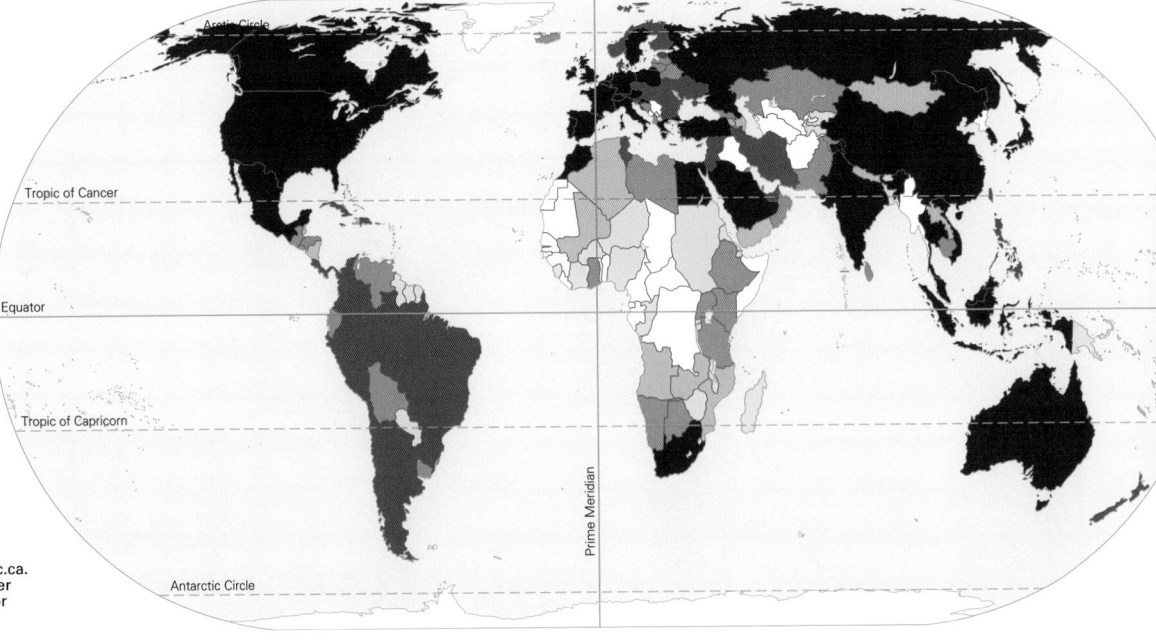

Eckert IV Projection   © Oxford University Press

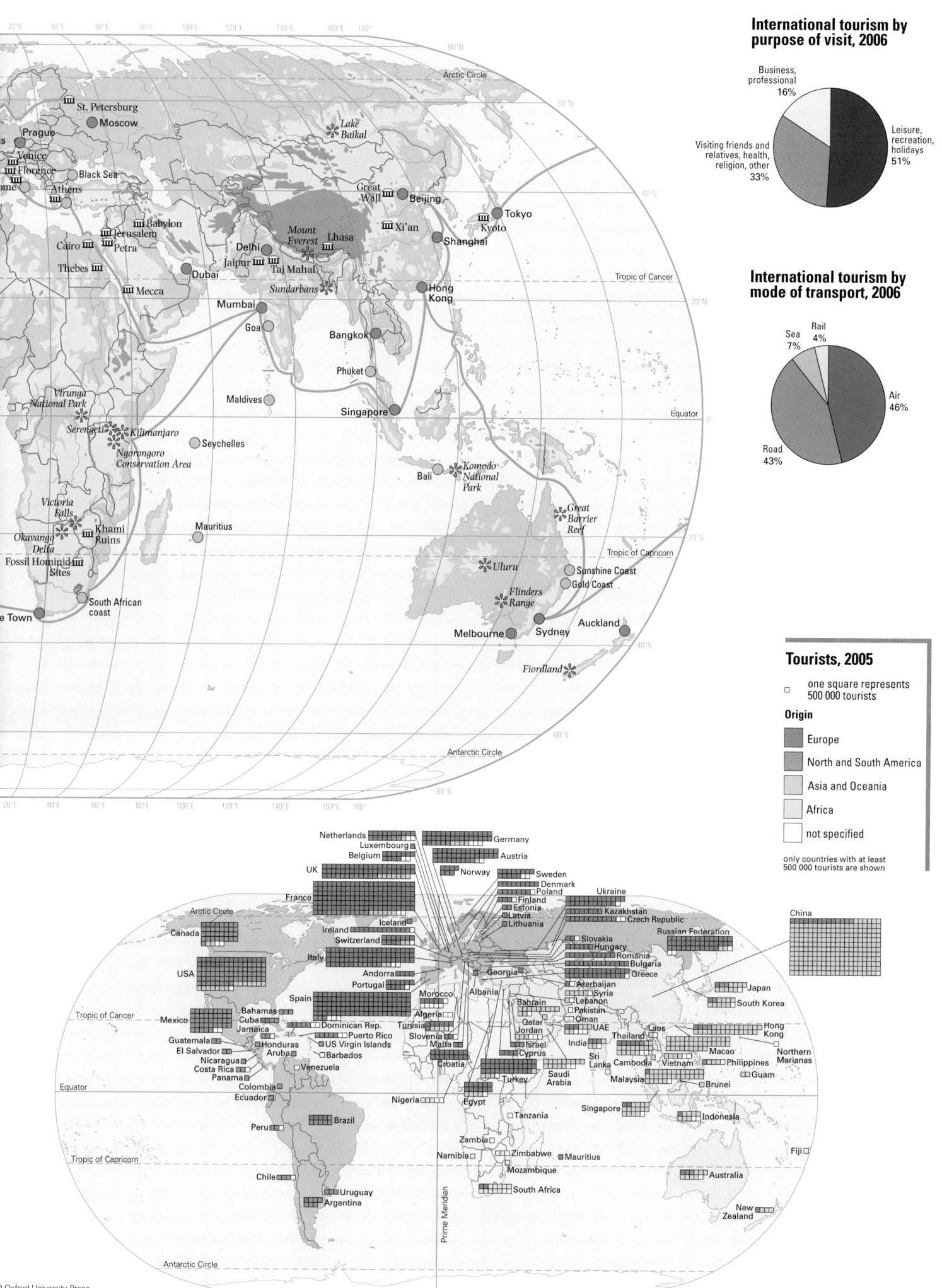

International tourism by purpose of visit, 2006

Business, professional 16%

Visiting friends and relatives, health, religion, other 33%

Leisure, recreation, holidays 51%

International tourism by mode of transport, 2006

Sea 7%

Rail 4%

Air 46%

Road 43%

Tourists, 2005

□ one square represents 500 000 tourists

Origin

- Europe
- North and South America
- Asia and Oceania
- Africa
- not specified

only countries with at least 500 000 tourists are shown

© Oxford University Press

Selected tourist sites

The locations shown represent a limited selection of important tourism sites.

- 𝍇 cultural/historical centres
- ✳ sites of natural beauty and wildlife
- ● National Parks†
- ● ● coastal tourism areas and resorts
- △ ski and mountain areas and resorts
- ★ leisure parks

land height

metres
2000
500
0

† All Canadian parks and reserves are shown on page 27.

Florida Scale 1: 8 000 000

Jacksonville
St. Augustine
Marineland
Daytona Beach
John F. Kenedy Space Centre
Cape Canaveral
Orlando
Universal Studios
Walt Disney World Resort Complex
Busch Gardens
Clearwater
St. Petersburg
Tampa
Tampa Bay
Sarasota
Fort Myers
Naples
Charlotte Harbour
Lake Okeechobee
Palm Beach
Fort Lauderdale
Miami Beach
Miami
Biscayne National Park
Big Cypress National Preserve
The Everglades
Everglades National Park
Key Largo
Florida Keys
Key West
Straits of Florida
FLORIDA
Gulf of Mexico

The Caribbean Scale 1: 18 000 000

West Indies

Leeward Islands
Virgin Is. (UK/USA)
Cane Garden Bay (UK/USA)
Trunk Bay
St. John (USA)
St. Croix (USA)
Anguilla
Shoal Bay
St. Maarten
St. Jean
ANTIGUA AND BARBUDA
Barbuda
Antigua
Guadeloupe (Fr.)
Grande Terre
DOMINICA
Marie Galante
Martinique (Fr.)
Le Diamant
ST. LUCIA
ST. VINCENT AND THE GRENADINES
St. Vincent
GRENADA
Grand Anse Beach
Tobago
TRINIDAD AND TOBAGO
Port-of-Spain
BARBADOS
Montserrat (UK)
ST. KITTS AND NEVIS
Windward Islands
Lesser Antilles

Puerto Rico (USA)
San Juan
Luquillo Beach
Santo Domingo
DOMINICAN REPUBLIC
HAITI
Port-au-Prince
Punta Cana
La Romana
Puerto Plata
Turks and Caicos Is. (UK)
Great Inagua
Mayaguana
Acklins I.
Crooked I.
Long Island
Great Exuma
THE BAHAMAS
Santa Lucia
Cayo Santa Maria
Varadero
CUBA
Havana
Cayo Largo
Isla de la Juventud
Cayman Islands (UK)
Grand Cayman
Seven Mile Beach
JAMAICA
Montego Bay
Negril Beach
Kingston
Greater Antilles
Windward Passage
Caicos Passage
Turks I. Passage

Netherland Antilles
Curaçao (Neths.)
Bonaire (Neths.)
Aruba (Neths.)

CARIBBEAN SEA
Lesser Antilles
Antilles

Main map Scale 1: 40 000 000 (main map)

CANADA
Arctic Circle
Queen Elizabeth Islands
Aulavik National Park
Tuktut Nogait National Park
Nahanni National Parkreserve
Wood Buffalo National Park
Wapusk National Park
Batoche
Batoche Battlefield
Columbia Icefield
Canadian Rocky Mountain Parks
Banff
Lake Louise
Golden
Fernie
Vancouver
Whistler
Kluane National Park
Kuane National Park
Glacier Bay National Park
Denali National Park
L'Anse aux Meadows
Icebergs
Gros Morne
St. John's
Cape Breton Highlands National Park
Louisbourg
whale watching
Halifax
Bay of Fundy
White Mts.
Montreal
Quebec
Mont Tremblant
Muskoka
Haliburton
Agawa Canyon
Great Lakes
Paramount Canada's Wonderland
Chicago
Niagara Falls
Adirondack Mountains
Killington
Boston
New England
New York
Washington D.C.
Escarpment Falls
Cedar Point
Kings Island
Grand Ole Opry
Memphis
Blue Ridge
Great Smoky Mountains National Park
Kings Dominion
Six Flags Over Georgia
Busch Gardens
Myrtle Beach
Fort Sumter National Museum
Walt Disney World
see inset
Universal Studios
Everglades National Park
New Orleans
Houston
Astro World
Six Flags Fiesta Texas
Alamo
Camp Snoopy
Six Flags Great America
Mount Rushmore
Little Bighorn Battlefield
Yellowstone National Park
Rocky Mountain National Park
Winter Park
Copper Mountain
Vail
Aspen
Steamboat
Salt Lake City
Navajo and Apache lands
Grand Canyon National Park
Fort Garry
Six Flags Great Adventure

UNITED STATES

San Francisco
Squaw Valley
Sea World
Santa Cruz Beach
Universal Studios
Los Angeles
Sun Valley
Alpental
Seattle
whale watching
Heavenly
Mammoth Mountain
Yosemite National Park
Death Valley
Las Vegas
Knott's Berry Farm
Tijuana

MEXICO
Chihuahua
Monterrey
Guadalajara
Guanajuato
San Miguel de Allende
Querétaro
Tula
Teotihuacán
Mexico City
Morelia
Lago de Pátzcuaro
Lago de Chapala
Ixtapa-Zihuatanejo
Acapulco
Puerto Escondido
Huatulco
Oaxaca
Palenque
San Cristóbal de las Casas
Yucatán Peninsula
Uxmal
Chichén Itzá
Cancún
Isla de Cozumel
Tulum
Puerto Vallarta
San Blas
Mazatlán
Guaymas
Cabo San Lucas
Baja California
Tropic of Cancer

ATLANTIC OCEAN
PACIFIC OCEAN
Gulf of Mexico

Scale 1: 17 000 000

Selected tourist sites

The locations shown represent a limited selection of important tourism sites.

Tuscany sites of natural beauty

⌶⌶⌶	cultural/historical centres
•⁘•	archaeological sites
●	coastal tourism areas and resorts
△	ski and mountain areas and resorts
★	leisure parks

land height

metres	
2000	
500	
0	

Flight times from London

typical non-stop flight times, 2007

hours

4 — ✈ Moscow
  — ✈ Athens

3 — ✈ Helsinki

  — ✈ Lisbon
  — ✈ Rome
2 — ✈ Vienna ✈ Madrid
  — ✈ Stockholm
  — ✈ Prague
  — ✈ Copenhagen ✈ Berlin

  — ✈ Dublin ✈ Edinburgh
1 — ✈ Amsterdam ✈ Paris
  — ✈ Brussels

  — 45 minutes

  — 30 minutes

  — 15 minutes

0 — ✈ **London**

Map labels

FINLAND — Finnish Lakeland — Helsinki

RUSSIA — St. Petersburg

SWEDEN — Stockholm

NORWAY — Oslo — Bergen — Norwegian Fjords

DENMARK — Copenhagen — Tivoli — Legoland — Dyrehavsbakken — Liseberg

ESTONIA
LATVIA — Jurmala
LITHUANIA — Vilnius — RUSSIA
BELARUS
UKRAINE — Kiev
MOLDOVA

POLAND — Warsaw — Krakow — Auschwitz

GERMANY — Berlin — Dresden — Weimar — Cologne — Lübeck — Amsterdam

NETHERLANDS — De Efteling
BELGIUM — Brussels — Bruges — Antwerp — Ardennes
LUXEMBOURG

CZECH REPUBLIC — Prague — Bohemia — Moravia
SLOVAKIA — Tatra
HUNGARY — Budapest
ROMANIA — Constanţa
BULGARIA — Varna

AUSTRIA — Vienna — Salzburg — Salzkammergut — Kitzbühel — Tirol
SWITZERLAND — Bern — Geneva
LIECHTENSTEIN
SLOVENIA
CROATIA — Dubrovnik — Dalmatian Coast
BOSNIA-HERZEGOVINA
SERBIA
MONTENEGRO
KOSOVO
FYRO MACEDONIA
ALBANIA

ITALY — Venice — Bologna — Verona — Florence — Siena — St. Gimignano — Tuscany — San Marino — Rome — Naples — Neapolitan Riviera — Amalfi Coast — Dolomites — Italian Lakes — Gardaland

FRANCE — Paris — Euro Disney — Reims — Chateaux of the Loire — Normandy — D-Day beaches — Brittany — Carnac — Lascaux Caves — Dordogne — Massif Central — Pont du Gard — Languedoc — Provence — Avignon — Lyons — Burgundy — Rhône Valley — Côte d'Azur — Riviera — MONACO

UNITED KINGDOM — London — York — Oxford — Stratford — Bath — Stonehenge — Alton Towers — Ironbridge Gorge — Bellewaerde — Lake District — Hadrian's Wall — Edinburgh — St. Andrews — SCOTTISH HIGHLANDS AND ISLANDS — Scottish Lowlands — Blackpool Pleasure Beach — Wales — Snowdonia — West Country — English Riviera — Vimy Ridge — Euro

REPUBLIC OF IRELAND — Dublin — The Burren — Aran Islands — Giant's Causeway — Antrim Coast — Ring of Kerry

SPAIN — Madrid — Segovia — Avila — Salamanca — Toledo — Córdoba — Seville — Granada — SIERRA NEVADA — Málaga — Costa del Sol — Marbella — Torremolinos — Guadalquivir — Tagus — Barcelona — Port Aventura — Costa Brava — Minorca — Majorca — Ibiza — Benidorm — Benicàssim — Alicante — ANDORRA — PYRENEES

PORTUGAL — Lisbon — Oporto — Viana do Castelo — Santiago de Compostela — Faro — Algarve

GREECE — Athens — Delphi — Mycenae — Olympia — Corfu — Ionian Islands — Thessaloniki — Halkidiki — Mykonos — Cyclades — Santorini — Knossós — Dodecanese — Rhodes

TURKEY — Istanbul — Troy — Ephesus — Turquoise Coast

AEGEAN SEA — IONIAN SEA — ADRIATIC SEA — Adriatic Riviera — BLACK SEA — BALTIC SEA — NORTH SEA — ATLANTIC OCEAN — MEDITERRANEAN SEA

Sicily — Sardinia — Corsica — Malta

Rhine — Elbe — Danube — Seine — Meuse — Rhône — Black Forest — Europa Park

Prime Meridian

© Oxford University Press   Conical Orthomorphic Projection

Scale 1: 55 000 000 (main map)

Selected tourist sites

The locations shown represent a limited selection of important tourism sites.

- ⛪ cultural/historical centres
- ∴ archaeological sites
- ✳ sites of natural beauty
- ⬤ National Parks and wildlife reserves
- ⬤ coastal tourism areas and resorts

land height

metres
2000
500
0

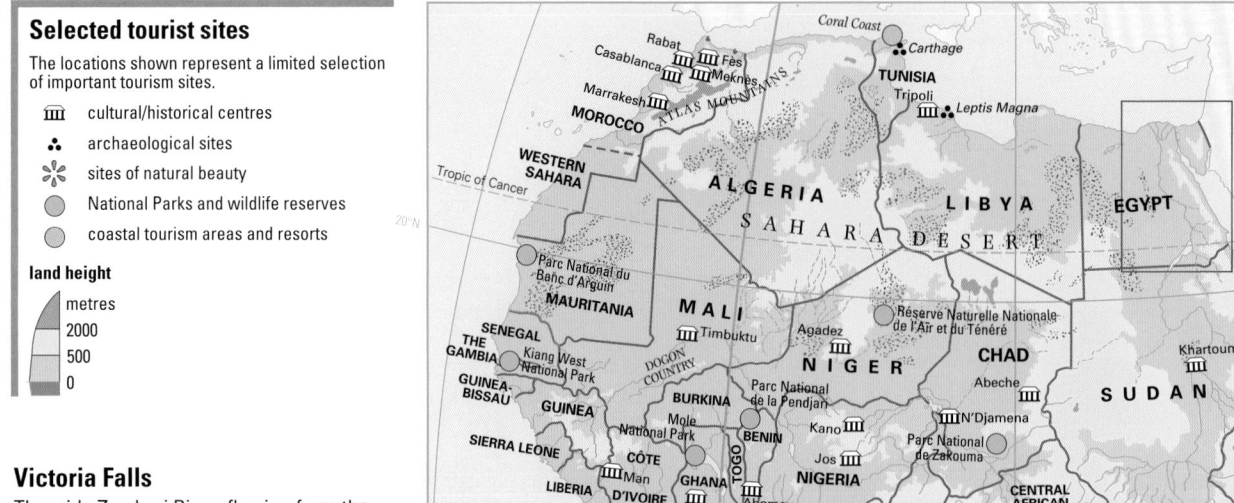

Victoria Falls

The wide Zambezi River, flowing from the top-left of the image, suddenly plunges 130 metres into the narrow gorge below. The tourist town of Victoria Falls (V) can be seen near the gorge.

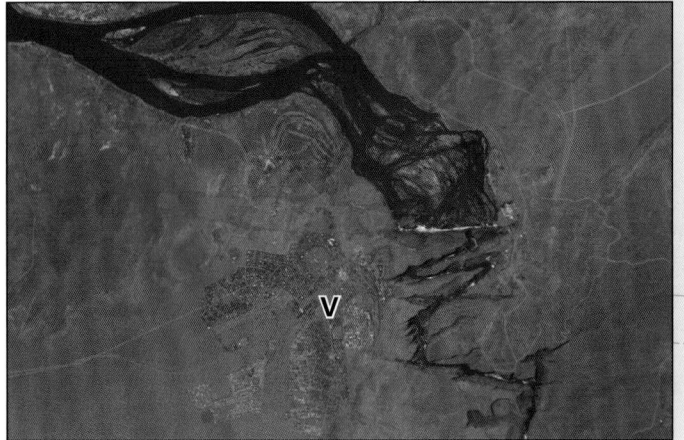

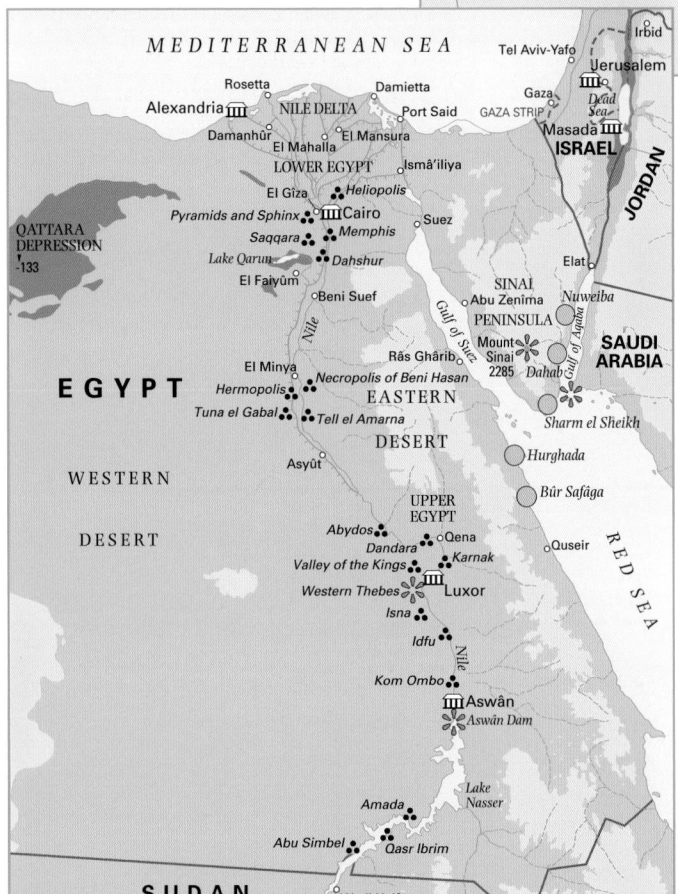

Nile Valley and Eastern Egypt Scale 1: 10 000 000

Kenya Scale 1: 10 000 000

Zenithal Equal Area Projection

© Oxford University Press

Land

1. Land and Freshwater Area

Province or Territory	Total Area (km²)	Land (km²)	Fresh Water (km²)	% of Total Area
Newfoundland & Labrador	405 212	373 872	31 340	4.1
Prince Edward Island	5 660	5 660	—	0.1
Nova Scotia	55 284	53 338	1 946	0.6
New Brunswick	72 908	71 450	1 458	0.7
Quebéc	1 542 056	1 365 128	176 928	15.4
Ontario	1 076 395	917 741	158 654	10.8
Manitoba	647 797	553 556	94 241	6.5
Saskatchewan	651 036	591 670	59 366	6.5
Alberta	661 848	642 317	19 531	6.6
British Columbia	944 735	925 186	19 549	9.5
Yukon	482 443	474 391	8 052	4.8
Northwest Territories	1 346 106	1 183 085	163 021	13.5
Nunavut	2 093 190	1 936 113	157 077	21.0
Canada	**9 984 670**	**9 093 507**	**891 163**	**100.0**

SOURCE: Adapted from Natural Resources Canada, "Facts about Canada—Land and Freshwater Areas" http://atlas.nrcan.gc.ca/site/english/learningresources/facts/surfareas.html. 2001 data courtesy of Natural Resouces Canada, Canada Centre for Remote Sensing.

Population

3. Total Population Growth, 1851 to 2006

Year	Population (000)	Average Annual Rate of Population Growth (%)
1851	2 436.3	—
1861	3 229.6	2.9
1871	3 689.3	1.3
1881	4 324.8	1.6
1891	4 833.2	1.1
1901	5 371.3	1.1
1911	7 206.6	3.0
1921	8 787.9	2.0
1931	10 376.8	1.7
1941	11 506.7	1.0
1951[1]	14 009.4	1.7
1961	18 238.2	2.5
1971	21 568.3	1.5
1981	24 343.2	1.1
1991	27 296.9	1.5
2001	30 007.1	1.0
2006	31 612.9	1.1

— = nil
NOTE: On 1 January 2008, Statistics Canada estimated Canada's population to be 33 143 610.
[1]Newfoundland included for the first time. [2]Data from Statistics Canada 2001 Census.
SOURCE: Adapted from Statistics Canada, *Canada Year Book*, Catalogue 11-402, 1992; Census of Canada, various years.

2. Primary Land Cover in Canada

Land Cover Class	Predominant Cover in the Class	Area[1] (000 km²)	% of Canada Total
Forest and taiga	Closed canopy forest and/or open stands of trees with secondary occurrences of wetland, barren land, or others	4 218	42.2
Tundra/sparse vegetation	Well-vegetated to sparsely vegetated or barren land, mostly in arctic or alpine environments	2 303	23.0
Wetland	Treed and non-treed fens, bogs, swamps, marshes, shallow open water, and coastal and shore marshes	1 396	14.0
Fresh water	Lakes, rivers, streams, and reservoirs	891	8.9
Cropland	Cropland, pasture land and orchards	681	6.6
Rangeland	Generally nonfenced pasture land, grazing land; includes natural grassland that is not necessarily used for agriculture	203	2.0
Ice/snow	Permanent ice and snow fields (glaciers, ice caps)	199	2.0
Built-up	Urban and industrial land	94	1.0
Total		**9 985**	**100.0**

NOTE: Data for this table are derived from satellite imagery and may deviate slightly from other sources of data. [1]Includes the area of all land and fresh water.
SOURCE: Derived from a variety of sources (1991 to 2002), including: Environment Canada, *The State of Canada's Environment*, 1996

4. Components of Population Growth, 1960 to 2006

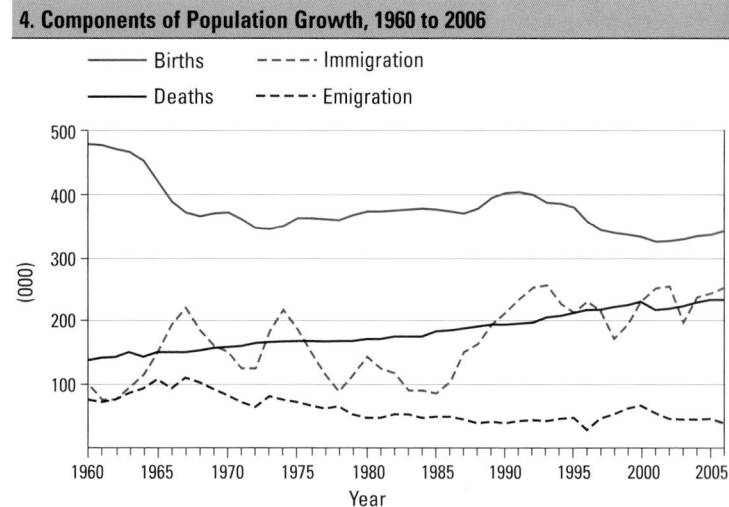

SOURCE: Adapted from Statistics Canada, *Annual Demographic Estimates: Canada Provinces and Territories* 2005-2006, Catalogue 91-215, tables 4.1 -4.4, 27 September 2006, http://www.statcan.ca/english/freepub/91-215-XIE/91-215-XIE2006000.pdf

5. Population Growth, 1961, 1971, 1981, 1991, 2001, 2006, and Population Density, 2006, by Province and Territory

Province or Territory	1961	1971	1981	1991	2001	2006	Population Density (km²) 2006
Newfoundland & Labrador	457 853	522 104	567 181	568 474	512 930	505 469	1.4
Prince Edward Island	104 629	111 641	122 506	129 765	135 294	135 851	23.9
Nova Scotia	737 007	788 960	847 882	899 942	908 007	913 462	17.3
New Brunswick	597 936	634 557	696 403	723 900	729 498	729 997	10.2
Québec	5 259 211	6 027 764	6 438 403	6 895 963	7 237 479	7 546 131	5.6
Ontario	6 236 092	7 703 106	8 625 107	10 084 885	11 410 046	12 160 282	13.4
Manitoba	921 686	988 247	1 026 241	1 091 942	1 119 583	1 148 401	2.1
Saskatchewan	925 181	926 242	968 313	988 928	978 933	968 157	1.6
Alberta	1 331 944	1 627 874	2 237 724	2 545 553	2 974 807	3 290 350	5.1
British Columbia	1 629 082	2 184 021	2 744 467	3 282 061	3 907 738	4 113 487	4.4
Yukon	14 628	18 388	23 153	27 797	28 674	30 372	0.06
Northwest Territories	22 998	34 807	45 741	57 649	37 360	41 464	0.04
Nunavut	n.a.	n.a.	n.a.	n.a.	26 745	29 474	0.02
Canada	**18 238 247**	**21 568 310**	**24 343 181**	**27 296 859**	**30 007 094**	**31 612 897**	**3.5**

n.a. = not available
SOURCE: Adapted from Statistics Canada: *Canada Year Book*, Catalogue 11-402, various years; "A National Overview—Population and Dwelling Counts", 1996 Census of Population, Catalogue 93-357, April 1997; "Population and Dwelling Counts" 2006 Census, Catalogue 97-550-XWE2006002, July 2007, http://www.statcan.ca/bsolc/english/bsolc?catno=97-550-X2006002; Census of Canada, various years.

6. Approximate Geographic Distribution of the Population

Selected Parallels of Latitude	%
South of 49°	70.0
Between 49° and 54°	27.6
Between 54° and 60°	2.1
North of 60°	0.3

Selected Distances North of Canada–US Border	
0–150 km	72.0
151–300 km	13.4
301–600 km	10.4
Over 600 km	4.2

SOURCE: Adapted from Statistics Canada, "Census of Population", 1986 Census.

7. Percentage of People Who are Bilingual (English and French), 1971, 1981, 2006

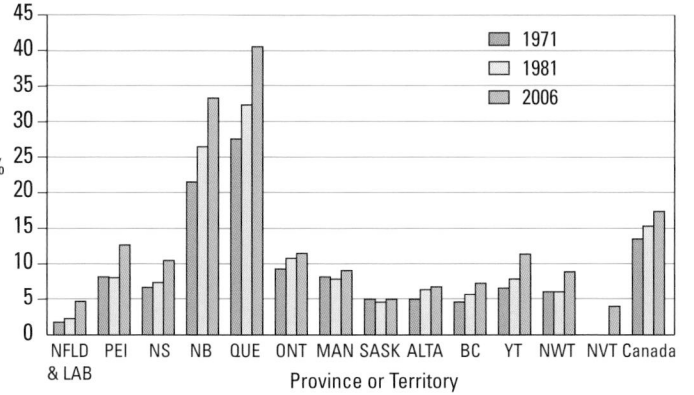

SOURCE: Adapted from Statistics Canada, *The Daily*, Catalogue 11-001, 2 December 1997, http://www.statcan. a/Daily/English/971202/d971202.htm; and "Detailed Mother Tongue (186), Knowledge of Official Languages (5), Age Groups (17A) and Sex (3) for the Population of Canada, Provinces, Territories, Census Metropolitan Areas and Census Agglomerations, 2001 and 2006 Censuses", Catalogue 97-555-XCB2006015, 4 December, 2007, http://www.statcan.ca/bsolc/english/bsolc?catno=97-555-X2006015.

8. Population by Mother Tongue,[1] 1991, 2001, 2006

Official Language	1991	2001	2006
English	16 169 875	17 352 315	18 232 200
French	6 502 860	6 703 325	6 970 405
Non-Official Language			
Chinese	498 845	853 745	1 034 085
Indo-European[2]	301 335	627 860	1 018 960
Italian	510 990	469 485	476 905
German	466 245	438 080	466 655
Spanish	177 425	245 500	362 120
Arabic	107 750	199 940	286 790
Tagalog (Filipino)	99 715	174 060	266 445
Portuguese	212 090	213 815	229 280
Aboriginal[3]	172 610	187 675	222 185
Polish	189 815	208 375	217 605
Vietnamese	78 570	122 055	146 410
Ukrainian	187 010	148 090	141 805
Russian	35 300	94 555	136 235
Dutch	149 870	128 670	133 240
Korean	36 185	85 070	128 120
Greek	126 205	120 365	123 575
Romanian	—	—	80 245
Hungarian	79 770	75 555	75 595
Total single response	26 686 850	29 257 885	30 848 270
Total multiple response	307 190	381 145	392 760
Canada	**26 994 045**	**29 639 035**	**31 241 030**

NOTE: Data is listed in order of 2006 population values.
[1]The mother tongue is the language learned at home in childhood and still understood by the individual at the time of the census. Also note that "mother tongue" is the official term used in the census.
[2]Includes the following principal languages: Panjabi (Punjabi) 382 585; Urdu 156 420; Persian (Farsi) 138 075; Tamil 122 020; Gujarati 86 285; Hindi 85 500; Bengali 48 075. [3]Thirty-six Aboriginal languages are listed separately in the 2006 Census, of which Cree with 84 905 speakers, Inuktitut with 32 580, and Ojibway with 25 575 are the largest. SOURCE: Adapted from Statistics Canada, "1991 and 2001 Census"; and "Detailed Mother Tongue (148), Single and Multiple Language Responses (3) and Sex (3) for the Population of Canada, Provinces, Territories, Census Metropolitan Areas and Census Agglomerations", 2006 Census, Catalogue 97-555-XCB2006007, 4 December 2007, http://www.statcan.ca/bsolc/english/bsolc?catno=97-555-X2006007.

9. Interprovincial Migration[1], 1976 to 2006

Years	NFLD & LAB	PEI	NS	NB	QUE	ONT	MAN	SASK	ALTA	BC	YT	NWT	NVT[2]
1976-1981	-19 860	-15	-8 420	-8 505	-141 725	-78 070	-43 600	5 820	197 645	110 930	-545	-2 015	n.a.
1981-1986	-16 550	1 540	6 275	1 370	-63 295	99 355	-1 555	-2 830	-27 675	9 515	-2 655	-755	n.a.
1986-1991	-13 945	-850	-4 885	-6 060	-25 560	46 965	-35 260	-60 365	-25 005	125 870	790	-1 695	n.a.
1991-1996	-23 240	1 455	-6 450	-1 950	-37 430	-47 025	-19 390	-19 780	3 575	149 935	685	-465	n.a.
1996-2001	-31 055	135	-1 275	-8 425	-57 315	51 905	-18 560	-24 940	119 420	-23 630	-2 760	-3 170	-330
2001-2006	-15 137	-105	-8 131	-8 683	-20 119	-33 497	-25 646	-37 070	140 272	10 265	-186	-1 774	-386

n.a. = not available
[1]Difference between the number of incoming and outgoing migrants.
[2]Nunavut became a territory in 1999.
SOURCE: Adapted from Statistics Canada, 2001 Census: analysis series, Profile of the Canadian population by mobility status: Canada, a nation on the move. Table: Net migrants and net migration rates, provinces and territories, 1976 to 2001 (page 20). Catalogue: 96F0030XIE2001006. http://www12.statcan.ca/english/census01/products/analytic/companion/mob/pdf/96F0030XIE2001006.pdf.

10. Births, Deaths, Migration, Infant Mortality, and Life Expectancy, 2006

Demographic Category	NFLD & LAB	PEI	NS	NB	QUE	ONT	MAN	SASK	ALTA	BC	YT	NWT	NVT	Canada
Birth rate/1000	8.5	9.7	9.0	9.0	10.9	10.6	12.0	12.1	13.4	9.9	10.0	16.0	24.1	10.9
Death rate/1000	8.9	9.3	9.3	8.8	7.3	7.1	8.7	9.2	6.2	7.2	5.8	3.9	4.3	7.3
Number of immigrants (000)	0.5	0.3	2.2	1.4	42.0	133.1	8.9	2.1	19.9	43.9	0.08	0.07	0.01	251.7
Number of emigrants (000)	0.14	0.14	0.8	0.3	6.1	16.6	1.4	0.5	5.3	7.1	0.02	0.02	0.02	38.6
Interprovincial in-migration (000)	10.5	3.4	16.5	12.1	25.6	64.2	14.2	16.0	109.7	55.8	1.5	2.2	1.1	332.8
Interprovincial out-migration (000)	14.9	3.5	20.4	15.9	33.8	85.6	22.9	25.1	52.6	52.0	1.7	3.6	1.0	332.8
Infant mortality rate/1000[1]	5.1	4.3	4.6	4.3	4.6	5.5	7.0	6.2	5.8	11.0	0.0		16.1	5.3
Life expectancy at birth (in years)[2] M	75	76	76	76	76	77	76	76	77	78	72[3]	72[3]	72[3]	77
Life expectancy at birth (in years)[2] F	81	82	81	82	82	82	81	82	82	83	77[3]	77[3]	77[3]	82

[1]2004 data. [2]2000–2002 data. [3]Data combined for all three territories.
SOURCE: Adapted from Statistics Canada, *Annual Demographic Estimates: Canada Provinces and Territories*, Catalogue 91-215, 2005–2006, pages 27, 29-30, tables 4-3, 4-4, 4-8, 4-9, 27 September 2006, http://www.statcan.ca/english/ reepub/91-215-XIE/91-215-XIE2006000.pdf; "Life Tables, Canada, Provinces and Territories", Catalogue 84-537, tables 2a-13b, http://www.statcan.ca/english/freepub/84-537-XIE/tables.htm; "Deaths and death rate, by province and territory", http://www40.statcan.ca/l01/cst01/demo07b.htm; & "Births and birth rate, by province and territory", http://www40.statcan.ca/l01/cst01/demo04b.htm.

11. Canadian Family and Household Structure, 2006

Province or Territory	Total Families	Married Families		Common-law Families		Lone-parent Families		% Couples with Children[1]	% Couples without Children[2]	% One-person Households	% Other[3]
		Number	%	Number	%	Number	%				
NFLD & LAB	155 730	114 630	73.6	16 935	10.9	24 165	15.5	30.4	34.0	20.2	15.4
PEI	39 185	28 700	73.2	4 085	10.4	6 400	16.3	29.6	30.9	24.1	15.5
NS	267 415	187 420	70.1	34 705	13.0	45 290	16.9	25.5	31.9	26.5	16.1
NB	217 795	151 210	69.4	30 995	14.2	35 585	16.3	26.9	32.9	24.3	15.9
QUE	2 121 610	1 156 930	54.5	611 855	28.8	352 825	16.6	25.7	28.7	30.7	14.9
ONT	3 422 315	2 530 560	73.9	351 040	10.3	540 715	15.8	31.2	28.3	24.3	16.3
MAN	312 810	225 875	72.2	33 720	10.8	53 210	17.0	27.6	28.2	28.6	15.5
SASK	267 460	194 165	72.6	28 850	10.8	44 445	16.6	26.4	29.9	28.8	14.9
ALTA	904 845	658 900	72.8	115 685	12.8	130 265	14.4	30.5	28.7	24.6	16.3
BC	1 161 425	844 430	72.7	141 830	12.2	175 165	15.1	26.3	29.6	28.0	16.1
YT	8 335	4 640	55.7	1 965	23.6	1 725	20.7	26.1	24.9	30.9	18.2
NWT	10 880	5 555	51.1	2 990	27.5	2 330	21.4	34.4	22.0	21.7	21.9
NVT	7 035	2 890	41.1	2 205	31.3	1 940	27.6	42.0	10.9	18.3	28.8
Canada	**8 896 840**	**6 105 910**	**68.6**	**1 376 870**	**15.5**	**1 414 060**	**15.9**	**28.5**	**29.0**	**26.8**	**15.8**

[1]Refers to households containing a couple with at least one child aged 24 and under at home. [2]Includes households containing a couple with all children aged 25 and over at home. [3]Includes lone-parent households, multiple-family households, and non-family households other than one-person households.
SOURCE: Adapted from Statistics Canada, "Family portrait: Continuity and change in Canadian families and households in 2006: Findings", Analysis Series, 2006 Census, Catalogue 97-553, 12 September 2007, Table 4 and 5, http://www12.statcan.ca/english/census06/analysis/famhouse/provterr.cfm.

12. Population by Sex and Age Group, 2006

Age Group	Total	Male	Female
0–4	1 690 540	864 600	825 940
5–9	1 809 370	926 860	882 515
10–14	2 079 925	1 065 865	1 014 065
15–24	4 220 875	2 143 235	2 077 645
25–34	4 005 805	1 963 660	2 042 145
35–44	4 818 730	2 369 030	2 449 705
45–54	4 977 905	2 449 095	2 528 805
55–64	3 674 490	1 806 530	1 867 960
65–74	2 288 360	1 087 270	1 201 095
75–84	1 526 280	637 905	888 375
85+	520 605	161 920	358 685
Median age[1]	39.5	38.6	40.4
Total	**31 612 895**	**15 475 970**	**16 136 930**

[1]The median age is an age 'x', such that exactly one half of the population is older than 'x' and the other half is younger than 'x'.
SOURCE: Adapted from Statistics Canada, "Age Groups (13) and Sex (3) for the Population of Canada, Provinces and Territories, 1921 to 2006 Censuses", 2006 Census, Catalogue 97-551-XCB2006005, 17 July 2007, http://www.statcan.ca/bsolc/english/bsolc?catno=97-551-X2006005.

14. Population Totals and Future Projection for Age Categories "Less than 15 Years" and "65 Years and Over"

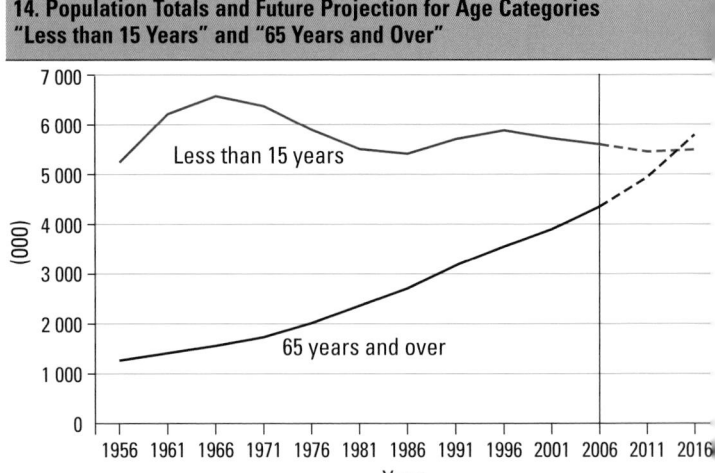

SOURCE: Adapted from Statistics Canada, "Portrait of the Canadian Population in 2006, by Age and Sex: National portrait", Analysis Series, 2006 Census, Catalogue 97-551-XWE2006001, 17 July 2007, Figure 1, http://www12.statcan.ca/english/census06/analysis/agesex/natlportrait1.cfm, accessed 17 July 2007.

13. Aging of the Canadian Population, 1921 to 2006

Year	Age 0–64 %	65 and Over %	Ratio of 65 and Over to 0–64 %	Average Annual Change %
1921	95.2	4.8	5.0	—
1931	94.4	5.6	5.9	0.86
1941	93.3	6.7	7.1	1.27
1951	92.2	7.8	8.4	1.26
1956	92.3	7.7	8.4	-0.04
1961	92.4	7.6	8.3	-0.25
1966	92.3	7.7	8.3	0.15
1971	91.9	8.1	8.8	0.93
1976	91.3	8.7	9.5	1.48
1981	90.3	9.7	10.7	2.40
1986	89.3	10.7	11.9	2.38
1991	88.4	11.6	13.1	2.42
1996	87.8	12.2	13.8	2.60
2001	87.0	13.0	14.9	2.04
2006	86.8	13.2	15.2	2.01

— = nil
SOURCE: Adapted from Statistics Canada: "Age, Sex and Marital Status", 1991 census, Catalogue 93-310, 6 July 1992, http://www.statcan.ca/bsolc/english/bsolc?catno=93-310-X; Report on the Demographic Situation in Canada, Catalogue 91-209, 1991 and 2001, http://www.statcan.ca/bsolc/english/bsolc?catno=91-209-XIE#formatdisp; and the CANSIM database, http://cansim2.statcan.ca, Table 051-0001, accessed 17 October 2007.

15. Aboriginal Population, 2006

Province or Territory	Aboriginal population[1]	First Nation[2]	Métis[2]
Newfoundland and Labrador	23 450	7 765	6 470
Prince Edward Island	1 730	1 230	385
Nova Scotia	24 175	15 240	7 680
New Brunswick	17 655	12 385	4 270
Québec	108 430	65 090	27 980
Ontario	242 495	158 395	73 605
Manitoba	175 395	100 645	71 805
Saskatchewan	141 890	91 400	48 115
Alberta	188 365	97 275	85 500
British Columbia	196 075	129 580	59 445
Yukon	7 580	6 275	805
Northwest Territories	20 635	12 640	3 580
Nunavut	24 920	100	130
Canada	**1 172 790**	**698 025**	**389 785**

[1]This total includes an additional 34 500 persons who reported more than one Aboriginal identity group, and also includes those who reported being a Registered Indian and/or Band member in the census without reporting an Aboriginal identity. The Inuit population of 50 485 is also included in this total (see Table 17).
[2]Includes only persons who reported a First Nation (North American Indian on the census) or Métis identity.
SOURCE: Adapted from Statistics Canada, "Aboriginal Peoples Highlight Tables, 2006 Census", Highlight tables, 2006 Census, Catalogue 97-558-XWE2006002, 15 January 2008, Table 1, http://www.statcan.ca/bsolc/english/bsolc?catno=97-558-X2006002.

16. Population of Census Metropolitan Areas, 1961, 1971, 1981, 1991, 2001, 2006

Census Metropolitan Area	Area (km²) 2006	1961	1971	1981	1991	2001	2006
Toronto	5 904	1 919 409	2 628 043	3 130 392	3 893 046	4 682 897	5 113 149
Montreal	4 259	2 215 627	2 743 208	2 862 286	3 127 242	3 426 350	3 635 571
Vancouver	2 877	826 798	1 082 352	1 268 183	1 602 502	1 986 965	2 116 581
Ottawa–Gatineau	5 716	457 038	602 510	743 821	920 857	1 063 664	1 130 761
Calgary	5 107	279 062	403 319	625 966	754 033	951 395	1 079 310
Edmonton	9 418	359 821	495 702	740 882	839 924	937 845	1 034 945
Québec	3 277	379 067	480 502	583 820	645 550	682 757	715 515
Winnipeg	5 303	476 543	540 262	592 061	652 354	671 274	694 668
Hamilton	1 372	401 071	498 523	542 095	599 760	662 401	692 911
London	2 665	226 669	286 011	326 817	381 522	432 451	457 720
Kitchener	827	154 864	226 846	287 801	356 421	414 284	451 235
St. Catharines–Niagara	1 398	257 796	303 429	342 645	364 552	377 009	390 317
Halifax	5 496	193 353	222 637	277 727	320 501	359 183	372 858
Oshawa	903	n.a.	120 318	186 446	240 104	296 298	330 594
Victoria	695	155 763	195 800	241 450	287 897	311 902	330 088
Windsor	1 023	217 215	258 643	250 885	262 075	307 877	323 342
Saskatoon	5 207	95 564	126 449	175 058	210 023	225 927	233 923
Regina	3 408	113 749	140 734	173 226	191 692	192 800	194 971
Sherbrooke	1 232	n.a.	n.a.	125 183	139 194	153 811	186 952
St. John's	804	106 666	131 814	154 835	171 859	172 918	181 113
Barrie	897	n.a.	n.a.	n.a.	n.a.	n.a.	177 061
Kelowna	2 904	n.a.	n.a.	n.a.	n.a.	n.a.	162 276
Abbotsford	626	n.a.	n.a.	n.a.	n.a.	n.a.	159 020
Greater Sudbury	3 382	127 446	155 424	156 121	157 613	155 601	158 258
Kingston	1 907	n.a.	n.a.	n.a.	136 401	146 838	152 385
Saguenay	1 754	127 616	133 703	158 229	160 928	154 938	151 643
Trois-Rivières	880	n.a.	n.a.	125 343	136 303	137 507	141 529
Guelph	379	n.a.	n.a.	n.a.	n.a.	n.a.	127 009
Moncton	2 406	n.a.	n.a.	n.a.	n.a.	n.a.	126 424
Brantford	1 073	n.a.	n.a.	n.a.	n.a.	n.a.	124 607
Thunder Bay	2 550	102 085	112 093	121 948	124 427	121 986	122 907
Saint John	3 359	98 083	106 744	121 012	124 981	122 678	122 389
Peterborough	1 506	n.a.	n.a.	n.a.	n.a.	n.a.	116 570

NOTE: Data is listed in order of 2006 population values. n.a. = not available
SOURCE: Adapted from Statistics Canada, "Population and dwelling counts, for census metropolitan areas, 2006 and 2001 censuses", Highlight Tables, 2006 Census, Catalogue 97-550-XWE2006002, 12 July 2007, http://www12.statcan.ca/english/census06/data/popdwell/Table.cfm?T=205&RPP=50.

17. Inuit Population, 2006

Region	Inuit Population
Inuit Nunaat[1]	
Nunatsiavut	2 160
Nunavik	9 565
Nunavut	24 635
Inuvialuit	3 115
Total	**39 475**
Outside Inuit Nunaat	
Rural	2 610
Urban	8 395
Total	**11 005**
Canada	**50 480**

[1]"Inuit Nunaat" is an Inuktitut expression for "Inuit homeland", an area comprising more than one-third of Canada's land mass. The Inuit population map on page 38 shows the regions of Inuit Nunaat.
SOURCE: Adapted from Statistics Canada, http://www12.statcan.ca/english/census06/analysis/aboriginal/inuit.cfm.

18. Aboriginal Languages, 2006

Language	Aboriginal Mother Tongue[1]	Knowledge of an Aboriginal Language[2]
Cree	76 460	87 285
Ojibway	24 410	30 255
Oji-Cree	11 605	12 435
Montagnais-Naskapi	10 470	11 080
Dene	8 495	9 250
Mi'kmaq	7 685	8 540
Siouan languages (Dakota/Sioux)	5 675	6 285
Atikamekw	5 140	5 320
Blackfoot	3 270	4 760
Salish languages n.i.e.	1 990	2 800
Algonquin	2 020	2 560
Dogrib	2 055	2 540
Carrier	1 800	2 320
South Slave	1 575	2 160
Inuktituk	32 380	34 345

n.i.e. = not included elsewhere
[1]"Mother tongue" is the first language learned at home in childhood and still understood. [2]"Knowledge" refers to a language in which the respondent can conduct a conversation.
SOURCE: Adapted from Statistics Canada, "Aboriginal Peoples in Canada in 2006: Inuit, Métis and First Nations, 2006 Census", Analysis Series, 2006 Census, Catalogue 97-551-XWE2006001, 15 January 2008, Table 24, http://www12.statcan.ca/english/census06/analysis/aboriginal/share.cfm.

19. Population by Ethnic Origin, 2006[1] (000)

Ethnic Origin	NFLD & LAB	PEI	NS	NB	QUE	ONT	MAN	SASK	ALTA	BC	YT	NWT	NVT	Canada
Canadian	241.5	52.4	368.9	380.9	4 474.1	2 768.9	206.4	172.4	667.4	720.4	6.1	6.1	1.2	10 066.3
British Isles	285.3	91.3	542.1	332.3	712.0	4 911.3	431.3	411.4	1 488.1	1 860.7	15.4	13.2	4.3	11 098.6
European	19.5	16.8	186.1	75.4	930.1	4 379.6	568.6	541.9	1 588.2	1 591.1	12.1	8.9	1.6	9 919.8
Western European	9.7	11.8	131.5	49.0	219.2	1 685.7	282.7	325.8	862.5	783.1	6.7	4.5	0.7	4 372.8
German	7.4	7.1	101.9	33.8	131.8	1 144.6	216.8	286.1	679.7	561.6	4.8	3.5	0.6	3 179.4
Dutch	2.1	4.6	37.0	15.5	23.0	491.0	55.4	35.4	172.9	196.4	1.5	1.0	0.1	1 036.0
Eastern European	3.1	2.3	25.3	9.0	186.4	1 171.2	265.3	225.7	609.8	493.4	3.5	2.8	0.4	2 998.2
Ukrainian	1.0	0.8	7.5	2.5	32.0	336.4	167.2	129.3	332.2	197.3	1.6	1.4	0.2	1 209.1
Polish	1.0	0.8	11.0	3.1	62.8	465.6	82.4	56.9	170.9	128.4	0.9	0.8	0.1	984.6
Russian	0.6	0.3	3.2	1.3	40.2	167.4	45.6	35.1	92.0	114.1	0.6	0.3	0.07	500.6
Southern European	4.3	2.0	25.3	11.6	505.2	1 642.0	51.2	19.6	168.7	291.3	1.2	1.1	0.2	2 723.7
Greek	0.3	0.2	2.9	1.0	66.0	132.4	3.5	2.5	11.9	21.8	0.07	0.05	0.02	242.7
Italian	1.4	1.0	13.5	5.9	299.7	868.0	21.4	8.0	82.0	143.2	0.6	0.6	0.1	1 445.3
Portuguese	0.9	0.2	3.1	1.7	57.5	282.9	11.1	1.1	17.6	34.7	0.07	0.1	0.05	410.9
Northern European	3.3	1.9	13.8	9.6	20.9	245.6	77.8	112.5	308.4	322.0	2.7	1.9	0.4	1 120.8
Norwegian	1.5	0.4	4.7	2.6	6.4	53.8	18.4	68.7	144.6	129.4	1.3	0.7	0.06	432.5
Jewish	0.5	0.2	3.3	1.4	71.4	177.3	13.2	2.1	14.8	30.8	0.1	0.03	0.03	315.1
French[2]	30.6	30.9	176.4	216.1	2 184.7	2 580.1	148.8	118.5	391.7	364.3	4.3	4.5	1.0	5 000.4
Eastern and Southeastern Asia	2.4	0.5	8.2	4.9	173.3	1 047.1	65.3	19.0	238.8	650.1	1.0	1.5	0.2	2 212.3
Chinese	1.7	0.3	5.1	2.9	91.9	644.5	17.9	11.1	137.6	432.2	0.5	0.5	0.08	1 346.5
Filipino	0.3	0.03	0.8	0.6	25.7	215.8	39.2	4.2	54.3	94.3	0.3	0.8	0.08	436.2
Aboriginal	37.3	3.7	48.2	35.2	264.2	403.8	186.7	149.8	244.6	250.9	7.8	20.9	25.2	1 678.2
South Asian	1.8	0.3	4.8	2.6	77.0	833.3	17.8	5.5	107.7	265.6	0.2	0.2	0.06	1 316.8
East Indian	1.3	0.3	3.9	2.2	41.6	573.3	14.9	4.5	88.2	232.4	0.2	0.1	0.04	962.7
Pakistani	0.3	0.0	0.5	0.3	11.7	91.2	1.1	0.5	11.2	8.0	0.01	0.03	0.0	124.7
Caribbean	0.7	0.3	3.5	1.0	133.6	390.0	8.5	2.1	21.0	17.6	0.08	0.1	0.05	578.7
Jamaican	0.3	0.2	1.0	0.3	11.9	197.6	3.3	0.8	8.7	6.9	0.05	0.07	0.02	231.1
Arab	1.4	0.9	10.6	3.8	202.2	188.0	4.4	2.9	37.9	18.3	0.07	0.2	0.03	470.6
African	1.0	0.5	11.1	3.1	78.0	235.9	11.9	5.0	41.2	32.9	0.1	0.4	0.2	421.2
Latin etc	0.5	0.2	1.5	1.1	101.1	166.3	10.2	3.3	34.5	41.1	0.02	0.1	0.03	360.2
West Asian	0.3	0.05	1.8	0.9	58.3	174.0	3.4	1.8	17.2	44.6	0.03	0.1	0.02	302.6
Oceania	0.1	0.2	0.7	0.2	1.7	16.2	0.9	1.1	9.5	27.7	0.09	0.1	0.02	58.5
Total[3]	**500.6**	**134.2**	**903.1**	**719.7**	**7 435.9**	**12 028.9**	**1 133.5**	**953.9**	**3 256.4**	**4 074.4**	**30.2**	**41.1**	**29.3**	**31 241.0**

[1]"Ethnic origin" refers to the the ethnic or cultural origins of the respondent's ancestors. For example, of the 4 911.3 in Ontario who reported origins in the British Isles, 3 736.6 reported another origin, and many would have reported "Canadian".
[2] Includes both French and Acadian responses.
[3] Represents total population. The sum of specific groups is not equal to the total population due to multiple counts.
SOURCE: Adapted from Statistics Canada, Ethnic origins, 2006 counts, for Canada, provinces and territories - 20% sample data (table). Ethnocultural Portrait of Canada Highlight Tables. 2006 Census. Statistics Canada Catalogue no. 97-562-XWE2006002. Ottawa, 2 April 2008, http://www12.statcan.ca/english/census06/data/highlights/ethnic/index.cfm?Lang=E, accessed 10 April 2008.

20. Immigration of Permanent Residents by Top Ten Source Countries and Source Area, 1997 to 2006

Source Countries	1997	1998	1999	2000	2001	2002	2003	2004	2005	2006
China	18 526	19 790	29 148	36 750	40 365	33 307	36 256	36 429	42 292	33 080
India	19 615	15 375	17 457	26 123	27 904	28 838	24 593	25 575	33 148	30 753
Philippines	10 872	8 184	9 205	10 119	12 928	11 011	11 989	13 303	17 525	17 717
Pakistan	11 239	8 089	9 303	14 201	15 354	14 173	12 351	12 795	13 575	12 332
United States	5 030	4 776	5 533	5 828	5 911	5 294	6 013	7 507	9 262	10 943
Iran	7 486	6 775	5 909	5 617	5 746	7 889	5 651	6 063	5 502	7 073
United Kingdom	4 657	3 899	4 478	4 649	5 360	4 725	5 199	6 062	5 865	6 542
South Korea	4 001	4 917	7 217	7 639	9 608	7 334	7 089	5 337	5 819	6 178
Colombia	571	922	1 296	2 228	2 967	3 226	4 273	4 438	6 031	5 813
France	2 858	3 867	3 923	4 345	4 428	3 963	4 127	5 028	5 430	4 915
Total for top ten only	**118 070**	**87 490**	**98 461**	**121 520**	**134 285**	**123 228**	**119 055**	**123 757**	**144 449**	**135 346**
Total other countries	**97 968**	**86 705**	**91 496**	**105 939**	**116 356**	**105 823**	**102 296**	**112 067**	**117 790**	**116 303**
Total	**216 038**	**174 195**	**189 957**	**227 459**	**250 641**	**229 051**	**221 351**	**235 824**	**262 239**	**251 649**
Source Area										
Asia and Pacific	117 070	84 202	96 581	120 739	132 944	119 059	113 733	114 575	138 057	126 479
Africa and the Middle East	37 795	32 592	33 557	40 909	48 238	46 340	43 678	49 531	49 279	51 863
Europe	38 674	38 538	38 991	42 963	43 295	38 869	37 570	41 902	40 908	37 946
South and Central America	17 422	14 045	15 279	17 007	20 211	19 473	20 349	22 255	24 639	24 306
United States	5 029	4 776	5 532	5 828	5 911	5 294	6 013	7 507	9 262	10 942
not stated		8	17	1	6	34	13	6	52	94	111
Total	**216 038**	**174 195**	**189 957**	**227 459**	**250 641**	**229 051**	**221 351**	**235 824**	**262 239**	**251 649**

NOTE: Data is listed in order of 2006 values.
SOURCE: Adapted from Citizenship and Immigration Canada: "Facts and Figures 2006 Immigration Overview: Permanent Residents: Canada—Permanent Residents by Top Source Countries" http://www.cic.gc.ca/english/resources/statistics/facts2006/permanent/12.asp; "Facts and Figures 2006 Immigration Overview: Permanent Residents: Canada—Permanent Residents by Gender and Source Area" http://www.cic.gc.ca/english/resources/statistics/facts2006/permanent/09.asp. Adapted and reproduced with the permission of the Minister of Public Works and Government Services Canada, 2008.

21. Total Population by Visible Minority, 2001 and 2006

	Total Population, 2006	Total Visible Minorities[1,2]		South Asian[3]		Chinese		Black		Filipino	
		2001	2006	2001	2006	2001	2006	2001	2006	2001	2006
NFLD & LAB	500 605	3 850	5 720	1 005	1 590	920	1 325	845	905	260	305
PEI	134 205	1 180	1 830	110	130	205	250	370	640	35	30
NS[4]	903 090	34 525	37 680	2 895	3 810	3 290	4 300	19 670	19 230	655	700
NB	719 650	9 425	13 345	1 415	1 960	1 530	2 450	3 845	4 455	355	530
QUE[4]	7 435 905	497 975	654 355	59 505	72 845	56 830	79 830	152 195	188 070	18 550	24 200
ONT[4]	12 028 895	2 153 045	2 745 205	554 870	794 170	481 505	576 980	411 090	473 765	156 515	203 220
MAN[4]	1 133 510	87 115	109 095	12 880	16 560	11 930	13 705	12 820	15 660	30 490	37 790
SASK[4]	953 845	27 580	33 900	4 090	5 130	8 085	9 505	4 165	5 090	3 025	3 770
ALTA[4]	3 256 355	329 925	454 200	69 585	103 885	99 100	120 275	31 390	47 075	33 940	51 090
BC[4]	4 074 385	836 445	1 008 855	210 290	262 290	365 490	407 225	25 460	28 315	64 005	88 080
YT[4]	30 195	1 020	1 220	205	195	225	325	120	125	235	210
NWT	41 060	1 545	2 270	190	210	255	320	175	375	465	690
NVT[4]	29 325	210	420	25	80	40	80	65	100	35	75
Canada[4]	**31 241 030**	**3 983 845**	**5 068 090**	**917 070**	**1 262 865**	**1 029 395**	**1 216 570**	**662 215**	**783 795**	**308 575**	**410 695**

[1]The *Employment Equity Act* defines visible minorities as "persons, other than Aboriginal peoples, who are non-Caucasian in race or non-white in colour." [2]Visible minorities included in the total but not listed separately include people from Latin America and Southeast Asia.[3]For example, "East Indian", "Pakistani", "Sri Lankan", etc. [4]Excludes census data for one or more incompletely enumerated Indian reserves or Indian settlements. SOURCE: Statistics Canada. "Visible Minority Groups (15) and Sex (3) for Population, for Canada, Provinces, Territories, Census Metropolitan Areas and Census Agglomerations, 2001 Census - 20% Sample Data", Catalogue 97F0010, January 23, 2003; Visible minority groups, 2006 counts, for Canada, provinces and territories - 20% sample data (table). Ethnocultural Portrait of Canada Highlight Tables. 2006 Census. Statistics Canada Catalogue no. 97-562-XWE2006002. Ottawa. Released April 2, 2008. http://www12. statcan.ca/english/census06/data/highlights/ethnic/index.cfm?Lang=E (accessed April 10, 2008).

22. Numbers of Immigrants and Immigration Rates, Canada, 1944 to 2006

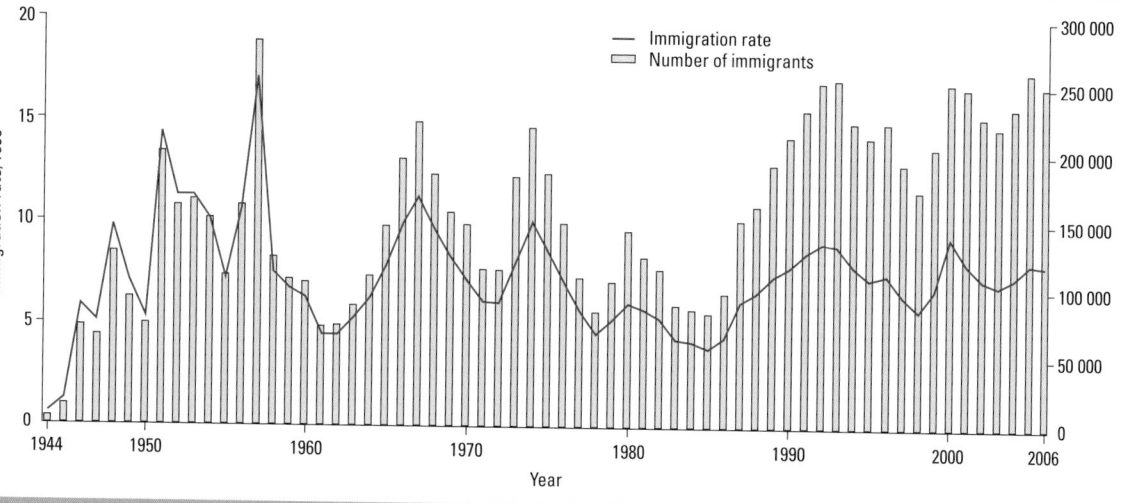

SOURCE: Adapted from Statistics Canada, "Report on the Demographic Situation in Canada", Catalogue 91-209, 2001-2004, http://www.statcan.ca/bsolc/english/bsolc?catno=91-209-X&CHROPG=1; Citizenship and Immigration Canada, "Facts and Figures 2006 Immigration Overview: Permanent and Temporary Residents: Canada --Permanent Residents by Category (No Backlog Reallocation)" http://www.cic.gc.ca/english/resources/statistics/facts2006/overview/01.asp. Adapted and reproduced with the permission of the Minister of Public Works and Government Services Canada, 2008.

23. Immigration of Permanent Residents by Category, 1997 to 2006

Category	1997	1998	1999	2000	2001	2002	2003	2004	2005	2006
Spouses and partners	29 775	28 062	32 790	35 293	37 761	32 742	38 736	43 999	45 406	45 280
Parents and grandparents	20 153	14 164	14 481	17 768	21 341	22 234	19 384	12 732	12 474	20 006
Others (including children)	9 610	8 370	7 956	7 550	7 691	7 304	6 993	5 529	5 479	5 222
Total family class	**59 538**	**50 596**	**55 227**	**60 611**	**66 793**	**62 280**	**65 113**	**62 260**	**63 359**	**70 508**
Skilled workers[1]	104 924	80 811	92 372	118 561	137 200	122 706	105 215	113 445	130 242	105 949
Business immigrants	19 924	13 777	13 018	13 665	14 587	11 022	8 100	9 759	13 469	12 077
Provincial/territorial nominees	47	0	477	1 252	1 275	2 127	4 418	6 248	8 047	13 336
Live-in caregivers	2 718	2 867	3 260	2 782	2 625	1 985	3 304	4 292	4 552	6 895
Total economic immigrants	**127 613**	**97 455**	**109 127**	**136 260**	**155 687**	**137 840**	**121 037**	**133 744**	**156 310**	**138 257**
Government-assisted refugees	7 660	7 387	7 443	10 671	8 697	7 505	7 506	7 411	7 416	7 316
Privately sponsored refugees	2 580	2 140	2 330	2 922	3 571	3 039	3 251	3 115	2 976	3 337
Refugees landed in Canada	10 429	10 059	11 780	12 993	11 897	10 546	11 265	15 901	19 935	15 892
Refugee dependants[2]	3 194	2 919	2 805	3 494	3 749	4 021	3 959	6 259	5 441	5 947
Total refugees	**23 863**	**22 505**	**24 358**	**30 080**	**27 914**	**25 111**	**25 981**	**32 686**	**35 768**	**32 492**
Retirees	46	8	9	0	0	n.a.	0	0	0	0
DROC and PDRCC[3]	3 233	2 486	1 020	460	206	125	79	53	20	23
Temporary resident permit holders	0	0	0	0	0	n.a.	97	148	123	136
Humanitarian and compassionate cases / Public policy	0	0	0	0	0	3 652	9 032	6 932	6 651	10 223
Total other	**3 279**	**2 494**	**1 029**	**460**	**206**	**3 787**	**9 208**	**7 133**	**6 794**	**10 382**
Total immigrants/refugees	**214 293**	**173 050**	**189 741**	**227 411**	**250 600**	**229 018**	**221 339**	**235 823**	**262 231**	**251 639**

[1]Includes independents and assisted relatives. [2]Dependants of refugees landed in Canada including spouses and partners. [3]Deferred removal orders and post-determination refugee claimants. SOURCE: Adapted from Citizenship and Immigration Canada, "Facts and Figures 2006 Immigration Overview: Permanent and Temporary Residents: Canada—Permanent Residents by Category (No Backlog Reallocation)" http://www.cic.gc.ca/english/resources/statistics/facts2006/overview/01.asp. Adapted and reproduced with the permission of the Minister of Public Works and Government Services Canada, 2008.

24. Immigration of Permanent Residents by Category and Source Area, 2006

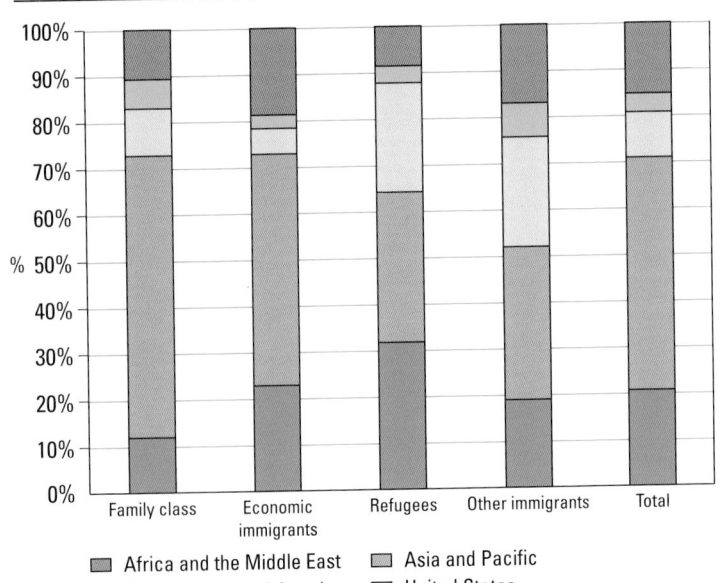

Legend:
- ■ Africa and the Middle East
- ■ Asia and Pacific
- □ South and Central America
- ■ United States
- ■ Europe and the United Kingdom

SOURCE: Adapted from Citizenship and Immigration Canada, "Facts and Figures 2006 Immigration Overview: Permanent Residents: Canada—Permanent Residents by Category and Source Area" http://www.cic.gc.ca/english/resources/statistics/facts2006/permanent/10.asp. Adapted and reproduced with the permission of the Minister of Public Works and Government Services Canada, 2008.

26. Employment by Industry and by Sex, 2006

Industry	Number Employed (000)		
	Both Sexes	Men	Women
Agriculture	346.4	239.5	107.0
Forestry, fishing, mining, oil and gas	330.1	269.1	60.9
Utilities	122.0	92.5	29.5
Construction	1 069.7	946.8	122.9
Manufacturing	2 117.7	1 517.8	599.9
Trade	2 633.5	1 340.4	1 293.2
Transportation and warehousing	802.2	616.2	186.0
Finance, insurance, real estate, and leasing	1 040.5	442.7	597.8
Professional, scientific, and technical services	1 089.9	620.1	469.9
Business, building, and other support services	690.0	366.1	323.9
Educational services	1 158.4	410.4	748.0
Health care and social assistance	1 785.5	312.8	1 472.7
Information, culture, and recreation	745.0	394.2	350.8
Accommodation and food services	1 015.0	402.2	612.8
Other services	701.0	327.9	373.1
Public administration	837.4	428.4	409.0
Total all industries	**16 484.3**	**8 727.1**	**7 757.2**

SOURCE: Adapted from Statistics Canada, http://www40.statcan.ca/l01/cst01/labor10a.htm, accessed 23 August 2007.

25. Individuals by Total Income Level, 2001 to 2005

	2001	2002	2003	2004	2005
Under $5 000	2 396 540	2 373 740	2 375 060	2 323 290	2 210 370
$5 000 and over	20 313 370	20 425 240	20 695 140	21 085 590	21 505 290
$10 000 and over	17 629 360	17 807 080	18 119 380	18 572 830	19 129 110
$15 000 and over	14 773 880	14 994 700	15 370 750	15 879 220	16 431 080
$20 000 and over	12 379 840	12 587 440	12 926 300	13 390 830	13 923 310
$25 000 and over	10 475 810	10 698 800	11 041 800	11 493 990	11 999 020
$35 000 and over	7 105 400	7 361 260	7 706 720	8 146 710	8 630 290
$50 000 and over	3 806 950	4 025 790	4 285 870	4 631 570	5 006 340
$75 000 and over	1 335 790	1 450 590	1 589 290	1 788 240	2 020 810
$100 000 and over	611 610	654 580	704 380	791 580	904 600
$150 000 and over	243 760	252 270	267 360	297 810	334 140
$200 000 and over	140 400	143 160	151 740	169 220	188 950
$250 000 and over	92 550	94 020	99 880	112 060	124 890
Total	**22 709 910**	**22 798 980**	**23 070 200**	**23 408 890**	**23 715 660**
Median total income	**22 600**	**23 100**	**23 600**	**24 400**	**25 400**

SOURCE: Adapted from Statistics Canada, http://www40.statcan.ca/l01/cst01/famil105a.htm?sdi=income%20canada, accessed 22 November 2007.

27. Persons in Low Income Before Tax, 1987, 1991, 2001, 2005 (000)

Persons and Age Group	1987	1991	2001	2005
All persons	**4 148**	**4 794**	**4 711**	**4 821**
Under 18 years of age	1 132	1 331	1 191	1 132
18 to 64 years of age	2 342	2 789	2 971	3 112
65 years of age and over	674	675	550	577
Persons in economic families	**2 883**	**3 268**	**3 076**	**3 040**
Under 18 years of age	1 132	1 331	1 191	1 132
18 to 64 years of age	1 542	1 769	1 757	1 770
65 years of age and over	208	168	129	138
Unattached individuals	**1 265**	**1 526**	**1 635**	**1 780**
Under 65 years of age	800	1 019	1 214	1 342
65 years of age and over	465	507	421	438

SOURCE: Adapted from Statistics Canada, http://www40.statcan.ca/l01/cst01/famil41b.htm, accessed 29 January 2008, and http://www40.statcan.ca/l01/cst01/famil41h.htm, accessed 13 May 2008.

28. Employment, Unemployment, and Participation Rates,[1] 2007

Province or Territory	Population Over 15 Years (000)	Labour Force (000)	Employed (000)	Unemployed (000)	Participation Rate (%)	Unemployment Rate (%)
Newfoundland and Labrador	423.1	247.2	213.8	33.5	58.4	13.6
Prince Edward Island	113.4	76.9	68.8	8.1	67.8	10.5
Nova Scotia	764.2	485	442.4	42.6	63.5	8.8
New Brunswick	613.1	390.4	362.2	28.2	63.7	7.2
Québec	6 317.7	4 143.7	3 858.5	285.2	65.6	6.9
Ontario	10 366.6	7 049.9	6 584.7	465.2	68.0	6.6
Manitoba	899.2	621.0	594.9	26.1	69.1	4.2
Saskatchewan	751.1	521.9	496.8	25.1	69.5	4.8
Alberta	2 748.8	2 037.0	1 968.9	68.1	74.1	3.3
British Columbia	3 572.6	2 355.3	2 257.6	97.7	65.9	4.1
Yukon	21.3	16.0	15.3	0.7	75.1	4.4
Northwest Territories	30.8	24.4	22.9	1.6	79.2	6.6
Nunavut	14.2	10.2	9.2	1.0	71.5	9.7
Canada[2]	**26 569.9**	**17 928.3**	**16 848.6**	**1 079.8**	**67.5**	**6.0**

[1]The participation rate is the percentage of the population over 15 years of age in the labour force and includes both employed and unemployed. [2]Values for the provinces and territories may not add up to the totals for Canada, due to rounding and the use of estimated data in some cases.
SOURCE: Adapted from Statistics Canada, *Labour Force Information*, Catalogue 71-001, Issue of July 15 to 21, 2007, pages 23, 25-26, 48, tables 1, 3, 6.2, 10 August 2007, http://www.statcan.ca/bsolc/english/bsolc?catno=71-001-X&CHROPG=1.

29. Distribution of Employed People by Industry and by Province, 2006

Province[1]	Employees (000)													
	All Industries	Agriculture	Forestry, Fishing, Mining, Oil and Gas, Utilities	Construction	Manufacturing	Trade Transportation and Warehousing	Finance, Insurance, Real Estate, and Leasing	Professional Scientific, and Technical Services	Business, Building, and Other Support Services	Educational Services	Health Care and Social Assistance	Information, Culture, and Recreation	Accommodation, Food, and Other Services	Public Administration
Newfoundland & Labrador	215.7	1.9	18.6	12.9	15.7	49.3	6.5	6.7	8.5	16.6	30.1	8.8	24.7	15.3
Prince Edward Island	68.6	3.9	2.7	5.7	6.6	12.1	2.1	2.8	2.8	4.6	7.9	2.6	8.5	6.3
Nova Scotia	441.8	4.7	14.5	27.3	39.1	96.9	22.3	18.4	28.8	34.7	59.1	16.3	50.5	29.2
New Brunswick	355.4	6.2	13.0	21.1	36.9	76.7	16.4	14.5	21.8	27.2	45.3	160.4	42.7	21.7
Québec	3765.4	65.1	68.5	186.1	581.3	795.7	222.3	241.7	139.8	260.9	454.1	319.6	373.9	215.6
Ontario	6492.7	100.4	87.7	405.2	1 007.2	1 311.8	476.8	453.8	295.8	444.5	638.2	319.6	637.2	314.5
Manitoba	587.0	29.4	12.1	29.9	66.6	126.4	34.2	23.4	18.3	45.5	79.6	23.7	62.9	35.0
Saskatchewan	491.6	47.8	26.0	29.6	29.3	104.9	25.7	18.9	12.6	38.1	59.5	20.2	51.4	27.5
Alberta	1870.7	52.3	156.4	172.6	137.5	388.6	96.2	142.2	62.7	130.4	179.5	68.3	202.8	81.1
British Columbia	2195.5	34.7	52.4	179.3	197.5	473.2	138.0	167.6	98.8	156.0	232.2	113.2	261.3	91.3
Canada	**16 484.3**	**346.4**	**452.1**	**1 069.7**	**2 117.7**	**3 435.7**	**1 040.5**	**1 089.9**	**690.0**	**1 158.4**	**1 785.5**	**745.0**	**1 716.0**	**837.4**

[1]Data for the three territories is not available.
SOURCE: Adapted from Statistics Canada, "Distribution of employed people, by industry, by province", http://www40.statcan.ca/l01/cst01/labor21a.htm, accessed 15 October 2007.

Agriculture

30. Farm Cash Receipts from Farming Operations, 2006[1] ($000)

	NFLD & LAB	PEI	NS	NB	QUE	ONT	MAN	SASK	ALTA	BC	Canada[2]
Wheat[3]	—	3 671	1 194	324	14 641	279 735	361 157	1 336 020	810 623	5 373	2 812 738
Oats	—	548	96	334	16 410	5 511	98 353	175 367	33 384	1 967	331 970
Barley[3]	—	5 071	493	1 072	14 622	6 625	39 678	214 339	133 028	2 235	417 163
Liquidations	—	—	—	—	—	—	75 214	208 797	121 831	4 924	410 766
Flaxseed	—	—	—	—	—	0	22 198	128 770	3 326	0	154 294
Canola	—	—	—	—	2 777	3 107	384 485	1 114 878	991 041	5 321	2 501 609
Soybeans	—	1 380	—	—	114 650	546 620	17 413	—	—	—	680 063
Corn	—	—	1 586	—	288 047	448 589	14 725	—	550	—	753 497
Potatoes	2 861	201 411	8 160	110 773	118 175	98 054	125 897	28 564	154 147	51 200	899 242
Greenhouse vegetables	216	x	4 533	x	58 709	426 202	x	735	30 459	236 457	758 243
Other vegetables	3 152	13 077	15 363	5 957	251 335	423 859	38 603	1 152	46 582	126 198	925 278
Apples	0	185	10 260	1 682	28 427	56 092	x	x	x	37 420	134 132
Other tree fruits	3	x	366	x	256	45 245	—	x	x	30 787	76 742
Strawberries	480	760	4 400	1 680	22 715	15 300	1 300	500	911	4 280	52 326
Other berries and grapes	137	4 946	25 536	14 724	66 236	75 440	481	926	837	139 994	329 257
Floriculture and nursery	8 377	2 209	37 058	50 406	240 965	987 121	46 031	30 563	146 101	401 656	1 950 488
Tobacco	—	0	0	0	143	178 378	—	—	—	—	178 521
Ginseng	0	0	0	0	0	56 562	0	0	0	7 802	64 364
Lentils	—	—	—	—	—	—	0	206 677	1 543	—	208 220
Dry beans	—	—	—	—	7 424	70 375	41 821	—	23 568	—	143 188
Dry peas	—	—	—	—	0	0	7 483	247 159	71 950	333	326 925
Chick peas	—	—	—	—	—	—	—	44 482	6 763	—	51 245
Forage and grass seed	0	0	0	0	598	2 313	23 750	23 660	21 214	1 375	72 910
Hay and clover	43	510	359	422	13 032	34 186	14 651	24 417	39 072	11 938	138 631
Maple products	—	0	1 159	10 853	152 256	11 007	—	—	—	—	175 275
Forest products	94	x	12 268	x	41 672	19 172	x	x	x	16 534	109 362
Christmas trees	330	242	10 636	6 692	49 261	5 151	121	177	82	562	73 254
Total crops	**15 991**	**237 395**	**134 335**	**215 530**	**1 506 706**	**3 821 883**	**1 275 343**	**3 636 866**	**2 551 378**	**1 086 684**	**14 482 106**
Cattle	1 511	20 175	22 797	20 489	294 950	944 925	450 378	803 450	2 979 307	206 485	5 744 469
Calves	172	354	1 429	2 237	218 910	70 806	82 053	262 447	38 913	73 224	750 546
Hogs	1 167	23 630	22 880	20 454	838 946	851 218	827 838	312 170	495 315	34 391	3 428 012
Lambs	527	388	2 221	1 263	32 604	41 878	5 663	8 729	19 196	9 212	121 681
Dairy	38 778	63 087	107 660	84 365	1 846 187	1 590 920	188 801	133 433	382 095	395 346	4 830 672
Hens and chickens	x	x	53 399	43 238	409 524	495 414	62 980	56 686	137 995	259 767	1 545 233
Turkeys	x	x	6 392	4 669	56 437	127 271	18 047	9 662	23 826	31 932	278 304
Eggs	12 112	3 724	24 735	15 672	98 101	213 511	59 780	20 932	44 320	67 643	560 530
Honey	—	114	1 600	400	6 716	13 972	30 951	44 902	34 699	3 156	136 510
Furs	3 527	1 927	54 280	1 429	3 121	16 797	x	18	2 646	x	96 599
Miscellaneous livestock	540	1 954	6 071	3 486	27 136	44 425	21 334	65 058	108 966	49 011	327 981
Total livestock	**78 973**	**121 106**	**303 621**	**200 379**	**3 849 170**	**4 442 960**	**1 784 444**	**1 728 934**	**4 299 995**	**1 150 406**	**17 959 991**
Stabilization, insurance, income disaster programs, and other payments	815	21 343	14 509	33 637	896 181	662 134	626 087	1 267 192	945 115	105 146	4 572 159
Total receipts	**95 779**	**379 844**	**452 465**	**449 546**	**6 252 057**	**8 926 977**	**3 685 874**	**6 632 992**	**7 796 488**	**2 342 236**	**37 014 256**

x = confidential to meet secrecy requirements of the Statistics Act; — = nil
[1]Those listed have total production exceeding $60 million. [2]Information about the territories is excluded because of the small number of farms. [3]Includes durum wheat; includes Canadian Wheat Board payments.
SOURCE: Adapted from Statistics Canada, *Farm Cash Receipts: Agriculture Economic Statistics*, Catalogue 21-011, May 2007 issue, vol. 6 no. 1, p. 34. table 1-26, 28 May 2007, http://www.statcan.ca/english/freepub/21-011-XIE/2007001/t027_en.htm.

31. Cash Receipts from Farming by Province, 1983, 1989, 1995, 2000, 2006

Province[1]	Cash Receipts ($000 000)				
	1983	1989	1995	2000	2006
Newfoundland & Labrador	35	58	67	73	96
Prince Edward Island	172	256	311	326	380
Nova Scotia	236	315	329	414	453
New Brunswick	200	272	287	366	450
Québec	2 710	3 649	4 379	5 423	6 252
Ontario	4 990	5 663	6 158	7 579	8 927
Manitoba	1 798	2 102	2 461	3 137	3 686
Saskatchewan	4 026	4 475	5 250	5 781	6 633
Alberta	3 751	4 509	5 846	7 337	7 797
British Columbia	915	1 164	1 527	2 077	2 342
Canada	**18 832**	**22 462**	**26 614**	**32 513**	**37 014**

[1]Information about the territories is excluded because of the small number of farms.
SOURCE: Adapted from Statistics Canada: *Agriculture Economic Statistics*, May 2002, Catalogue 21-603, 28 June 2002, http://www.statcan.ca/bsolc/english/bsolc?catno=21-603-UPE#formatdisp; *Net Farm Income: Agriculture Economic Statistics*, Catalogue 21-011, May 2007 issue, vol. 6, no. 1, page 13, table 1-6, 28 May 2007, http://www.statcan.ca/english/freepub/21-011-XIE/2007001/t027_en.htm.

32. Farm Cash Receipts, 2006 ($000 000)

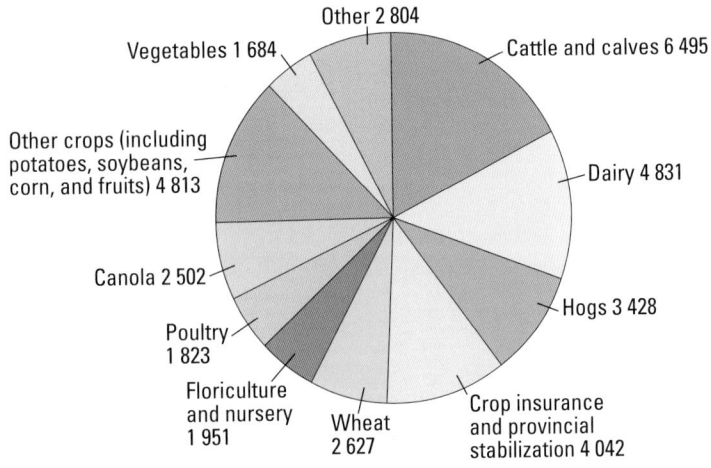

Other 2 804
Cattle and calves 6 495
Vegetables 1 684
Other crops (including potatoes, soybeans, corn, and fruits) 4 813
Dairy 4 831
Canola 2 502
Poultry 1 823
Hogs 3 428
Floriculture and nursery 1 951
Wheat 2 627
Crop insurance and provincial stabilization 4 042

Total cash receipts 2006 = 37 014

SOURCE: Adapted from Statistics Canada, *Farm Cash Receipts: Agriculture Economic Statistics*, Catalogue 21-011, May 2007 issue, vol. 6 no. 1, p. 34. table 1-26, 28 May 2007, http://www.statcan.ca/english/freepub/21-011-XIE/2007001/t027_en.htm.

33. Number of Farms and Average Size, Canada, 1901 to 2006

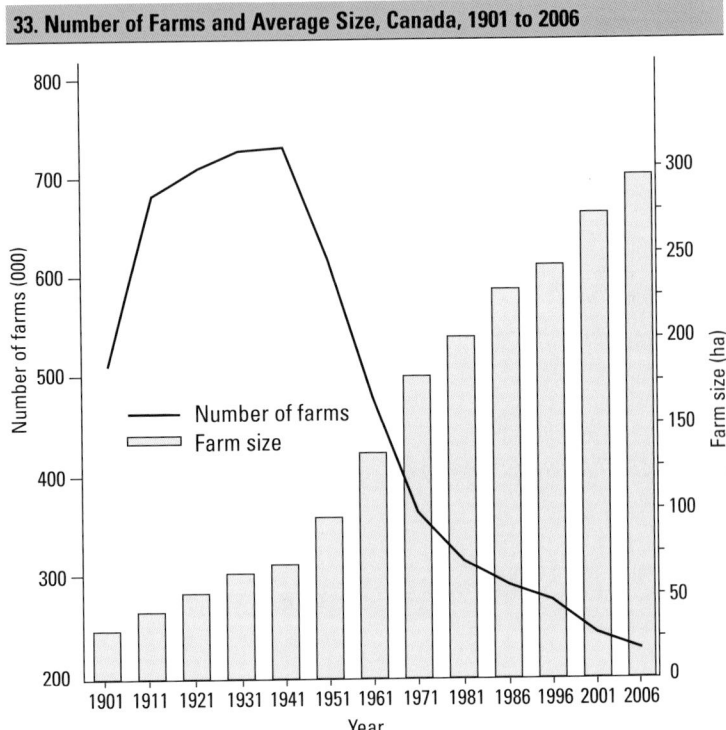

SOURCE: Adapted from Statistics Canada: 1996, 2001, and 2006 Census of Agriculture; "2006 Census of Agriculture: Farm operations and operators" from *The Daily*, Catalogue 11-001, 16 May 2007, http://www.statcan.ca/Daily/English/070516/d070516a.htm.

34. Agricultural Land Use, 2006

Province[1]	Farmland Area (000 ha)	% Change 1996 to 2006	% Classed as Class 1, 2, or 3 (1996)	Number of Farms	Average Farm Size (ha)	% Change in Farm Size 2001 to 2006	Cropland Area (000 ha)	Summer Fallow Area (000 ha)	Natural & Seeded Pasture (000 ha)
Newfoundland & Labrador	39.2	-10.5	0.005	558	65	+3.2	9.2	0.07	12.6
Prince Edward Island	250.9	-5.4	71.2	1 700	148	+4.2	171.3	0.2	23.2
Nova Scotia	403.0	-5.7	20.7	3 795	106	+1.9	116.6	1.1	55.1
New Brunswick	395.2	nil	17.9	2 776	142	+10.9	152.0	0.9	42.0
Québec	3 462.9	-0.2	1.4	30 675	113	+6.6	1 933.3	4.2	306.0
Ontario	5 386.5	-4.1	6.8	57 211	94	+2.2	1 788.9	11.9	753.7
Manitoba	7 718.6	-0.2	8.0	19 054	405	+12.2	4 701.0	126.6	2 046.5
Saskatchewan	26 002.6	-2.1	25.0	44 329	587	+13.1	14 960.1	2 428.6	7 138.0
Alberta	21 095.4	-0.3	16.2	49 431	427	+8.7	9 621.6	906.3	9 013.6
British Columbia	2 835.5	-12.1	1.0	19 844	143	+11.7	586.2	25.6	1 745.4
Canada[2]	**67 586.7**	**-0.7**	**4.6**	**229 373**	**295**	**+8.1**	**35 912.3**	**3 505.5**	**21 136.1**

[1]Information about the territories is excluded because of the small number of farms. [2]Values for the provinces and territories may not add up to the totals for Canada, due to rounding and the use of estimated data in some cases.
SOURCE: Adapted from Statistics Canada, 1996, 2001, and 2006 Census of Agriculture and "Farm Data and Farm Operator Data", 2006 Census of Agriculture, Catalogue 95-629, released 16 May 2007, Table 4, http://www.statcan.ca/english/freepub/95-629-XIE/2007000/landuse.htm#landuse.

35. Wheat Statistics,[1] 1994–2006

	1994-1995	1995-1996	1996-1997	1997-1998	1998-1999	1999-2000	2000-2001	2001-2002	2002-2003	2003-2004	2004-2005	2005-2006
Carryover from previous crop year	11 118	5 680	6 727	9 046	6 009	7 425	7 699	9 666	6 549	5 725	6 080	7 922
Production	22 920	24 989	29 801	24 280	24 082	26 941	26 519	20 568	16 198	23 552	25 860	25 748
Total supply	34 040	30 689	36 647	33 378	30 171	34 380	34 279	30 331	22 925	29 295	31 955	25 748
Exports	20 771	16 198	19 366	19 366	14 723	18 313	17 108	16 214	9 191	15 726	14 812	33 696
Domestic use	7 589	7 764	8 235	7 373	8 023	8 328	7 512	7 388	8 008	7 488	9 221	15 786
Carryover at the end of the crop year	5 680	6 727	9 046	6 009	7 425	7 739	9 658	6 729	5 725	6 080	7 922	9 698

[1]The crop year begins August 1 and ends July 31.
SOURCE: Adapted from Statistics Canada: *Grain Trade of Canada 1998-1999*, Catalogue 22-201, Table 2 "Supply and Disposition of Principal Grains, Canada, by Crop Year" http://www.statcan.ca/english/freepub/22-201-XIB/0009922-201-XIB.pdf; *Grain Trade of Canada 2000-2001*, Catalogue 22-201, Table 2 "Supply and Disposition of Principal Grains, Canada, by Crop Year" http://www.statcan.ca/english/freepub/22-201-XIB/0000122-201-XIB.pdf; *Cereals and Oilseeds Review*, Vols 24-30, Catalogue 22-007, Table 1, "Supply and disposition of wheat, Canada, by crop year".

36. Canadian Bulk Wheat (including durum) Exports,[1] 1996 to 2006 (000 t)

Country or Region	Average 1996 to 2006	2005/2006
United States	1 597	1 582
Japan	1 390	1 224
Sri Lanka	207	1 048
South Korea	426	1 045
Indonesia	797	996
Italy	625	911
Mexico	785	886
Venezuela	660	581
Iran	1 222	515
Algeria	1 106	358
China	896	160
Total all countries	**15 873**	**15 473**

[1]The crop year begins August 1 and ends July 31.
SOURCES: Canadian Wheat Board, 2005-2006 Statistical Tables, Table 12

37. World Wheat Imports and Exports, 1990, 1998, 2006

Country or Region	Imports (000 000 t)			
	1990	1998	2006	10-Year Average 1996 to 2006
European Union	n.a.	5.1	7.6	7.1
Egypt	6.0	7.1	7.8	7.0
Brazil	2.8	5.7	6.2	6.4
Japan	5.5	6.2	5.5	5.9
Algeria	3.5	5.2	5.5	4.9
Indonesia	2.0	3.7	5.0	4.1
South Korea	4.1	3.9	3.9	3.8
Iran	4.1	3.6	1.1	3.6
Mexico	n.a.	2.2	3.6	2.9
Philippines	n.a.	2.0	3.0	2.7
Iraq	0.2	2.5	4.8	2.6
World total[1]	**90.6**	**104.5**	**113.7**	**108.0**

Country or Region	Exports (000 000 t)			
	1990	1998	2006	10-Year Average 1996 to 2006
United States	28.3	28.3	27.4	27.9
European Union	18.5	16.3	15.0	16.4
Canada	21.9	20.0	15.8	16.1
Australia	11.9	15.4	15.2	15.7
Argentina	5.1	9.8	8.3	9.9
Russian Federation	n.a.	1.1	10.7	4.3
Ukraine	n.a.	1.4	6.5	3.2
World total	**90.6**	**104.5**	**113.7**	**108.0**

NOTE: Data is listed in order of 10-year average values.
n.a. = not available
[1]Morocco, United States, Nigeria, Yemen, the Russian Federation, and China imported between 2 and 3 million tonnes a year on average between 1996 and 2006.
SOURCE: (1990 data) Canadian Wheat Board, *CWB Annual Report*, 1990-1991; (1998-2006 data) Canadian Wheat Board, 2005-2006 Statistical Tables, Tables 30 and 31..

38. World Wheat Production, 1990, 1996, 2000, 2005 (000 000 t)

Country or Region	1990	1996	2000	2005
European Union	84.6	118.0	124.2	122.6
China	98.2	110.6	99.6	97.5
India	49.7	62.1	76.4	68.6
USA	74.5	62.0	60.0	57.3
Russian Federation	108.0	34.9	34.5	47.7
Canada	32.7	29.8	26.5	26.8
Australia	15.1	22.9	22.1	24.5
Pakistan	14.4	16.9	21.1	21.5
Ukraine	n.a	13.6	10.2	18.7
Turkey	20.0	16.0	18.0	18.0
Iran	n.a.	11.0	8.0	14.5
Argentina	11.4	15.9	16.2	13.0
World total	**592.4**	**582.6**	**581.5**	**618.9**

NOTE: Data is listed in order of 2005 production values.
SOURCE: Adapted from: (1990 data) CWB Annual Report, 1990-1991; (1996-2005 data) Canadian Wheat Board, 2005-2006 Statistical Tables, Table 29.

39. Natural Resources Summary, 2005[1,2]

	Forestry	Minerals	Energy	Geomatics[3]	Total Natural Resources	Canada
Gross Domestic Product ($ billion)	$37.6 (3.0%)	$50.7 (4.0%)	$75.2 (5.9%)	$2.4 (0.2%)	$165.9 (13.0%)	$1 276.6 (100%)
Direct employment (thousands of people)	340 (2.1%)	388 (2.4%)	250 (1.5%)	27 (0.01%)	1 005 (6.2%)	16 169 (100%)
New capital investments ($ billion)	$3.5 (1.3%)	$7.4 (2.8%)	$56.4 (21.3%)	n.a.	$67.3 (25.4%)	$265.5 (100%)
Trade ($ billion)						
Domestic exports (excluding re-exports)	$41.9 (10.3%)	$62.1 (15.2%)	$84.8 (20.8%)	$0.5 (0.1%)	$189.3 (46.4%)	$408.1 (100%)
Imports	$10.2 (2.7%)	$56.7 (14.9%)	$34.1 (9.0%)	n.a.	$101 (26.5%)	$380.8 (100%)
Balance of trade[4] (including re-exports)	+$31.9	+$7.5	+$50.7	n.a.	+$90.1	+$55.2

[1]The data reported for each of the natural resource sectors reflect the value of the primary industries and related downstream manufacturing industries as of September 2006. [2]The minerals industry now includes mineral extraction and concentrating, smelting and refining, non-metals and metals-based semi-fabricating industries, and metals fabricating industries. Minerals include uranium mining; energy includes coal mining. [3]Geomatics: The science and technology of gathering, analyzing, interpreting, distributing, and using geographic information. [4]Balance of trade shown in this table is the merchandise balance, which represents the difference between the total exports and imports of goods. Services and capital flows are excluded.
SOURCE: Adapted from *Important Facts on Canada's Natural Resources* (as of October 2005), Catalogue M2-6/2005, ISBN 0-662-69659-X [2006]. Reproduced with the permission of the Minister of Public Works and Government Services Canada, courtesy of Natural Resources Canada, 2007.

Forestry and Fishing

40. Forest Land, Harvests, and Forest Fires, 2005

Province or Territory	Total Land Area (000 000 ha)	Area of Forest and Other Wooded Land (000 000 ha)	Area Defoliated by Insects and Beetles (000 ha)	Total Area Harvested (000 ha)	Total Volume of Roundwood Harvested (000 000 m³)	Area Burned (000 ha)
Newfoundland & Labrador	40.3	20.1	57.9	22.9	2.4	22.8
Prince Edward Island	0.58	0.27	1.1	2.0	0.6	v.s.
Nova Scotia	5.3	4.4	n.a.	54.3	6.3	0.5
New Brunswick	7.3	6.2	nil	111.3 (2004)	11.4 (2004)	0.4
Québec	151.9	84.6	143.2	356.9	38.5	800.1
Ontario	107.5	68.3	1 403.6	225.2	23.4	42.3
Manitoba	63.6	36.4	47.2	13.7	2.1 (2004)	70.0
Saskatchewan	65.2	24.3	196.5	29.9	5.3	213.5
Alberta	65.4	36.4	2 700.0	79.8 (2004)	27.6	60.8
British Columbia	94.6	64.3	11 293.9	197.6	87.0	35.1
Yukon	48.5	22.8	82.6	v.s.	v.s.	170.7
Northwest Territories	128.1	33.4	35.0	0.13	v.s.	218.1
Nunavut	200.6	0.94	nil	nil	nil	nil
Canada	**979.1**	**402.1**	**15 960.9**	**1 108.4**	**191.0**	**1 885.3**

NOTE: Values for the provinces and territories may not add up to the totals for Canada, due to rounding and the use of estimated data in some cases.
— = nil; n.a. = not available; v.s. = very small
[1]Any forested area may be defoliated by more than one insect. Therefore, there can be considerable overlap in the reported figures. The area within which there is moderate to severe defoliation can also include roads, cultivated areas, small lakes, or burned areas. Areas reported as defoliated may include patches of different severity classes. Also, some areas of defoliation may be missed in the overall surveys.
SOURCE: Adapted from Natural Resources Canada, *The State of Canada's Forests 2005-2006* / "Canada's Forests" website, canadaforests.nrcan.gc.ca. Reproduced with the permission of the Minister of Public Works and Government Services, 2008, and the courtesy of the Canadian Forest Service.

41. Wood Pulp Market in Canada, 1995 to 2005

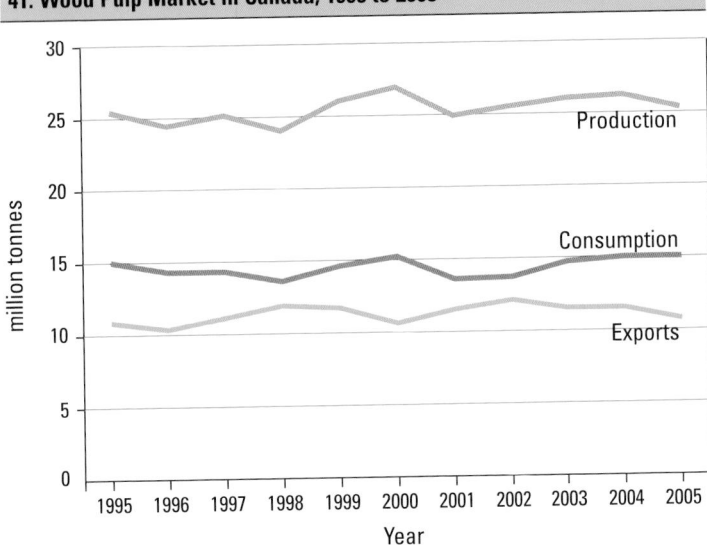

SOURCE: Adapted from Natural Resources Canada, *The State of Canada's Forests 2005–2006* / "Canada's Forests" website, http://canadaforests.nrcan.gc.ca. Reproduced with the permission of the Minister of Public Works and Government Services, 2008, and the courtesy of the Canadian Forest Service.

43. Softwood Lumber Market in Canada, 1995 to 2005

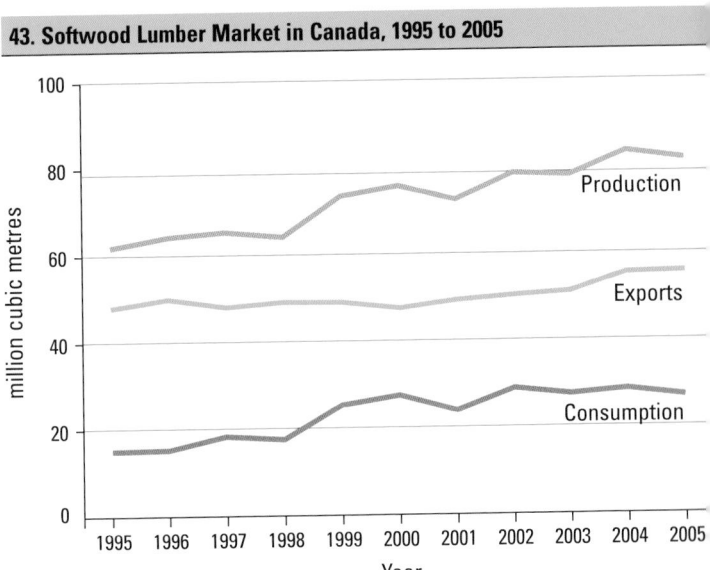

SOURCE: Adapted from Natural Resources Canada, *The State of Canada's Forests 2005–2006* / "Canada's Forests" website, http://canadaforests.nrcan.gc.ca. Reproduced with the permission of the Minister of Public Works and Government Services, 2008, and the courtesy of the Canadian Forest Service.

42. Newsprint Market in Canada, 1995 to 2005

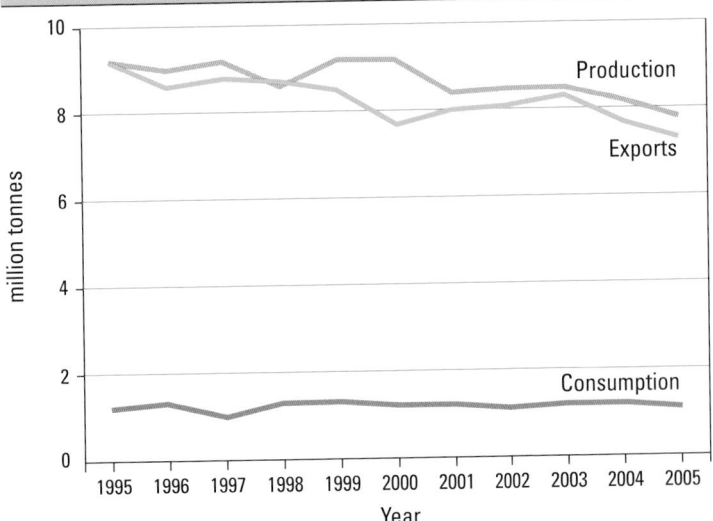

SOURCE: Adapted from Natural Resources Canada, *The State of Canada's Forests 2005–2006* / "Canada's Forests" website, http://canadaforests.nrcan.gc.ca. Reproduced with the permission of the Minister of Public Works and Government Services, 2008, and the courtesy of the Canadian Forest Service.

44. Printing and Writing Paper Market in Canada, 1995 to 2005

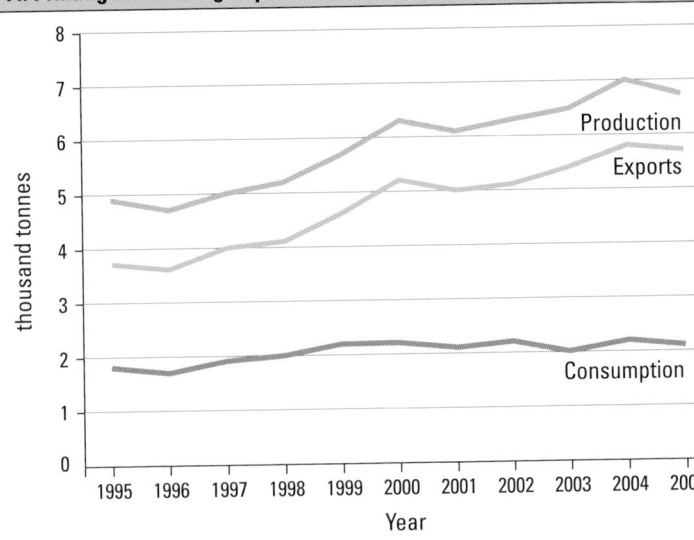

SOURCE: Adapted from Pulp and Paper Products Council (PPPC), *Canadian Pulp and Paper Industry Key Statistics* 2006, p. 3.

45. Commercial Fish Catches, 2000 and 2005[1]

	2000		2005	
	Quantity (tonnes, live weight)	Value ($000)	Quantity (tonnes, live weight)	Value ($000)
Sea fisheries				
Newfoundland and Labrador	278 141	584 319	357 472	517 626
PEI	54 712	129 808	45 873	140 076
Nova Scotia	336 216	704 551	268 211	731 681
New Brunswick	125 570	178 770	119 261	204 951
Québec	60 666	171 548	57 306	152 316
Total Atlantic seafisheries	**855 305**	**1 768 996**	**848 124**	**1 746 650**
Total Pacific seafisheries	**148 195**	**368 797**	**248 520**	**330 121**
Total seafisheries	**1 003 500**	**2 137 793**	**1 096 645**	**2 076 771**
Freshwater fisheries				
New Brunswick	1 611	691	—	—
Québec	1 508	3 960	—	—
Ontario	14 215	40 822	13 384	35 133
Manitoba	15 892	31 954	11 446	22 031
Saskatchewan	4 422	5 305	2 777	2 799
Alberta	1 752	2 508	1 679	2 024
Northwest Territories	1 173	1 580	906	814
Total freshwater fisheries	**40 573**	**86 820**	**30 192**	**62 801**
Total Canada	**1 044 073**	**2 224 613**	**1 126 837**	**2 139 572**

— = nil

[1]Aquaculture in 2004 produced an additional 146 thousand tonnes valued at $527 million.

SOURCE: Adapted from Fisheries and Oceans Canada website: "Summary of Canadian Commercial Catches and Values" 2000-2003, http://www.dfo-mpo.gc.ca/communic/statistics/commercial/landings/sum0003_e.htm; "Summary of Canadian Commercial Catches and Values" 2004-2005, http://www.dfo-mpo.gc.ca/communic/statistics/commercial/landings/sum0407_e.htm. Reproduced with the permission of Her Majesty the Queen in Right of Canada, 2008.

Mining

46. Production of Leading Minerals, 2006[1] ($000 000)

Mineral	NFLD & LAB	PEI	NS	NB	QUE	ONT	MAN	SASK	ALTA	BC	YT	NWT	NVT	Canada
Nickel	1 270.8	—	—	—	628.1	3 269.0	1 008.5	—	—	—	—	—	—	6 176.4
Copper	236.4	—	—	74.0	144.6	1 453.0	423.1	9.6	—	2 259.3	—	—	—	4 600.0
Iron ore	1 543.1	—	—	—	x	—	—	—	—	x	—	—	—	2 584.2
Gold	—	—	—	5.5	508.3	1 246.6	76.1	32.7	1.3	338.8	37.5	—	—	2 246.8
Zinc	—	—	—	902.4	319.0	378.8	369.7	1.9	—	115.4	—	—	—	2 087.3
Uranium	—	—	—	—	—	—	—	1 430.5	—	—	—	—	—	1 430.5
Platinum group	—	—	—	—	x	x	x	—	—	—	—	—	—	492.3
Silver	—	—	—	87.7	74.2	73.5	16.5	0.1	—	146.5	.2	—	—	398.8
Lead	—	—	—	112.9	—	—	—	—	—	3.7	—	—	—	116.6
Cobalt	25.1	—	—	—	13.8	55.3	19.0	—	—	—	—	—	—	113.2
Total metals	**3 075.4**	**—**	**—**	**1 185.3**	**3 213.4**	**6 898.8**	**1 959.0**	**1 475.0**	**1.3**	**3 297.8**	**37.7**	**55.7**	**0**	**21 199.3**
Potash	—	—	—	x	—	—	—	x	—	—	—	—	—	2 212.1
Cement	—	—	x	—	329.0	667.0	—	—	x	310.6	—	—	—	1 702.9
Diamonds	—	—	—	—	—	—	—	—	—	—	—	1 561.5	29.2	1 590.7
Stone	32.9	—	82.9	37.3	366.8	626.5	23.9	—	9.0	81.7	—	6.0	—	1 267.1
Sand and gravel	9.9	x	x	15.6	89.9	431.9	58.8	37.1	306.8	203.7	5.4	5.8	—	1 189.2
Lime	—	—	—	x	x	120.0	x	—	x	x	—	—	—	271.7
Salt	—	—	x	x	x	260.0	x	47.5	21.3	—	—	—	—	439.1
Clay products	—	—	x	—	x	184.9	—	x	x	x	—	—	—	230.9
Peat	x	x	x	74.8	63.1	—	x	x	26.8	x	—	—	—	211.2
Sulphur, elemental	x	—	—	—	—	x	—	2.3	141.3	x	—	—	—	158.4
Gypsum	x	—	105.4	—	—	x	x	—	—	x	—	—	—	123.9
Total non-metals	**46.5**	**3.9**	**x**	**x**	**1 515.1**	**2 492.2**	**127.1**	**x**	**x**	**672.7**	**5.4**	**1 573.3**	**29.2**	**10 199.0**
Total all minerals	**3 121.9**	**3.9**	**309.1**	**1 485.2**	**4 728.5**	**9 390.9**	**2 086.1**	**3 834.1**	**1 321.9**	**5 620.4**	**43.1**	**1 629.0**	**29.2**	**33 603.3**

— = nil; x = confidential to meet secrecy requirements of the Statistics Act.

Preliminary.

SOURCE: Adapted from Statistics Canada, *Canada's Mineral Production: Preliminary Estimates 2006*, Catalogue 26-202, Table 1, 6 June 2007, http://www.statcan.ca/bsolc/english/bsolc?catno=26-202-X.

47. Mineral Reserves 1994 to 2005

Mineral	Reserves						Production
	1994	1996	1998	2001	2003	2005	2005
Crude petroleum (000 000 m³)[1]	1 259.0	1 372.0	1 448.0	644.7	590.0	752.3	146.2[4]
Natural gas (000 000 000 m³)[1]	2 232.2	1 929.0	1 809.0	1 591.2	1 504.4	1 553.7	170.7
Crude bitumen (000 000 m³)[1]	158.8	197.5	229.8	1 830.0	1 720.0	1 620.0	n.a.[5]
Coal (megatonnes)[1]	8 623.0	8 623.0	8 623.0	4 555.3	4 423.1	4 291.8	65.3
Copper (000 t)[2]	9 533.0	9 667.0	8 402.0	6 666.0	6 037.0	6 589.0	595.4
Nickel (000 t)[2]	5 334.0	5 632.0	5 683.0	4 335.0	4 303.0	3 960.0	199.9
Lead (000 t)[2]	3 861.0	3 450.0	1 845.0	970.0	749.0	552.0	79.3
Zinc (000 t)[2]	14 514.0	13 660.0	10 159.0	7 808.0	6 251.0	5 063.0	666.7
Molybdenum (000 t)[2]	148.0	144.0	121.0	96.0	78.0	95.0	7.7
Silver (t)[2]	19 146.0	18 911.0	15 738.0	12 593.0	9 245.0	6 990.0	1 123.8
Gold (t)[2]	1 513.0	1 510.0	1 415.0	1 070.0	1 009.0	971.0	119.6
Uranium (000 t)[3]	397.0	369.0	312.0	452.0	429.0	n.a.	12.6

n.a. = not available
[1]Proved reserves recoverable with present technology and prices. [2]Proven and probable reserves. [3]Reserves recoverable from mineable ore. [4]Includes crude bitumen. [5]Included in the production data for crude petroleum.
SOURCE: Adapted from: Statistics Canada, http://www40.statcan.ca/l01/cst01/phys09.htm, accessed in 2002; and Natural Resources Canada, *Canadian Minerals Yearbook 2006*, © Her Majesty the Queen in Right of Canada, 2007.
Reproduced with permission.

48. Canada's World Role as a Producer of Certain Important Minerals, 2006

Mineral	Values (% of World Total)	World Total	Rank of Five Leading Countries				
			1	2	3	4	5
Uranium (U metal content) (mine production)	t (%)	41 827	**Canada** **11 627** **(27.8)**	Australia 9 559 (22.9)	Kazakhstan 4 357 (10.4)	Russia 3 431 (8.2)	Namibia 3 147 (7.5)
Potash (K₂O equivalent) (mine production)	000 t (%)	31 000	**Canada** **10 700** **(34.5)**	Russia 5 000 (16.1)	Belarus 4 500 (14.5)	Germany 3 800 (12.3)	Israel 2 100 (6.8)
Nickel (mine production)	000 t (%)	1449	Russia 300 (20.7)	**Canada** **198** **(13.7)**	Australia 189 (13.0)	Indonesia 148 (10.2)	New Caledonia 112 (7.7)
Cobalt (mine production)	t (%)	54 262	Congo D.R. 22 000 (40.5)	**Canada** **5 533** **(10.2)**	Zambia 5 422 (10.0)	Russia 4 748 (8.8)	Brazil 4 300 (7.9)
Magnesium (metal)	000 t (%)	722	China 468 (64.7)	USA 118 (16.3)	**Canada** **65** **(9.0)**	Russia 38 (5.3)	Israel 28 (3.8)
Titanium concentrate	000 t (%)	4 800	Australia 1 140 (23.8)	South Africa 952 (19.8)	**Canada** **809** **(16.9)**	China 400 (8.3)	Norway 380 (7.9)
Platinum group metals (mine metal content)	kg (%)	495 628	South Africa 299 964 (60.5)	Russia 137 600 (26.3)	**Canada** **21 456** **(5.6)**	USA 18 400 (3.7)	Zimbabwe 8 811 (1.9)
Aluminum (primary metal)	000 t (%)	31 955	China 7 806 (24.4)	Russia 3 647 (11.4)	**Canada** **2 894** **(9.1)**	USA 2 481 (7.8)	Australia 1 903 (6.0)
Gypsum (mine production)	000 t (%)	110 000	USA 17 500 (15.9)	Iran 11 000 (10.0)	**Canada** **9 500** **(8.6)**	Thailand 8 000 (7.3)	Spain/China 7 500 (6.8)
Chrysotile (asbestos) (mine production)	000 t (%)	2 200	Russia 875 (39.8)	China 360 (16.4)	Kazakhstan 350 (15.9)	**Canada** **240** **(10.9)**	Brazil 195 (8.9)
Cadmium (metal)	t (%)	18 440	China 3 000 (16.3)	South Korea 2 582 (14.0)	Japan 2 297 (12.5)	**Canada** **1 703** **(9.2)**	Mexico 1 627 (8.8)
Zinc (mine production)	000 t (%)	10 107	China 2 525 (25.0)	Australia 1 367 (13.5)	Peru 1 202 (11.9)	USA 748 (7.4)	**Canada** **667** **(6.6)**
Molybdenum (Mo content) (mine production)	t (%)	161 570	USA 56 900 (35.2)	Chile 45 500 (28.2)	China 28 500 (17.6)	Peru 9 700 (6.0)	**Canada** **7 910** **(4.9)**
Salt (mine production)	000 t (%)	210 000	USA 45 900 (21.9)	China 38 000 (18.1)	Germany 18 700 (8.9)	India 15 500 (7.4)	**Canada** **13 300** **(6.3)**
Lead (mine production)[1]	000 t (%)	3 333	China 1 023 (30.7)	Australia 767 (23.0)	USA 437 (13.1)	Peru 319 (9.6)	Mexico 134 (4.0)
Gold (mine production)[2]	t (%)	2 441	South Africa 297 (12.2)	Australia 263 (10.8)	USA 261 (10.7)	China 225 (9.2)	Peru 208 (8.5)
Silver[3]	t (%)	20 501	Peru 3 193 (15.6)	Mexico 2 894 (14.1)	China 2 500 (12.2)	Australia 2 407 (11.7)	Chile 1 400 (6.8)
Copper (mine production)[4]	000 t (%)	15 016	Chile 5 321 (35.4)	USA 1 140 (7.6)	Indonesia 1 064 (7.1)	Peru 1 010 (6.7)	Australia 927 (6.2)

[1]Canada ranked 6th. [2]Canada ranked 8th. [3]Canada ranked 8th. [4]Canada ranked 8th. SOURCE: Adapted from Natural Resources Canada, *Canadian Minerals Yearbook 2006*, © Her Majesty the Queen in Right of Canada, 2007. Reproduced with permission.

Energy

49. Coal,[1] Supply and Demand, 1960, 1970, 1980, 1991, 2001, 2005 (10^6 t)

	1960	1970	1980	1991	2000	2005
Production	10.0	15.1	36.7	71.1	70.5	65.3
Imports	11.5	18.0	15.6	12.4	25.4	16.3
Total supply	**21.5**	**33.1**	**52.3**	**83.5**	**95.9**	**81.7**
Domestic	20.4	25.7	37.3	49.4	57.3	57.2
Exports	0.9	4.3	15.3	34.1	30.2	25.4
Total demand	**21.3**	**30.0**	**52.6**	**83.5**	**87.5**	**82.6**

[1]Includes bituminous, sub-bituminous, and lignite.
SOURCE: Adapted from Statistics Canada, *Canada Year Book*, Catalogue 11-402, 1997, 5 November 1997; *Coal and Coke Statistics*, Catalogue 45-002, various years, http://www.statcan.ca/bsolc/english/bsolc?catno= 45-002-X&CHROPG=1; and *Energy Statistics Handbook*, Catalogue 57-601, January–March 2007, 17 August 2007, http://www.statcan.ca/english/freepub/57-601-XIE/57-601-XIE2007001.htm.

50. Marketable Natural Gas, Supply and Demand, 1960, 1970, 1980, 1991, 2001, 2005 (10^9 m^3)

	1960	1970	1980	1991	2000	2005
Production	12.5	52.9	69.8	105.2	171.4	170.7
Imports	0.2	0.3	5.6	0.3	3.9	9.5
Total supply	**12.7**	**53.2**	**75.4**	**105.5**	**175.3**	**180.2**
Domestic	9.4	29.5	43.3	54.8	85.5	73.9
Exports	3.1	22.1	22.6	47.6	108.2	106.3
Total demand	**12.5**	**51.6**	**75.4**	**102.4**	**193.7**	**180.2**

SOURCE: Adapted from Statistics Canada, *Canada Year Book*, Catalogue 11-402, 1997, Released November 5, 1997; *Supply and Disposition of Crude Oil and Natural Gas*, Catalogue 26-006, various years; and *Energy Statistics Handbook*, Catalogue 57-601, January–March 2007, 17 August 2007, http://www.statcan.ca/english/freepub/57-601-XIE/57-601-XIE2007001.htm.

51. Electricity, Supply and Demand, 1960, 1970, 1980, 1991, 2000, 2005 (10^9 kWh)

	1960	1970	1980	1991	2000	2005
Production	114.0	204.7	367.3	489.2	585.8	604.2
Imports	1.0	3.2	2.9	6.2	15.3	19.7
Total supply	**115.0**	**207.9**	**370.2**	**495.4**	**601.1**	**623.9**
Domestic	109.0	202.3	239.9	470.8	550.2	580.4
Exports	6.0	5.6	30.3	24.6	50.6	43.5
Total demand	**115.0**	**207.9**	**370.2**	**495.4**	**600.8**	**623.9**

SOURCE: Adapted from Statistics Canada, *Canada Year Book*, Catalogue 11-402, 1997, 5 November 1997; *Electric Power Statistics*, Catalogue 57-001, various years, http://www.statcan.ca/bsolc/english/bsolc?catno= 57-001-X&CHROPG=1; and *Energy Statistics Handbook*, Catalogue 57-601, January–March 2007, 17 August 2007, http://www.statcan.ca/english/freepub/57-601-XIE/57-601-XIE2007001.htm.

52. Crude Oil and Equivalent, Supply and Demand, 1960, 1970, 1980, 1991, 2001, 2005 (10^6 m^3)

	1960	1970	1980	1991	2000	2005
Production	36.5	80.2	89.5	96.7	129.0	146.2
Imports	21.2	33.1	32.2	31.5	53.5	53.8
Total supply	**57.7**	**113.3**	**121.7**	**128.2**	**182.5**	**200.0**
Domestic	46.8	74.3	109.8	84.4	103.1	108.4
Exports	10.7	38.9	11.9	44.2	79.6	91.6
Total demand	**57.5**	**113.2**	**121.7**	**128.6**	**182.7**	**200.0**

SOURCE: Adapted from Statistics Canada, *Canada Year Book*, Catalogue 11-402, 1997, 5 November 1997; *Electric Power Statistics*, Catalogue 57-001, various years, http://www.statcan.ca/bsolc/english/bsolc?catno=57-001-X&CHROPG=1; and *Energy Statistics Handbook*, Catalogue 57-601, January–March 2007, 17 August 2007, http://www.statcan.ca/english/freepub/57-601-XIE/57-601-XIE2007001.htm.

53. Electricity Production and Consumption, 1960, 1970, 1980, 2000, 2005 (GWh)

Province or Territory	1960 Production	1960 Consumption	1970 Production	1970 Consumption	1980 Production	1980 Consumption	2000 Production	2000 Consumption	2005 Production	2005 Consumption
Newfoundland & Labrador	1 512	1 427	4 854	4 770	46 374	8 545	43 598	11 817	42 136	11 947
Prince Edward Island	79	79	250	250	127	518	48	1 037	46	1 198
Nova Scotia	1 814	1 733	3 511	3 706	6 868	6 814	11 625	11 505	12 477	12 595
New Brunswick	1 738	1 684	5 142	4 221	9 323	8 838	19 295	16 134	21 063	15 880
Québec	50 433	44 002	75 877	69 730	97 917	118 254	179 757	191 819	180 296	206 909
Ontario	35 815	37 157	63 857	69 488	110 283	106 509	153 221	153 696	158 750	159 161
Manitoba	3 742	4 021	8 449	8 601	19 468	13 927	32 500	21 051	37 049	21 918
Saskatchewan	2 204	2 124	6 011	5 402	9 204	9 827	17 488	18 629	20 020	19 512
Alberta	3 443	3 472	10 035	9 880	23 451	23 172	54 535	59 363	63 636	62 207
British Columbia	13 409	13 413	26 209	25 761	43 416	42 789	68 683	64 052	67 773	65 732
Yukon	89	89	224	220	381	381	298	298	343	343
Northwest Territories	100	100	304	308	494	494	765[1]	765[1]	635	635
Nunavut	—	—	—	—	—	—	—	—	142	142
Canada	**114 378**	**109 304**	**204 723**	**202 337**	**367 306**	**340 068**	**581 813**	**550 166**	**604 500**	**580 649**

NOTE: Values for the provinces and territories may not add up to the totals for Canada, due to rounding and the use of estimated data in some cases. [1]Includes Nunavut.
SOURCE: Adapted from Statistics Canada, *Electric Power Statistics*, Catalogue 57-001, various years, http://www.statcan.ca/bsolc/english/bsolc?catno=57-001-X&CHROPG=1; and *Electric Power Generation, Transmission and Distribution*, Catalogue 57-202, 2005, 26 November 2007, http://www.statcan.ca/bsolc/english/bsolc?catno=57-202-X&CHROPG=1.

54. Primary Energy Production, 1990 to 2005 (petajoules)

Year	Coal	Crude Oil	Natural Gas	Gas Plant Natural Gas Liquids (NGLs)	Primary Electricity, Hydro & Nuclear	Steam & Biomass	Total
1990	1 673.1	3 765.2	4 183.8	390.3	1 305.9	16.0	11 495.4
1991	1 748.0	3 765.4	4 406.0	399.6	1 387.6	20.6	11 887.9
1992	1 553.5	3 931.7	4 864.5	433.5	1 401.8	12.6	12 196.2
1993	1 651.3	4 116.9	5 348.0	484.9	1 472.7	6.8	13 077.8
1994	1 735.3	4 299.9	5 831.3	500.5	1 542.3	4.0	13 913.3
1995	1 800.8	4 457.8	6 129.3	582.3	1 530.0	2.6	14 489.2
1996	1 832.3	4 590.7	6 343.4	589.1	1 583.1	2.5	14 800.3
1997	1 897.3	4 842.6	6 409.5	603.1	1 530.7	1.2	15 284.4
1998	1 651.5	5 021.7	6 664.1	605.2	1 426.2	0	15 368.7
1999	1 589.3	4 788.8	6 857.1	641.4	1 481.7	0	15 358.2
2000	1 509.9	4 999.6	7 062.1	672.2	1 524.6	0	15 768.4
2001	1 533.0	5 056.2	7 202.1	655.8	1 447.9	0	15 894.9
2002	1 429.9	5 359.6	7 249.9	626.2	1 505.3	0	16 171.0
2003	1 326.1	5 679.6	7 065.2	642.9	1 457.1	0	16 170.9
2004	1 415.7	5 869.4	7 095.7	650.7	1 522.2	0	16 553.7
2005	1 400.5	5 632.4	7 249.9	655.8	1 608.7	0	16 547.3

SOURCE: Adapted from Statistics Canada, *Energy Statistics Handbook*, Catalogue 57-601, January-March 2007, p. 30, table 2.1-1, 17 August 2007, http://www.statcan.ca/english/freepub/57-601-XIE/57-601-XIE2007001.htm.

55. Energy Summary, 1994, 2000 and 2005 (petajoules[1])

	1994	2000	2005
Primary production[2]	13 941	15 768	16 547
Net supply[3]	8 418	9 426	9 990
Producer's own consumption	976	1 257	1 355
Non-energy use	745	789	982
Energy use (final demand)	6 697	7 379	7 654
Industrial	2 086	2 287	2 283
Transportation	2 027	2 280	2 389
Agriculture	195	232	209
Residential	1 277	1 288	1 296
Public administration	145	131	137
Commercial and institutional	967	1 162	1 340

[1]A 30-litre gasoline fill-up contains about one gigajoule of energy. A petajoule is one million gigajoules. [2]Primary energy sources: coal, crude oil, natural gas, natural gas liquids, hydro, and nuclear energy. [3]Net supply of primary and secondary sources. In 2005, Canada exported 8 662 petajoules and imported 3 007.
SOURCE: Adapted from Statistics Canada *Canada Year Book*, Catalogue 11-402, 1997, 5 November 1997; "Energy Summary", http://www.statcan.ca/english/Pgdb/manuf19.htm, accessed 2002; and "Energy supply and demand", http://www40.statcan.ca/l01/cst01/prim71.htm, accessed 21 August 2007.

56. Installed Electrical Generating Capacity by Fuel Type and Region, 1970, 1990, 2000, 2004

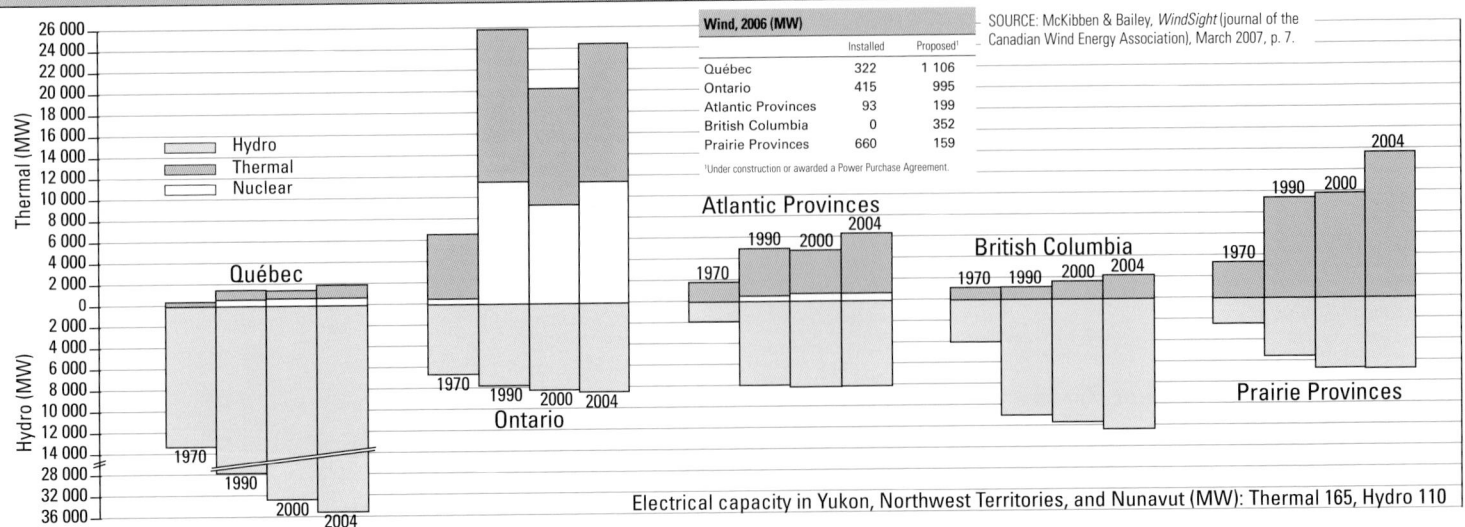

Wind, 2006 (MW)		
	Installed	Proposed[1]
Québec	322	1 106
Ontario	415	995
Atlantic Provinces	93	199
British Columbia	0	352
Prairie Provinces	660	159

[1]Under construction or awarded a Power Purchase Agreement.

SOURCE: McKibben & Bailey, *WindSight* (journal of the Canadian Wind Energy Association), March 2007, p. 7.

Electrical capacity in Yukon, Northwest Territories, and Nunavut (MW): Thermal 165, Hydro 110

SOURCE: Adapted from Statistics Canada, *Electric Power Generation, Transmission and Distribution*, Catalogue 57-202, 2000, 2 May 2002; and 2004, 29 August 2006, page 8-9, Table 1, http://www.statcan.ca/bsolc/english/bsolc?catno=57-202-X&CHROPG=1.

57. Top World Oil Producers, 2006

Country	Production (thousand barrels per day)
Saudi Arabia	10 719
Russia	9 668
United States	8 367
Iran	4 146
China	3 836
Mexico	3 706
Canada	3 289
United Arab Emirates	2 938
Venezuela	2 802
Norway	2 785
Kuwait	2 674
Nigeria	2 443
Brazil	2 163
Algeria	2 122
Iraq	2 008

SOURCE: Energy Information Administration: Official Energy Statistics from the US Government, "Top World Oil Producers and Consumers" 2006. http://www.eia.doe.gov/emeu/cabs/topworldtables1_2.htm.

58. Top World Oil Consumers, 2006

Country	Consumption (thousand barrels per day)
United States	20 588
China	7 274
Japan	5 222
Russia	3 103
Germany	2 630
India	2 534
Canada	2 218
Brazil	2 183
South Korea	2 157
Saudi Arabia	2 068
Mexico	2 030
France	1 972
United Kingdom	1 816
Italy	1 709
Iran	1 627

SOURCE: Energy Information Administration: Official Energy Statistics from the US Government, "Top World Oil Producers and Consumers" 2006. http://www.eia.doe.gov/emeu/cabs/topworldtables1_2.htm.

59. Conventional Crude Oil and Equivalent, Remaining Established Reserves in Canada, 2005 (000 m³)

	Remaining Reserves at 31 Dec 2004	2005 Gross Additions	2005 Net Production	Remaining Reserves at 31 Dec 2005	Net Change in Reserves during 2005
Crude Oil					
British Columbia	22 162	1 237	1 928	21 471	-691
Alberta	276 632	27 193	33 060	270 765	-5 867
Saskatchewan	187 902	34 264	24 515	197 651	9 749
Manitoba	3 861	893	812	3 942	81
Ontario	1 947	-214	138	1 595	-352
Québec	0	n.a.	n.a.	0	0
New Brunswick	0	n.a.	n.a.	0	0
Mainland territories	6 788	n.a.	1 089	5 699	-1 089
Eastcoast offshore	138 699	151 851	17 685	272 865	134 166
Total crude oil	**637 991**	**215 224**	**79 227**	**773 988**	**135 997**
Mackenzie/Beaufort	53 950	n.a.	n.a.	53 950	0
Arctic islands	0	n.a.	n.a.	0	0
Total frontier areas	**53 950**	**0**	**0**	**53 950**	**0**
Total crude oil	**691 941**	**215 224**	**79 227**	**827 938**	**135 997**
Pentanes plus					
British Columbia	6 477	629	466	6 640	163
Alberta	53 536	9 076	8 830	53 782	246
Saskatchewan	262	61	76	247	-15
Manitoba	0	n.a.	n.a.	0	0
Mainland territories	2 731	n.a.	55	2 676	-55
Eastcoast offshore	7 548	n.a.	185	7 363	-185
Total pentanes plus	**70 554**	**9 766**	**9 612**	**70 708**	**154**
Total crude oil & equivalent	**762 495**	**224 990**	**88 839**	**898 646**	**136 151**

n.a. = not available
SOURCE: Adapted from Canadian Association of Petroleum Producers, *Technical Report, Statistical Handbook for Canada's Upstream Petroleum Industry*, September 2007, 2006-9999, table 2.1a.

60. Marketable Natural Gas, Remaining Established Reserves in Canada, 2005

Area	Remaining Reserves at 31 Dec 2004	2005 Gross Additions	2005 Net Production	Remaining Reserves at 31 Dec 2005	Net Changes in Reserves during 2005
	(000 000 m³ at 101.325 kPa and 15°C)				
British Columbia	289 432	86 354	27 953	347 833	58 401
Alberta	1 175 892	113 301	135 713	1 153 480	-22 412
Saskatchewan	85 007	13 512	6 905	91 614	6 607
Ontario	11 456	1 912	347	13 021	1 565
Québec	105	—	—	105	0
New Brunswick	0	—	—	0	0
Mainland territories	11 872	-125	487	11 260	-612
Eastcoast offshore	19 278	—	4 031	15 247	-4 031
Total	**1 593 042**	**214 954**	**175 436**	**1 632 560**	**39 518**

SOURCE: Adapted from Canadian Association of Petroleum Producers, *Technical Report, Statistical Handbook for Canada's Upstream Petroleum Industry*, September 2007, 2006-9999, table 2.2a.

61. Developed Non-Conventional Oil, Remaining Established Reserves in Canada, 2005 (000 m³)

	Remaining Reserves at 31 Dec 2004	2005 Gross Additions	2005 Net Production	Remaining Reserves at 31 Dec 2005	Net Changes in Reserves during 2005
Mining—upgraded and bitumen[1] (Alberta)	841 235	163 633	31 553	973 315	132 080
In-situ—bitumen[2] (Alberta)	330 868	87 940	25 555	393 253	62 385
Total developed non-conventional oil	**1 172 103**	**251 573**	**57 108**	**1 366 568**	**194 465**
Total conventional & non-conventional oil	**1 934 598**	**476 563**	**145 947**	**2 265 214**	**330 616**

[1]Developed synthetic crude oil reserves are those recoverable from developed commercial projects. [2]Developed bitumen reserves are those recoverable from developed experimental/demonstration and commercial projects.
SOURCE: Adapted from Canadian Association of Petroleum Producers, *Technical Report, Statistical Handbook for Canada's Upstream Petroleum Industry*, September 2007, 2006-9999, table 2.5a.

62. Liquified Petroleum Gases, Remaining Established Reserves in Canada, 2005 (000 m³)

	Ethane, Propane, & Butanes				
	Remaining Reserves at 31 Dec 2004	2005 Gross Additions	2005 Net Production	Remaining Reserves at 31 Dec 2005	Net Change in Reserves during 2005
British Columbia	11 658	3 437	1 667	13 428	1 770
Alberta	113 269	16 064	18 532	110 801	-2 468
Saskatchewan	888	207	244	851	-37
Manitoba	0	0	n.a.	0	0
Total	**125 815**	**19 708**	**20 443**	**125 080**	**-735**

n.a. = not available
SOURCE: Adapted from Canadian Association of Petroleum Producers, *Technical Report, Statistical Handbook for Canada's Upstream Petroleum Industry*, September 2007, 2006-9999, table 2.3a.

63. Energy Supply and Demand, by Fuel Type, 2005 (petajoules)

	Coal	Crude Oil	Natural Gas	Natural Gas[1] Liquids (NGLs)	Primary Electricity, Hydro & Nuclear	Refined Petroleum Products
Production	**1 400.5**	**5 632.4**	**7 249.9**	**655.8**	**1 608.7**	**4 698.8**
Exports	659.6	3 541.3	4 065.9	238.7	156.7	974.5
Imports	486.0	2 072.3	364.4	13.9	70.8	632.4
Energy availability	1 272.3	4 507.1	3 543.1	465.0	1 522.8	4 246.4
Transformed to electricity by utilities	1 077.4	n.a.	280.6	n.a.	n.a.	162.7
Transformed to electricity by industry	0.04	0	67.1	n.a.	n.a.	16.9
Transformed to coke and manufactured gases	125.5	n.a.	n.a.	n.a.	n.a.	n.a.
Transformed to refined petroleum products	n.a.	4 507.1	26.4	60.0	n.a.	n.a.
Transformed to steam generation	0.01	n.a.	24.7	n.a.	0	5.9
Net supply	**70.2**	**0**	**3 144.3**	**405.0**	**1 522.8**	**4 123.0**
Producer consumption	5.8	0	714.5	28.6	152.3	453.7
Non-energy use	10.7	n.a.	162.0	321.3	n.a.	487.3
Energy use, final demand	53.7	0	2 267.8	108.3	1 936.7	3 128.7
Total industrial	52.8	n.a.	896.6	52.2	858.6	265.4
Total transportation	n.a.	n.a.	200.0	10.3	15.3	2 163.2
Agriculture	n.a.	n.a.	19.8	7.0	36.9	144.9
Residential	0.9	n.a.	646.6	12.3	543.6	92.7
Public administration	0.005	n.a.	22.4	0	50.3	63.3
Commercial and other institutional	0	n.a.	482.4	26.5	432.0	399.2

n.a. = not available
[1]Includes propane, butane, and ethane produced by gas plant.
SOURCE: Adapted from Statistics Canada, "Energy supply and demand, by fuel type", http://www40.statcan.ca/l01/cst01/prim72.htm, accessed 21 August 2007.

64. Canadian Imports and Exports of Selected Energy Materials

	1990 ($000 000)		1995 ($000 000)		2000 ($000 000)		2005 ($000 000)	
	Import	Export	Import	Export	Import	Export	Import	Export
Coal	611.4	2 110.3	475.2	2 212.1	946.5	1 659.7	1 265.0	3 182.7
Crude petroleum[1, 2]	5 300.2	5 528.5	5 707.9	8 956.3	13 668.6	19 589.3	21 925.3	29 926.8
Natural gas[2]	0.5	3 276.7	45.4	5 515.6	227.2	20 136.0	3 625.5	35 252.0
Petroleum products	1 583.2	2 651.2	1 167.3	2 562.0	2 351.9	5 598.9	5 790.2	11 454.3
Electricity	557.6	538.3	75.0	1 174.9	621.2	4 059.0	1 233.1	3 121.6
Total	**8 524.0**	**15 180.2**	**8 024.7**	**23 023.2**	**18 482.9**	**53 771.7**	**34 678.5**	**86 977.8**

[1]Main exporting countries 2005: Norway, 25.9%; Algeria, 17.6%; United Kingdom, 15.7%; Saudi Arabia, 8.2%; Iraq, 7.1%. [2]Over 95% of Canada's exports of petroleum and natural gas go to the United States.
SOURCE: Adapted from Statistics Canada, *Imports by Commodity*, 65-007, (Jan-Dec 2006 for 2006 data); *Exports by Commodity*, 65-004 (Jan-Dec 2006 for 2006 data).

Manufacturing

65. Summary Statistics, Annual Census of Manufacturers, 1965, 1970, 1975, 1980, 1984, 1990, 1994, 1999, 2005

Year	Number of Establishments[1]	Production and Related Workers		Cost of Fuel & Electricity ($000 000)	Cost of Materials & Supplies Used ($000 000)	Value of Shipments of Goods of Own Manufacture ($000 000)	Value Added ($000 000)
		Number	Wages ($000 000)				
1965	33 310	1 115 892	5 012	676	18 622	33 889	14 928
1970	31 928	1 167 063	7 232	903	25 700	46 381	20 048
1975	30 100	1 271 786	12 699	1 805	51 178	88 427	36 106
1980	35 495	1 346 187	22 162	4 449	99 898	168 059	65 852
1984	36 464	1 240 816	28 295	7 306	136 134	230 070	88 668
1990	39 864	1 393 324	40 407	7 936	168 664	298 919	122 973
1994	31 974	1 243 026	41 405	9 152	202 655	352 835	142 859
1999	29 822	1 487 098	53 164	11 018	277 803	488 729	202 930
2005	32 582	1 312 484	55 045	16 958	357 040	584 266	211 047

[1]The increase in the number of establishments between 1975 and 1980 was largely a result of the addition of 4 962 small establishments by improved coverage.
SOURCE: Adapted from Statistics Canada, *Manufacturing Industries of Canada, National and Provincial Areas*, Catalogue 31-203, various years; *Canada Year Book*, Catalogue 11-202E, 1976-77; Canada Year Book, Catalogue 11-402, 1992, 21 October 1991; and CANSIM database, http://cansim2.statcan.ca, table number 301-0006, extracted 23 August 2007.

66. Principal Statistics on Manufacturing Industries by Province and Territory, 2005

Province or Territory	Number of Establishments	Number of Production Workers	Production Workers' Wages ($000 000)	Cost of Energy and Water Utility ($000 000)	Cost of Materials, and Supplies ($000 000)	Revenue from Goods Manufactured ($000 000)	Manufacturing Value Added ($000 000)
Newfoundland & Labrador	369	14 136	352.5	140.8	1 290.5	2 407.0	934.4
Prince Edward Island	196	4 973	134.0	33.6	814.8	1 278.9	460.2
Nova Scotia	707	29 867	980.4	335.8	5 390.7	9 598.2	3 874.5
New Brunswick	631	28 028	837.3	438.0	11 225.6	15 542.4	3 981.4
Québec	8 059	342 379	13 047.0	4 212.2	76 924.3	133 791.5	52 742.7
Ontario	13 451	609 718	28 128.6	6 750.4	185 433.9	298 342.8	106 407.1
Manitoba	995	46 432	1 572.1	327.4	7 231.3	13 240.3	5 762.7
Saskatchewan	767	20 071	775.7	371.5	6 343.9	9 728.0	3 019.5
Alberta	3 100	99 697	4 137.6	2 891.5	39 931.9	60 348.5	17 812.5
British Columbia	4 241	116 737	5 064.5	1 454.9	22 377.5	39 875.8	16 015.1
Yukon	35	159	5.0	0.4	9.8	22.5	12.3
Northwest Territories	20	204	9.5	0.4	63.6	83.9	21.3
Nunavut	11	83	1.1	0.6	2.5	5.9	2.8
Canada	**32 582**	**1 312 484**	**55 045.4**	**16 957.5**	**357 040.3**	**584 265.7**	**211 046.6**

SOURCE: Adapted from Statistics Canada, *Manufacturing Industries of Canada, National and Provincial Areas*, 1999, Catalogue 31-203, 18 June 2002; and CANSIM database, http://cansim2.statcan.ca, table number 301-0006, extracted 23 August 2007.

67. Manufacturing Sales, by Subsector, 2002 and 2006 ($000 000)

	2002	2006
Food	64 089.5	72 138.0
Beverage and tobacco products	12 074.4	11 196.7
Textile mills	4 260.6	2 561.6
Textile product mills	2 950.4	2 442.3
Leather and allied products	933.6	459.1
Paper	34 284.4	31 422.4
Printing and related support activities	12 155.3	10 868.4
Petroleum and coal products	33 690.1	61 219.4
Chemicals	40 469.2	53 046.1
Plastics and rubber products	25 286.6	27 808.9
Clothing	8 024.4	5 309.9
Wood products	32 801.6	29 465.4
Non-metallic mineral products	11 630.8	13 945.7
Primary metals	36 074.9	51 273.6
Fabricated metal products	32 210.5	35 411.5
Machinery	27 448.5	31 424.7
Computer and electronic products	22 656.3	19 560.7
Electrical equipment, appliances, and components	10 135.9	10 520.1
Transportation equipment	126 451.6	118 449.0
Furniture and related products	13 916.5	13 358.9
Miscellaneous manufacturing	8 357.6	9 161.9
All manufacturing industries	**559 902.7**	**611 044.4**

SOURCE: Adapted from Statistics Canada, http://www40.statcan.ca/l01/cst01/manuf11.htm, accessed 25 October 2007.

Trade

68. Exports from Canada, Principal Nations, 1991, 1995, 2001, 2006 ($000 000)

Country or Region	1991	1995	2001	2006
United States	103 449	196 161	325 034	336 152
Japan	7 111	11 857	8 067	9 248
United Kingdom	2 920	3 748	4 700	9 150
China	1 849	3 212	3 920	7 183
Mexico	n.a.	1 107	2 353	4 026
Germany	2 125	3 150	2 691	3 484
South Korea	1 861	2 695	1 950	3 189
Netherlands	1 655	1 584	1 541	2 783
France	1 350	1 888	2 035	2 417
Belgium	1 073	1 823	1 837	2 204
Norway	n.a.	n.a.	n.a.	1 883
Italy	1 017	1 768	1 550	1 815
Australia	628	1 139	954	1 691
India	n.a.	n.a.	n.a.	1 529
Hong Kong	817	1 377	1 063	1 309
Taiwan	n.a.	1 683	965	1 308
Total all countries	**138 079**	**247 703**	**373 554**	**410 584**

NOTE: Data is listed in order of 2006 export values.
n.a. = not available
SOURCE: Adapted from Statistics Canada, *Exports by Country*, Catalogue 65-003, various years.

69. Imports to Canada, Principal Nations, 1991, 1995, 2001, 2006 ($000 000)

Country or Region	1991	1995	2001	2006
United States	86 235	150 705	218 408	217 597
China	1 852	4 639	12 712	34 473
Mexico	2 574	5 341	12 110	15 982
Japan	10 249	12 103	14 647	15 334
Germany	3 734	4 801	7 955	11 115
United Kingdom	4 182	5 470	11 631	10 843
South Korea	2 110	3 204	4 601	5 763
Norway	n.a.	2 314	3 500	5 445
France	2 670	3 125	5 510	5 175
Italy	1 792	3 270	4 034	4 916
Taiwan	2 212	2 792	4 410	3 877
Malaysia	n.a.	1 549	1 894	2 938
Ireland	n.a.	189	n.a.	2 550
Sweden	n.a.	1 305	1 708	2 356
Thailand	n.a.	1 014	1 689	2 251
Total all countries	**135 284**	**225 493**	**343 056**	**396 443**

NOTE: Data is listed in order of 2006 export values.
n.a. = not available
SOURCE: Adapted from Statistics Canada, *Imports by Country*, Catalogue 65-006, various years.

The Economy

70. Principal Commodities Imported and Exported, 2006 ($000 000)

Commodity	Imports	Exports[2]
Mineral fuels	36 273	86 258
Vehicles, rolling stock, parts	67 770	72 202
Wood and articles thereof	3 559	17 313
Machinery[1]	63 520	29 526
Electrical machinery and parts	39 085	16 522
Iron and steel products	18 234	11 759
Plastic products	13 860	14 206
Aircraft and parts	5 965	9 613
Pharmaceutical products	10 148	5 004
Paper and paperboard	6 268	14 218
Precious stones and metals	6 009	8 651
Organic chemicals	7 520	5 141
Aluminum and articles thereof	4 283	12 107
Optical equipment	11 396	4 596
Furniture and related products	7 522	7 172
Pulp wood and cellulose	439	6 649
Clothing and apparel	6 969	2 329
Rubber and articles thereof	5 552	3 639
Total, all commodities	**396 443**	**410 584**

[1]Includes nuclear reactors, boilers, machinery, and mechanical appliances and parts. [2]Nickel and related articles exports $5 820. SOURCE: Adapted from Statistics Canada, *Imports by Country*, Catalogue 65-006, vol. 63 no. 04, Jan to Dec 2006, 19 Feb 2007; and *Exports by Country*, Catalogue 65-003, vol. 63 no. 04, Jan to Dec 2006, 5 March 2007.

71. Gross Domestic Product by Industry,[1] Canada, 1980, 1990, 2001, 2006

Industry	1980 (%)	1990 (%)	2001 (%)	2006 (%)
Agricultural, fishing, trapping, and forestry	2.3	3.0	2.3	2.3
Mining	4.1	4.0	3.9	4.8
Manufacturing	17.7	18.1	17.3	15.6
Construction	5.7	6.4	5.3	6.2
Trade (wholesale and retail)	11.4	11.5	11.5	11.5
Finance, insurance, and real estate	13.4	15.7	19.6	19.3
Transportation	4.6	4.7	4.6	4.6
Professional, community, and personal services	22.2	23.1	22.3	23.9
Public administration	7.2	6.7	5.6	5.6
Other (utilities, and information and cultural industries)	11.4	6.8	7.6	6.2

[1]Based on per cent of Canada's GDP.
SOURCE: Adapted from Statistics Canada, *Canadian Economic Observer*, Catalogue 11-010, various years; and "Gross domestic product at basic prices, by industry", http://www40.statcan.ca/l01/cst01/econ41.htm, accessed 21 August 2007.

72. Inflation Rates, 1915 to 2006

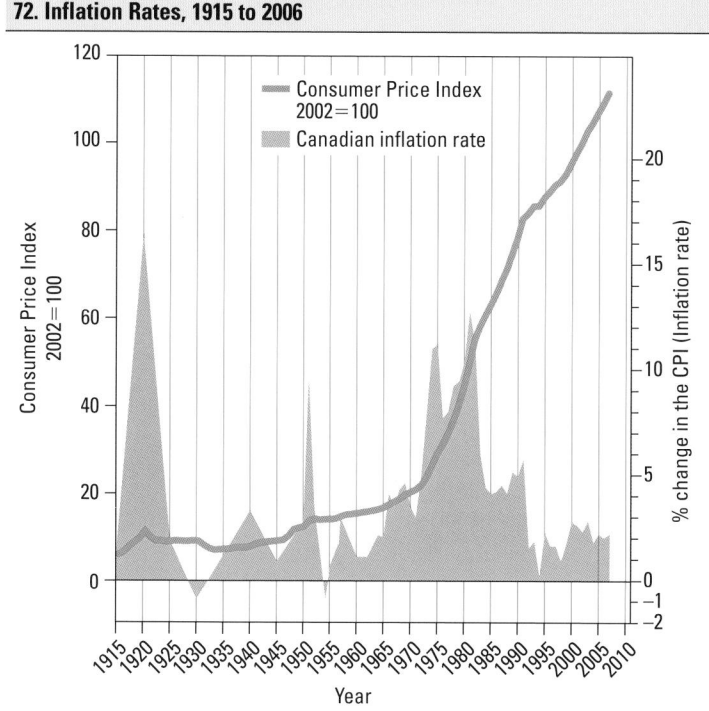

Year

NOTE: Prior to 1950, data was compiled every five years. Since 1950, data has been compiled annually.
SOURCE: Adapted from Statistics Canada, "Consumer Price Index, historical summary", http://www40.statcan.ca/l01/cst01/econ46a.htm

73. Gross Domestic Product by Province and Territory,[1] 1970, 1980, 1990, 2001, 2006

Province or Territory	1970	1980	1990	2001	2006
NFLD & LAB	1.4	1.3	1.3	1.3	1.7
PEI	0.3	0.3	0.3	0.3	0.3
NS	2.5	2.0	2.5	2.3	2.2
NB	1.9	1.6	2.0	1.7	1.8
QUE	25.5	23.3	23.1	21.0	19.7
ONT	42.0	37.1	40.8	40.6	38.7
MAN	4.2	3.6	3.5	3.2	3.1
SASK	3.4	4.0	3.1	3.1	3.1
ALTA	8.0	13.9	10.7	13.9	16.4
BC	10.6	12.4	12.2	12.0	12.5
YT, NWT & NVT	0.3	0.4	0.5	0.6	0.5

[1]Based on per cent of Canada's GDP, expenditure based. SOURCE: Adapted from Statistics Canada, *Canadian Economic Observer*, Catalogue 11-010, various years. "Gross domestic product, expenditure-based, by province and territory", http://www40.statcan.ca/l01/cst01/econ15.htm, accessed 21 August 2007.

74. Foreign Investment in Canada, 1970, 1990, 2000, 2006 ($000 000)

Country or Region	1970	1990	2000	2006
US	22 054	84 311	185 238	273 705
UK	2 641	18 217	19 268	39 012
Other EU	1 617	14 339	58 653	79 353
Japan	103	5 203	8 442	11 309
Other OECD[1]	580	5 871	9 229	19 359
Total	**27 374**	**130 932**	**291 520**	**448 858**

NOTE: Data is listed in order of 2006 investment values.
[1]OECD = Organization for Economic Cooperation and Development. Member countries are shown on the map on page 147.
SOURCE: Adapted from Statistics Canada, Table 376-0053, "International investment position, Canadian direct investment abroad and foreign direct investment in Canada, by industry and country, annual (dollars)", CANSIM (database), Using E-STAT (distributor), http://estat.statcan.ca/cgi-win/cnsmcgi.exe?Lang=E&EStatFile=EStat\English\CII_1_E.htm&RootDir=EStat/, http://estat.statcan.ca/cgi-win/cnsmcgi.exe?Lang=E&EStatFile=EStat\English\CII_2_E.htm&RootDir=EStat/, accessed 16 April 2008.

Transportation and Tourism

75. Principal Seaway Ports,[1] 1995, 2001, and 2006 (000 t)[2]

	Inbound Cargo			Outbound Cargo				Inbound Cargo			Outbound Cargo		
	1995	2001	2006	1995	2001	2006		1995	2001	2006	1995	2001	2006
Canadian ports	**30 289**	**26 022**	**28 230**	**26 622**	**24 471**	**28 664**	**US ports**	**11 986**	**9 941**	**12 867**	**16 375**	**12 449**	**12 416**
Thunder Bay	9	v.s.	—	6 702	6 145	6 203	Toledo	264	229	3 458	3 579	2 673	2 487
Port Cartier	4 664	2 733	2 045	2 113	2 068	3 686	Duluth	230	270	204	4 510	3 613	1 952
Sept-Îles	821	217	292	3 950	2 222	3 029	Sandusky	v.s.	v.s.	—	1 660	992	1 597
Québec City	2 247	955	1 837	1 008	883	2 412	Chicago	1 168	871	747	1 357	429	840
Hamilton	11 044	9 947	10 889	702	666	1 725	Ashtabula	710	563	242	660	1 186	604
Goderich	v.s.	v.s.	n.a.	758	1 046	1 599	Milwaukee	228	141	224	769	363	471
Pointe-Noire	380	263	—	3 845	3 753	1 588	Cleveland	2 044	1 692	1 834	400	339	404
Toronto[3]	798	3 751	3 361	19	1 623	1 417	Burns Harbor	3 047	1 735	1 968	566	225	376
Windsor	179	v.s.	382	1 373	773	885	Detroit	1 935	2 311	1 736	472	130	231
Sarnia	—	—	303	—	—	812	Gary	—	—	541	—	—	188
Meldrum Bay	—	—	—	—	—	633	Essexville	n.a.	400	438	n.a.	v.s.	—
Sault Ste Marie	—	—	—	—	—	504							
Picton	239	182	340	567	491	487							
Montreal[4]	2 198	1 775	1 785	96	442	451							
Nanticoke	n.a.	477	390	n.a.	304	265							
Sorel	404	307	537	116	133	187							
Baie-Comeau	2 643	1 248	2 136	v.s.	v.s.	—							
Trois-Rivieres	803	424	413	78	v.s.	—							

NOTE: Data is listed in order of 2006 cargo totals.
v.s. = very small/unreported; n.a. = not available
[1]Area includes all ports or installations within a 20 km radius of the main harbour. [2]Tonnage figures are limited to cargo volumes moved through seaway lock structures. [3]Includes Port Credit, Lakeview, Bowmanville, Clarkson, Oakville, and Oshawa. [4]Includes Côte Ste. Catherine.
SOURCE: The St. Lawrence Seaway Management Corporation, *St. Lawrence Seaway Traffic Report*, 1995, 2001, and 2006 Navigation Seasons.

76. The St. Lawrence Seaway

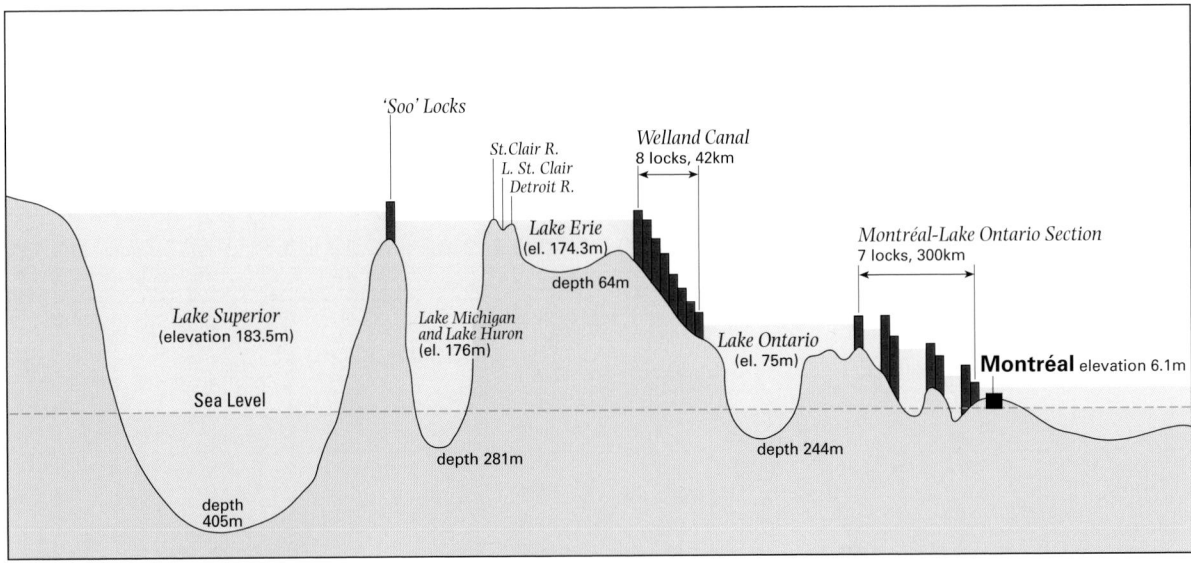

The St. Lawrence Seaway Authority was established in 1951 for the purpose of constructing, operating, and maintaining a deep waterway between the Port of Montréal and Lake Erie, replacing an earlier network of shallow-draught canals. Two of the seven seaway locks along the St. Lawrence River, in the United States, are operated by the US St. Lawrence Seaway Development Corporation.

The St. Lawrence Seaway was officially opened in 1959. It allows navigation by ships not exceeding 222.5 m in length, 23.2 m in width, and loaded to a maximum draught of 7.9 m in a minimum water depth of 8.2 m.

Beginning at Montréal, the Seaway naturally divides into four sections:

1. The Lachine Section required the construction of the 33 km South Shore Canal, to bypass the Lachine Rapids.

The St. Lambert and Côte Ste. Catherine locks provide a lift 13.7 m to Lake St. Louis.

2. The Soulanges Section contains the two Beauharnois locks, bypassing the Beauharnois hydroelectric plant to reach Lac Saint-François.

3. The Lac Saint-François Section extends to a point just east of Cornwall, Ontario.

4. The International Rapids Section was developed simultaneously for hydro-electric power generation and navigation. Ontario and the State of New York jointly built the Moses–Saunders Power Dam, the Long Sault and Iroquois control dams, and undertook the flooding of the river above the power dam to form Lake St. Lawrence, the 'head pond' of the generating station.

The Wiley–Dondero Canal and the Snell and Eisenhower locks allow ships to bypass the Moses–Saunders power station. The Iroquois lock and adjacent control dam are used to adjust the level of Lake St. Lawrence to that of Lake Ontario.

The Welland Canal joins lakes Ontario and Erie and allows ships to bypass Niagara Falls by means of eight locks. The present Welland Canal, completed in 1932, was later deepened to ensure 7.9 m draught navigation throughout the Seaway.

The final section consists of four parallel locks, the 'Soo' locks, on the St. Mary's River and connects Lake Superior to Lake Huron. This section is not part of the St. Lawrence Seaway Authority.

77. Cargo Loaded and Unloaded at Leading Canadian Ports, Major Commodities, 2004 (000 t)

Port	Domestic Cargo		International Cargo		Total
	Loaded	Unloaded	Loaded	Unloaded	
Vancouver	1 416	281	64 453 (potash, coal, wheat, sulphur)	8 849 (machinery/equipment)	74 998
Come-by-Chance	1 817 (crude petroleum)	15 579 (crude petroleum)	18 708 (crude petroleum)	5 948 (crude petroleum)	42 051
Saint John	1 158 (fuel oil)	1 430	10 772 (fuel oil, gasoline)	12 798 (crude petroleum)	26 158
Port Hawksbury	446	70	13 115 (crude petroleum)	10 343 (crude petroleum)	23 973
Montréal–Contrecoeur	1 209	3 877 (iron ore)	6 659 (wheat, food products)	11 521 (manufactured and miscellaneous goods, fuels)	23 265
Québec-Lévis	2 214 (fuel oil)	1 944 (wheat)	4 599 (wheat, iron ore)	12 891 (crude petroleum)	21 648
Port Cartier	3 684 (iron ore)	1 425 (wheat)	11 322 (iron ore)	1 167 (fodder and feed)	17 597
Sept-Îles–Pointe-Noire	1 730 (iron ore)	568	13 573	1 141 (alumina)	17 011
Newfoundland offshore	15 986 (crude petroleum)	372	0	0	16 359
Fraser River	5 434 (wood chips)	2 914 (limestone)	3 694 (logs, lumber, wood pulp)	2 816 (iron, steel)	14 857
Halifax	1 632	1 283	2 915	5 614	14 208
Nanticoke	671	932 (Manufactured and miscellaneous goods)	654	10 114 (coal)	12 371
Hamilton	625	5 005	643	5 645	11 917

SOURCE: Adapted from Statistics Canada, *Shipping in Canada*, Catalogue 54-205, 2004, p. 62, table 13, 20 July 2007, http://www.statcan.ca/bsolc/english/bsolc?catno=54-205-X.

78. St Lawrence Seaway Traffic by Commodity and by Nationality, 2006[1]

Commodities	Upbound (000 t)	Sources and Destinations of Upbound Commodities (%)	Downbound (000 t)	Sources and Destinations of Downbound Commodities (%)
Corn	—	—	1 729.3	Can to Can 5; US to Can 19; US to For 76
Flaxseed	—	—	467.7	Can to Can 2; Can to For 93; US to For 5
Wheat	11.7	Can to US 100	6 434.9	Can to Can 74; Can to For 6; US to Can 2; US to For 18
Soy beans	—	—	1 583.9	Can to Can 16; Can to For 9; US to Can 39; US to For 36
Canola	—	—	478.9	Can to Can 11; Can to For 89
Beans and peas	—	—	445.4	Can to Can 29; Can to For 49; US to Can 4; US to For 18
Total agricultural	**54.3**		**11 532.3**	
Iron ore	9 150.9	Can to Can 44; Can to US 56	1 859.1	US to Can 89; US to For 11
Bitumenous coal	—	—	3 714.5	Can to Can 12; US to Can 88
Salt	52.9	Can to Can 100	2 891.2	Can to Can 68; Can to US 6; US to Can 26
Coke	785.7	Can to Can 23; Can to US 56; For to Can 8; For to US 13	1 209.9	Can to Can 11; Can to For 4; US to Can 73; US to For 11
Gypsum	927.1	Can to Can 99; Can to US 1	—	—
Stone	443.0	Can to Can 4; Can to US 96	718.3	Can to Can 100
Total mine	**11 819.5**		**11 084.8**	
Iron and steel	3 447.0	Can to Can 1; For to Can 36; For to US 63	18.6	Can to For 98
Fuel oil	525.6	Can to Can 79; Can to US 21	700.9	Can to Can 73; Can to US 6; Can to For 4; US to Can 17
Cement	1 154.7	Can to Can 3; Can to US 97	52.1	Can to Can 100
Furnace slags	632.1	Can to Can 21; Can to US 56; For to US 22	433.3	Can to Can 83; Can to US 17
Cement clinker	1 064.5	Can to US 100	—	—
Steel slab	985.9	Can to Can 9; For to Can 59; For to US 32	—	—
Gasoline	621.0	Can to Can 96; US to Can 3	164.7	Can to Can 15; US to Can 85
Chemicals	391.9	Can to Can 1; US to Can 17; For to Can 74; For to US 9	338.4	Can to Can 7; Can to US 7; Can to For 68; US to Can 18
Total manufactures[2]	**10 463.4**	**Can to Can 16; Can to US 29; For to Can 25; For to US 29**	**2 135.3**	**Can to Can 55; Can to US 7; Can to For 18; US to Can 19**
Grand total	**22 386.7**	**Can to Can 31; Can to US 41; For to Can 13; For to US 15**	**24 777.5**	**Can to Can 40; Can to US 1; Can to For 9; US to Can 34; US to For 16**

— = nil
[1]Includes traffic through both the Montreal–Lake Ontario section and the Welland Canal section. [2]Includes unclassified cargoes.
SOURCE: The St. Lawrence Seaway Management Corporation, *The St. Lawrence Seaway Traffic Report 2006 Navigation Season*.

79. Visits and Expenditures of Canadian Residents in Selected Countries (other than the US), 2005

Country or Region	Visits (000)	Spending ($000 000)	Average Spending per Person per Visit ($)
Austria	152	80	525
Belgium	131	83[1]	629
France	684	834	1 219
Germany	409	279	682
Greece	146	144[1]	992
Ireland (Republic of)	127	146	1 151
Italy	423	618	1 460
Netherlands	266	135	507
Spain	216	225	1 038
Switzerland	164	123	750
United Kingdom	968	1 093	1 129
Other	914	619	1 761
Total Europe	**4 600**	**4 377**	**952**
Total Africa	**253**	**382**	**1 511**
China	170	305	1 795
Hong Kong	171	210	1 231
Japan	151	221	1 464
Other	696	817	2 677
Total Asia	**1 187**	**1 552**	**1 308**
Total Central America	**197**	**115**	**584**
Cuba	518	470	908
Dominican Republic	519	458	881
Other	1 225	522	426
Total Bermuda and Caribbean	**2 262**	**1 450**	**641**
Total South America	**233**	**266**	**1 144**
Mexico	1 007	926	919
Total North America	**1 016**	**928**	**913**
Australia	124	263	2 127
Total Oceania & other ocean islands	**179**	**383**	**2 136**
Total	**9 927**	**9 454**	**952**

[1]Use data with caution.
SOURCE: Adapted from Statistics Canada, *International Travel*, Catalogue 66-201, 2005, p. 49, table 27, 22 December 2006, http://www.statcan.ca/english/freepub/66-201-XIE/2005000/t034_en.htm.

80. Visits and Expenditures of Canadian Residents Returning from the US, by Selected States, 2005

State	Visits (000)	Spending ($000 000)
Arizona	516	437.5
California	1 258	867.6
Florida	2 207	2 353.3
Georgia	903	114.6
Idaho	475	45.5
Illinois	814	174.4
Indiana	534	63.1
Kentucky	498	38.2
Maine	949	186.7
Maryland	620	46.3
Massachusetts	736	208.4
Michigan	2 202	273.1
Minnesota	906	172.1
Montana	564	105.4
Nevada	1 010	777.6
New Hampshire	864	75.2
New York	4 445	696.2
North Carolina	861	107.5
North Dakota	556	86.3
Ohio	879	121.4
Oregon	420	97.7
Pennsylvania	1 439	136.2
South Carolina	784	261.6
Tennessee	517	79.4
Vermont	1 453	119.3
Virginia	897	96.3
Washington	2 057	321.7
West Virginia	462	16.9
Other states	3 671	1 550.0
Total	**33 496**	**9 653.6**

SOURCE: Adapted from Statistics Canada, *International Travel*, Catalogue 66-201, 2005, p. 47, table 25, 22 December 2006, http://www.statcan.ca/english/freepub/66-201-XIE/2005000/t032_en.htm.

81. Trip Characteristics of US Residents Entering Canada, Staying One or More Nights in Provinces Visited, 2005

	Atlantic Provinces[1]	Québec	Ontario	Manitoba	Saskatchewan	Alberta	British Columbia[2]	Canada
Person-visits (000)	989	2 196	7 214	293	181	961	3 793	15 627
Spending in province ($000 000)	461	1 299	2 932	146	125	626	1 875	7 463
Average spending per person-visit ($)	466	591	406	499	691	651	494	478
Person-nights (000)	4 220	7 946	25 320	1 057	692	4 489	13 606	57 331
Average number of nights per visit	4.3	3.6	3.5	3.6	3.8	4.7	3.6	3.7
Average spending per person-night ($)	109	163	116	138	181	139	138	130
Region of Residence (000)								
New England	431	782	348	x	x	39	71	1 682
Middle Atlantic	116	588	1 962	x	x	60	215	2 967
South Atlantic	132	270	708	27[3]	253	130	307	1 598
East North Central	113	205	2 886	35	28	107	237	3 611
West North Central	35[3]	65	526	161	54	105	164	1 111
East South Central	12[3]	34[3]	94	x	x	23[3]	603	231
West South Central	x	64	227	x	93	57	186	604
Mountain	36[3]	51	154	16[1]	23	189	349	818
Pacific	59	135	301	18	12	219	2 042	2 786
Total	**989**	**2 196**	**7 214**	**293**	**181**	**961**	**3 793**	**15 627**
Purpose of Trip (000)								
Business, convention, or employment	57	371	1 027	35	213	171	368	2 050
Visiting friends or relatives	274	378	1 412	63	50	211	594	2 981
Other pleasure, recreation, or holiday	598	1 244	4 029	151	82	448	2 427	8 978
Other	60	203	747	43	293	131	404	1 617
Total	**989**	**2 196**	**7 214**	**293**	**181**	**961**	**3 793**	**15 627**

continued ▶

81. Trip Characteristics of US Residents Entering Canada, Staying One or More Nights in Provinces Visited, 2005 (continued)

	Atlantic Provinces[1]	Québec	Ontario	Manitoba	Saskatchewan	Alberta	British Columbia[2]	Canada
Quarter of Entry (000)								
First	42	399	991	36	10	126	556	2 159
Second	204	552	1 928	85	49	234	982	4 034
Third	623	807	3 054	118	87	462	1 692	6 842
Fourth	121	438	1 241	54	35	139	563	2 591
Total	**989**	**2 196**	**7 214**	**293**	**181**	**961**	**3 793**	**15 627**
Length of Stay (000)								
1 night	164	295	1 789	76	67	126	894	3 412
2 to 6 nights	650	1 700	4 487	175	77	606	2 452	10 148
7 to 13 nights	151	173	788	38	32	202	383	1 768
14 nights and over	23	273	150	x	x	263	65	300
Total	**989**	**2 196**	**7 214**	**293**	**181**	**961**	**3 793**	**15 627**

x = data too small and/or unreliable to be published.
[1]Includes sum of visits to Newfoundland and Labrador, New Brunswick, Nova Scotia, and Prince Edward Island. [2]Includes sum of visits to British Columbia, Yukon Territory, Northwest Territories, and Nunavut. [3]Use data with caution.
SOURCE: Adapted from Statistics Canada, *International Travel*, Catalogue 66-201, 2005, p. 31, table 13, 22 December 2006, http://www.statcan.ca/english/freepub/66-201-XIE/2005000/t014_en.htm.

82. Trip Characteristics of Residents of Countries Other than the US Entering Canada, Staying One or More Nights in Provinces Visited, 2005

	Atlantic Provinces[1]	Québec	Ontario	Manitoba	Saskatchewan	Alberta	British Columbia[2]	Canada
Person-visits (000)	291	1 062	1 989	72	47	821	1 504	5 786
Spending in province ($000 000)	241	1 071	1 792	89	34	829	1 709	5 766
Average spending per person-visit ($)	828	1 009	901	1 235	724	1 010	1 137	997
Person-nights (000)	2 616	12 293	24 247	1 237	540[5]	7 906	19 486	68 325
Average number of nights per visit	9	12	12	17	11[5]	10	13	12
Average spending per person-night ($)	92	87	74	72	63	105	88	84
Area of Residence (000)								
Europe	189	703	1 048	37	30	451	638	3 096
France[3]	x	282	108	x	x	18[5]	21	446
Germany	43	67	123	6[5]	x	87	128	460
Netherlands	9	17	50	x	x	35	50	166
United Kingdom[4]	81	133	430	21	16	226	305	1 211
Other Europe	41	205	337	x	x	84	135	813
Africa	x	35	31	x	x	9	9[5]	91
Asia	39[5]	173	566	17	x	273	634	1 711
China	x	32	64	x	x	18	65	184
Hong Kong	x	11[5]	48	x	x	15	62	139
Japan	x	44	174	10[5]	x	110	213	578
South Korea	x	18[5]	69	x	x	43	107	241
Taiwan	x	x	9[5]	x	x	46	91	150
Other Asia	x	6 4	201	x	x	42	95	418
Central America, Bermuda, and Caribbean	19[5]	27[5]	110	x	x	x	x	173
South America	x	30	84	x	x	7[5]	17[5]	152
North America	16	57	83	x	x	17	59	235
Mexico	x	53	82	x	x	17	59	216
Oceania and other ocean islands	17[5]	37	66	x	x	59	137	327
Australia	15[5]	32	59	x	x	44	114	274
Total	**291**	**1 062**	**1 989**	**72**	**47**	**821**	**1 504**	**5 786**
Purpose of Trip (000)								
Business, convention, or employment	30	206	344	x	6[5]	89	146	826
Visiting friends or relatives	76	303	728	36	18[5]	157	332	1 650
Other pleasure, recreation, or holiday	160	474	733	26	18[5]	515	864	2 790
Other	26	79	184	5[5]	x	60	163	521
Total	**291**	**1 062**	**1 989**	**72**	**47**	**821**	**1 504**	**5 786**
Length of Stay (000)								
1 to 6 nights	164	557	939	30	29	464	783	2 966
7 to 13 nights	75	265	497	13[5]	x	206	359	1 423
14 nights and over	52	240	553	29	11[5]	151	362	1 398
Total	**291**	**1 062**	**1 989**	**72**	**47**	**821**	**1 504**	**5 786**
Quarter of Entry (000)								
First	22	136	224	x	x	106	246	746
Second	85	265	549	19	18	245	400	1 581
Third	161	464	839	30	19[5]	364	626	2 503
Fourth	23	197	376	18	x	105	232	957
Total	**291**	**1 062**	**1 989**	**72**	**47**	**821**	**1 504**	**5 786**

x = data too small and/or unreliable to be published. [1]Includes sum of visits to Newfoundland and Labrador, New Brunswick, Nova Scotia, and Prince Edward Island. [2]Includes sum of visits to British Columbia, Yukon Territory, Northwest Territories, and Nunavut. [3]Includes Andorra and Monaco. [4]Includes Gibraltar. [5]Use data with caution. SOURCE: Adapted from Statistics Canada, *International Travel*, Catalogue 66-201, 2005, p. 36, table 18, 22 December 2006, http://www.statcan.ca/english/freepub/66-201-XIE/2005000/t019_en.htm.

83. Trip Characteristics of Canadian Residents Returning from Countries Other than the US, After a Stay of One or More Nights, by Province of Residence, 2005

	Atlantic Provinces[1]	Québec	Ontario	Manitoba	Saskatchewan	Alberta	British Columbia[2]	Canada
Person-trips (000)	239	1 275	2 975	146	82	569	941	6 229
Spending ($000 000)	342	1 756	4 471	239	127	891	1 602	9 428
Average spending per person-trip ($)	1 430	1 377	1 503	1 630	1 541	1 567	1 702	1 514
Person-nights (000)	3 735	19 954	48 691	2 583	1 420	9 823	20 471	106 676
Average number of nights per trip	15.6	15.6	16.4	17.6	17.2	17.3	21.8	17.1
Average spending per person-night ($)	92	88	92	92	89	91	78	88
Area of Destination (000)								
Europe	83	483	1 249	43[3]	28[3]	155	334	2 375
Africa	x	x	49	x	x	x	14[3]	129
Asia	15[3]	67	357	x	x	85	199	745
Central America	x	x	53[3]	x	x	x	x	83
Bermuda and Caribbean	82	426	671	22[3]	13[3]	99	93	1 406
South America	x	x	70	x	x	x	x	146
Other areas	29[3]	139	305	49	25	151	203	902
Cruises	x	72[3]	219	x	x	44[3]	77	437
Total	**239**	**1 275**	**2 975**	**146**	**82**	**569**	**941**	**6 229**
Purpose of Trip (000)								
Business, convention, or employment	35[3]	141	301	x	x	68	82	647
Visiting friends or relatives	30[3]	124	671	x	x	89	231	1 183
Other pleasure, recreation, or holiday	165	979	1 799	102	54	377	554	4 030
Other	x	x	204	x	x	34[3]	74[3]	369
Total	**239**	**1 275**	**2 975**	**146**	**82**	**569**	**941**	**6 229**
Sex (000								
Male	104	508	1 234	69	33	238	401	2 585
Female	116	633	1 492	66	42	279	470	3 097
Not stated	x	135	250	x	x	52	70	546
Total	**239**	**1 275**	**2 975**	**146**	**82**	**569**	**941**	**6 229**
Age Group (000								
Under 12 years	x	50[3]	114	x	x	25[3]	38[3]	246
12 to 19 years	16[3]	49[3]	115	10[3]	x	30	62	284
20 to 24 years	x	36[3]	98	8[3]	x	29[3]	32[3]	212
25 to 34 years	22[3]	169	315	17[3]	13[3]	70	95	701
35 to 44 years	27	188	371	16[3]	x	75	117	804
45 to 54 years	49	273	545	40	16[3]	128	188	1 238
55 to 64 years	63	259	644	26[3]	19[3]	94	192	1 298
65 years and over	29[3]	116	524	x	10[3]	66	147	901
Not stated	x	135	250	x	x	52	70	546
Total	**239**	**1 275**	**2 975**	**146**	**82**	**569**	**941**	**6 229**
Length of Stay (000)								
1 to 6 nights	x	71	287	x	x	25[3]	33[3]	446
7 to 13 nights	111	581	1 302	72	37	231	319	2 653
14 to 20 nights	56	409	702	33[3]	26[3]	175	285	1 686
21 nights and over	49[3]	214	685	37[3]	x	138	305	1 444
Total	**239**	**1 275**	**2 975**	**146**	**82**	**569**	**941**	**6 229**
Quarter of Re-Entry (000)								
First	76	459	949	71	41	192	281	2 069
Second	80	302	692	32[3]	19[3]	142	218	1 485
Third	54[3]	298	722	x	x	125	229	1 458
Fourth	29[3]	216	613	24[3]	x	110	214	1 217
Total	**239**	**1 275**	**2 975**	**146**	**82**	**569**	**941**	**6 229**

x = data too small and/or unreliable to be published.
[1]Includes Newfoundland and Labrador, New Brunswick, Nova Scotia, and Prince Edward Island. [2]Also includes Yukon Territory, Northwest Territories and Nunavut. [3]Use data with caution.
SOURCE: Adapted from Statistics Canada, *International Travel*, Catalogue 66-201, 2005, p. 46, table 24-3, 22 December 2006, http://www.statcan.ca/english/freepub/66-201-XIE/2005000/t031_en.htm.

84. Trips of One or More Nights between Canada and the US, 1996 to 2005

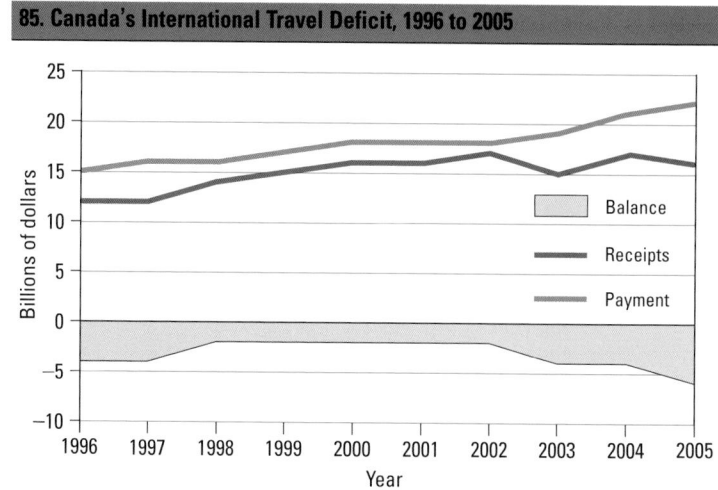

SOURCE: Adapted from Statistics Canada, *International Travel*, Catalogue 66-201, 2005, p. 46, table 6 & p. 26, table 8, 22 December 2006, http://www.statcan.ca/english/freepub/66-201-XIE/2005000/tablesectionlist.htm.

85. Canada's International Travel Deficit, 1996 to 2005

SOURCE: Adapted from Statistics Canada, *International Travel*, Catalogue 66-201, 2005, p. 15, chart 4, 22 December 2006, http://www.statcan.ca/english/freepub/66-201-XIE/2005000/ct004_en.htm.

Environment

86. Biophysical Characteristics of Terrestrial Ecozones

Terrestrial Ecozone	Land Area (km²)	Landforms	Vegetation/Productivity	Surface Materials/Soils	Climate Characteristics
Boreal Shield	1 876 142	Plains; some hills	Evergreen forest; mixed evergreen-deciduous forest	Canadian Shield rock; moraine; lacustrine; podzols;[1] brunisols[2]	Cold; moist
Taiga Shield	1 367 722	Plains; some hills	Open evergreen-deciduous trees; some lichen-shrub tundra	Canadian Shield rock; moraine; cryosols;[3] brunisols[2]	Cold; moist to semi-arid; discontinuous permafrost
Atlantic Maritime	202 619	Hills and coastal plains	Mixed deciduous-evergreen forest stands	Moraine; colluvium; marine; brunisols;[2] podzols;[1] luvisols[4]	Cool; wet
Arctic Cordillera	244 584	Mountains	Mainly unvegetated; some shrub-herb tundra	Ice; snow; colluvium; rock; cryosols[3]	Extremely cold; dry; continuous permafrost
Northern Arctic	1 529 827	Plains; hills	Herb-lichen tundra	Moraine; rock; marine; cryosols[3]	Very cold; dry; continuous permafrost
Southern Arctic	851 673	Plains; hills	Shrub-herb tundra	Moraine; rock; marine; cryosols[3]	Cold; dry; continuous permafrost
Mixedwood Plains	113 971	Plains; some hills	Mixed deciduous-evergreen forest	Moraine; marine; rock; luvisols;[4] brunisols[2]	Cool to mild; moist
Hudson Plains	374 270	Plains	Wetlands; some herb-moss-lichen tundra; evergreen forest	Organic; marine; cryosols[3]	Cold to mild; semi-arid; discontinuous permafrost
Boreal Plains	704 719	Plains; some foothills	Mixed evergreen-deciduous forest	Moraine, lacustrine; organic; luvisols;[4] brunisols[2]	Cold; moist
Prairies	464 070	Plains; some hills	Grass; scattered deciduous forest (aspen parkland)	Moraine; chernozems[5]	Cold; semi-arid
Taiga Plains	610 541	Plains; some foothills	Open to closed mixed evergreen-deciduous forest	Organic; moraine; lacustrine; cryosols;[3] brunisols[2]	Cold; semi-arid to moist; discontinuous permafrost
Montane Cordillera	490 234	Mountains; interior plains	Evergreen forest; alpine tundra; interior grassland	Moraine; colluvium; rock; luvisols;[4] brunisols[2]	Moderately cold; moist to arid
Pacific Maritime	213 000	Mountains; minor coastal plains	Coastal evergreen forest	Colluvium; moraine; rock; podzols;[1] brunisols[2]	Mild; temperate; very wet to cold alpine
Boreal Cordillera	470 476	Mountains; some hills	Largely evergreen forest; some tundra; open woodland	Colluvium; moraine; rock; podzols;[1] cryosols[3]	Moderately cold; moist
Taiga Cordillera	267 283	Mountains	Shrub-herb-moss-lichen tundra	Colluvium; moraine; rock; cryosols;[3] gleysols[6]	Very cold winters; cool summers; minimal precipitation

NOTE: See the maps illustrating Canada's terrestrial ecozones on page 26.
[1]Podzols are acid and well-weathered soils. [2]Brunisols are soils with minimal weathering. [3]Cryosols are frozen soils. [4]Luvisols are temperate-region soils with clay-rich sublayers. [5]Chernozems are organically rich, relatively fertile grassland soils. [6]Gleysols are soils developed under wet conditions and characterized by reduced iron and other elements.
SOURCE: Adapted from: Government of Canada, 1996, *The State of Canada's Environment Part II: Canadian Ecozones*, Minister of Public Works and Government Services Canada, http://www1.ec.gc.ca/~soer/SOE; © Her Majesty The Queen in Right of Canada, Environment Canada, 1996. Reproduced with the permission of the Minister of Public Works and Government Services Canada; Wiken, E.B. et al, 1996, *A Perspective on Canada's Ecosystems: An Overview of the Terrestrial and Marine Ecozones*, Canadian Council on Ecological Areas, Occasional paper No. 14, Ottawa.

87. Greenhouse Gas Emission Trends by Sector, 1990 to 2004

GHG Source/Sink Categories	(megatonnes of CO_2-equivalent emissions)				
	1990	1995	2000	2003	2004
Energy	**475**	**517**	**596**	**622**	**620**
Stationary combustion sources	283	296	347	368	360
Electricity and heat generation	95	101	132	139	130
Fossil fuel industries	53	56	70	77	79
Mining	6	8	10	16	15
Manufacturing industries	55	53	53	50	51
Construction	2	1	1	1	1
Commercial and institutional	26	29	33	38	38
Residential	44	45	45	45	43
Agriculture and forestry	2	3	3	2	2
Transportation[1]	150	160	180	190	190
Domestic aviation	6	6	7	7	8
Road transportation	107	119	131	140	145
Railways	7	6	7	6	6
Domestic marine	5	4	5	6	7
Others	20	30	30	30	30
Fugitive sources	43	57	65	66	67
Coal mining	2	2	0.9	1	1
Oil and natural gas	41	55	64	65	66
Industrial processes	**53**	**56**	**50**	**50**	**54**
Mineral production	8	9	10	9	10
Chemical industry	15	17	7	7	10
Metal production	20	19	19	17	18
Consumption of halocarbons and SF_6	2	2	5	6	6
Other and undifferentiated production	8	9	10	11	12
Solvent and other product use	**0.4**	**0.4**	**0.5**	**0.5**	**0.5**
Agriculture	**45**	**49**	**51**	**53**	**55**
Enteric fermentation	18	21	22	23	24
Manure management	7	7	8	8	8
Agricultural soils	20	21	22	22	22
Waste	**25**	**26**	**28**	**29**	**29**
Solid waste disposal on land	23	25	27	27	27
Wastewater handling	1	1	1	1	1
Waste incineration	0.4	0.3	0.3	0.2	0.3
Land use, land-use change, and forestry	**-82**	**190**	**-130**	**-11**	**81**
Forest land	-110	180	-140	-20	73
Cropland	14	7	3	0.8	0.1
Grassland	-	-	-	-	-
Wetlands	6	3	2	1	1
Settlements	8	7	7	7	7
Total[2]	**599**	**649**	**725**	**754**	**758**

NOTE: Totals may not add due to rounding.
[1]Emissions from fuel ethanol are reported within the gasoline transportation subcategories. [2]National totals exclude all GHGs from the "Land use, land-use change, and forestry" sector.
SOURCE: Adapted from Environment Canada, "National Inventory Report, 1990-2004—Greenhouse Gas Sources and Sinks in Canada", http://www.ec.gc.ca/pdb/ghg/inventory_report/2004_report/ts_3_e.cfm, © Her Majesty The Queen in Right of Canada, Environment Canada, 2006. Reproduced with the permission of the Minister of Public Works and Government Services Canada.

88. Species Extinct, Extirpated, and at Risk in Canada, 2005[1]

Status	Terrestrial Mammals	Marine Mammals	Birds	Fish	Amphibians	Reptiles	Molluscs	Arthropods[2]	Plants	Lichens	Mosses	Total
Extinct	1	1	3	6	0	0	1	0	0	0	1	13
Extirpated	2	2	2	3	1	4	2	3	2	0	1	22
Endangered	9	9	24	26	6	8	12	8	74	2	6	184
Threatened	7	10	10	24	5	13	2	6	48	1	3	129
Special concern	16	12	22	36	7	9	4	2	35	5	4	152
Total	**35**	**34**	**61**	**95**	**19**	**34**	**21**	**19**	**159**	**8**	**15**	**500**

[1]The Status categories are defined on page 25. [2]Formerly described as "lepidopterans".
SOURCE: Adapted from Environment Canada, Canadian Wildlife Service, Committee on the Status of Endangered Wildlife in Canada, 2005, *Canadian Species at Risk*, www.cosewic.gc.ca/eng/sct0/rpt/rpg_csar_e.cfm (accessed March 6, 2006).

89. Selected Environmental Impacts by Type of Transport

	Air	Land	Water	Solid Waste	Noise	Other
Cars and trucks	Air pollution and greenhouse gas emissions	Land taken for highways, roads, parking lots, and other infrastructure; extraction of road building materials; habitat disturbance; corridor creation; release of contaminants (spills, road salt)	Surface and groundwater pollution; modification of water systems through road building	Waste oil, tires and other materials; road vehicles and parts taken out of service	Noise and vibration in cities and along main roads	Animal kills; congestion
Trains	Air pollution and greenhouse gas emissions	Land taken for terminals, track, and rights of way; habitat disturbance; corridor creation	Modification of water systems in railway construction	Rolling stock and related equipment taken out of service	Noise and vibration around terminals and along railway lines	Animal kills
Planes	Air pollution and greenhouse gas emissions	Land taken for terminals and runways; habitat disturbance	Modification of water systems in airport construction	Aircraft and parts taken out of service	Noise and vibration around airports	Bird kills
Water transport	Air pollution and greenhouse gas emissions	Land taken for ports and other infrastructure; habitat disturbance	Release of substances into water (discharge of ballast water, oil spills); modification of water systems in port construction, canal cutting,	Vessels and parts taken out of service	Noise and vibration around terminals and port facilities	Animal kills; introduction of invasive species

SOURCE: United Nations Environment Programme, "Transport and the Environment: Facts and Figures, 1993", *Industry and Environment*, Vol. 16 (January-June), pp. 1-2, as found in Statistics Canada, *Human Activity and the Environment 2000*, Catalogue 11-509.

90. Water Resource Characteristics by Major River Basin

Major River Basin	Total area[1] (km²)	Mean Annual Streamflow		Mean Annual Precipitation		Dams	
		Rate (m³/second)	Total (km³)	Rate (mm)	Volume (km³)	Number	Generating Capacity[2] (MW)
Pacific Coastal	334 452	16 390	516.9	1 354	451	50	1 648
Fraser–Lower Mainland	233 105	3 972	125.3	670	156	24	848
Okanagan–Similkameen	15 603	74	2.3	466	7	3	594
Columbia	87 321	2 009	63.4	776	68	56	5 153
Yukon	332 906	2 506	79.0	346	115	10	76
Peace–Athabasca	485 146	2 903	91.5	497	241	17	3 427
Lower Mackenzie	1 330 481	7 337	231.4	365	486	18	83
Arctic Coast–Islands	1 764 279	8 744	275.8	189	333	0	0
Missouri	27 097	12	0.4	390	11	2	13
North Saskatchewan	150 151	234	7.4	443	67	6	504
South Saskatchewan	177 623	239	7.5	419	74	21	310
Assiniboine–Red	190 705	50	1.6	450	86	3	168
Winnipeg	107 654	758	23.9	683	74	98	905
Lower Saskatchewan–Nelson	360 883	1 911	60.3	508	183	60	4 941
Churchill	313 572	701	22.1	480	151	12	119
Keewatin–Southern Baffin Island	939 568	5 383	169.8	330	310	0	0
Northern Ontario	691 811	5 995	189.1	674	466	60	1 116
Northern Québec	940 194	16 830	530.8	698	656	66	15 238
Great Lakes–St. Lawrence	582 945	7 197	227.0	957	556	623	12 515
North Shore–Gaspé	369 094	8 159	257.3	994	367	129	10 785
Saint John–St. Croix	41 904	779	24.6	1 147	48	54	1 864
Maritime Coastal	122 056	3 628	114.4	1 251	153	60	411
Newfoundland and Labrador	380 355	9 324	294.0	1 030	392	90	6 693
Canada	**9 978 904**	**105 135**	**3 315.5**	**545**	**5 451**	**1 462**	**67 411**

[1]Area includes the Canadian portion of the Great Lakes. [2]The generating capacity refers to the maximum power capability from hydro plants. The survey coverage for those plants is limited to those utilities and companies which have at least one plant with a total generating capacity of over 500 kilowatts.

SOURCE: Environment Canada, 2003, Canadian Climate Normals, 1971 to 2000, Meteorological Service of Canada, *climate.weatheroffice.ec.gc.ca/climate_normals/index_e.html* (accessed 23 Feb 2005). Pearse, P.H., F. Bertrand and J.W. MacLaren, 1985, Currents of Change: Final Report of the Inquiry on Federal Water Policy, Environment Canada, Ottawa. Fernandes, R., G. Pavlic, W. Chen and R. Fraser, 2001, Canada-wide 1-km2 water fraction, National Topographic Database, Natural Resources Canada, *www.nrcan.gc.ca/ess/_portal_esst.cache/gc_ccrs_e* (accessed 23 Feb 2005). Laycock, A.H., 1987, "The Amount of Canadian Water and its Distribution", in Canadian Aquatic Resources, no. 215 of Canadian Bulletin of Fisheries and Aquatic Sciences, M.C. Healey and R.R. Wallace (eds.), 13–42, Fisheries and Oceans Canada, Ottawa. Natural Resources Canada, GeoAccess Division, 2003, 1:1 Million Digital Drainage Area Framework, version 4.8b. Statistics Canada, 2001 Census of Population. "Electric Power Generating Stations", catalogue no. 57-206-X.; Statistics Canada, *Human Activity and the Environment: Annual Statistics 2006*, Catalogue 16-201, pp. 44–45, 9 November 2006, http://www.statcan.ca/english/freepub/16-201-XIE/16-201-XIE2006000.pdf

91. Total Area Protected, by Province and Territory, 1989 and 2003

Province or Territory	1989		2003		Change in Protected Area as a Share of Total Land, 1989 to 2003
	Total Area Protected[1] (ha)	Protected Area as a Share of Total Land (%)	Total Area Protected[1] (ha)	Protected Area as a Share of Total Land (%)	
Newfoundland and Labrador	367 500	0.9	1 701 412	4.3	3.4
Prince Edward Island	6 000	1.0	14 780	2.6	1.5
Nova Scotia	138 700	2.4	465 363	8.2	5.7
New Brunswick	88 800	1.2	233 443	3.1	1.9
Québec	622 800	0.4	5 217 586	3.5	3.1
Ontario	5 152 900	5.2	9 142 039	9.2	4.0
Manitoba	315 400	0.5	5 402 416	8.5	8.0
Saskatchewan	1 936 000	3.0	2 243 230	3.5	0.5
Alberta	5 642 000	8.7	8 009 229	12.3	3.6
British Columbia	4 958 300	5.4	12 017 617	13.0	7.6
Yukon Territory	3 218 300	6.8	5 678 119	12.0	5.2
Northwest Territories and Nunavut	6 978 550	2.0	31 752 615	9.3	7.2
Canada	**29 425 250**	**3.0**	**81 877 849**	**8.4**	**5.4**

[1] Defined by World Wildlife Fund Canada as those areas that are permanently protected through legislation and that prohibit industrial uses such as logging, mining, hydro-electric development, oil and gas and other large scale developments.
SOURCE: World Wildlife Fund Canada, 2000, *Endangered Spaces: The Wilderness Campaign that Changed the Canadian Landscape 1989-2000*, Toronto; World Wildlife Fund Canada, 2003, *The Nature Audit: Setting Canada's Conservation Agenda for the 21st Century*, Toronto; as found in Statistics Canada, Human Activity and the Environment: Annual Statistics 2006, Catalogue 16-201.

Climate

92. Annual Average "Number of Days with" and Hours of Bright Sunshine

Station	Average[1] Number of Days with:[2]								Bright Sunshine[3] (hours)
	Winds (>63 km/h)	Hail[4]	Thunder[5]	Fog[6]	Freezing Temperatures[7]	Freezing Precipitation[8]	Rain[9]	Snow[10]	
Goose Bay	1	*	9	14	215	13	102	97	1 564.9
St. John's	23	*	3	124	176	38	156	88	1 497.4
Charlottetown	6	*	9	47	169	17	124	68	1 818.4
Halifax	3	*	9	122	163	19	125	64	1 885.0
Saint John	6	*	11	106	173	12	124	59	1 865.3
Kuujjuarapik	3	*	6	45	243	10	83	100	1 497.8
Québec	*	*	24	35	180	15	115	73	1 851.7
Sept-Îles	9	*	7	51	206	8	93	72	1 990.6
Montreal	1	*	25	20	155	13	114	62	2 054.0
Ottawa	*	*	24	35	165	16	107	62	2 008.5
Thunder Bay	*	*	26	38	204	8	88	61	2 202.8
Toronto	*	*	27	35	155	10	99	47	2 045.4
Windsor	2	*	33	37	136	9	105	45	n.a.
The Pas	*	*	23	15	209	12	65	73	2 167.5
Winnipeg	1	3	27	20	195	12	72	57	2 321.4
Churchill	11	*	7	48	258	19	58	100	1 827.9
Regina	9	1	23	29	204	14	59	58	2 331.1
Saskatoon	*	*	19	25	202	9	57	59	2 449.7
Calgary	6	3	25	22	201	5	58	62	2 314.4
Edmonton	*	3	22	17	185	8	70	59	2 263.7
Penticton	*	*	12	1	129	1	78	29	2 032.2
Vancouver	*	*	6	45	55	1	156	15	1 919.6
Prince Rupert	4	8	2	37	107	0	218	35	1 224.1
Alert	10	0	0	46	338	5	10	93	1 767.4
Inuvik	*	*	1	24	267	6	36	99	1 898.8
Yellowknife	*	*	5	21	226	13	46	82	2 276.6
Whitehorse	*	*	6	16	224	1	52	120	1 843.8
Resolute	25	0	*	62	324	13	20	82	1 505.1

* = a value less than 0.5 (but not zero); n.a. = not available
[1] Average, mean, or normal refer to the value of the particular element averaged over the period from 1951-1980. [2] A "day with" is counted once per day regardless of the number of individual occurrences of that phenomenon that day. [3] Bright sunshine is reported in hours and tenths. [4] Hail is a piece of ice with a diameter of 5 mm or more. [5] Thunder is reported when thunder is heard or lightning or hail is seen. [6] Fog is a suspension of small water droplets in air that reduces the horizontal visibility at eye level to less than 1 km. [7] Freezing temperature is a temperature below 0°C. [8] Freezing precipitation is rain or drizzle of any quantity that freezes on impact. [9] Rain is a measurable amount of liquid water (rain, showers, or drizzle) equal to or greater than 0.2 mm. [10] Snow is a measurable amount of solid precipitation (snow, snow grains, ice crystals, or ice and snow pellets) equal to or greater than 0.2 cm.
SOURCE: Adapted from David Phillips, *The Climates of Canada*, Catalogue EN56-1/1990E, Ottawa: Canadian Government Publishing, 1990 and the Environment Canada publications *Canadian Climate Normals 1961-1990* and *Principal Station Data*.

93. Average Monthly Precipitation[1] (mm)

Station	Jan	Feb	Mar	Apr	May	June	July	Aug	Sept	Oct	Nov	Dec	Annual
Goose Bay	64.9	57.0	68.6	57.1	66.4	100.9	119.4	98.3	90.6	78.8	79.9	77.6	959.5
St. John's West	179.4	154.9	146.3	124.5	107.0	93.5	77.8	113.8	117.0	149.0	152.8	163.5	1 579.5
Charlottetown	97.1	82.3	83.1	88.3	94.2	87.5	78.5	90.1	91.9	112.4	115.0	116.7	1 137.1
Halifax	146.9	119.1	122.6	124.4	110.5	98.4	96.8	109.6	94.9	128.9	154.4	167.0	1 473.5
Saint John	128.3	102.6	109.9	109.7	123.1	104.8	103.7	103.0	111.3	122.5	146.2	167.6	1 432.8
Kuujjuarapik	28.1	21.1	21.1	25.1	36.4	57.3	72.7	89.0	93.6	73.3	62.1	35.1	614.9
Québec	90.0	74.4	85.0	75.5	99.9	110.2	118.5	119.6	123.7	96.0	106.1	108.9	1 207.7
Sept-Îles	86.8	68.9	80.9	93.4	96.3	92.4	90.8	99.6	111.5	100.8	99.6	107.0	1 127.9
Montreal	63.3	56.4	67.6	74.8	68.3	82.5	85.6	100.3	86.5	75.4	93.4	85.6	939.7
Ottawa	50.8	49.7	56.6	64.8	76.8	84.3	86.5	87.8	83.6	74.7	81.0	72.9	869.5
Thunder Bay	32.4	25.6	40.9	47.1	69.3	84.0	79.9	88.5	86.4	60.9	49.4	39.3	703.5
Toronto	55.2	52.6	65.2	65.4	68.0	67.0	71.0	82.5	76.2	63.3	76.1	76.5	818.9
Windsor	50.3	53.7	72.0	80.3	75.7	97.0	85.3	85.7	86.7	57.9	75.4	81.6	901.6
The Pas	16.6	15.1	21.0	26.2	33.6	63.1	69.1	65.0	58.3	37.5	26.6	19.8	451.9
Winnipeg	19.3	14.8	23.1	35.9	59.8	83.8	72.0	75.3	51.3	29.5	21.2	18.6	504.4
Churchill	17.3	12.8	18.3	22.6	30.5	44.5	50.7	60.5	52.6	46.5	35.5	19.7	411.6
Regina	14.7	13.0	16.5	20.4	50.8	67.3	58.9	40.0	34.4	20.3	11.7	15.9	364.0
Saskatoon	15.9	12.9	16.0	19.7	44.2	63.4	58.0	36.8	32.1	16.9	14.1	17.2	347.2
Calgary	12.2	9.9	14.7	25.1	52.9	76.9	69.9	48.7	48.1	15.5	11.6	13.2	398.8
Edmonton	22.9	15.5	15.9	21.8	42.8	76.1	101.0	69.5	47.5	17.7	16.0	19.2	465.8
Penticton	27.3	20.6	20.4	25.8	33.0	34.4	23.3	28.4	23.0	15.7	24.3	32.1	308.5
Vancouver	149.8	123.6	108.8	75.4	61.7	45.7	36.1	38.1	64.4	115.3	169.9	178.5	1 167.4
Prince Rupert	250.8	216.5	188.2	181.0	142.0	119.5	112.9	162.8	244.7	378.9	284.4	269.8	2 551.6
Alert	7.8	5.2	6.8	9.4	9.9	12.7	25.0	23.8	24.3	13.2	8.8	7.4	154.2
Inuvik	15.6	11.1	10.8	12.6	19.1	22.2	34.1	43.9	24.2	29.6	17.5	16.8	257.4
Yellowknife	14.9	12.6	10.6	10.3	16.6	23.3	35.2	41.7	28.8	34.8	23.9	14.7	267.3
Whitehorse	16.9	11.9	12.1	8.3	14.4	31.2	38.5	39.3	35.2	23.0	18.9	18.9	268.8
Resolute	3.5	3.2	4.7	6.2	8.3	12.7	23.4	31.5	22.8	13.1	5.7	4.6	139.6

These are statistics for the 1961–1990 period.
SOURCE: Adapted from Environment Canada website http://www.msc-smc.ec.gc.ca/climate/climate_normals/index_e.cfm (accessed 2002). © Her Majesty The Queen in Right of Canada, Environment Canada, 2002. Reproduced with the permission of the Minister of Public Works and Government Services Canada.

94. Average Daily Temperature[1] (°C)

Station	Jan	Feb	Mar	Apr	May	June	July	Aug	Sept	Oct	Nov	Dec	Annual
Goose Bay	-17.3	-15.5	-9.2	-1.8	5.1	10.9	15.5	14.2	9.0	2.5	-4.0	-13.4	-0.3
St. John's West	-4.0	-4.6	-2.0	1.8	6.4	11.3	15.8	15.6	11.8	7.3	3.3	-1.4	5.1
Charlottetown	-7.2	-7.5	-3.0	2.7	9.2	14.8	18.8	18.4	14.0	8.6	3.1	-3.6	5.7
Halifax	-5.8	-6.0	-1.7	3.6	9.4	14.7	18.3	18.1	13.8	8.5	3.2	-3.0	6.1
Saint John	-8.2	-7.7	-2.6	3.2	9.1	13.8	16.9	16.7	12.7	7.5	2.1	-5.0	4.9
Kuujjuarapik	-22.8	-23.1	-17.5	-7.1	1.2	6.3	10.2	10.6	7.2	2.1	-5.0	-16.6	-4.5
Québec	-12.4	-11.0	-4.6	3.3	10.8	16.3	19.1	17.6	12.5	6.5	-0.5	-9.1	4.0
Sept-Îles	-14.6	-13.0	-6.8	0.0	5.9	11.6	15.2	14.2	9.2	3.4	-2.7	-11.0	0.9
Montreal	-10.3	-8.8	-2.4	5.7	12.9	18.0	20.8	19.4	14.5	8.3	1.6	-6.9	6.1
Ottawa	-10.7	-9.2	-2.6	5.9	13.0	18.1	20.8	19.4	14.7	8.3	1.5	-7.2	6.0
Thunder Bay	-15.0	-12.8	-5.6	2.7	9.0	13.9	17.7	16.4	11.2	5.4	-2.6	-11.3	2.4
Toronto	-4.5	-3.8	1.0	7.5	13.8	18.9	22.1	21.1	16.9	10.7	4.9	-1.5	8.9
Windsor	-5.0	-3.9	1.7	8.1	14.4	19.7	22.4	21.3	17.4	10.9	4.7	-1.9	9.1
The Pas	-21.4	-17.5	-10.0	0.5	8.7	14.8	17.7	16.4	9.9	3.5	-7.7	-18.0	-0.3
Winnipeg	-18.3	-15.1	-7.0	3.8	11.6	16.9	19.8	18.3	12.4	5.7	-4.7	-14.6	2.4
Churchill	-26.9	-25.4	-20.2	-10.0	-1.1	6.1	11.8	11.3	5.5	-1.4	-12.5	-22.7	-7.1
Regina	-16.5	-12.9	-6.0	4.1	11.4	16.4	19.1	18.1	11.6	5.1	-5.1	-13.6	2.6
Saskatoon	-17.5	-13.9	-7.0	3.9	11.5	16.2	18.6	17.4	11.2	4.8	-6.0	-14.7	2.0
Calgary	-9.6	-6.3	-2.5	4.1	9.7	14.0	16.4	15.7	10.6	5.7	-3.0	-8.3	3.9
Edmonton	-14.2	-10.8	-5.4	3.7	10.3	14.2	16.0	15.0	9.9	4.6	-5.7	-12.2	2.1
Penticton	-2.0	0.7	4.5	8.7	13.3	17.6	20.3	19.9	14.7	8.7	3.2	-1.1	9.0
Vancouver	3.0	4.7	6.3	8.8	12.1	15.2	17.2	17.4	14.3	10.0	6.0	3.5	9.9
Prince Rupert	0.8	2.5	3.7	5.5	8.4	10.9	12.9	13.3	11.3	8.0	3.8	1.7	6.9
Alert	-31.9	-33.6	-33.1	-25.1	-11.6	-1.0	3.4	1.0	-9.7	-19.5	-27.0	-29.5	-18.1
Inuvik	-28.8	-28.5	-24.1	-14.1	-0.7	10.6	13.8	10.5	3.3	-8.2	-21.5	-26.1	-9.5
Yellowknife	-27.9	-24.5	-18.5	-6.2	5.0	13.1	16.5	14.1	6.7	-1.4	-14.8	-24.1	-5.2
Whitehorse	-18.7	-13.1	-7.2	0.3	6.6	11.6	14.0	12.3	7.3	0.7	-10.0	-15.9	-1.0
Resolute	-32.0	-33.0	-31.2	-23.5	-11.0	-0.6	4.0	1.9	-5.0	-15.2	-24.3	-29.0	-16.6

These are statistics for the 1961–1990 period.
SOURCE: Adapted from Environment Canada website http://www.msc-smc.ec.gc.ca/climate/climate_normals/index_e.cfm (accessed 2002). © Her Majesty The Queen in Right of Canada, Environment Canada, 2002. Reproduced with the permission of the Minister of Public Works and Government Services Canada.

The datasets below are explained on pages 190/1

	Land		Population									Employment		
	Area	Arable and permanent crops	Total	Density	Change	Births	Deaths	Fertility	Infant mortality	Life expectancy	Urban	Agriculture	Industry	Services
			2007	2007	1997–2007	2007	2007	2007	2007	2007	2007			
	thousand km²	% of total	millions	persons per km²	%	births per 1000	deaths per 1000	children per mother	per 1000 live births	years	%	%	%	%
Afghanistan	652	12.4	31.9	48.9	43.5	47	21	6.8	166	42	20	∘∘∘	∘∘∘	∘∘∘
Albania	29	24.3	3.6	124.2	5.0	14	6	1.8	8	75	45	55	23	22
Algeria	2382	3.5	33.3	14.0	14.7	21	4	2.4	30	72	58	26	31	43
Andorra	0.5	2.2	0.1	143.6	11.2	11	4	1.3	3	∘∘∘	91	∘∘∘	∘∘∘	∘∘∘
Angola	1247	2.6	12.3	9.8	24.4	49	22	6.8	141	41	40	75	8	17
Antigua and Barbuda	0.4	22.7	0.1	173.7	7.3	21	6	2.3	20	72	39	∘∘∘	∘∘∘	∘∘∘
Argentina	2780	12.6	40.3	14.5	11.3	19	8	2.5	14	75	89	12	32	56
Armenia	30	18.8	3.0	99.1	-2.9	15	9	1.7	26	71	64	18	43	39
Australia	7741	6.3	20.4	2.6	10.1	13	6	1.8	5	81	91	6	26	68
Austria	84	17.4	8.2	97.6	1.6	9	9	1.4	4	80	67	8	38	54
Azerbaijan	87	23.2	8.1	93.3	5.8	18	6	2.1	10	72	52	31	29	40
Bahamas, The	14	0.9	0.3	21.8	8.6	16	7	1.9	13	71	90	5	16	79
Bahrain	0.7	8.5	0.7	1012.2	18.4	21	3	2.6	9	74	100	2	30	68
Bangladesh	144	58.5	150.4	1044.8	22.0	27	8	3.0	65	62	23	65	16	19
Barbados	0.4	39.5	0.3	702.4	4.0	14	8	1.9	14	76	53	14	30	56
Belarus	208	30.4	9.7	46.8	-4.0	9	14	1.2	7	70	73	20	40	40
Belgium	33	25.4	10.4	314.9	1.9	11	10	1.7	4	79	97	3	28	69
Belize	23	4.4	0.3	12.8	28.6	27	5	3.3	25	70	50	33	19	48
Benin	113	25.0	8.1	71.5	33.2	42	12	5.7	98	56	39	63	8	29
Bhutan	47	3.5	2.3	49.5	24.1	20	7	2.9	40	64	31	94	2	4
Bolivia	1099	2.8	9.1	8.3	18.5	29	8	3.7	51	65	63	47	18	35
Bosnia-Herzegovina	51	21.3	4.6	89.3	26.2	9	9	1.2	7	74	46	∘∘∘	∘∘∘	∘∘∘
Botswana	582	0.7	1.8	3.1	17.6	26	27	3.1	56	34	54	46	20	34
Brazil	8547	7.8	190.0	22.2	12.7	21	6	2.3	27	72	81	23	23	54
Brunei	6	1.2	0.4	62.4	23.6	19	3	2.3	7	75	72	2	24	74
Bulgaria	111	32.3	7.3	66.0	-9.2	10	15	1.4	10	73	71	13	48	39
Burkina	274	16.1	14.3	52.3	38.4	45	15	6.2	81	51	16	92	2	6
Burundi	28	48.5	8.4	299.7	37.1	46	16	6.8	107	49	10	92	3	5
Cambodia	181	21.0	14.0	77.3	19.4	26	9	3.4	71	63	15	74	8	18
Cameroon	475	15.1	18.1	38.0	26.4	37	14	4.9	74	50	53	70	9	21
Canada	9971	4.6	33.1	3.5	10.2	11	7	1.5	5	80	81	3	25	72
Cape Verde	4	11.2	0.4	105.9	9.1	30	5	3.5	28	71	56	30	30	40
Central African Republic	623	3.2	4.4	7.0	18.2	38	19	5.0	102	43	38	80	3	17
Chad	1284	2.8	9.9	7.7	36.1	47	16	6.5	102	51	21	83	4	13
Chile	757	3.0	16.3	21.5	11.5	15	5	2.0	8	78	88	19	25	56
China	9598	16.0	1321.9	137.7	6.6	12	7	1.6	27	72	44	72	15	13
Colombia	1139	3.4	44.4	39.0	17.5	20	6	2.4	19	72	72	27	23	50
Comoros	2	59.2	0.7	355.7	34.7	37	7	4.9	59	64	37	78	9	13
Congo	342	0.7	3.8	11.1	35.7	41	14	5.3	75	52	60	49	15	36
Congo, Dem. Rep.	2345	3.3	65.8	28.0	37.0	50	19	6.7	120	45	32	68	13	19
Costa Rica	51	10.3	4.1	81.1	17.5	16	4	1.9	10	79	59	26	27	47
Côte d'Ivoire	322	21.4	18.0	55.9	23.2	38	14	5.0	104	51	47	60	10	30
Croatia	57	28.1	4.5	78.8	1.1	10	12	1.4	6	75	56	16	34	50
Cuba	111	34.2	11.4	102.6	4.0	11	8	1.5	6	77	76	19	30	51
Cyprus	9	12.2	0.8	87.6	6.0	12	6	1.5	6	78	62	14	30	56
Czech Republic	79	41.9	10.2	129.5	-0.7	10	10	1.3	3	76	74	11	45	44
Denmark	43	53.0	5.5	127.2	3.5	12	10	1.9	4	78	72	6	28	66
Djibouti	23	0.04	0.5	21.6	18.8	30	12	4.2	67	54	82	∘∘∘	∘∘∘	∘∘∘
Dominica	0.8	26.7	0.1	90.5	3.0	24	7	3.0	22	74	73	∘∘∘	∘∘∘	∘∘∘
Dominican Republic	49	32.8	9.4	191.1	16.9	24	5	2.9	30	72	65	25	29	46
Ecuador	284	10.5	13.8	48.4	15.5	26	6	3.1	25	75	62	33	19	48
Egypt	1001	3.4	80.3	80.3	21.5	27	6	3.1	33	71	43	40	22	38
El Salvador	21	43.3	6.9	330.9	20.1	25	6	2.9	25	71	59	36	21	43
Equatorial Guinea	28	8.2	0.6	19.7	25.3	40	16	5.6	101	49	39	66	11	23
Eritrea	118	4.3	4.9	41.6	20.9	40	10	5.3	59	57	19	80	5	15

∘∘∘	no data	
per capita	for each person	

Wealth | Energy and trade | Quality of life

GNI	Purchasing power	Growth of PP	Energy consumption	Imports	Exports	Aid received (given)	Human Development Index	Health care	Food consumption	Safe water	Illiteracy male	Illiteracy female	Higher education	Internet users	
2005	2005	2005	2005	2006	2006	2005	2005	2004	2005	2004	2005	2005	2005	2007	
billion US$	US$	annual %	kg oil equivalent per capita	US$ per capita	US$ per capita	million US$		doctors per 100 000 people	daily calories per capita	% access	%	%	students per 100 000 people	users per 10 000 people	
7.0	ooo	ooo	16	95	14	ooo	ooo	ooo	ooo	ooo	ooo	ooo	ooo	111	Afghanistan
8.1	5316	5.2	925	850	220	319	0.801	131	2918	96	1	2	1694	609	Albania
89.3	7062	1.1	1084	652	1660	371	0.733	113	3510	85	20	40	2411	573	Algeria
22.5	2335	1.5	236	967	2917	442	0.446	8	2518	53	17	46	302	64	Angola
															Andorra
0.9	12 500	1.5	2512	8429	929	7	0.815	17	2045	91	ooo	ooo	ooo	4007	Antigua and Barbuda
72.7	14 280	1.1	1892	856	1167	100	0.869	301	2985	96	3	3	ooo	3400	Argentina
4.4	4945	4.4	1597	731	335	193	0.775	359	2380	92	0	1	2872	546	Armenia
73.2	31 794	2.5	6754	6860	6072	(1680)	0.962	247	3330	100	ooo	ooo	5040	7019	Australia
06.2	33 700	1.9	4680	17 105	17 122	(1573)	0.948	338	4023	100	ooo	ooo	2969	5661	Austria
10.6	5016	ooo	1977	650	787	223	0.746	355	2744	77	1	2	1534	803	Azerbaijan
ooo	18 380	0.4	4282	8747	2227	ooo	0.845	105	2521	97	5	5	ooo	6348	Bahamas, The
ooo	21 482	2.3	15 769	12 778	16 518	ooo	0.866	109	ooo	ooo	11	16	2593	2098	Bahrain
66.7	2053	2.9	122	109	80	1321	0.547	26	2309	74	46	59	643	27	Bangladesh
ooo	17 297	1.5	1858	5287	1283	-2	0.892	121	2988	100	0	0	ooo	5985	Barbados
27.0	7918	2.2	2789	2278	2014	54	0.804	455	2885	100	0	1	5406	3507	Belarus
78.7	32 119	1.7	6162	34 012	35 497	(1963)	0.946	449	3109	ooo	ooo	ooo	3718	4850	Belgium
1.0	7109	2.3	1278	2250	887	13	0.778	105	2921	91	ooo	ooo	247	1217	Belize
4.3	1141	1.4	101	125	71	349	0.437	4	2437	67	52	77	ooo	551	Benin
0.8	ooo	5.6	747	139	152	90	0.579	5	ooo	62	ooo	ooo	ooo	308	Bhutan
9.3	2819	1.3	574	313	429	583	0.695	122	2128	85	7	19	3769	506	Bolivia
10.5	7032	12.7	1630	1623	736	546	0.803	134	3068	97	1	6	ooo	1726	Bosnia-Herzegovina
9.8	12 387	4.8	775	1975	2919	71	0.654	40	ooo	95	20	18	620	317	Botswana
25.7	8402	1.1	1252	510	731	192	0.800	115	3244	90	12	11	2293	1720	Brazil
ooo	28 161	-0.8	7593	4325	19 250	ooo	0.894	101	2610	ooo	5	10	1344	3346	Brunei
27.1	9032	1.5	2930	3126	2036	ooo	0.824	356	2839	99	1	2	3074	2867	Bulgaria
5.6	1213	1.3	35	104	32	660	0.370	5	2593	61	69	83	211	52	Burkina
0.7	699	-2.8	25	53	7	365	0.413	3	1693	79	33	48	224	50	Burundi
6.1	2727	5.5	15	353	273	538	0.598	16	2370	41	15	36	404	26	Cambodia
16.4	2299	0.6	135	169	202	414	0.532	19	2634	66	23	40	612	141	Cameroon
52.6	33 375	2.2	11 075	10 805	11 769	(3756)	0.961	214	3486	100	ooo	ooo	4108	6782	Canada
1.0	5803	3.4	203	1355	53	161	0.736	49	2875	80	12	25	771	587	Cape Verde
1.4	1224	-0.6	35	56	28	95	0.384	8	2105	75	35	67	155	33	Central African Republic
4.2	1427	1.7	7	126	379	380	0.388	4	2190	42	59	87	107	45	Chad
98.4	12 027	3.8	1921	2386	3610	152	0.867	109	3079	95	4	4	4073	4235	Chile
73.0	6757	8.8	1279	599	734	1757	0.777	106	2951	77	5	14	1158	1040	China
05.0	7304	0.6	688	597	559	511	0.791	135	2745	93	7	7	2683	1288	Colombia
0.4	1993	-0.4	61	157	16	25	0.561	15	1766	86	36	36	296	293	Comoros
3.8	1262	-1.0	149	459	1730	1449	0.548	20	2026	58	10	21	ooo	132	Congo
6.9	714	-5.2	42	45	37	1828	0.411	11	1398	46	19	46	ooo	23	Congo, Dem. Rep.
20.2	10 180	2.3	1041	2810	2004	30	0.846	132	2618	97	5	5	2559	2048	Costa Rica
15.3	1648	-0.5	156	300	476	119	0.432	12	2268	84	39	61	ooo	99	Côte d'Ivoire
37.1	13 042	2.6	2349	4775	2306	125	0.850	244	2811	100	1	3	2739	3295	Croatia
ooo	6000	3.5	1016	825	235	88	0.838	591	3547	91	0	0	4187	167	Cuba
ooo	22 699	2.3	3990	8660	1666	ooo	0.903	234	3295	100	1	5	2650	3356	Cyprus
14.1	20 538	1.9	4347	9139	9321	ooo	0.891	351	3303	100	ooo	ooo	3286	4995	Czech Republic
61.8	33 973	1.9	3837	15 686	16 864	(2109)	0.949	293	3494	100	ooo	ooo	4288	6918	Denmark
0.8	2178	-2.7	830	692	100	79	0.516	18	2674	73	20	20	214	126	Djibouti
0.3	6393	1.3	678	2357	557	15	0.798	50	3083	97	ooo	ooo	ooo	3462	Dominica
21.8	8217	3.9	774	1216	700	77	0.779	188	2673	95	13	13	3300	1620	Dominican Republic
34.7	4341	0.8	753	892	938	210	0.772	148	2770	94	8	10	ooo	801	Ecuador
92.9	4337	2.4	929	261	174	926	0.708	54	3274	98	17	41	3504	690	Egypt
16.8	5255	1.6	460	1122	517	199	0.735	124	2680	84	18	21	1779	955	El Salvador
2.7	7874	16.6	2492	5000	17 200	39	0.642	30	ooo	43	7	20	ooo	62	Equatorial Guinea
0.8	1109	0.3	61	113	2	355	0.483	5	ooo	60	29	29	105	188	Eritrea

The datasets below are explained on pages 190/1■

	ooo	no data
	per capita	for each person

	Land		Population									Employment		
	Area	Arable and permanent crops	Total	Density	Change	Births	Deaths	Fertility	Infant mortality	Life expectancy	Urban	Agriculture	Industry	Services
			2007	2007	1997–2007	2007	2007	2007	2007	2007	2007			
	thousand km²	% of total	millions	persons per km²	%	births per 1000	deaths per 1000	children per mother	per 1000 live births	years	%	%	%	%
Estonia	45	14.0	1.3	29.2	-6.9	11	13	1.6	4	73	69	14	41	45
Ethiopia	1104	9.7	76.5	69.3	27.8	40	15	5.4	77	49	16	86	2	12
Fiji	18	15.6	0.9	51.0	15.1	21	6	2.5	16	68	51	46	15	39
Finland	338	6.5	5.2	15.5	2.0	11	9	1.8	3	79	62	8	31	61
France	552	35.5	63.7	115.4	5.7	13	9	2.0	4	81	77	5	29	66
French Guiana	91	0.1	0.2	2.2	ooo	31	4	4.0	10	75	76	ooo	ooo	ooo
Gabon	268	1.8	1.5	5.4	29.2	28	12	3.4	62	57	84	51	16	33
Gambia, The	11	22.6	1.7	153.5	36.6	38	11	5.1	75	58	50	82	8	10
Georgia	70	15.3	4.6	66.4	-4.9	11	10	1.3	20	73	52	26	31	43
Germany	357	33.6	82.4	230.8	0.5	8	10	1.3	4	79	75	4	38	58
Ghana	239	26.5	22.9	95.9	24.1	33	10	4.4	59	59	44	59	13	28
Greece	132	29.1	10.7	81.1	1.9	10	9	1.3	4	79	59	23	27	50
Greenland	342	ooo	0.1	0.2	0.5	16	8	2.4	11	70	83	ooo	ooo	ooo
Grenada	0.3	35.3	0.1	299.9	0.0	19	7	2.1	17	65	31	ooo	ooo	ooo
Guatemala	109	17.5	12.7	116.8	21.3	34	6	4.4	34	69	47	52	17	31
Guinea	246	6.3	9.9	40.4	23.6	42	14	5.7	113	54	30	87	2	11
Guinea-Bissau	36	15.2	1.5	40.9	23.3	50	19	7.1	117	46	30	85	2	13
Guyana	215	2.4	0.8	3.6	3.0	21	9	2.7	48	65	28	22	25	53
Haiti	28	39.6	8.7	310.9	24.0	29	11	4.0	57	58	36	68	9	23
Honduras	112	12.7	7.5	66.8	27.5	27	6	3.3	23	71	48	41	20	39
Hungary	93	51.6	10.0	107.1	-2.8	10	13	1.3	6	73	65	15	38	47
Iceland	103	0.07	0.3	2.9	11.3	15	6	2.1	2	81	93	ooo	ooo	ooo
India	3288	51.7	1129.9	343.6	18.7	24	8	2.9	58	64	28	64	16	20
Indonesia	1905	17.7	234.7	123.2	14.8	21	7	2.4	34	69	42	55	14	31
Iran	1633	10.4	65.4	40.0	5.6	18	6	2.0	32	70	67	39	23	38
Iraq	438	13.9	27.5	62.8	32.4	36	11	4.9	94	57	67	16	18	66
Ireland	70	16.0	4.1	58.7	12.0	15	7	1.9	4	78	60	14	29	57
Israel	21	19.2	6.4	306.0	16.2	21	6	2.8	4	80	92	4	29	67
Italy	301	36.7	58.1	193.2	1.2	10	9	1.4	4	81	68	9	31	60
Jamaica	11	25.8	2.8	252.7	9.8	17	6	2.1	24	72	49	25	23	52
Japan	378	12.6	127.4	337.1	1.2	9	9	1.3	3	82	79	7	34	59
Jordan	89	4.5	6.1	68.0	33.7	28	4	3.5	24	72	82	15	23	62
Kazakhstan	2717	8.0	15.3	5.6	-1.3	20	10	2.5	29	66	57	22	32	46
Kenya	580	8.9	36.9	63.6	29.7	40	12	4.9	77	53	19	80	7	13
Kiribati	0.7	50.7	0.1	154.0	25.9	31	8	4.2	43	62	47	ooo	ooo	ooo
Kuwait	18	0.8	2.5	139.2	41.9	21	2	2.6	8	78	98	1	25	74
Kyrgyzstan	199	7.1	5.3	26.6	13.3	23	7	2.8	50	66	35	32	27	41
Laos	237	4.2	6.5	27.5	27.9	36	12	4.8	85	55	21	78	6	16
Latvia	65	28.8	2.3	34.8	-7.2	10	14	1.4	8	72	68	16	40	44
Lebanon	10	30.1	3.9	392.6	14.4	19	5	2.3	17	71	87	7	31	62
Lesotho	30	11.0	2.1	70.8	6.8	28	25	3.5	91	36	13	40	28	32
Liberia	111	5.4	3.2	28.8	45.2	50	19	6.8	138	45	58	ooo	ooo	ooo
Libya	1760	1.2	6.0	3.4	26.8	24	4	3.0	21	73	85	11	23	66
Liechtenstein	0.2	25.0	0.03	171.2	9.4	11	6	1.4	3	80	15	ooo	ooo	ooo
Lithuania	65	45.8	3.6	55.0	-2.4	9	13	1.3	7	71	67	18	41	41
Luxembourg	3	ooo	0.5	160.1	14.1	12	8	1.7	3	78	83	ooo	ooo	ooo
Macedonia, FYRO*	26	23.8	2.1	79.1	3.6	11	9	1.4	13	74	59	21	40	39
Madagascar	587	6.0	19.4	33.1	35.3	40	12	5.2	79	57	26	78	7	15
Malawi	118	20.6	13.6	115.3	26.7	46	18	6.3	96	40	17	87	5	8
Malaysia	330	23.0	24.8	75.2	21.2	23	5	2.9	10	74	62	27	23	50
Maldives	0.3	40.0	0.4	1230.1	34.5	19	3	2.8	15	70	27	32	31	37
Mali	1240	3.8	12.0	9.7	28.0	48	16	6.6	96	53	31	86	2	12
Malta	0.3	31.3	0.4	1339.6	4.9	10	8	1.4	6	80	95	ooo	ooo	ooo
Marshall Islands	0.2	16.7	0.1	309.1	21.6	38	5	4.9	29	70	68	ooo	ooo	ooo
Mauritania	1026	0.5	3.3	3.2	33.8	35	9	4.8	74	62	40	55	10	35

* Former Yugoslav Republic of Macedonia

Wealth | Energy and trade | Quality of life

GNI	Purchasing power	Growth of PP	Energy consumption	Imports	Exports	Aid received (given)	Human Development Index	Health care	Food consumption	Safe water	Illiteracy male	Illiteracy female	Higher education	Internet users	
2005	2005	2005	2005	2006	2006	2005	2005	2004	2005	2004	2005	2005	2005	2007	
billion US$	US$	annual %	kg oil equivalent per capita	US$ per capita	US$ per capita	million US$		doctors per 100 000 people	daily calories per capita	% access	%	%	students per 100 000 people	users per 10 000 people	
12.8	15 478	4.2	4337	10 213	7284	ooo	0.860	448	2744	100	0	0	5034	5176	Estonia
11.3	1055	1.5	31	61	14	1937	0.406	3	1582	22	50	77	268	22	Ethiopia
2.7	6049	1.4	767	2002	754	64	0.762	34	3197	47	4	4	1500	807	Fiji
196.9	32 153	2.5	6012	13 245	14 814	(902)	0.952	316	3387	100	ooo	ooo	5833	6229	Finland
169.2	30 386	1.6	4695	8783	8052	(10 026)	0.952	337	3681	100	ooo	ooo	3593	5027	France
ooo	ooo	ooo	1851	ooo	ooo	ooo	ooo	ooo	ooo	ooo	ooo	ooo	ooo	2049	French Guiana
6.1	6954	-0.4	708	1234	4000	54	0.677	29	2705	88	12	20	ooo	458	Gabon
0.4	1921	0.1	68	159	6	58	0.502	11	2537	82	50	50	101	325	Gambia, The
5.8	3365	0.2	829	783	211	310	0.754	409	1797	82	ooo	ooo	3894	400	Georgia
2875.6	29 461	1.4	4398	11 027	13 495	(10 082)	0.935	337	3472	100	ooo	ooo	ooo	6117	Germany
10.0	2480	2.0	168	244	165	1120	0.553	15	3098	75	34	50	541	184	Ghana
220.3	23 381	2.5	3196	5905	1953	(384)	0.926	438	3706	ooo	2	6	5823	3351	Greece
ooo	ooo	ooo	3632	ooo	ooo	ooo	ooo	ooo	ooo	ooo	ooo	ooo	ooo	6629	Greenland
0.4	7843	2.5	840	3167	222	45	0.777	50	2310	95	ooo	ooo	1881	ooo	Grenada
30.3	4568	1.3	383	954	482	254	0.689	90	2239	95	25	37	ooo	763	Guatemala
3.9	2316	1.2	60	96	100	182	0.456	11	2428	50	57	82	253	61	Guinea
0.3	827	-2.6	82	79	54	79	0.374	12	1949	59	40	40	ooo	208	Guinea-Bissau
0.8	4508	3.2	734	1106	751	137	0.750	48	2853	83	1	1	969	1806	Guyana
3.9	1663	-2.0	80	201	60	515	0.529	25	1945	54	44	44	ooo	712	Haiti
8.0	3430	0.5	399	742	264	681	0.700	57	2435	87	20	20	1705	381	Honduras
102.9	17 887	3.1	2858	7696	7448	ooo	0.874	333	3272	99	ooo	ooo	4322	3039	Hungary
14.4	36 510	2.2	12 238	20 050	11 527	ooo	0.968	362	3189	100	ooo	ooo	5112	8627	Iceland
804.1	3452	4.2	370	157	108	1724	0.619	60	2417	86	27	52	1076	354	India
277.1	3843	2.1	608	347	446	2524	0.728	13	2893	77	6	13	1660	802	Indonesia
177.3	7968	2.3	2660	786	1134	104	0.759	87	3082	94	12	23	3115	1065	Iran
ooo	ooo	ooo	1192	1042	1104	ooo	ooo	ooo	ooo	ooo	ooo	ooo	1630	13	Iraq
171.1	38 505	6.2	3960	17 758	27 089	(719)	0.959	279	3679	ooo	ooo	ooo	4486	5019	Ireland
128.7	25 864	1.5	3080	7810	7258	ooo	0.932	382	3695	100	2	2	4491	5112	Israel
772.9	28 529	1.3	3445	7528	7067	(5091)	0.941	420	3730	ooo	1	2	3438	5166	Italy
9.1	4291	0.7	1505	2017	707	36	0.736	85	2826	93	26	14	ooo	3937	Jamaica
4976.5	31 267	0.8	4416	4546	5097	(13 147)	0.953	198	2679	100	ooo	ooo	3161	6708	Japan
13.5	5530	1.6	1318	1940	877	622	0.773	203	2741	97	5	13	3980	1171	Jordan
44.6	7857	2.0	4686	1642	2663	229	0.794	354	3200	86	0	1	4973	273	Kazakhstan
18.5	1240	-0.1	135	204	96	768	0.521	14	1881	61	22	30	300	317	Kenya
0.1	ooo	ooo	115	634	63	ooo	ooo	ooo	2333	ooo	ooo	ooo	ooo	214	Kiribati
77.7	26 321	0.6	11 476	6663	23 197	ooo	0.891	153	ooo	ooo	6	9	1524	2564	Kuwait
2.3	1927	-1.3	1004	330	153	269	0.696	251	3052	77	1	2	4286	515	Kyrgyzstan
2.6	2039	3.8	120	166	137	296	0.601	ooo	3064	51	23	39	801	43	Laos
15.6	13 646	3.6	1985	5004	2675	ooo	0.855	301	2586	99	0	0	5682	4519	Latvia
22.1	5584	2.8	1655	2474	722	243	0.772	325	3009	100	6	6	4633	1536	Lebanon
1.7	3335	2.3	90	733	347	69	0.549	5	ooo	79	26	10	441	171	Lesotho
0.4	ooo	ooo	57	148	60	ooo	ooo	ooo	1943	ooo	ooo	ooo	ooo	3	Liberia
34.7	10 335	ooo	3332	1178	6695	24	0.818	129	2892	ooo	7	25	6407	326	Libya
ooo	ooo	ooo	ooo	ooo	ooo	ooo	ooo	ooo	ooo	ooo	ooo	ooo	ooo	6176	Liechtenstein
23.6	14 494	1.9	2414	5361	3920	ooo	0.862	397	3196	ooo	0	0	5723	3589	Lithuania
31.4	60 228	3.3	11 060	53 310	45 690	(256)	0.944	266	ooo	100	ooo	ooo	666	6799	Luxembourg
5.7	7200	-0.1	1471	1792	1143	230	0.801	219	2631	ooo	2	6	2427	1909	Macedonia, FYRO*
5.4	923	-0.7	57	79	50	929	0.533	29	2148	50	24	35	242	53	Madagascar
2.1	667	1.0	51	91	41	575	0.437	2	1729	73	25	46	39	45	Malawi
126.1	10 882	3.3	2511	5375	6585	32	0.811	70	3013	99	8	15	2884	4781	Malaysia
0.8	5261	3.8	802	2361	563	67	0.741	92	2791	83	4	4	22	545	Maldives
5.2	1033	2.2	22	159	115	692	0.380	8	2306	50	68	84	241	55	Mali
5.5	19 189	2.7	2522	9940	6663	ooo	0.878	318	3451	100	14	11	2340	3165	Malta
0.2	ooo	ooo	ooo	ooo	ooo	ooo	ooo	ooo	ooo	ooo	ooo	ooo	ooo	397	Marshall Islands
1.8	2234	0.3	341	304	403	190	0.550	11	2371	53	41	57	285	68	Mauritania

The datasets below are explained on pages 190/19

	○○○ no data
	per capita for each person

	Land		Population									Employment		
	Area	Arable and permanent crops	Total	Density	Change	Births	Deaths	Fertility	Infant mortality	Life expectancy	Urban	Agriculture	Industry	Services
			2007	2007	1997–2007	2007	2007	2007	2007	2007	2007			
	thousand km²	% of total	millions	persons per km²	%	births per 1000	deaths per 1000	children per mother	per 1000 live births	years	%	%	%	%
Mauritius	2	52.0	1.3	625.4	8.8	14	7	1.7	14	72	42	17	43	40
Mexico	1958	13.9	108.7	55.5	13.4	21	5	2.4	21	75	75	28	24	48
Micronesia, Fed. States	0.7	51.4	0.1	154.1	0.9	26	6	4.1	40	67	22	○○○	○○○	○○○
Moldova	34	64.3	4.3	127.3	-2.0	11	12	1.3	12	69	45	33	30	37
Mongolia	1567	0.8	3.0	1.9	16.2	18	6	2.0	41	66	59	32	22	46
Montenegro	14	○○○	0.7	48.9	-1.1	12	9	1.6	10	73	64	○○○	○○○	○○○
Morocco	447	20.8	33.8	75.5	18.3	21	6	2.4	38	70	55	45	25	30
Mozambique	802	5.5	20.9	26.1	24.7	41	20	5.4	108	43	35	83	8	9
Myanmar	677	15.7	47.4	70.0	10.6	20	10	2.3	75	60	29	73	10	17
Namibia	824	1.0	2.1	2.5	15.8	27	13	3.6	55	52	33	49	15	36
Nauru	0.02	○○○	0.01	676.4	21.7	26	7	3.4	42	62	100	○○○	○○○	○○○
Nepal	147	22.4	28.9	196.6	25.7	28	9	3.1	51	62	14	94	0	6
Netherlands	41	22.9	16.6	404.2	6.2	11	8	1.7	4	80	65	5	26	69
New Zealand	271	12.5	4.1	15.2	12.0	14	7	2.0	5	80	86	10	25	65
Nicaragua	130	16.6	5.7	43.7	23.1	28	5	3.2	26	71	59	28	26	46
Niger	1267	3.6	12.9	10.2	33.4	48	15	7.1	126	56	17	90	4	6
Nigeria	924	35.7	135.0	146.1	27.1	43	18	5.9	100	47	44	43	7	50
Northern Marianas	0.5	17.4	0.1	169.1	35.5	17	2	1.2	7	75	90	○○○	○○○	○○○
North Korea	121	22.4	23.3	192.6	8.0	16	7	2.0	21	71	60	38	32	30
Norway	324	2.7	4.6	14.3	5.0	13	9	1.9	3	80	78	6	25	69
Oman	213	0.3	3.2	15.0	40.3	25	3	3.4	10	74	71	44	24	32
Pakistan	796	27.8	164.7	207.0	23.0	31	8	4.1	78	62	34	52	19	29
Palau	0.5	21.7	0.02	41.7	17.4	14	7	2.1	18	71	77	○○○	○○○	○○○
Panama	76	9.2	3.2	42.7	18.6	20	4	2.4	15	75	64	26	16	58
Papua New Guinea	463	1.9	5.8	12.5	26.8	32	10	4.1	64	57	13	79	7	14
Paraguay	407	7.7	6.7	16.4	29.2	27	6	3.5	36	71	57	39	22	39
Peru	1285	3.4	28.7	22.3	15.9	21	6	2.5	24	70	73	36	18	46
Philippines	300	35.7	91.1	303.6	21.4	27	5	3.4	27	69	48	46	15	39
Poland	323	45.5	38.5	119.3	-0.4	10	10	1.3	6	75	62	27	36	37
Portugal	92	29.4	10.6	115.7	4.8	10	10	1.4	4	78	55	18	34	48
Qatar	11	1.9	0.9	82.5	35.9	17	2	2.8	7	73	100	3	32	65
Romania	238	41.5	22.3	93.6	-1.3	10	12	1.3	14	71	55	24	47	29
Russian Federation	17 075	7.4	141.4	8.3	-4.5	10	15	1.3	10	65	73	14	42	44
Rwanda	26	52.6	9.9	381.1	30.7	43	16	6.1	86	47	17	92	3	5
St. Kitts and Nevis	0.4	22.2	0.04	98.4	0.1	18	9	2.3	15	70	32	○○○	○○○	○○○
St. Lucia	0.6	29.0	0.2	284.4	13.2	15	7	1.7	19	74	28	○○○	○○○	○○○
St. Vincent & the Grenadines	0.4	35.9	0.1	295.4	4.2	18	7	2.0	18	71	45	○○○	○○○	○○○
Samoa	3.0	45.4	0.2	71.4	12.8	29	6	4.4	20	73	22	○○○	○○○	○○○
San Marino	0.06	16.7	0.03	493.6	15.1	10	6	1.2	3	81	84	○○○	○○○	○○○
Sao Tome and Principe	1.0	56.3	0.2	199.6	37.1	35	8	4.1	77	64	58	○○○	○○○	○○○
Saudi Arabia	2150	1.8	27.6	12.8	30.0	30	3	4.1	16	75	81	19	20	61
Senegal	197	12.7	12.5	63.6	31.4	39	10	5.3	61	62	41	77	8	15
Serbia*	88	○○○	10.2	115.3	-1.8	11	12	1.8	13	72	52	○○○	○○○	○○○
Seychelles	0.5	15.6	0.1	163.8	5.0	17	8	2.1	11	72	53	○○○	○○○	○○○
Sierra Leone	72	8.4	6.1	85.3	34.2	46	23	6.1	158	48	36	68	15	17
Singapore	1	1.6	4.6	4553.0	19.7	10	4	1.3	3	80	100	0	36	64
Slovakia	49	31.8	5.4	111.2	1.2	10	10	1.3	7	74	56	12	32	56
Slovenia	20	9.8	2.0	100.5	-0.1	9	9	1.3	3	78	49	6	46	48
Solomon Islands	29	2.6	0.6	19.5	33.6	34	8	4.5	48	62	17	77	7	16
Somalia	638	1.7	9.1	14.3	37.5	46	17	6.8	117	48	34	○○○	○○○	○○○
South Africa	1221	12.9	44.0	36.0	2.7	23	15	2.7	43	51	53	14	32	54
South Korea	99	18.9	49.0	495.4	6.2	9	5	1.1	5	79	82	12	35	47
Spain	506	37.0	40.4	79.9	1.5	11	8	1.4	4	80	77	12	33	55
Sri Lanka	66	29.2	20.9	317.1	10.9	18	7	2.0	11	74	15	48	21	31
Sudan	2506	6.6	39.4	15.7	24.7	33	11	4.5	69	58	41	70	8	22

* includes data for the Republic of Kosovo

Wealth | Energy and trade | Quality of life

GNI	Purchasing power	Growth of PP	Energy consumption	Imports	Exports	Aid received (given)	Human Development Index	Health care	Food consumption	Safe water	Illiteracy male	Illiteracy female	Higher education	Internet users	
2005	2005	2005	2005	2006	2006	2005	2005	2004	2005	2004	2005	2005	2005	2007	
billion US$	US$	annual %	kg oil equivalent per capita	US$ per capita	US$ per capita	million US$		doctors per 100 000 people	daily calories per capita	% access	%	%	students per 100 000 people	users per 10 000 people	
6.5	12 715	3.8	1120	3025	1811	32	0.804	106	3097	100	12	20	1355	2398	Mauritius
52.8	10 751	1.5	1668	2497	2332	189	0.829	198	3117	97	7	10	2313	2132	Mexico
0.3	○○○	○○○	○○○	○○○	○○○	○○○	○○○	○○○	○○○	○○○	○○○	○○○	○○○	1454	Micronesia, Fed. States
3.3	2100	-3.5	823	626	245	192	0.708	264	2953	92	0	1	2818	1476	Moldova
1.9	2107	2.2	885	531	551	212	0.700	263	1995	62	2	3	4848	1031	Mongolia
2.0	○○○	○○○	○○○	2544	921	○○○	○○○	○○○	2679	○○○	○○○	○○○	○○○	1757	Montenegro
52.6	4555	1.5	463	710	383	652	0.646	51	3256	81	34	60	1216	1506	Morocco
6.2	1242	4.3	199	137	117	1286	0.384	3	2392	43	45	75	143	68	Mozambique
○○○	1027	6.6	125	52	90	145	0.583	36	3305	78	6	14	○○○	55	Myanmar
6.0	7586	1.4	727	1460	1324	123	0.650	30	○○○	87	13	17	668	360	Namibia
○○○	○○○	○○○	4448	○○○	○○○	○○○	○○○	○○○	○○○	○○○	○○○	○○○	○○○	263	Nauru
7.4	1550	2.0	60	74	27	428	0.534	21	2341	90	37	65	○○○	87	Nepal
42.0	32 684	1.9	6496	25 239	28 025	(5115)	0.953	315	3427	100	○○○	○○○	3462	7332	Netherlands
6.3	24 996	2.1	5201	6447	5471	(274)	0.943	237	3337	○○○	○○○	○○○	5855	7486	New Zealand
4.9	3674	1.8	342	534	183	740	0.710	37	2402	79	23	23	○○○	246	Nicaragua
3.4	781	-0.5	30	76	43	515	0.374	2	1897	46	57	85	77	23	Niger
3.1	1128	0.8	203	165	394	6437	0.470	28	2848	48	22	40	981	308	Nigeria
○○○	○○○	○○○	○○○	○○○	○○○	○○○	○○○	○○○	○○○	○○○	○○○	○○○	○○○	1187	Northern Marianas
○○○	○○○	○○○	1023	○○○	○○○	○○○	○○○	○○○	2291	○○○	○○○	○○○	○○○	○○○	North Korea
31.5	41 420	2.7	11 318	13 939	26 414	(2786)	0.968	313	3366	100	○○○	○○○	4627	6742	Norway
○○○	15 602	1.8	4650	3521	6963	31	0.814	132	○○○	○○○	13	27	1889	1162	Oman
8.2	2370	1.3	362	180	102	1667	0.551	74	2446	91	36	65	502	715	Pakistan
0.2	○○○	○○○	○○○	○○○	○○○	○○○	○○○	○○○	○○○	○○○	○○○	○○○	○○○	○○○	Palau
5.0	7605	2.2	1791	1520	328	20	0.812	150	2681	90	8	9	3907	946	Panama
4.1	2563	0.2	294	395	723	266	0.530	5	○○○	39	37	49	○○○	276	Papua New Guinea
6.7	4642	-0.6	1748	904	293	51	0.755	111	3101	86	6	7	2528	348	Paraguay
4.0	6039	2.2	570	542	828	398	0.773	117	2411	83	6	18	3251	1591	Peru
7.2	5137	1.6	402	576	526	562	0.771	58	2497	85	8	6	2893	896	Philippines
2.8	13 847	4.3	2398	3273	2865	○○○	0.870	247	3596	○○○	○○○	○○○	5550	2991	Poland
1.3	20 410	2.1	2631	6285	4087	(377)	0.897	342	3547	○○○	4	8	3611	7384	Portugal
○○○	27 664	○○○	26 555	18 266	37 834	○○○	0.875	222	○○○	100	11	11	1201	2657	Qatar
2.8	9060	1.6	2002	2292	1450	○○○	0.813	190	4125	57	2	4	3415	2335	Romania
9.3	10 845	-0.1	5292	1153	2143	○○○	0.802	425	3005	97	0	1	6291	1653	Russian Federation
2.1	1206	0.1	34	52	14	576	0.452	5	1980	74	29	40	292	56	Rwanda
0.4	13 307	2.9	967	7000	782	4	0.821	119	2798	100	○○○	○○○	○○○	2539	St. Kitts and Nevis
0.8	6707	0.9	818	2960	300	11	0.795	517	2159	98	○○○	○○○	1333	3243	St. Lucia
0.4	6568	1.6	699	2750	200	5	0.761	87	○○○	○○○	○○○	○○○	○○○	794	St. Vincent & the Grenadines
0.4	6170	2.5	357	1094	53	44	0.785	70	3093	88	1	2	○○○	433	Samoa
○○○	○○○	○○○	○○○	○○○	○○○	○○○	○○○	○○○	○○○	○○○	○○○	○○○	○○○	5200	San Marino
○○○	2178	0.5	232	354	19	32	0.654	49	○○○	79	8	22	○○○	1453	Sao Tome and Principe
9.2	15 711	0.1	7198	2456	7759	26	0.812	137	2631	○○○	13	24	2611	1055	Saudi Arabia
8.2	1792	1.2	173	281	127	689	0.499	6	2228	76	49	71	507	488	Senegal
6.0	○○○	○○○	○○○	1304	636	○○○	○○○	○○○	2679	○○○	○○○	○○○	○○○	1388	Serbia
0.7	16 106	1.5	3922	7640	4230	19	0.843	151	2992	88	9	8	○○○	3541	Seychelles
1.2	806	-1.4	78	65	36	343	0.336	3	○○○	57	53	76	○○○	19	Sierra Leone
5.6	29 663	3.6	11 649	53 034	60 394	○○○	0.922	140	○○○	100	3	11	○○○	5319	Singapore
3.6	15 871	2.8	3716	8494	7726	○○○	0.863	318	2615	100	○○○	○○○	3368	4647	Slovakia
4.9	22 273	3.2	3953	12 052	11 629	○○○	0.917	225	3087	○○○	0	0	5610	5553	Slovenia
0.3	2031	-2.4	141	333	201	198	0.602	13	2262	70	○○○	○○○	○○○	171	Solomon Islands
○○○	○○○	○○○	32	74	33	○○○	○○○	○○○	○○○	○○○	○○○	○○○	○○○	72	Somalia
5.8	11 110	0.6	2688	1748	1322	700	0.674	77	2874	88	16	19	1568	1027	South Africa
6.9	22 029	4.5	4802	6340	6669	○○○	0.921	157	2969	92	○○○	○○○	6678	6651	South Korea
5.9	27 169	2.5	3795	7833	5086	(3018)	0.949	330	3285	100	○○○	○○○	4169	4392	Spain
2.9	4595	3.7	271	496	333	1189	0.743	55	2200	79	8	11	○○○	141	Sri Lanka
3.4	2083	3.5	113	196	137	1829	0.526	22	2444	70	29	48	○○○	765	Sudan

	○○○	no data
	per capita	for each person

Land

Population

Employment

	Area	Arable and permanent crops	Total	Density	Change	Births	Deaths	Fertility	Infant mortality	Life expectancy	Urban	Agriculture	Industry	Service
			2007	2007	1997–2007	2007	2007	2007	2007	2007	2007			
	thousand km²	% of total	millions	persons per km²	%	births per 1000	deaths per 1000	children per mother	per 1000 live births	years	%	%	%	%
Suriname	163	0.4	0.5	2.9	13.9	21	7	2.5	20	69	74	21	18	61
Swaziland	17	10.9	1.1	66.7	7.5	28	29	3.6	73	33	23	40	22	38
Sweden	450	6.0	9.0	20.1	1.5	12	10	1.9	3	81	84	○○○	○○○	○○○
Switzerland	41	10.5	7.6	184.3	5.0	10	8	1.4	4	81	68	6	35	59
Syria	185	29.3	19.3	104.4	28.1	28	4	3.5	19	73	50	33	24	43
Taiwan	36	○○○	22.9	635.0	5.6	9	6	1.1	5	77	78	○○○	○○○	○○○
Tajikistan	143	7.4	7.1	49.5	20.7	26	7	3.4	65	64	26	41	23	36
Tanzania	945	5.4	39.4	41.7	26.7	40	15	5.4	78	50	23	84	5	11
Thailand	513	37.7	65.1	126.8	8.1	14	7	1.7	20	71	33	64	14	22
Togo	57	46.3	5.7	100.0	32.0	38	10	5.1	91	58	40	66	10	24
Tonga	0.8	64.0	0.1	146.2	20.0	27	6	3.6	12	71	24	○○○	○○○	○○○
Trinidad and Tobago	5	23.8	1.1	211.3	-7.2	14	8	1.6	15	69	12	11	31	58
Tunisia	164	30.0	10.3	62.7	11.3	17	6	2.0	20	74	65	28	33	39
Turkey	775	36.8	71.2	91.8	12.9	19	6	2.2	23	72	66	53	18	29
Turkmenistan	488	3.9	5.1	10.4	19.5	25	8	2.9	74	62	47	37	23	40
Tuvalu	0.02	○○○	0.01	599.6	15.6	27	10	3.7	35	64	47	○○○	○○○	○○○
Uganda	241	29.9	30.3	125.6	38.4	48	16	6.7	83	47	12	85	5	10
Ukraine	604	55.7	46.3	76.7	-8.1	10	16	1.3	10	68	68	20	40	40
United Arab Emirates	84	3.2	4.4	52.9	61.8	17	2	2.7	9	79	74	8	27	65
United Kingdom	245	23.9	60.8	248.1	3.3	12	10	1.8	5	79	90	2	29	69
United States of America	9364	18.5	301.1	32.2	10.3	14	8	2.1	7	78	79	3	28	69
Uruguay	177	7.6	3.5	19.6	5.9	15	9	2.1	15	75	93	14	27	59
Uzbekistan	447	10.8	27.8	62.1	17.7	24	7	2.7	58	67	36	34	25	41
Vanuatu	12	9.8	0.2	17.7	18.1	31	6	4.0	27	67	21	○○○	○○○	○○○
Venezuela	912	3.7	26.0	28.5	16.4	22	5	2.7	18	73	88	12	27	61
Vietnam	332	26.8	85.3	256.8	12.1	19	5	2.1	18	72	27	71	14	15
Western Sahara	252	0.008	0.4	1.5	36.6	28	8	2.9	49	65	92	○○○	○○○	○○○
Yemen	528	3.2	22.2	42.1	40.4	40	9	6.2	75	60	26	61	17	22
Zambia	753	7.0	11.5	15.2	20.4	41	22	5.5	100	38	35	75	8	17
Zimbabwe	391	8.6	12.3	31.5	7.9	31	21	3.8	60	37	36	68	8	24

Explanation of datasets

Land

Area is a country's total area, including areas under inland bodies of water and coastal waterways

Arable and permanent crops percentage of total land area used for arable and permanent crops

Population

Total estimate for mid 2007

Density the total population of a country divided by its land area

Change percentage change in population between 1997 and 2007. Negative numbers indicate a decrease

Births number of births per one thousand people in one year

Deaths number of deaths per one thousand people in one year

Fertility average number of children born to child bearing women

Infant mortality number of deaths of children under one year per 1000 live births

Life expectancy number of years a baby born now can expect to live

Urban percentage of the population living in towns and cities

Employment

Agriculture percentage of the labour force employed in agriculture

Industry percentage of the labour force employed in industry

Services percentage of the labour force employed in services

Wealth | Energy and trade | Quality of life

GNI million US$	Purchasing power US$	Growth of PP annual %	Energy consumption kg oil equivalent per capita	Imports US$ per capita	Exports US$ per capita	Aid received (given) million US$	Human Development Index	Health care doctors per 100 000 people	Food consumption daily calories per capita	Safe water % access	Illiteracy male %	Illiteracy female %	Higher education students per 100 000 people	Internet users users per 10 000 people	
2005	2005	2005	2005	2006	2006	2005	2005	2004	2005	2004	2005	2005	2005	2007	
1.1	7722	1.1	2204	1640	2400	44	0.774	45	3424	92	8	13	ooo	632	Suriname
2.5	4824	0.2	422	2000	1873	46	0.547	16	ooo	62	19	22	521	307	Swaziland
69.1	32 525	2.1	6481	14 082	16 375	(3362)	0.956	328	3108	100	ooo	ooo	4729	7565	Sweden
11.4	35 633	0.6	4272	18 850	19 661	(1767)	0.955	361	3306	100	ooo	ooo	2685	6776	Switzerland
27.0	3808	1.4	1039	512	463	78	0.724	140	2906	93	12	26	ooo	564	Syria
ooo	ooo	ooo	4912	8827	9729	ooo	ooo	ooo	ooo	ooo	ooo	ooo	ooo	6304	Taiwan
2.2	1356	-4.0	1073	250	203	241	0.673	203	ooo	59	0	1	1834	7	Tajikistan
12.7	744	1.7	47	114	45	1505	0.467	2	2131	62	23	38	133	86	Tanzania
74.6	8677	2.7	1411	1991	2025	-171	0.781	37	2657	99	5	10	3673	1252	Thailand
2.1	1506	ooo	146	200	112	87	0.512	4	1895	52	31	62	ooo	543	Togo
0.2	8177	1.9	439	1194	117	32	0.819	34	ooo	100	1	1	642	298	Tonga
14.2	14 603	4.3	12 624	5895	12 861	-2	0.814	79	2805	91	1	2	1296	1203	Trinidad and Tobago
28.8	8371	3.3	897	1457	1129	377	0.766	134	3484	93	17	35	3107	921	Tunisia
42.2	8407	1.7	1297	1964	1214	464	0.775	135	3212	96	5	20	2923	2109	Turkey
ooo	3838	-6.8	4419	811	1052	28	0.713	418	3112	72	1	2	ooo	52	Turkmenistan
ooo	ooo	ooo	ooo	1900	170	ooo	ooo	ooo	ooo	ooo	ooo	ooo	ooo	1724	Tuvalu
8.0	1454	3.2	36	86	34	1198	0.505	8	2392	60	23	42	ooo	175	Uganda
72.6	6848	-2.4	3297	966	823	410	0.788	295	2865	96	0	1	5533	1152	Ukraine
ooo	25 514	-0.9	12 702	37 598	53 597	ooo	0.868	202	2446	100	11	12	1504	3509	United Arab Emirates
73.7	33 238	2.5	4157	10 221	7398	(10 767)	0.946	230	3424	100	ooo	ooo	3798	6229	United Kingdom
12.9	41 890	2.1	8493	6432	3479	(27 622)	0.951	256	3637	100	ooo	ooo	5827	6991	United States of America
15.1	9962	0.8	1118	1399	1163	15	0.852	365	3066	100	4	3	2987	2042	Uruguay
13.8	2063	0.3	2060	146	206	172	0.702	274	2074	82	ooo	ooo	1558	331	Uzbekistan
0.3	3225	ooo	158	700	250	40	0.674	11	2187	60	ooo	ooo	452	337	Vanuatu
31.2	6632	-1.0	2951	1308	2537	49	0.792	194	2509	83	7	7	3950	1284	Venezuela
51.3	3071	5.9	368	526	469	1905	0.733	53	2762	85	6	13	1630	1754	Vietnam
ooo	ooo	ooo	344	ooo	ooo	ooo	ooo	ooo	ooo	ooo	ooo	ooo	ooo	ooo	Western Sahara
13.8	930	1.5	306	230	339	336	0.508	33	1590	67	27	65	959	103	Yemen
5.8	1023	-0.3	261	258	326	945	0.434	12	ooo	58	24	40	ooo	201	Zambia
4.5	2038	-2.1	391	184	160	368	0.513	16	1870	81	7	14	ooo	968	Zimbabwe

Explanation of datasets

Wealth

GNI   Gross National Income (GNI) is the total value of goods and services produced in a country plus income from abroad.

Purchasing power   Gross Domestic Product (GDP) is the total value of goods and services produced in a country. Purchasing power parity (PPP) is GDP per person, adjusted for the local cost of living

Growth of PP   average annual growth (or decline, shown as a negative value in the table) in purchasing power. This figure shows whether people are becoming better or worse off

Energy and trade

Energy consumption   consumption of commercial energy per person shown as the equivalent in kilograms of oil

Imports   total value of imports per person shown in US dollars

Exports   total value of exports per person shown in US dollars

Aid received (given)   amount of economic aid a country has received. Negative values indicate that the repayment of loans exceeds the amount of aid received. Figures in brackets show aid given

Quality of life

HDI   Human Development Index (HDI) measures the relative social and economic progress of a country. It combines life expectancy, adult literacy, average number of years of schooling, and purchasing power. Economically more developed countries have an HDI approaching 1.0. Economically less developed countries have an HDI approaching 0.

Health care   number of doctors in each country per 100 000 people

Food consumption   average number of calories consumed by each person each day

Safe water   percentage of the population with access to safe drinking water

Illiteracy   percentage of men and women who are unable to read and write

Higher education   number of students in higher education per 100 000 people

Internet users   the number of internet users per 10 000 people

How to use the gazetteer

To find a place on an atlas map use either the grid code or latitude and longitude.

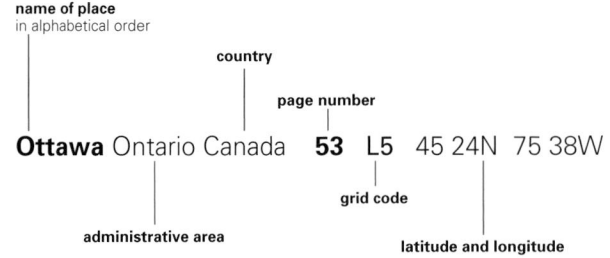

name of place
in alphabetical order

country

page number

Ottawa Ontario Canada **53** L5 45 24N 75 38W

administrative area

grid code

latitude and longitude

Grid code

Ottawa Ontario Canada **53** | L5 | 45 24N 75 38W

Ottawa is in grid square L5

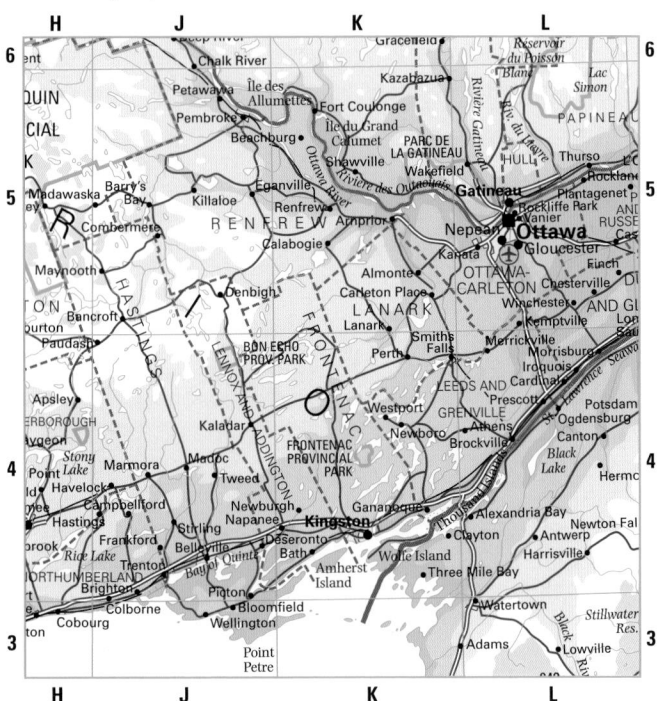

Latitude and longitude

Ottawa Ontario Canada **53** L5 | 45 24N 75 38W |

Ottawa is at latitude 45 degrees, 24 minutes north and 75 degrees, 38 minutes west

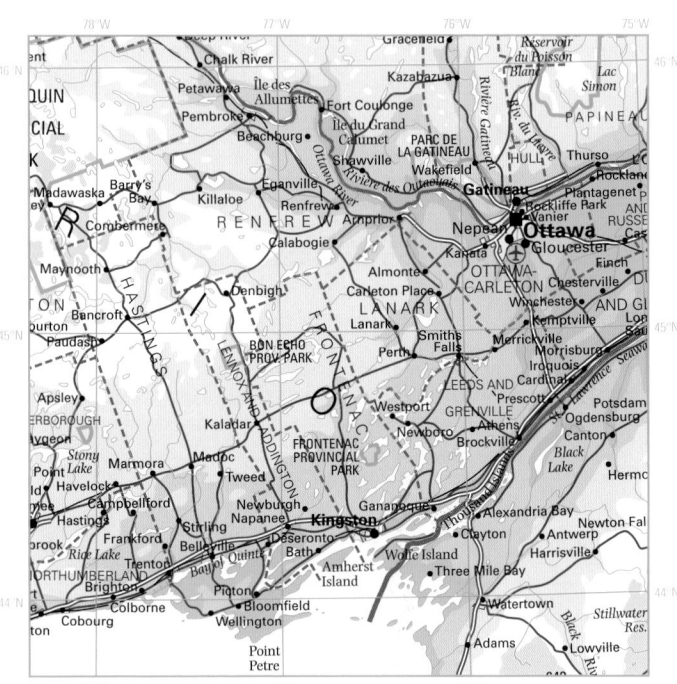

Abbreviations used in the gazetteer

admin.	administrative area	*mt.*	mountain, peak, or spot height
Aust.	Australia		
b.	bay or harbour	*mts.*	mountains
Bahamas	The Bahamas	Neths.	Netherlands
bor.	borough	NZ	New Zealand
c.	cape, point, or headland	*p.*	peninsula
can.	canal	Philippines	The Philippines
CAR	Central African Republic	*plat.*	plateau
CDR	Congo Democratic Republic	PNG	Papua New Guinea
		Port.	Portugal
Col.	Colombia	*r.*	river
Czech Rep.	Czech Republic	*res.*	reservoir
d.	desert	RoI	Republic of Ireland
dep.	depression	RSA	Republic of South Africa
Dom. Rep.	Dominican Republic	Russia	Russian Federation
Eq. Guinea	Equatorial Guinea	*salt l.*	salt lake
est.	estuary	*sd.*	sound, strait, or channel
Fr.	France	Sp.	Spain
g.	gulf	St.	Saint
geog. reg.	geographical region	Ste.	Sainte
hist. site	historical site	Switz.	Switzerland
i.	island	*tn.*	town
in.	inlet	UAE	United Arab Emirates
I.R.	Indian Reservation	UK	United Kingdom
is.	islands	USA	United States of America
ist.	isthmus	*vol.*	volcano
l.	lake, lakes, lagoon	W. Indies	West Indies
m.s.	manned meteorological station	Yemen	Yemen Republic

Abbreviations used on the maps

A.C.T.	Australian Capital Territory	P.	Pulau
Arch.	Archipelago	Peg.	Pegunungan
Arq.	Arquipelago	Pen.; Penin.	Peninsula
Aust.	Australia	Pk.	Peak
C.	Cape; Cabo; Cap	Port.	Portugal
Col.	Colombia	P.P.	Provincial Park
Cr.	Creek	PROV. PARK	Provincial Park
Czech Rep.	Czech Republic	Pt.	Point
D.C.	District of Columbia	Pte.	Pointe
E.	East	Pto.	Porto; Puerto
Eq. Guinea	Equatorial Guinea	R.	River; Rio
Fr.	France	Ra.	Range
FYROM	Former Yugoslav Republic of Macedonia	R.A.	Recreational Area
		Res	Reservoir
G.	Gunung; Gebel; Gulf	RÉS. FAUN.	Réserve Faunique
Hwy.	Highway	Riv.	Rivière
I.	Island; Île; Isla; Ilha	RSA	Republic of South Afri
Is.	Islands; Îles; Islas; Ilhas	Russia	Russian Federation
Kep.	Kepulauan	S.	South
L.	Lake; Lac; Lago	Sd.	Sound
Mt.	Mount; Mountain; Mont	Sp.	Spain
Mts.	Mountains; Monts	St.	Saint
N.	North	Sta.	Santa
NAT. PARK	National Park	Ste.	Sainte
Neths	Netherlands	UK	United Kingom
N.P.	National Park	USA	United States of Amer
NZ	New Zealand	Yemen	Yemen Republic

A

Abbotsford British Columbia 42 H4 49 02N 122 18W
Abitibi *admin.* Québec 53 K8/L8 48 20N 76 00W
Abitibi-De Troyes Provincial Park Ontario 51 L5 48 50N 80 40W
Abitibi River Ontario 51 L5 49 40N 81 20W
Acton Ontario 54 B2 43 38N 80 04W
Acton Vale Québec 53 P5 45 40N 72 35W
Adams Lake British Columbia 43 L2 51 10N 119 30W
Adams River British Columbia 43 L2 51 40N 119 00W
Adlatok River Newfoundland and Labrador 60 D7 55 28N 62 50W
Adlavik Islands Newfoundland and Labrador 60 F7 54 55N 58 40W
Admiralty Inlet Nunavut 65 N5 72 30N 86 00W
Advocate Harbour *tn.* Nova Scotia 61 M12 45 20N 64 45W
Agassiz Ice Cap Nunavut 65 Q7 80 15N 76 00W
Agassiz Provincial Forest Manitoba 49 D1 49 50N 96 20W
Aguasabon River Ontario 51 H5 48 50N 87 00W
Ailsa Craig *tn.* Ontario 54 A2 43 08N 81 34W
Ainslie, Lake Nova Scotia 61 M12 46 10N 61 10W
Airdrie Alberta 46 E2 51 20N 114 00W
Ajax Ontario 54 C2 43 48N 79 00W
Akimiski Island Nunavut 65 P1 52 30N 81 00W
Akimiski Island Bird Sanctuary Nunavut 65 P1 53 00N 81 00W
Akimiski Strait Nunavut/Ontario 50 L7 52 40N 82 00W
Akłarvik *(Aklavik)* Northwest Territories 64 D4 68 15N 135 02W
Akpatok Island Nunavut 56 F9 60 30N 68 00W
Akulivik Québec 56 A9 60 53N 78 15W
Albany Island Ontario 50 L7 52 15N 81 34W
Albany River Ontario 50 K6 51 40N 83 20W
Albany River Provincial Park Ontario 50 G6 51 30N 88 30W
Alberni Inlet *admin.* British Columbia 42 H4 49 05N 124 52W
Albert *admin.* New Brunswick 61 L12 45 40N 65 10W
Alberta *province* 46
Alberton Prince Edward Island 61 M12 46 50N 64 08W
Aldershot Ontario 54 C2 43 17N 79 51W
Aldersyde Alberta 46 F2 50 44N 113 53W
Alert Bay *tn.* British Columbia 43 G2 50 34N 126 58W
Alexandria Ontario 53 M5 45 19N 74 38W
Alexis Creek *tn.* British Columbia 43 J3 52 05N 123 12W
Alexis River Newfoundland and Labrador 60 G6 52 50N 57 40W
Alfred Ontario 53 M5 45 34N 74 53W
Alfred, Mount British Columbia 42 H5 50 13N 124 07W
Algoma *admin.* Ontario 52 C6/D6 48 00N 84 00W
Algonquin Provincial Park Ontario 52 H5 45 50N 78 30W
Alix Alberta 46 F3 52 25N 113 11W
Allan Saskatchewan 47 D2 51 54N 106 02W
Allan Water *tn.* Ontario 50 F6 50 14N 90 12W
Alliston Ontario 54 C3 44 09N 79 51W
Alma New Brunswick 61 M12 45 36N 64 58W
Alma Québec 57 E3 48 32N 71 41W
Almonte Ontario 53 K5 45 14N 76 12W
Alouette Lake British Columbia 42 H4 49 22N 121 22W
Alsask Saskatchewan 47 C2 51 22N 110 00W
Alsek Ranges *mts.* British Columbia 42 A6/B6 59 30N 137 30W
Altona Manitoba 49 D1 49 06N 97 35W
Alvin British Columbia 42 H4 49 25N 122 34W
Amadjuak Lake Nunavut 65 R3 65 00N 71 08W
Amaranth Manitoba 49 C2 50 36N 98 43W
Amberley Ontario 54 A3 44 02N 81 44W
Amery Manitoba 49 E5 56 45N 94 00W
Amherst Nova Scotia 61 M12 45 50N 64 14W
Amherstburg Ontario 52 C2 42 06N 83 07W
Amherst Island Ontario 53 K4 44 08N 76 43W
Amisk Lake Saskatchewan 47 F4 54 30N 102 15W
Amos Québec 57 A3 48 04N 78 08W
Amqui Québec 57 G3 48 30N 67 30W
Amund Ringnes Islands Nunavut 65 L6 78 00N 96 00W
Amundsen Gulf Northwest Territories 64 E5 70 30N 125 00W
Anahim Lake *tn.* British Columbia 43 H3 52 25N 125 18W
Ancaster Ontario 54 C2 43 13N 79 58W
Anderson River Northwest Territories 64 E4 69 42N 129 01W
Anderson River Delta Bird Sanctuary Northwest Territories 64 E4 69 50N 128 00W
Andrew Alberta 46 F3 53 52N 112 14W
Andrew Gordon Bay Nunavut 65 R3 60 27N 75 30W
Angers Québec 59 L3 45 32N 75 29W
Angikuni Lake Nunavut 65 L3 62 00N 99 45W
Angling Lake *I.R.* Ontario 50 G7 53 50N 89 30W
Anguille, Cape Newfoundland and Labrador 61 F3 47 55N 59 24W
Angus Ontario 54 C3 44 19N 79 53W
Anjou Québec 58 N5 45 36N 73 34W
Annacis Island British Columbia 44 G3 49 09N 122 59W
Annapolis *admin.* Nova Scotia 61 L11 44 40N 65 20W
Annapolis Royal Nova Scotia 61 L11 44 44N 65 32W
Annieville British Columbia 44 G3 49 10N 122 54W
Antigonish Nova Scotia 61 M12 45 39N 62 00W
Antigonish *admin.* Nova Scotia 61 M12 45 30N 62 10W
Anvil Range Yukon Territory 64 D3 62 25N 133 15W
Apsley Ontario 52 H4 44 45N 78 06W
Arborfield Saskatchewan 47 F3 53 06N 103 39W
Arborg Manitoba 49 D2 50 55N 97 12W
Arcola Saskatchewan 47 F1 49 38N 102 26W
Arctic Red River Northwest Territories 64 D4 66 00N 132 00W
Ardmore Alberta 46 G4 54 20N 110 29W
Argenteuil *admin.* Québec 53 M5 45 50N 74 40W
Argentia Newfoundland and Labrador 61 J3 47 17N 53 59W
Arichat Nova Scotia 61 M12 45 31N 61 00W
Aristazabal Island British Columbia 42 F3 52 40N 129 40W
Armstrong British Columbia 43 L2 50 27N 119 14W
Armstrong Ontario 50 G6 50 20N 89 02W
Arnold's Cove *tn.* Newfoundland and Labrador 61 H3 47 45N 54 00W
Arnot Manitoba 49 D4 55 46N 96 42W
Arnprior Ontario 53 K5 45 26N 76 21W
Aroland Ontario 50 H6 50 14N 86 59W
Aroostook New Brunswick 61 B3 46 45N 67 40W
Arran Lake Ontario 54 A3 44 29N 81 16W
Arrowsmith, Mount British Columbia 42 H4 49 00N 124 00W
Arthabaska *admin.* Québec 53 P5 45 58N 72 11W
Arthur Ontario 54 B2 43 50N 80 32W
Artillery Lake Northwest Territories 64 J3 63 09N 107 52W
Arviat *(Eskimo Point)* Nunavut 65 M3 61 10N 94 05W
Asbestos Québec 53 Q5 45 46N 71 56W
Ashcroft British Columbia 43 K2 50 41N 121 17W
Ashern Manitoba 49 C2 51 10N 98 20W
Asheweig River Ontario 50 H7 53 50N 87 50W
Ashihik Lake Yukon Territory 64 C3 61 00N 135 05W
Ashuanipi Newfoundland and Labrador 60 B6 52 46N 66 05W
Ashuanipi Lake Newfoundland and Labrador 60 B6 52 45N 66 15W
Ashuanipi River Newfoundland and Labrador 60 B6 53 50N 66 30W
Aspy Bay Nova Scotia 61 M12 46 50N 60 20W
Asquith Saskatchewan 47 D3 52 08N 107 12W
Assiniboia Saskatchewan 47 E1 49 39N 105 59W
Assiniboine River Manitoba/Saskatchewan 49 C1 49 40N 98 50W
Aston, Cape Nunavut 65 S5 70 00N 67 15W
Astray Newfoundland and Labrador 60 B7 54 36N 66 42W
Astray Lake Newfoundland and Labrador 60 B7 54 36N 66 42W
Athabasca Alberta 46 F4 54 44N 113 15W
Athabasca, Lake Alberta/Saskatchewan 47 C6 59 00N 109 00W
Athabasca River Alberta 46 G5 57 30N 111 40W
Athabasca Sand Dunes Provincial Wilderness Park Saskatchewan 47 C6 59 10N 108 30W
Athens Ontario 53 L4 44 38N 75 57W
Atherley Ontario 54 C3 44 36N 79 21W
Athol Nova Scotia 61 M12 45 40N 64 10W
Atikaki Provincial Park Manitoba 49 E2 51 30N 95 30W
Atik Lake Manitoba 49 D4 55 20N 96 10W
Atikokan Ontario 50 F5 48 45N 91 38W
Atikonak Lake Newfoundland and Labrador 60 C6 52 40N 64 32W
Atikonak River Newfoundland and Labrador 60 C6 53 20N 64 50W
Atkinson, Point British Columbia 44 E4 49 20N 123 16W
Atlin British Columbia 42 D6 59 31N 133 41W
Atlin Lake British Columbia 42 D6 59 31N 133 41W
Atlin Provincial Park British Columbia 42 D6 59 10N 133 50W
Atna Peak British Columbia 43 F3 53 53N 128 07W
Attawapiskat Ontario 50 K7 53 00N 82 30W
Attawapiskat Lake Ontario 50 H7 52 18N 87 54W
Attawapiskat River Ontario 50 K7 53 00N 84 00W
Aubry, Lake Northwest Territories 64 E4 67 23N 126 30W
Auden Ontario 50 H6 50 14N 87 54W
Aujuittuq *(Grise Fiord) tn.* Nunavut 65 P6 76 25N 82 57W
Aulac New Brunswick 61 M12 45 50N 64 20W
Aulavik National Park Northwest Territories 64 G5 73 30N 118 00W
Aulneau Peninsula Ontario 50 D5 49 23N 94 29W
Aupaluk Québec 56 F8 59 12N 69 35W
Aurora Ontario 54 C3 43 00N 79 28W
Ausable River Ontario 54 A2 43 06N 81 36W
Austin Channel Nunavut 65 K6 75 35N 103 25W
Auyuittuq National Park Reserve Nunavut 65 S4 67 00N 67 00W
Avalon Peninsula Newfoundland and Labrador 61 J3 47 30N 53 30W
Avalon Wilderness Reserve Newfoundland and Labrador 61 J3 47 10N 52 40W
Avola British Columbia 43 L2 51 47N 119 19W
Avon River Ontario 54 A2 43 20N 81 10W
Awenda Provincial Park Ontario 54 B3 44 50N 80 00W
Axel Heiberg Island Nunavut 65 M6 80 00N 90 00W
Aylmer Ontario 54 B1 42 47N 80 58W
Aylmer Québec 59 K2 45 23N 75 49W
Aylmer Lake Northwest Territories 64 J3 64 05N 108 30W
Ayr Ontario 54 B2 43 17N 80 26W
Azure Lake British Columbia 43 K3 52 22N 120 07W

B

Babine Lake British Columbia 43 H4 54 45N 125 05W
Babine Mountains Provoncial Park British Columbia 43 G4 54 50N 126 55W
Babine River British Columbia 43 G4 55 44N 127 29W
Bache Peninsula Nunavut 65 Q6 79 08N 76 00W
Backbone Ranges *mts.* Northwest Territories 64 E3 64 30N 130 00W
Back River Nunavut 64 J4 65 00N 105 00W
Baddeck Nova Scotia 61 M12 46 06N 60 45W
Badger Newfoundland and Labrador 61 G4 49 00N 56 04W
Baffin Bay Nunavut 65 S5 72 00N 64 00W
Baffin Island Nunavut 65 Q5 70 00N 75 00W
Baie-Comeau *tn.* Québec 57 F3 49 12N 68 10W
Baie des Chaleurs *b.* Québec/New Brunswick 57 H2 47 59N 65 50W
Baie de Valois *b.* Québec 58 M4 45 27N 73 17W
Baie d'Ungava Québec/Nunavut 56 G8 59 00N 67 30W
Baie James *b.* Québec/Nunavut 57 A5 52 00N 79 00W
Baie Lafontaine *b.* Ontario 59 L3 45 32N 75 18W
Baie-St.-Paul *tn.* Québec 53 R7 47 27N 70 30W
Baie-Trinité *tn.* Québec 57 G3 49 25N 67 20W
Baie Vert *b.* Nova Scotia 61 M12 46 00N 64 00W
Baie Vert *tn.* Newfoundland and Labrador 61 G4 49 55N 56 12W
Baie Verte Peninsula Newfoundland and Labrador 61 G4 49 45N 56 15W
Bailey Creek Ontario 54 C3 44 01N 79 56W
Baillie Island Northwest Territories 64 E5 70 35N 128 10W
Baillie River Northwest Territories/Nunavut 64 J3 64 40N 105 50W
Baird Peninsula Nunavut 65 Q4 68 55N 76 04W
Baker Lake Nunavut 65 L3 64 00N 95 00W
Balcarres Saskatchewan 47 F2 50 49N 103 32W
Baldock Lake Manitoba 49 C5 56 30N 98 25W
Baldy Mountain Manitoba 49 B2 51 27N 100 45W
Balgonie Saskatchewan 47 E2 50 31N 104 15W
Ballantyre Strait Northwest Territories 64 G6 77 25N 114 20W
Balmertown Ontario 50 E6 51 04N 93 41W
Balsam Lake Ontario 54 D3 44 37N 78 51W
Balsam Lake Provincial Park Ontario 54 D3 44 30N 78 50W
Bamaji Lake Ontario 50 F6 51 09N 91 25W
Bancroft Ontario 52 J5 45 03N 77 51W
Banff Alberta 46 E2 51 10N 115 34W
Banff National Park Alberta 46 D2/E2 51 00N 116 00W
Banks Island British Columbia 42 E3 53 30N 130 00W
Banks Island Northwest Territories 64 F4 73 15N 121 30W
Banks Island No 1 Bird Sanctuary Northwest Territories 64 F4 72 30N 124 50W
Banks Island No 2 Bird Sanctuary Northwest Territories 64 F4 73 30N 124 00W
Barachois Pond Provincial Park Newfoundland and Labrador 61 F4 48 28N 58 20W
Baring, Cape Northwest Territories 64 G5 70 02N 117 20W
Barkerville British Columbia 43 K3 53 06N 121 35W
Barkley Sound British Columbia 42 G4 48 58N 125 11W
Barnes Ice Cap Nunavut 65 R5 70 00N 74 00W
Barnfield British Columbia 42 G4 48 50N 125 07W
Barnston Island British Columbia 44 H3 49 11N 122 42W
Barrage Daniel-Johnson Québec 57 F4 50 39N 68 45W
Barraute Québec 57 B3 48 26N 72 15W
Barr'd Islands *tn.* Newfoundland and Labrador 61 H4 49 44N 54 11W
Barrhaven Ontario 59 J2 45 16N 75 47W
Barrhead Alberta 46 E4 54 10N 114 22W
Barrie Ontario 54 C3 44 22N 79 42W
Barrie Island Ontario 52 D5 45 56N 82 39W
Barrière British Columbia 43 K2 51 10N 120 07W
Barrington Nova Scotia 61 L11 43 34N 65 35W
Barrington Lake Manitoba 49 B5 57 00N 100 15W
Barrow Bay Ontario 54 A3 44 58N 81 11W
Barrows Manitoba 49 B2 52 50N 101 26W
Barrow Strait Nunavut 65 M5 74 24N 94 10W
Barry's Bay *tn.* Ontario 52 J5 45 27N 77 41W
Bashaw Alberta 46 F3 52 35N 112 58W
Basin Lake Saskatchewan 47 E3 52 40N 105 10W
Bassano Alberta 46 F2 50 47N 112 28W
Bass Lake Ontario 54 C3 44 36N 79 31W
Bass Lake Provincial Park Ontario 54 C3 44 30N 79 40W
Batchawana Bay *tn.* Ontario 51 J4 46 53N 84 36W
Batchawana Mountain Ontario 51 J4 47 04N 84 24W
Bath New Brunswick 61 B3 46 30N 67 36W
Bath Ontario 53 K4 44 11N 76 47W
Bathurst, Cape Northwest Territories 64 E5 70 31N 127 53W
Bathurst New Brunswick 61 C3 47 37N 65 40W
Bathurst Inlet Nunavut 64 J4 66 49N 108 00W
Bathurst Island Nunavut 65 K6 76 00N 100 00W
Batoche National Historic Site Saskatchewan 47 E3 52 45N 106 00W
Battle Creek Saskatchewan 47 C1 49 20N 109 30W
Battleford Saskatchewan 47 C3 52 45N 108 20W
Battle Harbour *tn.* Newfoundland and Labrador 60 H6 52 16N 55 35W
Battle River Alberta/Saskatchewan 47 C3 52 50N 109 10W
Bauld, Cape Newfoundland and Labrador 60 H5 51 40N 55 25W
Bay Bulls *tn.* Newfoundland and Labrador 61 J3 47 19N 52 50W
Bay de Verde *tn.* Newfoundland and Labrador 61 J4 48 03N 52 54W
Bay du Nord Wilderness Reserve Newfoundland and Labrador 61 H4 48 10N 54 55W
Bayers Lake Nova Scotia 59 Q6 44 38N 63 39W
Bayfield Ontario 54 A2 43 33N 81 41W
Bayfield River Ontario 54 A2 43 34N 81 38W
Bay Roberts *tn.* Newfoundland and Labrador 61 J3 47 36N 53 16W
Beachburg Ontario 53 K5 45 44N 76 51W
Beaconsfield Québec 58 M4 45 26N 73 50W
Beale, Cape British Columbia 42 G4 48 46N 125 10W
Beamsville Ontario 54 C2 43 10N 79 31W
Bear *r.* Ontario 59 L2 45 22N 75 29W
Beardmore Ontario 51 H5 49 36N 87 59W
Bear Island Nunavut 50 L8 64 01N 83 13W
Bear Lake Manitoba 49 D4 55 10N 96 30W
Bear River *tn.* Nova Scotia 61 L11 44 34N 65 40W
Bearskin Lake *I.R.* Ontario 50 F7 53 50N 90 55W
Beatton River British Columbia 43 K5 57 18N 121 15W
Beatty Saugeen River Ontario 54 B3 44 08N 80 54W
Beauce *admin.* Québec 53 R6 46 15N 71 00W
Beauceville Québec 53 R6 46 12N 70 45W
Beaufort Sea 64 C5 72 00N 139 30W
Beauharnois Québec 53 N5 45 18N 73 52W
Beaupré Québec 53 R7 47 03N 70 56W
Beauséjour Manitoba 49 D2 50 04N 96 30W
Beauval Saskatchewan 47 D4 55 09N 107 35W
Beaver Bank Nova Scotia 59 Q7 44 48N 63 39W
Beaver Creek Ontario 55 C2 43 51N 79 23W
Beaver Creek *tn.* Yukon Territory 64 B3 60 20N 140 45W
Beaverdell British Columbia 43 L1 49 25N 119 09W
Beaverhill Lake Alberta 46 F3 53 27N 112 32W
Beaver Hill Lake Manitoba 49 E4 54 20N 95 20W
Beaverlodge Alberta 46 C4 55 13N 119 26W
Beaver River Alberta/Saskatchewan 47 C4 54 20N 108 40W
Beaver River Ontario 54 B3 44 21N 80 33W
Beaverton Ontario 54 C3 44 25N 79 10W
Beaverton River Ontario 54 C3 44 08N 79 06W
Bécancour Québec 53 P6 46 20N 72 30W
Beckwith Island Ontario 54 B3 44 53N 80 06W
Bedford Nova Scotia 61 M11 44 44N 61 41W
Bedford Basin Nova Scotia 59 Q6 44 41N 63 37W
Beechey Head *c.* British Columbia 42 H4 48 19N 123 39W
Beechville Nova Scotia 59 Q6 44 37N 63 42W
Beeton Ontario 54 C3 44 04N 79 46W
Beiseker Alberta 46 F2 51 23N 113 32W
Belair Provincial Forest Manitoba 49 D2 50 38N 96 40W
Belcher Islands Nunavut 65 Q2 56 00N 79 30W
Bella Bella British Columbia 43 F3 52 06N 128 06W
Bella Coola British Columbia 43 G3 52 30N 126 50W
Bella Coola River British Columbia 43 G3 52 22N 126 35W
Bellcarra British Columbia 44 G4 49 19N 122 56W
Belle Bay Newfoundland and Labrador 61 H3 47 37N 55 18W
Bellechasse *admin.* Québec 53 R6 46 40N 70 50W
Belledune New Brunswick 61 C3 47 50N 65 45W
Belle Isle *i.* Newfoundland and Labrador 60 H5 51 57N 55 21W
Belle Isle, Strait of Newfoundland and Labrador 60 G5 51 30N 56 30W
Belle River *tn.* Ontario 52 D2 42 18N 82 43W
Belleville Ontario 53 J4 44 10N 77 23W
Bell-Irving River British Columbia 42 F5 56 42N 129 40W
Bell Island Newfoundland and Labrador 60 H5 50 50N 55 50W
Bell Peninsula Nunavut 65 P3 63 00N 82 00W
Bells Corners Ontario 59 J2 45 19N 75 49W
Belly River Alberta 46 F1 49 10N 113 40W
Belmont Ontario 54 A1 42 52N 81 06W
Beloeil Québec 53 N5 45 34N 73 15W
Belwood, Lake Ontario 54 B2 43 46N 80 20W
Benedict Mountains Newfoundland and Labrador 60 F7 54 45N 58 45W
Bengough Saskatchewan 47 E1 49 25N 105 10W
Benito Manitoba 49 B2 51 55N 101 30W
Bentley Alberta 46 E3 52 28N 114 04W
Berens River Manitoba/Ontario 49 D3 52 10N 96 40W
Berens River *tn.* Manitoba 49 D3 52 22N 97 00W
Beresford New Brunswick 61 C3 47 40N 65 40W
Bergland Ontario 50 D5 48 57N 94 23W
Bernier Bay Nunavut 65 N5 71 05N 88 15W
Berthier *admin.* Québec 53 M7 47 40N 75 20W
Bertrand New Brunswick 61 C3 47 45N 65 05W
Berwick Nova Scotia 61 M12 45 03N 64 44W
Berwyn Alberta 46 D5 56 09N 117 44W
Besnard Lake Saskatchewan 47 D4 55 30N 106 10W
Betsiamites Québec 57 F3 48 56N 68 40W
Bible Hill *tn.* Nova Scotia 61 M12 45 20N 63 10W
Bienfait Saskatchewan 47 F1 49 09N 102 48W
Big Bay *tn.* British Columbia 42 G5 50 24N 125 08W
Big Creek Ontario 54 B1 42 43N 80 33W
Big Creek Provincial Park British Columbia 43 J2 51 10N 123 10W
Biggar Saskatchewan 47 D3 52 03N 107 59W
Bighead River Ontario 54 B3 44 30N 80 47W
Big Indian Lake Nova Scotia 59 Q6 44 35N 63 42W
Big Island Nunavut 65 R3 62 43N 70 43W
Big Island Ontario 50 D5 49 10N 94 30W
Big Muddy Lake Saskatchewan 47 E1 49 10N 104 50W
Big Otter Creek Ontario 54 B1 42 46N 80 51W
Big River Newfoundland and Labrador 60 F7 54 50N 59 40W
Big River *tn.* Saskatchewan 47 D3 53 50N 107 01W

Big Salmon Range *mts.* Yukon Territory	64	D3	62 40N	134 59W
Big Sand Lake Manitoba	49	C5	57 50N	99 30W
Big Silver Creek British Columbia	42	H4	49 50N	121 50W
Bigstick Lake Saskatchewan	47	C2	50 20N	109 50W
Bigstone Lake Manitoba	49	E3	53 30N	95 50W
Big Trout Lake Ontario	50	F7	53 50N	90 00W
Big Trout Lake *tn.* Ontario	50	G7	53 40N	89 50W
Birch Cove Lakes Nova Scotia	59	Q6	44 40N	63 39W
Birch Hills *tn.* Saskatchewan	47	E3	53 00N	105 00W
Birch Island Manitoba	49	C3	52 20N	99 50W
Birch Lake Alberta	46	G3	53 19N	111 35W
Birch Lake Ontario	50	E6	51 20N	92 20W
Birch Mountains Alberta	46	F5	57 20N	113 55W
Birch Mountains Wildland Provincial Park Alberta	46	F5	57 30N	113 00W
Birch River Alberta	46	F6	58 20N	113 20W
Birds Hill *tn.* Manitoba	48	C2	49 58N	96 59W
Birken British Columbia	42	H5	50 29N	112 36W
Birtle Manitoba	49	B2	50 26N	101 04W
Biscotasing Ontario	51	K4	47 17N	82 06W
Bishop's Falls *tn.* Newfoundland and Labrador	61	H4	49 01N	55 30W
Bistcho Lake Alberta	46	C6	59 45N	118 50W
Bjorne Peninsula Nunavut	65	N6	77 37N	87 00W
Black Bear Island Lake Saskatchewan	47	E4	55 45N	105 50W
Black Birch Lake Saskatchewan	47	D5	56 55N	107 25W
Blackburn Hamlet Ontario	59	K2	45 26N	75 33W
Black Diamond Alberta	46	E2	50 45N	114 12W
Blackfalds Alberta	46	F3	52 23N	113 47W
Black Lake Saskatchewan	47	E6	59 10N	104 30W
Black Lake *tn.* Québec	53	Q6	46 03N	71 21W
Black Lake *tn.* Saskatchewan	47	E6	59 05N	105 35W
Black River Ontario	54	C3	44 48N	79 08W
Blacks Harbour New Brunswick	61	B2	45 03N	66 49W
Black Tickle Newfoundland and Labrador	60	D8	53 27N	55 49W
Blackville New Brunswick	61	C3	46 44N	65 51W
Blackwater Lake Northwest Territories	64	F3	64 00N	123 05W
Blaine Lake *tn.* Saskatchewan	47	D3	52 50N	106 54W
Blainville Québec	53	N5	45 39N	73 52W
Blair Ontario	54	B2	43 23N	80 23W
Blanc-Sablon Québec	56	L4	51 26N	57 08W
Blenheim Ontario	52	E2	42 20N	82 00W
Blind River *tn.* Ontario	52	D6	46 10N	82 58W
Bloodvein River Manitoba	49	D2	51 50N	96 40W
Bloomfield Ontario	53	J3	43 59N	77 14W
Blossom Park *tn.* Ontario	59	K2	45 21N	75 37W
Blubber Bay *tn.* British Columbia	42	H4	49 48N	124 37W
Bluenose Lake Nunavut	64	G4	68 30N	119 35W
Blue Ridge *tn.* Alberta	46	E4	54 08N	115 22W
Blue River *tn.* British Columbia	43	L3	52 05N	119 09W
Blyth Ontario	54	A2	43 43N	81 26W
Blyth Brook Ontario	54	A2	43 45N	81 31W
Bobcaygeon Ontario	52	H4	44 32N	78 33W
Boisbriand Québec	58	M5	45 35N	73 51W
Boissevain Manitoba	49	B1	49 14N	100 02W
Bolton Ontario	54	C2	43 53N	79 44W
Bonavista Newfoundland and Labrador	61	J4	48 39N	53 07W
Bonavista Bay Newfoundland and Labrador	61	J4	48 45N	53 30W
Bonavista Peninsula Newfoundland and Labrador	61	J4	48 30N	53 30W
Bon Echo Provincial Park Ontario	53	J4	44 55N	77 15W
Bonnet Plume River Yukon Territory	64	D4	65 25N	135 00W
Bonnyville Alberta	46	G4	54 16N	110 44W
Boothia, Gulf of Nunavut	65	N4	69 00N	88 00W
Boothia Peninsula Nunavut	65	M5	70 30N	94 30W
Borden-Carleton Prince Edward Island	61	M12	46 20N	63 40W
Borden Island Northwest Territories/Nunavut	64	H6	78 30N	111 30W
Borden Peninsula Nunavut	65	P5	73 00N	82 30W
Boston Bar British Columbia	43	K1	49 52N	121 25W
Botwood Newfoundland and Labrador	61	H4	49 09N	55 21W
Bouctouche New Brunswick	61	M12	46 30N	64 40W
Boundary Range *mts.* British Columbia	42	D6	58 00N	133 00W
Bowden Alberta	46	E2	51 55N	114 02W
Bowen Island British Columbia	42	H4	49 23N	123 26W
Bow Island *tn.* Alberta	46	G1	49 52N	111 22W
Bowman Bay Wildlife Sanctuary Nunavut	65	R4	66 00N	74 00W
Bowmanville Ontario	54	D2	43 55N	78 43W
Bowmanville Creek Ontario	54	D3	44 02N	78 47W
Bow River Alberta	46	F2	50 47N	111 55W
Bowron Lake Provincial Park British Columbia	43	K3	53 00N	121 00W
Bowron River British Columbia	43	K3	53 38N	121 40W
Bowser British Columbia	42	H4	49 26N	124 41W
Boyle Alberta	46	F4	54 35N	112 49W
Boyne River Ontario	54	B3	44 07N	80 07W
Bracebridge Ontario	52	G5	45 02N	79 19W
Bradford Ontario	54	C3	44 07N	79 34W
Bralorne British Columbia	43	J2	50 46N	122 51W
Bramalea Ontario	54	C2	43 44N	79 44W
Brampton Ontario	54	C2	43 42N	79 46W
Brandon Manitoba	49	C1	49 50N	99 57W
Brant *admin.* Ontario	54	B2	43 03N	80 29W
Brantford Ontario	54	B2	43 09N	80 17W
Bras d'Or Lake Nova Scotia	61	M12	45 50N	60 50W
Brazeau, Mount Alberta	46	D3	52 33N	117 21W
Brazeau River Alberta	46	D3	52 50N	116 20W
Brechin Ontario	54	C3	44 32N	79 11W
Brent Ontario	52	H6	46 02N	78 29W
Breton Cove *tn.* Nova Scotia	61	M12	46 30N	60 30W
Brevoort Island Nunavut	65	T3	63 19N	64 08W
Bridge River British Columbia	43	J2	50 55N	123 25W
Bridgetown Nova Scotia	61	L11	44 50N	65 20W
Bridgewater Nova Scotia	61	M11	44 23N	64 32W
Brier Island Nova Scotia	61	L11	44 20N	66 20W
Brighton Ontario	52	J4	44 07N	77 45W
Brisay Québec	56	E6	54 25N	70 42W
Bristol New Brunswick	61	B3	46 28N	67 38W
Britannia Beach *tn.* British Columbia	42	H4	49 38N	123 10W
British Columbia *province*	42/43			
British Empire Range *mts.* Nunavut	65	P7	82 30N	84 50W
British Mountains	64	B4	69 00N	141 00W
Britt Ontario	52	F5	45 46N	80 33W
Broadview Saskatchewan	47	F2	50 22N	102 31W
Brochet Manitoba	49	B5	57 55N	101 40W
Brockville Ontario	53	L4	44 35N	75 41W
Brodeur Peninsula Nunavut	65	N5	72 00N	87 30W
Brome *admin.* Québec	53	P5	45 10N	72 10W
Bromont Québec	53	P5	45 18N	72 38W
Bronte Ontario	54	C2	43 23N	79 43W
Brookfield Nova Scotia	61	M12	45 15N	63 18W
Brooklyn Nova Scotia	61	M11	44 04N	64 42W
Brooks Alberta	46	G2	50 35N	111 54W
Brooks Peninsula British Columbia	43	G2	50 05N	127 45W
Brooks Peninsula Provincial Park British Columbia	43	G2	50 15N	127 50W
Brown Lake Nunavut	65	M4	65 54N	91 15W
Bruce *admin.* Ontario	54	A3	44 15N	81 24W
Bruce Creek Ontario	55	C2	43 55N	79 20W
Bruce Mines *tn.* Ontario	52	C6	46 18N	83 48W
Bruce Peninsula Ontario	54	A3/A4	45 00N	81 20W
Bruce Peninsula National Park Ontario	54	A4	45 00N	81 20W
Bruderheim Alberta	46	F3	53 47N	112 56W
Brunette Island Newfoundland and Labrador	61	H3	47 16N	55 55W
Bruno Saskatchewan	47	E3	52 17N	105 31W
Brussels Ontario	54	A2	43 44N	81 15W
Buchan Gulf Nunavut	65	R5	71 47N	74 16W
Buchans Newfoundland and Labrador	61	G4	48 49N	56 53W
Buckingham Québec	57	C1	45 35N	75 24W
Buckinghorse River *tn.* British Columbia	43	J5	57 25N	122 50W
Buffalo Head Hills Alberta	46	E5	57 25N	115 55W
Buffalo Head Prairie Alberta	46	D6	58 04N	116 30W
Buffalo Lake Alberta	46	F3	52 27N	112 54W
Buffalo Narrows *tn.* Saskatchewan	47	C4	55 52N	108 28W
Buffalo River Alberta	46	E6	59 25N	114 35W
Buffalo Trail Alberta	46	G2	51 45N	110 35W
Bulkley River British Columbia	43	G4	55 00N	127 10W
Buntzen Lake British Columbia	44	G4	49 20N	124 51W
Burden, Mount British Columbia	43	J5	56 10N	123 09W
Burford Ontario	54	B2	43 46N	80 25W
Burgeo Newfoundland and Labrador	61	G3	47 37N	57 37W
Burin Newfoundland and Labrador	61	H3	47 02N	55 10W
Burin Peninsula Newfoundland and Labrador	61	H3	47 00N	55 40W
Burk's Falls *tn.* Ontario	52	G5	45 37N	79 25W
Burlington Ontario	54	C2	43 19N	79 48W
Burnaby British Columbia	42	H4	49 16N	122 58W
Burnaby Lake British Columbia	44	G3	49 14N	122 57W
Burns Bog Park Reserve British Columbia	44	G3	46 07N	122 58W
Burnside Nova Scotia	59	Q6	44 41N	63 35W
Burnside River Nunavut	64	J4	66 20N	109 30W
Burns Lake *tn.* British Columbia	43	H4	54 14N	125 45
Burnt Islands *tn.* Newfoundland and Labrador	61	F3	47 50N	58 00W
Burnt Lake Québec	57	J5	52 15N	63 50W
Burnt River Ontario	54	D3	44 41N	78 43W
Burntwood Lake Manitoba	49	B4	55 20N	100 10W
Burntwood River Manitoba	49	D4	55 50N	97 40W
Burquitlam British Columbia	44	G4	49 15N	122 56W
Burrard Inlet British Columbia	44	F4	49 19N	123 14W
Burstall Saskatchewan	47	C2	50 40N	109 56W
Bushell Park *tn.* Saskatchewan	47	E2	50 25N	105 30W
Butedale British Columbia	43	F3	53 12N	128 45W
Bute Inlet British Columbia	42	H5	50 31N	124 59W
Buttle Lake British Columbia	42	G4	49 47N	125 30W
Button Bay Manitoba	49	E6	58 50N	94 30W
Button Islands Nunavut	56	H9	60 35N	64 40W
Buttonville Ontario	55	C2	43 51N	79 22W
Byam Channel Nunavut	65	K6	75 10N	105 00W
Byam Martin Island Nunavut	65	K6	75 15N	104 15W
Bylot Island Nunavut	65	Q5	73 30N	79 00W
Byron Bay Newfoundland and Labrador	60	G7	54 40N	57 40W
C				
Cabano Québec	57	F2	47 40N	68 56W
Cabot Head Ontario	54	A4	45 15N	81 17W
Cabot Lake Newfoundland and Labrador	60	D8	56 09N	62 37W
Cabot Strait Nova Scotia/Newfoundland and Labrador	61	F3	47 10N	59 30W
Cabri Saskatchewan	47	C2	50 38N	108 28W
Cache Creek *tn.* British Columbia	43	K2	50 46N	121 17W
Cadotte Lake *tn.* Alberta	46	D5	56 25N	116 28W
Calabogie Ontario	53	K5	45 18N	76 43W
Calais New Brunswick	61	B2	45 10N	67 15W
Caledon East Ontario	54	C2	43 52N	79 53W
Caledonia Nova Scotia	61	L11	44 24N	65 02W
Caledonia Ontario	54	C2	43 05N	79 57W
Caledon Village Ontario	54	C2	43 51N	79 59W
Calgary Alberta	46	E2	51 05N	114 05W
Callander Ontario	52	G6	46 13N	79 22W
Calling Lake Alberta	46	F4	55 15N	113 20W
Calmar Alberta	46	F3	53 16N	113 49W
Calvert Island British Columbia	43	F2	51 30N	128 00W
Cambridge Ontario	54	B2	43 22N	80 20W
Cambridge-Narrows New Brunswick	61	C2	45 50N	65 55W
Cameron Hills Alberta	46	C6	59 48N	118 00W
Campbell Dam Saskatchewan	47	F3	53 40N	103 20W
Campbellford Ontario	52	J4	44 18N	77 48W
Campbell Lake British Columbia	42	G4	49 59N	125 30W
Campbell, Mount Yukon Territory	64	C3	64 23N	138 43W
Campbell River *tn.* British Columbia	42	G5	50 00N	125 18W
Campbells Cove *tn.* Prince Edward Island	61	M12	46 30N	62 15W
Campbellton New Brunswick	61	B3	48 00N	66 41W
Campbellton Newfoundland and Labrador	61	H4	49 17N	54 56W
Campbellville Ontario	54	C2	43 29N	79 59W
Camperville Manitoba	49	B2	51 00N	100 08W
Campobello Island New Brunswick	61	B2	44 50N	66 50W
Camrose Alberta	46	F3	53 01N	112 50W
Camsell Portage Saskatchewan	47	C6	59 39N	109 12W
CANADA	12/13			
Canal Flats *tn.* British Columbia	43	N2	50 09N	115 50W
Canal Lake Ontario	54	C3	44 34N	79 02W
Candiac Québec	58	N4	45 24N	73 31W
Candle Lake Saskatchewan	47	E3	53 55N	105 10W
Candle Lake *tn.* Saskatchewan	47	E3	53 50N	105 10W
Caniapiscau Québec	56	F6	54 58N	69 47W
Canmore Alberta	46	E2	51 07N	115 18W
Canning Nova Scotia	61	M12	45 10N	64 26W
Canoe Lake Saskatchewan	47	C4	55 10N	108 30W
Canoe Narrows Saskatchewan	47	C4	55 10N	108 09W
Canora Saskatchewan	47	F2	51 38N	102 28W
Canso Nova Scotia	61	M12	45 20N	61 00W
Canso, Cape Nova Scotia	61	M12	45 19N	60 59W
Cap-aux-Meules *tn.* Québec	61	E3	47 25N	62 00W
Cap-Chat *tn.* Québec	57	G3	49 06N	66 42W
Cap de Nouvelle-France *c.* Québec	56	D10	61 30N	73 45W
Cap Dufferin *c.* Québec	56	A8	58 35N	78 32W
Cape Breton *admin.* Nova Scotia	61	M12	45 50N	60 00W
Cape Breton Highlands National Park Nova Scotia	61	M12	46 45N	60 40W
Cape Breton Island Nova Scotia	61	M12	46 45N	60 00W
Cape Charles *tn.* Newfoundland and Labrador	60	H6	52 13N	55 38W
Cape Croker *tn.* Ontario	54	A3	44 56N	81 01W
Cape Dorset Sanctuaries Nunavut	65	Q3	63 50N	77 00W
Cape Le Havre Island Nova Scotia	61	M11	44 10N	64 20W
Cape North *tn.* Nova Scotia	61	M12	46 55N	60 30W
Cape Parry *m.s.* Northwest Territories	64	F5	70 08N	124 34W
Cape Sable Island Nova Scotia	61	L11	43 30N	65 40W
Cape St. George *tn.* Newfoundland and Labrador	61	F4	48 28N	59 15W
Cape Scott Provincial Park British Columbia	43	F2	50 42N	128 20W
Cape Smith *tn.* Nunavut	56	A9	60 44N	78 29W
Cape Tormentine *tn.* New Brunswick	61	M12	46 08N	63 47W
Cap Gaspé *c.* Québec	57	H3	48 46N	64 10W
Cap Hopes Advance *c.* Québec	56	F9	61 00N	69 40W
Capilano Lake British Columbia	44	F4	49 22N	123 06W
Cap Pelé *tn.* New Brunswick	61	M12	46 10N	64 10W
Cap Prince-de-Galles *c.* Québec	56	E9	61 42N	71 30W
Cap-Saint-Ignace *c.* Québec	53	R7	47 00N	70 29W
Capstick Nova Scotia	61	M12	47 00N	60 31W
Caramat Ontario	51	H5	49 37N	86 09W
Caraquet New Brunswick	61	C3	47 48N	64 59W
Carberry Manitoba	49	C1	49 52N	99 20W
Carbon Alberta	46	F2	51 29N	113 11W
Carbonear Newfoundland and Labrador	61	J3	47 44N	53 13W
Carcross Yukon Territory	64	D3	60 11N	134 41W
Cardigan Prince Edward Island	61	M12	46 14N	62 37W
Cardinal Ontario	53	L4	44 47N	75 23W
Cardston Alberta	46	F1	49 12N	113 18W
Cariboo Mountains British Columbia	43	K3	53 20N	120 50W
Cariboo Mountains Provincial Park British Columbia	43	K3	53 00N	120 30W
Caribou Manitoba	49	D6	59 20N	97 50W
Caribou Mountains Alberta	46	E6	59 00N	115 30W
Caribou Mountains Wildland Provincial Park Alberta	46	E6	59 10N	115 00W
Caribou River Manitoba	49	E6	59 30N	95 30W
Caribou River Provincial Park Manitoba	49	D6	59 30N	96 40W
Carleton–St-Omer Québec	57	G3	48 08N	66 10W
Carleton *admin.* New Brunswick	61	B3	46 10N	66 52W
Carleton, Mount New Brunswick	61	B3	47 24N	66 52W
Carleton Place Ontario	53	K5	45 15N	75 45W
Carlsbad Springs Ontario	59	L2	45 22N	75 29W
Carlson Landing Alberta	46	G6	58 59N	111 45W
Carlyle Saskatchewan	47	F1	49 39N	102 18W
Carmacks Yukon Territory	64	C3	62 04N	136 21W
Carman Manitoba	49	D1	49 32N	97 59W
Carmanah Walbran Provincial Park British Columbia	42	H4	48 37N	124 35W
Carmanville Newfoundland and Labrador	61	H4	49 24N	54 18W
Carnduff Saskatchewan	47	G1	49 11N	101 50W
Caronport Saskatchewan	47	E2	50 27N	105 49W
Carp Lake British Columbia	43	J4	54 48N	123 20W
Carp Lake Provincial Park British Columbia	43	J4	54 08N	123 30W
Carrot River Manitoba	49	D4	54 50N	96 40W
Carrot River Saskatchewan	47	E3	53 05N	104 15W
Carrot River *tn.* Saskatchewan	47	F3	53 18N	103 32W
Carstairs Alberta	46	E2	51 34N	114 06W
Cartmel, Mount British Columbia	43	F5	57 45N	129 12W
Cartwright Newfoundland and Labrador	60	G6	53 42N	57 01W
Cascade Range *mts.* British Columbia	42	H4	50 48N	121 15W
Cascade Recreation Area British Columbia	42	H4	49 16N	120 56W
Cascumpec Bay Prince Edward Island	61	M12	46 45N	64 00W
Casselman Ontario	53	L5	45 19N	78 07W
Cassiar Highway British Columbia	42	F5	57 30N	130 10W
Cassier Mountains British Columbia	42/43	E6/F6	59 50N	131 50W
Castlegar British Columbia	43	M1	49 18N	117 41W
Castor Alberta	46	G3	52 13N	111 53W
Catalina Newfoundland and Labrador	61	J4	48 31N	53 05W
Cat Arm Reservoir Newfoundland and Labrador	61	G5	50 10N	56 40W
Cathedral Provincial Park British Columbia	43	K1	49 05N	120 11W
Cat Lake Ontario	50	F6	51 30N	91 50W
Cat Lake *I.R.* Ontario	50	F6	51 40N	91 50W
Caubvick, Mt. Newfoundland and Labrador	60	D9	58 50N	64 40W
Causapscal Québec	57	G3	48 22N	67 14W
Cavendish Prince Edward Island	61	M12	46 30N	63 20W
Cayuga Ontario	54	C1	42 57N	79 50W
Cecil Lake *tn.* British Columbia	43	K5	56 19N	120 40W
Cedar Lake Manitoba	49	B3	53 40N	100 30W
Central Bedeque Prince Edward Island	61	M12	46 20N	63 40W
Central Butte Saskatchewan	47	D2	50 50N	106 30W
Central Patricia Ontario	50	F6	51 30N	90 09W
Central Saanich British Columbia	42	H4	48 32N	123 25W
Centreville Newfoundland and Labrador	61	J4	49 01N	53 53W
Centreville Nova Scotia	61	M12	45 10N	64 30W
C.F.B. Borden Ontario	54	C3	44 18N	79 53W
C.F.B. Suffield Alberta	46	G2	50 35N	110 47W
Chalk River *tn.* Ontario	53	J6	46 01N	77 27W
Chambly Québec	53	N5	45 27N	73 19W
Champlain *admin.* Québec	53	N7	48 20N	74 20W
Chandler Québec	57	H3	48 21N	64 41W
Channel-Port aux Basques Newfoundland and Labrador	61	F3	47 34N	59 09W
Chantrey Inlet Nunavut	65	L4	67 48N	96 20W
Chapais Québec	57	C3	49 47N	74 54W
Chapleau Ontario	51	K4	47 50N	83 24W
Chapleau-Nemegosenda River Provincial Park Ontario	51	K5	48 25N	83 00W
Chaplin Saskatchewan	47	D2	50 29N	106 40W
Chaplin Lake Saskatchewan	47	D2	50 25N	106 30W
Charles Island Nunavut	65	R3	62 39N	74 15W
Charles Lake Alberta	46	G6	59 50N	110 33W
Charles, Lake Nova Scotia	59	Q6	44 43N	63 32W
Charlevoix-Est *admin.* Québec	53	R7	47 50N	70 20W
Charlevoix-Ouest *admin.* Québec	53	R7	47 57N	71 05W
Charlo New Brunswick	61	B3	47 55N	66 20W
Charlotte *admin.* New Brunswick	61	B2	45 20N	67 20W
Charlotte Lake British Columbia	43	H3	52 11N	125 19W
Charlottetown Newfoundland and Labrador	60	G6	52 06N	56 07W
Charlottetown Prince Edward Island	61	M12	46 14N	63 09W
Charlton Island Nunavut	50	M7	52 00N	79 30W
Charny Québec	57	E2	46 43N	71 16W
Charron Lake Manitoba	49	E3	52 40N	95 40W
Chase British Columbia	43	L2	50 49N	119 41W
Chase Provincial Park British Columbia	43	H5	56 30N	125 10W
Chasm British Columbia	43	K2	51 13N	121 28W
Châteauguay Québec	53	N5	45 20N	73 42W
Chateh Alberta	46	C6	58 42N	118 55W

Place	Page	Grid	Latitude	Longitude
Chatham Ontario	52	D2	42 24N	82 11W
Chatham Sound British Columbia	42	E4	54 30N	130 30W
Chatsworth Ontario	54	B3	44 27N	80 54W
Chedabucto Bay Nova Scotia	61	M12	45 20N	61 10W
Cheepay River Ontario	50	K6	50 50N	83 40W
Chelsea Québec	59	J2	45 29N	75 48W
Chelsea Brook Québec	59	J3	45 31N	75 51W
Chemainus British Columbia	42	H4	48 54N	123 42W
Chemainus River British Columbia	42	H4	48 58N	124 09W
Cheslatta Lake British Columbia	43	H3	53 44N	125 20W
Chesley Ontario	54	A3	44 18N	81 07W
Chester Nova Scotia	61	M11	44 33N	64 16W
Chesterfield Inlet Nunavut	65	M3	63 21N	90 42W
Chesterville Ontario	53	L5	45 06N	75 14W
Cheticamp Nova Scotia	61	M12	46 37N	60 59W
Cheticamp Island Nova Scotia	61	M12	46 40N	61 05W
Chetwynd British Columbia	43	K4	55 38N	121 40W
Chevery Québec	56	L4	50 29N	59 41W
Chibougamau Québec	57	C3	49 56N	72 24W
Chicoutimi Québec	57	E3	48 26N	71 03W
Chicoutimi *admin.* Québec	53	R8	48 10N	71 10W
Chidley, Cape Newfoundland and Labrador	60	C10	60 23N	64 26W
Chignecto Bay Nova Scotia	61	M12	45 40N	64 40W
Chignecto, Cape Nova Scotia	61	M12	45 20N	64 55W
Chignecto Game Sanctuary Nova Scotia	61	M12	45 30N	64 35W
Chilanko Forks British Columbia	43	H3	52 04N	124 00W
Chilcotin River British Columbia	43	J2	51 54N	123 20W
Chilko Lake British Columbia	43	H2	51 15N	124 59W
Chilko River British Columbia	43	J2	51 59N	124 05W
Chilliwack British Columbia	42	H4	49 06N	121 56W
Chilliwack Lake British Columbia	42	H4	49 04N	121 22W
Chilliwack River British Columbia	42	H4	49 04N	121 52W
Chin, Cape Ontario	54	A4	45 05N	81 17W
Chinchaga River Alberta	46	C5	57 30N	119 00W
Chinchaga Wildland Provincial Park Alberta	46	C5	57 10N	119 40W
Chip Lake Alberta	46	E3	53 40N	115 23W
Chipman New Brunswick	61	C3	46 11N	65 54W
Chippawa Ontario	54	C2	43 03N	79 04W
Chisasibi Québec	57	A5	53 50N	79 01W
Chitek Lake Park Reserve Manitoba	49	C3	52 30N	99 30W
Choiceland Saskatchewan	47	E3	53 30N	104 33W
Chomedey Québec	58	M5	45 32N	73 46W
Chorkbak Inlet Nunavut	65	R3	64 30N	74 25W
Chown, Mount Alberta	46	C3	53 24N	119 25W
Christian Island Ontario	54	B3	44 50N	80 14W
Christian Island *tn.* Ontario	54	B3	44 49N	80 10W
Christie Bay Northwest Territories	64	H3	62 32N	111 10W
Christina River Alberta	46	G4	55 50N	111 59W
Churchbridge Saskatchewan	47	G2	50 55N	101 38W
Churchill Manitoba	49	E6	58 45N	94 00W
Churchill, Cape Manitoba	49	F6	59 00N	93 00W
Churchill Falls *tn.* Newfoundland and Labrador	60	D6	53 35N	64 00W
Churchill Lake Saskatchewan	47	C5	56 05N	108 15W
Churchill Peak British Columbia	43	H6	58 20N	125 02W
Churchill River Manitoba/Saskatchewan	49	E6	58 00N	95 00W
Churchill River Newfoundland and Labrador	60	D6	53 20N	63 40W
Churn Creek Provincial Park British Columbia	43	J2	51 25N	122 30W
Chute-aux-Outardes Québec	57	F3	49 17N	68 25W
Cirque Mountain Newfoundland and Labrador	60	D9	58 56N	63 33W
City View Ontario	59	K2	45 21N	75 44W
Claire, Lake Alberta	46	F6/G6	58 30N	112 00W
Clarence Head *c.* Nunavut	65	Q6	76 47N	77 47W
Clarence-Steepbank Lakes Provincial Wilderness Park Saskatchewan	47	E4	54 15N	105 10W
Clarenville Newfoundland and Labrador	61	J4	48 10N	53 58W
Claresholm Alberta	46	F2	50 04N	113 29W
Clarke City Québec	57	G4	50 11N	66 39W
Clark's Harbour *tn.* Nova Scotia	61	L11	43 25N	65 38W
Clarkson Ontario	54	C2	43 30N	79 38W
Clavet Saskatchewan	47	D3	51 59N	106 21W
Clayoquot Sound British Columbia	43	G1	49 12N	126 05W
Clear Hills Alberta	46	C5	56 40N	119 30W
Clearwater British Columbia	43	K2	51 37N	120 03W
Clearwater Bay *tn.* Ontario	50	D5	49 39N	94 48W
Clearwater Lake British Columbia	43	K3	52 13N	120 20W
Clearwater Lake Manitoba	49	B4	53 50N	101 40W
Clearwater Lake Provincial Park Manitoba	49	B4	54 00N	101 00W
Clearwater River Alberta	46	E2	51 59N	115 20W
Clearwater River Alberta	46	G5	56 47N	110 59W
Clearwater River Provincial Park Saskatchewan	47	C5	57 10N	108 10W
Clendinning Provincial Park British Columbia	43	J2	50 25N	123 45W
Clifford Ontario	54	B2	43 58N	80 00W
Clinton British Columbia	43	K2	51 05N	121 38W
Clinton Ontario	54	A2	43 36N	81 33W
Clinton-Colden Lake Northwest Territories	64	J3	64 58N	107 27W
Cloridorme Québec	57	H3	49 10N	64 51W
Close Lake Saskatchewan	47	E5	57 50N	104 40W
Cloverdale British Columbia	44	H3	49 05N	122 46W
Cluff Lake Mine *tn.* Saskatchewan	47	C6	58 20N	109 35W
Coaldale Alberta	46	F1	49 43N	112 37W
Coalhurst Alberta	46	F1	49 45N	112 56W
Coal River British Columbia	43	G6	59 56N	127 11W
Coast Mountains British Columbia	42/43	E5/H2	58 10N	132 40W
Coates Creek Ontario	54	B3	44 22N	80 07W
Coaticook Québec	53	Q5	45 08N	71 40W
Coats Island Nunavut	65	P3	63 30N	83 00W
Cobalt Ontario	51	M4	47 24N	79 41W
Cobble Hill *tn.* British Columbia	42	H4	48 41N	123 39W
Cobequid Bay Nova Scotia	61	M12	45 20N	63 50W
Cobequid Mountains Nova Scotia	61	M12	45 30N	64 50W
Cobourg Ontario	51	M2	43 58N	78 11W
Cochrane Alberta	46	E2	51 11N	114 28W
Cochrane Ontario	51	L5	49 04N	81 02W
Cochrane River Manitoba/Saskatchewan	47	F6	58 50N	102 20W
Cockburn Island Ontario	52	C5	45 55N	83 22W
Cod Island Newfoundland and Labrador	60	E8	57 47N	61 47W
Colborne Ontario	52	J4	44 00N	77 53W
Colchester *admin.* Nova Scotia	61	M12	45 30N	63 30W
Cold Lake Alberta	46	G4	54 00N	110 00W
Cold Lake *tn.* Alberta	46	G4	54 28N	110 15W
Cold Lake Air Weapons Range Alberta	46	G4	55 10N	110 25W
Coldspring Head Nova Scotia	61	M12	45 55N	63 50W
Coldstream British Columbia	43	L2	50 10N	119 12W
Coldwater Ontario	52	G4	44 43N	79 39W
Cole Harbour Nova Scotia	59	R6	44 40N	63 27W
Cole Harbour *tn.* Nova Scotia	59	R6	44 40N	63 30W
Colin-Cornwall Lakes Wildland Provincial Park Alberta	46	G6	59 35N	110 10W
Collingwood Ontario	54	B3	44 30N	80 14W
Collins Ontario	50	G6	50 17N	89 27W
Colonsay Saskatchewan	47	E3	52 00N	105 52W
Colpoys Bay Ontario	54	A3	44 48N	81 04W
Columbia, Mount British Columbia/Alberta	46	D3	52 09N	117 25W
Columbia Mountains British Columbia	43	K3/M2	53 12N	120 49W
Columbia River British Columbia	43	M2	51 15N	116 58W
Colville Lake Northwest Territories	64	E4	67 10N	126 00W
Colwood British Columbia	42	H4	48 27N	123 28W
Combermere Ontario	52	J5	45 22N	77 37W
Comma Island Newfoundland and Labrador	60	E7	55 20N	60 20W
Committee Bay Nunavut	65	N4	68 30N	86 30W
Comox British Columbia	42	H4	49 41N	124 56W
Comox Lake British Columbia	42	G4	49 37N	125 10W
Compton *admin.* Québec	53	Q5	45 20N	71 40W
Conception Bay Newfoundland and Labrador	61	J3	47 45N	53 00W
Conception Bay South *tn.* Newfoundland and Labrador	61	J3	47 30N	53 00W
Conche Newfoundland and Labrador	60	H5	50 53N	55 54W
Conestogo Lake Ontario	54	B2	43 47N	80 44W
Conestogo River Ontario	54	B2	43 41N	80 42W
Conne River *tn.* Newfoundland and Labrador	61	H3	47 50N	55 20W
Consort Alberta	46	G3	52 01N	110 46W
Contrecoeur Québec	53	N5	45 51N	73 15W
Contwoyto Lake Nunavut	64	J4	65 42N	110 50W
Cook's Bay Ontario	54	C3	44 53N	79 31W
Cookstown Ontario	54	C3	44 12N	79 42W
Coppermine River Nunavut	64	H4	67 10N	115 00W
Coquihalla Highway British Columbia	42	H4	49 25N	121 20W
Coquitlam British Columbia	44	G4	49 15N	122 52W
Coquitlam Lake British Columbia	44	G4	49 21N	122 46W
Coquitlam River British Columbia	44	G4	49 17N	122 45W
Cormorant Manitoba	49	B4	54 14N	100 35W
Cormorant Lake Manitoba	49	B4	54 10N	101 30W
Cormorant Provincial Forest Manitoba	49	B4	54 10N	100 50W
Corner Brook *tn.* Newfoundland and Labrador	61	G4	48 58N	57 58W
Cornwall Ontario	53	M5	45 02N	74 45W
Cornwall Prince Edward Island	61	M12	46 10N	63 10W
Cornwallis Island Nunavut	65	L6	75 00N	97 30W
Coronach Saskatchewan	47	E1	49 06N	105 29W
Coronation Alberta	46	G3	52 05N	111 27W
Coronation Gulf Nunavut	64	H4	68 15N	112 30W
Cortes Island British Columbia	42	H5	50 07N	125 01W
Couchiching, Lake Ontario	54	C3	44 39N	79 22W
Courtenay British Columbia	42	H4	49 40N	124 58W
Courtice Ontario	54	D2	43 57N	78 48W
Courtright Ontario	52	D2	42 49N	82 28W
Coutts Alberta	46	G1	49 00N	112 00W
Cove Island Ontario	54	A4	45 19N	81 44W
Cowansville Québec	53	P5	45 13N	72 44W
Cow Bay Nova Scotia	59	R6	44 36N	63 26W
Cow Head *tn.* Newfoundland and Labrador	61	G4	49 55N	57 48W
Cowichan Bay *tn.* British Columbia	42	H4	48 44N	123 40W
Cowichan Lake British Columbia	42	H4	48 50N	124 04W
Cowichan River British Columbia	42	H4	48 48N	123 58W
Cox's Cove *tn.* Newfoundland and Labrador	61	F4	49 07N	58 04W
Craigellachie British Columbia	43	L2	50 59N	118 38W
Craigleith Provincial Park Ontario	54	B3	44 30N	80 15W
Craik Saskatchewan	47	E2	51 03N	105 50W
Cranberry Junction British Columbia	43	F4	55 35N	128 36W
Cranberry Portage Manitoba	49	B4	54 36N	101 22W
Cranbrook British Columbia	43	N1	49 29N	115 48W
Crane Lake Saskatchewan	47	C2	50 10N	109 20W
Crane River Ontario	54	A4	45 53N	81 31W
Crane River *tn.* Manitoba	49	C2	51 30N	99 18W
Credit River Ontario	54	B2	43 50N	80 02W
Cree Lake Saskatchewan	47	D5	57 30N	106 30W
Creemore Ontario	54	B3	44 20N	80 07W
Cree River Saskatchewan	47	D5	58 00N	106 30W
Creighton Saskatchewan	47	G4	54 46N	101 50W
Cresswell Bay Nunavut	65	M5	72 40N	93 30W
Creston British Columbia	43	M1	49 05N	116 32W
Croker, Cape Ontario	54	B3	44 58N	80 59W
Crossfield Alberta	46	E2	51 26N	114 02W
Cross Lake Manitoba	49	D4	54 50N	97 20W
Cross Lake *tn.* Manitoba	49	D4	54 38N	97 45W
Crow Lake Ontario	50	E5	49 10N	93 56W
Crowsnest Highway Alberta	46	G1	49 50N	111 55W
Crowsnest Pass Alberta/British Columbia	43	N1	49 40N	114 41W
Crumlin Ontario	54	A2	43 01N	81 08W
Crystal Bay Ontario	59	J2	45 21N	75 51W
Crystal Beach *tn.* Ontario	54	C1	42 52N	79 03W
Cub Hills, The Saskatchewan	47	E4	54 20N	104 40W
Cudworth Saskatchewan	47	E3	52 31N	105 44W
Cumberland British Columbia	42	H4	49 37N	124 59W
Cumberland Ontario	59	L3	45 31N	75 23W
Cumberland *admin.* Nova Scotia	61	M12	45 30N	64 10W
Cumberland House *tn.* Saskatchewan	47	F3	53 57N	102 20W
Cumberland Lake Saskatchewan	47	F4	54 10N	102 30W
Cumberland Peninsula Nunavut	65	T4	67 00N	65 00W
Cumberland Sound Nunavut	65	S4	65 30N	66 00W
Cummins Lakes Provincial Park British Columbia	43	L3	52 10N	118 00W
Cupar Saskatchewan	47	E2	50 57N	104 12W
Cushing, Mount British Columbia	43	G5	57 36N	126 51W
Cut Knife Saskatchewan	47	C3	52 45N	109 01W
Cypress Hills Alberta/Saskatchewan	46	G1	49 30N	110 00W
Cypress Hills Provincial Park Alberta/Saskatchewan	46	G1	49 38N	110 00W

D

Place	Page	Grid	Latitude	Longitude
Dalhousie New Brunswick	61	B4	48 03N	66 22W
Dalhousie, Cape Northwest Territories	64	E5	70 14N	129 42W
Dalmeny Saskatchewan	47	D3	52 22N	106 46W
Dalrymple Lake Ontario	54	C3	44 41N	79 07W
Daniel's Harbour *tn.* Newfoundland and Labrador	61	G5	50 14N	57 35W
Danville Québec	53	P5	45 48N	72 01W
Darlington Provincial Park Ontario	54	D2	44 00N	78 50W
Darnley Bay Northwest Territories	64	F4	69 30N	123 30W
Dartmouth Nova Scotia	61	M11	44 40N	63 35W
Dauphin Manitoba	49	B2	51 09N	100 05W
Dauphin, Cape Nova Scotia	61	M12	46 20N	60 25W
Dauphin Lake Manitoba	49	C2	51 10N	99 30W
Dauphin River Manitoba	49	D2	51 50N	98 20W
Dauphin River *tn.* Manitoba	49	D2	51 50N	98 00W
Davidson Saskatchewan	47	E2	51 15N	105 59W
David Thompson Highway Alberta	46	D3	52 15N	116 35W
Davin Lake Saskatchewan	47	F5	56 45N	103 40W
Davis Strait Greenland/Nunavut	65	T4	65 00N	65 00W
Davy Lake Saskatchewan	47	C6	58 50N	108 10W
Dawson Bay Manitoba	49	B3	52 50N	100 50W
Dawson City Yukon Territory	64	C3	64 04N	139 24W
Dawson Creek *tn.* British Columbia	43	K4	55 44N	120 15W
Dawson, Mount British Columbia	43	M2	51 08N	117 26W
Dawson Range *mts.* Yukon Territory	64	C3	63 00N	139 30W
Dawsons Landing British Columbia	43	G2	51 28N	127 33W
Daysland Alberta	46	F3	52 52N	112 15W
Ddhaw Gro Habitat Protection Area Yukon Territory	64	C3	62 25N	135 50W
Dean Channel British Columbia	43	G3	52 18N	127 35W
Dean River British Columbia	43	G3	52 45N	122 30W
Dease Arm *b.* Northwest Territories	64	F4	66 52N	122 00W
Dease Lake British Columbia	42	E6	58 05N	130 04W
Dease Lake *tn.* British Columbia	42	E6	58 28N	130 00W
Dease River British Columbia	42	F6	59 05N	129 40W
Dease Strait Nunavut	64	J4	68 40N	108 00W
Deas Island British Columbia	44	F3	49 07N	123 04W
Déception Québec	56	C10	62 10N	74 45W
Dee Lake British Columbia	44	G3	49 14N	122 59W
Deep Cove British Columbia	44	G4	49 19N	122 58W
Deep Inlet Newfoundland and Labrador	60	E7	55 22N	60 14W
Deep River *tn.* Ontario	53	J6	46 06N	77 30W
Deer Island New Brunswick	61	B2	45 00N	67 00W
Deer Lake Ontario	50	D7	52 38N	94 25W
Deer Lake *tn.* Newfoundland and Labrador	61	G4	49 11N	57 27W
Delhi Ontario	54	B1	42 51N	80 30W
Déline *(Fort Franklin)* Northwest Territories	64	F4	65 11N	123 26W
Delisle Saskatchewan	47	D2	51 56N	107 10W
Deloraine Manitoba	49	B1	49 11N	100 30W
Delta British Columbia	42	H4	49 06N	123 01W
Dempster Highway Yukon Territory	64	C4	65 30N	138 10W
Denare Beach Saskatchewan	47	F4	54 39N	102 06W
Denbigh Ontario	53	J5	45 08N	77 15W
Denetiah Provincial Park British Columbia	43	G6	58 30N	127 30W
Deninue Kúé *(Fort Resolution)* Northwest Territories	64	H3	61 10N	113 39W
Denman Island British Columbia	42	H4	49 32N	124 49W
Deschambault Lake Saskatchewan	47	F4	54 50N	103 50W
Deseronto Ontario	53	J4	44 12N	77 03W
Desmaraisville Québec	57	B3	49 30N	76 18W
Desolation Sound Marine Park British Columbia	42	H5	50 08N	124 45W
Destruction Bay *tn.* Yukon Territory	64	C3	61 16N	138 50W
Détroit de Jacques-Cartier *sd.* Québec	57	J3	50 10N	64 10W
Détroit d'Honguedo *sd.* Québec	57	H3	49 30N	64 20W
Détroit d'Hudson *sd.* Québec/Nunavut	56	F9	62 00N	70 00W
Deux-Montagnes Québec	58	M5	45 32N	73 56W
Deux Rivières Ontario	52	H6	46 15N	78 17W
Devil's Glen Provincial Park Ontario	54	B3	44 20N	80 30W
Devon Alberta	46	F3	53 22N	113 44W
Devon Island Nunavut	65	N6	75 47N	88 00W
Dewar Lakes Nunavut	65	R4	68 30N	71 20W
Dewey Soper Bird Sanctuary Nunavut	65	R4	66 20N	68 50W
Diamond Jennes Peninsula Northwest Territories	64	G5	71 20N	117 00W
Didsbury Alberta	46	E2	51 40N	114 08W
Diefenbaker, Lake Saskatchewan	47	D2	51 10N	107 30W
Dieppe New Brunswick	61	M12	46 10N	64 40W
Digby Nova Scotia	61	L11	44 37N	65 47W
Digby *admin.* Nova Scotia	61	L11	44 20N	65 40W
Digby Neck *p.* Nova Scotia	61	L11	44 30N	66 00W
Dillon Saskatchewan	47	C6	55 56N	108 54W
Dingwall Nova Scotia	61	M12	46 50N	60 30W
Dinorwic Ontario	50	E5	49 41N	92 30W
Dinosaur Provincial Park Alberta	46	G2	50 47N	111 25W
Disappointment Lake Newfoundland and Labrador	60	D6	53 49N	62 31W
Dismal Lakes Nunavut	64	G4	67 26N	117 07W
Disraeli Québec	53	Q5	45 54N	71 22W
Dixon Entrance *sd.* British Columbia/USA	42	D4/E4	54 28N	132 50W
Doaktown New Brunswick	61	B3	46 34N	66 06W
Dobie River Ontario	50	F6	51 30N	90 05W
Dodge Lake Saskatchewan	47	E6	59 50N	105 25W
Dog Creek *tn.* British Columbia	43	J2	51 35N	122 18W
Dog (High) Island Newfoundland and Labrador	60	E8	56 38N	61 10W
Dog Lake Manitoba	49	C2	51 00N	98 20W
Dog Lake Ontario	51	G5	48 50N	89 30W
Dolbeau-Mistassini Québec	57	D3	48 52N	72 15W
Dollarton British Columbia	44	G4	49 18N	122 58W
Dolphin and Union Strait Nunavut	64	G4	69 05N	114 45W
Dominion Nova Scotia	61	M12	46 14N	60 01W
Dominion Lake Newfoundland and Labrador	60	E6	52 40N	61 43W
Domino Newfoundland and Labrador	60	H6	53 29N	55 48W
Don Mills Ontario	55	C1	43 44N	79 22W
Donnacona Québec	53	Q6	46 41N	71 45W
Don River Ontario	54	C2	43 48N	79 24W
D'Or, Cape Nova Scotia	61	M12	45 20N	64 50W
Dorcas Bay Ontario	54	A4	45 10N	81 38W
Dorchester New Brunswick	61	M12	45 54N	64 32W
Dorchester *admin.* Québec	53	R6	46 20N	70 40W
Dorchester, Cape Nunavut	65	Q4	65 27N	77 27W
Dore Lake Saskatchewan	47	D4	54 50N	107 20W
Dorion Ontario	51	G5	48 49N	88 33W
Dorval Québec	58	N4	44 27N	73 45W
Dorval-Lodge Québec	57	B2	47 27N	77 05W
Double Mer *in.* Newfoundland and Labrador	60	F7	54 04N	59 10W
Douglas Island British Columbia	44	G3	49 13N	122 46W
Dowling Lake British Columbia	46	F2	51 44N	112 00W
Downtown, Mount British Columbia	43	H3	52 45N	124 53W
Dows Lake Ontario	59	K2	45 24N	75 42W
Drayton Ontario	54	B2	43 45N	80 40W
Drayton Valley *tn.* Alberta	46	E3	53 13N	114 59W
Dresden Ontario	52	D2	42 34N	82 11W
Driftwood Ontario	51	L5	49 08N	81 20W
Drowning River Ontario	50	J6	50 30N	86 00W
Drumheller Alberta	46	F2	51 28N	112 40W
Drummond *admin.* Québec	53	P5	45 50N	72 40W

Drummondville Québec 53 P5 45 52N 72 30W
Dryden Ontario 50 E5 49 48N 92 48W
Drylake *tn.* Newfoundland and Labrador 60 C7 52 38N 65 59W
Dubawnt Lake Nunavut 65 K3 63 15N 102 00W
Dubreuilville Ontario 51 J5 48 21N 84 32W
Duck Bay *tn.* Manitoba 49 B3 52 10N 100 10W
Duck Lake *tn.* Saskatchewan 47 D3 52 52N 106 12W
Duck Mountain Provincial Forest Manitoba 49 B2 51 20N 100 50W
Duck Mountain Provincial Park Manitoba 49 B2 51 40N 101 00W
Duck Mountain Provincial Park Saskatchewan 47 G2 51 40N 101 40W
Dufferin *admin.* Ontario 54 B3 44 00N 80 20W
Duncan British Columbia 42 H4 48 46N 123 40W
Duncan, Cape Nunavut 50 L7 52 40N 80 50W
Duncan Lake British Columbia 43 M2 50 23N 116 57W
Dundalk Ontario 54 B3 44 10N 80 24W
Dundas Ontario 54 C2 43 16N 79 57W
Dundas Island British Columbia 42 E4 54 33N 131 20W
Dundas Peninsula Northwest Territories 64 H5 74 50N 111 30W
Dundurn Saskatchewan 47 D2 51 49N 106 30W
Dune Za Keyih Provincial Park British Columbia 43 G6/H6 58 20N 126 00W
Dunnville Ontario 54 C1 42 54N 79 36W
Dunville Newfoundland and Labrador 61 J3 47 16N 53 54W
Duparquet Québec 57 A3 48 32N 79 14W
Durham Ontario 54 B3 44 11N 80 49W
Durham *admin.* Ontario 54 C3/D3 44 04N 79 11W
Durrell Newfoundland and Labrador 61 H4 49 40N 54 44W
Dutton Ontario 54 A1 42 39N 81 30W
Duvernay Québec 58 N5 45 34N 73 41W
Dyer, Cape Nunavut 65 T4 66 37N 61 16W
Dyer's Bay Ontario 54 A4 45 10N 81 18W
Dyer's Bay *tn.* Ontario 54 A4 45 09N 81 20W
Dyke Lake Newfoundland and Labrador 60 B7 54 30N 66 18W

E

Eabamet Lake Ontario 50 H6 51 32N 87 46W
Eagle Lake Ontario 50 E5 49 35N 93 00W
Eagle Plains *tn.* Yukon Territory 64 C4 66 30N 136 50W
Eagle River Newfoundland and Labrador 60 G6 53 10N 58 00W
Eagle River Saskatchewan 47 D2 51 35N 107 40W
Eagle River *tn.* Ontario 50 E5 49 50N 93 12W
Ear Falls *tn.* Ontario 50 E6 50 38N 93 13W
Earl Rowe Provincial Park Ontario 54 C3 44 15N 79 45W
East Angus Québec 53 Q5 45 30N 71 40W
East Bay Bird Sanctuary Nunavut 65 P3 66 20N 74 00W
East Chezzetcook Nova Scotia 61 M11 44 34N 63 14W
Eastend Saskatchewan 47 C1 49 32N 108 50W
Eastern Passage *tn.* Nova Scotia 59 R6 44 36N 63 29W
Easterville Manitoba 49 C3 53 00N 99 40W
East Lake Nova Scotia 59 R7 44 46N 63 29W
Eastmain Québec 57 A5 52 10N 78 30W
East Point Prince Edward Island 61 M12 46 27N 61 59W
Eastport Newfoundland and Labrador 61 J4 48 39N 53 45W
East Thurlow Island British Columbia 42 G5 50 24N 125 26W
East York Ontario 55 C2 43 43N 79 20W
Eatonia Saskatchewan 47 C2 51 13N 109 22W
Echaot'ine Kúé *(Fort Liard)* Northwest Territories 64 F3 60 14N 123 28W
Echoing River Ontario 50 F8 54 30N 92 00W
Eclipse Sound Nunavut 65 Q5 72 38N 79 00W
Ecum Secum Nova Scotia 61 M11 44 58N 62 08W
Eddies Cove *tn.* Newfoundland and Labrador 60 G5 51 25N 56 27W
Edehon Lake Nunavut 65 L3 60 25N 97 15W
Edgerton Alberta 46 G3 52 46N 110 27W
Edgewood British Columbia 43 L1 49 47N 118 08W
Edmonton Alberta 46 F3 53 34N 113 25W
Edmund Lake Manitoba 49 F4 54 50N 93 30W
Edmundston New Brunswick 61 A3 47 22N 68 20W
Edson Alberta 46 D3 53 35N 116 26W
Eduni, Mount Northwest Territories 64 E3 64 13N 128 10W
Edwards Ontario 59 L2 45 19N 75 48W
Edziza, Mount British Columbia 42 E5 57 43N 130 42W
Edzo Northwest Territories 64 G3 63 50N 116 00W
Eganville Ontario 53 J5 45 32N 77 06W
Eglinton Island Northwest Territories 64 G6 75 48N 118 30W
Egmont British Columbia 42 H4 49 45N 123 55W
Egmont Bay Prince Edward Island 61 M12 46 30N 64 20W
Egmont, Cape Nova Scotia 61 M12 46 50N 60 20W
Eileen Lake Northwest Territories 64 J3 62 16N 107 37W
Ekwan Point Ontario 50 K7 53 20N 82 10W
Ekwan River Ontario 50 K7 53 30N 83 40W
Elaho River British Columbia 42 H5 50 14N 123 33W
Elbow Saskatchewan 47 D2 51 08N 106 36W
Elbow River Alberta 44 A1 50 59N 114 13W
Elgin *admin.* Ontario 54 A1 42 38N 81 36W
Elkford British Columbia 43 N2 50 02N 114 55W
Elkhorn Manitoba 49 B1 49 58N 101 14W
Elk Island Manitoba 49 D2 50 50N 96 40W
Elk Island National Park Alberta 46 F3 53 36N 112 53W
Elk Lake *tn.* Ontario 51 L4 47 44N 80 20W
Elk Lakes Provincial Park British Columbia 43 N2 50 00N 115 00W
Elk Point *tn.* Alberta 46 G3 53 54N 110 54W
Ellef Ringnes Island Nunavut 65 K6 78 30N 102 00W
Ellesmere Island Nunavut 65 P6 77 30N 82 30W
Ellice River Nunavut 64 J4 66 20N 105 00W
Elliot Lake *tn.* Ontario 52 D6 46 25N 82 40W
Elm Creek *tn.* Manitoba 49 D1 49 41N 97 59W
Elmira Ontario 54 B2 43 36N 80 34W
Elmira Prince Edward Island 61 M12 46 26N 62 05W
Elmvale Ontario 54 C3 44 35N 79 52W
Elora Ontario 54 B2 43 42N 80 26W
Elrose Saskatchewan 47 C2 51 12N 108 01W
Elsa Yukon Territory 64 C3 63 55N 135 29W
Elvira, Cape Nunavut 64 J5 73 16N 107 10W
Embree Newfoundland and Labrador 61 H4 49 18N 55 02W
Emerald Island Northwest Territories 64 H6 76 48N 114 10W
Emerson Manitoba 49 D1 49 00N 97 11W
Endako British Columbia 43 H4 54 10N 125 21W
Enderby British Columbia 43 L2 50 32N 119 10W
Enfield Nova Scotia 61 M11 44 56N 63 34W
Englee Newfoundland and Labrador 60 G5 50 44N 56 06W
Englehart Ontario 51 M4 47 50N 79 52W
English Bay British Columbia 44 F4 49 17N 123 12W
English River Ontario 50 D6 50 20N 94 50W
Ennadai Lake Nunavut 65 K3 60 58N 101 20W
Enterprise Northwest Territories 64 G3 60 34N 116 15W
Entiaco Provincial Park British Columbia 43 H3 53 15N 125 30W
Eramosa River Ontario 54 B2 43 33N 80 11W
Erieau Ontario 52 E2 42 16N 81 56W
Erie Beach *tn.* Ontario 52 D2 42 16N 82 00W
Erie Beach *tn.* Ontario 54 D1 42 53N 78 56W
Erie, Lake Ontario/USA 52 E2 42 15N 81 00W
Eriksdale Manitoba 49 C2 50 52N 98 07W
Erin Ontario 54 B2 43 48N 80 04W
Escuminac, Point New Brunswick 61 C3 47 04N 64 49W
Esker Siding Newfoundland and Labrador 60 B6 53 53N 66 25W
Eskimo Lakes Northwest Territories 64 D4 68 30N 132 30W
Espanola Ontario 52 E6 46 15N 81 46W
Esquimalt British Columbia 42 H4 48 25N 123 29W
Essex Ontario 52 D2 42 10N 82 49W
Essex *admin.* Ontario 52 D2 42 10N 82 50W
Esterhazy Saskatchewan 47 F2 50 40N 102 02W
Estevan Saskatchewan 47 F1 49 09N 103 00W
Eston Saskatchewan 47 C2 51 09N 108 42W
Etawney Lake Manitoba 49 D5 57 50N 96 40W
Ethelbert Manitoba 49 B2 51 32N 100 25W
Etobicoke Ontario 55 B1 43 38N 79 30W
Etobicoke Creek Ontario 55 A1 43 43N 79 47W
Eugenia Lake Ontario 54 B3 44 20N 80 30W
Eureka *m.s.* Nunavut 65 N6 79 59N 85 57W
Eureka River *tn.* Alberta 46 C5 56 25N 118 48W
Eutsuk Lake British Columbia 43 G3 53 12N 126 32W
Evansburg Alberta 46 E3 53 36N 115 01W
Evans, Mount Alberta 46 C3 52 26N 118 07W
Evans Strait Nunavut 65 P3 63 15N 82 30W
Exeter Ontario 54 A2 43 21N 81 30W
Exploits River Newfoundland and Labrador 61 G4 48 40N 56 30W
Eyehill River Saskatchewan 47 C3 52 25N 109 50W

F

Faber Lake Northwest Territories 64 G3 63 56N 117 15W
Fairchild Creek Ontario 54 B2 43 13N 80 11W
Fairview Alberta 46 C5 56 03N 118 28W
Fairweather Mountain British Columbia/USA 42 B6 58 50N 137 55W
Falcon Lake *tn.* Manitoba 49 E1 49 44N 95 18W
Falher Alberta 46 D4 55 44N 117 12W
Fallowfield Ontario 59 J2 45 17N 75 51W
Fall River *tn.* Nova Scotia 61 M11 44 49N 63 36W
False Creek British Columbia 44 F4 49 16N 123 08W
Family Lake Manitoba 49 E2 51 50N 95 40W
Farewell Newfoundland and Labrador 57 B3 48 26N 72 15W
Farnham Québec 53 P5 45 17N 72 59W
Farnham, Mount British Columbia 43 M2 50 27N 116 37W
Faro Yukon Territory 64 D3 62 30N 133 00W
Fathom Five National Marine Park Ontario 54 A4 54 20N 81 35W
Fauquier Ontario 51 L5 49 19N 81 59W
Fawn River Ontario 50 G8 54 20N 88 40W
Fawn River Provincial Park Ontario 50 G8 54 10N 89 25W
Felix, Cape Nunavut 65 L4 69 54N 97 58W
Fenelon Falls *tn.* Ontario 54 D3 44 32N 78 45W
Fergus Ontario 54 B2 43 43N 80 24W
Ferland Ontario 50 G6 50 18N 88 25W
Ferme-Neuve Québec 53 L6 46 42N 75 28W
Fermont Québec 57 G5 52 00N 68 00W
Fernie British Columbia 43 N1 49 30N 115 00W
Ferryland Newfoundland and Labrador 61 J3 47 01N 54 53W
Field British Columbia 43 M2 51 23N 116 29W
Fife Lake Saskatchewan 47 E1 49 10N 105 55W
Finch Ontario 53 L5 45 08N 75 05W
Finger-Tatuk Provincial Park British Columbia 43 H3 53 30N 124 15W
Finlay Ranges *mts.* British Columbia 43 H5 57 10N 126 00W
Finlay River British Columbia 43 G5 57 20N 125 40W
Finlay-Russel Provincial Park British Columbia 43 G5/H5 57 20N 126 00W
Fiordland Recreation Area British Columbia 43 F3 52 00N 127 00W
Firebag Hills Saskatchewan 47 C5 57 15N 109 50W
Firebag River Alberta 46 G5 57 30N 110 40W
Fish Creek Alberta 44 A1 50 55N 114 10W
Fish Creek Provincial Park Alberta 44 A1 50 55N 114 04W
Fisher Bay Manitoba 49 D2 51 30N 97 30W
Fisher Branch *tn.* Manitoba 49 D2 51 04N 97 38W
Fisher, Mount British Columbia 43 N1 49 35N 115 20W
Fisher Strait Nunavut 65 P3 63 00N 84 00W
Fishing Branch Game Reserve Yukon Territory 64 C4 66 30N 139 30W
Fishing Lake Manitoba 49 E3 52 10N 95 40W
Fitzgerald Alberta 46 G6 59 51N 111 36W
Fitzwilliam Island Ontario 52 E5 45 29N 81 45W
Fjord Alluviaq Québec 56 H8 59 30N 65 30W
Flamborough Ontario 54 C2 43 20N 79 57W
Flathead River British Columbia 43 N1 48 30N 114 10W
Flesherton Ontario 54 B3 44 16N 80 32W
Fletchers Lake Nova Scotia 59 Q7 44 51N 63 35W
Fleur de Lys Newfoundland and Labrador 61 G5 50 07N 56 08W
Fleuve Saint-Laurent *r.* Québec 57 F3 48 20N 69 20W
Flin Flon Manitoba 49 B4 54 50N 102 00W
Florenceville New Brunswick 61 B3 46 20N 67 20W
Flores Island British Columbia 43 G1 49 20N 126 10W
Flour Lake Newfoundland and Labrador 60 C6 53 44N 64 50W
Foam Lake *tn.* Saskatchewan 47 F2 51 38N 103 31W
Foch British Columbia 42 H5 50 07N 124 31W
Foch-Gitnadoix Provincial Park British Columbia 43 F3 54 00N 129 15W
Fogo Newfoundland and Labrador 61 H4 49 43N 54 17W
Fogo Island Newfoundland and Labrador 61 H4 49 40N 54 10W
Foleyet Ontario 51 K5 48 05N 82 26W
Fond du Lac Saskatchewan 47 D6 59 20N 107 09W
Fond du Lac River Saskatchewan 47 E6 59 05N 104 40W
Fontas River British Columbia 43 K6 58 20N 121 25W
Fonthill *tn.* Ontario 54 C2 43 02N 79 17W
Forbes, Mount Alberta 46 D2 51 52N 116 55W
Foremost Alberta 46 G1 49 29N 111 25W
Forest Ontario 52 E3 43 06N 82 00W
Forestburg Alberta 46 G3 52 35N 112 04W
Forest Hill Ontario 55 C1 43 42N 79 25W
Forestville Québec 57 F3 48 45N 69 04W
Forks of the Credit Provincial Park Ontario 54 B2 43 49N 80 02W
Forrest Lake Saskatchewan 47 C5 57 35N 109 10W
Fort Albany Ontario 50 L7 52 12N 81 40W
Fort Babine British Columbia 43 G4 55 20N 126 35W
Fort Chipewyan Alberta 46 G6 58 46N 111 09W
Fort Coulange Québec 53 K5 45 51N 76 46W
Forteau Newfoundland and Labrador 60 G5 51 28N 56 58W
Fort Erie Ontario 54 D1 42 55N 78 56W
Fort Frances Ontario 50 E5 48 37N 93 23W
Fort Fraser British Columbia 43 H4 54 03N 124 30W
Fort Garry Manitoba 48 B2 49 49N 97 10W
Fort Hope *I.R.* Ontario 50 H6 51 37N 87 55W
Fort Langley British Columbia 42 H4 49 11N 122 38W
Fort MacKay Alberta 46 G5 57 11N 111 37W
Fort Mackenzie Québec 56 F7 56 50N 68 56W
Fort Macleod Alberta 46 F1 49 44N 113 24W
Fort McMurray Alberta 46 G5 56 45N 111 27W
Fort Nelson British Columbia 43 J6 58 48N 122 44W
Fort Nelson River British Columbia 43 J6 59 20N 124 05W
Fort Qu'Appelle Saskatchewan 47 F2 50 46N 103 54W
Fort Rouge Manitoba 48 B2 49 52N 97 07W
Fort St. James British Columbia 43 H4 54 26N 124 15W
Fort St. John British Columbia 43 K5 56 14N 120 55W
Fort Saskatchewan Alberta 46 F3 53 42N 113 12W
Fort Severn Ontario 50 H9 56 00N 87 40W
Fortune Newfoundland and Labrador 61 H3 47 04N 55 50W
Fortune Bay Newfoundland and Labrador 61 H3 47 15N 55 30W
Fort Vermilion Alberta 46 E6 58 22N 115 59W
Fort Ware British Columbia 43 H5 57 30N 125 43W
Fort Whyte Manitoba 48 B2 49 49N 97 12W
Fosheim Peninsula Nunavut 65 P6 80 00N 85 00W
Foster, Mount British Columbia 42 C6 59 49N 135 35W
Foster River Saskatchewan 47 E5 56 20N 105 45W
Fourchu Nova Scotia 61 M12 45 43N 60 17W
Fox Creek *tn.* Alberta 46 D4 54 24N 116 48W
Foxe Basin *b.* Nunavut 65 P4 66 20N 79 00W
Foxe Channel Nunavut 65 P3 64 40N 80 00W
Foxe Peninsula Nunavut 65 Q3 65 00N 76 00W
Fox Mine *tn.* Manitoba 49 B5 56 39N 101 38W
Fox River Manitoba 49 F5 56 00N 93 50W
Fox Valley *tn.* Saskatchewan 47 C2 50 29N 109 29W
Frances Lake Yukon Territory 64 E3 61 20N 129 30W
François Lake British Columbia 43 H3 54 00N 125 47W
Frankford Ontario 52 J4 44 12N 77 36W
Franklin Bay Northwest Territories 64 E5 69 45N 126 00W
Franklin Lake Nunavut 65 L4 66 56N 96 03W
Franklin Mountains Northwest Territories 64 F3 61 15N 123 50W
Fraserdale Ontario 51 L5 49 51N 81 37W
Fraser Lake Newfoundland and Labrador 60 D7 54 24N 63 40W
Fraser Lake *tn.* British Columbia 43 H4 54 00N 124 50W
Fraser Plateau British Columbia 43 J3 52 32N 124 10W
Fraser River British Columbia 43 J2 51 36N 122 25W
Fraser River Newfoundland and Labrador 60 D8 56 50N 63 50W
Fredericton New Brunswick 61 B2 45 57N 66 40W
Fredericton Junction New Brunswick 61 B2 45 40N 66 38W
Freels, Cape Newfoundland and Labrador 61 J4 49 15N 53 29W
Freeport Nova Scotia 61 L11 44 17N 66 19W
Frenchman River Saskatchewan 47 D1 49 30N 108 00W
Frenchman's Cove *tn.* Newfoundland and Labrador 61 F4 49 04N 58 10W
French River Ontario 52 F6 46 00N 81 00W
French River *tn.* Ontario 52 F6 46 03N 80 34W
Freshwater Newfoundland and Labrador 61 J3 47 15N 53 59W
Frobisher Bay Nunavut 65 S3 62 15N 65 00W
Frobisher Lake Saskatchewan 47 C5 57 00N 108 00W
Frog Lake Alberta 46 G3 53 55N 110 20W
Frontenac *admin.* Ontario 53 K4 44 40N 76 45W
Frontenac *admin.* Québec 53 R5 45 40N 70 50W
Frontenac Provincial Park Ontario 53 K4 44 32N 76 29W
Frozen Strait Nunavut 65 P4 66 08N 85 00W
Fruitvale British Columbia 43 M1 49 08N 117 28W
Fundy, Bay of New Brunswick/Nova Scotia 61 L11 45 00N 66 00W
Fundy National Park New Brunswick 61 L12 45 40N 65 10W
Fury and Hecla Strait Nunavut 65 P4 69 56N 84 00W

G

Gabarus Bay Nova Scotia 61 M12 45 50N 60 10W
Gabriola Island British Columbia 42 H4 49 10N 123 51W
Gage, Cape Prince Edward Island 61 M12 46 50N 64 20W
Gagetown New Brunswick 61 B2 45 46N 66 29W
Gagnon Québec 57 F4 51 56N 68 16W
Galiano Island British Columbia 42 H4 48 57N 123 25W
Galt Ontario 54 B2 43 21N 80 19W
Gambier Island British Columbia 42 H4 49 30N 123 25W
Gambo Newfoundland and Labrador 61 H4 48 46N 54 14W
Gamet *(Red Lakes) tn.* Northwest Territories 64 G3 64 10N 117 20W
Gananoque Ontario 53 K4 44 20N 76 10W
Gander Newfoundland and Labrador 61 H4 48 57N 54 34W
Gander Lake Newfoundland and Labrador 61 H4 48 55N 54 35W
Ganges British Columbia 42 H4 48 51N 123 31W
Garden Creek *tn.* Alberta 46 F6 58 42N 113 53W
Garden Hill *tn.* Manitoba 49 E3 53 52N 94 37W
Gardiner Dam Saskatchewan 47 D2 51 15N 106 40W
Gardner Canal British Columbia 42 F3 53 30N 128 50W
Garibaldi Lake British Columbia 42 H4 49 55N 122 57W
Garibaldi, Mount British Columbia 42 H4 49 53N 123 00W
Garibaldi Provincial Park British Columbia 42 H4 49 58N 122 45W
Garnish Newfoundland and Labrador 61 H3 47 14N 55 22W
Garry Lake Nunavut 65 K4 66 20N 100 00W
Garry Point British Columbia 52 F3 49 07N 123 14W
Gaspé Québec 57 H3 48 50N 64 30W
Gaspereau Lake Nova Scotia 61 M11 44 50N 64 30W
Gataga River British Columbia 43 G6 58 30N 126 40W
Gateshead Island Nunavut 65 K5 70 36N 100 26W
Gatineau Québec 53 L5 45 29N 75 39W
Gatineau *admin.* Québec 53 L6 45 47N 76 05W
Gauer Lake Manitoba 49 D5 57 10N 97 30W
Gaultois Newfoundland and Labrador 61 H3 47 36N 55 54W
Geikie River Saskatchewan 47 E5 57 20N 104 40W
George, Cape Nova Scotia 61 M12 45 50N 61 50W
George Island Newfoundland and Labrador 60 G7 54 16N 57 20W
Georgetown Ontario 54 C2 43 39N 79 56W
Georgetown Prince Edward Island 61 M12 46 12N 62 32W
Georgian Bay Ontario 52 E5 45 00N 81 00W
Georgian Bay Islands National Park Ontario 52 G4 44 53N 79 52W
Georgia, Strait of British Columbia 42 H4 49 39N 124 34W
Georgina Island Ontario 54 C3 44 22N 79 17W
Geraldton Ontario 51 H5 49 44N 86 59W
Germansen Landing British Columbia 43 H4 55 47N 124 42W
Giant's Causeway Northwest Territories 64 F6 75 46N 121 11W
Giants Tomb Island Ontario 54 B3 44 55N 80 00W

Gibsons *tn.* British Columbia 42 H4 49 24N 123 30W
Gifford Island British Columbia 43 G2 50 45N 126 20W
Gift Lake *tn.* Alberta 46 E4 55 50N 115 50W
Gilbert Plains *tn.* Manitoba 49 B2 51 09N 100 28W
Gil Island British Columbia 42 F3 53 10N 129 15W
Gillam Manitoba 49 E5 56 25N 94 45W
Gillies Bay *tn.* British Columbia 42 H4 49 42N 124 28W
Gimli Manitoba 49 D2 50 39N 97 00W
Gitnadoix River Provincial Park British Columbia 43 F4 54 05NN 129 00W
Glace Bay *tn.* Nova Scotia 61 M12 46 11N 59 58W
Glacial Mountain British Columbia 42 F6 58 15N 129 25W
Glacier National Park British Columbia 43 M2 51 00N 117 00W
Gladstone Manitoba 49 C2 50 14N 98 56W
Gladstone Provincial Park British Columbia 43 L1 49 15N 118 10W
Gladys Lake British Columbia 42 D6 59 50N 132 52W
Glaslyn Saskatchewan 47 C3 53 23N 108 22W
Glenboro Manitoba 49 C1 49 35N 99 20W
Glen Cairn Ontario 59 J2 45 15N 75 45W
Glencoe Ontario 54 A1 42 45N 81 44W
Glenmore Reservoir Alberta 44 A1 50 58N 114 08W
Glenwood Newfoundland and Labrador 61 H4 48 59N 54 53W
Gloucester Ontario 53 L5 45 21N 75 39W
Gloucester *admin.* New Brunswick 61 C3 47 30N 65 50W
Glover Island Newfoundland and Labrador 61 G4 48 46N 57 43W
Glovertown Newfoundland and Labrador 61 H4 48 41N 54 02W
Goat Island British Columbia 42 H5 50 03N 124 28W
Goat Range Provincial Park British Columbia 43 M2 50 15N 117 15W
Goderich Ontario 54 A2 43 43N 81 43W
Gods Lake Manitoba 49 E4 54 40N 94 20W
Gods Lake *tn.* Manitoba 49 E4 54 45N 94 00W
Gods Mercy, Bay of Nunavut 65 N3 63 30N 88 10W
Gods River Manitoba 49 F4 56 20N 92 50W
Gogama Ontario 51 L4 47 40N 81 43W
Goldboro Nova Scotia 61 M12 45 12N 61 35W
Gold Bridge British Columbia 43 J2 50 51N 122 51W
Golden British Columbia 43 M2 51 19N 116 55W
Golden Ears Provincial Park British Columbia 42 H4 49 28N 122 25W
Golden Hinde *mt.* British Columbia 43 H1 49 35N 125 40W
Gold River British Columbia 43 G1 49 41N 125 59W
Goldsmith Channel Nunavut 64 J5 73 00N 106 00W
Golfe du Saint-Laurent Québec 57 J3 48 40N 63 20W
Goodeve Saskatchewan 47 F2 51 03N 103 11W
Good Hope British Columbia 43 G2 50 59N 124 01W
Good Hope Lake British Columbia 43 F6 56 15N 129 20W
Good Hope Mountain British Columbia 43 J2 51 08N 124 10W
Goodsoil Saskatchewan 47 C4 54 24N 109 12W
Goose Bay *tn.* Newfoundland and Labrador 60 E6 53 15N 60 20W
Goose River Newfoundland and Labrador 60 E6 53 30N 61 50W
Gordon Horne Peak British Columbia 43 L2 51 47N 118 50W
Gordon Lake Alberta 46 G5 56 30N 110 25W
Gordon Pittock Reservoir Ontario 54 B2 43 11N 80 43W
Gordon River British Columbia 42 H4 48 38N 124 25W
Gore Bay *tn.* Ontario 52 D5 45 55N 82 28W
Goshen Nova Scotia 61 M12 45 20N 62 55W
Gowganda Ontario 51 L4 47 39N 80 46W
Gracefield Québec 53 K6 46 05N 76 05W
Grady Harbour *tn.* Newfoundland and Labrador 60 G6 53 48N 56 25W
Graham Island British Columbia 42 D3 53 50N 132 40W
Graham Island Nunavut 65 M6 77 25N 90 30W
Graham Laurier Provincial Park British Columbia 43 J5 56 30N 123 30W
Granby Québec 53 P5 45 22N 72 43W
Granby Provincial Park British Columbia 43 L1 49 45N 118 30W
Granby River British Columbia 43 L1 49 27N 118 25W
Grand Bank Newfoundland and Labrador 61 H3 47 06N 55 46W
Grand Bay-Westfield *tn.* New Brunswick 61 L12 45 19N 66 14W
Grand Bend Ontario 52 E3 43 21N 81 45W
Grande-Anse New Brunswick 61 C3 47 50N 65 10W
Grande-Anse Québec 53 P7 47 05N 72 55W
Grande Cache Alberta 46 C3 53 50N 119 08W
Grande Pointe Manitoba 48 B2 49 45N 97 03W
Grande Prairie Alberta 43 L4 55 10N 118 40W
Grande-Rivière *tn.* Québec 57 H3 48 23N 64 31W
Grande Rivière de la Baleine *r.* Québec 56 C6 55 15N 77 00W
Grand Étang Nova Scotia 61 M12 46 00N 61 00W
Grande-Vallée *tn.* Québec 57 H3 49 15N 65 10W
Grand Falls/Grand Sault *tn.* New Brunswick 61 B3 47 02N 67 46W
Grand Falls-Windsor *tn.* Newfoundland and Labrador 61 H4 48 56N 55 40W
Grand Forks British Columbia 43 L1 49 02N 118 30W
Grandin, Lake Northwest Territories 64 G3 63 50N 119 50W
Grand Jardin Newfoundland and Labrador 61 F4 48 28N 59 13W
Grand Lake New Brunswick 61 B2 46 00N 66 40W
Grand Lake Newfoundland and Labrador 60 E6 53 40N 60 30W
Grand Lake Newfoundland and Labrador 61 G4 49 00N 57 20W
Grand Manan *tn.* New Brunswick 61 L11 44 41N 66 46W
Grand Manan Island New Brunswick 61 L11 44 45N 66 40W
Grand Marais Manitoba 49 D2 50 30N 96 35W
Grand-Mère Québec 53 P6 46 36N 72 41W
Grand Narrows *tn.* Nova Scotia 61 M12 45 55N 60 50W
Grand Prairie *tn.* Alberta 46 C4 55 10N 118 52W
Grand Rapids *tn.* Manitoba 49 C3 53 12N 99 19W
Grand-Remous Québec 57 C2 46 37N 75 56W
Grand River Ontario 54 C1 42 51N 79 34W
Grand Valley *tn.* Ontario 54 B2 43 54N 80 10W
Grandview Manitoba 49 B2 51 11N 100 51W
Granisle British Columbia 43 G4 54 56N 126 18W
Granite Bay *tn.* British Columbia 42 G5 50 00N 125 00W
Granite Lake Newfoundland and Labrador 61 G4 48 11N 57 01W
Granville Falls Manitoba 49 B5 56 10N 100 20W
Granville Lake Manitoba 49 B5 56 00N 101 00W
Grasslands National Park Saskatchewan 47 D1 49 10N 107 30W
Grass River Manitoba 49 C4 54 50N 99 20W
Grass River Provincial Park Manitoba 49 B4 54 40N 101 40W
Grassy Narrows *I.R.* Ontario 50 E6 50 10N 93 55W
Gravelbourg Saskatchewan 47 D1 49 53N 106 33W
Gravenhurst Ontario 52 G4 44 55N 79 22W
Grayling River British Columbia 43 H6 59 43N 125 55W
Greasy Lake Northwest Territories 64 F3 62 55N 122 15W
Great Bear Lake Northwest Territories 64 F4 66 00N 120 00W
Great Central Lake British Columbia 42 G4 49 22N 125 10W
Greater Sudbury Ontario 52 E6 46 30N 81 01W
Great Plain of the Koukdjuak Nunavut 65 R4 66 25N 72 50W
Great Pubnico Lake Nova Scotia 61 L11 43 50N 65 30W
Great Sand Hills Saskatchewan 47 C2 50 35N 109 20W
Great Slave Lake Northwest Territories 64 H3 62 00N 114 00W
Great Village Nova Scotia 61 M12 45 25N 63 36W
Greely Ontario 59 K2 45 16N 75 33W
Greely Fiord Nunavut 65 P7 80 30N 85 00W
Green Creek Ontario 59 K2 45 25N 75 35W
Green Gables Prince Edward Island 61 M12 46 28N 63 20W
Green Lake British Columbia 43 K2 51 26N 121 12W
Green Lake *tn.* Saskatchewan 47 D4 54 18N 107 49W
Greenville British Columbia 42 F4 55 05N 129 35W
Greenwater Lake Provincial Park Saskatchewan 47 F3 52 35N 103 25W
Greenwood British Columbia 43 L1 49 08N 118 41W
Greenwood Nova Scotia 61 M11 45 00N 64 50W
Grenfell Saskatchewan 47 F2 50 24N 102 56W
Grenville Québec 53 M5 45 40N 74 38W
Gretna Manitoba 49 D1 49 01N 97 34W
Grey *admin.* Ontario 54 B3 44 22N 80 33W
Grey Islands Newfoundland and Labrador 60 H5 50 50N 55 35W
Grey, Point British Columbia 44 E4 49 16N 123 17W
Grey River Newfoundland and Labrador 61 G3 47 50N 56 50W
Griffith Island Ontario 54 B3 44 50N 80 54W
Grimsby Ontario 54 C2 43 12N 79 35W
Grimshaw Alberta 46 D5 56 11N 117 36W
Grinnell Peninsula Nunavut 65 L6 76 40N 95 00W
Grizzly Bear Hills Saskatchewan 47 C4 55 50N 109 30W
Groais Island Newfoundland and Labrador 60 H5 50 57N 55 36W
Gros Morne *mt.* Newfoundland and Labrador 61 G4 49 36N 57 47W
Gros Morne National Park Newfoundland and Labrador 61 G4 49 40N 58 40W
Groswater Bay Newfoundland and Labrador 60 G7 54 20N 57 40W
Grouard Mission Alberta 46 D4 55 30N 116 10W
Groundhog River Ontario 51 K5 49 00N 82 10W
Guelph Ontario 54 B2 43 34N 80 16W
Gull Bay *I.R.* Ontario 50 G5 49 50N 89 00W
Gull Lake Alberta 46 F3 52 34N 114 00W
Gull Lake *tn.* Saskatchewan 47 C2 50 05N 108 30W
Gunisao Lake Manitoba 49 D3 53 30N 96 40W
Gunisao River Manitoba 49 D3 53 30N 96 50W
Guysborough Nova Scotia 61 M12 45 23N 61 30W
Guysborough *admin.* Nova Scotia 61 M12 45 20N 61 40W
Gwaii Haanas National Park Reserve British Columbia 42 E3 52 30N 130 40W
Gwillim Lake Provincial Park British Columbia 43 K4 55 00N 121 00W
Gypsumville Manitoba 49 C2 51 47N 98 38W
Gyrfalcon Islands Nunavut 56 F8 59 05N 69 00W

H

Habay Alberta 46 C6 58 49N 118 44W
Hadley Bay Nunavut 64 J5 72 22N 108 30W
Hagensborg British Columbia 43 G3 52 30N 126 30W
Hague Saskatchewan 47 D3 52 30N 106 25W
Haileybury Ontario 51 M4 47 27N 79 38W
Haines Junction Yukon Territory 64 C3 60 45N 137 21W
Hakai Recreation Area British Columbia 43 G2 50 40N 128 00W
Haldimand-Norfolk *admin.* Ontario 54 B1/C1 42 37N 80 39W
Halfway Point *tn.* Newfoundland and Labrador 61 F4 48 59N 58 06W
Halfway River British Columbia 43 J5 56 42N 122 30W
Haliburton Ontario 52 H5 45 03N 78 31W
Haliburton *admin.* Ontario 52 H5 45 05N 78 50W
Halifax Nova Scotia 61 M11 44 40N 63 41W
Halifax *admin.* Nova Scotia 61 M12 45 00N 63 00W
Halifax Harbour Nova Scotia 59 Q6 44 39N 63 33W
Hall Peninsula Nunavut 65 S3 68 40N 66 00W
Halls Harbour Nova Scotia 61 M12 45 12N 64 37W
Halton *admin.* Ontario 54 C2 43 26N 79 57W
Hamber Provincial Park British Columbia 43 M3 53 20N 117 55W
Hamilton Ontario 54 C2 43 15N 79 50W
Hamilton Harbour Ontario 54 C2 43 16N 80 50W
Hamilton Inlet Newfoundland and Labrador 60 F6 54 18N 57 30W
Hamilton Sound Newfoundland and Labrador 61 H4 49 30N 54 15W
Hamilton-Wentworth *admin.* Ontario 54 B2/C2 43 14N 80 09W
Hamiota Manitoba 49 B2 50 11N 100 38W
Hampden Newfoundland and Labrador 61 G4 49 33N 56 51W
Hampton New Brunswick 61 L12 45 30N 65 50W
Hampton Ontario 54 D2 43 52N 78 43W
Hanley Saskatchewan 47 D2 51 37N 106 26W
Hanna Alberta 46 G2 51 38N 111 56W
Hannah Bay Ontario 51 L6/M6 51 20N 80 00W
Hanover Ontario 54 A3 44 10N 81 03W
Hanson Lake Road Saskatchewan 47 E4 54 20N 104 35W
Hants *admin.* Nova Scotia 61 M12 45 10N 63 40W
Hantsport Nova Scotia 61 M12 45 04N 64 12W
Happy Valley-Goose Bay Newfoundland and Labrador 60 E6 53 18N 60 16W
Harbour Breton *tn.* Newfoundland and Labrador 61 H3 47 29N 55 50W
Harbour Deep *tn.* Newfoundland and Labrador 61 G5 50 22N 56 31W
Harbour Grace *tn.* Newfoundland and Labrador 61 J3 47 42N 53 13W
Hardisty Alberta 46 G3 52 40N 111 18W
Hardisty Lake Northwest Territories 64 G3 64 30N 117 45W
Hare Bay Newfoundland and Labrador 60 H5 51 15N 55 45W
Hare Bay *tn.* Newfoundland and Labrador 61 J4 48 51N 54 00W
Hare Indian River Northwest Territories 64 E4 66 40N 128 00W
Haro Strait British Columbia 42 H4 48 36N 123 17W
Harp Lake Newfoundland and Labrador 60 E7 55 05N 61 50W
Harrington Harbour *tn.* Québec 56 L4 50 31N 59 30W
Harrison, Cape Newfoundland and Labrador 60 G7 54 57N 57 57W
Harrison Hot Springs *tn.* British Columbia 42 H4 49 17N 121 47W
Harrison Lake British Columbia 42 H4 49 30N 122 10W
Harriston Ontario 54 B2 43 54N 80 52W
Harrow Ontario 52 D2 42 02N 82 55W
Harrowby Manitoba 49 B2 50 45N 101 28W
Harry Gibbons Bird Sanctuary Nunavut 65 N3 63 50N 86 00W
Hartland New Brunswick 61 B3 46 18N 67 31W
Hartney Manitoba 49 B1 49 29N 100 31W
Hart River Yukon Territory 64 C4 65 40N 137 10W
Hastings Ontario 52 J4 44 18N 77 57W
Hastings *admin.* Ontario 52 J4/J5 44 45N 77 40W
Hatchet Lake Saskatchewan 47 F6 58 50N 103 30W
Haultain River Saskatchewan 47 D5 56 20N 106 20W
Havelock Ontario 52 J4 44 26N 77 53W
Havre-Aubert Québec 61 E3 47 15N 61 51W
Havre Saint-Pierre Québec 57 J4 50 20N 63 38W
Hawkes Bay *tn.* Newfoundland and Labrador 61 G5 50 36N 57 10W
Hawkesbury Ontario 53 M5 45 36N 74 37W
Hay Camp Alberta 46 G6 59 31N 111 23W
Hay, Cape Northwest Territories 64 H5 74 25N 113 00W
Hayes River Manitoba 49 F4 55 20N 93 50W
Hay Lake Alberta 46 C6 58 52N 119 20W
Hay River Alberta/Northwest Territories 46 C6 58 20N 119 00W
Hazeldean Ontario 59 J2 45 18N 75 55W
Hazelton British Columbia 43 G4 55 17N 127 42W
Hazen Strait Northwest Territories/Nunavut 64 J6 77 00N 110 00W
Head of Bay d'Espoir Newfoundland and Labrador 61 H3 47 56N 55 45W
Hearst Ontario 51 K5 49 42N 83 40W
Heart's Content Newfoundland and Labrador 61 J3 47 53N 53 22W
Hebron Newfoundland and Labrador 60 D9 58 12N 62 38W
Hebron Nova Scotia 61 L11 43 57N 66 03W
Hebron Fiord *in.* Newfoundland and Labrador 60 D9 58 09N 62 45W
Hecate Strait British Columbia 42 E3 53 40N 131 10W
Hecla and Griper Bay Northwest Territories/Nunavut 64 H6 76 25N 113 00W
Hecla/Grindstone Provincial Park Manitoba 49 D2 51 10N 96 30W
Hecla Island Manitoba 49 D2 51 00N 96 30W
Height of the Rockies Provincial Park British Columbia 43 N2 50 15N 115 00W
Henrietta Island Newfoundland and Labrador 60 F7 54 05N 58 28W
Henrietta Maria, Cape Ontario 50 K8 55 00N 82 30W
Henry Kater Peninsula Nunavut 65 S4 69 20N 67 20W
Hensall Ontario 54 A2 43 26N 81 31W
Hepburn Saskatchewan 47 D3 52 30N 106 45W
Hepworth Ontario 54 A3 44 37N 81 09W
Herbert Saskatchewan 47 D2 50 26N 107 12W
Heriot Bay *tn.* British Columbia 42 G5 50 06N 125 12W
Hermitage Sandyville Newfoundland and Labrador 61 H3 47 33N 55 56W
Heron Bay *I.R.* Ontario 51 H5 48 40N 86 17W
Herring Cove Nova Scotia 61 M11 44 35N 63 35W
Herschel Yukon Territory 64 C4 69 34N 139 00W
Herschel Island Yukon Territory 64 C4 69 34N 139 00W
Hespeler Ontario 54 B2 43 26N 80 20W
Hess River Yukon Territory 64 D3 63 25N 133 50W
Hibbard Québec 53 M7 47 53N 74 03W
Hickman, Mount British Columbia 42 E5 57 15N 131 07W
Highlands British Columbia 42 H4 48 30N 123 30W
High Level *tn.* Alberta 46 D6 58 10N 117 20W
High Prairie *tn.* Alberta 46 D4 55 26N 116 29W
High River *tn.* Alberta 46 F2 50 35N 113 52W
Highrock Manitoba 49 B4 55 50N 100 22W
Highrock Lake Manitoba 49 B4 55 45N 100 20W
Highrock Lake Saskatchewan 47 E5 57 00N 105 20W
Hillsborough New Brunswick 61 M12 45 56N 64 40W
Hillsburgh Ontario 54 B2 43 46N 80 10W
Hilton Beach *tn.* Ontario 52 C6 46 16N 83 56W
Hinds Lake Reservoir Newfoundland and Labrador 61 G4 49 10N 56 50W
Hines Creek *tn.* Alberta 46 C5 56 15N 118 36W
Hinton Alberta 46 D3 53 25N 117 34W
Hoare Bay Nunavut 65 T4 65 17N 62 55W
Hodgeville Saskatchewan 47 D2 50 07N 106 58W
Hog Island Prince Edward Island 61 M12 46 53N 63 50W
Holden Alberta 46 F3 53 14N 112 14W
Holland Landing Ontario 54 C3 44 05N 79 29W
Holland River Ontario 54 C3 44 01N 79 39W
Holyrood Newfoundland and Labrador 61 J3 47 23N 53 08W
Homathko River British Columbia 43 H2 51 00N 125 05W
Home Bay Nunavut 65 S4 69 00N 87 00W
Home Island Newfoundland and Labrador 60 C10 60 10N 64 14W
Hope British Columbia 42 H4 49 21N 121 28W
Hope Bay Ontario 54 A3 44 55N 81 14W
Hopedale Newfoundland and Labrador 60 E7 55 28N 60 13W
Hope Island British Columbia 43 G2 50 55N 127 55W
Hope Island Ontario 54 B3 44 54N 80 11W
Hopes Advance Bay Québec 56 F8 59 20N 69 40W
Hopewell Nova Scotia 61 M12 45 29N 62 41W
Hopewell Islands Nunavut 56 A8 58 20N 78 10W
Hornaday River Northwest Territories 64 F4 69 00N 123 00W
Hornby Island British Columbia 42 H4 49 31N 124 40W
Hornepayne Ontario 51 J5 49 13N 84 47W
Horner Creek Ontario 54 B2 43 12N 80 35W
Horn Mountains Northwest Territories 64 G3 62 15N 119 15W
Horsefly Lake British Columbia 43 K3 52 25N 121 00W
Horse Islands Newfoundland and Labrador 61 H5 50 13N 55 48W
Horseshoe Bay *tn.* British Columbia 42 H4 49 22N 123 17W
Horseshoe Valley Ontario 54 C3 44 34N 79 41W
Horton River Northwest Territories 64 F4 68 50N 123 50W
Horwood Lake Ontario 51 K5 48 00N 82 20W
Hottah Lake Northwest Territories 64 G4 65 04N 118 30W
Houston British Columbia 43 G4 54 24N 126 39W
Houston Point Nunavut 50 L7 58 20N 81 00W
Howe Sound British Columbia 42 H4 49 30N 123 25W
Howie Centre Nova Scotia 61 M12 46 05N 60 15W
Howley Newfoundland and Labrador 61 G4 49 10N 57 07W
Hubbards Nova Scotia 61 M11 44 38N 64 03W
Hubbart Point Manitoba 49 E6 59 21N 94 41W
Hudson Bay *(Baie d'Hudson)* Canada 65 N3/P2 60 00N 85 00W
Hudson Bay *tn.* Saskatchewan 47 F3 52 45N 102 45W
Hudson's Hope British Columbia 43 K5 56 00N 121 59W
Hudson Strait *(Detroit d'Hudson)* Nunavut 65 R3 62 00N 70 00W
Hudwin Lake Park Reserve Manitoba 49 E3 53 15N 95 00W
Hugh Keenleyside Dam British Columbia 43 M1 49 33N 118 00W
Hull Québec 59 K2 45 25N 75 44W
Hull *admin.* Québec 53 L5 45 40N 75 40W
Humber Bay Ontario 54 C2 43 36N 79 27W
Humber River Ontario 54 C2 43 58N 79 37W
Humboldt Saskatchewan 47 E3 52 12N 105 07W
150 Mile House British Columbia 43 K3 52 05N 121 56W

100 Mile House British Columbia 43 K2 51 36N 121 18W
Hunter Island British Columbia 43 F2 51 57N 128 05W
Hunter River *tn.* Prince Edward Island 61 M12 46 20N 63 20W
Huntingdon Québec 53 M5 45 05N 74 11W
Huntingdon *admin.* Québec 53 M5 45 00N 74 20W
Huntingdon Island Newfoundland and Labrador 60 G6 53 47N 56 55W
Hunt River Newfoundland and Labrador 60 E7 55 20N 61 10W
Huntsville Ontario 52 G5 45 20N 79 13W
Hurd, Cape Ontario 54 A4 45 14N 81 44W
Huron *admin.* Ontario 54 A2 43 27N 81 35W
Huron, Lake Ontario/USA 52 D4/D5 45 00N 83 00W
Hyde Park Ontario 54 A2 43 00N 81 20W
Hythe Alberta 46 C4 55 18N 119 33W

I

Igluligaarjuk *(Chesterfield Inlet) tn.* Nunavut 65 M3 63 21N 90 42W
Iglulik *(Igloolike)* Nunavut 65 P4 69 23N 81 46W
Iglusuaktalialuk Island Newfoundland and Labrador 60 E8 57 20N 61 30W
Ignace Ontario 50 F5 49 26N 91 40W
Ikaahuk *(Sachs Harbour) tn.* Northwest Territories 64 E5 71 59N 125 13W
Ikpiarjuk *(Arctic Bay) tn.* Nunavut 65 N5 73 05N 85 20W
Île-à-la-Crosse *tn.* Saskatchewan 47 D4 55 28N 107 53W
Île aux Coudres *i.* Québec 53 R7 47 23N 70 20W
Île aux Herons Québec 58 N4 45 26N 73 35W
Île Bizard *i.* Québec 58 M4 45 29N 73 54W
Île d'Anticosti *i.* Québec 57 J3 49 20N 62 30W
Île de Montréal *i.* Québec 58 M4 45 30N 73 43W
Île des Allumettes *i.* Québec 53 J5 45 55N 77 08W
Île des Soeurs *i.* Québec 58 N4 45 28N 73 33W
Île d'Orléans *i.* Québec 53 R6 46 55N 71 00W
Île Dorval *i.* Québec 58 N4 45 26N 73 44W
Île Jésus *i.* Québec 58 N5 45 35N 73 45W
Île Kettle *i.* Québec 59 K2 45 28N 75 39W
Île Lamèque *i.* New Brunswick 61 C3 47 50N 64 40W
Île Lynch *i.* Québec 58 M4 45 25N 73 54W
Île Ste. Hélène *i.* Québec 58 N5 45 31N 73 32W
Île Sainte-Thérèse *i.* Québec 58 P5 45 39N 73 28W
Îles-de-Boucherville *is.* Québec 58 P5 45 36N 73 28W
Îles de la Madeleine *is.* Québec 61 E3 47 40N 61 50W
Îles du Grand Calumet *is.* Québec 53 K5 45 30N 76 35W
Ilford Manitoba 49 E5 56 04N 95 40W
Indian Arm *b.* British Columbia 44 G4 49 19N 122 55W
Indian Arm Provincial Park British Columbia 42 H4 49 22N 122 45W
Indian Cabins Alberta 46 D6 59 52N 117 02W
Indian Head *tn.* Saskatchewan 47 F2 50 35N 103 37W
Indian Tickle Newfoundland and Labrador 60 H6 53 34N 56 00W
Ingenika River British Columbia 43 G5 56 48N 126 11W
Ingersoll Ontario 54 B2 43 03N 80 53W
Ingonish Nova Scotia 61 M12 46 42N 60 22W
Inklin River British Columbia 42 D6 58 54N 132 50W
Inner Bay Ontario 54 B1 42 35N 80 26W
Innisfail Alberta 46 F3 52 01N 113 59W
Inside Passage British Columbia 42/43 F3 53 38N 129 40W
Inukjuak Québec 56 A8 58 40N 78 15W
Inuvik Northwest Territories 64 D4 68 16N 133 40W
Inverhuron Provincial Park Ontario 54 A3 44 20N 81 30W
Invermere British Columbia 43 M2 50 30N 116 00W
Inverness Nova Scotia 61 M12 46 14N 61 19W
Inverness *admin.* Nova Scotia 61 M12 46 00N 61 30W
Ioco *tn.* British Columbia 44 G4 49 18N 122 51W
Iqaluit Nunavut 65 S3 60 00N 65 00W
Iqaluktuutiaq *(Cambridge Bay) tn.* Nunavut 64 K4 69 09N 105 00W
Irma Alberta 46 G3 52 55N 111 14W
Iron Bridge *tn.* Ontario 52 C6 46 17N 83 14W
Ironside Québec 59 J2 45 27N 75 46W
Iroquois Ontario 53 L4 44 51N 75 19W
Iroquois Falls *tn.* Ontario 51 L5 48 47N 80 41W
Irvine Alberta 46 G1 49 57N 110 17W
Irvines Landing British Columbia 42 H4 49 37N 124 02W
Isaac Lake Ontario 54 A3 44 46N 81 13W
Isachsen Nunavut 65 K6 78 47N 103 30W
Ishpatina Ridge Ontario 51 L4 47 19N 80 44W
Iskut River British Columbia 42 E5 56 45N 131 10W
Island Falls Dam Saskatchewan 47 F4 55 30N 102 20W
Island Lake Manitoba 49 E3 53 50N 94 00W
Island Lake *tn.* Manitoba 49 E3 53 50N 94 00W
Island of Ponds *tn.* Newfoundland and Labrador 60 H6 53 20N 55 50W
Islands, Bay of Newfoundland and Labrador 60 F7 55 09N 59 49W
Islands, Bay of Newfoundland and Labrador 61 F4 49 10N 58 14W
Isle aux Morts *tn.* Newfoundland and Labrador 61 F3 47 35N 58 59W
Isle Madame *i.* Nova Scotia 61 M12 45 30N 60 50W
Isle Royale *i.* Ontario 51 G4 48 10N 88 30W
Isle Royale National Park Ontario 51 G4 48 10N 88 30W
Islington Ontario 55 B1 43 38N 79 32W
Itcha Ilgachuz Provincial Park British Columbia 43 H3 52 50N 125 00W
Itchen Lake Northwest Territories 64 H4 65 33N 112 50W
Ituna Saskatchewan 47 F2 51 09N 103 24W
Ivujivik Québec 56 B10 62 25N 77 54W
Ivvavik National Park Yukon Territory 64 C4 69 20N 139 30W

J

Jackfish Lake Manitoba 49 C2 50 30N 99 20W
Jackson's Arm *tn.* Newfoundland and Labrador 61 G4 49 53N 56 47W
Jacksons Point *tn.* Ontario 54 C3 44 18N 79 22W
Jaffray Melick Ontario 50 D5 49 49N 94 25W
Jakes Corner *tn.* Yukon Territory 64 D3 60 20N 133 58W
James Bay Ontario/Québec 50 L7/M7 53 45N 81 00W
James Ross, Cape Northwest Territories 64 H4 74 40N 114 25W
James Ross Strait Nunavut 65 L4 69 40N 96 00W
Jans Bay *tn.* Saskatchewan 47 C4 55 09N 108 08W
Jarvis Ontario 54 B1 42 52N 80 08W
Jasper Alberta 46 C3 52 55N 118 05W
Jasper National Park Alberta 46 C3/D3 53 00N 118 00W
Jellicoe Ontario 51 H5 49 41N 87 31W
Jennings River British Columbia 42 E6 59 33N 131 40W
Jenpeg Manitoba 49 C4 54 30N 98 00W
Jervis Inlet British Columbia 42 H4 49 47N 124 04W
Jock River Ontario 59 J2 45 15N 75 46W
Joe Batt's Arm *tn.* Newfoundland and Labrador 61 H4 49 44N 54 10W
Joggins Nova Scotia 61 M12 45 42N 64 27W
John D'or Prairie Alberta 46 E6 58 30N 115 08W
John E. Pearce Provincial Park Ontario 54 A1 42 37N 81 27W
John Hart Highway British Columbia 43 K4 55 40N 121 38W
Johnsons Crossing *tn.* Yukon Territory 64 D3 60 29N 133 17W
Johnstone Strait British Columbia 43 G2/H2 50 23N 126 30W
Joliette Québec 53 N6 46 02N 73 27W
Joliette *admin.* Québec 53 L7 47 40N 75 40W
Jones Ontario 50 D5 49 59N 94 05W
Jones Sound Nunavut 65 N6 76 00N 88 00W
Jonquière Québec 57 E3 48 25N 71 14W
Jordan Lake Nova Scotia 61 L11 44 05N 65 20W
Jordan River *tn.* British Columbia 42 H4 48 26N 123 59W
Juan de Fuca Strait British Columbia 42 H4 48 30N 124 31W
Judique Nova Scotia 61 M12 45 55N 61 30W

K

Kabania Lake Ontario 50 G7 52 12N 88 20W
Kabinakagami, Lake Ontario 51 J5 48 54N 84 25W
Kabinakagami River Ontario 51 J5 49 10N 84 10W
Kagawong Ontario 52 D5 45 54N 82 15W
K'ágee *(Kakisa)* Northwest Territories 64 G3 60 58N 117 30W
K'áhbamítúe *(Colville Lake) tn.* Northwest Territories 64 E4 67 02N 126 07W
Kahnawake Québec 58 N4 45 25N 73 42W
Kaipokok Bay Newfoundland and Labrador 60 F7 54 00N 59 35W
Kakabeta Falls *tn.* Ontario 51 G5 48 24N 89 40W
Kakkiviak, Cape Newfoundland and Labrador 60 C10 60 05N 64 15W
Kakwa Provincial Park British Columbia 43 K4 54 05N 120 20W
Kakwa River Alberta 46 C4 54 15N 119 45W
Kaladar Ontario 53 J4 44 39N 77 07W
Kaleden British Columbia 43 L1 49 20N 119 38W
Kamilukuak Lake Nunavut 65 K3 62 22N 101 40W
Kaminak Lake Nunavut 65 M3 62 10N 95 00W
Kamloops British Columbia 43 K2 50 39N 120 24W
Kamloops Lake British Columbia 43 K2 50 45N 120 40W
Kamouraska Québec 53 S7 47 34N 69 51W
Kamouraska *admin.* Québec 53 S7 47 10N 69 50W
Kamsack Saskatchewan 47 G2 51 34N 101 51W
Kamuchawie Lake Saskatchewan 47 F5/G5 56 20N 102 20W
Kanata Ontario 53 L5 45 20N 75 53W
Kangiqsualujjuaq Québec 56 G8 58 48N 66 08W
Kangiqsujuaq Québec 56 E9 61 40N 71 59W
Kangiqtinq *(Rankin Inlet)* Nunavut 65 M3 62 49N 92 05W
Kangiqtugaapik *(Clyde River)* Nunavut 65 S5 70 30N 68 30W
Kangirsuk Québec 56 E9 60 00N 70 00W
Kapiskau River Ontario 50 K7 52 30N 82 50W
Kapuskasing Ontario 51 K5 49 25N 82 26W
Kapuskasing River Ontario 51 K5 48 40N 82 50W
Kasabonika *I.R.* Ontario 50 G7 53 32N 88 37W
Kasabonika Lake Ontario 50 G7 53 35N 88 35W
Kasba Lake Northwest Territories/Nunavut 65 K3 60 18N 102 07W
Kashechewan *I.R.* Ontario 50 L7 52 18N 81 37W
Kaskattama River Manitoba 49 G5 56 25N 91 10W
Kaslo British Columbia 43 M1 49 54N 116 57W
Kasmere Lake Manitoba 49 B6 59 30N 101 10W
Katannilik Territorial Park Nunavut 65 S3 63 00N 69 55W
Kates Needle *mt.* British Columbia 42 D5 57 02N 132 05W
Kátł'odeeche *(Hay River)* Northwest Territories 64 G3 60 51N 115 42W
Kaumajet Mountains Newfoundland and Labrador 60 D8 57 48N 61 51W
Kawawachikamach Québec 56 G6 54 50N 67 00W
Kazabazua Québec 53 K5 45 56N 76 01W
Kearney Ontario 52 G5 45 35N 79 17W
Kechika River British Columbia 43 G6 58 44N 127 25W
Kedgwick New Brunswick 61 B3 47 38N 67 21W
Keele Peak Yukon Territory 64 D3 63 25N 130 17W
Keele River Northwest Territories 64 E3 64 15N 126 00W
Keewatin Ontario 50 D5 49 47N 94 30W
Keewatin River Manitoba 49 B5 56 59N 100 59W
Keg River *tn.* Alberta 46 D5 57 46N 117 39W
Keith Arm *b.* Northwest Territories 64 F4 65 20N 122 15W
Kejimkujik National Park Nova Scotia 61 L11 44 20N 65 20W
Kekerton Territorial Park Nunavut 65 S4 65 40N 65 15W
Keller Lake Northwest Territories 64 F3 64 00N 121 30W
Kellett, Cape Northwest Territories 64 E5 71 59N 126 00W
Kellett Strait Northwest Territories 64 G6 75 45N 117 30W
Kelliher Saskatchewan 47 F2 51 15N 103 41W
Kelowna British Columbia 43 L1 49 50N 119 29W
Kelsey Manitoba 49 D5 56 04N 96 30W
Kelsey Bay *tn.* British Columbia 43 H2 50 22N 125 29W
Kelvington Saskatchewan 47 F3 52 10N 103 30W
Kemano British Columbia 43 G3 53 39N 127 58W
Kempenfelt Bay Ontario 54 C3 44 22N 79 39W
Kemptville Ontario 53 L5 45 01N 75 38W
Kenamu River Newfoundland and Labrador 60 E6 52 50N 60 20W
Kenaston Saskatchewan 47 D2 51 30N 106 15W
Kendall Island Bird Sanctuary Northwest Territories 64 C4 69 30N 135 00W
Kennebecasis River New Brunswick 61 L12 45 30N 65 55W
Kennedy Lake British Columbia 42 G4 49 12N 125 32W
Kennetcook Nova Scotia 61 M12 45 10N 63 43W
Kenney Dam British Columbia 43 H3 53 38N 124 59W
Kenogami River Ontario 51 J6 50 50N 84 30W
Kenogamissi Lake Ontario 51 L5 48 15N 81 33W
Kenora Ontario 50 D5 49 47N 94 26W
Kensington Prince Edward Island 61 M12 46 26N 63 39W
Kent *admin.* New Brunswick 61 C3 46 30N 65 20W
Kent *admin.* Ontario 52 D2 42 25N 82 10W
Kent Peninsula Nunavut 64 J4 68 30N 106 00W
Kentville Nova Scotia 61 M12 45 04N 64 30W
Keremeos British Columbia 43 L1 49 12N 119 50W
Kerrobert Saskatchewan 47 C2 51 56N 109 09W
Kesagami Lake Ontario 51 L6 50 00N 80 00W
Kesagami Provincial Park Ontario 51 L6 50 30N 80 10W
Kesagami River Ontario 51 L6 50 30N 80 10W
Keswick Ontario 54 C3 44 15N 79 28W
Kettle Creek Ontario 54 A1 42 47N 81 13W
Kettle Rapids *tn.* Manitoba 49 E5 56 25N 94 30W
Kettle River British Columbia 43 L1 49 10N 119 02W
Kettle River Manitoba 49 H5 56 40N 89 50W
Kettlestone Bay Québec 56 B9 61 20N 77 54W
Keyano Québec 56 D5 53 52N 73 30W
Key Lake Mine *tn.* Saskatchewan 47 E5 57 10N 105 30W
Khutzeymafeen Provincial Park British Columbia 42 F4 54 45N 129 50W
Kicking Horse Pass Alberta/British Columbia 43 M2 51 28N 116 23W
Kiglapait, Cape Newfoundland and Labrador 60 E9 57 06N 61 22W
Kiglapait Mountains Newfoundland and Labrador 60 E8 57 06N 61 35W
Kikerk Lake Nunavut 64 H4 66 55N 113 20W
Kikkertarjote Island Newfoundland and Labrador 60 E8 57 30N 61 28W
Kikkertavak Island Newfoundland and Labrador 60 E8 56 22N 61 35W
Killaloe Ontario 53 J5 45 33N 77 26W
Killam Alberta 46 G3 52 47N 111 51W
Killarney Manitoba 49 C1 49 12N 99 40W
Killarney Ontario 52 E5 45 59N 81 30W
Killarney Provincial Park Ontario 52 E6 46 00N 81 00W
Killiniq Nunavut 56 H9 60 30N 64 50W
Killiniq Island Newfoundland and Labrador/Nunavut 60 C10 60 24N 64 31W
Kimberley British Columbia 43 N1 49 40N 115 58W
Kimmirut *(Lake Harbour)* Nunavut 65 S3 62 50N 69 50W
Kinbasket Lake British Columbia 43 M2 51 57N 118 02W
Kincardine Ontario 54 A3 44 11N 81 38W
Kincolith British Columbia 42 F4 55 00N 129 57W
Kincora Prince Edward Island 61 M12 46 20N 63 40W
Kindersley Saskatchewan 47 C2 51 27N 109 08W
King Christian Island Nunavut 65 K6 77 45N 102 00W
King City Ontario 54 C2 43 54N 79 31W
Kingcome Inlet British Columbia 43 G2 50 58N 125 15W
Kingfisher Lake Ontario 50 G7 53 05N 89 49W
Kingfisher Lake *I.R.* Ontario 50 G7 53 02N 89 50W
Kinggauk *(Bathurst Inlet) tn.* Nunavut 64 J4 66 50N 108 01W
King George, Mount British Columbia 43 N2 50 36N 115 26W
King Island British Columbia 43 G3 52 10N 127 35W
Kingnait *(Cape Dorset) tn.* Nunavut 65 Q3 64 10N 76 40W
Kings *admin.* New Brunswick 61 L12 45 30N 65 40W
Kings *admin.* Nova Scotia 61 M11 44 50N 64 50W
Kings *admin.* Prince Edward Island 61 M12 46 20N 62 40W
Kingsburg Nova Scotia 61 M11 44 20N 64 10W
Kings Landing New Brunswick 61 B2 45 50N 67 00W
Kingsmere Québec 59 J2 45 29N 75 50W
Kingston Ontario 53 K4 44 14N 76 30W
Kingsville Ontario 52 D2 42 02N 82 45W
Kingurutik Lake Newfoundland and Labrador 60 D8 56 49N 62 20W
King William Island Nunavut 65 L4 69 00N 97 30W
Kinistino Saskatchewan 47 E3 52 28N 105 01W
Kinoje River Ontario 50 L6 51 40N 81 50W
Kinoosao Saskatchewan 47 F5 57 07N 102 02W
Kinsac Lake Nova Scotia 59 Q7 44 50N 63 38W
Kinusheseo River Ontario 50 K8 54 30N 83 50W
Kiosk Ontario 52 H6 46 05N 78 53W
Kipahigan Lake Manitoba 49 B4 55 20N 101 50W
Kipling Saskatchewan 47 F2 50 08N 102 40W
Kirkland Lake Ontario 51 L5 48 10N 80 02W
Kirkpatrick Lake Alberta 46 G2 51 52N 111 18W
Kiskittogisa Lake Manitoba 49 C4 54 10N 98 50W
Kiskitto Lake Manitoba 49 C4 54 20N 98 50W
Kispiox British Columbia 43 G4 55 21N 127 41W
Kississing Lake Manitoba 49 B4 55 10N 101 30W
Kistigan Lake Manitoba 49 F4 54 50N 92 40W
Kitamaat Village British Columbia 43 F3 53 58N 128 38W
Kitchener Ontario 54 B2 43 27N 80 03W
Kitimat British Columbia 42 F4 54 05N 128 38W
Kitlope Heritage Conservancy Park British Columbia 43 G3 53 00N 127 30W
Klappan River British Columbia 42 F6 57 50N 129 40W
Kleinburg Ontario 55 B2 43 50N 79 36W
Klemtu British Columbia 43 F3 52 32N 128 24W
Klinaklini River British Columbia 43 H2 51 18N 125 45W
Klondike Highway Yukon Territory 64 C3 62 55N 136 10W
Klondike River Yukon Territory 64 C3 64 20N 138 50W
Kluane Lake Yukon Territory 64 C3 62 20N 139 00W
Kluane National Park Yukon Territory 64 C3 60 30N 139 00W
Kluane Wildlife Sanctuary Yukon Territory 64 B3 61 30N 139 50W
Kluskoil Lake Provincial Park British Columbia 43 J3 53 15N 124 00W
Knee Lake Manitoba 49 E4 55 10N 94 40W
Knight Inlet British Columbia 43 H2 50 45N 125 36W
Knox, Cape British Columbia 42 D4 54 09N 133 05W
Koch Island Nunavut 65 Q4 69 38N 78 15W
Kogaluc Bay Québec 56 B8 56 10N 63 30W
Kogaluk River Newfoundland and Labrador 60 D8 56 10N 63 30W
Kokanee Glacier Park British Columbia 43 M1 49 45N 117 10W
Komoka Ontario 54 A1 42 56N 81 26W
Kootenay Lake British Columbia 43 M1 49 35N 116 30W
Kootenay National Park British Columbia 43 M2 51 15N 116 25W
Kopka River Ontario 50 G6 50 00N 90 00W
Kotcho Lake British Columbia 43 K6 59 05N 121 10W
Kouchibouguac National Park New Brunswick 61 C3 46 45N 64 50W
Koukdjuak River Nunavut 65 R4 66 50N 72 50W
Kovik Bay Québec 56 B9 61 35N 77 54W
Kugaaruk *(Pelly Bay)* Nunavut 65 N4 68 32N 89 48W
Kugluktuk *(Coppermine)* Nunavut 64 H4 65 00N 110 00W
Kunghit Island British Columbia 42 E3 52 02N 131 02W
Kuujjuaq Québec 56 F8 58 25N 68 55W
Kuujjuarapik Québec 56 B6 55 15N 77 41W
Kwadacha Wilderness Provincial Park British Columbia 43 H5 57 35N 125 30W
Kwataboahegan River Ontario 51 K6 51 10N 82 30W
Kyle Saskatchewan 47 C2 50 50N 108 02W
Kyuquot Sound British Columbia 43 G1 50 02N 127 22W

L

La Baie Québec 57 E3 48 20N 70 52W
Labelle Québec 53 M6 46 17N 74 45W
Labelle *admin.* Québec 53 L6 46 30N 75 40W
Laberge, Lake Yukon Territory 64 D3 61 10N 134 59W
Labrador *geog. reg.* Newfoundland and Labrador 60 D6/E6 54 00N 64 00W
Labrador City Newfoundland and Labrador 60 B6 52 57N 66 55W
Labrador Sea 65 T2/U2 59 30N 60 00W
Lac Abitibi *l.* Ontario/Québec 51 M5 48 40N 79 40W
Lac Albanel *l.* Québec 57 D4 51 N 73 20W
Lac à l'Eau Claire *l.* Québec 56 C7 56 20N 74 30W
Lac Anuc *l.* Québec 56 C8 59 15N 75 10W
Lac Assinica *l.* Québec 57 C4 50 20N 75 12W
Lac au Goéland *l.* Québec 57 B3 49 45N 76 55W

Lac Aylmer *l.* Québec	53	Q5	45 50N	71 20W
Lac Bacqueville *l.* Québec	56	D8	58 05N	74 00W
Lac Batiscan *l.* Québec	53	Q7	47 23N	71 53W
Lac Bécard *l.* Québec	56	D9	60 05N	73 45W
Lac Belot *l.* Northwest Territories	64	E4	66 53N	126 16W
Lac Bérard *l.* Québec	56	E8	58 25N	70 05W
Lac Bermen *l.* Québec	56	F5	53 40N	69 00W
Lac Berté *l.* Québec	57	F4	50 52N	68 35W
Lac Bienville *l.* Québec	56	D6	55 30N	73 00W
Lac Bourdel *l.* Québec	56	C7	56 42N	74 15W
Lac Boyd *l.* Québec	57	B5	52 45N	76 45W
Lac Brochet *l.* Manitoba	49	B6	58 40N	101 20W
Lac Brochet *tn.* Manitoba	49	B6	58 45N	101 30W
Lac Brome *l.* Québec	53	P5	45 15N	72 30W
Lac Brome *tn.* Québec	53	P5	45 13N	72 30W
Lac Burton *l.* Québec	56	A6	54 45N	79 25W
Lac Cambrien *l.* Québec	56	F7	56 30N	69 22W
Lac Cananée *l.* Québec	56	H7	56 05N	64 05W
Lac Chaconipau *l.* Québec	56	F7	56 20N	68 45W
Lac Champdoré *l.* Québec	56	H5	55 50N	65 50W
Lac Champlain *l.* Québec/USA	53	N4	45 08N	73 08W
Lac Châtelain *l.* Québec	56	C9	60 20N	74 20W
Lac Chavigny *l.* Québec	56	C8	58 10N	75 10W
Lac Chibougamau *l.* Québec	57	C3	49 55N	74 20W
Lac Couture *l.* Québec	56	C9	60 00N	75 20W
Lac de Gras *l.* Northwest Territories	64	J3	64 10N	109 00W
Lac de la Hutte Sauvage *l.* Québec	56	H7	56 18N	65 00W
Lac des Bois *l.* Northwest Territories	64	E4	65 00N	127 00W
Lac des Commissaires *l.* Québec	53	P8	48 09N	72 13W
Lac des Deux Montagnes *l.* Québec	58	M4	45 30N	73 58W
Lac des Loups Marins *l.* Québec	56	D7	56 30N	73 30W
Lac des Mille Lacs *l.* Ontario	50	F5	48 53N	90 22W
Lac des Quinze *l.* Québec	57	A2	47 45N	79 15W
Lac des Trente et Un Milles *l.* Québec	53	L6	46 18N	75 43W
Lac d'Iberville *l.* Québec	56	D6	55 55N	73 25W
Lac du Bonnet *l.* Manitoba	49	E2	50 30N	95 50W
Lac du Bonnet *tn.* Manitoba	49	D2	50 16N	96 03W
Lac Duncan *l.* Québec	57	A5	53 25N	78 00W
Lac du Sable *l.* Québec	56	G6	54 25N	67 59W
Lac Édouard *l.* Québec	53	P7	47 40N	72 16W
Lac-Etchemin *tn.* Québec	53	R6	46 23N	70 32W
Lac Faribault *l.* Québec	56	E8	59 10N	72 00W
Lac Fleur-de-May *l.* Newfoundland and Labrador	60	C6	52 00N	65 02W
Lac Goatanaga *l.* Québec	53	J7	47 42N	77 28W
Lac Guillaume-Delisle *l.* Québec	56	B7	56 15N	77 20W
Lachute Québec	53	M5	51 00N	71 00W
Lac Île-à-la Crosse *l.* Saskatchewan	47	D4	55 40N	107 30W
Lac Jeannin *l.* Québec	56	G7	56 25N	66 30W
Lac-John Québec	56	G6	54 49N	66 47W
Lac Joseph *l.* Newfoundland and Labrador	60	C6	52 45N	65 18W
Lac Kempt *l.* Québec	53	M7	47 28N	74 08W
Lac Kénogami *l.* Québec	57	E3	48 22N	71 25W
Lac Kipawa *l.* Québec	51	M4	46 55N	79 06W
Lac Klotz *l.* Québec	56	D9	60 30N	73 30W
Lac la Biche *l.* Alberta	46	F4	54 55N	112 58W
Lac la Biche *tn.* Alberta	46	G4	54 46N	111 58W
Lac la Croix *l.* Ontario	51	F5	48 21N	92 09W
Lac la Loche *l.* Saskatchewan	47	C5	56 30N	109 40W
Lac la Martre *l.* Northwest Territories	64	G3	63 20N	118 30W
Lac la Plonge *l.* Saskatchewan	47	D4	55 05N	107 00W
Lac la Ronge *l.* Saskatchewan	47	E4	55 10N	105 00W
Lac la Ronge Provincial Park Saskatchewan	47	E4	55 20N	104 45W
Lac le Moyne *l.* Québec	56	F7	57 10N	68 33W
Lac Le Roy *l.* Québec	56	C8	58 35N	75 25W
Lac Lesdiguière *l.* Québec	56	C9	60 00N	74 20W
Lac Magpie *l.* Québec	57	H4	51 00N	64 40W
Lac Maicasagi *l.* Québec	57	B4	50 00N	76 45W
Lac Manitou *l.* Québec	57	H4	50 50N	65 20W
Lac Manouane *l.* Québec	57	E4	50 45N	70 45W
Lac Matagami *l.* Québec	57	B3	49 55N	77 50W
Lac Maunoir *l.* Northwest Territories	64	E4	67 30N	125 55W
Lac-Mégantic *tn.* Québec	53	R5	45 34N	70 53W
Lac Memphrémagog *l.* Québec	53	P5	45 05N	72 13W
Lac Mesgouez *l.* Québec	57	C4	51 25N	75 00W
Lac Minto *l.* Québec	56	C7	57 5N	75 00W
Lac Mistassini *l.* Québec	57	D4	51 00N	73 20W
Lac Mistinibi *l.* Québec	56	H6	55 50N	64 20W
Lac Mitchinamécus *l.* Québec	53	M7	47 20N	75 00W
Lac Musquaro *l.* Québec	57	K4	50 50N	60 50W
Lac Nantais *l.* Québec	56	C9	61 10N	74 20W
Lac Naococane *l.* Québec	57	E5	52 53N	70 40W
Lac Nichicapau *l.* Québec	56	F7	56 42N	68 28W
Lac Nichicun *l.* Québec	57	E5	53 05N	71 05W
Lacombe Alberta	46	F3	52 28N	113 44W
Lac Opiscotéo *l.* Québec	57	F5	53 15N	68 20W
Lac Otelnuk *l.* Québec	56	F7	56 10N	68 20W
Lac Parent *l.* Québec	53	J8	48 30N	77 08W
Lac Payne *l.* Québec	56	C8	59 25N	74 25W
Lac Pélican *l.* Québec	56	D8	59 57N	73 40W
Lac Péribonka *l.* Québec	57	E4	50 10N	71 23W
Lac Plétipi *l.* Québec	57	E4	51 0N	70 10W
Lac Poncheville *l.* Québec	57	B4	50 12N	77 00W
Lac Potherie *l.* Québec	56	D8	58 50N	72 25W
Lac Qilalugalik *l.* Québec	56	B8	58 35N	76 00W
Lac Ramusio *l.* Québec	56	J6	55 10N	63 59W
Lac Résolution *l.* Québec	56	H6	55 15N	64 40W
La Crete Alberta	46	D6	58 11N	116 30W
Lac Roberts *l.* Québec	56	E9	60 25N	70 25W
Lac Saindon *l.* Québec	56	D6	55 35N	73 30W
Lac Sainte-Anne *l.* Québec	57	G4	50 5N	68 00W
Lac Saint-François *l.* Québec	53	Q5	45 56N	71 08W
Lac Saint-Jean *l.* Québec	57	D3/E3	48 35N	72 00W
Lac-St.-Jean-Est *admin.* Québec	53	Q8	48 20N	71 40W
Lac-St.-Jean-Ouest *admin.* Québec	53	N8/P8	48 20N	72 20W
Lac Saint-Louis *l.* Québec	58	M4	45 25N	73 49W
Lac Saint-Patrice *l.* Québec	53	J6	46 20N	77 30W
Lac Saint-Pierre *l.* Québec	53	P6	46 12N	72 49W
Lac Sakami *l.* Québec	57	B5	53 20N	76 50W
Lac Seul *l.R.* Ontario	50	E6	50 15N	92 15W
Lac Seul *l.* Ontario	50	E6	50 20N	92 00W
Lac Simard *l.* Québec	57	A2	47 40N	78 50W
Lac Simon *l.* Québec	53	L5	45 55N	75 05W
Lac Soscumica *l.* Québec	57	B4	50 15N	77 35W
Lac Tasiaalujjuak *l.* Québec	56	E8	59 35N	71 59W
Lac Tasiat *l.* Québec	56	C8	59 05N	75 25W
Lac Tasiataq *l.* Québec	56	E8	58 40N	71 40W
Lac Tassialouc *l.* Québec	56	D8	58 59N	74 00W
Lac Témiscaminque *l.* Québec	57	A2	47 28N	79 30W
Lac Tiblemont *l.* Québec	53	J8	48 17N	77 20W
Lac Tudor *l.* Québec	56	H6	55 58N	65 30W
Lac Wakuach *l.* Québec	56	G6	55 35N	67 40W
Lac Waswanipi *l.* Québec	57	B3	49 35N	76 36W
Lac Wayagamac *l.* Québec	53	P7	47 23N	72 35W
Lac Whitegull *l.* Québec	56	H6	55 25N	64 30W
Ladner British Columbia	42	H4	49 06N	123 05W
Lady Evelyn-Smoothwater Provincial Park Ontario	51	L4	47 20N	80 30W
Ladysmith British Columbia	42	H4	48 57N	123 50W
Laflèche Saskatchewan	47	D1	49 44N	106 32W
Lagoon City Ontario	54	C3	44 31N	79 11W
La Grande 2 *dam* Québec	57	B5	53 45N	77 38W
La Grande 3 *dam* Québec	57	B5	53 40N	76 09W
La Grande 4 *dam* Québec	56	D5	53 59N	72 50W
La Grande Rivière *r.* Québec	57	C5	53 34N	74 36W
La Guadeloupe Québec	53	R5	45 58N	70 57W
Lake Country *tn.* British Columbia	43	L2	50 02N	119 25W
Lake Cowichan *tn.* British Columbia	42	H4	48 50N	124 04W
Lake Echo *tn.* Nova Scotia	59	R6	44 44N	63 24W
Lakefield Ontario	52	H4	44 26N	78 16W
Lakeland Provincial Park Alberta	46	G4	54 45N	112 25W
Lakeland Provincial Recreation Area Alberta	46	G4	54 45N	111 15W
Lake Louise *tn.* Alberta	46	D2	51 25N	116 14W
Lake of Bays *tn.* Ontario	52	G5	45 00N	79 00W
Lake of the Rivers Saskatchewan	47	E1	49 50N	105 30W
Lakeside Nova Scotia	59	Q6	44 38N	63 42W
Lake Superior National Marine Conservation Area Ontario	51	G5/H5	48 30N	87 30W
Lake Superior Provincial Park Ontario	51	J4	47 35N	85 45W
Lakeview Newfoundland and Labrador	61	J3	47 20N	54 10W
Lakeview Ontario	59	J2	45 20N	75 48W
La Loche Saskatchewan	47	C5	56 31N	109 27W
La Malbaie Québec	53	R7	47 39N	70 11W
Lamaline Newfoundland and Labrador	61	H3	46 52N	55 49W
Lambeth Ontario	54	A1	42 54N	81 20W
Lambton *admin.* Ontario	52	D2	42 45N	82 05W
Lambton, Cape Northwest Territories	64	F4	71 05N	123 09W
Lamèque New Brunswick	61	C3	47 45N	64 40W
Lampman Saskatchewan	47	F1	49 23N	102 48W
Lanark Ontario	53	K5	45 01N	74 30W
Lanark *admin.* Ontario	53	K5	45 05N	76 20W
Lancaster Ontario	53	M5	45 08N	74 30W
Lancaster Sound Nunavut	65	N5	74 00N	87 30W
Land's End Northwest Territories	64	F6	76 22N	122 33W
Langenburg Saskatchewan	47	G2	50 50N	101 42W
Langham Saskatchewan	47	D3	52 22N	106 55W
Langley British Columbia	42	H4	49 06N	122 38W
Lanigan Saskatchewan	47	E2	51 50N	105 01W
L'Annonciation Québec	53	M6	46 24N	74 52W
Lansdowne House *tn.* Ontario	50	H7	52 05N	88 00W
L'Anse-au-Loup Newfoundland and Labrador	60	G5	51 31N	56 45W
L'Anse aux Meadows National Historic Site Newfoundland and Labrador	60	H5	51 36N	55 32W
L'Anse Pleureuse Québec	57	H3	49 15N	65 40W
Lantzville British Columbia	42	H4	49 15N	124 05W
La Pocatière Québec	53	R7	47 22N	70 03W
La Poile Newfoundland and Labrador	61	F3	47 41N	58 42W
La Prairie Québec	58	P4	45 25N	73 29W
Larder Lake *tn.* Ontario	51	M5	48 05N	79 38W
L'Ardoise Nova Scotia	61	M12	45 37N	60 46W
Lark Harbour *tn.* Newfoundland and Labrador	61	F4	49 06N	58 23W
La Ronge Saskatchewan	47	E4	55 07N	105 18W
Larrys River *tn.* Nova Scotia	61	M12	45 15N	61 25W
Larsen Sound Nunavut	65	L5	70 35N	98 00W
La Salle Ontario	52	C2	42 15N	83 05W
LaSalle Québec	58	N4	44 26N	73 37W
La Salle River Manitoba	48	B1	49 42N	97 16W
La Sarre Québec	57	A3	48 50N	79 20W
La Scie Newfoundland and Labrador	61	H4	49 57N	55 36W
Lashburn Saskatchewan	47	C3	53 08N	109 36W
Lasqueti Island British Columbia	42	H4	49 28N	124 20W
Last Mountain Lake Saskatchewan	47	E2	51 40N	106 55W
La Tabatière–Gros Mecatina Québec	56	L4	50 50N	58 57W
Latchford Ontario	51	M4	47 20N	79 49W
La Tuque Québec	53	P7	47 26N	72 47W
Laurie River Manitoba	49	B5	56 30N	101 30W
Lauzon Québec	53	Q6	46 49N	71 10W
Laval Québec	53	N5	45 38N	73 45W
Laval-des-Rapides Québec	58	N5	45 33N	73 42W
Laval-Ouest Québec	58	M5	45 33N	73 50W
Lawn Newfoundland and Labrador	61	H3	46 57N	55 32W
Lawrencetown Nova Scotia	61	L11	44 54N	65 10W
Lax Kw'aiaams British Columbia	42	E4	54 32N	130 25W
Leader Saskatchewan	47	C2	50 55N	109 31W
Leading Tickles Newfoundland and Labrador	61	H4	49 30N	55 28W
Leaf Rapids *tn.* Manitoba	49	B5	56 30N	100 00W
Leamington Ontario	52	D2	42 03N	83 36W
Leaside Ontario	55	C1	43 44N	79 15W
Lebel-sur-Quévillon Québec	57	B3	49 05N	77 08W
Leduc Alberta	46	F3	53 17N	113 30W
Leeds and Grenville *admin.* Ontario	53	K4/L4	44 35N	76 00W
Le Havre River Nova Scotia	61	M11	44 30N	64 30W
Leitrim Ontario	59	K2	45 20N	75 35W
Lemieux Islands Nunavut	65	T3	63 40N	64 20W
Lennox and Addington *admin.* Ontario	53	J4	44 30N	77 00W
Lenore Lake Saskatchewan	47	E3	52 50N	104 40W
Leoville Saskatchewan	47	D3	53 39N	107 33W
Lesser Slave Lake Alberta	46	E4	55 25N	115 25W
Lethbridge Alberta	46	F1	49 43N	112 48W
Level Mountain British Columbia	42	E6	58 33N	131 25W
Lévis Québec	53	Q6	46 47N	71 12W
Lewis Hill *mt.* Newfoundland and Labrador	61	F4	49 48N	58 30W
Lewisporte Newfoundland and Labrador	61	H4	49 15N	55 03W
Liard River Northwest Territories	64	F3	60 00N	120 00W
Liard River *tn.* British Columbia	43	G6	59 28N	126 18W
Liard River Corridor Provincial Park British Columbia	43	H6	59 20N	125 30W
Liddon Gulf Northwest Territories	64	H6	75 03N	113 00W
Líídlı Kúé *(Fort Simpson)* Northwest Territories	64	F3	61 46N	121 15W
L'Île-Michon *tn.* Québec	57	J4	50 13N	62 02W
L'Île-Perrot *i.* Québec	58	M4	45 24N	73 55W
Lillooet British Columbia	43	K2	50 41N	121 59W
Lillooet Lake British Columbia	42	H5	50 15N	122 38W
Lillooet River British Columbia	42	H4	49 59N	122 25W
Limbour Québec	59	K2	45 29N	75 44W
Lindsay Ontario	54	D3	44 21N	78 44W
Linzee, Cape Nova Scotia	61	M12	46 00N	61 30W
Lions Bay *tn.* British Columbia	42	H4	49 28N	123 13W
Lions Head *tn.* Ontario	54	A3	44 59N	81 16W
Lipton Saskatchewan	47	F2	50 55N	103 49W
Liscomb Game Sanctuary Nova Scotia	61	M12	45 10N	62 40W
L'Islet *admin.* Québec	53	R7	47 00N	70 20W
L'Isle-Verte Québec	53	S8	48 00N	69 21W
Lismore Nova Scotia	61	M12	45 42N	62 16W
Listowel Ontario	54	B2	43 44N	80 57W
Little Abitibi River Provincial Park Ontario	51	L5	49 45N	81 00W
Little Bow River Alberta	46	F2	50 20N	113 40W
Little Buffalo River Alberta	46	F6	59 45N	113 30W
Little Churchill River Manitoba	49	E5	56 40N	96 00W
Little Current *tn.* Ontario	52	E5	45 58N	81 56W
Little Current River Provincial Park Ontario	50	H6	50 45N	86 15W
Little Dover Nova Scotia	61	M12	45 20N	61 05W
Little Grand Rapids *tn.* Manitoba	49	E3	52 10N	95 30W
Little Maitland River Ontario	54	A2	43 48N	81 10W
Little Mecatina River Newfoundland and Labrador	60	E6	52 40N	61 30W
Little Narrows *tn.* Nova Scotia	61	M12	45 59N	61 00W
Little River *tn.* British Columbia	42	H4	49 45N	124 56W
Little Rouge Creek Ontario	55	D2	43 54N	79 14W
Little Sachigo Lake Ontario	50	E8	54 09N	92 11W
Little Smoky River Alberta	46	D4	54 05N	117 45W
Liverpool Nova Scotia	61	M11	44 03N	64 43W
Liverpool Bay Northwest Territories	64	D4	69 45N	130 00W
Livingstone Cove *tn.* Nova Scotia	61	M12	45 52N	61 58W
Lloyd George, Mount British Columbia	43	H5	57 50N	124 58W
Lloyd Lake Alberta	44	A1	50 52N	114 10W
Lloyd Lake Saskatchewan	47	C5	57 20N	108 40W
Lloydminster Saskatchewan	47	C3	53 18N	110 00W
Lobstick Lake Newfoundland and Labrador	60	C7	54 00N	65 00W
Lockeport Nova Scotia	61	E6	43 40N	65 10W
Lockport Manitoba	49	D2	50 04N	97 00W
Lodge Creek Alberta/Saskatchewan	46	G1	49 15N	110 05W
Logan Lake *tn.* British Columbia	43	K2	50 28N	120 50W
Logan, Mount Yukon Territory	64	B3	60 34N	140 25W
Logan Mountains Yukon Territory	64	E3	60 30N	128 30W
London Ontario	54	A1	42 58N	81 15W
Long Beach *tn.* Ontario	54	C1	42 51N	79 23W
Long Cove *tn.* Newfoundland and Labrador	61	J3	47 34N	53 40W
Long Creek Saskatchewan	47	F1	49 20N	103 55W
Long Harbour *tn.* Newfoundland and Labrador	61	J3	47 26N	53 48W
Long Island Nova Scotia	61	L11	44 20N	66 15W
Longlac Ontario	51	H5	49 47N	86 34W
Long Lake New Brunswick	61	B3	47 00N	66 50W
Long Lake Nova Scotia	59	Q6	44 37N	63 37W
Long Lake Ontario	51	H5	49 00N	87 00W
Long Lake *l.R.* Ontario	51	H5	49 45N	86 32W
Long Lake Provincial Park Nova Scotia	59	Q6	44 36N	63 38W
Long Point Manitoba	49	C3	52 50N	98 20W
Long Point Ontario	54	B1	42 33N	80 04W
Long Point *tn.* Ontario	54	B1	42 34N	80 15W
Long Point Bay Ontario	54	B1	42 40N	80 14W
Long Point Provincial Park Ontario	54	B1	42 40N	80 15W
Long Pond Newfoundland and Labrador	61	H4	48 00N	55 52W
Long Range Mountains Newfoundland and Labrador	61	F3	50 00N	57 00W
Long Sault Ontario	53	M5	45 02N	74 53W
Longueuil Québec	53	N5	45 32N	73 31W
Longview Alberta	46	E2	50 32N	114 14W
Lookout, Cape Ontario	50	K8	55 18N	83 56W
Loon Lake Nova Scotia	59	Q6	44 42N	63 30W
Loon Lake *tn.* Alberta	46	E5	56 32N	115 24W
Loon Lake *tn.* Saskatchewan	47	C4	54 00N	109 10W
Loon River Alberta	46	E5	56 40N	115 20W
L'Original Ontario	53	M5	45 37N	74 42W
Loring Ontario	52	F5	45 56N	80 00W
Lorne Park *tn.* Ontario	54	C2	43 31N	79 36W
Lorraine Québec	58	M5	45 38N	73 47W
Lotbinière *admin.* Québec	53	Q6	46 20N	71 65W
Lougheed Island Nunavut	65	J6	77 26N	105 06W
Louisbourg Nova Scotia	61	N12	45 56N	59 58W
Louisbourg National Historic Site Nova Scotia	61	N12	45 55N	60 00W
Louise Island British Columbia	42	E3	52 59N	131 50W
Louiseville Québec	53	P6	46 16N	72 56W
Lourdes Newfoundland and Labrador	61	F4	48 39N	59 00W
Low, Cape Nunavut	65	N3	63 07N	85 18W
Lower Arrow Lake British Columbia	43	L1	49 40N	118 09W
Lower Foster Lake Saskatchewan	47	E5	56 30N	105 10W
Lower Manitou Lake Ontario	50	E5	49 15N	93 00W
Lower Post British Columbia	43	F6	59 56N	128 09W
Lower Sackville Nova Scotia	61	M11	44 40N	63 40W
Lubicon Lake Alberta	46	E5	56 23N	115 56W
Lucan Ontario	54	A2	43 11N	81 24W
Lucknow Ontario	54	A2	43 58N	81 31W
Lucky Lake *tn.* Saskatchewan	47	D2	50 59N	107 10W
Lulu Island British Columbia	44	F3	49 09N	123 09W
Lumby British Columbia	43	L2	50 15N	118 58W
Lumsden Saskatchewan	47	E2	50 39N	104 52W
Lund British Columbia	42	H4	49 59N	124 46W
Lundar Manitoba	49	C2	50 41N	98 01W
Lundbreck Alberta	46	E1	49 36N	114 10W
Lunenburg Nova Scotia	61	M11	44 23N	64 21W
Lunenburg *admin.* Nova Scotia	61	M11	44 35N	64 30W
Luseland Saskatchewan	47	C3	52 06N	109 24W
Luther Lake Ontario	54	B2	43 52N	80 26W
Łutselk'e *(Snowdrift)* Northwest Territories	64	H3	62 24N	110 44W
Lyall, Mount Alberta/British Columbia	46	E2	50 05N	114 42W
Lyell Islands British Columbia	42	E3	52 00N	131 00W
Lynn Lake *tn.* Manitoba	49	B5	56 51N	101 01W
Lynx Lake Northwest Territories	64	J3	62 25N	106 15W
Lytton British Columbia	43	K2	50 12N	121 34W

M

Maaset British Columbia	42	D4	54 00N	132 01W
Mabel Lake British Columbia	43	L2	50 35N	118 40W
Mabou Nova Scotia	61	M12	46 04N	61 22W
McAdam New Brunswick	61	B2	45 34N	67 20W
MacAlpine Lake Nunavut	65	K4	66 45N	130 00W
Macamic Québec	57	A3	48 46N	79 02W
McBride British Columbia	43	K3	53 21N	120 19W
McCabe Lake Nova Scotia	59	Q7	44 47N	63 43W
Maccan Nova Scotia	61	M12	45 43N	64 16W
McClintock Manitoba	49	E5	57 50N	94 10W
McConnell River Bird Sanctuary Nunavut	65	M3	60 30N	94 00W
McCreary Manitoba	49	C2	50 45N	99 30W
Macdiarmid Ontario	51	G5	49 23N	88 08W
MacDowell Ontario	50	E7	52 10N	92 40W
MacDowell Lake Ontario	50	E7	52 15N	92 42W
McFarlane River Saskatchewan	47	D5	57 50N	107 55W
McGivney New Brunswick	61	B3	46 22N	66 34W
MacGregor Manitoba	49	C1	49 57N	98 48W
McGregor Lake Alberta	46	F2	50 25N	112 52W
Macgregor Point Provincial Park Ontario	54	A3	44 25N	81 27W
McGregor River British Columbia	43	K4	54 10N	121 20W
McKay Lake Newfoundland and Labrador	60	C6	53 44N	65 37W
Mackay Lake Northwest Territories	64	H3	63 55N	110 25W

McKeller Ontario 52 G5 45 30N 79 00W
Mackenzie British Columbia 43 J4 55 18N 123 10W
Mackenzie Bay Yukon Territory 64 C4 69 00N 137 30W
Mackenzie Bison Sanctuary Northwest Territories 64 G3 61 30N 116 30W
McKenzie Creek Ontario 54 B2 43 02N 80 17W
Mackenzie Highway Alberta 46 D5 57 55N 117 40W
Mackenzie King Island Northwest Territories/Nunavut 64 H6 77 45N 111 00W
Mackenzie Mountains Yukon Territory/Northwest Territories 64 E3 66 00N 132 00W
Mackenzie River Northwest Territories 64 E4 66 20N 125 55W
Mackey Ontario 52 J6 46 10N 77 49W
Macklin Saskatchewan 47 C3 52 20N 109 58W
Maclean Strait Nunavut 65 K6 77 30N 102 30W
McLeese Lake *tn.* British Columbia 43 J3 52 25N 122 20W
McLennan Alberta 46 D4 55 42N 116 54W
McLeod Lake *tn.* British Columbia 43 J4 55 00N 123 00W
McLeod River Alberta 46 E3 53 40N 116 20W
M'Clintock Channel Nunavut 65 K5 72 00N 102 00W
M'Clure, Cape Northwest Territories 64 F4 74 32N 121 19W
M'Clure Strait Northwest Territories 64 G5 74 59N 120 10W
Macmillan Pass Yukon Territory 64 D3 63 25N 130 00W
Macmillan River Yukon Territory 64 D3 63 00N 134 00W
McNabs Island Nova Scotia 59 Q6 44 37N 63 31W
McNutt Island Nova Scotia 61 L11 43 40N 65 20W
Macoun Lake Saskatchewan 47 F5 56 30N 103 40W
Macrae Point Provincial Park Ontario 54 C3 44 30N 79 10W
McTavish Arm *b.* Northwest Territories 64 G4 66 06N 118 04W
MacTier Ontario 52 G5 45 08N 79 47W
McVicar Arm *b.* Northwest Territories 64 F3 65 20N 120 10W
Madawaska Ontario 52 J5 45 30N 77 59W
Madawaska *admin.* New Brunswick 61 A3/B3 47 30N 68 00W
Madawaska River Ontario 51 N3 45 10N 77 30W
Madoc Ontario 53 J4 44 30N 77 29W
Mad River Ontario 54 B3 44 18N 80 02W
Madsen Ontario 50 E6 50 58N 93 55W
Maelpaeg Réservoir Newfoundland and Labrador 61 G4 48 20N 56 40W
Magnetawan Ontario 52 G5 45 40N 79 39W
Magnetawan River Ontario 52 F5 45 46N 80 37W
Magog Québec 53 P5 45 16N 72 09W
Magpie River Ontario 51 J5 48 00N 84 50W
Magrath Alberta 46 F1 49 27N 112 52W
Maguse Lake Nunavut 65 M3 61 40N 95 10W
Mahone Bay Nova Scotia 61 M11 44 25N 64 15W
Mahone Bay *tn.* Nova Scotia 61 M11 44 27N 64 24W
Mahood Creek British Columbia 44 G3 49 09N 122 50W
Maidstone Saskatchewan 47 C3 53 06N 109 18W
Main Brook *tn.* Newfoundland and Labrador 60 G5 51 11N 56 01W
Main Channel Ontario 52 E5 45 00N 82 00W
Maitland River Ontario 54 A2 43 50N 81 28W
Major, Lake Nova Scotia 59 R6 44 45N 63 30W
Makkovik Newfoundland and Labrador 60 F7 55 05N 59 11W
Makoop Lake Ontario 50 F7 53 24N 90 50W
Malartic Québec 57 A3 48 09N 78 09W
Malaspina Strait British Columbia 42 H4 49 47N 124 30W
Mallet River Ontario 54 B2 43 51N 80 42W
Mallikjuaq Territorial Park Nunavut 65 Q3 64 14N 76 34W
Malpeque Bay Prince Edward Island 61 M12 46 35N 63 50W
Malton Ontario 54 C2 43 42N 79 38W
Manicouagan Québec 57 F4 50 40N 68 46W
Manigotagan Manitoba 49 D2 51 00N 96 10W
Manigotagan River Manitoba 49 E2 51 00N 96 10W
Manitoba *province* 49
Manitoba, Lake Manitoba 49 C2 50 30N 98 15W
Manito Lake Saskatchewan 47 C3 52 40N 109 20W
Manitou Manitoba 49 C1 49 15N 98 32W
Manitou Lake Ontario 51 E5 45 48N 82 00W
Manitoulin *admin.* Ontario 52 C5/D5 45 45N 82 30W
Manitoulin Island Ontario 52 D5 45 50N 82 20W
Manitouwadge Ontario 51 J5 49 10N 85 55W
Maniwaki Québec 53 L6 46 22N 75 58W
Manning Alberta 46 D5 56 55N 117 37W
Manning Provincial Park British Columbia 42 H4 49 09N 120 50W
Manotick Ontario 59 K1 45 14N 75 43W
Mansel Island Nunavut 65 Q3 62 00N 80 00W
Manson Creek *tn.* British Columbia 43 H4 55 40N 124 32W
Maple Ontario 54 C2 43 50N 79 30W
Maple Creek *tn.* Saskatchewan 47 B1 49 55N 109 28W
Maple Ridge British Columbia 42 H4 49 13N 122 36W
Mara Provincial Park Ontario 54 C3 44 30N 79 15W
Marathon Ontario 51 H5 48 44N 86 23W
Margaree Forks Nova Scotia 61 M12 46 20N 61 10W
Margaree Harbour *tn.* Nova Scotia 61 M12 46 26N 61 08W
Margaret Lake Alberta 46 E6 58 56N 115 25W
Margaretville Nova Scotia 61 L12 45 05N 65 05W
Marguerite River Wildland Provincial Park Alberta 46 G5 57 35N 110 10W
Maria Québec 57 H3 48 10N 65 59W
Marieville Québec 53 N5 45 27N 73 08W
Markdale Ontario 54 B3 44 19N 80 39W
Markham Ontario 54 C2 43 53N 79 14W
Markham Bay Nunavut 65 R3 63 02N 72 00W
Marmora Ontario 52 J4 44 29N 77 41W
Marten Falls *I.R.* Ontario 50 J6 51 40N 85 55W
Martensville Saskatchewan 47 D3 52 10N 106 30W
Mary's Harbour *tn.* Newfoundland and Labrador 60 H6 52 19N 55 50W
Marystown Newfoundland and Labrador 61 H3 47 10N 55 09W
Marysville New Brunswick 61 B2 45 58N 66 35W
Mascouche Québec 53 N5 45 47N 73 49W
Mashteuiatsh Québec 57 D3 48 34N 72 15W
Maskinongé *admin.* Québec 53 M7 47 40N 74 50W
Massasauga Provincial Park Ontario 52 F5 45 12N 80 02W
Massey Ontario 52 D6 46 12N 82 05W
Massey Sound Nunavut 65 L6 78 00N 95 00W
Matachewan Ontario 51 L4 47 56N 80 39W
Matagami Québec 57 B3 49 40N 77 40W
Matane Québec 57 G3 48 50N 67 31W
Matapédia Québec 57 G2 47 59N 66 58W
Matheson Ontario 51 L5 48 32N 80 28W
Matimekosh Québec 56 G6 54 49N 66 48W
Matsqui British Columbia 42 H4 49 05N 122 22W
Mattagami Lake Ontario 51 L4 47 54N 81 35W
Mattagami River Ontario 51 L5 49 00N 81 50W
Mattawa Ontario 52 H6 46 19N 78 42W
Mattice Ontario 51 K5 49 36N 83 16W
Maurelle Island British Columbia 42 G5 50 16N 125 11W
Mayerthorpe Alberta 46 E3 53 57N 115 08W
Mayne Island British Columbia 42 H4 48 50N 123 18W
Maynooth Ontario 52 J5 45 14N 77 57W
Mayo Yukon Territory 64 C3 63 34N 135 52W
Mayo Lake Yukon Territory 64 C3 135 00N 63 50W
Mayson Lake Saskatchewan 47 D5 57 50N 107 30W
Meadow Lake *tn.* Saskatchewan 47 C4 54 09N 108 26W
Meadow Lake Provincial Park Saskatchewan 47 C4 54 30N 108 00W
Meadowvale West Ontario 54 C2 43 35N 79 45W
Meaford Ontario 54 B3 44 36N 80 35W
Meaghers Grant Nova Scotia 61 M11 44 57N 63 15W
Mealy Mountains Newfoundland and Labrador 60 F6 53 10N 60 00W
Meander River *tn.* Alberta 46 D6 59 02N 117 42W
Meath Park *tn.* Saskatchewan 47 E3 53 27N 105 22W
Medicine Hat Alberta 46 G2 50 03N 110 41W
Meductic New Brunswick 61 B2 45 55N 67 30W
Medway Creek Ontario 54 A2 43 07N 81 18W
Medway River Nova Scotia 61 M11 44 15N 64 50W
Mégantic *admin.* Québec 53 Q6 46 10N 71 40W
Meighen Island Nunavut 65 L7 80 00N 99 30W
Melbourne Island Nunavut 64 J4 68 30N 104 45W
Meldrum Bay *tn.* Ontario 52 C5 45 56N 83 06W
Melfort Saskatchewan 47 E3 52 52N 104 38W
Melita Manitoba 49 B1 49 16N 101 00W
Melville Saskatchewan 47 F2 50 57N 102 49W
Melville Hills Northwest Territories/Nunavut 64 F4 69 00N 121 00W
Melville Island Northwest Territories/Nunavut 64 H6 75 30N 112 00W
Melville, Lake Newfoundland and Labrador 60 F6 53 45N 59 00W
Melville Peninsula Nunavut 65 P4 68 00N 84 00W
Melville Sound Nunavut 64 J4 68 05N 107 30W
Melville Sound Ontario 54 A3 43 00N 81 04W
Menihek Lakes Newfoundland and Labrador 60 B6 53 50N 66 50W
Menihek Siding Newfoundland and Labrador 60 B7 54 28N 66 36W
Mercier Québec 53 N5 45 20N 73 45W
Mercy Bay Northwest Territories 64 G5 74 05N 119 00W
Merigomish Nova Scotia 61 M12 45 37N 62 25W
Merrickville Ontario 53 L4 44 55N 75 50W
Merritt British Columbia 43 K2 50 09N 120 49W
Mersey River Nova Scotia 61 M11 44 10N 65 00W
Messines Québec 57 B2 46 15N 76 01W
Metabetchouane Québec 53 Q8 48 26N 71 52W
Meta Incognita Peninsula Nunavut 65 S3 63 30N 70 00W
Metcalfe Ontario 59 L1 45 14N 75 29W
Metchosin British Columbia 42 H4 48 22N 123 32W
Meteghan Nova Scotia 61 L11 44 12N 66 10W
Meziadin Junction British Columbia 43 F5 56 10N 129 15W
Mica Creek *tn.* British Columbia 43 L3 52 00N 118 28W
Mica Dam British Columbia 43 L3 52 04N 118 28W
Michaud Point Nova Scotia 61 M12 45 35N 60 40W
Michel Peak British Columbia 43 G3 53 30N 126 25W
Michikamats Lake Newfoundland and Labrador 60 C7 54 38N 64 19W
Michikamau Lake Newfoundland and Labrador 60 D6 54 00N 64 00W
Michipicoten Island Ontario 51 J4 47 45N 85 45W
Michipicoten River *tn.* Ontario 51 J4 47 56N 84 52W
Micmac, Lake Nova Scotia 59 Q6 44 41N 63 32W
Midale Saskatchewan 47 F1 49 23N 103 21W
Middle Arm Newfoundland and Labrador 61 G4 49 42N 56 06W
Middle Maitland River Ontario 54 A2 43 43N 81 11W
Middle Ridge Newfoundland and Labrador 61 H4 48 20N 55 15W
Middle Ridge Wilderness Reserve Newfoundland and Labrador 61 H4 48 30N 55 15W
Middle Sackville Nova Scotia 61 M11 44 47N 63 41W
Middlesex *admin.* Ontario 54 A2 42 46N 81 46W
Middleton Nova Scotia 61 L11 44 56N 65 04W
Midhurst Ontario 54 C3 44 26N 79 45W
Midland Ontario 52 G4 44 45N 79 53W
Midway British Columbia 43 L1 49 02N 118 45W
Midway Mountains British Columbia 43 L1 49 25N 118 45W
Mikkwa River Alberta 46 E5 57 40N 114 08W
Mildmay Ontario 54 A3 44 03N 81 08W
Milestone Saskatchewan 47 E1 49 59N 104 31W
Milk River Alberta 46 G1 49 10N 110 05W
Milk River *tn.* Alberta 46 F1 49 09N 112 05W
Millbrook Ontario 52 H4 44 09N 78 28W
Miller Lake Nova Scotia 59 Q7 44 49N 63 35W
Millet Alberta 46 F3 53 06N 113 28W
Mill Island Nunavut 65 Q3 64 00N 78 00W
Milltown Newfoundland and Labrador 61 H3 47 54N 55 46W
Mill Village Nova Scotia 61 M11 44 10N 64 40W
Millville New Brunswick 61 B3 46 08N 67 12W
Milo Alberta 46 F2 50 34N 112 53W
Milton Nova Scotia 61 M11 44 04N 64 44W
Milton Ontario 54 C2 43 31N 79 53W
Milton Prince Edward Island 61 M12 46 20N 63 10W
Milverton Ontario 54 B2 43 34N 80 55W
Miminegash Prince Edward Island 61 M12 46 54N 64 15W
Minaki Ontario 50 D5 50 00N 94 40W
Minas Basin Nova Scotia 61 M12 45 15N 64 15W
Minas Channel Nova Scotia 61 M12 45 10N 64 50W
Minden Ontario 52 H4 44 56N 78 44W
Minipi Lake Newfoundland and Labrador 60 E6 52 25N 60 45W
Miniss Lake Ontario 50 F6 50 48N 90 50W
Minitonas Manitoba 49 B3 52 04N 101 02W
Minnedosa Manitoba 49 C2 50 14N 99 50W
Minnitaki Lake Ontario 50 F5 49 58N 92 00W
Minonipi Lake Newfoundland and Labrador 60 E6 52 50N 60 50W
Minto New Brunswick 61 B3 46 05N 66 05W
Minto Yukon Territory 64 C3 62 34N 136 50W
Minto Inlet Northwest Territories 64 G5 71 20N 117 00W
Mira Bay Nova Scotia 61 N12 46 05N 59 50W
Mirabel Québec 53 M5 45 41N 74 20W
Miramichi New Brunswick 61 C3 46 55N 65 35W
Miramichi Bay New Brunswick 61 C3 47 05N 65 00W
Mira River Nova Scotia 61 M12 46 00N 60 10W
Miscouche Prince Edward Island 61 M12 46 26N 63 52W
Miscou Island New Brunswick 61 C3 47 50N 64 30W
Misery Point Newfoundland and Labrador 60 H6 52 01N 55 18W
Mishkeegogamang Ontario 50 F6 50 52N 90 13W
Missanabie Ontario 51 J5 48 19N 84 05W
Missinaibi Lake Ontario 51 K5 48 23N 83 40W
Missinaibi River Ontario 51 K5 49 30N 83 20W
Missinaibi River Provincial Park Ontario 51 K6 50 00N 83 15W
Mission British Columbia 42 H4 49 08N 122 20W
Missisa Lake Ontario 50 J7 52 18N 85 12W
Mississagi River Ontario 51 K4 46 10N 83 01W
Mississagi River Provincial Park Ontario 51 K4 47 10N 82 35W
Mississauga Ontario 54 C2 43 38N 79 36W
Missouri Coteau *hills* Saskatchewan 47 D2 50 40N 106 30W
Mistastin Lake Newfoundland and Labrador 60 D7 55 50N 63 00W
Mistissini Québec 57 D4 50 25N 73 50W
Mitchell Ontario 54 A2 43 27N 81 13W
Mitchells Brook *tn.* Newfoundland and Labrador 61 J3 47 08N 53 31W
Mittimatalik (*Pond Inlet*) *tn.* Nunavut 65 Q5 72 40N 77 59W
Mobert *I.R.* Ontario 51 J5 48 40N 85 40W
Moisie Québec 57 G4 50 12N 66 06W
Molson Lake Manitoba 49 D4 54 20N 96 50W
Monarch Mountain British Columbia 43 H2 51 55N 125 57W
Monashee Mountains British Columbia 43 L2 51 30N 118 50W
Monashee Provincial Park British Columbia 43 L2 50 30N 118 15W
Moncton New Brunswick 61 M12 46 04N 64 50W
Monkman Pass British Columbia 43 K4 54 30N 121 10W
Monkman Provincial Park British Columbia 43 K4 54 00N 121 10W
Mono Cliffs Provincial Park Ontario 54 B3 44 02N 80 03W
Mono Mills Ontario 54 C2 43 55N 79 57W
Montague Prince Edward Island 61 M12 46 10N 62 39W
Montcalm *admin.* Québec 53 L7 47 40N 76 15W
Mont D'Iberville *mt.* Québec/Newfoundland 60 D9 58 50N 64 40W
Mont Jacques-Cartier *mt.* Québec 57 H3 49 00N 66 00W
Mont-Joli *tn.* Québec 57 F3 48 36N 68 14W
Mont-Laurier *tn.* Québec 53 L6 46 33N 75 31W
Montmagny Québec 53 R6 46 58N 70 34W
Montmagny *admin.* Québec 53 R6 46 50N 70 20W
Montmartre Saskatchewan 47 F2 50 13N 103 26W
Montmorency *admin.* Québec 53 Q7 47 34N 71 20W
Montréal Québec 53 N5 45 32N 73 36W
Montreal Lake Saskatchewan 47 E4 54 15N 105 30W
Montreal River Ontario 51 J4 47 20N 84 20W
Montreal River Saskatchewan 47 E4 54 50N 105 30W
Montreal River *tn.* Ontario 51 J4 47 14N 84 39W
Montrose British Columbia 43 M1 49 06N 117 30W
Monts Chic-Chocs *mts.* Québec 57 G3 49 00N 66 40W
Monts Notre Dame *mts.* Québec 57 F3 48 00N 69 00W
Monts Otish *mts.* Québec 57 E5 52 30N 70 20W
Monts Povungnituk *mts.* Québec 56 C9 61 30N 75 59W
Monts Torngat *mts.* Québec/Newfoundland 56 H8 59 00N 64 15W
Mont Tremblant Québec 57 C2 46 07N 74 35W
Moose Creek Provincial Forest Manitoba 49 D2 51 30N 96 45W
Moose Factory Ontario 51 L6 51 16N 80 37W
Moose Jaw Saskatchewan 47 E2 50 23N 105 35W
Moosejaw River Saskatchewan 47 E2 50 15N 105 10W
Moose Lake *tn.* Manitoba 49 B3 53 43N 100 20W
Moose Mountain Creek Saskatchewan 47 F2 50 15N 103 25W
Moose Mountain Provincial Park Saskatchewan 47 F1 49 50N 102 20W
Moose River *tn.* Ontario 51 L6 50 48N 81 18W
Moosomin Saskatchewan 47 G2 50 09N 101 41W
Moosonee Ontario 51 L6 51 18N 80 39W
Morden Manitoba 49 C1 49 12N 98 05W
Morell Prince Edward Island 61 M12 46 25N 62 42W
Moresby Camp British Columbia 42 D3 53 05N 132 04W
Moresby Island British Columbia 42 D3 53 00N 132 00W
Morice Lake British Columbia 43 G3/G4 53 55N 127 30W
Moricetown British Columbia 43 G4 55 02N 127 20W
Morinville Alberta 46 F3 53 48N 113 39W
Morris Manitoba 49 D1 49 22N 97 21W
Morrisburg Ontario 53 L4 44 54N 75 11W
Morse Saskatchewan 47 D2 50 24N 107 00W
Morson Ontario 50 D5 49 03N 94 19W
Moser River *tn.* Nova Scotia 61 M11 44 58N 62 18W
Mostoos Hills Saskatchewan 47 C4 55 20N 109 30W
Mould Bay *m.s.* Northwest Territories 64 G6 76 14N 119 20W
Mountain Lake Ontario 54 A3 44 42N 81 02W
Mount Albert *tn.* Ontario 54 C3 44 07N 79 18W
Mount Blanchet Provincial Park British Columbia 43 H4 55 15N 125 55W
Mount Burke British Columbia 44 H4 49 18N 122 42W
Mount Carleton Provincial Park New Brunswick 61 B3 47 20N 66 30W
Mount Edziza Provincial Park British Columbia 42 E5 57 40N 131 40W
Mount Forest *tn.* Ontario 54 B2 43 58N 80 44W
Mount Hope *tn.* Ontario 54 C2 43 09N 79 54W
Mount Pearl *tn.* Newfoundland and Labrador 61 J3 47 31N 52 47W
Mount Revelstoke National Park British Columbia 43 L2/M2 50 40N 118 00W
Mount Robson Provincial Park British Columbia 43 L3 52 50N 118 40W
Mount Brydges *tn.* Ontario 54 A1 42 54N 81 30W
Mount Seymour Provincial Park British Columbia 42 G4 49 22N 122 56W
Mount Stewart *tn.* Prince Edward Island 61 M12 46 22N 62 52W
Mount Uniacke *tn.* Nova Scotia 61 M11 44 54N 63 50W
Mud Bay British Columbia 44 G3 49 04N 122 53W
Mudjatik River Saskatchewan 47 D5 56 40N 107 10W
Mud Lake *tn.* Newfoundland and Labrador 60 E6 53 19N 60 10W
Mukutawa River Manitoba 49 D3 53 10N 97 10W
Mulgrave Nova Scotia 61 M12 45 36N 61 25W
Muncho Lake British Columbia 43 H6 59 05N 125 47W
Muncho Lake *tn.* British Columbia 43 H6 59 00N 125 46W
Muncho Lake Provincial Park British Columbia 43 H6 58 50N 125 40W
Mundare Alberta 46 F3 53 36N 112 20W
Murdochville Québec 57 H3 48 57N 65 30W
Murray Harbour *tn.* Prince Edward Island 61 M12 46 00N 62 32W
Murray River *tn.* Prince Edward Island 61 M12 46 00N 62 38W
Murtle Lake British Columbia 43 L3 52 09N 119 40W
Musgrave Harbour Newfoundland and Labrador 61 J4 49 27N 53 58W
Musgravetown Newfoundland and Labrador 61 J4 48 24N 53 53W
Muskoka Falls *tn.* Ontario 52 G4 44 59N 79 16W
Muskrat Dam Lake Ontario 50 F7 53 25N 91 40W
Muskwa River British Columbia 43 J6 58 30N 123 20W
Musquodoboit Harbour Nova Scotia 61 M11 44 48N 63 10W
Muzon, Cape British Columbia 42 D4 54 41N 132 40W
Myles Bay Ontario 54 A3 44 56N 81 23W
Myrnam Alberta 46 G3 53 40N 111 14W

N

Nachvak Fiord *in.* Newfoundland and Labrador 60 D9 59 03N 63 45W
Nackawic New Brunswick 61 B2 46 00N 67 15W
Nagagami Lake Ontario 51 J5 49 25N 85 01W
Nagagami River Ontario 51 J5 49 30N 84 50W

Nahanni National Park Reserve Northwest Territories 64 E3 61 30N 126 00W
Nahatlatch River British Columbia 42 H4 49 55N 121 59W
Nahlin River British Columbia 42 E6 58 58N 131 30W
Naicam Saskatchewan 47 E3 52 26N 104 31W
Naikoon Provincial Park British Columbia 42 E3 53 59N 131 35W
Nain Newfoundland and Labrador 60 E8 56 32N 61 41W
Nakina Ontario 50 H6 50 11N 86 43W
Nakina River British Columbia 42 D6 59 07N 132 59W
Nakusp British Columbia 43 M2 50 15N 117 45W
Nanaimo British Columbia 42 H4 49 08N 123 58W
Nanaimo River British Columbia 42 H4 49 08N 123 54W
Nanisivik Nunavut 65 P5 73 00N 79 58W
Nansen Sound Nunavut 65 M7 81 00N 90 35W
Nanticoke Ontario 54 B1 42 48N 80 04W
Nanticoke Creek Ontario 54 B1 42 56N 80 16W
Nanton Alberta 46 F2 50 21N 113 46W
Napaktokh (Black Duck) Bay Newfoundland and Labrador 60 D9 58 01N 62 19W
Napaktulik Lake Nunavut 64 H4 66 30N 112 50W
Napanee Ontario 53 K4 44 15N 76 57W
Naramata British Columbia 43 L1 49 36N 119 36W
Nares Strait 65 R6 78 30N 72 30W
Narrow Hills Provincial Park Saskatchewan 47 E4 54 10N 103 30W
Narrows, The *sd.* Nova Scotia 59 Q6 44 40N 63 35W
Naskaupi River Newfoundland and Labrador 60 D7 54 20N 62 40W
Nass River British Columbia 42 F4 55 10N 129 20W
Nastapoka Islands Nunavut 56 B7 56 50N 76 50W
Natashquan Québec 57 K4 50 10N 61 50W
Natashquan River Newfoundland and Labrador 60 D6 52 30N 62 50W
Nation Lakes British Columbia 43 H4 55 08N 125 15W
Nation River British Columbia 43 H4 55 11N 124 25W
Natuashish Newfoundland and Labrador 60 E7 55 51N 62 04W
Naujat *(Repulse Bay)* Nunavut 65 N4 66 32N 86 15W
Nauwigewauk New Brunswick 61 L12 45 28W 65 53W
Nazko British Columbia 43 J3 53 00N 123 37W
Nechako Plateau British Columbia 43 H4/J4 54 40N 124 40W
Nechako River British Columbia 43 H3 53 35N 124 50W
Neeb Saskatchewan 47 D4 54 00N 107 50W
Neepawa Manitoba 49 C2 50 14N 99 29W
Neguac New Brunswick 61 C3 47 14N 65 03W
Neilburg Saskatchewan 47 C3 52 50N 109 38W
Nejanilini Lake Manitoba 49 D6 59 50N 97 20W
Nelson British Columbia 43 M1 49 29N 117 17W
Nelson Forks *tn.* British Columbia 43 H6 59 30N 124 00W
Nelson House *tn.* Manitoba 49 C4 55 49N 98 51W
Nelson Island British Columbia 42 H4 49 43N 124 03W
Nelson River Manitoba 49 F5 56 50N 93 40W
Némiscau Québec 57 B4 51 20N 77 01W
Nepean Ontario 53 L5 45 16N 75 48W
Nepewassi Lake Ontario 52 F6 46 22N 80 38W
Nepisiguit River New Brunswick 61 B3 47 20N 66 30W
Nesselrode, Mount British Columbia 42 C6 58 55N 134 20W
Nestor Falls *tn.* Ontario 50 E5 49 05N 93 55W
Nettilling Lake Nunavut 65 R4 66 30N 71 10W
Neustadt Ontario 54 A3 44 04N 81 00W
New Aiyansh British Columbia 43 F4 55 15N 129 02W
Newboro Ontario 53 K4 44 39N 76 19W
New Brunswick *province* 61 B3/C3
Newburgh Ontario 53 K4 44 19N 76 52W
New Carlisle Québec 57 H3 48 00N 65 22W
New Denver British Columbia 43 M1 49 59N 117 22W
Newell, Lake Alberta 46 G2 50 26N 111 55W
Newfoundland *i.* Newfoundland and Labrador 61 G4 53 51N 56 56W
Newfoundland and Labrador *province* 60/61
New Germany Nova Scotia 61 M11 44 34N 64 44W
New Glasgow Nova Scotia 61 M12 45 36N 62 38W
New Hazelton British Columbia 43 G4 55 15N 127 30W
New Liskeard Ontario 51 M4 47 31N 79 41W
Newmarket Ontario 54 C3 44 03N 79 27W
New Minas Nova Scotia 61 M12 45 00N 64 30W
New Richmond Québec 57 H3 48 12N 65 52W
New Ross Nova Scotia 61 M11 44 44N 64 27W
Newton British Columbia 44 G3 49 07N 122 50W
New Waterford Nova Scotia 61 M12 46 17N 60 05W
New Westminster British Columbia 42 H4 49 10N 122 58W
New-Wes-Valley Newfoundland and Labrador 61 J4 49 12N 53 31W
Niagara *admin.* Ontario 54 C2 43 02N 79 34W
Niagara Escarpment Ontario 54 B3 44 30N 80 45W
Niagara Falls *tn.* Ontario 54 C2 43 05N 79 06W
Niagara-on-the-Lake Ontario 54 C2 43 14N 79 16W
Nicolet Québec 53 P6 46 14N 72 36W
Nicolet *admin.* Québec 53 P6 46 00N 72 30W
Nicomekl *r.* British Columbia 44 H3 49 05N 122 43W
Nictau New Brunswick 61 B3 47 16N 67 11W
Night Hawk Lake Ontario 51 L5 48 28N 80 58W
Ningunsaw Provincial Park British Columbia 42 E5 56 50N 130 00W
Nipawin Saskatchewan 47 E3 53 23N 104 01W
Nipigon Ontario 51 G5 49 02N 88 26W
Nipigon Bay Ontario 51 G5 48 50N 88 10W
Nipigon, Lake Ontario 50 G5 49 50N 88 30W
Nipishish Lake Newfoundland and Labrador 60 E7 54 10N 60 30W
Nipissing Ontario 52 G6 46 05N 79 31W
Nipissing *admin.* Ontario 52 G6/H6 46 00N 79 00W
Nipissing, Lake Ontario 52 G6 46 17N 80 00W
Nirjutiqavvik National Wildlife Area Nunavut 65 Q6 76 00N 79 55W
Nisgara Memorial Lava Bed Park British Columbia 43 F4 55 15N 128 55W
Nisling Range *mts.* Yukon Territory 64 C3 62 00N 138 40W
Nitchequon Québec 57 E5 53 10N 70 58W
Nith River Ontario 54 B2 43 12N 80 22W
Nitinat Lake British Columbia 42 H4 48 45N 124 42W
Nitinat River British Columbia 42 H4 49 06N 124 35W
Niverville Manitoba 49 D1 49 39N 97 03W
Nobleton Ontario 54 C2 43 53N 79 39W
Nokomis Saskatchewan 47 E2 51 30N 105 00W
Nokomis Lake Saskatchewan 47 F5 56 55N 103 00W
Nootka Island British Columbia 43 G1 49 45N 126 50W
Nootka Sound British Columbia 43 G1 49 34N 126 39W
Nopiming Provincial Park Manitoba 49 E2 50 40N 95 10W
Noralee British Columbia 43 G3 53 59N 126 26W
Norman Bay *tn.* Newfoundland and Labrador 60 G6 52 55N 56 10W
Norman, Cape Newfoundland and Labrador 60 H5 51 38N 55 54W
Normandale Ontario 54 B1 42 41N 80 19W
Normansland Point Ontario 50 L7 52 00N 81 00W
Normétal Québec 57 A3 48 59N 79 53W
Norquay Saskatchewan 47 F2 51 52N 102 00W
Norris Arm *tn.* Newfoundland and Labrador 61 H4 49 05N 55 15W
Norris Point *tn.* Newfoundland and Labrador 61 G4 49 31N 57 53W
North Arm *b.* Northwest Territories 64 G3 62 05N 114 40W
North Arm *r.* British Columbia 44 F3 49 12N 123 05W
North Aulatsivik Island Newfoundland and Labrador 60 C9 59 46N 64 05W
North Battleford Saskatchewan 47 C3 52 47N 108 19W
North Bay *tn.* Ontario 52 G6 46 20N 79 28W
North, Cape Nova Scotia 61 M12 47 10N 60 00W
North Cape Prince Edward Island 61 M12 47 10N 64 00W
North Caribou Lake Ontario 50 F7 52 50N 90 40W
North Castor *r.* Ontario 59 K2 45 18N 75 31W
North Channel Ontario 52 C6/D6 46 00N 83 00W
North Cowichan British Columbia 42 H4 48 51N 123 41W
Northern Indian Lake Manitoba 49 D5 57 30N 97 30W
Northern Peninsula Newfoundland and Labrador 60 G5 50 30N 57 00W
Northern Rocky Mountains Provincial Park British Columbia 43 H6 58 00N 124 00W
Northern Woods and Water Route Canada 47 D4 54 10N 107 20W
North French River Ontario 51 L6 50 20N 81 00W
North Head *tn.* New Brunswick 61 L11 44 46N 66 45W
North Kent Island Nunavut 65 M6 76 40N 90 14W
North Knife Lake Manitoba 49 D6 58 10N 96 40W
North Knife River Manitoba 49 E6 58 40N 95 50W
North Moose Lake Manitoba 49 B4 54 00N 100 10W
North Pender Island British Columbia 42 H4 48 49N 123 17W
North River *tn.* Manitoba 49 E6 58 55N 94 30W
North River *tn.* Newfoundland and Labrador 60 F7 53 49N 57 05W
North River Bridge *tn.* Nova Scotia 61 M12 46 19N 60 40W
North Rustico Prince Edward Island 61 M12 46 26N 63 20W
North Saskatchewan River Alberta/Saskatchewan 47 D3 52 40N 106 40W
North Saugeen River Ontario 54 A3 44 18N 81 10W
North Seal River Manitoba 49 B6 59 00N 100 30W
North Spirit Lake Ontario 50 E7 52 31N 92 55W
North Spirit Lake *tn.* Ontario 50 E7 52 31N 93 01W
North Sydney Nova Scotia 61 M12 46 13N 60 15W
North Thames River Ontario 54 A2 43 02N 81 14W
North Thompson River British Columbia 43 L2 51 32N 120 00W
North Tweedsmuir Provincial Park British Columbia 43 G3 53 30N 126 30W
North Twin Island Nunavut 50 M7 53 20N 80 00W
Northumberland *admin.* New Brunswick 61 B3 47 10N 66 30W
Northumberland Strait Atlantic Provinces 61 M12 46 30N 64 30W
North Vancouver British Columbia 42 H4 49 21N 123 05W
North Wabasca Lake Alberta 46 F5 56 10N 113 55W
Northwest Angle Provincial Park Manitoba 49 E1 49 20N 95 30W
Northwest Bay *tn.* Ontario 50 E5 48 50N 93 38W
Northwest Gander River Newfoundland and Labrador 61 H4 48 30N 55 40W
Northwest Passage Territorial Park Nunavut 65 L4 68 35N 50 29W
North West River *tn.* Newfoundland and Labrador 60 E6 53 32N 60 08W
Northwest Territories *territory* 64
North York Ontario 55 C2 43 46N 79 26W
Norton New Brunswick 61 L12 45 38N 65 43W
Norway House *tn.* Manitoba 49 D3 53 59N 97 50W
Norwich Ontario 54 B1 42 59N 80 36W
Nose Creek Alberta 44 A2 51 08N 114 02W
Nose Hill Alberta 44 A2 51 06N 114 07W
Notekwin River Alberta 46 C5 56 55N 118 20W
Notre Dame Bay Newfoundland and Labrador 61 H4 49 45N 55 00W
Notre-Dame-des-Champs Ontario 59 L2 45 25N 75 28W
Nottawasaga Bay Ontario 54 B3 44 40N 80 30W
Nottawasaga River Ontario 54 C3 43 27N 79 53W
Nottingham Island Nunavut 65 Q3 63 05N 78 00W
Nova Scotia *province* 61 C1/E3
Nueltin Lake Manitoba/Nunavut 49 C6 60 00N 99 55W
Numaykoos Lake Provincial Park Manitoba 49 D5 57 55N 96 00W
Nunaksaluk Island Newfoundland and Labrador 60 E7 55 49N 60 20W
Nunavut *territory* 64/65
Nunsti Provincial Park British Columbia 43 J2 51 40N 123 50W
Nutak Newfoundland and Labrador 60 E8 57 28N 61 52W
Nut Mountain Saskatchewan 47 F3 52 20N 102 50W

O

Oakbank Manitoba 49 D1 49 57N 96 54W
Oak Bay British Columbia 42 H4 48 27N 123 18W
Oak Bluff Manitoba 48 A1 49 46N 97 18W
Oak Island Nova Scotia 61 M11 44 30N 63 55W
Oak Lake *tn.* Manitoba 49 B1 49 40N 100 45W
Oak Ridges Ontario 54 C2 44 55N 79 27W
Oakville Manitoba 49 C1 49 56N 98 00W
Oakville Ontario 54 C2 43 27N 79 41W
Oakwood Ontario 54 D3 44 20N 78 52W
Obabika River Provincial Park Ontario 51 L4 47 00N 80 30W
Obaska Québec 53 J8 48 12N 77 20W
O'Briens Landing Ontario 50 F5 49 50N 91 10W
Observatory Inlet British Columbia 42 F4 55 05N 129 59W
Ocean Falls *tn.* British Columbia 43 G3 52 24N 127 42W
Odei River Manitoba 49 C4 55 50N 98 00W
Ogidaki Mountain Ontario 51 K4 46 57N 83 59W
Ogilvie Mountains Yukon Territory 64 C4 65 05N 139 00W
Ogoki Ontario 50 J6 51 38N 85 57W
Ogoki Lake Ontario 50 H6 50 50N 87 10W
Ogoki Reservoir Ontario 50 G6 50 48N 88 18W
Ogoki River Ontario 50 H6 51 10N 86 30W
Oil Springs *tn.* Ontario 52 D2 42 47N 82 07W
Okak Bay Newfoundland and Labrador 60 D8 57 28N 62 20W
Okak Islands Newfoundland and Labrador 60 E8 57 30N 61 50W
Okanagan Lake British Columbia 43 L2 49 45N 119 32W
Okotoks Alberta 46 F2 50 44N 113 59W
Old Crow Yukon Territory 64 C4 67 34N 139 43W
Old Crow River Yukon Territory 64 C4 68 00N 140 00W
Oldman River Alberta 46 G1 49 50N 112 00W
Old Perlican Newfoundland and Labrador 61 J4 48 05N 53 01W
Olds Alberta 46 E2 51 50N 114 06W
Old Wives Lake Saskatchewan 47 D2 50 15N 106 40W
O'Leary Prince Edward Island 61 M12 46 43N 64 15W
Oliphant Ontario 54 A3 44 44N 81 16W
Oliver British Columbia 43 L1 49 10N 119 37W
Omemee Ontario 52 H4 44 19N 78 33W
Omineca Mountains British Columbia 43 G5/H4 57 15N 127 50W
Omineca Provincial Park British Columbia 43 H4 55 50N 124 45W
Omineca River British Columbia 43 H4 56 02N 126 00W
Onaman Lake Ontario 50 H6 50 00N 87 26W
Onaping Lake Ontario 51 L4 46 57N 81 30W
Ontario *province* 50
Ontario, Lake Ontario/USA 52/53 H3/K3
Ootsa Lake British Columbia 43 G3 53 40N 126 30W
Ootsa Lake *tn.* British Columbia 43 H3 53 42N 125 56W
Opasatika Ontario 51 K5 49 32N 82 52W
Opasquia Provincial Park Ontario 50 E7 53 30N 93 10W
Opeongo Lake Ontario 51 M3 45 42N 78 23W
Opinnagau River Ontario 50 K8 54 20N 83 50W
Orangeville Ontario 54 B2 43 55N 80 06W
Orillia Ontario 54 C3 44 36N 79 26W
Orleans Ontario 59 K2 45 28N 75 34W
Ormand's Creek *tn.* Manitoba 48 A2 49 58N 97 16W
Ormatown Québec 53 M5 45 08N 74 02W
Oromocto New Brunswick 61 B2 45 50N 66 28W
Orono Ontario 54 D2 43 59N 78 36W
Oshawa Ontario 54 D2 43 53N 78 51W
Oskélanéo Québec 53 L8 48 07N 75 14W
Osler Saskatchewan 47 D3 52 22N 106 32W
Osoyoos British Columbia 43 L1 49 00N 119 29W
Ospika River British Columbia 43 J5 56 55N 124 10W
Ossokmanuan Reservoir Newfoundland and Labrador 60 C6 53 25N 65 00W
Otoskwin-Attawapiskat Provincial Park Ontario 50 G6 52 15N 88 00W
Otoskwin River Ontario 50 G6 51 50N 89 40W
Ottawa Ontario 53 L5 45 24N 75 38W
Ottawa-Carleton *admin.* Ontario 53 L5 45 31N 75 22W
Ottawa Islands Nunavut 65 P2 59 10N 80 25W
Ottawa River Ontario/Québec 53 K5 45 34N 76 30W
Otter Lake Saskatchewan 47 E4 55 35N 104 30W
Otter Rapids *tn.* Ontario 51 L6 50 12N 81 40W
Outer Harbour East Headland Ontario 55 C1 43 38N 79 19W
Outlook Saskatchewan 47 D2 51 30N 107 03W
Owen Sound Ontario 54 B3 44 38N 80 56W
Owen Sound *tn.* Ontario 54 B3 44 34N 80 56W
Owl River Manitoba 49 F5 57 50N 93 20W
Oxbow Saskatchewan 47 F1 49 16N 102 12W
Oxford Nova Scotia 61 M12 45 43N 63 52W
Oxford *admin.* Ontario 54 B2 43 06N 80 59W
Oxford House *tn.* Manitoba 49 E4 54 58N 95 17W
Oxford Lake Manitoba 49 E4 54 40N 95 50W
Oyen Alberta 46 G2 51 22N 110 28W
Oyster River British Columbia 42 G4 49 50N 125 42W
Ozhiski Lake Ontario 50 G7 52 01N 88 30W

P

Pacific Rim National Park Reserve British Columbia 42 G4 48 52N 125 35W
Packs Harbour *tn.* Newfoundland and Labrador 60 G6 53 51N 56 59W
Pacquet Newfoundland and Labrador 61 H4 49 59N 55 53W
Paddle Prairie *tn.* Alberta 46 D5 57 57N 117 29W
Paint Lake Provincial Park Manitoba 49 D4 55 30N 97 40W
Paisley Ontario 54 A3 44 17N 81 16W
Pakashkan Lake Ontario 50 F5 49 21N 90 15W
Pakowki Lake Alberta 46 G1 49 20N 111 55W
Pakwash Lake Ontario 50 E6 50 45N 93 30W
Palmerston Ontario 54 B2 43 50N 80 50W
Panache Lake Ontario 52 E6 46 15N 81 20W
Panmure Island Prince Edward Island 61 M12 46 10N 62 30W
Panniqtuuq *(Pangnirtung)* Nunavut 65 S4 66 05N 65 45W
Papineau *admin.* Québec 53 L5 45 40N 75 30W
Paradise Hill *tn.* Saskatchewan 47 C3 53 32N 109 26W
Paradise River Newfoundland and Labrador 60 G6 52 50N 57 50W
Paradise River *tn.* Newfoundland and Labrador 60 G6 53 27N 57 17W
Parc de Conservation du Saguenay Québec 53 R8 48 15N 70 45W
Parc de la Gatineau Québec 53 K5 45 31N 75 53W
Parc de Récréation des Îles-de-Boucherville Québec 58 P5 45 36N 73 27W
Parc Marin du Saguenay–Saint-Laurent Québec 57 F3 48 00N 69 38W
Parc National d'Aiguebelle Québec 57 A3 48 30N 78 50W
Parc National d'Anticosti Québec 57 H3/J3 49 25N 62 58W
Parc National de Forillon Québec 57 H3 49 00N 64 00W
Parc National de Frontenac Québec 53 Q5 45 52N 71 17W
Parc National de la Gaspésie Québec 57 G3 48 52N 65 57W
Parc National de la Jacques-Cartier Québec 53 Q7 47 23N 71 30W
Parc National de la Mauricie Québec 53 N6/P6 46 50N 73 05W
Parc National des Grands-Jardins Québec 53 R7 47 47N 70 59W
Parc National des Pingualuit Québec 56 D9 61 25N 73 30W
Parc National du Mont-Tremblant Québec 53 M6 46 20N 74 43W
Parc québecois d'Oka Québec 58 M4 45 24N 73 58W
Parent Québec 53 M7 47 55N 74 36W
Paris Ontario 54 B2 43 12N 80 25W
Parke Lake Newfoundland and Labrador 60 F6 53 10N 58 50W
Parkhill Ontario 54 A2 43 10N 81 41W
Parksville British Columbia 42 H4 49 20N 124 19W
Parrsboro Nova Scotia 61 M12 45 25N 64 21W
Parry Island Ontario 52 F5 45 17N 80 11W
Parry Islands Northwest Territories/Nunavut 64 H6 75 30N 110 00W
Parry Sound *admin.* Ontario 52 F5/G5 45 22N 80 08W
Parry Sound *tn.* Ontario 52 F5 45 21N 80 03W
Parson's Pond *tn.* Newfoundland and Labrador 61 G5 50 02N 57 43W
Pasadena Newfoundland and Labrador 61 G4 49 01N 57 36W
Pasfield Lake Saskatchewan 47 E6 58 20N 105 45W
Pasqui Hills Saskatchewan 47 F3 53 10N 103 00W
Pass Lake Ontario 51 G5 48 34N 88 44W
Pattullo, Mount British Columbia 42 F5 56 15N 129 43W
Patuanak Saskatchewan 47 D4 55 53N 107 38W
Paudash Ontario 52 J4 44 56N 78 04W
Paulatuuq *(Paulatuk)* Northwest Territories 64 F4 69 49N 123 59W
Paul Island Newfoundland and Labrador 60 E8 56 30N 61 25W
Payne Bay Québec 56 F8 60 00N 70 01W

Peace Point *tn.* Alberta	46	F6	59 07N	112 27W
Peace River Alberta	46	E6	58 40N	114 30W
Peace River *tn.* Alberta	46	D5	56 15N	117 18W
Peachland British Columbia	43	L1	49 49N	119 48W
Peary Channel Nunavut	65	K6	79 40N	101 30W
Peawanuk Ontario	50	J8	55 00N	85 30W
Pedzéh Kį *(Wrigley)* Northwest Territories	64	F3	63 16N	123 39W
Peel *admin.* Ontario	54	C2	43 49N	79 57W
Peel River Yukon Territory	64	C4	66 05N	136 00W
Peel River Game Reserve Northwest Territories	64	D4	66 30N	134 00W
Peel Sound Nunavut	65	L5	73 15N	96 30W
Peerless Lake Alberta	46	E5	56 40N	114 35W
Pefferlaw Ontario	54	C3	44 18N	79 14W
Pefferlaw Brook Ontario	54	C3	44 10N	79 15W
Peggys Cove *tn.* Nova Scotia	61	M11	44 30N	63 50W
Pelee Island Ontario	52	D1	41 47N	82 40W
Pelee Island *tn.* Ontario	52	D1	41 45N	82 40W
Pelee Point Ontario	52	D1	41 45N	82 39W
Pelham Ontario	54	C2	43 02N	79 19W
Pelican Bay Manitoba	49	B3	52 40N	100 30W
Pelican Lake Manitoba	49	B3	52 30N	100 30W
Pelican Mountains Alberta	46	E4	55 35N	114 00W
Pelican Narrows *tn.* Saskatchewan	47	F4	55 12N	102 55W
Pelly Bay Nunavut	65	N4	68 53N	89 51W
Pelly Crossing Yukon Territory	64	C3	62 48N	136 30W
Pelly Mountains Yukon Territory	64	D3	62 10N	134 10W
Pelly Point British Columbia	44	F3	49 06N	123 13W
Pelly River Yukon Territory	64	D3	62 30N	134 50W
Pemberton British Columbia	42	H5	50 19N	122 49W
Pembina Alberta	46	E3	53 08N	115 09W
Pembina River Alberta	46	E3	53 15N	116 05W
Pembina River Manitoba	49	C1	49 10N	99 10W
Pembroke Ontario	53	J5	45 49N	77 08W
Penetanguishene Ontario	52	G4	44 47N	79 56W
Penhold Alberta	46	F3	52 08N	113 52W
Péninsule de la Gaspésie *p.* Québec	57	H3	48 30N	65 30W
Péninsule d'Ungava *p.* Québec	56	C8/C9	60 50N	76 00W
Penticton British Columbia	43	L1	49 30N	119 38W
Percé Québec	57	H3	48 32N	64 14W
Percé, Cape Nova Scotia	61	N12	46 10N	59 40W
Perdue Saskatchewan	47	D3	52 05N	107 33W
Perrault Falls *tn.* Ontario	50	E6	50 20N	93 08W
Perry Island *tn.* Nunavut	65	K4	67 48N	102 33W
Perth Ontario	53	K4	44 54N	76 15W
Perth *admin.* Ontario	54	A2	43 22N	81 10W
Perth Andover New Brunswick	61	B3	46 45N	67 42W
Petawawa Ontario	53	J5	45 54N	77 17W
Peterborough Ontario	52	H4	44 19N	78 20W
Peterborough *admin.* Ontario	52	H4	44 40N	78 30W
Peter Pond Lake Saskatchewan	47	C5	56 00N	108 50W
Petitcodiac New Brunswick	61	L12	45 57N	65 11W
Petite Rivière *tn.* Nova Scotia	61	M11	44 15N	64 25W
Petite Rivière de la Baleine *r.* Québec	56	C6	55 55N	75 58W
Petit Étang Nova Scotia	61	M12	46 39N	61 00W
Petit Jardin Nova Scotia	61	F4	48 28N	59 14W
Petit Lac de Loups Marins *l.* Québec	56	D7	56 30N	73 30W
Petit Lac Manicouagan *l.* Québec	57	G4	52 10N	67 40W
Petitot River British Columbia	43	K6	59 55N	122 15W
Petitsikapau Lake Newfoundland and Labrador	60	B7	54 37N	66 25W
Petre, Point Ontario	53	J3	43 50N	77 09W
Petrolia Ontario	52	D2	42 52N	82 09W
Phelps Lake Saskatchewan	47	F6	59 20N	102 55W
Philpots Island Nunavut	65	Q5	74 57N	79 58W
Pickerel Lake Ontario	51	F5	48 37N	91 19W
Pickering Ontario	54	C2	43 48N	79 11W
Pickering Village Ontario	54	C2	43 51N	79 02W
Pickle Lake *tn.* Ontario	50	F6	51 28N	90 12W
Pic River Ontario	51	H5	48 50N	86 20W
Picton Ontario	53	J4	44 00N	77 07W
Pictou Nova Scotia	61	M12	45 41N	62 42W
Pictou *admin.* Nova Scotia	61	M12	45 30N	62 40W
Pictou Island Nova Scotia	61	M12	45 41N	62 42W
Picture Butte *tn.* Alberta	46	F1	49 53N	112 47W
Pie Island Ontario	51	G5	48 15N	89 06W
Pierceland Saskatchewan	47	C4	54 20N	109 40W
Pigeon Lake Alberta	46	E3	53 01N	114 02W
Pigeon River Manitoba	49	D3	52 10N	96 50W
Pigeon River Ontario	54	D3	44 13N	78 42W
Pikangikum *I.R.* Ontario	50	E6	51 48N	93 59W
Pikangikum Lake Ontario	50	E6	51 48N	94 00W
Pikwitonei Manitoba	49	D4	55 35N	97 11W
Pilot Butte *tn.* Saskatchewan	47	E2	50 29N	104 29W
Pilot Mound *tn.* Manitoba	49	C1	49 13N	98 52W
Pinawa Manitoba	49	E2	50 13N	95 56W
Pincher Creek *tn.* Alberta	46	F1	49 29N	113 57W
Pinchi Lake British Columbia	43	H4	54 36N	124 25W
Pinecone Burke Provincial Park British Columbia	42	H4	49 30N	122 40W
Pine Falls *tn.* Manitoba	49	D2	50 33N	96 14W
Pinehouse Lake Saskatchewan	47	D4	55 35N	106 50W
Pinehouse Lake *tn.* Saskatchewan	47	D4	55 31N	106 36W
Pineimuta River Ontario	50	F7	52 10N	90 40W
Pine Le Moray Provincial Park British Columbia	43	J4	55 20N	122 30W
Pine Pass British Columbia	43	J4	55 30N	122 25W
Pine River British Columbia	43	K4	55 50N	121 50W
Pine River Ontario	54	B3	44 18N	80 06W
Pinery Provincial Park Ontario	52	E3	43 16N	81 50W
Pinsent Arm Newfoundland and Labrador	60	H6	52 41N	55 53W
Pinto Butte *mt.* Saskatchewan	47	B1	49 21N	107 25W
Pinware Newfoundland and Labrador	60	G5	51 37N	56 42W
Pipestone River Ontario	50	F7	52 20N	90 10W
Pipestone River Provincial Park Ontario	50	G7	52 55N	90 00W
Pistolet Bay Newfoundland and Labrador	60	H5	51 35N	55 45W
Pitman River British Columbia	43	G6	58 00N	128 15W
Pitt Island British Columbia	42	F3	53 38N	129 59W
Pitt Lake British Columbia	42	H4	49 25N	122 33W
Pitt Meadows *tn.* British Columbia	42	H4	49 13N	122 42W
Pitt River British Columbia	42	H4	49 42N	122 40W
Placentia Newfoundland and Labrador	61	J3	47 14N	53 58W
Placentia Bay Newfoundland and Labrador	61	H3	47 00N	54 30W
Plamondon Alberta	46	F4	54 51N	112 20W
Plantagenet Ontario	53	L5	45 32N	75 00W
Plaster Rock *tn.* New Brunswick	61	B3	46 55N	67 24W
Playgreen Lake Manitoba	49	C3	53 50N	98 10W
Pleasant Bay *tn.* Nova Scotia	61	M12	46 50N	60 48W
Pledger Lake Ontario	51	K6	50 53N	83 42W
Plum Coulee Manitoba	49	D1	49 12N	97 45W
Plum Point *tn.* Newfoundland and Labrador	60	G5	51 04N	56 53W
Pohénégamook Québec	53	S7	47 28N	69 17W
Pointe au Baril Station *tn.* Ontario	52	F5	45 36N	80 22W
Pointe aux Pins Ontario	52	E2	42 29N	84 28W
Pointe-aux-Trembles Québec	58	N5	45 38N	73 30W
Pointe de l'Est *c.* Québec	57	K3	49 00N	64 00W
Pointe Louis-XIV *c.* Québec	65	P1	54 38N	79 45W
Point Farms Provincial Park Ontario	54	A2	43 48N	81 42W
Point Lake Northwest Territories	64	H4	65 15N	113 04W
Point Pelee National Park Ontario	52	D1	41 57N	82 31W
Points North Landing Saskatchewan	47	E6	58 20N	104 10W
Polar Bear Provincial Park Ontario	50	J8	54 50N	84 30W
Pomquet Nova Scotia	61	M12	45 34N	61 50W
Pond Inlet Nunavut	65	Q5	72 41N	78 00W
Ponhook Lake Nova Scotia	61	M11	44 50N	64 10W
Ponoka Alberta	46	F3	52 42N	113 33W
Ponteix Saskatchewan	47	D1	49 45N	107 20W
Pontiac *admin.* Québec	52	K6	46 28N	77 40W
Pont Rouge Québec	53	Q5	46 45N	71 43W
Pont-Viau Québec	58	N5	45 33N	73 41W
Poplar Hill *tn.* Ontario	50	D7	52 05N	94 18W
Poplar/Nanowin Rivers Park Reserve Manitoba	49	D3	53 00N	96 50W
Poplar River Manitoba	49	D3	52 50N	97 00W
Porcher Island British Columbia	42	E3	54 00N	130 30W
Porcupine, Cape Newfoundland and Labrador	60	G6	53 56N	57 08W
Porcupine Hills Manitoba/Saskatchewan	47	G3	52 30N	101 40W
Porcupine Plain *tn.* Saskatchewan	47	F3	52 36N	103 15W
Porcupine Provincial Forest Manitoba	49	B3	52 30N	101 20W
Portabello Nova Scotia	59	Q6	44 44N	63 32W
Portage Prince Edward Island	61	M12	46 42N	64 08W
Portage la Prairie Manitoba	49	C1	49 58N	98 20W
Port Alberni British Columbia	42	H4	49 11N	124 49W
Port Alice British Columbia	43	G2	50 23N	127 24W
Port au Choix Newfoundland and Labrador	61	G5	50 43N	57 22W
Port au Port Peninsula Newfoundland and Labrador	61	F4	48 35N	59 00W
Port Bickerton *tn.* Nova Scotia	61	M12	45 10N	61 40W
Port Blandford *tn.* Newfoundland and Labrador	61	H4	48 21N	54 10W
Port Bruce Ontario	54	A1	42 40N	81 00W
Port Bruce Provincial Park Ontario	54	A1	42 40N	81 00W
Port Burwell Ontario	54	B1	42 39N	80 47W
Port Burwell Provincial Park Ontario	54	B1	42 40N	80 45W
Port Carling Ontario	52	G5	45 07N	79 35W
Port Cartier Québec	57	G4	50 02N	66 58W
Port Clements British Columbia	42	D3	53 41N	132 11W
Port Colborne Ontario	54	C1	42 53N	79 16W
Port Coquitlam British Columbia	42	H4	49 16N	122 45W
Port Credit Ontario	54	C2	43 33N	79 36W
Port Dover Ontario	54	B1	42 47N	80 12W
Port Edward British Columbia	42	E4	54 11N	130 16W
Port Elgin New Brunswick	61	M12	46 03N	64 08W
Port Elgin Ontario	54	A3	44 25N	81 23W
Porter Lake Saskatchewan	47	D5	56 20N	107 10W
Port Essington British Columbia	42	F4	54 08N	129 58W
Port Hammond British Columbia	44	H3	49 12N	122 40W
Port Hardy British Columbia	43	G2	50 37N	127 15W
Port Hawkesbury Nova Scotia	61	M12	45 36N	61 22W
Port Hood Nova Scotia	61	M12	46 00N	61 32W
Port Hope Ontario	51	M2	43 58N	78 18W
Port Hope Simpson Newfoundland and Labrador	60	G6	52 33N	56 18W
Port Kells British Columbia	44	H3	49 09N	122 43W
Portland Inlet British Columbia	42	E4	54 40N	130 30W
Port Lorne Nova Scotia	61	L11	44 50N	65 20W
Port McNeill British Columbia	43	G2	50 30N	127 01W
Port Maitland Nova Scotia	61	L11	43 59N	66 04W
Port Maitland Ontario	54	C1	42 51N	79 33W
Port Mellon British Columbia	42	H4	49 31N	123 30W
Port Menier Québec	57	H3	49 50N	64 20W
Port Moody British Columbia	42	H4	49 13N	122 57W
Port Mouton Nova Scotia	61	M11	43 58N	64 50W
Port Nelson Manitoba	49	F5	57 10N	92 35W
Portneuf *admin.* Québec	53	P7	46 50N	72 20W
Port Perry Ontario	54	D3	44 06N	78 58W
Port Renfrew British Columbia	42	H4	48 00N	124 00W
Port Rowan Ontario	54	B1	42 38N	80 27W
Port Royal Nova Scotia	61	L11	44 45N	65 40W
Port Saunders Newfoundland and Labrador	61	G5	50 39N	57 18W
Port Stanley Ontario	54	A1	42 40N	81 14W
Postville Newfoundland and Labrador	60	F7	54 54N	59 47W
Pouce Coupé British Columbia	43	K4	55 40N	120 08W
Pouch Cove *tn.* Newfoundland and Labrador	61	J3	47 46N	52 46W
Powassan Ontario	52	G6	46 05N	79 22W
Powell Lake British Columbia	42	H5	50 08N	124 26W
Powell River *tn.* British Columbia	42	H4	49 54N	124 34W
Powerview Manitoba	49	D2	50 30N	96 10W
Preeceville Saskatchewan	47	F2	51 58N	102 40W
Prescott Ontario	53	L4	44 43N	75 33W
Prescott and Russell *admin.* Ontario	53	M5	45 30N	74 45W
Preston Nova Scotia	59	R6	44 41N	63 26W
Preston Ontario	54	B2	43 23N	80 21W
Price Island British Columbia	43	F3	52 25N	128 40W
Prim, Point Prince Edward Island	61	M12	46 10N	63 00W
Primrose Lake Saskatchewan	47	C4	54 50N	109 30W
Primrose Lake Air Weapons Range Saskatchewan	47	C4	55 00N	109 00W
Prince *admin.* Prince Edward Island	61	M12	46 30N	64 00W
Prince Albert Saskatchewan	47	E3	53 13N	105 45W
Prince Albert National Park Saskatchewan	47	D3/D4	54 00N	106 00W
Prince Albert Peninsula Northwest Territories	64	H5	72 30N	117 00W
Prince Albert Sound Northwest Territories	64	G5	70 15N	117 30W
Prince Alfred, Cape Northwest Territories	64	F5	74 20N	124 46W
Prince Charles Island Nunavut	65	Q4	67 40N	77 00W
Prince Edward Island *province*	61	M12		
Prince Edward Island National Park Prince Edward Island	61	M12	46 10N	63 10W
Prince George British Columbia	43	J3	53 55N	122 49W
Prince Gustaf Adolf Sea Nunavut	65	J6	78 30N	107 00W
Prince of Wales Icefield Nunavut	65	Q6	78 00N	80 00W
Prince of Wales Island Nunavut	65	L5	73 00N	98 00W
Prince of Wales Strait Northwest Territories	64	G5	71 00N	119 50W
Prince Patrick Island Northwest Territories	64	G6	77 00N	120 00W
Prince Regent Inlet Nunavut	65	M5	72 40N	91 00W
Prince Rupert British Columbia	42	E4	54 09N	130 20W
Princess Margaret Range *mts.* Nunavut	65	M6	81 00N	92 30W
Princess Royal Island British Columbia	43	F3	53 04N	129 00W
Princeton British Columbia	43	K1	49 25N	120 35W
Princeville Québec	53	Q6	46 10N	71 52W
Prophet River British Columbia	43	J6	58 20N	123 00W
Prophet River *tn.* British Columbia	43	J6	58 20N	122 50W
Provost Alberta	46	G3	52 21N	110 16W
Pubnico Nova Scotia	61	L11	43 42N	65 48W
Pugwash Nova Scotia	61	M12	45 52N	63 40W
Pukaskwa National Park Ontario	51	J5	48 20N	85 40W
Pukatawagan Manitoba	49	B4	55 46N	101 14W
Pukeashun Mountain British Columbia	43	L2	51 12N	119 14W
Purcell Mountains British Columbia	43	M2	50 58N	116 59W
Purcell's Cove *tn.* Nova Scotia	59	Q6	44 35N	63 33W
Purcell Wilderness Conservancy British Columbia	43	M2	50 00N	116 00W
Purtuniq Québec	56	D9	61 52N	74 00W
Puvirnituq Québec	56	B9	59 45N	77 20W

Q

Qamanittuaq *(Baker Lake) tn.* Nunavut	65	L3	64 20N	96 10W
Qaummaarviit Territorial Park Nunavut	65	S3	63 45N	69 00W
Qausuittuq *(Resolute)* Nunavut	65	M5	74 40N	95 00W
Qikiqtarjuaq *(Broughton Island)* Nunavut	65	T4	67 40N	63 50W
Quadra Island British Columbia	42	G5	50 11N	125 20W
Qualicum Beach *tn.* British Columbia	42	H4	49 21N	124 27W
Qu'Appelle Saskatchewan	47	F2	50 33N	103 54W
Qu'Appelle Dam Saskatchewan	47	D2	50 55N	106 20W
Qu'Appelle River Saskatchewan	47	F2	50 30N	102 20W
Quaqtaq Québec	56	F9	61 00N	69 40W
Quathiaski Cove *tn.* British Columbia	42	G5	50 03N	125 11W
Quatsino Sound British Columbia	43	G2	50 25N	128 55W
Québec Québec	53	Q6	46 49N	71 13W
Québec *admin.* Québec	53	P7/Q7	47 50N	72 30W
Québec *province*	56/57			
Queen Bess, Mount British Columbia	43	H2	51 13N	124 35W
Queen Charlotte British Columbia	42	D3	53 18N	132 04W
Queen Charlotte Islands British Columbia	42	D3/E3	53 30N	131 50W
Queen Charlotte Sound British Columbia	43	F2	51 48N	129 25W
Queen Charlotte Strait British Columbia	43	G2	51 00N	127 55W
Queen Elizabeth Foreland Nunavut	65	T3	62 23N	64 28W
Queen Elizabeth Islands Northwest Territories	64	G6	77 30N	120 00W
Queen Maud Gulf Nunavut	65	K4	68 00N	101 00W
Queen Maud Gulf Migratory Bird Sanctuary Nunavut	65	K4	67 30N	103 20W
Queens *admin.* New Brunswick	61	C3	45 50N	65 50W
Queens *admin.* Nova Scotia	61	L11	44 10N	65 10W
Queens *admin.* Prince Edward Island	61	M12	46 20N	63 10W
Queenston Ontario	54	C2	43 09N	79 03W
Queenswood Heights Ontario	59	L2	45 28N	75 29W
Quesnel British Columbia	43	J3	53 03N	122 31W
Quesnel Lake British Columbia	43	K3	52 30N	121 20W
Quesnel River British Columbia	43	J3	52 58N	122 29W
Quetico Provincial Park Ontario	51	F5	48 30N	91 30W
Quill Lake *tn.* Saskatchewan	47	E3	52 03N	104 12W
Quill Lakes Saskatchewan	47	E2	52 03N	104 12W
Quince, Bay of Ontario	53	J4	44 07N	77 32W
Quirke Lake Ontario	51	K4	46 28N	82 33W
Quispamsis New Brunswick	61	L12	45 25N	65 55W
Quoich River Nunavut	65	M3	64 50N	94 40W
Quttinirpaaq National Park Nunavut	65	R7	82 00N	72 30W

R

Raanes Peninsula Nunavut	65	N6	78 30N	85 45W
Rabbit Lake Mine Saskatchewan	47	F2	58 10N	103 42W
Rabbit River British Columbia	43	G6	59 20N	127 20W
Race, Cape Nova Scotia	61	J3	46 39N	53 04W
Rádeyįlįkǫ́é *(Fort Good Hope)* Northwest Territories	64	E4	66 16N	128 37W
Radisson Québec	57	B5	53 43N	77 46W
Radisson Saskatchewan	47	D3	52 27N	107 24W
Radium Hot Springs British Columbia	43	L2	50 39N	116 09W
Radville Saskatchewan	47	E1	49 28N	104 19W
Rae Northwest Territories	64	G3	62 50N	116 03W
Rae River Nunavut	64	G4	68 10N	116 50W
Rae Strait Nunavut	65	L4	68 50N	95 00W
Ragged Lake Nova Scotia	59	Q6	44 37N	63 39W
Rainbow Lake Alberta	46	C6	58 17N	119 16W
Rainbow Lake *tn.* Alberta	46	C6	58 30N	119 23W
Rainy Lake Ontario	50	E5	48 00N	93 00W
Rainy River Ontario	50	D5	48 40N	94 10W
Rainy River *tn.* Ontario	50	D5	48 44N	94 33W
Ralston Alberta	46	G2	50 15N	111 10W
Ralz, Mount British Columbia	42	D5	57 24N	132 19W
Ramah Newfoundland and Labrador	60	D9	58 50N	63 12W
Ramea Newfoundland and Labrador	61	G3	47 31N	57 23W
Ramea Islands Newfoundland and Labrador	61	G3	47 31N	57 22W
Ramsey Lake Ontario	51	K4	47 13N	82 15W
Rankin Inlet Nunavut	65	M3	62 45N	92 05W
Rapide-Blanc-Station Québec	53	N7	47 00N	73 00W
Rapide-des-Cèdres Québec	57	B3	49 00N	77 09W
Rapides de Lachine Québec	58	N4	45 26N	73 39W
Rat Lake Manitoba	49	C5	56 10N	99 40W
Rat River Manitoba	49	C5	56 10N	99 20W
Ray, Cape Newfoundland and Labrador	61	F3	47 37N	59 19W
Raymond Alberta	46	F1	49 27N	112 39W
Raymore Saskatchewan	47	E2	51 24N	104 32W
Razorback *mt.* British Columbia	43	H2	51 28N	124 35W
Read Island British Columbia	42	G5	50 11N	125 05W
Red Bay *tn.* Newfoundland and Labrador	60	G5	51 44N	56 25W
Red Bay *tn.* Ontario	54	A3	44 47N	81 19W
Redberry Lake Saskatchewan	47	D3	52 45N	107 20W
Redcliff Alberta	46	G2	50 05N	110 47W
Red Deer Alberta	46	F3	52 15N	113 48W
Red Deer Lake Manitoba	49	B3	52 50N	101 30W
Red Deer River Alberta	46	F2	51 20N	112 35W

Red Deer River Saskatchewan 47 F3 52 50N 103 05W
Red Earth Creek *tn.* Alberta 46 E5 56 33N 115 15W
Redfern-Keily Creek Provincial Park British Columbia 43 J5 57 25N 124 00W
Red Indian Lake Newfoundland and Labrador 61 G4 48 40N 57 10W
Red Lake Ontario 50 E6 51 10N 93 50W
Red Lake *tn.* Ontario 50 E6 51 01N 93 50W
Red Lake Road *tn.* Ontario 50 E5 49 59N 93 22W
Redonda Island British Columbia 42 H5 50 15N 124 50W
Red River British Columbia 43 F6 59 23N 128 14W
Red River Manitoba 49 D1 49 30N 97 20W
Red Rock Ontario 51 G5 48 55N 88 15W
Redstone River Northwest Territories 64 E3 63 47N 128 00W
Red Sucker Lake Manitoba 49 F4 54 10N 94 10W
Red Sucker Lake *tn.* Manitoba 49 F4 54 11N 93 34W
Redvers Saskatchewan 47 G1 49 34N 101 42W
Redwater Alberta 46 F3 53 57N 113 06W
Red Wine River Newfoundland and Labrador 60 E7 54 10N 62 00W
Reed Lake Manitoba 49 B4 54 30N 100 10W
Refuge Cove *tn.* British Columbia 42 H5 50 07N 124 51W
Regina Saskatchewan 47 E2 50 30N 104 38W
Regina Beach *tn.* Saskatchewan 47 E2 50 49N 105 00W
Reindeer Grazing Reserve Northwest Territories 64 D4 69 00N 132 00W
Reindeer Island Manitoba 49 D3 52 30N 97 20W
Reindeer Lake Saskatchewan/Manitoba 47 F5 57 30N 102 30W
Reindeer River Saskatchewan 47 F5 56 10N 103 10W
Reliance Northwest Territories 64 J3 62 42N 109 08W
Renews Newfoundland and Labrador 61 J3 46 56N 52 56W
Renfrew Ontario 53 K5 45 28N 76 44W
Renfrew *admin.* Ontario 53 J5/K5 45 28N 76 41W
Rennie Lake Northwest Territories 64 J3 61 32N 105 35W
Repentigny Québec 53 N5 45 44N 73 27W
Réserve de la Rivière Matamec Québec 57 H4 50 30N 65 30W
Réserve du Parc National de l'Archipelago de Mingan Québec 57 J4 50 10N 62 30W
Réserve Faunique Ashuapmushuan Québec 57 D3 49 00N 73 30W
Réserve Faunique Assinica Québec 57 C4 50 48N 75 40W
Réserve Faunique Duchénier Québec 57 F3 48 08N 68 40W
Réserve Faunique de Dunière Québec 57 G3 48 30N 66 40W
Réserve Faunique de Matane Québec 57 G3 48 45N 67 00W
Réserve Faunique de Papineau-Labelle Québec 53 L6 46 20N 75 21W
Réserve Faunique de Port-Cartier–Sept-Îles Québec 57 G4 50 30N 67 30W
Réserve Faunique de Portneuf Québec 53 P7 47 10N 72 20W
Réserve Faunique de Port-Daniel Québec 57 H3 48 13N 65 00W
Réserve Faunique de Rimouski Québec 57 F3 48 00N 68 20W
Réserve Faunique des Chic-Chocs Québec 57 H3 49 10N 65 10W
Réserve Faunique des Laurentides Québec 53 Q7 47 50N 71 47W
Réserve Faunique des Lacs-Albanel-Mistassini-et-Waconichi Québec 57 C4 50 10N 74 20W
Réserve Faunique du Saint-Maurice Québec 53 N7 47 08N 73 18W
Réserve Faunique la Vérendrye Québec 53 J7/K7 47 08N 73 18W
Réserve Faunique Mastigouche Québec 53 N6 46 35N 73 47W
Réserve Faunique Rouge-Matawin Québec 53 M6 46 52N 74 35W
Réservoir Baskatong *res.* Québec 53 L6 47 00N 76 00W
Réservoir Blanc *res.* Québec 53 N7 47 49N 73 06W
Réservoir Cabonga *res.* Québec 53 K7 47 31N 76 45W
Réservoir Caniapiscau *res.* Québec 56 F6 54 10N 69 10W
Réservoir de La Grande 2 *res.* Québec 57 B5 53 38N 78 40W
Réservoir de La Grande 3 *res.* Québec 56 C5 54 10N 72 30W
Réservoir de La Grande 4 *res.* Québec 56 D5 53 59N 72 50W
Réservoir Dozois *res.* Québec 53 J7 47 30N 77 26W
Réservoir du Poisson Blanc *res.* Québec 53 L6 46 05N 75 50W
Réservoir Eastmain 1 *res.* Québec 57 C5 52 10N 75 45W
Réservoir Evans *res.* Québec 57 B4 50 45N 76 50W
Réservoir Gouin *res.* Québec 57 C3 48 30N 74 00W
Réservoir Kiamika *res.* Québec 53 L6 46 40N 75 05W
Réservoir Laforge 1 *res.* Québec 56 E6 54 20N 71 50W
Réservoir Laforge 2 *res.* Québec 56 E6 54 30N 71 20W
Réservoir Manic 2 *res.* Québec 57 F3 49 30N 68 25W
Réservoir Manic 3 *res.* Québec 57 F4 50 00N 68 40W
Réservoir Manicouagan *res.* Québec 57 F4 51 00N 58 00W
Réservoir Opinaca *res.* Québec 57 B5 52 30N 75 30W
Réservoir Outardes 4 *res.* Québec 57 F4 50 20N 69 20W
Réservoir Pipmuacan *res.* Québec 57 E3 49 30N 70 10W
Réservoir Soscumica-Matagami *res.* Québec 57 B4 50 10N 77 32W
Réservoir Taureau *res.* Québec 53 N6 46 47N 73 47W
Resolution Island Nunavut 65 T3 61 18N 64 53W
Restigouche *admin.* New Brunswick 61 B3 47 40N 67 10W
Restigouche River New Brunswick 61 B3 47 35N 67 30W
Reston Manitoba 49 B1 49 33N 101 05W
Revelstoke British Columbia 43 L2 51 02N 118 12W
Revelstoke, Lake British Columbia 43 L2 51 32N 118 40W
Rexton New Brunswick 61 C3 46 41N 64 56W
Ribstone Creek Alberta 46 G3 52 10N 111 55W
Rice Lake Ontario 52 H4 44 12N 78 10W
Richard Collinson Inlet Northwest Territories 64 H5 72 45N 113 55W
Richards Island Northwest Territories 64 C4 69 20N 134 30W
Richardson Mountains Yukon Territory/Northwest Territories 64 C4 67 50N 137 00W
Richardson River Alberta 46 G6 58 15N 110 55W
Rich, Cape Ontario 54 B3 44 43N 80 39W
Richibucto New Brunswick 61 C3 46 42N 64 54W
Richmond British Columbia 42 H4 49 09N 123 09W
Richmond Québec 53 P5 45 40N 72 10W
Richmond *admin.* Nova Scotia 61 M12 45 40N 60 40W
Richmond *admin.* Québec 53 P5 45 30N 72 10W
Richmond Hill *tn.* Ontario 54 C2 43 53N 79 26W
Rideau River Ontario 51 P3 44 50N 76 00W
Rideau River and Canal Ontario 59 K2 45 16N 75 43W
Ridgetown Ontario 52 E2 42 26N 81 54W
Riding Mountain Manitoba 49 B2 50 40N 100 40W
Riding Mountain National Park Manitoba 49 B2 50 50N 100 30W
Rigolet Newfoundland and Labrador 60 F7 54 11N 58 26W
Rimbey Alberta 46 E3 52 38N 114 41W
Rimouski Québec 57 F3 48 27N 68 32W
Riondel British Columbia 43 M1 49 46N 116 51W
Riou Lake Saskatchewan 47 D6 59 00N 106 30W
Ripley Ontario 54 A3 44 04N 81 34W
River Herbert *tn.* Nova Scotia 61 M12 45 42N 64 25W
River John *tn.* Nova Scotia 61 M12 45 44N 63 03W
Rivers *tn.* Manitoba 49 B2 50 02N 100 14W
Riverside-Albert New Brunswick 61 M12 45 40N 64 40W
Rivers Inlet British Columbia 43 G2 51 30N 127 30W
Riverton Manitoba 49 D2 51 00N 97 00W
Riverview New Brunswick 61 M12 46 06N 64 51W
Rivière Aguanus *r.* Québec 57 J4 51 15N 62 05W
Rivière à la Baleine *r.* Québec 56 G7 57 00N 67 40W
Rivière à l'Argent *r.* Québec 57 F4 50 30N 69 40W
Rivière Arnaud *r.* Québec 56 D8 59 37N 72 55W
Rivière Ashuapmushuan *r.* Québec 57 D3 49 22N 73 25W
Rivière aux Feuilles *r.* Québec 56 D8 57 45N 73 00W
Rivière aux Mélèzes *r.* Québec 56 D7 56 50N 72 15W
Rivière aux Outardes *r.* Québec 57 F4 51 38N 69 55W
Rivière-aux-Rats *tn.* Québec 53 P7 47 11N 72 52W
Rivière Bécancour *r.* Québec 53 P6/Q6 46 15N 72 20W
Rivière Bell *r.* Québec 57 B3 49 30N 77 30W
Rivière Betsiamites *r.* Québec 57 F3 49 27N 69 30W
Rivière Blanche *r.* Québec 59 K3 45 32N 75 38W
Rivière Broadback *r.* Québec 57 A4 51 15N 78 42W
Rivière Caniapiscau *r.* Québec 56 F7 56 38N 69 15W
Rivière Capitachouane *r.* Québec 53 K7 47 42N 76 49W
Rivière Casapédia *r.* Québec 57 G3 48 45N 66 20W
Rivière Chaudière *r.* Québec 53 Q6 46 30N 71 10W
Rivière Chicoutimi *r.* Québec 53 Q8 48 11N 71 29W
Rivière Chukotat *r.* Québec 56 B9 61 02N 77 15W
Rivière Coats *r.* Québec 56 B6 55 30N 76 50W
Rivière Coulonge *r.* Québec 53 J6 46 44N 77 10W
Rivière d'Argent *r.* Québec 53 L7 46 59N 75 00W
Rivière Delay *r.* Québec 56 E7 56 50N 71 10W
Rivière de Pas *r.* Québec 56 H6 55 12N 65 35W
Rivière de Rupert *r.* Québec 57 A4 51 22N 78 10W
Rivière des Mille Îles *r.* Québec 58 M5 45 37N 73 47W
Rivière des Outaouais *r.* Ontario/Québec 52 H6 45 35N 76 30W
Rivière des Prairies *r.* Québec 58 N5 45 36N 73 37W
Rivière du Chêne *r.* Québec 58 M5 45 34N 73 59W
Rivière du Gué *r.* Québec 56 E7 56 48N 72 00W
Rivière du Lièvre *r.* Québec 53 L5 45 50N 75 39W
Rivière-du-Loup *admin.* Québec 53 S7 47 50N 69 20W
Rivière-du-Loup *tn.* Québec 53 S7 47 49N 69 32W
Rivière Dumoine *r.* Québec 52 J6 46 20N 77 52W
Rivière du Petit Mécatina *r.* Québec 57 K4 51 50N 60 10W
Rivière du Sable *r.* Québec 56 F6 55 28N 68 20W
Rivière du Vieux Comptoir *r.* Québec 57 A5 52 33N 78 40W
Rivière Eastmain *r.* Québec 57 D5 52 20N 73 00W
Rivière False *r.* Québec 56 F7 57 40N 68 30W
Rivière Ford *r.* Québec 56 H8 58 20N 65 30W
Rivière Gatineau *r.* Québec 53 L5 45 58N 75 52W
Rivière George *r.* Québec 56 H7 57 50N 65 30W
Rivière Harricana *r.* Québec 57 A4 50 40N 79 20W
Rivière Innuksuac *r.* Québec 56 B8 58 40N 77 30W
Rivière Kanaaupscow *r.* Québec 56 C6 54 40N 75 00W
Rivière Kitchigama *r.* Québec 57 A4 50 50N 78 10W
Rivière Kogaluc *r.* Québec 56 B8 59 33N 76 18W
Rivière Koksoak *r.* Québec 56 F7 57 50N 69 10W
Rivière Koroc *r.* Québec 56 H8 58 40N 65 20W
Rivière Kovik *r.* Québec 56 B9 61 50N 77 20W
Rivière Magpie *r.* Québec 57 H4 50 42N 64 25W
Rivière Malbaie *r.* Québec 53 R7 48 01N 70 40W
Rivière Manicouagan *r.* Québec 57 F4 50 51N 68 55W
Rivière Manitou *r.* Québec 57 H4 51 08N 65 20W
Rivière Manouane *r.* Québec 57 E4 50 05N 70 59W
Rivière Maquatua *r.* Québec 57 A5 53 05N 78 40W
Rivière Mariet *r.* Québec 56 B8 59 05N 77 30W
Rivière Matapédia *r.* Québec 57 G3 48 30N 67 30W
Rivière Matawin *r.* Québec 53 N6 46 55N 73 39W
Rivière-Matawin *tn.* Québec 53 P6 46 54N 72 55W
Rivière Mégiscane *r.* Québec 57 B3 48 17N 76 50W
Rivière Métabetchouane *r.* Québec 53 P7 47 59N 72 05W
Rivière Mistanipiscou *r.* Québec 57 J4 51 50N 62 25W
Rivière Mistassibi *r.* Québec 57 D4 50 20N 72 15W
Rivière Mistassibi Nord-Est *r.* Québec 57 E4 50 01N 71 59W
Rivière Mistassini *r.* Québec 57 D4 50 20N 72 40W
Rivière Moisie *r.* Québec 57 G4 50 52N 66 33W
Rivière Montmorency *r.* Québec 53 Q7 47 19N 71 12W
Rivière Mucaliq *r.* Québec 56 G8 58 15N 67 30W
Rivière Nabisipi *r.* Québec 57 J4 50 59N 62 32W
Rivière Nastapoca *r.* Québec 56 C7 56 52N 75 30W
Rivière Natashquan *r.* Québec 57 K4 51 00N 61 35W
Rivière Nicolet *r.* Québec 53 P6 46 14N 72 35W
Rivière Nipissis *r.* Québec 57 H4 50 30N 66 00W
Rivière Noire *r.* Québec 53 J6 46 40N 77 23W
Rivière Nottaway *r.* Québec 57 A4 51 05N 78 20W
Rivière Olomane *r.* Québec 57 K4 50 58N 60 35W
Rivière Opinaca *r.* Québec 57 A5 52 20N 78 00W
Rivière Pentecôte *r.* Québec 57 G4 50 18N 67 35W
Rivière Peribonka *r.* Québec 57 E3 48 58N 71 30W
Rivière Pons *r.* Québec 56 F6 55 50N 69 50W
Rivière Pontax *r.* Québec 57 B4 51 50N 77 05W
Rivière Racine de Bouleau *r.* Québec 57 F5 52 00N 68 40W
Rivière Richelieu *r.* Québec 53 N5 45 03N 73 25W
Rivière Romaine *r.* Québec 57 J4 51 10N 63 40W
Rivière Saguenay *r.* Québec 57 E3 48 20N 70 43W
Rivière Saint-Augustin *r.* Québec 56 L4 51 58N 60 10W
Rivière Sainte-Anne *r.* Québec 53 P6 46 40N 72 11W
Rivière Sainte-Marguerite *r.* Québec 57 G4 51 20N 66 59W
Rivière Saint-François *r.* Québec 53 Q5 45 40N 71 30W
Rivière Saint-Jean *r.* Québec 57 H4 50 50N 64 03W
Rivière Saint-Maurice *r.* Québec 53 N7 47 55N 73 46W
Rivière Saint-Paul *r.* Québec 56 M4 51 55N 57 59W
Rivière Sakami *r.* Québec 57 D5 53 05N 73 15W
Rivière Sérigny *r.* Québec 56 F6 55 30N 69 59W
Rivière Témiscamie *r.* Québec 57 D4 51 15N 72 40W
Rivière Vachon *r.* Québec 56 D9 60 40N 72 25W
Rivière Vermillion *r.* Québec 53 N7 47 19N 73 22W
Rivière-Verte *tn.* New Brunswick 61 A3 47 19N 68 09W
Rivière Wacouna *r.* Québec 57 H4 50 57N 65 40W
Rivière Wheeler *r.* Québec 56 G7 56 25N 67 35W
Rivière Yamaska *r.* Québec 53 P5 45 40N 73 00W
Robert's Arm *tn.* Newfoundland and Labrador 61 H4 49 29N 55 49W
Roberts Creek *tn.* British Columbia 42 H4 49 25N 123 37W
Roberval Québec 57 D3 48 31N 72 16W
Roblin Manitoba 49 B2 51 15N 101 20W
Robson, Mount British Columbia 43 L3 53 08N 118 18W
Rock Bay *tn.* British Columbia 42 G5 50 18N 125 31W
Rockcliffe Park Ontario 53 L5 45 27N 75 39W
Rockglen Saskatchewan 47 E1 49 11N 105 57W
Rockland Ontario 53 L5 45 33N 75 18W
Rock Point Provincial Park Ontario 54 C1 42 50N 79 30W
Rockwood Ontario 54 B2 43 37N 80 10W
Rocky Bay *I.R.* Ontario 51 G5 49 26N 88 08W
Rocky Harbour *tn.* Newfoundland and Labrador 61 G4 49 39N 57 55W
Rocky Island Lake Ontario 51 K4 46 55N 83 04W
Rocky Lake Nova Scotia 59 Q7 44 45N 63 36W
Rocky Mountain House Alberta 46 E3 52 22N 114 55W
Rocky Mountains Forest Reserve Alberta 46 D3/E2 52 30N 116 30W
Rocky Mountain Trench British Columbia 43 H5 57 50N 126 00W
Rocky Saugeen River Ontario 54 B3 44 13N 80 52W
Roddickton Newfoundland and Labrador 60 G5 50 52N 56 08W
Rodney Ontario 52 E2 42 34N 81 41W
Roes Welcome Sound Nunavut 65 N3 63 30N 87 30W
Rogers Pass British Columbia 43 M2 51 23N 117 23W
Rogersville New Brunswick 61 C3 46 44N 65 28W
Romaine River Newfoundland and Labrador 60 D6 52 30N 64 00W
Rondeau Provincial Park Ontario 52 E2 42 17N 81 51W
Root River Ontario 50 F6 50 50N 91 40W
Rorketon Manitoba 49 C2 51 24N 99 35W
Roseau River Manitoba 49 D1 49 10N 96 50W
Rose Blanche Newfoundland and Labrador 61 F3 47 37N 58 41W
Rosedale Alberta 46 F2 51 26N 112 38W
Rosedale Ontario 54 D3 44 34N 78 47W
Rosemère Québec 58 M5 45 38N 73 49W
Rose Point British Columbia 42 E4 54 11N 131 39W
Rosetown Saskatchewan 47 D2 51 34N 107 59W
Rose Valley *tn.* Saskatchewan 47 F3 52 19N 103 49W
Ross Bay Junction *tn.* Newfoundland and Labrador 60 B6 53 03N 66 12W
Rossburn Manitoba 49 B2 50 40N 100 49W
Rosseau Ontario 52 G5 45 16N 79 39W
Rosseau, Lake Ontario 52 G5 45 10N 79 35W
Rossignol, Lake Nova Scotia 61 L11 44 10N 65 20W
Ross Island Manitoba 49 D4 54 20N 97 50W
Rossland British Columbia 43 M1 49 05N 117 48W
Rossport Ontario 51 H5 48 50N 87 31W
Ross River *tn.* Yukon Territory 64 D3 62 02N 132 28W
Rosswood British Columbia 43 F4 54 49N 128 42W
Rosthern Saskatchewan 47 D3 52 40N 106 20W
Rothesay New Brunswick 61 L12 45 23N 66 00W
Rouge River Ontario 54 C2 43 52N 79 15W
Rouleau Saskatchewan 47 E2 50 12N 104 56W
Round Pond Newfoundland and Labrador 61 H4 48 10N 55 50W
Route Jacques-Cartier Québec 57 H4 50 20N 66 00W
Rouyn-Noranda Québec 57 A3 48 15N 79 00W
Rowley Island Nunavut 65 Q4 69 06N 77 52W
Royston British Columbia 42 H4 49 39N 124 57W
Russell Manitoba 49 B2 50 47N 101 17W
Russell, Cape Northwest Territories 64 G6 75 15N 117 35W
Russell Point *c.* Northwest Territories 64 H5 73 30N 115 00W
Rycroft Alberta 46 C4 55 45N 118 43W

S

SaambaTu *(Trout Lake) tn.* Northwest Territories 64 F3 61 00N 121 30W
Saanich British Columbia 42 H4 48 28N 123 22W
Sabine Peninsula Nunavut 64 J6 76 20N 109 30W
Sable, Cape Nova Scotia 61 C1 43 23N 65 37W
Sable Island Nova Scotia 41 Z2 43 57N 60 00W
Sable River *tn.* Nova Scotia 61 L11 43 50N 65 05W
Sachigo *I.R.* Ontario 50 E7 53 50N 92 10W
Sachigo Lake Ontario 50 E7 53 49N 92 08W
Sachigo River Ontario 50 F8 54 50N 90 50W
Sackville New Brunswick 61 M12 45 54N 64 23W
Sacré-Coeur Québec 53 S8 48 26N 68 35WE
Saglek Bay Newfoundland and Labrador 60 D9 58 30N 63 00W
Saglek Fiord Newfoundland and Labrador 60 D9 58 29N 63 15W
Saguenay Québec 53 R8 48 25N 71 04W
Saguenay *admin.* Québec 53 S8 48 20N 70 00W
Saint-Agapit Québec 53 Q6 46 34N 71 26W
St. Albans Newfoundland and Labrador 61 H3 47 52N 55 51W
St. Albert Alberta 46 F3 53 38N 113 38W
Saint-Ambroise Québec 57 E3 48 33N 71 20W
St. Andrews New Brunswick 61 B2 45 05N 67 04W
St. Anthony Newfoundland and Labrador 60 H5 51 22N 55 35W
Saint-Antoine New Brunswick 61 M12 46 22N 64 50W
St. Antoine Québec 53 M5 45 47N 74 01W
St. Barbe Newfoundland and Labrador 60 G5 51 13N 56 45W
St. Bernard's Newfoundland and Labrador 61 H3 47 32N 54 47W
St. Boniface Manitoba 48 B2 49 53N 97 06W
St. Bride's Newfoundland and Labrador 61 H3 46 55N 54 10W
St. Catharines Ontario 54 C2 43 10N 79 15W
St. Clair, Lake Ontario/USA 52 D2 42 28N 82 40W
Saint-Constant Québec 57 D1 45 22N 73 33W
St. Croix River New Brunswick 61 B2 45 30N 67 40W
Saint-Donat Québec 53 M6 46 19N 74 15W
Sainte-Agathe-des-Monts Québec 53 M6 46 03N 74 19W
Ste. Anne Manitoba 49 D1 49 40N 96 40W
Ste. Anne de Beaupré Québec 53 R7 47 02N 70 58W
Sainte-Anne-des-Monts Québec 57 G3 49 07N 66 29W
Sainte-Anne-du-Lac Québec 53 L6 46 54N 75 20W
Sainte-Catherine Québec 58 N4 45 25N 73 35W
Sainte-Claire Québec 53 R6 46 37N 70 51W
Sainte-Croix Québec 53 Q6 46 38N 71 43W
Sainte-Dorothée Québec 58 M5 45 32N 73 49W
Sainte-Eustache Québec 58 M5 45 33N 73 54W
Sainte-Hyacinthe Québec 53 P5 45 38N 72 57W
St. Eleanors Prince Edward Island 61 M12 46 30N 63 50W
Saint Elias Mountains Yukon Territory 64 C3 60 12N 140 57W
Sainte-Marie Québec 53 Q6 46 26N 71 00W
Sainte-Marthe-sur-le-Lac Québec 58 M5 45 31N 73 55W

Sainte-Rose Québec 58 M5 45 36N 73 47W
Ste. Rose du Lac Manitoba 49 C2 51 04N 99 31W
Sainte-Thérèse Québec 53 N5 45 38N 73 50W
Saint-Félicien Québec 57 D3 48 38N 72 29W
St. Francis Harbour *tn.* Nova Scotia 61 M12 45 30N 61 20W
St. Francis, Lake Québec 53 M5 45 05N 74 30W
Saint-François Québec 58 N5 45 38N 73 35W
St. George New Brunswick 61 B2 45 08N 66 50W
St. George's Newfoundland and Labrador 61 F4 48 26N 58 29W
Saint-Georges Québec 53 P6 46 38N 72 35W
Saint-Georges Québec 53 R6 46 08N 70 40W
St. George's Bay Newfoundland and Labrador 61 F4 48 28N 59 16W
St. Georges Bay Nova Scotia 61 M12 45 40N 61 40W
St. Germain Manitoba 48 B2 49 46N 97 07W
St. Ignace Island Ontario 51 H5 48 45N 87 55W
St. Jacobs Ontario 54 B2 43 32N 80 33W
Saint-Jacques New Brunswick 61 A3 47 20N 68 28W
St. James, Cape British Columbia 42 E2 51 58N 131 00W
St. Jean Baptiste Manitoba 49 D1 49 15N 97 20W
Saint-Jean-Port-Joli Québec 53 R7 47 13N 70 16W
Saint-Jean-sur-Richelieu Québec 53 N5 45 18N 73 18W
St.-Jerôme Québec 53 M5 45 47N 74 01W
Saint John New Brunswick 61 L12 45 16N 66 03W
Saint John *admin.* New Brunswick 61 L12 45 20N 65 50W
St. John Bay Newfoundland and Labrador 60 G5 50 55N 57 09W
St. John, Cape Newfoundland and Labrador 61 H4 50 00N 55 32W
St. John, Lake Ontario 54 C3 44 38N 79 19W
St. John's Newfoundland and Labrador 61 J3 47 34N 52 43W
St. Joseph New Brunswick 61 M12 45 59N 64 30W
St. Joseph Island Ontario 52 C6 46 13N 83 57W
St. Joseph, Lake Ontario 50 F6 51 05N 90 35W
Saint-Laurent Québec 58 N5 45 31N 73 42W
St. Lawrence Newfoundland and Labrador 61 H3 46 55N 55 24W
St. Lawrence, Cape Nova Scotia 61 M12 47 10N 60 40W
St. Lawrence, Gulf of Québec 57 J3 48 40N 63 20W
St. Lawrence River Québec 57 C1 45 00N 75 00W
St. Lawrence Seaway Ontario/Québec/USA 53 L4 44 38N 78 34W
Saint Léonard New Brunswick 61 B3 47 10N 67 55W
Saint Leonard Québec 58 N5 45 34N 73 35W
St. Lewis Newfoundland and Labrador 60 H6 52 22N 55 41W
St. Lewis River Newfoundland and Labrador 60 G6 52 20N 56 50W
Saint-Lin-Laurentides Québec 57 D1 45 51N 73 45W
Saint-Louis de-Kent New Brunswick 61 C3 46 50N 65 00W
St. Lunaire Newfoundland and Labrador 60 H5 51 30N 55 29W
St. Malo Manitoba 49 D1 49 20N 96 55W
St. Margarets Bay Nova Scotia 61 M11 44 30N 64 50W
St. Martin, Lake Manitoba 49 C2 51 40N 98 20W
St. Martins New Brunswick 61 L12 45 20N 65 30W
St. Mary, Cape Nova Scotia 61 L11 44 10N 66 10W
St. Mary's Newfoundland and Labrador 61 J3 46 55N 53 34W
St. Marys Ontario 54 A2 43 15N 81 09W
St. Mary's Bay Newfoundland and Labrador 61 J3 46 50N 53 45W
St. Mary's Bay Nova Scotia 61 L11 44 20N 66 10W
St. Mary's River Nova Scotia 61 M12 45 20N 62 30W
St.-Maurice *admin.* Québec 53 M7 47 40N 74 30W
Saint-Michel-des-Saints Québec 53 N6 46 40N 73 55W
Saint-Nicéphore Québec 57 D1 45 51N 72 27W
St. Norbert Manitoba 48 B2 49 46N 97 12W
Saint-Pacôme Québec 53 S7 47 24N 69 58W
St.-Pamphile Québec 53 S6 46 58N 69 48W
Saint-Pascal Québec 53 S7 47 32N 69 48W
St. Paul Alberta 46 G4 53 59N 111 17W
St. Peters Nova Scotia 61 M12 45 40N 60 53W
St. Peters Prince Edward Island 61 M12 46 26N 62 35W
St. Pierre-Jolys Manitoba 49 D1 49 28N 96 58W
Saint-Prosper Québec 53 R6 46 12N 70 29W
Saint-Quentin New Brunswick 61 B3 47 30N 67 20W
Saint-Raymond Québec 53 Q6 46 54N 71 50W
St. Romauld Québec 53 Q6 46 52N 71 49W
Saint-Siméon Québec 53 S7 47 50N 69 55W
St. Stephen New Brunswick 61 B2 45 12N 67 18W
St. Stephens Newfoundland and Labrador 61 J3 46 47N 53 37W
St. Theresa Point *tn.* Manitoba 49 E3 53 45N 94 50W
St. Thomas Ontario 54 A1 42 46N 81 12W
Saint-Tite Québec 53 P6 46 44N 72 34W
Saint-Vincent-de-Paul Québec 58 N5 45 38N 73 39W
St. Walburg Saskatchewan 47 C3 53 38N 109 12W
Sakami Québec 57 B5 53 50N 76 10W
Salaberry-de-Valleyfield Québec 53 M5 45 16N 74 11W
Salisbury New Brunswick 61 L12 46 02N 65 03W
Salisbury Island Nunavut 65 Q3 63 10N 77 20W
Salliq *(Coral Harbour)* *tn.* Nunavut 65 P3 64 10N 83 15W
Salluit Québec 56 C10 62 20N 75 40W
Salmo British Columbia 43 M1 49 11N 117 16W
Salmon Arm *tn.* British Columbia 43 L2 50 41N 119 18W
Salmon Inlet British Columbia 42 H4 49 39N 123 47W
Salmon River New Brunswick 61 C3 46 10N 65 50W
Salmon River *tn.* Nova Scotia 61 L11 44 10N 66 10W
Saltcoats Saskatchewan 47 F2 51 03N 102 12W
Saltery Bay *tn.* British Columbia 42 H4 49 47N 124 10W
Saltspring Island British Columbia 42 H4 48 50N 123 30W
Sambro, Cape Nova Scotia 61 M11 44 30N 63 30W
San Cristoval Mountains British Columbia 42 E3 52 30N 131 30W
Sandilands Provincial Forest Manitoba 49 D1/E1 49 30N 96 00W
Sand Lakes Provincial Park Manitoba 49 C5 58 00N 98 30W
Sandspit British Columbia 42 E3 53 14N 131 50W
Sandy Bay *tn.* Saskatchewan 47 F4 55 30N 102 10W
Sandy Lake Newfoundland and Labrador 61 G4 49 20N 56 50W
Sandy Lake Nova Scotia 59 Q6 44 44N 63 40W
Sandy Lake Ontario 50 E7 53 02N 93 00W
Sandy Lake *I.R.* Ontario 50 E7 53 04N 93 20W
Sanikiluaq *(Sanikilluaq)* Nunavut 65 Q2 56 32N 79 14W
Sanirajak *(Hall Beach)* *tn.* Nunavut 65 P4 68 46N 81 12W
San Juan River British Columbia 42 H4 48 37N 124 20W
Sardis British Columbia 42 H4 49 07N 121 57W
Sarnia Ontario 52 D2 42 58N 82 23W
Sasaginnigak Lake Manitoba 49 E2 51 30N 95 30W
Sasamat Lake British Columbia 44 G4 49 19N 122 52W
Saskatchewan *province* 47
Saskatchewan River Manitoba/Saskatchewan 47 F3 53 50N 103 10W
Saskatoon Saskatchewan 47 D3 52 10N 106 40W
Saturna Island British Columbia 42 H4 48 47N 123 07W
Sauble Beach *tn.* Ontario 54 A3 44 38N 81 17W
Sauble Falls Provincial Park Ontario 54 A3 44 40N 81 15W
Sauble River Ontario 54 A3 44 36N 81 09W
Saugeen River Ontario 54 A3 44 23N 81 18W
Sault Ste. Marie Ontario 51 J4 46 31N 84 20W
Savant Lake Ontario 50 F6 50 30N 90 25W
Savant Lake *tn.* Ontario 50 F6 50 14N 90 43W
Sawbill Newfoundland and Labrador 60 B6 53 37N 66 21W
Sayabec Québec 57 G3 48 35N 67 41W
Sayward British Columbia 43 H2 50 19N 125 58W
Scarborough Ontario 55 D2 43 46N 79 14W
Scarborough Bluffs Ontario 55 D1 43 42N 79 15W
Scaterie Island Nova Scotia 61 N12 46 00N 59 40W
Schefferville Québec 56 G6 54 47N 66 48W
Schreiber Ontario 51 H5 48 48N 87 17W
Schultz Lake Nunavut 65 L3 64 45N 97 30W
Scotsburn Nova Scotia 61 M12 45 40N 62 51W
Scott Islands British Columbia 43 F2 50 48N 128 38W
Scott Lake Saskatchewan 47 D6 59 50N 106 30W
Scudder Ontario 52 D1 41 47N 82 39W
Scugog Island Ontario 54 D3 44 10N 78 52W
Scugog, Lake Ontario 54 D3 44 10N 78 51W
Scugog River Ontario 54 D3 44 16N 78 46W
Seaforth Ontario 54 A2 43 03N 81 24W
Sea Island British Columbia 44 F3 49 11N 123 11W
Seal Cove *tn.* Newfoundland and Labrador 61 G3 47 30N 56 00W
Seal Cove *tn.* Newfoundland and Labrador 61 G4 49 56N 56 23W
Seal Cove *tn.* Nova Scotia 61 L11 44 38N 66 52W
Seal Harbour *tn.* New Brunswick 61 M12 45 10N 61 30W
Seal Lake Newfoundland and Labrador 60 E7 54 20N 61 40W
Seal River Manitoba 49 D6 58 50N 97 00W
Sechelt British Columbia 42 H4 49 28N 123 46W
Sechelt Peninsula British Columbia 42 H4 49 45N 123 58W
Seine River Manitoba 48 C2 49 46N 97 02W
Selkirk Manitoba 49 D2 50 10N 96 52W
Selkirk Ontario 54 C1 42 50N 79 55W
Selkirk Mountains British Columbia 43 M2 51 40N 118 20W
Selkirk Provincial Park Ontario 54 C1 42 50N 80 00W
Selwyn Lake Northwest Territories 64 K3 60 05N 104 25W
Selwyn Mountains Yukon Territory 64 D3 64 30N 134 50W
Semchuck Trail Saskatchewan 47 C5 57 35N 109 20W
Senneterre Québec 53 J8 48 24N 77 16W
Sentinel Peak British Columbia 43 K4 54 56N 121 59W
Serpentine River British Columbia 44 G3 49 06N 122 46W
Seseganaga Lake Ontario 50 F6 50 00N 90 28W
Setting Lake Manitoba 49 C4 55 10N 98 50W
Seven Sisters Bay Newfoundland and Labrador 60 D9 59 25N 63 45W
Seven Sisters Provincial Park British Columbia 43 F4 55 00N 128 10W
70 Mile House British Columbia 43 K2 51 21N 121 25W
Severn Lake Ontario 50 F7 53 54N 90 48W
Severn River Ontario 50 H8 55 30N 88 30W
Severn River Provincial Park Ontario 50 F8 54 15N 90 30W
Sexsmith Alberta 46 C4 55 21N 118 47W
Seymour Creek British Columbia 44 F4 49 18N 123 01W
Seymour Inlet British Columbia 43 G2 51 03N 127 05W
Shabaqua Ontario 51 G5 48 35N 89 54W
Shabo Newfoundland and Labrador 60 B6 53 19N 66 12W
Shabogamo Lake Newfoundland and Labrador 60 B6 53 15N 66 30W
Shag Harbour *tn.* Nova Scotia 61 L11 43 30N 65 40W
Shakespeare Ontario 54 B2 43 22N 80 50W
Shaler Mountains Northwest Territories 64 H5 72 10N 111 00W
Shallow Lake *tn.* Ontario 54 A3 44 38N 81 06W
Shamattawa Manitoba 49 F4 55 51N 92 05W
Shamattawa River Ontario 50 J8 54 05N 85 50W
Shapio Lake Newfoundland and Labrador 60 E7 55 00N 61 18W
Sharon Ontario 54 C3 44 06N 79 26W
Shaunavon Saskatchewan 47 C1 49 40N 108 25W
Shawinigan Québec 53 P6 46 34N 72 45W
Shawinigan Lake *tn.* British Columbia 42 H4 48 38N 123 39W
Shawville Québec 53 K5 45 36N 76 30W
Shebandowan Ontario 51 F5 48 38N 90 04W
Shediac New Brunswick 61 M12 46 13N 64 35W
Sheet Harbour *tn.* Nova Scotia 61 M11 44 56N 62 31W
Shefford *admin.* Québec 53 P5 45 30N 72 45W
Shelburne Nova Scotia 61 M11 43 37N 65 20W
Shelburne Ontario 54 B3 44 05N 80 13W
Shelburne *admin.* Nova Scotia 61 L11 43 50N 65 30W
Sheldon Creek Ontario 54 B3 44 05N 80 06W
Shellbrook Saskatchewan 47 D3 53 14N 106 24W
Shelsey River British Columbia 42 E6 58 33N 132 02W
Shelter Bay *tn.* British Columbia 43 M2 50 38N 117 59W
Shepherd Bay Nunavut 65 M4 65 00N 90 00W
Sherbrooke Nova Scotia 61 M12 45 10N 61 58W
Sherbrooke Québec 53 Q5 45 24N 71 54W
Sherbrooke *admin.* Québec 53 P5 45 20N 72 10W
Sherbrooke Lake Nova Scotia 61 M11 44 40N 64 40W
Sherridon Manitoba 49 B4 55 07N 101 05W
Sherwood Park *tn.* Alberta 46 F3 53 31N 113 19W
Sheshatshui Newfoundland and Labrador 60 E6 53 30N 60 10W
Shibogama Lake Ontario 50 G7 53 35N 88 15W
Shipiskan Lake Newfoundland and Labrador 60 D7 54 39N 62 19W
Shippagan New Brunswick 61 C3 47 45N 64 44W
Shirleys Bay Ontario 59 J2 45 22N 75 54W
Shoal Bay *tn.* Newfoundland and Labrador 61 H4 49 41N 54 12W
Shoal Harbour *tn.* Newfoundland and Labrador 61 J4 48 11N 53 59W
Shoal Lake Ontario/Manitoba 50 D5 49 33N 95 01W
Shoal Lake *tn.* Manitoba 49 B2 50 28N 100 35W
Shoal Lakes Manitoba 49 D2 50 25N 97 35W
Shubenacadie Nova Scotia 61 M12 45 05N 63 25W
Shubenacadie Grand Lake Nova Scotia 59 Q7 44 53N 63 37W
Shubenacadie River Nova Scotia 61 M12 45 20N 63 30W
Shunacadie Nova Scotia 61 M12 46 00N 60 40W
Shuswap Lake British Columbia 43 L2 51 00N 119 00W
Sibbald Point Provincial Park Ontario 54 C3 44 15N 79 20W
Sicamous British Columbia 43 L2 50 50N 119 00W
Sidney British Columbia 42 H4 48 39N 123 25W
Sidney Bay Ontario 54 A3 44 55N 81 04W
Sifton Manitoba 49 B2 51 21N 100 09W
Sifton Pass British Columbia 43 G5 57 51N 126 17W
Sikanni Chief British Columbia 43 J5 57 11N 122 43W
Sikanni Chief River British Columbia 43 J5 57 16N 125 25W
Silver Dollar Ontario 50 F5 49 50N 91 15W
Silverthrone Mountain British Columbia 43 G2 51 30N 126 03W
Silvertip Mountain British Columbia 42 H4 49 09N 121 12W
Simcoe Ontario 54 B1 42 50N 80 19W
Simcoe *admin.* Ontario 54 C3 44 32N 79 54W
Simcoe, Lake Ontario 54 C3 44 23N 79 18W
Simonette River Alberta 46 C4 54 25N 118 20W
Simpson Bay Nunavut 64 H4 69 00N 113 40W
Simpson Peninsula Nunavut 65 N4 68 34N 88 45W
Simpson Strait Nunavut 65 L4 68 27N 97 45W
Sioux Lookout Ontario 50 F6 50 07N 91 54W
Sioux Narrows Ontario 50 D5 49 23N 94 08W
Sipiwesk Manitoba 49 D4 55 27N 97 24W
Sipiwesk Lake Manitoba 49 D4 55 10N 97 50W
Sir Alexander, Mount British Columbia 43 K3 53 52N 120 25W
Sir James McBrien, Mount Yukon Territory 64 E3 62 15N 128 01W
Sirmilik National Park Nunavut 65 P5/Q5 73 00N 80 00W
Sir Wilfred Laurier, Mount British Columbia 43 L3 52 45N 119 40W
Sisipuk Lake Manitoba 49 B4 55 30N 101 40W
Skagit Valley Recreation Area British Columbia 42 H4 49 06N 121 09W
Skeena Mountains British Columbia 42/43 F5 57 30N 129 59W
Skeena River British Columbia 43 F4 54 15N 129 15W
Skidegate British Columbia 42 E3 53 13N 132 02W
Skihist Mountain British Columbia 43 K2 50 12N 122 53W
Skownan Manitoba 49 C2 51 58N 99 35W
Slave Lake *tn.* Alberta 46 E4 55 17N 114 43W
Slave River Alberta/Northwest Territories 64 H3 60 30N 112 50W
Sleeping Giant (Sibley) Provincial Park Ontario 51 G5 48 10N 88 50W
Slocan British Columbia 43 M1 49 46N 117 28W
Slocan Lake British Columbia 43 M1 49 50N 117 20W
Smallwood Reservoir Newfoundland and Labrador 60 C7 54 10N 64 00W
Smeaton Saskatchewan 47 E3 53 30N 104 50W
Smith Alberta 46 E4 55 10N 114 02W
Smith Arm *b.* Northwest Territories 64 F4 66 15N 124 00W
Smith Bay Nunavut 65 Q6 77 12N 78 50W
Smithers British Columbia 43 G4 54 45N 127 10W
Smith Island Nunavut 56 A9 60 44N 78 30W
Smith Point Nova Scotia 61 M12 45 52N 63 25W
Smith River British Columbia 43 G6 59 56N 126 28W
Smiths Falls *tn.* Ontario 53 K4 44 45N 76 01W
Smithville Ontario 54 C2 43 06N 79 32W
Smoky, Cape Nova Scotia 61 M12 46 40N 60 20W
Smoky Lake *tn.* Alberta 46 F4 54 07N 112 28W
Smoky River Alberta 46 C4 55 30N 118 00W
Smooth Rock Falls *tn.* Ontario 51 L5 49 17N 81 38W
Smoothrock Lake Ontario 50 G6 50 30N 89 30W
Smoothstone Lake Saskatchewan 47 D4 54 40N 106 30W
Snake Creek Ontario 54 A3 44 23N 81 16W
Snake River Yukon Territory 64 D4 65 20N 133 30W
Snegamook Lake Newfoundland and Labrador 60 E7 54 33N 61 27W
Snowbird Lake Northwest Territories 65 K3 60 41N 102 56W
Snow Lake *tn.* Manitoba 49 B4 54 56N 100 00W
Snug Harbour *tn.* Newfoundland and Labrador 60 H6 52 53N 55 52W
Soldier Lake Nova Scotia 59 Q7 44 49N 63 33W
Sǫmbak'è *(Yellowknife)* Northwest Territories 64 H3 62 30N 114 29W
Somerset Manitoba 49 C1 49 26N 98 39W
Somerset Island Nunavut 65 M5 73 15N 93 30W
Sonora Island British Columbia 42 G5 50 21N 125 13W
Sooke British Columbia 42 H4 48 20N 123 42W
Sorel Québec 53 N6 46 03N 73 06W
Soulanges *admin.* Québec 53 M5 45 15N 74 20W
Sounding Creek Alberta 46 G2 51 40N 111 05W
Sounding Lake Alberta 46 G3 52 08N 110 29W
Souris Manitoba 49 B1 49 38N 100 17W
Souris Prince Edward Island 61 M12 46 22N 62 16W
Souris River Manitoba/USA 49 B1 49 30N 100 50W
Southampton Ontario 54 A3 44 29N 81 22W
Southampton Island Nunavut 65 P3 64 50N 85 00W
South Aulatsivik Island Newfoundland and Labrador 60 E8 56 46N 61 30W
South Bay *tn.* Ontario 50 E6 51 03N 92 45W
South Brookfield Nova Scotia 61 M11 44 23N 64 58W
Southend Saskatchewan 47 F5 56 20N 103 14W
Southern Indian Lake Manitoba 49 C5 57 00N 98 00W
Southey Saskatchewan 47 E2 50 57N 104 33W
South Gloucester Ontario 59 K2 45 17N 75 34W
South Hazelton British Columbia 43 G4 55 12N 127 42W
South Henik Lake Nunavut 65 L3 61 30N 97 30W
South Indian Lake *tn.* Manitoba 49 C5 56 48N 98 55W
South Knife River Manitoba 49 D6 58 20N 96 10W
South Maitland River Ontario 54 A2 43 39N 81 27W
South Moose Lake Manitoba 49 B3 53 40N 100 10W
South Nahanni River Northwest Territories 64 E3 61 30N 123 22W
South Porcupine Ontario 51 L5 48 28N 81 13W
South River *tn.* Ontario 52 G5 45 50N 79 23W
South Saskatchewan River Saskatchewan 47 C2 50 50N 110 00W
South Saugeen River Ontario 54 B3 44 00N 80 45W
South Seal River Manitoba 49 C5 58 00N 99 10W
South Tweedsmuir Provincial Park British Columbia 43 H3 52 30N 126 00W
South Twin Island Nunavut 50 M7 53 10N 79 50W
Southwest Miramichi River New Brunswick 61 B3 46 30N 66 50W
Spallumcheen British Columbia 43 L2 50 24N 119 14W
Spanish Ontario 52 D6 46 12N 82 12W
Spanish River Ontario 52 E6 46 32N 81 57W
Sparwood British Columbia 43 N1 49 55N 114 53W
Spatsizi Plateau Wilderness Park British Columbia 43 F5/G5 57 30N 128 30W
Speed River Ontario 54 B2 43 29N 80 17W
Spicer Islands Nunavut 65 Q4 63 19N 71 52W
Spirit River *tn.* Alberta 46 C4 55 46N 118 51W
Spiritwood Saskatchewan 47 D3 53 24N 107 33W
Split, Cape Nova Scotia 61 M12 45 20N 64 30W
Split Lake Manitoba 49 E5 56 10N 95 50W
Split Lake *tn.* Manitoba 49 D5 56 16N 96 08W
Spotted Island Newfoundland and Labrador 60 H6 53 31N 55 47W
Sprague Manitoba 49 E1 49 02N 95 36W
Springdale Newfoundland and Labrador 61 G4 49 30N 56 04W
Springfield Nova Scotia 61 M11 44 37N 64 52W
Springfield Ontario 54 B1 42 49N 80 57W
Springhill Nova Scotia 61 M12 45 40N 64 04W
Spring Water Provincial Park Ontario 54 C3 44 30N 79 45W
Sproat Lake British Columbia 42 G4 49 16N 125 05W
Spruce Grove Alberta 46 F3 53 32N 113 55W

Spruce Woods Provincial Forest Manitoba 49 C1 49 40N 99 40W
Spruce Woods Provincial Park Manitoba 49 C1 49 40N 99 10W
Spryfield Nova Scotia 59 L3 44 36N 63 40W
Spry Harbour *tn.* Nova Scotia 61 M11 44 50N 62 45W
Spuzzum British Columbia 43 K1 49 40N 121 25W
Squamish British Columbia 42 H4 49 41N 123 11W
Squamish River British Columbia 42 H5 49 42N 123 11W
Square Islands Newfoundland and Labrador 60 H6 52 45N 55 52W
Stanley New Brunswick 61 B3 46 17N 66 45W
Stanley Mission Saskatchewan 47 E4 55 24N 104 34W
Stanstead *admin.* Québec 53 P5 45 10N 72 10W
Starbuck Manitoba 49 D1 49 47N 97 38W
Star City Saskatchewan 47 E3 52 52N 104 20W
Stave Lake British Columbia 42 H4 49 21N 122 19W
Stayner Ontario 54 B3 44 25N 80 06W
Steele River Provincial Park Ontario 51 H5 49 25N 86 40W
Steen River *tn.* Alberta 46 D6 59 38N 117 10W
Stefansson Island Nunavut 65 K5 73 20N 105 00W
Steinbach Manitoba 49 D1 49 32N 96 40W
Stein Valley Provincial Park British Columbia 43 J2 50 10N 122 10W
Stellarton Nova Scotia 61 M12 45 34N 62 40W
Stephens Lake Manitoba 49 E5 56 30N 95 00W
Stephenville Newfoundland and Labrador 61 F4 48 33N 57 32W
Stephenville Crossing Newfoundland and Labrador 61 F4 48 30N 58 26W
Stettler Alberta 46 F3 52 19N 112 43W
Stevenson Lake Manitoba 49 E3 53 50N 95 50W
Steveston British Columbia 44 F3 49 07N 123 10W
Stewart British Columbia 42 F4 55 07N 129 58W
Stewart Yukon Territory 64 C3 63 15N 139 15W
Stewart Crossing Yukon Territory 64 C3 60 37N 128 37W
Stewart River Yukon Territory 64 C3 63 40N 138 20W
Stewiacke Nova Scotia 61 M12 45 09N 63 22W
Stikine British Columbia 42 E5 56 42N 131 45W
Stikine Range *mts.* British Columbia 42 E6/F6 57 00N 127 20W
Stikine River British Columbia 42 E5 58 00N 131 20W
Stikine River Recreation Area British Columbia 43 F5 58 07N 129 35W
Stirling Alberta 46 F1 49 34N 112 30W
Stirling Ontario 53 J4 44 18N 77 33W
Stittsville Ontario 59 J2 45 16N 75 54W
Stokes Bay Ontario 54 A3 45 00N 81 23W
Stone Mountain Provincial Park British Columbia 43 H6 58 35N 124 40W
Stonewall Manitoba 49 D2 50 08N 97 20W
Stoney Creek *tn.* Ontario 54 C2 43 13N 79 46W
Stony Lake Manitoba 49 C6 58 50N 98 30W
Stony Lake Ontario 52 H4 44 33N 78 06W
Stony Plain *tn.* Alberta 46 E3 53 32N 114 00W
Stony Rapids *tn.* Saskatchewan 47 E6 59 14N 105 48W
Stony Swamp Conservation Area Ontario 59 J2 45 15N 75 49W
Storkerson Peninsula Nunavut 64 J5 72 30N 106 30W
Stormont, Dundas and Glengarry *admin.* Ontario 53 M5 45 10N 75 00W
Stormy Lake Ontario 50 E5 49 23N 92 18W
Stouffville Ontario 54 C2 43 59N 79 15W
Stoughton Saskatchewan 47 F1 49 40N 103 00W
Stout Lake Ontario 50 D7 52 08N 94 35W
Strasbourg Saskatchewan 47 E2 51 05N 104 58W
Stratford Ontario 54 B2 43 07N 81 00W
Strathcona Provincial Park British Columbia 42 G4 49 40N 125 30W
Strathmore Alberta 46 F2 51 03N 113 23W
Strathroy Ontario 54 A1 42 57N 81 40W
Streetsville Ontario 54 C2 43 25N 79 44W
Stuart Island *tn.* British Columbia 42 G5 50 22N 125 09W
Stuart Lake British Columbia 43 H4 54 35N 124 40W
Stuart River British Columbia 43 J4 54 10N 124 05W
Stupart River Manitoba 49 E4 55 30N 94 30W
Sturgeon Bay Manitoba 49 D3 51 50N 98 00W
Sturgeon Falls *tn.* Ontario 52 G6 46 22N 79 57W
Sturgeon Lake Alberta 46 D4 55 06N 117 32W
Sturgeon Lake Ontario 50 F5 50 00N 91 00W
Sturgeon Lake Ontario 54 D3 44 30N 78 43W
Sturgeon Landing Saskatchewan 47 G4 54 18N 101 49W
Sturgeon Point *tn.* Ontario 54 D3 44 28N 78 42W
Sturgeon River Ontario 51 L4 47 00N 80 30W
Sturgeon River Saskatchewan 47 D3 53 30N 106 20W
Sturgeon River Provincial Park Ontario 51 L4 47 00N 80 50W
Sturgis Saskatchewan 47 F2 51 58N 102 32W
Styx River Ontario 54 B3 44 15N 80 58W
Sudbury *admin.* Ontario 52 E6 47 10N 82 00W
Sudbury, Regional Municipality of Ontario 52 E6 46 32N 81 00W
Suggi Lake Saskatchewan 47 F4 54 20N 103 10W
Sullivan Bay *tn.* British Columbia 43 G2 50 55N 126 52W
Sullivan Lake Alberta 46 F3 52 00N 112 00W
Sultan Ontario 51 K4 47 36N 82 45W
Summer Beaver Ontario 50 G7 52 50N 88 30W
Summerford Newfoundland and Labrador 61 H4 49 29N 54 47W
Summerland British Columbia 43 L1 49 35N 119 41W
Summerside Prince Edward Island 61 M12 46 24N 63 46W
Summerville Newfoundland and Labrador 61 J4 48 27N 53 33W
Sunbury *admin.* New Brunswick 61 B2 45 50N 66 40W
Sundre Alberta 46 E2 51 48N 114 38W
Sundridge Ontario 52 G5 45 46N 79 24W
Sunnyside Newfoundland and Labrador 61 J3 47 51N 53 55W
Superb Saskatchewan 47 C2 51 56N 109 25W
Superior, Lake Ontario/USA 51 G4/H4 48 00N 88 00W
Surrey British Columbia 42 H4 49 08N 122 50W
Sussex New Brunswick 61 L12 45 43N 65 32W
Sussex Corner New Brunswick 61 L12 45 40N 65 30W
Sustut Provincial Park British Columbia 43 G5 56 20N 126 50W
Sutton Ontario 54 C3 44 18N 79 22W
Sutton Québec 53 P5 45 05N 72 36W
Sutton Lake Ontario 50 J8 54 15N 84 44W
Sutton River Ontario 50 J8 54 50N 84 30W
Svendsen Peninsula Nunavut 65 P6 77 45N 84 00W
Sverdrup Islands Nunavut 65 L6 79 00N 96 00W
Swan Hills Alberta 46 E4 54 45N 115 45W
Swan Hills *tn.* Alberta 46 E4 54 43N 115 24W
Swan Lake Manitoba 49 B3 52 20N 100 50W
Swan Lake/Kispoix River Provincial Park British Columbia 43 F4 55 55N 128 25W
Swannell Range British Columbia 43 H5 56 38N 126 10W
Swan Pelican Provincial Forest Manitoba 49 B3 52 30N 100 30W
Swan River *tn.* Manitoba 49 B3 52 06N 101 17W
Swift Current *tn.* Saskatchewan 47 D2 50 17N 107 49W
Swift Current Creek Saskatchewan 47 C1 49 40N 108 30W
Swinburne, Cape Nunavut 65 L5 71 13N 98 33W
Swindle Island British Columbia 43 F3 52 33N 128 25W
Sydenham River Ontario 52 D2 42 40N 82 20W
Sydenham River Ontario 54 B3 44 32N 80 57W
Sydney Nova Scotia 61 M12 46 10N 60 10W
Sydney Mines *tn.* Nova Scotia 61 M12 46 16N 60 15W
Sylvan Lake *tn.* Alberta 46 E3 52 19N 114 05W
Sylvia Grinnell Territorial Park Nunavut 65 S3 63 45N 68 38W

T

Taber Alberta 46 F1 49 48N 112 09W
Table Bay Newfoundland and Labrador 60 G6 53 40N 56 25W
Tadoule Lake Manitoba 49 C6 58 30N 98 50W
Tadoussac Québec 53 S8 48 09N 69 43W
Tagish Yukon Territory 64 D3 60 18N 134 16W
Tagish Lake British Columbia 42 C6 59 50N 134 33W
Tahiryauk Lake Northwest Territories 64 H5 70 56N 112 15W
Tahoe Lake Nunavut 64 J4 70 15N 108 45W
Tahsis British Columbia 43 G1 49 50N 126 39W
Tahtsa Lake British Columbia 43 G3 53 41N 127 30W
Takla Lake British Columbia 43 H4 55 12N 125 45W
Takla Landing British Columbia 43 H4 55 27N 125 59W
Taku Arm *l.* British Columbia 42 C6 60 10N 134 05W
Taku River British Columbia 42 D6 58 43N 133 20W
Talbot Lake Manitoba 49 C4 54 00N 99 40W
Taloyoak *(Spence Bay)* Nunavut 65 M4 69 30N 93 20W
Taltson River Northwest Territories 64 H3 60 40N 111 30W
Tamaarvik Territorial Park Nunavut 65 Q5 72 35N 77 28W
Tantalus Provincial Park British Columbia 42 H4 49 50N 123 16W
Tara Ontario 54 A3 44 29N 81 09W
Taseko Mountain British Columbia 43 J2 51 12N 123 07W
Taseko River British Columbia 43 J2 51 35N 123 40W
Tasisuak Lake Newfoundland and Labrador 60 D8 56 45N 62 46W
Tasiujaq Québec 56 F8 58 40N 70 00W
Tasu Sound British Columbia 42 D3 52 40N 132 03W
Tatamagouche Nova Scotia 61 M12 45 43N 63 19W
Tatamagouche Bay Nova Scotia 61 M12 45 45N 63 15W
Tathlina Lake Northwest Territories 64 G3 60 33N 117 39W
Tatla Lake British Columbia 43 H3 51 59N 124 25W
Tatlatui Provincial Park British Columbia 43 G5 57 00N 127 20W
Tatlayoko Lake British Columbia 43 H2 51 39N 124 23W
Tatnam, Cape Manitoba 49 G5 57 25N 91 00W
Tatogga British Columbia 42 F5 57 45N 129 58W
Tatshenshini River British Columbia 42 B6 59 30N 137 30W
Tavistock Ontario 54 B2 43 19N 80 50W
Taylor British Columbia 43 K5 56 09N 120 40W
Taylor Head *p.* Nova Scotia 61 M11 44 40N 62 30W
Tazin Lake Saskatchewan 47 C6 59 50N 109 10W
Tazin River Saskatchewan 47 D6 59 50N 108 00W
Tecumseh Ontario 52 D2 42 18N 82 49W
Teeswater Ontario 54 A2 43 59N 81 18W
Teeswater River Ontario 54 A3 44 07N 81 22W
Teetl'it Zheh *(Fort McPherson)* Northwest Territories 64 D4 67 29N 134 50W
Tehek Lake Nunavut 65 L3 64 55N 95 38W
Telegraph Creek *tn.* British Columbia 42 E5 57 56N 131 11W
Telkwa British Columbia 43 G4 54 44N 127 05W
Temagami Ontario 51 M4 47 04N 79 47W
Temagami, Lake Ontario 51 L4 47 00N 80 05W
Témiscamingue *admin.* Québec 52 H6 46 44N 79 06W
Templeton Québec 59 K2 45 29N 75 36W
Terence Bay Nova Scotia 61 M11 44 20N 63 40W
Terrace British Columbia 43 F4 54 31N 128 32W
Terrace Bay *tn.* Ontario 51 H5 48 47N 87 06W
Terra Cotta Ontario 54 C2 43 42N 79 55W
Terra Nova National Park Newfoundland and Labrador 61 H4 48 40N 54 20W
Terrebonne Québec 53 N5 45 42N 73 37W
Terrebonne *admin.* Québec 53 M6 46 00N 74 30W
Terrenceville Newfoundland and Labrador 61 H3 47 40N 54 44W
Teslin Yukon Territory 64 D3 60 10N 132 42W
Teslin Lake British Columbia/Yukon Territory 64 D3 59 50N 132 25W
Teslin River British Columbia 42 E6 59 20N 131 50W
Tetachuk Lake British Columbia 43 H3 53 38N 127 40W
Teulon Manitoba 49 D2 50 26N 97 18W
Texada Island British Columbia 42 H4 49 30N 124 30W
Thamesford Ontario 54 A2 43 03N 81 00W
Thames River Ontario 52 E2 42 19N 82 27W
Thelon River Northwest Territories 64 K3 64 40N 102 30W
Thelon Wildlife Sanctuary Northwest Territories/Nunavut 65 K3 64 30N 103 00W
The Pas Manitoba 49 B3 53 49N 101 14W
Thesiger Bay Northwest Territories 64 E5 71 30N 124 05W
Thessalon Ontario 52 C6 46 15N 83 34W
Thetford Mines *tn.* Québec 53 Q6 46 06N 71 18W
Thicket Portage Manitoba 49 D4 55 20N 97 42W
Thirty Thousand Islands Ontario 52 F5 45 56N 80 57W
Thlewiaza River Nunavut 65 L3 60 50N 98 00W
Thomas Hubbard, Cape Nunavut 65 M6 81 45N 90 10W
Thomlinson, Mount British Columbia 43 G4 55 30N 127 30W
Thompson Manitoba 49 D4 55 45N 97 54W
Thompson River British Columbia 43 K2 50 12N 121 30W
Thomsen River Northwest Territories 64 G5 73 00N 119 50W
Thorah Island Ontario 54 C3 44 27N 79 13W
Thorhild Alberta 46 F4 54 10N 113 07W
Thornbury Ontario 54 B3 44 34N 80 27W
Thornhill *tn.* Ontario 54 C2 43 49N 79 26W
Thornloe Ontario 51 M4 47 42N 79 41W
Thorold Ontario 54 C2 43 08N 79 14W
Thorsby Alberta 46 E3 53 14N 114 03W
Thousand Islands Ontario 53 K4/L4 44 22N 75 55W
Three Hills *tn.* Alberta 46 F2 51 42N 113 16W
Three Mile Plains *tn.* Nova Scotia 61 M11 44 55N 64 10W
Thunder Bay *tn.* Ontario 51 G5 48 27N 89 12W
Thurso Québec 53 L5 45 38N 75 19W
Thutade Lake British Columbia 43 G5 56 59N 126 40W
Tide Head *tn.* New Brunswick 61 B3 47 58N 66 49W
Tignish Prince Edward Island 61 M12 46 58N 64 03W
Tikkoatokak Bay Newfoundland and Labrador 60 D8 56 42N 62 12W
Tilbury Ontario 52 D2 42 16N 82 26W
Tilbury Island British Columbia 44 F3 49 08N 123 02W
Tilden Lake *tn.* Ontario 52 G6 46 37N 79 39W
Tillsonburg Ontario 54 B1 42 53N 80 44W
Timber Bay Saskatchewan 47 E4 54 09N 105 40W
Timberlea Nova Scotia 61 M11 44 40N 63 45W
Timiskaming Québec 51 M4 46 44N 79 05W
Timiskaming, Lake Ontario 51 M4 46 52N 79 15W
Timmins Ontario 51 L5 48 30N 81 20W
Tinniswood, Mount British Columbia 42 H5 50 19N 123 47W
Tip Top Mountain Ontario 51 J5 48 16N 85 59W
Tirya River British Columbia 42 E6 58 46N 130 50W
Tisdale Saskatchewan 47 E3 52 51N 104 01W
Tiverton Ontario 54 A3 44 15N 81 33W
Tłegǫhłį *(Norman Wells) tn.* Northwest Territories 64 E4 65 19N 126 46W
Toad River *tn.* British Columbia 43 H6 58 50N 125 12W
Toba Inlet British Columbia 42 H5 50 25N 124 30W
Toba River British Columbia 42 H5 50 31N 124 18W
Tobeatic Wildlife Management Area Nova Scotia 61 L11 44 12N 65 25W
Tobermory Ontario 54 A4 45 15N 81 39W
Tobin Lake Saskatchewan 47 F3 53 30N 103 30W
Tofield Saskatchewan 46 F3 53 22N 112 40W
Tofino British Columbia 43 H1 49 05N 125 51W
Tombstone Territorial Park Yukon Territory 64 C3 64 30N 138 15W
Torbay Newfoundland and Labrador 61 J3 47 40N 52 44W
Tor Bay Nova Scotia 61 M12 45 15N 61 15W
Torch River Saskatchewan 47 F3 53 40N 103 50W
Tornado Mountain Alberta/British Columbia 43 N1 49 57N 114 35W
Torngat Mountains Newfoundland and Labrador 60 C9 59 00N 63 40W
Torngat Mountains National Park Reserve Newfoundland and Labrador 60 C9/D9 59 00N 63 30W
Toronto Ontario 54 C2 43 42N 79 46W
Toronto Islands Ontario 54 C2 43 42N 79 25W
Tottenham Ontario 54 C3 44 02N 79 48W
Touraine Québec 59 K2 45 29N 75 42W
Tracadie Nova Scotia 61 M12 45 38N 61 40W
Tracadie-Sheila New Brunswick 61 C3 47 32N 64 57W
Tracy New Brunswick 61 B2 45 41N 66 42W
Tracy Québec 53 N5 45 59N 73 04W
Trail British Columbia 43 M1 49 04N 117 39W
Trans-Canada Highway Canada 47 C2 50 10N 108 30W
Transcona Manitoba 48 C2 49 54N 97 01W
Treherne Manitoba 49 C1 49 39N 98 41W
Trembleur Lake British Columbia 43 H4 54 50N 124 55W
Trenton Nova Scotia 61 M12 45 37N 62 38W
Trenton Ontario 52 J4 44 07N 77 34W
Trent-Severn Waterway Ontario 54 C3 44 20N 79 23W
Trepassey Newfoundland and Labrador 61 J3 46 45N 53 20W
Trinity Bay Newfoundland and Labrador 61 J3 47 50N 53 40W
Trinity East Newfoundland and Labrador 61 J4 48 23N 53 20W
Triton Newfoundland and Labrador 61 H4 49 30N 55 30W
Trochu Alberta 46 F2 51 50N 113 13W
Trois-Pistoles Québec 53 S8 48 08N 69 10W
Trois-Rivières *tn.* Québec 53 P6 46 21N 72 34W
Trout Creek *tn.* Ontario 52 G5 45 59N 79 22W
Trout Lake Ontario 50 E6 51 20N 93 20W
Trout Lake *tn.* Alberta 46 E5 56 30N 114 32W
Trout River *tn.* Newfoundland and Labrador 61 H4 49 29N 58 08W
Troy Nova Scotia 61 M12 45 40N 61 30W
Truro Nova Scotia 61 M12 45 24N 63 18W
Tsawwassen British Columbia 42 H4 49 03N 123 06W
Tsiigehtchic *(Arctic Red River)* Northwest Territories 64 D4 67 27N 133 46W
Ts'yl-os Provincial Park British Columbia 43 H2 51 10N 123 50W
Tthebacha *(Fort Smith)* Northwest Territories 64 H3 60 01N 111 55W
Tthenáágóo *(Nahanni Butte) tn.* Northwest Territories 64 F3 61 30N 123 20W
Tthets'éhk'édéli *(Jean Marie River) tn.* Northwest Territories 64 F3 61 32N 120 38W
Tuchitua Yukon Territory 64 E3 61 20N 129 00W
Tuktut Nogait National Park Northwest Territories 64 F4 69 00N 121 50W
Tuktuujaqrtuuq *(Tuktoyaktuk)* Northwest Territories 64 D4 69 24N 133 01W
Tulemalu Lake Nunavut 65 L3 62 58N 99 25W
Tulit'a *(Fort Norman)* Northwest Territories 64 E3 64 55N 125 29W
Tumbler Ridge *tn.* British Columbia 43 K4 55 10N 121 01W
Tungsten Northwest Territories 64 E3 61 59N 128 09W
Tunungayualok Island Newfoundland and Labrador 60 E8 56 05N 61 05W
Turkey Point Ontario 54 B1 42 37N 80 20W
Turkey Point *tn.* Ontario 54 B1 43 41N 80 20W
Turkey Point Provincial Park Ontario 54 B1 42 45N 80 20W
Turnagain River British Columbia 43 F6 58 25N 129 08W
Turnavik Island Newfoundland and Labrador 60 F7 55 18N 59 21W
Turner Valley *tn.* Alberta 46 E2 50 40N 114 17W
Turnor Lake Saskatchewan 47 C5 56 35N 109 10W
Turnor Lake *tn.* Saskatchewan 47 C5 56 25N 108 40W
Turtleford Saskatchewan 47 C3 53 25N 108 588W
Turtle Mountain Provincial Park Manitoba 49 B1 49 00N 100 10W
Turtle River-White Otter Provincial Park Ontario 50 E5 49 15N 92 10W
Tusket Nova Scotia 61 L11 43 53N 65 58W
Tuxedo Manitoba 48 B2 49 51N 97 13W
Tuya Mountains Provincial Park British Columbia 42 E6 59 18N 130 35W
Tweed Ontario 53 J4 44 29N 77 19W
Twenty Mile Creek Ontario 54 C2 43 09N 79 48W
Twillingate Newfoundland and Labrador 61 H4 49 39N 54 46W
Twin Falls *tn.* Newfoundland and Labrador 60 C6 53 30N 64 32W
Twin Islands Nunavut 50 M7 53 20N 80 10W
Two Hills *tn.* Alberta 46 G3 53 43N 11 45W
Tyne Valley *tn.* Prince Edward Island 61 M12 46 36N 63 57W

U

Uashat Québec 57 G4 50 10N 66 00W
Ucluelet British Columbia 42 G4 48 55N 125 34W
Ugjoktok Bay Newfoundland and Labrador 60 E7 55 08N 60 30W
Uivak, Cape Newfoundland and Labrador 60 D9 58 29N 62 34W
Ukasiksalik Island Newfoundland and Labrador 60 E7 55 55N 60 47W
Ukkusiksalik National Park Nunavut 65 M4/N4 65 48N 90 00W
Uluqsaqnuq *(Holman)* Northwest Territories 64 G5 70 44N 117 44W
Umingmaktok Nunavut 64 J4 65 00N 105 00W
Umiujaq Québec 56 B7 56 00N 76 44W
Ungava Bay *(Baie d'Ungava)* Québec 65 S2 58 00N 72 30W
Unionville Ontario 54 C2 43 51N 79 19W
United States Range *mts.* Nunavut 65 R7 82 25N 68 00W

Unity Saskatchewan	47	C3	52 27N	109 10W
Upper Arrow Lake British Columbia	43	M2	50 25N	117 56W
Upper Campbell Lake British Columbia	42	G4	49 57N	125 36W
Upper Foster Lake Saskatchewan	47	E5	56 40N	105 35W
Upper Liard Yukon Territory	64	E3	60 00N	129 20W
Upper Lillooet Provincial Park British Columbia	43	J2	51 35N	123 40W
Upper Musquodoboit Nova Scotia	61	M12	45 10N	62 58W
Upper Sackville Nova Scotia	59	Q7	44 48N	63 42W
Upper Salmon Reservoir Newfoundland and Labrador	61	G4	48 20N	55 30W
Upper Windigo Lake Ontario	50	F7	52 30N	91 35W
Uqsuqtuq *(Gjoa Haven)* Nunavut	65	L4	68 39N	96 09W
Uranium City Saskatchewan	47	C6	59 32N	108 43W
Utikuma Lake Alberta	46	E4	55 50N	115 25W
Uxbridge Ontario	54	C3	44 07N	79 09W

V

Valdes Island British Columbia	42	H4	49 05N	123 40W
Val-d'Or Québec	57	B3	48 07N	77 47W
Valemount British Columbia	43	L3	52 50N	119 15W
Valhalla Provincial Park British Columbia	43	L1	49 00N	118 00W
Valleyview Alberta	46	D4	55 04N	117 17W
Val Marie Saskatchewan	47	D1	49 15N	107 44W
Val-Paradis Québec	57	A3	49 10N	79 17W
Vancouver British Columbia	42	H4	49 13N	123 06W
Vancouver Island British Columbia	42	G4/H4	48 55N	124 33W
Vanderhoof British Columbia	43	H3	54 00N	124 00W
Vanier Ontario	53	L5	45 27N	75 40W
Vankleek Hill Ontario	53	M5	45 31N	74 39W
Vanscoy Saskatchewan	47	D3	52 01N	106 59W
Vansittart Island Nunavut	65	P4	65 50N	84 00W
Varennes Québec	53	N6	45 39N	73 26W
Vaudreuil *admin.* Québec	53	M5	45 20N	74 20W
Vaughan Ontario	55	B2	43 39N	79 25W
Vauxhall Alberta	46	F2	50 04N	112 07W
Vegreville Alberta	46	F3	53 30N	112 03W
Verdun Québec	58	N4	44 28N	73 35W
Vermilion Alberta	46	G3	53 22N	110 51W
Vermilion Bay Ontario	50	E5	49 51N	93 21W
Vermilion Pass Alberta/British Columbia	46	D2	51 14N	116 03W
Vermilion River Alberta	46	G3	53 40N	111 25W
Vernon British Columbia	43	L2	50 17N	119 19W
Victoria British Columbia	42	H4	48 26N	123 20W
Victoria Newfoundland and Labrador	61	J3	47 46N	53 14W
Victoria Prince Edward Island	61	M12	46 10N	63 30W
Victoria *admin.* New Brunswick	61	B3	47 10N	67 30W
Victoria *admin.* Nova Scotia	61	M12	46 30N	60 30W
Victoria *admin.* Ontario	54	D3	44 45N	79 03W
Victoria Bridge Nova Scotia	61	M12	45 50N	60 20W
Victoria Harbour Ontario	52	G4	44 45N	79 45W
Victoria Island Northwest Territories/Nunavut	64	H5	70 45N	115 00W
Victoria Lake Newfoundland and Labrador	61	G4	48 18N	57 20W
Victoria River Newfoundland and Labrador	61	G4	48 30N	57 50W
Victoriaville Québec	53	Q6	46 04N	71 57W
Vienna Ontario	54	B1	42 39N	80 47W
Vieux Fort Québec	57	M4	51 59N	57 59W
Viking Alberta	46	G3	53 06N	111 488W
Virden Manitoba	49	B1	49 50N	100 57W
Virgil Ontario	54	C2	43 13N	79 07W
Virginiatown Ontario	51	M5	48 08N	79 35W
Viscount Melville Sound Northwest Territories/Nunavut	64	H5	74 10N	105 00W
Voisey's Bay Newfoundland and Labrador	60	E8	56 15N	61 50W
Voisey's Bay Mine Newfoundland and Labrador	60	D8	54 41N	62 12W
Vulcan Alberta	46	F2	50 24N	113 15W
Vuntut National Park Yukon Territory	64	C4	69 30N	139 30W

W

Wabakimi Lake Ontario	50	G6	50 38N	89 45W
Wabakimi Provincial Park Ontario	50	G6	50 30N	90 00W
Wabana Newfoundland and Labrador	61	J3	47 38N	52 57W
Wabasca-Desmarais Alberta	46	F4	55 59N	113 50W
Wabasca River Alberta	46	E5	57 30N	115 15W
Wabowden Manitoba	49	C4	54 57N	98 38W
Wabuk Point Ontario	50	J8	55 20N	85 05W
Wabush Newfoundland and Labrador	60	B6	52 55N	66 52W
Wabush Lake Newfoundland and Labrador	60	B6	53 05N	66 52W
Wabuskasing Ontario	50	E6	50 20N	93 10W
W.A.C. Bennet Dam British Columbia	43	J4	55 00N	122 11W
Waddington, Mount British Columbia	43	H2	51 22N	125 14W
Wade Lake Newfoundland and Labrador	60	C7	54 20N	65 38W
Wadena Saskatchewan	47	F2	51 57N	103 58W
Wager Bay Nunavut	65	N4	66 00N	89 00W
Waglisla British Columbia	43	F3	52 05N	128 10W
Wainfleet Ontario	54	C1	42 52N	79 22W
Wainwright Alberta	46	G3	52 49N	110 52W
Wakaw Saskatchewan	47	E3	52 40N	105 45W
Wakefield Québec	53	K5	45 39N	75 56W
Waldheim Saskatchewan	47	D3	52 39N	106 40W
Wales Island Nunavut	65	N4	68 01N	86 40W
Walker Lake Manitoba	49	D4	54 40N	96 40W
Walkerton Ontario	54	A3	44 08N	81 10W
Wallace Nova Scotia	61	M12	45 48N	63 26W
Wallaceburg Ontario	52	D2	42 34N	82 22W
Walton Nova Scotia	61	M12	45 14N	64 00W
Wanapitei Lake Ontario	51	L4	46 45N	80 45W
Wanless Manitoba	49	B4	54 11N	101 21W
Wapawekka Hills Saskatchewan	47	E4	54 50N	104 30W
Wapawekka Lake Saskatchewan	47	E4	55 00N	104 30W
Wapella Saskatchewan	47	G2	50 16N	101 59W
Wapikopa Lake Ontario	50	G7	52 54N	87 50W
Wapiti River Alberta	46	C4	54 40N	119 50W
Wapusk National Park Manitoba	49	F5	57 45N	93 20W
Wardsville Ontario	52	E2	42 39N	81 45W
Warman Saskatchewan	47	D3	52 19N	104 34W
Warner Alberta	46	F1	49 17N	112 12W
Warrender, Cape Nunavut	65	P5	74 28N	81 46W
Warren Landing *tn.* Manitoba	49	D3	53 42N	97 54W
Wasaga Beach *tn.* Ontario	54	B3	44 31N	80 02W
Wasaga Beach Provincial Park Ontario	54	B3	44 30N	80 05W
Wascana Creek Saskatchewan	47	E2	50 20N	104 20W
Wasekiu Lake *tn.* Saskatchewan	47	D3	53 55N	106 00W
Waskaganish Québec	57	A4	51 30N	79 45W
Waskaiowaka Lake Manitoba	49	D5	56 40N	96 40W
Waskamio Lake Saskatchewan	47	C5	56 50N	108 30W
Waskatenau Alberta	46	F4	54 06N	112 48W
Waswanipi Québec	57	C3	49 41N	75 57W
Waterbury Lake Saskatchewan	47	E6	58 10N	104 55W
Waterdown Ontario	54	C2	43 20N	79 54W
Waterford Ontario	54	B1	42 55N	80 19W
Waterhen Manitoba	49	C2	51 50N	99 30W
Waterhen Lake Manitoba	49	C3	52 00N	99 20W
Waterhen River Saskatchewan	47	C4	54 25N	108 50W
Waterloo Ontario	54	B2	43 28N	80 32W
Waterloo *admin.* Ontario	54	B2	43 30N	80 46W
Waterton Lakes National Park Alberta	46	F1	49 00N	114 45W
Watford Ontario	52	E2	42 57N	81 53W
Wathaman Lake Saskatchewan	47	F5	57 00N	104 10W
Wathaman River Saskatchewan	47	E5	56 50N	104 50W
Watrous Saskatchewan	47	E2	51 40N	105 29W
Watson Saskatchewan	47	E3	52 09N	104 31W
Watson Lake *tn.* Yukon Territory	64	E3	60 07N	128 49W
Waverley Nova Scotia	61	M11	44 48N	63 38W
Waverley Game Sanctuary Nova Scotia	59	Q7	44 49N	63 31W
Wawa Ontario	51	J4	48 00N	84 49W
Wawota Saskatchewan	47	G1	49 56N	102 00W
Weagamow Lake *tn.* Ontario	50	F7	52 53N	91 22W
Weaver Lake Manitoba	49	D3	52 40N	96 40W
Webbwood Ontario	52	E6	46 16N	81 53W
Webequie Ontario	50	H7	52 59N	87 21W
Wedge Mountain British Columbia	42	H5	50 07N	122 49W
Wedgeport Nova Scotia	61	L11	43 44N	66 00W
Wekusko Manitoba	49	C4	54 31N	99 45W
Wekusko Lake Manitoba	49	C4	54 30N	99 40W
Wekweti *(Snare Lakes)* Northwest Territories	64	H3	64 10N	114 20W
Weldon Saskatchewan	47	E3	53 00N	105 08W
Welland Ontario	54	C1	42 59N	79 14W
Welland Canal Ontario	54	C2	43 14N	79 13W
Welland River Ontario	54	C2	43 05N	79 46W
Wellesley Ontario	54	B2	43 27N	80 46W
Wellington Nova Scotia	59	Q7	44 50N	63 38W
Wellington Ontario	53	J3	43 57N	77 21W
Wellington *admin.* Ontario	54	B2	43 46N	80 41W
Wellington Channel Nunavut	65	L6	75 00N	93 00W
Wells British Columbia	43	K3	53 00N	121 30W
Wells Gray Provincial Park British Columbia	43	K3	52 00N	120 00W
Wells Lake Manitoba	49	B5	57 10N	100 30W
Wembley Alberta	46	C4	55 09N	119 08W
Wemindji Québec	57	A5	52 59N	78 50W
Wenebegon Lake Ontario	51	K4	47 23N	83 06W
Wentworth Nova Scotia	61	M12	45 39N	63 35W
Werner Lake Ontario	50	D6	50 27N	94 54W
Wesleyville Newfoundland and Labrador	61	J4	49 09N	53 34W
West Bay *tn.* Newfoundland and Labrador	60	G7	54 08N	57 26W
West Bay *tn.* Nova Scotia	61	M12	45 40N	61 10W
West Don River Ontario	55	B2	43 49N	79 31W
West Duffins Creek Ontario	55	D2	43 53N	79 10W
Western River Nunavut	64	J4	66 40N	107 00W
Westham Island British Columbia	44	F3	49 05N	123 10W
West Highland Creek Ontario	55	C2	43 46N	79 15W
West Humber River Ontario	55	B1	43 48N	79 43W
Westlock Alberta	46	F4	54 09N	113 52W
West Lorne Ontario	54	A1	42 36N	81 35W
Westmorland *admin.* New Brunswick	61	M12	46 10N	64 50W
Westmount Nova Scotia	61	M12	46 10N	60 10W
Westmount Québec	58	N4	44 29N	73 36W
West Nose Creek Alberta	44	A2	51 15N	114 11W
West Point Prince Edward Island	61	M12	46 38N	64 26W
Westport Nova Scotia	61	L11	44 20N	66 20W
Westport Ontario	53	K4	44 41N	76 24W
West Road River British Columbia	43	H3	53 12N	123 50W
West St. Modeste Newfoundland and Labrador	60	G5	51 36N	56 42W
West Thurlow Island British Columbia	42	G5	50 27N	125 35W
West Twin Provincial Park British Columbia	43	K3	53 20N	120 30W
West Vancouver British Columbia	42	H4	49 22N	123 11W
Westville Nova Scotia	61	M12	45 34N	62 44W
Wetaskiwin Alberta	46	F3	52 57N	113 20W
Weyburn Saskatchewan	47	F1	49 39N	103 51W
Weymouth Nova Scotia	61	L11	44 26N	66 00W
Whale Cove *(Tikirarjuaq) tn.* Nunavut	65	M3	62 10N	92 36W
Whaletown British Columbia	42	G5	50 06N	125 02W
What *(Lac la Martre)* Northwest Territories	64	G3	63 00N	117 30W
Wheatley Ontario	52	D2	42 06N	82 27W
Wheeler River Saskatchewan	47	E5	57 30N	105 10W
Whippoorwill Bay Ontario	54	A4	45 01N	81 15W
Whirl Creek Ontario	54	A2	43 29N	81 07W
Whistler British Columbia	42	H5	50 08N	122 58W
Whitby Ontario	54	D2	43 52N	78 56W
White Bay Newfoundland and Labrador	61	G5	50 00N	56 32W
White Bear Island Newfoundland and Labrador	60	E8	57 54N	61 42W
White Bear Lake Newfoundland and Labrador	60	F7	54 32N	59 30W
White City Saskatchewan	47	E2	50 35N	104 20W
Whitecourt Alberta	46	E4	54 10N	115 41W
Whitedog Ontario	49	D6	50 09N	94 55W
Whitefish Ontario	52	E6	46 23N	81 22W
Whitefish Bay Ontario	51	J4	46 38N	84 33W
Whitefish Lake Northwest Territories	64	J3	62 30N	106 40W
Whitefish Lake Ontario	51	J5	48 05N	84 10W
Whitefox River Saskatchewan	47	E3	53 25N	104 55W
White Handkerchief, Cape Newfoundland and Labrador	60	D9	59 17N	63 23W
Whitehorse Yukon Territory	64	C3	60 41N	135 08W
White Lake Ontario	51	J5	48 50N	85 30W
Whitemouth Manitoba	49	E1	49 58N	95 59W
Whitemouth Lake Manitoba	49	E1	49 10N	96 00W
Whitemouth River Manitoba	49	E1	49 50N	97 10W
White Otter Lake Ontario	50	F5	49 07N	91 52W
White Pass British Columbia	42	C6	59 37N	135 07W
White River Ontario	51	J5	48 30N	86 20W
White River Yukon Territory	64	B3	62 25N	140 05W
White River *tn.* Ontario	51	J5	48 35N	85 16W
White Rock British Columbia	42	H4	49 02N	122 50W
Whitesail Lake British Columbia	43	G3	53 25N	127 10W
Whitesand River Alberta	46	E6	59 00N	115 00W
Whiteshell Provincial Forest Manitoba	49	E1	49 50N	95 40W
Whiteshell Provincial Park Manitoba	49	E2	50 00N	95 20W
Whitewater Creek Saskatchewan/USA	47	D1	48 50N	107 40W
Whitewater Lake Ontario	50	G6	50 40N	89 30W
Whitewood Saskatchewan	47	F2	50 19N	102 16W
Whitney Ontario	52	H5	45 29N	78 15W
Whitworth Québec	53	S7	47 42N	69 17W
Wholdaia Lake Northwest Territories	64	K3	60 43N	104 10W
Whycocomagh Nova Scotia	61	M12	45 58N	61 08W
Wiarton Ontario	54	A3	44 44N	81 19W
Wildcat Hill Provincial Wilderness Area Saskatchewan	47	F3	53 20N	102 20W
Wildwood Alberta	46	E3	53 37N	115 14W
Wilkie Saskatchewan	47	C3	52 27N	108 42W
William, Lake Nova Scotia	59	Q7	44 46N	63 34W
William River Saskatchewan	47	C6	58 50N	108 55W
Williams Lake *tn.* British Columbia	43	J3	52 08N	122 07W
Williston Lake British Columbia	43	J4	56 00N	124 00W
Willmore Wilderness Park Alberta	46	C3	53 40N	119 30W
Will, Mount British Columbia	43	F5	57 30N	128 44W
Willowbunch Lake Saskatchewan	47	D1	49 20N	105 50W
Willow Lake Northwest Territories	64	G3	60 00N	115 00W
Winchester Ontario	53	L5	45 06N	75 21W
Windermere Lake Ontario	51	K4	47 58N	83 47W
Windigo Québec	53	N7	47 45N	73 22W
Windigo Lake Ontario	50	F7	52 35N	91 32W
Windsor Nova Scotia	61	M11	45 00N	64 09W
Windsor Ontario	52	C2	42 18N	83 00W
Windsor Québec	53	P5	45 35N	72 01W
Windsor Junction Nova Scotia	59	Q7	44 48N	63 38W
Winefred Lake Alberta	46	G4	55 30N	110 31W
Wingham Ontario	54	A2	43 54N	81 19W
Winisk Lake Ontario	50	H7	52 55N	87 22W
Winisk River Ontario	50	H7	54 50N	86 10W
Winisk River Provincial Park Ontario	50	H7	52 50N	87 30W
Winkler Manitoba	49	C1	49 12N	97 55W
Winnipeg Manitoba	49	D1	49 53N	97 10W
Winnipeg Beach *tn.* Manitoba	49	D2	50 30N	97 00W
Winnipeg, Lake Manitoba	49	C3/D3	53 00N	97 00W
Winnipegosis Manitoba	49	C2	51 40N	99 59W
Winnipegosis, Lake Manitoba	49	B3	52 10N	100 00W
Winnipeg River Manitoba	49	E2	50 20N	95 30W
Winokapau Lake Newfoundland and Labrador	60	D6	53 10N	62 52W
Winona Ontario	54	C2	43 12N	79 38W
Witless Bay *tn.* Newfoundland and Labrador	61	J3	47 16N	52 50W
Wolfe *admin.* Québec	53	Q5	45 40N	71 40W
Wolfe Island Ontario	53	K4	44 31N	75 59W
Wolfville Nova Scotia	61	M12	45 06N	64 22W
Wollaston, Cape Northwest Territories	64	G5	71 06N	118 04W
Wollaston Lake Saskatchewan	47	F6	58 20N	103 00W
Wollaston Lake *tn.* Saskatchewan	47	F6	58 05N	103 38W
Wollaston Peninsula Northwest Territories/Nunavut	64	H4	70 00N	115 00W
Wolseley Saskatchewan	47	F2	50 25N	103 15W
Woodbridge Ontario	54	C2	43 47N	79 36W
Wood Buffalo National Park Alberta/Northwest Territories	46	F6	59 00N	112 30W
Woodfibre British Columbia	42	H4	49 36N	123 00W
Wood Islands Prince Edward Island	61	M12	45 50N	62 40W
Woodland Caribou Provincial Park Ontario	50	D6	51 10N	94 20W
Wood Mountain Saskatchewan	47	D1	49 15N	106 20W
Woodside Nova Scotia	59	Q6	44 39N	63 31W
Woods Lake Newfoundland and Labrador	60	C7	54 30N	65 13W
Woods, Lake of the Ontario	50	D5	49 15N	94 45W
Woodstock New Brunswick	61	B3	46 10N	67 36W
Woodstock Ontario	54	B2	43 07N	80 46W
Woodville Ontario	54	D3	44 24N	78 44W
Wrong Lake Manitoba	49	E3	52 40N	96 10W
Wunnummin Lake Ontario	50	G7	52 55N	89 10W
Wynniatt Bay Northwest Territories	64	H5	72 45N	110 30W
Wynyard Saskatchewan	47	E2	51 50N	104 10W

Y

Yale British Columbia	42	H4	49 31N	121 29W
Yamaska *admin.* Québec	53	P5	46 00N	72 50W
Yarmouth Nova Scotia	61	L11	43 50N	66 08W
Yarmouth *admin.* Nova Scotia	61	L11	44 50N	65 40W
Yates River Alberta	46	D6	59 40N	116 25W
Yathkyed Lake Nunavut	65	L3	62 40N	98 00W
Yellow Grass Saskatchewan	47	E1	49 49N	104 11W
Yellowhead Highway Alberta	46	G3	53 20N	110 45W
Yellowhead Pass Alberta/British Columbia	46	C3	52 53N	118 28W
Yellowknife River Northwest Territories	64	H3	62 35N	114 10W
Yoho National Park British Columbia	43	M2	51 00N	116 00W
York New Brunswick	61	B3	46 10N	66 50W
York *admin.* Ontario	54	C2	43 57N	79 39W
York Ontario	55	C2	43 41N	79 28W
York, Cape Nunavut	65	N5	73 48N	87 00W
York Factory Manitoba	49	F5	57 08N	92 25W
York Landing Manitoba	49	E5	56 05N	95 59W
Yorkton Saskatchewan	47	F2	51 12N	102 29W
Youbou British Columbia	42	H4	48 52N	124 12W
Young Saskatchewan	47	E2	51 45N	105 45W
Yukon River Yukon Territory/USA	64	C3	63 00N	138 50W
Yukon Territory *territory*	64			

Z

Zama City Alberta	46	C6	59 08N	118 43W
Zeballos British Columbia	43	G1	49 57N	126 10W
Zhahti Koé *(Fort Providence)* Northwest Territories	64	G3	61 03N	117 40W
Zürich Ontario	54	A2	43 25N	81 37W

A

Aachen Germany 86 J9 50 46N 6 06E
Aalst Belgium 86 H9 50 57N 4 03E
Aba Nigeria 108 F9 5 06N 7 21E
Abādān Iran 97 E5 30 20N 48 15E
Abadla Algeria 108 D14 31 01N 2 45W
Abaetetuba Brazil 80 H13 1 45S 48 54W
Abakan Russia 95 M7 53 43N 91 25E
Abakan *r.* Russia 95 L7 52 00N 90 00E
Abancay Peru 80 C11 13 37S 72 52W
Abashiri Japan 102 D3 44 02N 114 17E
Abbe, Lake Ethiopia 108 N10 11 00N 44 00E
Abbeville Fr. 86 F9 50 06N 1 51E
'Abd al Kūrī *i.* Yemen 97 F1 11 55N 52 20E
Abéché Chad 108 J10 13 49N 20 49E
Abeokuta Nigeria 108 E9 7 10N 3 26E
Aberdeen UK 86 D12 57 10N 2 04W
Aberdeen HK China 100 B1 22 14N 114 09E
Aberdeen Maryland USA 73 B1 39 31N 76 10N
Aberdeen South Dakota USA 71 G6 45 28N 98 30W
Aberdeen Washington USA 70 B6 46 58N 123 49W
Aberystwyth UK 86 C10 52 25N 4 05W
Abhā Saudi Arabia 96 D2 18 14N 42 31E
Abidjan Côte d'Ivoire 108 D9 5 19N 4 01W
Abilene Texas USA 70 G3 32 27N 99 49W
Absaroka Range *mts.* USA 70 D6/E5 45 00N 110 00W
Abu Dhabi UAE 97 F3 24 28N 54 25E
Abu Hamed Sudan 108 L11 19 32N 33 20E
Abuja Nigeria 108 F9 9 10N 7 11E
Ālbū Kamāl Syria 96 D5 34 29N 40 56E
Abu Kebîr Egypt 109 R3 30 44N 31 48E
Abunã Brazil 80 D12 9 41S 65 20W
Acambaro Mexico 74 D3 20 00N 100 42W
Acaponeta Mexico 74 C4 22 30N 105 25W
Acapulco Mexico 74 E3 16 51N 99 56W
Acarigua Venezuela 80 D15 9 35N 69 12W
Acatlán Mexico 74 E3 18 12N 98 02W
Acayucán Mexico 74 E3 17 59N 94 58W
Accra Ghana 108 D9 5 33N 0 15W
Achacachi Bolivia 80 D10 16 01S 68 44W
Achinsk Russia 95 M8 56 20N 90 33E
Acklins Island Bahamas 75 K4 22 30N 74 30W
Aconcagua *mt.* Argentina 81 C7 32 40S 70 02W
Acre Israel 96 N11 32 55N 35 04E
Acre *admin.* Brazil 80 C12 8 30S 71 30W
Ada Oklahoma USA 71 G3 34 47N 96 41W
Adaga *r.* Sp. 87 C4 40 45N 4 45W
Adams New York USA 53 K3 43 49N 76 01W
Adana Turkey 96 C6 37 00N 35 19E
Ad Dakhla Western Sahara 108 A12 23 50N 15 58W
Ad Dammām Saudi Arabia 97 F4 26 25N 50 06E
Ad Dilam Saudi Arabia 97 E3 23 59N 47 06E
Ad Dir'īyah Saudi Arabia 97 E3 24 45N 46 32E
Addis Ababa Ethiopia 108 M9 9 03N 38 42E
Addison New York USA 53 J2 42 06N 77 14W
Ad Dīwānīyah Iraq 96 D5 32 00N 44 57E
Adelaide Aust. 110 F3 34 56S 138 36E
Adelanto California USA 72 E2 34 35N 117 24W
Adelie Land *geog. reg.* Antarctica 117 70 00S 135 00E
Aden Yemen 96 E1 12 50N 45 03E
Aden, Gulf of Indian Ocean 97 E1 12 30N 47 30E
Adirondack Mountains New York USA 71 M5 43 15N 74 40W
Admiralty Island Alaska USA 42 C5 57 45N 134 30W
Admiralty Island National Monument Alaska USA 42 C6 58 05N 134 00W
Admiralty Islands PNG 110 H9 2 30S 147 00E
Adoni India 98 D3 15 38N 77 16E
Adra Sp. 87 D2 36 45N 3 01W
Adrar Algeria 108 D13 27 51N 0 19W
Adrian Michigan USA 51 J1 41 54N 84 02W
Adriatic Sea Mediterranean Sea 89 E5 43 00N 15 00E
Ādwa Ethiopia 108 M10 14 12N 38 56E
Aegean Sea Mediterranean Sea 89 K3 39 00N 24 00E
AFGHANISTAN 97 H5/K6
Afyon Turkey 96 B6 38 46N 30 32E
Agadez Niger 108 F11 17 00N 7 56E
Agadir Morocco 108 C14 30 30N 9 40W
Agano *r.* Japan 102 C2 37 50N 139 30E
Agartala India 99 G4 23 49N 91 15E
Agen Fr. 87 F6 44 12N 0 38E
Ágios Nikólaos Greece 89 K1 35 11N 25 43E
Agout *r.* Fr. 87 G5 43 50N 1 50E
Agra India 98 D5 27 09N 78 00E
Agri *r.* Italy 89 F4 40 00N 16 00E
Ağri Daği *mt.* Turkey 96 D6 39 44N 44 15E
Agrigento Italy 89 D2 37 19N 13 35E
Agrínio Greece 89 H3 38 38N 21 25E
Aguadas Col. 80 B15 5 36N 75 30W
Aguadilla Puerto Rico 75 L3 18 27N 67 08W
Agua Prieta Mexico 74 C6 31 20N 109 32W
Aguascalientes Mexico 74 D4 21 51N 102 18W
Agueda *r.* Sp. 87 B4 40 50N 6 50W
Aguilas Sp. 87 E2 37 25N 1 35W
Aguiles Serdan Mexico 74 C5 28 40N 105 57W
Agulhas Basin Indian Ocean 113 A2 45 00S 20 00E
Agulhas, Cape RSA 109 J1 34 50S 20 00E
Ahmadabad India 98 C4 23 03N 72 40E
Ahmadnagar India 98 C3 19 08N 74 48E
Ahuachapán El Salvador 74 G2 13 57N 89 49W
Ahvāz Iran 97 E5 31 17N 48 43E
Ain *r.* Fr. 87 H7 46 30N 5 30E
Aïn Sefra Algeria 108 D14 32 45N 0 35W
Aïr *mts.* Niger 108 F11 19 10N 8 20E
Aire-sur-l'Adour Fr. 87 E5 43 42N 0 15W
Aix-en-Provence Fr. 87 H5 43 31N 5 27E
Aizawl India 99 M9 23 43N 92 47E
Aizu-wakamatsu Japan 102 C2 37 30N 139 58E
Ajaccio France 87 K4 41 55N 8 43E
Ajay *r.* India 99 J9 23 50N 88 00E
Ajdabiya Libya 108 J14 30 46N 20 14E
'Ajlūn Jordan 96 N11 32 20N 35 35E
Ajman UAE 97 G4 25 23N 55 26E
Ajmer India 98 C5 26 29N 74 40E
Ajo Arizona USA 70 D3 32 24N 112 51W
Akabira Japan 102 D3 43 40N 141 55E
Akaroa NZ 111 D3 43 49S 172 58E
Akashi Japan 102 B1 34 39N 135 00E
Aketi CDR 108 J8 2 42N 23 51E
Akita Japan 102 D2 39 44N 140 05E
Akobo Sudan 108 L9 7 50N 33 05E
Akola India 98 D4 20 49N 77 05E
Ákra Akrítas *c.* Greece 89 H2 36 43N 21 52E
Ákra Kafiréas *c.* Greece 89 K3 38 10N 24 35E
Ákra Maléas *c.* Greece 89 J2 36 27N 23 12E
Ákra Taínaro *c.* Greece 89 J2 36 23N 22 29E
Akron Ohio USA 71 K5 41 04N 81 31W
Aktau Kazakhstan 94 H5 43 37N 51 11E
Aktyubinsk Kazakhstan 94 H7 50 16N 57 13E
Alabama *r.* Alabama USA 71 J3 31 00N 88 00W
Alabama *state* USA 71 J3 32 00N 87 00W
Alagoas *admin.* Brazil 80 K12 9 30S 37 00W
Alagoinhas Brazil 80 K11 12 09S 38 21W
Alagón *r.* Sp. 87 B3 40 00N 6 30W
Alajuela Costa Rica 75 H2 10 00N 84 12W
Al 'Amārah Iraq 97 E5 31 51N 47 10E
Alamo Nevada USA 72 F3 37 23N 115 10W
Alamosa Colorado USA 70 E4 37 28N 105 54W
Åland *is.* Finland 88 G14 60 15N 20 00E
Alanya Turkey 96 B6 36 32N 32 02E
Al Artāwīyah Saudi Arabia 96 E4 26 31N 45 21E
Ala Shan *mts.* China 101 J6/J7 40 00N 102 30E
Alaska *state* USA 42 C5 58 00N 135 00W
Alaska, Gulf of Alaska USA 115 M13 58 00N 147 00W
Alaska Range *mts.* Alaska USA 64 A3/B3 62 30N 145 00W
Al 'Ayn UAE 97 G3 24 10N 55 43E
Alay Range *mts.* Asia 94 K4 39 00N 70 00E
Albacete Sp. 87 E3 39 00N 1 52W
Alba Iulia Romania 89 J7 46 04N 23 33E
ALBANIA 89 G4/H4
Albany Aust. 110 B3 34 57S 117 54E
Albany Georgia USA 71 K3 31 37N 84 10W
Albany New York USA 71 M5 42 40N 73 49W
Albany Oregon USA 70 B5 44 38N 123 07W
Al Başrah Iraq 97 E5 30 30N 47 50E
Al Bayda Libya 108 J14 32 00N 21 30E
Albert, Lake Uganda/CDR 108 L8 2 00N 31 00E
Albert Lea Minnesota USA 71 H5 43 38N 93 16W
Albi Fr. 87 G5 43 56N 2 08E
Albion Michigan USA 52 B2 42 14N 84 45W
Albion New York USA 52 H3 43 14N 78 11W
Al Bi'r Saudi Arabia 96 C4 28 50N 36 16E
Ålborg Denmark 88 B12 57 05N 9 50E
Albuquerque New Mexico USA 70 E4 35 05N 106 38W
Al Buraymī Oman 97 G3 24 16N 55 48E
Alcalá de Henares Sp. 87 D4 40 28N 3 22W
Alcamo Italy 89 D2 37 58N 12 58E
Alcañiz Sp. 87 E4 41 03N 0 09W
Alcázar de San Juan Sp. 87 D3 39 24N 3 12W
Alcira Sp. 87 E3 39 10N 0 27W
Alcoy Sp. 87 E3 38 42N 0 29W
Aldabra Islands Indian Ocean 113 D6 9 00S 46 00E
Aldama Mexico 74 E4 22 54N 98 05W
Aldan Russia 95 Q8 58 44N 124 22E
Aldan *r.* Russia 95 R8 59 00N 132 30E
Alderney *i.* British Isles 86 D8 49 43N 2 12W
Alegrete Brazil 81 F8 29 45S 55 40W
Aleksandrovsk-Sakhalinskiy Russia 95 S7 50 55N 142 12E
Alençon Fr. 86 F8 48 25N 0 05E
Alenuihaha Channel *sd.* Hawaiian Islands 115 Y18 20 20N 156 20W
Aleppo Syria 96 C6 36 14N 37 10E
Alès Fr. 87 H6 44 08N 4 05E
Alessándria Italy 89 B6 44 55N 8 37E
Aleutian Basin Pacific Ocean 114 J13 54 00N 178 00W
Aleutian Islands Pacific Ocean 114 H13 52 00N 178 00W
Aleutian Ridge Pacific Ocean 114 H13 53 55N 178 00W
Aleutian Trench Pacific Ocean 114 H13 50 55N 178 00W
Alexander Archipelago *is.* Alaska USA 42 B5/D4 57 00N 137 30W
Alexander Bay *tn.* RSA 109 H2 28 40S 16 30E
Alexander Island Antarctica 117 71 00S 70 00W
Alexandra NZ 111 B2 45 15S 169 23E
Alexandria Egypt 108 K14 31 13N 29 55E
Alexandria Romania 89 K5 43 59N 25 19E
Alexandria Louisiana USA 71 H3 31 19N 92 29W
Alexandria Bay *tn.* New York USA 51 P3 44 20N 75 55W
Alexandroúpoli Greece 89 K4 40 51N 25 53E
Alfambra *r.* Sp. 87 E4 40 40N 1 00W
Alfeiós *r.* Greece 89 H2 37 30N 21 45E
Al Fuḩayḩil Kuwait 97 E4 29 07N 47 02E
Algeciras Sp. 87 C2 36 08N 5 27W
ALGERIA 108 C13
Alghero Italy 89 B4 40 34N 8 19E
Algiers Algeria 108 E15 36 50N 3 00E
Al Hadīthah Iraq 96 D5 34 06N 42 25E
Al Hariq Saudi Arabia 97 E3 23 34N 46 35E
Al Ḩasakah Syria 96 D6 36 32N 40 44E
Al Ḩillah Iraq 96 D5 32 28N 44 29E
Al Hufūf Saudi Arabia 97 E4 25 20N 49 34E
Aliákmanas *r.* Greece 89 J4 40 00N 22 00E
Alicante Sp. 87 E3 38 21N 0 29W
Alice Texas USA 71 G2 27 45N 98 06W
Alice Springs *tn.* Aust. 110 E5 23 42S 133 52E
Aligarh India 98 D5 27 54N 78 04E
Aling Kangri *mt.* China 100 E5 32 51N 81 03E
Alipur Duar India 99 K11 26 27N 89 38E
Al Jahrah Kuwait 97 E4 29 22N 47 40E
Al Jawf Libya 108 J12 24 12N 23 18E
Al Jawf Saudi Arabia 96 C4 29 49N 39 52E
Al Jubayl Saudi Arabia 97 E4 26 59N 49 40E
Aljustrel Port. 87 A2 37 52N 8 10W
Al Karāmah Jordan 96 N10 31 58N 35 34E
Al Khums Libya 108 G14 32 39N 14 16E
Al Kufrah Oasis Libya 108 J12 24 10N 23 15E
Al Kūt Iraq 96 E5 32 30N 45 51E
Allagash River Maine USA 53 S6 46 45N 69 20W
Allahabad India 98 E5 25 27N 81 50E
Allegheny River Pennsylvania USA 52 G1 41 40N 79 30W
Allegheny Mountains Pennsylvania USA 73 A2 40 30N 78 25W
Allegheny Reservoir Pennsylvania/New York USA 51 M1 41 52N 79 00W
Allende Mexico 74 D5 28 22N 100 50W
Allentown Pennsylvania USA 71 L5 40 37N 75 30W
Alleppey India 98 D1 9 30N 76 22E
Alliance Nebraska USA 70 F5 42 08N 102 54W
Allier *r.* Fr. 87 G7 46 40N 3 00E
Al Līth Saudi Arabia 96 D3 20 10N 40 20E
Alma Michigan USA 52 B3 43 23N 84 40W
Almada Port. 87 A3 38 40N 9 09W
Almadén Sp. 87 C3 38 47N 4 50W
Almansa Sp. 87 E3 38 52N 1 06W
Almanzora *r.* Sp. 87 D2 37 15N 2 10W
Almaty Kazakhstan 94 K5 43 19N 76 55E
Almería Sp. 87 D2 36 50N 2 26W
Älmhult Sweden 88 E12 56 32N 14 10E
Almodôvar Port. 87 A2 37 31N 8 03W
Al Mubarraz Saudi Arabia 97 E4 25 26N 49 37E
Al Mukhā Yemen 96 D1 13 20N 43 16E
Al Muqdādīyah Iraq 96 D5 33 58N 44 58E
Alor *i.* Indonesia 103 G2 8 15S 124 30E
Alor Setar Malaysia 103 C5 6 07N 100 21E
Alpena Michigan USA 51 K3 45 03N 83 27W
Alpes Maritimes *mts.* Fr./Italy 87 J5/J6 44 15N 6 45E
Alpi Carniche *mts.* Europe 89 D7 46 00N 13 00E
Alpi Cozie *mts.* Europe 87 J6 45 00N 8 00E
Alpi Dolomitiche *mts.* Italy 89 C7 46 00N 12 00E
Alpi Graie *mts.* Europe 89 A6 45 00N 7 00E
Alpi Lepontine *mts.* Switz. 87 K7 46 26N 8 30E
Alpine Texas USA 70 F3 30 22N 103 40W
Alpi Pennine *mts.* Italy/Switz. 87 J7 45 55N 7 30E
Alpi Retiche *mts.* Switz. 87 K7/L7 46 25N 9 45E
Alps *mts.* Europe 87 J6/L7 46 00N 7 30E
Al Qāmishlī Syria 96 D6 37 03N 41 15E
Al Qunayţirah Syria 96 N11 33 08N 35 49E
Al Qunfudhah Saudi Arabia 96 D2 19 09N 41 07E
Alsek River Alaska USA 42 A6 59 15N 138 40W
Alta Gracia Argentina 81 E7 31 42S 64 25W
Altai *mts.* Mongolia 100 G8 47 00N 92 30E
Altamaha *r.* Georgia USA 71 K3 32 00N 82 00W
Altamira Brazil 80 G13 3 13S 52 15W
Altamura Italy 89 F4 40 49N 16 34E
Altay China 100 F8 47 48N 88 07E
Altay *mts.* Russia 95 L7 51 00N 89 00E
Alto Molocue Mozambique 109 M4 15 38S 37 42E
Altoona Pennsylvania USA 71 L5 40 32N 78 32W
Alto Purus *r.* Peru 80 C11 10 30S 72 00W
Altun Shan *mts.* China 100 E6/F6 37 30N 86 00E
Altus Oklahoma USA 70 G3 34 39N 99 21W
Alva Oklahoma USA 71 G4 36 48N 98 40W
Al Wajh Saudi Arabia 96 C4 26 16N 36 28E
Alwar India 98 D5 27 32N 76 35E
Amadeus, Lake Aust. 110 E5 24 00S 132 30E
Amadi Sudan 108 L9 5 32N 30 20E
Amagasaki Japan 102 C1 34 42N 135 23E
Amakusa-shotō *is.* Japan 102 B1 32 50N 130 05E
Amapá Brazil 80 G14 2 00N 50 50W
Amapá *admin.* Brazil 80 G14 2 00N 52 30W
Amargosa Desert Nevada USA 72 E3 36 45N 116 37W
Amargosa Valley *tn.* Nevada USA 72 E3 36 40N 116 22W
Amarillo Texas USA 70 F4 35 14N 101 50W
Amazonas *admin.* Brazil 80 D13 4 30S 65 00W
Amazonas *r.* Brazil 80 G13 2 00S 53 00W
Amazon, Mouths of the *est.* Brazil 80 G14 1 00N 51 00W
Ambala India 98 D6 30 19N 76 49E
Ambarchik Russia 95 U10 69 39N 162 37E
Ambato Ecuador 80 B13 1 18S 78 39W
Ambon Indonesia 103 H3 3 41S 128 10E
Ambovombe Madagascar 109 P2 25 10S 46 06E
Amboy California USA 72 F2 34 33N 115 44W
Amderma Russia 94 J10 66 44N 61 35E
Amdo China 100 G5 32 22N 91 07E
Ameca Mexico 74 D4 20 34N 104 03W
American Falls *tn.* Idaho USA 70 D5 42 47N 112 50W
American Samoa Pacific Ocean 115 K6 15 00S 170 00W
Amery Ice Shelf Antarctica 117 70 00S 70 00E
Amfípoli Greece 89 J4 40 48N 23 52E
Amga Russia 95 R9 61 51N 131 59E
Amga *r.* Russia 95 R9 60 30N 130 00E
Amgun' *r.* Russia 95 R7 52 00N 137 00E
Amiens Fr. 86 G8 49 54N 2 18E
Amindivi Islands India 98 C2 11 23N 72 23E
Amirante Islands Seychelles 113 E6 5 00S 55 00E
Amman Jordan 96 C5 31 04N 46 17E
Amorgós *i.* Greece 89 K2 36 50N 25 55E
Ampana Indonesia 103 G3 0 54S 121 35E
Amravati India 98 D4 20 58N 77 50E
Amritsar India 98 C6 31 35N 74 56E
Amsterdam Neths. 86 H10 52 22N 4 54E
Amsterdam New York USA 73 C3 42 57N 74 11W
Amstetten Austria 88 E8 48 08N 14 52E
Am Timan Chad 108 J10 10 59N 20 18E
Amudar'ya *r.* Asia 94 J4/J5 40 00N 64 00E
Amundsen Sea Southern Ocean 117 72 00S 130 00W
Amur *r.* Asia 101 P9 52 30N 126 30E
Amursk Russia 95 R7 50 16N 136 55E
Anabar *r.* Russia 95 P11 71 30N 113 00E
Anacapa Islands California USA 72 D2 34 01N 119 23W
Anaconda Montana USA 70 D6 46 09N 112 56W
Anacortes Washington USA 42 H4 48 29N 122 35W
Anadolu Dağlari *mts.* Turkey 96 C7/D7 40 30N 38 30E
Anadyr' Russia 95 V9 64 50N 178 00E
Anadyr' *r.* Russia 95 V10 65 00N 175 00E
Anadyr', Gulf of Russia 95 W9 65 00N 178 00W
Anáfi *i.* Greece 89 K2 36 20N 25 45E
Anaheim California USA 72 E1 33 50N 117 54W
Anai Mudi *mt.* India 98 D2 10 20N 77 15E
Anan Japan 102 B1 33 54N 134 40E
Ananindeua Brazil 80 H13 1 22S 48 20W
Anantapur India 98 D2 14 42N 77 05E
Anápolis Brazil 80 H10 16 19S 48 58W
Ancona Italy 89 D5 43 37N 13 31E
Andaman and Nicobar *admin.* India 99 G1 12 30N 92 45E
Andaman Islands India 99 G2 12 00N 94 00E
Anderson South Carolina USA 71 K3 34 30N 82 39W
Anderson Indiana USA 71 J5 40 05N 85 41W
Andes *mts.* South America 80/81 B14 10 00S 77 00W
Andhra Pradesh *admin.* India 98 D3 16 00N 79 00E
Andizhan Uzbekistan 94 K5 40 40N 72 12E
Andkhvoy Afghanistan 97 J6 36 59N 65 08E
ANDORRA 87 F5
Andorra la Vella Andorra 87 F5 42 30N 1 30E
Andros *i.* Bahamas 75 J4 24 00N 78 00W
Ándros *i.* Greece 89 K2 37 49N 24 54E
Androscoggin River Maine USA 57 E1 44 27N 70 50W
Andújar Sp. 87 C3 38 02N 4 03W
Andulo Angola 109 H5 11 29S 16 43E
Angara *r.* Russia 95 M8 58 00N 97 30E
Angarsk Russia 95 N7 52 31N 103 55E
Angel de la Guarda *i.* Mexico 74 B5 29 00N 113 30W
Angelholm Sweden 88 D12 56 15N 12 50E
Angels Camp California USA 72 C4 38 04N 120 34W
Angers Fr. 87 E7 47 29N 0 32W
Anglesey *i.* UK 86 C10 53 18N 4 25W
ANGOLA 109 H5
Angola Indiana USA 51 J1 41 38N 84 59W
Angola New York USA 52 G2 42 39N 79 02W
Angola Basin Atlantic Ocean 116 J5 15 00S 3 00E
Angoon Alaska USA 42 C5 57 30N 133 35W
Angoulême Fr. 87 F6 45 40N 0 10E
Anguilla *i.* Leeward Islands 74 P10 18 14N 63 05W
Anjō Japan 102 C1 34 56N 137 05E
Ankara Turkey 96 B6 39 55N 32 50E
Ankaratra *mt.* Madagascar 109 P4 19 25S 47 12E
'Annaba Algeria 108 F15 36 55N 7 47E
An Nabk Saudi Arabia 96 C5 31 21N 37 20E
An Nabk Syria 96 C5 34 02N 36 43E
An Nafud *d.* Saudi Arabia 96 D4 28 20N 40 30E
An Najaf Iraq 96 D5 31 59N 44 19E
Annapolis Maryland USA 71 L4 38 59N 76 30W
Annapurna *mt.* Nepal 98 E5 28 34N 83 50E
Ann Arbor Michigan USA 51 K2 42 17N 83 45W
An Nāsirīyah Iraq 96 E5 31 04N 46 17E
Annecy Fr. 87 J6 45 54N 6 07E
Annette Island Alaska USA 42 E4 55 10N 131 30W
Anniston Alabama USA 71 J3 33 38N 85 50W
Annotto Bay *tn.* Jamaica 75 U14 18 16N 76 47W
Anqing China 101 M5 30 46N 119 40E
Ansbach Germany 88 C8 49 18N 10 36E
Anshan China 101 N7 41 05N 122 58E
Anshun China 101 K4 26 15N 105 51E
Antakya Turkey 96 C6 36 12N 36 10E
Antalya Turkey 96 B6 36 53N 30 42E
Antananarivo Madagascar 109 P4 18 52S 47 30E
Antarctica 117
Antarctic Peninsula Antarctica 117 68 00S 65 00W
Antequera Sp. 87 C2 37 01N 4 34W
Antibes Fr. 87 J5 43 35N 7 07E
Antigua Guatemala 74 F2 14 33N 90 42W
Antigua *i.* Antigua & Barbuda 74 Q9 17 09N 61 49W
ANTIGUA AND BARBUDA 74 Q9
Antioch California USA 72 C4 38 00N 121 49W
Antipodes Islands Southern Ocean 114 H3 49 42S 178 50E
Antofagasta Chile 80 C9 23 40S 70 23W
Antsiranana Madagascar 109 P5 12 19S 49 17E

Antwerp New York USA	53	L4	44 13N	75 38W
Antwerpen Belgium	86	H9	51 13N	4 25W
Anuradhapura Sri Lanka	98	E1	8 20N	80 25E
Anxi China	100	H7	40 32N	95 57E
Anyang China	101	L6	36 04N	114 20E
Anza California USA	72	E1	33 33N	116 41W
Anzhero-Sudzhensk Russia	95	L8	56 10N	86 01E
Aomori Japan	102	D3	40 50N	140 43E
Aosta Italy	89	A6	45 43N	7 19E
Aozou Strip Chad	108	H12	23 00N	17 00E
Apaporis *r.* Col.	80	C14	1 00N	72 30W
Aparri Philippines	103	G7	18 22N	121 40E
Apatity Russia	94	F10	67 32N	33 21E
Apatzingán Mexico	74	D3	19 05N	102 20W
Apostle Islands Wisconsin USA	51	F4	47 02N	90 30W
Appalachian Mountains USA	71	K4	37 00N	82 00W
Appennini *mts.* Italy	89	B6/E4	43 00N	12 30E
Appennino Abruzzese *mts.* Italy	89	D5/E4	42 00N	14 00E
Appennino Ligure *mts.* Italy	89	B6	44 00N	9 00E
Appennino Lucano *mts.* Italy	89	E4	40 30N	15 30E
Appennino Tosco-Emiliano *mts.* Italy	89	C6/D5	44 00N	12 00E
Appleton Wisconsin USA	71	J5	44 17N	88 24W
Apure *r.* Venezuela	80	D15	7 40N	68 00W
'Aqaba Jordan	96	C5	29 32N	35 00E
Aqaba, Gulf of Middle East	96	N9	28 40N	34 40E
Aquidauana Brazil	80	F9	20 27S	55 45W
Aquidauana *r.* Brazil	80	F10	20 00S	56 00W
Arabian Basin Indian Ocean	113	F7/F8	10 00N	65 00E
Arabian Sea Indian Ocean	113	F8	17 00N	60 00E
Aracaju Brazil	80	K11	10 54S	37 07W
Aracati Brazil	80	K13	4 32S	37 45W
Arad Romania	89	H7	46 10N	21 19E
Arafura Sea Indonesia	103	J2	8 00S	132 00E
Aragón *r.* Sp.	87	E5	42 15N	1 40W
Araguaia *r.* Brazil	80	H12	7 20S	49 00W
Araguaína Brazil	80	H12	7 16S	48 18W
Araguari Brazil	80	H10	18 38S	48 13W
Arāk Iran	97	E5	34 05N	49 42E
Aral Sea *l.* Asia	94	H5/J6	45 00N	60 00E
Aral'sk Kazakhstan	94	J6	46 56N	61 43E
Arambag India	99	K9	22 50N	87 59E
Aranda de Duero Sp.	87	D4	41 40N	3 41W
Aran Islands RoI	86	A10	53 10N	9 50W
Aranjuez Sp.	87	D4	40 02N	3 37W
Arapiraca Brazil	80	K12	9 45S	36 40W
Ar'ar Saudi Arabia	96	D5	30 58N	41 03E
Araraquara Brazil	80	H9	21 46S	48 08W
Ararat, Mount Turkey	96	D6	39 44N	44 15E
Aras *r.* Turkey	96	D7	40 00N	43 30E
Arauca Col.	80	C15	7 04N	70 41W
Arauca *r.* Venezuela	80	D15	7 10N	68 30W
Araxá Brazil	80	H10	19 37S	46 50W
Araz *r.* Iran	96	E6	38 40N	46 30E
Arbil Iraq	96	D6	36 12N	44 01E
Arcachon Fr.	87	E6	44 40N	1 11W
Arcade New York USA	52	H2	42 32N	78 25W
Arctic National Wildlife Refuge Alaska USA	40	F7/G7	68 30N	144 30W
Arctic Ocean	117			
Arda *r.* Bulgaria	89	K4	41 30N	26 00E
Ardabil Iran	97	E6	38 15N	48 18E
Ardennes *mts.* Belgium	86	H9/J9	50 10N	5 45E
Ardila *r.* Sp.	87	B3	38 15N	6 50W
Ardmore Oklahoma USA	71	G3	34 11N	97 08W
Arendal Norway	86	K13	58 27N	8 56E
Arequipa Peru	80	C10	16 25S	71 32W
Arezzo Italy	89	C5	43 28N	11 53E
Argentan Fr.	86	E8	48 45N	0 01W
ARGENTINA	81	D6		
Argentine Basin Atlantic Ocean	116	J3	42 00S	45 00W
Argeș *r.* Romania	89	K6	44 00N	26 00E
Argun *r.* Asia	101	M9	51 30N	120 00E
Argyle, Lake Aust.	110	D6	17 00S	128 30E
Århus Denmark	88	C12	56 15N	10 10E
Arica Chile	80	C10	18 30S	70 20W
Arima Trinidad and Tobago	75	V15	10 38N	61 17W
Aripuanã *r.* Brazil	80	E12	7 00S	60 30W
Ariquemes Brazil	80	E12	9 55S	63 06W
Arizona *state* USA	70	D3	34 00N	112 00W
Arizpe Mexico	74	B6	30 20N	110 11W
Arjona Col.	80	B16	10 14N	75 22W
Arkalyk Kazakhstan	94	J7	50 17N	66 51E
Arkansas *r.* USA	70	G4	36 00N	99 00W
Arkansas *state* USA	71	H3	34 00N	93 00W
Arkansas City Kansas USA	71	G4	37 03N	97 02W
Arkhangel'sk Russia	94	G9	64 32N	40 40E
Arklow RoI	86	B10	52 48N	6 09W
Arlanza *r.* Sp.	87	D5	42 00N	3 30W
Arlanzón *r.* Sp.	87	D5	42 00N	4 00W
Arles Fr.	87	H5	43 41N	4 38E
Arlington Washington USA	42	H4	48 08N	122 15W
Arlit Niger	108	F11	18 50N	7 00E
Arlon Belgium	86	H8	49 41N	5 49E
Armagh UK	86	B11	54 21N	6 39W
Armavir Russia	94	G5	44 59N	41 40E
ARMENIA	94	G5		
Armenia Col.	80	B14	4 32N	75 40W
Armenia Mountain Pennsylvania USA	53	K1	41 45N	76 55W
Armidale Aust.	110	J3	30 32S	151 40E
Arnhem Neths.	86	H9	52 00N	5 53E
Arnhem Land *geog. reg.* Aust.	110	E7	13 00S	133 00E
Arno *r.* Italy	89	C5	43 00N	10 00E
Arnold California USA	72	C4	38 15N	120 20W
Aroostook River Maine USA	57	F2	46 48N	68 30W
Arquipélago dos Bijagós *is.* Guinea-Bissau	108	A10	11 20N	16 40W
Ar Ramādī Iraq	96	D5	33 27N	43 19E
Ar Ramlah Jordan	96	N9	29 28N	25 58E
Arran *i.* UK	86	C11	55 35N	5 15W
Ar Raqqah Syria	96	C6	35 57N	39 03E
Arras Fr.	86	G9	50 17N	2 46E
Arroyo Grande California USA	72	C2	35 08N	120 34W
Árta Greece	89	H3	39 10N	20 59E
Artigas Uruguay	81	F7	30 25S	56 28W
Arua Uganda	108	L8	3 02N	30 56E
Aruba *i.* Neths.	80	C16	12 30N	70 00W
Arunachal Pradesh *admin.* India	99	G5/H5	28 00N	95 00E
Arusha Tanzania	108	M7	3 23S	36 40E
Aruwimi *r.* CDR	108	K8	2 00N	25 00E
Arvika Sweden	88	D13	59 41N	12 38E
Arvin California USA	72	D2	35 11N	118 50W
Asahi-dake *mt.* Japan	102	D3	43 42N	142 54E
Asahikawa Japan	102	D3	43 46N	142 23E
Asamankese Ghana	108	D9	5 45N	0 45W
Asansol India	99	F4	23 40N	86 59E
Asbury Park *tn.* New Jersey USA	73	C2	40 14N	74 00W
Ascension Island Atlantic Ocean	116	G6	7 57S	14 22W
Ascoli Piceno Italy	89	D5	42 52N	13 35E
Assab Eritrea	108	N10	13 01N	42 47E
Asenovgrad Bulgaria	89	K4	42 00N	24 53E
Ashburton NZ	111	C3	43 54S	171 45E
Ashburton *r.* Aust.	110	B5	22 30S	116 00E
Ashdod Israel	96	N10	31 48N	34 48E
Asheville North Carolina USA	71	K4	35 35N	82 35W
Ash Fork Arizona USA	70	D4	35 13N	112 29W
Ashgabat Turkmenistan	94	H4	37 58N	58 24E
Ashikaga Japan	102	C2	36 21N	139 26E
Ashizuri-misaki *c.* Japan	102	B1	32 42N	133 00E
Ashland Kentucky USA	71	K4	38 28N	82 40W
Ashland Oregon USA	70	B5	42 14N	122 44W
Ashland Wisconsin USA	51	F4	46 35N	90 53W
Ashqelon Israel	96	N10	31 40N	34 35E
Ash Springs *tn.* Nevada USA	72	F3	37 32N	115 12W
Ashtabula Ohio USA	51	L1	41 52N	80 48W
Askim Norway	86	L13	59 15N	11 10E
Asmara Eritrea	108	M11	15 20N	38 58E
Assam *admin.* India	99	G5	26 20N	92 00E
As Samāwah Iraq	96	E5	31 18N	45 18E
Assis Brazil	80	G9	22 37S	50 25W
Assisi Italy	89	D5	43 04N	12 37E
As Sulaymaniyah Iraq	96	E6	35 32N	45 27E
As Sūq Saudi Arabia	96	D3	21 55N	42 02E
As Suwaydā' Syria	96	P11	32 43N	36 33E
Astana Kazakhstan	94	K7	51 10N	71 28E
Asti Italy	89	B6	44 54N	8 13E
Astoria Oregon USA	70	B6	46 12N	123 50W
Astrakhan' Russia	94	G6	46 22N	48 04E
Astypálaia *i.* Greece	89	L2	36 30N	26 20E
Asunción Paraguay	80	F8	25 15S	57 40W
Aswa *r.* Uganda	108	L8	3 30N	32 30E
Aswân Egypt	108	L12	24 05N	32 56E
Aswân Dam Egypt	108	L12	23 40N	31 50E
Asyût Egypt	108	L13	27 14N	31 07E
Atar Mauritania	108	B12	20 32N	13 08W
Atascadero California USA	72	C2	35 30N	120 40W
Atbara Sudan	108	L11	17 42N	34 00E
Atbara *r.* Sudan	108	M11	17 28N	34 30E
Atbasar Kazakhstan	94	J7	51 49N	68 18E
Atchison Kansas USA	71	G4	39 33N	95 09W
Athens Greece	89	J2	38 00N	23 44E
Athens Georgia USA	71	K3	33 57N	83 24W
Athens Pennsylvania USA	53	K1	41 57N	76 31W
Athlone RoI	86	B10	53 25N	7 56W
Athol Springs *tn.* New York USA	54	D1	42 45N	78 49W
Áthos *mt.* Greece	89	K4	40 10N	24 19E
Ati Chad	108	H10	13 11N	18 20E
Atlanta Georgia USA	71	K3	33 45N	84 23W
Atlanta Michigan USA	51	J3	45 00N	84 08W
Atlantic City New Jersey USA	71	M4	39 23N	74 27W
Atlantic-Indian Ridge Atlantic Ocean	116	H1/K1	53 00S	3 00E
Atlantic Ocean	116			
Atlas Saharien *mts.* Algeria	108	D14	33 30N	1 00E
Atrai *r.* India/Bangladesh	99	K10	25 10N	88 50E
At Tā'if Saudi Arabia	96	D3	21 15N	40 21E
Attica New York USA	52	H2	42 52N	78 17W
Atyrau Kazakhstan	94	H6	47 08N	51 59E
Aubagne Fr.	87	H5	43 17N	5 35E
Aubenas Fr.	87	H6	44 37N	4 24E
Auburn Indiana USA	52	A1	41 22N	85 02W
Auburn Maine USA	71	M5	44 04N	70 27W
Auburn Massachusetts USA	73	E3	42 11N	71 51W
Auburn New York USA	71	L5	42 57N	76 34W
Auburn Reservoir California USA	72	C4	39 05N	120 55W
Auch Fr.	87	F5	43 40N	0 36E
Auckland NZ	111	E6	36 51S	174 46E
Auckland Islands Southern Ocean	114	G2	50 35S	116 00E
Aude *r.* Fr.	87	G5	43 00N	2 00E
Au Gres Michigan USA	52	C3	44 03N	83 40W
Augsburg Germany	88	C8	48 21N	10 54E
Augusta Aust.	110	B3	34 19S	115 09E
Augusta Georgia USA	71	K3	33 29N	82 00W
Augusta Maine USA	71	N5	44 17N	69 50W
Aulne *r.* Fr.	86	D8	48 10N	4 00W
Aurangābād India	98	D3	19 52N	75 22E
Aurillac Fr.	87	G6	44 56N	2 26E
Au Sable Michigan USA	51	K3	44 23N	83 20W
Au Sable *r.* Michigan USA	51	J3	44 39N	84 08W
Austin Nevada USA	72	E4	39 30N	117 05W
Austin Texas USA	71	G3	30 18N	97 47W
AUSTRALIA	110			
Australian Capital Territory *admin.* Aust.	110	H2	35 00S	144 00E
AUSTRIA	88/89	D7/E7		
Autlán Mexico	74	D3	19 48N	104 20W
Autun Fr.	87	H7	46 58N	4 18E
Auxerre Fr.	86	G7	47 48N	3 35E
Avallon Fr.	87	G7	47 30N	3 54E
Avalon California USA	72	D1	33 21N	118 19W
Avawatz Mountains California USA	72	E2	35 32N	116 30W
Aveiro Port.	87	A4	40 38N	8 40W
Avellaneda Argentina	81	F7	34 40S	58 20W
Avenal California USA	72	C3	36 00N	120 10W
Avesta Sweden	88	F14	60 09N	16 10E
Aveyron *r.* Fr.	87	G6	44 30N	2 05E
Avezzano Italy	89	D5	42 02N	13 26E
Avila Sp.	87	C4	40 39N	4 42W
Avilés Sp.	87	C5	43 33N	5 55W
Avon Lake *tn.* Ohio USA	52	D1	41 31N	82 01W
Avranches Fr.	86	E8	48 42N	1 21W
Awali *r.* Lebanon	96	N11	33 35N	35 32E
Awash Ethiopia	108	N9	9 01N	41 10E
Awash *r.* Ethiopia	108	N9	10 00N	40 00E
Awa-shima *i.* Japan	102	C2	38 40N	139 15E
Awbārī Libya	108	G13	26 35N	12 46E
Ayacucho Peru	80	C11	13 10S	74 15W
Ayaguz Kazakhstan	94	L6	47 59N	80 27E
Ayamonte Sp.	87	B2	37 13N	7 24W
Ayan Russia	95	R8	56 29N	138 07E
Ayaviri Peru	80	C11	14 53S	70 35W
Ayers Rock *mt.* Aust.	110	E4	25 18S	131 18E
'Aynūnah Saudi Arabia	96	C4	28 06N	35 08E
Ayod Sudan	108	L9	8 08N	31 24E
Ayon *i.* Russia	95	U10	69 55N	169 10E
Ayr UK	86	C11	55 28N	4 38W
Ayutthaya Thailand	103	C6	14 20N	100 35E
AZERBAIJAN	94	G4		
Aziscohos Lake Maine USA	53	R5	45 08N	70 59W
Azogues Ecuador	80	B13	2 46S	78 56W
Azores *is.* Atlantic Ocean	116	F10	38 30N	28 00W
Azoum *r.* Chad	108	J10	12 00N	21 00E
Azuero, Peninsula de Panama	75	H1	7 40N	81 00W
Azul Argentina	81	F6	36 46S	59 50W
Azurduy Bolivia	80	E10	20 00S	64 29W
Az Zabadānī Syria	96	P11	33 42N	36 03E

B

Ba'albek Lebanon	96	P12	34 00N	36 12E
Babahoyo Ecuador	80	B13	1 53S	79 31W
Bab el Mandab *sd.* Red Sea	108	N10	12 30N	47 00E
Babylon *hist. site* Iraq	96	D5	32 33N	44 25E
Bacabal Brazil	80	J13	4 15S	44 45W
Bacău Romania	89	L7	46 33N	26 58E
Bacolod Philippines	103	G6	10 38N	122 58E
Badajoz Sp.	87	B3	38 53N	6 58W
Badalona Sp.	87	G4	41 27N	2 15E
Bad Axe Michigan USA	51	K2	43 48N	82 59W
Baden Austria	88	F7	48 01N	16 14E
Badulla Sri Lanka	98	E1	6 59N	81 03E
Bafoussam Cameroon	108	G9	5 31N	10 25E
Bāfq Iran	97	G5	31 35N	55 21E
Bagé Brazil	81	G7	31 22S	54 06W
Baghdad Iraq	96	D5	33 20N	44 26E
Baghlān Afghanistan	97	J6	36 11N	68 44E
BAHAMAS, THE	75	J4		
Baharampur India	99	K10	24 06N	88 15E
Bahawalpur Pakistan	98	C5	29 24N	71 47E
Bahia *admin.* Brazil	80	J11	12 00S	42 30W
Bahía Blanca Argentina	81	E6	38 45S	62 15W
Bahía Blanca *b.* Argentina	81	E6	39 00S	61 00W
Bahía de Campeche *b.* Mexico	74	E4/F4	20 00N	95 00W
Bahía Grande *b.* Argentina	81	D3	51 30S	68 00W
Bahra el Manzala Lake Egypt	109	R4	31 18N	31 54E
Bahraich India	98	E5	27 35N	81 36E
BAHRAIN	97	F4		
Bahrain, Gulf of The Gulf	97	F4	25 55N	50 30E
Bahr el Abiad *r.* Sudan	108	L10	14 00N	32 20E
Bahr el Arab *r.* Sudan	108	K9	10 00N	27 30E
Bahr el Azraq *r.* Sudan	108	L10	13 30N	33 45E
Bahr el Baqar *r.* Egypt	109	S3	30 54N	32 02E
Bahr el Ghazal *r.* Chad	108	H10	14 00N	16 00E
Bahr Faqus *r.* Egypt	109	R3	30 42N	31 42E
Bahr Hadus *r.* Egypt	109	R4	31 01N	31 43E
Bahr Saft *r.* Egypt	109	R3	30 57N	31 48E
Baia Mare Romania	88	J7	47 39N	23 36E
Baicheng China	101	N8	45 37N	122 48E
Baie de la Seine *b.* Fr.	86	E8	49 40N	0 30W
Baja Hungary	89	G7	46 11N	18 58E
Baja California *p.* Mexico	74	A6/C4	27 30N	113 00W
Baker California USA	72	E2	35 16N	116 06W
Baker Oregon USA	70	C5	44 46N	117 50W
Baker Island Alaska USA	42	D4	55 30N	133 30W
Baker Islands Pacific Ocean	114	J8	0 30N	173 00W
Baker, Mount Washington USA	42	H4	48 48N	121 50W
Baker River Washington USA	42	H4	48 40N	121 30W
Bakersfield California USA	70	C4	35 25N	119 00W
Balaghat India	98	E4	21 48N	80 16E
Balaghat Range *mts.* India	98	D3	18 45N	77 00E
Balakovo Russia	94	G7	52 04N	47 46E
Balama Mozambique	109	M5	13 19S	38 35E
Bala Morghab Afghanistan	97	H6	35 35N	63 21E
Balassagyarmat Hungary	88	G7	48 06N	19 17E
Balaton *l.* Hungary	89	F7	47 00N	17 30E
Balboa Panama	75	J1	8 57N	79 33W
Balclutha NZ	111	B1	46 14S	169 44E
Balearic Islands Mediterranean Sea	87	F3/H3	40 00N	2 00E
Bali *i.* Indonesia	103	E2/F2	8 30S	115 00E
Balikesir Turkey	96	A6	39 37N	27 51E
Balikpapan Indonesia	103	F3	1 15S	116 50E
Balipar India	99	M11	27 00N	92 30E
Balkhash Kazakhstan	94	K6	46 50N	74 57E
Ballarat Aust.	110	G2	37 36S	143 58E
Balleny Islands Southern Ocean	114	G1	66 30S	164 00E
Ballymena UK	86	B11	54 52N	6 17W
Balsas Mexico	74	E3	18 00N	99 44W
Balta Ukraine	88	M7	47 58N	29 39E
Bălți Moldova	88	L7	47 44N	28 41E
Baltic Sea Europe	88	G12	55 15N	17 00E
Baltimore Maryland USA	71	L4	39 18N	76 38W
Baluchistan *geog. reg.* Pakistan	98	A5	27 30N	65 00E
Balurghat India	99	K10	25 12N	88 50E
Bam Iran	97	G4	29 07N	58 20E
Bamako Mali	108	C10	12 40N	7 59W
Bambari CAR	108	J9	5 40N	20 37E
Bamberg Germany	88	C8	49 54N	10 54E
Bamenda Cameroon	108	G9	5 55N	10 09E
Banas *r.* India	98	D5	26 00N	75 00E
Banda Aceh Indonesia	103	B5	5 30N	95 20E
Bandama Blanc *r.* Côte d'Ivoire	108	C9	8 00N	5 45W
Bandar-e 'Abbās Iran	97	G4	27 12N	56 15E
Bandar-e Lengeh Iran	97	F4	26 34N	54 52E
Bandar-e Torkeman Iran	97	F6	36 55N	54 01E
Bandar Khomeynī Iran	97	E5	30 40N	49 08E
Bandar Seri Begawan Brunei	103	F4	4 53N	115 00E
Banda Sea Indonesia	103	H2	5 50S	126 00E
Bandirma Turkey	96	A7	40 21N	27 58E
Bandundu CDR	108	H7	3 20S	17 24E
Bandung Indonesia	103	D2	6 57S	107 34E
Banfora Burkina	108	D10	10 36N	4 45W
Bangalore India	98	D2	12 58N	77 35E
Bangassou CAR	108	J8	4 41N	22 48E
Bangkok Thailand	103	C6	13 44N	100 30E
BANGLADESH	99	F4/G4		
Bangor Wales UK	86	C10	53 13N	4 08W
Bangor Northern Ireland UK	86	C11	54 40N	5 40W
Bangor Maine USA	71	N5	44 49N	68 47W
Bangui CAR	108	H8	4 23N	18 37E
Bangweulu, Lake Zambia	109	K5	11 15S	29 45E
Banja Luka Bosnia-Herzegovina	89	F6	44 47N	17 11E
Banjarmasin Indonesia	103	E3	3 22S	114 33E
Banjul The Gambia	108	A10	13 28N	16 39W
Banmi Pakistan	98	C6	33 00N	70 30E
Banning California USA	72	E1	33 55N	116 52W
Banská Bystrica Slovakia	88	G8	48 44N	19 10E
Banyuwangi Indonesia	103	E2	8 12S	114 22E
Baoding China	101	M6	38 54N	115 26E
Baoji China	101	K5	34 23N	107 16E
Baotou China	101	K7	40 38N	109 59E
Ba'qūbah Iraq	96	D5	33 45N	44 40E
Baracaldo Sp.	87	D5	43 17N	2 59W
Barahona Dom. Rep.	75	K3	18 13N	71 07W
Barakpur India	99	K9	22 45N	88 23E
Baral *r.* Bangladesh	99	K10	24 20N	89 05E
Baranof Alaska USA	42	C5	57 05N	134 50W
Baranof Island Alaska USA	42	C5	57 30N	135 00W
Barbacena Brazil	80	J9	21 13S	43 47W
BARBADOS	74	S11		
Barbastro Sp.	87	F5	42 02N	0 07E
Barbuda *i.* Antigua & Barbuda	74	Q9	17 41N	61 48W
Barcaldine Aust.	110	H5	23 31S	145 15E
Barcellona Italy	89	E3	38 10N	15 15E
Barcelona Sp.	87	G4	41 25N	2 10E
Barcelona Venezuela	80	E16	10 08N	64 43W
Barcelonnette Fr.	87	J6	44 24N	6 40E
Barcelos Brazil	80	E13	0 59S	62 58W
Barcoo *r.* Aust.	110	G5	24 00S	144 00E
Barcs Hungary	89	F6	45 58N	17 30E
Barddhaman India	99	F4	23 20N	88 00E
Bareilly India	98	D5	28 20N	79 24E
Barents Sea Arctic Ocean	117		75 00N	40 00E
Barge Canal New York USA	52	H3	43 14N	78 23W
Barharwa India	99	J10	24 51N	87 49E
Bari Italy	89	F4	41 07N	16 52E
Barinas Venezuela	80	C15	8 36N	70 15W
Barisal Bangladesh	99	L9	22 41N	90 20E
Barkly Tableland *geog. reg.* Aust.	110	F6	17 30S	137 00E
Bârlad Romania	89	L7	46 14N	27 40E
Bar-le-Duc Fr.	86	H8	48 46N	5 10E
Barlee, Lake Aust.	110	B4	28 30S	120 00E
Barletta Italy	89	F4	41 20N	16 17E
Barnaul Russia	95	L7	53 21N	83 45E
Barnstaple UK	86	C9	51 05N	4 04W
Barpeta Road *tn.* India	99	L11	26 27N	90 56E
Barquisimeto Venezuela	80	D16	10 03N	69 18W
Barra do Corba Brazil	80	H12	5 30S	45 12W
Barrancabermeja Col.	80	C15	7 06N	73 54W
Barrancas Venezuela	80	E15	8 45N	62 13W
Barranquilla Col.	80	C16	11 10N	74 50W
Barre Vermont USA	71	M5	44 13N	72 31W
Barreiras Brazil	80	J11	12 09S	44 58W
Barreiro Port.	87	A3	38 40N	9 05W
Barron Wisconsin USA	51	F3	45 24N	91 50W
Barrow Alaska USA	40	D8	71 18N	156 43W

Barrow *r.* RoI	**86**	B10	52 38N	6 58W
Barrow-in-Furness UK	**86**	D11	54 07N	3 14W
Barrow Island Aust.	**110**	B5	21 00S	115 00E
Barry UK	**86**	D9	51 24N	3 18W
Barstow California USA	**70**	C3	34 55N	117 01W
Bartlesville Oklahoma USA	**71**	G4	36 44N	95 59W
Bartolome, Cape Alaska USA	**42**	D4	55 15N	133 39W
Basalt Nevada USA	**72**	D3	38 02N	118 18W
Basalt Island HK China	**100**	D1	22 18N	114 21E
Basel Switz.	**87**	J7	47 33N	7 36E
Basingstoke UK	**86**	E9	51 16N	1 05W
Basirhat India	**99**	K9	22 39N	88 52E
Bassas da India *i.* Mozambique Channel	**109**	M3	22 00S	40 00E
Bassein Myanmar	**103**	A7	16 46N	94 45E
Basse Terre Lesser Antilles	**74**	Q9	16 00N	61 20W
Basseterre St. Kitts and Nevis	**74**	P9	17 18N	62 43W
Basse Terre *i.* Lesser Antilles	**74**	Q9	16 10N	61 40W
Bass Strait Aust.	**110**	H2	40 00S	145 00E
Basswood Lake Minnesota USA	**51**	F5	48 00N	91 50W
Bastia Fr.	**87**	K5	42 14N	9 26E
Bastogne Belgium	**86**	H8	50 00N	5 43E
Bastrop Louisiana USA	**71**	H3	32 49N	91 54W
Bata Eq. Guinea	**108**	F8	1 51N	9 49E
Batakan Indonesia	**103**	E3	4 03S	114 39E
Batala India	**98**	D6	31 48N	75 17E
Batang China	**101**	H5	30 02N	99 01E
Batangafo CAR	**108**	H9	7 27N	18 11E
Batangas Philippines	**103**	G6	13 46N	121 01E
Batavia New York USA	**51**	M2	42 59N	78 10W
Batdâmbâng Cambodia	**103**	C6	13 06N	103 13E
Bath UK	**86**	D9	51 23N	2 22W
Bath New York USA	**53**	J2	42 20N	77 18W
Batha *r.* Chad	**108**	H10	13 00N	19 00E
Bathinda India	**98**	C6	30 10N	74 58E
Bathurst Aust.	**110**	H3	33 27S	149 35E
Bathurst Island Aust.	**110**	E7	12 00S	130 00E
Batna Algeria	**108**	F15	35 34N	6 10E
Baton Rouge Louisiana USA	**71**	H3	30 30N	91 10W
Batroûn Lebanon	**96**	N12	36 16N	35 40E
Batticaloa Sri Lanka	**98**	E1	7 43N	81 42E
Battle Creek *tn.* Michigan USA	**71**	J5	42 20N	85 21W
Bat Yam Israel	**96**	N10	31 59N	34 45E
Baubau Indonesia	**103**	G2	5 30S	122 37E
Bauchi Nigeria	**108**	F10	10 16N	9 50E
Baudette Minnesota USA	**49**	E1	48 42N	94 34W
Bauru Brazil	**80**	H9	22 19S	49 07W
Bautzen Germany	**88**	E9	51 11N	14 29E
Bayamo Cuba	**75**	J4	20 23N	76 39W
Bay City Michigan USA	**71**	K5	43 35N	83 52W
Bay City Texas USA	**71**	G2	28 59N	96 00W
Baydhabo Somalia	**108**	N8	3 08N	43 34E
Bayerische Alpen *mts.* Germany	**89**	C7	47 00N	11 00E
Bayeux Fr.	**86**	E8	49 16N	0 42W
Baykonur Kazakhstan	**94**	J6	47 50N	66 03E
Bayonne Fr.	**87**	E5	43 30N	1 28W
Bayonne New Jersey USA	**73**	H1	40 39N	74 07W
Bayreuth Germany	**88**	C8	49 27N	11 35E
Bay Ridge *tn.* New York USA	**73**	H1	40 37N	74 02W
Baytown Texas USA	**71**	H2	29 43N	94 59W
Baza Sp.	**87**	D2	37 30N	2 45W
Bcharre Lebanon	**96**	P12	34 15N	36 00E
Bear Lake USA	**70**	D5	42 00N	111 20W
Beatrice Nebraska USA	**71**	G5	40 17N	96 45W
Beatty Nevada USA	**70**	C4	36 54N	116 45W
Beaufort South Carolina USA	**71**	K3	32 26N	80 40W
Beaufort Island HK China	**100**	C1	22 11N	114 15E
Beaumont Texas USA	**71**	H3	30 04N	94 06W
Beaune Fr.	**87**	H7	47 02N	4 50E
Beauvais Fr.	**86**	G8	49 26N	2 05E
Beaver Island Michigan USA	**51**	J3	45 39N	85 30W
Béchar Algeria	**108**	D14	31 35N	2 17W
Beckley West Virginia USA	**71**	K4	37 46N	81 12W
Bedford UK	**86**	E10	52 08N	0 29W
Bedford Pennsylvania USA	**73**	A2	40 01N	78 31W
Beersheba Israel	**96**	N10	31 15N	34 47E
Beeville Texas USA	**71**	G2	28 25N	97 47W
Behbehān Iran	**97**	F5	30 34N	50 18E
Behm Canal *sd.* Alaska USA	**42**	D4/E5	56 00N	131 00W
Bei'an China	**101**	P8	48 16N	126 36E
Beihai China	**101**	K3	21 29N	109 10E
Beijing China	**101**	M6	39 55N	116 26E
Beira Mozambique	**109**	L4	19 49S	34 52E
Beirut Lebanon	**96**	N11	33 52N	35 30E
Beja Port.	**87**	B3	38 01N	7 52W
Bejaïa Algeria	**108**	F15	36 49N	5 03E
Béjar Sp.	**87**	C4	40 24N	5 45W
Békescsaba Hungary	**89**	H7	46 45N	21 09E
Bela Pakistan	**98**	B5	26 12N	66 20E
BELARUS	**94**	E7		
Belém Brazil	**80**	H13	1 27S	48 29W
Belfast UK	**86**	C11	54 35N	5 55W
Belfast Maine USA	**57**	F1	44 26N	69 01W
Belfort Fr.	**87**	J7	47 38N	6 52E
Belgaum India	**98**	C3	15 54N	74 36E
BELGIUM	**86**	G9/H9		
Belgorod Russia	**94**	F7	50 38N	36 36E
Belgrade Serbia	**89**	H6	44 50N	20 30E
BELIZE	**74**	G3		
Belize Belize	**74**	G3	17 29N	88 10W
Bellac Fr.	**87**	F7	46 07N	1 04E
Bellaire Michigan USA	**52**	A4	44 59N	85 12W
Bellary India	**98**	D3	15 11N	76 54E
Bella Vista Argentina	**81**	F8	28 31S	59 00W
Belle-Île *i.* Fr.	**87**	D7	47 20N	3 10W
Bellingham Washington USA	**70**	B6	48 45N	122 29W
Bellingshausen Sea Southern Ocean	**117**		71 00S	85 00W
Bello Col.	**80**	B15	6 20N	75 41W
Belluno Italy	**89**	D7	46 08N	12 13E
Belmopan Belize	**74**	G3	17 13N	88 48W
Belogorsk Russia	**95**	Q7	50 55N	128 26E
Belo Horizonte Brazil	**80**	J10	19 54S	43 54W
Belted Range *mts.* Nevada USA	**72**	E3	37 28N	116 05W
Belyy *i.* Russia	**94**	K11	73 00N	70 00E
Belyy Yar Russia	**95**	L8	58 28N	85 03E
Bembézar *r.* Sp.	**87**	C2/C3	38 00N	5 15W
Bemidji Minnesota USA	**71**	H6	47 29N	94 52W
Benavente Sp.	**87**	C4	42 00N	5 40W
Bend Oregon USA	**70**	B5	44 04N	121 20W
Bender-Bayla Somalia	**108**	Q9	9 30N	50 50E
Bendigo Aust.	**110**	G2	36 48S	144 21E
Benevento Italy	**89**	E4	41 08N	14 46E
Bengal, Bay of Indian Ocean	**99**	F3	17 00N	88 00E
Bengbu China	**101**	M5	32 56N	117 27E
Benghazi Libya	**108**	J14	32 07N	20 04E
Bengkulu Indonesia	**103**	C3	3 46S	102 16E
Benguela Angola	**109**	G5	12 34S	13 24E
Beni *r.* Bolivia	**80**	D11	13 00S	67 30W
Beni Abbès Algeria	**108**	D14	30 11N	2 14W
Benicarló Sp.	**87**	F4	40 25N	0 25E
Beni Mellal Morocco	**108**	C14	32 22N	6 29W
BENIN	**108**	E10		
Benin, Bight of *b.* West Africa	**108**	E9	5 50N	2 30E
Benin City Nigeria	**108**	F9	6 19N	5 41E
Beni Suef Egypt	**108**	L13	29 05N	31 05E
Benjamin Constant Brazil	**80**	C13	4 23S	69 59W
Ben Macdui *mt.* UK	**86**	D12	57 04N	3 40W
Ben Nevis *mt.* UK	**86**	C12	56 40N	5 00W
Bennington Vermont USA	**73**	D3	42 53N	73 12W
Benson Arizona USA	**70**	D3	31 58N	110 19W
Benton Harbor *tn.* Michigan USA	**71**	J5	42 07N	86 27W
Benue *r.* Nigeria/Cameroon	**108**	F9	8 00N	7 40E
Benxi China	**101**	N7	41 21N	123 45E
Beppu Japan	**102**	B1	33 18N	131 30E
Bequia *i.* Lesser Antilles	**74**	R11	13 01	61 13W
Berat Albania	**89**	H4	40 43N	19 46E
Berber Sudan	**108**	L11	18 01N	34 00E
Berbera Somalia	**108**	P10	10 28N	45 02E
Berbérati CAR	**108**	H8	4 19N	15 51E
Berck Fr.	**86**	F9	50 24N	1 35E
Berdychiv Ukraine	**88**	M8	49 54N	28 39E
Beregovo Ukraine	**88**	J8	48 13N	22 39E
Berezniki Russia	**94**	H8	59 26N	56 49E
Berezovo Russia	**94**	J9	63 58N	65 00E
Bérgamo Italy	**89**	B6	45 42N	9 40E
Bergerac Fr.	**87**	F6	44 50N	0 29E
Ber Harbor *tn.* Maine USA	**57**	F1	44 24N	68 10W
Bering Sea Pacific Ocean	**114/115**	H13	60 00N	175 00W
Berkakit Russia	**95**	Q8	56 36N	124 49E
Berkeley California USA	**72**	B3	37 53N	122 17W
Berkner Island Antarctica	**117**		80 00S	45 00W
Berlin Germany	**88**	D10	52 32N	13 25E
Berlin New Hampshire USA	**71**	M5	44 27N	71 13W
Bermejo *r.* Argentina	**80**	E8	25 00S	61 00W
Bermuda *i.* Atlantic Ocean	**116**	B10	32 50N	64 20W
Bern Switz.	**87**	J7	46 57N	7 26E
Berner Alpen *mts.* Switz.	**87**	J7/K7	46 25N	7 30E
Berryessa, Lake California USA	**72**	B4	38 37N	122 15W
Bertoua Cameroon	**108**	G8	4 34N	13 42E
Berwick Pennsylvania USA	**73**	B2	41 04N	76 15W
Berwick-upon-Tweed UK	**86**	E11	55 46N	2 00W
Besançon Fr.	**87**	H7	47 14N	6 02E
Beskidy Zachodnie *mts.* Poland	**88**	H8	50 00N	20 00E
Bethel Alaska USA	**40**	C6	60 48N	161 50W
Bethesde Maryland USA	**73**	B1	38 58N	77 06W
Bethlehem Middle East	**96**	N10	31 42N	35 12E
Bethlehem Pennsylvania USA	**73**	C2	40 37N	75 23W
Béthune Fr.	**86**	G9	50 32N	2 38E
Betsiboka *r.* Madagascar	**109**	P4	17 00S	46 30E
Beyla Guinea	**108**	C9	8 42N	8 39W
Beyşehir Gölü *l.* Turkey	**96**	B6	37 40N	31 43E
Béziers Fr.	**87**	G5	43 21N	3 13E
Bhadravati India	**98**	D2	13 54N	75 38E
Bhagalpur India	**99**	F5	25 14N	86 59E
Bhairab Bazar Bangladesh	**99**	L10	24 04N	91 00E
Bhandara India	**98**	D4	21 10N	79 41E
Bhanga Bangladesh	**99**	L9	23 24N	89 58E
Bharatpur India	**98**	D5	27 14N	77 29E
Bharuch India	**98**	C4	21 40N	73 02E
Bhatpara India	**99**	K9	22 51N	88 24E
Bhavnagar India	**98**	C4	21 46N	72 14E
Bhilwara India	**98**	C5	25 23N	74 39E
Bhima *r.* India	**98**	D3	17 00N	76 00E
Bhopal India	**98**	D4	23 17N	77 28E
Bhubaneshwar India	**99**	F4	20 13N	85 50E
Bhuj India	**98**	B4	23 12N	69 54E
Bhusawal India	**98**	D4	21 01N	75 50E
BHUTAN	**99**	G5		
Biała Podlaska Poland	**88**	J9	52 03N	23 05E
Białystok Poland	**88**	J10	53 09N	23 10E
Biarritz Fr.	**87**	E5	43 29N	1 33W
Bibai Japan	**102**	D3	43 21N	141 53E
Bida Nigeria	**108**	F9	9 06N	5 59E
Biddeford Maine USA	**71**	M5	43 29N	70 27W
Biebrza *r.* Poland	**88**	J10	53 00N	22 00E
Biel Switz.	**87**	J7	46 27N	8 13E
Bielefeld Germany	**88**	B10	52 02N	8 32E
Biella Italy	**89**	B6	45 34N	8 04E
Bielsko-Biała Poland	**88**	G8	49 50N	19 00E
Bielsk Podlaski Poland	**88**	J10	52 47N	23 11E
Biferno *r.* Italy	**89**	E4	41 00N	14 00E
Big Bay De Noc *b.* Michigan USA	**51**	H3	45 55N	86 50W
Big Black *r.* Mississippi USA	**71**	H3	33 00N	90 00W
Bigelow Mountain Maine USA	**53**	R5	45 10N	70 18W
Bighorn *r.* USA	**70**	E6	45 00N	108 00W
Bighorn Mountains USA	**70**	E5	44 00N	108 00W
Big Lake Maine USA	**57**	G1	44 10N	67 45W
Big Muddy Creek *r.* Montana USA	**47**	E1	48 50N	105 20W
Big Pine California USA	**72**	D3	37 10N	118 18W
Big Rapids *tn.* Michigan USA	**51**	J2	43 42N	85 29W
Big Sioux *r.* Minnesota/South Dakota USA	**71**	G5	44 00N	96 00W
Big Smokey Valley Nevada USA	**72**	E4	38 52N	117 08W
Big Spring *tn.* Texas USA	**70**	F3	32 15N	101 30W
Big Sur California USA	**72**	C3	36 15N	121 47W
Bihać Bosnia-Herzegovina	**89**	E6	44 49N	15 53E
Bihar *admin.* India	**99**	F5	24 40N	86 00E
Biharamulo Tanzania	**108**	L7	2 37S	31 20E
Bijapur India	**98**	D3	16 47N	75 48E
Bījār Iran	**97**	E6	35 52N	47 39E
Bikaner India	**98**	C5	28 01N	73 22E
Bilaspur India	**98**	E4	27 51N	82 00E
Bila Tserkva Ukraine	**88**	N8	49 49N	30 10E
Bilbao Sp.	**87**	D5	43 15N	2 56W
Bilibino Russia	**95**	U10	68 00N	166 15E
Billings Montana USA	**70**	E6	45 47N	108 30W
Biloxi Mississippi USA	**71**	J3	30 24N	88 55W
Binghampton New York USA	**71**	L5	42 06N	75 55W
Bintulu Malaysia	**103**	E4	3 10N	113 02E
Bioko *i.* Eq. Guinea	**108**	F8	3 00N	8 20E
Birao CAR	**108**	J10	10 11N	22 49E
Biratnagar Nepal	**99**	F5	26 27N	87 17E
Birch Lake Minnesota USA	**51**	F4	47 35N	91 55W
Birdsville Aust.	**110**	F4	25 50S	139 20E
Bīrjand Iran	**97**	G5	32 55N	59 10E
Birkenhead UK	**86**	D10	53 24N	3 02W
Birmingham UK	**86**	E10	52 30N	1 50W
Birmingham Alabama USA	**71**	J3	33 30N	86 55W
Birnin Kebbi Nigeria	**108**	E10	12 30N	4 11E
Birobidzhan Russia	**95**	R6	48 49N	132 54E
Birzai Lithuania	**88**	K12	56 12N	24 48E
Biscay, Bay of Atlantic Ocean	**87**	D6	45 30N	2 50W
Bishkek Kyrgyzstan	**94**	K5	42 53N	74 46E
Bismarck North Dakota USA	**70**	F6	46 50N	100 48W
Bismarck Archipelago *is.* PNG	**110**	H9/J9	2 00S	146 00E
Bismarck Sea PNG	**110**	H9	3 30S	148 00E
Bissau Guinea-Bissau	**108**	A10	11 52N	15 39W
Bistriţa Romania	**89**	K7	47 08N	24 30E
Bistriţa *r.* Romania	**89**	K7	47 00N	25 00E
Bitola FYROM	**89**	H4	41 01N	21 21E
Bitterroot Range *mts.* USA	**70**	D6	46 00N	114 00W
Biwa-ko *l.* Japan	**102**	C2	35 20N	135 20E
Biysk Russia	**95**	L7	52 35N	85 16E
Bizerte Tunisia	**108**	F15	37 18N	9 52E
Blackall Aust.	**110**	H5	24 23S	145 27E
Blackburn UK	**86**	D10	53 45N	2 29W
Black Lake Michigan USA	**52**	B5	45 30N	84 20W
Black Lake New York USA	**53**	L4	44 30N	75 30W
Black Point *c.* HK China	**100**	A2	22 25N	113 54E
Blackpool UK	**86**	D10	53 50N	3 03W
Black River Michigan USA	**52**	D3	43 25N	82 35W
Black River New York USA	**53**	L3	43 47N	75 30W
Black River *tn.* Jamaica	**75**	U14	18 02N	77 52W
Black Volta *r.* Africa	**108**	D9	9 00N	2 40W
Blackwell Oklahoma USA	**71**	G4	36 47N	97 18W
Blagoevgrad Bulgaria	**89**	J5	42 01N	23 05E
Blagoveshchensk Russia	**95**	Q7	50 19N	127 30E
Blaine Washington USA	**42**	H4	49 00N	122 44W
Blantyre Malawi	**109**	L4	15 46S	35 00E
Blenheim NZ	**111**	D4	41 31S	173 57E
Blida Algeria	**108**	E15	36 30N	2 50E
Bligh Water *sd.* Fiji	**114**	T16	17 00S	178 00E
Bloemfontein RSA	**109**	K2	29 07S	26 14E
Bloomfield New Jersey USA	**73**	H2	40 37N	74 10W
Bloomington Illinois USA	**71**	J5	40 29N	89 00W
Bloomington Indiana USA	**71**	J4	39 10N	86 31W
Bloomsburg Pennsylvania USA	**73**	B2	41 00N	76 27W
Bluefield West Virginia USA	**71**	K4	37 14N	81 17W
Bluefields Nicaragua	**75**	H2	12 00N	83 49W
Blue Mountains Jamaica	**75**	U14	18 00N	76 30W
Bluff NZ	**111**	B1	46 36S	168 20E
Bluff Island HK China	**100**	D1	22 19N	114 21E
Blumenau Brazil	**80**	H8	26 55S	49 07W
Blyth UK	**86**	E11	55 07N	1 30W
Blythe California USA	**70**	D3	33 38N	114 35W
Bo Sierra Leone	**108**	B9	7 58N	11 45W
Boa Vista Brazil	**80**	E14	2 49N	60 40W
Bobo Dioulasso Burkina	**108**	D10	11 11N	4 18W
Bocholt Germany	**88**	A9	51 49N	6 37E
Bodega Head *c.* California USA	**72**	B4	38 18N	123 06W
Bodélé *dep.* Chad	**108**	H11	17 00N	17 50E
Bodensee *l.* Switz.	**87**	K7	47 40N	9 30E
Bogalusa Louisiana USA	**71**	J3	30 56N	89 53W
Bogor Indonesia	**103**	D2	6 34S	106 45E
Bogotá Col.	**80**	C14	4 38N	74 05W
Bo Hai *b.* China	**101**	M6	38 30N	118 30E
Böhmer Wald *mts.* Germany	**88**	D8	49 00N	13 00E
Bohol *i.* Philippines	**103**	G5	10 00N	124 00E
Bois Blanc Island Michigan USA	**52**	B5	45 45N	84 30W
Boise Idaho USA	**70**	C5	43 38N	116 12W
Boise City Oklahoma USA	**70**	F4	36 44N	102 31W
Bokaro India	**99**	F4	23 46N	85 55E
Boké Guinea	**108**	B10	10 57N	14 13W
Bolesławiec Poland	**88**	E9	51 16N	15 34E
Bolgatanga Ghana	**108**	D10	10 44N	0 53W
Bolhrad Ukraine	**89**	M6	45 42N	28 35E
BOLIVIA	**80**	D10		
Bolmen *l.* Sweden	**88**	D12	57 00N	13 30E
Bologna Italy	**89**	C6	44 30N	11 20E
Bolzano Italy	**89**	C7	46 30N	11 22E
Boma CDR	**109**	G6	5 50S	13 03E
Bom Jesus da Lapa Brazil	**80**	J11	13 16S	43 23W
Bomu *r.* Central Africa	**108**	J8	4 50N	24 00E
Bonaire *i.* Lesser Antilles	**75**	L2	12 15N	68 27W
Bonaparte Archipelago *is.* Aust.	**110**	D7	19 00S	126 00E
Bondo CDR	**108**	J8	1 22N	23 54E
Bongor Chad	**108**	H10	10 18N	15 20E
Bonifacio Fr.	**87**	K4	41 23N	9 10E
Bonifacio, Strait of Fr./Sp.	**87**	K4	41 20N	8 45E
Bonn Germany	**88**	A9	50 44N	7 06E
Bonners Ferry *tn.* Idaho USA	**43**	M1	48 41N	116 20W
Bonny, Bight of *b.* West Africa	**108**	F8	2 10N	7 30E
Bonthe Sierra Leone	**108**	B9	7 32N	12 30W
Boosaaso Somalia	**108**	P10	11 18N	49 10E
Bor Sudan	**108**	L9	6 18N	31 34E
Borås Sweden	**88**	D12	57 44N	12 55E
Bordeaux Fr.	**87**	E6	44 50N	0 34W
Borgholm Sweden	**88**	F12	56 51N	16 40E
Borislav Ukraine	**88**	J8	49 18N	23 28E
Borneo *i.* Indonesia/Malaysia	**103**	D3/F5	1 00N	113 00E
Bornholm *i.* Denmark	**88**	E11	55 02N	15 00E
Borūjerd Iran	**97**	E5	33 55N	48 48E
Borzya Russia	**95**	P7	50 24N	116 35E
Bosna *r.* Bosnia-Herzegovina	**89**	G6	45 00N	18 00E
BOSNIA-HERZEGOVINA	**89**	F6/H6		
Bossangoa CAR	**108**	H9	6 27N	17 21E
Bosso Niger	**108**	G10	13 43N	13 19E
Boston Massachusetts USA	**71**	M5	42 20N	71 05W
Boston Mountains Arkansas USA	**71**	H4	36 00N	94 00W
Botoşani Romania	**88**	L7	47 44N	26 41E
BOTSWANA	**109**	J3/K3		
Bottineau North Dakota USA	**49**	B1	48 48N	100 28W
Bouaké Côte d'Ivoire	**108**	D9	7 42N	5 00W
Bouar CAR	**108**	H9	5 58N	15 35E
Bouârfa Morocco	**108**	D14	32 30N	1 59W
Bougainville Island PNG	**114**	F7	5 58N	15 35E
Bougouni Mali	**108**	C10	11 25N	7 28W
Boulder Colorado USA	**70**	E5	40 02N	105 16W
Boulevard California USA	**72**	E1	32 39N	116 15W
Boulogne-sur-Mer Fr.	**86**	F9	50 43N	1 37E
Boundary Bald Mountain Maine USA	**53**	R5	45 45N	70 14W
Bourem Mali	**108**	D11	16 59N	0 20W
Bourges Fr.	**87**	G7	47 05N	2 23E
Bourke Aust.	**110**	H3	30 09S	145 59E
Bournemouth UK	**86**	E9	50 43N	1 54W
Bou Saâda Algeria	**108**	F15	35 10N	4 09E
Bousso Chad	**108**	H10	10 32N	16 45E
Bouvet Island Atlantic Ocean	**116**	J1	54 26S	3 24E
Bowbells North Dakota USA	**47**	F1	48 53N	102 15W
Bowen Aust.	**110**	H5	20 00S	148 10E
Bowling Green Kentucky USA	**71**	J4	37 00N	86 29W
Bowling Green Missouri USA	**71**	H4	39 21N	91 11W
Bowling Green Ohio USA	**51**	K1	41 22N	83 39W
Bowman North Dakota USA	**70**	F6	46 11N	103 26W
Boyne City Michigan USA	**52**	B5	45 13N	85 00W
Boyoma Falls CDR	**108**	J8	0 18N	25 30E
Bozeman Montana USA	**70**	D6	45 40N	111 00W
Bozoum CAR	**108**	H9	6 16N	16 22E
Brač *i.* Croatia	**89**	F5	43 00N	16 00E
Bradenton Florida USA	**71**	K2	27 29N	82 33W
Bradford UK	**86**	D10	53 48N	1 45W
Bradford Pennsylvania USA	**52**	H1	41 57N	78 38W
Brady Texas USA	**70**	G3	31 08N	99 22W
Braemar UK	**86**	D12	57 01N	3 23W
Braga Port.	**87**	A4	41 32N	8 26W
Bragança Brazil	**80**	H13	1 02S	46 46W
Bragança Port.	**87**	B4	41 47N	6 46W
Brahman Baria Bangladesh	**99**	L9	23 58N	91 04E
Brahmaputra *r.* India/Bangladesh	**99**	G5	26 40N	93 00E
Brăila Romania	**89**	L6	45 17N	27 58E
Brainerd Minnesota USA	**71**	H6	46 20N	94 10W
Branco *r.* Brazil	**80**	E14	0 00	62 00W
Brandenburg Germany	**88**	D10	52 25N	12 34E
Brasileia Brazil	**80**	D11	10 59S	68 45W
Brásília Brazil	**80**	H10	15 45S	47 57W
Braşov Romania	**89**	K6	45 39N	25 35E
Bratislava Slovakia	**88**	F8	48 10N	17 10E
Bratsk Russia	**95**	N8	56 20N	101 50E
Bratsk Vodokhrahnilishche *res.* Russia	**95**	N8	56 00N	102 00E
Brattleboro Vermont USA	**73**	D3	42 51N	72 34W

Braunschweig Germany	88	C10	52 15N	10 30E
Brawley California USA	70	C3	32 59N	115 30W
BRAZIL	80	F11		
Brazil Basin Atlantic Ocean	116	F5/F6	10 00S	26 00W
Brazos *r.* Texas USA	71	G3	32 00N	97 00W
Brazzaville Congo	108	H7	4 14S	15 14E
Breda Neths.	86	H9	51 35N	4 46E
Bremen Germany	88	B10	53 05N	8 48E
Bremerhaven Germany	88	B10	53 33N	8 35E
Bremerton Washington USA	70	B6	47 34N	122 40W
Brenham Texas USA	71	G3	30 09N	96 24W
Brenner Pass Austria/Italy	89	C7	47 02N	11 32E
Brescia Italy	89	C6	45 33N	10 13E
Brest Belarus	88	J10	52 08N	23 40E
Brest Fr.	86	C8	48 23N	4 30W
Brewer Maine USA	57	F1	44 52N	68 01W
Brewerton New York USA	51	N2	43 14N	76 08W
Bria CAR	108	J9	6 32N	22 00E
Briançon Fr.	87	J6	44 53N	6 39E
Bridgeport California USA	72	D4	38 14N	119 15W
Bridgeport Connecticut USA	71	M5	41 12N	73 12W
Bridgeton New Jersey USA	73	C1	39 26N	75 14W
Bridgetown Barbados	74	S11	13 06N	59 37W
Bridgwater UK	86	D9	51 08N	3 00W
Briey Fr.	86	H8	49 15N	5 57E
Brigham City Utah USA	70	D5	41 30N	112 02W
Brighton UK	86	E9	50 50N	0 10W
Brighton Beach *tn.* New York USA	73	J1	40 34N	73 58W
Bríndisi Italy	89	F4	40 37N	17 57E
Brisbane Aust.	110	J4	27 30S	153 00E
Bristol UK	86	D9	51 27N	2 35W
Bristol Channel UK	86	C9/D9	51 20N	3 50W
Bristol Lake California USA	72	F2	34 30N	115 40W
Brive-la-Gaillarde Fr.	87	F6	45 09N	1 32E
Brno Czech Rep.	88	F8	49 13N	16 40E
Brockport New York USA	52	J3	43 13N	77 56W
Brockton Massachusetts USA	71	M5	42 06N	71 01W
Brody Ukraine	88	K9	50 05N	25 08E
Broken Hill *tn.* Aust.	110	G3	31 57S	141 30E
Broken Ridge Indian Ocean	113	J3	30 00S	93 00E
Bronx *admin.* New York USA	73	D2	40 48N	73 50W
Brookings South Dakota USA	71	G5	44 19N	96 47W
Brooklyn *admin.* New York USA	73	D2	40 41N	73 57W
Broome Aust.	110	C6	17 58S	122 15E
Browning Montana USA	70	D6	48 33N	113 00W
Brownsville Texas USA	71	G2	25 54N	97 30W
Brownwood Texas USA	71	G3	31 42N	98 59W
Bruay-en-Artois Fr.	86	G9	50 29N	2 33E
Brugge Belgium	86	G9	51 13N	3 14E
BRUNEI	103	E4/F4		
Brunswick Georgia USA	71	K3	31 09N	81 30W
Brussels Belgium	86	H9	50 50N	4 21E
Bryan Ohio USA	52	B1	41 30N	84 34W
Bryan Texas USA	71	G3	30 41N	96 24W
Bryansk Russia	94	F7	53 15N	34 09E
Brzeg Poland	88	F9	50 52N	17 27E
Bucaramanga Col.	80	C15	7 08N	73 10W
Bucharest Romania	89	L6	44 25N	26 07E
Buchanan Liberia	108	B9	5 57N	10 02W
Budapest Hungary	89	G7	47 30N	19 03E
Budjala CAR	108	H8	2 38N	19 48E
Buellton California USA	72	C2	34 37N	120 11W
Buenaventura Col.	80	B14	3 54N	77 02W
Buenaventura Mexico	74	C5	29 50N	107 30W
Buena Vista Lake California USA	72	D2	35 13N	119 18W
Buenos Aires Argentina	81	F7	34 40S	58 30W
Buenos Aires, Lake Argentina/Chile	81	C4	47 00S	72 00W
Buffalo New York USA	71	L5	42 52N	78 55W
Buffalo Wyoming USA	70	E5	44 21N	106 40W
Buhusi Romania	89	L7	46 44N	26 41E
Bujumbura Burundi	108	K7	3 22S	29 19E
Bukachacha Russia	95	P7	53 00N	116 58E
Bukama CDR	109	K6	9 13S	25 52E
Bukavu CDR	108	K7	2 30S	28 50E
Bukhara Uzbekistan	94	J4	39 47N	64 26E
Bukittinggi Indonesia	103	C3	0 18S	100 20E
Bukoba Tanzania	108	L7	1 19S	31 49E
Bula Indonesia	103	J3	3 07S	130 27E
Bulawayo Zimbabwe	109	K3	20 10S	28 43E
BULGARIA	89	J5/K5		
Bullion Mountains California USA	72	E2	34 30N	116 15W
Bull Shoals Lake USA	71	H4	36 00N	93 00W
Bulun Russia	95	Q11	70 45N	127 20E
Bumba CDR	108	J8	2 10N	22 30E
Bunbury Aust.	110	B3	33 20S	115 34E
Bundaberg Aust.	110	J5	24 50S	152 21E
Bungo-suidō *sd.* Japan	102	B1	33 00N	132 30E
Bunia CDR	108	L8	1 33N	30 13E
Buôn Mê Thuôt Vietnam	103	D6	12 41N	108 02E
Bura Kenya	108	M7	1 06S	39 58E
Buraydah Saudi Arabia	96	D4	26 20N	43 59E
Burbank California USA	72	D2	34 10N	118 17W
Burdur Turkey	96	B6	37 44N	30 17E
Bureya *r.* Russia	95	R7	52 00N	133 00E
Būr Fu'ad Egypt	109	S4	31 50N	32 19E
Burgas Bulgaria	89	L5	42 30N	27 29E
Burgos Sp.	87	D5	42 21N	3 41W
Burgsvik Sweden	88	G12	57 03N	18 19E
Burhanpur India	98	D4	21 18N	76 08E
BURKINA	108	D10		
Burlington Colorado USA	70	F4	39 17N	102 17W
Burlington Iowa USA	71	H5	40 50N	91 07W
Burlington Vermont USA	71	M5	44 28N	73 14W
Burlington Washington USA	42	H4	48 26N	122 20W
Burnie Aust.	110	H1	41 03S	145 55E
Bursa Turkey	96	A7	40 12N	29 04E
Bûr Safâga Egypt	108	L13	26 43N	33 55E
Bûr Taufiq Egypt	109	T1	29 57N	32 34E
Burt Lake Michigan USA	52	B5	45 30N	84 40W
Buru *i.* Indonesia	103	H3	3 30S	126 30E
BURUNDI	108	K7/L7		
Burwell Nebraska USA	70	G5	41 48N	99 09W
Būshehr Iran	97	F4	28 57N	50 52E
Busira *r.* CDR	108	H7/J7	1 00S	20 00E
Busto Arsizio Italy	89	B6	45 37N	8 51E
Buta CDR	108	J8	2 49N	24 50E
Butare Rwanda	108	K7	2 35S	29 44E
Buthidaung Myanmar	99	M8	20 49N	92 34E
Buton *i.* Indonesia	103	G2/G3	5 00S	122 45E
Butte Montana USA	70	D6	46 00N	112 31W
Butuan Philippines	103	H5	8 56N	125 31E
Buulobarde Somalia	108	P8	3 50N	45 33E
Buzău Romania	89	L6	45 09N	26 49E
Bydgoszcz Poland	88	F10	53 16N	18 00E
Bygland Norway	86	J13	58 50N	7 49E
Byrranga Mountains Russia	95	M11	75 00N	100 00E
Bytom Poland	88	G9	50 21N	18 51E
C				
Cabanatuan Philippines	103	G7	15 30N	120 58E
Cabimas Venezuela	80	C16	10 26N	71 27W
Cabinda *admin.* Angola	108	G6	5 30S	12 20E
Cabinet Mountains Montana USA	43	N1	48 15N	115 45W
Cabo Brazil	80	K12	8 16S	35 00W
Cabo Blanco *c.* Costa Rica	75	G1	9 36N	85 06W
Cabo Catoche *c.* Mexico	74	G4	21 38N	87 08W
Cabo Corrientes *c.* Col.	80	B15	5 29N	77 36W
Cabo Corrientes *c.* Mexico	74	C4	20 25N	105 42W
Cabo de Gata *c.* Sp.	87	D2	36 44N	2 10W
Cabo de Hornos *c.* Chile	81	D2	56 00S	67 15W
Cabo de la Nao *c.* Sp.	87	F3	38 44N	0 14E
Cabo Delgado *c.* Mozambique	109	N5	10 45S	40 45E
Cabo de Palos *c.* Sp.	87	E2	37 38N	0 40W
Cabo de Peñas *c.* Sp.	87	C5	43 39N	5 50W
Cabo de São Vicente *c.* Port.	87	A2	37 01N	8 59W
Cabo de Tortosa *c.* Sp.	87	F4	40 44N	0 54E
Cabo Dos Bahías *c.* Argentina	81	D5	45 00S	65 30W
Cabo Espichel *c.* Port.	87	A3	38 24N	9 13W
Cabo Finisterre *c.* Sp.	87	A5	42 52N	9 16W
Cabo Gracias á Dios *c.* Nicaragua	75	H3	15 00N	83 10W
Cabo Orange *c.* Brazil	80	G14	4 25N	51 32W
Cabo Ortegal *c.* Sp.	87	B5	43 46N	7 54W
Cabora Bassa Dam Mozambique	109	L4	16 00S	33 00E
Caborca Mexico	74	B6	30 42N	112 10W
Cabo San Juan *c.* Argentina	81	E3	54 45S	63 46W
Cabo San Lucas Mexico	74	C4	22 50N	109 52W
Cabo Santa Elena *c.* Costa Rica	74	G2	10 54N	85 56W
Cabo Vírgenes *c.* Argentina	81	D3	52 20S	68 00W
Cabrera *i.* Sp.	87	G3	39 00N	2 59E
Cabriel *r.* Sp.	87	E3	39 20N	1 15W
Čačak Serbia	89	H5	43 54N	20 22E
Cáceres Brazil	80	F10	16 05S	57 40W
Cáceres Sp.	87	B3	39 29N	6 23W
Cachoeira Brazil	80	K11	12 35S	38 59W
Cachoeira do Sul Brazil	81	G7	30 03S	52 52W
Cachoeiro de Itapemirim Brazil	80	J9	20 51S	41 07W
Cadillac Michigan USA	51	J3	44 14N	85 23W
Cadiz Philippines	103	G6	10 57N	123 18E
Cádiz Sp.	87	B2	36 32N	6 18W
Cádiz, Gulf of Sp.	87	B2	36 30N	7 15W
Cadiz Lake California USA	72	F2	34 17N	115 23W
Caen Fr.	86	E8	49 11N	0 22W
Caernarfon UK	86	C10	53 08N	4 16W
Cagayan de Oro Philippines	103	G5	8 29N	124 40E
Cágliari Italy	89	B3	39 13N	9 08E
Caguas Puerto Rico	75	L3	18 41N	66 04W
Cahors Fr.	87	F6	44 28N	0 26E
Caicos Passage *sd.* W. Indies	75	K4	22 20N	72 30W
Cairns Aust.	110	H6	16 51S	145 43E
Cairo Egypt	108	L13	30 00N	31 15E
Cairo Illinois USA	71	J4	37 01N	89 09W
Cajamarca Peru	80	B12	7 09S	78 32W
Cajàzeiras Brazil	80	K12	6 52S	38 31W
Cakovec Croatia	89	F7	46 24N	16 26E
Calabar Nigeria	108	F8	4 56N	8 22E
Calahorra Sp.	87	E5	46 19N	1 58W
Calais Fr.	86	F9	50 57N	1 52E
Calais Maine USA	57	G1	44 11N	67 16W
Calama Chile	80	D9	22 30S	68 55W
Calamar Col.	80	C16	10 16N	74 55W
Calamian Group *is.* Philippines	103	F6/G6	12 00N	120 00E
Calamocha Sp.	87	E4	40 54N	1 18W
Calapan Philippines	103	G6	13 23N	121 10E
Calatayud Sp.	87	E4	41 21N	1 39W
Calçoene Brazil	80	G14	2 30N	50 55W
Caldas da Rainha Port.	87	A3	39 24N	9 08W
Caldwell Idaho USA	70	C5	43 39N	116 40W
Caledonia New York USA	52	J2	42 58N	77 51W
Calexico California USA	72	F1	32 40N	115 30W
Cali Col.	80	B14	3 24N	76 30W
Calicut India	98	D2	11 15N	75 45E
Caliente Nevada USA	70	D4	37 36N	114 31W
California *state* USA	70	C4	35 00N	119 00W
Calistoga California USA	72	B4	38 36N	122 35W
Callao Peru	80	B11	12 05S	77 08W
Caltanissetta Italy	89	E2	37 29N	14 04E
Calvi Fr.	87	K5	42 34N	8 44E
Calvinia RSA	109	H1	31 25S	19 47E
Camaçari Brazil	80	K11	12 44S	38 16W
Camacupa Angola	109	H5	12 03S	17 50E
Camagüey Cuba	75	J4	21 25N	77 55W
CAMBODIA	103	C6/D6		
Cambrai Fr.	86	G9	50 10N	3 14E
Cambria California USA	72	C2	35 34N	121 05W
Cambrian Mountains UK	86	D10	52 15N	3 45W
Cambridge NZ	111	E6	37 53S	175 28E
Cambridge UK	86	F10	52 12N	0 07E
Cambridge Maryland USA	71	L4	38 34N	76 04W
Camden New Jersey USA	73	C1	39 57N	75 07W
CAMEROON	108	G9		
Cametá Brazil	80	H13	2 12S	49 30W
Camiri Bolivia	80	E9	20 08S	63 33W
Camocim Brazil	80	J13	2 55S	40 50W
Camorta Island Nicobar Islands	99	G1	7 30N	93 30E
Campbell Island Southern Ocean	114	G2	52 30S	169 10E
Campbeltown UK	86	C11	55 26N	5 36W
Campeche Mexico	74	F3	19 50N	90 30W
Câmpina Romania	89	K6	45 08N	25 44E
Campina Grande Brazil	80	K12	7 15S	35 50W
Campinas Brazil	80	H9	22 54S	47 06W
Campoalegre Col.	80	B14	2 49N	75 19W
Campobasso Italy	89	E4	41 33N	14 39E
Campo Grande Brazil	80	G9	20 24S	54 35W
Campo Maior Brazil	80	J13	4 50S	42 12W
Campo Mourão Brazil	80	G9	24 01S	52 24W
Campos Brazil	80	J9	21 46S	41 21W
Camptonville California USA	72	C4	39 28N	121 01W
Cam Rahn Vietnam	103	D6	11 54N	109 14E
Canadian *r.* USA	70	F4	35 00N	104 00W
Canajoharie New York USA	73	C3	42 55N	74 46W
Canakkale Turkey	96	A7	40 09N	26 25E
Canal du Midi Fr.	87	G5	43 20N	2 00E
Canandaigua New York USA	53	J2	42 53N	77 17W
Canandaigua Lake New York USA	53	J2	42 50N	77 17W
Cananea Mexico	74	B6	30 59N	110 20W
Canary Basin Atlantic Ocean	116	E9/F9	26 20N	30 00W
Canary Islands Sp.	108	A13	28 30N	15 10W
Canaveral, Cape Florida USA	71	K2	28 28N	80 28W
Canberra Aust.	110	H2	35 18S	149 08E
Cancún Mexico	74	G4	21 09N	86 45W
Cangamba Angola	109	H5	13 40S	19 47E
Cangzhou China	101	M6	38 19N	116 54E
Canisteo New York USA	52	J2	42 16N	77 37W
Cannanore India	98	D2	11 53N	75 23E
Cannanore Islands India	98	C2	10 05N	72 10E
Cannes Fr.	87	J5	43 33N	7 00E
Cannonsville Reservoir New York USA	53	L2	42 05N	75 20W
Canõas Brazil	81	G8	28 55S	51 10W
Canouan *i.* Lesser Antilles	74	R11	12 43N	61 20W
Canterbury UK	86	F9	51 17N	1 05E
Canterbury Plains NZ	111	C2/D3	43 45S	171 56E
Can Tho Vietnam	103	D6	10 03N	105 46E
Canton New York USA	51	P3	44 36N	75 10W
Canton Ohio USA	71	K5	40 48N	81 23W
Canton East Pennsylvania USA	53	K1	41 38N	76 50W
Cap Corse *c.* Fr.	87	K5	43 00N	9 21E
Cap d'Ambre *c.* Madagascar	109	P5	12 00S	49 15E
Cap de Creus *c.* Sp.	87	G5	42 19N	3 19E
Cap de la Hague *c.* Fr.	86	E8	49 44N	1 56W
Cape Basin Atlantic Ocean	116	J3	36 00S	6 00E
Cape Coast *tn.* Ghana	108	D9	5 10N	1 13W
Cape Cod Bay Massachusetts USA	73	E2	41 00N	70 00W
Cape Girardeau *tn.* Missouri USA	71	J4	37 19N	89 31W
Cape May *tn.* New Jersey USA	73	C1	38 56N	74 54W
Cape Rise Atlantic Ocean	116	K2	42 00S	11 00E
Cape Town RSA	109	H1	33 56S	18 28E
CAPE VERDE	116	E8		
Cape Verde Basin Atlantic Ocean	116	E8	11 00N	35 00W
Cape York Peninsula Aust.	110	G7	12 30S	142 30E
Cap-Haïtien Haiti	75	K3	19 47N	72 17W
Capo Carbonara *c.* Italy	89	B3	39 07N	9 33E
Capo Passero *c.* Italy	89	E2	36 42N	15 09E
Capo Santa Maria di Leuca *c.* Italy	89	G3	39 47N	18 22E
Capo San Vito *c.* Italy	89	D3	38 12N	12 43E
Capri *i.* Italy	89	E4	40 33N	14 15E
Capricorn Channel Aust.	110	J5	23 00S	152 30E
Caprivi Strip *geog. reg.* Namibia	109	J4	17 30S	27 50E
Cap Ste. Marie *c.* Madagascar	109	P2	25 34S	45 10E
Cap Vert *c.* Senegal	108	A10	14 43N	17 33W
Caqueta *r.* Col.	80	C13	0 05S	72 30W
Caracal Romania	89	K6	44 07N	24 18E
Caracas Venezuela	80	D16	10 35N	66 56W
Caratinga Brazil	80	J10	19 50S	42 06W
Caravelas Brazil	80	K10	17 45S	39 15W
Carbondale Pennsylvania USA	53	L1	41 35N	75 31W
Carcassonne Fr.	87	G5	43 13N	2 21E
Cardamom Hills India	98	D1	9 50N	77 00E
Cárdenas Mexico	74	E4	22 00N	99 41W
Cardiff UK	86	D9	51 30N	3 13W
Cardigan Bay UK	86	C10	52 30N	4 30W
Carei Romania	88	J7	47 40N	22 28E
Cargados Carajos Shoals Indian Ocean	113	E5	16 00S	60 00E
Cariacica Brazil	80	J10	20 15S	40 23W
Caribbean Sea Central America	75	J3/L3	15 00N	75 00W
Caribou Maine USA	57	F2	46 52N	68 01W
Caripito Venezuela	80	E16	10 07N	63 07W
Carlisle UK	86	D11	54 54N	2 55W
Carlsbad California USA	72	E1	33 09N	117 20W
Carlsbad New Mexico USA	70	F3	32 25N	104 14W
Carlsberg Ridge Indian Ocean	113	F7	5 00N	65 00E
Carmarthen UK	86	C9	51 51N	4 20W
Carmen Col.	80	B15	9 46N	75 06W
Carmichael California USA	72	C4	38 36N	121 20W
Carnarvon Aust.	110	A5	24 51S	113 45E
Carnegie, Lake Aust.	110	C4	27 00S	124 00E
Carnegie Ridge Pacific Ocean	115	T7	1 30S	95 00W
Car Nicobar Island Nicobar Islands	99	G1	9 00N	93 00E
Carnot CAR	108	H8	4 59N	15 56E
Caro *r.* Michigan USA	52	C3	43 29N	83 24W
Carolina Brazil	80	H12	7 20S	47 25W
Caroline Island Kiribati	115	M7	10 00S	150 00W
Caroline Islands Pacific Ocean	114	E8	8 00N	148 00E
Caroni *r.* Venezuela	80	E15	7 00N	62 30W
Carpathians *mts.* Europe	88/89	G8/K7	49 00N	22 00E
Carpatii Meridionali *mts.* Romania	89	J6/K6	45 00N	24 00E
Carpentaria, Gulf of Aust.	110	F6/F7	13 30S	138 00E
Carpentras Fr.	87	H6	44 03N	5 03E
Carriacou *i.* Lesser Antilles	74	R11	12 30N	61 27W
Carrion *r.* Sp.	87	C5	42 30N	4 45W
Carson *r.* Nevada USA	72	D4	39 15N	119 36W
Carson City Nevada USA	70	C4	39 10N	119 46W
Cartagena Col.	80	B16	10 24N	75 33W
Cartagena Sp.	87	E2	37 36N	0 59W
Cartago Costa Rica	75	H1	9 50N	83 52W
Carteret New Jersey USA	73	H1	40 34N	74 13W
Caruarú Brazil	80	K12	8 15S	35 55W
Carúpano Venezuela	80	E16	10 39N	63 14W
Casablanca Morocco	108	C14	33 39N	7 35W
Casa Grande Arizona USA	70	D3	32 52N	111 46W
Cascade Range *mts.* North America	70	B5/B6	48 00N	121 00W
Cascais Port.	87	A3	38 41N	9 25W
Cascavel Brazil	80	K13	4 10S	38 15W
Caserta Italy	89	E4	41 04N	14 20E
Casper Wyoming USA	70	E5	42 50N	106 20W
Cassino Italy	89	D4	41 29N	13 50E
Cass River Michigan USA	52	C3	43 30N	83 30W
Castellane Fr.	87	J5	43 50N	6 30E
Castellón de la Plana Sp.	87	E3	39 59N	0 03W
Castelo Branco Port.	87	B3	39 50N	7 30W
Castlebar RoI	86	A10	53 52N	9 17W
Castle Peak HK China	100	A2	22 23N	113 57E
Castres Fr.	87	G5	43 36N	2 14E
Castries St. Lucia	74	R12	14 02N	60 59W
Castrovillari Italy	89	F3	39 48N	16 12E
Catamarca Argentina	81	D8	28 28S	65 46W
Catánia Italy	89	E2	37 31N	15 06E
Catanzaro Italy	89	F3	38 54N	16 36E
Cataract, 1st Egypt	108	L12	24 00N	32 45E
Cataract, 2nd Sudan	108	L12	21 40N	31 12E
Cataract, 3rd Sudan	108	L11	19 45N	30 25E
Cataract, 5th Sudan	108	L11	18 25N	33 52E
Cathedral Provincial Park Washington USA	43	K1/L1	48 55N	120 00W
Cat Island Bahamas	75	J4	24 30N	75 30W
Catskill Mountains New York USA	71	L5	42 10N	74 20W
Cattaraugus New York USA	52	H2	42 20N	78 50W
Cattaraugus Creek New York USA	52	H2	42 28N	78 30W
Caucaia Brazil	80	K13	3 44S	38 45W
Caura *r.* Venezuela	80	E15	6 00N	64 00W
Cauvery *r.* India	98	D2	11 05N	78 15E
Cavalier North Dakota USA	49	D1	48 47N	97 38W
Caxias Brazil	80	J13	4 53S	43 20W
Caxias do Sul Brazil	81	G8	29 14S	51 10W
Cayenne French Guiana	80	G14	4 55N	52 18W
Cayman Trench Caribbean Sea	116	A8	15 00N	80 00W
Cayuga Lake New York USA	51	N2	42 40N	76 50W
Ceará *admin.* Brazil	80	J12	5 30S	40 00W
Cebu Philippines	103	G6	10 17N	123 56E
Cedar *r.* Iowa USA	71	H5	42 00N	92 00W
Cedar City Utah USA	70	D4	37 40N	113 04W
Cedar Creek *r.* North Dakota USA	70	F6	46 00N	102 00W
Cedar Grove New Jersey USA	73	H2	40 51N	74 14W
Cedar Rapids *tn.* Iowa USA	71	H5	41 59N	91 39W
Cedros *i.* Mexico	74	A5	28 00N	115 00W
Ceduna Aust.	110	E3	32 07S	133 42E
Ceerigaabo Somalia	108	P10	10 40N	47 20E
Cegléd Hungary	89	G7	47 10N	19 47E
Celaya Mexico	74	D4	20 32N	100 48W
Celebes Sea Indonesia	103	G4	3 00N	122 00E
Celje Slovenia	89	E7	46 15N	15 16E
Celle Germany	88	C10	52 37N	10 05E

CENTRAL AFRICAN REPUBLIC	108	H9/J9		
Central District HK China	100	C1	22 17N	114 10E
Central Pacific Basin Pacific Ocean	114	J8	10 00N	177 00W
Central Siberian Plateau Russia	95	N10	65 00N	110 00E
Cerro de Pasco Peru	80	B11	10 43S	76 15W
Cesis Latvia	88	K12	57 18N	25 18E
České Budějovice Czech Rep.	88	E8	48 58N	14 29E
Ceuta *territory* Sp.	87	C1	35 53N	5 19W
Cévennes *mts.* Fr.	87	G6	44 20N	3 30E
Ceyhan *r.* Turkey	96	C6	37 45N	36 45E
Cèze *r.* Fr.	87	H6	44 30N	4 00E
Chachapoyas Peru	80	B12	6 13S	77 54W
CHAD	108	H10		
Chad, Lake West Africa	108	G10	13 50N	14 00E
Chagai Hills Afghanistan/Pakistan	98	A5	29 30N	63 00E
Chaghcharan Afghanistan	97	J5	34 28N	65 03E
Chagos Archipelago Indian Ocean	113	G6	6 00S	73 00E
Chagos-Laccadive Ridge Indian Ocean	113	G6	0 00	75 00E
Chāh Bahār Iran	97	H4	25 16N	60 41E
Chaine des Mitumba *mts.* CDR	109	K6	7 30S	27 30E
Chai Wan HK China	100	C1	22 16N	114 14E
Chalkída Greece	89	J3	38 28N	23 36E
Chalkidikí *p.* Greece	89	J4	40 30N	23 00E
Chalkyitsik Alaska USA	64	B4	66 38N	143 49W
Challenger Fracture Zone Pacific Ocean	115	R4/T4	33 30S	100 00W
Châlons-sur-Marne Fr.	86	H8	48 58N	4 22E
Chalon-sur-Saône Fr.	87	H7	46 47N	4 51E
Chaman Pakistan	98	B6	30 55N	66 27E
Chambal *r.* India	98	D5	26 00N	77 00E
Chamberlain Lake Maine USA	53	S6	46 15N	69 20W
Chambersburg Pennsylvania USA	73	B1	39 56N	77 39W
Chambéry Fr.	87	H6	45 34N	5 55E
Chamo, Lake Ethiopia	108	M9	5 55N	37 35E
Champaign Illinois USA	71	J5	40 07N	88 14W
Champlain New York USA	53	N4	44 59N	73 29W
Champlain, Lake Vermont USA	53	N4	44 53N	73 10W
Champotón Mexico	74	F3	19 20N	90 43W
Chānaral Chile	80	C8	26 23S	70 40W
Chandigarh India	98	D6	30 44N	76 54E
Chandigarh *admin.* India	98	D6	30 44N	76 54E
Chandpur Bangladesh	99	L9	23 15N	90 40E
Chandrapur India	98	D3	19 58N	79 21E
Changara Mozambique	109	L4	16 50S	33 17E
Changchun China	101	P7	43 53N	125 20E
Changde China	101	L4	29 03N	111 35E
Chang Jiang *r.* China	101	K5	31 00N	110 00E
Changsha China	101	L4	28 10N	113 00E
Changzhi China	101	L6	36 05N	113 12E
Changzhou China	101	N5	31 39N	120 45E
Chaniá Greece	89	K1	35 31N	24 01E
Channel Island National Park California USA	72	C2	34 04N	120 00W
Channel Islands British Isles	86	D8	49 30N	2 30W
Chaoyang China	101	N7	41 36N	120 25E
Chaozhou China	101	M3	23 42N	116 36E
Chapada Diamantina *mts.* Brazil	80	J11	12 30S	42 30W
Chapecó Brazil	80	G8	27 14S	52 41W
Chardzhev Turkmenistan	94	J4	39 09N	63 34E
Chari *r.* Chad/Sudan	108	H10	11 00N	16 00E
Charikar Afghanistan	97	J5	35 01N	69 11E
Charleroi Belgium	86	H9	50 25N	4 27E
Charleston South Carolina USA	71	L3	32 48N	79 58W
Charleston West Virginia USA	71	K4	38 23N	81 40W
Charleston Peak *mt.* Nevada USA	72	F3	36 16N	115 41W
Charlestown Rhode Island USA	73	E2	41 23N	71 39W
Charleville-Mézières Fr.	86	H8	49 46N	4 43E
Charlevoix Michigan USA	51	J3	45 18N	85 15W
Charlotte North Carolina USA	71	K4	35 03N	80 50W
Charlottesville Virginia USA	71	L4	38 02N	78 29W
Charlotteville Trinidad and Tobago	75	V15	11 16N	60 36W
Charters Towers Aust.	110	H5	20 02S	146 20E
Chartres Fr.	86	F8	48 27N	1 30E
Chateaubelair St. Vincent and the Grenadines	74	R11	13 17N	61 15W
Châteaubriant Fr.	86	E7	47 43N	1 22W
Chateaugay New York USA	53	M4	44 55N	74 06W
Châteauroux Fr.	87	F7	46 49N	1 41E
Château-Thierry Fr.	86	G8	49 03N	3 24E
Châtellerault Fr.	87	F7	46 49N	0 33E
Chatham Alaska USA	42	C5	57 30N	135 00W
Chatham Massachusetts USA	73	F2	41 41N	69 58W
Chatham Rise Pacific Ocean	114	H3	45 00S	175 00E
Chatham Strait *sd.* Alaska USA	42	C5	57 45N	134 50W
Châtillon-sur-Seine Fr.	86	H7	47 52N	4 35E
Chattanooga Tennessee USA	71	J4	35 02N	85 18W
Chattisgarh *admin.* India	98	E4	22 30N	82 30E
Chaumont Fr.	86	H8	48 07N	5 08E
Chautauqua Lake New York USA	52	G2	42 12N	79 30W
Chazy New York USA	53	N4	44 53N	73 29W
Cheb Czech Rep.	88	D9	50 08N	12 28E
Cheboksary Russia	94	G8	56 08N	47 12E
Cheboygan Michigan USA	51	J3	45 39N	84 28W
Cheju do *i.* South Korea	101	P5	33 00N	126 30E
Chek Lap Kok *i.* HK China	100	A1	22 18N	113 56E
Chelan, Lake Washington USA	42	H4	48 06N	120 20W
Chelan National Recreation Area Washington USA	42	H4	48 25N	120 30W
Chełm Poland	88	J9	51 08N	23 29E
Chelmsford UK	86	F9	51 44N	0 28E
Chelsea Michigan USA	52	B2	42 19N	84 01W
Cheltenham UK	86	D9	51 54N	2 04W
Chelyabinsk Russia	94	J8	55 12N	61 25E
Chemnitz Germany	88	D9	50 50N	12 55E
Chemung River New York USA	53	K2	42 02N	76 50W
Chenab *r.* Pakistan	98	C6	32 30N	74 00E
Chenango River New York USA	53	L2	42 28N	75 40W
Chengde China	101	M7	40 59N	117 52E
Chengdu China	101	J5	30 37N	104 06E
Chennai India	98	E2	13 05N	80 18E
Cher *r.* Fr.	87	F7	47 17N	0 50E
Cherbourg Fr.	86	E8	49 38N	1 37W
Cheremkhovo Russia	95	N7	53 08N	103 01E
Cherepovets Russia	94	F8	59 09N	37 50E
Chernihiv Ukraine	88	N9	51 30N	31 18E
Chernivtsi Ukraine	88	K8	48 19N	25 52E
Chernyakhovsk Russia	88	H11	54 36N	21 48E
Cherokee Iowa USA	71	G5	42 45N	95 32W
Cherskogo Range *mts.* Russia	95	R10/S9	66 30N	140 00E
Chervonograd Ukraine	88	K9	50 25N	24 10E
Chesaning Michigan USA	52	B3	43 12N	84 08W
Chesapeake Virginia USA	71	L4	36 45N	76 15W
Chesapeake Bay Maryland USA	71	L4	39 00N	76 20W
Chester UK	86	D10	53 12N	2 54W
Chester Maryland USA	73	B1	38 59N	76 17W
Chesuncook Lake Maine USA	53	S6	46 00N	69 22W
Chetumal Mexico	74	G3	18 30N	88 17W
Cheung Chau *i.* HK China	100	B1	22 10N	114 02E
Cheung Sha HK China	100	A1	22 14N	113 57E
Chewack River Washington USA	42	H4	48 45N	120 10W
Chewelah Washington USA	43	M1	48 17N	117 44W
Cheyenne Wyoming USA	70	F5	41 08N	104 50W
Cheyenne *r.* USA	70	F5	44 00N	102 00W
Chhatak Bangladesh	99	L10	25 02N	91 38E
Chhukha Bhutan	99	K11	27 01N	89 35E
Chiai Taiwan	101	N3	23 09N	120 11E
Chiang Mai Thailand	103	B7	18 48N	98 59E
Chiba Japan	102	D2	35 38N	140 07E
Chicago Illinois USA	71	J5	41 50N	87 45W
Chicapa *r.* Angola/CDR	109	J6	8 00S	20 30E
Chichagof Island Alaska USA	42	C5	57 40N	136 00W
Chickasha Oklahoma USA	71	G4	35 03N	97 57W
Chicken Alaska USA	64	B3	64 04N	142 00W
Chiclayo Peru	80	B12	6 47S	79 47W
Chico California USA	70	B4	39 46N	121 50W
Chico *r.* Argentina	81	D4	49 00S	70 00W
Chico *r.* Argentina	81	D5	45 00S	67 30W
Chienti *r.* Italy	89	D5	43 00N	14 00E
Chieti Italy	89	E5	42 21N	14 10E
Chihuahua Mexico	74	C5	28 40N	106 06W
CHILE	80/81	C5/C8		
Chile Basin Pacific Ocean	115	T4	36 00S	84 00W
Chile Chico Chile	81	C4	46 34S	71 44W
Chile Rise Pacific Ocean	115	S4	40 00S	92 00W
Chillán Chile	81	C6	36 37S	72 10W
Chilpancingo Mexico	74	E3	17 33N	99 30W
Chilumba Malawi	109	L5	10 25S	34 18E
Chilung Taiwan	101	N4	25 10N	121 43E
Chi Ma Wan Peninsula HK China	100	A1	22 14N	113 58E
Chimborazo *mt.* Ecuador	80	B13	1 29S	78 52W
Chimbote Peru	80	B12	9 04S	78 34W
CHINA	100/101			
China Lake California USA	72	E2	35 45N	117 36W
Chinandega Nicaragua	74	G2	12 35N	87 10W
Chincha Alta Peru	80	B11	13 25S	76 07W
Chinchilla Aust.	110	J4	26 42S	150 35E
Chinde Mozambique	109	M4	18 35S	36 28E
Chinese Turkestan *geog. reg.* China	100	D6	40 00N	80 00E
Chingola Zambia	109	K5	12 31S	27 53E
Chinju South Korea	101	P6	35 10N	128 06E
Chinko *r.* CAR	108	J9	5 00N	24 00E
Chinook Montana USA	47	C1	48 36N	109 14W
Chíos Greece	89	L3	38 23N	26 07E
Chíos *i.* Greece	89	K3/L3	38 00N	26 00E
Chippewa Falls *tn.* Wisconsin USA	51	F3	44 56N	91 23W
Chippewa River Michigan USA	52	B3	43 36N	84 45W
Chiquimula Guatemala	74	G2	14 48N	89 32W
Chirchik Uzbekistan	94	J5	41 28N	69 31E
Chişinău Moldova	89	M7	47 00N	28 50E
Chita Russia	95	P7	52 03N	113 35E
Chitembo Angola	109	H5	13 33S	16 47E
Chitral Pakistan	98	C7	35 52N	71 58E
Chittagong Bangladesh	99	L9	22 20N	91 48E
Chittoor India	98	D2	13 13N	79 06E
Chocolate Mountains California USA	72	F1	33 30N	115 30W
Choiseul *i.* Solomon Islands	114	F7	5 58N	153 15E
Chojnice Poland	88	F10	53 42N	17 32E
Cholet Fr.	87	E7	47 04N	0 53W
Choluteca Honduras	74	G2	13 15N	87 10W
Chone Ecuador	80	A13	0 44S	80 04W
Chongjin North Korea	101	P7	41 50N	129 55E
Chongju South Korea	101	P6	36 39N	127 27E
Chongqing China	101	K4	29 30N	106 35E
Chonju South Korea	101	P6	35 50N	127 50E
Chornobyl Ukraine	88	N9	51 17N	30 15E
Chott El Jerid *salt l.* Tunisia	108	F14	30 00N	9 00E
Chott Melrhir *salt l.* Algeria	108	F14	33 30N	6 10E
Chowchilla California USA	72	C3	37 07N	120 14W
Choybalsan Mongolia	101	L8	48 02N	114 32E
Christchurch NZ	111	D3	43 32S	172 38E
Christmas Island Aust.	103	D1	10 15S	106 00E
Chu *r.* Asia	94	K5	45 00N	72 30E
Chubut *r.* Argentina	81	D5	43 30S	67 30W
Chūgoku-sanchi *mts.* Japan	102	B1	35 00N	133 00E
Chukchi Sea Arctic Ocean	117		70 00N	170 00W
Chuk Kok HK China	100	C2	22 21N	114 15E
Chukotsk Peninsula Russia	95	W10	66 00N	175 00W
Chukotsk Range *mts.* Russia	95	V10	68 00N	175 00E
Chulucanas Peru	80	A12	5 08S	80 10W
Chulym *r.* Russia	95	L8	57 30N	87 30E
Chumphon Thailand	103	B6	10 30N	99 11E
Chuna *r.* Russia	95	M8	57 30N	98 00E
Chunchon South Korea	101	P6	37 56N	127 40E
Chunchura India	99	K9	22 55N	88 15E
Ch'ungju South Korea	101	P6	36 59N	127 53E
Chunya *r.* Russia	95	N9	62 00N	101 00E
Chur Switz.	87	K7	46 52N	9 32E
Ciego de Avila Cuba	75	J4	21 51N	78 47W
Ciénaga Col.	80	C16	11 01N	74 15W
Cienfuegos Cuba	75	H4	22 10N	80 27W
Cimarron *r.* USA	70	F4	37 00N	103 00W
Cimislia Moldova	89	M7	46 30N	28 50E
Cinca *r.* Sp.	87	F4	41 45N	0 15E
Cincinnati Ohio USA	71	K4	39 10N	83 30W
Circle Alaska USA	64	B4	65 50N	144 11W
Cirebon Indonesia	103	D2	6 46S	108 33E
Cisco Texas USA	70	G3	32 23N	98 59W
Cisneros Col.	80	B15	6 32N	75 04W
Citlaltépetl *mt.* Mexico	74	E3	19 00N	97 18W
City Island New York USA	73	J2	40 51N	73 48W
Ciucea Romania	89	J7	46 58N	22 50E
Ciudad Acuna Mexico	74	D5	29 20N	100 58W
Ciudad Bolívar Venezuela	80	E15	8 06N	63 36W
Ciudad Camargo Mexico	74	C5	27 41N	105 10W
Ciudad del Carmen Mexico	74	F3	18 38N	91 50W
Ciudad del Este Paraguay	80	G8	25 32S	54 34W
Ciudadela Sp.	87	G3	40 00N	3 50E
Ciudad Guayana Venezuela	80	E15	8 22N	62 37W
Ciudad Juárez Mexico	74	C6	31 42N	106 29W
Ciudad Lerdo Mexico	74	D5	25 34N	103 30W
Ciudad Madero Mexico	74	E4	22 19N	97 50W
Ciudad Manté Mexico	74	E4	22 44N	98 59W
Ciudad Obregón Mexico	74	C5	27 28N	109 59W
Ciudad Real Sp.	87	D3	38 59N	3 55W
Ciudad Rodrigo Sp.	87	B4	40 36N	6 33W
Ciudad Victoria Mexico	74	E4	23 43N	99 10W
Civitavecchia Italy	89	C5	42 05N	11 47E
Cizre Turkey	96	D6	37 21N	42 11E
Clan Alpine Mountains Nevada USA	72	E4	39 34N	117 53W
Clare Michigan USA	52	B3	43 49N	84 47W
Claremont New Hampshire USA	73	D3	43 22N	72 20W
Clarence Island South Shetland Islands	81	G1	61 10S	54 00W
Clarence Strait *sd.* Alaska USA	42	D4	56 00N	133 30W
Clarendon Pennsylvania USA	52	G1	41 46N	79 06W
Clarion Fracture Zone Pacific Ocean	115	N9	18 00N	130 00W
Clark Fork *r.* Montana USA	43	N1	48 00N	115 55W
Clark Hill Lake South Carolina USA	71	K3	33 00N	82 00W
Clarksburg West Virginia USA	71	K4	39 16N	80 22W
Clarks Ferry *tn.* Pennsylvania USA	73	B2	40 25N	77 56W
Clarksville Tennessee USA	71	J4	36 31N	87 21W
Clayton New York USA	53	K4	44 15N	76 06W
Clearfield Pennsylvania USA	73	A2	41 01N	78 26W
Clear Lake California USA	72	B4	39 04N	122 48W
Clearwater Florida USA	71	K2	27 57N	82 48W
Clearwater *r.* Idaho USA	70	C6	46 00N	116 00W
Clermont-Ferrand Fr.	87	G6	45 47N	3 05E
Cleveland Ohio USA	71	K5	41 30N	81 41W
Cleveland Peninsula Alaska USA	42	D4	55 30N	132 00W
Clinton Iowa USA	71	H5	41 51N	90 12W
Clinton Oklahoma USA	70	G4	35 32N	98 59W
Clipperton Fracture Zone Pacific Ocean	115	P8/Q9	10 00N	120 00W
Clipperton Island Pacific Ocean	115	R9	10 20N	109 13W
Cloncurry Aust.	110	G5	20 41S	140 30E
Clonmel RoI	86	B10	52 21N	7 42W
Cloppenburg Germany	88	B10	52 52N	8 02E
Cloquet Minnesota USA	51	E4	46 43N	92 27W
Cloverdale California USA	72	B4	38 47N	123 01W
Clovis California USA	72	D3	36 47N	119 43W
Clovis New Mexico USA	70	F3	34 14N	103 13W
Cluj-Napoca Romania	89	J7	46 47N	23 37E
Clyde Ohio USA	52	D1	41 17N	82 58W
Clydebank UK	86	C11	55 54N	4 24W
Coaldale Nevada USA	72	E4	38 02N	117 52W
Coalinga California USA	72	C3	36 08N	120 22W
Coari Brazil	80	E13	4 08S	63 07W
Coast Ranges *mts.* California USA	70	B4/B6	41 00N	123 00W
Coatepec Mexico	74	E3	19 29N	96 59W
Coats Land *geog. reg.* Antarctica	117		77 00S	25 00W
Coatzacoalcos Mexico	74	F3	18 10N	94 25W
Cobán Guatemala	74	F3	15 28N	90 20W
Cobar Aust.	110	H3	31 32S	145 51E
Cobija Bolivia	80	D11	11 01S	68 45W
Coburg Germany	88	C9	50 15N	10 58E
Cochabamba Bolivia	80	D10	17 26S	66 10W
Cochin India	98	D1	9 56N	76 15E
Cochrane Chile	81	C4	47 16S	72 33W
Cochranton Pennsylvania USA	52	F1	41 32N	80 03W
Cocos Basin Indian Ocean	113	J6	5 00S	96 00E
Cocos Islands Indian Ocean	113	J5	12 30S	97 00E
Cocos Ridge Pacific Ocean	115	S8	4 00N	90 00W
Codajás Brazil	80	E13	3 55S	62 00W
Cod, Cape Massachusetts USA	71	N5	42 05N	70 12W
Codó Brazil	80	J13	4 28S	43 51W
Codrington Antigua and Barbuda	74	Q9	17 43N	61 49W
Coeur d'Alene Idaho USA	70	C6	47 40N	116 46W
Cognac Fr.	87	E6	45 42N	0 19W
Coihaique Chile	81	C4	45 35S	72 08W
Coimbatore India	98	D2	11 00N	76 57E
Coimbra Port.	87	A4	40 12N	8 25W
Colchester UK	86	F9	51 54N	0 54E
Cold Springs *tn.* Nevada USA	72	E4	39 22N	117 53W
Coldwater Michigan USA	51	J1	41 56N	84 59W
Coleen River Alaska USA	64	B4	67 30N	142 30W
Coleraine UK	86	B11	55 08N	6 40W
Colima Mexico	74	D3	19 14N	103 41W
College Alaska USA	64	A3	64 54N	147 55W
Collie Aust.	110	B3	33 20S	116 06E
Collingwood NZ	111	D4	40 41S	172 41E
Colmar Fr.	86	J8	48 05N	7 21E
Cologne Germany	88	A9	50 56N	6 57E
COLOMBIA	80	C14		
Colombo Sri Lanka	98	D1	6 55N	79 52E
Colón Panama	75	J1	9 21N	79 54W
Colorado *r.* Argentina	81	D6	37 30S	69 00W
Colorado *r.* North America	70	D3	33 00N	114 00W
Colorado *r.* Texas USA	71	G2	29 00N	96 00W
Colorado *state* USA	70	E4/F4	39 00N	106 00W
Colorado Desert California USA	72	E1/F1	33 18N	116 00W
Colorado Plateau Arizona USA	70	D4	36 00N	111 00W
Colorado River Aqueduct California USA	72	E1	34 00N	116 30W
Colorado Springs *tn.* Colorado USA	70	F4	38 50N	104 50W
Columbia Missouri USA	71	H4	38 58N	92 20W
Columbia South Carolina USA	71	K3	34 00N	81 00W
Columbia *r.* North America	70	B6	46 00N	120 00W
Columbus Georgia USA	71	K3	32 28N	84 59W
Columbus Indiana USA	71	J4	39 12N	85 57W
Columbus Mississippi USA	71	J3	33 30N	88 27W
Columbus Nebraska USA	71	G5	41 27N	97 21W
Columbus Ohio USA	71	K5	39 59N	83 03W
Columbus Salt Marsh Nevada USA	72	E4	38 06N	117 57W
Colville Washington USA	43	M1	48 33N	117 55W
Colvocoresses Bay Antarctica	117		66 00S	120 00E
Comilla Bangladesh	99	L9	23 28N	91 10E
Comitán Mexico	74	F3	16 18N	92 09W
Como Italy	89	B6	45 48N	9 05E
Comodoro Rivadavia Argentina	81	D4	45 50S	67 30W
COMOROS	109	N5		
Compiègne Fr.	86	G8	49 25N	2 50E
Comrat Moldova	89	M7	46 18N	28 40E
Conakry Guinea	108	B9	9 30N	13 43W
Concepción Chile	81	C5	36 50S	73 03W
Concepción Mexico	74	D4	24 38N	101 25W
Concepción Paraguay	80	F9	23 22S	57 26W
Concepción del Uruguay Argentina	81	F7	32 30S	58 15W
Conchos *r.* Mexico	74	C5	27 30N	107 00W
Concord California USA	72	B3	37 59N	122 03W
Concord New Hampshire USA	71	M5	43 13N	71 34W
Concordia Argentina	81	F7	31 25S	58 00W
Concordia Kansas USA	71	G4	39 35N	97 39W
Concrete Washington USA	42	H4	48 30N	121 45W
Condom Fr.	87	F5	43 58N	0 23E
Conduit *r.* Israel	96	N11	32 25N	35 00E
Conecuh *r.* Alabama USA	71	J3	31 00N	87 00W
Conesus Lake New York USA	52	J2	42 48N	77 44W
Coney Island New York USA	73	J1	40 34N	74 00W
CONGO	108	H7		
Congo *r.* Congo/CDR	108	H7	2 00S	17 00E
CONGO DEMOCRATIC REPUBLIC	108	H7		
Conneaut Ohio USA	52	F1	41 58N	80 34W
Connecticut *r.* North America	71	M5	43 00N	72 00W
Connecticut *state* USA	71	M5	41 00N	73 00W
Constanţa Romania	89	M6	44 12N	28 40E
Constantine Algeria	108	F15	36 22N	6 40E
Constitución Chile	81	C6	31 05S	57 51W
Contamana Peru	80	B12	7 19S	75 04W

Drôme *r.* Fr. 87 H6 44 50N 5 00E
Dronning Maud Land *geog. reg.* Antarctica 117 73 00S 10 00E
Drummond Island Michigan USA 51 K3 46 00N 83 50W
Dubai UAE 97 G4 25 14N 55 17E
Dubbo Aust. 110 H3 32 16S 148 41E
Dublin RoI 86 B10 53 20N 6 15W
Dublin Georgia USA 71 K3 32 31N 82 54W
Dubno Ukraine 88 K9 50 28N 25 40E
Du Bois Pennsylvania USA 73 A2 41 07N 78 48W
Dubrovnik Croatia 89 G5 42 40N 18 07E
Dubuque Iowa USA 71 H5 42 31N 90 41W
Dudhanai India 99 L10 25 57N 90 47E
Dudinka Russia 95 L10 69 27N 86 13E
Duero *r.* Sp./Port. 87 B4 41 25N 6 30W
Dugi Otok *i.* Croatia 89 E5/E6 44 00N 15 00E
Duisburg Germany 88 A9 51 26N 6 45E
Duke Island Alaska USA 42 E4 54 50N 131 30W
Dulce *r.* Argentina 81 E8 29 00S 63 00W
Duluth Minnesota USA 71 H6 46 45N 92 10W
Dumfries UK 86 D11 55 04N 3 37W
Duna *r.* Hungary 89 G6/G7 46 00N 19 00E
Dunaújváros Hungary 89 G7 47 00N 18 55E
Dunav *r.* Serbia/Bulgaria 89 J5 45 00N 20 00E
Duncan Oklahoma USA 71 G3 34 30N 97 57W
Dundalk RoI 86 B11 54 01N 6 25W
Dundee UK 86 D12 56 28N 3 00W
Dunedin NZ 111 C2 45 53S 170 30E
Dunfermline UK 86 D12 56 04N 3 29W
Dungeness Washington USA 42 H4 48 07N 123 06W
Dunkerque Fr. 86 G9 51 02N 2 23E
Dunkirk New York USA 71 L5 42 29N 79 21W
Dún Laoghaire RoI 86 B10 53 17N 6 08W
Dunnigan California USA 72 C4 38 53N 121 57W
Duque de Caxias Brazil 80 J9 22 46S 43 18W
Durand Michigan USA 52 C2 42 55N 83 58W
Durango Mexico 74 D4 24 01N 104 40W
Durango Colorado USA 70 E4 37 16N 107 53W
Durant Oklahoma USA 71 G3 33 59N 96 24W
Durazno Uruguay 81 F7 33 22S 56 31W
Durban RSA 109 L2 29 53S 31 00E
Durgapur India 99 F4 24 47N 87 44E
Durg-Bhilai India 98 E4 21 12N 81 20E
Durham UK 86 E11 54 47N 1 34W
Durham North Carolina USA 71 L4 36 00N 78 54W
Durrës Albania 89 G4 41 18N 19 28E
Dushanbe Tajikistan 94 J4 38 38N 68 51E
Düsseldorf Germany 88 A9 51 13N 6 47E
Duyun China 101 K4 26 16N 107 29E
Dzhetygara Kazakhstan 94 J7 52 14N 61 10E
Dzhugdzhur Range *mts.* Russia 95 R8 57 00N 137 00E

E

Eagle Alaska USA 64 B3 64 46N 141 20W
Eagle Crags *mt.* California USA 72 E2 35 25N 117 04W
Eagle Lake Maine USA 53 S6 46 25N 69 20W
Eagle Mountain Minnesota USA 51 F4 47 54N 90 31W
Eagle Pass *tn.* Texas USA 70 F2 28 44N 100 31W
Eagle River *tn.* Wisconsin USA 51 G3 45 55N 89 14W
East Aurora New York USA 52 H2 42 46N 78 37W
Eastbourne UK 86 F9 50 46N 0 17E
East Cape NZ 111 G6 37 41S 178 33E
East Caroline Basin Pacific Ocean 114 E8 4 00N 148 00E
East China Sea China/Japan 101 N5/N6 32 00N 126 00E
Easter Island Pacific Ocean 115 R5 27 05S 109 20W
Easter Island Fracture Zone Pacific Ocean 115 R5 24 00S 100 00W
Eastern Ghats *mts.* India 98 D2/E3 15 00N 80 00E
Eastern Group *is.* Fiji 114 V16 17 40S 178 30W
Eastern Sayan *mts.* Russia 95 M7 53 00N 97 30E
East Falkland *i.* Falkland Islands 81 F3 52 00S 58 50W
East Glacier Park *tn.* Montana USA 46 F1 48 27N 113 13W
East Lamma Channel HK China 100 B1 22 14N 114 09E
East Lansing Michigan USA 51 J2 42 44N 84 29W
East London RSA 109 K1 33 00S 27 54E
East Marianas Basin Pacific Ocean 114 F9 13 00N 153 00E
East Pacific Basin Pacific Ocean 115 L9 16 00N 153 00E
East Pacific Ridge Pacific Ocean 115 Q4/R7 20 00S 113 00W
East Pacific Rise Pacific Ocean 115 R9 13 00N 103 00W
Eastport Maine USA 57 G1 44 55N 67 01W
East Rift Valley East Africa 108 M8 6 00N 37 00E
East River New York USA 73 J2 40 48N 73 55W
East Siberian Sea Arctic Ocean 117 72 00N 165 00E
Eastsound Washington USA 42 H4 48 43N 123 05W
EAST TIMOR 103 H2
East Walker *r.* Nevada USA 72 D4 38 48N 119 03W
Eaton Rapids *tn.* Michigan USA 52 B2 42 30N 84 40W
Eau Claire *tn.* Wisconsin USA 71 H5 44 50N 91 30W
Eauripik-New Guinea Rise Pacific Ocean 114 E8 2 00N 142 00E
Ebensburg Pennsylvania USA 73 A2 40 29N 78 44W
Eberswalde-Finow Germany 88 D10 52 50N 13 53E
Ebinur Hu *l.* China 100 E7 45 00N 83 00E
Ebolowa Cameroon 108 G8 2 56N 11 11E
Ebro *r.* Sp. 87 F4 43 00N 4 30W
Ech Cheliff Algeria 108 E15 36 05N 1 15E
Ecija Sp. 87 C2 37 33N 5 04W
ECUADOR 80 B13
Ed Damer Sudan 108 L11 17 37N 33 59E
Ed Debba Sudan 108 L11 18 02N 30 56E
Edéa Cameroon 108 G8 3 47N 10 13E
Eden New York USA 54 D1 42 39N 78 55W
Eden North Carolina USA 71 L4 36 30N 79 46W
Eder *r.* Germany 88 B9 51 00N 9 00E
Edessa Greece 89 J4 40 48N 22 03E
Edgecombe, Cape Alaska USA 42 C5 57 00N 135 45W
Edgewood Maryland USA 73 B1 39 25N 76 18W
Edinboro Pennsylvania USA 51 L1 41 52N 80 08W
Edinburgh UK 86 D11 55 57N 3 13W
Edward, Lake CDR/Uganda 108 K7 0 30S 29 00E
Edwards Plateau Texas USA 70 F3 31 00N 100 00W
Eger Hungary 88 H7 47 53N 20 28E
Eğirdir Gölü *l.* Turkey 96 B6 37 52N 30 51E
Egmont, Mount NZ 111 E5 39 18S 174 04E
EGYPT 108 K13
Eifel *plat.* Germany 88 A9 50 00N 7 00E
Eight Degree Channel Indian Ocean 98 C1 8 00N 73 30E
Eighty Mile Beach Aust. 110 C6 19 00S 121 00E
Eindhoven Neths. 86 H9 51 26N 5 30E
Eisenach Germany 88 C9 50 59N 10 19E
Eketahuna NZ 111 E4 40 39S 175 42E
Ekibastuz Kazakhstan 94 K7 51 50N 75 10E
Eksjö Sweden 88 E12 57 40N 15 00E
El Arco Mexico 74 B5 28 00N 113 25W
Elat Israel 96 B4 29 33N 34 57E
Elâziğ Turkey 96 C6 38 41N 39 14E
El Bahr el Saghîr Egypt 109 R4 31 38N 31 39E
El Ballâh Egypt 109 S3 30 47N 32 19E
El Banco Col. 80 C15 9 04N 73 59W
Elbasan Albania 89 H4 41 07N 20 05E
El Bayadh Algeria 108 E14 33 40N 1 00E
Elbe *est.* Europe 88 B10 54 00N 9 00E
Elbert, Mount Colorado USA 70 E4 39 05N 106 27W
Elbląg Poland 88 G11 54 10N 19 25E
Elburz Mountains Iran 97 F6 36 15N 51 00E
El Cajon California USA 72 E1 32 48N 116 58W
El Callao Venezuela 80 E15 7 18N 61 50W
El Cap Egypt 109 S3 30 55N 32 23E
El Centro California USA 70 C3 32 47N 115 33W
Elche Sp. 87 E3 38 16N 0 41W
Elda Sp. 87 E3 38 29N 0 47W
El Dorado Arkansas USA 71 H3 33 12N 92 40W
El Dorado Kansas USA 71 G4 37 51N 96 52W
Eldoret Kenya 108 M8 0 31N 35 17E
Elephant Island South Shetland Islands 81 F1 62 00S 55 00W
El Faiyûm Egypt 108 L13 29 19N 30 50E
El Fasher Sudan 108 K10 13 37N 25 22E
El Ferrol del Caudillo Sp. 87 A5 43 29N 8 14W
El Firdân Egypt 109 S3 30 42N 32 20E
El Fuerte Mexico 74 C5 26 28N 108 35W
Elgin UK 86 D12 57 39N 3 20W
El Giza Egypt 108 L13 30 01N 31 12E
El Golea Algeria 108 E14 30 35N 2 51E
Elgon, Mount Uganda/Kenya 108 L8 1 07N 34 35E
Elista Russia 94 G6 46 18N 44 14E
Elizabeth Aust. 110 F3 34 45S 138 39E
Elizabeth New Jersey USA 73 H1 40 39N 74 13W
Elizabeth City North Carolina USA 71 L4 36 18N 76 16W
El Jadida Morocco 108 C14 33 19N 8 35W
El Jafr Jordan 96 P10 30 16N 36 11E
Elk Poland 88 J10 53 51N 22 20E
Elk California USA 72 B4 39 08N 123 43W
Elk City Oklahoma USA 70 G4 34 25N 99 26W
Elk Creek *tn.* California USA 72 B4 39 36N 122 34W
Elk Grove California USA 72 C4 38 26N 121 26W
El Khârga Egypt 108 L13 25 27N 30 32E
Elkhart Indiana USA 71 J5 41 52N 85 56W
Elkhorn *r.* Nebraska USA 71 G5 42 00N 98 00W
Elkland Pennsylvania USA 53 J1 42 00N 77 20W
Elko Nevada USA 70 C5 40 50N 115 46W
Ellis Island New Jersey USA 73 H1 40 42N 74 02W
Ellsworth Maine USA 57 F1 44 34N 68 24W
Ellsworth Land *geog. reg.* Antarctica 117 75 00S 80 00W
El Mahalla El Kubra Egypt 108 L14 30 59N 31 10E
El Manzala Egypt 109 R4 31 09N 31 57E
El Matarîya Egypt 109 S4 31 10N 32 02E
El Médano Mexico 74 B4 24 35N 111 29W
Elmhurst Pennsylvania USA 73 C2 41 20N 75 32W
el Milk *r.* Sudan 108 K11 17 00N 29 00E
El Minya Egypt 108 L13 28 06N 30 45E
Elmira New York USA 71 L5 42 06N 76 50W
El Muglad Sudan 108 K10 11 01N 27 50E
El Obeid Sudan 108 L10 13 11N 30 10E
El Paso Texas USA 70 E3 31 45N 106 30W
El Porvenir Mexico 74 C6 31 15N 105 48W
El Progreso Honduras 74 G3 15 20N 87 50W
El Puerto de Santa Maria Sp. 87 B2 36 36N 6 14W
El Qantara Egypt 109 S3 30 53N 32 20E
El Reno Oklahoma USA 71 G4 35 32N 97 57W
El Sâlhîya Egypt 109 R3 30 47N 31 59E
El Salto Mexico 74 C4 23 47N 105 22W
EL SALVADOR 74 G2
El Shallûfa Egypt 109 T2 30 06N 32 33E
El Sueco Mexico 74 C5 29 54N 106 22W
Eltanin Fracture Zone Pacific Ocean 115 M3 52 00S 135 00W
El Tigre Venezuela 80 E15 8 44N 64 18W
El Tina Egypt 109 S4 31 03N 32 19E
El Toro California USA 72 E1 33 36N 117 40W
Eluru India 98 E3 16 45N 81 10E
Elvas Port. 87 B3 38 53N 7 10W
Ely Nevada USA 70 D4 39 15N 114 53W
Elyria Ohio USA 71 K5 41 22N 82 06W
Emāmrūd Iran 97 F6 36 15N 54 59E
Emba Kazakhstan 94 H6 48 47N 58 05E
Emba *r.* Kazakhstan 94 H6 47 30N 56 00E
Embalse de Guri *l.* Venezuela 80 E15 7 30N 62 30W
Emden Germany 88 A10 53 23N 7 13E
Emerald Aust. 110 H5 23 30S 148 08E
Emi Koussi *mt.* Chad 108 H11 19 52N 18 31E
Empalme Mexico 74 B5 28 00N 110 49W
Emperor Seamounts Pacific Ocean 114 G12 42 00N 169 00E
Emporia Kansas USA 71 G4 38 24N 96 10W
Emporium Pennsylvania USA 52 H1 41 30N 78 14W
Ems *r.* Germany 88 A10 53 00N 7 00E
Encarnación Paraguay 80 F8 27 20S 55 50W
Encinitas California USA 72 E1 33 04N 117 17W
Endeh Indonesia 103 G2 8 51S 121 40E
Enderby Land *geog. reg.* Antarctica 117 65 00S 45 00E
Endicott New York USA 53 K2 42 06N 76 00W
Engel's Russia 94 G7 51 30N 46 07E
England *admin.* UK 86 D11 53 00N 2 00W
Enid Oklahoma USA 71 G4 36 24N 97 54W
Enna Italy 89 E2 37 34N 14 16E
En Nahud Sudan 108 K10 12 41N 28 28E
Enniskillen UK 86 B11 54 21N 7 38W
Enns *r.* Austria 88 E7 48 00N 14 40E
Enosburg Falls *tn.* Vermont USA 53 P4 44 55N 72 49W
Enschede Neths. 86 J10 52 13N 6 55E
Ensenada Mexico 74 A6 31 53N 116 38W
Entebbe Uganda 108 L8 0 04N 32 27E
Enugu Nigeria 108 F9 6 20N 7 29E
Épernay Fr. 86 G8 49 02N 3 58E
Épinal Fr. 86 J8 48 10N 6 28E
EQUATORIAL GUINEA 108 F8
Erechim Brazil 80 G8 27 35S 52 15W
Erenhot China 101 L7 43 50N 112 00E
Erfurt Germany 88 C9 50 58N 11 02E
Erg Chech *geog. reg.* Algeria 108 D12 24 30N 3 00W
Erg Iguidi *geog. reg.* Algeria 108 C13 26 00N 6 00W
Erie Pennsylvania USA 71 K5 42 07N 80 05W
Erimo-misaki *c.* Japan 102 D3 41 55N 143 13E
ERITREA 108 N10
Erode India 98 D2 11 21N 77 43E
Erris Head *c.* RoI 86 A11 54 20N 10 00W
Er Roseires Sudan 108 L10 11 52N 34 23E
Erzgebirge *mts.* Europe 88 D9 50 00N 13 00E
Erzincan Turkey 96 C6 39 44N 39 30E
Erzurum Turkey 96 D6 39 57N 41 17E
Esashi Japan 102 D3 41 54N 140 09E
Esbjerg Denmark 88 B11 55 20N 8 20E
Escanaba Michigan USA 71 J6 45 47N 87 04W
Escárcega Mexico 74 F3 18 39N 90 43W
Escobal Panama 75 Y2 9 11N 79 59W
Escondido California USA 70 C3 33 07N 117 05W
Eşfahān Iran 97 F5 32 41N 51 41E
Eskilstuna Sweden 88 F13 59 22N 16 31E
Eskişehir Turkey 96 B6 39 46N 30 30E
Esmeraldas Ecuador 80 B14 0 56N 79 40W
Esparto California USA 72 B4 38 42N 122 00W
Esperance Aust. 110 C3 33 49S 121 52E
Espírito Santo *admin.* Brazil 80 J10 18 40S 40 00W
Espoo Finland 88 K14 60 10N 24 40E
Esquel Argentina 81 C5 42 55S 71 20W
Es Semara Western Sahara 108 B13 26 25N 11 30W
Essen Germany 88 A9 51 27N 6 57E
Essequibo *r.* Guyana 80 F14 2 30N 58 00W
Essex California USA 72 F2 34 45N 115 15W
Estância Brazil 80 K11 11 15S 37 28W
ESTONIA 88 J13
Estrecho de Magallanes *sd.* Chile 81 C3 53 00S 71 00W
Etawah India 98 D5 26 46N 79 01E
ETHIOPIA 108 M9
Etna, Mount Italy 89 E2 37 45N 15 00E
Etolin Island Alaska USA 42 D5 56 10N 132 30W
Etosha Pan *salt l.* Namibia 109 H4 18 30S 16 30E
Eucla Aust. 110 D3 31 40S 128 51E
Euclid Ohio USA 51 L1 41 34N 81 32W
Eugene Oregon USA 70 B5 44 03N 123 04W
Euphrates *r.* Iraq/Syria/Turkey 96 D5 34 40N 42 00E
Eureka California USA 70 B5 40 49N 124 10W
Eureka Montana USA 43 N1 48 56N 115 05W
Eureka Nevada USA 72 F4 39 49N 115 58W
Evansville Indiana USA 71 J4 38 00N 87 33W
Eveleth Minnesota USA 51 E4 47 28N 92 32W
Everest, Mount China/Nepal 99 F5 27 59N 86 56E
Everett Washington USA 70 B6 47 59N 122 14W
Evora Port. 87 B3 38 46N 7 41W
Evreux Fr. 86 F8 49 03N 1 11E
Evvoia *i.* Greece 89 K3 38 00N 24 00E
Excelsior Mountains Nevada USA 72 D4 38 15N 118 30W
Exeter UK 86 D9 50 43N 3 31W
Exeter California USA 72 D3 36 18N 119 08W
Exmoor *hills* UK 86 D9 51 08N 3 40W
Exmouth Aust. 110 A5 21 54S 114 10E
Eyasi, Lake Tanzania 108 M7 4 00S 35 00E
Eyre Creek Aust. 110 F4 26 00S 138 00E
Eyre, Lake Aust. 110 F4 28 00S 136 00E
Eyre Peninsula Aust. 110 F3 34 00S 136 00E

F

Fada Chad 108 J11 17 14N 21 32E
Faeroes *i.* Atlantic Ocean 116 H13 62 00N 7 00W
Fafan *r.* Ethiopia 108 N9 7 30N 44 00E
Fagersta Sweden 88 E13 59 59N 15 49E
Fairbanks Alaska USA 64 A3 64 50N 147 50W
Fairfield California USA 72 B4 38 14N 122 03W
Fair Isle *i.* UK 86 E13 59 32N 1 38W
Fairmont West Virginia USA 71 K4 39 28N 80 08W
Fairview Park HK China 100 B2 22 29N 114 03E
Faisalabad Pakistan 98 C6 31 25N 73 09E
Faizabad India 98 E5 26 46N 82 08E
Fakfak Indonesia 103 J3 2 55S 132 17E
Falam Myanmar 100 G3 22 58N 93 45E
Falfurrias Texas USA 71 G2 27 17N 98 10W
Falkenburg Sweden 88 D12 56 55N 12 30E
Falkirk UK 86 D11 55 59N 3 48W
Falkland Islands South Atlantic Ocean 81 E3/F3 52 30S 60 00W
Falköping Sweden 88 D13 58 10N 13 32E
Fallon Nevada USA 72 D4 39 29N 118 46W
Fall River *tn.* Massachusetts USA 71 M5 41 41N 71 08W
Falmouth Antigua and Barbuda 74 Q9 17 01N 61 46W
Falmouth Jamaica 75 U14 18 29N 77 39W
Falmouth Massachusetts USA 73 E2 41 34N 70 37W
Famagusta Cyprus 96 B6 35 07N 33 57E
Fan Lau HK China 100 A1 22 12N 113 51E
Fanling HK China 100 B2 22 29N 114 07E
Fâqûs Egypt 109 R3 30 44N 31 48E
Farafangana Madagascar 109 P3 22 50S 47 50E
Farāh Afghanistan 97 H5 32 22N 62 07E
Farah Rud *r.* Afghanistan 97 H5 32 00N 62 00E
Fargo North Dakota USA 71 G6 46 52N 96 49W
Faridabad India 98 D5 28 24N 77 18E
Faridpur Bangladesh 99 K9 23 29N 89 31E
Farmington Maine USA 53 R4 44 41N 70 11W
Farmington New Mexico USA 70 E4 36 43N 108 12W
Farnham New York USA 54 C1 42 36N 79 05W
Faro Port. 87 B2 37 01N 7 56W
Farquhar Islands Seychelles 109 Q6 9 00N 50 00E
Fastov Ukraine 88 M9 50 08N 29 59E
Fatehgarh India 98 D5 27 22N 79 38E
Faya-Largeau Chad 108 H11 17 58N 19 06E
Fayetteville Arkansas USA 71 H4 36 03N 94 10W
Fayetteville North Carolina USA 71 L4 35 03N 78 53W
Fâyid Egypt 109 S2 30 18N 31 19E
Fderik Mauritania 108 B12 22 30N 12 30W
Fécamp Fr. 86 F8 49 45N 0 23E
FEDERATED STATES OF MICRONESIA 114 E8/F8
Feilding NZ 111 E4 40 14S 175 34E
Feira de Santana Brazil 80 K11 12 17S 38 53W
Felipe Carrillo Puerto Mexico 74 G3 19 51N 88 02W
Feni Bangladesh 99 L9 23 00N 91 24E
Fenton Michigan USA 52 C2 42 48N 83 42W
Fergana Uzbekistan 94 K5 40 23N 71 19E
Fergus Falls *tn.* Minnesota USA 71 G6 46 18N 96 07W
Ferndale Washington USA 42 H4 48 50N 122 35W
Fernley Nevada USA 72 D4 39 36N 119 17W
Ferrara Italy 89 C6 44 50N 11 38E
Ferreñafe Peru 80 B12 6 42S 79 45W
Fès Morocco 108 C14 34 05N 5 00W
Fethiye Turkey 96 A6 36 37N 29 06E
Feyzābād Afghanistan 97 K6 37 06N 70 34E
Fianarantsoa Madagascar 109 P3 21 27S 47 05E
Fier Albania 89 G4 40 44N 19 33E
Figeac Fr. 87 G6 44 32N 2 01E
Figueira da Foz Port. 87 A4 40 09N 8 51W
Figueres Sp. 87 G5 42 16N 2 57E
FIJI 114
Filchner Ice Shelf Antarctica 117 80 00S 37 00W
Findlay Ohio USA 51 K1 41 01N 83 39W
FINLAND 94 E9
Finland, Gulf of Finland/Russia 88 J13 59 40N 23 30E
Fiordland NZ 111 A2 45 09S 167 18E
Firat *r.* Turkey/Syria/Iraq 96 C6 37 30N 38 00E
Firozabad India 98 D5 27 09N 78 24E
Firth of Clyde *est.* UK 86 C11 55 30N 5 00W
Firth of Forth *est.* UK 86 D12 56 05N 3 00W
Firth of Lorn *est.* UK 86 B12 56 15N 6 00W
Fish *r.* Namibia 109 H2 26 30S 17 30E
Fishguard UK 86 C9 51 59N 4 59W
Fitchburg Massachusetts USA 73 E3 42 35N 71 48W
Fitzroy *r.* Aust. 110 C6 18 00S 124 00E
Flagstaff Arizona USA 70 D4 35 12N 111 38W
Flagstaff Lake Maine USA 53 R5 45 14N 70 20W
Flambeau River Wisconsin USA 51 F3 45 59N 90 30W
Flamborough Head *c.* UK 86 E11 54 06N 0 04W

Flatbush New York USA 73 J1 40 38N 73 56W
Flathead Lake Montana USA 70 D6 47 55N 114 05W
Flathead River Montana USA 46 E1 48 55N 114 30W
Flatlands New York USA 73 J1 40 37N 73 54W
Flattery, Cape Washington USA 70 B6 48 24N 124 43W
Flekkefjord Norway 86 J13 58 17N 6 40E
Flensburg Germany 88 B11 54 47N 9 27E
Flers Fr. 86 E8 48 45N 0 34W
Fletcher Pond *l.* Michigan USA 52 C4 44 59N 83 53W
Flinders *r.* Aust. 110 G6 19 00S 141 30E
Flinders Range *mts.* Aust. 110 F3 32 00S 138 00E
Flint Michigan USA 71 K5 43 03N 83 40W
Flint *r.* Georgia USA 71 K3 31 00N 84 00W
Flint River Michigan USA 52 C3 43 12N 83 50W
Florence Italy 89 C5 43 47N 11 15E
Florence Alabama USA 71 J3 34 48N 87 40W
Florence South Carolina USA 71 L3 34 12N 79 44W
Florence Wisconsin USA 51 G3 45 55N 88 15W
Florencia Col. 80 B14 1 37N 75 37W
Flores Guatemala 74 G3 16 58N 89 50W
Flores *i.* Indonesia 103 G2 8 30S 121 00E
Flores Sea Indonesia 103 F2/G2 7 00S 119 00E
Floresti Moldova 88 M7 47 52N 28 12E
Floriano Brazil 80 J12 6 45S 43 00W
Florianópolis Brazil 81 H8 27 35S 48 31W
Florida Uruguay 81 F7 34 04S 56 14W
Florida *state* USA 71 K2 28 00N 82 00W
Florida Bay Florida USA 71 K2 25 00N 81 00W
Florida Keys *is.* Florida USA 71 K1 25 00N 80 00W
Flórina Greece 89 H4 40 48N 21 26E
Florissant Missouri USA 71 H4 38 49N 90 24W
Flushing New York USA 73 J2 40 45N 73 49W
Focşani Romania 89 L6 45 41N 27 12E
Fóggia Italy 89 H4 41 28N 15 33E
Fohnsdorf Austria 89 E7 47 13N 14 40E
Foix Fr. 87 F5 42 57N 1 35E
Folkestone UK 86 F9 51 05N 1 11E
Fond du Lac Wisconsin USA 71 J5 43 48N 88 27W
Fontainebleau Fr. 86 G8 48 24N 2 42E
Fonte Boa Brazil 80 D13 2 33S 65 59W
Foresthill *tn.* California USA 72 C4 39 02N 120 49W
Forest Hills *tn.* New York USA 73 J1 40 43N 73 51W
Forli Italy 89 D6 44 13N 12 02E
Formentera *i.* Sp. 87 F3 38 41N 1 30E
FORMER YUGOSLAV REPUBLIC OF MACEDONIA (FYROM) 89 H4/J4
Formosa Argentina 80 F8 26 07S 58 14W
Formosa Brazil 80 H10 15 30S 47 22W
Forrest Aust. 110 D3 30 49S 128 03E
Fortaleza Brazil 80 K13 3 45S 38 35W
Fort Bragg California USA 70 B4 39 29N 123 46W
Fort Collins Colorado USA 70 E5 40 35N 105 05W
Fort-de-France Lesser Antilles 74 R12 14 36N 61 05W
Fort Dodge Iowa USA 71 H5 42 31N 94 10W
Fortescue *r.* Aust. 110 B5 21 30S 117 30E
Fort Kent Maine USA 57 F2 47 15N 68 35W
Fort Lauderdale Florida USA 71 K2 26 08N 80 08W
Fort Myers Florida USA 71 K2 26 39N 81 51W
Fort Peck Lake Montana USA 70 E6 48 01N 106 28W
Fort Pierce Florida USA 71 K2 27 28N 80 20W
Fort Portal Uganda 108 L8 0 40N 30 17E
Fort Scott Kansas USA 71 H4 37 52N 94 43W
Fort Smith Arkansas USA 71 H4 35 22N 94 27W
Fort Stockton Texas USA 70 F3 30 54N 102 54W
Fort Sumner New Mexico USA 70 F3 34 27N 104 16W
Fortuna North Dakota USA 47 F1 48 58N 103 49W
Fort Walton Beach *tn.* Florida USA 71 J3 30 25N 86 38W
Fort Wayne Indiana USA 71 J5 41 05N 85 08W
Fort Worth Texas USA 71 G3 32 45N 97 20W
Fort Yukon Alaska USA 64 A4 66 35N 145 20W
Foshan China 101 L3 23 03N 113 08E
Fostoria Ohio USA 51 K1 41 09N 83 24W
Fougères Fr. 86 E8 48 21N 1 12W
Foula *i.* UK 86 D14 60 08N 2 05W
Foumban Cameroon 108 G9 5 43N 10 50E
Fouta Djallon *geog. reg.* Guinea 108 B10 12 00N 13 10W
Foz do Iguaçú Argentina 80 G8 25 33S 54 31W
Framingham Massachusetts USA 73 E3 42 17N 71 25W
Franca Brazil 80 H9 20 33S 47 27W
FRANCE 86/87
Francis Case, Lake South Dakota USA 70 G5 43 00N 99 00W
Francistown Botswana 109 K3 21 11S 27 32E
Frankenmuth Michigan USA 52 C3 43 19N 83 44W
Frankfort Kentucky USA 71 K4 38 11N 84 53W
Frankfurt am Main Germany 88 B9 50 06N 8 41E
Frankfurt an der Oder Germany 88 E10 52 20N 14 32E
Fränkische Alb *mts.* Germany 88 C8 49 00N 11 00E
Franklin D. Roosevelt Lake Washington USA 70 C6 48 05N 118 15W
Franklinville New York USA 52 H2 42 20N 78 27W
Franz Josef Land *is.* Russia 94 G13 80 00N 50 00E
Fraserburgh UK 86 E12 57 42N 2 00W
Frederick Maryland USA 73 B1 39 25N 77 25W
Fredericksburg Virginia USA 71 L4 38 18N 77 30W
Frederick Sound Alaska USA 42 C5/D5 57 00N 134 00W
Frederikshavn Denmark 88 C12 57 28N 10 33E
Fredonia New York USA 52 G2 42 27N 79 22W
Fredrikstad Norway 86 L13 59 20N 10 50E
Freeport Texas USA 71 G2 28 56N 95 20W
Freetown Sierra Leone 108 B9 8 30N 13 17W
Freewood Acres New Jersey USA 73 C2 40 10N 74 14W
Freiburg im Breisgau Germany 88 A7 48 00N 7 52E
Fréjus Fr. 87 J5 43 26N 6 44E
Fremantle Aust. 110 B3 32 07S 115 44E
Fremont California USA 72 C3 37 32N 121 59W
Fremont Ohio USA 51 K1 41 21N 83 07W
French Creek *r.* Pennsylvania USA 52 F1 41 40N 80 10W
French Guiana *territory* Fr. 80 G14 5 00N 53 00W
Frenchman Fork *r.* USA 70 F5 40 00N 103 00W
Frenchman Lake Nevada USA 72 F3 36 50N 115 58W
French Polynesia Pacific Ocean 115 M6 21 00S 150 00W
Fresnillo Mexico 74 D4 23 10N 102 54W
Fresno California USA 70 C4 36 41N 119 47W
Fresno Reservoir Montana USA 47 B1/C1 48 42N 110 00W
Friday Harbor *tn.* Washington USA 42 H4 48 36N 123 05W
Frontera Mexico 74 F3 18 32N 92 39W
Frosinone Italy 89 D4 41 38N 13 22E
Frýdek-Místek Czech Rep. 88 G8 49 42N 18 20E
Fuerteventura *i.* Canary Islands 108 B13 28 25N 14 00W
Fuji Japan 102 C2 35 10N 138 37E
Fujinomiya Japan 102 C2 35 16N 138 33E
Fuji-san *mt.* Japan 102 C2 35 23N 138 42E
Fujisawa Japan 102 C2 35 20N 139 29E
Fukui Japan 102 C2 36 04N 136 12E
Fukuoka Japan 102 B1 33 39N 130 21E
Fukushima Japan 102 D2 37 44N 140 28E
Fukuyama Japan 102 B1 34 29N 133 21E
Fulda Germany 88 B9 50 33N 9 41E
Fulton New York USA 73 B3 43 19N 76 25W
Funabashi Japan 102 C2 35 42N 139 59E
Funchal Madeira 108 A14 32 40N 16 55W
Furneaux Group *is.* Aust. 110 H1 45 00S 148 00E
Furukawa Japan 102 D2 38 34N 140 56E
Fushun China 101 N7 41 50N 123 54E
Fu Tau Fan Chau *i.* HK China 100 D2 22 20N 114 22E
Fuxin China 101 N7 42 04N 121 39E
Fuzhou China 101 M4 26 09N 119 17E
Fyn *i.* Denmark 88 C11 55 30N 10 00E

G

Gaalkacyo Somalia 108 P9 6 47N 47 12E
Gabbs Nevada USA 72 E4 38 53N 117 57W
Gabès Tunisia 108 G14 33 52N 10 06E
GABON 108 G7
Gaborone Botswana 109 K3 24 45S 25 55E
Gabrovo Bulgaria 89 K5 42 52N 25 19E
Gadsden Alabama USA 71 J3 34 00N 86 00W
Gaeta Italy 89 D4 41 13N 13 36E
Gafsa Tunisia 108 F14 34 28N 8 43E
Gagnoa Côte d'Ivoire 108 C9 6 04N 5 55W
Gaillard Cut Panama 75 Y2 9 05N 79 40W
Gainesville Florida USA 71 K2 29 37N 82 21W
Gainesville Texas USA 71 G3 33 09N 97 38W
Gairdner, Lake Aust. 110 F3 32 50S 136 00E
Gajol India 99 K10 25 10N 88 14E
Galápagos Rise Pacific Ocean 115 T6 12 00S 87 00W
Galashiels UK 86 D11 55 37N 2 49W
Galata Montana USA 46 G1 48 27N 111 20W
Galaţi Romania 89 M6 45 27N 28 02E
Galeota Point Trinidad and Tobago 75 V15 10 09N 60 00W
Galera Point Trinidad and Tobago 75 V15 10 49N 60 54W
Galesburg Illinois USA 71 H5 40 58N 90 22W
Galeton Pennsylvania USA 52 J1 41 44N 77 40W
Galle Sri Lanka 98 E1 6 01N 80 13E
Gallego *r.* Sp. 87 E4/E5 41 55N 0 56W
Gallipoli Italy 89 G4 40 03N 17 59E
Gallup New Mexico USA 70 E4 32 32N 108 46W
Galveston Texas USA 71 H2 29 17N 94 48W
Galway RoI 86 A10 53 16N 9 03W
Galway Bay RoI 86 A10 53 15N 9 15W
Gambia *r.* Senegal/The Gambia 108 B10 13 45N 13 15W
GAMBIA, THE 108 A10
Gambier Islands Pacific Ocean 115 N5 23 10S 135 00W
Gamboa Panama 75 Y2 9 08N 79 42W
Gandak *r.* India 99 E5 26 30N 85 00E
Gandhi Sagar *l.* India 98 D4 24 30N 75 30E
Ganga *r.* India 98 E5 25 00N 83 30E
Ganga, Mouths of the *est.* Bangladesh/India 99 F4 21 30N 89 00E
Ganganagar India 98 C5 29 54N 73 56E
Gangdisê Shan *mts.* China 100 E5 31 00N 82 30E
Gangtok India 99 F5 27 20N 88 39E
Ganzhou China 101 L4 25 45N 114 51E
Gao Mali 108 D11 16 19N 0 09W
Gap Fr. 87 J6 44 33N 6 05E
Garanhuns Brazil 80 K12 8 53S 36 28W
Gard *r.* Fr. 87 H5 44 05N 4 20E
Garden City Kansas USA 70 F4 37 57N 100 54W
Gardēz Afghanistan 97 J5 33 37N 69 07E
Gardner Island Kiribati 114 J7 4 40S 174 32W
Garissa Kenya 108 M7 0 27S 39 39E
Garland Texas USA 71 G3 32 55N 96 37W
Garonne *r.* Fr. 87 E6 44 45N 0 15E
Garoua Cameroon 108 G9 9 17N 13 22E
Gary Indiana USA 71 J5 41 34N 87 20W
Garzón Col. 80 B14 2 14N 75 37W
Gascoyne *r.* Aust. 110 A5 25 00S 114 00E
Gastonia North Carolina USA 71 K4 35 14N 81 12W
Gateshead UK 86 E11 54 58N 1 35W
Gates of the Arctic National Park Alaska USA 40 E7 67 30N 155 00W
Gatún Panama 75 Y2 9 16N 79 55W
Gatún Lake Panama 75 Y2 9 15N 79 50W
Gávdos *i.* Greece 89 K1 34 00N 24 00E
Gaya India 99 F4 24 48N 85 00E
Gaylord Michigan USA 51 J3 45 01N 84 41W
Gaza Middle East 96 N10 31 30N 34 28E
Gaza *territory* Middle East 96 N10 31 28N 34 05E
Gaziantep Turkey 96 C6 37 04N 37 21E
Gbarnga Liberia 108 C9 7 02N 9 26W
Gdańsk Poland 88 G11 54 22N 18 41E
Gdańsk, Gulf of Baltic Sea 88 G11 54 00N 19 00E
Gdynia Poland 88 G11 54 31N 18 30E
Gedaref Sudan 108 M10 14 01N 35 24E
Gediz *r.* Turkey 96 A6 38 40N 27 30E
Geelong Aust. 110 G2 38 10S 144 26E
Gejiu China 101 J3 23 25N 103 05E
Gela Italy 89 E2 37 04N 14 15E
Genale *r.* Ethiopia 108 N9 6 00N 40 00E
Geneina Sudan 108 J10 13 27N 22 30E
Geneseo New York USA 52 J2 42 48N 77 49W
Geneseo River New York USA 51 M2 42 40N 78 00W
Geneva Switz. 87 J7 46 13N 6 09E
Geneva New York USA 51 N2 42 51N 77 01W
Geneva Ohio USA 52 F1 41 48N 80 57W
Genil *r.* Sp. 87 C2 37 20N 4 45W
Genk Belgium 86 H9 50 58N 5 30E
Genoa Italy 89 B6 44 24N 8 56E
Gent Belgium 86 G9 51 02N 3 42E
Georgetown Guyana 80 F15 6 46N 58 10W
George Town Malaysia 103 C5 5 25N 100 20E
Georgetown South Carolina USA 71 L3 33 23N 79 18W
George V Land *geog. reg.* Antarctica 117 70 00S 150 00E
GEORGIA 94 G5
Georgia *state* USA 71 K3 33 00N 83 00W
Gera Germany 88 D9 50 51N 12 11E
Geraldton Aust. 110 A4 28 49S 144 36E
GERMANY 88 A9
Gerona Sp. 87 G4 41 59N 2 49E
Getafe Sp. 87 D4 40 18N 3 44W
Gettysburg Pennsylvania USA 73 B1 39 49N 77 14W
Gettysburg National Military Park Pennsylvania USA 73 B1 39 57N 77 15W
Ghadamis Libya 108 F14 30 08N 9 30E
Ghaghara *r.* India/Nepal 98 E5 27 20N 81 30E
GHANA 108 D9
Ghanzi Botswana 109 J3 21 42S 21 39E
Ghardaïa Algeria 108 E14 32 20N 3 40E
Gharyan Libya 108 G14 32 10N 13 01E
Ghat Libya 108 G12 24 58N 10 11E
Ghaziabad India 98 D5 28 39N 77 26E
Ghazni Afghanistan 97 J5 33 33N 68 26E
Ghisonaccia Fr. 87 K5 42 01N 9 24E
Gibraltar *territory* U.K. 87 C2 36 09N 5 21W
Gibraltar, Strait of Sp./Morocco 87 C1 35 58N 5 30W
Gibson Desert Aust. 110 C5 25 00S 123 00E
Gidole Ethiopia 108 M9 5 38N 37 28E
Gifu Japan 102 C2 35 27N 136 46E
Gigüela *r.* Sp. 87 D3 39 40N 3 15W
Gijón Sp. 87 C5 43 32N 5 40W
Gila *r.* USA 70 D3 33 00N 114 00W
Gila Bend Arizona USA 70 D3 32 56N 112 42W
Gilbert *r.* Aust. 110 G6 17 00S 142 30E
Gilbert Islands Pacific Ocean 114 H7/H8 0 00 173 00E
Gildford Montana USA 46 G1 48 39N 110 35W
Gilgit Kashmir 98 C7 35 54N 74 20E
Gillette Wyoming USA 70 E5 44 18N 105 30W
Gilroy California USA 72 C3 37 01N 121 38W
Gineifa Egypt 109 S2 30 12N 32 26E
Ginir Ethiopia 108 N9 7 06N 40 40E
Gippsland *geog. reg.* Aust. 110 H2 37 30S 147 00E
Girard Pennsylvania USA 52 F2 42 01N 80 20W
Girardot Col. 80 C14 4 19N 74 47W
Girga Egypt 108 L13 26 17N 31 58E
Gironde *r.* Fr. 87 E6 45 30N 0 45W
Girvan UK 86 C11 55 15N 4 51W
Gisborne NZ 111 G5 38 40S 178 01E
Giurgiu Romania 89 K5 43 53N 25 58E
Gizhiga Russia 95 U9 62 00N 160 34E
Gjirokastër Albania 89 H4 40 05N 20 10E
Glacier Washington USA 42 H4 48 53N 121 57W
Glacier Bay *r.* Alaska USA 42 B6 58 45N 136 15W
Glacier Bay National Park Alaska USA 42 B6 58 45N 136 30W
Glacier National Park Montana USA 46 E1/F1 48 50N 114 00W
Gladstone Aust. 110 J5 23 52S 151 16E
Gladwin Michigan USA 51 J2 43 59N 84 30W
Glasgow UK 86 C11 55 53N 4 15W
Glendale California USA 72 D2 34 09N 118 16W
Glen Ridge New Jersey USA 73 H2 40 47N 74 13W
Glens Falls *tn.* New York USA 71 M5 43 17N 73 41W
Gliwice Poland 88 G9 50 20N 18 40E
Globe Arizona USA 70 D3 33 23N 110 48W
Głogów Poland 88 F9 51 40N 16 06E
Gloucester UK 86 D9 51 53N 2 14W
Gloucester Massachusetts USA 73 E3 42 37N 70 40W
Gloversville New York USA 73 C3 43 03N 74 20W
Gniezno Poland 88 F10 52 32N 17 32E
Goa *admin.* India 98 C3 15 00N 74 00E
Goalpara India 99 L11 26 08N 90 36E
Gobabis Namibia 109 H3 22 30S 18 58E
Gobi Desert Mongolia 101 H7 48 30N 100 00E
Godavari *r.* India 98 C3 20 00N 75 00E
Godhra India 98 C4 22 49N 73 40E
Goiânia Brazil 80 H10 16 43S 49 18W
Goiás Brazil 80 G10 15 57S 50 07W
Goiás *admin.* Brazil 80 H11 14 00S 48 00W
Golan Heights *territory* Middle East 96 N11 33 00N 35 55E
Gold Coast *tn.* Aust. 110 J4 27 59S 153 22E
Goldfield *tn.* Nevada USA 72 E3 37 42N 117 15W
Goldsboro North Carolina USA 71 L4 35 23N 78 00W
Goldsworthy Aust. 110 B5 20 20S 119 31E
Goleta California USA 72 D2 34 26N 119 50W
Golfe de Gabès *g.* Tunisia 108 G14 34 20N 10 30E
Golfe de St-Malo *g.* Fr. 86 D8 48 55N 2 30W
Golfe du Lion *g.* Fr. 87 G5/H5 43 10N 4 00E
Golfo de California *g.* Mexico 74 B5/C4 27 00N 111 00W
Golfo de Guayaquil *g.* Ecuador 80 A13 3 00S 81 30W
Golfo de Honduras *g.* Caribbean Sea 74 G3 17 00N 87 30W
Golfo del Darién *g.* Col./Panama 75 J1 9 00N 77 00W
Golfo de San Jorge *g.* Argentina 81 D4 47 00S 66 00W
Golfo de Tehuantepec *g.* Mexico 74 E3/F3 15 30N 95 00W
Golfo de Venezuela *g.* Venezuela 80 C16 12 00N 71 30W
Golfo di Cágliari *g.* Italy 89 B3 39 00N 9 00E
Golfo di Catania *g.* Italy 89 E2 37 30N 15 20E
Golfo di Gaeta *g.* Italy 89 D4 41 00N 13 00E
Golfo di Genova *g.* Italy 89 B6 44 00N 9 00E
Golfo di Squillace *g.* Italy 89 F3 38 30N 17 00E
Golfo di Táranto *g.* Italy 89 F4 40 00N 17 00E
Golfo di Venézia *g.* Adriatic Sea 89 D6 45 00N 13 00E
Golfo San Matías *g.* Argentina 81 E5 42 00S 64 00W
Golmud China 100 G6 36 22N 94 55E
Gomati *r.* India 98 E5 26 50N 81 00E
Gomera *i.* Canary Islands 108 A13 28 08N 17 14W
Gómez Palacio Mexico 74 D5 25 39N 103 30W
Gonder Ethiopia 108 M10 12 39N 37 29E
Gondia India 98 E4 21 23N 80 14E
Good Hope, Cape of RSA 109 H1 34 30S 19 00E
Goodland Kansas USA 70 F4 39 20N 101 43W
Goondiwindi Aust. 110 J4 28 30S 150 17E
Gorakhpur India 98 E5 26 45N 83 23E
Gora Narodnaya *mt.* Russia 94 J10 65 02N 60 01E
Gora Pobeda *mt.* Russia 95 S10 65 10N 146 00E
Gorda Rise Pacific Ocean 115 N12 43 00N 130 00W
Gore Ethiopia 108 M9 8 10N 35 29E
Gore NZ 111 B1 46 06S 168 56E
Gorgān Iran 97 F6 36 50N 54 29E
Gorizia Italy 89 D6 45 57N 13 37E
Görlitz Germany 88 E9 51 09N 15 00E
Goroka PNG 110 H8 6 02S 145 22E
Gorontalo Indonesia 103 G4 0 33N 123 05E
Gory Kamen' *mt.* Russia 95 M10 69 06N 94 59E
Goryn' *r.* Ukraine 88 L9 51 00N 26 00E
Gorzów Wielkopolski Poland 88 E10 52 42N 15 12E
Gostivar FYROM 89 H4 41 47N 20 55E
Göta älv *r.* Sweden 88 C12 58 00N 12 00E
Göteborg Sweden 86 C12 57 45N 12 00E
Gotha Germany 88 C9 50 57N 10 43E
Gotland *i.* Sweden 88 G12 57 30N 18 40E
Göttingen Germany 88 B9 51 32N 9 57E
Gough Island Atlantic Ocean 116 H2 40 20S 10 00W
Goulburn Aust. 110 H3 34 47S 149 43E
Gouré Niger 108 G10 13 59N 10 15E
Governador Valadares Brazil 80 J10 18 51S 41 57W
Govind Ballash Pant Sagar *l.* India 98 E4 24 30N 82 30E
Gowanda New York USA 52 H2 42 27N 78 56W
Grafton Aust. 110 J4 29 40S 152 56E
Graham Texas USA 71 G3 33 07N 98 36W
Graham Land *geog. reg.* Antarctica 117 67 00S 64 00W
Grahamstown RSA 109 K1 33 18S 26 32E
Grampian Pennsylvania USA 73 A2 40 58N 78 37W
Grampian Mountains UK 86 C12 56 45N 4 00W
Granada Nicaragua 74 G2 11 58N 85 59W
Granada Sp. 87 D2 37 10N 3 35W
Gran Canaria *i.* Canary Islands 108 A13 28 00N 15 35W
Gran Chaco *geog. reg.* Argentina 80 E8/E9 25 00S 62 30W
Grand *r.* South Dakota USA 70 F6 46 00N 102 00W
Grand Bahama *i.* Bahamas 75 J5 27 00N 78 00W
Grand Canyon USA 70 D4 36 04N 112 07W
Grand Canyon Village Arizona USA 70 D4 36 02N 112 09W
Grand Cayman *i.* Caribbean Sea 75 H3 19 20N 81 15W
Grand Coulee Dam Washington USA 70 C6 47 59N 118 58W
Grande *r.* Bolivia 80 E10 18 00S 65 00W
Grande *r.* Brazil 80 G10 20 00S 50 00W

Grand Erg Occidental *geog. reg.* Algeria 108 E14 30 35N 0 30E
Grand Erg Oriental *geog. reg.* Algeria 108 F14 30 15N 6 45E
Grande Terre *i.* Lesser Antilles 74 Q9 17 00N 61 40W
Grand Forks North Dakota USA 71 G6 47 57N 97 05W
Grand Island *tn.* Nebraska USA 71 G5 40 56N 98 21W
Grand Junction *tn.* Colorado USA 70 E4 39 04N 108 33W
Grand Ledge Michigan USA 52 B2 42 45N 84 44W
Grand Marais Minnesota USA 51 F4 47 45N 90 20W
Grand Rapids *tn.* Michigan USA 71 J5 42 57N 86 40W
Grand Rapids *tn.* Minnesota USA 71 H6 47 13N 93 31W
Grand Rapids *tn.* Ohio USA 52 C1 41 23N 83 52W
Grand River Michigan USA 52 A2 42 55N 85 15W
Grand River Ohio USA 52 C1 41 25N 80 57W
Grand Traverse Bay Michigan USA 51 J3 45 00N 85 30W
Grandyle New York USA 54 D2 43 01N 78 57W
Granite Peak Montana USA 70 E6 45 10N 109 50W
Grant, Mount Nevada USA 72 D4 38 34N 118 48W
Grant Range *mts.* Nevada USA 72 F4 38 24N 115 27W
Grants Pass *tn.* Oregon USA 70 B5 42 26N 123 20W
Grasse Fr. 89 J3 43 40N 5 56E
Grass Island HK China 100 D2 22 29N 114 22E
Grass Valley *tn.* California USA 72 C4 39 13N 121 04W
Grassy Hill *mt.* HK China 100 B2 22 25N 114 10E
Gravesend New York USA 73 J1 40 36N 73 58W
Gravina Island Alaska USA 42 55 25N 131 45W
Grayling Michigan USA 51 J3 44 39N 84 43W
Graz Austria 89 E7 47 05N 15 22E
Great Abaco *i.* Bahamas 75 J5 26 40N 77 00W
Great Astrolabe Reef Fiji 114 U15 18 45S 178 50E
Great Australian Bight *b.* Aust. 110 D3/E3 33 00S 130 00E
Great Barrier Island NZ 111 E6 36 13S 175 24E
Great Barrier Reef Aust. 110 G7/H6 15 00S 146 00E
Great Basin *dep.* Nevada USA 70 C4 40 00N 117 00W
Great Bend Kansas USA 71 G4 38 22N 98 47W
Great Bitter Lake Egypt 109 S2 30 22N 32 22E
Great Dividing Range *mts.* Aust. 110 G7/H2 35 00S 148 00E
Greater Antilles *is.* W. Indies 75 H4/L3 19 00N 78 00W
Great Exuma *i.* Bahamas 75 J4 23 30N 76 00W
Great Falls *tn.* Montana USA 70 D6 47 30N 111 16W
Great Inagua *i.* Bahamas 75 K4 21 40N 73 00W
Great Karoo *mts.* RSA 109 J1 32 30S 22 30E
Great Neck New York USA 73 K2 40 48N 72 44W
Great Nicobar *i.* Nicobar Islands 99 G1 6 30N 94 00E
Great Salt Lake Utah USA 70 D5 41 10N 112 40W
Great Sand Sea *d.* Sahara Desert 108 J13 27 00N 25 00E
Great Sandy Desert Aust. 110 C5/D5 21 00S 124 00E
Great Sea Reef Fiji 114 T16 16 30S 178 00E
Great Victoria Desert Aust. 110 D4/E4 28 00S 130 00E
Great Wall China 101 L6 40 00N 111 00E
Great Yarmouth UK 86 F10 52 37N 1 44E
Great Zab *r.* Iraq 96 D6 36 00N 44 00E
GREECE 89 H3/K3
Greeley Colorado USA 70 F5 40 26N 104 43W
Green *r.* USA 70 D5 42 00N 110 00W
Green *r.* USA 70 E4 39 00N 110 00W
Green Bay Wisconsin USA 71 J6 45 00N 87 00W
Green Bay *tn.* Wisconsin USA 71 J5 44 32N 88 00W
Greenbush Minnesota USA 49 D1 48 42N 96 11W
Greenfield Massachusetts USA 73 D3 42 36N 72 36W
GREENLAND 65 U6
Greenland Basin Atlantic Ocean 116 H14 72 00N 0 00
Greenland Sea Arctic Ocean 117 76 00N 5 00W
Green Mountains Vermont USA 71 M5 43 00N 73 00W
Greenock UK 86 C11 55 57N 4 45W
Greensboro North Carolina USA 71 L4 36 03N 79 50W
Greenville Liberia 108 C9 5 01N 9 03W
Greenville Maine USA 53 S5 45 28N 69 36W
Greenville Mississippi USA 71 H3 33 23N 91 03W
Greenville South Carolina USA 71 K3 34 52N 82 25W
Greenville Texas USA 71 G3 33 09N 96 06W
Greenwood Mississippi USA 71 H3 33 31N 90 10W
Grenå Denmark 88 C12 56 25N 10 53E
GRENADA 74 R11
Grenoble Fr. 87 H6 45 11N 5 43E
Greymouth NZ 111 C3 42 27S 171 12E
Grey Range *mts.* Aust. 110 G4 27 00S 144 00E
Gridley California USA 72 C4 39 24N 121 42W
Griffin Georgia USA 71 K3 33 15N 84 17W
Grimsby UK 86 E10 53 35N 0 05W
Grindstone Lake Wisconsin USA 51 F3 45 59N 91 20W
Groningen Neths. 86 J10 53 13N 6 35E
Groom Lake Nevada USA 72 F3 37 18N 115 49W
Groote Eylandt *i.* Aust. 110 F7 14 00S 137 00E

Grootfontein Namibia 109 H4 19 32S 18 05E
Grosseto Italy 89 C5 42 46N 11 07E
Gross Glockner *mt.* Austria 89 D7 47 05N 12 44E
Groveland California USA 72 C3 37 43N 120 56W
Grover City California USA 72 C2 35 08N 120 35W
Groznyy Russia 94 G5 43 21N 45 42E
Grudziądz Poland 88 G10 53 29N 18 45E
Guadalajara Mexico 74 D4 20 40N 103 20W
Guadalajara Sp. 87 D4 40 37N 3 10W
Guadalcanal *i.* Solomon Islands 114 G7 9 30S 160 00E
Guadalope *r.* Sp. 87 E4 40 50N 0 30W
Guadalquivir *r.* Sp. 87 C2 37 45N 5 30W
Guadalupe *i.* Mexico 74 A5 29 00N 118 24W
Guadeloupe *i.* Lesser Antilles 74 Q9 16 30N 61 30W
Guadeloupe Passage *sd.* Caribbean Sea 74 Q9 16 40N 61 50W
Guadiana *r.* Sp./Port. 87 B3 38 30N 7 30W
Guadix Sp. 87 D2 37 19N 3 08W
Guainía *r.* Col./Venezuela 80 D14 2 30N 67 30W
Guajará Mirim Brazil 80 D11 10 50S 65 21W
Gualala California USA 72 B4 38 45N 123 31W
GUAM 114 E9
Guamúchil Mexico 74 C5 25 28N 108 10W
Guangzhou China 101 L3 23 08N 113 20E
Guantánamo Cuba 75 J4 20 09N 75 14W
Guaporé *r.* Brazil/Bolivia 80 E11 13 00S 62 00W
Guaqui Bolivia 80 D10 16 38S 68 50W
Guarapuava Brazil 80 G8 25 22S 51 28W
Guarda Port. 87 B4 40 32N 7 17W
Guardiana *r.* Sp. 87 C2 39 00N 4 00W
Guasdualito Venezuela 80 C15 7 15N 70 40W
GUATEMALA 74 F3
Guatemala Basin Pacific Ocean 115 S9 12 00N 95 00W
Guatemala City Guatemala 74 F2 14 38N 90 22W
Guaviare *r.* Col. 80 C14 3 00N 70 00W
Guayaquil Ecuador 80 A13 2 13S 79 54W
Guaymas Mexico 74 B5 27 59N 110 54W
Guéret Fr. 87 F7 46 10N 1 52E
Guernsey *i.* British Isles 86 D8 49 27N 2 35W
Guildford UK 86 E9 51 14N 0 35W
Guilin China 101 L4 25 21N 110 11E
Guimarães Port. 87 A4 41 26N 8 19W
GUINEA 108 B10
Guinea Basin Atlantic Ocean 116 H7 1 00N 8 00W
GUINEA-BISSAU 108 A10
Güines Cuba 75 H4 22 50N 82 02W
Güiria Venezuela 80 E16 10 37N 62 21W
Guiyang China 101 K4 26 35N 106 40E
Gujarat *admin.* India 98 C4 23 20N 72 00E
Gujranwala Pakistan 98 C6 32 06N 74 11E
Gujrat Pakistan 98 C6 32 35N 74 06E
Gulbarga India 98 D3 17 22N 76 47E
Gulfport Mississippi USA 71 J3 30 21N 89 08W
Gulu Uganda 108 L8 2 46N 32 21E
Gunnison *r.* Colorado USA 70 E4 38 00N 107 00W
Guntersville Lake Alabama USA 71 J3 34 00N 86 00W
Guntur India 98 E3 16 20N 80 27E
Gunung Kinabalu *mt.* Malaysia 103 F5 6 03N 116 32E
Gurgueia *r.* Brazil 80 J12 9 00S 44 00W
Gurupi *r.* Brazil 80 H13 4 00S 47 00W
Gusev Russia 88 J11 54 32N 22 12E
Gushgy Turkmenistan 97 H6 36 03N 62 43E
Güstrow Germany 88 D10 53 48N 12 11E
Guthrie Oklahoma USA 71 G4 35 53N 97 26W
Guwahati India 99 G5 26 10N 91 45E
GUYANA 80 F14
Guyana Basin Atlantic Ocean 116 D7 8 00N 50 00W
Gwalior India 98 D5 26 12N 78 09E
Gweru Zimbabwe 109 K4 19 27S 29 49E
Gyda Peninsula Russia 95 K11 70 00N 77 30E
Gympie Aust. 110 J4 26 10S 152 35E
Gyöngyös Hungary 88 G7 47 46N 20 00E
Győr Hungary 89 F7 47 41N 17 40E

H

Haapsalu Estonia 88 J13 58 58N 23 32E
Haarlem Neths. 86 H10 52 23N 4 39E
Haast NZ 111 B3 43 53S 169 03E
Hab *r.* Pakistan 98 B5 25 20N 67 00E
Habbān Yemen 97 E1 14 21N 47 04E
Haboro Japan 102 D3 44 23N 141 43E
Hachinohe Japan 102 D3 40 30N 141 30E
Hackensack River New Jersey USA 73 H2 40 47N 74 06W
Hadejia Nigeria 108 G10 12 30N 10 03E
Hadejia *r.* Nigeria 108 F10 4 10N 9 30E
Hadera Israel 96 N11 32 26N 34 55E
Haderslev Denmark 88 B11 55 15N 9 30E
Hadhramaut *geog. reg.* Yemen 97 E2 15 40N 47 30E
Hadiboh Yemen 97 F1 12 36N 53 59E
Hadraibari India 99 23 55N 91 50E
Haeju North Korea 101 P6 38 04N 125 40E
Hagerstown Maryland USA 71 L4 39 39N 77 44W
Ha Giang Vietnam 101 J3 22 50N 105 00E
Haifa Israel 96 N11 32 49N 34 59E
Haikou China 101 L3 20 00N 110 25E
Hā'il Saudi Arabia 96 D4 27 31N 41 45E
Hailar China 101 M8 49 15N 119 41E
Hainan Dao *i.* China 101 K2/L2 18 50N 109 50E
Haines Alaska USA 42 C6 59 11N 135 23W
Hai Phong Vietnam 101 K3 20 50N 106 41E
HAITI 75 K3
Hakodate Japan 102 D3 41 46N 140 44E
Halaib Sudan 108 M12 22 12N 36 35E

Hegang China 101 Q8 47 36N 130 30E
Hegura-jima *i.* Japan 102 C2 37 52N 136 56E
Heidelberg Germany 88 B8 49 25N 8 42E
Heilbronn Germany 88 B8 49 08N 9 14E
Hei Ling Chau *i.* HK China 100 B1 22 15N 114 02E
Hekou China 101 J3 22 30N 104 00E
Helan Shan *mts.* China 101 K6 38 00N 106 00E
Helena Montana USA 70 D6 46 35N 112 00W
Helendale California USA 72 E2 34 45N 117 19W
Heligoland Bight *b.* Germany 88 B11 54 00N 8 00E
Hellín Sp. 87 E3 38 31N 1 43W
Helmand *r.* Afghanistan 97 H5 30 00N 62 30E
Helsingborg Sweden 88 D12 56 03N 12 43E
Helsingør Denmark 88 D12 56 03N 12 38E
Helsinki Finland 88 K14 60 08N 25 00E
Hemet California USA 72 E1 33 45N 116 58W
Henares *r.* Sp. 87 D4 40 45N 3 10W
Henderson Nevada USA 70 D4 36 01N 115 00W
Henderson Island Pacific Ocean 115 N5 23 00S 127 00W
Hengelo Neths. 86 J10 52 16N 6 46E
Hengyang China 101 L4 26 58N 112 31E
Henryetta Oklahoma USA 71 G4 35 27N 96 00W
Henzada Myanmar 103 B7 17 36N 95 26E
Herāt Afghanistan 97 H5 34 20N 62 12E
Hérault *r.* Fr. 87 G5 43 50N 3 30E
Hereford UK 86 D10 52 04N 2 43W
Hermel Lebanon 96 P12 34 25N 36 23E
Hermon New York USA 53 L4 44 28N 75 12W
Hermon, Mount Lebanon/Syria 96 N11 33 24N 35 50E
Hermosillo Mexico 74 B5 29 15N 110 59W
Herning Denmark 88 B12 56 08N 8 59E
Hesperia California USA 72 E2 34 25N 117 19W
Hetch Hetchy Aqueduct California USA 72 C3 37 35N 121 45W
Hetch Hetchy Reservoir California USA 72 D3 37 57N 119 45W
Hibbing Minnesota USA 51 E4 47 25N 92 56W
Hickory North Carolina USA 71 K4 35 44N 81 23W
Hicksville Ohio USA 52 B1 41 18N 84 45W
Hidalgo Mexico 74 24 16N 99 28W
Hidalgo del Parral Mexico 74 C5 26 58N 105 40W
High Island HK China 100 D2 22 21N 114 21E
High Island Reservoir HK China 100 D2 22 22N 114 20E
High Point *tn.* North Carolina USA 71 L4 35 58N 80 00W
High Veld *mts.* RSA 109 K4 28 00S 28 00E
Hiiumaa *i.* Estonia 88 J13 58 55N 22 30E
Hiko Nevada USA 72 F3 37 36N 115 14W
Hildesheim Germany 88 B10 52 09N 9 58E
Hillsdale Michigan USA 52 B1 41 56N 84 37W
Hilo Hawaiian Islands 115 Z17 19 42N 155 04W
Hilton New York USA 52 B1 43 17N 77 47W
Hilversum Neths. 86 H10 52 14N 5 10E
Himachal Pradesh *admin.* India 98 D6 32 00N 77 30E
Himalaya *mts.* Asia 98/99 D6 28 00N 85 00E
Himeji Japan 102 B1 34 50N 134 40E
Hinckley Lake New York USA 53 L3 43 20N 75 10W
Hindu Kush *mts.* Afghanistan 97 J5/K6 35 00N 70 00E
Hirakud Reservoir India 98 E4 21 40N 83 40E
Hirosaki Japan 102 D3 40 34N 140 28E
Hiroshima Japan 102 B1 34 23N 132 27E
Hisar India 98 D5 29 10N 75 45E
Hispaniola *i.* W. Indies 75 K3/L3 18 00N 70 00W
Hitachi Japan 102 D2 36 35N 140 40E
Hjørring Denmark 88 B12 57 28N 9 59E
Ho Ghana 108 E9 6 38N 0 38E
Hobart Aust. 110 H1 42 54S 147 18E
Hoboken New Jersey USA 73 H1 40 44N 74 02W
Hobyo Somalia 108 P9 5 20N 48 30E
Hô Chi Minh Vietnam 101 K2 10 46N 106 43E
Ho Chung HK China 100 C2 22 22N 114 14E
Hodeida Yemen 96 D1 14 50N 42 58E
Hódmezővásárhely Hungary 89 H7 46 26N 20 21E
Hof Germany 88 C9 50 19N 11 56E
Hofu Japan 102 B1 34 02N 131 34E
Hogeland Montana USA 47 C1 48 51N 108 39W
Hoggar *mts.* Algeria 108 F12 23 45N 6 00E
Hohhot China 101 L7 40 49N 111 37E
Hoi Ha HK China 100 C2 22 28N 114 20E
Hokitika NZ 111 C3 42 43S 170 58E
Hokkaidō *i.* Japan 102 D3 43 30N 143 00E
Holbaek Denmark 88 C11 56 33N 10 19E
Holguín Cuba 75 J4 20 54N 76 15W
Hollister California USA 72 C3 36 47N 121 25W
Holly Michigan USA 52 C2 42 48N 83 37W
Holstebro Denmark 88 B12 56 22N 8 38E
Holston *r.* USA 71 K4 37 00N 82 00W
Holyoke Massachusetts USA 73 D3 42 13N 72 38W
Homestead Florida USA 71 K2 25 29N 80 29W
Homs Syria 96 C5 34 42N 36 40E
Honda Col. 80 C15 5 15N 74 50W
HONDURAS 74 G2
Hønefoss Norway 88 L14 60 10N 10 16E
Honesdale Pennsylvania USA 53 L1 41 34N 75 15W
Hong Kong *admin.* China 101 L3 23 00N 114 00E
Hong Kong Island HK China 100 B1/C1 22 15N 114 12E
Hong Lok Yuen HK China 100 B2 22 27N 114 08E
Honokaa Hawaiian Islands 115 Z18 20 04N 155 27W
Honolulu Hawaiian Islands 115 Y18 21 19N 157 50W
Honshū *i.* Japan 102 C2 36 00N 139 00E
Hood, Mount Oregon USA 70 B6 45 24N 121 41W
Hoolehua Hawaiian Islands 115 Y18 21 11N 157 06W

Hoonah Alaska USA 42 C6 58 06N 135 25W
Hopkinsville Kentucky USA 71 J4 36 50N 87 30W
Ho Pui HK China 100 B2 22 24N 114 04E
Ho Pui Reservoir HK China 100 B2 22 25N 114 05E
Hormuz, Strait of The Gulf 97 G4 26 35N 56 30E
Hornell New York USA 52 J2 42 20N 77 40W
Horsens Denmark 88 B11 55 53N 9 53E
Horsham Aust. 110 G2 36 45S 142 15E
Hospet India 98 D3 15 16N 76 20E
Hospitalet Sp. 87 G4 41 21N 2 06E
Hotan China 100 D6 37 07N 79 57E
Hotan He *r.* China 100 E6 39 00N 80 30E
Hot Springs *tn.* Arkansas USA 71 H3 34 30N 93 02W
Houghton Michigan USA 51 G4 47 07N 88 35W
Houghton Lake Michigan USA 52 B4 44 20N 84 45W
Houghton Lake *tn.* Michigan USA 52 B4 44 17N 84 45W
Houhara NZ 111 D7 34 48S 173 06E
Houlton Maine USA 57 G2 46 09N 67 50W
Houma China 101 L6 35 36N 111 15E
Houma Louisiana USA 71 H2 29 35N 90 44W
Houston Texas USA 71 G2 29 45N 95 25W
Hovd Mongolia 100 G8 48 00N 91 43E
Hövsgöl Nuur *l.* Mongolia 101 J9 51 00N 100 30E
Howar *r.* Sudan 108 K11 17 00N 25 00E
Howard City Michigan USA 51 J2 43 23N 85 28W
Howe, Cape Aust. 110 H2 37 20S 149 59E
Howland Islands Pacific Ocean 114 J8 2 00N 177 00W
Hoy *i.* UK 86 D13 58 48N 3 20W
Hradec Králové Czech Rep. 88 E9 50 13N 15 50E
Hrodna Belarus 88 J10 53 40N 23 50E
Hron *r.* Slovakia 88 G8 48 00N 18 00E
Hsinchu Taiwan 101 N3 24 48N 120 59E
Huacho Peru 80 B11 11 05S 77 36W
Huaide China 101 N7 43 30N 124 48E
Huainan China 101 M5 32 41N 117 06E
Huajuápan de León Mexico 74 E3 17 50N 97 48W
Huambo Angola 109 H5 12 44S 15 47E
Huancayo Peru 80 B11 12 05S 75 12W
Huang He *r.* China 101 L6 38 00N 111 00E
Huangshi China 101 M5 30 13N 115 05E
Huanuco Peru 80 B12 9 55S 76 11W
Huaráz Peru 80 B12 9 33S 77 31W
Huascaran *mt.* Peru 80 B12 9 08S 77 36W
Huashixia China 101 H6 35 13N 99 12E
Hubbard Lake Michigan USA 52 C4 44 50N 83 30W
Huddersfield UK 86 E10 53 39N 1 47W
Hudson River New York USA 73 D2/D3 42 00N 73 55W
Huê Vietnam 103 D7 16 28N 107 35E
Huelva Sp. 87 B2 37 15N 6 56W
Huelva *r.* Sp. 87 B2 37 50N 6 30W
Huesca Sp. 87 E5 42 08N 0 25W
Hughenden Aust. 110 G5 20 50S 144 10E
Hugli *r.* India 99 K8 22 00N 88 00E
Hugo Oklahoma USA 71 G3 34 01N 95 31W
Huixtla Mexico 74 F3 15 09N 92 30W
Huizhou China 101 L3 23 08N 114 28E
Humaitá Brazil 80 E12 7 33S 63 01W
Humboldt *r.* Nevada USA 70 C5 41 00N 118 00W
HUNGARY 88/89 F7
Hungnam North Korea 101 P6 39 49N 127 40E
Hung Shui Kiu HK China 100 A2 22 25N 113 59E
Hunjiang China 101 P7 41 54N 126 23E
Hunsrück *mts.* Germany 88 J8/J9 50 00N 7 00E
Hunter Trench Pacific Ocean 114 H5 23 00S 175 00E
Huntington West Virginia USA 71 K4 38 24N 82 26W
Huntington Beach *tn.* California USA 72 D1 33 40N 118 00W
Huntly NZ 111 E6 37 34S 175 10E
Huntsville Alabama USA 71 J3 34 44N 86 35W
Huntsville Texas USA 71 G3 30 43N 95 34W
Hurghada Egypt 108 L13 27 17N 33 47E
Hurley Wisconsin USA 51 F4 46 26N 90 10W
Huron River Michigan USA 52 C2 42 10N 83 15W
Huskvarna Sweden 88 E12 57 47N 14 15E
Husn Jordan 96 N11 32 29N 35 53E
Hutchinson Kansas USA 71 G4 38 03N 97 56W
Huzhou China 101 N5 30 56N 120 04E
Hvar *i.* Croatia 89 F5 43 00N 17 00E
Hwange Zimbabwe 109 K4 18 22S 26 29E
Hyder Alaska USA 42 E4 55 45N 130 10W
Hyderabad India 98 D3 17 22N 78 26E
Hyderabad Pakistan 98 B5 25 23N 68 24E

I

Ialomiţa *r.* Romania 89 L6 44 00N 27 00E
Iaşi Romania 89 L7 47 09N 27 38E
Ibadan Nigeria 108 E9 7 23N 3 56E
Ibagué Col. 80 B14 4 25N 75 20W
Ibarra Ecuador 80 B14 0 23N 78 05W
Ibb Yemen 96 D1 14 03N 44 10E
Ibi Nigeria 108 F9 8 11N 9 44E
Ibiza Sp. 87 F3 38 54N 1 26E
Ibiza *i.* Sp. 87 F3 39 00N 1 20E
Ibotirama Brazil 80 J11 12 13S 43 12W
Ibri Oman 97 G3 23 15N 56 35E
Ica Peru 80 B11 14 02S 75 48W
Icacos Point Trinidad and Tobago 75 V15 10 41N 61 42W
ICELAND 116 F13
Ichalkaranji India 98 C3 16 40N 74 33E
Ichinomiya Japan 102 C2 35 18N 136 48E
Icy Strait *sd.* Alaska USA 42 C6 58 20N 135 45W
Idaho *state* USA 70 D5 44 00N 115 00W
Idaho Falls *tn.* Idaho USA 70 D5 43 30N 112 01W
Idfu Egypt 108 L12 24 58N 32 50E
Igarka Russia 95 L10 67 31N 86 33E
Iglesias Italy 89 B3 39 19N 8 32E
Iguaçu *r.* Brazil 80 G8 26 00S 51 00W
Iguala Mexico 74 E3 18 21N 99 31W
Iguape Brazil 80 H9 24 37S 47 30W
Iguatu Brazil 80 K12 6 22S 39 20W
Ihavandiffulu Atoll *i.* Maldives 98 C1 7 00N 72 55E
Ihosy Madagascar 109 P3 22 23S 46 09E
Iida Japan 102 C2 35 32N 137 48E
IJsselmeer *l.* Neths. 86 H10 52 50N 5 15E
Ikaría *i.* Greece 89 L2 37 35N 26 10E
Ikela CDR 108 J7 1 06S 23 06E
Iki *i.* Japan 102 A1 33 50N 129 40E
Ilagan Philippines 103 G7 17 07N 121 53E
Île Amsterdam *i.* Indian Ocean 113 G3 37 56S 77 40E
Ilebo CDR 108 J7 4 20S 20 35E
Ile de Jerba *i.* Tunisia 108 G14 33 40N 11 00E
Île de l'Europe *i.* Mozambique Channel 109 N3 22 20S 40 20E
Île de Ré *i.* Fr. 87 E7 46 10N 1 26W
Île d'Oléron *i.* Fr. 87 E6 45 55N 1 16W
Île d'Ouessant *i.* Fr. 86 C8 48 28N 5 05W
Île d'Yeu *i.* Fr. 87 D7 46 43N 2 20W
Ilesa Nigeria 108 E9 7 39N 4 38E
Île St. Paul *i.* Indian Ocean 113 G3 38 44S 77 30E
Îles Crozet *is.* Indian Ocean 113 E2 46 27S 52 00E
Îles d'Hyères *is.* Fr. 87 J5 43 10N 6 25E
Îles Kerguelen *is.* Indian Ocean 113 F2 49 30S 69 30E
Îles Loyauté *is.* Pacific Ocean 114 G5 21 00S 167 00E
Ilha Bazaruto *i.* Mozambique 109 M3 21 40S 35 30E
Ilha de Marajó *i.* Brazil 80 G13 1 30S 50 00W
Ilha Fernando de Noronha *i.* Brazil 80 L13 3 50S 32 25W
Ilhéus Brazil 80 K11 14 50S 39 06W
Ili *r.* Asia 94 K5 44 00N 78 00E
Iligan Philippines 103 G5 8 12N 124 13W
Illapel Chile 81 C7 31 40S 71 13W
Illinois *state* USA 71 J5 40 00N 89 00W
Illizi Algeria 108 F13 26 45N 8 30E
Iloilo Philippines 103 G6 10 41N 122 33E
Ilorin Nigeria 108 E9 8 32N 4 34E
Imabari Japan 102 B1 34 04N 132 59E
Imi Ethiopia 108 N9 6 28N 42 10E
Imperatriz Brazil 80 H12 5 32S 47 28W
Imperia Italy 89 B5 43 53N 8 03E
Impfondo Congo 108 H8 1 36N 18 00E
Imphal India 99 G4 24 47N 93 55E
Inangahua NZ 111 C4 41 52S 171 57E
Inca Sp. 87 G3 39 43N 2 54E
Inchon South Korea 101 P6 37 30N 126 38E
Independence California USA 72 D3 36 48N 118 14W
Independence Kansas USA 71 G4 37 13N 95 43W
INDIA 98/99 B4/F4
Indiana *state* USA 71 J5 40 00N 86 00W
Indian Antarctic Basin Southern Ocean 114 A2 57 00S 113 00E
Indian-Antarctic Ridge Southern Ocean 114 A3 51 00S 124 00E
Indianapolis Indiana USA 71 J4 39 45N 86 10W
Indian Ocean 113
Indian Springs *tn.* Nevada USA 72 F3 36 33N 115 40W
Indigirka *r.* Russia 95 S10 70 00N 147 30E
Indio California USA 72 E1 33 44N 116 14W
INDONESIA 103 C3/H3
Indravati *r.* India 98 E3 19 00N 81 30E
Indre *r.* Fr. 87 F7 46 50N 1 25E
Indus *r.* Pakistan 98 B5 28 00N 69 00E
Indus, Mouths of the *est.* Pakistan 98 B4 24 00N 67 00E
Ingham Aust. 110 H6 18 35S 146 12E
Inglewood California USA 72 D1 33 58N 118 22W
Ingolstadt Germany 88 C8 48 46N 11 27E
Ingraj Bazar India 99 K10 24 59N 88 10E
Inhambane Mozambique 109 M3 23 51S 35 29E
Inírida *r.* Col. 80 D14 2 30N 70 00W
Inn *r.* Europe 89 C7 48 00N 12 00E
Innisfail Aust. 110 H6 17 30S 146 00E
Innsbruck Austria 89 C7 47 17N 11 25E
Inongo CDR 108 H7 1 55S 18 20E
Inowrocław Poland 88 G10 52 49N 18 12E
In Salah Algeria 108 E13 27 20N 2 03E
Insein Myanmar 103 B7 16 54N 96 08E
Inta Russia 94 J10 66 04N 60 01E
Inubō-zaki *c.* Japan 102 D2 35 41N 140 52E
Invercargill NZ 111 B1 46 25S 168 22E
Inverness UK 86 C12 57 27N 4 15W
Inyo Range *mts.* California USA 72 D3 36 37N 117 52W
Ioánnina Greece 89 H3 39 40N 20 51E
Ione Washington USA 43 M1 48 45N 117 25W
Ionia Michigan USA 52 A2 42 58N 85 06W
Ionia Nisiá Greece 89 G3 39 00N 20 00E
Ionian Sea Mediterranean Sea 89 F2/G2 38 00N 27 00E
Íos *i.* Greece 89 K2 36 00N 25 00E
Iowa *state* USA 71 H5 42 00N 94 00W
Iowa City Iowa USA 71 H5 41 39N 91 31W
Ipatinga Brazil 80 J10 19 32S 42 30W
Ipiales Col. 80 B14 0 52N 77 38W
Ipoh Malaysia 103 C4 4 36N 101 05E
Ipswich UK 86 F10 52 04N 1 10E
Ipu Brazil 80 J13 4 32S 40 44W
Iquique Chile 80 C9 20 15S 70 08W
Iquitos Peru 80 C13 3 51S 73 13W
Irákleio Greece 89 K1 35 20N 25 08E
IRAN 97 F5/G5
Irānshahr Iran 97 H4 27 15N 60 41E
Irapuato Mexico 74 D4 20 40N 101 30W
IRAQ 96 D5
Irbid Jordan 96 C5 32 33N 35 51E
Irecê Brazil 80 J11 11 22S 41 51W
Irian Jaya *admin.* Indonesia 103 J3 3 00S 133 00E
Iriri *r.* Brazil 80 G13 5 00S 54 50W
Irkutsk Russia 95 N7 52 18N 104 15E
Iron Knob *tn.* Aust. 110 F3 32 44S 137 08E
Iron Mountain *tn.* Michigan USA 51 G3 45 49N 88 04W
Ironwood Michigan USA 71 H6 46 25N 90 08W
Irrawaddy *r.* Myanmar 103 A8 20 00N 95 00E
Irtysh *r.* Asia 94 K8 57 30N 72 30E
Irún Sp. 87 E5 43 20N 1 48W
Irving Texas USA 71 G3 32 49N 96 57W
Irvington New Jersey USA 73 H1 40 44N 74 15W
Isabella Reservoir California USA 72 D2 35 41N 118 28W
Ise Japan 102 C1 34 29N 136 41E
Isère *r.* Fr. 87 H6 45 17N 5 47E
Ishikari *r.* Japan 102 D3 43 20N 141 45E
Ishikari-wan *b.* Japan 102 D3 43 30N 141 00E
Ishim *r.* Russia 94 J8 56 00N 69 00E
Ishinomaki Japan 102 D2 38 25N 141 18E
Isiro CDR 108 K8 2 50N 27 40E
Iskenderun Turkey 96 C6 36 37N 36 08E
Iskŭr *r.* Bulgaria 89 K5 43 30N 24 00E
Isla Asinara *i.* Italy 89 B4 41 00N 8 00E
Isla de Chiloé *i.* Chile 81 C5 42 30S 74 00W
Isla de Coco *i.* Costa Rica 115 S8 4 00N 85 00W
Isla de Coiba *i.* Panama 75 H1 7 40N 82 00W
Isla de Cozumel *i.* Mexico 74 G4 20 30N 87 00W
Isla de la Juventud *i.* Cuba 75 H4 22 00N 82 30W
Isla d'Elba *i.* Italy 89 C5 42 00N 10 00E
Isla de los Estados *i.* Argentina 81 E3 55 00S 64 00W
Isla Grande de Tierra del Fuego *i.* Chile/Argentina 81 D3 54 00S 67 30W
Islamabad Pakistan 98 C6 33 40N 73 08E
Isla Margarita *i.* Venezuela 80 E16 11 30N 64 00W
Islampur India 99 K11 26 16N 88 11E
Island Beach New Jersey USA 73 C1 39 55N 74 05W
Isla San Felix *i.* Chile 115 U5 26 23S 80 05W
Islas de la Bahia *is.* Honduras 74 G3 16 40N 86 00W
Islas Galápagos *i.* Ecuador 115 S7 0 05S 90 00W
Islas Juan Fernández *is.* Chile 115 T4 33 30S 80 00W
Islas Marias *is.* Mexico 74 C4 22 00N 107 00W
Islas Revillagigedo *is.* Pacific Ocean 74 B3 19 00N 112 30W
Isla Wellington *i.* Chile 115 U3 48 50S 79 00W
Islay *i.* UK 86 B11 55 48N 6 12W
Isle of Man British Isles 86 C11 54 15N 4 15W
Isle of Wight *i.* UK 86 E9 50 40N 1 20W
Isle Royale *i.* Michigan USA 51 G4 48 00N 89 0W
Isle Royale National Park Michigan USA 51 G4 48 00N 89 0W
Ismâ'ilîya Egypt 109 S3 30 36N 32 16E
Isoka Zambia 109 L5 10 09S 32 39E
Isola Lipari *is.* Italy 89 E3 38 00N 14 00E
ISRAEL 96 N9
Istanbul Turkey 96 A7 41 02N 28 57E
Istmo de Tehuantepec *ist.* Mexico 74 F3 17 20N 93 10W
Istres Fr. 87 H5 43 30N 4 59E
Itabaiana Brazil 80 K11 10 42S 37 37W
Itabuna Brazil 80 K11 14 48S 39 18W
Itacoatiara Brazil 80 F13 3 06S 58 22W
Itagüí Col. 80 B15 6 13N 75 40W
Itaituba Brazil 80 F13 4 15S 55 56W
Itajaí Brazil 80 H8 26 50S 48 39W
ITALY 89 C5/D5
Itapipoca Brazil 80 K13 3 29S 39 35W
Itaqui Brazil 81 F8 29 10S 56 30W
Ithaca New York USA 53 K2 42 27N 76 30W
Itui *r.* Brazil 80 C12 5 30S 71 00W
Ivano-Frankivs'k Ukraine 88 K8 48 40N 24 40E
Ivanovo Russia 94 G8 57 00N 41 00E
Ivdel' Russia 94 J9 60 45N 60 30E
Iwaki Japan 102 D2 37 03N 140 58E
Iwakuni Japan 102 B1 34 10N 132 09E
Iwamizawa Japan 102 D3 43 12N 141 47E
Iwanai Japan 102 D3 43 01N 140 32E
Iwo Nigeria 108 E9 7 38N 4 11E
Ixtaccihuati *mt.* Mexico 74 E3 19 11N 98 38W
Ixtapa-Zihuatanejo Mexico 74 D3 17 39N 101 35W
Ixtepec Mexico 74 E3 16 32N 95 10W
Iyo-nada *b.* Japan 102 B1 33 50N 132 00E
Izhevsk Russia 94 H8 56 49N 53 11E
Izhma *r.* Russia 94 H9 64 00N 54 00E
Izmayil Ukraine 89 M6 45 20N 28 48E
Izmir Turkey 96 A6 38 25N 27 10E
Izra' Syria 96 P11 32 52N 36 15E
Izu-shotō *is.* Japan 102 C1 34 20N 139 20E

J

Jabal Akhdar *mt.* Oman 97 G3 24 00N 56 30E
Jabal al Akhdar *mts.* Libya 108 J14 33 00N 22 00E
Jabal as Sawdā' *mts.* Libya 108 G13 29 00N 15 00E
Jabalpur India 98 D4 23 10N 79 59E
Jablonec Czech Rep. 88 E9 50 44N 15 10E
Jaboatão Brazil 80 K12 8 05S 35 00W
Jackman Maine USA 53 R5 45 37N 70 16W
Jack Mountain Washington USA 42 H4 48 45N 120 55W
Jackson California USA 72 C4 38 19N 120 47W
Jackson Michigan USA 71 K5 42 15N 84 24W
Jackson Mississippi USA 71 H3 32 20N 90 11W
Jackson Tennessee USA 71 J4 35 37N 88 50W
Jackson Wyoming USA 70 D5 43 28N 110 45W
Jackson Heights New York USA 73 J2 40 45N 73 52W
Jacksonville Florida USA 71 K3 30 20N 81 40W
Jacksonville North Carolina USA 71 L3 34 45N 77 26W
Jacksonville Beach *tn.* Florida USA 71 K3 30 18N 81 24W
Jack Wade Alaska USA 64 B3 64 05N 141 35W
Jacmel Haiti 75 K3 18 18N 72 32W
Jacobabad Pakistan 98 B5 28 16N 68 30E
Jacobina Brazil 80 J11 11 13S 40 30W
Jaén Sp. 87 D2 37 46N 3 48W
Jaffna Sri Lanka 98 E1 9 40N 80 01E
Jagdalpur India 98 E3 19 04N 82 05E
Jahrom Iran 97 F4 28 29N 53 32E
Jaintiapur Bangladesh 99 M10 25 06N 92 08E
Jaipur India 98 D5 26 53N 75 50E
Jakarta Indonesia 103 D2 6 08S 106 45E
Jalālābād Afghanistan 97 C6 34 26N 70 25E
Jalandhar India 98 D6 31 18N 75 40E
Jalapa Enriquez Mexico 74 E3 19 32N 96 56W
Jalgaon India 98 D4 21 01N 75 39E
Jalón *r.* Sp. 87 E4 41 30N 1 35W
Jalpaiguri India 99 K11 26 29N 88 47E
Jālū Libya 108 J13 29 02N 21 33E
JAMAICA 75 J3
Jamaica New York USA 73 J1 40 42N 73 48W
Jamaica Bay New York USA 73 J1 40 37N 73 50W
Jambi Indonesia 103 C3 1 34S 103 37E
James *r.* South Dakota USA 71 G5 44 00N 98 00W
James *r.* Virginia USA 71 L4 37 00N 77 00W
Jamestown New York USA 71 L5 42 05N 79 15W
Jamestown North Dakota USA 71 G6 46 54N 98 42W
Jamiltepec Mexico 74 E3 16 18N 97 51W
Jammu India 98 C6 32 43N 74 54E
Jammu and Kashmir *state* Southern Asia 98 D6 29 40N 76 30E
Jamnagar India 98 C4 22 28N 70 06E
Jamshedpur India 99 F4 22 47N 86 12E
Jamuna *r.* Bangladesh 99 K10 25 00N 89 40E
Janesville Wisconsin USA 71 J5 42 42N 89 02W
Jangipur India 99 K10 24 27N 88 04E
Jan Mayen *i.* Arctic Ocean 117 71 00N 9 00W
Januária Brazil 80 J10 15 28S 44 23W
JAPAN 102
Japan, Sea of Pacific Ocean 102 C2 39 00N 137 00E
Japan Trench Pacific Ocean 114 E11 35 00N 143 00E
Japurá *r.* Brazil 80 D13 2 00S 67 30W
Jari *r.* Brazil 80 G14 2 00N 54 00W
Jarú Brazil 80 E11 10 24S 62 45W
Jarvis Islands Pacific Ocean 115 K8 0 00 163 00W
Jāsk Iran 97 G4 25 40N 57 46E
Jasło Poland 88 H8 49 45N 21 28E
Jastrowie Poland 88 F10 53 25N 16 50E
Jaunpur India 98 E5 25 44N 82 41E
Java *i.* Indonesia 103 D2/E2 7 00S 110 00E
Java Sea Indonesia 103 E2 5 00S 112 00E
Java Trench Indian Ocean 113 L5 10 00S 110 00E
Jayapura Indonesia 110 G9 2 37S 140 39E
Jaynagar Manzilpur India 99 K9 22 10N 88 24E
Jaza'īr Farasān *is.* Saudi Arabia 96 D2 16 45N 42 10E
Jean Nevada USA 72 F2 35 46N 115 20W
Jebel Abyad Plateau Sudan 108 K11 18 00N 28 00E
Jebel Marra *mts.* Sudan 108 J10 13 00N 24 00E
Jedda Saudi Arabia 96 C3 21 30N 39 10E
Jefferson Ohio USA 52 F1 41 44N 80 46W
Jefferson City Missouri USA 71 H4 38 33N 92 10W
Jefferson, Mount Nevada USA 72 E4 38 47N 116 58W
Jelenia Góra Poland 88 E9 50 55N 15 45E
Jelgava Latvia 88 J12 56 39N 23 40E
Jena Germany 88 C9 50 56N 11 35E
Jenin Jordan 96 N11 32 28N 35 18E
Jequié Brazil 80 J11 13 52S 40 06W
Jequitinhonha *r.* Brazil 80 J10 16 00S 41 00W
Jérémie Haiti 75 K3 18 40N 74 09W
Jerez de la Frontera Sp. 87 B2 36 41N 6 08W
Jerez de los Caballeros Sp. 87 B3 38 20N 6 45W
Jericho Middle East 96 N10 31 51N 35 27E
Jersey *i.* British Isles 86 D8 49 13N 2 07W
Jersey City New Jersey USA 73 C2 40 43N 74 06W
Jerusalem Israel/Jordan 96 N10 31 47N 35 13E
Jessore Bangladesh 99 K9 23 10N 89 12E
Jezioro Sniardwy *l.* Poland 88 H10 53 00N 21 00E
Jhang Maghiana Pakistan 98 C6 31 19N 72 22E
Jhansi India 98 D5 25 27N 78 34E
Jharkhand *admin.* India 99 E4/F4 23 50N 85 00E
Jhelum *r.* Pakistan 98 C6 32 30N 72 30E
Jhenida Bangladesh 99 K9 23 32N 89 09E
Jiamusi China 101 Q8 46 59N 130 29E
Ji'an China 101 M4 27 08N 115 00E
Jiangmen China 101 L3 22 40N 113 05E
Jiaxing China 101 N5 30 15N 120 52E
Jiayuguan China 101 H6 39 47N 98 14E
Jihlavá Czech Rep. 88 E8 49 24N 15 34E
Jilin China 101 P7 43 53N 126 35E
Jiloca *r.* Sp. 87 E4 41 08N 1 45W
Jima Ethiopia 108 M9 7 39N 36 47E
Jinan China 101 M6 36 41N 117 00E
Jingdezhen China 101 M4 29 17N 117 12E
Jinhua China 101 M4 29 06N 119 40E

Jining China 101 L7 40 58N 113 01E
Jining China 101 M6 35 25N 116 40E
Jinja Uganda 108 L8 0 27N 33 14E
Jinsha Jiang *r.* China 101 J4 27 30N 103 00E
Jinxi China 101 N7 40 46N 120 47E
Jinzhou China 101 N7 41 07N 121 06E
Jiparaná *r.* Brazil 80 E12 8 00S 62 30W
Jiu *r.* Romania 89 J6 44 00N 24 00E
Jiujiang China 101 M4 29 41N 116 03E
Jixi China 101 Q8 45 17N 131 00E
Jīzān Saudi Arabia 96 D2 16 56N 42 33E
João Pessoa Brazil 80 K12 7 06S 34 53W
Jodhpur India 98 C5 26 18N 73 08E
Jõetsu Japan 102 C2 37 06N 138 15E
Jogighopa India 99 L11 26 12N 90 34E
Johannesburg RSA 109 K2 26 10S 28 02E
John Day *r.* Oregon USA 70 B5/C5 45 00N 120 00W
John H. Kerr Reservoir USA 71 L4 37 00N 78 00W
Johnson City Tennessee USA 71 K4 36 20N 82 23W
Johnston Atoll *is.* Pacific Ocean 115 K9 17 00N 168 00W
Johnstown Pennsylvania USA 71 L5 40 20N 78 56W
Johor Bahru Malaysia 103 C4 1 27N 103 45E
Joinville Brazil 80 H8 26 20S 48 55W
Jonesboro Arkansas USA 71 H4 35 50N 90 41W
Jonesville Michigan USA 52 B1 41 59N 84 39W
Jönköping Sweden 88 E12 57 45N 14 10E
Joplin Missouri USA 71 H4 37 04N 94 31W
JORDAN 96 C5
Jordan *r.* Middle East 96 N11 32 15N 32 10E
Jos Nigeria 108 F9 9 54N 8 53E
Joseph Bonaparte Gulf Aust. 110 D7 14 00S 128 30E
Joshua Tree *tn.* California USA 72 E2 34 09N 116 20W
Joshua Tree National Monument California USA 72 F1 33 54N 116 00W
Jos Plateau Nigeria 108 F9 9 30N 8 55E
Joünié Lebanon 96 N11 33 58N 35 38E
Jowai India 99 M10 25 26N 92 16E
Juan de Fuca Strait North America 70 B6 48 00N 124 00W
Juàzeiro Brazil 80 J12 9 25S 40 30W
Juàzeiro do Norte Brazil 80 K12 7 10S 39 18W
Juba Sudan 108 L8 4 50N 31 35E
Jubba *r.* Somalia 108 N8 3 00N 42 30E
Jubilee Reservoir HK China 100 B2 22 23N 114 09E
Júcar *r.* Sp. 87 E3 39 08N 1 50W
Juchitán Mexico 74 E3 16 27N 95 05W
Juiz de Fora Brazil 80 J9 21 47S 43 23W
Juliaca Peru 80 C10 15 29S 70 09W
Julijske Alpe *mts.* Europe 89 D7 46 00N 13 00E
Junagadh India 98 C4 21 32N 70 32E
Junction City Kansas USA 71 G4 39 02N 96 51W
Jundiaí Brazil 80 H9 23 10S 46 54W
Juneau Alaska USA 42 C6 58 20N 134 20W
Jungfrau *mt.* Switz. 87 J7 46 33N 7 58E
Junggar Pendi China 100 E7/G7 44 00N 87 30E
Junipero Serra Peak *mt.* California USA 72 C3 36 09N 121 26W
Junk Bay HK China 100 C1 22 18N 114 15E
Jur *r.* Sudan 108 K9 8 00N 28 00E
Jura *i.* UK 86 C11/C12 55 55N 6 00W
Jura *mts.* Fr./Switz. 87 H7/J7 46 30N 6 00E
Jura Krakowska *mts.* Poland 88 G9/H9 50 00N 20 00E
Jurmala Latvia 88 J12 56 59N 23 35E
Juruá *r.* Brazil 80 C12 9 30S 73 00W
Juruá *r.* Brazil 80 D13 4 30S 67 00W
Juruena *r.* Brazil 80 F11 10 00S 57 40W

K

K2 *mt.* China/India 100 D6 35 47N 76 30E
Kabrit Egypt 109 S2 30 16N 32 29E
Kābul Afghanistan 97 J5 34 30N 69 10E
Kabwe Zambia 109 K5 14 29S 28 25E
Kachchh, Gulf of India 98 B4 22 40N 69 30E
Kadoma Zimbabwe 109 K4 18 21N 29 55E
Kaduna Nigeria 108 F10 10 28N 7 25E
Kaduna *r.* Nigeria 108 F10 10 00N 6 30E
Kaédi Mauritania 108 B11 16 12N 13 32W
Kaesong South Korea 101 P6 37 59N 126 30E
Kafue Zambia 109 K4 15 44S 28 10E
Kafue *r.* Zambia 109 K5 16 00S 27 00E
Kagoshima Japan 102 B1 31 37N 130 32E
Kahoolawe *i.* Hawaiian Islands 115 Y18 20 30N 156 40W
Kahuku Point *c.* Hawaiian Islands 115 Y18 21 42N 158 00W
Kaiapoi NZ 111 D3 43 23S 172 39E
Kaifeng China 101 L5 34 47N 114 20E
Kaikohe NZ 111 D7 35 25S 173 48E
Kaikoura NZ 111 D3 42 24S 173 41E
Kailua Hawaiian Islands 115 Z17 19 43N 155 59W
Kaimana Indonesia 103 J3 3 39S 133 44E
Kainji Reservoir Nigeria 108 E10 10 25N 4 56E
Kaipara Harbour NZ 111 E6 36 12S 174 06E
Kairouan Tunisia 108 G14 35 42N 10 01E
Kaiserslautern Germany 88 A8 49 27N 7 47E
Kaitaia NZ 111 D7 35 07S 173 16E
Kaiwi Channel *sd.* Hawaiian Islands 115 Y18 21 20N 157 30W
Kākināda India 98 E3 16 59N 82 20E
Kalae *c.* Hawaiian Islands 115 Z17 18 58N 155 24W
Kalahari Desert Southern Africa 109 J3 23 30S 23 00E
Kalamáta Greece 89 J2 37 02N 22 07E
Kalamazoo Michigan USA 71 J5 42 17N 85 36W
Kalambo Falls Tanzania/Zambia 109 L6 8 35S 31 13E
Kalat Pakistan 98 B5 29 01N 66 38E
Kalémié CDR 109 K6 5 57S 29 10E
Kalgoorlie Aust. 110 C3 30 49S 121 29E
Kalimantan *admin.* Indonesia 103 E3 0 00 115 00E
Kalindri *r.* India 99 J10 25 30N 88 00E
Kaliningrad Russia 88 H11 54 40N 20 30E
Kaliningrad *admin.* Russia 88 H11 54 40N 21 00E
Kalispell Montana USA 70 D6 48 12N 114 19W
Kalisz Poland 88 G9 51 46N 18 02E
Kalmar Sweden 88 F12 56 39N 16 20E
Kalni *r.* Bangladesh 99 L10 24 45N 91 15E
Kalomo Zambia 109 K4 17 02S 26 29E
Kaluga Russia 94 F7 54 31N 36 16E
Kalundborg Denmark 88 C11 55 42N 11 06E
Kama *r.* Russia 94 H8 57 00N 55 00E
Kamaishi Japan 102 D2 39 18N 141 52E
Kamarān *i.* Yemen 96 D2 15 21N 42 40E
Kambara *i.* Fiji 114 V15 18 57S 178 58W
Kamchatka *p.* Russia 95 T7 57 30N 160 00E
Kamchatka Bay Russia 95 U7 55 00N 164 00E
Kamchiya *r.* Bulgaria 89 L5 43 00N 27 00E
Kamensk-Ural'skiy Russia 94 J8 56 29N 61 49E
Kamet *mt.* India 98 D6 30 55N 79 36E
Kamina CDR 109 K6 8 46S 25 00E
Kampala Uganda 108 L8 0 19N 32 35E
Kâmpóng Cham Cambodia 103 D6 11 59N 105 26E
Kâmpóng Chhnăng Cambodia 103 C6 12 16N 104 39E
Kam Tin HK China 100 B2 22 26N 114 04E
Kam'yanets'-Podil's'kyy Ukraine 88 L8 48 40N 26 36E
Kamyshin Russia 94 G7 50 05N 45 24E
Kananga CDR 109 J6 5 53S 22 26E
Kanazawa Japan 102 C2 36 35N 136 38E
Kanbe Myanmar 103 B7 16 45N 96 04E
Kandahār Afghanistan 97 J5 31 35N 65 45E
Kandalaksha Russia 94 F10 67 09N 32 31E
Kandavu *i.* Fiji 114 U15 19 10S 178 30E
Kandavu Passage *sd.* Fiji 114 T15 18 50S 178 00E
Kandi Benin 108 E10 11 05N 2 59E
Kandla India 98 C4 23 03N 70 11E
Kandy Sri Lanka 98 E1 7 17N 80 40E
Kane Pennsylvania USA 52 H1 41 41N 78 49W
Kaneohe Hawaiian Islands 115 Y18 21 25N 157 48W
Kangan Iran 97 F4 27 51N 52 07E
Kangar Malaysia 103 C5 6 27N 100 11E
Kangaroo Island Aust. 110 F2 35 50S 137 50E
Kangnung South Korea 101 P6 37 48N 127 52E
Kaniet Islands PNG 110 H9 0 53S 145 30E
Kanin Peninsula Russia 94 G10 68 00N 45 00E
Kankakee Illinois USA 71 J5 41 08N 87 52W
Kankan Guinea 108 C10 10 22N 9 11W
Kannapolis North Carolina USA 71 K4 35 30N 80 36W
Kano Nigeria 108 F10 12 00N 8 31E
Kanoya Japan 102 B1 31 22N 130 50E
Kanpur India 98 E5 26 27N 80 14E
Kansas *state* USA 70/71 G4 38 00N 98 00W
Kansas City Missouri USA 71 H4 39 02N 94 33W
Kansk Russia 95 M8 56 11N 95 48E
Kanye Botswana 109 J3 24 59S 25 19E
Kaohsiung Taiwan 101 N3 22 36N 120 17E
Kaolack Senegal 108 A10 14 09N 16 08W
Kapaa Hawaiian Islands 115 X19 22 04N 159 20W
Kapfenberg Austria 89 E7 47 27N 15 18E
Kapingamarangi Rise Pacific Ocean 114 F8 3 00N 154 00E
Kaposvár Hungary 89 F7 46 21N 17 49E
Kara Bogaz Gol *b.* Turkmenistan 94 H5 42 00N 53 00E
Karabük Turkey 96 B7 41 12N 32 36E
Karachi Pakistan 98 B4 24 51N 67 02E
Karaganda Kazakhstan 94 K6 49 53N 73 07E
Karaginskiy *i.* Russia 95 U8 58 00N 164 00E
Karaj Iran 97 F6 35 48N 50 58E
Karak Jordan 96 N10 31 11N 35 42E
Karakoram Pass China/Kashmir 98 D7 35 33N 77 51E
Kara Kum *geog. reg.* Turkmenistan 94 H4/J4 40 00N 60 00E
Karasburg Namibia 109 H2 28 00S 18 43E
Kara Sea Russia 95 K11 75 00N 70 00E
Karatoya *r.* Bangladesh 99 K10 25 15N 89 15E
Karbalā' Iraq 96 D5 32 37N 44 03E
Karcag Hungary 89 H7 47 19N 20 53E
Kariba Dam Zambia/Zimbabwe 109 K4 16 31S 28 50E
Kariba, Lake Zambia/Zimbabwe 109 K4 17 00S 28 00E
Karibib Namibia 109 H3 21 59S 15 51E
Karimganj India 99 M10 24 50N 92 21E
Karisimbi, Mount Rwanda/CDR 108 K7 1 32S 29 27E
Karlino Poland 88 E11 54 02N 15 52E
Karlovac Croatia 89 E6 45 30N 15 34E
Karlovy Vary Czech Rep. 88 D9 50 13N 12 52E
Karlshamn Sweden 88 E12 56 10N 14 50E
Karlskoga Sweden 88 E13 59 19N 14 33E
Karlskrona Sweden 88 E12 56 10N 15 35E
Karlsruhe Germany 88 B8 49 00N 8 24E
Karlstad Sweden 88 D13 59 24N 13 32E
Karnafuli Reservoir Bangladesh 99 M9 22 30N 92 20E
Karnataka *admin.* India 98 D2 14 40N 75 30E
Kárpathos *i.* Greece 89 L1 35 30N 27 12E
Karpenísi Greece 89 H3 38 55N 21 47E
Kars Turkey 96 D7 40 35N 43 05E
Karsakpay Kazakhstan 94 J6 47 47N 66 43E
Karwar India 98 C2 14 50N 74 09E
Kasai *r.* Angola/CDR 108 H7 4 00S 19 00E
Kasama Zambia 109 L5 10 10S 31 11E
Kasaragod India 98 C2 12 30N 74 59E
Kasempa Zambia 109 K5 13 28S 25 48E
Kasese Uganda 108 L8 0 10N 30 06E
Kāshān Iran 97 F5 33 59N 51 35E
Kashi China 100 D6 39 29N 76 02E
Kashinatpur Bangladesh 99 K9 23 58N 89 37E
Kashiwazaki Japan 102 C2 37 22N 138 33E
Kásos *i.* Greece 89 L1 35 20N 26 55E
Kassala Sudan 108 M11 15 24N 36 30E
Kassel Germany 88 B9 51 18N 9 30E
Kastamonu Turkey 96 B7 41 22N 33 47E
Kastoriá Greece 89 H4 40 33N 21 15E
Kasur Pakistan 98 C6 31 07N 74 30E
Kataba Zambia 109 K4 16 02S 25 03E
Katchall Island India 99 G1 7 57N 93 22E
Kateríni Greece 89 J4 40 15N 22 30E
Katha Myanmar 100 H3 24 11N 96 20E
Katherine Aust. 110 E7 14 29S 132 20E
Kathiawar *p.* India 98 C4 21 10N 71 00E
Kathmandu Nepal 99 F5 27 42N 85 19E
Katmai National Park Alaska USA 40 D5/E5 58 15N 155 00W
Katowice Poland 88 G9 50 15N 18 59E
Katrineholm Sweden 88 F13 58 59N 16 15E
Katsina Nigeria 108 F10 13 00N 7 32E
Katsina Ala Nigeria 108 F9 7 10N 9 30E
Kattegat *sd.* Denmark/Sweden 88 C12 57 00N 11 00E
Kauai *i.* Hawaiian Islands 115 X18 22 00N 159 30W
Kauai Channel *sd.* Hawaiian Islands 115 X18 21 45N 158 50W
Kaula *i.* Hawaiian Islands 115 W18 21 35N 160 40W
Kaulakahi Channel *sd.* Hawaiian Islands 115 X18 21 58N 159 50W
Kaunas Lithuania 88 J11 54 52N 23 55E
Kaura Namoda Nigeria 108 F10 12 39N 6 38E
Kau Sai Chau *i.* HK China 100 C2 22 22N 114 19E
Kau Yi Chau *i.* HK China 100 B1 22 17N 114 04E
Kavajë Albania 89 G4 41 11N 19 33E
Kavála Greece 89 K4 40 56N 24 25E
Kavaratti India 98 C2 10 33N 72 39E
Kawagoe Japan 102 C2 35 55N 139 30E
Kawaihae Hawaiian Islands 115 Z18 20 02N 155 05W
Kawasaki Japan 102 C2 35 30N 139 45E
Kawerau NZ 111 F5 38 05S 176 42E
Kaya Burkina 108 D10 13 04N 1 09W
Kayes Mali 108 B10 14 26N 11 28W
Kayseri Turkey 96 C6 38 42N 35 28E
Kazach'ye Russia 95 R11 70 46N 136 15E
KAZAKHSTAN 94 H6/J6
Kazakh Upland Kazakhstan 94 K6 47 00N 75 00E
Kazan' Russia 94 G8 55 45N 49 10E
Kazanlŭk Bulgaria 89 K5 42 37N 25 23E
Kazatin Ukraine 88 M8 49 41N 28 49E
Kāzerūn Iran 97 F4 29 35N 51 40E
Kazym *r.* Russia 94 J9 63 00N 67 30E
Kéa *i.* Greece 89 K2 37 00N 24 00E
Kearney Nebraska USA 70 G5 40 42N 99 04W
Kearny New Jersey USA 73 H2 40 45N 74 07W
Kecskemét Hungary 89 G7 46 56N 19 43E
Kediri Indonesia 103 E2 7 45S 112 01E
Keene New Hampshire USA 73 D3 42 56N 72 17W
Keetmanshoop Namibia 109 H2 26 36S 18 08E
Kefallonia *i.* Greece 89 H3 38 00N 20 00E
Kei Ling Ha Hoi *b.* HK China 100 C2 22 26N 114 17E
K'elafo Ethiopia 108 N9 5 37N 44 10E
Kelkit *r.* Turkey 96 C7 40 20N 37 40E
Kelseyville California USA 72 B4 38 58N 122 50W
Kelso California USA 72 F2 35 01N 115 39W
Kemerovo Russia 95 L8 55 25N 86 05E
Kemp Land *geog. reg.* Antarctica 117 65 00S 60 00E
Kempten Germany 88 C7 47 44N 10 19E
Kenai Fjords National Park Alaska USA 40 E5/F5 60 00N 150 00W
Kendal UK 86 D11 54 20N 2 45W
Kendari Indonesia 103 G3 3 57S 122 36E
Kenema Sierra Leone 108 B9 7 57N 11 11W
Kengtung Myanmar 101 H3 21 15N 99 40E
Keningau Malaysia 103 F5 5 21N 116 11E
Kénitra Morocco 108 C14 34 20N 6 34W
Kenmare North Dakota USA 47 F1 48 40N 101 59W
Kennebec River Maine USA 53 S5 45 10N 69 42W
Kennebunk Maine USA 73 E3 43 24N 70 31W
Kennedy Town HK China 100 B1 22 17N 114 07E
Kenosha Wisconsin USA 71 J5 42 34N 87 50W
Kentucky *state* USA 71 J4 37 00N 85 00W
Kentwood Michigan USA 51 J2 42 54N 85 35W
KENYA 108 M7
Kenya, Mount Kenya 108 L13 0 10S 37 19E
Kepulauan Anambas *is.* Indonesia 103 D4 3 00N 106 20E
Kepulauan Aru *is.* Indonesia 103 J2 6 00S 134 30E
Kepulauan Babar *is.* Indonesia 103 H2 7 50S 129 30E
Kepulauan Batu *is.* Indonesia 103 B3 0 18S 98 29E
Kepulauan Kai *is.* Indonesia 103 J2 5 30S 132 30E
Kepulauan Lingga *is.* Indonesia 103 C3 0 10S 104 30E
Kepulauan Mentawai *is.* Indonesia 103 B3 2 00S 99 00E
Kepulauan Obi *is.* Indonesia 103 H3 1 30S 127 30E
Kepulauan Riau *is.* Indonesia 103 C4 0 30N 104 30E
Kepulauan Sangir *is.* Indonesia 103 H4 3 00N 125 30E
Kepulauan Sula *is.* Indonesia 103 G3 1 50S 124 50E
Kepulauan Tanimbar *is.* Indonesia 103 J2 7 30S 131 30E
Kerala *admin.* India 98 D1/D2 10 10N 76 30E
Kerema PNG 110 H8 7 59S 145 46E
Keren Eritrea 108 M11 15 46N 38 30E
Kerguelen Plateau Indian Ocean 113 G1 55 00S 80 00E
Kérkyra *i.* Greece 89 G3 39 00N 19 00E
Kermadec Islands Pacific Ocean 114 J5 30 00S 178 30W
Kermadec Trench Pacific Ocean 114 J4 33 00S 177 00W
Kermān Iran 97 G5 30 18N 57 05E
Kermānshāh Iran 97 E5 34 19N 47 04E
Kern *r.* California USA 72 D2 36 00N 118 28W
Kerrville Texas USA 70 G3 30 03N 99 09W
Kerulen *r.* Mongolia 101 L8 47 30N 112 30E
Ket' *r.* Russia 95 L8 58 30N 87 00E
Ketapang Indonesia 103 E3 1 50S 110 00E
Ketchikan Alaska USA 42 E4 55 25N 131 40W
Ketrzyn Poland 88 H10 54 05N 21 24E
Kettle Creek *r.* Pennsylvania USA 52 J1 41 30N 77 40W
Keuka Lake New York USA 53 J2 42 30N 77 10W
Kevin Montana USA 46 G1 48 45N 111 57W
Keweenaw Bay Michigan USA 51 G4 47 05N 88 15W
Keweenaw Peninsula Michigan USA 71 J6 47 00N 88 00W
Key West Florida USA 71 K1 24 34N 81 48W
Khabarovsk Russia 95 R6 48 32N 135 08E
Khalig el Tina Egypt 109 T4 31 08N 32 36E
Khambhat India 98 C4 22 19N 72 39E
Khambhat, Gulf of India 98 C4 20 30N 72 00E
Khammam India 98 E3 17 15N 80 11E
Khānābād Afghanistan 97 J6 36 42N 69 08E
Khānaqīn Iraq 96 E5 34 22N 45 22E
Khandwa India 98 D4 21 49N 76 23E
Khanty-Mansiysk Russia 94 J9 61 01N 69 00E
Khān Yūnis Middle East 96 N10 31 21N 34 18E
Kharagpur India 99 F4 22 23N 87 22E
Kharan Pakistan 98 B5 28 32N 65 26E
Khārg *i.* Iran 97 F4 29 14N 50 20E
Khartoum Sudan 108 L11 15 33N 32 35E
Khāsh Iran 97 H4 28 14N 61 15E
Khash *r.* Afghanistan 97 H5 31 30N 62 30E
Khasi Hills *mts.* India 99 L10 25 34N 91 30E
Khaskovo Bulgaria 89 K4 41 57N 25 32E
Khatanga Russia 95 N11 71 59N 102 31E
Khatanga *r.* Russia 95 N11 72 30N 102 30E
Khaybar Saudi Arabia 96 C4 25 50N 39 00E
Khemisset Morocco 108 C14 33 50N 6 03W
Kheta *r.* Russia 95 M11 71 30N 95 00E
Khilok *r.* Russia 95 N7 51 00N 107 30E
Khiva Uzbekistan 94 J5 41 25N 60 49E
Khmel'nyts'kyy Ukraine 88 L8 49 25N 26 59E
Kholmsk Russia 95 S6 47 02N 142 03E
Khorog Tajikistan 94 K4 37 22N 71 32E
Khorramābād Iran 97 E5 33 29N 48 21E
Khorramshahr Iran 97 E5 30 25N 48 09E
Khotin Ukraine 88 L8 48 30N 26 31E
Khouribga Morocco 108 C14 32 54N 6 57W
Khowai India 99 L10 24 05N 91 36E
Khulna Bangladesh 99 K9 22 49N 89 34E
Khyber Pass Afghanistan/Pakistan 98 C6 34 06N 71 05E
Kibombo CDR 108 K7 3 58S 25 54E
Kiel Germany 88 C11 54 20N 10 08E
Kielce Poland 88 H9 50 51N 20 39E
Kiev Ukraine 88 N9 50 25N 30 30E
Kigali Rwanda 108 L7 1 56S 30 04E
Kigoma Tanzania 108 K7 4 52S 29 36E
Kii-suidō *sd.* Japan 102 B1 34 00N 134 45E
Kikinda Serbia 89 H6 45 50N 20 30E
Kikori PNG 110 G8 7 25S 144 13E
Kikwit CDR 108 H6 5 02S 18 51E
Kilanea Hawaiian Islands 115 X19 22 05N 159 35W
Kilimanjaro *mt.* Tanzania 108 M7 3 04S 37 22E
Kilkenny RoI 86 B10 52 39N 7 15W
Kilkís Greece 89 J4 40 59N 22 52E
Killarney RoI 86 A10 52 03N 9 30W
Killeen Texas USA 71 G3 31 08N 97 44W
Kilmarnock UK 86 C11 55 36N 4 30W
Kilwa Masoko Tanzania 109 M6 8 55S 39 31E
Kimberley RSA 109 J2 28 45S 24 46E
Kimberley Plateau Aust. 110 D6 17 30S 126 00E
Kimchaek North Korea 101 P7 40 41N 129 12E
Kindia Guinea 108 B10 10 03N 12 49W
Kindu CDR 108 K7 3 00S 25 56E
King City California USA 72 C3 36 13N 121 09W
King George Island South Shetland Islands 81 F1 62 00S 58 00W
King Island Aust. 110 G2 40 00S 144 00E
Kingman Arizona USA 70 D4 35 12N 114 02W
Kings *r.* California USA 72 D3 36 32N 119 30W
Kings Canyon National Park California USA 72 D3 36 45N 118 30W
King's Lynn UK 86 F10 52 45N 0 24E
King Sound Aust. 110 C6 16 00S 123 00E
Kings Point *tn.* New York USA 73 J2 40 49N 73 45W
Kingsport Tennessee USA 71 K4 36 33N 82 34W
Kingston Jamaica 75 U13 17 58N 76 48W
Kingston New York USA 73 C2 41 56N 74 00W
Kingston upon Hull UK 86 E10 53 45N 0 20W
Kingstown St. Vincent and The Grenadines 74 R11 13 12N 61 14W
Kingsville Texas USA 71 G2 27 32N 97 53W
Kinkala Congo 108 G7 4 18S 14 49E
Kinleith NZ 111 E5 38 15S 175 56E

Kinshasa CDR	**108**	H7	4 18S	15 18E
Kipili Tanzania	**109**	L6	7 30S	30 39E
Kirensk Russia	**95**	N8	57 45N	108 02E
KIRIBATI	**114/115**	H8/L7		
Kirikkale Turkey	**96**	B6	39 51N	33 32E
Kiritimati Island Kiribati	**115**	L8	2 10N	157 00W
Kirkcaldy UK	**86**	D12	56 07N	3 10W
Kirkcudbright UK	**86**	C11	54 50N	4 03W
Kirksville Missouri USA	**71**	H5	40 12N	92 35W
Kirkūk Iraq	**96**	D6	35 28N	44 26E
Kirkwall UK	**86**	D13	58 59N	2 58W
Kirov Russia	**94**	G8	58 00N	49 38E
Kiryū Japan	**102**	C2	36 26N	139 18E
Kisangani CDR	**108**	K8	0 33N	25 14E
Kishiwada Japan	**102**	C1	34 28N	135 22E
Kiskunfélegyháza Hungary	**89**	G7	46 42N	19 52E
Kiskunhalas Hungary	**89**	G7	46 26N	19 29E
Kismaayo Somalia	**108**	N7	0 25S	42 31E
Kisumu Kenya	**108**	L7	0 08S	34 47E
Kita-Kyūshu Japan	**102**	B1	33 52N	130 49E
Kitami Japan	**102**	D3	43 51N	143 54E
Kittery Maine USA	**73**	E3	43 06N	70 46W
Kitwe Zambia	**109**	K5	0 08S	30 30E
Kivu, Lake CDR/Rwanda	**108**	K7	2 00S	29 00E
Kızıl Irmak *r.* Turkey	**96**	B7	40 30N	34 00E
Kykládes *is.* Greece	**89**	K2	37 00N	25 00E
Kladno Czech Rep.	**88**	E9	50 10N	14 07E
Klagenfurt Austria	**89**	E7	46 38N	14 20E
Klaipėda Lithuania	**88**	H11	55 43N	21 07E
Klamath *r.* USA	**70**	B5	42 00N	123 00W
Klamath Falls *tn.* Oregon USA	**70**	B5	42 14N	121 47W
Klatovy Czech Rep.	**88**	D8	49 24N	13 17E
Klerksdorp RSA	**109**	K2	26 52S	26 39E
Klintehamn Sweden	**88**	G12	57 24N	18 14E
Kłodzko Poland	**88**	F9	50 28N	16 40E
Klukwan Alaska USA	**42**	C6	59 25N	135 55W
Klyuchevskaya Sopka *mt.* Russia	**95**	U8	56 03N	160 38E
Knokke-Heist Belgium	**86**	G9	51 21N	3 19E
Knoxville Tennessee USA	**71**	K4	36 00N	83 57W
Kōbe Japan	**102**	C1	34 40N	135 12E
Koblenz Germany	**88**	A9	50 21N	7 36E
Kobryn Belarus	**88**	K10	52 16N	24 22E
Kocaeli Turkey	**96**	A7	40 47N	29 55E
Koch Bihar India	**99**	F5	26 18N	89 32E
Kōchi Japan	**102**	B1	33 33N	133 32E
Kodiak Alaska USA	**40**	E5	57 46N	152 30W
Kodiak Island Alaska USA	**115**	L13	57 20N	153 40W
Kodok Sudan	**108**	L9	9 51N	32 07E
Koforidua Ghana	**108**	D9	6 01N	0 12W
Kōfu Japan	**102**	C2	35 42N	138 34E
Kohat Pakistan	**98**	C6	33 37N	71 30E
Kohima India	**99**	G5	25 40N	94 08E
Koh-i-Mazar *mt.* Afghanistan	**97**	J5	32 30N	66 23E
Kokand Uzbekistan	**94**	K5	40 33N	70 55E
Kokomo Indiana USA	**71**	J5	40 30N	86 09W
Kokshetau Kazakhstan	**94**	J7	53 18N	69 25E
Kola Peninsula Russia	**94**	F10	67 30N	37 30E
Kolar Gold Fields *tn.* India	**98**	D2	12 54N	78 16E
Kolding Denmark	**88**	B11	55 29N	9 30E
Kolguyev *i.* Russia	**94**	G10	69 00N	49 30E
Kolhapur India	**98**	C3	16 40N	74 20E
Kolin Czech Rep.	**88**	E9	50 02N	15 11E
Kolka Latvia	**88**	J12	57 44N	22 27E
Kolkata India	**99**	F4	22 30N	88 20E
Kolobrzeg Poland	**88**	E11	54 10N	15 35E
Kolomyya Ukraine	**88**	K8	48 31N	25 00E
Kolosib India	**99**	M10	24 05N	92 50E
Kolpashevo Russia	**95**	L8	58 21N	82 59E
Kolwezi CDR	**109**	K5	10 45S	25 25E
Kolyma *r.* Russia	**95**	T10	66 30N	152 00E
Kolyma Lowland Russia	**95**	T10	69 00N	155 00E
Kolyma Range *mts.* Russia	**95**	T9	63 00N	160 00E
Komandorskiye Ostrova *is.* Russia	**114**	G13	60 00N	175 00W
Komárno Slovakia	**88**	G7	47 46N	18 05E
Komatsu Japan	**102**	C2	36 25N	136 27E
Komotiní Greece	**89**	K4	41 06N	25 25E
Kômpóng Saôm Cambodia	**103**	C6	10 38N	103 28E
Komsomol'sk-na-Amure Russia	**95**	R7	50 32N	136 59E
Kondūz Afghanistan	**97**	J6	36 45N	68 51E
Kongolo CDR	**108**	K6	5 20S	27 00E
Kongsvinger Norway	**88**	C14	60 12N	12 01E
Konin Poland	**88**	G10	52 12N	18 12E
Konosha Russia	**94**	G9	60 58N	40 08E
Konstanz Germany	**88**	B7	47 40N	9 10E
Konya Turkey	**96**	B6	37 51N	32 30E
Koocanusa, Lake Montana USA	**43**	N1	48 55N	115 10W
Koper Slovenia	**89**	D6	45 31N	13 44E
Kopychintsy Ukraine	**88**	K8	49 10N	25 58E
Korçë Albania	**89**	H4	40 38N	20 44E
Korčula *i.* Croatia	**89**	F5	43 00N	17 00E
Korea Bay China/North Korea	**101**	N6	39 00N	124 00E
Korea Strait Japan/South Korea	**101**	P5/Q6	33 00N	129 00E
Korhogo Côte d'Ivoire	**108**	C9	9 22N	5 31W
Korinthiakós Kólpos *g.* Greece	**89**	J3	38 00N	22 00E
Kórinthos Greece	**89**	J2	37 56N	22 55E
Kōriyama Japan	**102**	D2	37 23N	140 22E
Korla China	**100**	F7	41 48N	86 10E
Koro *i.* Fiji	**114**	U16	17 20S	179 25E
Koro Sea Fiji	**114**	U16	17 35S	180 00
Korosten' Ukraine	**88**	M9	51 00N	28 30E
Korsakov Russia	**95**	S6	46 36N	142 50E
Kortrijk Belgium	**86**	G9	50 50N	3 17E
Koryak Range *mts.* Russia	**95**	V9	62 00N	170 00E
Kós *i.* Greece	**89**	L2	36 45N	27 10E
Kosciusko Island Alaska USA	**42**	D4	56 00N	133 45W
Kosciusko, Mount Aust.	**110**	H2	36 28S	148 17E
Košice Slovakia	**88**	H8	48 44N	21 15E
KOSOVO	**89**	H5		
Kosovska Mitrovica Kosovo	**89**	H5	42 54N	20 52E
Kosti Sudan	**108**	L10	13 11N	32 28E
Kostroma Russia	**94**	G8	57 46N	40 59E
Koszalin Poland	**88**	F11	54 10N	16 10E
Kota India	**98**	D5	25 11N	75 58E
Kota Bharu Malaysia	**103**	C5	6 08N	102 14E
Kota Kinabalu Malaysia	**103**	F5	5 59N	116 04E
Kotlas Russia	**94**	G9	61 15N	46 35E
Kotri Pakistan	**98**	B5	25 22N	68 18E
Kotto *r.* CAR	**108**	J9	7 00N	22 30E
Kotuy *r.* Russia	**95**	N10	67 30N	102 00E
Koudougou Burkina	**108**	D10	12 15N	2 23W
Koulamoutou Gabon	**108**	G7	1 12S	12 29E
Koulikoro Mali	**108**	C10	12 55N	7 31W
Koumra Chad	**108**	H9	8 56N	17 32E
Kourou French Guiana	**80**	G15	5 08N	52 37W
Kovel' Ukraine	**88**	K9	51 12N	24 48E
Kowloon HK China	**100**	C1	22 19N	114 11E
Kowloon Peak *mt.* HK China	**100**	C2	22 20N	114 14E
Kowloon Reservoirs HK China	**100**	B2	22 21N	114 09E
Kowloon Tong HK China	**100**	C2	22 20N	114 11E
Kozáni Greece	**89**	H4	40 18N	21 48E
Kpalimé Togo	**108**	E9	6 55N	0 44E
Kragujevac Serbia	**89**	H5	44 01N	20 55E
Kraków Poland	**88**	G9	50 03N	19 55E
Kraljevo Serbia	**89**	H5	43 44N	20 41E
Kranj Slovenia	**89**	E7	46 15N	14 20E
Krasnodar Russia	**94**	F6	45 02N	39 00E
Krasnovodsk Turkmenistan	**94**	H5	40 01N	53 00E
Krasnoyarsk Russia	**95**	M8	56 05N	92 46E
Krefeld Germany	**88**	A9	51 20N	6 32E
Kremenets Ukraine	**88**	K9	50 05N	25 48E
Krems Austria	**88**	E8	48 25N	15 36E
Kribi Cameroon	**108**	F8	2 56N	9 56E
Krishna *r.* India	**98**	D3	16 00N	77 30E
Krishnanagar India	**99**	K9	23 25N	88 30E
Kristiansand Norway	**86**	J13	58 08N	8 01E
Kristianstad Sweden	**88**	E12	56 02N	14 10E
Kristinehamn Sweden	**88**	E13	59 17N	14 09E
Kríti *i.* Greece	**89**	K1	35 00N	25 00E
Krk *i.* Croatia	**89**	E6	45 00N	14 00E
Krosno Poland	**88**	J8	49 40N	21 46E
Kruševaç Serbia	**89**	H5	43 34N	21 20E
Kruzof Island Alaska USA	**42**	C5	57 15N	135 40W
Kuala Lumpur Malaysia	**103**	C4	3 09N	101 42E
Kuala Terengganu Malaysia	**103**	C5	5 20N	103 09E
Kuantan Malaysia	**103**	C4	3 48N	103 19E
Kuching Malaysia	**103**	E4	1 35N	110 21E
Kuito Angola	**109**	H5	12 25S	16 56E
Kuiu Island Alaska USA	**42**	C5/D5	56 45N	134 00W
Kujū-san *mt.* Japan	**102**	B1	33 07N	131 14E
Kukës Albania	**89**	H5	42 05N	20 24E
Kuldiga Latvia	**88**	H12	56 58N	21 58E
Kuma *r.* Russia	**94**	G5	45 00N	45 00E
Kumagaya Japan	**102**	C2	36 09N	139 22E
Kumamoto Japan	**102**	B1	32 50N	130 42E
Kumanovo FYROM	**89**	H5	42 07N	21 40E
Kumasi Ghana	**108**	D9	6 45N	1 35W
Kumba Cameroon	**108**	F8	4 39N	9 26E
Kumbakonam India	**98**	D2	10 59N	79 24E
Kunar *r.* Afghanistan/Pakistan	**97**	K6	34 50N	71 05E
Kunashir *i.* Russia	**102**	E3	44 30N	146 20E
Kundat Malaysia	**103**	F5	6 54N	116 50E
Kungrad Uzbekistan	**94**	H5	43 06N	58 54E
Kunlun Shan *mts.* China	**100**	E6/F6	36 30N	85 00E
Kunming China	**101**	J4	25 04N	102 41E
Kunsan South Korea	**101**	P6	35 57N	126 42E
Kununurra Aust.	**110**	D6	15 42S	128 50E
Kupa *r.* Croatia	**89**	E6	45 30N	15 00E
Kupang Indonesia	**103**	G1	10 13S	123 38E
Kupreanof Island Alaska USA	**42**	D5	56 50N	133 30W
Kurashiki Japan	**102**	B1	34 36N	133 43E
Kure Japan	**102**	B1	34 14N	132 32E
Kuressaare Estonia	**88**	J13	59 22N	28 40E
Kureyka *r.* Russia	**95**	M10	67 30N	91 00E
Kurgan Russia	**94**	J8	55 30N	65 20E
Kuria Muria Islands Oman	**97**	G2	17 30N	56 00E
Kurigram Bangladesh	**99**	K10	25 49N	89 39E
Kuril Islands Russia	**95**	T6	50 00N	155 00E
Kuril Ridge Pacific Ocean	**114**	F12	47 50N	152 00E
Kuril Trench Pacific Ocean	**114**	F12	45 40N	154 00E
Kurnool India	**98**	D3	15 51N	78 01E
Kursk Russia	**94**	F7	51 45N	36 14E
Kurskiy Zaliv *g.* Russia	**88**	H11	55 00N	21 00E
Kurtalan Turkey	**96**	D6	37 55N	41 44E
Kurume Japan	**102**	B1	33 20N	130 29E
Kushiro Japan	**102**	D3	42 58N	144 24E
Kustanay Kazakhstan	**94**	J7	53 15N	63 40E
Kütahya Turkey	**96**	A6	39 25N	29 56E
Kutno Poland	**88**	G10	52 13N	19 20E
Kutubdia Island Bangladesh	**99**	L8	21 50N	91 52E
Kuvango Angola	**109**	H5	14 27S	16 20E
KUWAIT	**97**	E4		
Kuwait Kuwait	**97**	E4	29 20N	48 00E
Kuytun China	**100**	E7	44 30N	85 00E
Kwai Chung HK China	**100**	B2	22 22N	114 07E
Kwangju South Korea	**101**	P6	35 07N	126 52E
Kwango *r.* CDR	**109**	H6	6 00S	17 00E
Kwekwe Zimbabwe	**109**	K4	18 55S	29 49E
Kwilu *r.* CDR	**109**	H6	6 00S	19 00E
Kwun Tong HK China	**100**	C1	22 18N	114 13E
Kwu Tung HK China	**100**	B3	22 31N	114 06E
Kyburz California USA	**72**	C4	38 47N	120 19W
Kyle of Lochalsh UK	**86**	C12	57 17N	5 43W
Kyoga, Lake Uganda	**108**	L8	2 00N	34 00E
Kyōga-misaki *c.* Japan	**102**	C2	35 48N	135 12E
Kyōto Japan	**102**	C2	35 02N	135 45E
Kyparissiakós Kólpos *g.* Greece	**89**	H2	37 00N	21 00E
KYRGYZSTAN	**94**	K5		
Kythira *i.* Greece	**89**	J2	36 00N	23 00E
Kýthnos *i.* Greece	**89**	K2	37 25N	24 25E
Kyūshū *i.* Japan	**102**	B1	32 20N	131 00E
Kyushu-Palau Ridge Pacific Ocean	**114**	D9	15 00N	135 00E
Kyustendil Bulgaria	**89**	J5	42 26N	22 40E
Kyzyl Russia	**95**	M7	51 45N	94 28E
Kyzyl Kum *d.* Asia	**94**	J5	43 00N	65 00E
Kzylorda Kazakhstan	**94**	J5	44 25N	65 28E

L

Laascaanood Somalia	**108**	P9	8 35N	46 55E
Laâyoune Western Sahara	**108**	B13	27 10N	13 11W
la Baule-Escoublac Fr.	**87**	D7	47 18N	2 22W
Labé Guinea	**108**	B10	11 17N	12 11W
Labrador Basin Atlantic Ocean	**116**	C12	58 00N	50 00W
Lábrea Brazil	**80**	E12	7 20S	64 46W
La Brea Trinidad and Tobago	**75**	V15	10 14N	61 37W
Labytnangi Russia	**94**	J10	66 43N	66 28E
Lac Alaotra *l.* Madagascar	**109**	P4	17 30S	54 00E
Laccadive Islands India	**98**	C1/C2	11 00N	72 00E
La Ceiba Honduras	**74**	G3	15 45N	86 45W
Lac Fitri *l.* Chad	**108**	H10	13 00N	17 30E
Lachlan *r.* Aust.	**110**	H3	34 00S	145 00E
La Chorrera Panama	**75**	Y1	8 51N	79 46W
Lackawanna New York USA	**54**	D1	42 49N	78 49W
Lac Léman *l.* Switz.	**87**	J7	46 20N	6 20E
Lac Mai-Ndombe *l.* CDR	**108**	H7	2 00S	18 20E
La Coruña Sp.	**87**	A5	43 22N	8 24W
La Crosse Wisconsin USA	**71**	H5	43 48N	91 04W
Lacul Razim *l.* Romania	**89**	M6	45 00N	29 00E
Ladakh Range *mts.* Kashmir	**98**	D6	34 30N	78 30E
Ladozhskoye Ozero *l.* Russia	**94**	F9	61 00N	30 00E
Ladysmith RSA	**109**	K2	28 34S	29 47E
Ladysmith Wisconsin USA	**51**	F3	45 28N	91 06W
Lae PNG	**110**	H8	6 43S	147 01E
La Esmeralda Venezuela	**80**	D14	3 11N	65 33W
Lafayette Indiana USA	**71**	J5	40 25N	86 54W
Lafayette Louisiana USA	**71**	H3	30 12N	92 18W
La Fé Cuba	**75**	H4	22 02N	84 15W
Laghouat Algeria	**108**	E14	33 49N	2 55E
Lago Argentino *l.* Argentina	**81**	C3	50 10S	72 30W
Lago de Chapala *l.* Mexico	**74**	D4	20 05N	103 00W
Lago de Maracaibo *l.* Venezuela	**80**	C15	9 50N	71 30W
Lago de Nicaragua *l.* Nicaragua	**75**	G2	11 50N	86 00W
Lago de Poopó *l.* Bolivia	**80**	D10	18 30S	67 20W
Lago di Bolsena *l.* Italy	**89**	C5	42 00N	12 00E
Lago di Como *l.* Italy	**89**	B6	46 00N	9 00E
Lago di Garda *l.* Italy	**89**	C6	45 00N	10 00E
Lago Maggiore *l.* Italy	**89**	B6	46 00N	8 00E
Lagos Nigeria	**108**	E9	6 27N	3 28E
Lagos Port.	**87**	A2	37 05N	8 40W
Lago Titicaca *l.* Peru/Bolivia	**80**	C10	16 00S	69 30W
La Grande Oregon USA	**70**	C6	45 21N	118 05W
La Grange Georgia USA	**71**	J3	33 02N	85 02W
La Guaira Venezuela	**80**	D16	10 38N	66 55W
Laguna Caratasca *l.* Honduras	**75**	H3	15 05N	84 00W
Laguna de Perlas *l.* Nicaragua	**75**	H2	12 30N	83 30W
Laguna Madre *l.* Mexico	**74**	E4	25 00N	98 00W
Laguna Mar Chiquita *l.* Argentina	**81**	E7	30 30S	62 30W
Lagunillas Venezuela	**80**	C16	10 07N	71 16W
Lahaina Hawaiian Islands	**115**	Y18	20 23N	156 40W
Lahontan Reservoir Nevada USA	**72**	D4	39 22N	119 08W
Lahore Pakistan	**98**	C6	31 34N	74 22E
Lai Chi Wo HK China	**100**	C3	22 32N	114 15E
Lajes Brazil	**81**	G8	27 48S	50 20W
La Junta Colorado USA	**70**	F4	37 59N	103 34W
Lake Alpine *tn.* California USA	**72**	D4	38 30N	120 00W
Lake Charles *tn.* Louisiana USA	**71**	H3	30 13N	93 13W
Lake City *tn.* Michigan USA	**51**	J3	44 19N	85 13W
Lake Gogebic Michigan USA	**51**	G4	46 30N	89 30W
Lake Isabella *tn.* California USA	**72**	D2	35 37N	118 28W
Lakeland Florida USA	**71**	K2	28 02N	81 59W
Lakemba Passage *sd.* Fiji	**114**	V16	18 10S	179 00W
Lake Orion *tn.* Michigan USA	**52**	C2	42 47N	83 13W
Lakeport California USA	**70**	B4	39 04N	122 56W
Lake Success California USA	**72**	D3	36 07N	118 55W
Lake Timsâh Egypt	**109**	S3	30 34N	32 18E
Lakeview Oregon USA	**70**	B5	42 13N	120 21W
Lake View *tn.* New York USA	**54**	D1	42 43N	78 56W
Lakshadweep *admin.* India	**98**	C1/C2	9 30N	73 00E
La Línea de la Concepción Sp.	**87**	C2	36 10N	5 21W
Lalitpur India	**98**	D4	24 42N	78 24E
Lalmanir Hat Bangladesh	**99**	K10	25 51N	89 34E
La Maddalena Italy	**89**	B4	41 13N	9 25E
La Mancha *admin.* Sp.	**87**	D3	39 10N	2 45W
Lamar Colorado USA	**70**	F4	38 04N	102 37W
Lambaréné Gabon	**108**	G7	0 41S	10 13E
Lambasa Fiji	**114**	U16	16 25S	179 24E
Lambert Glacier Antarctica	**117**		73 00S	70 00E
Lambertville New Jersey USA	**73**	C2	40 22N	74 57W
Lamego Port.	**87**	B4	41 05N	7 49W
La Mesa California USA	**72**	E1	32 45N	117 00W
Lamía Greece	**89**	J3	38 55N	22 26E
Lamma Island HK China	**100**	B1	22 12N	114 08E
Lampazos Mexico	**74**	D5	27 00N	100 30W
Lam Tei Hong Kong China	**100**	A2	22 25N	113 59E
Lamu Kenya	**108**	N7	2 17S	40 54E
Lanai *i.* Hawaiian Islands	**115**	Y18	20 50N	156 55W
Lanai City Hawaiian Islands	**115**	Y18	20 50N	156 56W
Lancang Jiang *r.* China	**101**	H4/H5	30 00N	98 00E
Lancaster UK	**86**	D11	54 03N	2 48W
Lancaster California USA	**70**	C3	34 42N	118 09W
Lancaster Ohio USA	**71**	K4	39 43N	82 37W
Lancaster Pennsylvania USA	**71**	L5	40 01N	76 19W
Land's End *c.* UK	**86**	C9	50 03N	5 44W
Landshut Germany	**88**	D8	48 31N	12 10E
Landskrona Sweden	**88**	D12	55 53N	12 50E
Langdon North Dakota USA	**49**	C1	48 50N	98 25W
Langon Fr.	**87**	E6	44 33N	0 14W
Langres Fr.	**86**	H7	47 53N	5 20E
Lannion Fr.	**86**	D8	48 44N	3 27W
L'Anse Michigan USA	**51**	G4	46 45N	88 26W
Lansing Michigan USA	**71**	K5	42 44N	85 34W
Lantau Channel HK China	**100**	A1	22 11N	113 52E
Lantau Island HK China	**100**	A1	22 15N	113 56E
Lantau Peak *mt.* HK China	**100**	A1	22 15N	113 55E
Lanzarote *i.* Canary Islands	**108**	B13	29 00N	13 38W
Lanzhou China	**101**	J6	36 01N	103 45E
Laoag Philippines	**103**	G7	18 14N	120 36E
Lao Cai Vietnam	**101**	J3	22 30N	103 57E
Laon Fr.	**86**	G8	49 34N	3 37E
La Oroya Peru	**80**	B11	11 36S	75 54W
LAOS	**103**	C7/D7		
La Paz Bolivia	**80**	D10	16 30S	68 10W
La Paz Mexico	**74**	B4	24 10N	110 17W
Lapeer Michigan USA	**51**	K2	43 03N	83 19W
La Pesca Mexico	**74**	E4	23 46N	97 47W
La Plata Argentina	**81**	F6	34 52S	57 55W
Laptev Sea Arctic Ocean	**117**		76 00N	125 00E
Laptev Strait Russia	**95**	S11	73 00N	141 00E
L'Aquila Italy	**89**	D5	42 22N	13 24E
Lār Iran	**97**	F4	27 42N	54 19E
Larache Morocco	**108**	C15	35 12N	6 10W
Laramie Wyoming USA	**70**	E5	41 20N	105 38W
Lärbro Sweden	**88**	G12	57 47N	18 50E
Laredo Texas USA	**70**	G2	27 32N	99 22W
La Rioja Argentina	**81**	D8	29 26S	66 50W
Lárisa Greece	**89**	J3	39 38N	22 25E
Larkana Pakistan	**98**	B5	27 32N	68 18E
Larnaca Cyprus	**96**	B5	34 54N	33 29E
Larne UK	**86**	C11	54 51N	5 49W
la Rochelle Fr.	**87**	E7	46 10N	1 10W
la Roche-sur-Yon Fr.	**87**	E7	46 40N	1 25W
La Romana Dom. Rep.	**75**	L3	18 27N	68 57W
Larsen Ice Shelf Antarctica	**117**		67 00S	62 00W
Las Cruces New Mexico USA	**70**	E3	32 18N	106 47W
La Serena Chile	**81**	C8	29 54S	71 18W
la Seyne-sur-Mer Fr.	**87**	H5	43 06N	5 53E
Lashio Myanmar	**101**	H3	22 58N	97 48E
Las Marismas *geog. reg.* Sp.	**87**	B2/C2	36 55N	6 00W
Las Palmas Canary Islands	**108**	A13	28 08N	15 27W
La Spézia Italy	**89**	B6	44 07N	9 48E
Las Vegas Nevada USA	**70**	C4	36 10N	115 10W
Las Vegas New Mexico USA	**70**	E4	35 36N	105 15W
Latacunga Ecuador	**80**	B13	0 58S	78 36W
Latakia Syria	**96**	C6	35 31N	35 47E
Latina Italy	**89**	D4	41 28N	12 53E
Latur India	**98**	D3	18 24N	76 34E
LATVIA	**88**	J12		
Lau Fau Shan HK China	**100**	A2	22 28N	113 59E
Launceston Aust.	**110**	H1	41 25S	147 07E
Laurel Mississippi USA	**71**	J3	31 41N	89 09W
Laurie Island South Orkney Islands	**81**	J1	61 30S	46 00W
Lausanne Switz.	**87**	J7	46 32N	6 39E
Laut *i.* Indonesia	**103**	F3	4 40S	116 00E
Lautoka Fiji	**114**	T16	17 36S	177 28E
Laval Fr.	**86**	E8	48 04N	0 45W
La Vega Dom. Rep.	**75**	K3	19 15N	70 33W
Laverton Aust.	**110**	C4	28 49S	122 25E
La Victoria Venezuela	**80**	D16	10 16N	67 21W
Lawrence Kansas USA	**71**	G4	38 58N	95 15W
Lawrence Massachusetts USA	**73**	E3	42 41N	71 11W
Lawrence Park *tn.* Pennsylvania USA	**52**	F2	42 08N	80 02W
Lawton Oklahoma USA	**71**	G3	34 36N	98 25W
Laylá Saudi Arabia	**97**	E3	22 16N	46 45E
Laysan *i.* Hawaiian Islands	**114**	J10	25 46N	171 44W
Laytonville California USA	**72**	B4	39 41N	123 29W
LEBANON	**96**	N11/P12		
Lebanon Missouri USA	**71**	H4	37 40N	92 40W
Lebanon Pennsylvania USA	**73**	B2	40 23N	76 20W
Lebu Chile	**81**	C6	37 38S	73 43W
Lecce Italy	**89**	G4	40 21N	18 11E
Leeds UK	**86**	E10	53 50N	1 35W
Leeuwarden Neths.	**86**	H10	53 12N	5 48E
Leeuwin, Cape Aust.	**110**	B3	34 24S	115 09E
Lee Vining California USA	**72**	D3	37 58N	119 09W
Leeward Islands Lesser Antilles	**75**	M3	17 30N	64 00W

Lefkáda *i.* Greece 89 H3 38 45N 20 40E
Le François Martinique 74 R12 14 37N 60 54W
Leganés Sp. 87 D4 40 20N 3 46WE
Legnica Poland 88 F9 51 12N 16 10E
le Havre Fr. 86 F8 49 30N 0 06E
Leicester UK 86 E10 52 38N 1 05W
Leiden Neths. 86 H10 52 10N 4 30E
Leipzig Germany 88 D9 51 20N 12 25E
Leiria Port. 87 A3 39 45N 8 49W
Leivadiá Greece 89 J3 38 26N 22 53E
Leizhou Bandao *p.* China 101 L3 21 00N 110 00E
Lek *r.* Neths. 86 H9 51 48N 4 47E
le Mans Fr. 86 F7 48 00N 0 12E
Lemoore California USA 72 D3 36 18N 119 47W
Lena *r.* Russia 95 Q10 70 00N 125 00E
Leninogorsk Kazakhstan 95 L7 50 23N 83 32E
Leninsk-Kuznetskiy Russia 95 L7 54 44N 86 13E
Lens Fr. 86 G9 50 26N 2 50E
Lensk Russia 95 P9 60 48N 114 55E
Leoben Austria 89 E7 47 23N 15 06E
León Mexico 74 D4 21 10N 101 42W
León Nicaragua 74 G2 12 24N 86 52W
León Sp. 87 C5 42 35N 5 34W
Leon *r.* Texas USA 71 G3 32 00N 98 00W
Leonora Aust. 110 C4 28 54S 121 20E
le Puy Fr. 87 G6 45 03N 3 53E
Léré Chad 108 G9 9 41N 14 17E
Le Roy New York USA 52 J2 42 59N 77 59W
Lerwick UK 86 E14 60 09N 1 09W
Les Abymes Guadeloupe 74 Q9 16 15N 61 31W
Les Cayes Haiti 75 K3 18 15N 73 46W
Leskovac Serbia 89 J5 43 00N 21 57E
LESOTHO 109 K2
les Sables-d'Olonne Fr. 87 E7 46 30N 1 47W
Lesser Antilles *is.* W. Indies 75 L2 18 00N 65 00W
Lésvos *i.* Greece 89 L3 39 00N 26 00E
Leszno Poland 88 F9 51 51N 16 35E
Leticia Col. 80 C13 4 09S 69 57W
le Tréport Fr. 86 F9 50 04N 1 22E
Leuven Belgium 86 H9 50 53N 4 42E
Lévêque, Cape Aust. 110 C6 16 25S 122 55E
Levice Slovakia 88 G8 48 14N 18 35E
Levin NZ 111 E4 40 37S 175 17E
Levuka Fiji 114 U16 17 42N 178 50E
Lewis *i.* UK 86 B12 58 15N 6 30W
Lewiston Idaho USA 70 C6 46 25N 117 00W
Lewiston Maine USA 71 M5 44 08N 70 14W
Lewiston New York USA 51 M2 43 10N 79 02W
Lewistown Montana USA 70 E6 47 04N 109 26W
Lewistown Pennsylvania USA 73 B2 40 36N 77 34W
Lexington Kentucky USA 71 K4 38 03N 84 30W
Lexington Heights *tn.* Michigan USA 52 D3 43 15N 82 32W
Leyte *i.* Philippines 103 G6/H6 11 00N 125 00E
Lezhë Albania 89 G4 41 47N 19 39E
Lhasa China 100 G4 29 41N 91 10E
Lhaze China 100 F4 29 08N 87 43E
Lianyungang China 101 M5 34 37N 119 10E
Liaoyang China 101 N7 41 16N 123 12E
Liaoyuan China 101 P7 42 53N 125 10E
Libby Montana USA 43 N1 48 25N 115 33W
Libenge CDR 108 H8 3 39N 18 39E
Liberal Kansas USA 70 F4 37 03N 100 56W
Liberec Czech Rep. 88 E9 50 48N 15 05E
LIBERIA 108 B9/C9
Liberty New York USA 73 C2 41 48N 74 44W
Libourne Fr. 87 E6 44 55N 0 14W
Libreville Gabon 108 F8 0 30N 9 25E
LIBYA 108 G13
Libyan Desert North Africa 108 J13 25 00N 25 00E
Libyan Plateau Egypt 108 K14 31 00N 26 00E
Licata Italy 89 D2 37 07N 13 57E
Lichinga Mozambique 109 M5 13 19S 35 13E
Lidköping Sweden 88 D13 58 30N 13 10E
LIECHTENSTEIN 87 K7
Liège Belgium 86 H9 50 38N 5 35E
Lienz Austria 89 D7 46 51N 12 50E
Liepaja Latvia 88 H12 56 30N 21 00E
Ligurian Sea Mediterranean Sea 89 B5 44 00N 9 00E
Lihue Hawaiian Islands 115 X18 21 59N 159 23W
Likasi CDR 109 K5 10 58S 26 47E
Lille Fr. 86 G9 50 39N 3 05E
Lilongwe Malawi 109 L5 13 58S 33 49E
Lim *r.* Europe 89 G5 43 00N 19 00E
Lima Peru 80 B11 12 04S 77 03W
Lima Ohio USA 71 K5 40 43N 84 06W
Lima *r.* Port. 87 A4 42 00N 8 30W
Limassol Cyprus 96 B5 34 04N 33 03E
Limay *r.* Argentina 81 D6 39 30S 69 30W
Limbe Cameroon 108 F8 3 58N 9 10E
Limerick RoI 86 A10 52 04N 8 38W
Limfjorden *sd.* Denmark 88 B12 57 00N 8 50E
Límnos *i.* Greece 89 K3 39 00N 25 00E
Limoges Fr. 87 F6 45 50N 1 15E
Limón Costa Rica 75 H2 10 00N 83 01W
Limoux Fr. 87 G5 43 03N 2 13E
Limpopo *r.* Southern Africa 109 L3 22 30S 32 00E
Linares Mexico 74 E4 24 54N 99 38W
Linares Sp. 87 D3 38 05N 3 38W
Lincoln UK 86 E10 53 14N 0 33W
Lincoln Nebraska USA 71 G5 40 49N 96 41W
Linden Guyana 80 F15 5 59N 58 19W
Linden New Jersey USA 73 H1 40 37N 74 13W
Line Islands Kiribati 115 L7 0 00 155 00W
Linhares Brazil 80 K10 19 22S 40 04W
Linköping Sweden 88 E13 58 25N 15 35E
Linton North Dakota USA 70 F6 46 17N 100 14W
Lin Tong Mei HK China 100 B2 22 29N 114 06E
Linxia China 101 J6 35 31N 103 08E
Linz Austria 88 E8 48 19N 14 18E
Lipetsk Russia 94 F7 52 37N 39 36E
Lisbon Port. 87 A3 38 44N 9 08W
Lisburn UK 86 B11 54 31N 6 03W
Lisianski *i.* Hawaiian Islands 114 J10 26 04N 173 58W
Lisieux Fr. 86 F8 49 09N 0 14E
Lismore Aust. 110 J4 28 48S 153 17E
Litāni *r.* Lebanon 96 N11 33 35N 35 40E
Lithgow Aust. 110 J3 33 30S 150 09E
LITHUANIA 88 J11
Little Aden Yemen 96 D1 12 47N 44 55E
Little Andaman *i.* Andaman Islands 99 G2 10 30N 92 40E
Little Bitter Lake Egypt 109 T2 30 14N 32 33E
Little Colorado *r.* Arizona USA 70 D4 36 00N 111 00W
Little Falls *tn.* Minnesota USA 71 H6 45 58N 94 20W
Little Missouri *r.* USA 70 F6 46 00N 104 00W
Little Nicobar *i.* Nicobar Islands 99 G1 7 00N 94 00E
Little Rock Kansas USA 71 H3 34 42N 92 17W
Little Sioux *r.* USA 71 G5 42 00N 96 00W
Little Snake *r.* USA 70 E5 41 00N 108 00W
Little Traverse Bay Michigan USA 52 A5 45 25N 85 00W
Liuzhou China 101 K3 24 17N 109 15E
Livermore California USA 72 C3 37 40N 121 46W
Liverpool UK 86 D10 53 25N 2 55W
Livingston Montana USA 70 D6 45 40N 110 33W
Livingstone Zambia 109 K4 17 50S 25 53E
Livingston Island South Shetland Islands 81 E1 62 38S 60 30W
Livorno Italy 89 C5 43 33N 10 18E
Liwale Tanzania 109 M6 9 47S 38 00E
Lizard Point UK 86 C8 49 56N 5 13W
Ljubljana Slovenia 89 E7 46 04N 14 30E
Ljungby Sweden 88 D12 56 49N 13 55E
Llanelli UK 86 C9 51 42N 4 10W
Llanos *geog. reg.* Venezuela 80 D15 7 30N 67 30W
Lleida Sp. 87 F4 41 37N 0 38E
Lobatse Botswana 109 K2 25 11S 25 40E
Lobito Angola 109 G5 12 20S 13 34E
Loch Ness *l.* UK 86 C12 57 02N 4 30W
Loch Tay *l.* UK 86 D12 56 31N 4 10W
Lockhart Texas USA 71 G2 29 54N 97 14W
Lock Haven *tn.* Pennsylvania USA 73 B2 41 09N 77 28W
Lockport New York USA 51 M2 43 10N 78 42W
Lod Israel 96 N10 31 57N 34 54E
Lodi California USA 72 C4 38 07N 121 18W
Łodz Poland 88 G9 51 49N 19 28E
Lo Fu Tau *mt.* HK China 100 A1 22 18N 114 00E
Logan Utah USA 70 D5 41 45N 111 50W
Logan, Mount Washington USA 42 H4 48 30N 121 00W
Logone *r.* Chad 108 G10 11 00N 15 00E
Logroño Sp. 87 D5 42 28N 2 26W
Loir *r.* Fr. 87 F7 47 30N 0 35E
Loire *r.* Fr. 87 E7 47 20N 1 20W
Loja Ecuador 80 B13 3 59S 79 16W
Loja Sp. 87 C2 37 10N 4 09W
Lok Ma Chau HK China 100 B3 22 31N 114 05E
Lokoja Nigeria 108 F9 7 49N 6 44E
Lol *r.* Sudan 108 K9 9 00N 28 00E
Lolland *i.* Denmark 88 C11 54 45N 12 20E
Lomami *r.* CDR 108 K6 5 30S 25 30E
Lomblen *i.* Indonesia 103 G2 8 30S 123 30E
Lombok *i.* Indonesia 103 F2 8 30S 116 30E
Lomé Togo 108 E9 6 10N 1 21E
Lomela CDR 108 J7 2 19S 23 15E
Lomela *r.* CDR 108 J7 3 00S 23 00E
Lompoc California USA 72 C2 34 39N 120 27W
Łomza Poland 88 J10 53 11N 22 04E
London UK 86 E9 51 30N 0 10W
Londonderry UK 86 B11 54 59N 7 19W
Londrina Brazil 80 G9 23 18S 51 13W
Lone Pine California USA 72 D3 36 35N 118 04W
Long Beach *tn.* California USA 70 C3 33 47N 118 15W
Long Beach Island New Jersey USA 73 C1 39 40N 74 15W
Long Branch New Jersey USA 71 M5 40 17N 73 59W
Longfellow Mountains Maine USA 53 R5/S5 45 10N 70 00W
Longford RoI 86 B10 53 44N 7 47W
Long Island Bahamas 75 J4/K4 23 20N 75 00W
Long Island New York USA 73 D2 40 43N 73 05W
Long Island City New York USA 73 J2 40 46N 73 55W
Long Island Sound New York USA 73 D2 40 50N 73 05W
Long Lake Maine USA 57 F2 47 14N 68 18W
Longreach Aust. 110 G5 23 30S 144 15E
Longview Texas USA 71 H3 32 20N 94 45W
Longview Washington USA 70 B6 46 08N 122 56W
Longwy Fr. 86 H8 49 32N 5 46E
Lopez, Cape Gabon 108 F7 0 36S 8 45E
Lopez Island Washington USA 42 H4 48 25N 123 05W
Lop Nur *l.* China 100 G7 40 15N 90 20E
Lorain Ohio USA 71 K5 41 28N 82 11W
Lorca Sp. 87 E2 37 40N 1 41W
Lord Howe Rise Pacific Ocean 114 F5 27 30S 162 00E
Lorient Fr. 86 D7 47 45N 3 21W
Los Alamos Mexico USA 70 E4 35 52N 106 19W
Los Andes Chile 81 C6 37 28S 72 23W
Los Angeles California USA 70 C3 34 00N 118 15W
Los Angeles Aqueduct California USA 72 D2 35 12N 118 08W
Los Banos California USA 72 C3 37 03N 120 53W
Los Gatos California USA 72 C3 37 13N 121 57W
Los Mochis Mexico 74 C5 25 48N 109 00W
Los Teques Venezuela 80 D16 10 25N 67 01W
Lot *r.* Fr. 87 F6 44 35N 1 10E
Louangphrabang Laos 103 C7 19 53N 102 10E
Loubomo Congo 108 G7 4 09S 12 47E
Loudéac Fr. 86 D8 48 11N 2 45W
Lough Corrib *l.* RoI 86 A10 53 10N 9 10W
Lough Derg *l.* RoI 86 A10 52 55N 8 15W
Lough Mask *l.* RoI 86 A10 53 40N 9 30W
Lough Neagh *l.* UK 86 B11 54 35N 6 30W
Lough Ree *l.* RoI 86 B10 53 35N 8 00W
Louisade Archipelago *is.* PNG 110 J7 12 00S 153 00E
Louisiana *state* USA 71 H3 32 00N 92 00W
Louis Trichardt RSA 109 K3 23 01S 29 43E
Louisville Kentucky USA 71 J4 38 13N 85 48W
Lourdes Fr. 87 E5 43 06N 0 02W
Lowell Massachusetts USA 71 M5 42 38N 71 19W
Lower Bay New York USA 73 H1 40 32N 74 04W
Lower Hutt NZ 111 E4 41 13S 174 55E
Lower Lake *tn.* California USA 72 B4 38 55N 122 37W
Lower Lough Erne *l.* UK 86 B11 54 30N 7 45W
Lower Red Lake Minnesota USA 71 H6 48 00N 95 00W
Lowestoft UK 86 F10 52 29N 1 45E
Łowicz Poland 88 G10 52 06N 19 55E
Lo Wu HK China 100 B3 22 32N 114 07E
Lowville New York USA 51 P2 43 47N 75 29W
Loznica Serbia 89 G6 44 31N 19 14E
Lualaba *r.* CDR 108 K7 4 00S 26 30E
Luanda Angola 109 G6 8 50S 13 15E
Luangwa *r.* Zambia 109 L5 12 00S 32 30E
Luanshya Zambia 109 K5 13 09S 28 24E
Luarca Sp. 87 B5 43 33N 6 31W
Luau Angola 109 J5 10 42S 22 12E
Lubango Angola 109 G5 14 55S 13 30E
Lubbock Texas USA 70 F3 33 35N 101 53W
Lübeck Germany 88 C10 53 52N 10 40E
Lubilash *r.* CDR 109 J6 4 00S 24 00E
Lublin Poland 88 J9 51 18N 22 31E
Lubumbashi CDR 109 K5 11 41S 27 29E
Lucena Sp. 87 C2 37 25N 4 29W
Luckenwalde Germany 88 D10 52 05N 13 11E
Lucknow India 98 E5 26 50N 80 54E
Lucusse Angola 109 J5 12 38S 20 52E
Lüderitz Namibia 109 H2 26 38S 15 10E
Ludhiana India 98 D6 30 56N 75 52E
Ludington Michigan USA 51 H2 43 57N 86 26W
Luena Angola 109 H5 11 47S 19 52E
Lufkin Texas USA 71 H3 31 21N 94 47W
Lugo Sp. 87 B5 43 00N 7 33W
Lugoj Romania 89 H6 45 41N 21 57E
Luiana *r.* Angola 109 J4 17 00S 21 00E
Luk Keng HK China 100 C3 22 32N 114 13E
Łuków Poland 88 J9 51 57N 22 21E
Lulua *r.* CDR 109 J6 9 00S 22 00E
Lumberton North Carolina USA 71 L3 34 37N 79 03W
Lummi Island Washington USA 42 H4 48 40N 122 36W
Lund Sweden 88 D12 55 42N 13 10E
Lund Nevada USA 72 F4 38 53N 115 01W
Lüneburg Germany 88 C10 53 15N 10 24E
Lunéville Fr. 86 J8 48 35N 6 30E
Lung Kwu Chau *i.* HK China 100 A2 22 23N 113 53E
Lunglei India 99 M9 22 54N 92 49E
Lungue Bungo *r.* Angola/Zambia 109 J5 13 00S 22 00E
Luni *r.* India 98 C5 26 00N 73 00E
Luoshan China 101 L5 31 12N 114 30E
Luoyang China 101 L5 34 47N 112 26E
Lurgan UK 86 B11 54 28N 6 20W
Lurio *r.* Mozambique 109 M5 14 00S 39 00E
Lusaka Zambia 109 K4 15 26S 28 20E
Lusambo CDR 108 J7 4 59S 23 26E
Lüshun China 101 N6 38 46N 121 15E
Luton UK 86 E9 51 53N 0 25W
Luts'k Ukraine 88 K9 50 42N 25 15E
Luuq Somalia 108 N8 2 52N 42 34E
LUXEMBOURG 86 H8
Luxembourg Luxembourg 86 J8 49 37N 6 08E
Luxor Egypt 108 L13 25 41N 32 24E
Luzern Switz. 87 K7 47 03N 8 17E
Luzhou China 101 K4 28 55N 105 25E
Luziânia Brazil 80 H10 16 16S 47 57W
Luzon *i.* Philippines 103 G7 15 00N 122 00E
Luzon Strait China/Philippines 103 G8 20 00N 121 30E
L'viv Ukraine 88 K8 49 50N 24 00E
Lyna *r.* Poland 88 H11 54 00N 20 00E
Lynchburg Virginia USA 71 L4 37 24N 79 09W
Lynden Washington USA 42 H4 48 56N 122 28W
Lynn Massachusetts USA 73 E3 42 28N 70 58W
Lynn Canal *sd.* Alaska USA 42 C6 58 50N 135 05W
Lyons Fr. 87 H6 45 46N 4 50E
Lyons New York USA 51 N2 43 04N 76 59W
Lyttelton NZ 111 D3 43 36S 172 42E

M

Ma'ān Jordan 96 C5 30 11N 35 43E
Ma'anshan China 101 M5 31 49N 118 32E
Maastricht Neths. 86 H9 50 51N 5 42E
Mabalane Mozambique 109 L3 23 51S 32 38E
McAlester Oklahoma USA 71 G3 34 56N 95 46W
McAllen Texas USA 71 G2 26 13N 98 15W
Macao China 101 L3 22 10N 113 40E
Macapá Brazil 80 G14 0 04N 51 04W
Macarata Italy 89 D5 43 18N 13 27E
McClure, Lake California USA 72 C3 37 38N 120 16W
McComb Mississippi USA 71 H3 31 13N 90 29W
McCook Nebraska USA 70 F5 40 13N 100 35W
McDonald, Lake Montana USA 46 E1/F1 48 50N 114 00W
Macdonnell Ranges *mts.* Aust. 110 E5 24 00S 132 30E
Maceió Brazil 80 K12 9 40S 35 44W
Machala Ecuador 80 B13 3 20S 79 57W
Machanga Mozambique 109 L3 20 58N 35 01E
Machias Maine USA 57 G1 44 50N 67 20W
Machiques Venezuela 80 C16 10 04N 72 37W
Mackay Aust. 110 H5 21 10S 149 10E
Mackay, Lake Aust. 110 D5 22 30S 128 00E
Mackinac, Straits of *sd.* Michigan USA 52 B5 45 48N 84 43W
Mackinaw City Michigan USA 71 K6 45 47N 84 43W
McKinney Texas USA 71 G3 33 14N 96 37W
Macleod, Lake Aust. 110 A5 24 00S 113 30E
Mâcon Fr. 87 H7 46 18N 4 50E
Macon Georgia USA 71 K3 32 49N 83 37W
McPherson Kansas USA 71 G4 38 22N 97 41W
Macquarie Island Southern Ocean 114 F2 54 29S 158 58E
Macquarie Ridge Southern Ocean 114 F2 55 00S 160 00E
Mādabā Jordan 96 N10 31 44N 35 48E
MADAGASCAR 109 P2/P5
Madagascar Basin Indian Ocean 113 E4 25 00S 55 00E
Madagascar Ridge Indian Ocean 113 D3 30 00S 45 00E
Madang PNG 110 H8 5 14S 145 45E
Madaripur Bangladesh 99 L9 23 09N 90 11E
Madden Lake Panama 75 Y2 9 15N 79 35W
Madeira *r.* Brazil 80 E12 6 00S 61 30W
Madeira Islands Atlantic Ocean 108 A14 32 45N 17 00W
Madera California USA 72 C3 36 59N 120 12W
Madhya Pradesh *admin.* India 98 D4/E4 23 00N 78 30E
Madīnat ash Sha'b Yemen 96 D1 12 50N 44 56E
Madison Maine USA 53 S4 44 48N 69 53W
Madison Wisconsin USA 71 J5 43 04N 89 22W
Madiun Indonesia 103 E2 7 37S 111 33E
Mado Gashi Kenya 108 M8 0 45N 39 11E
Madre de Dios *r.* Bolivia 80 D11 12 00S 68 00W
Madrid Sp. 87 D4 40 25N 3 43W
Madura *i.* Indonesia 103 E2 7 00S 113 00E
Madurai India 98 D1 9 55N 78 07E
Maebashi Japan 102 C2 36 24N 139 04E
Maevantanana Madagascar 109 P4 16 57S 46 50E
Mafia Island Tanzania 109 M6 7 00S 39 00E
Mafikeng RSA 109 K2 25 53S 25 39E
Mafraq Jordan 96 C5 32 20N 36 12E
Magadan Russia 95 T8 59 38N 150 50E
Magangué Col. 80 C15 9 14N 74 47W
Magdalena Mexico 74 B6 30 38N 110 59W
Magdalena *r.* Col. 80 C15 8 00N 73 30W
Magdeburg Germany 88 C10 52 08N 11 37E
Magelang Indonesia 103 E2 7 28S 110 11E
Magnitogorsk Russia 94 H7 53 28N 59 06E
Mahadeo Hills India 98 D4 22 30N 78 30E
Mahajanga Madagascar 109 P4 15 40S 46 20E
Mahanadi *r.* India 99 E4 21 00N 85 00E
Maharashtra *admin.* India 98 C3 19 30N 75 00E
Mahón Sp. 87 H3 39 54N 4 15E
Maiduguri Nigeria 108 G10 11 53N 13 16E
Main *r.* Germany 88 B8 50 00N 8 00E
Maine *state* USA 71 N6 45 00N 70 00W
Mainland *i.* Orkney Islands UK 86 D13 59 00N 3 15W
Mainland *i.* Shetland Islands UK 86 E14 60 15N 1 20W
Maintirano Madagascar 109 N4 18 01S 44 03E
Mainz Germany 88 B8 50 00N 8 16E
Mai Po Hong Kong China 100 B2 22 29N 114 03E
Maiquetía Venezuela 80 D16 10 38N 66 59W
Maiskhal Island Bangladesh 99 L8 21 36N 91 53E
Maitland Aust. 110 J3 32 33S 151 33E
Maizuru Japan 102 C2 35 30N 135 20E
Majene Indonesia 103 F3 3 33S 118 59E
Maji Ethiopia 108 M9 6 12N 35 32E
Makassar Strait *sd.* Indonesia 103 F3/F4 0 00 119 00E
Makeni Sierra Leone 108 B9 8 57N 12 02W
Makgadikgadi Salt Pan Botswana 109 K3 21 00S 26 00E
Makhachkala Russia 94 G5 42 59N 47 30E
Makó Hungary 89 H7 46 11N 20 30E
Makokou Gabon 108 G8 0 38N 12 47E
Makurdi Nigeria 108 F9 7 44N 8 35E
Malabar Coast India 98 C2/D1 12 00N 74 00E
Malabo Eq. Guinea 108 F8 3 45N 8 48E
Malacca, Strait of Indonesia 103 B5/C4 4 00N 100 00E
Málaga Sp. 87 C2 36 43N 4 25W
Malaga New Jersey USA 73 C1 39 34N 75 03W
Malaita *i.* Solomon Islands 114 G7 9 00S 161 00E
Malakal Sudan 108 L9 9 31N 31 40E
Malang Indonesia 103 E2 7 59S 112 45E
Malanje Angola 109 H6 9 32S 16 20E
Mälaren *l.* Sweden 88 F13 59 30N 17 00E
Malaspina Glacier Alaska USA 64 B2 59 50N 140 40W
Malatya Turkey 96 C6 38 22N 38 18E
MALAWI 109 L5
MALAYSIA 103 C5/E5
Malbork Poland 88 G11 54 02N 19 01E
MALDIVES 113 G7
Maldonado Uruguay 81 G7 34 57S 54 59W
Malegaon India 98 C4 20 32N 74 38E
Malema Mozambique 109 M5 14 57S 37 25E

Mitchell South Dakota USA 71 G5 43 40N 98 01W
Mitchell *r.* Aust. 110 G6 16 00S 142 30E
Mitkof Island Alaska USA 42 D5 56 40N 132 45W
Mito Japan 102 D2 36 22N 140 29E
Mitú Col. 80 C14 1 07N 70 05W
Miyako Japan 102 D2 39 38N 141 59E
Miyakonojō Japan 102 B1 31 43N 131 02E
Miyazaki Japan 102 B1 31 56N 131 27E
Mizen Head *c.* Rol 86 A9 51 30N 9 50W
Mizoram *admin.* India 99 G4 23 40N 93 30E
Mjölby Sweden 88 E13 58 19N 15 10E
Mladá Boleslav Czech Rep. 88 E9 50 26N 14 55E
Mława Poland 88 H10 53 08N 20 20E
Moala *i.* Fiji 114 U15 18 34S 179 56E
Mobaye CAR 108 J8 4 19N 21 11E
Mobile Alabama USA 71 J3 30 40N 88 05W
Moçambique Mozambique 109 N4 15 03S 40 45E
Mocuba Mozambique 109 M4 16 52S 36 57E
Módena Italy 89 C6 44 39N 10 55E
Modesto California USA 70 B4 37 37N 121 00W
Moe Aust. 110 H2 38 09S 146 22E
Mogadishu Somalia 108 P8 2 02N 45 21E
Mogocha Russia 95 P7 53 44N 119 45E
Mogollon Rim *plat.* Arizona USA 70 D3 34 00N 111 00W
Mohall North Dakota USA 47 G1 48 50N 101 34W
Mohe China 101 N9 52 55N 122 20E
Mohyliv-Podil's'kyy Ukraine 88 L8 48 29N 27 49E
Mojave California USA 70 C4 35 02N 118 11W
Mojave *r.* California USA 72 E2 34 47N 117 15W
Mojave Desert California USA 72 E2 35 08N 117 21W
Mokau NZ 111 E5 38 42S 174 37E
Mokelumne *r.* California USA 72 C4 38 13N 121 05W
Mokolo Cameroon 108 G10 10 49N 13 54E
Mokp'o South Korea 101 P5 34 50N 126 25E
Molango Mexico 74 E4 20 48N 98 44W
MOLDOVA 88/89 M7
Moldova *r.* Romania 89 L7 47 00N 26 00E
Molepolole Botswana 109 K3 24 25S 25 30E
Mollendo Peru 80 C10 17 00S 72 00W
Molokai *i.* Hawaiian Islands 115 Y18 21 40N 155 55W
Molopo *r.* Southern Africa 109 J2 26 30S 22 30E
Molucca Sea Indonesia 103 G3 0 30S 125 30E
Mombasa Kenya 108 M7 4 04S 39 40E
MONACO 87 J5
Monahans Texas USA 70 F3 31 35N 102 54W
Monbetsu Japan 102 D3 42 28N 142 10E
Monbetsu Japan 102 D3 44 23N 143 22E
Monção Brazil 80 H13 3 30S 45 15W
Mönchengladbach Germany 88 A9 51 12N 6 25E
Monclova Mexico 74 D5 26 55N 101 25W
Mondego *r.* Port. 87 A4 40 30N 8 15W
Mondovi Italy 89 A6 44 23N 7 49E
Monemvasia Greece 89 J2 36 41N 23 03E
Mong Kok HK China 100 B1 22 19N 114 09E
MONGOLIA 100/101 F8
Mongu Zambia 109 J4 15 13S 23 09E
Mono Lake California USA 72 D4 38 00N 119 00W
Monopoli Italy 89 F4 40 57N 17 18E
Monroe Louisiana USA 71 H3 32 31N 92 06W
Monroe Michigan USA 51 K1 41 54N 83 24W
Monrovia Liberia 108 B9 6 20N 10 46W
Montana Bulgaria 89 J5 43 25N 23 11E
Montana *state* USA 70 E6 47 00N 111 00W
Montañas de León *mts.* Sp. 87 B5 42 30N 6 15E
Montargis Fr. 86 G7 48 00N 2 44E
Montauban Fr. 87 F6 44 01N 1 20E
Montauk Point New York USA 73 E2 41 05N 71 55W
Montbéliard Fr. 87 J7 47 31N 6 48E
Mont Blanc *mt.* Fr./Italy 87 J6 45 50N 6 52E
Mont Cameroun *mt.* Cameroon 108 F8 4 13N 9 10E
Montclair New Jersey USA 73 H2 40 48N 74 12W
Mont-de-Marsan Fr. 87 E5 43 54N 0 30W
Monte Cinto *mt.* Fr. 87 K5 42 23N 8 57E
Montego Bay *tn.* Jamaica 75 U14 18 27N 77 56W
Montélimar Fr. 87 H6 44 33N 4 45E
MONTENEGRO 89 G5
Monterey California USA 70 B4 36 35N 121 55W
Monterey Bay California USA 72 C3 36 46N 121 51W
Montería Col. 80 B15 8 45N 75 54W
Montero Bolivia 80 E10 17 20S 63 15W
Monte Roraima *mt.* Guyana 80 E15 5 14N 60 44W
Monterrey Mexico 74 D5 25 40N 100 20W
Montes Claros *tn.* Brazil 80 J10 16 45S 43 52W
Montes de Toledo *mts.* Sp. 87 C3 39 35N 4 30W
Montevideo Uruguay 81 F7 34 55S 56 10W
Montgomery Alabama USA 71 J3 32 22N 86 20W
Monti del Gennargentu *mts.* Italy 89 B3/B4 40 00N 9 30E
Monti Nebrodi *mts.* Italy 89 E2 37 00N 14 00E
Montluçon Fr. 87 G7 46 20N 2 36E
Montmorillon Fr. 87 F7 46 26N 0 52E
Monto Aust. 110 J5 24 53S 151 06E
Montpelier Ohio USA 52 B1 41 35N 84 35W
Montpellier Fr. 87 G5 43 36N 3 53E
Montreux Switz. 87 J7 46 27N 6 55E
Montrose UK 86 D12 56 43N 2 29W
Montrose Colorado USA 70 E4 38 29N 107 53W
Monts d'Auvergne *mts.* Fr. 87 G6 45 30N 2 50E
Montserrat *i.* Lesser Antilles 74 P9 16 45N 62 14W
Monts Nimba *mts.* Guinea/Liberia 108 C9 7 39N 8 30W
Monywa Myanmar 100 H3 22 05N 95 12E
Monza Italy 89 B6 45 35N 9 16E
Moora Aust. 110 B3 30 40S 116 01E
Moore, Lake Aust. 110 B4 30 00S 117 30E
Moorhead Minnesota USA 71 G6 46 51N 96 44W
Moosehead Lake Maine USA 53 S5 45 40N 69 40W
Mooselookmeguntic Lake Maine USA 57 E1 44 56N 71 00W
Mopti Mali 108 D10 14 29N 4 10W
Moradabad India 98 D5 28 50N 78 45E
Morant Point Jamaica 75 U13 17 55N 76 12W
Moratuwa Sri Lanka 98 D1 6 47N 79 53E
Morava *r.* Europe 88 F8 48 00N 17 00E
Moray Firth *est.* UK 86 D12 57 45N 3 45W
Moreau *r.* South Dakota USA 70 F6 45 00N 102 00W
Moree Aust. 110 H4 29 29S 149 53E
Morelia Mexico 74 D3 19 40N 101 11W
Morenci Arizona USA 70 E3 33 05N 109 22W
Morgan Hill California USA 72 C3 37 05N 121 48W
Morgantown West Virginia USA 71 L4 39 38N 79 57W
Mori Japan 102 D3 42 07N 140 33E
Morioka Japan 102 D2 39 43N 141 08E
Morlaix Fr. 86 D8 48 35N 3 50W
Morne Diablotins *mt.* Dominica 74 Q8 15 30N 61 24W
MOROCCO 108 C14
Morogoro Tanzania 109 M6 6 49S 37 40E
Moro Gulf Philippines 103 G5 7 00N 123 00E
Morón Cuba 75 J4 22 08N 78 39W
Morondava Madagascar 109 N3 20 19S 44 17E
Moroni Comoros 109 N5 11 40S 43 16E
Morotai *i.* Indonesia 103 H4 2 30N 128 30E
Moroto Uganda 108 L8 2 32N 34 41E
Morrinsville NZ 111 E6 37 39S 175 32E
Morristown New Jersey USA 73 C2 40 49N 74 29W
Morro Bay *tn.* California USA 72 C2 35 22N 120 50W
Moscow Russia 94 F8 55 45N 37 42E
Moscow Idaho USA 70 C6 46 44N 117 00W
Mosel *r.* Germany/Fr. 88 A8 50 00N 7 00E
Moses Lake *tn.* Washington USA 70 C6 47 09N 119 20W
Mosgiel NZ 111 C2 45 53S 170 21E
Moshi Tanzania 108 M7 3 21S 37 19E
Mosquito Creek Lake *res.* Ohio USA 52 F1 41 20N 80 45W
Moss Norway 86 L13 59 26N 10 41E
Mossoró Brazil 80 K12 5 10S 37 18W
Most Czech Rep. 88 D9 50 31N 13 39E
Mostar Bosnia-Herzegovina 89 F5 43 20N 17 50E
Móstoles Sp. 87 D4 40 19N 3 53W
Mosul Iraq 96 D6 36 21N 43 08E
Motala Sweden 88 E13 58 34N 15 05E
Mothe *i.* Fiji 114 V15 18 39S 178 32W
Motherwell UK 86 D11 55 48N 3 59W
Motril Sp. 87 D2 36 45N 3 31W
Motueka NZ 111 D4 41 07S 173 01E
Mouila Gabon 108 B7 1 50S 11 02E
Moulins Fr. 87 G7 47 00N 3 48E
Moulmein Myanmar 103 B7 16 30N 97 39E
Moundou Chad 108 H9 8 35N 16 01E
Mount Darwin *tn.* Zimbabwe 109 L4 16 45S 31 39E
Mount Desert Island Maine USA 57 F1 44 22N 68 15W
Mount Gambier *tn.* Aust. 110 G2 37 51S 140 50E
Mount Hagen *tn.* PNG 110 G8 5 54S 144 13E
Mount Isa *tn.* Aust. 110 F5 20 50S 139 29E
Mount Magnet *tn.* Aust. 110 B4 28 06S 117 50E
Mount Morgan *tn.* Aust. 110 J5 23 40S 150 25E
Mount Pleasant *tn.* Michigan USA 51 J2 43 36N 84 46W
Mount Union *tn.* Pennsylvania USA 73 B2 40 22N 77 52W
Mount Vernon *tn.* Illinois USA 71 J4 38 19N 88 52W
Mount Vernon *tn.* Washington USA 42 H4 48 25N 122 20W
Moyale Kenya 108 M8 3 31N 39 04E
Moyobamba Peru 80 B12 6 04S 76 56W
MOZAMBIQUE 109 L3/M5
Mozambique Basin Indian Ocean 113 C3 35 00S 40 00E
Mozambique Channel Mozambique/Madagascar 109 N4 18 00S 42 00E
Mpanda Tanzania 109 L6 6 21S 31 01E
Mtwara Tanzania 109 N5 10 17S 40 11E
Muang Chiang Rai Thailand 103 B7 19 56N 99 51E
Muang Khon Kaen Thailand 103 C7 16 25N 102 50E
Muang Lampang Thailand 103 B7 18 16N 99 30E
Muang Nakhon Sawan Thailand 103 B7 15 42N 100 10E
Muang Phitsanulok Thailand 103 C7 16 49N 100 18E
Muchinga Mountains Zambia 109 L5 12 30S 32 30E
Mudanjiang China 101 P7 44 36N 129 42E
Mufulira Zambia 109 K5 12 30S 28 12E
Muğla Turkey 96 A6 37 13N 28 22E
Muir Woods National Monument California USA 72 B3 37 54N 122 32W
Mui Wo HK China 100 A1 22 16N 113 59E
Mukachevo Ukraine 88 J8 48 26N 22 45E
Mukalla Yemen 97 E1 14 34N 49 09E
Mulegé Mexico 74 B5 26 54N 112 00W
Mulhacén *mt.* Sp. 87 D2 37 04N 3 19W
Mulhouse Fr. 86 J7 47 45N 7 21E
Mull *i.* UK 86 B12 56 25N 6 00W
Mullett Lake Michigan USA 52 B5 45 30N 84 30W
Mullingar Rol 86 B10 53 32N 7 20W
Multan Pakistan 98 C6 30 10N 71 36E
Mumbai India 98 C3 18 56N 72 51E
Muna *i.* Indonesia 103 G2/G3 5 00S 122 20E
Muncie Indiana USA 71 J5 40 11N 85 22W
Muncy Pennsylvania USA 73 B2 41 12N 76 48W
Mundo *r.* Sp. 87 D3/E3 38 30N 2 00W
Mungbere CDR 108 K8 2 40N 28 25E
Mungla Bangladesh 99 K9 22 18N 89 34E
Munich Germany 88 C8 48 08N 11 35E
Munising Michigan USA 51 H4 46 24N 86 39W
Münster Germany 88 A9 51 58N 7 37E
Mur *r.* Europe 89 E7 48 00N 14 40E
Murat *r.* Turkey 96 D6 38 50N 40 20E
Murchison NZ 111 D4 41 50S 172 20E
Murchison *r.* Aust. 110 B4 26 00S 117 00E
Murcia Sp. 87 E2 37 59N 1 08W
Mureş *r.* Romania 89 J6 46 00N 22 00E
Murfreesboro Tennessee USA 71 J4 35 50N 86 25W
Müritz *l.* Germany 88 D10 53 00N 12 00E
Murmansk Russia 94 F10 68 59N 33 08E
Murom Russia 94 G8 55 34N 42 04E
Muroran Japan 102 D3 42 21N 140 59E
Muroto Japan 102 B1 33 13N 134 11E
Muroto-zaki *c.* Japan 102 B1 33 13N 134 11E
Murray *r.* Aust. 110 G2 35 30S 144 00E
Murray Bridge *tn.* Aust. 110 F2 35 10S 139 17E
Murray Seascarp Pacific Ocean 115 N11 32 00N 138 00W
Murrumbidgee *r.* Aust. 110 H3 34 30S 146 30E
Murupara NZ 111 F5 38 27S 176 42E
Murwara India 98 E4 23 49N 80 28E
Murzuq Libya 108 G13 25 55N 13 55E
Muş Turkey 96 D6 38 45N 41 30E
Muscat Oman 97 G3 23 37N 58 38E
Musgrave Ranges Aust. 110 E4 26 00S 132 00E
Mushin Nigeria 108 E9 6 30N 3 15E
Muskegon Michigan USA 71 J5 43 13N 86 15W
Muskegon River Michigan USA 52 A3 44 00N 85 05W
Muskogee Oklahoma USA 71 G4 35 35N 95 21W
Musselshell *r.* Montana USA 70 E6 47 00N 108 00W
Mustique *i.* Lesser Antilles 74 R11 12 39N 61 15W
Mutarara Mozambique 109 M4 17 30S 35 06E
Mutare Zimbabwe 109 L4 18 58N 32 40E
Mutsu Japan 102 D3 41 18N 141 15E
Mutsu-wan *b.* Japan 102 D3 41 05N 140 40E
Muyun Kum *d.* Kazakhstan 94 J5/K5 44 00N 70 00E
Muzaffarnagar India 98 D5 29 28N 77 42E
Muzaffarpur India 99 F5 26 07N 85 23E
Muzon, Cape Alaska USA 42 D4 54 41N 132 40W
Mwanza Tanzania 108 L7 2 31S 32 56E
Mweru, Lake CDR/Zambia 109 K6 8 30S 28 30E
MYANMAR 103 B7
Myitkyina Myanmar 101 H4 25 24N 97 25E
Mymensingh Bangladesh 99 L10 33 43N 78 54W
Myrtle Beach *tn.* USA 71 L3 22 50N 109 52W
Mys Chelyuskin *c.* Russia 95 N12 77 44N 103 55E
Mys Kanin Nos *c.* Russia 94 G10 68 38N 43 20E
Mys Navarin *c.* Russia 95 V9 62 17N 179 13E
Mys Olyutorskiy *c.* Russia 95 V9 59 58N 170 25E
Mysore India 98 D2 12 18N 76 37E
Mys Tolstoy *c.* Russia 95 T8 59 00N 155 00E
My Tho Vietnam 103 D6 10 21N 106 21E
Mytilíni Greece 89 L3 39 06N 26 34E
Mzuzu Malawi 109 L5 11 31S 34 00E

N

Naas Rol 86 B10 53 13N 6 39W
Naberezhnyye Chelny Russia 94 H8 55 42N 52 19E
Nablus Jordan 96 N11 32 13N 35 16E
Nacimiento Reservoir California USA 72 C2 34 45N 121 00W
Nacogdoches Texas USA 71 H3 31 36N 94 40W
Nadiad India 98 C4 22 42N 72 55E
Nador Morocco 108 D15 35 10N 3 00W
Nadym Russia 94 K10 65 25N 72 40E
Naestved Denmark 88 C11 55 14N 11 47E
Náfplio Greece 89 J2 37 34N 22 48E
Naga Philippines 103 G6 13 36N 123 12E
Nagaland *admin.* India 99 G5 26 00N 94 30E
Nagano Japan 102 C2 36 39N 138 10E
Nagaoka Japan 102 C2 37 27N 138 50E
Nagaon India 99 G5 26 20N 92 41E
Nagasaki Japan 102 A1 32 45N 129 52E
Nagato Japan 102 B1 34 22N 131 11E
Nagercoil India 98 D1 8 11N 77 30E
Nagornyy Russia 95 Q8 55 57N 124 54E
Nagoya Japan 102 C2 35 08N 136 53E
Nagpur India 98 D4 21 10N 79 12E
Nagykanizsa Hungary 89 F7 46 27N 17 00E
Nahariyya Israel 96 N11 33 01N 35 05E
Nairobi Kenya 108 M7 1 17S 36 50E
Najd *geog. reg.* Saudi Arabia 96 D4 25 40N 42 30E
Najrān Saudi Arabia 96 D2 17 37N 44 40E
Nakamura Japan 102 B1 33 02N 132 58E
Nakatsu Japan 102 B1 33 37N 131 11E
Nakhodka Russia 95 R5 42 53N 132 54E
Nakhon Ratchasima Thailand 103 C6 14 59N 102 06E
Nakhon Si Thammarat Thailand 103 B5 8 24N 99 58E
Nakuru Kenya 108 M7 0 16S 36 05E
Nal *r.* Pakistan 98 B5 26 10N 65 30E
Nal'chik Russia 94 G5 43 31N 43 38E
Namangan Uzbekistan 94 K5 40 59N 71 41E
Nam Dinh Vietnam 101 K3 20 25N 106 12E
Namib Desert Namibia 109 G3/H2 22 00S 14 00E
Namibe Angola 109 G4 15 10S 12 09E
NAMIBIA 109 H3
Nampa Idaho USA 70 C5 43 35N 116 34W
Nampo North Korea 101 P6 38 51N 125 10E
Nampula Mozambique 109 M4 15 09S 39 14E
Namtu Myanmar 101 H3 23 04N 97 26E
Namur Belgium 86 H9 50 28N 4 52E
Nam Wan HK China 100 B2 22 20N 114 05E
Nanao Japan 102 C2 37 03N 136 58E
Nanchang China 101 M4 28 33N 115 58E
Nanchong China 101 K5 30 54N 106 06E
Nancowry Island India 99 G1 7 59N 93 32E
Nancy Fr. 86 J8 48 42N 6 12E
Nanda Devi *mt.* India 98 D6 30 21N 79 58E
Nānded India 98 D3 19 11N 77 21E
Nanduri Fiji 114 U16 16 26S 179 08E
Nanjing China 101 M5 32 03N 118 47E
Nan Ling *mts.* China 101 L3 25 00N 112 00E
Nanning China 101 K3 22 50N 108 19E
Nanpan Jiang *r.* China 101 K3 25 00N 106 00E
Nanping China 101 M4 26 40N 118 07E
Nantes Fr. 87 E7 47 14N 1 35W
Nantong China 101 N5 32 06N 121 04E
Nantucket Island Massachusetts USA 71 M5 41 15N 70 05W
Nantucket Sound Massachusetts USA 73 E2 41 20N 70 08W
Nanuku Passage *sd.* Fiji 114 V15 16 40S 179 25W
Nanumea *is.* Tuvalu 114 H7 5 43S 176 00E
Nanyang China 101 L5 33 06N 112 31E
Nanyuki Kenya 108 M8 0 01N 37 05E
Naogaon Bangladesh 99 K10 24 49N 88 59E
Napa California USA 72 B4 38 18N 122 17W
Napier NZ 111 F5 39 30S 176 54E
Naples Italy 89 E4 40 50N 14 15E
Naples Florida USA 71 K2 26 09N 81 48W
Napo *r.* Peru 80 C13 2 30S 73 30W
Napolean Ohio USA 52 B1 41 24N 84 09W
Napoopoo Hawaiian Islands 115 Z17 19 29N 155 55W
Nara Japan 102 C1 34 41N 135 49E
Narail Bangladesh 99 K9 23 18N 89 45E
Narayanganj Bangladesh 99 L9 23 36N 90 28E
Narbonne Fr. 87 G5 43 11N 3 00E
Narcondam Island India 99 G2 13 15N 94 30E
Nares Deep Atlantic Ocean 116 B9 26 00N 61 10W
Narew *r.* Europe 88 H10 53 00N 21 00E
Narmada *r.* India 98 C4 22 00N 75 00E
Narrogin Aust. 110 B3 32 57S 117 07E
Nar'yan Mar Russia 94 H10 67 37N 53 02E
Nasca Ridge Pacific Ocean 115 T5 20 00S 81 00W
Naseby NZ 111 C2 45 02S 171 26E
Nashik India 98 C3 20 00N 73 52E
Nashua New Hampshire USA 71 M5 42 44N 71 28W
Nashville Tennessee USA 71 J4 36 10N 86 50W
Nassau Bahamas 75 J5 25 05N 77 20W
Nasser, Lake Egypt 108 L12 22 35N 31 40E
Nässjö Sweden 88 E12 57 40N 14 40E
Natal Brazil 80 K12 5 46S 35 15W
Natchez Mississippi USA 71 H3 31 32N 91 24W
Natewa Peninsula Fiji 114 U15 16 40S 180 00
National City California USA 72 E1 32 39N 117 05W
Natron, Lake Tanzania 108 M7 2 00S 36 00E
Natuna Besar *i.* Indonesia 103 D4 3 40N 108 00E
Naturaliste, Cape Aust. 110 B3 33 32S 115 01E
NAURU 114 G7
Nausori Fiji 114 U15 18 01S 178 31E
Navadwip India 99 K9 23 25N 88 22E
Navia *r.* Sp. 87 B5 43 10N 7 05W
Naviti *i.* Fiji 114 T16 17 08S 177 15E
Navoi Uzbekistan 94 J5 40 04N 65 20E
Navojoa Mexico 74 C5 27 04N 109 28W
Navsari India 98 C4 20 58N 73 01E
Nawabganj Bangladesh 99 K10 24 35N 88 21E
Náxos *i.* Greece 89 K2 37 00N 25 00E
Nayoro Japan 102 D3 44 21N 142 30E
Nazareth Israel 96 N11 32 41N 35 16E
Nazca Peru 80 C11 14 53S 74 54W
Nazwá Oman 97 G3 22 56N 57 33E
Ndélé CAR 108 J9 8 25N 20 38E
Ndjamena Chad 108 H10 12 10N 14 59E
Ndola Zambia 109 K5 13 00S 28 39E
Neah Bay *tn.* Washington USA 42 H4 48 20N 124 38W
Néapoli Greece 89 J2 36 31N 23 03E
Nebitdag Turkmenistan 94 H4 39 31N 54 24E
Nebraska *state* USA 70 F5 42 00N 102 00W
Neche North Dakota USA 49 D1 48 59N 97 33W
Neckei *i.* Hawaiian Islands 115 K10 23 25N 164 42W
Necochea Argentina 81 F6 38 31S 58 46W
Needles California USA 70 D3 34 51N 114 36W
Negele Ethiopia 108 M9 5 20N 39 35E
Negev *d.* Israel 96 N10 30 50N 30 45E
Negombo Sri Lanka 98 D1 7 13N 79 51E
Negritos Peru 80 A13 4 42S 81 18W
Negro *r.* Argentina 81 E6 40 00S 65 00W
Negro *r.* Brazil 80 D13 0 05S 67 00W
Negro *r.* Uruguay 81 F7 33 00S 57 30W
Negros *i.* Philippines 103 G5 10 00N 123 00E
Neijiang China 101 K4 29 32N 105 03E
Nei Mongol Zizhiqu *admin.* China 101 K7 42 30N 112 30E
Neiva Col. 80 B14 2 58N 75 15W
Nek'emte Ethiopia 108 M9 9 04N 36 30E
Nellore India 98 D2 14 29N 80 00E
Nelson NZ 111 D4 41 30S 172 30E
Neman *r.* Lithuania/Russia 88 J11 55 00N 22 00E
Nemuro Japan 102 E3 43 22N 145 36E
Nemuro-kaikyō *sd.* Japan 102 E3 44 00N 146 00E

Nenjiang China	**101**	P8	49 10N	125 15E
Nen Jiang *r.* China	**101**	P9	50 00N	125 00E
NEPAL	**98/99**	E5/F5		
Nerchinsk Russia	**95**	P7	52 02N	116 38E
Neretva *r.* Bosnia-Herzegovina	**89**	G5	43 30N	15 18E
Nerva Sp.	**87**	B2	37 41N	6 33W
Neryungri Russia	**95**	Q8	56 39N	124 38E
Netanya Israel	**96**	N11	32 20N	34 51E
Netcong New Jersey USA	**73**	C2	40 54N	74 42W
NETHERLANDS	**86**	H10		
Netzahualcóyotl Mexico	**74**	E3	19 24N	99 02W
Neubrandenburg Germany	**88**	D10	53 33N	13 16E
Neuchâtel Switz.	**87**	J7	46 55N	6 56E
Neufchâtel-en-Bray Fr.	**86**	F8	49 44N	1 26E
Neumünster Germany	**88**	B11	54 05N	9 59E
Neuquén Argentina	**81**	D6	38 55S	68 05W
Neuruppin Germany	**88**	D10	52 56N	12 49E
Neusiedler See *l.* Austria	**88**	F7	48 00N	16 00E
Neustrelitz Germany	**88**	D10	53 22N	13 05E
Nevada *state* USA	**70**	C4	39 00N	118 00W
Nevers Fr.	**87**	G7	47 00N	3 09E
Nevis *i.* St. Kitts and Nevis	**74**	P9	17 10N	62 34W
New *r.* USA	**71**	K4	37 00N	81 00W
New Albany Indiana USA	**71**	J4	38 17N	85 50W
New Amsterdam Guyana	**80**	F15	6 18N	57 30W
Newark New Jersey USA	**71**	M5	40 44N	74 24W
Newark New York USA	**53**	J3	43 02N	77 06W
Newark Ohio USA	**71**	K5	40 03N	82 25W
Newark Bay New Jersey USA	**73**	H1	40 40N	74 08W
New Bedford Massachusetts USA	**71**	M5	41 38N	70 55W
New Bern North Carolina USA	**71**	L4	35 05N	77 04W
Newberry Michigan USA	**51**	J4	46 21N	85 31W
New Braunfels Texas USA	**71**	G2	29 43N	98 09W
New Brighton New Jersey USA	**73**	H1	40 37N	74 06W
New Britain Connecticut USA	**73**	D2	41 40N	72 48W
New Britain *i.* PNG	**110**	H8/J8	4 45S	150 30E
New Brunswick New Jersey USA	**73**	C2	40 29N	74 26W
Newburgh New York USA	**71**	M5	41 30N	74 00W
New Caledonia *i.* Pacific Ocean	**114**	G5	22 00S	165 00E
Newcastle Aust.	**110**	J3	32 55S	151 46E
Newcastle Wyoming USA	**70**	F5	43 52N	104 14W
Newcastle upon Tyne UK	**86**	E11	54 59N	1 35W
New Delhi India	**98**	D5	28 37N	77 14E
New Dorp New York USA	**73**	H1	40 34N	74 06W
Newfane New York USA	**52**	H3	43 17N	78 42W
Newfoundland Basin Atlantic Ocean	**116**	D11	44 00N	40 00W
New Guinea *i.* Pacific Ocean	**110**	E9/H8	5 00S	141 00E
Newhalem Washington USA	**42**	H4	48 35N	121 20W
New Hampshire *state* USA	**71**	M5	43 00N	72 00W
New Hartford Connecticut USA	**73**	D2	41 52N	72 57W
New Haven Connecticut USA	**71**	M5	41 18N	72 55W
New Hebrides Trench Pacific Ocean	**114**	G6	15 00S	169 00E
New Iberia Louisiana USA	**71**	H2	30 00N	91 51W
New Ireland *i.* PNG	**110**	J9	3 15S	152 30E
New Jersey *state* USA	**71**	M4	40 00N	75 00W
New London Connecticut USA	**71**	M5	41 21N	72 06W
Newman Aust.	**110**	B5	23 20S	119 34E
New Mexico *state* USA	**70**	E3	35 00N	107 00W
New Milford Pennsylvania USA	**53**	L1	41 52N	75 44W
New Orleans Louisiana USA	**71**	H2	30 00N	90 03W
New Plymouth NZ	**111**	E5	39 04S	174 04E
Newport UK	**86**	D9	51 35N	3 00W
Newport Rhode Island USA	**73**	E2	41 29N	71 20W
Newport Vermont USA	**53**	P4	44 56N	72 13W
Newport Beach *tn.* California USA	**72**	E1	33 38N	117 55W
Newport News Virginia USA	**71**	L4	36 59N	76 26W
Newry UK	**86**	B11	54 11N	6 20W
New Siberian Islands Russia	**95**	R12/S12	75 00N	145 00E
New South Wales *state* Aust.	**110**	G3/H3	32 00S	145 00E
New Springville New York USA	**73**	H1	40 35N	74 10W
Newton Falls *tn.* New York USA	**53**	L4	44 13N	74 58W
New Ulm Minnesota USA	**71**	H5	44 19N	94 28W
New York New York USA	**71**	M5	40 40N	73 50W
New York *state* USA	**71**	L5	43 00N	76 00W
NEW ZEALAND	**111**			
Neyrīz Iran	**97**	F4	29 14N	54 18E
Neyshābūr Iran	**97**	G6	36 13N	58 49E
Ngami, Lake Botswana	**109**	J3	21 00S	23 00E
Ngau *i.* Fiji	**114**	U15	18 00S	179 16E
Ngong Ping HK China	**100**	A1	22 15N	113 54E
Nguigmi Niger	**108**	G10	14 19N	13 06E
Nguru Nigeria	**108**	G10	12 53N	10 30E
Nha Trang Vietnam	**103**	D6	12 15N	109 10E
Nhulunbuy Aust.	**110**	F7	12 30S	136 56E
Niagara Escarpment New York USA	**54**	D2	43 08N	78 50W
Niagara Falls *tn.* New York USA	**71**	L5	43 06N	79 04W
Niamey Niger	**108**	E10	13 32N	2 05E
Niangara CDR	**108**	K8	3 45N	27 54E
NICARAGUA	**75**	G2		
Nice Fr.	**87**	J5	43 42N	7 16E
Nicobar Islands India	**99**	G1	8 30N	94 00E
Nicosia Cyprus	**96**	B6	35 11N	33 23E
Niedere Tauern *mts.* Austria	**89**	D7	47 00N	14 00E
Nienburg Germany	**88**	B10	52 38N	9 13E
Nieuw Nickerie Suriname	**80**	F15	5 52N	57 00W
NIGER	**108**	E10		
Niger *r.* West Africa	**108**	F9	5 30N	6 15E
NIGERIA	**108**	F10		
Nihoa *i.* Hawaiian Islands	**115**	K10	23 03N	161 55W
Niigata Japan	**102**	C2	37 58N	139 02E
Niihama Japan	**102**	B1	33 57N	133 15E
Niihau *i.* Hawaiian Islands	**115**	W18	21 50N	160 11W
Nii-jima *i.* Japan	**102**	C1	34 20N	139 15E
Nijmegen Neths.	**86**	H9	51 50N	5 52E
Nikkō Japan	**102**	C2	36 45N	139 37E
Nikolayevsk-na-Amure Russia	**95**	S7	53 10N	140 44E
Nikšić Montenegro	**89**	G5	42 48N	18 56E
Niland California USA	**72**	F1	33 14N	115 30W
Nile *r.* Sudan/Egypt	**108**	L13	27 30N	31 40E
Nilgiri Hills India	**98**	D2	11 00N	76 30E
Nîmes Fr.	**87**	H5	43 50N	4 21E
Nimule Sudan	**108**	L8	3 35N	32 03E
Nim Wan HK China	**100**	A2	22 26N	113 56E
Nine Degree Channel *sd.* Maldives	**98**	C1	9 00N	73 00E
9 de Julio *tn.* Argentina	**81**	E6	35 28S	60 58W
Ninepin Group *is.* HK China	**100**	D1	22 15N	114 22E
Ninety East Ridge Indian Ocean	**113**	H4	20 00S	88 00E
Ninety Mile Beach NZ	**111**	D7	34 45S	172 58E
Nineveh *hist. site* Iraq	**96**	D6	36 24N	43 08E
Ningbo China	**101**	N4	29 54N	121 33E
Ninh Binh Vietnam	**101**	K3	20 14N	106 00E
Niobrara *r.* USA	**70**	F5	42 00N	102 00W
Nioro du Sahel Mali	**108**	C11	15 12N	9 35W
Niort Fr.	**87**	E7	46 19N	0 27W
Niš Serbia	**89**	H5	43 20N	21 54E
Niterói Brazil	**80**	J9	22 54S	43 06W
Nitra Slovakia	**88**	G8	48 19N	18 04E
Niue *i.* Pacific Ocean	**115**	K6	19 02S	169 55W
Nizamabad India	**98**	D3	18 40N	78 05E
Nizhneangarsk Russia	**95**	N8	55 48N	109 35E
Nizhnekamsk Russia	**94**	H8	55 38N	51 49E
Nizhnekolymsk Russia	**95**	U10	68 34N	160 58E
Nizhnevartovsk Russia	**94**	K9	60 57N	76 40E
Nizhniy Novgorod Russia	**94**	G8	56 20N	44 00E
Nizhniy Tagil Russia	**94**	J8	58 00N	59 58E
Nizhnyaya (Lower) Tunguska *r.* Russia	**95**	M9	64 00N	95 00E
Nízké Tatry *mts.* Slovakia	**88**	G8	49 00N	19 00E
Nkongsamba Cameroon	**108**	F8	4 59N	9 53E
Noakhali Bangladesh	**99**	L9	22 52N	91 03E
Nobeoka Japan	**102**	B1	32 36N	131 40E
Nogales Mexico	**74**	B6	31 20N	111 00W
Nogales Arizona USA	**70**	D3	31 20N	110 56W
Nojima-zaki *c.* Japan	**102**	C1	34 54N	139 54E
Nokrek Peak *mt.* India	**99**	L10	25 27N	90 21E
Nola CAR	**108**	H8	3 28N	16 08E
Nome Alaska USA	**40**	B6	64 32N	165 28W
Nordfriesische Inseln *is.* Germany	**88**	A11	54 00N	8 00E
Nordhausen Germany	**88**	C9	51 31N	10 48E
Nordvik Russia	**95**	P11	74 01N	111 30E
Nore *r.* RoI	**86**	B10	52 45N	7 21W
Norfolk Nebraska USA	**71**	G5	42 01N	97 25W
Norfolk Virginia USA	**71**	L4	36 54N	76 18W
Norfolk Island Pacific Ocean	**108**	G5	29 05S	167 59E
Norfolk Island Trough Pacific Ocean	**114**	F5	27 30S	166 00E
Norfolk Lake Arkansas USA	**71**	H4	36 00N	92 00W
Noril'sk Russia	**95**	L10	69 21N	88 02E
Normanton Aust.	**110**	G6	17 40S	141 05E
Norridgewock Maine USA	**53**	S4	44 43N	69 48W
Norris Lake Tennessee USA	**71**	K4	36 00N	84 00W
Norristown Pennsylvania USA	**73**	C2	40 07N	75 21W
Norrköping Sweden	**88**	F13	58 35N	16 10E
Norrtälje Sweden	**88**	G13	59 46N	18 43E
Norseman Aust.	**110**	C3	32 15S	121 47E
North Adams Massachusetts USA	**73**	D3	42 43N	73 12W
Northam Aust.	**110**	B3	31 40S	116 40E
North American Basin Atlantic Ocean	**116**	C10	34 00N	55 00W
Northampton Aust.	**110**	A4	28 27S	114 37E
Northampton UK	**86**	E10	52 14N	0 54W
Northampton Massachusetts USA	**73**	D3	42 20N	72 38W
North Andaman *i.* Andaman Islands	**99**	G2	13 00N	93 00E
North Australian Basin Indian Ocean	**113**	L5	14 00S	115 00E
North Bergen New Jersey USA	**73**	H2	40 46N	74 02W
North Canadian *r.* USA	**70**	F4	36 00N	100 00W
North Cape NZ	**111**	D7	34 25S	173 03E
North Carolina *state* USA	**71**	L4	36 00N	80 00W
North Cascades National Park Washington USA	**42**	H4	48 45N	121 20W
North Channel British Isles	**86**	C11	55 20N	5 50W
North Collins New York USA	**54**	D1	42 36N	78 57W
North Dakota *state* USA	**70/71**	F6	47 00N	102 00W
North East Pennsylvania USA	**52**	G2	42 13N	79 51W
Northern Ireland *admin.* UK	**86**	B11	54 40N	7 00W
NORTHERN MARIANAS	**114**	E9/F9		
Northern Territory *territory* Aust.	**110**	E5/E6	19 00S	132 00E
North Fiji Basin Pacific Ocean	**114**	H6	18 00S	173 00E
North Island NZ	**111**	D7/E4	39 00S	176 00E
NORTH KOREA	**101**	P6/P7		
North Little Rock Arkansas USA	**71**	H3	34 46N	92 16W
North Loup *r.* Nebraska USA	**70**	F5	42 00N	100 00W
North Platte Nebraska USA	**70**	F5	41 09N	100 45W
North Platte *r.* North America	**70**	F5	42 00N	103 00W
North Pole Arctic Ocean	**117**		90 00N	
North Stratford New Hampshire USA	**53**	Q4	44 46N	71 36W
North Uist *i.* UK	**86**	B12	57 04N	7 15W
North West Cape Aust.	**110**	A5	21 48S	114 10E
North West Christmas Island Ridge Pacific Ocean	**115**	K9	9 30N	170 00W
Northwestern Atlantic Basin Atlantic Ocean	**116**	A10	33 00N	70 00W
Northwest Highlands UK	**86**	C12	58 00N	5 00W
Northwest Pacific Basin Pacific Ocean	**114**	E11	35 00N	150 00E
North York Moors UK	**86**	E11	55 22N	0 45W
Norton Kansas USA	**70**	G4	39 51N	99 53W
Norwalk Connecticut USA	**73**	D2	41 08N	73 25W
Norwalk Ohio USA	**51**	K1	41 15N	82 36W
NORWAY	**86**	H13		
Norwegian Basin Atlantic Ocean	**116**	H13	67 00N	0 00
Norwegian Sea Arctic Ocean	**117**		70 00N	5 00E
Norwich UK	**86**	F10	52 38N	1 18E
Norwich Connecticut USA	**73**	D2	41 32N	72 05W
Norwich New York USA	**53**	L2	42 32N	75 32W
Noshiro Japan	**102**	D3	40 13N	140 00E
Nosop *r.* Southern Africa	**109**	J2	25 00S	20 30E
Nosy Bé *i.* Madagascar	**109**	P5	13 00S	47 00E
Notéc *r.* Poland	**88**	F10	53 00N	17 00E
Nottingham UK	**86**	E10	52 58N	1 10W
Nouadhibou Mauritania	**108**	A12	20 54N	17 01W
Nouakchott Mauritania	**108**	A11	18 09N	15 58W
Nova Friburgo Brazil	**80**	J9	22 16S	42 34W
Nova Iguaçu Brazil	**80**	J9	22 46S	43 23W
Novara Italy	**89**	B6	45 27N	8 37E
Nova Scotia Basin Atlantic Ocean	**116**	C10	39 00N	55 00W
Novato California USA	**72**	B4	38 05N	122 34W
Novaya Zemlya *is.* Russia	**94**	H11	74 00N	55 00E
Novgorod Russia	**94**	F8	58 30N	31 20E
Novi Pazar Serbia	**89**	H5	43 09N	20 29E
Novi Sad Serbia	**89**	G6	45 15N	19 51E
Novograd Volynskiy Ukraine	**88**	L9	50 34N	27 32E
Novo Hamburgo Brazil	**81**	G8	29 37S	51 07W
Novokazalinsk Kazakhstan	**94**	J6	45 48N	62 06E
Novokuznetsk Russia	**95**	L7	53 45N	87 12E
Novorossiysk Russia	**94**	F5	44 44N	37 46E
Novosibirsk Russia	**95**	L8	55 04N	83 05E
Novvy Port Russia	**94**	K10	67 38N	72 33E
Novvy Urengoy Russia	**94**	K10	66 00N	77 20E
Nowa Sól Poland	**88**	E9	51 49N	15 41E
Nowy Dwor Mazowiecki Poland	**88**	H10	52 27N	20 41E
Nowy Sącz Poland	**88**	H8	49 39N	20 40E
Noyes Island Alaska USA	**42**	D4	56 30N	133 45W
Nubian Desert Sudan	**108**	L12	21 00N	33 00E
Nueces *r.* Texas USA	**70**	G2	28 00N	99 00W
Nueva Rosita Mexico	**74**	D5	27 58N	101 11W
Nueva San Salvador El Salvador	**74**	G2	13 40N	89 18W
Nuevitas Cuba	**75**	J4	21 34N	77 18W
Nuevo Casas Grandes Mexico	**74**	C6	30 22N	107 53W
Nuevo Laredo Mexico	**74**	E5	27 39N	99 30W
Nu Jiang *r.* China/Myanmar	**101**	H3/H4	25 00N	99 00E
Nukus Uzbekistan	**94**	H5	42 28N	59 07E
Nullarbor Plain Aust.	**110**	D3	32 00S	128 00E
Numazu Japan	**102**	C2	35 08N	138 50E
Numedal *geog. reg.* Norway	**86**	K13	60 40N	9 00E
Nunivak Island Alaska USA	**115**	K13	60 00N	166 00W
Nuoro Italy	**89**	B4	40 20N	9 21E
Nuremberg Germany	**88**	C8	49 27N	11 05E
Nusaybin Turkey	**96**	D6	37 05N	41 11E
Nushki Pakistan	**98**	B5	29 33N	66 01E
Nyainqêntanglha Shan *mts.* China	**100**	F4/G5	30 00N	90 00E
Nyala Sudan	**108**	J10	12 01N	24 50E
Nyasa, Lake Southern Africa	**109**	L5	12 00S	35 00E
Nyíregyháza Hungary	**88**	H7	47 57N	21 43E
Nykøbing Denmark	**88**	C11	54 47N	11 53E
Nyköping Sweden	**88**	F13	58 45N	17 03E
Nyngan Aust.	**110**	H3	31 34S	147 14E
Nyons Fr.	**87**	H6	44 22N	5 08E
Nysa Poland	**88**	F9	50 30N	17 20E
Nysa *r.* Poland	**88**	E9	52 00N	14 00E
Nyūdō-zaki *c.* Japan	**102**	C2	40 00N	139 42E

O

Oahe, Lake USA	**70**	F6	45 00N	100 00W
Oahu *i.* Hawaiian Islands	**115**	X18	21 30N	158 10W
Oakdale California USA	**72**	C3	37 40N	120 53W
Oak Harbor *tn.* Ohio USA	**52**	C1	41 31N	83 10W
Oak Harbor *tn.* Washington USA	**42**	H4	48 20N	122 38W
Oakhurst California USA	**72**	D3	37 20N	119 39W
Oakland California USA	**70**	B4	37 50N	122 15W
Oak Ridge *tn.* Tennessee USA	**71**	K4	36 02N	84 12W
Oamaru NZ	**111**	C2	45 06S	170 58E
Oaxaca Mexico	**74**	E3	17 05N	96 41W
Ob' *r.* Russia	**94**	J10	65 30N	66 00E
Oban UK	**86**	C12	56 25N	5 29W
Ob', Gulf of Russia	**94**	K10	68 00N	74 00E
Obidos Brazil	**80**	F13	1 52S	55 30W
Obihiro Japan	**102**	D3	42 56N	143 10E
Ocala Florida USA	**71**	K2	29 11N	82 09W
Ocana Col.	**80**	C15	8 16N	73 21W
Ocatlán Mexico	**74**	D4	20 21N	102 42W
Oceanside California USA	**72**	E1	33 12N	117 23W
Ōda Japan	**102**	B2	35 10N	132 29E
Ōdate Japan	**102**	D3	40 18N	140 32E
Odawara Japan	**102**	C2	35 15N	139 08E
Odense Denmark	**88**	C11	55 24N	10 25E
Oder *r.* Europe	**88**	E10	52 00N	15 30E
Odessa Delaware USA	**73**	C1	39 27N	75 40W
Odessa Texas USA	**70**	F3	31 50N	102 23W
Odiel *r.* Sp.	**87**	B2	37 32N	7 00W
Odra *r.* Europe	**88**	E10	52 00N	15 00E
Oeno *i.* Pacific Ocean	**115**	N5	23 10S	132 00W
Ofanto *r.* Italy	**89**	E4/F4	41 00N	15 00E
Offenburg Germany	**88**	A8	48 29N	7 57E
Ōfunato Japan	**102**	D2	39 04N	141 43E
Ogaden *geog. reg.* Africa	**108**	P9	7 00N	51 00E
Ōgaki Japan	**102**	C2	35 22N	136 36E
Ogasawara Gunto *i.* Pacific Ocean	**114**	E10	27 30N	143 00E
Ogbomoso Nigeria	**108**	E9	8 05N	4 11E
Ogden Utah USA	**70**	D5	41 14N	111 59W
Ogdensburg New York USA	**51**	P3	44 05N	74 36W
Ogooué *r.* Gabon	**108**	F7	0 50S	9 50E
Ohai NZ	**111**	A2	45 56S	167 57E
Ōhata Japan	**102**	D3	41 22N	141 11E
Ohio *r.* USA	**71**	J4	38 00N	86 00W
Ohio *state* USA	**71**	K5	40 00N	83 00W
Ohridsko ezero *l.* Europe	**89**	H4	41 00N	21 00E
Oil City Pennsylvania USA	**52**	G1	41 26N	79 44W
Oildale California USA	**72**	D2	35 25N	119 00W
Oise *r.* Fr.	**86**	G8	49 10N	2 10E
Ōita Japan	**102**	B1	33 15N	131 36E
Ojinaga Mexico	**74**	D5	29 35N	104 26W
Okanagan *r.* North America	**70**	C6	49 00N	119 00W
Okanogan Washington USA	**43**	L1	48 22N	119 35W
Okanogan River North America	**43**	L1	49 00N	119 00W
Okara Pakistan	**98**	C6	30 49N	73 31E
Okavango *r.* Southern Africa	**109**	H4	17 50S	20 00E
Okavango Basin Botswana	**109**	J4	19 00S	23 00E
Okaya Japan	**102**	C2	36 03N	138 00E
Okayama Japan	**102**	B1	34 40N	133 54E
Okazaki Japan	**102**	C1	34 58N	137 10E
Okeechobee, Lake Florida USA	**71**	K2	27 00N	81 00W
Okha Russia	**95**	S7	53 35N	143 01E
Okhotsk Russia	**95**	S8	59 20N	143 15E
Okhotsk, Sea of Russia	**95**	S7/S8	55 00N	148 00E
Oki *is.* Japan	**102**	B2	36 05N	133 00E
Okinawa *i.* Japan	**101**	P4	26 30N	128 00E
Oklahoma *state* USA	**71**	G4	36 00N	98 00W
Oklahoma City Oklahoma USA	**71**	G4	35 28N	97 33W
Oktyabr'skiy Russia	**95**	T7	52 43N	156 14E
Okushiri-tō *i.* Japan	**102**	C3	42 15N	139 30E
Olancha California USA	**72**	D3	36 18N	118 00W
Öland *i.* Sweden	**88**	F12	56 45N	51 50E
Olbia Italy	**89**	B4	40 56N	9 30E
Olcott New York USA	**54**	D2	43 20N	78 40W
Oldenburg Germany	**88**	B10	53 08N	8 13E
Old Saybrook Connecticut USA	**73**	D2	41 18N	72 23W
Old Town Maine USA	**57**	F1	44 55N	68 41W
Olean New York USA	**51**	M2	42 05N	78 26W
Olekma *r.* Russia	**95**	Q8	59 00N	121 00E
Olekminsk Russia	**95**	Q9	60 25N	120 25E
Olenek Russia	**95**	P10	68 28N	112 18E
Olenek *r.* Russia	**95**	Q11	72 00N	122 00E
Olga Washington USA	**42**	H4	48 40N	123 05W
Olhâo Port.	**87**	B2	37 01N	7 50W
Olinda Brazil	**80**	K12	8 00S	34 51W
Olomouc Czech Rep.	**88**	F8	49 38N	17 15E
Olongapo Philippines	**103**	G6	14 49N	120 17E
Olsztyn Poland	**88**	H10	53 48N	20 29E
Olt *r.* Romania	**89**	K6	44 00N	24 00E
Olympia Washington USA	**70**	B6	47 03N	122 53W
Ólympos *mt.* Greece	**89**	J4	40 05N	22 21E
Olympus *mt.* Cyprus	**96**	B5	34 55N	32 52E
Olympus, Mount Washington USA	**70**	B6	47 49N	123 42W
Om' *r.* Russia	**94**	K8	55 30N	79 00E
Omagh UK	**86**	B11	54 36N	7 18W
Omaha Nebraska USA	**71**	G5	41 15N	96 00W
Omak Washington USA	**43**	L1	48 25N	119 30W
OMAN	**97**	F2/G3		
Oman, Gulf of Iran/Oman	**97**	G3	24 30N	58 30E
Omboué Gabon	**108**	F7	1 38S	9 20E
Omdurman Sudan	**108**	L11	15 37N	32 29E
Ommaney, Cape Alaska USA	**42**	C5	56 10N	134 40W
Omo *r.* Ethiopia	**108**	M9	7 00N	37 00E
Omolon *r.* Russia	**95**	U10	65 00N	160 00E
Omoloy *r.* Russia	**95**	R10	70 00N	132 00E
Omsk Russia	**94**	K8	55 00N	73 22E
Ōmuta Japan	**102**	B1	33 02N	130 26E
Onaway Michigan USA	**52**	B5	45 23N	84 14W

Oneida New York USA	**51**	P2	43 05N	75 39W
Oneida Lake New York USA	**51**	P2	43 14N	76 00W
Oneonta New York USA	**53**	L2	42 30N	75 04W
Onești Romania	**89**	L7	46 15N	26 45E
Onezhskoye Ozero *l.* Russia	**94**	F9	62 00N	40 00E
Ongea Levu *i.* Fiji	**114**	V15	19 11S	178 28W
Onitsha Nigeria	**108**	F9	6 10N	6 47E
Onomichi Japan	**102**	B1	34 25N	133 11E
Onon *r.* Russia/Mongolia	**101**	L9	51 00N	114 00E
Onslow Aust.	**110**	B5	21 41S	115 12E
Ontario California USA	**70**	C3	34 04N	117 38W
Ontonagon Michigan USA	**71**	J6	46 52N	89 18W
Oostende Belgium	**86**	G9	51 13N	2 55E
Opala CDR	**108**	J7	0 40S	24 20E
Opava Czech Rep.	**88**	F8	49 58N	17 55E
Opheim Montana USA	**47**	D1	48 56N	106 25W
Opole Poland	**88**	F9	50 40N	17 56E
Oporto Port.	**87**	A4	41 09N	8 37W
Opotiki NZ	**111**	F5	38 01S	177 17E
Oradea Romania	**89**	H7	47 03N	21 55E
Orai India	**98**	D5	26 00N	79 26E
Oran Algeria	**108**	D15	35 45N	0 38W
Orán Argentina	**80**	E9	23 07S	64 16W
Orange Aust.	**110**	H3	33 19S	149 10E
Orange Fr.	**87**	H6	44 08N	4 48E
Orange New Jersey USA	**73**	H2	40 45N	74 14W
Orange Texas USA	**71**	H3	30 05N	93 43W
Orange *r.* Southern Africa	**109**	H2	28 30S	17 30E
Orangeburg South Carolina USA	**71**	K3	33 28N	80 53W
Oravița Romania	**89**	H6	45 02N	21 43E
Orbigo *r.* Sp.	**87**	C5	42 15N	5 45W
Orcas Island Washington USA	**42**	H4	48 40N	123 05W
Orchard Park *tn.* New York USA	**52**	H2	42 46N	78 45W
Orcia *r.* Italy	**89**	C5	42 00N	11 00E
Ord Mountain California USA	**72**	E2	34 42N	116 50W
Ordu Turkey	**96**	C7	41 00N	37 52E
Örebro Sweden	**88**	E13	59 17N	15 13E
Oregon *state* USA	**70**	B5/C5	44 00N	120 00W
Oregon City Oregon USA	**70**	B6	45 21N	122 36W
Orël Russia	**94**	F7	52 58N	36 04E
Orem Utah USA	**70**	D5	40 20N	111 45W
Orenburg Russia	**94**	H7	51 50N	55 00E
Orense Sp.	**87**	B5	42 20N	7 52W
Orient New York USA	**73**	D2	41 09N	72 18W
Orihuela Sp.	**87**	E3	38 05N	0 56W
Orinoco *r.* Venezuela	**80**	E15	8 00N	64 00W
Orissa *admin.* India	**99**	E4	20 20N	83 00E
Oristano Italy	**89**	B3	39 54N	8 36E
Orizaba Mexico	**74**	E3	18 51N	97 08W
Orkney Islands UK	**86**	D13	59 00N	3 00W
Orlando Florida USA	**71**	K2	28 33N	81 21W
Orléans Fr.	**86**	F7	47 54N	1 54E
Oroville California USA	**72**	C4	39 32N	121 34W
Oroville Washington USA	**43**	L1	48 57N	119 27W
Orsk Russia	**94**	H7	51 13N	58 35E
Ortigueira Sp.	**87**	B5	43 43N	8 13W
Ortona Italy	**89**	E5	42 21N	14 24E
Orūmīyeh Iran	**96**	D6	37 40N	45 00E
Oruro Bolivia	**80**	D10	17 59S	67 08W
Osaka Japan	**102**	C1	34 40N	135 30E
O-shima *i.* Japan	**102**	C1	34 45N	139 25E
Oshkosh Wisconsin USA	**71**	J5	44 01N	88 32W
Oshogbo Nigeria	**108**	E9	7 50N	4 35E
Osijek Croatia	**89**	G6	45 33N	18 41E
Oskarshamn Sweden	**88**	F12	57 16N	16 25E
Oslo Norway	**86**	L13	59 56N	10 45E
Oslofjorden *fj.* Norway	**86**	L13	59 20N	10 37E
Osmaniye Turkey	**96**	C6	37 04N	36 15E
Osnabrück Germany	**88**	B10	52 17N	8 03E
Osorno Chile	**81**	C5	40 35S	73 14W
Ossa, Mount Aust.	**110**	H1	41 52S	146 04E
Osseo Wisconsin USA	**51**	F3	44 35N	91 13W
Ostfriesische Inseln *is.* Germany	**88**	A10	53 00N	7 00E
Ostrava Czech Rep.	**88**	G8	49 50N	18 15E
Ostróda Poland	**88**	G10	53 42N	19 59E
Ostrołęka Poland	**88**	H10	53 05N	21 32E
Ostrowiec Swietokrzyski Poland	**88**	H9	50 58N	21 22E
Ostrów Mazowiecka Poland	**88**	H10	52 50N	21 51E
Ostrów Wielkopolski Poland	**88**	F9	51 39N	17 50E
Osumi-kaikyo *sd.* Japan	**102**	B1	30 50N	131 00E
Oswego New York USA	**71**	L5	43 27N	76 31W
Otaki NZ	**111**	E4	40 46S	175 09E
Otaru Japan	**102**	D3	43 14N	140 59E
Otavalo Ecuador	**80**	B14	0 13N	78 15W
Otira NZ	**111**	C3	42 50S	171 34E
Otra *r.* Norway	**86**	J13	58 17N	7 30E
Otranto Italy	**89**	G4	40 08N	18 30E
Otranto, Strait of Adriatic Sea	**89**	G3/G4	40 00N	19 00E
Otsu Japan	**102**	C2	35 00N	135 50E
Ottawa Kansas USA	**71**	G4	38 35N	95 16W
Ottumwa Iowa USA	**71**	H5	41 02N	92 26W
Ouachita *r.* USA	**71**	H3	34 00N	93 00W
Ouachita Mountains USA	**71**	G3/H3	34 00N	95 00W
Ouadda CAR	**108**	J9	8 09N	22 20E
Ouagadougou Burkina	**108**	D10	12 20N	1 40W
Ouahigouya Burkina	**108**	D10	13 31N	2 20W
Ouargla Algeria	**108**	F14	32 00N	5 16E
Oubangui *r.* Central Africa	**108**	H8	0 00	17 30E
Oudtshoorn RSA	**109**	J1	33 35S	22 12E
Oued Dra *r.* Morocco	**108**	B13	28 10N	11 00W
Ouesso Congo	**108**	H8	1 38N	16 03E
Ouham *r.* CAR	**108**	H9	7 00N	17 30E
Oujda Morocco	**108**	D14	34 41N	1 45W
Ou-sanmyaku *mts.* Japan	**102**	D2	39 20N	141 00E
Oust *r.* Fr.	**86**	D7	47 50N	2 30W
Outer Hebrides *is.* UK	**86**	B12	58 00N	7 00W
Ovalau *i.* Fiji	**114**	U16	17 40S	178 47E
Ovalle Chile	**81**	C7	30 33S	71 16W
Oviedo Sp.	**87**	C5	43 21N	7 18W
Owando Congo	**108**	H7	0 27S	15 44E
Owego New York USA	**53**	K2	42 07N	76 16W
Owen Falls Dam Uganda	**108**	L8	0 29N	33 11E
Owen Fracture Zone Indian Ocean	**113**	E7	10 00N	55 00E
Owensboro Kentucky USA	**71**	J4	37 45N	87 05W
Owens Lake California USA	**70**	C4	36 25N	117 56W
Owen Stanley Range *mts.* PNG	**110**	H8	9 15S	148 30E
Owosso Michigan USA	**51**	J2	42 59N	84 10W
Owyhee *r.* USA	**70**	C5	43 00N	117 00W
Oxford UK	**86**	E9	51 46N	1 15W
Oxnard California USA	**70**	C3	34 11N	119 10W
Oyama Japan	**102**	C2	36 18N	139 48E
Oyapock *r.* Brazil	**80**	G14	3 00N	52 30W
Oyem Gabon	**108**	G8	1 34N	11 31E
Ozark Plateau Missouri USA	**71**	H4	37 00N	93 00W
Ozarks, Lake of the Missouri USA	**71**	H4	38 00N	93 00W
Ozero Alakol' *salt l.* Kazakhstan	**94**	L6	46 00N	82 00E
Ozero Balkhash *l.* Kazakhstan	**94**	K6	46 00N	75 00E
Ozero Baykal *l.* Russia	**95**	N7	54 00N	109 00E
Ozero Chany *salt l.* Russia	**94**	K7	55 00N	77 30E
Ozero Il'men' *l.* Russia	**94**	F8	58 00N	31 30E
Ozero Issyk-Kul' *salt l.* Kyrgyzstan	**94**	K5	42 30N	77 30E
Ozero Khanka *l.* Asia	**95**	R6	45 00N	132 30E
Ozero Taymyr *l.* Russia	**95**	N11	74 00N	102 30E
Ozero Tengiz *salt l.* Kazakhstan	**94**	J7	51 00N	69 00E
Ozero Zaysan *l.* Kazakhstan	**95**	L6	48 00N	84 00E
Ozieri Italy	**89**	B4	40 35N	9 01E

P

Pabianice Poland	**88**	G9	51 40N	19 20E
Pabna Bangladesh	**99**	K10	24 00N	89 15E
Pacasmayo Peru	**80**	B12	7 27S	79 33W
Pachuca Mexico	**74**	E4	20 10N	98 44W
Pacific-Antarctic Ridge Pacific Ocean	**115**	M1	55 00S	135 00W
Pacific Grove California USA	**70**	B4	36 36N	121 56W
Pacific Ocean	**114/115**			
Padang Indonesia	**103**	C3	1 00S	100 21E
Paderborn Germany	**88**	B9	51 43N	8 44E
Padilla Bolivia	**80**	E10	19 18S	64 20W
Padma *r.* Bangladesh	**99**	L9	23 25N	90 10E
Padua Italy	**89**	C6	45 24N	11 53E
Paducah Kentucky USA	**71**	J4	37 03N	88 36W
Paeroa NZ	**111**	E6	37 23S	175 40E
Pag *i.* Croatia	**89**	E6	44 00N	15 00E
Pagadian Philippines	**103**	G5	7 50N	123 30E
Pahala Hawaiian Islands	**115**	Z17	19 12N	155 28W
Pahute Mesa *mts.* Nevada USA	**72**	E3	37 15N	116 20W
Painesville Ohio USA	**51**	L1	41 43N	81 15W
Paisley UK	**86**	C11	55 50N	4 26W
Paita Peru	**80**	A12	5 11S	81 09W
Pakanbaru Indonesia	**103**	C4	0 33N	101 30E
PAKISTAN	**98**	B5/C5		
Pak Mong HK China	**100**	A1	22 18N	113 57E
Pakokku Myanmar	**100**	H3	21 20N	95 05E
Pak Tam Chung HK China	**100**	C2	22 24N	114 19E
Pakxé Laos	**103**	D6	15 00N	105 55E
Palana Russia	**95**	T8	59 05N	159 59E
Palangkaraya Indonesia	**103**	E3	2 16S	113 55E
PALAU	**114**	D8		
Palawan *i.* Philippines	**103**	F5/F6	10 00N	119 00E
Palembang Indonesia	**103**	C3	2 59S	104 45E
Palencia Sp.	**87**	C5	41 01N	4 32W
Palermo Italy	**89**	D3	38 08N	13 23E
Palestine Texas USA	**71**	G3	31 45N	95 39W
Palestine *geog. reg.* Middle East	**96**	N10/N11	32 00N	35 00E
Palghat India	**98**	D2	10 46N	76 42E
Palk Strait India	**98**	D1	10 00N	80 00E
Palma de Mallorca Sp.	**87**	G3	39 35N	2 39E
Palmar Sur Costa Rica	**75**	H1	8 57N	83 28W
Palmas, Cape Liberia	**108**	C8	4 25N	7 50W
Palmdale California USA	**72**	D2	34 35N	118 07W
Palmer Land *geog. reg.* Antarctica	**117**		72 00S	62 00W
Palmerston NZ	**111**	C2	45 29S	170 43E
Palmerston Atoll *i.* Pacific Ocean	**115**	K6	18 04S	163 10W
Palmerston North NZ	**111**	E4	40 22S	175 37E
Palmira Col.	**80**	B14	3 33N	76 17W
Palm Springs *tn.* California USA	**72**	E1	33 49N	116 33W
Palmyra Syria	**96**	C5	34 40N	38 10E
Palmyra New York USA	**53**	J3	43 04N	77 14W
Palmyra Pennsylvania USA	**73**	C2	40 19N	76 36W
Palmyra Atoll *i.* Pacific Ocean	**115**	L8	5 52N	162 05W
Palo Alto California USA	**72**	B3	37 26N	122 10W
Palomares Mexico	**74**	E3	17 10N	95 04W
Palopo Indonesia	**103**	G3	3 01S	120 12E
Palu Indonesia	**103**	F3	0 54S	119 52E
Pamiers Fr.	**87**	F5	43 07N	1 36E
Pampas *geog. reg.* Argentina	**81**	E6	36 00S	63 00W
Pamplona Col.	**80**	C15	7 24N	72 38W
Pamplona Sp.	**87**	E5	42 49N	1 39W
PANAMA	**75**	H1/J1		
Panama Canal Panama	**75**	J1	9 00N	80 00W
Panama City Panama	**75**	J1	8 57N	19 30W
Panama City Florida USA	**71**	J3	30 10N	85 41W
Panay *i.* Philippines	**103**	G6	11 00N	122 00E
Pancake Range *mts.* Nevada USA	**72**	F4	38 45N	115 55W
Pančevo Serbia	**89**	H6	44 52N	20 40E
Panevezys Lithuania	**88**	K11	55 44N	24 24E
Pangkalpinang Indonesia	**103**	D3	2 05S	106 09E
Panipat India	**98**	D5	29 24N	76 58E
Pantar *i.* Indonesia	**103**	G2	8 30S	124 00E
Pantelleria *i.* Italy	**89**	D2	36 00N	12 00E
Papa Hawaiian Islands	**115**	Z17	19 12N	155 53W
Pápa Hungary	**89**	F7	47 20N	17 29E
Papantla Mexico	**74**	E4	20 30N	97 21W
Papoose Lake Nevada USA	**72**	F3	37 08N	115 52W
Papua, Gulf of PNG	**110**	G8/H8	8 15S	144 45E
PAPUA NEW GUINEA	**110**	G8/H8		
Pará *admin.* Brazil	**80**	G13	4 30S	52 30W
Paraburdoo Aust.	**110**	B5	23 15S	117 45E
Paracel Islands South China Sea	**103**	E7	16 00N	113 30E
Paragua *r.* Bolivia	**80**	E11	14 00S	61 30W
Paragua *r.* Venezuela	**80**	E15	6 00N	63 30W
PARAGUAY	**80**	F9		
Paraguay *r.* Paraguay/Argentina	**80**	F8/F9	26 30S	58 00W
Paraiba *admin.* Brazil	**80**	K12	7 20S	37 10W
Parakou Benin	**108**	E9	9 23N	2 40E
Paramaribo Suriname	**80**	F15	5 52N	55 14W
Paramonga Peru	**80**	B11	10 42S	77 50W
Paraná Argentina	**81**	E7	31 45S	60 30W
Paraná *admin.* Brazil	**80**	G9	24 30S	53 00W
Paraná *r.* Paraguay/Argentina	**80**	F8	27 00S	56 00W
Paranaíba *r.* Brazil	**80**	H10	18 00S	49 00W
Parana Panema *r.* Brazil	**80**	G9	22 30S	52 00W
Paranguá Brazil	**80**	H8	25 32S	48 36W
Paraparaumu NZ	**111**	E4	40 55S	175 00E
Pardo *r.* Brazil	**80**	K10	15 10S	40 00W
Pardubice Czech Rep.	**88**	E9	50 03N	15 45E
Parepare Indonesia	**103**	F3	4 00S	119 40E
Parintins Brazil	**80**	F13	2 38S	56 45W
Paris Fr.	**86**	G8	48 52N	2 20E
Paris Texas USA	**71**	G3	33 41N	95 33W
Parish New York USA	**51**	N2	43 24N	76 08W
Parkersburg West Virginia USA	**71**	K4	39 17N	81 33W
Parma Italy	**89**	C6	44 48N	10 19E
Parma Ohio USA	**51**	L1	41 22N	81 44W
Parnaíba Brazil	**80**	J13	2 58S	41 46W
Parnaiba *r.* Brazil	**80**	J12	7 30S	45 00W
Parnassós *mt.* Greece	**89**	J3	38 30N	22 37E
Pärnu *r.* Estonia	**88**	K13	58 30N	24 30E
Paroo *r.* Aust.	**110**	G4	29 00S	144 30E
Páros Greece	**89**	K2	37 04N	25 06E
Parras Mexico	**74**	D5	25 30N	102 11W
Pasadena California USA	**72**	D2	34 10N	118 08W
Pasadena Texas USA	**71**	G2	29 42N	95 14W
Pascagoula Mississippi USA	**71**	J3	30 21N	88 32W
Pasco Washington USA	**70**	C6	46 15N	119 07W
Paso Robles California USA	**72**	C2	35 38N	120 42W
Passaic New Jersey USA	**73**	H2	40 50N	74 08W
Passaic River New Jersey USA	**73**	H2	40 46N	74 09W
Passau Germany	**88**	D8	48 35N	13 28E
Passo Fundo Brazil	**81**	G8	28 16S	52 20W
Pastaza *r.* Peru	**80**	B13	2 30S	77 00W
Pasto Col.	**80**	B14	1 12N	77 17W
Patagonia *geog. reg.* Argentina	**81**	C3	48 00S	70 00W
Patan India	**98**	C4	23 51N	72 11E
Patan Nepal	**99**	F5	27 40N	85 20E
Patchogue New York USA	**73**	D2	40 46N	73 01W
Patea NZ	**111**	E5	39 45S	174 28E
Pate Island Kenya	**108**	N7	2 05S	41 05E
Paterson New Jersey USA	**71**	M5	40 55N	74 08W
Pathankot India	**98**	D6	32 16N	75 43E
Patiala India	**98**	D6	30 21N	76 27E
Patna India	**99**	F5	25 37N	85 12E
Patos Brazil	**80**	K12	6 55S	37 15W
Patras Greece	**89**	H3	38 14N	21 44E
Patterson California USA	**72**	C3	37 29N	121 09W
Pau Fr.	**87**	E5	43 18N	0 22W
Pavia Italy	**89**	B6	45 12N	9 09E
Pavlodar Kazakhstan	**94**	K7	52 21N	76 59E
Pawtucket Rhode Island USA	**73**	E2	41 53N	71 23W
Paysandu Uruguay	**81**	F7	32 21S	58 05W
Pazardzhik Bulgaria	**89**	K5	42 10N	24 20E
Peake Deep Atlantic Ocean	**116**	G11	43 00N	20 05W
Pearl *r.* Mississippi USA	**71**	H3	32 00N	90 00W
Pearl Harbor Hawaiian Islands	**115**	X18	21 22N	158 00W
Peć Kosovo	**89**	H5	42 40N	20 19E
Pechora Russia	**94**	H10	65 14N	57 18E
Pechora *r.* Russia	**94**	H10	66 00N	52 00E
Pecos Texas USA	**70**	F3	30 00N	102 00W
Pecos *r.* USA	**70**	F3	30 00N	102 00W
Pécs Hungary	**89**	G7	46 04N	18 15E
Pedreiras Brazil	**80**	J13	4 32S	44 40W
Pedro Juan Caballero Paraguay	**80**	F9	22 30S	55 44W
Peekskill New York USA	**73**	D2	41 18N	73 50W
Pegu Myanmar	**103**	B7	17 18N	96 31E
Pegunungan Barisan *mts.* Indonesia	**103**	C3	2 30S	102 30E
Pegunungan Maoke *mts.* Indonesia	**110**	F9	4 00S	137 00E
Pegunungan Muller *mts.* Indonesia	**103**	E4	0 00	113 00E
Pegunungan Schwaner *mts.* Indonesia	**103**	E3	1 00S	111 00E
Pegunungan Van Rees *mts.* Indonesia	**110**	F9	2 45S	138 30E
Pekalongan Indonesia	**103**	D2	6 54S	109 37E
Pelée, Mount Martinique	**74**	R12	14 47N	61 04W
Pelican Point Namibia	**109**	G3	22 54S	14 25E
Pelješac *i.* Croatia	**89**	F5	43 00N	17 00E
Pelopónnisos *geog. reg.* Greece	**89**	H2/J2	37 00N	22 00E
Pelotas Brazil	**81**	G7	31 45S	52 20W
Pematangsiantar Indonesia	**103**	B4	2 59N	99 01E
Pemba Mozambique	**109**	N5	13 00S	40 30E
Pembina Minnesota USA	**49**	D1	48 59N	97 20W
Peñarroya-Pueblonuevo Sp.	**87**	C3	38 19N	5 16W
Pendleton Oregon USA	**70**	C6	45 40N	118 46W
Pend Oreille Lake Idaho USA	**43**	M1	48 10N	116 20W
Pend Oreille River Washington USA	**43**	M1	48 50N	117 25W
Penedo Brazil	**80**	K11	10 16S	36 33W
Peng Chau *i.* HK China	**100**	B1	22 17N	114 02E
Peninsula de Taitao Chile	**81**	B4	46 30S	75 00W
Peninsular Malaysia *admin.* Malaysia	**103**	C4	5 00N	102 00E
Penner *r.* India	**98**	D2	14 30N	79 30E
Pennines *hills* UK	**86**	C11	54 30N	2 10W
Pennsylvania *state* USA	**71**	L5	41 00N	78 00W
Penn Yan New York USA	**53**	J2	42 40N	77 03W
Penobscot River Maine USA	**57**	F1	44 15N	68 30W
Penonomé Panama	**75**	H1	8 30N	80 20W
Penrith UK	**86**	D11	54 40N	2 44W
Pensacola Florida USA	**71**	J3	30 26N	87 12W
Pentland Firth *sd.* UK	**86**	D13	58 45N	3 10W
Penza Russia	**94**	G7	53 11N	45 00E
Penzance UK	**86**	C9	50 07N	5 33W
Peoria Illinois USA	**71**	J5	40 43N	89 38W
Pereira Col.	**80**	B14	4 47N	75 46W
Périgueux Fr.	**87**	F6	45 12N	0 44E
Perm' Russia	**94**	H8	58 01N	56 10E
Pernambuco *admin.* Brazil	**80**	K12	8 00S	37 30W
Pernik Bulgaria	**89**	J5	42 36N	23 03E
Perpignan Fr.	**87**	G5	42 42N	2 54E
Perris California USA	**72**	E1	33 47N	117 14W
Perrysburg Ohio USA	**52**	C1	41 33N	83 39W
Persian Gulf Middle East	**97**	F4	27 20N	51 00E
Perth Aust.	**110**	B3	31 58S	115 49E
Perth UK	**86**	D12	56 42N	3 28W
Perth Amboy New Jersey USA	**73**	C2	40 31N	74 16W
PERU	**80**	B11		
Peru Basin Pacific Ocean	**115**	S6	18 00S	95 00W
Peru-Chile Trench Pacific Ocean	**115**	T7	13 00S	77 00W
Perugia Italy	**89**	D5	43 07N	12 23E
Pesaro Italy	**89**	D5	43 54N	12 54E
Pescadero California USA	**72**	B3	37 15N	122 24W
Pescara Italy	**89**	E5	42 27N	14 13E
Peshawar Pakistan	**98**	C6	34 01N	71 40E
Petah Tiqwa Israel	**96**	N11	32 05N	34 53E
Petaluma California USA	**70**	B4	38 13N	12 39W
Petare Venezuela	**80**	D16	10 31N	66 50W
Petauke Zambia	**109**	L5	14 15S	31 20E
Peterborough Aust.	**110**	F3	33 00S	138 51E
Peterborough UK	**86**	E10	52 35N	0 15W
Peterhead UK	**86**	E12	57 30N	1 46W
Petersburg Alaska USA	**42**	D5	56 49N	132 58W
Petersburg Virginia USA	**71**	L4	37 14N	77 24W
Petoskey Michigan USA	**51**	J3	45 22N	84 58W
Petra *hist. site* Jordan	**96**	N10	30 19N	35 26E
Petrolina Brazil	**80**	J12	9 22S	40 30W
Petropavlovsk Kazakhstan	**94**	J7	54 53N	69 13E
Petropavlovsk-Kamchatskiy Russia	**95**	T7	53 03N	158 43E
Petroșani Romania	**89**	J6	45 25N	23 22E
Petrozavodsk Russia	**94**	F9	61 46N	34 19E
Pevek Russia	**95**	V10	64 41N	170 19E
Phenix City Alabama USA	**71**	J3	32 28N	85 01W
Philadelphia Pennsylvania USA	**71**	L4	40 00N	75 10W
Philippine Sea Pacific Ocean	**114**	C10	21 00N	130 00E
PHILIPPINES, THE	**103**	G7		
Philippine Trench Pacific Ocean	**114**	C8/C9	12 00N	127 00E
Phillipsburg New Jersey USA	**73**	C2	40 42N	75 11W
Phnom Penh Cambodia	**103**	C6	11 35N	104 55E
Phoenix Arizona USA	**70**	D3	33 30N	112 03W
Phoenix Island Kiribati	**114**	J7	3 30S	174 30W
Phoenix Islands Kiribati	**114**	J7	4 40S	177 30W
Phôngsali Laos	**101**	J3	21 40N	102 06E
Phuket Thailand	**103**	B5	7 52N	98 22E
Piacenza Italy	**89**	B6	45 03N	9 41E
Piatra Neamț Romania	**89**	L7	46 53N	26 23E
Piauí *admin.* Brazil	**80**	J12	7 30S	43 00W
Pico Bolivar *mt.* Venezuela	**80**	C15	8 33N	71 03W
Pico Cristóbal *mt.* Col.	**80**	C16	10 53N	73 48W
Pico de Itambé *mt.* Brazil	**80**	J10	18 23S	43 21W
Picos Brazil	**80**	J12	7 05S	41 24W
Picton NZ	**111**	E4	41 18S	174 00E
Pidurutalagala *mt.* Sri Lanka	**98**	E1	7 01N	80 45E
Piedras Negras Mexico	**74**	D5	28 40N	100 32W
Pierre South Dakota USA	**70**	F5	44 23N	100 20W
Pierreville Trinidad and Tobago	**75**	V15	10 17N	61 01W
Pietermaritzburg RSA	**109**	L2	29 36S	30 24E
Pietersburg RSA	**109**	K3	23 54N	29 23E
Pigeon Michigan USA	**52**	C3	43 50N	83 15W
Pijijiapan Mexico	**74**	F3	15 42N	93 12W
Pikes Peak Colorado USA	**70**	E4	38 50N	105 03W
Pik Pobedy *mt.* Kyrgyzstan	**94**	L5	42 25N	80 15E

Name	Page	Grid	Lat	Long
Piła Poland	88	F10	53 09N	16 44E
Pilar Paraguay	80	F8	26 51S	58 20W
Pilcomayo r. Paraguay/Argentina	80	F9	24 00S	60 00W
Pilica r. Poland	88	H9	52 00N	21 00E
Pimenta Bueno Brazil	80	E11	11 40S	61 14W
Pimlico Sound North Carolina USA	71	L4	35 00N	76 00W
Pinang i. Malaysia	103	C5	5 25N	100 20E
Pinar del Río Cuba	75	H4	22 24N	83 42W
Pindhos mts. Greece	89	H3	40 00N	21 00E
Pine Bluff Arkansas USA	71	H3	34 13N	92 00W
Pine Creek r. Pennsylvania USA	53	J1	41 40N	77 25W
Pinecrest California USA	72	D4	38 13N	120 00W
Pine Flat Reservoir California USA	72	D3	36 52N	119 17W
Pine River Michigan USA	52	B3	43 23N	84 40W
Ping Chau i. HK China	100	D3	22 33N	114 26E
Ping Che HK China	100	C3	22 32N	114 10E
Pingdingshan China	101	L5	33 50N	113 20E
Ping Shan HK China	100	B2	22 27N	114 00E
Pingtung Taiwan	101	N3	22 40N	120 30E
Pingxiang China	101	K3	22 06N	106 44E
Pingxiang China	101	L4	27 35N	113 46E
Pinnacles National Monument California USA	72	C3	36 27N	121 12W
Piombino Italy	89	C5	42 56N	10 32E
Pioneer Ohio USA	52	B1	41 42N	84 33W
Piotrków Trybunalski Poland	88	G9	51 27N	19 40E
Pirapora Brazil	80	J10	17 20S	44 54W
Pireneos mts Sp./Fr.	87	E5/F5	42 50N	0 30E
Pirin Planina mts. Bulgaria	89	J4	41 00N	23 00E
Pisa Italy	89	C5	43 43N	10 24E
Pisco Peru	80	B11	13 46S	76 12W
Písek Czech Rep.	88	D8	49 18N	14 10E
Pisté Mexico	74	D3	20 44N	88 35W
Pistoia Italy	89	C5	43 56N	10 55E
Pitanga Brazil	80	G9	24 45S	51 43W
Pitcairn Islands Pacific Ocean	115	N5	25 04S	130 06W
Piteşti Romania	89	K6	44 51N	24 51E
Pittsburgh Pennsylvania USA	71	L5	40 26N	80 00W
Pittsfield Massachusetts USA	71	M5	42 27N	73 15W
Piura Peru	80	A12	5 15S	80 38W
Placervile California USA	72	C4	38 43N	120 50W
Plainfield New Jersey USA	73	C2	40 38N	74 24W
Plainview Texas USA	70	F3	34 12N	101 43W
Planada California USA	72	C3	37 18N	120 19W
Planalto de Mato Grosso geog. reg. Brazil	80	F11	13 00S	56 00W
Plasencia Sp.	87	B4	40 02N	6 05W
Plateau de Langres hills Fr.	87	H7	47 40N	4 55E
Plateau de Tchigaï Chad/Niger	108	G12	21 30N	15 00E
Plateau du Tademaït Algeria	108	E13	8 45N	2 00E
Plateaux du Limousin hills Fr.	87	F6	45 45N	1 15E
Platte r. USA	70	F5	41 00N	100 00W
Plattsburgh New York USA	71	M5	44 42N	73 29W
Plauen Germany	88	D9	50 29N	12 08E
Playa Azul Mexico	74	D3	18 00N	102 24W
Plenty, Bay of NZ	111	F6	37 48S	177 12E
Plentywood Montana USA	47	E1	48 51N	104 34W
Pleven Bulgaria	89	K5	43 25N	24 04E
Płock Poland	88	G10	52 32N	19 40E
Ploieşti Romania	89	K6	44 57N	26 01E
Plovdiv Bulgaria	89	K5	42 08N	24 45E
Plover Cove Reservoir HK China	100	C2	22 28N	114 15E
Plunge Lithuania	88	H11	55 52N	21 49E
Plymouth Montserrat	74	P9	16 42N	62 13W
Plymouth UK	86	C9	50 23N	4 10W
Plymouth Massachusetts USA	73	E2	41 58N	70 41W
Plzeň Czech Rep.	88	D8	49 45N	13 25E
Po r. Italy	89	C6	45 00N	10 00E
Pocatello Idaho USA	70	D5	42 35N	112 26W
Pochutla Mexico	74	E3	15 45N	96 30W
Podgorica Montenegro	89	G5	42 28N	19 17E
Podkamennaya (Stony) Tunguska r. Russia	95	M9	62 00N	97 30E
Podol'sk Russia	94	F8	55 23N	37 32E
Pohang South Korea	101	P6	36 00N	129 26E
Point Arena c. California USA	72	B4	39 57N	123 45W
Point Arguello c. California USA	72	C2	34 34N	120 39W
Point Buchon c. California USA	72	C2	35 15N	120 55W
Point Conception c. California USA	72	C2	34 27N	120 28W
Pointe-à-Pitre Guadeloupe	74	Q9	16 14N	61 32W
Point-Noire tn. Congo	108	G7	4 46S	11 53E
Point Reyes c. California USA	72	B4	38 00N	123 01W
Point Roberts c. Washington USA	42	H4	49 00N	123 06W
Point Sur c. California USA	72	C3	36 19N	121 53W
Poitiers Fr.	87	F7	46 35N	0 20E
Pokhara Nepal	98	E5	28 14N	83 58E
Pok Wai HK China	100	B2	22 28N	114 03E
POLAND	88	E10		
Pollensa Spain	87	G3	39 52N	3 01E
Polýgyros Greece	89	J4	40 23N	23 25E
Polynesia geog. reg. Pacific Ocean	115	K4	30 00S	166 00W
Pomeranian Bay Baltic Sea	88	E11	54 00N	14 00E
Pomona California USA	72	E2	34 04N	117 45W
Ponca City Oklahoma USA	71	G4	36 41N	97 04W
Ponce Puerto Rico	75	L3	18 01N	66 36W
Pondicherry India	98	D2	11 59N	79 50E
Pondicherry admin. India	98	D2	11 00N	79 45E
Ponferrada Sp.	87	B5	42 33N	6 35W
Ponta da Marca c. Angola	109	G4	16 33S	11 43E
Ponta das Salinas c. Angola	109	G5	12 50S	12 54E
Ponta Grossa Brazil	80	G8	25 07S	50 09W
Ponta Porã Brazil	80	F9	22 27S	55 39W
Pontchartrain, Lake Louisiana USA	71	H3	30 00N	90 00W
Ponte Leccia Fr.	87	K5	42 28N	9 12E
Pontevedra Sp.	87	A5	42 25N	8 39W
Pontiac Michigan USA	51	K2	42 38N	83 18W
Pontianak Indonesia	103	D3	0 05S	109 16E
Pontivy Fr.	86	D8	48 04N	2 58W
Poole UK	86	E9	50 43N	1 59W
Pool Malebo l. CDR	108	H7	5 00S	17 00E
Popacatepetl mt. Mexico	74	E3	19 02N	98 38W
Popayán Col.	80	B14	2 27N	76 32W
Poplar Bluff tn. Missouri USA	71	H4	36 16N	90 25W
Popondetta PNG	110	H8	8 45S	148 15E
Porbandar India	98	B4	21 04N	69 40E
Porcupine River Alaska USA	64	B4	67 15N	144 00W
Pordenone Italy	89	D6	45 58N	12 39E
Porirua NZ	111	E4	41 08S	174 50E
Poronaysk Russia	95	S6	49 13N	143 05E
Porsgrunn Norway	86	K13	59 10N	9 40E
Portadown UK	86	B11	54 26N	6 27W
Portal North Dakota USA	47	F1	49 01N	102 34W
Portalegre Port.	87	B3	39 17N	7 25W
Portales New Mexico USA	70	F3	34 12N	103 20W
Port Alexander Alaska USA	42	C5	56 13N	134 40W
Port Allegany tn. Pennsylvania USA	52	H1	41 49N	78 17W
Port Angeles Washington USA	70	B6	48 06N	123 26W
Port Antonio Jamaica	75	U14	18 10N	76 27W
Port Arthur Texas USA	71	H2	29 55N	93 56W
Port Augusta Aust.	110	F3	32 30S	137 27E
Port-au-Prince Haiti	75	K3	18 33N	72 20W
Port Austin Michigan USA	51	K3	44 02N	82 59W
Port Blair Andaman Islands	99	G2	11 40N	92 44E
Port Canning tn. India	99	K9	22 19N	88 40E
Port Chalmers NZ	111	C2	45 49S	170 37E
Port Clinton Ohio USA	51	K1	41 30N	82 56W
Port-de-Paix Haiti	75	K3	19 56N	72 52W
Port Elizabeth RSA	109	K1	33 58S	25 36E
Porterville California USA	72	D3	36 03N	119 08W
Port Gentil Gabon	108	F7	0 40S	8 50E
Port Harcourt Nigeria	108	F8	4 43N	7 05E
Port Hedland Aust.	110	B5	20 24S	118 36E
Port Huron Michigan USA	71	K5	42 59N	82 28W
Portimaõ Port.	87	A2	37 08N	8 32W
Port Island HK China	100	D2	22 30N	114 21E
Port Jervis New York USA	73	C2	41 23N	74 41W
Port Kaituma Guyana	80	F15	7 44N	59 53W
Portland Aust.	110	G2	38 21S	141 38E
Portland Maine USA	71	M5	43 41N	70 18W
Portland Michigan USA	52	B2	42 52N	84 53W
Portland Oregon USA	70	B6	45 32N	122 40W
Portland Canal sd. Alaska USA	42	E4	55 00N	130 10W
Portland Point Jamaica	75	U13	17 42N	77 11W
Portlaoise RoI	86	B10	53 02N	7 17W
Port Lincoln Aust.	110	F3	34 43S	135 49E
Port Macquarie Aust.	110	J3	31 28S	152 25E
Port Maria Jamaica	75	U14	18 22N	76 54W
Port Morant Jamaica	75	U13	17 53N	76 20W
Port Moresby PNG	110	H8	9 30S	147 07E
Port Nolloth RSA	109	H2	29 17S	16 51E
Porto Alegre Brazil	81	G7	30 03S	51 10W
Porto Amboim Angola	109	G5	10 47S	13 43E
Portobelo Panama	75	Y3	9 33N	79 37W
Port-of-Spain Trinidad and Tobago	75	V15	10 38N	61 31W
Pôrto Grande Brazil	80	G14	0 43N	51 23W
Porto Novo Benin	108	E9	6 30N	2 47E
Porto Tórres Italy	89	B4	40 51N	8 24E
Porto-Vecchio France	87	K4	41 35N	9 16E
Pôrto Velho Brazil	80	E12	8 45S	63 54W
Portoviejo Ecuador	80	A13	1 07S	80 28W
Port Pirie Aust.	110	F3	33 11S	138 01E
Portree UK	86	B12	57 24N	6 12W
Port Said Egypt	109	S4	31 17N	32 18E
Port Shelter b. HK China	100	C2	22 21N	114 18E
Portsmouth Dominica	74	Q8	15 35N	61 28W
Portsmouth UK	86	E9	50 48N	1 05W
Portsmouth New Hampshire USA	71	M5	43 03N	70 47W
Portsmouth Virginia USA	71	L4	36 50N	76 20W
Port Sudan Sudan	108	M11	19 38N	37 07E
PORTUGAL	87	A3		
Posadas Argentina	80	F8	27 27S	55 50W
Potenza Italy	89	E4	40 38N	15 48E
Potiskum Nigeria	108	G10	11 40N	11 03E
Po Toi i. HK China	100	C1	22 10N	114 16E
Potomac r. Maryland USA	71	L4	39 10N	77 30W
Potosí Bolivia	80	D10	19 34S	65 45W
Potsdam Germany	88	D10	52 24N	13 04E
Potsdam New York USA	51	P3	44 40N	74 59W
Poughkeepsie New York USA	71	M5	41 43N	73 56W
Pouthisat Cambodia	103	C6	12 27N	103 40E
Poway California USA	72	E1	32 57N	117 01W
Powell, Lake USA	70	D4	37 00N	110 00W
Powers Lake tn. North Dakota USA	47	F1	48 34N	102 39W
Poyang Hu l. China	101	M4	29 00N	116 30E
Poza Rica Mexico	74	E4	20 34N	97 26W
Poznań Poland	88	F10	52 25N	16 53E
Prague Czech Rep.	88	E9	50 06N	14 26E
Prairie Dog Town Fork r. USA	70	F3	34 00N	101 00W
Prato Italy	89	C5	43 53N	11 06E
Pratt Kansas USA	71	G4	37 40N	98 45W
Přerov Czech Rep.	88	F8	49 28N	17 30E
Prescott Arizona USA	70	D3	34 34N	112 28W
Presidencia Roque Sáenz Peña Argentina	80	E8	6 45S	60 30W
Presidente Prudente Brazil	80	G9	22 09S	51 24W
Prešov Slovakia	88	H8	49 00N	21 10E
Prespansko ezero l. Europe	89	H4	41 00N	21 00E
Presque Isle tn. Maine USA	71	N6	46 42N	68 01W
Preston UK	86	D10	53 46N	2 42W
Pretoria RSA	109	K2	25 45S	28 12E
Préveza Greece	89	H3	38 59N	20 45E
Příbram Czech Rep.	88	E8	49 42N	14 01E
Price Utah USA	70	D4	39 35N	110 49W
Price r. Utah USA	70	D4	39 00N	110 00W
Prieska RSA	109	J2	29 40S	22 45E
Priest Lake Idaho USA	43	M1	49 45N	116 50W
Priestly Mountain Maine USA	53	S6	46 34N	69 23W
Priest River tn. Idaho USA	43	M1	48 11N	116 55W
Prijedor Bosnia-Herzegovina	89	F6	45 00N	16 41E
Prilep FYROM	89	H4	41 20N	21 32E
Prince Edward Island Indian Ocean	113	C2	46 30S	37 20E
Prince of Wales Island Alaska USA	42	D4	56 00N	132 00W
Princess Elizabeth Land geog. reg. Antarctica	117		72 00S	80 00E
Príncipe i. Gulf of Guinea	108	F8	1 37N	7 27E
Prinzapolca Nicaragua	75	H2	13 19N	83 35W
Priština Kosovo	89	H5	42 39N	21 20E
Prizren Kosovo	89	H5	42 12N	20 43E
Probolinggo Indonesia	103	E2	7 45S	113 12E
Progreso Mexico	74	G4	21 20N	89 40W
Prokop'yevsk Russia	95	L7	53 55N	86 45E
Propriá Brazil	80	K11	10 15S	36 51W
Providence Rhode Island USA	71	M5	41 50N	71 28W
Providence, Cape NZ	111	A2	46 01S	166 28E
Provideniya Russia	95	W9	64 30N	73 11E
Provincetown Massachusetts USA	73	E3	42 03N	70 12W
Provo Utah USA	70	D5	40 15N	111 40W
Prudhoe Bay tn. Alaska USA	64	A5	70 05N	148 20W
Pruszków Poland	88	H10	52 10N	20 47E
Prut r. Romania	88	K8	47 00N	28 00E
Przemyśl Poland	88	J8	49 48N	22 48E
Przeworsk Poland	88	J9	50 04N	22 30
Przheval'sk Kyrgyzstan	94	K5	42 31N	78 22E
Pskov Russia	94	E8	57 48N	28 26E
Pucallpa Peru	80	C12	8 21S	74 33W
Puebla Mexico	74	E3	19 03N	98 10W
Pueblo Colorado USA	70	F4	38 17N	104 38W
Puerto Aisén Chile	81	C4	45 27S	72 58W
Puerto Armuelles Panama	75	H1	8 19N	82 51W
Puerto Ayacucho Venezuela	80	D15	5 39N	67 32W
Puerto Barrios Guatemala	74	G3	15 41N	88 32W
Puerto Berrio Col.	80	C15	6 28N	74 28W
Puerto Cabello Venezuela	80	D16	10 29N	68 02W
Puerto Cabezas Nicaragua	75	H2	14 02N	83 24W
Puerto Carreño Col.	80	D15	6 08N	69 27W
Puerto Cortés Honduras	74	G3	15 50N	87 55W
Puerto de Morelos Mexico	74	G4	20 49N	86 52W
Puerto Escondido Mexico	74	E3	15 52N	97 02W
Puerto La Cruz Venezuela	80	E16	10 14N	64 40W
Puertollano Sp.	87	C3	38 41N	4 07W
Puerto Maldonado Peru	80	D11	12 37S	69 11W
Puerto Montt Chile	81	C5	41 28S	73 00W
Puerto Natales Chile	81	C3	51 41S	72 15W
Puerto Penasco Mexico	74	B6	31 20N	113 35W
Puerto Pilón Panama	75	Y2	9 21N	79 48W
Puerto Plata Dom. Rep.	75	K3	19 47N	70 42W
Puerto Princesa Philippines	103	F5	9 46N	118 45E
PUERTO RICO	75	L3		
Puerto Rico Trench Atlantic Ocean	116	B9	21 00N	65 00W
Puerto Santa Cruz Argentina	81	D3	50 03S	68 35W
Puerto Vallarta Mexico	74	C4	20 36N	105 15W
Pukekohe NZ	111	E6	37 12S	174 54E
Pula Croatia	89	D6	44 52N	13 52E
Pulacayo Bolivia	80	D9	20 25S	66 41W
Pulau Bangka i. Indonesia	103	D3	2 30S	107 00E
Pulau Belitung i. Indonesia	103	D3	2 30S	107 30E
Pulau Dolak i. Indonesia	110	F8	7 45S	138 15E
Pulau Enggano i. Indonesia	103	C2	5 20S	102 20E
Pulau Nias i. Indonesia	103	B4	1 00N	97 30E
Pulau Simeulue i. Indonesia	103	B4	2 30N	96 00E
Pullman Washington USA	70	C6	46 46N	117 09W
Pune India	98	C3	18 34N	73 58E
Punjab admin. India	98	D6	30 40N	75 30E
Puno Peru	80	C10	15 53S	70 03W
Punta Alta Argentina	81	E6	38 50S	62 00W
Punta Arenas Chile	81	C3	53 10S	70 56W
Punta del Mona c. Nicaragua	75	H2	11 36N	83 37W
Punta Eugenia c. Mexico	74	A5	27 50N	115 05W
Punta Galera c. Ecuador	80	A14	0 49N	80 03W
Punta Gallinas c. Col.	80	C16	12 27N	71 44W
Punta Gorda Belize	74	G3	16 10N	88 45W
Punta Manzanillo c. Panama	75	Y3	9 37N	79 36W
Punta Negra c. Peru	80	A12	6 06S	81 09W
Puntarenas Costa Rica	75	H2	10 00N	85 00W
Puntcak Jaya mt. Indonesia	110	F9	4 05S	137 09E
Punto Fijo Venezuela	80	C16	11 50N	70 16W
Puquio Peru	80	C11	14 44S	74 07W
Pur r. Russia	95	K10	67 00N	77 30E
Puri India	99	F3	19 49N	85 54E
Purnia India	99	F5	25 47N	87 28E
Purus r. Brazil	80	D12	7 00S	65 00W
Pusan South Korea	101	P6	35 05N	129 02E
Putoran Mountains Russia	95	M10	68 00N	95 00E
Puttalam Sri Lanka	98	D1	8 02N	79 50E
Putumayo r. Col./Peru	80	C13	2 30S	72 30W
Puy de Sancy mt. Fr.	87	G6	45 32N	2 48E
Pyasina r. Russia	95	L11	71 00N	90 00E
Pyatigorsk Russia	94	G5	44 04N	43 06E
Pyè Myanmar	103	B7	18 50N	95 14E
Pyinmana Myanmar	103	B7	19 45N	96 12E
Pymatuning Lake res. Ohio/Pennsylvania USA	52	F1	41 35N	80 30W
Pyongyang North Korea	101	P6	39 00N	125 47E
Pyramid Lake Nevada USA	70	C5	40 00N	119 00W
Pyrénées mts. Fr./Sp.	87	F5	42 50N	0 30E
Pýrgos Greece	89	H2	37 40N	21 27E
Pýrgos Greece	89	K1	35 00N	25 10E
Pysht Washington USA	42	H4	48 08N	124 25W

Q

Name	Page	Grid	Lat	Long
Qaidam Pendi China	100	G6	37 30N	94 00E
Qanâ el Manzala can. Egypt	109	R4	31 21N	31 56E
Qasr-e-Shīrīn Iraq	96	E5	34 32N	45 35E
Qasr Farâfra Egypt	108	K13	27 03N	28 00E
QATAR	97	F4		
Qatrāna Jordan	96	P10	31 14N	36 03E
Qattara Depression Egypt	108	K13	24 00N	27 30E
Qazvīn Iran	97	E6	36 16N	50 00E
Qezi'ot Israel	96	N10	30 53N	34 28E
Qiemo China	100	F6	38 08N	85 33E
Qila Saifullah Pakistan	98	B6	30 42N	68 30E
Qilian Shan mts. China	101	H6	39 00N	98 00E
Qingdao China	101	N6	36 04N	120 22E
Qinghai Hu l. China	101	J6	37 00N	100 00E
Qingjiang China	101	M5	33 35N	119 02E
Qinhuangdao China	101	M6	39 55N	119 37E
Qin Ling mt. China	101	K5	34 00N	107 30E
Qionghai China	101	L2	19 17N	110 30E
Qiqihar China	101	N8	47 23N	124 00E
Qom Iran	97	F5	34 39N	50 57E
Qomisheh Iran	97	F5	32 01N	51 55E
Quang Ngai Vietnam	103	D7	15 00N	108 50E
Quang Tri Vietnam	103	D7	16 46N	107 11E
Quanzhou China	101	M3	24 53N	118 36E
Quarry Bay tn. HK China	100	C1	22 17N	114 13E
Queanbeyan Aust.	110	H2	35 24S	149 17E
Queen Mary Land geog. reg. Antarctica	117		70 00S	90 00E
Queens admin. New York USA	73	D2	40 47N	73 50W
Queensland state Aust.	110	G5	23 00S	143 00E
Queenstown Aust.	110	H1	42 07S	145 33E
Queenstown NZ	111	B2	45 02S	168 40E
Quelimane Mozambique	109	M4	17 53S	36 51E
Querétaro Mexico	74	D4	20 38N	100 23W
Quetta Pakistan	98	B6	30 15N	67 00E
Quezaltenango Guatemala	74	F2	14 50N	91 30W
Quezon City Philippines	103	G6	14 39N	121 02E
Quibala Angola	109	G5	10 48S	14 59E
Quibdó Col.	80	B15	5 40N	76 38W
Quiberon Fr.	87	D7	47 29N	3 07W
Quilá Mexico	74	C4	24 26N	107 11W
Quillacollo Bolivia	80	D10	17 26S	66 16W
Quilon India	98	D1	8 53N	76 38E
Quilpie Aust.	110	G4	26 35S	144 14E
Quimper Fr.	86	C7	48 00N	4 06W
Quincy Illinois USA	71	H4	39 55N	91 22W
Quincy Massachusetts USA	73	E3	42 15N	71 01W
Qui Nhon Vietnam	103	D6	13 47N	109 11E
Quito Ecuador	80	B13	0 14S	78 30W
Quixadá Brazil	80	K13	4 57S	39 04W
Qullai Garmo mt. Tajikistan	94	K4	38 59N	72 01E
Quseir Egypt	108	L13	26 04N	34 15E

R

Name	Page	Grid	Lat	Long
Raas Caseyr c. Somalia	108	Q10	11 50N	51 16E
Raba Indonesia	103	F2	8 27S	118 45E
Rabat-Salé Morocco	108	C14	34 02N	6 51W
Rabaul PNG	110	J9	4 13S	152 11E
Rabnabad Islands Bangladesh	99	L8	21 58N	90 24E
Rach Gia Vietnam	103	D5	10 00N	105 05E
Racibórz Poland	88	G9	50 05N	18 10E
Radford Virginia USA	71	K4	37 07N	80 34W
Radom Poland	88	H9	51 26N	21 10E
Radom Sudan	108	J9	9 58N	24 53E
Radomsko Poland	88	G9	51 04N	19 25E
Radstadt Austria	89	D7	47 23N	13 28E
Raeside, Lake Aust.	110	C4	29 00S	122 00E
Raetihi NZ	111	E5	39 26S	175 17E
Rafah Egypt	96	N10	31 18N	34 15E
Rafsanjān Iran	97	G5	30 25N	56 00E
Ragusa Italy	89	E2	36 56N	14 44E
Rahimyar Khan Pakistan	98	C5	28 22N	70 20E
Raichur India	98	D3	16 15N	77 20E
Raiganj India	99	K10	25 37N	88 12E
Raigarh India	98	E4	21 53N	83 28E
Railroad Valley Nevada USA	72	F4	38 18N	115 38W
Rainier, Mount Washington USA	70	B6	46 25N	121 45W

Raipur India 98 E4 21 16N 81 42E
Raisin, River Michigan USA 52 C1 41 55N 83 40W
Rajahmundry India 98 E3 17 01N 81 52E
Rajapalaiyam India 98 D1 9 26N 77 36E
Rajasthan *admin.* India 98 C5 26 30N 73 00E
Rajkot India 98 C4 21 18N 70 53E
Rajshahi Bangladesh 99 K10 24 24N 88 40E
Raleigh North Carolina USA 71 L4 35 46N 78 39W
Ralik Chain *is.* Pacific Ocean 114 G8 7 30N 167 30E
Ramat Gan Israel 96 N10 32 04N 34 48E
Ramgarh Bangladesh 99 L9 22 59N 91 43E
Râmnicu Vâlcea Romania 89 K6 45 06N 24 21E
Rampur Himachal Pradesh India 98 D6 31 26N 77 37E
Rampur Uttar Pradesh India 98 D5 28 50N 79 05E
Ramtha Jordan 96 N11 32 34N 36 00E
Rancagua Chile 81 C7 34 10S 70 45W
Ranchi India 99 F4 23 22N 85 20E
Randers Denmark 88 C12 56 28N 10 03E
Rangeley Maine USA 53 R4 44 58N 70 40W
Rangiora NZ 111 D3 43 19S 172 36E
Rangpur Bangladesh 99 K10 25 45N 89 21E
Rann of Kachchh *geog. reg.* India/Pakistan 98 B4/C4 24 00N 69 00E
Rapid City South Dakota USA 70 F5 44 06N 103 14W
Rapid River *tn.* Michigan USA 51 H3 45 56N 86 58W
Ra's al Hadd *c.* Oman 97 G3 22 31N 59 45E
Ra's al Khaymah UAE 97 G4 25 48N 55 56E
Râs Banâs *c.* Egypt 108 M12 23 58N 35 50E
Ras Dashen Terara *mt.* Ethiopia 108 M10 13 15N 38 27E
Râs el Barr Egypt 109 R5 31 32N 31 42E
Râs el 'Ish Egypt 109 S4 31 07N 32 18E
Ra's Fartak *c.* Yemen 97 F2 15 20N 52 12E
Rasht Iran 97 E6 37 18N 49 38E
Ras Lanuf Libya 108 H14 30 31N 18 34E
Ra's Madrakah *c.* Oman 97 G2 18 58N 57 50E
Ras Nouadhibou *c.* Mauritania 108 A12 20 53N 17 01W
Ratak Chain *is.* Pacific Ocean 114 H9 10 00N 172 30E
Rat Buri Thailand 103 B6 13 30N 99 50E
Ratlam India 98 D4 23 18N 75 06E
Ratno Ukraine 88 K9 51 40N 24 32E
Raton New Mexico USA 70 F4 36 45N 104 27W
Raurkela India 99 E4 22 16N 85 01E
Ravenna Italy 89 D6 44 25N 12 12E
Ravensburg Germany 88 B7 47 47N 9 37E
Ravensthorpe Aust. 110 C3 33 34S 120 01E
Ravi *r.* Pakistan 98 C6 31 00N 73 00E
Rawalpindi Pakistan 98 C6 33 40N 73 08E
Rawlins Wyoming USA 70 E5 41 46N 107 16W
Rawson Argentina 81 E5 43 15S 65 06W
Raymondville Texas USA 71 G2 26 30N 97 48W
Raystown Lake Pennsylvania USA 73 A2 40 10N 78 10W
Razgrad Bulgaria 89 L5 43 31N 26 33E
Reading UK 86 E9 51 28N 0 59W
Reading Pennsylvania USA 71 L5 40 20N 75 55W
Rebun-tō *i.* Japan 102 D4 45 25N 141 04E
Recherche, Archipelago of the *is.* Aust. 110 C3 35 00S 122 50E
Recife Brazil 80 L12 8 06S 34 53W
Reconquista Argentina 81 F8 29 08S 59 38W
Red *r.* USA 71 G3 34 00N 95 00W
Red *r.* USA 71 G6 46 00N 97 00W
Red Bluff California USA 70 B5 40 11N 122 16W
Redding California USA 70 B5 40 35N 122 24W
Redlands California USA 72 E2 34 03N 117 10W
Redon Fr. 86 D7 47 39N 2 05W
Redondo Beach *tn.* California USA 72 D1 33 51N 118 24W
Red Sea Middle East 96 C4/C2 27 00N 35 00E
Red Wing Minnesota USA 71 H5 44 33N 92 31W
Redwood City California USA 72 B3 37 28N 122 15W
Reed City Michigan USA 51 J2 43 53N 85 30W
Reedley California USA 72 D3 36 35N 119 27W
Reedsport Oregon USA 70 B5 43 42N 124 05W
Reefton NZ 111 C3 42 07S 171 52E
Regensburg Germany 88 D8 49 01N 12 07E
Reggio di Calabria Italy 89 E3 38 06N 15 39E
Reggio nell'Emilia Italy 89 C6 44 42N 10 37E
Rehovot Israel 96 N10 31 54N 34 46E
Reims Fr. 86 H8 49 15N 4 02E
Reinosa Sp. 87 C5 43 01N 4 09W
Rembang Indonesia 103 E2 6 45S 111 22E
Rendsburg Germany 88 B11 54 19N 9 39E
Rennes Fr. 86 E8 48 06N 1 40W
Reno Nevada USA 70 C4 39 32N 119 49W
Republic Washington USA 43 L1 48 39N 118 45W
REPUBLIC OF IRELAND 86 B10
REPUBLIC OF SOUTH AFRICA 109 J1/J2
Repulse Bay HK China 100 C1 22 14N 114 13E
Resistencia Argentina 80 F8 27 28S 59 00W
Reşiţa Romania 89 H6 45 16N 21 55E
Réthymno Greece 89 K1 35 23N 24 28E
Réunion *i.* Indian Ocean 113 E4 21 00S 55 30E
Reus Sp. 87 F4 41 10N 1 06E
Revillagigedo Island Alaska USA 42 E4 55 30N 131 30W
Rewa India 98 E4 24 32N 81 18E
Reykjanes Ridge Atlantic Ocean 116 E12 57 00N 33 00W
Reynosa Mexico 74 E5 26 05N 98 18W
Rhein *r.* Germany 88 A8 50 30N 8 00E
Rheine Germany 88 A10 52 17N 7 26E
Rhinelander Wisconsin USA 51 G3 45 38N 89 24W
Rhode Island *state* USA 71 M5 41 00N 71 00W
Rhône *r.* Switz./Fr. 87 H6 45 00N 4 50E
Ribe Denmark 88 B11 55 20N 8 47E
Ribeirão Prêto Brazil 80 H9 21 09S 47 48W
Riberalta Bolivia 80 D11 10 59S 66 06W
Richgrove California USA 72 D2 35 46N 119 04W
Richland Washington USA 70 C6 46 17N 119 17W
Richmond Aust. 110 G5 20 45S 143 05E
Richmond NZ 111 D4 41 31S 173 39E
Richmond California USA 70 B4 37 46N 122 20W
Richmond Indiana USA 71 K4 39 50N 84 51W
Richmond New York USA 73 H1 40 36N 74 10W
Richmond Virginia USA 71 L4 37 34N 77 27W
Richmondville New York USA 73 C3 42 38N 74 34W
Ridgecrest California USA 72 E2 35 37N 117 43W
Ridgeway Pennsylvania USA 52 H1 41 25N 78 40W
Riesa Germany 88 D9 51 18N 13 18E
Rieti Italy 89 D5 42 24N 12 51E
Riga Latvia 88 K12 56 53N 24 08E
Riga, Gulf of Estonia/Latvia 88 J12 57 30N 23 30E
Rijeka Croatia 89 E6 45 20N 14 27E
Rimini Italy 89 D6 44 03N 12 34E
Ringgold Isles *is.* Fiji 114 V16 16 10S 179 50W
Ringkøbing Denmark 88 B12 56 06N 8 15E
Ringkøbing Fjord Denmark 88 B11 56 00N 8 00E
Riobamba Ecuador 80 B13 1 44S 78 40W
Rio Branco *tn.* Brazil 80 D12 9 59S 67 49W
Río Cuarto *tn.* Argentina 81 E7 33 08S 64 20W
Rio de Janeiro *tn.* Brazil 80 I8 22 53S 43 17W
Rio de Janeiro *admin.* Brazil 80 J9 22 00S 42 30W
Río de la Plata *est.* Uruguay/Argentina 81 F6/F7 35 00S 57 00W
Rio de Para *r.* Brazil 80 H13 1 00S 48 00W
Río Gallegos *tn.* Argentina 81 D3 51 35S 68 10W
Rio Grande *r.* Mexico/USA 70 E3/F3 30 00N 105 00W
Río Grande *tn.* Argentina 81 D3 53 45S 67 46W
Rio Grande *tn.* Brazil 81 G7 32 03S 52 08W
Río Grande *tn.* Mexico 74 D4 23 50N 103 02W
Rio Grande do Norte *admin.* Brazil 80 K12 6 00S 37 00W
Rio Grande do Sul *admin.* Brazil 81 G8 28 00S 52 30W
Rio Grande Rise Atlantic Ocean 116 E3 32 00S 36 00W
Riohacha Col. 80 C16 11 34N 72 58W
Rio Verde *tn.* Brazil 80 G10 17 50S 50 55W
Río Verde *tn.* Mexico 74 D4 21 58N 100 00W
Rishiri-tō *i.* Japan 102 D4 45 10N 141 20E
Ritter, Mount California USA 70 C4 37 40N 119 15W
Rivera Uruguay 81 F7 30 52S 55 30W
River Cess *tn.* Liberia 108 C9 5 28N 9 32W
Riverside California USA 70 C3 33 59N 117 22W
Riverton NZ 111 B1 46 22S 168 01E
Rivière-Pilote *tn.* Martinique 74 R12 14 29N 60 54W
Rivne Ukraine 88 L9 50 39N 26 10E
Riyadh Saudi Arabia 97 E3 24 39N 46 46E
Roanne Fr. 87 H7 46 02N 4 05E
Roanoke Virginia USA 71 L4 37 15N 79 58W
Robertsport Liberia 108 B9 6 45N 11 22W
Robin's Nest *mt.* HK China 100 C3 22 33N 114 11E
Roca Alijos *is.* Mexico 115 Q10 24 59N 115 49W
Rochefort Fr. 87 E6 45 57N 0 58W
Roche Harbor *tn.* Washington USA 42 H4 48 38N 123 06W
Rochester Minnesota USA 71 H5 84 01N 92 27W
Rochester New Hampshire USA 73 E3 43 18N 70 59W
Rochester New York USA 71 L5 43 12N 77 37W
Rockall Bank Atlantic Ocean 116 G12 58 00N 15 00W
Rockaway Beach New York USA 73 J1 40 33N 73 55W
Rockaway Inlet New York USA 73 J1 40 34N 73 56W
Rockford Illinois USA 71 J5 42 16N 89 06W
Rockhampton Aust. 110 J5 23 22S 150 32E
Rock Hill *tn.* South Carolina USA 71 K3 34 55N 81 01W
Rockin California USA 72 C4 38 47N 121 18W
Rock Island *tn.* Illinois USA 71 H5 41 30N 90 34W
Rock Lake *tn.* North Dakota USA 49 C1 48 49N 99 13W
Rockport Washington USA 42 H4 48 27N 121 37W
Rock Springs *tn.* Wyoming USA 70 E5 41 35N 109 13W
Rockville Maryland USA 73 B1 39 04N 77 08W
Rocky Mount *tn.* North Carolina USA 71 L4 35 46N 77 48W
Rodez Fr. 87 G6 44 21N 2 34E
Rodopi Planina *mts.* Bulgaria 89 K4 41 00N 25 00E
Rodrigues *i.* Indian Ocean 113 F5 19 43S 63 26E
Rogers City Michigan USA 51 K3 45 25N 83 49W
Rogers Lake California USA 72 E2 34 55N 117 48W
Rolette North Dakota USA 49 C1 48 40N 99 51W
Rolla Missouri USA 71 H4 37 56N 91 55W
Rolla North Dakota USA 49 C1 48 52N 99 37W
Roman Romania 89 L7 46 56N 26 56E
ROMANIA 88 H6
Rome Italy 89 D4 41 53N 12 30E
Rome Georgia USA 71 J3 34 01N 85 02W
Rome New York USA 71 L5 43 13N 75 28W
Ronda Sp. 87 C2 36 45N 5 10W
Rondônia *admin.* Brazil 80 E11 11 30S 63 00W
Rondonópolis Brazil 80 G10 16 29S 54 37W
Ronne Ice Shelf Antarctica 117 77 00S 60 00W
Roosevelt Minnesota USA 49 E1 48 48N 95 06W
Roraima *admin.* Brazil 80 E14 2 30N 62 30W
Rosamond Lake California USA 72 D2 34 50N 118 05W
Rosario Argentina 81 E7 33 00S 60 40W
Rosário Brazil 80 J13 3 00S 44 15W
Rosario Mexico 74 A6 30 02N 115 46W
Rosario Mexico 74 C4 23 00N 105 51W
Rosario Strait *sd.* Washington USA 42 H4 48 25N 123 00W
Rosarito Mexico 74 B5 28 38N 114 02W
Roscoff Fr. 86 D8 48 43N 3 59W
Roscommon Michigan USA 51 J3 44 30N 84 35W
Roseau Dominica 74 Q8 15 18N 61 23W
Roseau Minnesota USA 49 E1 48 54N 95 43W
Roseburg Oregon USA 70 B5 43 13N 123 21W
Roselle New Jersey USA 73 H1 40 40N 74 16W
Rosenheim Germany 88 D7 47 51N 12 09E
Roseville California USA 72 C4 38 43N 121 20W
Roseville Michigan USA 52 D2 42 29N 82 52W
Rossano Italy 89 F3 39 35N 16 38E
Ross Ice Shelf Antarctica 117 80 00S 180 00
Ross Lake Washington USA 42 H4 48 50N 121 05W
Ross Lake National Recreation Area Washington USA 42 H4 48 50N 121 00W
Rosslare RoI 86 B10 52 15N 6 22W
Rosso Mauritania 108 A11 16 29N 15 53W
Ross Sea Antarctica 117 75 00S 180 00
Rostock Germany 88 D11 54 06N 12 09E
Rostov-na-Donu Russia 94 F6 47 15N 39 45E
Roswell New Mexico USA 70 F3 33 24N 104 33W
Rotorua NZ 111 F5 38 08S 176 14E
Rotterdam Neths. 86 H9 51 54N 4 28E
Roubaix Fr. 86 G9 50 42N 3 10E
Rouen Fr. 86 F8 49 26N 1 05E
Round Mountain *tn.* Nevada USA 72 E4 38 43N 117 03W
Rovigo Italy 89 C6 45 04N 11 47E
Rowta India 99 M11 26 50N 92 20E
Roxas Philippines 103 G6 11 36N 122 45E
Roxburgh NZ 111 B2 45 33S 169 19E
Royal Oak Michigan USA 52 C2 42 29N 83 09W
Royan Fr. 87 E6 45 38N 1 02W
Rub Al Khālī *d.* Saudi Arabia 97 E2 19 30N 48 00E
Rubtsovsk Russia 94 L7 51 43N 81 11E
Rudnyy Kazakhstan 94 J7 53 00N 63 05E
Rudyard Montana USA 46 G1 48 34N 110 33W
Rufiji *r.* Tanzania 109 M6 7 30S 38 40E
Rugao China 101 N5 32 27N 120 35E
Rugby UK 86 E10 52 23N 1 15W
Rügen *i.* Germany 88 D11 54 00N 14 00E
Rukwa, Lake Tanzania 109 L6 8 00S 33 00E
Rumford Maine USA 57 E1 44 33N 70 34W
Rumoi Japan 102 D3 43 57N 141 40E
Runanga NZ 111 C3 42 24S 171 15E
Ruse Bulgaria 89 L5 43 50N 25 59E
Rusk Texas USA 71 G3 31 49N 95 11W
Russas Brazil 80 K13 4 56S 38 02W
Russell NZ 111 E7 35 16S 174 07E
Russell Kansas USA 71 G4 38 54N 98 51W
Russian *r.* California USA 72 B4 38 52N 123 03W
RUSSIAN FEDERATION 94/95
Ruston Louisiana USA 71 H3 32 32N 92 39W
Ruth Nevada USA 70 D4 39 16N 114 59W
Rutland Vermont USA 71 M5 43 37N 72 59W
Rutog China 100 D5 33 27N 79 43E
Ruvuma *r.* Tanzania/Mozambique 109 M5 11 30S 38 00E
Ružomberok Slovakia 88 G8 49 04N 19 15E
RWANDA 108 K7
Ryazan' Russia 94 F7 54 37N 39 43E
Rybinsk Russia 94 F8 58 03N 38 50E
Rybinskoye Vodokhranilische *res.* Russia 94 F8 59 00N 38 00E
Rybnik Poland 88 G9 50 07N 18 30E
Ryukyu Islands Japan 101 N4 27 30N 127 30E
Ryukyu Ridge Pacific Ocean 114 C10 25 50N 128 00E
Rzeszów Poland 88 J9 50 04N 22 00E

S

Saalfeld Germany 88 C9 50 39N 11 22E
Saarbrücken Germany 88 A8 49 15N 6 58E
Saaremaa *i.* Estonia 88 J13 58 20N 22 00E
Šabac Serbia 89 G6 44 45N 19 41E
Sabadell Sp. 87 G4 41 33N 2 07E
Sabah *admin.* Malaysia 103 F4/F5 5 00N 115 00E
Sabaloka Cataract Sudan 108 L11 16 19N 32 40E
Sabhā Libya 108 G13 27 02N 14 26E
Sabi *r.* Zimbabwe/Mozambique 109 L3 20 30S 33 00E
Sabinas Mexico 74 D5 27 50N 101 09W
Sabinas Hidalgo Mexico 74 D5 26 33N 100 10W
Sabine *r.* USA 71 H3 30 00N 94 00W
Sable, Cape Florida USA 71 K2 25 08N 80 07W
Sabor *r.* Port. 87 B4 41 22N 6 50W
Sabyā Saudi Arabia 96 D2 17 07N 42 39E
Sabzevār Iran 97 G6 36 15N 57 38E
Sacramento California USA 70 B4 38 32N 121 30W
Sacramento *r.* California USA 72 C4 38 05N 121 35W
Sacramento Mountains USA 70 E3 33 00N 105 00W
Sadiya India 99 H5 27 49N 95 38E
Sado *r.* Port. 87 A3 38 15N 8 30W
Sadoga-shima *i.* Japan 102 C2 38 20N 138 30E
Säffle Sweden 88 D13 59 08N 12 55E
Safi Morocco 108 C14 32 20N 9 17W
Saga Japan 102 B1 33 16N 130 18E
Sagamihara Japan 102 C2 35 34N 139 22E
Sagamore Massachusetts USA 73 E2 41 46N 70 31W
Sagar India 98 D4 23 50N 78 44E
Sage Creek *r.* Montana USA 46 G1 48 45N 110 40W
Saginaw Michigan USA 71 K5 43 25N 83 54W
Saginaw Bay Michigan USA 71 K5 44 00N 84 00W
Sagua la Grande Cuba 75 H4 22 48N 80 06W
Sagunto Sp. 87 E3 39 40N 0 17W
Sahara Desert North Africa 108/109 C12
Saharanpur India 98 D5 29 58N 77 33E
Sahiwal Pakistan 98 C6 30 41N 73 11E
Sahuaripa Mexico 74 C5 29 00N 109 13W
Sahuayo Mexico 74 D4 20 05N 102 42W
Saidpur Bangladesh 99 K10 25 48N 89 00E
Saikhoa Ghat India 99 H5 27 40N 95 35E
Sai Kung HK China 100 C2 22 23N 114 16E
St. Albans UK 86 E9 51 46N 0 21W
St. Albans New York USA 73 J1 40 42N 73 45W
St. Albans Vermont USA 57 D1 44 49N 73 07W
St. Andrews UK 86 D12 56 20N 2 48W
St. Ann's Bay *tn.* Jamaica 75 U14 18 26N 77 12W
St. Augustine Florida USA 71 K2 29 54N 81 19W
St. Barthélémy *i.* Lesser Antilles 74 P9 17 55N 62 50W
St-Brieuc Fr. 86 D8 48 31N 2 45W
St. Cloud Minnesota USA 71 H6 45 34N 94 10W
St. Croix *i.* W. Indies 75 M3 22 45N 65 00W
St. Croix *r.* USA 71 H6 46 00N 93 00W
St-Dié Fr. 86 J8 48 17N 6 57E
St-Dizier Fr. 86 H8 48 38N 4 58E
St. Elias, Mount Alaska USA 64 B3 60 12N 140 57W
Ste. Marie Martinique 74 R12 14 47N 61 00W
Saintes Fr. 87 E6 45 44N 0 38W
St-Étienne Fr. 87 H6 45 26N 4 23E
St. Eustatius *i.* Lesser Antilles 74 P9 17 30N 62 55W
St. Francis *r.* USA 71 H4 35 00N 90 00W
St. Gallen Switz. 87 K7 47 25N 9 23E
St-Gaudens Fr. 87 F5 43 07N 0 44E
St. George's Grenada 74 R11 12 04N 61 44W
St. George's Channel British Isles 86 B9 52 00N 6 00W
St. Helena *i.* Atlantic Ocean 116 H5 15 58S 5 43W
St. Helena Bay RSA 109 H1 32 00S 17 30E
St. Ignace Michigan USA 71 K6 45 53N 84 44W
St. John North Dakota USA 49 C1 48 57N 99 43W
St. John *r.* Liberia 108 C9 6 30N 9 40W
Saint John *r.* USA 71 N6 46 00N 69 00W
St. John's Antigua and Barbuda 74 Q9 17 08N 61 50W
St. Johns Michigan USA 52 B3 43 01N 84 31W
St. Joseph Missouri USA 71 H4 39 45N 94 51W
St. Joseph River Indiana/Ohio USA 52 B1 41 12N 84 55W
St. Kitts *i.* St. Kitts and Nevis 74 P9 17 21N 62 48W
ST. KITTS AND NEVIS 74 P9
St. Laurent French Guiana 80 G15 5 29N 54 03W
St. Lawrence Island Alaska USA 115 J14 63 15N 169 50W
St-Lô Fr. 86 E8 49 07N 1 05W
St. Louis Senegal 108 A11 16 01N 16 30W
St. Louis Missouri USA 71 H4 38 40N 90 15W
St. Louis River Minnesota USA 51 E4 47 20N 92 40W
ST. LUCIA 74 R11
St. Lucia Channel *sd.* Caribbean Sea 74 R12 14 09N 60 57W
St. Maarten Lesser Antilles 74 P10 18 04N 63 04W
St-Malo Fr. 86 D8 48 39N 2 00W
St. Martin Lesser Antilles 74 P10 18 04N 63 04W
St. Mary Montana USA 46 F1 48 44N 113 26W
St. Marys Pennsylvania USA 52 H1 41 25N 78 33W
St. Moritz Switz. 87 K7 46 30N 9 51E
St-Nazaire Fr. 87 D7 47 17N 2 12W
St-Omer Fr. 86 G9 50 45N 2 15E
St. Paul Minnesota USA 71 H5 45 00N 93 10W
St. Paul *r.* Liberia 108 B9/C9 7 10N 10 05W
St. Paul Rocks Atlantic Ocean 116 F7 0 23N 29 23W
St. Petersburg Russia 94 F8 59 55N 30 25E
St. Petersburg Florida USA 71 K2 27 45N 82 40W
St. Pölten Austria 88 E8 48 13N 15 37E
St-Quentin Fr. 86 G8 49 51N 3 17E
St. Thomas *i.* W. Indies 75 L3 18 00N 65 30W
St-Tropez Fr. 87 J5 43 16N 6 39E
St. Vincent *i.* St. Vincent and The Grenadines 74 R11 13 15N 61 12W
ST. VINCENT AND THE GRENADINES 74 R11
St. Vincent Passage *sd.* St. Lucia 74 R11 13 30N 61 00W
Sakai Japan 102 C1 34 35N 135 28E
Sākākah Saudi Arabia 96 D4 29 59N 40 12E
Sakakawea, Lake North Dakota USA 70 F6 48 00N 103 00W
Sakarya Turkey 96 B7 40 47N 30 23E
Sakarya *r.* Turkey 96 B7 40 05N 30 15E
Sakata Japan 102 C2 38 55N 139 51E
Sakhalin *i.* Russia 95 S7 50 00N 143 00E
Sakhalin Bay Russia 95 S7 54 00N 141 00E
Saki Nigeria 108 E9 8 39N 3 25E
Sala Sweden 88 F13 59 55N 16 38E
Salado *r.* Argentina 81 D6 35 00S 66 30W
Salado *r.* Argentina 81 E8 28 30S 62 30W
Şalalah Oman 97 F2 17 00N 54 04E
Salamanca Mexico 74 D4 20 34N 101 12W
Salamanca Sp. 87 C4 40 58N 5 40W
Salamanca New York USA 52 H2 42 10N 78 43W
Salay Goméz *i.* Pacific Ocean 115 R5 26 28S 105 28W
Saldus Latvia 88 J12 56 38N 22 30E

Salekhard Russia	94	J10	66 33N	66 35E
Salem India	98	D2	11 38N	78 08E
Salem Massachusetts USA	71	M5	42 32N	70 53W
Salem Oregon USA	70	B5	44 57N	123 01W
Salerno Italy	89	E4	40 40N	14 46E
Salgótarján Hungary	88	G8	49 05N	19 47E
Salgueiro Brazil	80	K12	8 04S	39 05W
Salima Malawi	109	L5	13 45S	34 29E
Salina Kansas USA	71	G4	38 53N	97 36W
Salinas Ecuador	80	A13	2 15S	80 58W
Salinas California USA	70	B4	36 39N	121 40W
Salinas *r.* California USA	72	C3	36 30N	121 40W
Salinas Grandes *l.* Argentina	81	D7/E8	30 00S	65 00W
Saline Michigan USA	52	C2	42 12N	83 46W
Salisbury UK	86	E9	51 05N	1 48W
Salisbury Maryland USA	71	L4	38 22N	75 37W
Salisbury North Carolina USA	71	K4	35 20N	80 30W
Salmon Idaho USA	70	D6	45 11N	113 55W
Salmon *r.* Idaho USA	70	C6	45 00N	116 00W
Salmon Reservoir New York USA	53	L3	43 32N	75 50W
Salmon River Mountains Idaho USA	70	C5	45 00N	115 00W
Salonta Romania	89	H7	46 49N	21 40E
Salt Jordan	96	N11	32 03N	35 44E
Salt *r.* Arizona USA	70	D3	34 00N	110 00W
Salta Argentina	80	D9	24 46S	65 28W
Salt Fork *r.* Texas/Oklahoma USA	70	F3	35 00N	100 00W
Saltillo Mexico	74	D5	25 30N	101 00W
Salt Lake City Utah USA	70	D5	40 45N	111 55W
Salto Uruguay	81	F7	31 27S	57 50W
Salton Sea *l.* California USA	70	C3	33 00N	116 00W
Salvador Brazil	80	K11	12 58S	38 29W
Salween *r.* China/Myanmar	103	B8	20 00N	103 00E
Salzburg Austria	88	D7	47 48N	13 03E
Salzgitter Germany	88	C10	52 13N	10 20E
Samani Japan	102	D3	42 07N	142 57E
Samar *i.* Philippines	103	G6	12 00N	125 00E
Samara Russia	94	H7	53 10N	50 10E
Samarinda Indonesia	103	F3	0 30S	117 09E
Samarkand Uzbekistan	94	J4	39 40N	66 57E
Sāmarrā' Iraq	96	D5	34 13N	43 52E
Sambalpur India	99	E4	21 28N	84 04E
Sambas Indonesia	103	D4	1 22N	109 15E
Sambor Ukraine	88	J8	49 31N	23 10E
SAMOA	114	J6		
Sámos *i.* Greece	89	L2	37 45N	26 45E
Samothráki *i.* Greece	89	K4	40 00N	25 00E
Samsun Turkey	96	C7	41 17N	36 22E
San Mali	108	C10	13 21N	4 57W
Sana Yemen	96	D2	15 23N	44 14E
Sanaga *r.* Cameroon	108	G8	4 30N	12 20E
Sanandaj Iran	97	E6	35 18N	47 01E
San Andrés Tuxtla Mexico	74	E3	18 28N	95 15W
San Angelo Texas USA	70	F3	31 28N	100 28W
San Antonio Chile	81	C7	33 35S	71 39W
San Antonio Texas USA	71	G2	29 25N	98 30W
San Antonio *r.* Texas USA	71	G2	29 00N	97 00W
San Antonio Oeste Argentina	81	E5	40 45S	64 58W
San Benito *r.* California USA	72	C3	36 45N	121 18W
San Bernardino California USA	70	C3	34 07N	117 18W
San Bernardo Chile	81	C7	33 37S	70 45W
San Carlos Venezuela	80	D15	9 39N	68 35W
San Carlos Luzon Philippines	103	G7	15 59N	120 22E
San Carlos Negros Philippines	103	G6	10 30N	123 29E
San Carlos de Bariloche Argentina	81	C5	41 11S	71 23W
San Carlos del Zulia Venezuela	80	C15	9 01N	71 58W
San Clemente California USA	72	E1	33 26N	117 36W
San Clemente Island California USA	70	C3	33 26N	117 36W
San Cristóbal Argentina	81	E7	30 20S	61 14W
San Cristóbal Mexico	74	F3	16 45N	92 40W
San Cristóbal Venezuela	80	C15	7 46N	72 15W
Sancti Spíritus Cuba	75	J4	21 55N	79 28W
Sandakan Malaysia	103	F5	5 52N	118 04E
Sanday *i.* UK	86	D13	59 15N	2 30W
Sandefjord Norway	86	L13	59 00N	10 15E
San Diego California USA	70	C3	32 45N	117 10W
Sandpoint *tn.* Idaho USA	70	C6	48 17N	116 34W
Sandusky Ohio USA	51	K1	41 27N	82 43W
Sandusky Bay Ohio USA	52	D1	41 30N	82 50W
Sandwip Island Bangladesh	99	L9	22 30N	91 25E
Sandy River Maine USA	53	R4	44 45N	70 12W
San Felipe Mexico	74	B6	31 03N	114 52W
San Felipe Venezuela	80	D16	10 25N	68 40W
San Feliú de Guixols Sp.	87	G4	41 47N	3 02E
San Fernando Mexico	74	A5	29 59N	115 10W
San Fernando Sp.	87	B2	36 28N	6 12W
San Fernando Trinidad and Tobago	75	V15	10 16N	61 28W
San Fernando California USA	72	D2	34 17N	118 27W
San Fernando de Apure Venezuela	80	D15	7 53N	67 15W
Sanford Florida USA	71	K2	28 49N	81 17W
San Francisco Argentina	81	E7	31 29S	62 06W
San Francisco Dom. Rep.	75	K3	19 19N	70 15W
San Francisco California USA	70	B4	37 45N	122 27W
San Francisco Bay California USA	72	B3	37 37N	122 15W
San Francisco del Oro Mexico	74	C5	26 52N	105 50W
Sangar Russia	95	Q9	64 02N	127 30E
Sanger California USA	72	D3	36 42N	119 33W
Sangha *r.* Africa	108	H8	2 00N	17 00E
Sangli India	98	C3	16 55N	74 37E
Sangre de Cristo Mountains New Mexico USA	70	E4	37 00N	105 00W
Sangre Grande Trinidad and Tobago	75	V15	10 35N	61 08W
Sangu *r.* Bangladesh	99	M9	22 10N	92 15E
San Jacinto Peak *mt.* California USA	72	E1	33 48N	116 40W
San Javier Bolivia	80	E10	16 22S	62 38W
San Joaquin *r.* California USA	70	B4	37 00N	120 00W
San José Costa Rica	75	H1	9 59N	84 04W
San José Uruguay	81	F7	34 27S	56 40W
San José California USA	70	B4	37 20N	121 55W
San José del Cabo Mexico	74	C4	23 01N	109 40W
San Juan Argentina	81	D7	31 33S	68 31W
San Juan Peru	80	B10	15 22S	75 07W
San Juan Puerto Rico	75	L3	18 29N	66 08W
San Juan *r.* USA	70	D4	37 00N	110 00W
San Juan Islands Washington USA	42	H4	48 30N	123 05W
San Juan Mountains Colorado USA	70	E4	37 50N	107 50W
San Julián Argentina	81	D4	49 17S	67 45W
Sankosh *r.* India/Bhutan	99	K11	26 55N	90 00E
Sankuru *r.* CDR	108	J7	4 00S	23 30E
Sanliurfa Turkey	96	C6	37 08N	38 45E
Sanlúcar de Barrameda Sp.	87	B2	36 46N	6 21W
San Luis Argentina	81	D7	33 20S	66 23W
San Luis Obispo California USA	70	B4	35 16N	120 40W
San Luis Obispo Bay California USA	72	C2	35 03N	120 39W
San Luis Potosí Mexico	74	D4	22 10N	101 00W
San Marcos Texas USA	71	G2	29 54N	97 57W
SAN MARINO	89	D5	44 00N	12 00E
San Mateo California USA	72	B3	37 33N	122 22W
Sanmenxia China	101	L5	34 46N	111 17E
San Miguel El Salvador	74	G2	13 28N	88 10W
San Miguel *r.* Bolivia	80	E10	15 00S	63 30W
San Miguel de Tucumán Argentina	80	D8	26 47S	65 15W
San Miguel Island California USA	72	C2	34 03N	120 22W
Sanming China	101	M4	26 16N	117 35E
San Nicolas de los Arroyos Argentina	81	E7	33 25S	60 15W
San Nicolas Island California USA	72	D1	33 15N	119 30W
San Pablo Philippines	103	G6	14 03N	121 19E
San Pablo Bay California USA	72	B4	38 00N	122 15W
San Pedro Argentina	80	E9	24 12S	64 55W
San Pedro Côte d'Ivoire	108	C8	4 45N	6 37W
San Pedro Dom. Rep.	75	L3	18 30N	69 18W
San Pedro Channel California USA	72	D1	33 37N	118 30W
San Pedro de las Colonias Mexico	74	D5	25 50N	102 59W
San Pedro Sula Honduras	74	G3	15 26N	88 01W
San Rafael Argentina	81	D7	34 35S	68 24W
San Rafael California USA	70	B4	37 58N	122 30W
San Rafael Mountains California USA	72	D2	34 50N	119 40W
San Remo Italy	89	A5	43 48N	7 46E
San Salvador El Salvador	74	G2	13 40N	89 10W
San Salvador *i.* Bahamas	75	K4	24 00N	74 32W
San Salvador de Jujuy Argentina	80	D9	24 10S	65 48W
San Sebastián Sp.	87	E5	43 19N	1 59W
San Severo Italy	89	E4	41 41N	15 23E
Santa Ana Bolivia	80	D11	13 46S	65 37W
Santa Ana El Salvador	74	G2	14 00N	89 31W
Santa Ana California USA	70	C3	33 44N	117 54W
Santa Barbara Mexico	74	C5	26 48N	105 50W
Santa Barbara California USA	70	C3	33 29N	119 01W
Santa Barbara Channel California USA	72	C2	34 15N	120 00W
Santa Barbara Island California USA	72	D1	33 29N	119 02W
Santa Catalina, Gulf of California USA	72	D1	33 07N	118 00W
Santa Catalina Island California USA	70	C3	33 25N	118 25W
Santa Catarina *admin.* Brazil	80	G8	27 00S	51 00W
Santa Clara Cuba	75	J4	22 25N	79 58W
Santa Clara California USA	72	C3	37 21N	121 57W
Santa Clarita California USA	72	D2	34 23N	118 33W
Santa Cruz Bolivia	80	E10	17 50S	63 10W
Santa Cruz Canary Islands	108	A13	28 28N	16 15W
Santa Cruz California USA	70	B4	36 58N	122 03W
Santa Cruz *r.* Argentina	81	C3	50 00S	70 00W
Santa Cruz Island California USA	70	C3	34 00N	119 40W
Santa Cruz Islands Solomon Islands	114	G6	11 00S	167 00E
Santa Fé Argentina	81	E7	31 35S	60 50W
Santa Fe New Mexico USA	70	E4	35 41N	105 57W
Santa Isabel *i.* Solomon Islands	114	F7	7 30S	158 30E
Santa Maria Brazil	81	G8	29 45S	53 40W
Santa Maria California USA	70	B3	34 56N	120 25W
Santa Marta Col.	80	C16	11 18N	74 10W
Santa Monica California USA	72	D2	34 00N	118 28W
Santana do Livramento Brazil	81	F7	30 52S	55 30W
Santander Col.	80	B14	3 00N	76 25W
Santander Sp.	87	D5	43 28N	3 48W
Sant' Antioco Italy	89	B3	39 04N	8 27E
Santa Paula California USA	72	D2	34 20N	119 04W
Santarém Brazil	80	G13	2 26S	54 41W
Santarém Port.	87	A3	39 14N	8 40W
Santa Rosa Argentina	81	E6	36 37S	64 17W
Santa Rosa Honduras	74	G2	14 48N	88 43W
Santa Rosa California USA	70	B4	38 26N	122 43W
Santa Rosa New Mexico USA	70	F3	34 56N	104 42W
Santa Rosa Island California USA	70	B3	34 00N	120 05W
Santa Rosalia Mexico	74	B5	27 20N	112 20W
Santa Ynez Mountains California USA	72	C2	34 31N	120 00W
Santee California USA	72	E1	32 51N	116 59W
Santiago Chile	81	C7	33 30S	70 40W
Santiago Panama	75	H1	8 08N	80 59W
Santiago de Compostela Sp.	87	A5	42 52N	8 33W
Santiago de Cuba Cuba	75	J4	20 00N	75 49W
Santiago del Estero Argentina	81	E8	27 47S	64 15W
Santiago Ixcuintla Mexico	74	C4	21 50N	105 11W
San Tin HK China	100	B3	22 30N	114 04E
Santipur India	99	K9	23 16N	88 27E
Santo Andre Brazil	80	H9	23 39S	46 29W
Santo Domingo Dom. Rep.	75	L3	18 30N	69 57W
Santo Domingo de los Colorados Ecuador	80	B13	0 13S	79 09W
Santos Brazil	80	H9	23 56S	46 22W
San Vicente El Salvador	74	G2	13 38N	88 42W
San Wai Tsuen HK China	100	B2	22 28N	114 03E
Sanxia Shuiku *res.* China	101	K4/L5	31 27N	108 00S
Sanya China	101	K2	18 25N	109 27E
São Bernardo do Campo Brazil	80	H9	23 45S	46 34W
São Borja Brazil	81	F8	28 35S	56 01W
São Francisco *r.* Brazil	80	K12	8 30S	39 00W
São José Brazil	81	H8	27 35S	48 40W
São José do Rio Prêto Brazil	80	H9	20 50S	49 20W
São José dos Campos Brazil	80	H9	23 07S	45 52W
São Luís Brazil	80	J13	2 34S	44 16W
Saône *r.* Fr.	87	H7	46 28N	4 55E
São Paulo Brazil	80	H9	23 33S	46 39W
São Paulo *admin.* Brazil	80	G9	21 30S	50 00W
São Paulo de Olivença Brazil	80	D13	3 34S	68 55W
São Tomé *i.* Gulf of Guinea	108	F8	0 25N	6 35E
SÃO TOMÉ AND PRINCIPE	108	F8		
São Vicente Brazil	80	H9	23 57S	46 23W
Sapporo Japan	102	D3	43 05N	141 21E
Saqqez Iran	96	E6	36 14N	46 15E
Sarajevo Bosnia-Herzegovina	89	G5	43 52N	18 26E
Sarakhs Iran	97	H6	36 32N	61 07E
Saransk Russia	94	G7	54 12N	45 10E
Sarasota Florida USA	71	K2	27 20N	82 32W
Sarata Ukraine	89	M7	46 00N	29 40E
Saratoga Springs *tn.* New York USA	73	D3	43 05N	73 47W
Saratov Russia	94	G7	51 30N	45 55E
Saravan Iran	97	H4	27 25N	62 17E
Sarawak *admin.* Malaysia	103	E4	1 00N	111 00E
Sardindida Plain Kenya	108	M8	2 00N	40 00E
Sardinia *i.* Italy	89	B3/B4	40 00N	9 00E
Sar-e Pol Afghanistan	97	J6	36 15N	65 57E
Sargasso Sea Atlantic Ocean	116	B9	27 00N	66 00W
Sargodha Pakistan	98	C6	32 01N	72 40E
Sarh Chad	108	H9	9 08N	18 22E
Sarīr Calanscio *d.* Libya	108	J13	26 00N	22 00E
Sark *i.* British Isles	86	D8	49 26N	2 22W
Sarles North Dakota USA	49	C1	48 57N	98 59W
Sarmiento Argentina	81	D4	45 38S	69 08W
Sarny Ukraine	88	L9	51 21N	26 31E
Sarpsborg Norway	86	L13	59 17N	11 06E
Sarrebourg Fr.	86	J8	48 43N	7 03E
Sarreguemines Fr.	86	J8	49 06N	6 55E
Sartène France	87	K4	41 37N	8 58E
Sasebo Japan	102	A1	33 10N	129 42E
Sassandra Côte d'Ivoire	108	C8	4 58N	6 08W
Sassandra *r.* Côte d'Ivoire	108	C9	5 50N	6 55W
Sassari Italy	89	B4	40 43N	8 34E
Sassnitz Germany	88	D11	54 32N	13 40E
Satna India	98	E4	24 33N	80 50E
Satpura Range *mts.* India	98	C4/D4	21 40N	75 00E
Sattahip Thailand	103	C6	12 36N	100 56E
Satu Mare Romania	88	J7	47 48N	22 52E
SAUDI ARABIA	96/97	D3/F3		
Sault Ste. Marie Michigan USA	51	J4	46 29N	84 22W
Saumur Fr.	87	E7	47 16N	0 05W
Saurimo Angola	109	J6	9 39S	20 24E
Sava *r.* Europe	89	G6	45 00N	16 00E
Savannah Georgia USA	71	K3	32 04N	81 07W
Savannah *r.* USA	71	K3	33 00N	82 00W
Savannakhet Laos	103	C7	16 34N	104 45E
Savanna la Mar Jamaica	75	T14	18 13N	78 08W
Savona Italy	89	B6	44 18N	8 28E
Sawahlunto Indonesia	103	C3	0 41S	100 52E
Sawu Sea Indonesia	103	G2	9 00S	122 00E
Sayanogorsk Russia	95	M7	53 00N	91 26E
Saylac Somalia	108	N10	11 21N	43 30E
Saynshand Mongolia	101	L8	45 00N	111 10E
Sayre Pennsylvania USA	53	K1	41 58N	76 03W
Say'ūn Yemen	97	E2	15 59N	48 44E
Scarborough Trinidad and Tobago	75	V15	11 11N	60 44W
Scarborough UK	86	E11	54 17N	0 24W
Schenectady New York USA	71	M5	42 48N	73 57W
Schleswig Germany	88	B11	54 32N	9 34E
Schurz Nevada USA	72	D4	38 57N	118 48W
Schwäbisch Alb *mts.* Germany	88	B8	48 00N	9 00E
Schwarzwald *mts.* Germany	88	B8	47 00N	8 00E
Schweinfurt Germany	88	C9	50 03N	10 16E
Schwerin Germany	88	C10	53 38N	11 25E
Scilly, Isles of UK	86	B8	49 56N	6 20W
Scobey Montana USA	47	E1	48 50N	105 29W
Scotia Ridge Atlantic Ocean	116	C1	53 00S	50 00W
Scotia Sea Antarctica	117		55 00S	45 00W
Scotland *admin.* UK	86	C12	56 00N	4 00W
Scott Island Southern Ocean	114	G1	66 35S	180 00
Scottsbluff Nebraska USA	70	F5	41 52N	103 40W
Scranton Pennsylvania USA	71	L5	41 25N	75 40W
Searles Lake California USA	72	E2	35 42N	117 17W
Seaside California USA	72	C3	36 36N	121 51W
Seattle Washington USA	70	B6	47 35N	122 20W
Sebewaing Michigan USA	52	C3	43 44N	83 26W
Seboomook Lake Maine USA	53	S5	45 55N	69 50W
Sedalia Missouri USA	71	H4	38 42N	93 15W
Sedan Fr.	86	H8	49 42N	4 57E
Sedro Woolley Washington USA	42	H4	48 27N	122 18W
Ségou Mali	108	C10	13 28N	6 18W
Segovia Sp.	87	C4	40 57N	4 07W
Segre *r.* Sp.	87	F4	42 00N	1 10E
Segura *r.* Sp.	87	D3	38 00N	1 00W
Seine *r.* Fr.	86	F8	49 15N	1 15E
Sekiu Washington USA	42	H4	48 10N	124 30W
Sekondi Takoradi Ghana	108	D8	4 59N	1 43W
Selat Sunda *sd.* Indonesia	103	D2	5 50S	105 30E
Selemdzha *r.* Russia	95	R7	53 00N	132 00E
Selenge *r.* Mongolia	101	J8	49 00N	102 00E
Selima Oasis Sudan	108	K12	21 22N	29 19E
Selma Alabama USA	71	J3	32 24N	87 01W
Selma California USA	72	D3	36 34N	119 36W
Semarang Indonesia	103	E2	6 58S	110 29E
Seminoe Reservoir Wyoming USA	70	E5	42 00N	106 00W
Seminole Oklahoma USA	71	G4	35 15N	96 40W
Semipalatinsk Kazakhstan	94	L7	50 26N	80 16E
Semnān Iran	97	F6	35 30N	53 25E
Sendai Honshu Japan	102	D2	38 16N	140 52E
Sendai Kyushu Japan	102	B1	31 50N	130 17E
Seneca Falls *tn.* New York USA	53	K2	42 55N	76 48W
Seneca Lake New York USA	51	N2	42 40N	77 01W
SENEGAL	108	A10		
Sénégal *r.* Senegal/Mauritania	108	A11	16 45N	14 45W
Senhor do Bonfim Brazil	80	J11	10 28S	40 11W
Senj Croatia	89	E6	45 00N	14 55E
Sennar Sudan	108	L10	13 31N	33 38E
Sens Fr.	86	G8	48 12N	3 18E
Senyavin Islands Pacific Ocean	114	G8	7 00N	161 30E
Seoul South Korea	101	P6	37 32N	127 00E
Sepik *r.* PNG	110	G9	4 15S	143 00E
Sequoia National Park California USA	72	D3	36 23N	118 38W
Seram *i.* Indonesia	103	H3/J3	3 30S	129 30E
Seram Sea Indonesia	103	H3/J3	2 30S	130 00E
Serang Indonesia	103	D2	6 07S	106 09E
SERBIA	89	H5/H6		
Seremban Malaysia	103	C4	2 43N	102 57E
Serenje Zambia	109	L5	13 12S	30 15E
Sergino Russia	94	J9	62 30N	65 40E
Sergipe *admin.* Brazil	80	K11	11 00S	38 00W
Sergiyev Posad Russia	94	F8	56 20N	38 10E
Seria Brunei	103	E4	4 39N	114 23E
Serian Malaysia	103	E4	1 10N	110 35E
Sérifos *i.* Greece	89	K2	37 10N	24 25E
Serov Russia	94	J8	59 42N	60 32E
Serpent's Mouth *sd.* Trinidad and Tobago	75	V15	10 10N	61 58W
Serra Brazil	80	J10	20 06S	40 16W
Serra do Mar *mts.* Brazil	80/81	H8	27 30S	49 00W
Serra do Navio Brazil	80	G14	1 00N	52 05W
Serrania de Cuenca *mts.* Sp.	87	D4/E4	40 30N	2 15W
Serra Tumucumaque *mts.* Brazil	80	F14	2 00N	55 00W
Sérres Greece	89	J4	41 03N	23 33E
Sete Lagoas Brazil	80	J10	19 29S	44 15W
Setesdal *geog. reg.* Norway	86	J13	59 30N	7 10E
Sétif Algeria	108	F15	36 11N	5 24E
Setit *r.* Sudan	108	M10	14 20N	36 15E
Seto-naikai *sd.* Japan	102	B1	34 00N	132 30E
Settat Morocco	108	C14	33 04N	7 37W
Setúbal Port.	87	A3	38 31N	8 54W
Severn *r.* UK	86	D10	52 30N	3 15W
Severnaya (North) Dvina *r.* Russia	94	G9	63 00N	43 00E
Severnaya Sos'va *r.* Russia	94	J9	62 30N	62 00E
Severnaya Zemlya *is.* Russia	95	M13	80 00N	95 00E
Severodvinsk Russia	94	F9	64 35N	39 50E
Sevier *r.* Utah USA	70	D4	39 00N	113 00W
Seville Sp.	87	C2	37 24N	5 59W
SEYCHELLES	113	E6		

Seychelles Ridge Indian Ocean 113 E6 10 00S 60 00E
Seymchan Russia 95 T9 62 54N 152 26E
Sfântu Gheorghe Romania 89 K6 45 51N 25 48E
Sfax Tunisia 108 G14 34 45N 10 43E
Sha Chau *i.* HK China 100 A2 22 21N 113 53E
Shache China 100 D6 38 27N 77 16E
Shah Alam Malaysia 103 C4 3 02N 101 31E
Shahdol India 98 E4 23 19N 81 26E
Shahjahanpur India 98 D5 27 53N 79 55E
Sha Lo Wan HK China 100 A1 22 17N 113 54E
Sham Chung HK China 100 C2 22 26N 114 17E
Sham Chun River HK China 100 B3 22 30N 114 00E
Shamokin Pennsylvania USA 73 B2 40 47N 76 34W
Sham Shek Tsuen HK China 100 A1 22 17N 113 53E
Sham Shui Po HK China 100 C1 22 20N 114 10E
Shangani *r.* Zimbabwe 109 K4 19 00S 29 00E
Shanghai China 101 N5 31 06N 121 22E
Shangqui China 101 M5 34 27N 115 07E
Shangrao China 101 M4 28 28N 117 54E
Shannon RoI 86 A10 52 41N 8 55W
Shannon *r.* RoI 86 A10 52 45N 8 57W
Shannon, Lake Washington USA 42 H4 48 35N 121 45W
Shantou China 101 M3 23 23N 116 39E
Shaoguan China 101 L3 24 54N 113 33E
Shaoxing China 101 N5 30 02N 120 35E
Shaoyang China 101 L4 27 10N 111 25E
Shaqrā' Saudia Arabia 96 E4 25 18N 45 15E
Sharjah UAE 97 G4 25 20N 55 20E
Sharm el Sheikh Egypt 96 B4 27 52N 34 16E
Sharon Pennsylvania USA 71 K5 41 46N 80 30W
Sharp Island HK China 100 C2 22 22N 114 18E
Sharp Peak HK China 100 D2 22 26N 114 22E
Shashi China 101 L5 30 16N 112 20E
Shasta Lake California USA 70 B5 40 45N 122 20W
Shasta, Mount California USA 70 B5 41 25N 122 12W
Sha Tau Kok HK China 100 C3 22 33N 114 13E
Sha Tin HK China 100 C2 22 23N 114 11E
Shatsky Rise Pacific Ocean 114 G11 34 00N 160 00E
Shebele *r.* Ethiopia/Somalia 108 N9 6 00N 44 00E
Sheberghān Afghanistan 97 J6 36 41N 65 45E
Sheboygan Wisconsin USA 71 J5 43 46N 87 44W
Sheffield UK 86 E10 53 23N 1 30W
Sheffield Pennsylvania USA 52 G1 41 43N 79 02W
Shek Kong HK China 100 B2 22 26N 114 06E
Shek Kwu Chau *i.* HK China 100 A1 22 12N 113 59E
Shek O HK China 100 C1 22 14N 114 15E
Shek Pik HK China 100 A1 22 13N 113 53E
Shek Pik Reservoir HK China 100 A1 22 14N 113 54E
Shek Uk Shan *mt.* HK China 100 C2 22 26N 114 18E
Shek Wu Hui HK China 100 B3 22 30N 114 07E
Shelby Montana USA 70 D6 48 30N 111 52W
Shelekhov Bay Russia 95 T8/T9 60 00N 157 00E
Shell Lake Wisconsin USA 51 F3 45 45N 91 56W
Shelter Island HK China 100 C1 22 19N 114 19E
Shenandoah Iowa USA 71 G5 40 48N 95 22W
Shenandoah Mountains West Virginia USA 73 B1 39 20N 78 45W
Shenandoah National Park West Virginia/Virginia USA 73 B1 39 00N 78 00W
Shenyang China 101 N7 41 50N 123 26E
Shenzhen China 101 L3 22 31N 114 08E
Shepetovka Ukraine 88 L9 50 12N 27 01E
Sherburne New York USA 53 L2 42 41N 75 30W
Sheridan Wyoming USA 70 E5 44 48N 106 57W
's-Hertogenbosch Neths. 86 H9 51 41N 5 19E
Sherwood North Dakota USA 47 G1 48 57N 101 38W
Shetland Islands UK 86 E13/E14 60 00N 1 15W
Sheung Fa Shan HK China 100 B2 22 23N 114 06E
Sham Tseng HK China 100 B2 22 22N 114 03E
Sheung Shui HK China 100 B3 22 31N 114 08E
Shiawassee River Michigan USA 52 B3 43 05N 84 12W
Shihezi China 100 F7 44 19N 86 10E
Shijiazhuang China 101 L6 38 04N 114 28E
Shikarpur Pakistan 98 B5 27 58N 68 42E
Shikoku *i.* Japan 102 B1 33 40N 134 00E
Shikotan *i.* Japan 102 E3 43 47N 148 45E
Shiliguri India 99 F5 26 42N 88 30E
Shilka *r.* Russia 95 P7 52 30N 117 30E
Shillong India 99 G5 25 34N 91 53E
Shimizu Japan 102 C2 35 01N 138 29E
Shimla India 98 D6 31 07N 77 09E
Shimoga India 98 D2 13 56N 75 31E
Shimonoseki Japan 102 B1 33 59N 130 58E
Shinano *r.* Japan 102 C2 37 40N 139 00E
Shīndand Afghanistan 97 H5 33 16N 62 05E
Shingū Japan 102 C1 33 42N 136 00E
Shinjō Japan 102 D2 38 45N 140 18E
Shinyanga Tanzania 108 L7 3 40S 33 25E
Shiono-misaki *c.* Japan 102 C1 33 28N 135 47E
Shirakawa Japan 102 D2 37 07N 140 11E
Shiraoi Japan 102 D3 42 34N 141 19E
Shīrāz Iran 97 F4 29 38N 52 34E
Shiretoko-misaki *c.* Japan 102 E3 44 24N 145 20E
Shizuishan China 101 K6 39 04N 106 22E
Shizuoka Japan 102 C1 34 59N 138 24E
Shkodër Albania 89 G5 42 03N 19 01E
Shoshone California USA 72 E2 35 58N 116 17W
Shreveport Louisiana USA 71 H3 32 30N 93 46W
Shrewsbury UK 86 D10 52 43N 2 45W
Shuangliao China 101 N7 43 30N 123 29E
Shuangyashan China 101 Q8 46 42N 131 20E
Shuen Wan HK China 100 C2 22 28N 114 12E
Shui Tau HK China 100 B2 22 27N 114 04E
Shui Tsiu San Tsuen HK China 100 B2 22 26N 114 02E
Shuksan, Mount Washington USA 42 H4 48 52N 121 30W
Shumen Bulgaria 89 L5 43 17N 26 55E
Shunde China 101 L3 22 50N 113 16E
Shuqrā Yemen 97 E1 13 23N 45 44E
Shymkent Kazakhstan 94 J5 42 16N 69 05E
Sialkot Pakistan 98 C6 32 29N 74 35E
Siauliai Lithuania 88 J11 55 51N 23 20E
Šibenik Croatia 89 E5 43 45N 15 55E
Sibi Pakistan 98 B5 29 31N 67 54E
Sibiti Congo 108 G7 3 40S 13 24E
Sibiu Romania 89 K6 45 46N 24 09E
Sibolga Indonesia 103 B4 1 42N 98 48E
Sibu Malaysia 103 E4 2 19N 111 50E
Sibut CAR 108 H9 5 46N 19 06E
Sichuan Pendi China 101 J5/K5 32 00N 107 00E
Sicilian Channel Mediterranean Sea 89 D2 37 00N 12 00E
Sicily *i.* Italy 89 D2/E2 37 00N 14 00E
Sicuani Peru 80 C11 14 21S 71 13W
Sidi Barrani Egypt 108 K14 31 38N 25 58E
Sidi Bel Abbès Algeria 108 D15 35 15N 0 39W
Sidi Ifni Morocco 108 B13 29 24N 10 12W
Sidney Lanier, Lake Georgia USA 71 K3 34 00N 84 00W
Sidon Lebanon 96 N11 33 32N 35 22E
Siedlce Poland 88 J10 52 10N 22 18E
Siegen Germany 88 B9 50 52N 8 02E
Siena Italy 89 C5 43 19N 11 19E
Sierra Blanca *tn.* Texas USA 70 E3 31 10N 105 22W
Sierra de Maracaju *mts.* Brazil 80 F9 20 00S 55 00W
SIERRA LEONE 108 B9
Sierra Madre del Sur *mts.* Mexico 74 D3/E3 17 30N 100 00W
Sierra Madre Occidental *mts.* Mexico 74 C5/D4 26 00N 107 00W
Sierra Madre Oriental *mts.* Mexico 74 D5/E4 23 30N 100 00W
Sierra Morena *mts.* Sp. 87 B3/C3 38 05N 5 50W
Sierra Nevada *mts.* Sp. 87 D2 37 00N 3 20W
Sierra Nevada *mts.* California USA 70 C4 37 00N 119 00W
Sierras de Córdoba *mts.* Argentina 81 D7/E7 32 30S 65 00W
Sífnos *i.* Greece 89 K2 37 00N 24 40E
Sighetu Marmaţiei Romania 88 J7 47 56N 23 53E
Sighişoara Romania 89 K7 46 12N 24 48E
Sigüenza Sp. 87 D4 41 04N 2 38W
Siguiri Guinea 108 C10 11 28N 9 07W
Sikar India 98 D5 27 33N 75 12E
Sikasso Mali 108 C10 11 18N 5 38W
Sikhote-Alin' *mts.* Russia 95 R6 45 00N 137 00E
Sikkim *admin.* India 99 F5 27 30N 88 30E
Sil *r.* Sp. 87 B5 42 25N 7 05W
Silchar India 99 G4 24 49N 92 47E
Silifke Turkey 96 B6 36 22N 33 57E
Silistra Bulgaria 89 L6 44 06N 27 17E
Silkeborg Denmark 88 B12 56 10N 9 39E
Silute Lithuania 88 H11 55 21N 21 30E
Silver Bay *tn.* Minnesota USA 51 F4 47 18N 91 15W
Silver City New Mexico USA 70 E3 32 47N 108 16W
Silver Creek *tn.* New York USA 52 G2 42 32N 79 10W
Silver Peak Range *mts.* Nevada USA 72 E3 37 30N 117 45W
Silver Springs *tn.* Nevada USA 72 D4 39 25N 119 14W
Silves Port. 87 A2 37 11N 8 26W
Simi Valley *tn.* California USA 72 D2 34 16N 118 47W
Simpson Desert Aust. 110 F5 24 30S 137 30E
Sincelejo Col. 80 B15 9 17N 75 23W
Sind *geog. reg.* Pakistan 98 B5 26 20N 68 40E
Sines Port. 87 A2 37 58N 8 52W
SINGAPORE 103 C4
Singaraja Indonesia 103 F2 8 06S 115 04E
Singatoko Fiji 114 T15 18 10S 177 30E
Sinop Turkey 96 C7 42 02N 35 09E
Sintra Port. 87 A3 38 48N 9 22W
Sinuiju North Korea 101 N7 40 04N 124 25E
Sioux City Iowa USA 71 G5 42 30N 96 28W
Sioux Falls *tn.* South Dakota USA 71 G5 43 34N 96 42W
Siping China 101 N7 43 15N 124 25E
Sira *r.* Norway 86 J13 58 50N 6 40E
Siracusa Italy 89 E2 37 04N 15 19E
Sirajganj Bangladesh 99 K10 24 27N 89 42E
Siret *r.* Romania 88 L7 47 00N 26 00E
Sirte Libya 108 H14 31 13N 16 35E
Sirte Desert Libya 108 H14 30 00N 16 00E
Sirte, Gulf of Libya 108 H14 31 00N 17 00E
Sisak Croatia 89 F6 45 30N 16 22E
Sisophon Cambodia 103 C6 13 37N 102 58E
Sisteron Fr. 87 H6 44 16N 5 56E
Sitka Alaska USA 42 C5 57 05N 135 20W
Sitka Sound Alaska USA 42 C5 57 00N 135 50W
Sittwe Myanmar 100 G3 20 09N 92 55E
Sivas Turkey 96 C6 39 44N 37 01E
Siwa Egypt 108 K13 29 11N 25 31E
Sjaelland *i.* Denmark 88 C11 55 15N 11 30E
Skadarsko ezero *l.* Europe 89 G5 42 00N 19 00E
Skagen Denmark 88 C12 57 44N 10 37E
Skagerrak *sd.* Denmark/Norway 86 K12 57 30N 8 00E
Skagit River Washington USA 42 H4 48 30N 121 20W
Skagway Alaska USA 42 C6 59 23N 135 20W
Skien Norway 86 K13 59 14N 9 37E
Skierniewice Poland 88 H9 51 58N 20 10E
Skikda Algeria 108 F15 36 53N 6 54E
Skive Denmark 88 B12 56 34N 9 02E
Skopje FYROM 89 H4 42 00N 21 28E
Skövde Sweden 88 D13 58 24N 13 52E
Skovorodino Russia 95 Q7 54 00N 123 53E
Skowhegan Maine USA 53 S4 44 46N 69 44W
Skye *i.* UK 86 B12 57 20N 6 15W
Skýros *i.* Greece 89 K3 38 50N 24 35E
Slaney *r.* RoI 86 B10 52 24W 6 33W
Slatina Romania 89 K6 44 26N 24 22E
Slavonski Brod Croatia 89 F6 45 09N 18 02E
Sligo RoI 86 A11 54 17N 8 28W
Sliven Bulgaria 89 L5 42 40N 26 19E
SLOVAKIA 88 F8/H8
SLOVENIA 89 E6
Sluch' *r.* Ukraine 88 L9 50 00N 27 00E
Słupsk Poland 88 F11 54 28N 17 00E
Smederevo Serbia 89 H6 44 40N 20 56E
Smethport Pennsylvania USA 52 H1 41 48N 78 26W
Smoky Hills Kansas USA 70 G4 39 00N 100 00W
Smolensk Russia 94 F7 54 49N 32 04E
Smolyan Bulgaria 89 K4 41 34N 24 42E
Snake *r.* USA 70 C5 44 00N 118 00W
Snake River Plain USA 70 D5 43 00N 114 00W
Snowdon *mt.* UK 86 C10 53 04N 4 05W
Snowy Mountains Aust. 110 H2 36 50S 147 00E
Snyder Texas USA 70 F3 32 43N 100 54W
Soa-Siu Indonesia 103 H4 0 40N 127 30E
Sobat *r.* Sudan 108 L9 8 00N 33 00E
Sobral Brazil 80 J13 3 45S 40 20W
Sochi Russia 94 F5 43 35N 39 46E
Society Islands Pacific Ocean 115 L6 16 30S 153 00W
Socotra *i.* Yemen 97 F1 12 05N 54 10E
Soda Lake California USA 72 E2 35 09N 116 04W
Soda Springs *tn.* California USA 72 C4 39 19N 120 23W
Sodertälje Sweden 88 F13 59 11N 17 39E
Sodo Ethiopia 108 M9 6 49N 37 41E
Sodus New York USA 53 J3 43 14N 77 04W
Sofia Bulgaria 89 J5 42 40N 23 18E
Sogamoso Col. 80 C15 5 43N 72 56W
Sohâg Egypt 108 L13 26 33N 31 42E
Soissons Fr. 86 G8 49 23N 3 20E
Sok Kwu Wan HK China 100 B1 22 13N 114 08E
Sokodé Togo 108 E9 8 59N 1 11E
Soko Islands HK China 100 A1 22 10N 113 54E
Sokoto Nigeria 108 F10 13 02N 5 15E
Sokoto *r.* Nigeria 108 E10 13 02N 4 55E
So Kwun Wat HK China 100 B2 22 23N 114 00E
Solāpur India 98 D3 17 43N 75 56E
Soledad California USA 72 C3 36 25N 121 20W
Solikamsk Russia 94 H8 59 40N 56 45E
Solimões *r.* Brazil 80 D13 3 30S 69 00W
Söller Spain 87 G3 39 46N 2 42E
Sologne *geog. reg.* Fr. 87 F7 47 35N 1 47E
SOLOMON ISLANDS 114 G7
Solomon Sea PNG 110 J8 7 00S 150 00E
Solothurn Switz. 87 J7 47 13N 7 32E
Soltau Germany 88 B10 52 59N 9 50E
Solway Firth *est.* UK 86 D11 54 45N 3 40W
SOMALIA 108 N8
Somali Basin Indian Ocean 113 E7 5 00N 55 00E
Sombor Serbia 89 G6 45 46N 19 09E
Sombrerete Mexico 74 D4 23 38N 103 40W
Sombrero Channel *sd.* India 99 G1 7 41N 93 35E
Somerset Michigan USA 51 J2 42 03N 84 22W
Somme *r.* Fr. 86 F8 50 00N 1 45E
Sommen *l.* Sweden 88 E12 58 05N 15 15E
Somoto Nicaragua 74 G2 13 29N 86 36W
Son *r.* India 98 E4 24 00N 84 00E
Sønderborg Denmark 88 B11 54 55N 9 48E
Songea Tanzania 109 M5 10 42S 35 59E
Songhua Jiang *r.* China 101 P8 46 00N 128 00E
Songkhla Thailand 103 C5 7 12N 100 35E
Song-koi *r.* China/Vietnam 101 J3 22 30N 103 00E
Sonoita Mexico 74 B6 31 53N 112 52W
Sonora California USA 72 C3 37 59N 120 21W
Sonsonate El Salvador 74 G2 13 43N 89 44W
Sopot Poland 88 G11 54 27N 18 31E
Soria Sp. 87 D4 41 46N 2 28W
Soroca Moldova 88 M8 48 08N 28 12E
Sorong Indonesia 103 J3 0 50S 131 17E
Soroti Uganda 108 L8 1 42N 33 37E
Sorraia *r.* Port. 87 A3 38 55N 9 30W
Sosnowiec Poland 88 G9 50 16N 19 07E
Soufrière *mt.* Guadeloupe 74 Q9 16 03N 61 40W
Souillac Fr. 87 F6 44 53N 1 29E
Sousse Tunisia 108 G14 35 50N 10 38E
Southampton UK 86 E9 50 55N 1 25W
Southampton New York USA 73 D2 40 53N 72 24W
South Andaman *i.* Andaman Islands 99 G2 11 30N 93 00E
South Australia *state* Aust. 110 E3/F4 27 00S 135 00E
South Australian Basin Indian Ocean 113 M3 38 00S 125 00E
South Bend Indiana USA 71 J5 41 40N 86 15W
South Carolina *state* USA 71 K3 34 00N 81 00W
South China Sea Pacific Ocean 103 E6/F7 15 00N 110 00E
South Dakota *state* USA 70 F5 45 00N 102 00W
South East Cape Aust. 110 H1 43 38S 146 48E
Southeast Indian Basin Indian Ocean 113 K3 32 00S 108 00E
Southeast Indian Ridge Indian Ocean 113 H2 45 00S 90 00E
South East Pacific Basin Pacific Ocean 115 S3 53 00S 95 00W
Southend-on-Sea UK 86 F9 51 33N 0 43E
Southern Alps *mts.* NZ 111 B2/C3 43 07S 171 13E
Southern Honshu Ridge Pacific Ocean 114 E10 25 50N 142 30E
Southern Ocean 117
South Fiji Basin Pacific Ocean 114 H5 25 00S 176 50E
South Georgia *i.* Atlantic Ocean 116 E1 54 00S 36 30W
South Hatia Island Bangladesh 99 L9 22 19N 91 07E
South Indian Basin Indian Ocean 113 L1 55 00S 130 00E
South Island NZ 111 A1/D4 42 30S 172 00E
SOUTH KOREA 101 P6
South Lake Tahoe *tn.* California USA 72 D4 38 55N 119 58W
South Loup *r.* Nebraska USA 70 G5 42 00N 99 00W
South Negril Point *c.* Jamaica 75 T14 18 16N 78 22W
South Orkney Islands Southern Ocean 117 60 00S 45 00W
South Platte *r.* USA 70 F5 41 00N 103 00W
South Pole Antarctica 117 90 00S
South Sandwich Trench Atlantic Ocean 116 E2/F1 55 00S 30 00W
South San Francisco California USA 72 B3 37 39N 122 24W
South Shetland Islands Southern Ocean 117 62 00S 60 00W
South Sioux City Nebraska USA 71 G5 42 28N 96 24W
South Uist *i.* UK 86 B12 57 20N 7 15W
Southwest Cape NZ 111 A1 48 00S 168 00E
Southwest Indian Ridge Indian Ocean 113 C2 40 00S 50 00E
South West Pacific Basin Pacific Ocean 115 L4 35 00S 155 00W
Sovetsk Russia 88 H11 55 02N 21 50E
Sovetskaya Gavan' Russia 95 S6 48 57N 140 16E
SPAIN 87 C3/E3
Spanish Town Jamaica 75 U13 17 59N 76 58W
Sparks Nevada USA 70 B4/C4 39 34N 119 46W
Spartanburg South Carolina USA 71 K3 34 56N 81 57W
Spárti Greece 89 J2 37 05N 22 25E
Spassk-Dal'niy Russia 95 R5 44 37N 132 37E
Speightstown Barbados 74 S11 13 15N 59 39W
Spencer Iowa USA 71 G5 43 08N 95 08W
Spencer Gulf Aust. 110 F2 34 00S 137 00E
Spey *r.* UK 86 D12 57 35N 3 10W
Spitsbergen *i.* Arctic Ocean 94 D12 79 00N 15 00E
Spittal an der Drau Austria 89 D7 46 48N 13 30E
Split Croatia 89 F5 43 31N 16 28E
Spokane Washington USA 70 C6 47 40N 117 25W
Spoleto Italy 89 D5 42 44N 12 44E
Spratly Islands South China Sea 103 E5/F5 8 45N 111 54E
Springbok RSA 109 H2 29 44S 17 56E
Springdale Nevada USA 72 E3 37 02N 116 46W
Springfield NZ 111 C3 43 20S 171 56E
Springfield Illinois USA 71 J4 39 49N 89 39W
Springfield Massachusetts USA 71 M5 42 07N 72 35W
Springfield Missouri USA 71 H4 37 11N 93 19W
Springfield Ohio USA 71 K4 39 55N 83 48W
Springfield Oregon USA 70 B5 44 03N 123 01W
Springfield Vermont USA 73 D3 43 18N 72 29W
Spring Mountains Nevada USA 72 F3 36 22N 115 52W
Springsure Aust. 110 H5 24 09S 148 04E
Springville New York USA 73 A3 42 30N 78 40W
Spurn Head *c.* UK 86 F10 53 36N 0 07E
Sredinnyy Range *mts.* Russia 95 T7/T8 57 00N 158 00E
Srednekolymsk Russia 95 T10 67 27N 153 35E
Sretensk Russia 95 P7 52 15N 117 52E
Srikakulam India 99 E3 18 19N 84 00E
SRI LANKA 98 E1
Srinagar Kashmir 98 C6 34 08N 74 50E
Stafford UK 86 D10 52 48N 2 07W
Stamford Connecticut USA 73 D2 41 04N 73 33W
Standish Michigan USA 51 K2 43 59N 83 57W
Stanley Falkland Islands 81 F3 51 45S 57 56W
Stanley HK China 100 C1 22 12N 114 12E
Stanovoy Range *mts.* Russia 95 Q8 56 00N 122 30E
Stara Planina *mts.* Europe 89 J5/K5 43 00N 23 00E
Stara Zagora Bulgaria 89 K5 42 25N 25 37E
Stargard Szczeciński Poland 88 E10 53 21N 15 01E
Starogard Gdański Poland 88 G10 53 58N 18 30E
Start Point *c.* UK 86 D9 50 13N 3 38W
Staryy Oskol Russia 94 F7 51 20N 37 50E
State College Pennsylvania USA 71 L5 40 48N 77 52W
Staten Island New York USA 73 H1 40 35N 74 10W
Staunton Virginia USA 71 L4 38 10N 79 05W
Stavanger Norway 86 H13 58 58N 5 45E
Staveley NZ 111 C3 43 39S 171 26E
Stavropol' Russia 94 G6 45 03N 41 59E
Stehekin Washington USA 42 H4 48 25N 120 30W
Stendal Germany 88 C10 52 36N 11 52E
Stephens Passage *sd.* Alaska USA 42 D5 58 00N 134 00W
Sterling Colorado USA 70 F5 40 37N 103 13W

Sterlitamak Russia 94 H7 53 40N 55 59E
Steubenville Ohio USA 71 K5 40 22N 80 39W
Stewart Island NZ 111 A1 46 55S 167 55E
Steyr Austria 88 E7 48 04N 14 25E
Stillaguamish River Washington USA 42 H4 48 16N 122 00W
Stillwater Nevada USA 72 D4 39 31N 118 33W
Stillwater Reservoir New York USA 53 L3 43 55N 75 00W
Štip FYROM 89 J4 41 44N 22 12E
Stirling UK 86 D12 56 07N 3 57W
Stockbridge Massachusetts USA 73 D3 42 17N 73 19W
Stockholm Sweden 88 G13 59 20N 18 05E
Stockton California USA 70 B4 37 59N 121 20W
Stockton-on-Tees UK 86 E11 54 34N 1 19W
Stœng Trêng Cambodia 103 D6 13 31N 105 59E
Stoke-on-Trent UK 86 D10 53 00N 2 10W
Stonecutters Island HK China 100 B1 22 18N 114 08E
Stonyford California USA 72 B4 39 23N 122 34W
Stornoway UK 86 B13 58 12N 6 23W
Straits of Florida *sd.* Florida USA 71 K1 25 00N 80 00W
Stralsund Germany 88 D11 54 18N 13 06E
Stranraer UK 86 C11 54 55N 5 02W
Strasbourg Fr. 86 J8 48 35N 7 45E
Straubing Germany 88 D8 48 53N 12 35E
Stretto di Messina *sd.* Italy 89 E2 38 00N 15 00E
Strímonas *r.* Greece 89 J4 41 00N 23 00E
Stromboli *mt.* Italy 89 E3 38 48N 15 15E
Stroudsburg Pennsylvania USA 73 C2 40 59N 75 12W
Struma *r.* Bulgaria 89 J4 42 00N 23 00E
Stryy Ukraine 88 J8 49 16N 23 51E
Sturt Creek *r.* Aust. 110 D6 19 00S 127 30E
Stuttgart Germany 88 B8 48 47N 9 12E
Styr' *r.* Ukraine/Belarus 88 K9 51 30N 25 30E
Suakin Sudan 108 M11 19 08N 37 17E
Subotica Serbia 89 G7 46 04N 19 41E
Suceava Romania 88 L7 47 37N 26 18E
Sucre Bolivia 80 D10 19 05S 65 15W
SUDAN 108 K10
Sudety Reseniky *mts.* Europe 88 E9/F9 50 40N 16 00E
Sue *r.* Sudan 108 K9 7 00N 28 00E
Suez Egypt 109 T1 29 59N 32 33E
Suez Canal Egypt 109 S4 31 30N 32 20E
Suez, Gulf of Egypt 109 T1 29 56N 32 32E
Sugarloaf Mountain Maine USA 53 R5 45 02N 70 18W
Sühbaatar Mongolia 101 K9 50 10N 106 14E
Suiattle River Washington USA 42 H4 48 16N 121 20W
Sukabumi Indonesia 103 D2 6 55S 106 50E
Sukhona *r.* Russia 94 G9 60 00N 45 00E
Sukkur Pakistan 98 B5 27 42N 68 54E
Sulaiman Range *mts.* Pakistan 98 B5/C6 30 00N 70 00E
Sulawesi *i.* Indonesia 103 F3/G3 2 00S 120 00E
Sullana Peru 80 A13 4 52S 80 39W
Sulu Archipelago Philippines 103 G5 6 00N 121 00E
Sulu Sea Philippines/Malaysia 103 F5/G5 8 00N 120 00E
Sumas Washington USA 42 H4 49 00N 122 18W
Sumatra *i.* Indonesia 103 B4/C3 0 00 100 00E
Sumba *i.* Indonesia 103 F2/G1 10 00S 120 00E
Sumbawa *i.* Indonesia 103 F2 8 00S 118 00E
Sumburgh Head *c.* UK 86 E13 59 51N 1 16W
Summer Strait *sd.* Alaska USA 42 D5 56 30N 133 30W
Sunburst Montana USA 46 G1 48 56N 111 58W
Sunbury Pennsylvania USA 73 B2 40 52N 76 47W
Sunchon South Korea 101 P5 34 56N 127 28E
Sundarbans *geog. reg.* India/Bangladesh 99 K8 21 50N 88 50E
Sunderland UK 86 E11 54 55N 1 23W
Sung Kong *i.* HK China 100 C1 22 11N 114 17E
Sunnyvale California USA 72 C3 37 23N 122 00W
Sunset Peak HK China 100 A1 22 15N 113 57E
Sunshine Island HK China 100 B1 22 16N 114 03E
Suntar Russia 95 P9 62 10N 117 35E
Sunyani Ghana 108 D9 7 22N 2 18W
Suō-nada *b.* Japan 102 B1 33 50N 131 30E
Superior Wisconsin USA 71 H6 46 42N 92 05W
Sūr Oman 97 G3 22 34N 59 32E
Surabaya Indonesia 103 E2 7 14S 112 45E
Surakarta Indonesia 103 E2 7 32S 110 50E
Surat India 98 C4 21 10N 72 54E
Surat Thani Thailand 103 B5 9 09N 99 20E
Surgut Russia 94 K9 61 13N 73 20E
SURINAME 80 F14
Susquehanna River Pennsylvania USA 53 K1 41 45N 76 25W
Susuman Russia 95 S9 62 46N 148 08E
Sutlej *r.* Pakistan 98 C6 30 30N 73 00E
Suva Fiji 114 U15 18 08S 178 25E
Suwalki Poland 88 J11 54 06N 22 56E
Suzhou China 101 M5 33 38N 117 02E
Suzhou China 101 N5 31 21N 120 40E
Suzuka Japan 102 C1 34 52N 136 37E
Suzu-misaki *c.* Japan 102 C2 37 30N 137 21E
Svobodnyy Russia 95 Q7 51 24N 128 05E
Swale *r.* UK 86 E11 54 20N 2 00W
Swansea UK 86 D9 51 38N 3 57W
Swanton Ohio USA 52 C1 41 36N 83 54W
Swanton Vermont USA 53 N4 44 56N 73 08W
SWAZILAND 109 L2
SWEDEN 88 D13
Sweetwater *tn.* Texas USA 70 F3 32 27N 100 25W
Swellendam RSA 109 J1 34 01S 20 26E
Swiebodzin Poland 88 E10 52 15N 15 31E
Swindon UK 86 E9 51 34N 1 47W
Swinoujście Poland 88 E10 53 55N 14 18E
SWITZERLAND 87 J7/K7
Sydney Aust. 110 J3 33 55S 151 10E
Syktyvkar Russia 94 H9 61 42N 50 45E
Sylhet Bangladesh 99 L10 24 53N 91 51E
Sylt Germany 88 B11 54 00N 8 00E
Sylvania Ohio USA 51 K1 41 41N 83 37W
Syracuse New York USA 71 L5 43 03N 76 10W
Syr-Dar'ya *r.* Asia 94 J5 43 30N 66 30E
SYRIA 96 C6
Syrian Desert Middle East 96 C5 32 30N 39 20E
Syzran' Russia 94 G7 53 10N 48 29E
Szczecin Poland 88 E10 53 25N 14 32E
Szczecinek Poland 88 F10 53 42N 16 41E
Szeged Hungary 89 H7 46 15N 20 09E
Székesfehérvár Hungary 89 G7 47 11N 18 22E
Szolnok Hungary 89 H7 47 10N 20 10E
Szombathely Hungary 89 F7 47 14N 16 38E

T

Ţabas Iran 97 G5 33 37N 56 54E
Table Rock Lake Missouri USA 71 H4 36 38N 93 17W
Tábor Czech Rep. 88 E8 49 25N 14 39E
Tabora Tanzania 108 L7 5 01S 32 48E
Tabriz Iran 96 E6 38 04N 46 17E
Tabuaaran Island Kiribati 115 L8 4 00N 158 10W
Tabūk Saudi Arabia 96 C4 28 33N 36 36E
Tacloban Philippines 103 G6 11 15N 125 01E
Tacna Peru 80 C10 18 00S 70 15W
Tacoma Washington USA 70 B6 47 16N 122 30W
Taegu South Korea 101 P6 35 52N 128 36E
Taejon South Korea 101 P6 36 20N 127 26E
Tafila Jordan 96 N10 30 52N 35 36E
Taganrog Russia 94 F6 47 14N 38 55E
Tagus *r.* Sp./Port. 87 B3 39 30N 7 00W
Tahat, Mount Algeria 108 F12 23 18N 5 33E
Tahiti *i.* Pacific Ocean 115 M6 17 30S 148 30W
Tahoe, Lake California USA 70 C4 39 00N 120 00W
Tahoua Niger 108 F10 14 57N 5 19E
Tai'an China 101 M6 36 15N 117 10E
Taibei Taiwan 101 N4 25 05N 121 32E
Taichung Taiwan 101 N3 24 09N 124 40E
Taihape NZ 111 E5 39 41S 175 48E
Tai Lam Chung HK China 100 B2 22 22N 114 01E
Tai Lam Chung Reservoir HK China 100 B2 22 23N 114 01E
Tai Long HK China 100 D2 22 25N 114 22E
Tai Long Wan *b.* HK China 100 D2 22 24N 114 23E
Tai Mei Tuk HK China 100 C2 22 28N 114 14E
Tai Mong Tsai HK China 100 C2 22 23N 114 18E
Tai Mo Shan *mt.* HK China 100 B2 22 25N 114 07E
Tainan Taiwan 101 N3 23 01N 120 14E
Tai O HK China 100 A1 22 15N 113 52E
Tai Po HK China 100 C2 22 27N 114 10E
Tai Shui Hang HK China 100 B1 22 17N 114 01E
Tai Tam Resevoirs HK China 100 C1 22 15N 114 13E
Tai Tam Wan *b.* HK China 100 C1 22 13N 114 13E
Tai Wai HK China 100 C2 22 23N 114 10E
TAIWAN 101 N3
Taiwan Strait China/Taiwan 101 M3 24 00N 119 30E
Tai Wan Tau HK China 100 C1 22 17N 114 17E
Taiyuan China 101 L6 37 50N 112 30E
Ta'izz Yemen 96 D1 13 35N 44 02E
TAJIKISTAN 94 J4/K4
Tajo *r.* Sp./Port. 87 B3 39 00N 7 00W
Tak Thailand 103 B7 16 51N 99 08E
Takamatsu Japan 102 B1 34 20N 134 01E
Takaoka Japan 102 C2 36 47N 137 00E
Takapuna NZ 111 E6 36 48S 174 46E
Takasaki Japan 102 C2 36 20N 139 00E
Takayama Japan 102 C2 36 09N 137 16E
Takefu Japan 102 C2 35 54N 136 10E
Takêv Cambodia 103 C6 11 00N 104 46E
Taki India 99 K9 22 35N 88 56E
Taku Inlet Alaska USA 42 C6 58 30N 134 00W
Talara Peru 80 A13 4 38S 81 18W
Talavera de la Reina Sp. 87 C3 39 58N 4 50W
Talbot, Cape Aust. 110 D7 13 49S 126 42E
Talca Chile 81 C6 35 28S 71 40W
Talcahuano Chile 81 C6 36 40S 73 10W
Taldykorgan Kazakhstan 94 K6 45 02N 78 23E
Tallahassee Florida USA 71 K3 30 26N 84 16W
Tallinn Estonia 88 K13 59 22N 24 48E
Tall Kalakh Syria 96 P12 34 45N 36 17E
Talodi Sudan 108 L10 10 40N 30 25E
Talsi Latvia 88 J12 57 17N 22 37E
Taltal Chile 80 C8 25 26S 70 33W
Tamabo Range Malaysia 103 F4 4 00N 115 30E
Tamale Ghana 108 D9 9 26N 0 49W
Tamanrasset Algeria 108 F12 22 50N 5 28E
Tamazunchale Mexico 74 E4 21 18N 98 46W
Tambov Russia 94 G7 52 44N 41 28E
Tambre *r.* Sp. 87 A5 42 55N 8 50W
Tâmega *r.* Port. 87 B4 41 40N 7 45W
Tamil Nadu *admin.* India 98 D2 12 00N 78 30E
Tampa Florida USA 71 K2 27 58N 82 38W
Tampico Mexico 74 E4 22 18N 97 52W
Tamworth Aust. 110 J3 31 07S 150 57E
Tana *r.* Kenya 108 M7 0 30S 39 00E
Tanabe Japan 102 C1 33 43N 135 22E
Tanahmerah Indonesia 110 G8 6 08S 140 18E
Tana, Lake Ethiopia 108 M10 12 20N 37 20E
Tandil Argentina 81 F6 37 18S 59 10W
Tanega-shima *i.* Japan 102 B1 31 00N 131 00E
Tanezrouft *geog. reg.* Algeria 108 D12 24 00N 0 30W
Tanga Tanzania 108 M6 5 07S 39 05E
Tangail Bangladesh 99 K10 24 15N 89 55E
Tangan *r.* India 99 K10 25 30N 88 20E
Tanganyika, Lake East Africa 109 K6/L6 7 00S 30 00E
Tanggula Shan *mts.* China 100 G5 32 30N 92 30E
Tangier Morocco 108 C15 35 48N 5 45W
Tangshan China 101 M6 39 37N 118 05E
Tanjungkarang-Telukbetung Indonesia 103 D2 5 28S 105 16E
Tannu Ola *mts.* Russia 95 M7 51 00N 92 30E
Tanout Niger 108 F11 15 05N 8 50E
TANZANIA 108/109 L6
Tapachula Mexico 74 F2 14 54N 92 15W
Tapajós *r.* Brazil 80 F12 6 30S 57 00W
Tāpi *r.* India 98 D4 21 30N 76 30E
Tappi-zaki *c.* Japan 102 D3 41 14N 140 21E
Taquari *r.* Brazil 80 F10 18 00S 57 00W
Tarakan Indonesia 103 F4 3 20N 117 38E
Táranto Italy 89 F4 40 28N 17 15E
Tarapoto Peru 80 B12 6 31S 76 23W
Tarauacá Brazil 80 C12 8 06S 70 45W
Tarawera NZ 111 F5 38 15S 175 56E
Tarazona Sp. 87 E4 41 54N 1 44W
Tarbes Fr. 87 F5 43 14N 0 05E
Taree Aust. 110 J3 31 54S 152 26E
Tarfaya Morocco 108 B13 27 58N 12 55W
Târgovişte Romania 89 K6 44 56N 25 27E
Târgu-Jiu Romania 89 J6 45 03N 23 18E
Târgu Mureş Romania 89 K7 46 33N 24 34E
Tarija Bolivia 80 D9 21 33S 65 02W
Tarim He *r.* China 100 E7 41 00N 82 00E
Tarim Pendi China 100 E6/F6 39 00N 84 00E
Tarko-Sale Russia 94 K9 64 55N 77 50E
Tarkwa Ghana 108 D9 5 16N 1 59W
Tarn *r.* Fr. 87 G5 44 05N 1 40E
Tarnobrzeg Poland 88 H9 50 35N 21 40E
Tarnów Poland 88 H9 50 01N 20 59E
Tarragona Sp. 87 F4 41 07N 1 15E
Tarrasa Sp. 87 G4 41 34N 2 00E
Tarsus Turkey 96 B6 26 25N 34 52E
Tartary, Gulf of Russia 95 S6/S7 50 00N 141 00E
Tarţūs Syria 96 C5 34 55N 35 52E
Tashkent Uzbekistan 94 J5 41 16N 69 13E
Tasman Basin Southern Ocean 114 F3 48 00S 154 00E
Tasman Bay NZ 111 D4 41 00S 173 14E
Tasmania *state* Aust. 110 H1 43 00S 147 00E
Tasman Plateau Southern Ocean 114 E3 48 00S 147 00E
Tasman Sea Pacific Ocean 111 D6 40 00S 155 00E
Tassili N'Ajjer *mts.* Algeria 108 F13 26 00N 6 20W
Tatabánya Hungary 89 G7 47 31N 18 25E
Tateyama Japan 102 C1 34 59N 139 50E
Taumarunui NZ 111 E5 38 53S 175 16E
Taunggyi Myanmar 101 H3 20 55N 97 02E
Taunton UK 86 D9 51 01N 3 06W
Taunton Massachusetts USA 73 E2 41 54N 71 06W
Taupo NZ 111 F5 38 42S 176 05E
Taupo, Lake NZ 111 F5 38 55S 175 49
Tauranga NZ 111 F6 37 41S 176 10E
Tauva Fiji 114 T16 17 31S 177 53E
Tavda *r.* Russia 94 J8 58 00N 64 00E
Taveuni *i.* Fiji 114 U15 16 40S 180 00
Tavira Port. 87 B2 37 07N 7 39W
Tavoy Myanmar 103 B6 14 02N 98 12E
Tawas City Michigan USA 51 K3 44 16N 83 31W
Tawau Malaysia 103 F4 4 16N 117 54E
Taymā' Saudi Arabia 96 C4 27 37N 38 30E
Taymyr Peninsula Russia 95 M12 75 00N 100 00E
Tayshet Russia 95 M8 55 56N 98 01E
Taz *r.* Russia 95 L10 67 00N 82 00E
Taza Morocco 108 D14 34 16N 4 01W
Tchibanga Gabon 108 G7 2 49S 11 00E
Tczew Poland 88 G11 54 05N 18 46E
Te Anau, Lake NZ 111 A2 45 13S 167 45E
Te Aroha NZ 111 E6 37 32S 175 42E
Te Awamutu NZ 111 E5 38 01S 175 20E
Tébessa Algeria 108 F15 35 21N 8 06E
Tecopa California USA 72 E2 35 51N 116 13W
Tecuci Romania 89 L6 45 50N 27 27E
Tecumseh Michigan USA 52 C2 42 01N 83 56W
Tees *r.* UK 86 D11 54 40N 1 20W
Tefé Brazil 80 E13 3 24S 64 45W
Tefé *r.* Brazil 80 D12 4 30S 65 30W
Tegal Indonesia 103 D2 6 52S 109 07E
Tegucigalpa Honduras 74 G2 14 05N 87 14W
Tehachapi California USA 72 D2 35 08N 118 27W
Tehachapi Mountains California USA 72 D2 34 52N 118 45W
Tehran Iran 97 F6 35 40N 51 26E
Tehuacán Mexico 74 E3 18 30N 97 26W
Tehuantepec Mexico 74 E3 16 21N 95 13W
Teifi *r.* UK 86 C10 52 03N 4 30W
Tejo *r.* Port. 87 B3 39 30N 8 15W
Tekapo, Lake NZ 111 C3 43 53S 170 32E
Te Kuiti NZ 111 E5 38 20S 175 10E
Tel *r.* India 98 E4 20 30N 84 00E
Tela Honduras 74 G3 15 46N 87 25W
Tel Aviv-Yafo Israel 96 N11 32 05N 34 46E
Telemark *geog. reg.* Norway 86 K13 59 42N 8 00E
Telescope Peak *mt.* California USA 72 E3 36 11N 117 05W
Teles Pires *r.* Brazil 80 F12 8 00S 57 00W
Telford UK 86 D10 52 42N 2 28W
Telsiai Lithuania 88 J12 55 59N 22 17E
Teluk Bone *b.* Indonesia 103 G3 4 00S 121 00E
Teluk Cenderawasih *b.* Indonesia 110 E9 2 15S 135 30E
Teluk Intan Malaysia 103 C4 4 02N 101 01E
Teluk Tomini *b.* Indonesia 103 G3 0 20S 121 00E
Tema Ghana 108 E9 5 41N 0 00
Temecula California USA 72 E1 33 30N 117 08W
Temirtau Kazakhstan 94 K7 50 05N 72 55E
Tempio Pausania Italy 89 B4 40 54N 9 07E
Temple Texas USA 71 G3 31 06N 97 22W
Temuco Chile 81 C6 38 45S 72 40W
Temuka NZ 111 C2 44 15S 171 17E
Tenali India 98 E3 16 13N 80 36E
Ten Degree Channel Andaman Islands/Nicobar Islands 99 G1 10 00N 93 00E
Tenerife *i.* Canary Islands 108 A13 28 15N 16 35W
Tennant Creek *tn.* Aust. 110 E6 19 31S 134 15E
Tennessee *r.* USA 71 J4 35 00N 88 00W
Tennessee *state* USA 71 J4 35 00N 87 00W
Teófilo Otôni Brazil 80 J10 17 52S 41 31W
Tepatitlán Mexico 74 D4 20 50N 102 46W
Tepic Mexico 74 D4 21 30N 104 51W
Ter *r.* Sp. 87 G4 41 55N 2 30E
Teresina Brazil 80 J12 5 09S 42 46W
Teressa Island India 99 G1 8 15N 93 10E
Termez Uzbekistan 94 J4 37 15N 67 15E
Termim Imerese Italy 89 D2 27 59N 13 42E
Ternate Indonesia 103 H4 0 48N 127 23E
Terni Italy 89 D5 42 34N 12 39E
Ternopil' Ukraine 88 K8 49 35N 25 39E
Terpeniya Bay Russia 95 S6 48 00N 144 0E
Terracina Italy 89 D4 41 17N 13 15E
Terrasini Italy 89 D3 38 09N 13 05E
Terre Haute Indiana USA 71 J4 39 27N 87 24W
Teruel Sp. 87 E4 40 21N 1 06W
Teseney Eritrea 108 M11 15 10N 36 48E
Teshio Japan 102 D3 44 53N 141 46E
Testa del Gargano *c.* Italy 89 F4 41 50N 16 10E
Teteiev *r.* Ukraine 88 M9 50 00N 29 00E
Tétouan Morocco 108 C15 35 34N 5 22W
Tetovo FYROM 89 H5 42 00N 20 59E
Texarkana Arkansas USA 71 H3 33 28N 94 02W
Texas *state* USA 70 G3 31 00N 100 00W
Texel *i.* Neths. 86 H10 53 05N 4 45E
Texoma, Lake Oklahoma/Texas USA 71 G3 34 00N 97 00W
THAILAND 103 B7/C7
Thailand, Gulf of Southern Asia 103 C6 10 50N 101 00E
Thakhek Laos 103 C7 17 22N 104 50E
Thames NZ 111 E6 37 09S 175 33E
Thames *r.* UK 86 E9 51 32N 0 50W
Thane India 98 C3 19 14N 73 02E
Thanh Hoa Vietnam 103 D7 19 49N 105 48E
Thanjavur India 98 D2 10 46N 79 09E
Thar Desert India 98 C5 27 30N 72 00E
Thásos *i.* Greece 89 K4 40 00N 24 00E
Thayetmyo Myanmar 103 B7 19 20N 95 10E
The Brothers *is.* HK China 100 A2 22 20N 113 58E
The Dalles *tn.* Oregon USA 70 B6 45 36N 121 10W
The Everglades *swamp* Florida USA 71 K2 26 00N 81 00W
The Hague Neths. 86 H10 52 05N 4 16E
Thermaïkós Kólpos *g.* Greece 89 J3/J4 40 00N 22 50E
Thermopolis Wyoming USA 70 E5 43 39N 108 12W
Thessaloníki Greece 89 J4 40 38N 22 58E
The Valley Anguilla 74 P10 18 03N 63 04W
Thief River Falls *tn.* Minnesota USA 71 G6 48 12N 96 48W
Thiers Fr. 87 G6 45 51N 3 33E
Thiès Senegal 108 A10 14 49N 16 52W
Thimphu Bhutan 99 F5 27 32N 89 43E
Thionville Fr. 86 J8 49 22N 6 11E
Thíra *i.* Greece 89 K2 36 00N 25 00E
Thisted Denmark 88 B12 56 58N 8 42E
Thithia *i.* Fiji 114 V16 17 45S 179 20W
Thíva Greece 89 J3 38 19N 23 19E
Thomasville Georgia USA 71 K3 30 50N 83 59W
Thomson *r.* Aust. 110 G5 24 00S 141 00E
Thornapple River Michigan USA 52 A2/B2 42 38N 85 00W
Thousand Oaks California USA 72 D2 34 10N 118 50W
Three Kings Islands NZ 111 D7 34 10S 172 07E
Three Mile Bay *tn.* New York USA 51 N3 44 05N 76 10W
Three Points, Cape Ghana 108 D8 4 43N 2 06W
Thun Switz. 87 J7 46 46N 7 38E
Thunder Bay Michigan USA 52 C4 45 00N 83 25W
Thüringer Wald *hills* Germany 88 C9 50 00N 10 00E
Thurso UK 86 D13 58 35N 3 32W
Tianjin China 101 M6 39 08N 117 12E
Tianshui China 101 K5 34 25N 105 58E
Tiber *r.* Italy 89 D4 42 00N 12 00E
Tiberias Israel 96 N11 32 48N 35 32E
Tiberias, Lake Israel 96 N11 32 45N 35 30E
Tibesti *mts.* Chad 108 H12 21 00N 17 00E
Tiburón *i.* Mexico 74 B5 28 30N 112 30W
Ticul Mexico 74 G4 20 22N 89 31W
Tierra Blanca Mexico 74 E3 18 28N 96 21W
Tiffin Ohio USA 51 K1 41 07N 83 10W
Tighina Moldova 89 M7 46 50N 29 29E
Tikrīt Iraq 96 D5 34 36N 43 42E
Tijuana Mexico 74 A6 32 29N 117 10W
Tiksi Russia 95 Q11 71 40N 128 45E
Tilburg Neths. 86 H9 51 34N 5 05E
Timaru NZ 111 C2 44 24S 171 15E
Timimóun Algeria 108 E13 29 15N 0 14E
Timişoara Romania 89 H6 45 45N 21 15E
Timişul *r.* Romania/Serbia 89 H6 45 00N 21 00E
Timon Brazil 80 J12 5 08S 42 52W
Timor *i.* Indonesia 103 G1 9 00S 125 00E
Timor Sea Indonesia 103 H1 10 45S 126 00E
Tindouf Algeria 108 C13 27 42N 8 10W
Tinos *i.* Greece 89 K2 37 00N 25 00E
Tin Sam HK China 100 A2 22 26N 113 59E
Tinsukia India 99 H5 27 30N 95 22E
Tionesta Pennsylvania USA 52 G1 41 31N 79 30W

Tionesta Lake Pennsylvania USA	**52**	G1	41 30N	79 29W
Tiranë Albania	**89**	G4	41 20N	19 49E
Tir'at el Ismâ'iliya *can.* Egypt	**109**	R3	30 32N	31 48E
Tir'at el Mansûriya *r.* Egypt	**109**	R4	31 12N	31 38E
Tiraz Mountains Namibia	**109**	H2	25 30S	16 30E
Tirso *r.* Italy	**89**	B3	40 00N	9 00E
Tiruchchirappalli India	**98**	D2	10 50N	78 41E
Tirunelveli India	**98**	D1	8 45N	77 43E
Tirupati India	**98**	D2	13 39N	79 25E
Tiruppur India	**98**	D2	11 05N	77 20E
Tisza *r.* Hungary/Serbia	**89**	H7	46 00N	20 00E
Titovo Užice Serbia	**89**	G5	43 52N	19 50E
Titov Veles FYROM	**89**	H4	41 43N	21 49E
Tittabawassee River Michigan USA	**52**	B3	43 50N	84 25W
Titusville Pennsylvania USA	**52**	G1	41 37N	79 42W
Tiu Chung Chau *i.* HK China	**100**	C2	22 20N	114 19E
Tiverton Rhode Island USA	**73**	E2	41 38N	71 12W
Tivoli Italy	**89**	D4	41 58N	12 48E
Tizimín Mexico	**74**	G4	21 10N	88 09W
Tizi Ouzou Algeria	**108**	E15	36 44N	4 05E
Tiznit Morocco	**108**	C13	29 43N	9 44W
Tlemcen Algeria	**108**	D14	34 53N	1 21W
Toamasina Madagascar	**109**	P4	18 10S	49 23E
Tobago *i.* Trinidad and Tobago	**75**	V15	11 15N	60 40W
Tobi-shima *i.* Japan	**102**	C2	39 12N	139 32E
Tobol *r.* Russia	**94**	J8	57 00N	67 30E
Tobol'sk Russia	**94**	J8	58 15N	68 12E
Tocantins *admin.* Brazil	**80**	H11	12 00S	47 00W
Tocantins *r.* Brazil	**80**	H12	10 00S	49 00W
Toco Trinidad and Tobago	**75**	V15	10 49N	60 57W
Tocopilla Chile	**80**	C9	22 05S	70 10W
TOGO	**108**	E9		
Toi Tan HK China	**100**	C2	22 26N	114 19E
Toiyabe Range *mts.* Nevada USA	**72**	E4	39 20N	117 15W
Tok Alaska USA	**64**	B3	63 20N	142 59W
Tokelau Islands Pacific Ocean	**114**	J7	9 00S	168 00W
Tokushima Japan	**102**	B1	34 03N	134 34E
Tokuyama Japan	**102**	B1	34 03N	131 48E
Tokyo Japan	**102**	C2	35 40N	139 45E
Tolaga Bay *tn.* NZ	**111**	G5	38 22S	178 18E
Tôlanaro Madagascar	**109**	P2	25 01S	47 00E
Toledo Sp.	**87**	C3	39 52N	4 02W
Toledo Ohio USA	**71**	K5	41 40N	83 35W
Toliara Madagascar	**109**	N3	23 20S	43 41E
Tollhouse California USA	**72**	D3	37 01N	119 25W
Tolo Channel HK China	**100**	C2	22 28N	114 17E
Tolo Harbour *b.* HK China	**100**	C2	22 26N	114 13E
Tolosa Sp.	**87**	D5	43 09N	2 04W
Toluca Mexico	**74**	E3	19 20N	99 40W
Tol'yatti Russia	**94**	G7	53 32N	49 24E
Tomakomai Japan	**102**	D3	42 39N	141 33E
Tomaniivi *mt.* Fiji	**114**	U16	17 37S	178 01E
Tomar Port.	**87**	A3	39 36N	8 25W
Tomatlán Mexico	**74**	C3	19 54N	105 18W
Tombigbee *r.* USA	**71**	J3	32 00N	88 00W
Tombouctou Mali	**108**	D11	16 49N	2 59W
Tombua Angola	**109**	G4	15 49S	11 53E
Tom Price, Mount Aust.	**110**	B5	22 49S	117 51E
Tomsk Russia	**95**	L8	56 30N	85 05E
Tonalá Mexico	**74**	F3	16 08N	93 41W
Tonasket Washington USA	**43**	L1	48 42N	119 28W
Tonawanda New York USA	**51**	M2	43 01N	78 53W
Tonawanda Channel New York USA	**54**	D2	43 03N	78 55W
Tonawanda Creek *r.* New York USA	**52**	H3	43 08N	78 35W
TONGA	**114**	J5		
Tonga Trench Pacific Ocean	**114**	J5	20 00S	173 00E
Tongchuan China	**101**	K6	35 05N	109 02E
Tong Fuk HK China	**100**	A1	22 14N	113 56E
Tonghai China	**101**	J3	24 07N	104 45E
Tonghua China	**101**	P7	41 42N	125 45E
Tongking, Gulf of China/Vietnam	**101**	K2	19 00N	107 00E
Tongling China	**101**	M5	30 58N	117 48E
Tônlé Sab *l.* Cambodia	**103**	C6	12 00N	103 50E
Tonopah Nevada USA	**70**	C4	38 05N	117 15W
Tønsberg Norway	**86**	L13	59 16N	10 25E
Tooele Utah USA	**70**	D5	40 32N	112 18W
Toowoomba Aust.	**110**	J4	27 35S	151 54E
Topeka Kansas USA	**71**	G4	39 02N	95 41W
Torbay UK	**86**	D9	50 27N	3 30W
Tordesillas Sp.	**87**	C4	41 30N	5 00W
Tormes *r.* Sp.	**87**	C4	41 03N	5 58W
Tororo Uganda	**108**	L8	0 42N	34 12E
Toros Dağlari *mts.* Turkey	**96**	B6	37 10N	33 10E
Torre del Greco Italy	**89**	E4	40 46N	14 22E
Torrelavega Sp.	**87**	C5	43 21N	4 03W
Torrens, Lake Aust.	**110**	F3	31 00S	137 50E
Torreón Mexico	**74**	D5	25 34N	103 25W
Torres Strait Aust.	**110**	G7/G8	10 00S	142 30E
Torrington Connecticut USA	**73**	D2	41 48N	73 07W
Tortosa Sp.	**87**	F4	40 49N	0 31E
Torun Poland	**88**	G10	53 01N	18 35E
Tosa-wan *b.* Japan	**102**	B1	33 20N	133 40E
Totoya *i.* Fiji	**114**	V15	18 56S	179 50W
Tottori Japan	**102**	B2	35 32N	134 12E
Touggourt Algeria	**108**	F14	33 08N	6 04E
Toulon Fr.	**87**	H5	43 07N	5 55E
Toulouse Fr.	**87**	F5	43 33N	1 24E
Toungoo Myanmar	**103**	B7	18 57N	96 26E
Tournai Belgium	**86**	G9	50 36N	3 24E
Tours Fr.	**87**	F7	47 23N	0 42E
Towanda Pennsylvania USA	**53**	K1	41 46N	76 27W
Townsville Aust.	**110**	H6	19 13S	146 48E
Towson Maryland USA	**73**	B1	39 25N	76 36W
Toyama Japan	**102**	C2	36 42N	137 14E
Toyohashi Japan	**102**	C1	34 46N	137 22E
Toyota Japan	**102**	C2	35 05N	137 09E
Tozeur Tunisia	**108**	F14	33 55N	8 07E
Trabzon Turkey	**96**	C7	41 00N	39 43E
Tracy California USA	**72**	C3	37 39N	121 26W
Tralee RoI	**86**	A10	52 16N	9 42W
Tranås Sweden	**88**	E13	58 03N	15 00E
Transantarctic Mountains Antarctica	**117**		80 00S	155 00E
Trápani Italy	**89**	D3	38 02N	12 32E
Traverse City Michigan USA	**71**	J5	44 46N	85 38W
Treinta-y-Tres Uruguay	**81**	G7	33 16S	54 17W
Trelew Chile	**81**	D5	43 13S	65 15W
Trelleborg Sweden	**88**	D11	55 22N	13 10E
Trenčin Slovakia	**88**	G8	48 53N	18 00E
Trenque Lauquen Argentina	**81**	E6	35 56S	62 43W
Trent *r.* UK	**86**	E10	53 30N	0 50W
Trento Italy	**89**	C7	46 04N	11 08E
Trenton New Jersey USA	**71**	M5	40 15N	74 43W
Tres Arroyos Argentina	**81**	E6	38 26S	60 17W
Três Lagoas Brazil	**80**	G9	20 46S	51 43W
Treviso Italy	**89**	D6	45 40N	12 15E
Trichur India	**98**	D2	10 32N	76 14E
Trieste Italy	**89**	D6	45 39N	13 47E
Tríkala Greece	**89**	H3	39 33N	21 46E
Trincomalee Sri Lanka	**98**	E1	8 34N	81 13E
Trindale *i.* Atlantic Ocean	**116**	F4	20 30S	29 20W
Trinidad Bolivia	**80**	E11	14 46S	64 50W
Trinidad Cuba	**75**	H4	21 48N	80 00W
Trinidad Colorado USA	**70**	F4	37 11N	104 31W
Trinidad *i.* Trinidad and Tobago	**75**	V15	11 00N	61 30W
TRINIDAD AND TOBAGO	**75**	M2		
Trinity *r.* USA	**71**	G3	32 00N	96 00W
Trípoli Greece	**89**	J2	37 31N	22 22E
Tripoli Lebanon	**96**	N12	34 27N	35 50E
Tripoli Libya	**108**	G14	32 54N	13 11E
Tripura *admin.* India	**99**	G4	23 40N	92 00E
Tristan da Cunha *i.* Atlantic Ocean	**116**	G3	37 15S	12 30W
Trivandrum India	**98**	D1	8 30N	76 57E
Trnava Slovakia	**88**	F8	48 23N	17 35E
Trollhätten Sweden	**88**	D13	58 17N	12 20E
Trombetas *r.* Brazil	**80**	F14	1 30N	57 00W
Trona California USA	**72**	E2	35 46N	117 24W
Trouville Fr.	**86**	F8	49 22N	0 05E
Troy Alabama USA	**71**	J3	31 49N	86 00W
Troy Montana USA	**43**	N1	48 28N	115 55W
Troy New York USA	**71**	M5	42 43N	73 43W
Troy *hist. site* Turkey	**96**	A6	39 55N	26 17E
Troyes Fr.	**86**	H8	48 18N	4 05E
Trujillo Peru	**80**	B12	8 06S	79 00W
Trujillo Sp.	**87**	C3	39 28N	5 53W
Trujillo Venezuela	**80**	C15	9 20N	70 38W
Truk Islands Pacific Ocean	**114**	E8	7 30N	152 30E
Truro UK	**86**	C9	50 16N	5 03W
Tseung Kwan O HK China	**100**	C1	22 19N	114 14E
Tshane Botswana	**109**	J3	24 05S	21 54E
Tshuapa *r.* CDR	**108**	J7	1 00S	23 00E
Tsing Chau Tsai HK China	**100**	B2	22 20N	114 02E
Tsing Yi HK China	**100**	B2	22 21N	114 06E
Tsu Japan	**102**	C1	34 41N	136 30E
Tsuchiura Japan	**102**	D2	36 05N	140 11E
Tsuen Wan HK China	**100**	B2	22 22N	114 06E
Tsugaru-kaikyō *sd.* Japan	**102**	D3	41 30N	140 30E
Tsumeb Namibia	**109**	H4	19 13S	17 42E
Tsuruga Japan	**102**	C2	35 40N	136 05E
Tsuruoka Japan	**102**	C2	38 42N	139 50E
Tsushima *i.* Japan	**102**	A1	34 30N	129 20E
Tsuyama Japan	**102**	B2	35 04N	134 01E
Tua *r.* Port.	**87**	B4	41 20N	7 30W
Tuamotu Archipelago *is.* Pacific Ocean	**115**	N6	15 00S	145 00W
Tuamotu Ridge Pacific Ocean	**115**	M6	19 00S	144 00W
Tübingen Germany	**88**	B8	48 32N	9 04E
Tubruq Libya	**108**	J14	32 05N	23 59E
Tubuai Islands Pacific Ocean	**115**	M5	23 23S	149 27W
Tucson Arizona USA	**70**	D3	32 15N	110 57W
Tucumcari New Mexico USA	**70**	F4	35 11N	103 44W
Tucupita Venezuela	**80**	E15	9 02N	62 04W
Tucuruí Brazil	**80**	H13	3 42S	49 44W
Tudela Sp.	**87**	E5	42 04N	1 37W
Tuen Mun HK China	**100**	A2	22 24N	113 58E
Tukums Latvia	**88**	J12	56 58N	23 10E
Tula Russia	**94**	F7	54 11N	37 38E
Tula Mexico	**74**	E4	20 01N	99 21W
Tula Mexico	**74**	E4	23 00N	99 41W
Tulare California USA	**72**	D3	36 12N	119 21W
Tulare Lake California USA	**72**	D3	36 04N	119 45W
Tulcán Ecuador	**80**	B14	0 50N	77 48W
Tulcea Romania	**89**	M6	45 10N	28 50E
Tulkarm Jordan	**96**	N11	32 19N	35 02E
Tulle Fr.	**87**	F6	45 16N	1 46E
Tulsa Oklahoma USA	**71**	G4	36 07N	95 58W
Tuluá Col.	**80**	B14	4 05N	76 12W
Tulun Russia	**95**	N7	54 32N	100 35E
Tumaco Col.	**80**	B14	1 51N	78 46W
Tumbes Peru	**80**	A13	3 37S	80 27W
Tumkur India	**98**	D2	13 20N	77 06E
Tunduru Tanzania	**109**	M5	11 08S	27 21E
Tundzha *r.* Bulgaria	**89**	K5	42 00N	25 00E
Tungabhadra *r.* India	**98**	D3	15 00N	75 30E
Tung Lung Chau *i.* HK China	**100**	C1	22 15N	114 17E
Tunis Tunisia	**108**	G14	36 50N	10 13E
TUNISIA	**108**	F14		
Tunja Col.	**80**	C15	5 33N	73 23W
Tunkhannock Pennsylvania USA	**53**	L1	41 32N	75 46W
Tuolumne *r.* California USA	**72**	C3	37 53N	120 09W
Tupelo Mississippi USA	**71**	J3	34 15N	88 43W
Tupiza Bolivia	**80**	D9	21 27S	65 45W
Túquerres Col.	**80**	B14	1 06N	77 37W
Tura Russia	**95**	N9	64 20N	100 17E
Turda Romania	**89**	J7	46 35N	23 50E
Turgay *r.* Kazakhstan	**94**	J7	50 00N	64 00E
Turia *r.* Sp.	**87**	E3	39 45N	0 55W
Turin Italy	**89**	A6	45 04N	7 40E
Turkana, Lake Ethiopia/Kenya	**108**	M8	4 00N	36 00E
TURKEY	**96**	B6		
TURKMENISTAN	**94**	H4/J4		
Turks and Caicos Islands W. Indies	**75**	K4	21 30N	72 00W
Turks Island Passage *sd.* W. Indies	**75**	K4	21 30N	71 30W
Turlock California USA	**72**	C3	37 30N	120 53W
Turner Montana USA	**47**	C1	48 51N	108 25W
Turnu Măgurele Romania	**89**	K5	43 44N	24 53E
Turpan China	**100**	F7	42 55N	89 06E
Turpan Depression China	**100**	F7	42 40N	89 30E
Turukhansk Russia	**95**	L10	65 49N	88 00E
Tuscaloosa Alabama USA	**71**	J3	33 12N	87 33W
Tuticorin India	**98**	D1	8 48N	78 10E
Tuttlingen Germany	**88**	B7	47 59N	8 49E
TUVALU	**108**	H7		
Tuxpan Mexico	**74**	C4	21 58N	105 20W
Tuxpan Mexico	**74**	E4	20 58N	97 23W
Tuxtla Gutierrez Mexico	**74**	F3	16 45N	93 09W
Túy Sp.	**87**	A5	42 03N	8 39W
Tuz Gölü *l.* Turkey	**96**	B6	38 40N	33 35E
Tuzla Bosnia-Herzegovina	**89**	G6	44 33N	18 41E
Tver' Russia	**94**	F8	56 49N	35 57E
Tweed *r.* UK	**86**	D11	55 45N	2 10W
Twentynine Palms California USA	**72**	E2	34 09N	116 03W
Twin Falls *tn.* Idaho USA	**70**	D5	42 34N	114 30W
Twisp Washington USA	**43**	K1	48 22N	120 08W
Twisp River Washington USA	**42**	H4	48 30N	120 20W
Two Harbors *tn.* Minnesota USA	**51**	F4	47 02N	91 40W
Two Medicine River Montana USA	**46**	F1	48 27N	112 50W
Tyan-Shan' Kyrgyzstan	**94/95**	K5	41 00N	76 00E
Tyler Texas USA	**71**	G3	32 22N	95 18W
Tym *r.* Russia	**95**	L8	59 00N	82 30E
Tynda Russia	**95**	Q8	55 10N	124 35E
Tyne *r.* UK	**86**	E11	55 58N	2 43W
Tyre Lebanon	**96**	N11	33 16N	35 12E
Tyrone Pennsylvania USA	**73**	A2	40 41N	78 14W
Tyrrhenian Sea Europe	**89**	C4/D4	40 00N	12 00E
Tyumen' Russia	**94**	J8	57 11N	65 29E
Tyung *r.* Russia	**95**	P9	65 00N	119 00E
Tywi *r.* UK	**86**	D9	51 50N	4 25W

U

Uaupés Brazil	**80**	D13	0 07S	67 05W
Ubangi *r.* CAR	**108**	H8	4 00N	18 00E
Ube Japan	**102**	B1	33 57N	131 16E
Uberaba Brazil	**80**	H10	19 47S	47 57W
Uberlândia Brazil	**80**	H10	18 57S	48 17W
Ubly Michigan USA	**52**	D3	43 44N	82 58W
Ubon Ratchathani Thailand	**103**	C7	15 15N	104 50E
Ubort' *r.* Europe	**88**	L9	51 00N	27 00E
Ubundu CDR	**108**	K7	0 24S	25 30E
Ucayali *r.* Peru	**80**	C12	6 00S	74 00W
Uchiura-wan *b.* Japan	**102**	D3	42 30N	140 40E
Uda *r.* Russia	**95**	R7	54 00N	134 00E
Udaipur India	**98**	C4	24 36N	73 47E
Udaipur India	**99**	L9	23 32N	91 29E
Uddevalla Sweden	**88**	C13	58 20N	11 56E
Udine Italy	**89**	D7	46 04N	13 14E
Udon Thani Thailand	**103**	C7	17 25N	102 45E
Ueda Japan	**102**	C2	36 27N	138 13E
Uele *r.* CDR	**108**	K8	4 00N	27 00E
Uelen Russia	**95**	W10	66 13N	169 48W
Uelzen Germany	**88**	C10	52 58N	10 34E
Ufa Russia	**94**	H7	54 45N	55 58E
Ugab *r.* Namibia	**109**	H3	21 00S	15 00E
UGANDA	**108**	L7/L8		
Uinta Mountains Utah USA	**70**	D5	40 00N	111 00W
Uitenhage RSA	**109**	K1	33 46S	25 25E
Ujjain India	**98**	D4	23 11N	75 50E
Ujung Pandang Indonesia	**103**	F2	5 09S	119 28E
Ukhta Russia	**94**	H9	63 33N	53 44E
Ukiah California USA	**70**	B4	39 09N	123 12W
Ukiah California USA	**72**	B4	39 09N	123 12W
Ukmerge Lithuania	**88**	K11	55 14N	24 49E
UKRAINE	**88**	J8/N8		
Ulaangom Mongolia	**100**	G8	49 59N	92 00E
Ulan Bator Mongolia	**101**	K8	47 54N	106 52E
Ulan-Ude Russia	**95**	N7	51 55N	107 40E
Ulhasnagar India	**98**	C3	19 15N	73 08E
Uliastay Mongolia	**101**	H8	47 42N	96 52E
Ullapool UK	**86**	C12	57 54N	5 10W
Ulm Germany	**88**	C8	48 24N	10 00E
Ulsan South Korea	**101**	P6	35 32N	129 21E
Ulungur Hu *l.* China	**100**	F8	47 10N	87 10E
Ul'yanovsk Russia	**94**	G7	54 19N	48 22E
Uman' Ukraine	**88**	N8	48 45N	30 10E
Umbagog Lake New Hampshire/Maine USA	**53**	R4	44 45N	71 00W
Umm as Samīm *geog. reg.* Oman	**97**	G3	22 10N	56 00E
Umm Ruwaba Sudan	**108**	L10	12 50N	31 20E
Umtata RSA	**109**	K1	31 35S	28 47E
Umuarama Brazil	**80**	G9	23 43S	52 57W
Una *r.* Bosnia-Herzegovina/Croatia	**89**	F6	45 15N	16 15E
'Unayzah Saudi Arabia	**96**	D4	26 06N	43 58E
Union New Jersey USA	**73**	H1	40 42N	74 14W
Union *i.* Lesser Antilles	**74**	R11	12 36N	61 26W
Union City New Jersey USA	**73**	H2	40 45N	74 01W
Union City Pennsylvania USA	**52**	G1	41 56N	79 51W
Union City Reservoir Pennsylvania USA	**52**	G1	41 58N	79 54W
Uniontown Pennsylvania USA	**71**	L4	39 54N	79 44W
Unionville Michigan USA	**52**	C3	43 41N	83 29W
UNITED ARAB EMIRATES	**97**	F3		
UNITED KINGDOM	**86**			
UNITED STATES OF AMERICA	**70/71**			
Unst *i.* UK	**86**	E14	60 45N	0 55W
Upata Venezuela	**80**	E15	8 02N	62 25W
Upham North Dakota USA	**49**	B1	48 35N	100 44W
Upington RSA	**109**	J2	28 28S	21 14E
Upolu Point *c.* Hawaiian Islands	**115**	Z18	20 16N	155 52W
Upper Bay New Jersey USA	**73**	H1	40 40N	74 03W
Upper Hutt NZ	**111**	E4	41 07S	175 04E
Upper Lake *tn.* California USA	**72**	B4	39 10N	122 56W
Upper Lough Erne *l.* UK	**86**	B11	54 15N	7 30W
Upper Red Lake Minnesota USA	**71**	H6	48 04N	94 48W
Upper Sandusky Ohio USA	**51**	K1	40 50N	83 17W
Upplands Vasby Sweden	**88**	F13	59 30N	18 15E
Uppsala Sweden	**88**	F13	59 55N	17 38E
Ur *hist. site* Iraq	**96**	E5	30 56N	46 08E
Urakawa Japan	**102**	D3	42 10N	142 46E
Ural *r.* Asia	**94**	H6	48 00N	52 00E
Ural Mountains Russia	**94**	H7	57 00N	60 00E
Ural'sk Kazakhstan	**94**	H7	51 19N	51 20E
Uraricuera *r.* Brazil	**80**	E14	3 00N	62 30W
Urawa Japan	**102**	C2	35 52N	139 40E
Ure *r.* UK	**86**	E11	54 20N	1 55W
Urengoy Russia	**95**	K10	65 59N	78 30E
Urgench Uzbekistan	**94**	J5	41 35N	60 41E
Urmston Road *sd.* HK China	**100**	A2	22 23N	113 53E
Uroševac Kosovo	**89**	H5	42 21N	21 09E
Uruapan Mexico	**74**	D3	19 26N	102 04W
Urubamba Peru	**80**	C11	13 20S	72 07W
Uruguaiana Brazil	**81**	F8	29 45S	57 05W
URUGUAY	**81**	F7		
Uruguay *r.* Uruguay/Argentina	**81**	F7	32 00S	57 40W
Ürümqi China	**100**	F7	43 43N	87 38E
Urziceni Romania	**89**	L6	44 43N	26 39E
Usa *r.* Russia	**94**	H10	66 00N	60 00E
Ushuaia Argentina	**81**	D3	54 48S	68 19W
Usinsk Russia	**94**	H10	65 57N	57 27E
Üsküdar Turkey	**96**	A7	41 02N	29 02E
Usol'ye-Sibirskoye Russia	**95**	N7	52 48N	103 40E
Ussuri *r.* Russia	**95**	R6	47 00N	134 00E
Ussuriysk Russia	**95**	R5	43 48N	131 59E
Ustica *i.* Italy	**89**	D3	38 00N	13 00E
Ust'-Ilimsk Russia	**95**	N8	58 03N	102 39E
Ustí nad Labem Czech Rep.	**88**	E9	50 40N	14 02E
Ust'-Kamchatsk Russia	**95**	U8	56 14N	162 28E
Ust'-Kamenogorsk Kazakhstan	**95**	L6	49 58N	82 36E
Ust'-Kut Russia	**95**	N8	56 48N	105 42E
Ust'Maya Russia	**95**	R9	60 25N	134 28E
Ust'-Nera Russia	**95**	S9	64 35N	143 14E
Ust'Olenek Russia	**95**	P11	72 59N	119 57E
Ust Urt Plateau Asia	**94**	H5	43 30N	55 00E
Usulután Mexico	**74**	G2	13 20N	88 25W
Utah *state* USA	**70**	D4	39 00N	112 00W
Utah Lake Utah USA	**70**	D5	40 10N	111 50W
Utica New York USA	**71**	L5	43 06N	75 15W
Utrecht Neths.	**86**	H10	52 05N	5 07E
Utrera Sp.	**87**	C2	37 10N	5 47W
Utsunomiya Japan	**102**	C2	36 33N	139 52E
Uttaradit Thailand	**103**	C7	17 38N	100 05E
Uttaranchal *admin.* India	**98**	D5/D6	30 00N	78 00E
Uttar Pradesh *admin.* India	**98**	E5	27 00N	80 00E
Uvalde Texas USA	**70**	G2	29 14N	99 49W
Uvinza Tanzania	**108**	L6	5 08S	30 23E
Uvs Nuur *l.* Mongolia	**100**	G9	50 10N	92 30E
Uwajima Japan	**102**	B1	33 13N	132 32E
Uyuni Bolivia	**80**	D9	20 28S	66 47W
Uz *r.* Slovakia	**88**	H8	48 30N	22 00E
UZBEKISTAN	**94**	H5/J5		
Uzhgorod Ukraine	**88**	J8	48 37N	22 22E

V

Vaal *r.* RSA	**109**	K2	27 30S	25 30E
Vác Hungary	**88**	G7	47 46N	19 08E
Vacaville California USA	**72**	C4	38 21N	121 59W
Vadodara India	**98**	C4	22 19N	73 14E
Vaga *r.* Russia	**94**	G9	62 00N	43 00E
Váh *r.* Slovakia	**88**	F8	48 00N	18 00E
Vakh *r.* Russia	**95**	L9	61 30N	80 30E
Vakhsh *r.* Asia	**94**	J4	37 00N	68 00E
Valdepeñas Sp.	**87**	D3	38 46N	3 24W
Valdés, Peninsula Argentina	**81**	E5	42 30S	63 00W
Valdez Alaska USA	**40**	F6	61 07N	146 16W
Valdivia Chile	**81**	C6	39 46S	73 15W
Valdosta Georgia USA	**71**	K3	30 51N	83 51W
Valença Brazil	**80**	K11	13 22S	39 06W
Valence Fr.	**87**	H6	44 56N	4 54E

Valencia Sp. 87 E3 39 29N 0 24W
Valencia Venezuela 80 D16 10 14N 67 59W
Valencia, Gulf of Sp. 87 F3 39 30N 0 20E
Valenciennes Fr. 86 G9 50 22N 3 32E
Valera Venezuela 80 C15 9 21N 70 38W
Valjevo Serbia 89 G6 44 16N 19 56E
Valladolid Mexico 74 G4 20 40N 88 11W
Valladolid Sp. 87 C4 41 39N 4 45W
Valle de la Pascua Venezuela 80 D15 9 15N 66 00W
Valledupar Col. 80 C16 10 31N 73 16W
Valle Grande Bolivia 80 E10 18 30S 64 04W
Vallejo California USA 70 B4 38 05N 122 14W
Vallenar Chile 81 C8 28 36S 70 45W
Valletta Malta 89 E1 35 54N 14 32E
Valley Stream *tn.* New York USA 73 K1 40 39N 73 42W
Valmiera Latvia 88 K12 57 32N 25 29E
Valparaíso Chile 81 C7 33 05S 71 40W
Van Turkey 96 D6 38 28N 43 20E
Van Buren Maine USA 57 G2 47 10N 67 59W
Vancouver Washington USA 70 B6 45 38N 122 40W
Vänern *l.* Sweden 88 D13 59 00N 13 30E
Vänersborg Sweden 88 D13 58 23N 12 19E
Van Gölü *l.* Turkey 96 D6 38 33N 42 46E
Vannes Fr. 86 D7 47 40N 2 44W
Vanua Levu *i.* Fiji 114 U16 16 20S 179 00E
Vanua Levu Barrier Reef Fiji 114 U16 17 10S 179 00E
Vanua Mbalavu *i.* Fiji 114 V16 17 15S 178 55W
VANUATU 103 N7
Van Wert Ohio USA 51 J1 40 52N 84 35W
Varadero Cuba 75 H4 23 09N 81 16W
Varanasi India 98 E5 25 20N 83 00E
Varaždin Croatia 89 F7 46 18N 16 21E
Varberg Sweden 88 D12 57 07N 12 16E
Varna Bulgaria 89 L5 43 12N 27 57E
Värnamo Sweden 88 E12 57 11N 14 03E
Várzea Grande Brazil 80 J12 6 32S 42 05W
Vaslui Romania 89 L7 46 37N 27 46E
Vassar Michigan USA 52 C3 43 23N 83 33W
Västerås Sweden 88 F13 59 36N 16 32E
Västervik Sweden 88 F12 57 45N 16 40E
Vasyugan *r.* Russia 94 K8 59 00N 77 30E
Vättern *l.* Sweden 88 E13 58 20N 14 20E
Vatulele *i.* Fiji 114 T15 18 30S 177 38E
Vaupés *r.* Col. 80 C14 1 30N 72 00W
Växjö Sweden 88 E12 56 52N 14 50E
Vaygach *i.* Russia 94 H11 70 00N 59 00E
Vejle Denmark 88 B11 55 43N 9 33E
Velebit *mts.* Croatia 89 E6 44 00N 15 00E
Velikiye Luki Russia 94 F8 56 19N 30 31E
Veliko Tŭrnovo Bulgaria 89 K5 43 04N 25 39E
Vellore India 98 D2 12 56N 79 09E
VENEZUELA 80 D15
Venezuelan Basin Caribbean Sea 116 B8 14 00N 67 00W
Venice Italy 89 D6 45 26N 12 20E
Venta *r.* Latvia/Lithuania 88 J12 56 05N 21 50E
Ventspils Latvia 88 H12 57 22N 21 31E
Ventura California USA 70 C3 34 16N 119 18W
Veracruz Mexico 74 E3 19 11N 96 10W
Veraval India 98 C4 20 53N 70 28E
Vercelli Italy 89 B6 45 19N 8 26E
Verde *r.* Paraguay 80 F9 23 20S 60 00W
Verde *r.* Arizona USA 70 D3 34 00N 112 00W
Verdun-sur-Meuse Fr. 86 H8 49 10N 5 24E
Vereeniging RSA 109 K2 26 41S 27 56E
Verin Sp. 87 B4 41 55N 7 26W
Verkhoyansk Russia 95 R10 67 35N 133 25E
Verkhoyansk Range *mts.* Russia 95 Q10 65 00N 130 00E
Vermilion Ohio USA 52 D1 41 24N 82 21W
Vermillion Lake Minnesota USA 51 E4 47 35N 92 28W
Vermillion Range *mts.* Minnesota USA 51 F4 48 00N 91 00W
Vermont *state* USA 71 M5 44 00N 73 00W
Vernon Texas USA 70 G3 34 10N 99 19W
Véroia Greece 89 J4 40 32N 22 11E
Verona Italy 89 C6 45 26N 11 00E
Versailles Fr. 86 G8 48 48N 2 07E
Verviers Belgium 86 H9 50 36N 5 52E
Vesuvio *vol.* Italy 89 E4 40 49N 14 26E
Vetlanda Sweden 88 E12 57 26N 15 05E
Viano do Castelo Port. 87 A4 41 41N 8 50W
Viar *r.* Sp. 87 C2 37 45N 5 50W
Viborg Denmark 88 B12 56 28N 9 25E
Vicente Guerrero Mexico 74 A6 30 48N 116 00W
Vicenza Italy 89 C6 45 33N 11 32E
Vichy Fr. 87 G7 46 07N 3 25E
Vicksburg Mississippi USA 71 H3 32 21N 90 51W
Victoria Chile 81 C6 38 20S 72 30W
Victoria Texas USA 71 G2 28 49N 97 01W
Victoria *r.* Aust. 110 E6 16 00S 131 30E
Victoria *state* Aust. 110 G2/H2 37 00S 145 00E
Victoria de las Tunas Cuba 75 J4 20 58N 76 59W
Victoria Falls Zambia/Zimbabwe 109 K4 17 55S 25 51E
Victoria Harbour HK China 100 C1 22 18N 114 10E
Victoria, Lake East Africa 108 L7 2 00S 33 00E
Victoria Land *geog. reg.* Antarctica 117 75 00S 157 00E
Victoria Peak HK China 100 B1 22 17N 114 09E
Victoria West RSA 109 J1 31 25S 23 08E
Victorville California USA 72 E2 34 31N 117 18W
Vidin Bulgaria 89 J5 44 00N 22 50E
Viedma Argentina 81 E5 40 45S 63 00W
Vienna Austria 88 F8 48 13N 16 22E
Vienne Fr. 87 H6 45 32N 4 54E
Vientiane Laos 103 C7 17 59N 102 38E
Vierzon Fr. 87 G7 47 14N 2 03E
VIETNAM 103 D7
Vieux Fort St. Lucia 74 R11 13 44N 60 57W
Vigia Brazil 80 H13 0 50S 48 07W
Vigo Sp. 87 A5 42 15N 8 44W
Vijayawada India 98 E3 16 34N 80 40E
Vijosë *r.* Albania 89 H4 40 30N 20 00E
Vila Nova de Gaia Port. 87 A4 41 08N 8 37W
Vila Real Port. 87 B4 41 17N 7 45W
Vila Velha Brazil 80 J9 20 23S 40 18W
Vilhena Brazil 80 E11 12 40S 60 08W
Villach Austria 89 D7 46 37N 13 51E
Villa Constitución Mexico 74 B5 25 05N 111 45W
Villahermosa Mexico 74 F3 18 00N 92 53W
Villalba Sp. 87 B5 43 17N 7 41W
Villa María Argentina 81 E7 32 25S 63 15W
Villa Montes Bolivia 80 E9 21 15S 63 30W
Villanueva Mexico 74 D4 22 24N 102 53W
Villarrica Chile 81 C6 39 15S 72 15W
Villarrobledo Sp. 87 D3 39 16N 2 36W
Villa Unión Argentina 81 D8 29 27S 62 46W
Villa Unión Mexico 74 C4 23 10N 106 12W
Villavicencio Col. 80 C14 4 09N 73 38W
Villefranche-sur-Saône Fr. 87 H6 46 00N 4 43E
Villeneuve-sur-Lot Fr. 87 F6 44 25N 0 43E
Villeurbanne Fr. 87 H6 45 46N 4 54E
Vilyuy *r.* Russia 95 Q9 64 00N 123 00E
Vilyuysk Russia 95 Q9 63 46N 121 35E
Viña del Mar Chile 81 C7 33 02S 71 35W
Vinaroz Sp. 87 F4 40 29N 0 28E
Vincennes Indiana USA 71 J4 38 42N 87 30W
Vindhya Range *mts.* India 98 D4 23 00N 75 00E
Vineland New Jersey USA 71 L4 39 29N 75 02W
Vinh Vietnam 103 D7 18 42N 105 41E
Vinkovci Croatia 89 G6 45 16N 18 49E
Vinnytsya Ukraine 88 M8 49 11N 28 30E
Vinson Massif *mts.* Antarctica 117 78 02S 22 00W
Vipiteno Italy 89 C7 46 54N 11 27E
Virgin *r.* USA 70 D4 37 00N 114 00W
Virginia Minnesota USA 71 H6 47 30N 92 28W
Virginia *state* USA 71 L4 38 00N 77 00W
Virginia Beach *tn.* Virginia USA 71 L4 36 51N 75 59W
Virgin Islands W. Indies 75 M3 18 00N 64 30W
Virovitica Croatia 89 F6 45 50N 17 25E
Vis *i.* Croatia 89 F5 43 00N 16 00E
Visalia California USA 70 C4 36 20N 119 18W
Visby Sweden 88 G12 57 32N 18 15E
Vise *i.* Russia 95 K12 79 30N 77 00E
Viseu Port. 87 B4 40 40N 7 55W
Vishakhapatnam India 98 E3 17 42N 83 24E
Vista California USA 72 E1 33 12N 117 15W
Viterbo Italy 89 D5 42 24N 12 06E
Vitichi Bolivia 80 D9 20 14S 65 22W
Viti Levu *i.* Fiji 114 T15 18 10S 177 55E
Vitim Russia 95 P8 59 28N 112 35E
Vitim *r.* Russia 95 P8 58 00N 113 00E
Vitória Brazil 80 J9 20 20S 40 18W
Vitória da Conquista Brazil 80 J11 14 53S 40 52W
Vitoria Gasteiz Sp. 87 D5 42 51N 2 40W
Vitry-le-François Fr. 86 H8 48 44N 4 36E
Vityaz Trench Pacific Ocean 114 G7 9 30S 170 00E
Vivi *r.* Russia 95 M10 61 00N 96 00E
Vizianagaram India 98 E3 18 07N 83 30E
Vladikavkaz Russia 94 G5 43 02N 44 43E
Vladimir Russia 94 G8 56 08N 40 25E
Vladimir Volynskiy Ukraine 88 K9 50 51N 24 19E
Vladivostok Russia 95 R5 43 09N 131 53E
Vlissingen Neths. 86 G9 51 27N 3 35E
Vlorë Albania 89 G4 40 29N 19 29E
Vltava *r.* Czech Rep. 88 E8 49 00N 14 00E
Voi Kenya 108 M7 3 23S 38 35E
Volga *r.* Russia 94 G6 50 00N 45 00E
Volgodonsk Russia 94 G6 47 35N 42 08E
Volgograd Russia 94 G6 48 45N 44 30E
Vologda Russia 94 F8 59 10N 39 55E
Vólos Greece 89 J3 39 22N 22 57E
Volta, Lake Ghana 108 D9 7 30N 0 30W
Volturno *r.* Italy 89 E4 41 00N 14 00E
Volzhskiy Russia 94 G6 48 48N 44 45E
Vóreioi Sporádes *is.* Greece 89 J3/K3 39 00N 24 00E
Vorkuta Russia 94 J10 67 27N 64 00E
Voronezh Russia 94 F7 51 40N 39 13E
Vørterkaka Nunatak *mt.* Antarctica 117 71 45S 32 00E
Vosges *mts.* Fr. 86 J8 48 10N 6 50E
Vostochnyy Russia 95 R5 42 52N 132 56E
Vouga *r.* Port. 87 A4 40 45N 8 15W
Vranje Serbia 89 H5 42 33N 21 54E
Vratsa Bulgaria 89 J5 43 12N 23 32E
Vrbas *r.* Bosnia-Herzegovina 89 F6 44 00N 17 00E
Vršac Serbia 89 H6 45 07N 21 19E
Vryburg RSA 109 J2 26 57S 24 44E
Vukovar Croatia 89 G6 45 19N 19 01E
Vung Tau Vietnam 103 D6 10 21N 107 04E
Vunisea Fiji 114 U15 19 04S 178 09E
Vyatka *r.* Russia 94 G8 58 00N 50 00E
Vyborg Russia 94 E9 60 45N 28 41E
Vychegda *r.* Russia 94 H9 62 00N 52 00E

W

Wa Ghana 108 D10 10 07N 2 28W
Wabash *r.* USA 71 J4 38 00N 87 30W
Wabuska Nevada USA 72 D4 39 09N 119 13W
Waco Texas USA 71 G3 31 33N 97 10W
Waddeneilanden Neths. 86 H10 53 25N 5 15E
Waddenzee *sea* Neths. 86 H10 53 15N 5 15E
Wādī al 'Arabah *r.* Israel 96 N10 30 30N 35 10E
Wādī al Masīlah *r.* Yemen 97 F2 16 00N 50 00E
Wâdi el Gafra Egypt 109 R2 30 16N 31 46E
Wadi Halfa Sudan 108 L12 21 55N 31 20E
Wad Medani Sudan 108 L10 14 24N 33 30E
Wagga Wagga Aust. 110 H2 35 07S 147 24E
Wagin Aust. 110 B3 33 20S 117 15E
Waglan Island HK China 100 C1 22 11N 114 18E
Wah Pakistan 98 C6 33 50N 72 44E
Waha Libya 108 H13 28 10N 19 57E
Wahpeton North Dakota USA 71 G6 46 16N 96 36W
Waialua Hawaiian Islands 115 X18 21 35N 158 08W
Waigeo *i.* Indonesia 103 J3 0 15S 130 45E
Waihi NZ 111 E6 37 57S 175 44E
Wailuku Hawaiian Islands 115 Y18 20 54N 156 30W
Waimate NZ 111 C2 44 44S 171 03E
Waipara NZ 111 D3 43 04S 172 45E
Waipawa NZ 111 F5 39 57S 176 35E
Waipu NZ 111 F7 35 59S 174 27E
Wairoa NZ 111 F5 39 03S 177 25E
Waitara NZ 111 E5 39 00S 174 14E
Wajima Japan 102 C2 37 23N 136 53E
Wajir Kenya 108 M8 1 46N 40 05E
Wakasa-wan *b.* Japan 102 C2 35 40N 135 30E
Wakayama Japan 102 C1 34 12N 135 10E
Wakefield Rhode Island USA 73 E2 41 26N 71 30W
Wake Islands Pacific Ocean 114 G9 19 18N 166 36E
Wakkanai Japan 102 D4 45 26N 141 43E
Wałbrzych Poland 88 F9 50 48N 16 19E
Wales *admin.* UK 86 C10 52 40N 3 30W
Walhalla North Dakota USA 49 D1 48 55N 97 55W
Walker *r.* Nevada USA 72 D4 39 08N 119 00W
Walker Lake Nevada USA 70 C4 38 40N 118 43W
Wallaroo Aust. 110 F3 33 57S 137 36E
Walla Walla Washington USA 70 C6 46 05N 118 18W
Wallis and Futuna *is.* Pacific Ocean 114 J6 13 16S 176 15W
Walsenburg Colorado USA 70 F4 37 36N 104 48W
Waltham Massachusetts USA 73 E3 42 23N 71 14W
Walvis Bay *tn.* Namibia 109 G3 22 59S 14 31E
Walvis Ridge Atlantic Ocean 116 J3 30 00S 3 00E
Walyevo Fiji 114 V16 17 35S 179 58W
Wamba *r.* CDR 109 H6 6 30S 17 30E
Wanganui NZ 111 E5 39 56S 175 03E
Wang Chau *i.* HK China 100 D1 22 19N 114 22E
Wanxian China 101 K5 30 54N 108 20E
Warangal India 98 D3 18 00N 79 35E
Wardha *r.* India 98 D4 20 30N 79 00E
Warner Springs *tn.* California USA 72 E1 33 19N 116 38W
Warren Michigan USA 51 K2 42 30N 83 02W
Warren Ohio USA 71 K5 41 15N 80 49W
Warren Pennsylvania USA 52 G1 41 52N 79 09W
Warrnambool Aust. 110 G2 38 23S 142 03E
Warroad Minnesota USA 49 E1 48 59N 95 20W
Warsaw Poland 88 H10 52 15N 21 00E
Warta *r.* Poland 88 F10 52 00N 17 00E
Warwick Aust. 110 J4 28 12S 152 00E
Warwick Rhode Island USA 71 M5 41 42N 71 23W
Wasco California USA 72 D2 35 36N 119 20W
Washburn Wisconsin USA 51 F4 46 41N 90 53W
Washington *state* USA 70 B6/C6 47 00N 120 00W
Washington Crossing *tn.* New Jersey USA 73 C2 40 18N 74 52W
Washington D.C. District of Columbia USA 71 L4 38 55N 77 00W
Wash, The *b.* UK 86 F10 52 55N 0 10E
Watampone Indonesia 103 G3 4 33S 120 20E
Waterbury Connecticut USA 73 D2 41 34N 73 02W
Waterford RoI 86 B10 52 15N 7 06W
Waterloo Iowa USA 71 H5 42 30N 92 20W
Waterloo New York USA 53 K2 42 54N 76 53W
Watersmeet Michigan USA 51 G4 46 16N 89 10W
Watertown New York USA 71 L5 43 57N 75 56W
Watertown South Dakota USA 71 G5 44 54N 97 08W
Waterville Maine USA 71 N5 44 34N 69 41W
Waterville New York USA 53 L2 42 55N 75 24W
Waterville Ohio USA 52 C1 41 29N 83 44W
Watkins Glen *tn.* New York USA 53 K2 42 23N 76 53W
Watsonville California USA 72 C3 36 59N 121 47W
Wau PNG 110 H8 7 22S 146 40E
Wau Sudan 108 K9 7 40N 28 04E
Waukegan Illinois USA 71 J5 42 21N 87 52W
Waukesha Wisconsin USA 71 J5 43 01N 88 14W
Wausau Wisconsin USA 71 J5 44 58N 89 40W
Wawona California USA 72 D3 37 32N 119 39W
Waycross Georgia USA 71 K3 31 12N 82 22W
Webster New York USA 53 J3 43 13N 77 26W
Weddell Sea Southern Ocean 117 71 00S 40 00W
Weiden Germany 88 D8 49 40N 12 10E
Weifang China 101 M6 36 44N 119 10E
Wei He *r.* China 101 K5 34 00N 106 00E
Weipa Aust. 110 G7 12 35S 141 56E
Weirton West Virginia USA 71 K5 40 24N 80 37W
Wejherowo Poland 88 G11 54 36N 18 12E
Wellesley Islands Aust. 110 F6 16 30S 139 00E
Wellington NZ 111 E4 41 17S 174 46E
Wellington Kansas USA 71 G4 37 17N 97 25W
Wellington Nevada USA 72 D4 38 45N 119 23W
Wellsboro Pennsylvania USA 53 J1 41 45N 77 18W
Wellsford NZ 111 E6 36 18S 174 31E
Wellsville New York USA 52 J2 42 07N 77 56W
Wels Austria 88 D8 48 10N 14 02E
Wenzhou China 101 N4 28 02N 120 40E
Weser *r.* Germany 88 B10 53 00N 8 00E
West Australian Basin Indian Ocean 113 J4/J5 20 00S 100 00E
West Bank *territory* Israel 96 N10 32 00N 35 00E
West Bengal *admin.* India 99 F4 22 00N 88 00E
West Branch Michigan USA 51 J3 44 17N 84 16W
Westby Montana USA 47 E1 48 52N 104 04W
West Caroline Basin Pacific Ocean 114 D8 3 00N 136 00E
West Chester Pennsylvania USA 73 C1 39 57N 75 36W
Western Australia *state* Aust. 110 B2/D7 25 00S 117 00E
Western Ghats *mts.* India 98 C3/D2 15 30N 74 00E
WESTERN SAHARA 108 A12
Western Sayan *mts.* Russia 95 L7/M7 52 30N 92 30E
Westerwald *geog. reg.* Germany 88 A9/B9 50 00N 8 00E
West European Basin Atlantic Ocean 116 G11 47 00N 18 00W
West Falkland *i.* Falkland Islands 81 E3/F3 51 00S 60 40W
Westfield Massachusetts USA 73 D3 42 08N 72 45W
Westfield New York USA 52 G2 42 20N 79 34W
West Grand Lake Maine USA 57 F1 44 15N 68 00W
Westhope North Dakota USA 47 G1 48 57N 101 02W
West Indies *is.* Caribbean Sea 75 K4/L4 22 00N 69 00W
Westlake Ohio USA 52 E1 41 25N 81 54W
West Lamma Channel HK China 100 B1 22 14N 114 05E
West Marianas Basin Pacific Ocean 114 D9 16 00N 137 30E
West Memphis Arkansas USA 71 H4 35 09N 90 11W
West Palm Beach *tn.* Florida USA 71 K2 26 42N 80 05W
West Plains *tn.* Missouri USA 71 H4 36 44N 91 51W
Westport NZ 111 C4 41 45S 171 36E
Westport RoI 86 A10 53 48N 9 32W
Westport California USA 72 B4 39 39N 123 47
Westport Connecticut USA 73 D2 41 08N 73 21W
West Siberian Lowland Russia 94 K8/K9 60 00N 75 00E
West Virginia *state* USA 71 K4 39 00N 81 00W
Wetar *i.* Indonesia 103 H2 7 15S 126 45E
Wewak PNG 110 G9 3 35S 143 35E
Wexford RoI 86 B10 52 20N 6 27W
Weymouth UK 86 D9 50 37N 2 25W
Weymouth Massachusetts USA 73 E3 42 13N 70 59W
Whakatane NZ 111 F6 37 58S 176 59E
Whangarei NZ 111 E7 35 43S 174 19E
Wharfe *r.* UK 86 E11 54 10N 2 05W
Wharton Pennsylvania USA 52 H1 41 31N 78 00W
Wharton Basin Indian Ocean 113 J5 15 00S 100 00E
Whatconi, Lake Washington USA 42 H4 48 40N 122 26W
Wheeler Lake Alabama USA 71 J3 34 00N 87 00W
Wheeling West Viriginia USA 71 K5 40 05N 80 43W
Whidbey Island Washington USA 42 H4 48 20N 122 38W
White *r.* Arkansas USA 71 H4 35 00N 92 00W
White *r.* Nevada USA 72 F4 38 40N 115 10W
White *r.* South Dakota USA 70 F5 43 00N 103 00W
White Nile Dam Sudan 108 L11 14 18N 32 20E
White Sea Russia 94 F10 66 00N 37 30E
White Volta *r.* Ghana 108 D9 9 30N 1 30W
Whitewater Montana USA 47 D1 48 46N 107 37W
Whitewater Creek *r.* Montana USA 47 D1 48 46N 107 36W
Whitianga NZ 111 E6 36 49S 175 42E
Whitney, Mount California USA 70 C4 36 35N 118 17W
Whitney Point *tn.* New York USA 73 C3 42 20N 75 58W
Whyalla Aust. 110 F3 33 04S 137 34E
Wichita Kansas USA 71 G4 37 43N 97 20W
Wichita *r.* Texas USA 70 F3 33 00N 100 00W
Wichita Falls *tn.* Texas USA 71 G3 33 55N 98 30W
Wick UK 86 D13 58 26N 3 06W
Wickliffe Ohio USA 52 E1 41 38N 81 25W
Wicklow RoI 86 B10 52 59N 6 03W
Wicklow Mountains RoI 86 B10 53 00N 6 20W
Wiener Neustadt Austria 88 F7 47 49N 16 15E
Wieprz *r.* Poland 88 J9 51 00N 23 00E
Wiesbaden Germany 88 B9 50 05N 8 15E
Wildrose North Dakota USA 47 F1 48 38N 103 11W
Wilhelm II Land *geog. reg.* Antarctica 117 70 00S 90 00E
Wilhelmshaven Germany 88 B10 53 32N 8 07E
Wilkes-Barre Pennsylvania USA 71 L5 41 15N 75 50W
Wilkes Land *geog. reg.* Antarctica 117 68 00S 105 00E
Willemstad Curaçao 75 L2 12 12N 68 56W
Williams California USA 72 B4 39 09N 122 09W
Williams Minnesota USA 49 E1 48 45N 94 55W
Williamsport Pennsylvania USA 71 L5 41 16N 77 03W
Williston North Dakota USA 70 F6 48 09N 103 39W
Willits California USA 72 B4 39 23N 123 22W
Willmar Minnesota USA 71 G6 45 06N 95 03W
Willoughby Hills *tn.* Ohio USA 52 E1 41 35N 81 29W
Willow Creek *r.* Montana USA 46 G1 48 40N 111 20W

Willow River Michigan USA 52 D3 43 50N 82 58W
Willows California USA 72 B4 39 32N 122 10W
Willow Springs *tn.* Missouri USA 71 H4 36 59N 91 59W
Wilmington Delaware USA 71 L4 39 46N 75 31W
Wilmington North Carolina USA 71 L3 34 14N 77 55W
Wilson New York USA 54 D2 43 15N 78 50W
Wilson North Carolina USA 71 L4 35 43N 77 56W
Wiluna Aust. 110 C4 26 37S 120 12E
Winchendon Massachusetts USA 73 D3 42 41N 72 03W
Winchester UK 86 E9 51 04N 1 19W
Winchester Virginia USA 71 L4 39 11N 78 12W
Windhoek Namibia 109 H3 22 34S 17 06E
Wind River Range *mts.* Wyoming USA 70 E5 43 00N 109 00W
Windsor Locks *tn.* Connecticut USA 73 D2 41 55N 72 37W
Windward Islands Lesser Antilles 75 M2 12 30N 62 00W
Windward Passage *sd.* Cuba/Haiti 75 K3/K4 20 00N 73 00W
Winnemucca Nevada USA 70 C5 40 58N 117 45W
Winona Minnesota USA 71 H5 44 02N 91 37W
Winslow Arizona USA 70 D4 35 01N 110 43W
Winston-Salem North Carolina USA 71 K4 36 05N 80 18W
Winterthur Switz. 87 K7 47 30N 8 45E
Winthrop Washington USA 42 H4 48 35N 120 10W
Winton Aust. 110 G5 22 22S 143 00E
Wisconsin *r.* Wisconsin USA 71 H5 45 00N 90 00W
Wisconsin *state* USA 71 H6/J6 45 00N 90 00W
Wisconsin Rapids *tn.* Wisconsin USA 51 G3 44 23N 89 51W
Wisła *r.* Poland 88 G10 53 00N 19 00E
Wisłok *r.* Poland 88 J9 50 00N 22 00E
Wismar Germany 88 C10 53 54N 11 28E
Wittenberg Germany 88 D9 51 53N 12 39E
Wittenberge Germany 88 C10 52 59N 11 45E
Włocławek Poland 88 G10 52 39N 19 01E
Wolcott New York USA 53 K3 43 13N 76 49W
Wolfsberg Austria 89 E7 46 50N 14 50E
Wolfsburg Germany 88 C10 52 27N 10 49E
Wollongong Aust. 110 J3 34 25S 150 52E
Wolverhampton UK 86 D10 52 36N 2 08W
Wompah Aust. 110 G4 29 04S 142 05E
Wong Chuk Hang HK China 100 C1 22 15N 114 10E
Wonju South Korea 101 P6 37 24N 127 52E
Wonsan North Korea 101 P6 39 07N 127 26E
Woodfords California USA 72 D4 38 47N 119 50W
Woodland California USA 72 C4 38 42N 121 47W
Woodlark Island PNG 110 J8 9 10S 152 50E
Woodville NZ 111 E4 40 21S 175 52E
Woodward Oklahoma USA 70 G4 36 26N 99 25W
Woonsocket Rhode Island USA 73 E2 42 01N 71 30W
Worcester RSA 109 H1 33 39S 19 26E
Worcester UK 86 D10 52 11N 2 13W
Worcester Massachusetts USA 71 M5 42 17N 71 48W
Workington UK 86 D11 54 39N 3 33W
Worland Wyoming USA 70 E5 44 01N 107 58W
Worthing UK 86 E9 50 48N 0 23W
Worthington Minnesota USA 71 G5 43 37N 95 36W
Wrangel Island Russia 95 V11 61 30N 180 00
Wrangell Alaska USA 42 D5 56 28N 132 23W
Wrangell Island Alaska USA 42 D5 56 25N 132 05W
Wrangell Mountains Alaska USA 64 B3 62 00N 143 00W
Wrangell-St. Elias National Park Alaska USA 64 B3 62 00N 142 30W
Wrexham UK 86 D10 53 03N 3 00W
Wrights Corner New York USA 54 D2 43 10N 78 45W
Wrightsville Pennsylvania USA 73 B2 40 02N 76 32W
Wrocław Poland 88 F9 51 05N 17 00E
Wu Chau Tong HK China 100 C2 22 30N 114 18E
Wuhai China 101 K6 39 40N 106 40E
Wuhan China 101 L5 30 35N 114 19E
Wuhu China 101 M5 31 23N 118 25E
Wukari Nigeria 108 F9 7 49N 9 49E
Wu Kau Tang HK China 100 C3 22 30N 114 15E
Wuppertal Germany 88 A9 51 15N 7 10E
Wurno Nigeria 108 F10 13 18N 5 29E
Wurtsboro New York USA 73 C2 41 35N 74 29W
Würzburg Germany 88 B8 49 48N 9 57E
Wusul Jiang *r.* China 101 Q8 47 00N 134 00E
Wutongqiao China 101 J4 29 21N 103 48E
Wuxi China 101 N5 31 35N 120 19E
Wuyi Shan *mts.* China 101 M4 26 00N 116 30E
Wuzhou China 101 L3 23 30N 111 21E
Wyandotte Michigan USA 51 K2 42 11N 83 10W
Wye *r.* UK 86 D10 51 50N 2 40W
Wyndham Aust. 110 D6 15 30S 128 09E
Wyoming Michigan USA 51 J2 42 54N 85 44W
Wyoming *state* USA 70 E5 43 00N 108 00W

X
Xaafuun Somalia 108 Q10 10 27N 51 15E
Xam Hua Laos 101 J3 20 28N 104 05E
Xánthi Greece 89 K4 41 07N 24 56E
Xiamen China 101 M3 24 28N 118 05E
Xi'an China 101 K5 34 16N 108 54E
Xiangfan China 101 L5 32 05N 112 03E
Xiangkhoang Laos 103 C7 19 21N 102 23E
Xiangtan China 101 L4 27 48N 112 55E
Xianyang China 101 K5 34 22N 108 42E
Xigaze China 100 F4 29 18N 88 50E
Xi Jiang *r.* China 101 L3 23 30N 111 00E
Xingtai China 101 L6 37 08N 114 29E
Xingu *r.* Brazil 80 G12 5 00S 54 00W
Xining China 101 J6 36 35N 101 55E
Xinjiang Uygur Zizhiqu *admin.* China 100 E7/F7 41 00N 85 00E
Xinjin China 101 N6 39 25N 121 58E
Xiqing Shan *mts.* China 101 J5 34 00N 102 30E
Xizang Zizhiqu *admin.* China 100 E5/G5 33 30N 85 00E
Xochimilco Mexico 74 E3 19 08N 99 09W
Xuanhua China 101 M7 40 36N 115 01E
Xuchang China 101 L5 34 03N 113 48E
Xuwen China 101 L3 20 25N 110 08E
Xuzhou China 101 M5 34 17N 117 18E

Y
Yablonovy Range *mts.* Russia 95 N7/P7 51 30N 110 00E
Yabrūd Syria 96 P11 33 58N 36 39E
Yaizu Japan 102 C1 34 54N 138 20E
Yakima Washington USA 70 B6 46 37N 120 30W
Yakima *r.* Washington USA 70 B6 47 00N 120 00W
Yaku-shima *i.* Japan 102 B1 30 00N 130 30E
Yakutat Alaska USA 42 A6 59 50N 139 49W
Yakutat Bay Alaska USA 42 A6 59 50N 140 00W
Yakutsk Russia 95 Q9 62 10N 129 50E
Yalu *r.* China/North Korea 101 P7 41 00N 126 00E
Yamagata Japan 102 D2 38 16N 140 16E
Yamaguchi Japan 102 B1 34 10N 131 28E
Yamal Peninsula Russia 94 J11 72 00N 70 00E
Yambio Sudan 108 K8 4 34N 28 21E
Yambol Bulgaria 89 L5 42 28N 26 30E
Yamburg Russia 95 K10 68 19N 77 09E
Yamoussoukro Côte d'Ivoire 108 C9 6 50N 5 20W
Yamuna *r.* India 98 E5 26 00N 80 30E
Yamunanagar India 98 D6 30 07N 77 17E
Yana *r.* Russia 95 R10 69 00N 135 00E
Yanbu'al Baḩr Saudi Arabia 96 C3 24 07N 38 04E
Yangcheng China 101 N5 33 23N 120 10E
Yangon Myanmar 103 B7 16 47N 96 10E
Yangquan China 101 L6 37 52N 113 29E
Yanji China 101 P7 42 52N 129 32E
Yanjing China 101 H4 29 01N 98 38E
Yankton South Dakota USA 71 G5 42 53N 97 24W
Yantai China 101 N6 37 30N 121 22E
Yaoundé Cameroon 108 G8 3 51N 11 31E
Yap Islands Pacific Ocean 114 D8 9 30N 138 09E
Yap Trench Pacific Ocean 114 D8 10 00N 139 00E
Yaqui *r.* Mexico 74 C5 28 00N 109 50W
Yarlung Zangbo *r.* China 100 G4 29 00N 92 30E
Yaroslavl' Russia 94 F8 57 34N 39 52E
Yarumal Col. 80 B15 6 59N 75 25W
Yasawa *i.* Fiji 114 T16 16 50S 177 30E
Yasawa Group *is.* Fiji 114 T16 17 00S 177 40E
Yatsushiro Japan 102 B1 32 32N 130 35E
Yau Tong HK China 100 C1 22 18N 114 14E
Yavari *r.* Peru/Brazil 80 C13 5 00S 72 30W
Yawatahama Japan 102 B1 33 27N 132 24E
Yazd Iran 97 F5 31 54N 54 22E
Yazoo *r.* Mississippi USA 71 H3 33 00N 90 00W
Ye Myanmar 103 B7 15 15N 97 50E
Yekaterinburg Russia 94 J8 56 52N 60 35E
Yell *i.* UK 86 E14 60 35N 1 10W
Yellow Sea China 101 N6 35 30N 122 30E
Yellowstone *r.* USA 70 E6 46 00N 108 00W
Yellowstone Lake Wyoming USA 70 D5 44 30N 110 20W
YEMEN REPUBLIC 96/97 D2/E2
Yenisey *r.* Russia 95 L9 64 00N 87 30E
Yenisey, Gulf of Russia 95 K11 72 30N 80 00E
Yeniseysk Russia 95 M8 58 27N 92 13E
Yeppoon Aust. 110 J5 23 05S 150 42E
Yerington Nevada USA 72 D4 39 00N 119 11W
Yesilirmak *r.* Turkey 96 C7 41 00N 36 25E
Ye Xian China 101 M6 37 10N 119 55E
Yiannitsá Greece 89 J4 40 46N 22 24E
Yibin China 101 J4 28 42N 104 30E
Yichang China 101 L5 30 46N 111 20E
Yinchuan China 101 K6 38 30N 106 19E
Yingkou China 101 N7 40 40N 122 17E
Yining China 100 E7 43 50N 81 28E
Yi Pak HK China 100 B1 22 18N 114 01E
Yirga Alem Ethiopia 108 M9 6 48N 38 22E
Yiyang China 101 L4 28 39N 112 10E
Yoakum Texas USA 71 G2 29 18N 97 20W
Yogyakarta Indonesia 103 E2 7 48S 110 24E
Yoichi Japan 102 D3 43 14N 140 47E
Yokadouma Cameroon 108 H8 3 26N 15 06E
Yokkaichi Japan 102 C1 34 58N 136 38E
Yokohama Japan 102 C2 35 27N 139 38E
Yokosuka Japan 102 C2 35 18N 139 38E
Yokote Japan 102 D2 39 20N 140 31E
Yola Nigeria 108 G9 9 14N 12 32E
Yonago Japan 102 B2 35 27N 133 20E
Yonezawa Japan 102 D2 37 56N 140 06E
Yonkers New York USA 73 D2 40 58N 73 53W
Yonne *r.* Fr. 86 G8 48 00N 3 15E
York UK 86 E10 53 58N 1 05W
York Pennsylvania USA 71 L4 39 57N 76 44W
York, Cape Aust. 110 G7 10 42S 142 32E
Yosemite National Park California USA 72 D3 37 30N 119 00W
Yosu South Korea 101 P5 34 50N 127 30E
Youghal RoI 86 B9 51 51N 7 50W
You Jiang *r.* China 101 K3 23 30N 107 00E
Youngstown New York USA 52 G3 43 14N 79 01W
Youngstown Ohio USA 71 K5 41 05N 80 40W
Youngsville Pennsylvania USA 52 G1 41 52N 79 22W
Ypsilanti Michigan USA 52 C2 42 15N 83 36W
Ystad Sweden 88 D11 55 25N 13 50E
Yuba City California USA 70 B4 39 09N 121 36W
Yūbari Japan 102 D3 43 04N 141 59E
Yucatan *p.* Mexico 74 G3 19 00N 89 00W
Yucatan Basin Caribbean Sea 115 T9 20 00N 85 00W
Yucca Lake Nevada USA 72 F3 37 00N 116 02W
Yuci China 101 L6 37 40N 112 44E
Yuen Long HK China 100 B2 22 26N 114 02E
Yugakir Plateau Russia 95 T10 66 30N 156 00E
Yu Jiang *r.* China 101 K3 23 00N 109 00E
Yukon Flats National Wildlife Refuge Alaska USA 64 A4 66 30N 147 30W
Yuma Arizona USA 70 D3 32 40N 114 39W
Yumen China 101 H6 39 54N 97 43E
Yung Shue Wan *tn.* HK China 100 B1 22 13N 114 06E
Yurimaguas Peru 80 B12 5 54S 76 07W
Yuzhno-Sakhalinsk Russia 95 S6 46 58N 142 45E
Yverdon Switz. 87 J7 46 47N 6 38E
Yvetot Fr. 86 F8 49 37N 0 45E

Z
Zaanstad Neths. 86 H10 52 27N 4 49E
Zābol Iran 97 H5 31 00N 61 32E
Zabrze Poland 88 G9 50 18N 18 47E
Zacapa Guatemala 74 G3 15 00N 89 30E
Zacatecas Mexico 74 D4 22 48N 102 33W
Zacatecoluca El Salvador 74 G2 13 29N 88 51W
Zadar Croatia 89 E6 44 07N 15 14E
Zafra Sp. 87 B3 38 25N 6 25W
Żagań Poland 88 E9 51 37N 15 20E
Zagreb Croatia 89 E6 45 48N 15 58E
Zagros Mountains Iran 97 E5/F5 32 45N 48 50E
Zāhedān Iran 97 H4 29 32N 60 54E
Zahlé Lebanon 96 N11 33 50N 35 55E
Zakopane Poland 88 G8 49 17N 19 54E
Zákynthos *i.* Greece 89 H2 37 45N 20 50E
Zalaegerszeg Hungary 89 F7 46 53N 16 51E
Zalău Romania 89 J7 47 10N 23 04E
Zaltan Libya 108 H13 28 15N 19 52E
Zambeze *r.* Mozambique 109 L4 16 00S 34 00E
Zambezi Zambia 109 J5 13 33S 23 08E
Zambezi *r.* Zambia/Zimbabwe 109 J4 16 00S 23 00E
ZAMBIA 109 J5/L5
Zamboanga Philippines 103 G5 6 55N 122 05E
Zamora Sp. 87 C4 41 30N 5 45W
Zamość Poland 88 J9 50 43N 23 15E
Zanderij Suriname 80 F15 5 26N 55 14W
Zanesville Ohio USA 71 K4 39 55N 82 02W
Zanjān Iran 97 E6 36 40N 48 30E
Zanthus Aust. 110 C3 31 01S 123 32E
Zanzibar Tanzania 109 M6 6 10S 39 12E
Zanzibar *i.* Tanzania 108/109 M6 6 10S 39 13E
Zaozhuang China 101 M5 34 53N 117 38E
Zaragoza Sp. 87 E4 41 39N 0 54W
Zarand Iran 97 G5 30 50N 56 35E
Zaraza Venezuela 80 D15 9 23N 65 20W
Zarembo Island Alaska USA 42 D5 56 30N 132 50W
Zaria Nigeria 108 F10 11 01N 7 44E
Zarqa Jordan 96 C5 32 04N 36 05E
Zefat Israel 96 N11 32 57N 35 27E
Zell-am-See *tn.* Austria 89 D7 47 19N 12 47E
Zenica Bosnia-Herzegovina 89 F6 44 11N 17 53E
Zephyr Cove *tn.* Nevada USA 72 D4 39 07N 119 57W
Zeya Russia 95 Q7 53 48N 127 14E
Zeya *r.* Russia 95 Q7 53 00N 127 30E
Zêzere *r.* Port. 87 B3 39 50N 8 05W
Zgierz Poland 88 G9 51 52N 19 25E
Zgorzelec Poland 88 E9 51 10N 15 00E
Zhambyl Kazakhstan 94 K5 42 50N 71 25E
Zhangjiakou China 101 L7 40 51N 114 59E
Zhangzhou China 101 M3 24 31N 117 40E
Zhanjiang China 101 L3 21 10N 110 20E
Zhengzhou China 101 L5 34 45N 113 38E
Zhezkazgan Kazakhstan 94 J6 47 44N 67 42E
Zhigansk Russia 95 Q10 66 48N 123 27E
Zhmerynka Ukraine 88 M8 49 00N 28 02E
Zhob Pakistan 98 B6 31 30N 69 30E
Zhob *r.* Pakistan 98 B6 30 55N 68 01E
Zhoukou China 101 L5 33 35N 114 41E
Zhuzhou China 101 L4 27 53N 113 07E
Zhytomyr Ukraine 88 M9 50 18N 28 40E
Zibo China 101 M6 36 51N 118 01E
Zielona Góra Poland 88 E9 51 57N 15 30E
Zigong China 101 J4 29 25N 104 47E
Ziguinchor Senegal 108 A10 12 35N 16 20W
ZIMBABWE 109 K4/L4
Zinder Niger 108 F10 13 46N 8 58E
Ziqudukou China 100 H5 33 03N 95 51E
Zlatoust Russia 94 H8 55 10N 59 38E
Zlín Czech Rep. 88 F8 49 14N 17 40E
Znojmo Czech Rep. 88 F8 48 52N 16 04E
Zolochev Ukraine 88 K8 49 49N 24 53E
Zomba Malawi 109 M4 15 22S 35 22E
Zonguldak Turkey 96 B7 41 26N 31 47E
Zouar Chad 108 H12 20 30N 16 30E
Zouérate Mauritania 108 B12 22 44N 12 21W
Zrenjanin Serbia 89 H6 45 22N 20 23E
Zújar *r.* Sp. 87 C3 38 35N 5 30W
Zunyi China 101 K4 27 35N 106 48E
Zürich Switz. 87 K7 47 23N 8 33E
Zvishavane Zimbabwe 109 L3 20 20S 30 02E
Zwickau Germany 88 D9 50 43N 12 30E
Zyrardów Poland 88 H10 52 02N 20 28E
Zyryanka Russia 87 T10 65 42N 150 49E

Glossary

Ákra	cape (Greek)
Älv	river (Swedish)
Bahia	bay (Spanish)
Bahr	stream (Arabic)
Baie	bay (French)
Bugt	bay (Danish)
Cabo	cape (Portugese; Spanish)
Cap	cape (French)
Capo	cape (Italian)
Cerro	hill (Spanish)
Chaîne	mountain range (French)
Chapada	hills (Portugese)
Chott	salt lake (Arabic)
Co	lake (Chinese)
Collines	hills (French)
Cordillera	mountain range (Spanish)
Costa	coast (Spanish)
Côte	coast (French)
-dake	peak (Japanese)
Danau	lake (Indonesian)
Dao	island (Chinese)
Dasht	desert (Persian; Urdu)
Djebel	mountain (Arabic)
Do	island (Korean; Vietnamese)
Embalse	reservoir (Spanish)
Erg	dunes (Arabic)
Estrecho	strait (Spanish)
Estreito	strait (Portugese)
Gebel	mountain (Arabic)
Golfe	gulf; bay (French)
Golfo	gulf; bay (Italian; Spanish)
Gölü	lake (Turkish)
Gora	mountain (Russian)
Gunto	islands (Japanese)
Gunung	mountain (Indonesian; Malay)
Hafen	harbour (German)
Hai	sea (Chinese)
Ho	river (Chinese)
Hu	lake (Chinese)
Île; Isle	island (French)
Ilha	island (Portugese)
Inseln	islands (German)
Isla	island (Spanish)
Istmo	isthmus (Spanish)
Jabal; Jebel	mountain (Arabic)
Jezero	lake (Serb-Croat)
Jezioro	lake (Polish)
Jiang	river (Chinese)
-jima	island (Japanese)
-kaikyō	strait (Japanese)
Kamen'	rock (Russian)
Kap	cape (Danish)
Kepulauan	islands (Indonesian)
-ko	lake (Japanese)
Lac	lake (French)
Lago	lake (Italian; Portugese; Spanish)
Laguna	lagoon (Spanish)
Ling	mountain range (Chinese)
Llyn	lake (Welsh)
-misaki	cape (Japanese)
Mont	mountain (French)
Montagne	mountain (French)
Monts	mountains (French)
Monti	mountains (Italian)
More	sea (Russian)
Muang	city (Thai)
Mys	cape (Russian)
-nada	gulf; sea (Japanese)
-nama	cape (Japanese)
Ostrova	islands (Russian)
Ozero	lake (Russian)
Pergunungan	mountain range (Indonesian)
Pendi	basin (Chinese)
Pic	summit (French; Spanish)
Pico	summit (Spanish)
Pik	summit (Russian)
Planalto	plateau (Portugese)
Planina	mountain range (Bulgarian; Serb-Croat)
Poluostrov	peninsula (Russian)
Puerto	port (Spanish)
Pulau-pulau	islands (Indonesian)
Puncak	mountain (Indonesian)
Punta	cape (Italian; Spanish)
Ras; Râs	cape (Arabic)
Ra's	cape (Persian)
Rio	river (Portugese; Spanish)
Rivière	river (French)
Rubha	cape (Gaelic)
-saki	cape (Japanese)
Salina	salt pan (Spanish)
-san	mountain (Japanese)
-sanchi	mountains (Japanese)
-sanmyaku	mountain range (Japanese)
Sebkra	salt pan (Arabic)
See	lake (German)
Selat	strait (Indonesian)
Seto	strait (Japanese)
Shan	mountains (Chinese)
-shima	island (Japanese)
-shotō	islands (Japanese)
Sierra	mountain range (Spanish)
Song	river (Vietnamese)
-suidō	strait (Japanese)
Tassili	plateau (Berber)
Tau	island (Chinese)
Teluk	bay (Indonesian)
-tō	island (Japanese)
Tonle	lake (Cambodian)
-wan	bay (Japanese)
-zaki	cape (Japanese)
Zaliv	bay (Russian)

OXFORD
UNIVERSITY PRESS

8 Sampson Mews, Suite 204, Don Mills, Ontario, M3C 0H5
www.oupcanada.com

Oxford University Press is a department of the University of Oxford.
It furthers the University's objective of excellence in research,
scholarship, and education by publishing worldwide in

Oxford   New York
Auckland   Cape Town   Dar es Salaam   Hong Kong   Karachi
Kuala Lumpur   Madrid   Melbourne   Mexico City   Nairobi
New Delhi   Shanghai   Taipei   Toronto

With offices in
Argentina   Austria   Brazil   Chile   Czech Republic   France   Greece
Guatemala   Hungary   Italy   Japan   Poland   Portugal   Singapore
South Korea   Switzerland   Thailand   Turkey   Ukraine   Vietnam

Oxford is a trade mark of Oxford University Press in the UK and in
certain other countries

Published in Canada by Oxford University Press

Library and Archives Canada Cataloguing in Publication

Oxford University Press (Canada)
Canadian Oxford world atlas [cartographic material] / Quentin H.
Stanford, general editor. – 6th ed.

ISBN 978-0-19-542924-4 (bound). – ISBN 978-0-19-542929-9 (pbk.).

1. Atlases, Canadian. 2. Canada–Maps. I. Stanford, Quentin H. II. Title.

G1021.O88 2008   912   C2008-902692-6

Oxford University Press is committed to our environment. This
book is printed on Forest Stewardship Council certified paper,
harvested from a responsibly managed forest, and the text contains
10% post-consumer waste.

Printed and bound in Canada.

10 11 12 - 15 14 13

Credits
Contributor: Kingsley Hurlington

Cartographic Project Manager/Editor: Caleb Gould
Cartographic Editor: Karen Brittin
Cartographic Technician: Tracey Learoyd

Photo research: Suzanne Williams of pictureresearch (UK); Lynn McIntyre (Canada)

Every possible effort has been made to trace the original source of the material
contained in this book. Where the effort has been unsuccessful, the publisher would
be pleased to hear from the copyright holders to rectify any omission.

Photos
cover photo: Satellite image courtesy of WorldSat Int. Inc. 2008

Corbis **132** (desert/Dave G. Houser), **133** (tundra/Staffan Widstrand), **133** (semi-
desert/Charles & Josette Lenars); Courtesy Hubble data: NASA , ESA, and A. Zezas
(Harvard-Smithsonian Center for Astrophysics); GALEX data: NASA, JPL-Caltech,
GALEX Team, J. Huchra et al. (Harvard-Smithsonian Center for Astrophysics),
Spitzer data: NASA/JPL/Caltech/Harvard-Smithsonian Center for Astrophysics **10**
Earth in Space; Jean du Boisberranger / Getty Images **132** Mixed Forest Trois-
Rivieres, QC; NASA **154**; NASA Images courtesy of the MODIS Rapid Response
Team at Goddard Space Flight Center **81** (1986), **81** (2001); NASA / Science Source
/ First Light 7 Earth; NASA Visible Earth **152**; Courtesy National Snow and Ice Data
Center, NSIDC Arctic Snow and Ice News Fall 2007 / WorldSat International Inc. **64**
Polar ice; Photolibrary.com **132** (temperate grasslands/Sean Morris), **132** (tropical
rainforest/Michael Fogden), **132** (evergreen trees and shrubs/David Fox), **133**
(Coniferous Forest/David Tipling), **133** (mountains/Martyn Colbeck), **133** (tropical
grasslands/Stan Osolinski), **133** (thorn forest/Gerald Thompson); Science Photo
Library **99** (Cnes, 1990 Distribution Spot Image), **109** (M-Sat Ltd), **129** (NOAA), **131**
(NASA/Goddard Space Flight Center), **132** (ice/Simon Fraser); Courtesy of UNEP
130 (1989), **130** (2003); WorldSat International Inc. **9** Vancouver, looking North,
Edmonton, **44** Calgary, **45** Vancouver, Rocky Mountains-Kicking Horse Pass, Victoria,
48 Indian Head, SK, Winnipeg. **53** Golden Horse Shoe, **55** Toronto, **58** Montreal,
59 Ottawa, Halifax, **61** Beloeil, Québec, Québec City, Bobcaygeon, ON, Manicouagan
Reservoir, QC, **62** Dawson City, Yukon, Mackenzie Delta, L'Anse aux Meadows, NL,
St. John's, NL; **67** North America, **77** South America, **83** Europe, **91** Asia, **105** Africa.

12–13 Provincial and territorial flags courtesy of: Legislative Services, Tourism, Parks,
Recreation and Culture, Government of Alberta; Copyright © Province of British
Columbia. All rights reserved. Reprinted with permission of the Province of British
Columbia. www.ipp.gov.bc.ca; Communications Services Manitoba, Manitoba
Government; Government of Newfoundland and Labrador; Communications New
Brunswick; Legislative Assembly of the NWT; Crown Copyright Province of Nova
Scotia. Used with permission; Legislative Assembly of Nunavut; Government of
Ontario; Government of PEI, Provincial Treasury; Direction des communications,
Ministère du Conseil exécutif du Québec - Justice; Office of Protocol and Honours,
Saskatchewan Government Relations; Office of Protocol, Government of Yukon.

Maps
All maps in this atlas have been adapted from various sources. Following are credits
for major contributions:

Natural Resources Canada, *The Atlas of Canada*: **14** main map "Age of Rocks"; **22** right
"Soil Capability for Agriculture";

Natural Resources Canada, *The Atlas of Canada, 1st ed.*: **36** "Density of Population,
1901 [Eastern Canada]", "Density of Population, 1901 [Western Canada].

Natural Resources Canada, *The Atlas of Canada, 5th ed.*: **14** inset "Glaciers"; **15** main
map "Terrestrial Ecoregions, 1993", inset "Wetland Regions, 1986"; **16** top and
middle "Temperature—January and July; **17** top left "Precipitation", middle left:
"Snowfall"; **18** top "Heating Degree-days"; **19** "Climatic Regions: Thornthwaite
Classification Moisture Regions"; **28** "Energy and Minerals, 1985"; **38** "Indian and
Inuit Communities and Languages, 1980"

Natural Resources Canada, *The Atlas of Canada*, Agriculture: **23** top "Grape Area
in Production, 2001"; "Area Irrigated in Western Canada, 2001"; "Change in
Greenhouse Area, 1991-2001"; "Very Large Livestock Farms, 2001"; "Very Large
Livestock Farms, 2001 (Western Canada)"

39 Natural Resources Canada, *The Atlas of Canada, History, 1639 to 1949*:
"Territorial Evolution of Canada (1667 to 1949)"

24 Natural Resources Canada: various Natural Hazards maps at http://atlas.nrcan.
gc.ca/site/english/maps/environment/naturalhazards

17 bottom left: David Phillips, "Thunderstorms" in *The Climates of Canada*. (Ottawa:
Minister of Supply and Service Canada), © Her Majesty The Queen in Right of Canada,
Environment Canada, 1990. Reproduced with the permission of the Minister of
Public Works and Government Services Canada.

Statistics

Statistics Canada information is used with the permission of Statistics Canada. Users are forbidden to copy this material and/or redisseminate the data, in an original or modified form, for commercial purposes, without the expressed permission of Statistics Canada. Information on the availability of the wide range of data from Statistics Canada can be obtained from Statistics Canada's Regional Offices, its World Wide Web site at http://www.statcan.ca, and its toll-free access number 1-800-263-1136.

12–13 Statistics Canada, "Population and dwelling counts, for Canada, provinces and territories, 2006 and 2001 censuses - 100% data (table)", "Population and Dwelling Count Highlight Tables", 2006 Census, Catalogue no. 97-550-XWE2006002, Ottawa, 13 March 2007, http://www12.statcan.ca/english/census06/data/popdwell/Table.cfm?T=101&SR=1&S=0&O=A&RPP=25&PR=0&CMA=0, accessed 21 April 2008.

21 Fish catches by quantity and value Fisheries and Oceans Canada, "1990 Atlantic & Pacific Coasts Commercial Landings, by Province (metric tonnes, live weight)"; "2006 Atlantic & Pacific Coasts Commercial Landings, by Province (metric tonnes, live weight)"; "1990 Value of Atlantic & Pacific Coasts Commercial Landings, by Province (thousand dollars) 2006"; "Value of Atlantic & Pacific Coasts Commercial Landings, by Province (thousand dollars)"; Major world fishing countries, 2004 Food and Agriculture Organization of the United Nations, FishStat, 2001-2004; Aquaculture value by species, 2005 Adapted from Statistics Canada. "Aquaculture Statistics 2006", Table 1-15, 2005, Catalogue 23-222-X, http://www.statcan.ca/english/freepub/23-222-XIE/2006000/tablesectionlist.htm.

23 Farm types, 2006, Pasture land by province, Cropland by province, Canada farm land, 2006 Adapted from Statistics Canada, "2006 Census of Agriculture, Farm Data and Farm Operator Data", Catalogue 95-629-XWE, Table 4.3-2. http://www.statcan.ca/english/freepub/95-629-XIE/4/4.3-2_A.htm.

25 Greenhouse gas emissions by province, 2004 Environment Canada, *National Inventory Report, 1990–2004*, Greenhouse Gas Sources and Sinks in Canada, Annex 12: Provincial/Territorial Greenhouse gas emission tables, 1990-2004; **Greenhouse gas emissions by sector, 2004** Environment Canada, *National Inventory Report, 1990–2004*, Greenhouse Gas Sources and Sinks in Canada, Annex 8: Canada's Greenhouse Gas Emission Tables, 1990–2004, Table A8-2: Canada's 1990-2004 Greenhouse Gas Emissions by Sector http://www.ec.gc.ca/pdb/ghg/inventory_report/2004_report/ta8_2_e.cfm; **Contribution of Canadian greenhouse gas emissions to future global warming** Environment Canada, *National Inventory Report, 1990–2004*, Greenhouse Gas Sources and Sinks in Canada, Table S-2: Canada's GHG Emissions by Gas and Sector, 2004, http://www.ec.gc.ca/pdb/ghg/inventory_report/2004_report/ts_2_e.cfm; **Observed trends in temperature** Henry Hengeveld, Bob Whitewood, and Angus Fergusson, "Observed trends in temperatures across southern Canada since 1900 and all of Canada since 1948", Figure 1.9, in *An Introduction to Climate Change: A Canadian perspective.* (Downsview: Environment Canada, 2005), p. 10, www.msc.ec.gc.ca/education/scienceofclimatechange

26 Population by ecozone, 2001 Adapted from Statistics Canada, *Human Activity and the Environment: Annual Statistics, 2006*, Catalogue 16-201-XWE, Table 3.3 and Map 2.2. http://www.statcan.ca/english/freepub/16-201-XIE/2006000/t071_en.htm?.

28 Metallic mineral production of Canada, 2006; Nonmetallic mineral production of Canada, 2006 Adapted from Statistics Canada, *Canada's Mineral Production, Preliminary Estimates, 2006*, Catalogue 26-202-XIB, Table 1, http://www.statcan.ca/english/freepub/26-202-XIB/26-202-XIB2007000.pdf, accessed June 2007.

29 Coal imports and exports, Coal consumption by province Adapted from Natural Resources Canada, *Canadian Minerals Yearbook 2005*, pp. 20.1, 20.3-20.4, © Her Majesty the Queen in Right of Canada, 2007; **Crude oil transfers, Natural gas transfers** National Energy Board, *Annual Report 2005 to Parliament*, pp. 23, 27. Reproduced with the permission of the Minister of Public Works and Government Services Canada, 2008.

30 Electricity trade National Energy Board, *Annual Report 2005 to Parliament*, p.30. Reproduced with the permission of the Minister of Public Works and Government Services Canada, 2008.

31 provincial data Adapted from Statistics Canada, 2006, National and Provincial Principal Statistics from the Annual Survey of Manufactures and Logging (ASML), CANSIM Database http://cansim2.statcan.ca/, Tables 301-0006 and 301-0007; **CMA data** Adapted from Statistics Canada, Summary Statistics of Manufacturing Industries, by Census Metropolitan Areas (CMA), Annual Survey of Manufactures and Logging (ASML), 2003.

32–33 Trade (exports) and Trade (imports) Adapted from Statistics Canada, *Imports by Country*, Catalogue 65-006, vol. 63 no. 04, January to December 2006, 19 February 2007; *Exports by Country*, Catalogue 65-003, vol. 63 no. 04, January to December 2006, 5 March 2007.

36 Census Metropolitan Areas Adapted from Statistics Canada, "2006 Census of the Population, Population and Dwelling Count Highlight Tables, Population and dwelling counts for census metropolitan areas, 2006 and 2001 censuses—100% data", Catalogue 97-550-XWE2006002, http://www12.statcan.ca/english/census06/data/popdwell/Table.cfm?T=205&RPP=50.

37 Population, 2006 Adapted from Statistics Canada, "Age and Sex, 2006 counts for both sexes, for Canada, provinces and territories - 100% data (table)". Age and Sex Highlight Tables. 2006 Census, Catalogue 97-551-XWE2006002, Ottawa, 17 July 2007. http://www12.statcan.ca/english/census06/data/highlights/agesex/index.cfm?Lang=E, accessed 18 April 2008; **Population by mother tongue, 2006** Adapted from Statistics Canada, "Population by mother tongue and age groups, 2006 counts, for Canada, provinces and territories – 20% sample data (table)". Language Highlight Tables. 2006 Census, Catalogue 97-555-XWE2006002, Ottawa, 4 December 2007, http://www12.statcan.ca/english/census06/data/highlights/Language/Table401.cfm?Lang=E&T=401&GH=4&SC=1&S=99&O=A, accessed 18 April 2008; **Immigrant population for selected CMAs, 2006** Adapted from Statistics Canada, "Population by immigrant status and period of immigration, 2006 counts, for Canada and census metropolitan areas and census agglomerations – 20% sample data (table)". Immigration and Citizenship Highlight Tables. 2006 Census. Catalogue 97-557-XWE2006002, Ottawa, 4 December 2007, http://www12.statcan.ca/english/census06/data/highlights/Immigration/Table403.cfm?Lang=E&T=403&GH=8&SC=1&S=0&O=A, accessed 18 April 2008; **Immigrant population by province or territory, 2006** Adapted from Statistics Canada, "Population by immigrant status and period of immigration, 2006 counts, for Canada, provinces and territories – 20% sample data (table)". Immigration and Citizenship Highlight Tables. 2006 Census. Catalogue 97-557-XWE2006002, Ottawa, 4 December 2007, http://www12.statcan.ca/english/census06/data/highlights/Immigration/Table403.cfm?Lang=E&T=403&GH=4&SC=1&S=99&O=A, accessed 18 April 2008; **provincial pie charts** Adapted from Statistics Canada, "2001 Census of the Population, Ethnocultural Portrait of Canada: Highlight Tables, Ethnic Origins", Catalogue 97F0024XIE2001006; **map lower left Natural increase values** Adapted from Statistics Canada, "Population Change 2001-2006" Natural Increase - Annual Demographic Estimates: Canada, Provinces and Territories - 2005-2006, Table 4-11: Annual estimates of demographic components, national perspective-Natural increase, Catalogue 91-215; **map lower left Interprovincial migration values** Adapted from Statistics Canada "2001 Census: analysis series, Profile of the Canadian population by mobility status: Canada, a nation on the move", Table: "Net migrants and net migration rates, provinces and territories, 1976 to 2001" p. 20, Catalogue 96F0030XIE2001006, http://www12.statcan.ca/english/census01/products/analytic/companion/mob/pdf/96F0030XIE2001006.pdf; map lower left International migration values Adapted from Statistics Canada, "Population Change 2001-2006" Net international migration - Annual Demographic Estimates: Canada, Provinces and Territories - 2005-2006, Table 4-13: Annual estimates of demographic components, national perspective-Net international migration, Catalogue 91-215; **map lower left percentages for Immigrants arriving in Canada by place of birth, 2001-2006** Adapted from Statistics Canada, "Place of birth for the immigrant population by period of immigration, 2006 counts and percentage distribution, for Canada, provinces and territories – 20% sample data (table)". Immigration and Citizenship Highlight Tables. 2006 Census, Catalogue 97-557-XWE2006002, Ottawa, 4 December 2007, http://www12.statcan.ca/english/census06/data/highlights/Immigration/Table404.cfm?Lang=E&T=404&GH=4&SC=1&S=1&O=D, accessed 21 April 2008.

38 Aboriginal population, 2006; Aboriginal peoples, 2006, Where the aboriginal population live, 2006 Adapted from Statistics Canada, "Aboriginal Peoples Highlight Tables, 2006 Census", Catalogue 97-558-XWE2006002, Table 1: "Aboriginal identity population by age groups, median age and sex", http://www12.statcan.ca/english/census06/data/highlights/aboriginal/index.cfm?Lang=E

40–65 land area statistics "Facts about Canada—Land and Freshwater Areas", 2001 data courtesy of Natural Resources Canada, Canada Centre for Remote Sensing; **Census population** Adapted from Statistics Canada: "Population and Dwelling Counts", 2006 Census, Catalogue 97-550-XWE2006002, July 2007, http://www.statcan.ca/bsolc/english/bsolc?catno=97-550-X2006002; "Population urban and rural, by province and territory", http://www40.statcan.ca/l01/cst01/demo62a.htm; **Census Metropolitan Areas, 2006, Other important urban centres, 2006** Adapted from Statistics Canada, "Population and dwelling counts, for Canada, provinces and territories, 2006 and 2001 censuses - 100% data (table)". Population and Dwelling Count Highlight Tables, 2006 Census, Catalogue 97-550-XWE2006002, Ottawa, 13 March 2007. http://www12.statcan.ca/english/census06/data/popdwell/Table.cfm?T=101&SR=1&S=0&O=A&R PP=25&PR=0&CMA=0, accessed 18 April 2008; Gross Domestic Product Adapted from Statistics Canada, "Gross Domestic Product (GDP) at basic prices, by North American Industry Classification System (NAICS) and province, annual (dollars)", CANSIM 379-0025, http://cansim2.statcan.ca/cgi-win/CNSMCGI.PGM, accessed June 2007.

World Flags

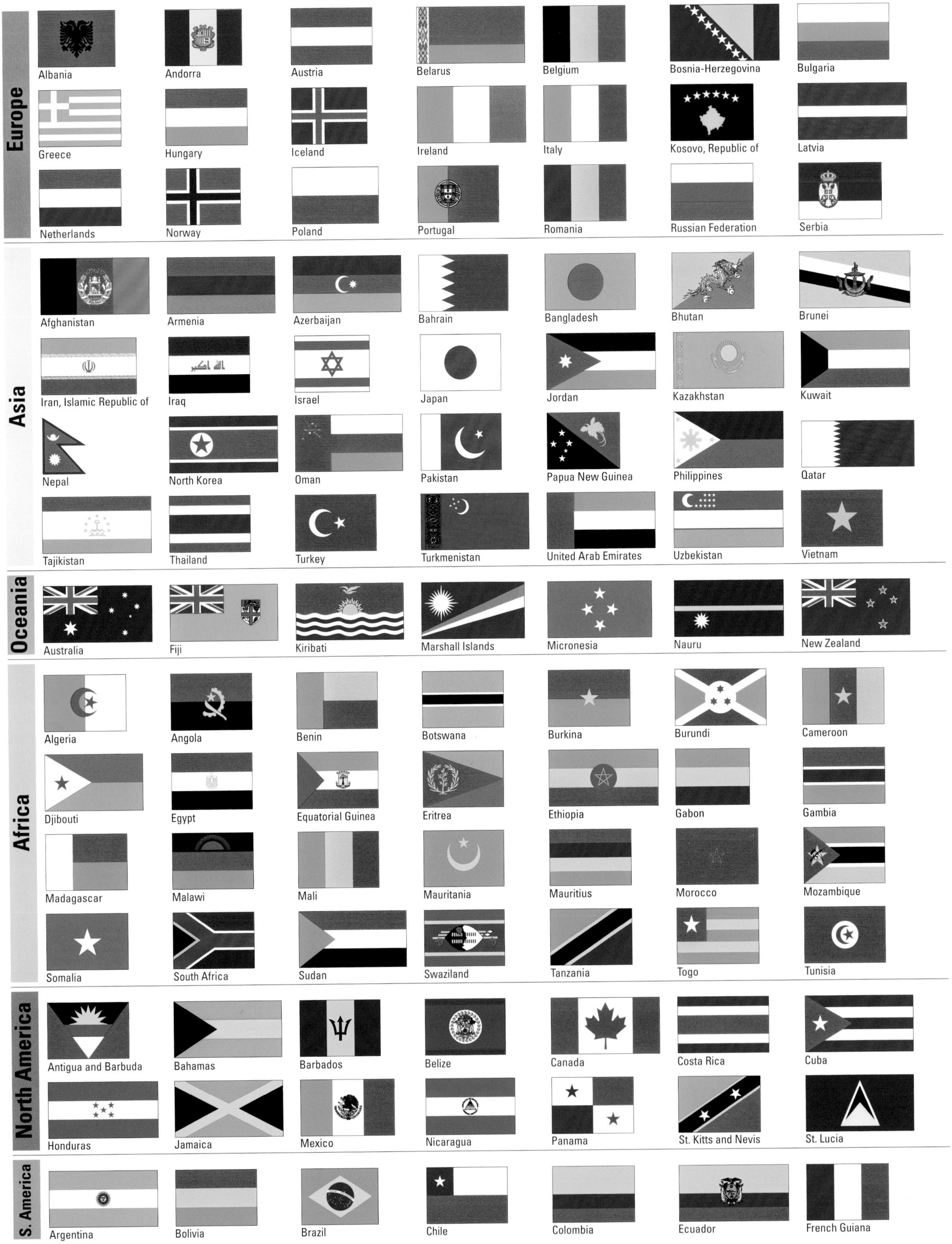

Europe

Albania

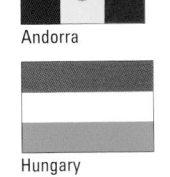
Andorra

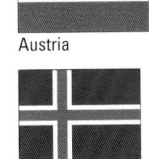
Austria

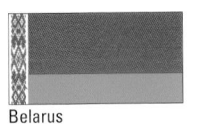
Belarus

Belgium

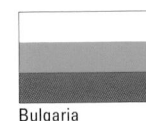
Bosnia-Herzegovina

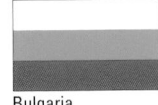
Bulgaria

Greece

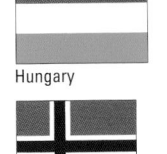
Hungary

Iceland

Ireland

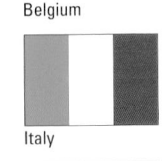
Italy

Kosovo, Republic of

Latvia

Netherlands

Norway

Poland

Portugal

Romania

Russian Federation

Serbia

Asia

Afghanistan

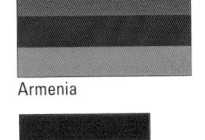
Armenia

Azerbaijan

Bahrain

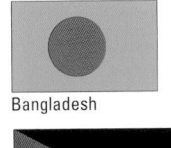
Bangladesh

Bhutan

Brunei

Iran, Islamic Republic of

Iraq

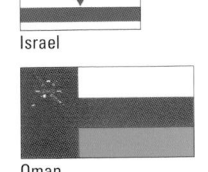
Israel

Japan

Jordan

Kazakhstan

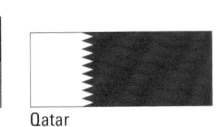
Kuwait

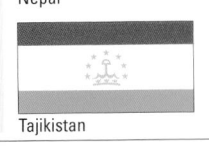
Nepal

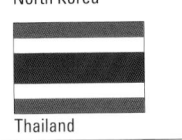
North Korea

Oman

Pakistan

Papua New Guinea

Philippines

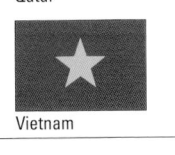
Qatar

Tajikistan

Thailand

Turkey

Turkmenistan

United Arab Emirates

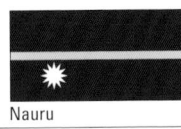
Uzbekistan

Vietnam

Oceania

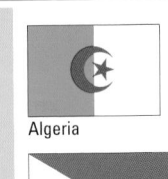
Australia

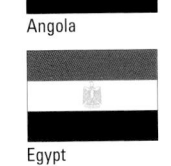
Fiji

Kiribati

Marshall Islands

Micronesia

Nauru

New Zealand

Africa

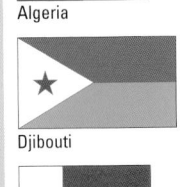
Algeria

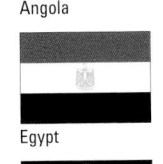
Angola

Benin

Botswana

Burkina

Burundi

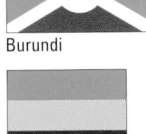
Cameroon

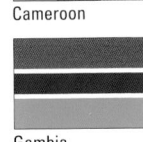
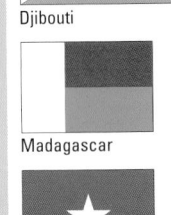
Djibouti

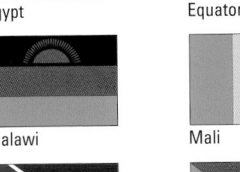
Egypt

Equatorial Guinea

Eritrea

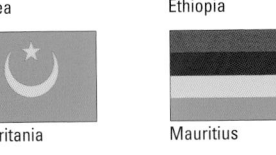
Ethiopia

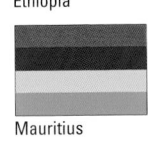
Gabon

Gambia

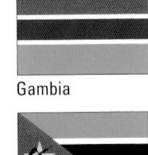
Madagascar

Malawi

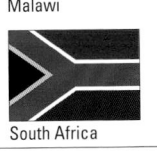
Mali

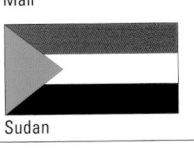
Mauritania

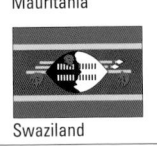
Mauritius

Morocco

Mozambique

Somalia

South Africa

Sudan

Swaziland

Tanzania

Togo

Tunisia

North America

Antigua and Barbuda

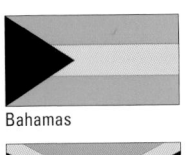
Bahamas

Barbados

Belize

Canada

Costa Rica

Cuba

Honduras

Jamaica

Mexico

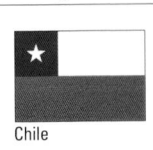
Nicaragua

Panama

St. Kitts and Nevis

St. Lucia

S. America

Argentina

Bolivia

Brazil

Chile

Colombia

Ecuador

French Guiana

Flags **World**

Europe

 Croatia
 Czech Republic
 Denmark
 Estonia
 Finland
 France
 Germany

 Liechtenstein
 Lithuania
 Luxembourg
 Macedonia, FYRO
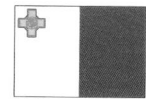 Malta
 Moldova
Montenegro

 Slovakia
Slovenia
 Spain
 Sweden
 Switzerland
Ukraine
United Kingdom

Asia

 Cambodia
 China
 Cyprus
 East Timor
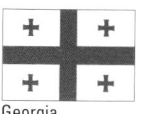 Georgia
 India
 Indonesia

 Kyrgyzstan
 Laos
 Lebanon
 Malaysia
 Maldives
 Mongolia
 Myanmar

 Saudi Arabia
Seychelles
 Singapore
 South Korea
 Sri Lanka
 Syria
 Taiwan

 Yemen

Oceania

 Northern Marianas
 Palau
 Samoa
 Solomon Islands
 Tonga
 Tuvalu
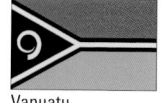 Vanuatu

Africa

 Cape Verde
Central African Republic
Chad
Comoros
Congo
Congo, Dem. Rep.
Côte d'Ivoire

 Ghana
Guinea
Guinea-Bissau
Kenya
Lesotho
Liberia
Libya

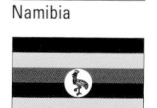 Namibia
Niger
Nigeria
Rwanda
Sao Tomé and Pirncipe
Senegal
Sierra Leone

 Uganda
Zambia
Zimbabwe

North America

Dominica
Dominican Republic
El Salvador
Greenland
Grenada
Guatemala
Haiti

St. Vincent & the Grenadines
Trinidad and Tobago
United States of America

S. America

 Guyana
Paraguay
Peru
Suriname
Uruguay
Venezuela